Operations Management

A supply chain approach

This book is dedicated to the memory of my parents and brother ...

Albert, Hilda, and Ken

... to my wife and children for their patience ...

Christine, Delphine, and Guillaume

... and to the following who guided me during my education and career ...

John Cooper of Chater School, for his implicit trust
Betty Preston of Rickmansworth Grammar School, for her patience and determination
Frank Manning of Marchon Products, for his direction and encouragement
Ken Peet of the University of Newcastle, for always being prepared to listen
Hugh Baird of C F Braun, for his enthusiasm and support

DEREK L WALLER, FEBRUARY 2002

Operations Management

A supply chain approach

SECOND EDITION

Derek L Waller

THOMSON

Australia • Canada • Mexico • Singapore • Spain • United Kingdom • United States

THOMSON

OPERATIONS MANAGEMENT: A SUPPLY CHAIN APPROACH,
2nd edition

Copyright © 2003 Derek L. Waller

The Thomson logo is a registered trademark used herein
under licence.

For more information, contact Thomson Learning, High
Holborn House, 50–51 Bedford Row, London, WC1R 4LR or visit
us on the World Wide Web at: http://www.thomsonlearning.co.uk

BRITISH LIBRARY CATALOGUING-IN-PUBLICATION DATA
A catalogue record for this book is available from the
British Library

ISBN 1-86152-803-5

First edition published in 1999 by International Thomson
Business Press

PUBLICATION TEAM
Typeset by Gray Publishing, Tunbridge Wells, Kent
Text designed by Malcolm Harvey Young
Printed in Italy by G. Canale & C.

Contents

Preface

About this book

This book is about operations management, which, of all management disciplines, is the key activity in both market-driven business firms and not-for-profit organizations. Operations are the wheels of the strategic direction of the firm. Being principally cost centres operation are closely linked with finance. Operations provide the tangible goods and services demanded by marketing. No organization can function without competent people and thus the overlap of operations with human resource management.

Now in its second edition, *Operations Management: A Supply Chain Approach* has maintained its authority as *the* comprehensive (some say encyclopaedic) pragmatic and integrated text of the operations management environment, covering it from a supply chain point of view. Now fully revised and updated to acknowledge the impact of information technology, e-commerce, outsourcing, and six-sigma quality control, the text addresses both services and manufacturing and gives a broad international perspective in four parts:

- Part I – Operations and strategic decisions
  Provides an introduction to the field of operations management, its link to the supply chain, and how it functions in the global business environment.
- Part II – Design in operations management
  Answers the question of how the supply chain system can be designed so that it meets the strategic objectives of the firm.
- Part III – Planning and organizing
  Gives complete coverage of the core functions of operations and the supply chain from sales forecasting, inventory management, enterprise resource planning, lean production, purchasing, through to project management.
- Part IV – System control and further analysis
  Because operations are both quantitative and qualitative, this part goes into more analytical depth and 'closes the loop' on the processes examined throughout the book.

How to use this book

Structure and content

The four principal parts of the text take the reader through the complete supply chain process. As illustrated in Figure P1, Operations management: A supply chain approach, we begin with an exploration of the concept of operations itself and the strategic decisions necessary to set the supply chain in motion. The figure then highlights the type of design considerations needed for inputs, progressing to the planning and organizing requirements necessary for successful transformations, before concluding with the system control and further analysis essential to 'close the loop'. This figure is repeated in each part of the book with the relevant chapter names affixed so that the reader can see exactly where specific topics fit into the overall supply chain process and thus the text itself.

PART I OPERATIONS AND STRATEGIC DECISIONS gives an overview of the operations management environment and details some of the strategic elements related to the field. Chapter 1, introduces the reader to the field of operations management, its link to the supply chain, how it functions in the global business environment, and the importance of the 'king' client. An organization, either services or manufacturing, is driven by top management's strategy, and it is this strategy that gives the direction and framework of the supply chain and the various operations. This is the thrust of Chapter 2, which gives an overview of corporate strategy, describes the market orientation, and highlights the synergy between the supply chain, operations, and strategic elements. Today, many firms are relocating away from their home country to low-cost labour areas and this is the essence of Chapter 3, regarding the strategy of where to locate the firm, taking into account factors such as cost, labour, supplier availability, transportation times, infrastructure, and other resource elements. Quality has to be incorporated into the strategic activities of the firm, as without an acceptable quality level, a firm would have difficulty sustaining its operations. This theme is covered in detail in Chapter 4. The ecological environment, not often found in other operations management texts, is presented in Chapter 5. Without a sound environmental policy in its strategy, a firm would eventually lose credibility, incur legal problems, and tarnish its image. In both Chapters 4 and 5 two international certifications, ISO-9000 for quality, and ISO-14000 for the environment, are reviewed.

PART II DESIGN IN OPERATIONS MANAGEMENT looks at the supply chain as a system that must be designed so that it meets the strategic objectives of the firm. These key design elements for the supply chain system are the thrust of the next four chapters. Chapter 6 explores the product design, whether a tangible or service product. It is the product that is the direct link between operations and the marketplace. The chapter deals with the product lifecycle, technology in product design, and product development and flexibility. Chapter 7 covers the systems for producing the product including operating capacity requirements, the advantages of vertical integration or disintegration of firms, automation, information technology in the process system, electronic commerce in both business-to-business and business-to-commerce transactions, and business process reengineering for process design improvement. No system will function without a trained and motivated workforce and this is the substance of Chapter 8, which discusses the people in operations who make it all happen. The chapter addresses job design, managing the workforce, the learning curve, labour rates, stress, and change. The last chapter in Part II is Chapter 9, which deals with the physical organization of the facility, whether a manufacturing or a service organization such as a restaurant, airport, or a design office. A poorly conceived physical arrangement can be detrimental to the smooth flow of material or communication within the supply chain.

PART III PLANNING AND ORGANIZING consists of nine chapters covering the core functions of the operations and supply chain. Chapter 10 is about forecasting, the trigger in the supply chain, which is that function that sets off all the operating activities to pull the product through the supply chain. Forecasting, since it involves 'managing' the external environment, is probably the most inexact and difficult activity for the firm. This chapter treats forecasting both from a qualitative and quantitative aspect including many statistical methods. Whether a firm manufactures, performs a distribution function, or is a retail outlet, there is inventory, and this is the essence of Chapter 11 that discusses the reasons for holding inventory, the requirements for good inventory management, inventory modelling, and the

impact of electronic commerce on inventory levels. Chapter 12 discusses how short-term capacity might be adjusted to meet demand, using inventory to buffer production and demand, backordering, and how the subsequent backlog can be used as a planning tool. The formulation of an aggregate plan is discussed in detail and the development and use of the master production schedule is presented. Chapter 13 details the development of manufacturing resource planning (MRP-I) for dependent inventory, presents methods for lot sizing, before moving onto (MRP-II) and then enterprise resource planning (ERP), the commercial business application software systems. Short-term scheduling is presented in Chapter 14, including the use of Gantt charts, the consequence of sequencing methods in scheduling, and various quantitative methods for scheduling. Chapter 15, covers lean production and just-in-time, dealing with how to be efficient in the operations and supply chain including designing pull systems, balancing a supply chain, Toyota's concept and the use of kanban cards, SMED, and determining overall workplace effectiveness. In the supply chain, the upstream purchasing and subcontracting activity is critical and for some firms may involve upto 80% of the costs of the finished product. This is the substance of Chapter 16, which underscores the international aspects of purchasing, organization of the function, sourcing, ethics, value analysis, outsourcing, and, again, the growing importance of electronic commerce. Chapter 17 deals with how to be effective in planning and controlling the supply chain including modelling the system, pipeline mapping, distribution requirements planning, the function of the distribution centre or warehouse, transportation modes, international considerations, and efficient organization of the supply chain function. A production or service operation is born as a project, and throughout the life of the operation there are project activities implemented to update, modify, or improve efficiency. This is the purpose of Chapter 18, which defines project work, the types of contracts, project organization and scheduling, and how CPM and PERT network diagrams can be used for effective planning and control.

PART IV SYSTEM CONTROL AND FURTHER ANALYSIS recognizes that operations are both quantitative and qualitative and although earlier chapters in this book present many quantitative approaches, the purpose of this final section is to go into more analytical depth. A well-conceived supply chain and all its operating activities will not run smoothly and be reliable if a good maintenance programme is not in place, a fact underscored in Chapter 19. The first part of this chapter presents series and parallel systems for reliability, FMECA for determining critical features in various failure modes, and, then, the following sections discuss maintenance programmes including emergency maintenance, preventive maintenance, total productive maintenance, and reliability-centred maintenance. Chapter 20 gives detailed coverage of the analytical control procedures for statistical process control, variation in a process, six-sigma quality control, and acceptance plans for product lots that have already been manufactured. This chapter is the complementary analytical component of Chapter 4 (Quality management). The theory of waiting lines, or queuing, which can be both a scheduling and capacity problem is presented in Chapter 21 and includes a practical illustration of the Monte Carlo computer simulation. Chapter 22 covers the theory of constraints for system improvement by examining bottlenecks in the supply chain, whether they be physical, in the sense of insufficient capacity, or virtual, due to poor system planning and control. Analytical techniques such as decision theory, marginal analysis, and a cost–benefit analysis for system optimization, and for minimizing risk, are covered in Chapter 23. Chapter 24 presents linear programming with a particular emphasis on the application of the Solver tool in Microsoft Excel. No business can be properly described without examining the financial aspects, and this is the thrust of Chapter 25, which covers product pricing, operating costs, the treatment of fixed assets, activity-based costing, and the economics of short and long run production costs. Auditing of the operations and supply chain is covered in Chapter 26, including customer satisfaction and the application of analytical tools presented throughout the text. Practical audit sheets are included with the chapter. Finally, Chapter 27 has the objective to refresh the reader's knowledge of the theory behind some of the statistical methods referred to in earlier chapters particularly those related to probability, dispersion, and distributions. This final chapter is conceived to 'close the loop' on this integrated operations management textbook with a supply chain approach.

Key features

Industry insights

Throughout the book, *Industry insights*, derived from leading business publications such as *The Economist, The Wall Street Journal Europe, Business Week*, and *The Sunday Times* use lively, real-world examples to illustrate the practical application of the material.

Summaries of key elements

At the end of each chapter you will find a *Summary of key elements* including concepts, basic definitions, and formulae, which provide an excellent resource for both exam preparation and general revision.

Review and discussion topics

Review and discussion topics are provided at the end of each chapter and these are intended to inspire the reader critically to consider what they have learned in that chapter. These are ideal as a starting point for tutorial discussions or as essay topics.

Demonstrating the concept

Demonstrating the concept portrays complete and thorough worked examples of selected processes and methods detailed throughout the text. Each demonstrates a concept step by step, providing the reader with practical clarification when new to a topic or for those requiring a revision aid.

Application exercises

Application exercises offer a basic outline of an operations requirement by a given situation, inviting the reader to provide the appropriate solution. Either directly linked to a *Demonstrating the concept* section, or specific to a topic outlined within the chapter, they offer the reader the chance to practise and assess their level of understanding and practical ability achieved from the chapter.

Case studies

A *Case study* is provided at the end of almost every chapter. The case study presents the reader with a detailed situation and encourages a critical and practical response to whatever that situation may require. Equipped with the knowledge gained from the chapter, the reader will be tested in the ability to respond effectively to the given situation. The case studies are of such a length to provide a great learning resource for tutorials.

Selected further reading

Broad *Further reading* recommendations are supplied to accompany each chapter, with reference to specialized and general textbooks as well as many journal articles and industry papers.

What's on the web?

Further learning resources are available at www.supplychain-online.com. This site is completely dedicated to this second edition of *Operations Management: A Supply Chain Approach* and is host to extensive supplementary learning and teaching resources to accompany the text. Some resources are specific to chapters in the book and these are detailed in the *What's on the web?* sections at the end of the chapter.

For more information about the site, see the section devoted to the website that follows.

Appendix

The *Appendix* contains a table of discoveries, inventions, and developments, beginning with the Industrial Revolution, which have had an impact on the operations environment in both manufacturing and services.

Glossary

A full *Glossary* of terms is supplied at the end of this book. The glossary has been updated since the previous edition and now includes nearly 800 entries.

Who should use this book?

This text will provide a comprehensive introduction to students of operations and supply chain management courses as well as undergraduates on business studies and other such related degrees, since no prior knowledge of the subject matter is assumed.

MBA students and other postgraduate students will note that the book provides critical coverage of all key operations and supply management issues, drawing on practical real-world examples from industry and the business world.

Practitioners in operations and supply chain management will be able to use this comprehensive text as an invaluable reference bible.

Website

Anyone using this book will find the accompanying website useful, since it is home to an array of supplementary materials to enhance learning when using this text.

The website www.supplychain-online.com has been produced by Thomson Learning as a dedicated learning centre for the second edition of *Operations Management: A Supply Chain Approach*. In addition to the chapter-specific resources as detailed in the what's on the web? sections, the site hosts an array of other resources for both students and lecturers using the book.

Part of the site is open access, where students and general readers can view the chapter-specific resources and much more. In addition, there is a password-protected area of the site accessible to lecturers only. The following chart gives a breakdown of what's available:

For students	For lecturers
Chapter-specific extra resources referred to throughout the text	Instructor's manual containing teaching notes for each chapter
Interactive objective multiple-choice concept tests	Suggested course outlines for teaching on a quarter or semester system
Related links	PowerPoint™ slides
	Objective multiple-choice concept tests
	Suggested responses to review and discussion topics
	Solutions to application exercises
	Suggested responses to the case studies

The website will be updated periodically.

Foreword

It gives me great satisfaction to write this foreword for the 2nd edition of *Operations Management: A Supply Chain Approach* by Derek Waller. Supply chain management, together with all the associated operating activities, is a fundamental function in business and if a global firm like IKEA did not pay strict attention to this activity we would certainly entail high costs, long lead times, and the quality of our products and our service would surely suffer.

IKEA is a Swedish-based distributor of home furnishing products involved in production, distribution and sale, either from its 154+ retail stores or by mail order. The company does not manufacture its products but uses over 1800 different worldwide subcontractors and suppliers from 55 countries, on every continent, who ship products to IKEA's distribution centres for eventual sale. This is the function of the IKEA distribution platform here in St Quentin Fallavier, part of a network of 17 distribution platforms in Europe, and which is of strategic importance to IKEA's retail activities in France and Spain. This facility is half a kilometre long, 150 metres wide with a maximum storage height of 18 metres allowing for over 100,000 cubic metres of effective storage capacity. The handling equipment includes 22 trans-stockers, which run in a circuit of some seven kilometres, and front-end loaders with retractable elevators and platforms for narrow spaces. In addition to the truck docks, there is a rail spur at the site where we can receive and dispatch trainload shipments.

Principal activities of IKEA at St Quentin Fallavier include the physical reception of finished products from suppliers, quantity and quality control, and registration of the units in our information technology (IT) database. Units are then stored at locations automatically designated by our IT system. When customer orders are received, the 'picking' activity includes removing items from storage, preparation, palletization, labelling, control and then transfer to the loading area. All the identification is performed with our laser-gun tracking and barcode system. Our expedition services covers the control and optimum loading of goods destined to the various retail outlets. In addition, we have a function that manages the in-flow activities, including purchasing and supplier contacts regarding planning, product delivery, daily vehicle reception, container and vehicle queuing and, when necessary, management of external warehouses. There is an out-flow management function which covers forecasting of product needs of the retail outlets, service agreements, transport route planning, and scheduling store reception. As such, the St Quentin facility encompasses numerous operational activities and is a key facility in the integrated supply chain of IKEA.

It is always a pleasure to receive Derek and his students here at our IKEA distribution centre where we are able to show them the real-world activities of the operations and supply chain environment. Further, as a practitioner of the subject, I believe his textbook presents a very comprehensive and pragmatic approach to the field, underscoring the importance of operations and supply chain management in business.

Eric MOREAU, Operations Manager
(Responsable d'Exploitation)
IKEA Distribution
St Quentin Fallavier, France
September 2002

Operations management: A supply chain approach

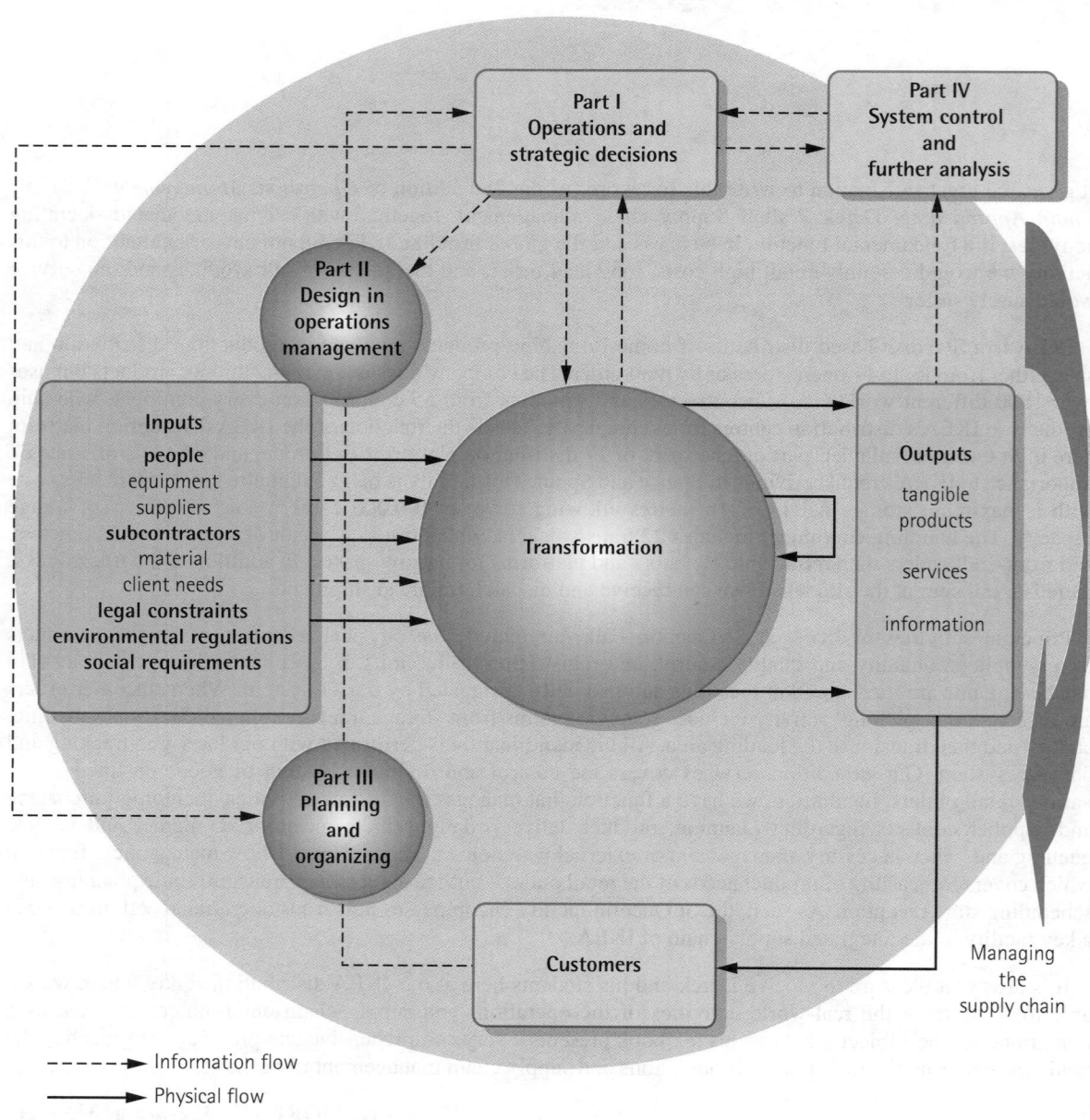

About the author

Derek Waller started early in the field of supply chain and operations management. From the age of 11 through his teenage years he had many regular odd jobs, including a grocery delivery boy, a butcher's assistant in charge of managing the inventory of meat, construction labourer installing sewage systems and mixing cement, postal sorter and mailman, and a scene changer in a theatre. As a student in the 1962 he had an internship with British Oxygen Co. in North London, working in a machine shop on drilling, lathes, and milling machines. The following year he worked as an operations assistant in southern Norway on a polyvinyl acetate plant used for the production of white glue.

After graduating with a PhD in chemical engineering in 1968 from the University of Newcastle, UK, Derek worked for Caltex Petroleum Co. (now Chevron-Texaco), first in London as a design engineer and then in Turkey in operations on the Izmit oil refinery. When he returned to England, he worked for a year for the Pritchard Co. on the operations and design of gas-treating plants for what was then Yugoslavia. In 1971 he decided to go west. With a one-way ticket on the liner *Queen Elizabeth*, and a three-month Greyhound bus pass in his pocket, he left England for New York. He crisscrossed the USA and Canada for several weeks learning the details of the schedules of the Greyhound buses, and the operation of the cheapest hotels, before he finally settled in southern California.

For the next 15 years Derek was employed by C F Braun & Co., an engineering, design, and construction firm just outside Los Angeles. During this period he worked first as a process engineer on oil refineries, metals-processing units, chemical plants, a brewery, food-processing plants, and nuclear power facilities. This work included operations and startups ensuring that the plants operated according to design specifications. From engineering he moved into sales. First he was involved on sales proposal development, working closely with purchasing agents, schedulers, quality assurance personnel, lawyers, and project managers. Later he was in line sales where clients included private firms and also units of the US government related to the design and operation of processing facilities. After line sales Derek became responsible for developing the company's strategic plan, which included measuring operating performance of Braun with the strategic plan, and also benchmarking activities with competitor firms. He later spent a period with the parent firm, Santa Fe, where he continued working on strategic planning and also financial analysis of the purchase and disposal of capital assets including oilrigs, drilling platforms, underwater pipe-laying vessels, and land pipelines. During his tenure with Braun and Santa Fe, Derek travelled extensively in the USA, Canada, Europe, the Middle East and Africa. He also studied part time to obtain a business management diploma for technical people from UCLA in 1976; an MBA, with an emphasis in finance, in 1980; and then, in 1988, a bachelor of arts in French.

Derek's move out of full-time industry activity began as a professor at the California State University in Los Angeles where he taught operations management, strategy, and quantitative methods in management using his industry experience as a base. In 1989 he moved to France to take a professorship at the Lyon Graduate School of Management in southeast France. Here he continues to teach operations and supply chain management, business statistics, and applied management science. He developed a specialized master's programme in operations management, and was nominated by students as one of the best professors in the MBA programme in 1995. In addition to teaching, he works closely with students on internships on operations and supply chain management with such firms as Renault, Nestlé, PepsiCo, Group Schneider, Alstom, Hewlett-Packard, 3M, General Motors, Aventis, Unilever, Novartis, and Schlumberger.

Derek is a member of the Institute of Operations Management, a chartered engineer; a member of the Institution of Chemical Engineers, and an editorial board member of *Greener Management International*, the journal of corporate environmental strategy and practice.

Acknowledgements

I would like to thank the following people who directly or indirectly, knowingly or unknowingly, helped in the preparation of the text by reviewing certain sections, providing useful information, organizing plant visits, or giving critical advice.

- Francis ARNOULD
- Hugh BAIRD; President C.F Braun & Co., Alhambra, Pasadena California, USA
- David FILLON; Toyota, Valenciennes, France
- Alain HAAG; Renault VI, Vénissieux, France
- Thierry LAVIALLE; Xerox, Lyon, France
- Alain MONTIER; Panzini, Lyon France
- Charles RAMMELOO; Pittance Constructors (retired), Dardilly, France
- Dan RANKIN; Pasadena, California, USA

Students from E M Lyon:

- Diane-Audrey CHANUT
- Anne CHEVILLARD
- Christelle CUIOC
- Laure GAILLARD
- Sidney GRÜNBERGY
- Régis LAFFONT
- Jocelyn NGUYEN
- Bertrand POISONNET
- Nathalie PUPIN
- Dominique SALAÜN
- Benoit STOS
- Christophe SURGEY
- Anne-Caroline ULRICH
- Christian WILD

Part I

Operations and strategic decisions

Part I introduces the reader to operations management and the supply chain, gives an overview of the function of operations management and its activities in the global business environment, and details some of the strategic elements related to the field, such as site selection, quality management, and environmental considerations.

> '*If a man does not know to what port he is steering,*
> *no wind is favourable to him.*'
>
> Seneca

Part I: Operations and strategic decisions

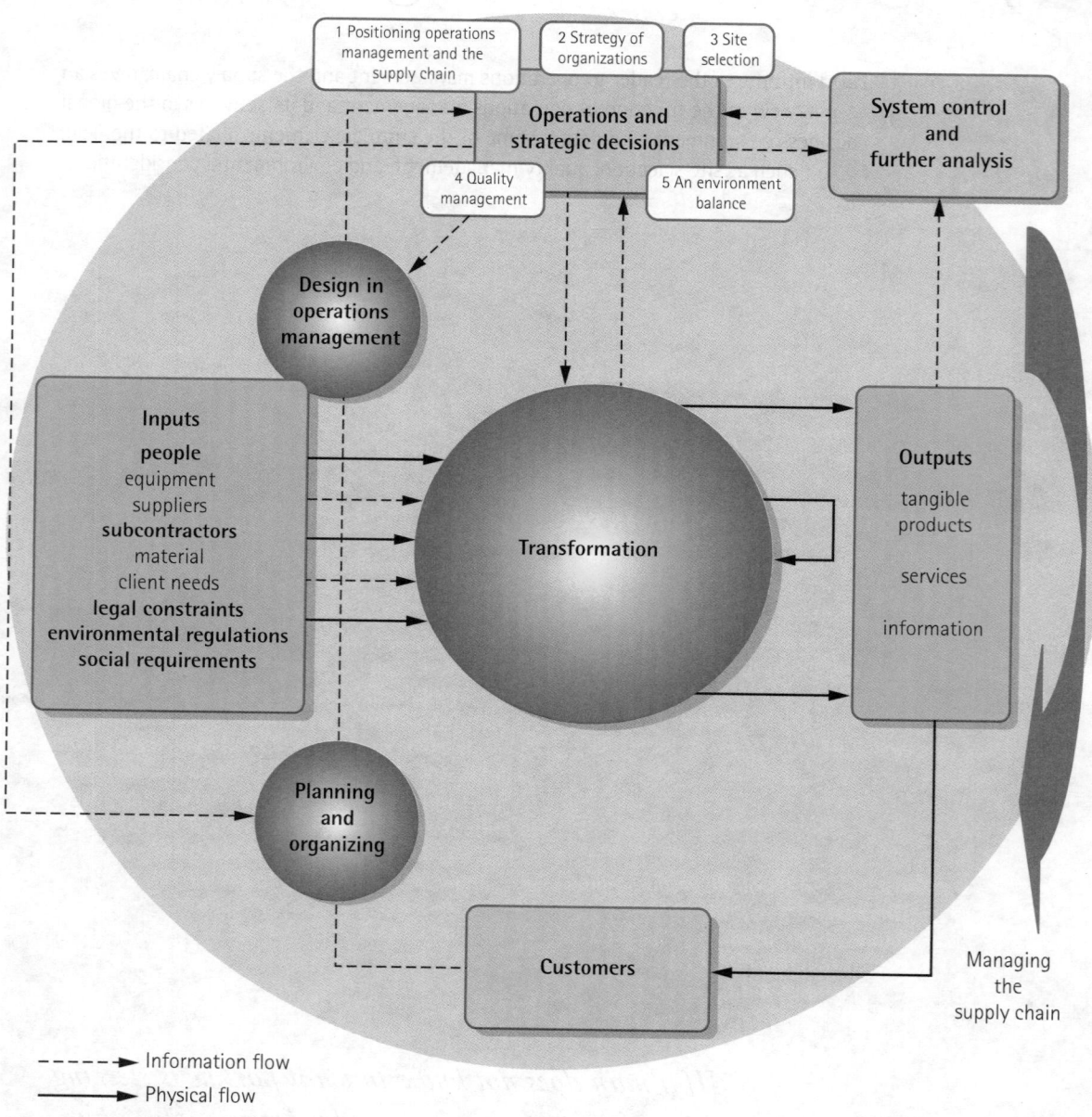

- - - - - ► Information flow
———————► Physical flow

1 *Positioning operations management and the supply chain*

Chapter overview

- **Defining operations management and the supply chain**
- **Classification of operating systems**
- **Operations are international**
- **Employment in operations**
- **Model of operations**
- **Productivity**
- **Management activities in operations**
- **Systems approach to operations**
- **Technology**

Defining operations management and the supply chain

Scope of operations management

We are constantly confronted with the operations environment. The daily repetitive activity from waking, showering, dressing, feeding the dog, reading the newspaper, having breakfast, dropping the children off at school, and catching the train to work represent several interrelated operations. Sometimes many of us try to *manage* these activities by optimizing, or minimizing the time necessary so that we can sleep in as late as possible, and still arrive to work on time! Further, the bed you sleep in, the water for washing, the clothes we wear, the breakfast we eat, the veterinary service for the dog, the news we hear on the radio, the newspaper that is delivered, the school the children attend, the train schedule for the commute, these are all products originating from the operations management environment.

The subject of operations management covers the effective planning, organizing, and control of all the resources and activities necessary to provide the market with tangible goods and services. The operations activities are vast and apply to manufacturing industries, and service firms in the private sector as well as non-profit organizations, and even to governments.

The integrated supply chain

An integrated supply chain model can generally be considered as containing three interrelated flow streams as illustrated in Figure 1.1. The first is a material flow stream which itself has three distinct stages: purchasing, transformation, and distribution. Purchasing is the buying from suppliers and/or subcontractors of the necessary raw materials, components and services. Transformation is the manufacturing and assembly in work centres of these raw materials and components into finished goods. These two stages together are often considered under the umbrella of materials management. The third stage in this material flow chain is the distribution of the finished product to the client and is often referred to as business logistics or physical distribution management.

The supply chain may be very complex with many subcontractors and suppliers, who may be located overseas and a long way from the final assembly plant. This is the case, for example, in the automobile, aircraft, computer, and chemical industries. Within the supply chain are business-to-business links and business-to-consumer links. In the automobile industry, for example, a chemical company would supply the plastic for making the fuel tank to an equipment manufacturer. This is a business-to-business link. The maker of this fuel tank would then supply his product to the automobile manufacturer, another business-to-business link. The automobile manufacturer, through a

Figure 1.1 **The supply chain**

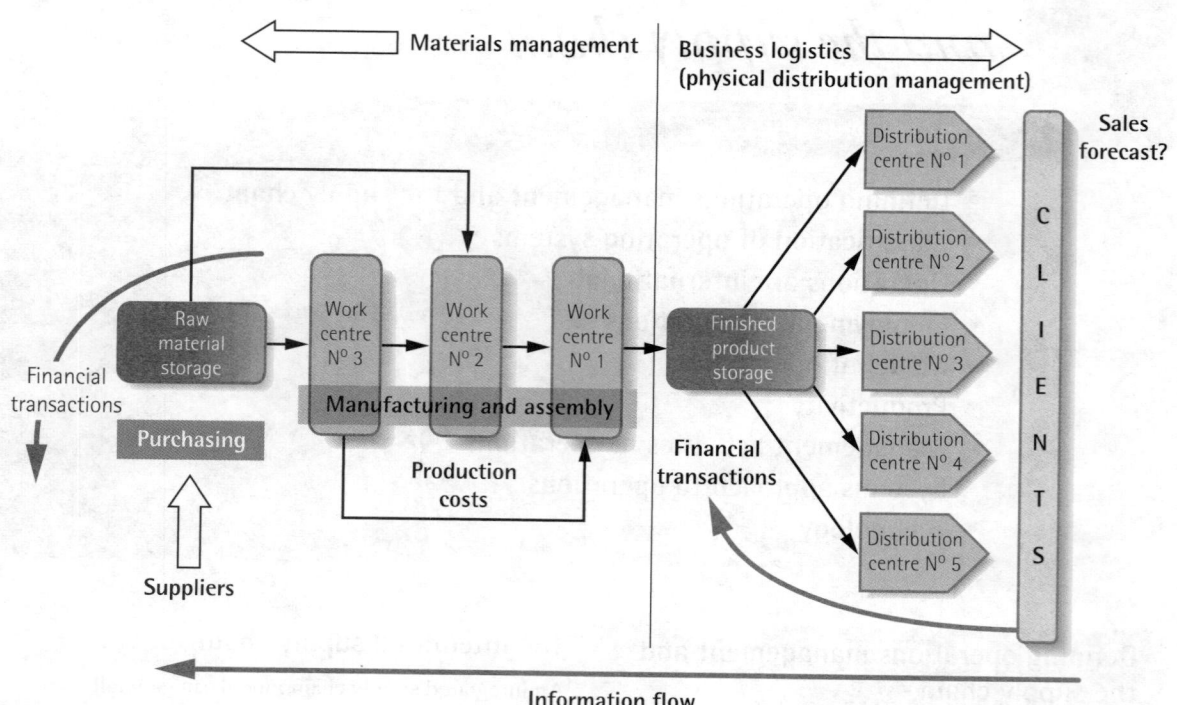

distributor, would then sell an automobile to a client. This is the business-to-consumer link.

Another flow stream in the supply chain, usually in reverse to the physical flow, is the information stream that specifies the needs and requirements of the purchasers, manufacturers, distributors and clients. Very often this information flow is by electronic data interchange (EDI) or website linkages. Finally, the third stream in the supply chain are the financial flows, which include the payment to suppliers and subcontractors for the goods and services and payment by the consumer to the retailer for the final product. In many instances these external financial flows occur using a global EDI system. In addition, internal to the firm are other financial flows such as the payment of employee salaries, which are necessary to keep the firm running.

Linkage supply chain and operations

Within each phase of the integrated supply chain are numerous operations necessary to keep the activity functioning efficiently. This is conceptualized in Figure 1.2, where the umbrella represents the supply chain that envelops the three stages of purchasing,

transformation, and distribution. Within these three stages are numerous operational activities such as sourcing, subcontractor selection, quality control in purchasing, operations planning and layout in transformation, and warehousing and transportation in distribution, etc. (These activities are covered in detail in subsequent chapters.) The three most important challenges to a firm are probably quality products, promised delivery times, and acceptable costs (or prices) so it is obvious that poor management or control of any of these operations can have a considerable impact on the performance of the integrated supply chain. The link operations and supply chain is critical when we consider that most business firms today are international and may have perhaps between 80 and 90% of their work performed by subcontractors, many of those, furthermore, located in other countries.

It is true that the supply chain is perhaps better conceptualized in manufacturing since there is physical flow of goods. However, a supply chain is very much present in the service sector such as airlines, financial institutions, consulting companies, distribution firms, retail outlets etc. which to be successful rely on timely information flow through a sophisticated communications network.

Figure 1.2 Operations and the supply chain

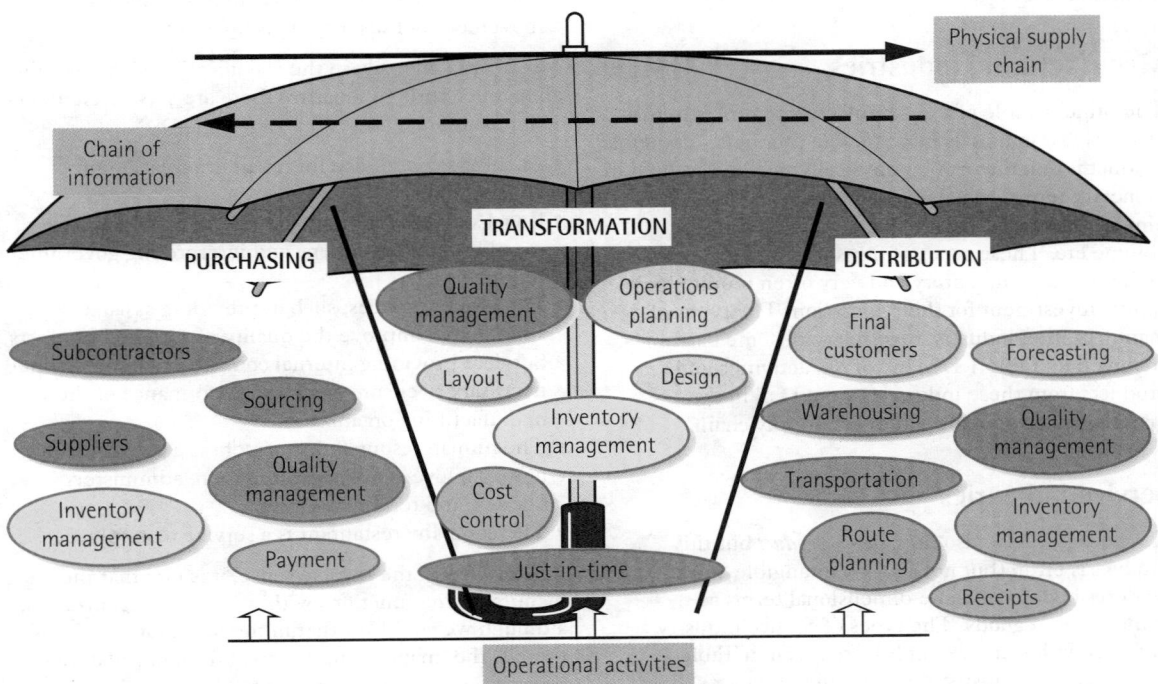

Serving the client

The ultimate driving force in a market-driven firm is to make a satisfactory profit, which implies satisfying the client. The client expects to have the product delivered at the right time, at an acceptable quality, at a reasonable price, and courteously. Even in a non-profit organization or government, although there is no commercial gain, there is a client. The client should be considered king!

Importance of operations management

Not far upstream of the client is the operations manager who has the responsibility of producing the product for the client. This might be a packaged holiday from a travel organization, an MBA course from a teaching institution, a sports car from an automobile manufacturer, or a medical procedure in a hospital. If the operations management function is not performed correctly, then the client will not be satisfied. Although operations management is often taught as an isolated subject, in practice it should be totally integrated with other business functions:

- In operations you must control the cost and this is where cost accounting plays a role.

- In all operations capital investment is required for the machinery, equipment, and buildings and so financial accounting is important.
- In operations you need motivated and productive people and this is the link with human resource management.
- Products that are made by operations have to conform to the customer requirements and hence the strong link with marketing.
- The operations of the firm are driven by the strategy of the organization hence there has to be a strong synergy between operations management and strategic management. For example, if a firm has a strategy to increase market share it has to have in place an effective operation in order to produce the right products that will satisfy the market.
- The operations of the firm have to abide by the current laws including worker safety, working hours, rules impacting the ecological environment, etc.

Classification of operating systems

Operations management covers market-driven firms, and non-profit organizations. The market-driven firms can be divided into manufacturing and service industries as follows.

Manufacturing industries

The principal role of the manufacturing firm is to turn physical raw materials into tangible products. A tangible product is one that can be physically touched, valued in monetary terms, visualized, and described by dimensional terms such as weight, length, height, volume etc. These types of firms use, and generate, a high volume of inventory and very often require high capital investment for their operation. The types of manufacturing industry, together with some examples, are given in Table 1.1. Many of the activities and products from these industries would fall in the materials management part of the supply chain.

Service industries

A service industry also provides a *product* but this product is often (but not always) intangible and cannot be described in the same dimensional terms as manufactured goods. The types of service industry, together with some examples, are given in Table 1.2. In the service industry, there is generally more client contact in all phases of the operating environment than there is in manufacturing. For example, the personnel in medical services, restaurants, and hotels have client contact on a continuing basis. This is not the case in the production of automobiles, the brewing industry, or light bulb manufacture, for example, where the client only makes an appearance on delivery of the finished product or perhaps at the start of the operation if the product is of new design. This client differentiation characteristic often gives a secondary classification in operations where those persons in services are more people oriented, as opposed to those in manufacturing where there is usually a higher proportion of technicians and engineers.

Classification anomalies

The separation of manufacturing and services is clearly not a black and white matter. Some service firms violate the *intangible product* rule as illustrated below:

- Engineering and construction service firms build bridges, oil refineries, and commercial complexes. These products can be touched, visualized, and have dimensions.
- Food service firms, or restaurants, provide meals or *inventory* that can be touched.
- Distribution firms handle finished goods inventory.

- Retail stores are service organizations involved in the sale of tangible end products that is to say, the movement of finished goods inventory.

A further anomaly in the classification is that within all manufacturing industries there are service elements, as for example:

- An after-sales service for repair or replacement of faulty products.
- Legal services for employee rights, problems with suppliers and customers, and interpreting government regulations.
- Purchasing services, such as providing assistance to suppliers to improve the quality of supplied products.
- Services providing internal company training deemed necessary to ensure effective performance of the manufacturing organization.
- The human resource department is a service. It hires new employees, follows promotion, administers salaries, and terminates people.
- The company restaurant is a service to employees.

However, in the reverse sense, it is rare that there are manufacturing functions within a service organization, although we could say that in the restaurant business there is the 'manufacture' of food from raw materials (bread, cakes, cooked meats, etc.).

Thus, since in many cases it is difficult to put business distinctly in one category or another, they might also be considered on a continuum where one moves from pure services such as insurance, to steel production, which is almost pure manufacturing as illustrated in Figure 1.3.

Not-for-profit organizations

In addition to market-driven operations, the economy also includes numerous not-for-profit (or non-profit) organizations, which for the most part are service organizations. Here the driving force is a desire to do good rather than to serve any commercial interest. However, although non-profit organizations are not constrained by the profit motive, they are nevertheless operations that need to be managed to use resources effectively, and to serve the end users of the services at a reasonable cost.

Not-for-profit organizations can be broadly classified into two groups. The first group includes those directly, or indirectly managed by national and local governments and are usually funded by tax receipts. The second group are those allowed a non-profit status by government because they serve the public at large to educate, inform, provide healthcare, support cultural events, provide social services, etc., which is something private industry is unable or not equipped to provide.

Table 1.1 Manufacturing firms according to industry

Manufacturing industry	Example
Aerospace	Airbus (France), Boeing, Bombardier (Canada)
Apparel	Benneton (Italy), Berkshire Hathaway, Levi Strauss
Beverages	Coca-Cola, Cadbury-Schweppes (UK), Heineken (Netherlands)
Building materials/glass	Corning, Pilkington (UK), Saint-Gobain (France)
Chemicals	Du Pont, Hoechst (Germany), ICI (UK)
Computers	Hewlett-Packard/Compaq, IBM, Dell
Electronics/electrical	Electrolux (Sweden), General Electric, Hitachi (Japan)
Food	Danône (France), General Mills, Nestlé (Switzerland)
Forest and paper	Fletcher Challenge (New Zealand), Stora (Sweden), Weyerhaeuser
Industrial/farm equipment	Caterpillar, Deere, Thyssen (Germany)
Jewellery and silverware	Citizen Watch (Japan), Seiko (Japan)
Metal products	Pechiney (France), Sandvik (Sweden), Sumitomo Electric (Japan)
Metals	Alcoa, Kobe Steel (Japan), Arcelor (France)
Mining	CRA (Australia), De Beers (South Africa), RTZ (UK)
Mobile phones	Ericsson (Sweden), Motorola, Nokia (Finland)
Motor vehicles	Daimler-Chrysler (Germany), Ford, General Motors, Toyota (Japan)
Petroleum refining	Exxon-Mobil, BP-Amoco (UK), Shell (UK/Netherlands)
Pharmaceuticals	Bristol-Myers Squibb, Glaxo-Wellcome (UK), Novartis (Switzerland)
Publishing and printing	Pearson (UK), Thomson (Canada), Reed Elsevier (UK/Netherlands)
Rubber and plastics	Firestone/Bridgestone (Japan), Goodyear, Michelin (France)
Scientific and photographic	Fuji Film (Japan), Kodak, Xerox
Soaps and cosmetics	Colgate-Palmolive, Henkel (Germany) L'Oréal (France)
Textiles	DMC (France), Coats Viyella (UK), Haci Ömer Sabanci (Turkey)
Tobacco	BAT Industries (UK), Philip Morris, RJR Nabisco
Toys	Nintendo (Japan), Yamaha (Japan)
Transportation equipment	Hyundai (South Korea), Kvaerner (Norway), Schlindler (Switzerland)
(Country of non-US firms in the parentheses)	

Funding for these groups might come from donations, foundations, revenue-generating activities within the organization, or partial government funding. Although these organizations may make a *net income*, all this income is ploughed back into the organization to offset costs and to benefit the service user.

Examples of organizations in these two categories are given in the following sections. The distinction is not

Table 1.2 Service firms according to industry

Service industry	Example
Airlines	British Airways (UK), Lufthansa (Germany), United Airlines
Banking	Citicorp, Crédit Suisse (Switzerland), Deutsche Bank (Germany)
Computer software	Microsoft, Oracle, SAP (Germany)
Diversified financials	American Express, ING (Netherlands), Morgan Stanley Dean Witter
Engineering/construction	Bechtel, Bouygues (France), Fluor, Technip (France)
Entertainment	AOL-Time Warner, Disney, Viacom
Food stores	Albertson, Carrefour (France), Ahold (Netherlands), Tesco (UK)
General merchandisers	K-Mart, Marks & Spencer (UK), Migros (Switzerland), Wal-Mart
Healthcare	Columbia/HCA Healthcare, Pacificare, United Healthcare
Hotels	Accor (France), Bass (UK), Marriot International
Insurance	Aetna, AXA (France), Prudential (UK), Sun Life (Canada)
Mail/package delivery	Deutsche Post (Germany), Federal Express, La Poste (France), UPS
Rail transportation	Burlington Northern Santa Fe, Deutsche Bahn (Germany), SNCF (France)
Restauration	Eurorest (France), Burger King (UK), Mcdonald's
Shipping	Stena Lines (Sweden), Peninsular & Orient (UK)
Telecommunications	AT&T, France Télécom (France), MCI, Vodaphone (UK)
Trading	Hyundai (South Korea), Misui (Japan), SHV Holdings (Netherlands)
Utilities	British Gas (UK), Duke Energy, EDF (France) PG&E
Waste management	WMX Technologies

(Country of non-US firms is in parentheses)

Figure 1.3 Content of the service function in business

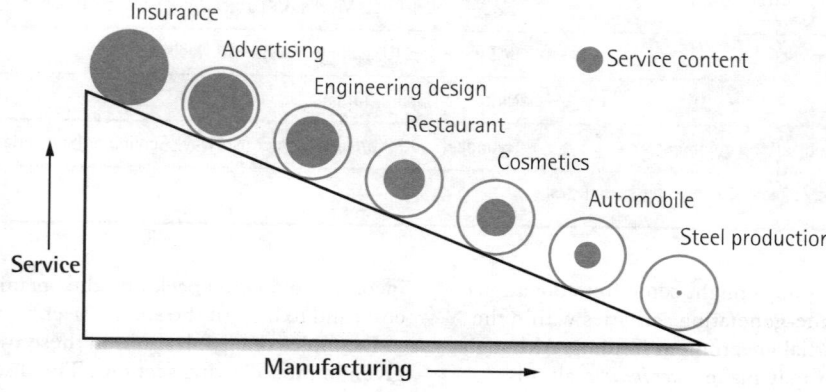

always clear-cut as for example some non-profit organizations may have their operations influenced by governments, particularly if they receive some government funding. Universities would be an example. Contrariwise, some government agencies might be relatively independent of government control. The United Nations, although entirely funded by governments, makes decisions entirely independently of governments.

Government or quasi-government

- Agencies within governments, such as those regulating transportation, trade, environmental, industrial, and transportation safety policies.
- Groups that provide personal safety such as the police, US Federal Bureau of Investigation (FBI), or the International Criminal Police Organization (Interpol).
- Health services and hospitals. (In the USA, some are 'for-profit' organizations.)
- Military services including the army, air force, and navy.
- National, state, and local governments themselves.
- North Atlantic Treaty Organization (NATO).
- Peace corps.
- Police, fire, and ambulance services.
- Postal service.
- Rail and bus services (in some countries).
- Schools (some are private and although having a similar curriculum are non-profit).
- United Nations Organization (UN).
- World Health Organization (WHO).

Non-profit status

- Boy and Girl Scouts' organizations.
- Humanitarian organizations such as the Salvation Army and the Red Cross.
- Libraries.
- Museums and cultural centres.
- Religious groups such as the Catholic and Protestant churches.
- Sports events such as the Olympic movement.
- The British Council.
- Town and village cultural centres that provide sport and cultural activities for the community.
- Universities (depending on the country these may be controlled by government).

Economic classification of operations

Economists divide operations including manufacturing, services and non-profit activities according to the following economic triad.

Primary sector

The primary sector covers extraction of primary mineral resources such as oil, coal, gold, and silver, and also agricultural activities such as wheat farming, cattle rearing, and fruit growing. Mineral extraction is classed as manufacturing, however farming is very often considered as a distinct operation separate from industrial activity.

Secondary sector

The secondary sector involves the transformation of primary resources into manufactured products. This might be steel into automobiles or washing machines, gold into jewellery, crude oil into gasoline or chemicals, wheat into bread, milk into yoghurt, and cattle into hamburgers, etc.

Tertiary sector

The tertiary sector covers activities where there is no transformation of material in the classic sense. In the market-driven firm this would include transportation, travel, distribution, and financial activities. Economists sometimes include not-for-profit organizations, as just described, in the tertiary sector.

Operations are international

Changes in the business environment

The operations environment has an increasing international content. Some of the reasons for this include the following:

- The reduction in trade barriers brought about by the creation of such entities as the European Union (EU) with its current 15 members, or the North Atlantic Free Trade Association (NAFTA) between the USA, Canada, and Mexico.
- Foreign labour is often less expensive than in industrialized countries such as the USA, Japan, Germany, Britain, France, Italy, and Canada.
- Domestic markets are saturated so that new markets are being developed away from the home country.
- The international transport of goods, services, and people has become easier, and cheaper. Road, rail, and air networks have mushroomed since 1950 and the cost has fallen in real terms.
- Relative stability and the democratization of the world have increased communication and the acceptance of new products and services.

Manufacturing firms

As conceptualized in Figure 1.4, a manufacturing firm may have:

- headquarters in New York, that provide top management and support services
- manufacturing facilities in Argentina, Ukraine, and Singapore

- product distribution centres in central USA, Columbia, Norway, and Western Australia
- purchasing activities in China and the Philippines
- clients throughout South America, California, Europe, eastern and western Europe.

The real-world international extent of manufacturing firms is illustrated in Industry insights 1.1, 1.2, and 1.3.

Figure 1.4 Operations are international

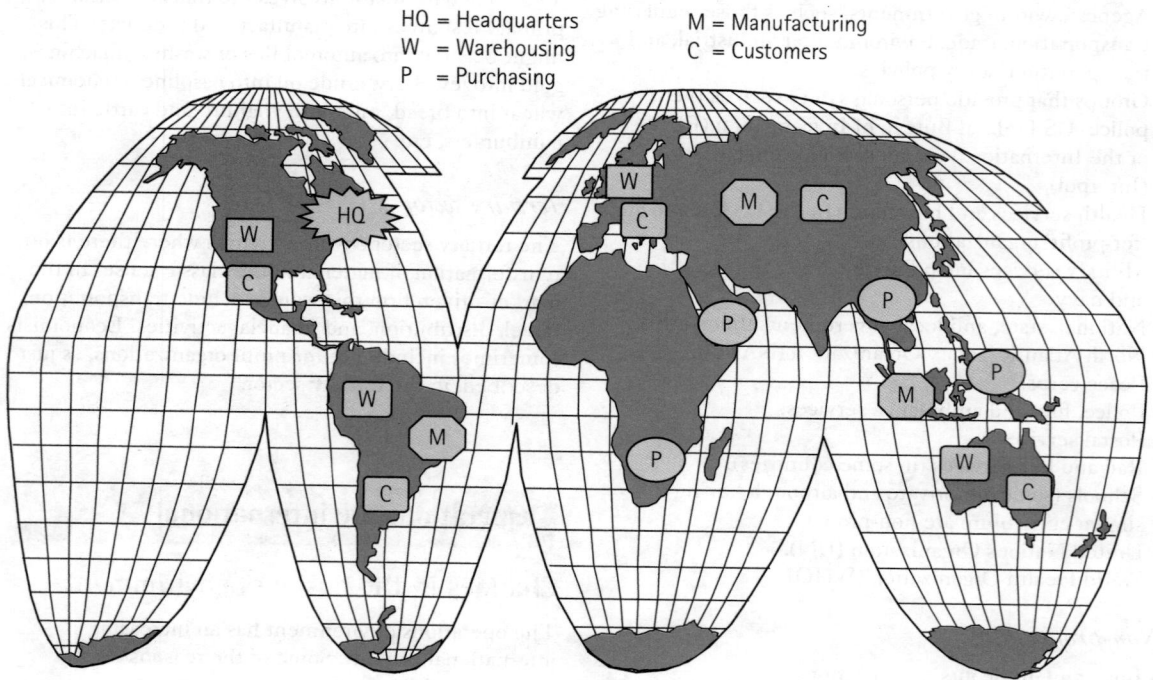

HQ = Headquarters
W = Warehousing
P = Purchasing

M = Manufacturing
C = Customers

ExxonMobil

Industry insight 1.1

ExxonMobil is the world's largest integrated oil company. It has upstream drilling activities for oil and gas in some 50 countries. Some of the major offshore discoveries in 2000 were in the Gulf of Mexico, Brazil, Trinidad, Azerbaijan, Angola, Norway, and in the Northwest Shelf of Australia. It has continuing production operations in Texas and Louisiana in the USA, in Canada in association with its majority-owned affiliate, Imperial Oil Ltd., including the provinces of Alberta and Newfoundland. In South America it produces in Argentina, Brazil, Venezuela, and Bolivia. It is present in the North Sea working in the British and Norwegian sectors plus in the Netherlands on the large Groningen

gas field. In Africa it has interests in Nigeria, Equatorial Guinea, Chad, Algeria, Cameroon, Egypt, Niger, and the Republic of Congo. Its activities in the vast Middle East reserves include Qatar, Abu Dhabi, Kuwait, and Saudi Arabia. There is growing activity in the former Soviet Union including Kazakhstan, Azerbaijan, Sakhalin Island, and Turkmenistan. In the Far East it is present in Indonesia, Australia, and Papua New Guinea.

Downstream in oil refining and distribution, ExxonMobil has ownership of 46 refineries in 26 countries. This includes seven in the USA, four in Canada, 12 in Europe, three in Saudi Arabia, five in Japan, six in the Far East, four in Africa, four in

South America and one in Martinique. At yearend 2000, the refining capacity was 6.2 million barrels a day and a lubricating oil capacity of 146 thousand barrels a day. In distribution, it has 64 crude oil and petroleum product tankers, over 25,000 miles of pipeline, and 320 major petroleum products terminals. ExxonMobil markets gasoline and other fuel products in 118 countries with 45,000 service stations worldwide. It has aviation facilities in more than 700 airports in 80 countries. Further, it has over one million industrial and wholesale customers around the globe and sells marine fuels at more than 300 ports in 70 countries.

Adapted from: ExxonMobil 2000, Financial and Operating Review[1]

The Boeing Company

Industry insight 1.2

The Boeing Company, based in Chicago, is the largest aerospace company and the world's largest manufacturer of commercial jetliners and military aircraft. It is also the USA's largest NASA contractor. In terms of sales, Boeing is the largest US exporter. Total company revenues for 2000 were $51 billion. The global reach of the company includes customers in 145 countries, employees in more than 60 countries and operations in 26 states. Worldwide, Boeing and its subsidiaries employed more than 198,000 people in 2000 having major production operations in the Seattle–Puget Sound area of Washington state, Southern California, Wichita, Kansas, and St Louis, Missouri. Boeing is organized into six major units which include Commercial Airplanes; Space and Communications; Military Aircraft and Missiles; Shared Services; Air Traffic Management; Connexion by Boeing[SM] and Boeing Capital Corporation.

Boeing has been the world leader in commercial flight for more than 40 years. The main commercial products consist of the 717, 737, 747, 757, 767, and 777 families of jetliners and the Boeing Business Jet. The company has more than 11,000 commercial jetliners in service worldwide. Boeing provides unsurpassed, round-the-clock technical support to help operators maintain their airplanes in peak operating conditions through its Boeing Customer Support unit. In addition, Boeing Airplane Services offers a full range of world-class engineering, modification, and logistics services to its global customer base. This includes the world's passenger and cargo airlines as well as maintenance, repair, and overhaul facilities. Boeing also provides training for maintenance and flight crews in the 100-seat and over airliner market through Flight Safety Boeing Training International, the world's largest and most comprehensive airline-training provider.

Adapted from: Boeing Overview[2]

Siemens

Industry insight 1.3

Siemens, with headquarters in Munich, Germany employs nearly 460,000 employees in over 190 countries. Its net income in 2000 was DM7.9 billion. Siemens is a leading manufacturer of high-technology industrial and consumer equipment. Its products include gas turbines, control systems, and transmission equipment for power generation; automatic and robotics equipment for industrial use such as automatic letter-sorting machines, and bottling machine systems; telecommunications equipment including telephones, networks, Internet applications, and server systems; transportation equipment such as the tramways used in Lisbon, Portugal, and Vienna; X-ray and echography testing equipment used in the medical field; semiconductors for the television and computer industry; and lighting and household equipment in collaboration with Bosch, another German company.

Siemens has worldwide manufacturing facilities in the United States, Canada, Venezuela, Columbia, Argentina, Brazil, South Africa, India, China, Australia, Russia, Turkey, and almost every country in Europe. In addition to the manufacturing sites, it has sales offices in just about every country of the world.

Adapted from: Siemens Corporate Overview[3]

Service firms

Major service firms survive simply by being international with offices, activities, and communication networks worldwide. Excerpt summaries of activities are illustrated by Industry insights 1.4, 1.5, and 1.6.

British Airways

In air transportation, British Airways is one of the world leaders for business and holiday travel. Its principal operations are based out of London's Heathrow and Gatwick airports in the south of England. At Manchester International Airport it has a substantial operation to serve customers in the northwest of England. The operation of flying airplanes encompasses numerous other operating activities from route planning, aircraft maintenance, restaurant services, booking, charter holiday travel, refuelling logistics, weather operations, cleaning, inventory management of parts, and the human resources element in dealing with passengers.

In addition to operating in its own right, British Airways global activities are aided by multinational alliances and franchises. This includes linkups with Aer Lingus (Ireland), American Airlines, America West Airlines, Cathay Pacific (Hong Kong), Crossair (Switzerland), Deutsche BA (Germany), Emirates, Finnair (Finland), Iberia (Spain), Lanchile (Chile), Lot Polish Airlines, Malev Hungarian Airlines, and Qantas (Australia). British Airways global operations, including its alliances, cover all the five continents to 474 scheduled destinations in 103 countries.[4]

Adapted from: British Airways[5]

Accor

In the hotel and restaurant service area, Accor of France also ranks as one of the world's leaders. In 2000 its revenues were € 7007 million, an increase of 14.8% from the previous period, and it employed 140,000 people in 140 countries. As of August 2001 it operated or controlled 3608 hotels with a total of 402,447 rooms in 90 countries. This included 1227 hotels in North America, 139 in South America, 1247 in France, 665 in the rest of Europe, 145 in Africa and the Middle East and 185 in the Asia-Pacific region. Its hotels in the economy and budget market include Formule 1, Motel 6, Etap Hotel, Red Roof Inns, and Ibis. In the mid-scale and upscale hotels it has Suitehotel, Mercure, Novotel, and Sofitel. As far as the operation of the hotels is concerned, 31% are group owned, 19% are under Accor management, 15% are franchised, and 35% are rented.

Other activities besides hotels include tourism, restaurants and casinos through its Carlson Wagonlit travel, Accor Tour, Frantour, Lenôtre, Compagnie des Wagon-Lits, and Accor Casinos. Accor Services, another branch of the firm, is present in 31 countries and realizes services such as food vouchers or restaurant tickets; Expense Management which helps businesses simplify the management of its operating expenses; and Social Services enabling public authorities to ensure efficient distribution of ticket services, milk tokens, service cards etc.

Adapted from: Accor Worldwide[6]

Crédit Suisse

Crédit Suisse, based in Zurich, Switzerland, is a world leading financial service groups with operating activities on every continent, and in all the world's major financial centres. In 2000 it had a net profit of SF5.8 billion ($3.6) up 11% from the previous year. Its worldwide staff as of 31 December 2000 was 80,000.

The Crédit Suisse Group is made up of four business units. Financial Services, which provides banking services to individual and corporate clients throughout Europe in 235 locations. Through its Winterthur Insurance subsidiary it provides health, accident, and life insurance in Europe and North America. It has a technology and services division within the financial services business unit where it provides IT service for the whole of the Crédit Suisse Group and is one of the largest software developers in Switzerland. The second business unit is Crédit Suisse Private Banking, which provides portfolio management and financial advice for high-net-worth clients worldwide. It has 48 operating units in Switzerland, and 42 locations elsewhere serving 300,000 clients. The third business unit is Crédit Suisse First Boston with three locations in Switzerland, and 95 internationally. This unit offers integrated services covering securities underwriting, sales and trading, investment and merchant banking and venture capital. The fourth business unit is Crédit Suisse Asset Management, which focuses on institutional mutual funds and private client investors in Switzerland, Europe, the Americas, Australia, and Japan.

Adapted from: The Crédit Suisse Group[7]

World Health Organization

The global objectives of the World Health Organization (WHO) include the attainment by all people of the highest level of health. Its operations involve assisting governments in providing technical assistance and emergency medical aid to governments, to establish international standards for biological and pharmaceutical products, to standardize diagnostic procedures, and to aid in the prevention and control of epidemic, endemic, and other diseases. Notable successes in this area have been the global eradication of smallpox, and the control and near-eradication of polio, guinea-worm disease, and leprosy.

WHO was established in 1946 after the United Nations agreed on the formation of an autonomous international health organization. The headquarters of the organization are in Geneva, Switzerland, and there are regional offices in Harare, Zimbabwe; Washington, DC, USA; Cairo, Egypt; Copenhagen, Denmark; New Delhi, India; Manila, Philippines; Kobe, Japan; and Lyon, France. As of 2001 there were 191 member countries, which included 45 in Africa, 35 in the Americas, ten in South-East Asia, 51 in Europe, 24 in the Eastern Mediterranean, and 27 in the Western Pacific region. For the period 1998–1999 the budget of WHO was $1.8 million which originated from member states (countries) and voluntary funding.

Adapted from: The World Health Organization[8]

Non-profit organizations

The arm of many non-profit organizations is worldwide if one considers, for example, the Catholic Church, NATO, the Salvation Army, and the Red Cross. Industry insight 1.7 gives the international scope of the World Health Organization.

Products are international

Besides the actual operations of a firm many of the manufactured products have international input even though they are assembled and sold in one country. As an illustration, Table 1.3 gives the different countries that supply some of the component parts for the Ford Escort assembled and marketed principally in Britain.[9]

Foreign sales and country size

Another characteristic concerning the international aspect of firms is that many of them, based in small countries, generate a large portion of their revenues internationally. As an illustration, of the world's biggest multinational firms, Nestlé (foods), Switzerland, Philips (electronics), Netherlands, and Asea Brown Boveri, (industrial equipment), also of Switzerland, generate some 90% of their revenues away from their home base. Japanese companies also obtain large portions of their revenue outside Japan. US companies, by way of contrast, although they have many big multinational firms, possess a bigger domestic market than European, or Japanese firms, and generally, with the exception of oil firms, generate a smaller proportion of their revenues overseas.

Table 1.3 **Supply of components for the Ford Escort**

Country of supply	Components supplied
Denmark	Cooling and air conditioning belts
The Netherlands	Tyres, paint, control systems
Switzerland	Carpeting, speedometer
Norway	Straps for exhaust system, tyres
Germany	Pistons, cylinder bolts, steering column
Austria	Tyres, radiator and heating lines
Japan	Starter, alternator, bearings
USA	Catalytic converter, wheel bolts, windows
Belgium	Inner tubes, seat cushions, brakes and linings
Sweden	Tubular columns, cylinder bolts, stamped sections
Italy	Engine block, carburettor, lights, de-icing system
Spain	Radiator and heater leads, air filters, batteries, rear mirrors
France	Master cylinder, brakes, gear box casing, waterproof joints
Canada	Windows, radio
Great Britain	Oil pumps, heating system, direction indicators, gasoline tank, steering wheel

Employment in operations

Manufacturing employment

In both Europe and the United States employment in manufacturing grew rapidly from the early 1800s as people moved from farming into industry. In the USA in the late 1800s, the principal industries included iron and steel destined for locomotives and railroad construction. In the early 1900s the automobile was born from manufacturing firms like General Motors and Ford of the USA, Daimler of Germany, and Panhard and Levassor of France. Labour demand in manufacturing continued to increase markedly through to the end of World War II, after which the growth rate declined. From about the early 1980s the absolute level of employment in manufacturing in the USA has declined (see Figure 1.5). In 2000 only about 30% of the labour force was employed in manufacturing, down from some 75% in 1939.[10]

Manufacturing output

Even though manufacturing employment in the USA has declined, manufacturing output has continued to increase, as illustrated in Figure 1.6. In the 50 years between 1950 and 2000 manufacturing output has increased by a factor of four and in the 20 years between 1980 and 2000 output has doubled. The principal reason for this is new technological developments, which have improved the efficiency of manufacturing and assembly operations, and also the fact that automated equipment has significantly replaced a large proportion of labour in manufacturing.

Service industries

Compared to manufacturing, service industries in the USA have grown very rapidly, absorbing a large portion of the labour force to manufacturing's detriment. This phenomenon is illustrated in Figure 1.5 and also in Figure 1.7. In 1982 employment in the service industries surpassed that in manufacturing and by 2000 almost 70% of the labour force was employed in services. Most notably these include the travel industry, financial services and medical care, partly as a result of the ageing population.

European Union and Japan

The employment profiles for the European Union and Japan follow similar trends as presented for the United States, in that service industries have either surpassed manufacturing as far as employment is concerned or are very close to it. (Britain now makes more money from its pop groups than it does from the steel industry.) Similar to the USA, technology has increased manufacturing output even though the absolute level of manufacturing employment has declined.

Developing regions

Developing regions, notably the Far East, Latin American countries, and former eastern European countries, have increased their manufacturing output. This is either because European and USA countries have moved some of their production operations to these low labour cost countries (see Chapter 3), or because the countries themselves have established their own manufacturing operations and have developed alternatives to US and European products as illustrated in Industry insight 1.8.

Figure 1.5 Employment levels in the USA

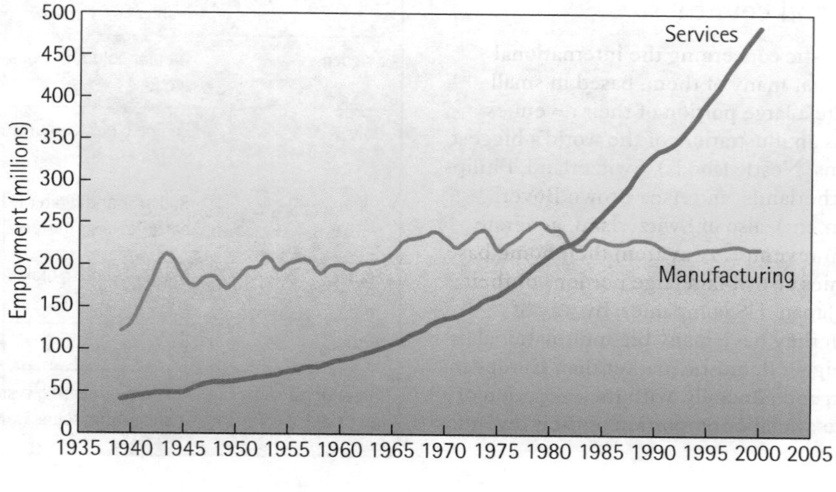

Figure 1.6 Manufacturing employment and output in the USA

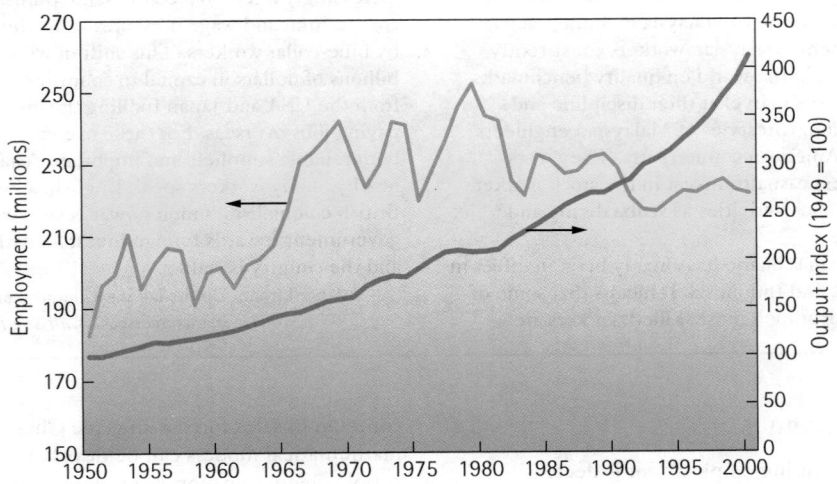

Figure 1.7 Proportion of US labour force in services and manufacturing

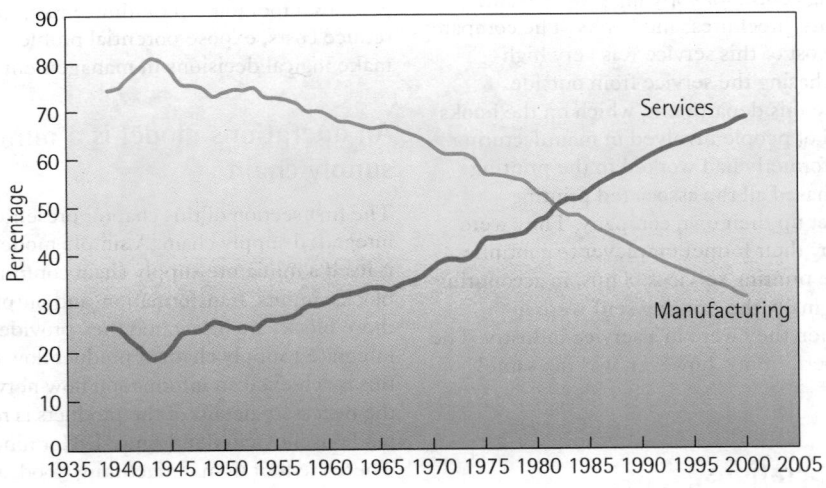

Industry insight 1.8

Brain drain from the USA

Yoon Chong Leong runs a team of Hewlett-Packard Co. engineers at its plant in Penang, Malaysia, and also at a Boise, Idaho, plant some halfway around the globe in the USA. When HP established itself in Penang in 1974 people expected Malaysia to be an unequal partner. Now US people work for Malaysians. American multinationals like HP came to Malaysia mainly for low wages but now they have bred a fast growing class of professionals and high-skilled technicians equivalent to the US labour force. Since the plant opened it has become more automated and autonomous. It no longer relies on US pilot lines or engineering support to solve production and design problems.

Intel Corp. also typifies the new Malaysia where its Penang factory has tripled its output over the last ten years with no increase in the labour force. One in every six is an engineer compared to one in 40 in 1980. Locals run every part of the plant. Further, design jobs, once the sole province of the Santa Clara, California, offices, have also come to Malaysia including new chip development. Malaysian workers consistently rank the highest in the world on quality benchmarks and US executives marvel at their discipline and group orientation. Lifestyles of Malaysian engineers emulate their American counterparts. They work long hours, dress casually, invest in the stock market, and relax with such activities as scuba diving and jogging.

The Malaysian scenario has already been in effect in Taiwan, China, and Indonesia. It means that some of America's and Europe's most skilled workers are increasingly likely to face the same punishing competition and wage pressures from abroad already felt by blue-collar workers. This shift in work is sending billions of dollars in capital to countries such as Malaysia from the USA and Japan fuelling the growth of high-paying jobs overseas. For these overseas operations, both reliable suppliers and important Asian markets are nearby; many workers speak English, a holdover from British colonialism; union power is very weak; the government rewards foreign investors with tax breaks; and the country is stable.

Adapted from: 'Up the ladder: US multinationals take brain work to plants overseas', *Wall Street Journal Europe*[11]

Accounting changes

Although manufacturing employment is decreasing, structural changes in companies also have modified the method of accounting for labour levels. For example, a large manufacturing company in the USA had a significant printing centre for copying, printing, and binding documents, brochures, and books. The company realized that the cost of this service was very high compared to purchasing the service from outside. It decided to close this department, which on the books reduced the level of people involved in manufacturing. Employees who formerly had worked in the printing department purchased all the associated printing equipment and set up their own company. They were then contracted by their former employer to continue performing all the printing services. Thus, in accounting employment, originally the printing staff were in manufacturing, then they were in a service industry. The work they were performing, however, was the same!

Model of operations

Models in management

A model is a representation of reality. In addition to a diagrammatic flow model there are physical models to help in design, production, or construction such as a model of a nuclear reactor, a skyscraper, or an airplane whose flight behaviour can be tested in a wind tunnel. A model might be a three-dimensional computer display using CAD systems such as used in automobile design and plant construction. There are also quantitative models, which use historical data, or assumed values to develop a mathematical model, which can then be used to estimate future values. Mathematical models are very common in sales forecasting (see Chapter 10) but other mathematical models can be developed to simulate the supply chain, transportation routes, inventory movements, or financial movements such as illustrated by pro-forma income statements. Whatever the type of model, its purpose is to present the system and also perhaps a tool to help minimize risk, improve planning, reduce costs, expose potential problems, and to help make logical decisions in management.

An operations model is a miniature supply chain

The first section of this chapter presented a model for an integrated supply chain. A simple model for any operation is itself a miniature supply chain comprising three basic blocks: inputs, transformation, and outputs. When all these blocks are integrated they provide the network or integrated supply chain of product flow to clients. Once this is achieved an information flow network providing all the necessary details of the products is required. Such a model is illustrated in Figure 1.8 for nine industry types. There are four in manufacturing (food, automobiles, chemicals, and textiles) and five in services (insurance, healthcare, distribution, engineering and construction, and the entertainment industry). In general:

- Inputs are where the raw materials are received by the operating firm. These may originate locally, nationally, or internationally.
- Transformation is where the state of the received raw materials is modified according to desired requirements. The transformation may be in a multitude of steps and occur at different locations.
- Outputs are where the desired product is finished and distributed to customers. The customers may be local, national or international and they may be another business or the final user of the product.

Figure 1.8 Operations model

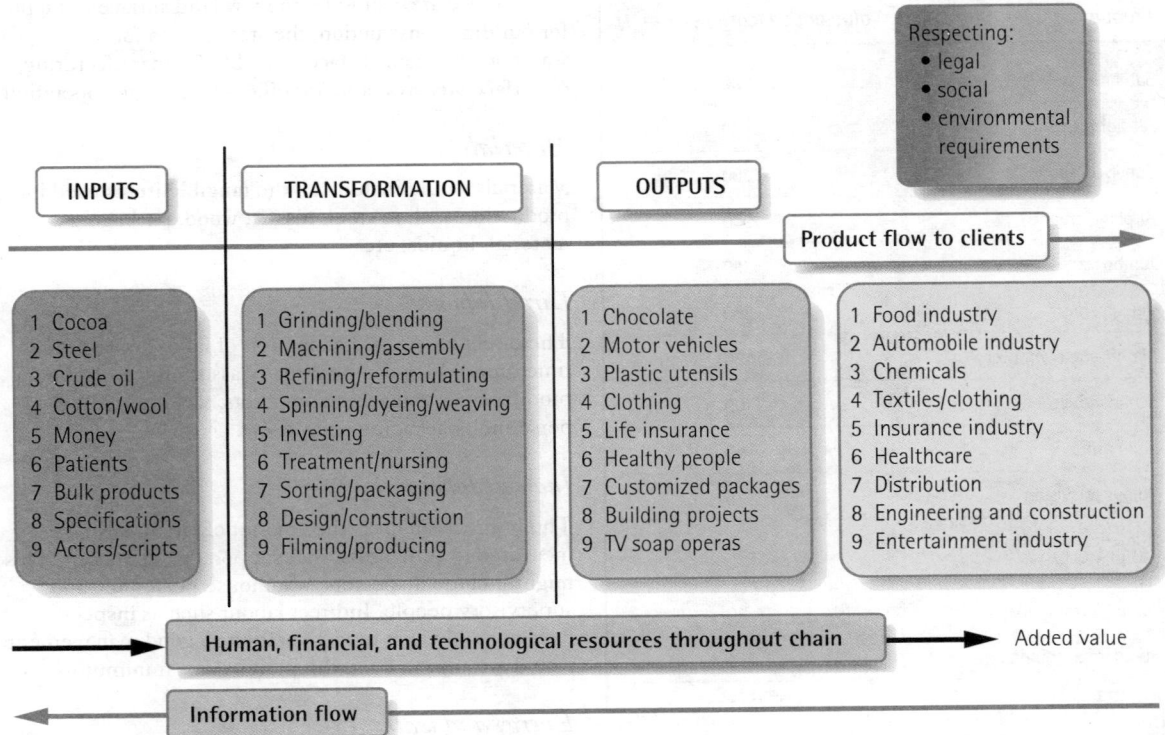

In order for the chain to function, and no matter the type of operation, it uses a combination of financial, human, and technological resources. At the same time the operation must be carried out respecting current legal, social, and environmental regulations.

Model economics

In any operation, as presented in the model, the economic value of the output must be greater than the economic value of the input or:

$$\frac{\text{Output value}}{\text{Input value}} > 1$$

From a marketing point of view, in the operation the margin obtained from the output product is greater than the margin that would be obtained from the input product. In the model examples shown:

- a slab of chocolate has a higher value than the input raw cocoa beans
- an automobile has a higher added value than raw steel

- a healthy patient has a higher value than one who is sick and going into hospital
- a life insurance policy has a greater value than non-invested cash
- a six pack of beer has a higher added value in a retail store than six cans of beer coming off the filling line in a brewery
- a graduating student has a higher economic value than a freshman.

Product added value

Another economic viewpoint of the operations model is to examine the value added to the operation which for the complete supply chain is given by the following relationship:

$$\text{Value added} = \begin{bmatrix} \text{Product value at the} \\ \text{end of the supply} \end{bmatrix} - \begin{bmatrix} \text{Value of inputs} \\ \text{at the beginning} \end{bmatrix}$$

It is this added value that translates into net income or profit for the firm. Different products have different

Table 1.4 Products and their value added

Product	Value added (cargo ship = 1)
Satellite	20,000
Jet fighter	2,500
Super computer	1,700
Airplane engine	900
Jumbo jet	350
Video camera	280
Mainframe computer	160
Semiconductor	100
Submarine	40
Colour television	16
Numerically controlled machine tool	10
Luxury automobile	10
Standard automobile	4
Cargo ship	1

added values, and companies which have multiple business units may have a marketing strategy to retain the production of those products that have the highest added value and discontinue those products that have a lower added value. Alternatively, in the production of the final product, they may outsource those operations that for them have a low added value and retain only those that have a high added value. Table 1.4, based on Japanese studies, illustrates that different products have different added values.[12] Here relative values are presented based on $/kg where the cargo ship has a value of unity.

Productivity

Resources in operations

The objective in any operation is productively to use available resources. High productivity translates into lower costs and, for a given price, higher profits. Resources might include the following elements.

Surface area

The surface area could be the raw land surface available for building construction, the storage area for warehousing, floor surface available for manufacturing, or surface area available for offices in a service operation.

Materials

Materials would include all the tangible items used in production such as steel, plastic, wood, packaging material, liquids, etc.

Direct labour

The direct labour is that amount of labour measured in time units which can be directly associated with the product such as machine operators, welders, wiring personnel, packaging people, etc.

Indirect labour

The indirect labour is the amount of labour, also measured in time units, that supports an operation. This might include inspectors, warehouse personnel, and supervisory people. Indirect labour such as inspection does not add value to an operation so good management would attempt to keep this activity to a minimum.

Energy and water

Energy includes oil, gas, electricity used directly in a production operation but also that used for space heating, cooling, or, say, refrigeration for the food industry. Water is the cooling water used, say, in a refinery operation, in a nuclear power plant or the actual water used in the production process such as in the food, paper, or chemical industry.

Financial resources

Financial resources in the broad sense include the cash needed to finance land purchase, building construction, new machines, pay salaries, purchasing of raw materials, maintenance expenditures, travel costs, etc.

Productivity ratio

Productivity is a measure of how resources are used. Globally, it is given by the ratio of the value of the output achieved to the inputs used, or, expressed more simply:

$$\text{Productivity} = \frac{\text{Output}}{\text{Input}}$$

Productivity in an operation increases if an amount of output has increased without increasing the

Table 1.5 Labour hours in car assembly (USA, 2000)

Constructor	Labour hours/unit
Daimler-Chrysler	32
Ford	26
General Motors	27
Honda	20
Nissan	17
Toyota	22

Table 1.6 Service firms and productivity ratio used

Airline industry	Passenger mile/airplanes in service
Engineering	Design hours per project
Hotel industry	Number of hotel rooms filled per period
Railways	Passengers per network mile
Television	Viewers per programme
Education	Students per professor
Fast food restaurant	Time to make a hamburger

corresponding amount of input. Productivity improvements are often a bargaining element in union contracts. An increase in productivity is one way a firm can afford to raise wages while still remaining competitive in an increasingly global economy.

The productivity ratio is somewhat analogous to the value-added ratio, but it is not the same. As an illustration, from the basic raw materials, an automobile built in Japan may have the same added value as one built in the UK. However, the productivity of arriving at the finished product may be different in the two countries. Alternatively, the perceived added value to a hotel customer may be the same with two companies, but the productivity of providing the service may be quite different. The way in which productivity is measured depends very much on the industry and particularly whether it is manufacturing and services as the following sections illustrate.

Manufacturing

Since manufacturing has historically been labour intensive (although this has changed considerably with automation), productivity is usually measured relative to the inputs of labour. The ratios used might be the number of units produced per employee, or the labour hours needed to produce one unit of product. As an illustration, Table 1.5 gives, for 2000, the estimated labour hours to assemble an automobile for major firms in the United States.[13]

Service firms

For service firms, using output per labour input is very often not an appropriate indicator of productivity. The ratio employed depends on the type of firm and Table 1.6 contains some illustrations. It should be noted that some of these are similar to capacity utilization, discussed in Chapter 12.

Some firms use revenues as the numerator in the productivity ratios as, for example, revenues per passenger mile in the travel industry, or revenues per design engineer. However, this is not really a good measure for analyzing the productivity since revenues can be increased by increasing price with no changes in the inputs.

Productivity changes

What is often of interest is not the absolute value of productivity, but the change over time such that one has a basis of comparison to see if improvements are being made. The change in productivity for the USA has already been presented by showing the change in output in Figure 1.6. In addition, Figure 1.9 shows the annual percentage change in productivity between 1996 and 2000. In this period the productivity of the USA and France as been high relative to Canada and Norway.[14]

Workweek and productivity

In Europe there has been a big push from some governments to reduce the workweek. France has already implemented a 35-hour week and there are moves in Italy to do the same. Compared to countries that have a 40-hour week, such as the USA, this lower workweek reduces the output or the effective productivity as Table 1.7 illustrates. The assumption is that a country used to have in place a 40-hour workweek and this has now been reduced to a 35-hour week.

If the cycle time of eight minutes per unit, established at the 40-hour week, cannot be changed (it means people have to work faster) then the production rate falls to 262.5 units a week (2100/8) or only 87.5% of the original 40-hour workweek. This reduction thus makes countries less competitive internationally.

Figure 1.9 Manufacturing productivity for various countries

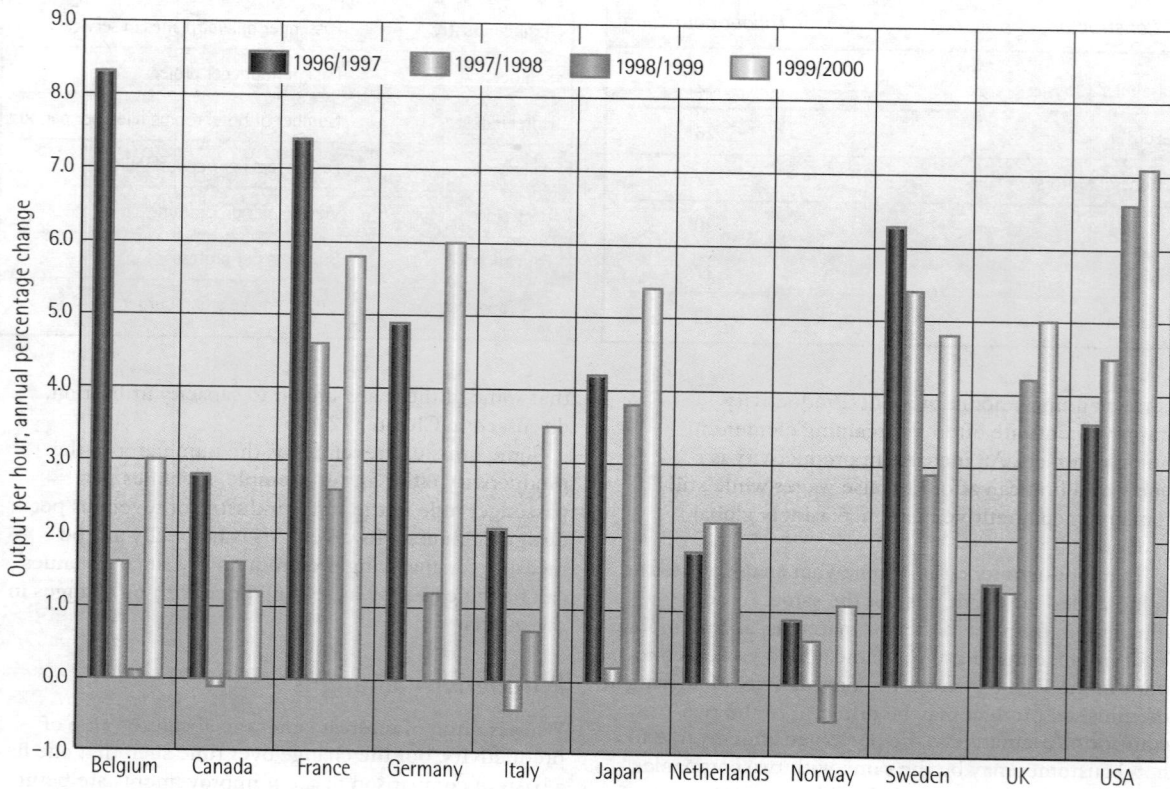

Table 1.7 Workweek and productivity

	Before	After
Hours a week	40	35
Required production rate, units/week	300	300
Minutes a week available	40 * 60 = 2400	35 * 60 = 2100
Cycle time, minutes/unit	2400/300 = 8.0	2100/300 = 7.0

Management activities in operations

The ultimate responsibility of the operations manager is to ensure that the objectives of the firm are met in terms of production output whether this involves manufactured goods or a service. To arrive at these objectives involves considerable interaction with other business functions as well as concentrating on specific operational activities as discussed as follows.

Interface with marketing

The operations manager would (or should) have a strong interface with all the marketing personnel including line sales and the market research group. This would include interpreting the correct response to sales forecasts for existing products and then translating these forecasts into a coherent production planning schedule. For new products, the operations manager would work with the market research people regarding client demands and the feasibility of translating these demands into production units.

Working with the finance department

All firms are cost conscious and the operations manager would work closely with financial and accounting personnel. This would include calculating meaningful product costs, to be sure that operating costs are conforming to budget levels and that inventory levels are kept low. Further, the operations department would work with financial people regarding purchase decision for raw materials, subcontractor services, and capital equipment.

Operations

Some of the key operational activities would include:

- Working with top management and financial persons to plan capacity requirements over the long range.
- Deciding what production capacity will be needed over the short range to satisfy client needs.
- Deciding what raw materials, parts, subassemblies, should be purchased or produced, at what time period, and in what quantity.
- Optimizing the levels of inventory to keep investment at a minimum.
- Implementing just-in-time production and other approaches in order to achieve 'lean manufacturing'.

Then, depending on the firm, other activities in the operations environment would involve some of the following specific activities.

Environment

This would include working with research and development personnel on what strategy the organization should adopt in order to minimize downstream pollution. This includes considering the product design, product lifecycle, minimizing use of toxic materials, recycling methods, and packaging materials. (See Chapter 5.)

Human resources

This would involve determining how effectively to use the personnel assigned to an operation, level of communicating, and motivation in a continually changing environment. It might also involve staff selection, and training of personnel who will work in the production and operations departments. (See Chapter 8.)

Layout

This would involve determining the optimum layout of machines, equipment, storage areas, or office space. With new evolving technologies and new products, design layouts are often changed. (See Chapter 9.)

Location or site selection

This would involve working with top management when new production facilities are to be added to decide where they should be located. (See Chapter 3.)

Maintenance

This would involve organization of the operation so that routine maintenance reduces the unplanned shutdowns and emergency situations. (See Chapter 19.)

Productivity

This would include analyzing the effective use of the resources and determining how productivity can be maintained, or improved.

Purchasing

This is working with suppliers and subcontractors so that quality, price, and delivery times are respected. (See Chapter 16.)

Scheduling

This involves deciding on the optimum method to schedule operations such as organizing machines, equipment, and personnel, to avoid bottlenecks and meet client demand. (See Chapters 14 and 22.)

Distribution

This involves working with warehouses and distribution centres in order properly to manage the finished goods inventory, which is ultimately supplied to the final client. This is the business logistics aspect. (See Chapter 17.)

Project management

When projects arrive in the operation this activity involves how they should be effectively managed, budgeted, and controlled. (See Chapter 18.)

Quality assurance

This is continually looking at quality in the operation to see how it can be improved and to ensure that methods and procedures are properly documented. (See Chapters 4 and 20.)

Information systems

This is working with computer personnel continually to update information systems to have an efficient and responsive supply chain.

Organization charts

An organization chart defines the relationships with functional departments in the organization. All businesses have organization charts although there is no one standard chart even for similar firms. For example, the organizational chart for one automobile firm might be quite different from another. Further some firms respect to the letter the organization chart whereas others allow a lot of flexibility. Figures 1.10–1.13

Figure 1.10 Organization chart for a food distribution centre

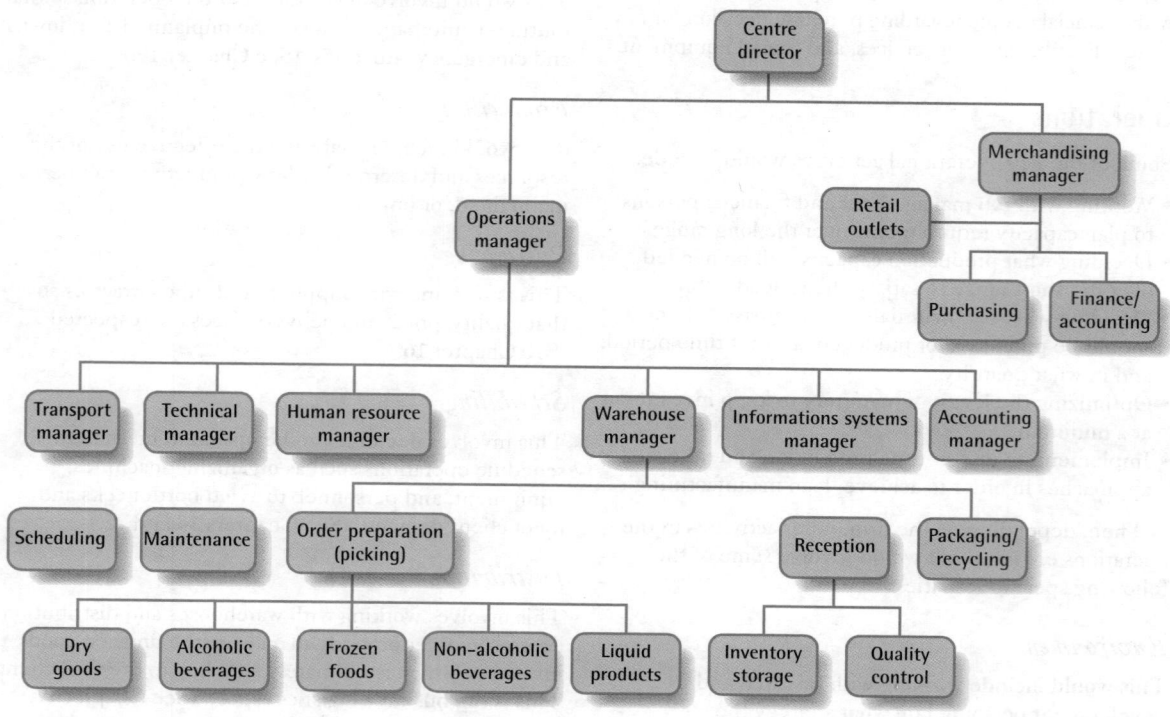

Figure 1.11 Organization chart for an airline company

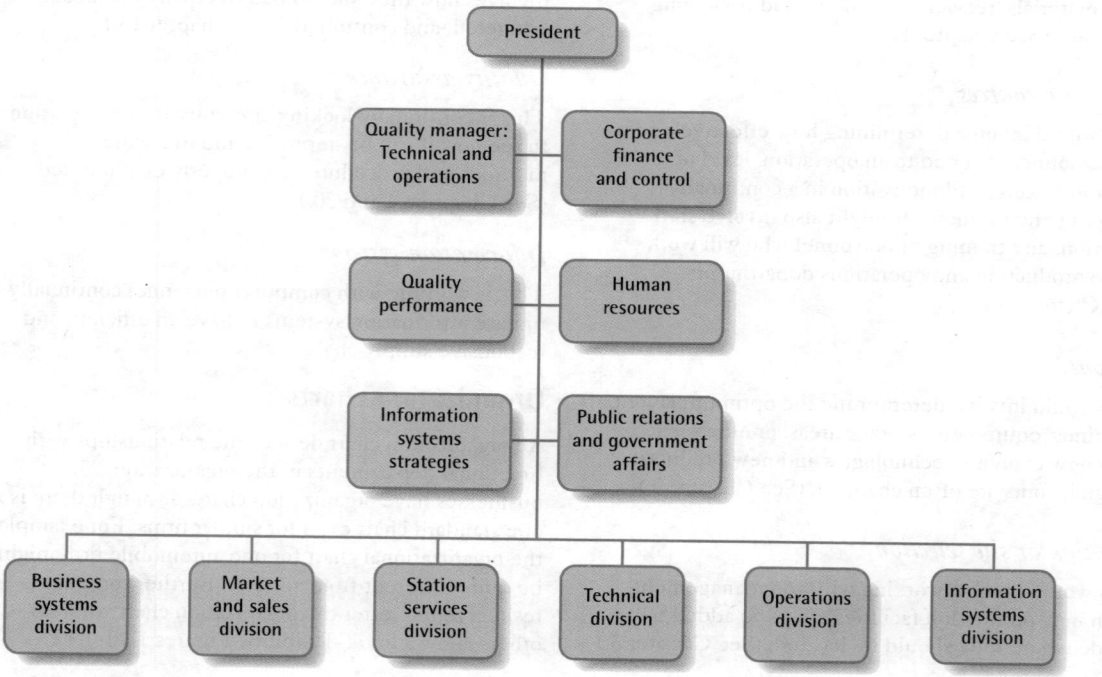

Figure 1.12 **Organization chart for a small pharmaceutical manufacturer**

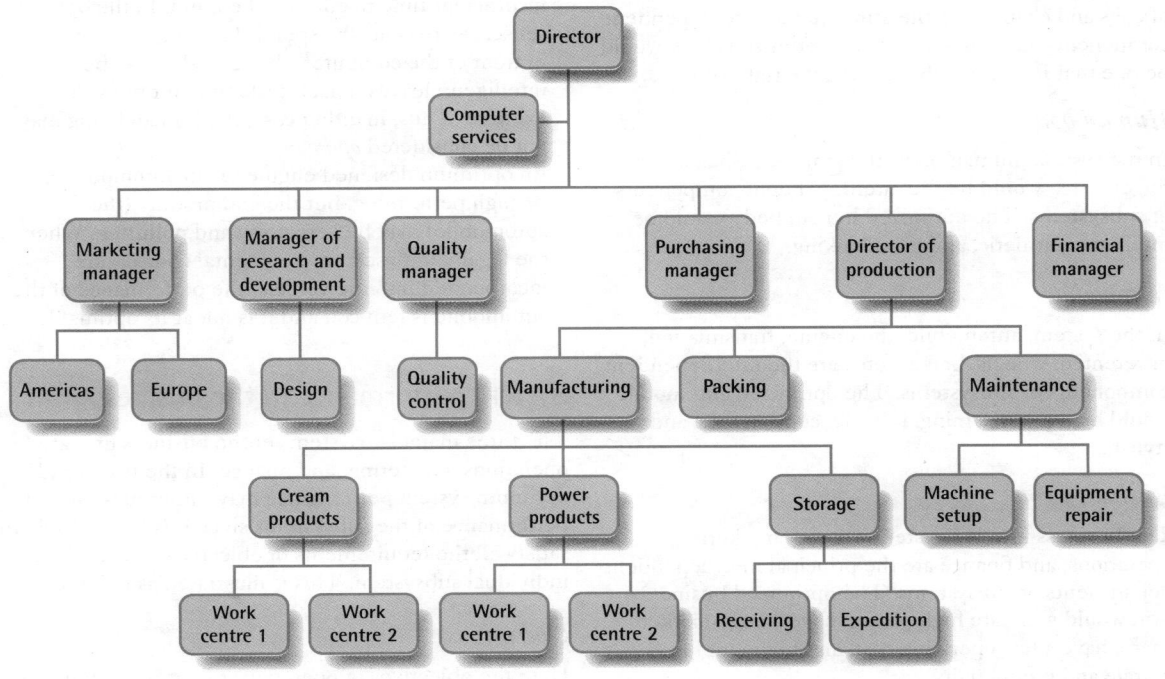

Figure 1.13 **Organization chart for part of an automobile constructor**

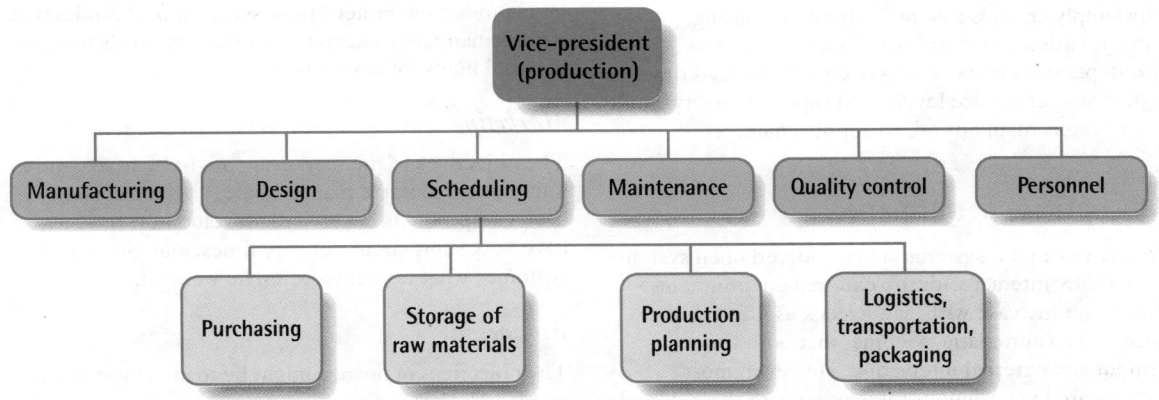

(two service firms and two manufacturing companies) indicate where some of the operations management activities fit into the overall business organization.

Systems approach to operations

Concept of a system

Any organization, be it manufacturing, services, or non-profit, can be considered a system. A system, a concept developed by Jay Forrester,[15] is a perhaps complex grouping of interdependent components, variables, activities, or subsystems. The objective of the complete system design is that the final output, performance, or appearance is optimized. The concept of a systems approach is directed at the business organization but it can be explained by a clock, the human body, a product such as an automobile, as well as the business firm, and ultimately the supply chain. This is explained as follows.

A clock

In the system of a clock, the pendulum, the mechanism of cogs and chains, and the arms are the interdependent components, or subsystems. The optimized clock would be one that is continually keeping the right time.

Human body

In the system, human body, the arms, legs, head, feet, fingers, etc., would be the interdependent components or subsystems. The optimized human body would be intelligent, athletic, and good looking.

Automobile

In the system, automobile, the engine, transmission, differential, wheels, brakes, etc., are the interdependent components or subsystems. The optimized automobile would be top performing, reliable, comfortable, and stylish.

Business firm

The business firm is a system wherein marketing, operations, and finance are the principal interdependent departments or subsystems. The optimized business firm would generate high profits, have a large market share, have a low operating cost, and high employee morale and productivity.

Supply chain

The supply chain is a system where purchasing, transformation and distribution are the major interdependent units or subsystems. Short lead times, high customer service levels, and superior quality would be indicators of an optimized supply chain.

Sub-optimal performance

For the most part, systems are considered open systems in that they interact with the external environment. This is not the case with, say, a clock as illustrated earlier, or an automatic machine, that both function without any external interaction. However, most systems are in continuous interaction with the external environment, which imposes on them certain constraints. As a result, a condition of sub-optimal performance probably exists. Sub-optimal is the condition when optimization of one component, or subsystem, results in less than optimal performance of the overall system, and vice versa. The following are illustrations based on the examples given earlier:

- The human body interacts with the external environment in order to be educated and physically fit. However, excessive attention to the body's physical performance for, say, an athlete, may give optimum physical performance but may leave insufficient time to educate the mind. In the opposite sense, the person who spends large amounts of time in front of the computer, although she may be intelligent, leaves herself little time for physical exercise. Thus, in either case, the human being may not be considered *optimum*.
- An optimum designed engine for an automobile may be high performing, but the end product (the automobile) may be very noisy and polluting. When the legally imposed environmental controls are incorporated into the vehicle, the performance of the automobile is reduced and it is not at its optimal level.

System performance in the business firm

The three major subsystems of the business firm are operations, marketing, and finance. In the real-world optimum system performance may imply sub-optimal performance of the subsystems since it is not possible to satisfy all the requirements or objectives of the individual subsystem. This is illustrated as follows.

Operations

Here the objectives of operations might be to minimize operating costs of the facility, minimize shutdowns, standardize product range or service designs, maintain a level production rather than a synchronized production with demand, or to keep high inventory levels to ensure material flows are always met.

Marketing

The objectives of the marketing might be to maximize units sold, maximize market share, develop custom-designed products or services, develop new products, have very short client delivery times, and give the customer what he wants, when he wants it.

Finance

The objectives of finance might be to maximize company profits, minimize any risky ventures, maintain a liquid cash position, maintain low inventory levels to keep working capital low, or to keep external borrowing low.

As a result of the conflicting objectives of each of these three subsystems, there is potential for sub-optimality to occur between the three functions because of the following:

- Production prefers to minimize costs by standardized designs whereas marketing wants to have more custom designs to satisfy the clients.

Figure 1.14 Interaction of major business functions in operations

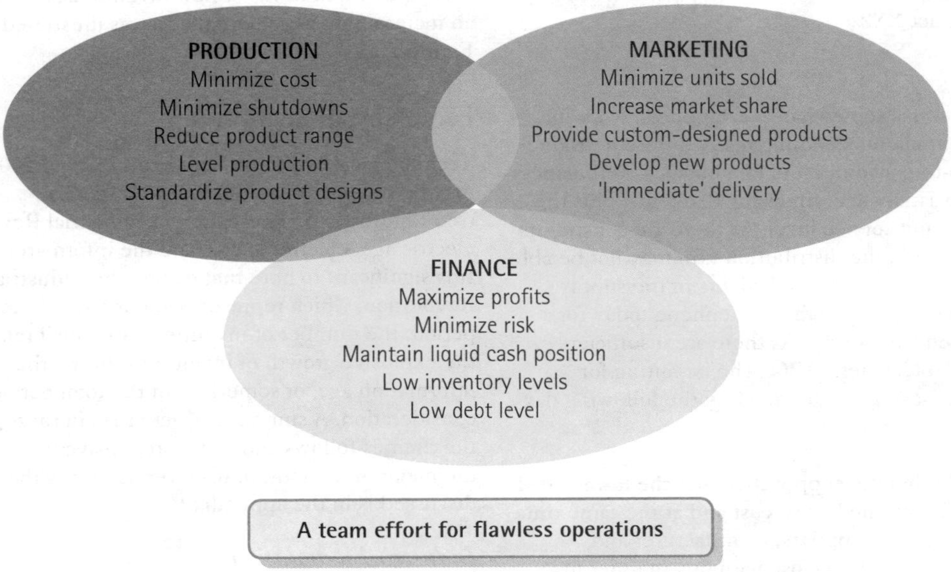

PRODUCTION
Minimize cost
Minimize shutdowns
Reduce product range
Level production
Standardize product designs

MARKETING
Minimize units sold
Increase market share
Provide custom-designed products
Develop new products
'Immediate' delivery

FINANCE
Maximize profits
Minimize risk
Maintain liquid cash position
Low inventory levels
Low debt level

A team effort for flawless operations

- Finance wants to keep investments in inventory low, while production wants to keep inventory high as a security measure to minimize the risk of shutdown.
- Marketing wants to expand the sales territory, but finance is hesitant because of the capital investment requirement.

Thus, in practice, marketing, production, and finance need to compromise on their particular objectives in order to arrive at an acceptable optimum for the business system. This implies that marketing, production, and finance have to work as an integrated team to ensure products or services conform to customer requirements, are ready on time, are at an acceptable price, and that the necessary investment is available for their development and commercialization. The goals of each subsystem must be properly tuned so that the output of the system (the firm) attains the desired objectives. This situation is summarized in Figure 1.14.

System performance in the supply chain

The three major subsystems of the supply chain are suppliers/subcontractors, transformation/manufacturing, and distribution. In a similar way to the business firm, the real-world optimum system performance of the supply chain may imply sub-optimal performance of the elements of the subsystem. Assume that we consider a particular, Product XYZ, moving through the supply chain whose ultimate destination is Client ABC.

Suppliers/subcontractors

Suppliers and subcontractors work for a host of different clients in a business-to-business link providing many different products that have to conform to cost (or price) requirements for each client, product specifications which differ from client to client, and stringent lead times for all these different clients. As a result, Product XYZ may not be supplied at the optimum requirement in terms of cost, specification, or lead time. Furthermore, the supplier would like to optimize its profit but because of the demands from its client's purchasing department it may be obligated to lower its price for Product XYZ in order to obtain the order.

Transformation/manufacturing

Manufacturing departments often have many different products to make, each with a demand on lead times, and manufacturing cost. The way manufacturing is scheduled may mean that the time by which Product XYZ is finished, and also perhaps its subsequent cost are not optimum for the downstream client. Manufacturing is a cost centre and will attempt to plan in order to minimize costs, and this may not correspond to lead times of Product XYZ.

Distribution

Distribution firms, somewhat like suppliers, work for many different clients handling many different product in a business-to-consumer link or a business-to-business link. It has to satisfy lead times for all clients, plus the quality, price, and service level. As there are constraints with the resources, the distribution firm may not be able to give maximum service to all clients in the supply chain. For example, three firms telephone today for a delivery of items tomorrow. As there are insufficient vehicles available, Client ABC, who is waiting for Product XYZ, has to wait for delivery the following day and suffers a stockout.

Thus, in order that the supply chain has the lowest lead time possible, with the lowest cost and at the same time maintaining quality, suppliers, manufacturer and distributors must work in close harmony in order to optimize the supply chain system.

Technology

Technological developments, probably more than any other single advance, have had the biggest impact on the operations management environment, both in terms of products and processes. The

Industrial Revolution is considered to have heralded in the technological movement and, since then, growth, in terms of new inventions, has followed an increasingly exponential curve as illustrated in Figure 1.15.[16]

Evolution of technology

Technological evolution between 1733 and 2002 may be broken down into four timeframes (see Figure 1.15). These are the Industrial Revolution, electric age, electronic age, and the information age. It is significant to note that during the Industrial Revolution, which represents about 54% of the time period, the number of inventions was small relative to the explosive growth of inventions during the information age, or some 11% of the total period in consideration. A summary of activities in these four timeframes follows and a comprehensive list of some of the major inventions, or discoveries during the periods discussed is in the appendix.[17]

Industrial Revolution

The Industrial Revolution (1733–1878) is considered to have started when, in 1733, British inventor John Kay invented the flying shuttle for weaving textiles. Other notable inventions in this period included the development of the steam engine by James Watt in 1765, and the cotton gin by Eli Whitney in 1793, which enabled to increase the rate at which seeds could be combed from cotton. In 1837 Samuel Morse patented the telegraph and in 1876 Alexander Graham Bell did the same for the telephone.

Figure 1.15 **Technological evolution**

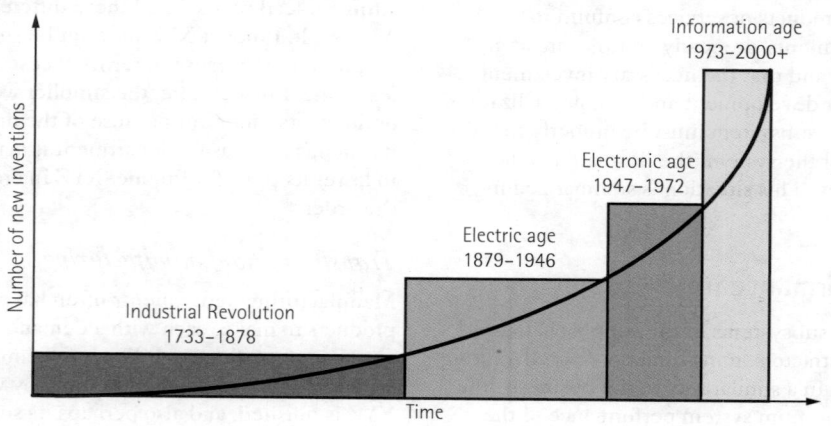

Electric age

The electric age (1879–1946) began with the invention of the electric light bulb by Thomas Edison and Joseph Swan. This period saw the development of the first successful gasoline-driven automobile by Karl Benz in 1885 and Marconi's invention of wireless telegraphy in 1895. At the turn of the century, in 1903, Orville and Wilbur Wright made the first extended airplane flight. Computers came on the scene in 1930 when Vannevar Bush invented the first analogue computer.

Electronic age

The period of the electronic age (1947–1972) included the development of the transistor at the Bell Laboratories (now Lucent Technologies) in 1947. In 1956 FORTRAN became the first computer programming language. Other inventions were the launching of the Telstar 1 commercial communications satellite in 1962, and, in the same year, the introduction of the compact cassette by Philips of the Netherlands. The invention of the first computers to use integrated circuits was made by the Burroughs Corporation in 1968 and the production of the first home video cassette recorder (VCR) in 1972.

Information age

The information age (1973–2002+) saw the explosion of information technology and includes such inventions as the ability to put 10,000 units on a one square centimetre computer chip in 1973, and the transmittal in six minutes of the first international fax in 1974. In 1977 Apple brought out the first personal computer with colour graphics and in 1981 IBM adopted the standard disk operating system (DOS) for its personal computers. In 1983 Motorola introduced the first cellular telephone and in 1984 Philips and Sony brought out the compact disc read-only memory (CD-ROM). In 1990 the Internet and World Wide Web was set up and, in 1995, Microsoft, under Bill Gates, introduced Windows 95, an upgrade of the operating system for most personal computers. This was followed by Windows 98 and then Windows 2000.

Operations and the 21st century

In the 20th century, some global technological developments that have played a major role in operations are illustrated in Figure 1.16. Some of the impact these technology changes have had on the operations environment include the following.

Figure 1.16 **Key technological developments in the 20th century**

Petrochemicals
(Exxon's commercialization of isopropyl alcohol in 1920)

Composite materials
(light, resists corrosion, inflammable, machines easily)
- Kevlar (Dupont) – electric cables, boat hulls
- Ceramic fibres – electrical/electronics
- Composite polymers – automobiles, computers
- Carbon fibre – skis, tennis rackets, golf clubs

Plastics
- Synthetic rubber – IG Farben
- Polyethylene – ICI
- Nylon – Dupont
- Polystyrene, silicones, polypropylene

Computers/automation/robots
- CAD/CAM
- Flexible manufacturing
- Automatic storage and retrieval

Electronic data interchange
(The Internet)
- Order processing/purchasing
- Collection/billing
- Logistics management
- Payroll

Expert systems
- Copying human logic

Virtual systems
- Simulations of the 'real thing'

Production processes

Automatic welding machines increase the speed, and accuracy of joining metal sheeting. Robots for painting improve the uniformity, and the quality of finishing on automobile bodywork. The automatic bottling and canning of fruits, vegetables, and meat is faster, better quality, and less prone to bacteriological contamination.

Service operations

Money can be withdrawn from the bank by using a simple plastic card. Compact discs store a wealth of information for insurance, banking, and other databases. Bar codes, and the associated electronic scanners, speed the process through a store checkout and inventory management.

Communication

Electronic mail allows worldwide communication at any hour of the day. Stock prices are available almost instantaneously. Portable phones can be used to telephone from anywhere. Money can be transferred internationally in seconds.

Transportation times

In the 1950s it took three weeks to travel from Europe to Australia by boat but now with jumbo jets it takes a matter of hours. Motorways, and improved technology of road construction, make delivery of food and other products much quicker. Bullet trains in France, Japan, and Germany reduce intercity travel time to a matter of hours.

Variety of products available

The number of drugs on the market for asthma, heart disease, and ulcers has multiplied. Clothing, in a variety of colours, styles, and sizes can be obtained in natural or synthetic materials. Model types, engine size, and colour of automobiles have come a long way since Henry Ford's Model T.

Job conditions

Automatic cutting and drilling machines have reduced the backbreaking work in mines. Thanks to automatic washing machines and dryers, gone is the scrubbing of clothes and turning them through the mangle. Computers have simplified and increased the speed of the reservation process in the travel industry.

Product and process quality

Paint colours on wallpaper, carpeting, and photography are more uniform, and the colour can be repeated. There is improved quality of results for medical treatment such as electrocardiographs, X-rays, and DNA tests. Computer programs improve quality (accuracy) of financial analyses. Furthermore, transportation, especially considering the enormous distances travelled, is much safer.

Product delivery time

Automation allows automobiles to be produced within days. Chemical feeds allow chickens, geese, and turkeys to be bred at a faster rate (is this, however, a good thing?). Microwave ovens allow airplane stewards rapidly to serve meals that approach restaurant quality. (Although not everybody would agree with this comment.)

Product prices

Production methods for the computer have put the price of computers within the range of most consumers. New construction materials have brought down the cost of home prices. The real cost of many drugs, and medical treatments have come down, making them available to a broader spectrum of patients.

Reduced labour needs

Labour needs on the assembly line have dropped. Tellers are not needed in the banking industry. Operators are not needed in the telephone industry. On certain metro lines in Europe, such as in Lyon, France, there are no train drivers.

Summary of key elements

- Operations management is the planning, organizing, and control of all the resources and activities to provide goods and services. It applies equally to manufacturing, and services in the private and public sector, and even government.

- The integrated supply chain is a material flow stream from purchasing, transformation through to distribution. In the reverse sense it is an information stream and within the supply chain there are financial flows to the suppliers and from the clients. Within the supply chain are numerous operating activities.

- The driving force in operations management is the 'king' client who requires products at the right time, at an acceptable quality, at a reasonable price, and courteously.

- A manufacturing firm turns physical raw materials into tangible products. These products can be seen and touched, described in dimensional terms such as weight, length, height, and volume, and have monetary value.

- Services provide a 'product', often intangible, which cannot be described in dimensional terms. Compared to manufacturing, there is more client contact and so operations personnel are often more people oriented.

- As well as market-driven firms there are non-profit service organizations. Here the driving force is a desire to do good rather than to serve commercial interests. Although not constrained by the profit motive, they are nevertheless operations that need to be managed effectively, and to serve end client users at a reasonable cost.

- Operations is increasingly international because of reduction in trade barriers, less expensive foreign labour, expanding markets in emerging economies, coupled with saturated domestic markets, and cheaper and easier international transportation.

- The employment level in manufacturing in developed nations continues to decline because of technology replacing labour, relocation to cheaper labour regions, and the explosive growth of service industries.

- An operations model is a supply chain network of three blocks – inputs, transformation, and outputs of end products – which is coupled, in the reverse sense, with an information flow. The economic value of the outputs is greater than that of inputs.

- The objective of operations is to use resources productively as this translates into both lower costs, and higher profits. Resources include surface area, materials, direct and indirect labour, energy and water, and finances. Globally speaking, productivity is the ratio of output to inputs.

- Operations involves activities related to sales, finance, the environment, human resources, facility layout, site selection, maintenance, productivity improvements, purchasing, scheduling, distribution, project management, quality assurance, and information systems.

- The firm, or organization, can be considered a system, of which operations, marketing and finance are the three subsystems. Optimizing the firm may lead to sub-optimization of the operations management function.

- The supply chain consisting of purchasing, transformation, and distribution is also a system where optimization of the system and subsystems may not be maximized.

- Technological developments have had a bigger impact than anything else on operations management, including the development of new products, process design, and the reduced requirement for labour.

Notes and references

1. http://www.exxonmobil.com
2. http://www.boeing.com
3. http://www.siemens.com
4. British Airways, Reports and Accounts, 1996–97
5. http://www.britishairways.com
6. http://www.accor.com
7. http://www.creditsuisse.com
8. http://www.who.int/home-page/
9. 'Les firmes multinationales' (international firms), *Mémo Larousse Encyclopédie*, Librairie Larousse, Paris, 1990, p. 600
10. US Bureau of Labor, http://stats.bls.gov
11. Zachary, G. Pascal, 'Up the ladder: US multinationals take brain work to plants overseas: Job competition and pressure on wages begin to reach America's labour elite', *Wall Street Journal Europe*, 30 September 1994, pp 1 and 7
12. *The Economist*, 2 December 1989
13. Welch, David, 'Why Detroit is going to pieces: Modular outsourcing is gaining converts – even among unions', *Business Week*, 3 September 2001, p. 60EU1
14. US Department of Labor
15. Forrester, Jay, *Industrial Dynamics*, MIT Press, Cambridge, Massachusetts, 1964
16. Based on Roach, Stephen S., 'Computers can do a great job – yours', *Time*, 13 November 1995, pp 22–3
17. *Mémo Larousse Encyclopédie*, Librairie Larousse, Paris, 1990 and others

Review and discussion topics

1. Link supply chain and operations

The supply chain refers to the purchasing, transformation, and delivery of finished goods to the client. All along the supply chain are 'clients'. The client is king! What is meant by this axiom in the supply chain? In your day-to-day living in dealing with businesses, university, stores, are you treated as 'King'? Discuss, in particular where you think improvements are warranted.

2. Distinction, services and manufacturing

The distinction is often made between manufacturing and services. What is the usefulness of such a distinction? Is it meaningful? What purpose does it serve? Illustrate your discussion with real companies or industries.

3. International firms

As regards the international scene, the text makes reference to ExxonMobil (an oil company), Boeing (aircraft manufacture), Siemens (industrial and consumer goods), British Airways (transportation), Accor (hotels), Crédit Suisse (banking) and the World Health Organization (non-profit). Discuss the supply chain as it applies globally and operations of these types of international industry from a point of view of personnel, materials, cost, and operations.

4. Employment

Manufacturing sector employment has dropped dramatically in favour of the service sector. Do you believe this trend will continue? What impact will it have on developed countries? Developing (emerging) countries? Discuss these trends in relationship to the high unemployment levels in France and Germany. Why is the unemployment level lower in Great Britain compared to Germany and France?

5. Modelling

Develop a simple flow scheme, or model of operations, for the following, indicating which is the main value-added step in the operation:
  (a) local grocery store
  (b) university or business school
  (c) dentist, or doctor's surgery
  (d) post office
  (e) large department store.

6. Productivity

Discuss how productivity would be measured in a:
  (a) plumbing service company which makes house calls
  (b) retail store
  (c) travel agent
  (d) milk-bottling company.

7. Managing technology

People often talk about 'Managing Technology' in business as technology is considered a resource. Discuss what you believe are the important elements to be considered in managing technology, taking into consideration the rapid change in techniques and methods in operations.

8. Technology in the firm

Consider the following operations:
  (a) the house in which you live
  (b) university or business school
  (c) medical centre
  (d) library
  (e) stores you use.
Where do you think technology would improve the efficiency, decrease the cost, and reduce the time in these operations? What would be the downside of adding your proposed technical innovations?

9. Technical change

Many people resent technical change. A classic illustration is the Luddites who, during the Industrial Revolution, smashed the weaving looms as they felt that, through them, their jobs were being lost. Unions often cite technological changes as a reduction in the workforce. People are 'afraid to use computers'. Do you believe people's fears are justified? Do you believe that the introduction of new technology is always a good thing? How do you think managers should cope with these changes in relation to their staff?

10. Operations, the supply chain, and the automobile industry

Present a flow scheme of the supply chain for the manufacture of automobiles, such as Citroën, Renault, Ford, General Motors, etc. This should start upstream from raw materials going through transformation, to the distribution of the finished product. Indicate on this flow sheet, or separately, the operations involved throughout the chain and present some of the challenges involved in these various operations.

Case study 1.1 Pangas

Situation*

Pangas, in Liverpool, England was created in 1976 and is now owned by the current president. Its business is the servicing, maintenance, and installation of electric and gas heating appliances. Its principal clients are individual homes, small businesses (printing shops, stores, car repair stores, etc.), and community-owned blocks of flats. In 1995 its revenues amounted to £1.5 million.

Pangas currently has 37 employees, of which 14 are administrative and 23 are technicians who perform the maintenance and installation work. The service area covers all of Liverpool and some of the surrounding areas. At present, the company has 18,500 maintenance contracts, of which one-third are for homes and flats and two-thirds are for small business. These contracts have been negotiated at a fixed price, and usually have a duration of three to five years.

Pangas' revenues are growing at about 2 to 3% a year although there is a lot of pressure on service price as a result of competitive pressure. The cost of the work for Pangas is as follows:

- 60% salaries
- 15% pieces purchased for the repair work
- 9% telephone, communications, vehicle maintenance, insurance, computer service charges, rent for office space
- 3% for taxes
- 1% depreciation
- 1% gasoline for service vehicles.

Operational activity

Pangas has several types of service activities. The maintenance contracts are serviced two to three times a year. The planning for this activity is entered into the computer system, which the administrators print out each day and enter into the planning for the service technicians. Installation of new equipment, which constitutes about 5% of the revenues, is usually planned about two to three weeks in advance. For this type of work, the appliances are purchased by the client, and the technicians' responsibility is the installation. However, there are often situations where the technicians have to buy additional parts because of special considerations. The other activity is emergency service work such as breakdown of appliances, poor operation, etc., which is difficult to plan, and often involves reorganizing the rescheduling of technicians' routing. In total, the technicians make about 35,000 visits every year. Not all of these are productive, because clients are not at home, keys for the house/flat cannot be located, or the technician does not have the correct parts in his van.

When a client has a problem he/she telephones Pangas and a telephone operator takes down the required information, and enters it directly into the computer system. With the client on the line she directly proposes a date and time for the service work. For this purpose, she has a planning programme for each technician, according to the geographic zone and the type of work. She would plan about four visits for the morning, and five for the afternoon. This information would be confirmed to the client by mail sent two to three weeks in advance of the service date. The telephone operators do not have full details regarding the competence of each technician and scheduling so sometimes modifications have to be made. When the job has been performed, the technicians fill out the necessary details of the job, have it signed by the client, and give this to accounting. Accounting bills the customer accordingly and asks for payment within 60 days if the work falls outside the contract terms. This might be when parts are not included, or the work is beyond the scope of the contract.

Required

1. Present how you believe this service firm would operate from reception of a client call to performing the work, to billing the customer. What problems do you think are likely to be encountered? (Bear in mind that these will be typical of many service organizations where house or small business visits are made.)
2. Develop an appropriate organization chart for Pangas.
3. How should company productivity be measured? Based on your ideas, how might the productivity be improved?

*Based on a study by Dominique Salaün and others, CESMA Groupe, ESC Lyon, 1996/97.

Selected further reading

Many of the references here include general textbooks on production and operations management. These reference books contain useful information related to many of the functional areas discussed in this book.

CHASE, Richard B., AQUILANO, Nicholas J. and JACOBS, F. Robert (2000) *Operations Management for Competitive Advantage*, 9th edition, McGraw-Hill.

GAITHER, Norman, FRAZIER, Greg and FRAZIER, Gregory (2001) *Operations Management with Operations Management Software CD-ROM and Microsoft Project 2000 CD-ROM*, 9th edition, South-Western.

HEIZER, Jay and RENDER, Barry (2001) *Production and Operations Management*, 6th edition, Prentice-Hall.

INGRASSIA, Paul and WHITE, Joseph B. (1995) *Comeback: The Fall and Rise of the American Automobile Industry*, Simon and Schuster.

KNOD, Edward M. and SCHONBERGER, Richard J. (2001) *Operations Management: Customer Focused Principles*, 7th edition, McGraw-Hill.

KRAJEWSKI, Lee J. and RITZMAN, Larry P. (2001) *Operations Management: Strategy and Analysis*, 6th edition, Prentice-Hall.

NAHMIAS, Steven (2000) *Production and Operations Analysis*, 4th edition, McGraw-Hill.

RUSSELL, Roberta S. and TAYLOR, Bernard W. III (2000) *Operations Management*, 3rd edition, Prentice-Hall.

SKINNER, Wickham (1985) *Manufacturing: The Formidable Competitive Weapon*, Wiley.

STEVENSON, William (1999) *Production Operations Management*, 6th edition, Irwin.

An extensive listing of other further reading can be found on the website.

What's on the web?

Further learning resources are available to lecturers and students at www.supplychain-online.com, including the following which are specific to *Positioning operations management and the supply chain*:

Resource	Subject
Chapter overview	Positioning operations management and the supply chain
Exam topics	Positioning operations management and the supply chain
Case study: Stena Line	Positioning operations management and the supply chain
More further reading	Positioning operations management and the supply chain

2 *Strategy of organizations*

Chapter overview

- Market-driven organizations
- Not-for-profit organizations
- The strategic plan
- Synergy strategy and operations
- Real-world corporate strategic objectives

Market-driven organizations

Every manufacturing or service firm must have a long-term objective. Globally, the objectives would encompass: Where do we want to be? Who do we want to be? What do we want to do? The strategy then includes the measures to take in order to arrive at the organization's stated objectives. Senior managers in the organization would have the ultimate responsibility for these measures. Once these objectives and strategies are established, they would then be the drivers for setting the strategies and objectives for the operations and supply chain functions. Objectives, and strategy, have their roots in wartime. The objectives of a nation are, of course, to win the war and the strategy is how the country mobilizes its resources in order to achieve this objective.

As discussed in Chapter 1, the firm is an open system, which interacts continually with the external environment. The external environment is constantly in a state of flux demographically, politically, economically, and socially. Markets and consumer needs change, laws are modified, trade barriers are falling, and technology is constantly being updated and improved. It is in this competitive environment that the firm operates and as such it has basically the following three options: to ignore the environment, adapt enough to survive, and grow by exploiting opportunities. These are described as follows.

Ignore the environment

In the long run, if the firm maintains its status quo, it will end in disaster. The failure of many firms is the result of complacency and ignoring the changing business environment. Eventually these firms are consumed by the changing events. Examples might be

Smith Corona (typewriters), and the shipbuilding industry in the United Kingdom.

Adapt enough to survive

Some conservative firms adhere to the familiar path because of the fear of taking risks. Firms in this category eventually find their market share dwindling and they are eventually swallowed. An example here might be the automobile industry in the United Kingdom where companies such as Jaguar, Bentley, Rolls-Royce, and Austin are now all owned by foreign firms.

Grow by exploiting opportunities

In order to grow, the firm must innovate and change. It must seize opportunities, but at the same time avoid dangers that are constantly being created by the ever changing environment. Every business enterprise makes decisions that ultimately decide its future. Choices are made that influence long-term outcomes and those made on accurate business environmental forecasts will lead to growth and profitability. Examples here are General Electric, Microsoft, and ExxonMobil, three of the world's biggest companies according to market capitalization.

Profit, return on investment, and cash flow

In the long run, the global objective of a business firm must be to make a profit. With this profit:

- Shareholders will receive dividends and may invest further in the business.
- Salaries can be increased, or employees might receive bonuses, which can have an indirect effect of motivating their work effort.

- Funds are available for capital expansion, which will lead to higher employment. Capital expansion would mean increasing business in the surrounding community to support the increased number of employees.

If the company does not continue to make a profit in the long run, it will fail. However, profit must not be a blind objective without taking other financial factors into consideration such as return on investment and cash flow. For example, a firm can invest heavily in new technology including robots, automated machinery, and information systems. If these increase the productivity of the firm then profits will increase. However, the return on this capital investment will be low. Further, if investment involves borrowing then repaying this debt may have an adverse impact on the firm's cash flow. It is conceivable for a firm to make a profit but have a negative cash flow. If a firm has a strong cash situation it is able to acquire other firms when the timing is right. This has been the case with General Electric, Ford Motor, and ExxonMobil.

Not-for-profit organizations

Like market-driven firms, not-for-profit or non-profit organizations are also open systems in that they interact with the surrounding environment. However, unlike market-driven firms they are not constrained by the push to generate profits or to battle competitors. Their existence is to provide to the public at large the service established according to their charter such as education, humanitarian aid, postal delivery, transportation services, etc. The objectives are overseen by a board of directors which would then establish a strategy for the operational personnel.

Regina E Herzlinger, at Harvard University, in a study of hundreds of non-profit organizations over the later years of the 20th century, developed the following four interrelated criteria to aid the board of directors achieve the objectives.[1]

Consistency with financial resources

Organizational goals should be consistent with the organization's financial resources. In broad terms these mean that if a large proportion of society is not benefiting by the service, it should be reduced, or curtailed. This philosophy was behind the actions of the British government's Dr Beeching, who, in March 1964, announced the closure of many rail services in the then nationalized British Railways system. The principal argument was that, although a public service, the operating cost of some lines was inconsistent with the number of users.[2] (This decision-making approach is similar to a cost benefit analysis described in Chapter 23.)

Equitable services for all generations

This guideline is that objectives of today should not jeopardize the services offered in the future, and vice versa. As an illustration, when a charity saves an excessively large proportion of its resources to help future users, it denies benefits to present users. Conversely, when it consumes virtually all its assets to serve present users, it denies the benefits of the organization's services to future users.

Sources and uses of funds should be matched

Non-profit organizations have expenses that are fixed in the sense that they are exceedingly difficult to reverse. The compensations of, say, a tenured professor at a university, a noted conductor at a symphony orchestra, or the head of a public hospital, represent fixed expenses. These fixed expenses should be funded by sources that can be readily controlled, and yield a steady stream of income. For example, the income from endowment capital, invested in a relatively risk-free portfolio, should be used to match fixed expenses. It would be inappropriate to match the salaries of a professor with research grants as, if these dry up, teaching capacity at universities has to be decreased.

Sustainability of the organization

If the first three criteria are satisfied, then normally the status quo of the organization can be sustained if it is maintained on an inflation-adjusted constant value. Preparation of a strategic plan, together with an associated pro-forma financial statement (discussed later), would demonstrate that continuation of present policies would enable the organization to survive in its present form. Illustrations of this are the government-managed social securities programmes of many major industrialized countries (USA, Britain, France, Germany, and Japan) that are technically 'bankrupted'. In this case the changing demographic environment is showing that the organization is unable to meet the first three criteria:

- Goals are not consistent with financial resources.
- It will be impossible to have equitable services for all generations.
- It is difficult to match sources and uses of funds.

As such many countries' social security programmes are not sustainable in their present forms.

Note that, contrary to the market-driven organization, the status quo of the non-profit organization is the major element in its sustainability. The Catholic Church, the Red Cross, or the elementary school has barely changed. However, compare this to the British coal industry, British shipbuilding, or Smith Corona Typewriters where all three were unable to adapt to the changing environment.

The strategic plan

A strategic plan is the detail of how an organization proposes to arrive at its desired objectives. Elements of the strategic plan depend on the particular organization but they would generally include such items as the timeframe, the mission of the firm, or, in the case of a non-profit organization, a charter. The strategic plan would attempt to analyze the current and future external environment, particularly those elements that would have a strong impact on the organization. Further, the plan would include a rigorous analysis of the organization's strengths and weaknesses, both internal and external to the environment.

Strategic plans for business firms are ultimately developed by top management personnel such as the president, and vice-presidents of marketing, finance, operations, and human resources, and they usually have to be approved by the board of directors. For non-profit firms it is often the board of directors which develops the plans. However, in all cases, strategic plans are built up from input provided by operating personnel.

Timeframe

A strategic plan is generally long term with a timeframe of nominally about five years, but, in reality, this depends on the organization. For non-profit organizations such as universities, hospitals, and the military, five years might be reasonable. However, for companies that are involved in activities that are strongly influenced by technology changes such as IBM (computers), AT&T (telecommunications), and Microsoft (software development), the strategic plans may be less than five years because the technology field changes so rapidly. Aircraft firms (Boeing and Airbus), nuclear power plant constructors, or oil companies have strategic plans which go beyond five years because of the enormous time needed for activities such as development, design, and product commercialization. Industry insight 2.1, which is written from a chronological basis concerning Mobil Oil (acquired by Exxon in 1999), illustrates the lengthy, costly (some $4.2 billion) and often rocky process of arriving at a company's objective. Here, there is a timeframe of almost 40 years.

Oil drilling   Industry insight 2.1

The Hibernia offshore oilfield, one of the largest in North America, lies some 310 kilometres southeast of St John's, Newfoundland, Canada. The area bears a geographic resemblance to the North Sea oilfields but oil companies ignored it for years because of its location in 'iceberg alley' or the region where the *Titanic* went down in 1912 after hitting a submerged iceberg.

In **1959** Don Axford, a retired Mobil executive, says that he first considered the region might hold promise during an executive meeting when he examined the location of Sable Island in the Atlantic Ocean, east of Nova Scotia and south of Hibernia's location. The executive was puzzled why a speck of an island could be sitting out there in the ocean by itself. He wondered whether it could be that it was a rocky dome formation called a 'high' that sometimes hold oil. A team of geologists spent months researching the prospect but Mobil's management (now ExxonMobil) twice turned down Axford's theory. After insisting, however,

Don Axford was given permission to buy up permits covering one million acres (400,000 hectares) beneath the glacial waters off eastern Canada. This was the first exploration permit in that area granted to a major oil company and Arthur Dutmar, then president of Mobil's Canadian unit, said this was 'just in case there is oil'.

Interest in the region grew and other oil companies began buying permits and sinking holes all over the Grand Banks where fishing had for years been the main occupation. In **1965** Mobil purchased a second batch of permits for just several cents an acre, including the terrain that became Hibernia, when new seismic data showed evidence of oil on the bottom of the ocean. (As a comparison Amoco Corp. spent $65.7 million in 1995 for a small exploration lease near Hibernia.)

Mobil started drilling first on Sable Island in **1967**. To do this, they loaded a drilling rig onto a World War II landing craft and ran it onto the beach and then dragged the rig to the middle of the island. They drilled straight down and hit gas. It wasn't in sufficient quantity to be commercial but it provided some evidence of energy resources in the region.

In **1973** Mobil drilled Adolphus N° 1 Well, the first in the Hibernia formation. The conditions were very treacherous with high waves and winds but the company struck oil. Again the quantity obtained was too small to be commercial and with better prospects elsewhere, including Alaska's Prudhoe Bay, geologists lost interest. In the meantime the federal and Newfoundland provincial governments of Canada began to argue over who owned the offshore mineral rights. The federal government argued that the province of Newfoundland ceded those rights in joining Canada in 1949. As a result, oil companies, in a defensive posture, began requesting permits from both governments. In some cases, the same acreage was leased to two companies. The then premier of Newfoundland, Brian Tobin, said that governments were fighting over spoils before any were found.

Mobil had taken up a partnership with Chevron Corp. and in **1979** they drilled the well that discovered commercial oil on the Hibernia field. This was the same year as the second Arab oil embargo. Oilmen, first ecstatic over a colossal strike in friendly waters during such a politically sensitive period, became disenchanted over the continuing bickering of the federal and provincial governments over mineral rights.

In February **1982** tragedy struck the Hibernia project. The *Ocean Ranger*, a semi-submersible drilling rig balanced on two giant pontoons, went down in a winter storm while exploring the Hibernia prospect. All 84 persons aboard the rig were killed. This accident persuaded operators to build an extraordinarily heavy platform that could withstand bad weather rather than the more typical floating rig.

In **1985** the dispute over mineral rights between the Canadian provincial and federal governments was resolved. The previous year Brian Mulroney had become prime minister and one of his most trusted cabinet members was John Crosbie from Newfoundland. Crosbie lobbied Mulroney to distribute the bulk of Hibernia's wealth to the province of Newfoundland. The subsequent 1985 accord ultimately granted all royalty rights to the Newfoundland government, as Mulroney was well aware of the poverty and hardship endured by the Newfoundland people. In addition, Mulroney's government took a tough negotiating stance with the oil companies insisting that Newfoundland be awarded some of the construction work.

As time went on oil prices began to fall and by **1988** Mobil was eager to delay the Hibernia project because of the poor economic viability. Arne Nielsen, then chief executive of Mobil's Canadian unit, told Canadian government officials at a tension-filled meeting in Montreal that Mobil and its partners were quitting plans to develop the Hibernia field. Newfoundland was desperately in need of the economic boost for its region and Marcel Masse, Canada's energy minister at the time, told Nielsen that the project was to go ahead and asked him what he needed to proceed. The response from Nielsen was that the Mobil consortium demanded that the Canadian government put up an enormous $700 million up front and guarantee loans for about one-third of the $4.2 billion capital cost. Mobil thought that this response would be the end of the Hibernia project, but the Canadian government agreed to the terms.

With all the parties finally in step with one another, design and construction plans got under way for the Hibernia field. Then in January **1992** there was another setback when Gulf Canada Resources Ltd, which had a 24% stake in the project, decided to pull out. Gulf, owned then by the financially strapped Reichmann family of Canada, was unable to keep up the payments. This left Mobil, Chevron, and its other consortium member, Petro-Canada, without one of its major partners. The pullout sparked fresh public criticism about the viability of the project and work stopped for a year while the consortium searched for a replacement for Gulf. Both the Royal Dutch/Shell Group and Exxon refused to join. Finally, the independent Murphy Oil of El Dorado Arkansas offered to pick up 6.5%, paying for the purchase with loans backed by the Canadian government. This offer inspired both Mobil and Chevron to pick up another 5% each, and the Canadian government, already up to its neck in loans and subsidies, took on an 8.5% interest.

In February **1997** two giant barges moved around the snow-crusted bluff of Come-By-Chance, a small town in southeastern Newfoundland, carrying the top of the production platform for Hibernia. The barges brought the section to a partially submerged pillar which was so big that workman poured concrete non-stop for more than 50 days in order to construct it. Once the top of the platform was in place, water, used as a ballast, was pumped out of the column allowing the concrete pillar to rise up underneath the platform lifting it into the air. The structure stood 60 storeys high, taller than the United Nations building in New York. In May the platform was floated out to the Hibernia location and by August it was anchored onto the ocean floor. Commercial production of oil started at the end of **1997** and as of yearend 1999 production was at 150,000 barrels a day according to the now ExxonMobil, which has a 33% interest in Hibernia.[3]

Adapted from: 'Old Gusher: Four decades later oilfield of Canada is ready to produce', *Wall Street Journal Europe*[4]

Mission statement

A mission statement globally defines the business and the objectives of an organization. It is the start point of the strategic plan. The following illustrations demonstrate what the mission statement of some organizations might be.

Railways

In the business of providing transportation services for people and goods at competitive prices with other transportation means.

Business school

To be one of the top ten international business schools, providing programmes at undergraduate, masters, executive, and doctorate level.

Engineering and construction

To provide top-quality services in the process, energy, and food industries, both domestically and internationally.

Hotel

In the business of providing accommodation and restaurant services to private and business clients in the international market.

Volkswagen (in 1937)

To manufacture and sell an automobile which is affordable to everyone.

SWOT analysis

A SWOT analysis is a strategic planning tool that attempts to match the internal strengths and weaknesses of the organization with external opportunities and threats. (SWOT is an acronym for strengths, weaknesses, opportunities, and threats.) The objective of the analysis is that if an organization carefully reviews such strengths, weaknesses, opportunities, and threats, then an appropriate strategy for meeting objectives can be developed. Several general considerations for an organization are illustrated in Figure 2.1.[5]

As a concrete example in a SWOT analysis, the following gives strengths and weaknesses an of an engineering and construction service company.

Strengths

- Ability, and the reputation to perform quality and innovative engineering in the petroleum refining, chemical process, pharmaceutical, and food industries.
- A documented record of completing projects within budget, and on schedule.

Figure 2.1 **Considerations for a SWOT analysis**

INTERNAL

Strengths
- Distinctive competence
- Strong financial resources
- Good employee skills
- Well thought of by suppliers
- Acknowledged market leader
- Access to economies of scale
- Proprietary technology
- Cost advantages
- Competitive advantages
- Product innovation abilities

Weaknesses
- No clear strategic direction
- Weak salesforce
- Obsolete facilities
- Poor quality image
- Lack of R&D capability
- Narrow product line
- Distance from markets
- Weak management
- Average age of employees high
- Narrow product line

EXTERNAL

Opportunities
- Overseas markets
- Acquisition possibilities
- Vertical integration
- Weakness among competition
- Drop in price of raw materials
- Technological innovations

Threats
- Adverse government policies
- Changing client needs
- Economic downturn
- Foreign competition
- Increase in interest rates
- Increase in union power

- Record of trouble free startups, and excellent first-year level of plant operation.
- Ability to offer a broad range of services in the oil and gas production area both on and offshore.
- Growing capability in the international arena.

Weaknesses

- Perception of a lack of flexibility in dealing with clients during contract negotiations, and the execution phase of the project.
- Lack of engineering design offices in strategic areas such as Asia, Europe, and the US gulf coast.
- Lack of cold climate (Alaska, Siberia, etc.) and harsh environment (Middle East, and Central America).
- Tendency to develop our own design systems and tools rather than investigating more efficient, and less expensive systems designed by others.

Opportunities

Examples of opportunities in the environment include the following.

Demographic changes For airlines, an increase in disposable income, more free time as a result of early retirement is significantly increasing the demand from vacation travellers. Alternatively, in the pharmaceutical industry, there is an increasing demand for certain medical products as a result of the growing ageing population.

New geographic markets New markets are opening in China, former eastern European countries with the fall of the Berlin Wall, South Africa now liberated from apartheid, and Central, and South America, which are more politically stable with democratic governments.

New products Government regulations on exhaust emissions are pushing the development of electric cars by such companies as Renault, General Motors, and Mercedes-Chrysler. New drugs are being developed by pharmaceutical companies to combat AIDS.

Government deregulation Government deregulation is opening up new markets, and permitting strategic alliances in, say, the airline industry (British Airways, Lufthansa, and certain US airlines) and in telecommunications (BT, France Télécom, and Deutsche Telekom).

Threats

Examples of threats in the environment include the following.

Government regulation Stricter regulations from governments for drug approval are making the introduction of new products a slow process for the pharmaceutical industry. Further, pressure to reduce medical costs, particularly in Europe, USA, and Japan, is cutting into profit margins.

Market saturation For automobile firms, market saturation, low level of vehicle replacement, plus route saturation pushing people into public transportation is cutting into sales of new vehicles.

Action plans to achieve objectives

Some of the long-range plans to meet the objectives of the strategic plan might include some of the following actions. (Many of these are discussed in further details in later chapters.)

New facilities

Constructing, or opening new facilities is one sure way of increasing market exposure. Examples would include BMW of Germany building a new automobile facility in the USA, BT of the UK opening telecommunication facilities in Europe, Formule 1 of France building hotels elsewhere in Europe, and the rapid expansion of fast food restaurants by McDonald's. (McDonald's hamburger chain is now present in over 100 countries.)

Expansion

As an alternative to the construction of a new facility, an existing one might be expanded. Oil refineries are often expanded, as are automobile manufacturing facilities, storage warehouses for distribution companies, and even supermarkets and other retail stores.

Acquisitions

Companies might resort to acquiring other companies as a route to market. Ford of the USA acquired Jaguar of the UK in 1989. Rhône Poulenc of France (now Rhodia in bulk chemicals and Aventis in life sciences after the combination with Hoechst of Germany) acquired Fisons of the UK in 1995. In the USA, Burlington Northern Railways swallowed Santa Fe Pacific and Wells Fargo bought First Interstate Bank in 1995/96. In France, as the government will not allow construction of new hypermarkets, acquisitions are occurring in the retail business. Auchan acquired Dock de France in 1996 and in September 1997 Promodes made a hostile bid for Casino.[6]

New technology

With the rapid pace of technological growth, firms have to update their facilities or products. This might include the installation of a new computer network for operations planning, telecommunication companies financing the launching of new communication satellites, automating an existing operating facility, or developing biotechnology methods for new pharmaceutical products.

Quantitative components of the strategic plan

In developing the strategic plan, it is necessary to quantify the objectives in the plan. Then, at the end of the plan period, one would be able to compare actual results with planned objectives.

Business firms

Market-driven organizations might have quantitative statements such as to:

- Increase market share by 15% in five years so that we are a market leader.
- Increase profits by 10% per year over the next five years.
- Have 5% of our business in China by 2000.

Non-profit organizations

Non-profit organizations might be able to quantity actions by such statements as to:

- Have a 95% literacy rate in a certain country within five years.
- Completely eradicate a disease in five years.
- Increase an intake of students by 25% over the next five years.

Pro-forma financial statements

Pro-forma financial statements are estimated income and balance sheet statements often prepared for each year during the planning period. They are developed by making estimates or forecasts of revenues, costs, and as such quantify in detail what are the expected outcomes from the defined strategic plan. (See the following section for further details on pro-forma income statements.)

Synergy strategy and operations

As mentioned, organizations develop global strategies and then plan, design, organize, and manage the operation in order to meet the strategic objectives. As such, strategies and operations are closely interwoven or there is a very strong synergy:

- For a desired strategy to be realized, all operating plans need to be in place.
- For operations to be successful, there has to be a well-defined strategy.

A strategy is very often long term, often unique, and is definable, although some organizations might have short-term strategies in, say, manufacturing, distribution, or sales in order to meet some well-defined objective. Opposed to these strategic elements are operations, which have a timeframe of usually less than one year, and are continuous and repetitive. Figure 2.2 illustrates the elements in the interface strategy/operations.

Figure 2.2 Synergy of the strategic and operating environments

The top part of the loop shows those activities that are principally strategic in nature. The bottom part of the loop gives those activities that are principally operational in nature. However, as the following indicates, the separation is not always clearly black and white:

- Quality management is a long-term activity but requires day-to-day attention.
- Environmental management is a long-term strategy but involves a day-to-day involvement.
- Facility layout is shown as operational because the design can be changed in the short term. However, changing the design is expensive and some firms might put the layout in a long-range plan.
- Project management is a daily activity but projects themselves can be long term.

Strategic importance of operations and the supply chain

In the previous chapter, a systems approach to the organization was presented highlighting that operations, marketing, and finance were the principal subsystems of the business firm. In this system, the strategic importance of operations, is illustrated with reference to the pro-forma income statement of Hershey, a US food company manufacturing food products including chocolate items (its principal products), sweets, and pasta. Figure 2.3 presents the actual 2000 income

statement[7] and then pro-forma statements based on three hypothetical assumptions concerning possible strategic objectives in each of the subsystems.

Marketing

The objective for the firm is that sales are to be increased by 50% above that obtained in 2000. In arriving at a new net income, cost of goods sold is assumed to increase by 50%, as are selling, marketing, and administrative expenses. All other costs and expenses and the tax rate remain the same. As illustrated in the pro-forma statement, this strategy would give an increase in net income of some 57%.

Finance

The objective for the firm is that the interest expense is to be reduced by 80% below that incurred in 2000. All other costs and expenses and the tax rate remain the same. As illustrated in the pro-forma statement, this strategy would give an increase in net income of 11%.

Operations

The objective for the firm is that operating costs are to be reduced by 25% below that incurred in 2000. In arriving at a new net income, sales are assumed to be unchanged and other expenses and the tax rate remain the same.

Figure 2.3 Strategic importance of operations

HERSHEY FOODS (all figures in $000s)	Actual 2000 income statement	Strategic options for various hypotheses		
		Increase sales by 50.00%	Reduce interest expense by 80.00%	Reduce operating costs by 25.00%
Sales	4,220,976	6,331,464	4,220,976	4,220,976
Cost of goods sold	2,471,151	3,706,727	2,471,151	1,853,363
Gross margin	1,749,825	2,624,738	1,749,825	2,367,613
Selling, marketing and administrative	1,127,175	1,690,763	1,127,175	1,127,175
Total cost and expenses	3,598,326	5,397,489	3,598,326	2,980,538
Income before interest and income taxes	622,650	933,975	622,650	1,240,438
Interest expense, net	76,011	76,011	15,202	76,011
Income before income taxes	546,639	857,964	607,448	1,164,427
Provision for income taxes	212,096	332,890	235,690	451,798
Net income	334,543	525,074	371,758	712,629
Tax rate on provision	38.80%	38.80%	38.80%	38.80%
Net income/sales	7.93%	8.29%	8.81%	16.88%
Increase in net income		190,531	37,215	378,086
Increase in net income (%)		56.95%	11.12%	113.02%

[for sales option, selling, marketing, and administrative expense increased by same proportion]

As illustrated in the pro-forma statement, this strategy would give an increase in net income of 113%.

Although it can be argued about the exact changes to the financial data, the direction is clear. The key entity in a company's strategy is its operations.

Responsibilities of the firm

Whether a firm is considering its strategies, or its operations, it has responsibilities to three principle parties as illustrated in Figure 2.4.

Employees

Poor employee relations as a result of the type of work, conditions in the production centre, salaries, and the like can reduce productivity. At the worst, a strike can stop production as Industry insight 2.2 illustrates.

Customers

Dissatisfied customers can reduce net income and market share, as customers turn to competitors.

Figure 2.4 Responsibilities of the firm

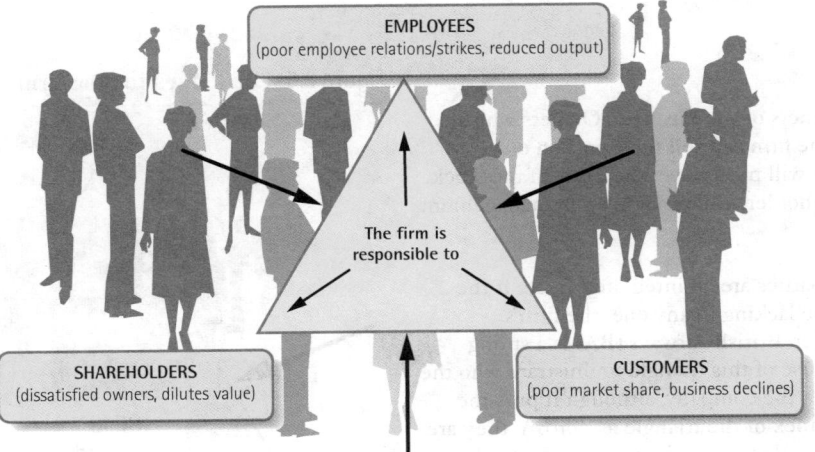

EMPLOYEES
(poor employee relations/strikes, reduced output)

The firm is responsible to

SHAREHOLDERS
(dissatisfied owners, dilutes value)

CUSTOMERS
(poor market share, business declines)

Industry insight 2.2

Strikes at Detroit

With a strike at a passenger car plant in its third week, General Motors faced a strike deadline late Tuesday at a Pontiac, Michigan, assembly plant that builds full-size trucks. A walkout by 5400 United Auto Workers, members at the Pontiac East plant, would halt production of GM's bread-and-butter pickups potentially biting into the N° 1 automaker's profits and hampering GM in the increasingly competitive pickup market. Officials of the UAW union (United Auto Workers) at the Pontiac plant contend that the automaker is violating a local 1995 union agreement that included promises to hire permanent assembly workers and slow the pace of work being farmed out to non-UAW suppliers. Under that agreement, which ended a six-day strike at the plant in the spring of 1995, GM has hired about 80 people and assigned them all to non-assembly jobs in the plant, according to

officials with Local 594. Meanwhile, GM is grappling with a strike at its Oklahoma City car assembly plant, which began 5 April and is recovering from a March strike at its Fort Wayne, Indiana, pickup truck assembly plant.

At the same time Chrysler (now Daimler-Chrysler) is contending with a two-week old strike at an engine plant that has crippled much of its light truck production. This strike by 1800 workers has crippled the N° 3 US automaker's ability to produce most of its highly profitable sports-utility vehicles and pickups. As this engine plant is part of the supply chain of 16 of Chrysler's truck plants, a total of 23,000 assembly and parts workers have been idle in the USA, Canada, and Mexico. Financial analysts say the strike has already reduced second-quarter earnings by 20 cents a share and is costing Chrysler $12 million a day in profit.

The main issue is the UAW's charge that Chrysler wants to outsource at least 300 jobs to an independent supplier. Chrysler contends that no jobs will be lost.

   These labour unrests suggest that even though the big three US automakers signed new three-year national labour pacts last fall, serious disagreements exist between the UAW and the automobile firms concerning staffing and outsourcing of work. (Ford Motor has been free of local strikes so far this year because it is relatively more productive than GM and Chrysler and thus is putting less pressure on the UAW.) Although the unions acknowledge that GM and Chrysler need to improve factory efficiency in order to remain competitive, they resist what they see as an excessively low staffing level in some plants. They also cite efforts by the automobile companies to skirt previous local agreements. National union contracts generally set broad guidelines for wages, benefits, training and grievances, but room is left for local unions to work out day-to-day plant operating details which are then ultimately spelled out in individual factory contracts. As a result, some powerful local unions can end up unravelling some of the automakers' gains in the national contract.

Adapted from: 'GM, Chrysler face strikes as local unrest remains', *Wall Street Journal Europe*[8]

Shareholders

These are the owners of the business. Owners who are not happy with the firm can sell their portion of ownership, which will push down the price of the stock. Dissatisfied shareholders can influence the management of the firm.

These principal parties are an integrated force. If the responsibilities are lacking to any one, the firm's activities will suffer. British Airways (BA) is a strong proponent of the use of this triangle to illustrate who the stakeholders are in the company, although it puts the customers at the apex of the triangle as, for BA, they are the most important element. British Airways says the customer is the product and if not treated correctly, they are perishable.[9] This type of triangle doesn't have the same importance to non-profit organizations, although there might be some similarities if one considers the government as a shareholder.

Challenges for the firm

Business firms have competitors and this jungle-type environment represents a challenge to the firm. No matter the product, or service, the major challenges revolve around quality, delivery, and cost and these can be represented by three axes (see Figure 2.5). A company which continually offers quality products will enhance its business. Delivery, the thrust of the supply chain, is meeting the planned time to market, or the due date promised to the client. The cost is either the producer's cost, or the price a consumer has to pay, or 'his cost'. These three are explicitly, or implicitly, part of the strategy. But they are also 'operational and supply' in that they are of daily concern.

Figure 2.5 Challenges for the firm

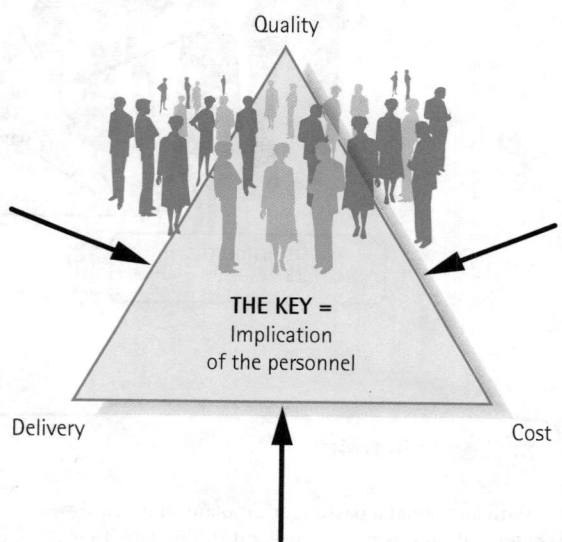

Real-world corporate strategic objectives

The following illustrates the real-world corporate objectives of some major corporations. They all stress the importance of the customer in the strategy.

Hewlett-Packard

This company, based in California, has seven corporate objectives as elaborated in the following.[10] The objectives stress the importance of profit, although this means profit integrated with other essential elements of a successful organization.

Profit

To achieve sufficient profit to finance our company growth and to provide the resources we need to achieve our other corporate objectives.

Customers

To provide products and services of the highest quality, and the greatest possible value to our customers, thereby gaining and holding their respect and loyalty.

Fields of interest

To participate in those fields of interest that build on our technology and customer base, that offer opportunities for continuing growth, and that enable us to make a needed and profitable contribution.

Growth

To let our growth be limited only by our profits and our ability to develop and produce innovative products that satisfy real customer needs.

Our people

- To help Hewlett-Packard people share in the company's success which they make possible.
- To provide employment security based on their performance.
- To ensure them a safe and pleasant work environment.
- To recognize their individual achievements.
- To help them gain a sense of satisfaction and accomplishment from their work.

Management

To foster initiative and creativity by allowing the individual great freedom of action in attaining well-defined objectives.

Citizenship

To honour our obligations to society by being an economic, intellectual, and social asset to each nation and each community in which we operate.

British Airways

This UK-based airline has four strategic objectives for its company.[11] They are elaborated in the following.

Inspired people

This is considered the dominant objective of the firm and relates to the company employees who need to be continually motivated, able to learn, and who benefit from the corporate success.

Customer choice

British Airways clients have a choice in the service offered by the airline.

Truly global

The company recognizes that it has to have presence internationally and this is one of the reasons why it is still pursuing an international alliance with American Airways. British Airways is the biggest European airline and American is the world's largest carrier. An alliance between the two was proposed in 1996 but was blocked by US and European regulators.[12]

Strong profitability

No firm can succeed without a strong balance sheet. Here, the cost is king! In the 1990s British Airways had been very profitable. However, at yearend 2000 it had a net loss of £97.8.[13]

To succeed in its strategy the company has a four-pronged approach:[14]

- Develop a marketing plan with universal appeal.
- Help employees understand the company's global vision.
- Benchmark mistakes that others may have made in the past.
- Select the right partners for joint ventures overseas.

IBM

Back in the late 1980s IBM was regarded as a national disaster. It was famous for blanketing big corporations with legions of pinstriped marketing and field engineering troops. It had become distant, arrogant, and unresponsive. Now with Louis V Gerstner Jr as Chairman and Chief Executive Officer, IBM is once again one of the most profitable computer makers. Gerstner's strategy is customer relationships, talking to customers, learning their needs, and figuring out how to satisfy them. Gerstner says:[15]

- You start the day with customers.
- You start thinking about a company around its customers.
- You organize around customers.

Summary of key elements

- The global strategic objectives of the market-based firm are to grow by exploiting opportunities. If firms ignore the external environment, or adapt only enough to survive, they will be eventually fail, or be swallowed.

- The global strategic objectives of a non-profit organization are essentially sustainability, and the status quo. Its operation must be consistent with financial resources, its sources and use of funds should be matched, and it should provide equitable services for all generations.

- The timeframe of a strategic plan is nominally five years but may vary according to the industry. New, high-technology firms may have a shorter time-frame, whereas established firms with high capital projects may have a much longer timeframe.

- A mission statement, or charter, describes in general terms the activity of the organization and it is the start point, or the root of the strategic plan.

- A SWOT analysis (strengths, weaknesses, opportunities, and threats) is a strategic planning tool to aid an organization to match its internal characteristics with the external environment.

- Action plans to achieve strategic objectives might be constructing new facilities, expansion of existing facilities, acquisitions of other companies, creating new markets, or the application of new technology.

- A strategic plan needs to quantify its expected outcome, which may be in terms of profit, market share, geographic territory, or unit measurements. Pro-forma financial statements are instruments useful for quantifying a strategic plan.

- A firm's strategy and operations are closely interwoven. Neither exists without the other. For a desired strategy to be realized, all the operating plans need to be properly defined. For operations to be successful, there has to be a well-defined strategy.

- In the integrated system – operations, marketing, and finance – operations plays a dominant role and cost reductions in this area can have the biggest impact on the firm's financial performance.

- The responsibilities of the firm are to its employees, its customers, and its shareholders.

- The principal challenges to the firm concern quality of products, processes or services, delivery time, and cost.

- Real-world strategic objectives have the customer in the pole position. This is often followed by profits, the people in the firm, and continued growth.

Notes and references

1. HERZLINGER, Regina E., 'Effective oversight: A guide for non-profit directors', *Harvard Business Review*, July–August 1994, pp 52–60
2. The reshaping of British Railways, *A British Railways Board Report*, Chairman Dr Beeching
3. ExxonMobil 1999 Annual Report, p. 11
4. SULLIVAN, Allana, 'Old Gusher: Four decades later, oilfield off Canada is ready to produce. Politics, money and nature put vast deposit on ice. Now it may last 50 years. Shot in the arm for the US', *Wall Street Journal Europe*, 2 April 1997
5. Based on CERTO, Samuel C., *Principles of Modern Management: Functions and Systems*, Allyn & Bacon, London, 4th edition, 1989, p. 144
6. 'Food fight: Promodes shakes up France in hostile bid for Casino, Rallye', *Wall Street Journal Europe*, 2 September 1997
7. Hershey, Pennsylvania, *Hershey Corp*, 2000 Annual Report.
8. CHRISTIAN, Nichole M., STERN, Gabriella, *Wall Street Journal Europe*, 23 April 1997
9. Presentation by COOPER, George, European Director of British Airways, at the G7 Management Conference, 16 May 1997, Lyon Graduate School of Business (with permission)
10. *The HP Way Hewlett-Packard*, company brochure 1994 (with permission)
11. COOPER, George, European Director of British Airways (with permission)
12. 'American and BA set course: Airlines revive plan for major alliance', *International Herald Tribune*, 4–5 August 2001, p. 11
13. Financial Times 500: The world's largest companies (The UK 500), 11 May 2001
14. 'Flying high, going global', *Fortune*, 7 July 1997, pp 87–9
15. 'How IBM became a growth company again: It's raking in new business, its stock is roaring, and it's regaining the respect of Corporate America. What's Gerstner's secret?', *Business Week*, 9 December 1996, p. 36

Review and discussion topics

1. Proactive or reactive
What firms do you believe today are pursuing a proactive strategy? A reactive strategy? Explain your reasoning. Do their financial results support your conclusions?

2. Mission statements
What do you believe would be the mission statement of:
(a) a medical centre
(b) hypermarket/supermarket firms like Tesco or Sainsbury's in the UK, Carrefour or Leclerc in France, or Albertson or Ralphs in the USA
(c) a law firm
(d) an armaments factory
(e) a cigarette company?

3. New business opportunities

Where do you believe are the new business opportunities today according to:
(a) geographical location
(b) new products?

4. Government policies and strategies

How do government policies affect the strategies of firms? Justify your reasoning and, where possible, give real illustrations.

5. Firm's responsibilities

The text indicates that a firm has a responsibility to its employees, clients, and owners. Some companies say that their responsibilities are solely to our owners, since it is they who provide the financing and who take the risk for the firm. Contrariwise, the argument goes that employees are remunerated with salaries so that our responsibilities are abrogated. Very often, when a company announces layoffs,

the market value, as indicated by the stock price, rises (Renault, AT&T, IBM). Similarly, useful products are provided to the client and this nullifies any further responsibility. What is your opinion?

6. SWOT analysis

You are studying at university or business school for a career. Develop a SWOT analysis for yourself. What do you perceive are your strengths and weaknesses? What are the opportunities and threats posed to you, taking into consideration your career objectives?

7. Operations and strategy

The basic supply chain of the automobile covers raw materials and components from suppliers, manufacturing and assembly, and distribution of the final product to customers. Using Figure 2.6, indicate what some of the operating elements are that would have an impact on the strategic objectives of the firm.

Figure 2.6 Cause and effect diagram: Synergy, strategy and operations

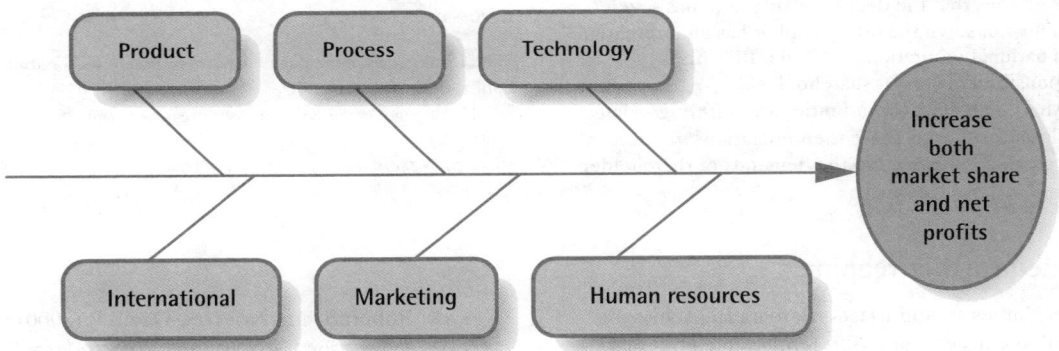

Case study 2.1 British Petroleum

Situation

Lima is a town in western Ohio, USA, some 100 kilometres from the Canadian border. It was in that region, in 1885, that Benjamin C Faurot discovers oil and, the following year, John D Rockefeller purchases 151 acres of navy bean fields for $200 to build the Solar oil refinery at Lima. In 1931, Standard Oil of Ohio (Sohio) bought the Lima refinery from Solar. In 1948 it carried out a $30 million refinery expansion and then, the following year, Sohio, jointly with Sun Oil start work on a 1600 km long pipeline from Texas to Ohio through Mid-Valley Pipeline Co., a jointly owned affiliate. These construction projects make Lima an important oil centre.

In 1967 Sohio spent another $75 million to expand the refinery and in the following two years British Petroleum

agreed with Sohio to trade part of its interest in the Alaska Prudhoe Bay oilfield for minority stock ownership in the Lima refinery. As production increased from Prudhoe Bay, BP's percentage ownership in the refinery increased. In 1987 purchase of the remaining Sohio stock for $7.6 billion made BP the sole owner of the Lima refinery.[1]

In January 1996 BP announced plans to rationalize its international refining system and this included closing its Lima refinery, even though productivity had risen 30%. In addition, it planned to close another facility at Lavera, in southern France, and also the Pernis section of the Nerefco refinery complex at Rotterdam in the Netherlands. BP's rationale was that there was overcapacity in its refineries and profit margins at these sites were low. BP said it would only operate refineries that are among the top 25% in efficiency and profitability in their respective regions. At the time the Lima facility, with a capacity of 160,000 barrels/day employed 455 people, Lavera, with a capacity of 200,000 bbl/day employed 620, and the Nerefco complex, of some 420,000 bbl/day, employed 875 people. BP said it hoped to minimize layoffs but would make no guarantee. In November 1996 BP announced that only three bids were received for the sale of the Lima facility, all of which were unacceptable. Thus, the refinery would be closed within two years and likely turned into a terminal. BP's stock price began climbing on the news of the closures.[2]

The impact on the small community of 48,000 at Lima was enormous. The city relied on the refinery not only for jobs, but it covers 260 hectares of real estate which generates $26 million annually in fees to utilities, plus $11 million to local businesses. The concern was that the land would become a wasteland. However, the response from BP's Vice President, David Atton was: 'BP realizes that the decision made here has severe ramifications. On the other hand, it has an international and national reputation to defend. BP's first responsibility is to our shareholders.'

More than ever, communities are suffering as large multinational firms cease their operations in efforts to cut costs, and respond to the demands of shareholders.

In Papendrecht, the Netherlands, 1200 people were made redundant when Daimler-Benz of Germany stopped funding NV Fokker Airplane Company in 1996. Similarly, in early 1997, the residents of Vilvoorde, Belgium, learned of a similar fate when 3100 workers and as many as 1000 suppliers were told they would be axed when Renault decided to close its automobile facility there.[3]

Required

Review this strategic decision to close down an operation and its impact:

(a) What are your opinions? Do you agree with management's decision?
(b) What is its impact?
(c) Do you believe there are any alternatives?
(d) Do you think international companies should have long-term obligations to local communities in which they establish operations?

Give as much detail and justification as you feel is necessary.

[1] The Lima News home page, http://www.limanews.com/bp/bphist.html, 28 April 1997.
[2] BP Homepage, http://www.bp.com/press/pr2.html, 28 April 1997.
[3] *Wall Street Journal Europe*, 25 March 1996.

Selected further reading

FLYNN, James E. and FLYNN, Barbara B. 'Achieving simultaneous cost and differentiation competitive advantages through continuous improvement: World class manufacturing as a competitive strategy', *Journal of Managerial Issues*, vol. 8, issue 3, autumn 1996, pp 360–79.

HILL, Terry (1999) *Manufacturing Strategy: Text and Cases*, 3rd edition, Irwin/McGraw-Hill.

KAPLAN, Robert S. and NORTON, David P. (2000) *The Strategy-Focused Organization: How Balanced Scorecard Companies Thrive in the New Business Environment*, Harvard Business School Press.

PORTER, Michael E. (1998) *Competitive Strategy: Techniques for Analyzing Industries and Competitors*, Free Press.

THOMPSON, John L. (1997) *Strategic Management*, 3rd edition, Thomson Learning.

An extensive listing of other further reading can be found on the website.

What's on the web?

Further learning resources are available to lecturers and students at www.supplychain-online.com, including the following which are specific to *Strategy of organizations*:

Resource	Subject
Chapter overview	Strategy of organizations
Case study: Group Michelin	Strategy of organizations
More further reading	Strategy of organizations

3 Site selection

Chapter overview

- Defining site selection
- Staffing
- Inherent local conditions
- Infrastructure
- Construction
- Factors that impact cash flow
- Financial aid
- Proximity of resources
- Quantitative approaches to site selection

Defining site selection

Site selection, or facility location, for either manufacturing or service organizations is deciding on a location for constructing, expanding, or acquiring, a physical entity of a firm in order to reach new markets, increase production capacity, and/or better serve clients. As illustrated in Figure 3.1, the physical entity may be a warehouse for raw materials, a manufacturing centre, a distribution centre for finished products, or a retail outlet. These would all represent physical plant in a material supply chain. Alternatively, the new facility may be an office block with communication equipment, an airport, a hospital, a school, a hotel, a restaurant etc., to better serve an expanding market. In the supply chain, the location of the operating facility is a critical factor regarding timely delivery of tangible products or services. Also, if a firm uses many suppliers and subcontractors when these are located close to the client firm lead times are shorter and transportation costs are lower.

Nature of the facility

A chosen site for a new facility may be grassroots, that is to say virgin land on which a completely new installation will be built. Alternatively, the location may contain an existing facility, which needs to be modified to serve the needs of the firm. Site selection may be relatively easy for a small regional company, or very complex for large

multinationals where many factors come into play. A selected site may be domestic, in the country where the parent company is based, or it may be international, located hundreds of miles away from the parent office in a foreign country. The following gives some illustrations.

Domestic site

- General Motors based in Detroit, in the USA, selects to build the new Saturn automobile facility in Spring Hill, Tennessee, 56 km south of Nashville.
- Valéo, a manufacturer of automobile parts based in Paris, France, constructs a facility for assembling starter motors in L'Isle d'Abeau near Lyon.
- British Petroleum, based in London, expands its ethylene capacity at its facility in Grangemouth, in Scotland, from 270,000 to 600,000 tons a year in 1992.
- Sainsbury's, a food company in the UK decides to build a new store in Watford, north of London in the 1990s.

International site

- Nissan of Japan locating an automobile facility in Smyrna, Tennessee, in 1981.
- The decision of Daimler-Benz (now Daimler-Chrysler) of Germany to build a factory in Tuscaloosa, Alabama, in September 1993.
- ABB/CEE a subsidiary of Switzerland's Asea Brown Boveri builds a power plant in Indonesia in 1989.
- Marks & Spencer, the British retail store, opens a store in Lyon, France, in the 1980s. However, it decides to close it in 2001!

Figure 3.1 Site selection

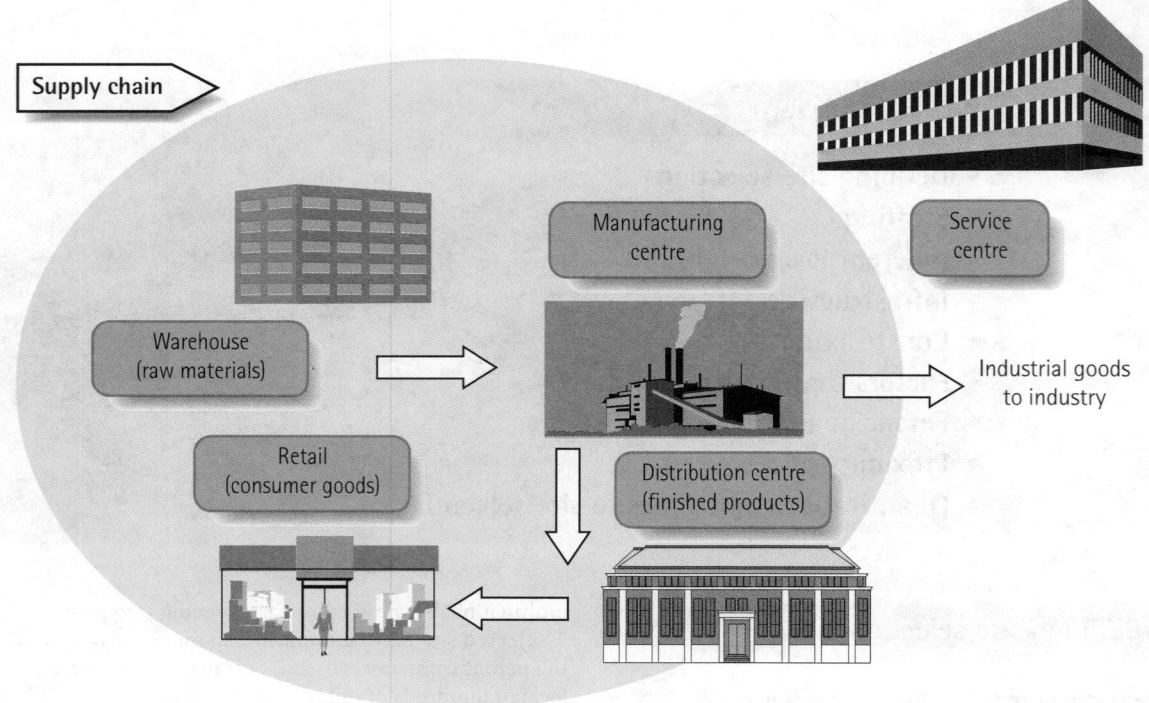

- Mckinsey Consulting of the USA opens up a new office in Osaka, Japan, in the late 1980s.
- McDonald's of the USA opens a new fast food restaurant in Beijing, China, in the 1990s.
- General Motors of the USA opens a new automobile factory near Gravatai in Rio Grande do Sul in Brazil in July 2000.

  The ultimate decision on site selection is based on such criteria as the level of revenues expected to be generated and the cost of operating the new facility. Site selection for a manufacturing facility is more complex than it is for an office facility, retail outlet, or a distribution centre, as there is a bigger capital investment, a higher content of labour requirements, and thus a greater downside risk. Deciding on a location for a new facility may take months because of the many variables to be taken into consideration.

Strategy and operations

Site selection is a strategic, long-term decision made at top management level. However, it is part of the

operations management environment because:

- Operations management personnel are solicited for their opinions concerning site selection.
- Operations management will be responsible for running the new facility once construction is finished.
- The choice of a site can mean the success or failure of an operation and the efficiency of the supply chain. Operations managers would need to respond to such considerations as:
  - Are cost controllable?
  - Is there stability in the region?
  - Is the labour force adaptable to the types of operation?
  - Are there suppliers located nearby and are they dependable regarding quality and delivery?
  - Are the energy sources reliable?
  - Is there a reliable transportation system?

Markets

The ultimate objective of a business firm is to sell the product or service, and thus the proximity and reliability of the final market is a key concern. That is, what is the expected risk? Even though potential markets exist, companies need to be able to evaluate the expected market growth, competition from local firms, and the expectation of new competitors moving into the area. For service companies such as financial institutions, restaurants, hotels, retail outlets, consulting firms, and the like the site selected has to be close to the client. For manufacturing firms this may not be so critical because physical products can be shipped from one location to another. Certainly, many manufacturing firms locate in low cost production areas, and then export their products to other regions.

Asia

Many companies are locating in emerging economies in Asia, particularly China, not necessarily because labour is cheaper but because that region is a target market. The criterion is that these areas represent a large untapped market relative to developed economies, which have a relatively stagnant market. Table 3.1 illustrates the potential size of the Asian market relative to other regions. Of the Asian population, China has about 1.2 billion people, or 22% of the world's population.[1]

As illustrations, automobile companies (General Motors, Toyota, and Group PSA), telecommunications firms (AT&T and British Telecom), construction companies (Bechtel, Fluor, and Bouygues) and nuclear plant designers and constructors (Electricité de France and Framatome) are some of the types of companies with facilities in China.

Table 3.1 Potential size of Asian market compared to other regions

	Millions	% of total
Asia	3,245	59
Africa	660	12
Europe	550	10
Former Soviet Union	330	6
Latin America	440	8
North America	275	5
Total	**5,500**	**100**

Strategic role of foreign factories

Kasra Ferdows, in the *Harvard Business Review*, developed a classification of foreign factories. He described how the strategic role of foreign factories could be divided into six types.[2]

Offshore factory

An offshore factory is one that is established to produce specific products, at a low cost, which are then later exported. At this site, there is little development or engineering.

Source factory

A source factory also produces at low cost but operations managers have a greater control over procurement, production planning, process planning, and design decisions.

Server factory

A server factory is set up to supply national or regional markets. This facility provides for the parent firm, a way to overcome tariffs, reduce taxes, minimize logistics costs, and to reduce the exposure to fluctuating currency exchange rates.

Contributor factory

Like the server factory, a contributor factory also serves national or regional markets, but it goes further in that its responsibilities extend to product design, process engineering, and supplier selection.

Outpost factory

The primary role of an outpost factory is to collect information for strategic purposes for the parent firm. As such, it is located in areas where there are competitors, research laboratories, and customers. Of course to justify its existence, the outpost factory is also a producer but this is often a secondary strategic role.

Lead factory

A lead factory creates new process, products, and technologies for the entire company. Operations managers in these facilities have a key role in the choice of suppliers and the type of development work.

Corporate towns

From the turn of the century up to the early 1950s, when companies were very paternalistic, site selection of facilities was often governed by offering employees a host of benefits in addition to employment. This phenomenon gave birth to company towns where the firm was in many respects able to control the life of the employees even when they were not in the work centre. Some examples are as follows:[3]

- *Corning*, a technology firm (Corning Glass), was established in a small town named Corning, in the Appalachians, in upstate New York. Half of the 12,000 inhabitants work for Corning, and many of the rest work for subsidiaries or dependants.
- *IBM* has its headquarters in Endicott, also in New York State. Here there are several manufacturing plants, the IBM golf course, and a street, Watson Boulevard, named after Thomas Watson, a former chairman.
- *Boeing* aircraft company had its headquarters in Seattle, Washington, USA. The firm once so dominated this city that Senator Henry Jackson was known as the senator from Boeing. In 2001 Boeing decided to relocate its corporate offices to Chicago.
- *Hitachi*, the engine maker, is at a site 160 km north of Tokyo called Hitachi City.
- *Ford Motor's* River Rouge plant outside Detroit was once one of the world's biggest company towns. In its day this modern factory, with some 100,000 workers, offloaded iron ore and sand from freighters at one end of the complex, and rolled out finished cars from the other made from its own smelted steel. Today, this icon of 20th-century manufacturing is little more than an industrial ghost town, employing around 10,000 people, with most of its facilities rusting, little used, or abandoned.[4]
- *Cadbury* (now Cadbury-Schweppes) was relocated on 18 June 1878 by its founder, George Cadbury, from the grime of Birmingham to Bourneville, four miles south of the centre of Birmingham, to escape from the 'unwholesomeness of city life'. Bourneville cocoa was once one of its main products.[5]
- *Lever Brothers*, founded by William Lever, the soap baron, selected a model site outside Liverpool called Port Sunlight to give a more rural lifestyle to his employees.
- *Rowntree*, started by Joseph Rowntree, built New Earswick, in England, as his company town. This was a traditional-looking village that one of his architects said 'gave life just that order, that crystalline structure it had in feudal times'.
- *Krupp* steel company chose a company site in Margaretenhohe, near Essen, Germany.
- *Pullman*, the railroad car builder started by George Pullman, built a beautiful town for his employees on the outskirts of Chicago in the 'belief that a rational

and aesthetic order would elevate the character of his workers'.
- *Broken Hill Proprietary Co.*, the Australian mining company, established Newman in a desolate part of Western Australia as its company town.
- *Philips Petroleum* chose Bartlesville, Oklahoma, USA as its company town because of crude oil in this region. Bartlesville has since fallen on hard times.
- *Phelps Dodge*, a copper-producing company, selected Tyrone, in a remote corner of New Mexico, USA, as the site of its company town.

Company towns are just about non-existent today as industries have merged, reorganization has taken place, other firms move into the area, or employees have become much less dependent on a single employer.

Factors in site selection

There are numerous factors to be considered in site selection such as staffing, local conditions, construction feasibility, financial concerns, proximity of subcontractors and suppliers, availability of energy and raw materials, etc. Within these are sub-considerations, which make the whole selection process complex. These are all discussed later in this chapter. However, this is not to say that site selection is sometimes made on a whim, or personal preference of owners, or top management personnel, as these examples demonstrate:

- A US managing director relocated his company from New York to Colorado, so that he could be close to the ski slopes.
- A British chairman insisted a distribution centre was close to the French Riviera where his yacht was berthed.
- A Japanese entrepreneur checked prospective sites in Europe that were closest to top golf courses.

Staffing

Staffing for a firm includes the hiring of all the types of personnel needed to run a facility including direct and indirect operating personnel and management. Some of the factors in staffing are now discussed.

Labour costs

The cost of direct wages is probably one of the most important criteria in site selection. It helps to explain why many international companies, based in the USA, Europe, and Japan have built facilities away from their own country. Labour costs enter directly into the cost of manufactured products, or the cost of providing a

Figure 3.2 Hourly labour costs in manufacturing (1999)

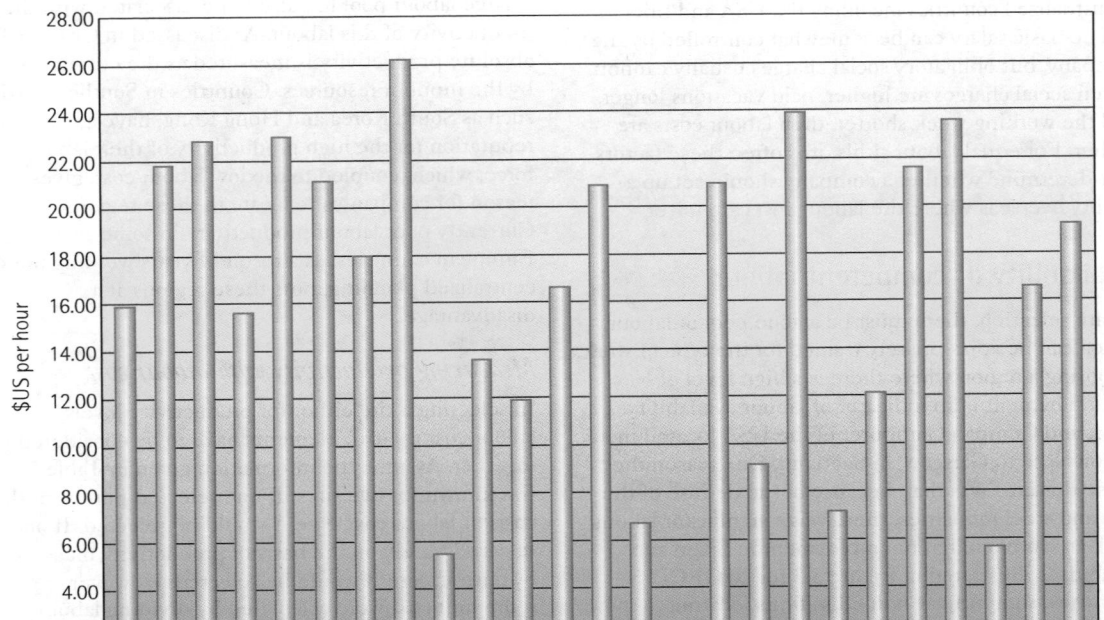

service. The higher the labour costs, the higher is the
product, or service cost. Labour costs include not only
the basic salary, or wages, but all social and other charges
(the burden) paid to the employee, or paid by the
employer to the government in the form of taxes for the
employee in question. Figure 3.2[6] gives data for labour
costs in 25 different countries, showing that for the
information presented, Germany is the most expensive
labour cost country with a cost of $26.18 an hour
whereas Mexico is the least expensive at $2.12 an hour.

Social charges

Social charges cover medical insurance, social security
payments, paid vacations, retirement benefits,
unemployment benefits, and, in some cases, paid
educational programmes. The law of the country
mandates these charges and this explains why countries
in Europe such as Germany, Norway, and Denmark
have such high labour costs. The impact of the social
charge can reverse the impact of the other. For example,
wages paid in Denmark are higher than in Germany, but
when German social charges are added, Germany has
the highest total cost.

Social laws

Social laws, which directly impact social charges, concern
labour flexibility such as the basic workweek, overtime
permitted, weekend working, hiring and termination laws.
Social laws are also a strong factor on deciding where a
company should locate. In 1992 the European Union
enacted the Social Chapter of the Maastricht Treaty
allowing it more flexibility in its employment practices.
The objectives of this chapter are, 'the promotion of
employment, improved living and working conditions,
proper social protection, dialogue between management
and labour, the development of human resources with a
view to lasting employment and the combating of social
exclusion'. The then prime minister of the Conservative
government, John Major, opted out of this social charter.
When it was signed, the Social Chapter was heralded as a
boon to workers, strengthening their rights, and social
protection. Although social protection is a worthy
objective it is very damaging to smaller firms and those
competing internationally and it is pricing Europe out
of the world market. Having all the social benefits in
the world is not very helpful if you don't have a job! A
further blow to Europe's competitiveness is the adoption

of the 35-hour week in France in 2000 (being considered by Italy) compared to the 40-hour week in many other industrialized countries including the USA and Britain.

The basic salary can be somewhat controlled by the company, but obligatory social charges usually cannot. When social charges are higher, paid vacations longer, and the working week shorter, then labour costs are higher. For equal labour skills, it is often these factors that determine whether a company should set up a facility overseas where the labour costs are lower.

Availability of competent labour

In site selection, there must be a good pool of labour, which can be appropriately trained for the type of work. Choosing a region where there is a high level of unemployment is an indicator of labour availability. IBM, and Compaq Computer of the USA located in a region close to Glasgow, in Scotland. One reason they chose this area was that, because of the demise of the coal and steel industries, there was a significant labour pool. In Europe, high unemployment in Spain and Ireland, as illustrated in Figure 3.3 for 20 OECD countries, significantly helped in firms locating to those countries. In Spain the unemployment rate was about 21% in 1997 forecasting to drop to 12% in 2002. Equivalent figures for Ireland are 11 and 4%.[7]

Productivity

A large labour pool has also to be associated with the productivity of this labour. As discussed in Chapter 1, absolute productivity is measured as the output divided by the input of resources. Countries in Southeast Asia, such as South Korea and Hong Kong, have a reputation for the high productivity of their labour force, which, coupled to the low labour cost, gives reason for companies to locate in these regions. Currently poor labour productivity in some eastern European countries, as a result of years working under centralized planning, puts these regions at a disadvantage.

Measuring productivity with labour cost

In selecting a site either for productivity levels, or labour cost the two elements have to be considered together. Assume the information given in Table 3.2 was known for two sites. If one selected purely on the basis of labour cost, Site A would be selected. If one selected purely on the basis of productivity measured by output, Site B would be selected. However, if the unit cost were calculated by dividing labour cost by productivity, there would be a trade-off between the two sites. There is a breakeven situation at £0.16 per unit.

Figure 3.3 Unemployment as a percentage of labour force

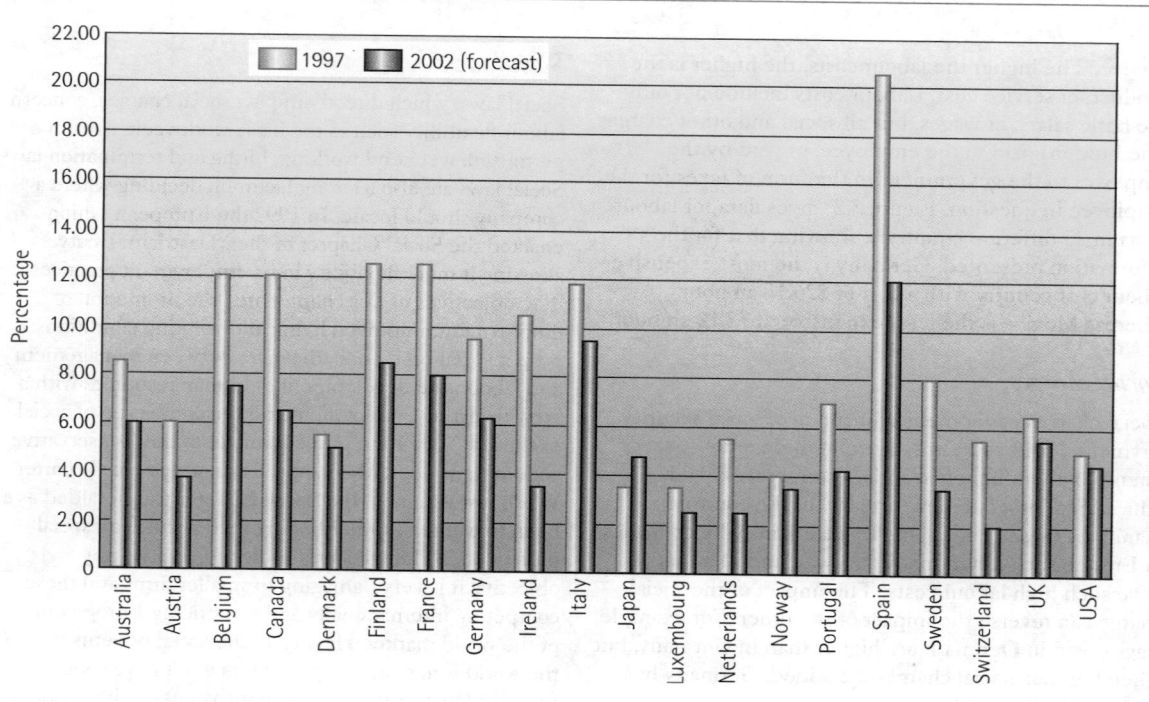

Trade unions

Strong trade union power in a country is a strong deterrent for a firm to locate in that region. Many trade unions in industrial countries, concerned about unemployment, are rigid, reluctant to modernize, unable to accept new technology, or to adopt labour enhancements to improve a firm's productivity. Tony Blair, UK Prime Minister, underscored these facts about union rigidity in a speech to the Trade Union Congress (TUC) in Brighton on 9 September 1997.[8]

Union membership

Overall, union membership in industrialized countries is declining, as illustrated in Figure 3.4,[9] for 17 OECD countries in 1980 and 1990. Only Finland and Sweden are exceptions. Trade union power suffered the biggest decline in Spain, where membership fell from 25% to

11% during the decade. Union membership was lowest in France where in 1990 only 10% of French workers belonged to a union. By contrast, 83% of Swedish workers belonged to a union in 1990. On average, trade union membership in OECD countries fell by 6.4 percentage points in the period 1980–1990. Some reasons for union decline is that:

- Service industries, which are usually non-unionized, are replacing manufacturing firms, which historically have been the bedrock of unions.
- Women, who make up a fast growing part of the labour force, are not eager to join unions that are almost exclusively run by men.
- Self-employed individuals, or small businesses that are a fast growing sector of the economy, do not, in most cases, belong to unions. These groups have to be *flexible* and *competitive* to survive and thus are not attracted by rhetoric that continually casts scorn on those two words.
- Young people are also thinly unionized. They are seemingly reluctant to join the ranks of the predominantly middle-aged union members.

Industrial action

Related to the union membership for site selection is the country's history of industrial action, or strikes, which is illustrated in Figure 3.5.[10] During the 1990s rich countries lost an annual average of 59 working days

Table 3.2 **Measuring productivity with labour cost**

Variable element	Site A	Site B
Labour cost, £/hour	16.00	20.00
Productivity, units/hour	100.00	125.00
Cost per unit, £/unit	0.16	0.16

Figure 3.4 **Trade union membership (1980 and 1990)**

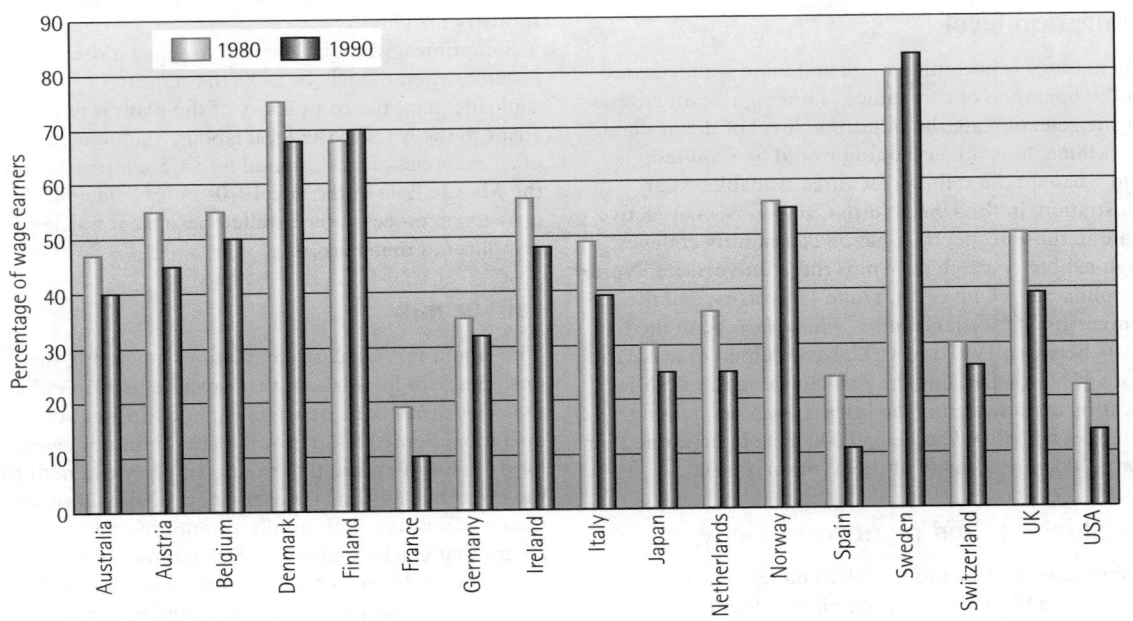

Figure 3.5 Labour disputes (1990–1999)

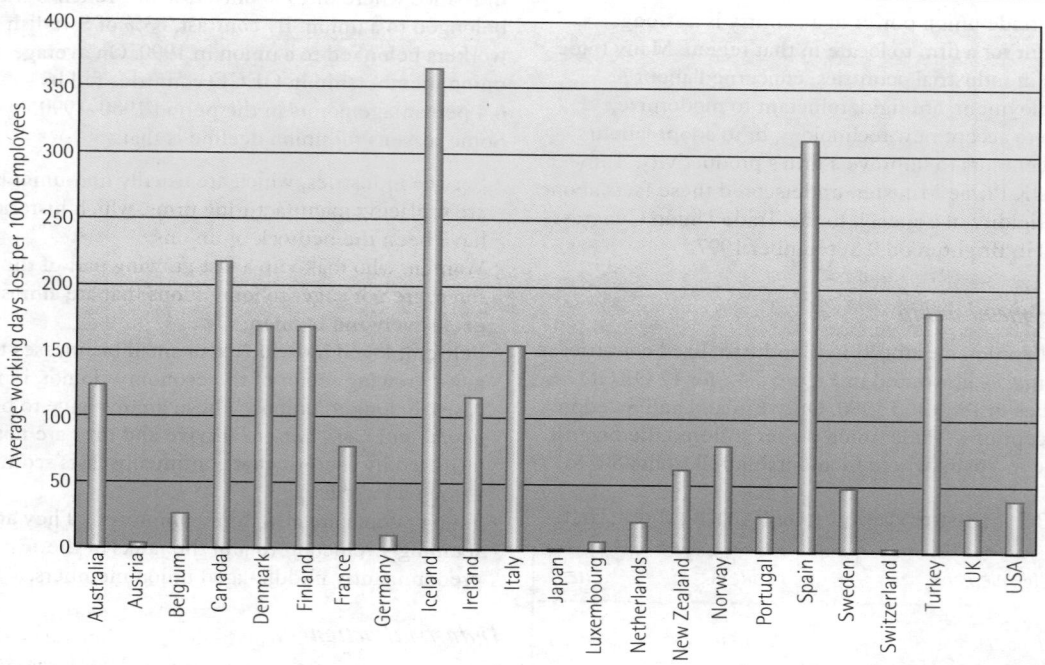

per 1000 employees in labour disputes. The three at the top end of the scale were Iceland, Spain, and Canada with respectively 364, 312, and 245 lost days and at the bottom end, Japan, Switzerland, and Austria with fewer than five days.

Education level

Technology is becoming more and more sophisticated in the operation of companies. Thus significant criteria in site selection are the education level of the available workforce, how much training would be required, and what are the training facilities available. As an illustration, in the USA, North Carolina is an attractive state in these respects. It has 58 community colleges, a high-calibre research park plus three universities; North Carolina State University, Duke University, and the University of North Carolina. These factors, in the five years between 1987 and 1992, have helped to make the state of North Carolina the first choice in the USA for locating manufacturing facilities. In worker training schemes since 1963 some 250,000 have been trained for some 3000 firms, many of them international.[11]

Local labour and plant technology

Continuous flow facilities such as oil refineries, chemical, and food processing plants often have complex process control systems that require a certain

sophistication of the operating labour. Problems can arise if the labour pool is unable to be adequately trained such that the facility can be operated according to specification design, including safety considerations. This was one of the factors cited as the reason for the Union Carbide accident at Bhopal, India, described in Industry insight 3.1.

Sometimes, when it is critical to select a site in a location when the labour lacks the required sophistication, the complexity of the plant is reduced to adapt to the level of the local labour. Such was the case of an ethylene plant designed by a US constructor for the Middle East in the late 1970s. A less efficient conversion process was installed because it was less complicated to manage.[12]

Labour mix

The labour mix concerns regulations governing the percentage of local labour that must be used in either the construction of a new facility, or its subsequent operation. Some countries stipulate minimum levels of local labour to ensure that their own people benefit from the economic advantages of the new facility. If this is the case, it puts a limit on the amount of expatriate labour that can be employed. Regulations such as these can cause problems for the country concerned if the local labour does not have the required educational capacity to perform the work. In the Bhopal situation

Industry insight 3.1

Union Carbide and Bhopal

Union Carbide of the USA built a pesticide facility in India in 1969, needed as a result of the increased production of wheat, rice, and corn. The pesticide plant used the highly toxic methyl isocyanate (MIC) as a raw material that initially was imported. To eliminate the need for imports, a methyl isocyanate plant was constructed at Bhopal, by Humphrey's & Glasgow of the UK between 1975 and 1980. In 1982 the facility was turned over to Indian personnel.

On 3 December 1984 personnel cleaned out a pipe in the MIC storage system without installing a slip blind (used to prevent backflow of fluid). This violated maintenance procedures. As a result, water entered the MIC storage tank causing an exothermic reaction. The temperature and pressure of the tank increased rapidly.

Refrigeration units used to cool tanks were inoperable since they had been shut down five months earlier as an economy measure. The gas pressure increased to such a level that the safety release valve opened, releasing MIC gas into the atmosphere. A safety scrubber used to neutralize MIC gas could not be used as that was down for maintenance. Similarly, the flare tower designed to burn off gases was also down for repairs. Emergency transfer tanks for the MIC could not be used, as they were full.

In two hours 45 tons of methyl isocyanate gas had leaked into the atmosphere. The result was an official death toll of 2347 and extensive injuries including blindness and respiratory ailments.

Adapted from: 'The Union Carbide Corporation and Bhopal', *Business, Government and Society*[13]

described in Industry insight 3.1, it was pressure from the Indian government, that, in 1982, required that the plant be turned over to Indian personnel as opposed to previously Union Carbide expatriate personnel.

Inherent local conditions

Inherent local conditions include factors such as climate, culture, and language, which are important not only to the personnel employed by the company, but also to the associated families. Some considerations are as follows.

Climate

Regions where there are many days of sunshine and good weather present attractive locations for facilities. People prefer to live in these regions and consequently it is easier to recruit personnel if a company is located in the sun belt. In the USA this explains the rapid growth of California, Florida, and Texas to the detriment of the harsher climate of the northeast. In Europe, Sophia-Antipolis, a science park created in 1969 on 2300 hectares on the French Mediterranean coast has proved to be a magnet for many industrial companies. It has attracted nearly 1000 different firms, including IBM, Cordis, a US medical company, and Tepar, an oil company joint venture including Texaco, and Elf Aquitaine. Even though it is an expensive area in which to live with high rents, and rigid planning controls, there is a waiting list for new occupants. Similarly, the agreeable climate is one of the reasons why Spain, Malta, and Greece are attractive.[14] However, Greece loses its attraction because of its poor labour relations.[15]

Besides the benefits to employees, a warmer climate translates into lower operating energy costs. Also, the cost of construction materials may be lower in warmer regions as insulation requirements are not as rigorous, and foundation depth can be lower if there is no danger of deep freezing. In addition, a new facility can be built more quickly in warmer climates because almost 12 months of the year are available for construction. In the northern climates the window may be reduced by four months or more because of bad weather. In Alaska, it is even worse where construction project planning is complicated because the window for construction is only about five months. This was one of the constraints presented to C F Braun, a southern Californian construction company, building an ammonia facility on the Kenai Peninsular in the 1970s.[16]

Climate was an important factor for the location of the Port Aventura theme park southwest of Barcelona, Spain, by the consortium of Anheuser-Busch (USA), and Tussauds' Group (UK) in 1995.[17] Euro Disney, with a similar product, chose the region around Paris even though Spain was originally a consideration. This region, with its relative proximity to the northern Europe population, and good transportation links for Disney Corporation overrode the negative impact of the northern French climate.

Culture

In the rapid expansion periods after World War II companies, particularly from the USA, employed large numbers of expatriate personnel in their overseas facilities. Expatriates are nationals of the country in which the head office is located, who are sent overseas on a time-limited contract. They are usually paid a premium on their salary according to the difficulty of the location. Saudi Arabia would be considered more difficult than England, for example. Using expatriates is very costly not only because of the salary premium, but also because housing and transportation has to be provided for the employee and, if married, his family. In addition, using expatriates is not always successful because either the employee is unable to adapt, or his wife and family cannot, and this puts a stress on the employee. Industry insight 3.2 gives three actual situations concerning cultural differences.[18] As a result of the high cost, finding the right individuals, and the requirement of foreign governments to use local people, the use of expatriate personnel has declined.

Ethics

Western companies whose ethical principles do not always match those of other countries have difficulties in adapting to different ethical cultures that are found in some Asian, Middle Eastern, and African countries. The US government's regulations on ethics can be a roadblock on American companies doing business in these regions. (See further in Chapter 16 regarding ethics.) In Europe, Italy puts itself at a disadvantage for possible investors because of its Mafia dealings and the French island of Corsica has similar problems. A measure of ethical values is illustrated in Figure 3.6. This index shows that for the data given, Finland, Sweden, and the UK are considered the least corrupt, or highly ethical, while at the lower end of the scale, Indonesia, Ukraine, and Russia are consider the most corrupt.[19]

Language

Although English is the language of business, in continental Europe it is necessary for employees to speak several languages if an international company is to be successful. One reason why the United Kingdom is attractive to US companies is the common language.

Problems of cultural adaptation

An engineer
In the late 1960s a single expatriate chemical engineer from England was sent on a two-year operating assignment in a Middle East oil refinery. He was housed in a sparsely furnished villa on a company-owned housing complex. Other residents included approximately 100 Moslem families, and five expatriate families, including the British general manager. He put in long hours at the refinery, including working Saturday morning, and doing several stints on the night shifts. He was highly regarded by the local engineers and the local refinery manager. Social life for a single person was extremely dull. The only café in the village seemed to be exclusively for men to drink tea, chat, and play cards. The engineer met a young American woman, a teacher from a nearby US military base. After a period, they lived together. Some local families on the complex strongly disapproved of this 'western behaviour' and registered a complaint to the expatriate general manager. The general manager called the engineer into his office and told him he had to stop living with the woman, as this type of behaviour was not acceptable to the host country. If not, he would have to leave the country. The engineer's response was: 'You can tell me what to do during work hours, but the evening time is mine.' The engineer's assignment was terminated shortly afterwards.

An operations manager
In the early 1970s a US-based company was constructing a petrochemical facility on the Gulf of Izmit in Turkey. One US expatriate operations manager from Texas was not adapting to the assignment and began drinking. He was very critical of the Turkish culture. One evening, at an important banquet where there were many senior personnel from the parent company present, he became very drunk. At one point, he stubbed his cigarette out in the mayonnaise. He was removed from his assignment the following day.

A marketing manager
In the late 1980s a large French food and retail group purchased a similar operation in southern California, USA. To understand the French operation better, a marketing manager from the southern California store was brought to France. He came with his wife and two children, ostensibly for a 2-year period. The company paid his travel, provided furnished accommodation in a comfortable villa in an agreeable part of France, paid expenses associated with the children's schooling, and provided two automobiles. Adapting was not easy because of the language and culture of middle France compared to southern California. The wife had great difficulty in adapting to the lifestyle, felt the quality of medical services was poor, and was critical of the education her children were receiving in French schools. She made many trips back to the USA leaving her husband behind. The whole family left the assignment before a year had expired.

Figure 3.6 **Corruption perception index (2001)**

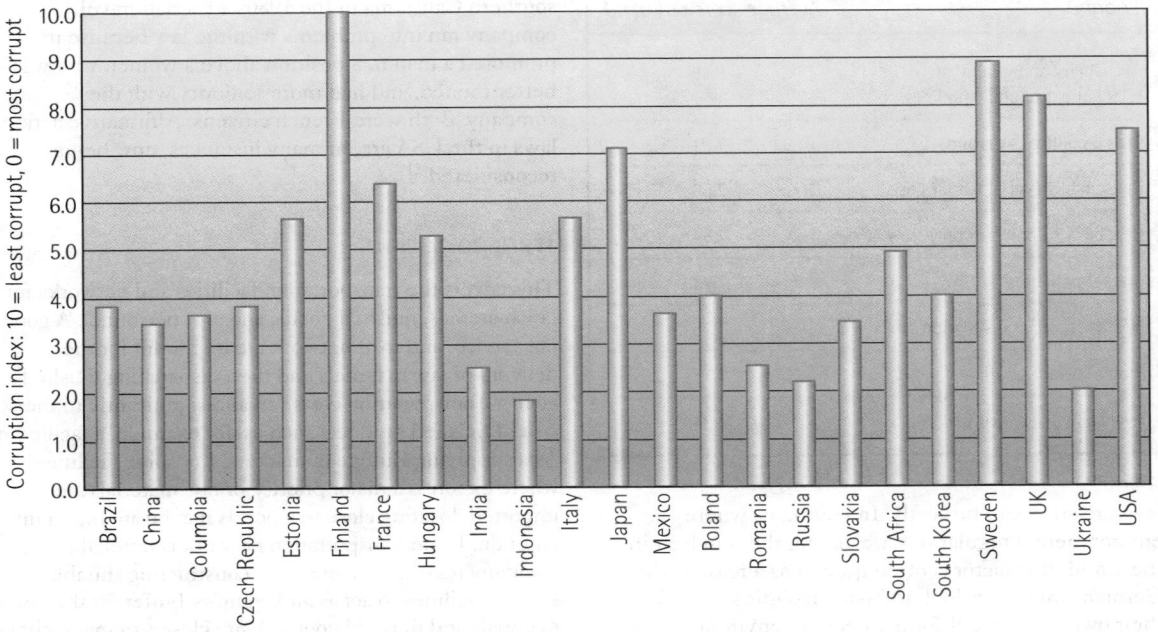

The UK is also attractive to Japanese companies for this reason, because English is the second language for the Japanese. Many companies are now looking to establish facilities in former communist countries of eastern Europe. One of their handicaps is to attract qualified personnel who speak German, Russian, or another appropriate language. On the other side of the Atlantic, the province of Quebec in Canada attracts French companies, again, because of the common language.

Infrastructure

Infrastructure in the broadest sense includes physical facilities put in place by the region, laws enacted by the government, or the business environment that has evolved, or perhaps declined, through the years as a result of that country's management.

Family services

Family services cover housing, schools, universities, shops, medical services etc., and are an element in attracting personnel. Schooling often presents a problem to expatriate families with children at the lycée or high school level. For those in the Middle East or Africa it often means leaving their children in boarding schools in their own country.

Communication

Communication covers telephone, fax lines, computer network facilities, and video conferencing, all of which imply the need for cable and satellite connections. Often locating a facility in a developing region presents a problem with communication links. In France in the early 1960s telephone communication was very difficult compared to other developed countries and this made firms non-competitive. President Valéry Giscard D'Estaing was instrumental in forging ahead rapidly with new telephone links in the 1970s, making France a leader in telecommunications. According to a survey by Plant Location International, in 1993, of 300 international companies questioned, the availability and quality of telephone, fax, and data lines was the most important criterion in the selection of facility location, as illustrated in the survey data presented in Table 3.3.[20]

Environmental regulations

Environmental regulations cover local, regional and national rules for air, water, land, and noise pollution. Locating a facility in an area where the environmental

Table 3.3 Communication in the infrastructure

Priority	Average score out of 10
Availability and quality of telephone, fax, and data lines	8.48
Stable political situation	7.91
Reasonable level of labour costs	7.68
Reliability of power supply	7.54
Market proximity	7.23
Healthy economic situation	7.15
Stable social climate	7.15
Availability of skilled workers	7.04

laws are strict can be costly. In Germany, where environmental regulations are among the toughest in the world, this factor is often quoted as a reason why German companies look to install facilities away from their own turf. In California, USA, an environmental impact statement has to be prepared before a company can construct. This document has to address all the possible effects that construction and operation may have on the environment. Preparation of such a report can be lengthy, entailing a delay longer than normal for the plant construction. For this reason, companies are shying away from California, preferring sites in neighbouring Arizona, and New Mexico. Changing environmental laws can impact an existing operating facility. Again in southern California, there are many oil refineries that were constructed before strong environmental regulations were put in place. Now, with the tighter regulations mandated by the Southern California Air Resources Board, companies have been obliged to install expensive pollution abatement equipment, or simply close down.

Legal framework

Litigation laws vary enormously from country to country. The USA has probably the severest liability laws, and damage claims for infringement such as faulty products, faulty operation, environmental spills and the like can run into millions of dollars. In addition, in the USA, companies are required to have in place affirmative action programmes whose objective is to stress the hiring and promotion of minority and disadvantaged individuals. These groups are based on race, sex, and physical disability. Affirmative action programmes arose

out of the US government's 1964 and 1972 Equal Employment Opportunity Commission (EEOC). In southern California in the 1980s a French travel company ran into problems with the law because it promoted a man to a position above a women who was better trained, and had more seniority with the company. Both were French citizens. Affirmative action laws in the USA are, in many instances, now being reconsidered.[21]

Transportation

This covers the transportation facilities and networks for raw materials, finished goods, and also personnel. A good rail service, and road network are important for the delivery of raw materials and then dispatching finished goods. Transportation costs can add significantly to the cost of finished products such as, for example, a facility in Asia supplying European markets. For some facilities where export is a major priority, or raw materials are imported, locating close to a port is maybe an important criterion. If the transportation network is unreliable the company may have to envisage constructing suitable storage facilities to act as an inventory buffer for the raw materials and finished goods. A site close to a major airport may be critical for companies where there is considerable movement of site personnel. Europe, recognizing the importance of a good transport network, for business, including the travel industry, is investing billions of euros in road and rail infrastructure.[22] Specifically, in the late 1980s and early 1990s, Spain considerably improved its road and rail network, which has been a positive factor in attracting foreign investment to its country. Conversely, the degradation of a transportation network such as due to frequent road bottlenecks is sometimes a reason for companies to relocate. Such has been the case for companies in New York and Los Angeles, and for companies in England who have moved their offices from Central London to Docklands, further east.

Rental costs

For service firms, office rental cost plays an important consideration in site selection since it increases the cost of the service (and hence the price to the consumer). Some companies, for example, who desire to locate to a particularly country, establish an office not in the capital city where rental rates are very high, but in adjacent towns where costs may be lower. Among the industrialized countries, London's West End is the most expensive location for offices with San Francisco, Silicon Valley in California, and Tokyo also very high on the list as illustrated in Figure 3.7.[23]

Figure 3.7 Office rents for prime business areas (2001)

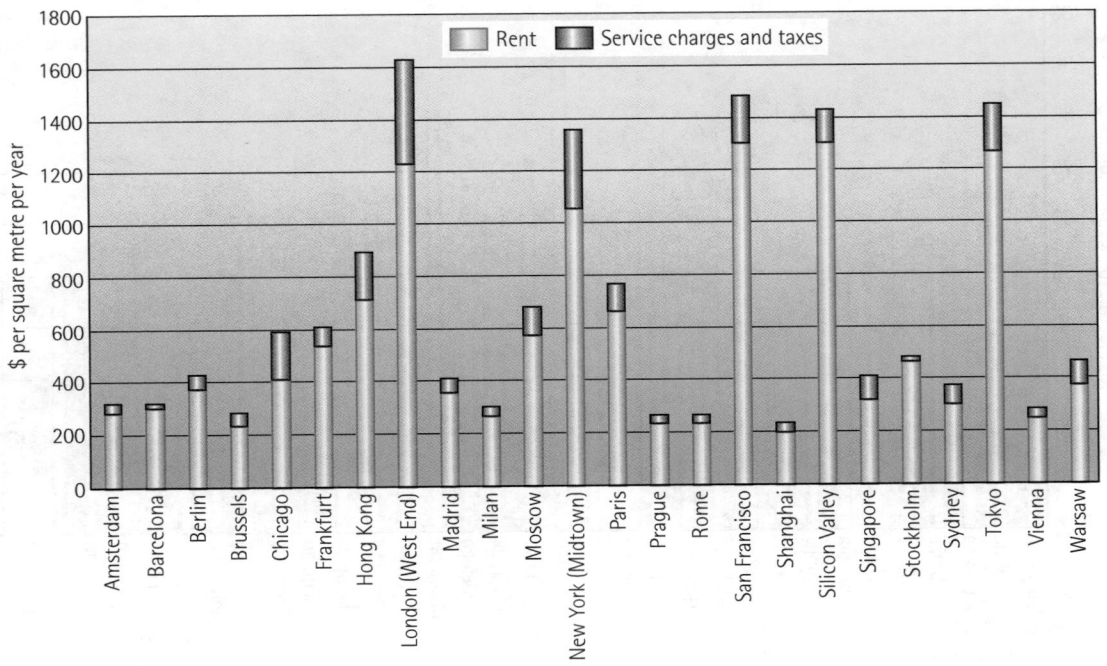

Figure 3.8 Cost of living internationally (1999)

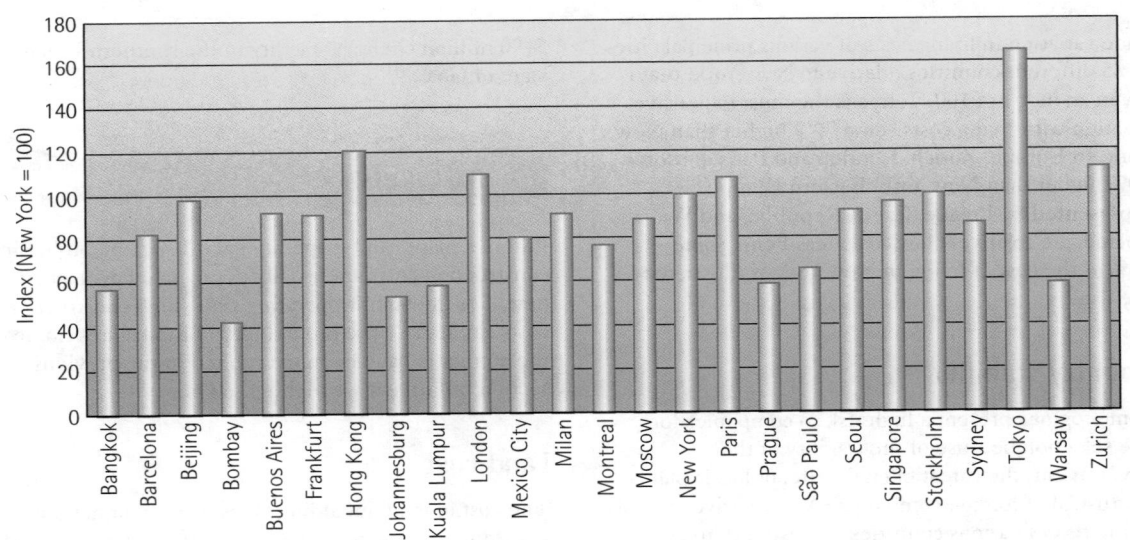

Living costs

Living costs cover all the expenses for employees to live in the area. Regions of high living cost may make it difficult to recruit the appropriate personnel because prospective employees find it prohibitive to relocate. Alternatively, if the company is responsible for paying the living cost then this is an added burden on the corporation. Figure 3.8 illustrates the

Figure 3.9 **Country risk (4th quarter, 2000)**

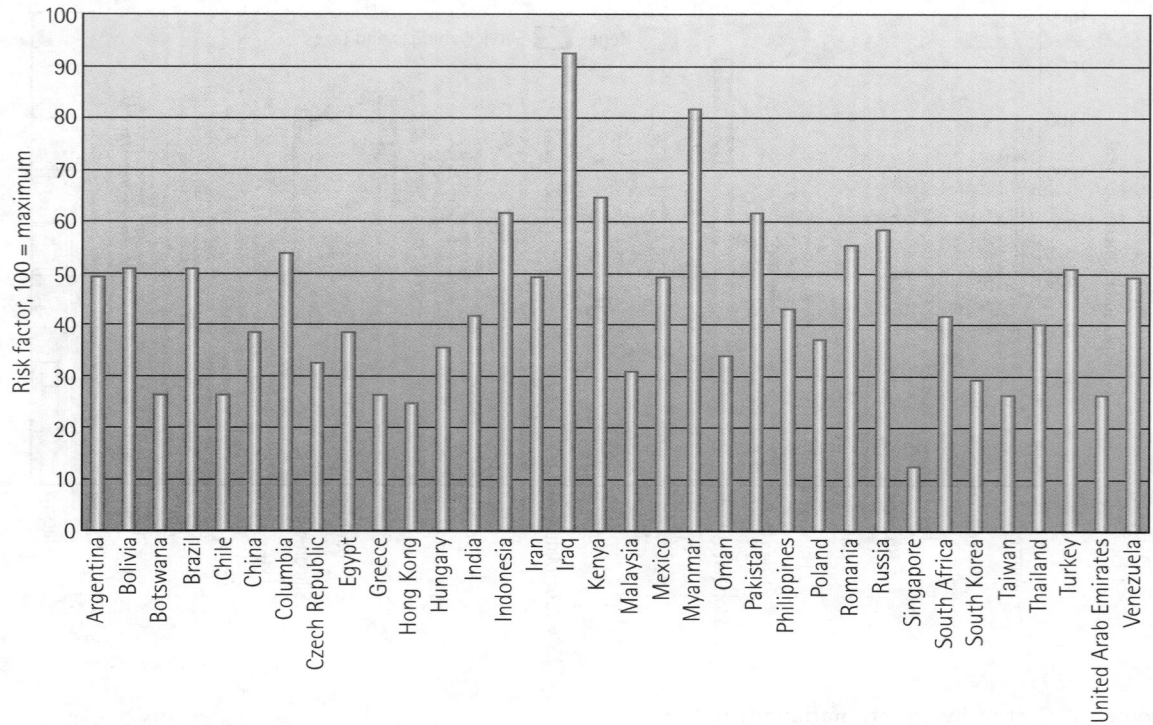

wide variation in living costs of various principal cities in 25 different countries relative to New York, that is given an index of 100. Tokyo is the most expensive location with living costs some 70% higher than New York. In Europe, Zurich, London and Paris are some 10% higher than New York. Eastern Europe, as represented by Prague, Czech Republic, and Warsaw, Poland, are relatively low cost areas being some 60% of the cost of living in New York as illustrated by the data.

Country stability

Some regions present a high risk to companies for site selection because of the fragility of the government, the threat of civil strife, or locals plainly distrustful of foreign companies. A qualitative analysis of the risk of various countries is illustrated in Figure 3.9.[25] This is a measure of the credit risk rating of countries in emerging markets, based on economic and political factors. Of the countries considered, Iraq is the most risky followed by Myanmar, Kenya, Pakistan, and India. Dupont, USA, has experienced difficulties in this respect, having tried to build a

$190 million chemical facility in the southern Indian state of Goa.

Construction

Before a plant can be operational it has to be built. Since construction costs are usually depreciated over a certain period of the plant's operating time, high construction costs can reduce the profitability of the facility. Some of the elements have been mentioned in the previous section but others are highlighted here.

Land cost

The cost of land, including taxes by local or national governments, is often high where land is scarce. Europe is high relative to many other regions. In the USA, land cost in southern California is high relative to the Mid-West. However, tax incentives by regional or national governments may make the ultimate land cost cheaper, as was the case for Disney Corp., which received tax incentives on the land at Marne La Vallée,

France, when it constructed the Euro Disney entertainment facility in the 1980s.

Construction labour

This covers the pool of construction labour available as opposed to operating labour for a facility once it is running. Even though there may be local regulations requiring a certain proportion of local labour in the construction activity the labour may not always be available and has to be imported. This is often the case in the Middle East where the construction labour often comes from Indonesia, China, Malaysia and other countries in East Asia.

Land preparation

Land preparation covers the work necessary to prepare land for the facility construction. Industrial parks, created by regional districts for the purpose of attracting companies, require little land preparation and often all the utility hook-ups are in place. This may not be the case in many developing regions such as the Philippines, Brazil, or the Middle East.

Expansion possibilities

After a company has built a new facility there may be need for expansion. Thus in selecting a site location, consideration needs to be given whether expansion possibilities exist. Hewlett-Packard which has a facility in Grenoble, France, has expanded its operation in that country considerably. However, on the original site there was no room for expansion and it had to purchase land in L'Isle d'Abeau, near Lyon, some 120 km from the plant at Grenoble. As a result, the company was obliged to put in place a daily delivery service between the two sites. Trucks deliver and collect components and finished products daily, which adds to the logistics and inventory planning.

Zoning regulations

These cover laws regarding the constructing in a particular area. In most countries, an area has to be designated an industrial zone before a plant can be constructed.

Environmental regulations

These may be included in the zoning regulations and would cover the type of plant being constructed. The environmental regulations would cover the construction phase, and then the operation phase once the plant is running. (Chapter 5 gives more information on environmental regulations.)

Material availability

Construction materials such as cement, fibreboard, wood, and construction steel may not be available locally and have to be imported, adding to costs.

Factors that impact cash flow

Most of the factors reviewed earlier enter the financial equation of site selection. Other financial considerations, which directly impact a firm's cash flow, are now discussed.

Fluctuating exchange rates

Currency stability is important in selecting a site for an operating company. Relative to the currency of the country of the parent company, wide variations can sharply impact the revenues realized, cost of raw materials, operating costs, and investment amounts needed. Figure 3.10[26] illustrates how countries' currencies have changed, including the 12 in the Eurozone (Austria, Belgium, Finland, France, Germany, Greece, Ireland, Italy, Luxembourg, Netherlands, Portugal, and Spain). For the data provided, with the exception of Mexico and Poland, all the currencies have weakened against the dollar. The impact during this period on revenues to a US company, say, with a facility in Turkey is that revenues accrued to the US parent in $US have decreased by some 51%. The change in operating cost, and raw material cost depends on what currency the cost is denominated in. Crude oil, which is the basic raw material for oil refineries, chemical plants, and also the energy source for facilities, is denominated in $US. Thus, when the dollar becomes stronger (it takes more foreign currency units to purchase one dollar) then the cost of oil increases which increases the cost of raw materials and energy with the effect of depressing net income.

A strong currency, although an indicator of the stability of a country, can also be a deterrent for investment in new facilities. The past strength of the former German mark (now replaced by the euro) is one reason why German companies such as Mercedes-Benz, Hoechst, and Deutsche Telekom opted to invest in facilities in the USA, rather than locally.

Figure 3.10 Currency exchange against the $US

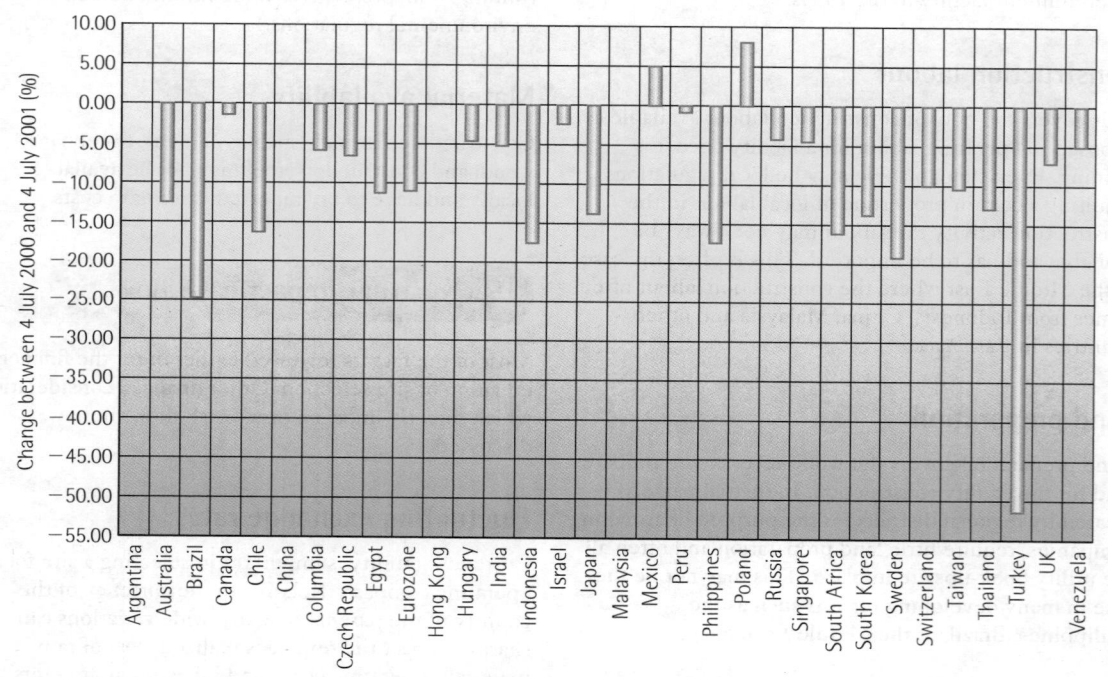

Figure 3.11 Corporate income tax (2000)

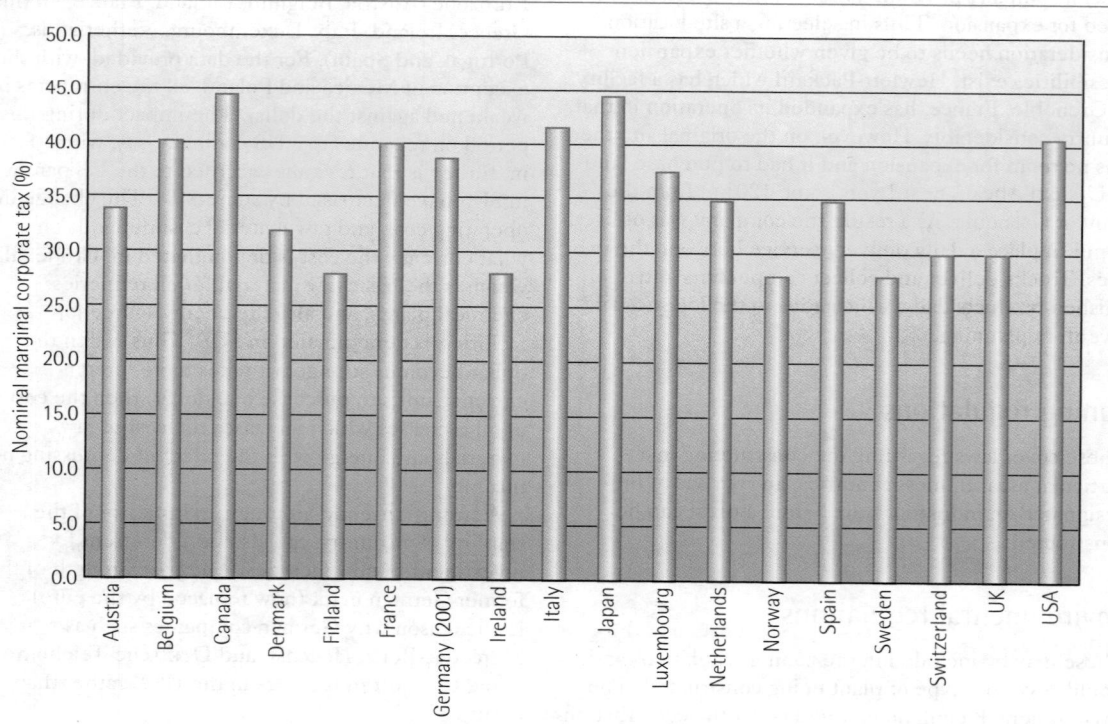

Repatriation of funds

Repatriation of funds concerns the ability of the parent company to repatriate the funds to the country where the headquarters are located. Some countries, particularly in emerging economies, have strict exchange controls so that transfer is not easy.

Taxes on operations

Countries levy taxes on companies that do business in their territory. Taxes paid will diminish the net return to the corporation. Figure 3.11[27] illustrates the maximum taxes on company profits including national, local, municipal, and other taxes in the OECD countries. Cross-country differences in tax rates on corporate profits can distort the investment decisions of multinational firms. Most Scandinavian countries have aligned their tax rates at 28%, thus reducing the risk of inefficient capital flows based purely on tax rates. Germany previously led most developed countries but it lowered its rate twice in the period 2000–2002 and its rate now corresponds closely to the rates of several neighbours, notably Luxembourg at 37.5%, France at 40%, and Belgium at 40.2%.

Financial aid

Financial aid from regional, local, or national governments can be a vital factor in the selection of a site. The financial aid might include direct cash grants, or tax incentives on the land, operation, or products produced. The following illustrates the point for the USA, the United Kingdom, and Germany.

USA

The USA has always been a magnet for investment by foreign companies because of its stability, large market, flexible hiring and termination practices, and low labour costs relative to other OECD countries. In particular, the southern states are attractive because of the climate and weak union membership and, as Industry insight 3.3 illustrates, attractive financial aid packages. Another, state in the USA which has been successful in attracting industry is Utah, where in addition to financial aid, the Utah Mormon culture offers a disciplined labour force.[28]

Alabama, USA

Industry insight 3.3

In April 1993 Mercedes-Benz of Germany (now Daimler-Chrysler) announced its plans to build a $300 million plant somewhere in the USA to produce a new four-wheel drive sports-utility vehicle. It began the site selection process by establishing a team advised by Fluor-Daniels, the Los Angeles-based engineering and construction company. This team established an initial list of 150 sites based in 30 states using criteria such as transport costs, quality of the workforce, and financial proposals from government agencies. The list was subsequently reduced to 64 sites, in 21 states, by considering distance to nearby residential areas, and distance to existing automotive operations as further evaluation criteria. Then, in-depth studies covering infrastructure, education, availability of the workforce, and productivity narrowed the selection to 20 sites in 11 states. When factors covering distance to suppliers, training programmes, and quality of life were added, this left just six sites in six states – Tennessee, Nebraska, South Carolina, North Carolina, Georgia, and Alabama.

A further detailed analysis then covered the proximity of universities and colleges, other companies in the area, the business climate, a re-evaluation of the workforce, operating, and investment costs. This then made a shortlist of three sites in three southern states – North Carolina, South Carolina, and Alabama. These three all presented the attraction of a relatively low-cost but skilled and abundant workforce, anti-union sentiments, affordable housing, attractive lifestyle, and good transport links with Europe. In addition, they all had governments willing to throw money at companies ready to locate in their state. The governments of the three states under consideration all offered attractive financial incentives. A site at Tuscaloosa, Alabama, was finally selected. The state's financial package amounted to incentives totalling to an upfront sum of $253 million including $17.4 million to purchase and develop the plant site for Mercedes, $42.6 million for building construction, $30 million for a training centre, $60 million to train Mercedes workers, and $77 million to develop the related infrastructure, such as roads and water lines. In addition, the package qualified Mercedes-Benz for tax breaks related to its profits and head count, which were estimated at $9.2 million per year for up to 25 years – an additional amount of some $230 million.

Adapted from: 'Locating in North America', *Financial Times*[29]

United Kingdom

In Europe, the United Kingdom has been successful in attracting foreign firms. Financial aid, as well as the language, cheap labour relative to the rest of Europe, and low social charges are incentives for foreign firms as Industry insight 3.4 illustrates.

Germany

In the years following the reunification of Germany in 1989, the former communist-governed East Germany suffered from very high unemployment, lack of capital investment, and a flight of labour from east to west. However, as Industry insight 3.5 illustrates financial aid from the German government may be helping to bring prosperity to ailing eastern Germany.

Wales, United Kingdom   Industry insight 3.4

A big investment that was attracted into the UK is a $2.6 billion project by South Korea's LG Group to build two electronic factories in a 100-hectare industrial park near Newport in southern Wales. When the facility is completed in 2002 the two plants will employ 6100 people in the biggest industrial programme in western Europe by a non-European company. As part of the deal with the British government and local authorities, LG is expected to benefit from subsidies running into hundreds of millions of dollars. Other attractions for LG are Britain's low labour cost compared to the rest of Europe, low tax rates, flexible labour conditions and the availability of a skilled workforce. Newport is on the western end of Britain's M4 motorway from London that in recent years has become a focus for many high-tech firms along what is known as the M4 corridor. The deal also offers LG a chance to tap the expertise of London University's Imperial College since the industrial park, where the factories are to be built, is a joint venture between Imperial College and local Welsh authorities. Officials expect the college to play a key role in training staff and providing research facilities for LG.

LG executives in Britain say the Newport project is part of a strategy to increase LG's worldwide sales fivefold to $360 billion by 2005. The Korean company plans to use Britain as a manufacturing base for everything from components to finished goods for distribution throughout western Europe and for export

to the USA. Even though Britain is not part of the Eurozone its membership in the Europe Union allow foreign manufacturers tariff-free access to the main Continental European markets. Part of the project includes a semiconductor plant to produce 360,000 20-centimetre chips a year for use in home appliances to control information and communication systems. Another is annually to produce two million computer monitors and three million wide-screen colour television tubes.

Why Britain? As one executive said: 'Most Korean people speak English, not French. If I go to France I imagine it would be terrible. In Italy the weather is better, but there's too much bribery. In the UK nothing changes. It's very, very stable, politically and economically. We know what to expect.'

Britain has been able to attract significant investment from foreign firms in the past years. In addition to this LG project others have been Siemens with an investment of £1.1 billion, and Toyota and Samsung each with £0.45 billion. Wales has been particularly successful for luring high-tech firms and hosts subsidiaries belonging to over 50 Japanese companies. Further, Wales is home to 23% of all consumer electronic jobs in the United Kingdom.

Adapted from: 'Shock therapy: Britain sends message on EU jobs by winning $2.6 billion investment', *Wall Street Journal Europe*[30]

Leipzig, Germany   Industry insight 3.5

In July 2001 the luxury carmaker Bayerische Motoren Werke AG (BMW) said it will spend €1 billion to build a new automobile plant in the city of Leipzig, creating 10,000 jobs in the depressed region. This includes 5500 direct employees and an estimated 4500 at supplier companies that are expected to spring up around the BMW facility. To win BMW as an investor, Leipzig had

to compete with more than 250 other applicants that included cities in France and the Czech Republic where labour cost are lower than in Germany.

The automakers' Chief Executive Officer, Joachim Milberg, said that Leipzig was chosen for its good infrastructure, its skilled local workforce and trade unions' consent to flexible workweeks that will vary with demand. This last factor of labour flexibility, reached with the consent of the powerful engineering union IG Metall, was a very strong point for BMW. It will allow workweeks that vary between four and six days and, as a result, it will be possible for machines at Leipzig to be manned for periods of up to 140 hours, or even 160 hours per week if warranted by client demand. These levels compare to 99 hours at BMW's other German plants. BMW said that other countries, including France and the Czech Republic, were simply not able to match this labour flexibility. Mr Milberg also said that state subsidies helped to sway BMW's decision in the site's favour, which is expected to cover around 28% of its investment costs. This high level of subsidy was a concern to some analysts as it is an indicator of the region's continued dependence on handouts by the state.

BMW plans to produce its popular 3-Series vehicles in the new factory, starting in 2005 with a target daily production of 650 cars. BMW's plant in the Bavarian town of Regensburg that currently produces the 3-Series cars will then switch to production of the smaller 1-Series vehicles.

The decision by BMW follows on the heels of General Motor's Opel unit, Volkswagen and Porsche, which have all invested in eastern Germany. The move is sending a strong signal of support to the region where unemployment is just under 17% of the workforce.

Adapted from: 'BMW chooses site in East Germany for its new plant', *Wall Street Journal Europe*[31]

Proximity of resources

Raw materials

For some facilities, particular process flow plants, proximity of raw materials and energy are critical factors regarding site selection. Processing facilities such as coal power stations are often located close to coalmines because it is cheaper to process the coal in situ rather than to ship the coal by rail to a power plant some distance away. Also, for environmental reasons, often the only feasible way to produce electricity is to burn the coal in a remote region and then to transmit to power by high-tension cable to the user area. An illustration is the power stations in the remote Four Corners area of New Mexico, USA, that transmit their power to Los Angeles.

Oil refineries, which produce gasoline, kerosene and diesel from crude oil, are sometimes located close to the oilfields and then the finished products are shipped to the customers. Similarly, metal-processing plants such as copper, iron ore, and aluminium smelters are most often located close to the mine because it is less expensive to ship the refined product rather than the raw material.

Process and utility water

Oil refineries, metal-processing plants, and paper companies use a large quantity of utility water for cooling and/or in the process itself. Thus these types of plant need to be located close to a reliable water supply, such as inland lakes or rivers or close to the sea.

For food processing plants, particularly the brewing and soft drinks industry the water supply is an integral part of the product and so the quality of the water is very important. Coors Beer of the USA has facilities in Colorado, as the quality of the mountain water is considered critical to the finished product. Other brewing facilities, for example, Heineken, the Netherlands, have water purification plants on their site, which upgrade the water before it is used in the process. Companies that sell bottled water (Evian, Contrex, Badoit, Perrier, etc.) have their processing facility at the water source.

Reliability of power supplies

Reliability of power supplies is important. In some emerging economies, such as Africa, electrical supplies are not always reliable. In this case, if a site in these areas is selected, backup power facilities need to be constructed close to the facility.

Suppliers or subcontractors

Companies may depend heavily on suppliers and subcontractors in their operation. In this case a consideration in site selection is that proposed suppliers of products or services are readily available so that in the supply chain production doesn't risk being interrupted. Reliability in delivery of goods is particularly important if a just-in-time production criterion is used at the company (see Chapter 15). Further, it might be a requirement that the quality of subcontracted work is certified by codes such as the European ISO-9000. (See Chapter 4.)

Quantitative approaches to site selection

If parameters and variables related to site selection can be estimated with some certainty, the following four quantitative methods might be used as a basis for selection:

1. weighting site criteria
2. breakeven analysis
3. uncertainty and risk
4. centre of gravity method.

These approaches are useful in that they quantitatively determine the 'best' location. However, they are not foolproof as the input data used might change, and thus alter results. The following explains the four methods, each given with a worked example.

Weighting the selection criteria

This method applies weighting factors to the criteria for site selection. The site with the highest overall value would be the preferred location. This method is similar to the weighting criteria used in supplier selection presented in Chapter 16.

Procedure

- Select the site criteria that are considered the most important for the site. These might be, for example, cost, labour availability, transport, etc.
- Assign a weighting factor, F, to all the site criteria according to their importance in the selection. The total weighting will be equal to unity.
- Apply a numerical score, S (out of 100 for example), for all the site criteria for each possible location being considered.
- Multiply the weighting factor by the numerical score, F * S for each site, and for each criterion.
- Sum the total F * S.
- The value $\Sigma(F * S)$ that is the maximum indicates the preferred site.

Demonstrating the concept 3.1 illustrates this method.

Breakeven analysis

Breakeven analysis is a common evaluation method when costs can be determined with some certainty. The technique is also illustrated in Chapter 16.

Procedure

- Determine the fixed and variable costs for each site.
- If a site has a variable cost higher than another site, but a lower fixed cost, then there will be a breakeven point. There will be no breakeven point if both the fixed costs and variable costs are higher than the corresponding costs at another location.

- Determine the production level expected from each site.
- The preferred site will be the one with the lowest total cost.

The concept of breakeven analysis is developed in Chapters 16 and 25.

Uncertainty and risk

Uncertainty and risk uses the decision methods described in Chapter 23.

Uncertainty

Uncertainty is when it is difficult to assign probabilities to a situation. In this case, the criteria of maximax, maximin, equally likely, minimax regret may be used depending on the approach of the decision maker.

- Maximax is an optimistic approach when the decision is to select that option which gives the maximum outcome.
- Maximin is a pessimistic approach in that the decision is to select the best of the worst possible outcomes.
- Equally likely is a middle of the road approach which selects the arithmetic mean of the possible outcomes.
- Minimax regret is the method which selects the option which has the least regret or disappointment when the decision is made.

Probabilities

If probabilities can be assigned, then this becomes a risk situation and the expected outcome of a particular site selection may be determined by weighting according to the various probabilities. For example if the probabilities of occurrence are denoted by P_1, P_2, and P_3, and the financial outcomes by R_1, R_2, and R_3, then the expected value of the possible outcome is given by the relationship:

$$P_1 * R_1 + P_2 * R_2 + P_3 * R_3$$

These two approaches are illustrated in Demonstrating the concept 3.2.

Centre of gravity

The centre of gravity method is a technique that may be used to establish, for example, the location of a primary central distribution centre, which supplies secondary distribution centres. The method takes into account the volume of goods shipped from the central to the secondary sites, and also the distance between sites. The assumption of the method is that unit shipping costs are the same, regardless of location. The object of this technique is to find the *centre of gravity* for the network, or to optimize the location of the site as far as shipping movements are concerned.

Procedure

• Position the network on a grid identified by an x and y coordinate. The units of the coordinates are not important but they must be created such that they are to scale with the network.
• The centre of gravity coordinates are then calculated by the following relationships:

$$X_c = \frac{\sum X_i Q_i}{\sum Q_i} \quad \text{and} \quad Y_c = \frac{\sum Y_i Q_i}{\sum Q_i}$$

where:

X_c and Y_c are the coordinates for the centre of gravity
X_i and Y_i are the coordinates for each of the supply centres
Q_i is the quantity delivered from the central, to the secondary centre.

This method is illustrated by Demonstrating the concept 3.3.

Summary of key elements

• Site selection is a market-driven strategic decision with considerable operations management involvement. Operations management personnel may have input to the site selection or they may ultimately be involved in operating the new facility.

• Foreign factories may be classified according to six strategic roles of the parent firm. This classification may be as an offshore factory, source factory, server factory, contributor factory, an outpost factory, or a lead factory.

• At the beginning of the 20th century, company paternalism led to the selection of sites that grew into corporate towns. However, their impact today is minimized as a result of mergers, acquisitions, and employee mobility.

• Labour costs, including social charges and labour flexibility is a key element in site selection. Additionally, areas with high unemployment, as a result of the loss of traditional industries such as coal mining and steel production, may represent a competent labour pool.

• Productivity of labour, as an element in site selection, must be considered in conjunction with labour costs. Rigidity of unions often weakens productivity.

• Regions with good training facilities present a magnet for countries to locate to, as it is important that local labour has the competence to handle sophisticated technology used by firms.

• Cultural differences, including language, often make it difficult for expatriates to adapt to the new environment. Further, emerging economies are demanding higher proportions of local labour in the operation from the company that selects a site in their country. This is often to the detriment of the use of expatriate labour.

• A warm climate, a developed infrastructure, political stability, reasonable living costs, balanced environmental regulations, and a manageable legal framework, are all positive considerations in site selection.

• In constructing a new facility on a virgin site, land costs, construction labour, amount of land preparation, expansion possibilities, zoning and environmental regulations, and material availability are important considerations.

• Fluctuating exchange rates, ease of repatriating funds, and taxes on operations have an impact on a firm's cash flow at foreign sites.

• All other factors being equal, the financial aid offered by local or national governments can swing the balance in site selection.

• Country instability, because of economic fragility, or political instability, is a strong negative factor in site selection.

• Other than labour costs in site selection for manufacturing firms, the proximity of raw materials, process and utility water, reliability of power supplies, closeness and reliability of suppliers are other important considerations.

• Quantitative methods for evaluating the location of a site include weighting the evaluation criteria, a financial breakeven analysis, a probability analysis of the various returns, and the centre of gravity method to balance distribution costs.

Notes and references

1. United Nations (published in *The Economist*, 12 March 1994)
2. 'Making the most of foreign factories', *Harvard Business Review*, March–April 1997, pp 73–88
3. 'Company towns. The strange death of corporationville: The company town was invented by the Industrial Revolution. Will it be killed off by the information age?', *The Economist*, 23 December 1995–5 January 1996, pp 77–80
4. 'Ford greens Rouge', *The Economist*, 25 November 2000, p. 92
5. 'The story of Cadbury Limited', *Time Traveller*, Cover Publishing Ltd and W H Smith Retail, 1998

6. US Bureau of Labor Statistics
7. 'Labour markets', *The Economist*, 2 December 2000
8. 'No return to industrial warfare: Join the real world, Blair tells unions', *The Times*, 10 September 1997
9. OECD (published in *The Economist*, 23 July 1994)
10. 'Economic and financial indicators: Labour disputes', *The Economist*, 12 May 2001, p. 112.
11. 'Locating in North America', *Financial Times*, 28 October 1993
12. Project worked on by the author
13. STEINER, George A. and STEINER, John F., 'The Union Carbide Corporation and Bhopal: A case study of management responsibility', in *Business, Government and Society. A Managerial Perspective*, Random House, London, 1988, 5th edition, p. 303
14. 'Business locations in Europe: The driving force behind much of the business location activity across Europe arises from the need to consolidate manufacturing, distribution, and management functions, and to adjust to a wider European market of 400 million people', *Financial Times*, 11 October 1993
15. 'Island getaway: Greek labor unrest, red tape drive out foreign companies. Siemens ponders withdrawal, possibly joining Goodyear, Levi Strauss and Pirelli', *Wall Street Journal Europe*, 14 October 1996
16. Author's experience
17. 'With one eye on Disneyland: A theme park may lift all Catalonia', *Business Week*, 27 March 1995, p. 5
18. Personal situations encountered by the author
19. 'A survey of Russia: At the grubby end', *The Economist*, 21 July 2001, p. 13
20. *Plant Location International* (published in *Financial Times*, 11 October 1993)
21. 'The battle of Piscataway', *The Economist*, 30 August 1997, p. 35
22. 'All aboard the supertrains', *Newsweek*, 31 July 1989
23. 'Economic indicators: Commercial property', *The Economist*, 20 January 2001, p. 110
24. 'Economic indicators: Cost of living', *The Economist*, 29 January 2000, p. 136
25. 'Emerging market indicators: Country risk', *The Economist*, 10 March 2001, p. 116
26. 'Economic and financial indicators', *The Economist*, 7 July 2001, pp 107–108
27. 'Financial indicators: Corporate tax rates', *The Economist*, 26 August 2000, p. 97
28. 'Utah's own Lehi wins high-tech plant: Micron joins slew of firms in Mormon country', *Wall Street Journal Europe*, 14 March 1995
29. DICKSON, Martin, 'Locating in North America', *Financial Times*, 28 October 1993
30. 'Shock therapy: Britain sends message on EU jobs by winning $2.6 billion investment. LG will build plants in Wales, reflecting firms' interest in labour-market reforms. The UK is very, very stable', *Wall Street Journal Europe*, 11 July 1996
31. ROHWEDDER, Cecile and BUCHENAU, Martin, 'BMW chooses site in East Germany for its new plant: Car maker gives lift to depressed region', *Wall Street Journal Europe*, 19 July 2001, pp 1 and 7

Review and discussion topics

1. Emerging economies
The following are emerging economies
(a) India
(b) China
(c) Mexico
(d) Korea.
What are the reasons why a corporation might establish a business in these regions? What are some of the risks that might be encountered?

2. Raw materials
How important is it today to locate a facility close to raw materials? Illustrate you arguments with actual industries.

3. Euro currency
By 2001, 11 European countries had adopted the euro as a common currency. The United Kingdom was not one of these. Discuss the advantages and disadvantages of site selection in Europe in the Eurozone.

4. Local authorities
Local authorities often make financial inducements to attract businesses, conferences (G7 in Denver, USA, in 1997), or major sporting events (the Winter Olympic Games to Albertville, France, in 1992). These inducements are paid out of local taxes. Not all residents approve of these decisions, particularly when the cost far exceeds revenues. What do you believe is correct? Discuss the pros and contras of these site selection decisions.

5. Quantitative methods
How might you use the quantitative approaches to site selection in conjunction with the qualitative approaches, reviewed in Chapter 3?

6. Weighting methods
What are the limitations of the weighting method for site selection?

7. Breakeven analysis
In using a breakeven analysis, in which of the two costs, fixed or variable, would you have more confidence? What is the danger of using this method in inflationary periods?

8. Uncertainty
In conditions of uncertainty estimates of future outcomes may be made. How are 'future outcomes' developed? How sensitive are these estimates to external situations? As a decision maker, would you tend to be optimistic or pessimistic in deciding the outcome of site selection using the relevant criteria? Justify your response.

9. Centre of gravity
Discuss the advantages, and disadvantages of using the centre of gravity method for site selection. What are some of the costs that are not considered with this method?

Demonstrating the concept 3.1   Steel King

Situation

Steel King, a company with corporate offices based in London, manufactures high-quality office furniture. Production capacity at the existing production centres is now saturated and the company has decided to construct a new production facility somewhere in Europe to satisfy its expanding market.

After a study of the possible locations, these five were the leading contenders:

1. Bari, Italy
2. Lille, France
3. Munich, Germany
4. Valence, Spain
5. Watford, England.

Steel King's Department of Strategic Planning proposed to use six comprehensive criteria for analyzing the various sites.

1. Productivity
This was based on data provided by an external consultant and covered such elements as union regulations, quality of work, turnover, absenteeism, and work ethic.

2. Construction cost
This covered the turnkey cost of construction the facility including land cost, construction time, and cost incentives provided by the region.

3. Labour cost
Included in the wage rates was the entire social charge, and costs of hiring and termination.

4. Proximity to clients
This was based on existing clients, and an estimation of new clients. Transportation costs were an important consideration in this factor.

5. Proximity to suppliers
Steel King ran its production operation on a just-in-time basis and so distance, as related to on-time delivery, was an important criterion in this factor. There were about 25 key suppliers who furnished the steel, wheels, tubing, locks, plastic components and the like.

6. Weather/quality of living
An agreeable environment, including weather, and surroundings for the workforce, was a consideration in the evaluation, albeit not a major one.

Table 3.4 gives:

- the various weighting factors, for a total of 10
- the numerical score assigned to each site.

The score was out of a maximum of 100. The higher the score, the more favourable the site. For example, labour costs at Bari were lower than at Munich, hence the weighting factor for Bari was higher. However, productivity at Munich was considered higher than at Bari, so the weighting factor for Munich was higher.

Required

1. Based on the data provided, determine the preferred location for the construction of a new production facility for Steel King.
2. If the labour cost value for Munich were re-evaluated at 30, and the construction cost for Watford re-evaluated to 50, would this change the decision based on the information given?
3. What can you say about the sensitivity of using this approach for site selection?

Solution

1. The weighting factor, F, is multiplied by the score, S, for each location and the total $\Sigma(F * S)$

Table 3.4 Steel King: Site selection procedure

Site criteria	Weighting factor F	Bari S	Lille S	Munich S	Valence S	Watford S
Productivity	2.75	25	65	90	60	75
Construction cost	1.35	60	50	30	70	40
Labour cost	2.50	70	30	25	35	50
Proximity to clients	1.25	40	75	85	60	55
Proximity to suppliers	1.15	30	65	55	35	45
Weather/quality of living	1.00	85	25	25	90	35
Total	10.00					

is determined. The values are given in the last line of Table 3.5. Based on the information given, Valence would be the preferred location.

2. The results are given in Table 3.5. Yes, in fact Watford, Munich, and Valence are hard to differentiate now.
3. This approach for selection is very sensitive to the weighting and scores given for each location.

Table 3.5 Steel King: Weighting factors

Case 1

Site criteria	Weighting factor, F	1. Bari		2. Lille		3. Munich		4. Valence		5. Watford	
		Score, S	F*S	Score, S	F*S	Score, S	F*S	Score, S	F*S	Score, S	F*S
Productivity	2.75	25	68.75	65	178.75	90	247.50	60	165.00	75	206.25
Construction cost	1.35	60	81.00	50	67.50	30	40.50	70	94.50	40	54.00
Labour cost	2.50	70	175.00	30	75.00	25	62.50	35	87.50	50	125.00
Proximity to clients	1.25	40	50.00	75	93.75	85	106.25	60	75.00	55	68.75
Proximity to suppliers	1.15	30	34.50	65	74.75	55	63.25	35	40.25	45	51.75
Weather/quality of living	1.00	85	85.00	25	25.00	25	25.00	90	90.00	35	35.00
Total	10.00		494.25		514.75		545.00		552.25		540.75

Maximum score   **552.25**
Preferred location   **4. Valence**

Case 2

Site criteria	Weighting factor, F	1. Bari		2. Lille		3. Munich		4. Valence		5. Watford	
		Score, S	F*S	Score, S	F*S	Score, S	F*S	Score, S	F*S	Score, S	F*S
Productivity	2.75	25	68.75	65	178.75	90	247.50	60	165.00	75	206.25
Construction cost	1.35	60	81.00	50	67.50	30	40.50	70	94.50	50	67.50
Labour cost	2.50	70	175.00	30	75.00	**30**	75.00	35	87.50	**50**	125.00
Proximity to clients	1.25	40	50.00	75	93.75	85	106.25	60	75.00	55	68.75
Proximity to suppliers	1.15	30	34.50	65	74.75	55	63.25	35	40.25	45	51.75
Weather/quality of living	1.00	85	85.00	25	25.00	25	25.00	90	90.00	35	35.00
Total	10.00		494.25		514.75		557.50		552.25		554.25

Maximum score   **557.50**
Preferred location   **3. Munich**

The higher the site factor, S, the more favourable the site location

Demonstrating the concept 3.2   Pike Company

Situation

The Pike Company, based in Germany, manufactures and distributes jogging shoes, principally in the European market. As a result of an unexpected increase in demand of its product, the company is considering four possibilities for capacity expansion:

1. a new facility in Mexico in a joint venture operation with a local company

2. a new facility in Hong Kong which will be 100% owned by Pike
3. a new relatively small facility in southern Europe
4. limited expansion of an existing facility in Poland.

An estimation of the profit over five years from each facility, in euros, is given in Table 3.6 according to various market changes. The numbers take into account all construction costs, transportation, risks associated with currency changes, and financial assistance from government, and regional authorities.

Table 3.6 Pike Company: Profit estimations

Market change over five years	50% increase	25% increase	Flat	10% decline
Mexico/joint venture	22,250,000	19,250,000	−625,000	−11,250,000
Hong Kong	26,290,000	15,500,000	−1,479,000	−18,925,000
Southern Europe	6,273,500	5,250,000	−1,790,000	−12,920,000
Expand existing	7,400,000	5,500,000	−50,000	−100,000

Required

1. Based on the data provided, what would be the preferred site:
   (a) if management were optimistic in its approach
   (b) if management were pessimistic in its approach
   (c) if management took a middle of the road approach
   (d) using the concept of minimax regret?
2. Assume that the probability of the market changes were estimated as shown in Table 3.7.
   Using expected values, what decision would be made for site selection?
3. After further analysis and consultation, the probabilities of the market changes were revised. The new data are as shown in Table 3.8.
   Using expected values, would the decision for site selection be modified?

Table 3.7 Pike Company: Probability of market changes

Market change over five years	50% increase	25% increase	Flat	10% decline
Probability of occurrence (%)	30	45	20	5

Table 3.8 Pike Company: Market changes revised for Pike Company

Market change over five years	50% increase	25% increase	Flat	10% decline
Probability of occurrence (%)	50	40	5	5

Solution

1. The results are given in Table 3.9.
   (a) If management were optimistic in its approach, this implies using a maximax approach, or selecting the alternative that has the maximum estimated return. In this case, management would select the Hong Kong site, which has an estimated profit of €26,290,000 based on a 50% market increase in five years.
   (b) If management were pessimistic in its approach, this implies using a maximin approach, or selecting the alternative that has the best estimated return of the worst possible outcomes. In this case management would elect to expand the existing facility because −€100,000 for the expansion is the best of all the worst possible outcomes.
   (c) If management took a middle of the road approach, one way of arriving at a decision is to take the simple average of the outcomes of all of the possible profit numbers, and to select the choice with the highest average. The average values are given in the last column of Table 3.9. On this basis, the preferred site would be in Mexico, under a joint venture with an average of all of the possible outcomes of €7,406,250.
   (d) In the minimax regret, the maximum regret is determined for each column. This value is the difference between the maximum outcome in that column, and the possible outcome for each cell. The maximum for each possible decision is determined. The minimum of this maximum is then chosen. In this case it is the Mexico joint venture.
2. The results are given in Table 3.10. The expected value is obtained by multiplying the probability of the market change by the estimated outcome, and then obtaining the sum. This information is given in the last column of the table.
   Based on this method, the preferred site is in Mexico as a joint venture which has an expected (weighted average value) of €14,650,000.
3. The results are given in Table 3.10. Based on this method, the preferred site is in Hong Kong which has an expected (weighted average value) of €18,324,800.

Table 3.9 Pike Company Uncertainty

Market change	50% increase	25% increase	Flat	10% decline	Outcome
Maximax (optimistic approach)					**Maximum**
Mexico/joint venture	22,250,000	19,250,000	−625,000	−11,250,000	22,250,000
Hong Kong	26,290,000	15,500,000	−1,479,000	−18,925,000	26,290,000
Europe	6,273,500	5,250,000	−1,790,000	−12,920,000	6,273,500
Expand existing	7,400,000	5,500,000	−50,000	−100,000	7,400,000
Maximum of maximum	26,290,000				

Preferred decision is to select **Hong Kong**

Market change	50% increase	25% increase	Flat	10% decline	Outcome
Maximin (pessimistic approach)					**Minimum**
Mexico/joint venture	22,250,000	19,250,000	−625,000	−11,250,000	−11,250,000
Hong Kong	26,290,000	15,500,000	−1,479,000	−18,925,000	−18,925,000
Europe	6,273,500	5,250,000	−1,790,000	−12,920,000	−12,920,000
Expand existing	7,400,000	5,500,000	−50,000	−100,000	−100,000
Maximum of minimum	−100,000				

Preferred decision is to select **Expand existing**

Market change	50% increase	25% increase	Flat	10% decline	Outcome
Equally likely (middle of the road)					**Average**
Mexico/joint venture	22,250,000	19,250,000	−625,000	−11,250,000	7,406,250
Hong Kong	26,290,000	15,500,000	−1,479,000	−18,925,000	5,346,500
Europe	6,273,500	5,250,000	−1,790,000	−12,920,000	−796,625
Expand existing	7,400,000	5,500,000	−50,000	−100,000	3,187,500
Maximum of average	7,406,250				

Preferred decision is to select **Mexico/joint venture**

Market change	50% increase	25% increase	Flat	10% decline	Outcome
Minimax regret matrix					**Maximum**
Mexico/joint venture	4,040,000	0	575,000	11,150,000	11,150,000
Hong Kong	0	3,750,000	1,429,000	18,825,000	18,825,000
Europe	20,016,500	14,000,000	1,740,000	12,820,000	20,016,500
Expand existing	18,890,000	13,750,000	0	0	18,890,000
Minimum of max regret	11,150,000				

Preferred decision is to select **Mexico/joint venture**

All financial data are in euros

Table 3.10 Pike Company Risk

Probability (%)	30	45	20	5	100
Market change	50% increase	25% increase	Flat	10% decline	Expected value
Mexico/joint venture	22,250,000	19,250,000	−625,000	−11,250,000	14,650,000
Hong Kong	26,290,000	15,500,000	−1,479,000	−18,925,000	13,619,950
Europe	6,273,500	5,250,000	−1,790,000	−12,920,000	3,240,550
Expand existing	7,400,000	5,500,000	−50,000	−100,000	4,680,000
Maximum of expected value	14,650,000				

Preferred decision is to select **Mexico/joint venture**

(Continued)

Table 3.10 (Continued)

Probability (%)	50	40	5	5	100
Market change	50% increase	25% increase	Flat	10% decline	Expected value
Mexico/joint venture	22,250,000	19,250,000	−625,000	−11,250,000	18,231,250
Hong Kong	26,290,000	15,500,000	−1,479,000	−18,925,000	18,324,800
Europe	6,273,500	5,250,000	−1,790,000	−12,920,000	4,501,250
Expand existing	7,400,000	5,500,000	−50,000	−100,000	5,892,500
Maximum of expected value	18,324,800				

Preferred decision is to select **Hong Kong**

All financial data are in euros

Demonstrating the concept 3.3   Prismode Co.

Situation

Prismode Co. is a large European retail outlet in France which is negotiating the merger with another major retailer in Spain. If the merger is completed, the new organization will provide a large distribution/sales network throughout Europe.

One of the decisions to be made in the new organization is where to locate the primary distribution centre to serve already established secondary distribution centres which are located in Rennes, France; Oporto, Portugal; Valencia, Spain; Naples, Italy; Frankfurt, Germany; Athens, Greece; Göteborg, Sweden; Bergen, Norway; and Birmingham, England. Initial studies have indicated that the average monthly delivery of consumer goods from the primary distribution centre to the secondary centres will be as shown in Table 3.11.

Required

1. Using the centre of gravity method, determine in the vicinity of the major city the central distribution

Table 3.11 **Prismode Co.: Average monthly delivery**

Secondary distribution centre	Units/month (000s)
Rennes	5,536
Oporto	5,784
Valencia	4,055
Naples	3,521
Frankfurt	2,420
Athens	5,130
Göteborg	1,431
Bergen	2,272
Birmingham	5,595

centre would best be located in. Assume that unit transportation costs between the central and secondary sites are the same.

2. In the merger proposal there is some uncertainty concerning the acquisition of the outlets in Frankfurt, Göteborg, and Birmingham. If these sites were not included in the merger proposal, and the unit deliveries at the other sites remained the same, near which major city would the centre of gravity method now suggest for locating the primary centre?

Solution

- The network is first located on a grid with x and y coordinates. This is given in Figure 3.12.
- From the map/grid, the corresponding x and y coordinates are established for each secondary distribution sites. These are given in columns 2 and 3 of Table 3.12.
- The product (coordinate * N° of units delivered) is then calculated for each site (columns 5 and 6).
- The centre of gravity coordinates are then determined from the relationship:

$$\frac{\sum \text{coordinate} * \text{quantity}}{\sum \text{quantity}}$$

1. The x coordinate is 6.00, and the y coordinate is 3.80. This puts the centre of gravity at about Lyon, France.
2. The x coordinate is 6.02, and the y coordinate is 2.86. This puts the centre of gravity at about Marseille, France.

As with all quantitative data, the final result is sensitive to the input data. A change in the number of units delivered could change the final result.

Figure 3.12 Prismode: Site selection

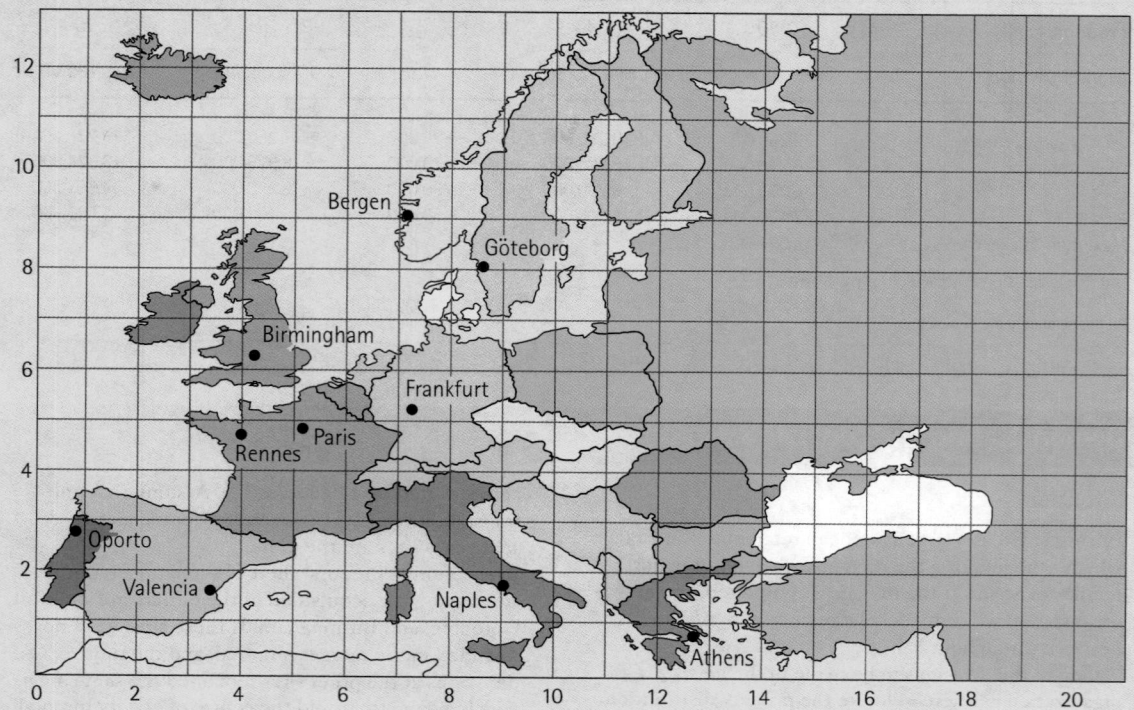

Table 3.12 Prismode Co.: Secondary sites

1	2	3	4	5	6
	X coordinate	Y coordinate	Units/month (000s)	X * Units (Col 2) * (Col 4)	Y * Units (Col 3) * (Col 4)
Rennes	4.2	4.8	5,536	23,253	26,574
Oporto	0.9	2.1	5,784	5,206	12,147
Valencia	3.5	1.4	4,055	14,193	5,677
Naples	9.2	1.8	3,521	32,396	6,338
Frankfurt	7.5	5.2	2,420	18,147	12,582
Athens	12.9	0.8	5,130	66,174	4,104
Göteborg	9.0	8.1	1,431	12,879	11,591
Bergen	7.5	9.0	2,272	17,041	20,449
Birmingham	4.5	6.5	5,595	25,175	36,365
Total			**35,744**	**214,464**	**135,827**
Centre of gravity Lyon, France				**6.00**	**3.80**

Table 3.12 **continued**

1	2	3	4	5	6
	X coordinate	Y coordinate	Units/month (000s)	X * Units (Col 2) * (Col 4)	Y * Units (Col 3) * (Col 4)
Rennes	4.2	4.8	5,536	23,253	26,574
Oporto	0.9	2.1	5,784	5,206	12,147
Valencia	3.5	1.4	4,055	14,193	5,677
Naples	9.2	1.8	3,521	32,396	6,338
Frankfurt	7.5	5.2	0	0	0
Athens	12.9	0.8	5,130	66,174	4,104
Göteborg	9.0	8.1	0	0	0
Bergen	7.5	9.0	2,272	17,041	20,449
Birmingham	4.5	6.5	0	0	0
Total			**26,299**	**158,262**	**75,289**
Centre of gravity Marseille, France				6.02	2.86

Application exercise 3.1 Ceramics

Situation

A ceramics company in Worcester, England, has its current
manufacturing capacity saturated and it is considering a new
site near Lisbon in Portugal or one near Madrid in Spain. The
firm is basing its analysis on two major product categories,
A and B. The products are sold internationally and are always
quoted in pounds sterling. The average sales price for Product
A is £19.00 a unit and £25.00 a unit for Product B. It is
estimated that the sales product mix will remain at 30% for
Product A and 70% for Product B.

At the site in Portugal, direct material costs for Product A
are budgeted at €6.60 a unit and direct labour costs at €8.25
a unit. For Product B, direct material costs are budgeted at
€8.25 a unit and direct labour costs at €4.95 a unit. Fixed
costs for one year at this site are estimated at €4.95 million.

At the site in Spain, direct material costs for Product A
are budgeted at €8.25 a unit and direct labour costs at
€10.73 a unit. For Product B, direct material costs are
budgeted at €7.43 a unit and direct labour costs at

€4.54 a unit. Fixed costs for one year at this site are estimated
at €5.28 million.

For conversion purposes a currency rate of £1 = €1.65
is used.

Required

1. Based on the information given, determine the preferred
production site according to a breakeven analysis. Assume that
the same sales mix is used throughout the analysis. Justify
your answer.
2. What is the breakeven point in units at both sites?
Give the information in total units and for Product A and
Product B. Show the information for both sites on a
breakeven graph.
3. What would the fixed costs at the site in Spain have to be
such that the number of breakeven units is the same as for the
site in Portugal? Assume that all other sales and cost data
remain the same.

Application exercise 3.2 Computers

Situation

A computer company based in the USA is considering four possibilities in new facilities for increasing its production capacity (see Table 3.13).

An estimation of the returns over five years from each facility, in US dollars, is given in Table 3.14 according to various market changes. The numbers take into account all construction costs, transportation, risks associated with currency changes, and financial assistance from government, and regional authorities.

Required

1. Based on the data provided, what would be the preferred site:

(a) if management were optimistic in its approach
(b) if management were pessimistic in its approach
(c) if management took a middle of the road approach
(d) using the concept of minimax regret?

2. Assume that the probability of the market changes were estimated as shown in Table 3.15.

Using expected values, what decision would be made for site selection?

3. If the probability of a 25% increase in the market and a flat market remained unchanged, to what level would the 50% increase in market have to decrease (at the expense of an increase in the 5% decline case) in order that the decision in question 2 should be changed? Do you believe this situation would be realistic?

Table 3.13 Potential increase in production capacity (computers)

USA (100% owned facility)
China (joint venture)
India (expansion of an existing facility)
Ireland (small new facility)

Table 3.15 Probability of market changes

Probability (%)	40	30	25	5
Market change	50% increase	25% increase	Flat	5% decline

Table 3.14 Returns over five years

Market change	50% increase	25% increase	Flat	5% decline
USA (100% owned)	40,500,000	27,250,000	−2,000,000	−18,500,000
China (JV)	29,500,000	13,500,000	−1,500,000	−8,000,000
India (expansion)	15,500,000	10,000,000	−1,000,000	−4,500,000
Ireland (new)	10,000,000	6,500,000	0	−1,000,000

Application exercise 3.3 Distribution centre

Situation

A company is considering establishing a new distribution platform in northern Europe to serve its retail outlets in the Benelux countries, France, and Germany. Table 3.16 shows the distribution outlets, and an estimate of the number of journeys a day from the distribution centre to the retail outlet.

Required

Using the centre of gravity method, determine in the vicinity of which major city the distribution centre would best be located. Assume that unit transportation costs between sites are the same.

Table 3.16 Distribution outlets and round trips undertaken daily

Retail outlet	Round trips/day
Paris, France	12
Rotterdam, Netherlands	12
Charleroi, Belgium	9
Nancy, France	8
Groningen, Netherlands	15
Cologne, Germany	8
Strasbourg, France	14

Application exercise 3.4 Textiles

Situation

A European-based company is considering developing a new textile facility for producing principally ladies' and children's clothing. There are five possible international locations: in

- China
- England
- France
- India
- Mexico

Part of the decision-making process is based on weighting various criteria for the five sites. This information is given in Table 3.17.

The table gives:

- the various weighting factors, for a total of ten
- the numerical value assigned to each site.

The numerical value is out of a maximum of 100. The higher the score, the more favourable is the site.

Required

1. Based on the data provided, determine the preferred location for the facility.
2. Illustrate the sensitivity of the weighted score for France according to the numerical value of the labour cost by a graph for numerical values of the labour cost from 45 to 100 in increments of five. Assume that the weighted score for the other entire sites remains constant at the values calculated in question 1. What would have to be the numerical values of the labour cost for France in order that it breaks even, that is the weighted score is the same as for the other sites?

Table 3.17 Decision–making criteria for a textile firm

		1	2	3	4	5
Site criteria	Weighting factor	China	England	France	India	Mexico
Productivity	3.00	70	85	80	65	70
Construction cost	2.00	55	35	25	60	60
Labour cost	3.00	90	55	45	75	80
Proximity to clients	1.50	50	90	100	60	50
Proximity to suppliers	0.50	50	30	60	55	45

Case study 3.1 Holger Co.

Situation

Franz Holger and his brother Roland began a company in the late 1800s making small machine tools in the Cologne area of Germany. Originally, these tools were destined for the coal mining industry in the Ruhr. The company grew rapidly and ventured into larger machines, which operated the mineshaft elevators, and the small trains used underground in the mine tunnels. In the 1930s the Holger Co. employed almost 1000 people including engineers, a large number of operating personnel, and sales agents. When the car industry began its accelerating growth, Holger started supplying machine components for Volkswagen and Mercedes. Holger had no debt. During this period it was privately owned and financed all its investment from internal operations.

As war in Europe loomed, Holger was forced to start providing machine tools, and components for the military, including tanks, and aircraft components. The Allies, familiar with Holger's war effort, targeted the manufacturing facility, and in 1944 the firm was heavily bombed. The result was that in 1945 Holger Co. was almost non-existent and the Allies were of the mind to liquidate the firm. However, after discussions, the Holger Co. (now in the hands of three of the sons of the founders) was allowed to continue with an infusion of 30% of the capital injected by a British group.

In the 1950s through to the late 1970s Holger Co. grew at an impressive pace. The company was well known for the quality of its products, prices were very competitive, and it provided excellent after-sales service. It remained in its core business of machine tools, and automated machines but also specialized components for the automobile industry. Whereas originally the firm's market had been Germany, now it had a broad territory in the European Union and a growing market in eastern Europe. However, its manufacturing facilities remained around Cologne.

In 1981 Holger received a large order from Hyundai in South Korea, which also required an infusion of capital into the Holger Co. This order, and subsequent work, gave a market distribution according to revenues of 20% in South Korea and other Asian countries, 70% in Europe, and 10% in North America. Capital ownership of Holger was now 60% German, 30% British, and 10% South Korean.

In the late 1980s profit margins for Holger started to decline. Business was getting very competitive, and the company was having difficulties controlling its manufacturing costs. In 1996 Holger's board, composed of personnel from the three countries, discussed a major strategic decision to move the manufacturing operations out of Germany. Discussions were acrimonious and difficult. Two serious possibilities were being considered: One was in northern England, at a new site close to Newcastle upon Tyne. Newcastle had itself been dependent on coal mining and also shipbuilding but both these industries had declined. The other site selection was at Inchon, a coastal town in South Korea, not far from the capital, Seoul. If the company moved to

England it was felt that about 90 key members of the company and their families would be asked to relocate. This would include design personnel, key operators, and management people in the commercial and manufacturing area. If South Korea were selected, it was believed that only about 50 of Holger's people would relocate. Whichever site were selected, termination in Germany would include some 850 people including work centre operators, maintenance people, and secretarial staff.

Required

1. Discuss what might have been some of the reasons for the high costs for the manufacturing operation in Germany.
2. What would be the impact in Germany if the company relocated its facility out of Germany?
3. What are the advantages to the firm in relocating to England? What do you believe could have been some of the inducements offered?
4. What are some of the disadvantages in relocating the operation to England?
5. What do you believe are some of the advantages to relocating to South Korea?
6. What are the disadvantages to relocating to South Korea?

Consider in your response the global impact of the operation including sales, products, personnel, and costs.

Selected further reading

BUCKNER, Robert W. (1998) *Site Selection: New Advancements in Methods and Technology*, C.H.I.P.S.

CHAN, Yupo (2000) *Location Theory and Decision Analysis with Facility-Location and Land-Use Models CD-ROM*, South-Western.

DREZNER, Zvi and HAMACHER, Horst W. (2001) *Facility Location: Applications and Theory*, Springer Verlag.

SALVANESCHI, Luigi and AKIN, Camille (ed.) (1996) *Location, Location, Location: How to Select the Best Site for Your Business* (Psi Successful Business Library), Oasis Press.

SULE, Dileep R., 'Logistics of Facility Location and Allocation', *Industrial Engineering*, vol 21, 2001.

An extensive listing of other further reading can be found on the website.

What's on the web?

Further learning resources are available to lecturers and students at www.supplychain-online.com, including the following which are specific to *Site selection*:

Resource	Subject
Chapter overview	Site selection
Industry insight: Moving from Germany to England	Staffing
Industry insight: Union rigidity	Staffing
Demonstrating the concept: Ramona	Quantitative approaches to site selection
Application exercise: Daunay	Breakeven analysis
Case study: Hoover Corporation	Site selection
More further reading	Site selection

4 *Quality management*

Chapter overview

- Quality concerns
- Definition of quality
- Total quality management
- Leading proponents of quality management
- Costs of quality and non–quality
- Quality control
- Quality-related tools and techniques
- International Organization for Standardization and ISO-9000
- European Foundation for Quality Management
- The UK Best Factory Awards
- Malcolm Baldrige National Quality Award
- Ethics and quality

Quality concerns

One issue, which is, or should be, a key concern to all organizations is quality of the goods, process, or services offered. To the consumer, or client, quality-related incidents occur all the time. The car wouldn't start in the morning. The train was late. The packaging was torn. The receptionist was rude. At the very least, quality problems can be irritating. At worst, they can be tragic as, for example, the DC-10 airplane accident in Chicago in 1979, which killed all the passengers and crew. The problem was in part due to a bad mounting assembly on one of the engines. (See further Chapter 19.)

Quality issues for specific industries

Some quality-related concerns in specific industries would include the following.

Travel

- Are customers treated courteously?
- Is the accommodation comfortable?
- Does the publicity conform to actuality?
- Is the transportation punctual?

Distribution

- Is the product delivered on time?
- Are the delivery agents courteous?
- Does the product arrive in good order?
- Is the product installed correctly?

Automobiles

- Does the vehicle perform as expected?
- Do the accessories work properly?
- Is it safe during operation?
- Does it conform to environmental regulations?

Education

- Are courses well structured?
- Is the professor competent?
- Is the material up to date?
- Is the teaching interactive?

Food

- Do products have an agreeable taste?
- Is processing under hygienic conditions?
- Do products have correct ingredients?
- Do products have a reasonable shelf life?

Fertilizers

- Is the chemical composition correct?
- Is the packaging durable?
- Do particle sizes meet specifications?
- Are use instructions clearly indicated?

Medical services

- Is the patient treated with understanding?
- Are visitors treated courteously?
- Is the prescribed treatment appropriate?
- Is the environment pleasing for recovery?

Quality is a strategic issue

Quality-related problems occur daily and, initially, we might put them at the operational level. However, the cause of quality is very deep rooted and ultimately can be traced to incorrect design, poor organization, and, in particular, related to people. Employees and managers who lack motivation become sloppy in their work, and this translates into errors in production, or a poor attitude in dealing with customers. Thus, quality involves long-term planning, an appropriate organizational structure for quality management, and continuing quality training programmes. As such, quality management is a strategic long-term issue but which has to be monitored and practised on a daily basis.

Quality and the supply chain

Quality issues have a strong impact on the material supply chain. Even though flow is efficient, and timely throughout the chain, poor quality at any point will impede success of the organization. This issue is discussed more fully in a later section in this chapter.

Customers drive quality

Customers judge quality. If a tangible product has a reputation for quality, customers will purchase. All else being equal, the company will benefit. German machine tools have a reputation for good quality and, as a consequence, enjoy a reasonably healthy market share. In the 1970s the then independent Jaguar Motor Company of the UK had a poor reputation for quality and this impacted their sales. The joke went: If you want a Jaguar, buy two: One to have as a spare while the other is in the garage for repairs! (Ford, USA now owns Jaguar.[1]) Service industries use quality aspects as a strong marketing tool. British Airways, partly as a result of a reputation for good service, enjoyed a strong growth period in the 1980s and 1990s and is a very successful airline. Harvard University of the USA enjoys a reputation for quality programmes, and producing quality graduates. It has minimal problems in recruitment, or obtaining industrial financing. Supermarkets that sell quality fresh produce and meat have a better customer following.

Net income and quality

Producing superior quality products, or providing a quality service, is vital to the continued growth and success of a firm as it:

- gives a positive company image
- improves competitive ability both nationally and internationally
- increases market share which translates into higher profits
- overall, reduces costs which then translates into a higher operating margin
- reduces, or eliminates, product liability problems, avoiding unnecessary costs and a poor company image
- creates an atmosphere for high employee moral which improves productivity.

In summary, as illustrated in Figure 4.1, quality has a direct impact on the bottom line.

Definition of quality

If you ask someone what they mean by quality, the response is certain to be different as people's appreciation or requirements of a product, or service, varies:

- For some, the Volvo stationwagon is considered a reliable and robust vehicle and this translates into a quality product. For others, the car is not stylish, and there is no quality message in the product.
- At a retail store a simple, 'No' from a salesperson might seem curt and disrespectful to some customers and thus is translated into poor quality service. Others may consider this response sufficient and not attach any importance to it.
- Some products are marked 'hand-crafted leather', 'hand painted', or 'hand sewn'. Some consider the manual labour input signifies good quality. Others may consider that hand-fabricated items are of a lesser quality than those made by machine because humans make errors and machines are more consistent in their operation.
- Students' evaluation of the quality of a university course can vary enormously. Some may consider a professor who is rigid and has a well-structured course excellent. Others might feel the course lacks flexibility, and the professor lacks warmth, so for them the quality is poor.

Figure 4.1 Quality increases net income

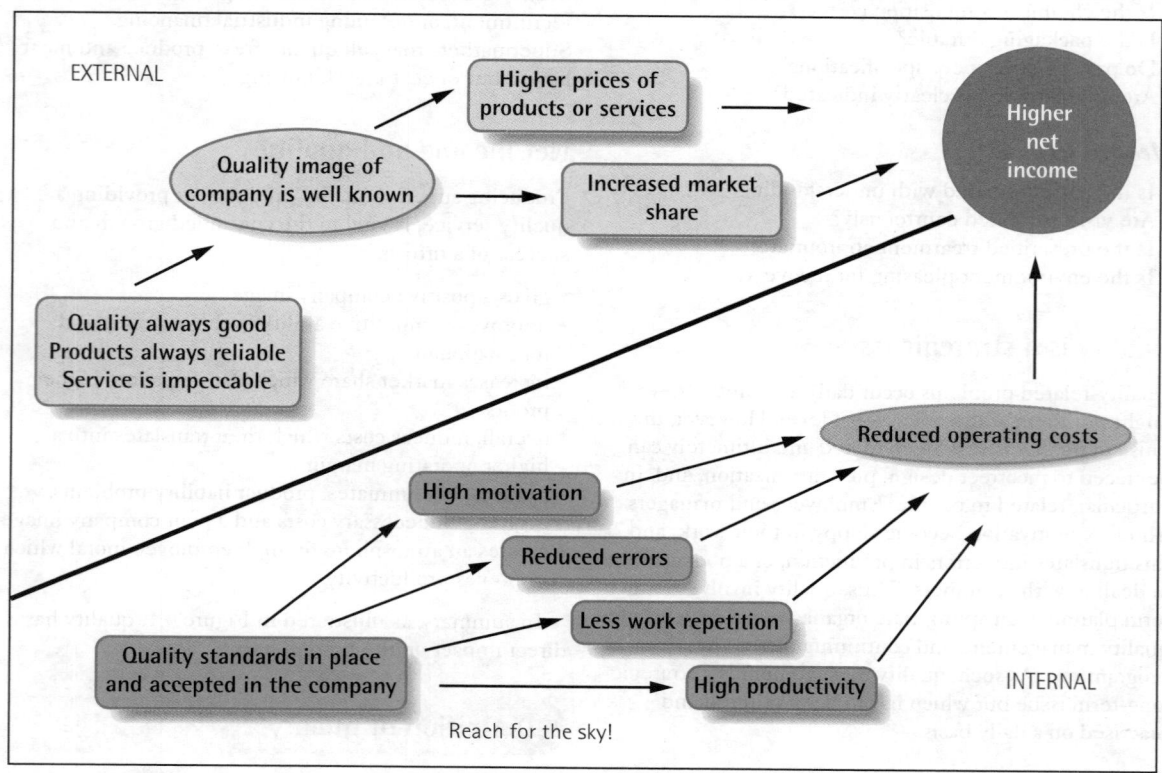

International Organization for Standardization

The International Organization for Standardization, ISO (presented in more detail later in the chapter) defines quality as, 'the totality of features and characteristics of a product, process, or service that bear on its ability to satisfy stated or implied needs'.[2] In this definition the following are implied.

Stated needs

Stated needs imply a contractual obligation for quality and would be specified in a written document such as the labelling on packaging. For example, the fertilizer contains 10% by weight of phosphorus, 5% potassium, and 15% nitrogen.

Implied needs

Implied needs are the expectations of the customer and these needs are probably not in writing. For example, one expects courteous service, food that is fresh, mail

delivered on time, and a lecture course that is relevant and well presented.

Evolution

Needs in the quality definition may change with time. This is particularly so with changing technology, and so product designs, and specifications have to be updated to satisfy the customer. As an illustration, automobile designs and safety features have evolved enormously over the years. Similarly, the range of services offered by a financial institution is now more than just simply checking services.

Specification

A specification, or standard in some countries, is the document that describes in detail the requirements with which the product, process, or service, has to conform. The specification includes drawings, patterns, and tables of dimensions or other relevant information. The document should also indicate the means, and criteria whereby conformity to the specifications can be checked. Sometimes a specification may be more precisely identified such as a:

- design specification
- manufacturing specification
- purchase specification
- quality system specification
- testing specification
- operating specification.

Grade

For many similar products there may be different levels of quality usually referred to as grades: A grade is an indicator of category, or rank, applied to products, processes, or services which are intended for the same functional use, but for an otherwise different set of needs as, for example:

- Porsche and Ford
- business class and first-class air travel
- Hilton Hotel and Formule 1 hotels
- Visa Gold Card, or regular card
- stainless steel and carbon steel
- full service or fast food restaurant.

The grade reflects a planned difference in requirements but if not planned then there is a recognized difference. The difference is often evidenced by the ratio of the cost to the functional use relationship and would be higher for the better grades. The concept is elaborated further as follows.

Travel

If the question is just getting to a destination, then flying first or second class makes no difference. A similar logic applies to if one drives from Rome to Milan in a Porsche or in a Ford. In both examples, the cost/function relationship of the first mode is higher.

Adequacy of quality

A high-grade article can be of inadequate quality for satisfying customer needs and vice versa. For example: a luxurious hotel which doesn't offer a porter, well-dressed waiters, and room service would not satisfy wealthy customers. Whereas a Formule 1 hotel offering these services would be totally out of place as the Formule 1 clients are not seeking these types of service. Clients' needs are different.

Numerical notation

Where grade is denoted numerically, it is common for the highest grade to have the number 1, and lower grades to have higher numbers such as 4 or 5. Although in a student exam the lowest points denotes the poorest grade.

Point score

When a point score denotes the grade then the lowest grade has the fewest points. In the star system for a hotel, the highest number would represent the best grade as, for example, a five-star hotel compared to a two-star hotel. The clothing company Pimkie in France has the following star system for denoting the quality control of its clothing articles:

*	rapid quality control
**	careful quality control
***	superior quality control
****	guaranteed high-quality control.

The prices of its articles are priced accordingly. One-star items are less expensive than the four-star items.

National origin

At one time quality in products or services could be identified by their country of origin:

- Germany for machine tools and automobiles
- France for wine, cuisine, and perfume
- USA for televisions and other consumer products
- Switzerland for watches and banking services
- Sweden for industrial engines and paper.

However, with the internationalization of many businesses, changes in cost structure, and the dominance of Japan in many industrial and consumer goods, this identification is no longer dominant. Further, as Industry insight 4.1 illustrates, the former eastern bloc countries are now moving into the picture.

Improving quality in the former eastern Europe

Firms in the former eastern European countries were not renowned for quality under communism. Now, after the fall of the Berlin Wall, more and more companies in central and eastern Europe are rapidly raising the quality of their products to conform to western standards. A good example is illustrated at Petofi Printing & Packaging Co. in Kecskemet, Hungary, a maker of cardboard boxes, wrappers, and other packaging. In the past, Petofi's employees drank beer and schnapps on the job and by mid-morning many were incapable of work. Not surprisingly, the absentee rate was very high. Product design was almost non-existent. A customer would give Petofi a sample to make and the production people didn't pay too much attention but would make something close to the sample. Managers told workers not to waste material even if that meant shipping junk. In production, flies became stuck in the paint and glue and subsequently ended up pressed onto the paperboard. The firm had no box-cutting machinery and instead employed a bunch of 50 burly women with rubber mallets pounding waste paper off the edges of the boxes. The product's quality and colour depended on which paints and material were available. If red paint were running low, orange would be supplemented. Very often containers were delivered in wrong colours and sizes. Only 7% of the products were exported and that went further east. The sales staff didn't make calls but set up visiting hours when customers could present their problems. However, customers rarely complained; instead they bribed the state company with chocolate and liquor.

Many of the past practices have changed. Petrofi was privatized in 1990 and is now partly owned by the Italian Cofinec Group. Using finance from the new owners, the World Bank, and the European Bank for Reconstruction and Development, Petrofi pumped $35 million into new equipment between 1990 and 1993 and called in western consultants. It installed 40 state-of-the-art machines including computer-controlled laser equipment to make prototypes, offset printers, computerized colour analyzers to mix the Wrigley green or Marlboro red, ultraviolet varnishing, and cameras to check for printing imperfections. It also established

quality assurance laboratories to check the quality of raw materials and terminated suppliers who were sending off-specification goods sometimes with the belief that a Hungarian firm would not care. Drinking on the job was forbidden and if any worker opened a beer on the job he lost one-third of his monthly wage. If the problem persisted he would be terminated. Petofi's top management was overhauled and the new management gave a 40% salary increase to workers, yearend bonuses and improved working conditions. Early retirement packages were offered to older workers who had difficulty changing their habits and this brought the average employee age down to 36. The new young workers went to trade shows to learn about the importance of quality. After this training, any products that were rejected by customers for quality problems were traced back to the worker whose wages were subsequently docked.

Now Petofi represents a big threat to western competitors. Most of Petrofi's products are exported to major customers such as Unilever, General Electric, Philip Morris, Pepsi Cola, Sara Lee and Henkel. According to the purchasing departments of these companies, Petrofi offers a very optimum cost/quality product. Petofi has won several awards from the World Packaging Organization and is certified ISO-9000. With the help of tax incentives and low labour costs the firm can undercut western competitive prices between 10 and 15%. Its market share is growing rapidly in what is a relatively flat European market. Petofi has profit margins around 30%, which is one-third higher than most western competitors.

Adapted from: 'New competitor: East Europe's industry is raising its quality and taking on the west', *Wall Street Journal Europe*[3]

Total quality management

Total quality management (TQM) or total quality control (TQC) is where attention to quality pervades the whole operation, and not just one particular sector. The driving wheel of TQM lies in the word management and, more precisely, top management.

Top management

A high proportion of quality problems can be traced to poor management. Top management *must* be the initiator of TQM. They have to provide leadership, direction, motivation, and support. If not, the system will break down. If assembly line workers are conscious of quality in their work, they will soon lose enthusiasm

if top management is not supportive. Management which does not respect meeting schedules, which is sloppy in organization, or does not pay attention to detail, will have difficulty in running a quality organization. Further, some managers who are afraid and anxious to defend their own position create a barrier to collaboration, communication, creativity, and employee advancement. This de-motivates employees and has its consequent adverse impact on quality. For TQM to function, top management, as the leaders of the organization, need to provide an appropriate work environment for employees, as illustrated in Figure 4.2.

Quality–related training

A key element in total quality management is that quality-related training must be available for everyone

Figure 4.2 **Quality and management:
The requirements**

- Furnish correct working tools
- Maintain small workgroups (maximizes identification)
- Provide training programmes
- Communicate
- Respect and show confidence
- Recognize employee contribution
- Develop/promote from within
- Permit certain amount of individual freedom
- Manage by objectives
- Discuss strategies and programmes
- Motivate
- Allow employees to share in financial success
- Encourage teamwork
- Dignify the job

Management is ultimately responsible for poor quality

in the company. This means from work centre, to boardroom, including line personnel, staff, and clerical people and must also include suppliers. Further, the company's quality programme must be transparent to customers. Training should be a continuous and integrated process, such as every month. A once-only training programme is soon forgotten and does not give evidence of a company's commitment to quality. Renault Automobiles in France, which introduced TQM in about 1988, continues to send employees on refresher quality-related training courses. This training (*formation*) consumes one-tenth of the training budget and is equivalent to a not inconsiderable 5% of the total wage bill.[4]

Manufacturing quality supply chain

Quality is also a supply chain operation as illustrated in Figure 4.3. For a tangible product, quality starts at conception and continues as the product moves from

Figure 4.3 **Quality chain in manufacturing**

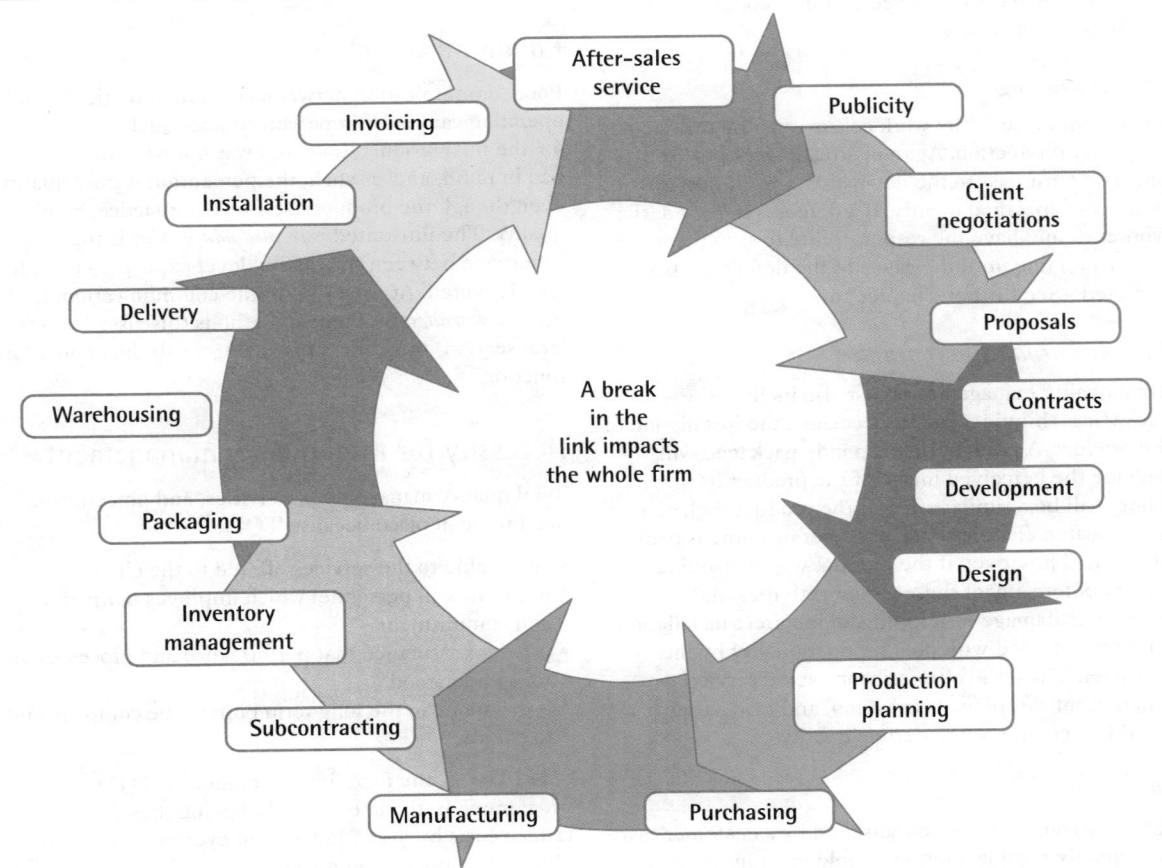

design to production, packaging, transportation to retail outlet, purchase, and use by the final customer. A break in the link of the chain impacts the whole firm. Some key considerations are now examined.

Development and design

Quality should be considered from the point at which a product is conceived and designed. It is difficult to rectify a poorly conceived product when it is at the production stage. The performance of the product, reliability, durability, the way the product is offered, will all be elements of quality to the final customer. Design engineers should work closely with operating personnel to ensure that the designed product can be properly manufactured in order to give the desired quality.

Purchased materials

Raw materials and purchased component parts must be according to specifications, if not they will impact the quality of the final product. Suppliers must be aware of a company's quality requirements. An important criterion in the selection of a supplier is the quality of the production process employed and the products. (See further Chapter 16.)

Manufacturing

Every employee in the work centre must be conscious of quality production. At an upstream work post the operator must pass to the downstream work post a product of specified quality. If a defect is detected, the worker should have the responsibility to stop the production line until the cause of the defect has been detected. (See further Chapter 15.)

Finished product to consumer

Total quality management must also include the packaging, shipping, and, if necessary, the installation of the product. A product that is poorly packaged will degrade the perceived image of the product itself. There will be a similar effect if the product such as a water heater, electric stove, or copier machine is badly installed. Thus, even if the product was of specification quality before any of these earlier activities, poor packaging, damage in shipping, or incorrect installation, might be equated with poor product quality by the customer. Thus, the often subcontracted service functions of shipping, distribution, and installation should be committed to perfect quality.

Invoicing

Sloppy accounting can be translated by a customer as a poor quality organization. I was told of an incident where a customer ordered 1000 cases of beer. He was invoiced for 2000! Not intentionally, of course, but as a result of poor communication within the organization.

Service quality chain

In a service industry the chain-like analogy exists, although the 'chain' is often shorter and the difference is that company personnel are dealing much more closely with the client than in the case of manufacturing. As such, quality in services covers how courteous company agents are with customers. Are they honest, responsive, have a smile, patient, etc? Illustrations of the chain-like reaction might include the following:

- Accounting errors in a banking operation can destroy the confidence of the client in that particular bank.
- Products delivered damaged will impact the image of a delivery firm.
- Poor food on an airline flight, perhaps subcontracted, can discredit the airline company.
- Unresponsive assistants in a retail store can tarnish the image of that retail firm.

Communication

Poor communication between concerned parties in an operation can result in perceived poor quality. In Figure 4.4 the final product delivered was not what the client had in mind, and, as such, the perception is poor quality even though the product itself was, in practice, good quality. The illustrated *perceived non-quality* is the difference between the quality level expected, and what was delivered. At each step in the communication, the quality *degrades*. In Taguchi methods (discussed in a later section) this concept is analogous to the quality loss function.

Necessity for total quality management

Total quality management activities, and procedures, need to be in place because TQM:

- adds value to the services offered to the client
- implicates all personnel which improves motivation and commitment
- provides assurance that performance and processes are well understood
- is economic in the long term both to the company and to clients.

H J Heinz, the food firm, introduced a TQM programme in the late 1980s, believing they could reduce costs by over $250 million over three years by eliminating waste, and rework.[5]

Figure 4.4 Quality level is reduced in the chain (communication)

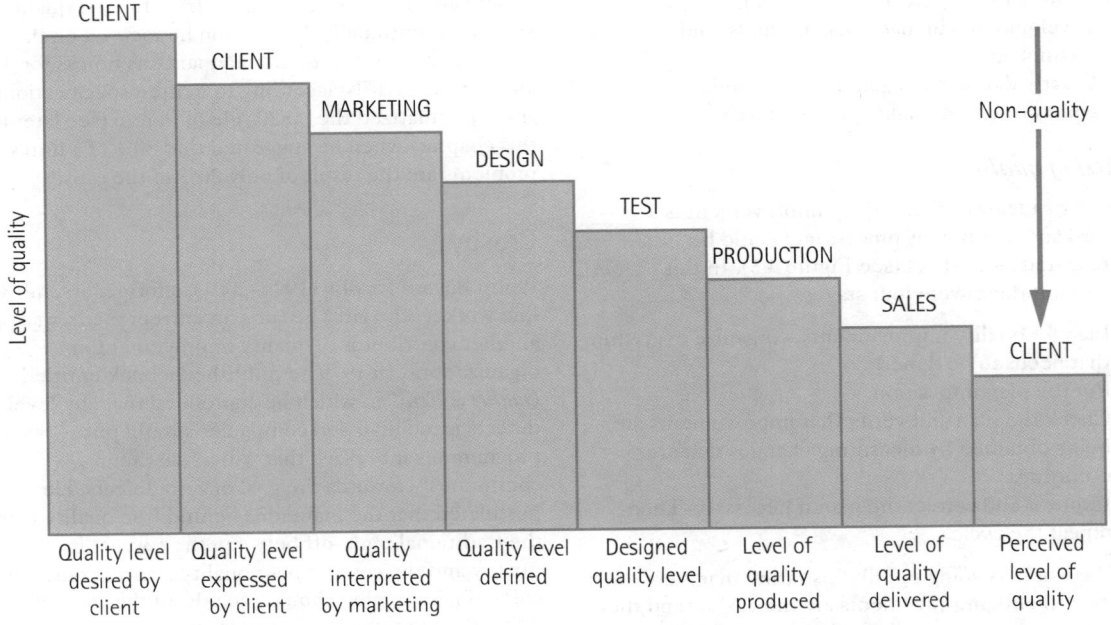

Leading proponents of quality management

There are many proponents who have developed concepts and ideas in quality management, most insisting that management accept responsibility for building good quality systems. Notable individuals include Deming, Juran, Crosby, and Feigenbaum of the USA and Taguchi and Ishikawa of Japan. The philosophies of the US gurus are presented here and the Taguchi and Ishikawa quality methods are discussed later in this chapter.

Deming

Dr W Edwards Deming, who died in 1994, was by training a statistician, a professor at New York University as well as being a consultant to industry. After World War II he was invited to Japan at the request of the government to help improve the quality of Japanese products. He worked extensively with Japanese industries, and was so successful that the government established the annual Deming prize for innovation in quality management. Deming is well known for establishing the following 14 criteria for quality improvement.[6]

Fourteen criteria for quality improvement

1. Create consistency of purpose toward product quality.
2. Refuse to allow commonly accepted levels of delay for mistakes, defective material, and defective workmanship.
3. Build quality into the product and stop depending on inspections to catch problems.
4. Build long-term relationships with suppliers, based on performance instead of awarding business on the basis of price.
5. Implement programmes for continuous improvements of costs, quality, service, and productivity.
6. Start training to make full use of all employees.
7. Focus supervision on helping people to do a better job. Provide the tools and techniques for people to have pride of workmanship.
8. Eliminate fear or stress in the workplace and encourage two-way communication.
9. Break down barriers between departments and encourage problem solving through teamwork.
10. Eliminate the use of numerical goals, slogans, and posters for the workforce.
11. Use statistical methods for continuing improvement of quality and productivity and eliminate all standards prescribing numerical quotas.

12. Remove barriers to pride of workmanship.
13. Institute a vigorous programme of education and training to keep people abreast of new developments in materials, methods, and technologies.
14. Clearly define management's permanent commitment to quality and productivity.

Wheel of quality

Deming's idea was that quality improvement is a cyclical and continuous process and could be represented by a wheel (see Figure 4.5). In this continuum there were four stages:[7]

1. Plan for quality improvements – organize everything that needs to be done.
2. Put the plan into action.
3. Check the plan and verify that improvements are being obtained by measuring changes that are occurring.
4. Improve and correct the plan if necessary. Then repeat the cycle.

The wheel is going uphill illustrating that, very often, the first quality improvements are the easiest and then become more and more difficult.

Juran

Joseph M Juran in the 1970s and 1980s was another pioneer in helping the Japanese to improve product

quality. Like Deming, he believed strongly in top management commitment, support, and involvement in quality and also in teamwork to strive to raise quality standards continually. In addition he focused on the customer in an effort to define quality as fitness for use and not necessarily according to written specifications. Juran popularized the 80/20 rule of Pareto (see later in this chapter) when he suggested that 80% of a firm's problems are the result of only 20% of the causes.

Crosby

Philip Bayard Crosby (1926–2001), a former assembly line worker who later became an entrepreneur, was another contributor to quality improvement in organizations. In 1979 he published a book entitled *Quality is Free*,[8] in which he contended that any level of defects is too high and companies should put programmes into place that will move them continuously towards the goal of zero defects. He postulated that the main idea behind free quality is that the traditional trade-off between the costs of improving quality and the costs of poor quality is erroneous. The costs of poor quality should include all the costs of not doing the job right the first time such as scrap, rework, lost labour hours, and machine-hours, the hidden costs of customer ill will, lost sales, and warranty costs. He strongly believed that the cost of poor quality is so understated that unlimited amounts can be profitably spent on improving quality. Among Crosby's clients were General Motors, Chrysler, Motorola, and Xerox.[9] (Quality-related costs are developed in more detail in the following section.)

Feigenbaum

Armand V Feigenbaum published a book entitled *Total Quality Control* in 1983, in which he emphasized that the responsibility for quality has to rest with the people who perform the associated work – secretaries, salespersons, machinists, suppliers etc.[10] This is referred to as quality at the source and discussed later (see Chapter 15).

Feigenbaum, together with his brother, created a consulting practice and worked extensively with US firms on quality issues. In their work they estimated that the quality failure costs (cost of non-quality) averages 10% of gross sales in world-class US companies but a high 25% in most other major US companies. To illustrate, as a result of work by the Feigenbaums, Union Pacific (US railroads) has eliminated more than $700 million a year in quality-related costs since 1988 by upgrading the scheduling, maintenance and customer service. Similarly, Tenneco (Energy) has increased operating yield by $250 million annually by improving quality.[11]

Figure 4.5 Deming's quality wheel: A continuous circular process

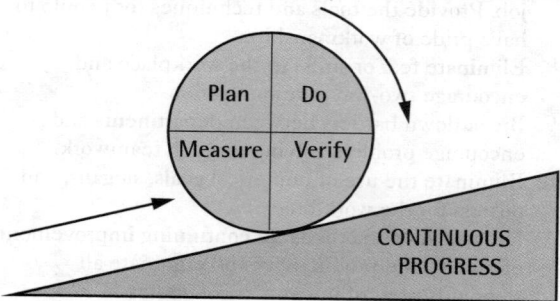

Plan: Organize everything that needs to be done
Do: Take action on those things that have been planned
Verify: Check that all the work has been done
Measure: Analyze the results
Are there any anomalies? Improve

Plan | Do
Measure | Verify

CONTINUOUS PROGRESS

Costs of quality and non-quality

The costs associated with quality, total quality costs, referred to in the previous section when discussing Crosby and the Feigenbaums, may be represented by an equation, as illustrated in Figure 4.6. This shows that total quality costs are the sum of four elements: external and internal costs, and evaluation and prevention costs. These are dealt with in more detail in the following and summarized in Figure 4.7.

Figure 4.6 Relationship for the cost of quality

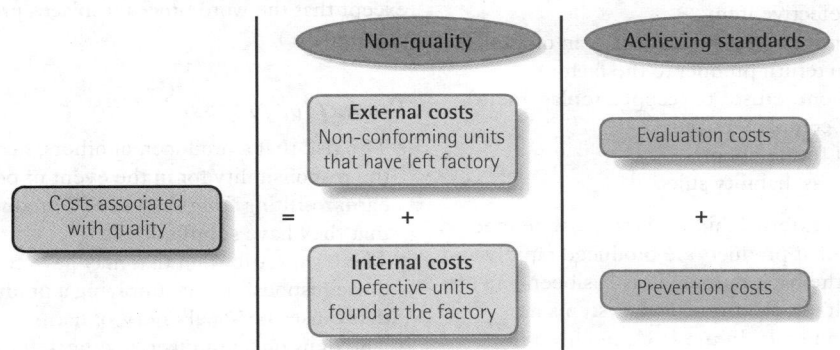

Figure 4.7 Costs associated with quality

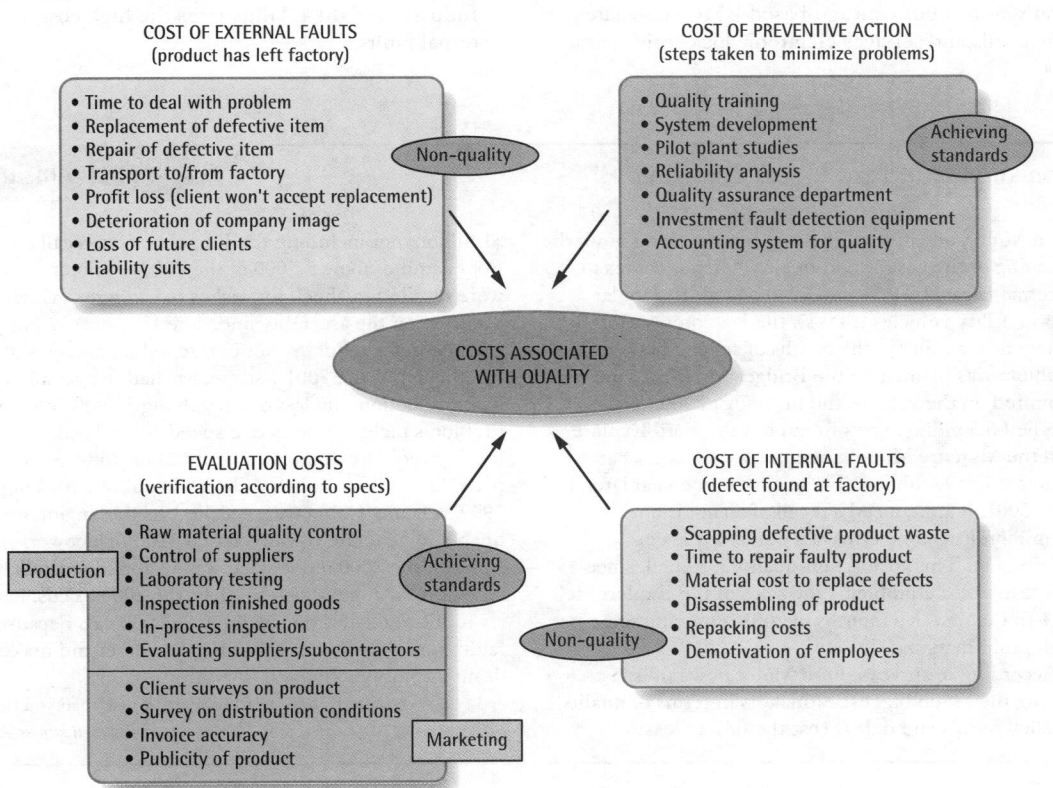

External faults

In an external fault, which is the cost of non-quality, a product has left the factory, and is subsequently found to be defective. The fault may be detected at the distribution level, the client determines the fault, or governments determine the product is faulty.

Costs resulting from external failure would include:

- time for an employee to deal with problem
- replacing the defective item
- use of repair service to put product back in order
- transport cost to return product to the factory
- loss of profit (client refuses to accept a replacement)
- deterioration of company image
- potential loss of future clients
- product, or process, liability suits.

A contributor to external failures is the rush to meet client demand so that products are produced rapidly and quality is put on the back burner. This has been one of the problems with the electronic lock systems now commonly used in hotels. In the USA, in only a few years, electronic locks have been installed in one-third of the nation's 3.2 million hotel rooms and poor quality is evidenced by guests being unable to get into their rooms, or worse, unable to get out! The precise failure rate isn't known but Chicago-based EMG Associates Inc. that sells and services electronic locks said that in

1995 it sold about 5000 electronic locks – and repaired about 5500.[12]

Product, or process liability is one of the severest quality-related repercussions to a producer arising from external faults. The limits of liability vary from country to country according to national legislation. In the USA, liability settlements are very much higher than in Europe. The definition of product and process liability is now given. (The definitions are identical except that the word process replaces product where appropriate.)

Product (or process) liability

- The risk that a producer, or others, may have to bear the responsibility for in the event of personal injury, or harm resulting from the use of a product (or process) that they have supplied.
- The legal retribution that may have to be made by those responsible for supplying a product (or process) that causes personal injury, or harm.
- The onus on a producer, or others, for the financial loss, or other harm suffered by the users of a product (or process) that they were responsible for putting into circulation.

Industry insight 4.2 illustrates the high cost of external faults.

Non-quality at Ford Motor Company   Industry insight 4.2

Ford Motor, one of the big three automakers, knows the meaning of the cost of non-quality when it comes to external faults. In 1999 and 2000 one of its popular sports-utility vehicles (SUVs), the Explorer, suffered rollovers, resulting in the deaths of several people. The problem was blamed on the Bridgestone/Firestone tyres mounted on the vehicle and in August 2000 Ford recalled 6.5 million tyres from both the Ford Explorer and the Mercury Mountaineer SUVs at a cost of an estimated $500 million. Then, almost one year later, in May 2001, it announced a recall of an additional 13 million Firestone tyres at a cost of a staggering $2.1 billion. This cost of non-quality is not all, since as a result of the problems the sales of the Explorer fell 21% in the first five months of 2001 removing some very high profit margins.

According to surveys, Ford Motor now ranks last among the seven biggest carmakers in terms of quality. In 2000 recalls and delays cost the firm at least

$1 billion, not including the Firestone tyre recalls. For example, some 52,000 of the 2002 Explorer SUVs were recalled to check for gashes in the tyres, which occurred on the assembly line. The US government said the defect could result in tyre failure and crashes. Another SUV, the 2001 Escape, has had five recalls since its introduction, the last one involving 51,000 vehicles. Problems included defective speed control cables, leaking fuel lines, and missing rivets on windshield parts. On its basic automobile models about 4000 of the 1999 Mustang Cobra were recalled, as the engine was unable to generate the advertised 320 horsepower. Further, the 2000 model year was scrapped entirely. One of their compact car models, the 2000 Focus, had six recalls, one of them covering 207,000 cars because of faulty hub nuts that could cause the wheel and brake drum assembly to fall off.

Adapted from: 'Ford: Why it's worse than you think',
Business Week[14]

Internal faults

An internal fault is also part of the cost of non-quality and this is where the defect is found before the product leaves the factory. The costs may include:

- scrapping the defective product so there would be material waste
- reprocessing time for employees to repair the faulty product
- material cost to replace the defective product
- disassembling the product
- repackaging costs
- management/employee irritation which could lead to reduced productivity.

Preventive measures

For preventive measures a firm develops methods to eliminate, or minimize quality problems and so these become costs to achieve quality. They may include:

- quality-related employee training programmes
- systems development for quality improvement
- pilot plant to use for quality programmes
- quality assurance department.

Detection and/or evaluation

Detection and/or evaluation would include activities associated with verifying that a product is according to specification quality and so, again, they represent costs to obtain quality. They might be divided into costs at the production stage, and costs at the marketing stage.

Production

Costs at the production stage would include:

- sampling of raw materials for conformity
- inspection of in-process products
- inspection of finished goods
- laboratory testing for conformity
- online quality detection equipment
- client surveys for opinion on the quality of manufactured products
- evaluating suppliers, licensees, or subcontractors for quality conformance.

Marketing

Costs at the marketing stage would include:

- client surveys for opinion on the quality of final products
- survey of distribution chain, including transportation systems

- accuracy of invoicing documents
- presentation and display of final products
- cost of the 'phantom customer' (see later in this chapter).

Percentage cost of quality

Considering these four elements in the cost of quality, then a mathematical relationship, as a percentage, is:

$$\text{Cost of quality} = \frac{C_e + C_i + C_d + C_p}{C_B + C_e + C_i + C_d + C_p} * 100$$

- C_e is the cost of external faults
- C_i is the cost of internal faults
- C_d is the cost of detection
- C_p is the cost of prevention
- C_B is the measured base production cost (no costs for quality).

In practice, it is difficult the separate all the costs, but even making an estimation would give a manufacturer or service operator some idea as to how much is involved. As an illustration, the following summarizes the costs associated with quality for a food packing and distribution firm in France.[13]

Food distribution firm

This company has two principal activities. One is the reception of bulk dry foods, including rice, beans, herbs, etc., and then packaging them on automatic filling machines into one and five kilogram sacks for delivery to supermarkets. The second activity is the mixing, processing, bottle filling and packaging of soft drinks such as cola, orange, lemon etc., also for supermarket clients.

The company recognized it had a quality problem and its first step in 1995 to tackle the situation was to determine the total cost of all the quality-related activities in the firm. To do this, it determined the time spent on quality problems for each department and multiplied this by average salary to come up with a cost. Prevention and detection costs were the time of all the associated laboratory work, and control studies spent in the packing area. The costs of non-quality was the time spent on activities such as:

- quality control of raw materials
- maintenance because of unplanned machine shutdowns

Figure 4.8 Cost of non–quality/quality for food packaging and distribution

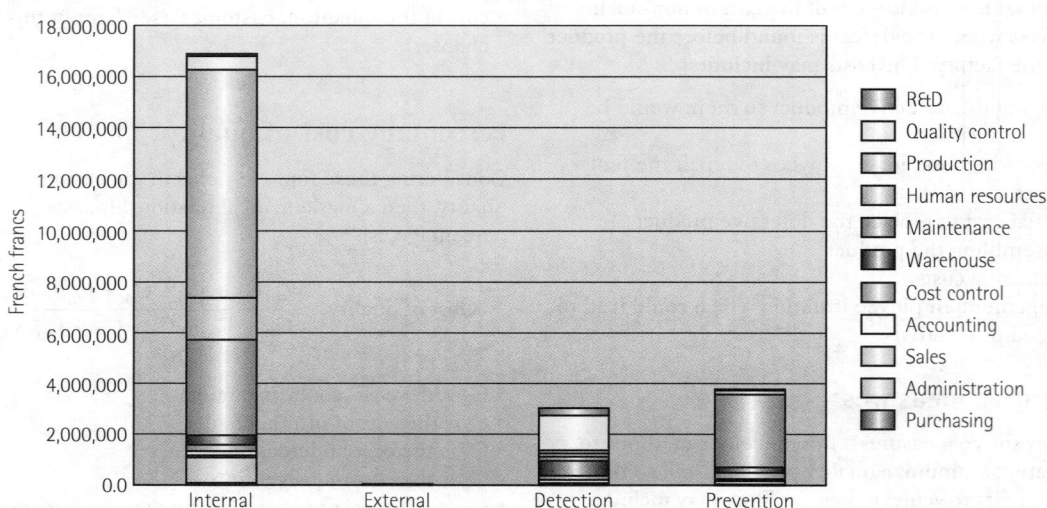

- taking back poor quality products from clients
- time lost in reception or production because bags would break.

Figure 4.8 summarizes the results. On a percentage basis these were:

- internal costs   71.1%
- prevention   15.9%
- detection   12.8%
- external costs   0.2%

and were equivalent to 8.2% of revenues, or 211,000 FF ($36) per employee.

Costs are long term

Changing levels of quality do not happen overnight. Improved results from training programmes, design modifications, or installing fault detection equipment take time. However, in the long run, the benefits are positive. Directional changes are shown in Figure 4.9. The explanation is as follows.

No quality programme

With no quality management programme in place, then additional manufacturing or service-related costs would be incurred arising from external and internal faults. This is represented by the upper curve labelled, Costs with no quality programme.

Figure 4.9 Long-term quality programmes reduce cost

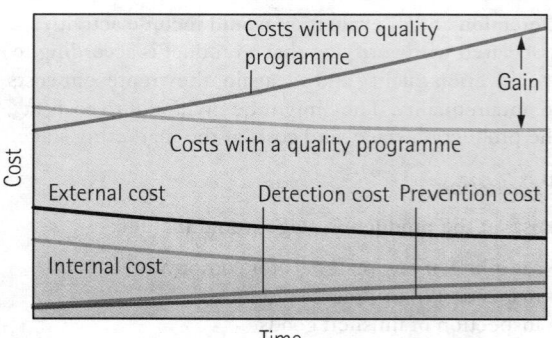

With a quality programme

If a quality programme were in place, then over time, both external and internal costs would decline as illustrated by the curve, Costs with a quality programme. By the same token, detection and prevention costs would generally increase although they would probably even up, as personnel were effective in managing the detection and prevention systems. The net result is that additional costs would be less than with no such quality programme, as illustrated by the vertical difference between the two curves.

Costs and the level of quality design

Quality has a cost and the more one improves a product through quality enhancements, the higher are production-related costs. These higher production costs are passed along to the consumer. However, there is a limit to how much a customer is willing to pay for a certain product. It makes no sense to 'gold plate' an article if it is priced out of the market.

The type of relationship between the product price, and the production cost is shown in Figure 4.10. The shape of the curve will differ according to the product, quality improvements, and the like. However, the relationship will be similar. The cost of improving the quality design will increase in an exponential form. The price a customer would be willing to pay will level out, as the additional quality enhancements add no marked increase in value in the eyes of the customer.

The following sections illustrate this.

Books

A hardback book is more attractive and durable, and to many represents better quality than the same text as a softback. Very often a publisher will price a hardback version higher than a soft. Customers, particularly students, may not necessarily be willing to pay for such hardback editions, when a softback will suffice. After all, it is the text inside which is important.

Automobile

An automobile can be fitted with leather upholstery, teak dashboard, stainless steel wheel mouldings and the like. However, this would price it out of the market for many people, who see a car as a basic utility vehicle. Only for clients who would pay a high price for a car such as a Bentley or Aston Martin are these fittings acceptable.

Jewellery

With new techniques, for most people it is hard to see the difference between costume and fine jewellery. For many customers the price and appearance of costume jewellery is sufficient as fine jewellery may be out of their budget.

Furniture

With furniture, new manufacturing techniques make possible a wide range of module furniture (as sold by IKEA; for instance) constructed from compressed wood chips or plywood. Finishing the product with oak, walnut, or teak laminations give it the appearance of solid wood.

Figure 4.10 **Limit to quality design**

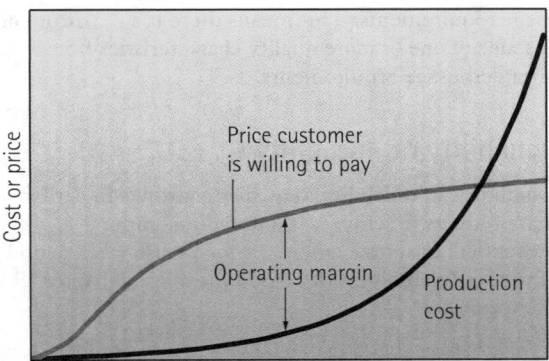

Matches

Matches are produced at low quality levels, low production costs per unit. People don't care as long as they light.

Nails and screws

Customers wouldn't pay the price for precision stainless steel nails or screws when simple carbon steel products do the same job.

Quality control

Quality control covers the operational techniques, and activities, used to satisfy quality requirements including monitoring a process and eliminating causes of unsatisfactory performances at all stages of the quality chain. The quality control programme depends very much on the industry but an organization might have in place a quality control programme for manufacturing, purchasing, customer relations, transportation, warehousing, etc. Quality control will almost certainly include statistical quality control, which is the analytical technique for verifying conformity for a process or for a product. (These are dealt with in detail in Chapter 20.) The purpose of this section is to highlight some of the terms and qualitative aspects related to quality control.

Defective product

A defective product can mean a broad range of problems. If, for example, the product is a television it might be defective because it plainly does not work, the reception is poor, it makes a strange noise, or, say, the screen has a scratch. The strict definition of a defective product is one where there is non-fulfilment of intended usage requirements. This means there is a departure or absence of one or more quality characteristics from intended usage requirements.

Reliability or durability

Durability, or reliability in quality control is to verify that products function, without failing, under prescribed, or stated conditions for a reasonable period of time. (Reliability is discussed further in Chapter 19.) For example:

- grocery bags that don't collapse when full of food items
- zippers on clothing that are reliable for the duration of the life of the garment
- filler caps on bottles that do not leak.

Reproducibility

Reproducibility in quality control is the ability to produce products that are reproducible in quality and their characteristics. For example, reproducibility according to colour might be applied to textiles, paint colours, photographic reprints, food dressing, wallpaper, and carpets.

Quality control departments

Historically, and even currently in some firms, manufacturing, or engineering and construction companies had quality control departments. Those in quality control were staff, as opposed to line personnel whose responsibility was to establish quality specifications, monitor, measure, and report on the quality of products or designs produced by the corresponding department, or work centre. In production, the principal responsibility was to maintain throughput, keep unit costs low, and to produce at an acceptable quality level. In many instances, the main criteria for judging production were quotas and costs. Thus, as a result quality took a back seat and this put production, and quality control departments in conflict. Quality control policed production to ensure quality was according to standards. Production tried to meet their quantity quotas, but the surveillance by quality control created stress in the organization. Quality control was not a line function, and they had no responsibility to shut down an operation, or to enforce a design change.

To manage an organization so that quality takes precedence, people must work as a team. Sales, design engineers, production, suppliers, maintenance, and the like have to take responsibility for the quality of their work. Their customer – whether the end user of the product, the next workstation, an industrial client, or a contractor – has to be provided with a product which meets the quality expectations or specifications. That is, quality at the source as espoused by Feigenbaum. To achieve quality at the source the following should be the rule, and not the exception.

Responsibility

Complete quality responsibility is assigned to the person performing the work. That is, quality becomes a line, rather than a staff, function.

Self-inspection

The production function is enlarged, so that workers inspect their own work. If workers are properly informed and trained, this makes the activity more motivating. In this case, the number of people related formally to quality control can be reduced and the excess reassigned to the value-added production operation.

Remove the policeman

The quality control department, rather than being a policeman, is responsible for establishing the quality specifications, to train personnel in quality control, and to provide whatever assistance is needed in quality matters. Today, quality control departments may be referred to as quality assurance departments.

Inspection in quality control

Ideally, no inspection is needed if quality work is produced 100% of the time. Unfortunately, this is not the case and so inspection, preferably at a minimum level, is performed in certain circumstances. The inspection covers all the activities such as measuring, examining, testing, or gauging one or more characteristics of a product, process, or service by sampling and then comparing these results with designated requirements. (See also Chapter 20.) Some tools for quality control inspection of products would include:

- surface finishing gauges to test surface finish
- weigh scales
- callipers to measure diameter
- chemical analysis
- electronic meters
- viscosity meter for the measuring pouring characteristics of lubricating oils.

Extent of inspection

The extent of inspection depends on the type of product produced. Where the product has a high value, every product coming from the production line is subjected to some level of final inspection. This is the case of automobiles, computers, and electrical switchgear for instance. In many cases, because of economics, not all final manufactured products are 100% inspected. This is the case of standard products coming off an assembly line such as canned beer, screws, or books. Where destructive testing is required, such as would be the case for ammunition, fire extinguishers, and concrete, 100% testing would destroy all output! In all these cases samples are selected at random, tested, and, using statistical analysis, decisions are made whether to accept, or reject the entire lot. (See Chapter 20.)

There is a risk in sampling. Some faulty items would be analyzed before they reach the customer but other faulty items would escape inspection and end up in with the customer. However, as there is a cost associated with inspection, there is an optimum level, or a balance between the amount of inspection employed and the cost associated with defective products reaching the marketplace, as illustrated in Figure 4.11. The larger the proportion of final products inspected, the greater the cost. However, in this case the risk of defective units being passed on to the customer is less, and so the cost of non-quality is less. On the opposite side, with little inspection, there is a lower inspection cost, but a greater chance of defective items being passed along to the customer. The graphical illustration is similar to inventory movements in balancing purchasing costs and holding costs presented in Chapter 11.

When and where to inspect

When it is uneconomical to inspect all products the following are some general guidelines when to inspect in an operation:

- Raw materials, and purchased parts at a supplier's facility. This will help to avoid reception of non-conforming products.

Figure 4.11 **Balance between inspection and cost**

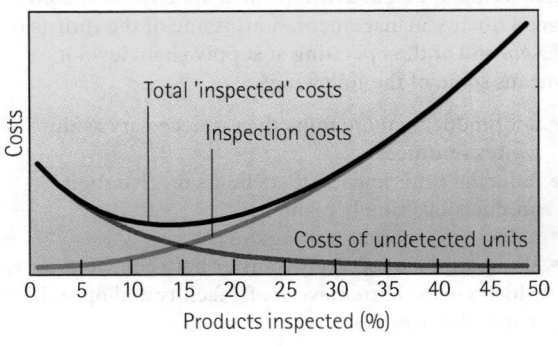

- On receipt of supplier's products if inspection at the supplier's location is not possible. Obviously, starting with faulty raw materials will be a bad start in the quality chain.
- After a new team has been working on an operation.
- At a licensee's facility to verify processing conditions, such as a brewery.
- At a franchise facility to verify quality standards such as a McDonald's fast food restaurant.
- Inspect after operations that are complex and are known to produce faulty items, such as intricate soldering or assembly.
- Inspect before costly operations. Do not waste costly labour or machine time on items that are already defective. In a book-printing/binding operation, to print a large quantity of books that have not been well proofed is very costly.
- Before an irreversible process. For example, a plastic such as polypropylene is made starting from propylene. If the propylene feed is not according to specification, then the final product will be off-specification.
- Inspect before operations that cover up defects. Painting, plating, soldering, and assembling often can hide defects.
- Inspect before assembly operations that cannot be undone.
- On automatic machines, inspect first and last on the production runs, but less in between.
- Inspect finished products if it is economical. Customer satisfaction is important, the firm's image is at stake, and the firm is liable for faulty products. Repairing, or replacing defective products in the field is more expensive than at the factory. If this occurs, the seller is probably responsible for shipping costs and a client may hold up final payments pending delivery of non-defective goods.
- Distributors or transport operators to verify their handling practices.

Traceability

Traceability in quality control is the ability to trace the history, application, or location of an item or activity by means of recorded identification. The identification may be a date stamp, lot number or, very often, a bar code. Traceability is a requirement of the ISO certification discussed later.

Quality-related tools and techniques

Companies can improve the quality of their products, services, processes, or organization by adopting certain practices. The following describes these various quality practices in alphabetical order. As indicated some of them are treated elsewhere in this book. Further, a summary tabulation is given in Chapter 26, as they are very useful in carrying out a diagnostic of the firm and not necessarily only in the area of quality.

ABC analysis

ABC analysis is a special form of Pareto or frequency analysis, used to determine the financial value of stocks relative to the quantity (Chapter 11) or perhaps number of suppliers relative to value of purchases (Chapter 16). Using this type of analysis improves the management of resources, which indirectly has a bearing on the quality of an operation.

Activity–based costing

Conventional cost management does not put a cost on reworking, delays, inventory storage, or bottlenecks. Activity-based costing (ABC) is a technique that measures costs at each step of the supply chain, or the production process, in a way that uncovers inefficiencies, and activities that do not add value, and often lead to poor overall quality. (The concept is reviewed in more detail in Chapter 25.)

Benchmarking

Benchmarking, in global terms, is the comparison of one firm's business practices with others'. From a quality point of view it is the comparison of the product quality between firms. For example, in a benchmarking study conducted in 1994 by J D Power and Associates, of new car defect rates in the first 90 days of ownership, Toyota scored 70 for every 100 vehicles to Chrysler's 125.[15] (Benchmarking is detailed in Chapter 26.)

Brainstorming

Brainstorming is a process where a small group of people in the company, often from different departments, meets, and without any inhibitions or preconceived notions, puts forward ideas related to company issues. It can be particularly useful to discuss quality-related problems in an organization. Brainstorming can be a precursor to an Ishikawa diagram described later. (See also Chapter 6.)

Failure mode, effect, and criticality analysis

A failure mode, effect and criticality analysis (FMECA) is the detailed study of a product design, manufacturing

Table 4.1 Problems in a food production unit

Production line	Problems in a week
Slab chocolate	12
Boiled candy	15
Soft candy	8
Mustard	4
Spices	3
Mixed chocolates	8
Total	**50**

operation, or distribution network to determine which features are critical to various modes of failure. (The method is covered in detail in Chapter 19.)

Frequency check sheets

A frequency check sheet can be used to indicate how often any problem might be occurring with a particular product. Table 4.1 presents a check sheet for problems occurring in a food production unit. It can be further developed into a Pareto analysis, as discussed later.

Hoshin

The Japanese term *hoshin* is short for *hoshin kanri*. The word *ho* means 'direction' and *shin* is 'needle' thus the literal translation of *hoshin* would be direction needle or compass. The word *kanri* can also be broken into two parts, *kan* means 'control or channelling' and *ri* means 'reason' or 'logic'. Thus, together *hoshin kanri* means 'focusing management and control of the firm in the right direction'. *Hoshin* to work relies on a system of forms and rules.

In any operation one should strive to minimize the non-value-added activities, which are criteria related to good quality management. This is one of the thrusts of *hoshin* and at the operating at supply chain level it means some of the following:

• not producing more units than is necessary as this wastes resources
• reducing lead times so that clients receive their products in a timely manner
• reducing inventory waiting times
• eliminating unnecessary transfer between work posts which means better layout of a facility and optimizing material movement

Table 4.2 Applying the concept of *hoshin*

Phase	Stage	Duration (example)
1	Selection of the work post, production line, etc.	Half-day
2	Formation of the task group for the *hoshin* study and providing the appropriate information	Half-day
3	Analysis, proposals for improvement, new process schemes, etc.	Two days
4	Implementing the proposed changes	One day
5	Fine-tuning the modifications	One day
6	Increasing the production throughput	Up to two weeks
7	Evaluation of modification	One day
8	Validating the new process or operation in terms of method and quality	One day

- optimizing transport between production sites and distribution centres
- eliminating rework of items.

In order that the concept of *hoshin* is successful it needs the cooperation of operators who must be supported morally by all supervisory and management staff. An example of applying the *hoshin* concept would be, say, to select a specific element or unit such as a production line or work post and undertake an analysis according to the steps in Table 4.2.

Improvement monitoring charts

In setting up programme to improve an operation, it is necessary to monitor if progress is being made. This has to be illustrated by comparing earlier results with current results. For example, assume the interest was to reduce the number of defective products being made in an assembly operation. The percent defectives would be the indicator. Periodic sampling would be made at specified periods, and results compared. If at the start of the quality programme the percent defects were 8%, three months later 6.5%, and then three months after that 4.7%, then a conclusion that is apparent is that the quality plan is working. Figure 4.12 illustrates a general situation of progress being made over time as the value of the indicator is decreasing. The indicators can be

Figure 4.12 **Operational improvements are shown by measuring changes**

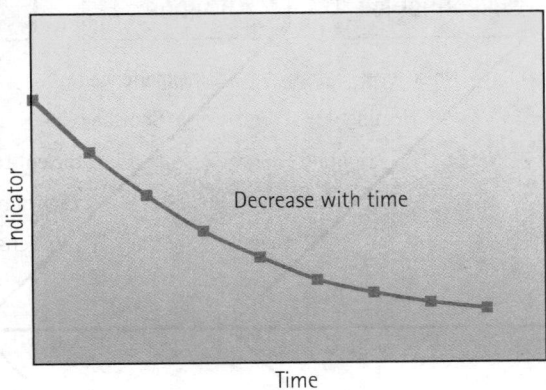

anything: employee absenteeism, product composition, delivery times, inventory levels, arrival times, the number of errors on billing statements, etc.

Ishikawa diagram

An Ishikawa diagram, named after its inventor, is also known as a fishbone diagram because of its shape, or a cause and effect diagram because of its use. It is a useful analytical tool for quality studies and can be appropriately adapted after brainstorming to first look at all eventualities.

Manufacturing operation

Figure 4.13 is a fishbone analysis that might be used to analyze why there is an excessive number of defective products being produced. In this example, there are six major generic potential problem areas together with identifiable situations within that area:

- physical work environment
- labour employed
- machines employed
- management
- methods
- materials.

Other areas that might be considered are financial – insufficient capital, inadequate cash flow, late payment by customers, high costs, and the like.

Service operation

Figure 4.14 gives some of the considerations in analysis of a service operation such as a restaurant. In this example, there are six major potential generic problem

Figure 4.13 Ishikawa diagram for a manufacturing operation

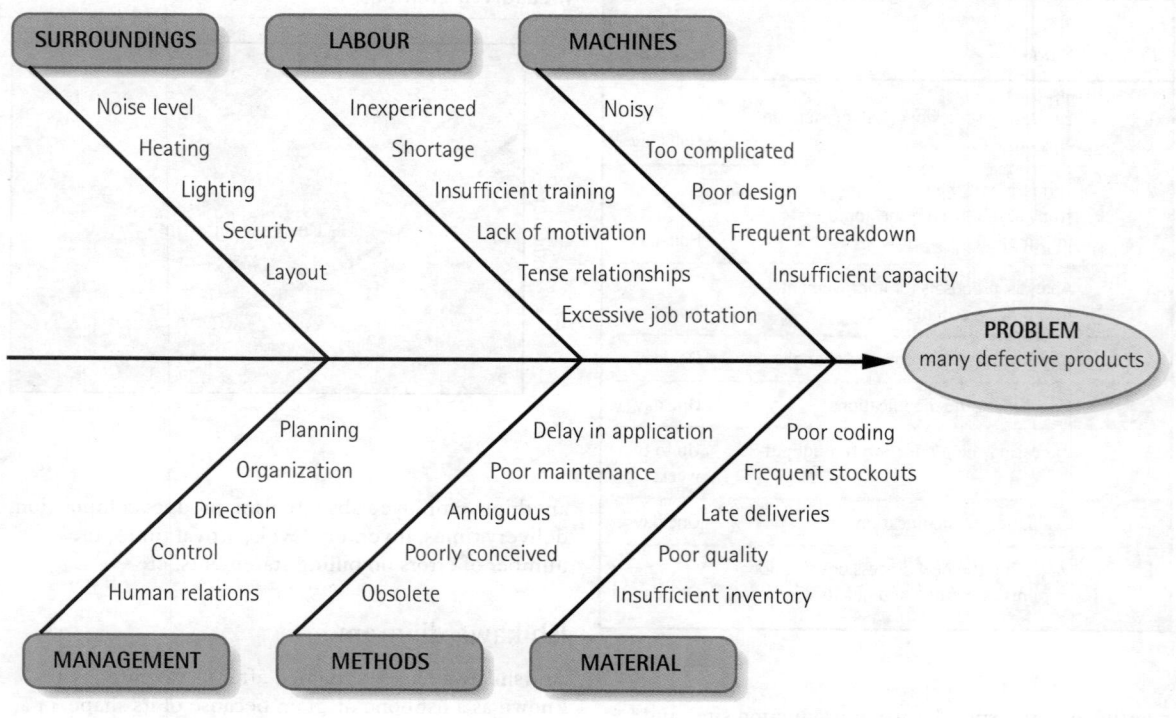

Figure 4.14 Ishikawa diagram for a restaurant

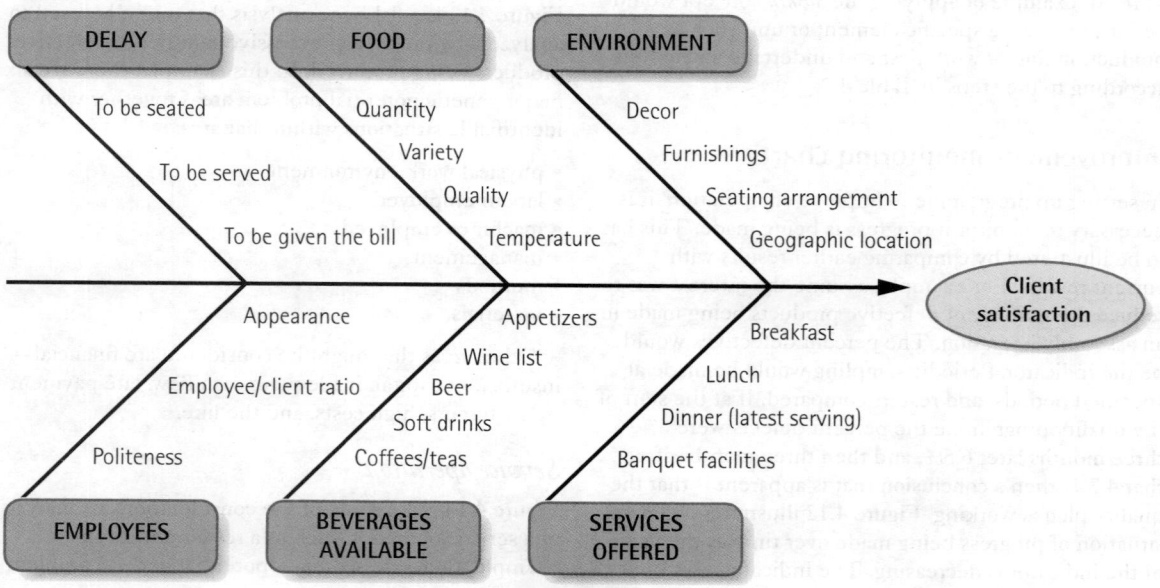

areas together with identifiable situations within that area:

- delay
- food
- environment
- employees
- beverages available
- services offered.

An Ishikawa diagram can be developed for just about every operation. As an analytical tool, it is best used in starting from the right-hand side (head of the fishbone), which is the principal indicator for the operation and then to work backwards identifying specific elements.

Just-in-time

Just-in-time production (covered in detail in Chapter 15) is a management practice where the exact quantities of a product are produced, or delivered, just when needed. Delay times and inventory levels are kept to an absolute minimum since the philosophy is that unnecessary inventories, or delays, are an inefficient use of resources. Thus, practising JIT enforces adherence to product quality.

Kaizen, or continuous improvement

A continuous improvement process (CIP) or kaizen, means continuously trying to establish higher levels of quality by, say, isolating sources of problems. The ultimate goal is zero defects, the objective espoused by Crosby. In kaizen the concept is: Don't always strive for new breakthrough products but try to improve on existing designs. This logic was very much evident in the production of the Volkswagen Beetle which was introduced in Germany in 1937 and, until production in Europe was stopped in 1978, over 22 million VW Beetles were sold – more than any other automobile in the world. The basic design and style remained essentially unchanged for close to half a century but quality-related improvements were continually added. Industry insight 4.3 illustrates the how the kaizen approach has helped an automotive supplier in modern-day Germany.

Keep designs simple

'Keep designs simple' is the philosophy of reducing the number of parts in a product, which helps to minimize the probability of error. The more parts there are in a

---

Practising the kaizen concept in Germany

Industry insight 4.3

In Zurich, Switzerland, is the Kaizen Institute, a consultancy firm that helps European manufacturers to put in place the concept of kaizen, a continuous improvement programme that was detailed in a book of the same name by the Japanese management guru, Masaaki Imai, in 1986. The methods of the Kaizen Institute have considerably helped the Edenkoben plant of Walker Gillet Europe GmbH, a subsidiary of Tenneco, USA, located some 120 kilometres southwest of Frankfurt, Germany. The firm makes automotive exhaust systems and is a supplier to General Motors, Porsche, and Volkswagen. Automotive suppliers worldwide are struggling and Walker Gillet is cutting away at fat by adopting this Japanese concept of kaizen for continuous improvement at its facility. For example, at one large U-shaped assembly line for welding together muffler housings there used to be as much as three days of work-in-process inventory accumulated along the line. After careful analysis, this has been reduced to one day. In addition, instead of parts being moved around in large quantities by a forklift truck, smaller quantities are placed in bins and moved around by hand. At another workstation the company was able to free up 20% more space, reduce the distance parts

had to travel between manufacturing steps by 42%, and increase output by 40% – all in one week. Throughout the plant, black floors that used to hide the oil leaks were replaced with colourful, easy-to-clean flooring. Work tools were colour coded corresponding to the section they were used in and they were located within arm's reach of the operator rather than in a central location. In addition, the setup time to change dies at one seaming station was cut to 12 hours from the original 80 and new preventive maintenance programmes reduced downtime of equipment and machinery. As a result of these improvements overall Walker Gillet has reduced end project reject rates by more than 5% and reduced inventories to between one and two days from a previous four to five. Output rose 15% in 1995 and returned the company to profitability after losing money in the previous two years. Walker Gillet has been so successful at cutting its own costs that one of its own workers, a veteran of 40 years of the 'old system' started conducting kaizen workshops at Walker Gillet's own suppliers.

Adapted from: 'On the line: Automotive suppliers in Germany take aim at years of inefficiency', *Wall Street Journal Europe*[16]

product, the more areas there are in which things can go wrong. (Chapter 19 analyzes this logic further.) Simple designs also reduce material cost, assembly time, and inventory costs. Two illustrations follow.

General Motors

They redesigned the rear bumper of the Seville automobile with the following results.[17]

- The number of parts was cut in half to 63.
- The assembly time was reduced by 57% to under eight minutes.
- The estimated annual labour savings was $462,000.

IBM

IBM's Laser Printer has fewer parts, and fewer screws, than the comparable Hewlett-Packard Laser Jet III.[18]

Overall equipment effectiveness

Chapter 15 examines this approach where analyzing the activities of a machine might include:

- operator breaks
- machine breakdowns
- unplanned interruptions
- machine setup
- speed less than design
- waste products.

The ultimate objective of analyzing the overall equipment effectiveness is to increase the throughput of the machine, or the work post.

Pareto analysis

A Pareto analysis, named after Vilfredo Pareto a 19th-century Italian economist, is a graphical representation showing the frequency of the causes of a problem (see also Chapter 27), and is a graphical representation of a frequency check sheet (discussed earlier). The following are three examples using a histogram for the exact frequency of occurrence, and a line graph giving the cumulative amounts.

Manufacturing

This is shown in Figure 4.15. Non-quality material is the major problem, which may be directly related to suppliers.

Distribution

This is given in Figure 4.16. Squashed fruit is the problem that occurs most frequently (about 40% of the time). However, bacteria on fruit might be a more critical problem (occurring about 3% of the time) in the case of the delivery of fresh fruit.

Services

This is given in Figure 4.17.[19] Peaceful surroundings are the most important, although communication and eating facilities are close behind.

The principle of a Pareto analysis is to concentrate, first, on solving the most critical, which are often the most frequently occurring activities, before devoting resources to the less frequently occurring areas.

Figure 4.15 **Pareto analysis: Lost time on a machine**

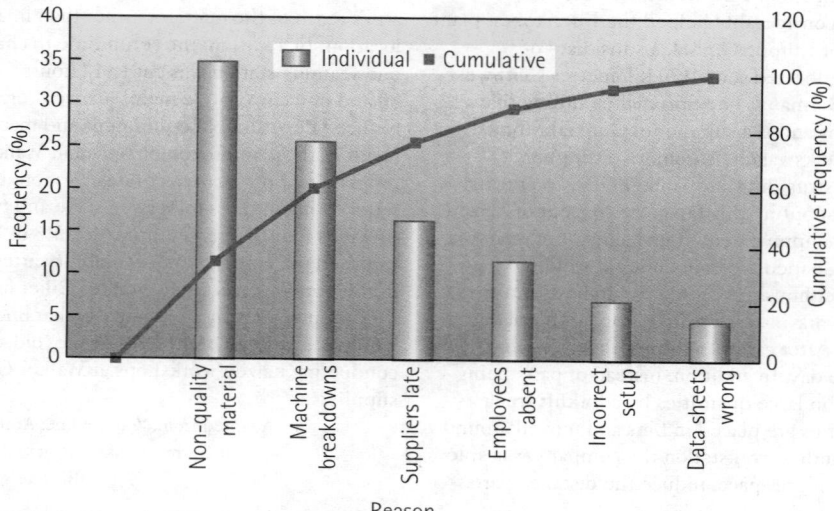

Phantom customer in services

Phantom customers are used, for example, in automobile dealerships, banks, retail stores, and restaurants to monitor the quality of its operations. At any unspecified time a *customer*, which is, in reality, a company employee or an outside consulting service, visits the site requesting a service. When the service is completed this customer evaluates the service outlet on quality of work, price, time, and the way the customer was treated. Industry insight 4.4 illustrates this activity in one European country. (However, this author is not in agreement with the comment that there is poor customer service in France.)

Figure 4.16 Pareto analysis: Distribution of chemical products

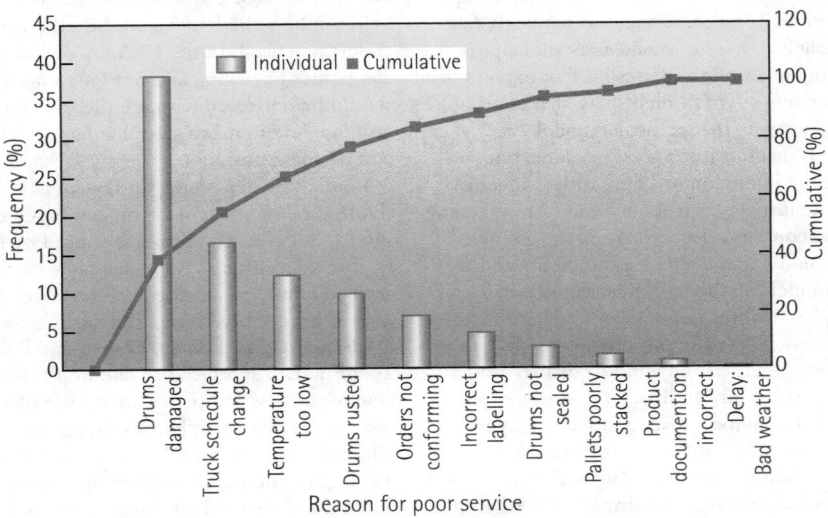

Figure 4.17 Pareto analysis: Most valuable benefits of airport executive lounges

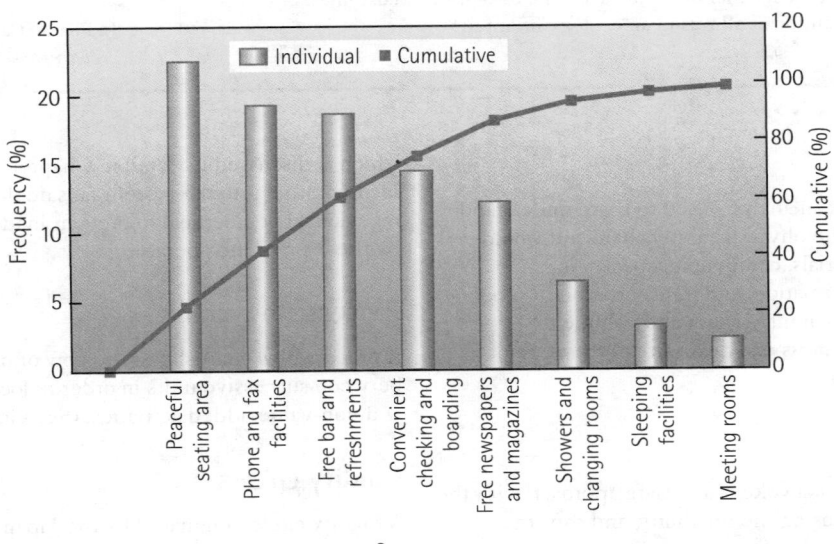

The work of the phantom customer

In his flannel shirt and leather jacket, Yannick Bichon could be just another 30-something customer seeking a yearend bargain here in a large shopping mall in La Defense, northwest of Paris. However, he has no intention of spending a franc, as he is a phantom customer, taking notes on how he is treated by the salespeople. Bichon is pretending to look for a computer printer in a large appliance store and after a ten-minute wait, he begins to chase any one of the red-blazered assistants to try to make eye contact. Eventually he corners one who quickly tells him to ask someone else. The second assistant he pins down shows a hint of a smile and uses his foot to point to a computer printer, one out of 21 on display, that he would recommend. Asking why that particular model, the assistant's retort is that it is just a good machine, but provides no backup information. Then, with a sigh, the assistant begins to inspect his nails and moves away telling Bichon to think about his selection. When the assistant had left, Bichon noted that the display counter was dirty and that no pamphlets on the machines were available.

In a mobile phone store, Yannick worked hard to keep a salesman's attention. For the salesman to remove the phone of interest from the front window display was apparently out of the question. In a large store selling parts for computers, compact discs and video players, the checkout person never made eye-to-eye contact and there was never a hello or goodbye. In another store, one salesperson who was rearranging a display looked at him with contempt when he asked how one particular item was used. When he asked for a book on dogs a young women heaved a sigh and walked over to the right shelf only to find the book out of stock. She made no attempt to secure the article for Bichon. The closest he came to getting any attention at all was in an ecology-oriented giftshop.

Being a customer in France, particularly in Paris, can be a humbling experience. The client is not yet king. Salespeople make it clear that their phone conversations should not be interrupted, handling the merchandise can be annoying, and if a customer asks a question they might have to wait until the assistant has finished tidying the shelf. Some storeowners complain that they are unable to work on their accounting books in the morning because customers bother them. Getting any help can be a challenge, and the sullen stare seems almost practised. In the USA, by way of contrast, companies have long taken it for granted that service should be delivered with a smile, and sending people into the field to make sure that happens is a common part of doing business.

Yannick Bichon works for Dynamic Mystery Shopping (DMS), a three-year old company based in Suresnes, a suburb of Paris. The firm was started by François Leaute who, after a visit to see his sister in the USA, noticed how pleasant the experience of shopping was. Aware that quality service can raise income, clients of DMS include Air France, Disneyland Paris, TotalFinaElf, and Jacadi, a children's clothing chain. One of the first companies to use the phantom customer service of DMS was Pharmactiv, an association of 550 pharmacies throughout France, which felt that service was highly important because all pharmacies sell pretty much the same product. Pharmacists who used the service were at first sceptical because they believed it was like using spies. Further, it was rather a cultural thing because although they believed in making money they were not worried about the feelings of the customer.

Adapted from: 'In France: Can I not help you', *International Herald Tribune*[20]

Pipeline map

A pipeline map is an analysis used to try to understand the activities in the physical supply chain and would include raw materials, components, packaging, reception, transformation, and transportation. A pipeline map is broken down into length and volume to represent the leanness and flexibility of the system. (See Chapter 17.)

Poka yoke

The concept of poka yoke is a failsafe approach with the objective of increasing the reliability, and thus the quality, of a product, process, or service. The concept, which is discussed in detail in Chapter 19, means incorporating into the system failsafe devices perhaps mechanical or electrical to prevent inadvertent mistakes by the user, or the operator.

Process flow chart

A process flow chart shows the flow of materials between successive units in order to locate the value and non-value-added activities. (See Chapter 7.)

Quality circles

A quality circle, originated by the Japanese, is a small group of employees (average number nine), who

Figure 4.18 Quality circles

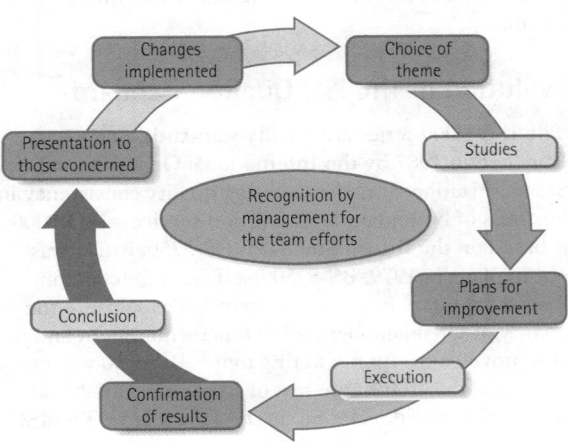

Figure 4.19 Quality attributes for a production operation

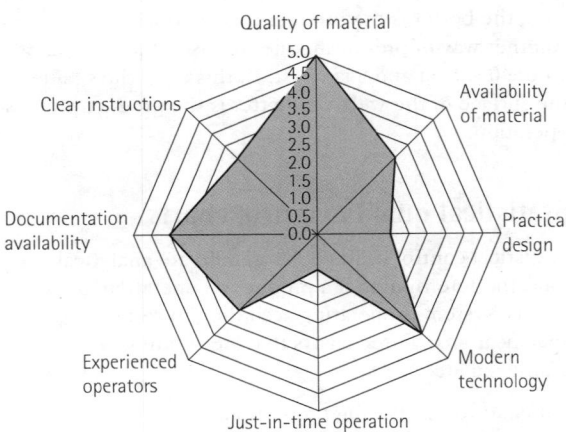

volunteer to meet regularly to analyze work-related projects, which have the objective of advancing the company, improving working conditions, and spurring mutual self-development, by using quality control concepts.[21] Participation is voluntary, and there are no direct cash incentives. The principal reason is personal satisfaction, and achievement, and recognition of improvements is given at regional, and national quality control meetings. The process is illustrated in Figure 4.18.

Quality function deployment

Quality function deployment (QFD) is an analytical method which focuses and coordinates capabilities within an organization in order to design, manufacture, and market goods that are desired by the customers. The concept is that products should be designed to reflect customers' preferences and priorities. As a result, marketing people, design engineers, operating personnel, and suppliers must work very closely together in order to produce a product that will meet these customer requirements. (See Chapter 6.)

Reengineering

Reengineering, or business process reengineering (BPR) is an idea that has its roots in late 1980's USA. It means a complete re-evaluation and shake-up of a firm with the ultimate objective to increase its performance, to be more flexible, more reactive, and more closely in touch with the needs of the client. With this increase in performance is included (it is hoped) improved quality

of products and services. (Reengineering is further reviewed in Chapter 7.)

Scatter diagram

A scatter diagram is a presentation of the dependent variable with an independent variable and the purpose of scatter diagram is to see if there is a correlation between the two. If so, perhaps a quantitative model can be developed which will forecast, or estimate, certain outcomes and indirectly improve the quality of decision making. As an illustration, Chapter 10 gives a scatter diagram for operator absenteeism as an independent variable against the number of poor quality units as the dependent variable. The objective to see if there is a correlation between the two measures and if so, what measures can be taken to rectify the quality problem.

Spider web

A spider web is a Pareto-type analysis where the information is presented on a graph which resembles a spider web, as illustrated in Figure 4.19. Here there are the eight criteria for analyzing the operation, both from a process and product viewpoint.

- quality of material
- availability of material
- practical design
- modern technology
- just-in-time operation
- experienced operators
- documentation availability
- clear instructions.

These criteria are given a numerical score from 0 to 5, with 5 being the best from a quality point of view. Thus, when the spider web is drawn, the bigger the area of the web, the better is the product/process operation. Another way of presenting the web is in the reverse, where 0 is best and 5 is worst. In this case, the smaller the surface of the web, the better is the product/process operation.

Statistical quality control charts

Statistical control charts (Chapter 20) are analytical tools for determining if a production operation, or service system is operating according to certain specifications. Three charts that are commonly employed are:

- p-chart for measuring proportions, or fraction units defectives
- c-chart for measuring the absolute number of defective units
- x-bar chart, together with a range chart for measuring the output of variables in an operation.

Taguchi methods

Taguchi methods, named after the Japanese Genichi Taguchi, are procedures aimed at quality improvement in both product and process design. They are based on making designs robust by building in tolerances for manufacturing variables known to be unavoidable. Taguchi's philosophy is that missing the quality target in a consistent manner can be better than hitting it a few times with the rest being scattered all over the board.[22] (The three basic concepts in the Taguchi methods are presented in Chapter 6.)

International Organization for Standardization and ISO-9000

International Organization for Standardization

The International Organization for Standardization or ISO is an international, non-governmental body whose principal goal is to decrease trade barriers by promoting worldwide product standardization. It was founded in 1947, with headquarters in Geneva, Switzerland, and there are some 120 member countries. The acronym ISO is used for the International Organization for Standardization rather than the seemingly logical IOS because in the Greek language *iso* means

equal and the ISO wanted to convey the idea of equality in the sense of placing organizations on an equal footing.

Evolution of the ISO Quality Standards

The ISO-9000 series are quality standards, first launched in 1987 by the International Organization for Standardization, aimed at assuring quality consistency in business of both manufacturing and services. ISO-9000 is based on the British Standards BS-5750, which was put in place in 1979. BS-5750 itself was modelled on Britain's military procurement standards to ensure the quality of UK-manufactured defence equipment and it also proved a useful marketing tool.[23] BS-5750 was initially introduced into the rest of Europe as EN 29000 from which was developed the ISO standards. The ISO standards were revised in 1994 and at that time there were the following three basic standards for which a firm could become ISO-certified based on verification by a third party auditor.

ISO-9001

The ISO-9001 was the fullest and most complete standard. It was a module that defined all the elements necessary for conformity throughout the whole supply chain operating cycle from design through development, production, installation and servicing. Within the module were the 20 detailed sections as given in Table 4.3.[24]

ISO-9002

ISO-9002 was the module for quality assurance in production and installation and was the more common standard for manufacturers. It applied where there was already an established design or specification which constitutes the specified product requirement. With the exception of design, and design changes, this standard was very similar to ISO-9001.

ISO-9003

This was a module that applied to firms in a contractual situation who wished to demonstrate capabilities for inspecting and testing products. It covered document control, product identification and marking, control of products that do not pass specified tests, a handling and storage system, control of measuring and test equipment, statistical techniques, and training.

In 2000 the ISO-9000 series were again revised and the above three certification standards were integrated and replaced by just one standard, now referred to as ISO-9001: 2000. This applies to all organizations including

Table 4.3 Sections in ISO–9001 (version 1994)

1. Management responsibility	Defines how a company should draw up an organization chart to identify the responsibilities of all staff that manage, or carry out, work associated with the quality activity
2. Quality system	Defines how a firm should establish and maintain procedures and instructions for a quality system to assure that products conform to specifications
3. Contract review	Defines and documents how firms must establish, and maintain current, the requirements for contract review and contract differences between concerned parties
4. Design control	Defines requirements and procedures to manage and verify product conception and design to ensure that defined specifications are achieved
5. Document control	Establishes procedures for document control, including approval, availability, logging of manuals, and diffusion to concerned parties
6. Purchasing	Defines procedures to ensure that a purchased product conforms to specifications including evaluation procedures for subcontractors
7. Purchaser-supplied product	Defines verification procedures for a supplier regarding storage and maintenance of purchased products
8. Product/service identification and traceability	Describes, when appropriate, how a supplier for the purpose of traceability must establish and keep up-to-date identification procedures, based on a product's original design, specifications, or other appropriate documents in all phases of production, delivery, and installation
9. Process control	Covers documentation of how a process should be carried out, including, where necessary, installation procedures. Written instructions must be given to the employee involved where appropriate and the process must be monitored
10. Inspection and testing	Covers procedures necessary to assure that the product is neither used nor put into service, until it has been inspected and tested according to written specifications
11. Inspection, measuring, and test equipment	Covers requirements for using, standardizing, and maintaining in good condition all inspection, measuring, and test equipment
12. Inspection and test status	Covers the status of inspection according to appropriate stamping, ticketing, markings, recording documents, follow-up instruction, and the like
13. Control of non-conforming product	Covers procedures in order to assure that a non-conforming product is not used or inadvertently installed. It covers identification procedures, documentation, and isolation of the product
14. Corrective action	Covers procedures for researching why a product does not conform, the corrective action necessary, and to eliminate potential problems that might arise because of non-conforming products
15. Handling, storage, packaging, and delivery	Covers procedures necessary for product handling to prevent damage, the type of storage areas, and storage environment to prevent product deterioration or damage. It also includes detailing procedures for types of packaging, the packaging methods, and delivery procedures to respect
16. Quality records	Covers requirements to be established for the identification, collection, indexing, organizing, and filing to keep up to date, or for destroying all records related to quality
17. Internal quality audits	Covers procedures necessary for carrying out internal quality audits
18. Training	Covers procedures to identify that appropriate training is available to all those people who might in some way have an incidence on the quality operation of the firm
19. Servicing	When after-sales service is identified in a contract, this section covers procedures to verify that the after-sales service is according to requirements
20. Statistical techniques	Where appropriate, this section covers statistical procedures necessary to verify that a product or process is according to specifications

services, manufacturing, and government and the standard gives all the requirements for certification. In addition to ISO-9001: 2000 there is also ISO-9000: 2000 which explains the fundamentals of certification and ISO-9004: 2000 which give the guidelines for performance improvements. The major reasons for the revisions in 2000 were to emphasize the need to monitor customer satisfaction; to develop more user-friendly documents; to assure consistency between quality management system requirements and guidelines; and to promote the use of generic quality management principles by organizations and, to enhance their compatibility with ISO-14000, the environmental standard (see Chapter 5). The new ISO-9001: 2000 standard means that firms that are currently certified ISO-9002 or ISO-9003, according to the 1994 version, now have to become certified ISO-9001: 2000. The deadline for updating to the new certification is 15 December 2003.

Basis of ISO-9000 standards

The purpose of the certification standard ISO-9001: 2000 is to establish a management system that provides confidence to the producing organization, and more importantly, to its clients, that products meet established or specified requirements. In this context, 'products' applies to services, processed material, and hardware and software intended for the customer. The ISO-9001: 2000 does not guarantee the quality of products and services because it is a process standard and not a product standard. Certification means that an organization's quality management processes have met ISO's requirements. These are the following five principle sections in ISO-9001: 2000, which replace the 20 sections in the previous ISO-9001 of 1994.

- Description of the activities used to supply the products
- Quality management system used
- Management responsibility
- Resource management
- Measurement, analysis and improvement.

Importance of certification

Some of the considered advantages of ISO-9000 certification are as follows.

International orientation

As of 31 December 1999, 343,653 ISO-9000 certificates were issued with 55% being to Europe; 3% to Central and South America; 13% to North America; 17% to the Far East; 7% to Australia and New Zealand; and 5% to Africa and West Asia.[25] Although the number is low for North America its acceptance is growing rapidly and there was an almost 35% increase in 1999 over 1998. This international orientation makes the ISO certification the logical choice for any organization that does business globally or that serves customers who demand an international standard of quality.

Marketing muscle

Companies which obtain ISO-9000 certification are permitted to display the appropriate certificate. As a result, in theory, a company that is certified is able to offer a superior product or service and this will give the company marketing muscle.

Contractor selection

If a company, say for example in Asia, is looking for a European subcontractor and it is not completely familiar with European business, it is more likely to select a partner that has the ISO certification.

Suppliers

Selecting a new supplier can be time consuming and costly (see Chapter 16). If a potential supplier is certified ISO-9000 then the selection process for a buyer firm can be considerably reduced. Suppliers in Europe, with European clients, are probably more likely to be selected if they have certification.

Criticism of certification

Obtaining certification is criticized by some as being costly, long (it may take up to three years to obtain certification), and bureaucratic.[26] Further, it is no guarantee that a company that is certified provides a quality service or product.

Quality certification only provides a book of procedures and not necessarily better quality. Many companies in the past, such as Hewlett Packard (computer products), C F Braun & Co., (engineering and construction), Suchard (chocolate and confectionery), and Marks & Spencer (retail), long enjoyed a reputation for quality before certification. Strong opponents of ISO-9000 say those who believe that achieving certification will result in the production of higher quality products and services is somewhat like believing that issuing driving licenses produces safer roads!

Within the organization, strictly adhering to the ISO certification is viewed as returning to the rigidity of Taylorism in the firm (see Chapter 8). It demotivates people because it puts a block on individual initiative.

Others say that the systematic controls and written procedures are considered as being unnecessary '*policing*' of activity. Policing is the criticism often thrown at the old Quality Control Departments. On the employment side, when all procedures are written, it limits the hiring, or the upward mobility of those unable to read clearly. (Some people in production may have a low level of education.)

European Foundation for Quality Management

Background

The European Foundation for Quality Management (EFQM) was founded by the presidents of 14 major European companies, with the endorsement of the European Commission. Jacques Delors, then President of the European Commission, signed the letter of intent to establish the EFQM in Brussels on 15 September 1988. The membership is in excess of 550 organizations across 23 European countries, ranging from multinational and national firms, research institutes, and universities.[27]

Mission of the EFQM

The mission of EFQM is twofold:

1. To stimulate and assist organizations throughout Europe to participate in improvement activities, leading ultimately to excellence in customer satisfaction, employee satisfaction, impact on society, and business results.

2. To support the managers of European organizations in accelerating the process of making total quality management a decisive factor for achieving global competitive advantage.

The European Quality Award programme and the EFQM model

The European Quality Award, which is part of the EFQM programme, was developed in 1991 to recognize those companies that show a high level of commitment to quality. Entry for the award is through a cascade process involving national quality organizations from each of the European countries. The criterion for making the award is based on a point system, using the EFQM model illustrated in Figure 4.20.[28] This model contains nine elements that can be used to assess an organization's progress towards excellence in business. Each of these elements examines how the organization is functioning (enablers, as shown in the figure) and what are the results (results, as shown in the figure) which require evidence of achievement in the nine model categories. The total possible points for the award are 1000 (500 for the enablers and 500 for the results). This, together with the required evidence, or proof, is explained as follows.[29]

Figure 4.20 The EFQM quality model

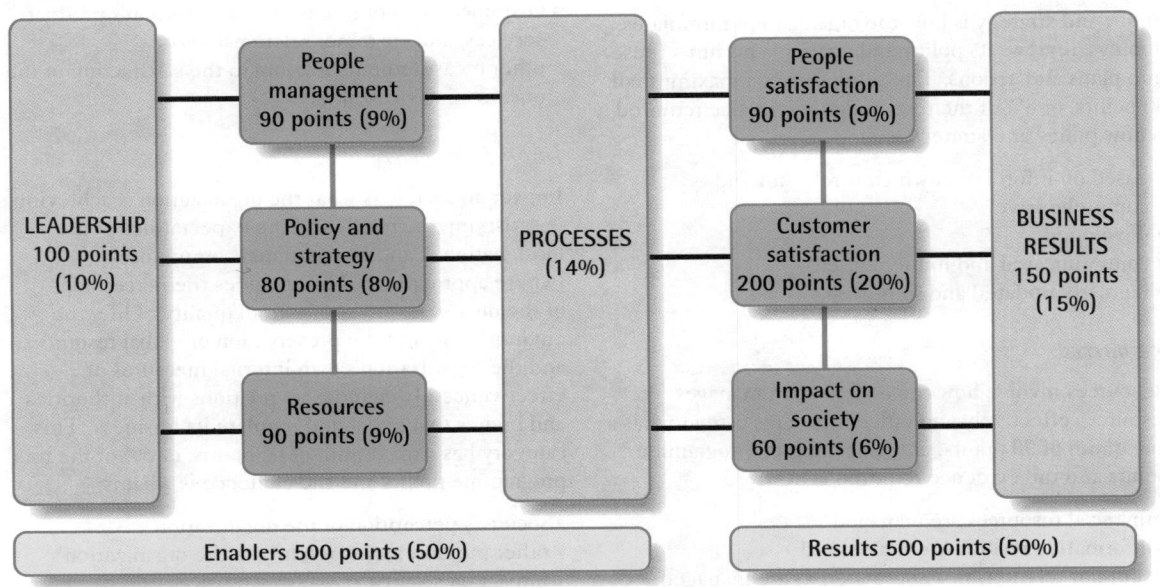

Leadership

Leadership is how the behaviour and actions of the executive team and all other leaders inspire, support and promote a culture of total quality management. This category has a maximum of 100 points, or 10% of the total programme points. The evidence required is how:

- Leaders visibly demonstrate their commitment to a culture of total quality management.
- Leaders support improvement and involvement by providing appropriate resources, and assistance.
- Leaders are involved with customers, suppliers, and other external organizations.
- Leaders recognize, and appreciate people's efforts and achievements.

People management

People management is how the organization releases the full potential of its people. This category has a maximum of 90 points, or 9% of the total programme points and the evidence required is how:

- People resources are planned and improved.
- People capabilities are sustained and developed.
- People are involved in targets and continuously review performance.
- People are involved, empowered, and recognized.
- People and the organization have an effective dialogue.
- People are cared for.

Policy and strategy

Policy and strategy is how the organization formulates, deploys, reviews its policy and strategy and turns these into plans and actions. The category has a maximum of 80 points, or 8% of the total and the evidence required is how policy and strategy are:

- based on information which is relevant and comprehensive
- developed
- communicated and implemented
- regularly updated and improved.

Resources

Resources involve how the organization manages resources effectively and efficiently. This category has a maximum of 90 points, or 9% of the total programme points and the evidence required is how:

- financial resources are managed
- information resources are managed
- supplier relationships and materials are managed

- buildings, equipment, and other assets are managed
- technology and intellectual property are managed.

Processes

Processes are how the organization identifies, manages, reviews and improves its processes. This category has a maximum of 140 points, or 14% of the total programme points and the evidence required is how processes:

- that are key to the success of the business are identified
- are systematically managed
- are reviewed, and targets are set for improvement
- are improved using innovation and creativity
- are changed and the benefits evaluated.

People satisfaction

People satisfaction is what the organization is achieving in relation to the satisfaction of its people. This category has a maximum of 90 points, or 9% of the total programme points and the evidence is what is:

- people's perception of the organization
- other measurements relating to people satisfaction.

Customer satisfaction

Customer satisfaction is what the organization is achieving in relation to the satisfaction of its external customers. This category is the most important and has a maximum of 200 points, or 20% of the total programme points. The evidence required is what are:

- customers' perception of the organization's products, services, and customer relationships
- other measurements relating to the satisfaction of the organization's customers.

Impact on society

Impact on society is what the organization is achieving in satisfying the needs and the expectations of the local, national, and international community (where appropriate). This includes the perception of the organization's approach to quality of life, the environment, and the preservation of global resources, and the organization's own internal measures of effectiveness. It includes its relations with authorities and bodies that affect and regulate its business. This category has a maximum of 60 points, or 6% of the total programme points and the evidence is what is:

- society's perception of the organization
- other measurements relating to the organization's impact on society.

Table 4.4 European Quality Award winners (2000)

Company	Category
Nokia Mobile Phones, Europe and Africa (Finland)	Large business
Inland Revenue, Account Office, (Cumbernauld, Scotland)	Public sector
Burton-Apta Refractory Manufacturing Ltd (Hungary)	Small and medium enterprises

Business results

Business results are what the organization is achieving in relation to its planned business objectives and in satisfying the needs and expectations of everyone with a financial interest or stake in the organization. This category has a maximum of 150 points, or 15% of the total programme points and the evidence is what is:

- the financial measurements of the organization's performance
- other measurements relating to the organization's performance.

Award winners

The award winners for 2000 are given in Table 4.4.[30]

The UK Best Factory Awards

Background

The Best Factory Awards is a programme developed by *Management Today*, the leading UK management publication, in association with Cranfield School of Management, and in its present form has been run since 1992. Its purpose is to identify those manufacturing facilities in the United Kingdom, which, in operational terms, are considered leaders in their field in quality, service, efficiency, and cost. One of its aims is to promote manufacturing excellence in the UK.

Evaluation criteria

The evaluation criteria are comprehensive and evaluation is based on a 16-page questionnaire covering such operating criteria as:[31]

- worldwide activity
- customer lead times
- cost structure
- profit margins

- product types
- processing time
- control elements
- setup times and associated costs
- customer network
- supplier network
- delivery frequency of materials

- inventory levels/stock turns
- employee characteristics (direct and indirect)
- employee turnover
- employee training provided
- new product innovation
- management involvement
- customer service.

Timetable of award process

The following is the timetable of the award process:

January–April	— Participating firms carry out a self-administered audit.
May	— Preparation of benchmark reports and selection of finalists.
June–July	— Benchmarking reports distributed to all participants.
	— Teams of assessors make visits to the facilities of the finalists.
July	— Selection of award winners.
November	— Winners announced at a luncheon sponsored by *Management Today*.

Award categories and winners

There are several award categories each of which is sponsored by a specific business. These categories and the 1999 winners are given in Table 4.5.[32]

Malcolm Baldrige National Quality Award

Malcolm Baldrige and the award

Malcolm Baldrige was the US Secretary of Commerce under President Reagan from 1981 until his death in a rodeo accident in 1987. In that year an award entitled the Malcolm Baldrige National Quality Award was established by Congress and signed into law on 20 August 1987 as Public Law 100-107. Its purpose is to raise awareness about quality management and to recognize US companies that have successful quality management systems.[33]

Background of the award

The award was established because of the following analysis, studies, and criteria concerning US industry.[34]

Table 4.5 UK Best Factory Award winners (1999)

Award	Recipient
Factory of the year – The best engineering factory	Britax Wingard, Porchester
Best engineering factory – Highly commended	Black & Decker, County Durham
Best process factory	Reckitt & Colman, Hull
Best process factory – Highly commended	Henkel Consumer Adhesives, Cheshire
Best electronics and electrical factory	Lucas Automotive Electronics, Birmingham
Best electronics and electrical factory – Highly commended	Caradon Trend, West Sussex
Best household and general products factory	Nichols Foods, St Helens
Best small factory	Giroflex, Mid-Glamorgan
Best small factory – Highly commended	Medical Support Systems, Cardiff
Most improved factory	Alenia Marconia Systems, Portsmouth
Judges' special award	Bespak, Norfolk

US leadership

The leadership of the United States in product and process quality has been challenged strongly (and sometimes successfully) by foreign competition, and the nation's productivity has improved less than competitors over the last two decades.

Cost of quality

American business and industry are beginning to understand that poor quality costs companies as much as 20% of sales revenues nationally, and that improved quality of goods and services goes hand in hand with improved productivity lower costs, and increased profitability.

Strategic planning

Strategic planning for quality and quality improvement programmes, through a commitment to excellence in manufacturing and services, are becoming more and more essential to the well-being of the US economy and its ability to compete effectively in the global marketplace.

Manufacturing

Improved management and understanding of the factory floor, worker involvement in quality, and greater emphasis on statistical process control can lead to dramatic improvements in the cost of quality of manufactured products.

All operations

The concept of quality improvement is directly applicable to small companies as well as large, to service industries as well as manufacturing, and to the public sector as well as private enterprise.

Management led and customer oriented

In order to be successful, quality improvement programmes must be management led and customer oriented, and this may require fundamental changes in the way companies and agencies do business.

Other countries

Several major industrial nations have successfully coupled rigorous private sector quality audits with national awards giving special recognition to those enterprises the audits identify as the very best.

Purpose of the quality award

A national quality award programme in the USA was considered helpful for improving quality and productivity by:

• Helping to stimulate American companies to improve quality and productivity for the pride of recognition while obtaining a competitive edge through increased profits.

- Recognizing the achievements of those companies that improve the quality of their goods and services and providing examples to others.
- Establishing guidelines and criteria that can be used by business, industrial, governmental, and other organizations to evaluate their own quality improvement efforts.
- Providing specific guidance for other American organizations that wish to learn how to manage for high quality by making available detailed information on how winning organizations were able to change their cultures and achieve eminence.

Award criteria

The award programme focuses on quality as a strategic integral part of business management and the award's criteria are widely accepted as the standard for quality excellence. They are designed to help companies deliver ever improving value to customers and to improve overall company performance, and capabilities. For many companies having quality as a strategic element, the result is better employee relations, higher productivity, greater customer satisfaction, increased market share, and improved profitability. (This further underscores why quality is a strategic component.)

The US Commerce Department's National Institute of Standards and Technology (NIST) manages the awards in close cooperation with the private sector. The examiners evaluate a company's quality management system by looking for achievements and improvements in the following seven areas.

Leadership

- Have the senior leaders clearly defined the company's values, goals, and ways to achieve the goals?
- Are senior executives personally involved?
- Does this involvement include communicating quality excellence to groups outside the company?

Information analysis

- Is the information used to guide the company's quality management system reliable, timely, and accessible?

Strategic planning

- How does the company plan strengthen its competitive position?
- How are these plans integrated into its overall business planning?

Human resource development and management

- How does the company develop the full potential of its workforce?

Process management

- How are products and services designed?
- How are product and service production and delivery processes managed?
- How does the company assure that suppliers meet its performance requirements?

Business results

- How is the company performing in key business areas and what are their plans for improving?

Customer focus and satisfaction

- Does the customer define quality?

Figure 4.21 illustrates various stages leading up to the award.

Award winners

The award winners for 2000 are given in Table 4.6.[35]

Ethics and quality

Correlation between quality and ethical situations

In Chapter 16 ethics is discussed related to behaviour of some purchasing agents and their suppliers. Ethics is also an issue when it comes to quality control. Consider the following.[36]

US military

While practising at 4500 metres over Wisconsin, USA, says Lt Col Richard Van Roo, his A-10 attack jet suddenly began 'bouncing and skidding' through the sky. One of the two bolts fastening a 225-kilogram Maverick missile to the wing had broken, leaving the missile swinging under the wing, attached only by the other bolt.

The pilot declared an emergency. Fire engines rushed to the runway. The pilot touched down and rolled to a safe stop with just ten centimetres to spare between the dangling missile and the runway.

This was no isolated incident. Numerous bolts holding Maverick missiles have broken, either in mid-air or while the missiles were being loaded onto planes.

Figure 4.21 The Malcolm Baldrige Quality Award process

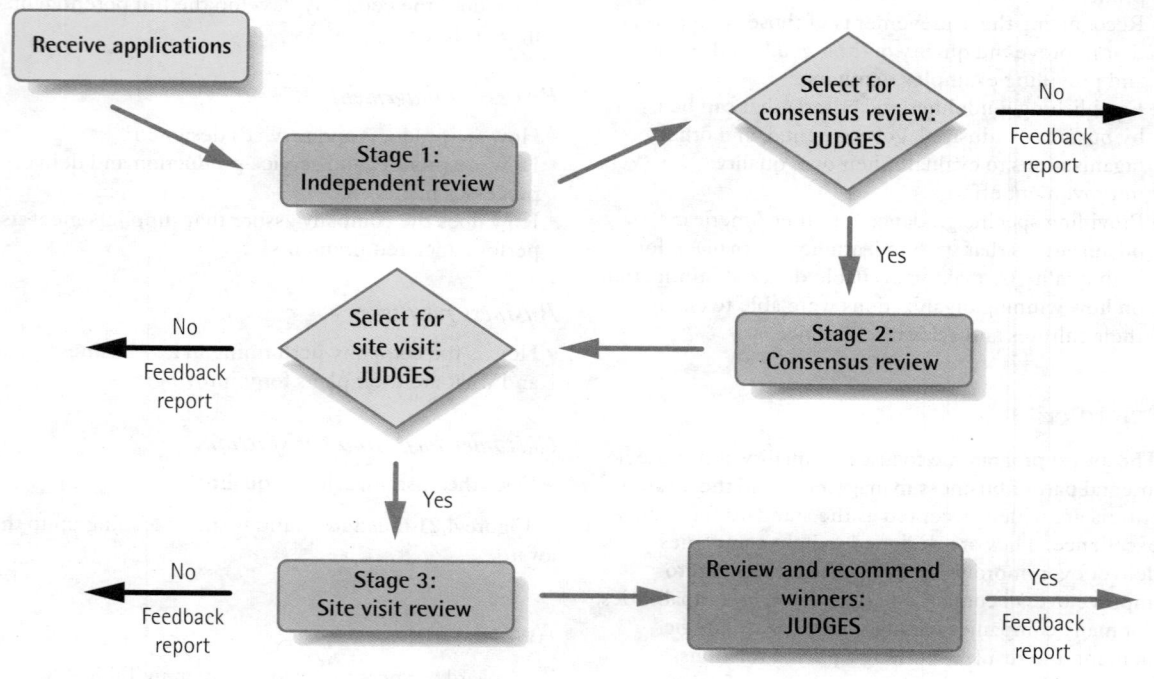

Table 4.6 Malcolm Baldrige Quality Award winners (2000)

Company	Activity
Dan Corporation-Spicer Driveshaft Division, Toledo, Ohio	Manufacturer of drive shafts for light, medium, heavy duty and off-highway vehicles
Karlee Company, Garland, Texas	Manufacturer of precision sheet metal and machined components for the telecommunications, semiconductor, and medical equipment industries
Operations Management International, Inc., Greenwood Village, Colorado	Operates and maintains more than 160 public and private sector wastewater and water treatment facilities worldwide
Los Alamos National Bank, Los Alamos, New Mexico	Independent community bank in northern and central New Mexico

The manufacturer of the bolts, United Telecontrol Electronics Inc., New Jersey, has been charged in US Federal Court with violating quality control regulations including:

• using bolts with cracks, or lack of plating needed to guard against corrosion
• using other components with surface cracks that workers would grind off at night when inspectors weren't around

• using parts that failed inspections, but workers manipulated computer-controlled measurements to produce passing reports.

Lucas Industries

A US unit of this British manufacturer pleaded guilty in US courts in 1995 to falsifying quality records for gearboxes that drive electrical oil and fuel systems on Navy F-18 fighters. Prosecutors said that when 150 of the gearboxes were taken apart, 100% failed inspection. Faulty gearboxes were blamed for 71 emergency landings, several in-flight fires, as well as the loss of an F-18 during the Persian Gulf War.

Philips

A US unit of Philips Electronic NV pleaded guilty in 1995 to submitting false tests of resistors that control electric current in weapon systems. When resistors showed signs of failing engineers would secretly replace them with fresh resistors to pass the tests.

Summary of key elements

• Quality problems occur frequently and the cause, usually deep rooted, can be traced to incorrect design, poor organization, and is often people related. Quality management involves long-term planning, training and organization, and thus is a strategic issue.

• Customers judge quality. If a tangible product, or service, has a reputation for quality, customers will buy and all else being equal, the company will benefit financially.

• Providing a quality service or products gives a positive company image, improves competitive ability and market share, which translates into improved profits.

• The International Organization for Standardization (ISO) defines quality as 'the totality of features and characteristics of a product, process, or service that bear on its ability to satisfy stated or implied needs'.

• A specification is the document that describes in detail the requirements with which the product, process or service, has to perform.

• Total quality management (TQM) is where attention to quality pervades the whole operation, and not just one particular sector. The driving wheel of TQM lies in the word management and more precisely, top management.

• There exists a quality supply chain analogous to a physical supply chain. A break in the link, including poor communication, can impact final quality.

• Leading quality management authorities include Edwards Deming, Joseph Juran, Philip Crosby, Armand Feigenbaum, Kaoru Ishikawa, and Genichi Taguchi.

• Quality-related costs include external and internal faults, which are the costs of non-quality. Then there are evaluation and prevention activities, which are the costs of quality.

• Quality control is all activities to satisfy quality requirements including process monitoring and eliminating causes of poor performances at all stages in the supply chain. It is a non-value-added activity and as such a firm should have a total quality management system in place to minimize the level of the quality control needed.

• Tools and techniques to improve quality include benchmarking, brainstorming, FMECA, *hoshin*, Ishikawa diagram, just-in-time, kaizen, keep designs simple, overall equipment effectiveness, Pareto analysis, phantom customer, pipeline map, poka yoke, quality circles, quality function deployment, statistical quality control, and Taguchi methods.

• The ISO-9000 is a series of internationally accepted quality standards aimed at improving the quality of manufacturing services and government. The standard that covers all organizations is ISO-9001:2000.

• The EFQM has a quality model based on nine elements, which serve as a basis for an award programme. The model underscores the importance of the customer in quality issues.

• Cranfield Business School has a Best Factory Award programme for quality in the UK.

• The Malcolm Baldrige Award is a US programme to raise awareness about quality and to recognize US firms with successful quality management systems.

• The differences between ISO-9000 and a quality award is that ISO is a way to improve quality, whereas an award is once-only quality recognition.

• Ethical issues are very often intertwined with quality problems.

Notes and references

1. 'Jaguar factory tries to blend automation with best traditions of hand-crafted work', *Wall Street Journal Europe*, 25 July 1991
2. *International Organization for Standardization*, ISO-8402
3. 'New competitor: East Europe's industry is raising its quality and taking on the west: Swift change in work habits yields exportable goods while costs remain low. A halt to drinking on the job', *Wall Street Journal Europe*, 22 September 1994
4. 'Statecraft at Renault: Does state control always limit a manager? Renault's Louis Schweitzer has held the state at bay. Until now', *The Economist*, 27 May 1995
5. 'Cost cutting, how to do it right', *Fortune*, 9 April 1990, p. 28
6. DEMING, W. E., 'Philosophy continues to flourish', *APICS–The Performance Advantage*, 1, no 4, October 1991, p. 20

7. DEMING, W. E. Edwards. *Out of the Crisis*, Center for Advanced Engineering Study, Cambridge, Massachusetts, 2000

8. CROSBY, Philip B., *Quality is Free*, McGraw-Hill, New York, 1979

9. CROSBY, Philip Bayard, 'Advocate of zero defects', *International Herald Tribune*, 23 August 2001, p. 4

10. FEIGENBAUM, A. V., *Total Quality Control: Engineering and Management*, McGraw-Hill, New York, 1983

11. 'Never mind the buzzwords. Roll up your sleeves. The Feigenbaum brothers' advice is pragmatic, and it saves companies big bucks', *Business Week*, 22 January 1996, pp 50–1

12. 'Hotel lock failures may mean, No Exit. Key cards foil prowlers, and also guests', *Wall Street Journal Europe*, 15 April 96, p. 4

13. From a confidential study directed by Derek Waller

14. MULLER, Joann, 'Ford: Why it's worse than you think. Quality, morale, and market share are down. Can Jacques Nasser get this company out of reverse?', *Business Week*, 25 June 2001, pp 48–55

15. 'An embarrassment of glitches galvanises Chrysler: With its vaunted turnaround threatened, No 3 gets serious about quality', *Business Week*, 17 April 1995, pp 58–9

16. 'On the line: Automotive suppliers in Germany take aim at years of inefficiency: Facing likely shakeout, plants try Japanese techniques to boost competitiveness. Catching up is common sense', *Wall Street Journal Europe*, 6 February 1996

17. 'The quality imperative', *Business Week*, 2 December 1991

18. 'IBM discovers a simple pleasure', *Fortune*, 21 May 90, p. 45

19. *Wall Street Journal Europe*, 11/12 October 1996

20. Adapted from DALEY, Suzanne, 'In France: Can I not help you? In shops, firm checks service, or lack of it', *International Herald Tribune*, 27 December 2000, p. 16

21. OAKLAND, John S., *Total Quality Management*, Heinemann, London, 1990, p. 252

22. American Supplier Institute, *Taguchi Methods: Selected Papers on Methodology and Applications*, ASI Press, Dearborn, Michigan, USA, 1988

23. SHIPMAN, Alan, 'ISO-9000', *International Management*, May 1993

24. Norme Européene, Comité Européen de Normalisation, Brussels, Belgium

25. http://www.praxiom.com (update 2002)

26. 'A victim of its own success', *Financial Times*, 21 July 1993

27. 'Histoire d'une adhésion', *European Foundation for Quality Management*, Brussels, Belgium, http://www.efqm.org

28. QUAGLIA, Giovanni, 'Model development', *Quality Link. European Foundation for Quality Management*, vol. 9, no 49, September 1997, p. 11

29. 'Le Prix Européen de la Qualité', information brochure, 1997, *European Foundation for Quality Management*, Brussels, Belgium

30. http//www.efqm.org/

31. NEW, Colin C. and SZWEJCZEWSKI, Marek, *Best Factory Awards Audit, 1997* (the questionnaire document published by *Management Today* in association with Cranfield School of Management)

32. http://www.logisticseurope.haynet.com/awards/1999.html

33. National Institute of Standards and Technology, Route 270 and Quince Orchard Road, Administration Building, Room A537, Gaitjersburg, MD, USA 20899-0001

34. Findings and Purpose Section of US Public Law 100–107

35. http://www.nist.gov/public_affairs/releases/g00-187.htm

36. 'Bombs away: US military contractor gets tough scrutiny for defective products: Missile bolt snaps in midair; Federal prosecutors find a high-level coverup. Other probes hit Lucas, Philips', *Wall Street Journal Europe*, 4 March 1996

Review and discussion topics

1. Service operation

In your day-to-day life, you encounter some of the following operations:

(a) business school
(b) shops
(c) post office
(d) medical centre
(e) cinema
(f) bus company.

What is your opinion of the quality of the services offered by these operations? Do you think improvements could be made? Describe.

2. Quality and accidents

Can you cite any illustrations when quality defects resulted in accidents, either minor or major, in operations and supply?

3. Quality and value added

For many, quality is a non-value-added activity since the client does 'not see quality in a product or service'. The client expects quality. Others believe quality is, indeed, a value-added activity. Discuss, justifying your reasoning.

4. Limit to quality design

Discuss the 'idea of a limit to quality design'. Can you give illustrations where you believe there is too much quality in a product or service offered?

5. Quality chain

Considering the start of the operation to the finish, develop a quality chain for:

(a) a university or business school
(b) a hospital
(c) a restaurant
(d) a packaged ski trip
(e) a supermarket
(f) a flight from Paris to Los Angeles
(g) a case of wine
(h) an automobile

(i) a new house

(j) a bag of fertilizer.

6. Quality is free

Some management theorists believe 'quality is free'. Do you agree with them? Justify your reasoning.

7. Elements of quality

You are the manager of a firm. In order that the company produces products and services of acceptable quality, what should be:

(a) the organization and attitudes of the firm

(b) the tools and methods used?

Case study 4.1 Mitsubishi

Situation

You could call Motohiro Kaibara a Mitsubishi man. He works as a mechanic at his family's Mitsubishi Motors dealership in Kitakyushu, a city in southern Japan, and he will only drive a Mitsubishi. However, Kaibara's faith in Mitsubishi began to unravel when in May 1999 a customer nearly ran down his own grandchild while attempting to park his $33,000 1998 Mitsubishi Diamante. The driver had just put the car into reverse when it lurched backward, barely missing the child before crashing into a gate. In July 1999 Mitsubishi tested the vehicle at its regional technical centre and insisted that nothing fundamental was wrong. In subsequent months, the incident happened twice more to the same driver almost causing an accident on both occasions. Kaibara checked the car himself. To his surprise the vehicle shot back a metre on shifting into reverse.

This was not an isolated case. In September 1999 Shigeo Toyoda, the 57-year-old president of a small business in western Japan was parking his four-month old Diamante on a Tokyo street. Before he could turn the engine off the car jumped back suddenly hitting an empty van. Then, Shigeji Tsugahara, a taxi driver in Saitama with 35 years' driving experience, was backing into a parking spot in June 2000 when the engine of his new Diamante revved up unexpectedly and he rammed into another car parked three metres behind him. The following month, Sadao Ito was backing his Diamante into a space on the fifth floor of a Tokyo supermarket parking lot. When he put the car into reverse, the car jumped back, veering to the right and crashed into a pillar. But for the pillar, the car would have smashed through a railing and fallen 15 metres to the ground.

These, and other incidents, come in the wake of revelations that over the last two decades Mitsubishi Motors has covered up thousands of complaints about glitches with its vehicles. Since August 2000 the company has announced the recall of 620,000 vehicles. Already Mitsubishi's reputation is suffering. Its sales in Japan slumped 3.9% in August 2000 from the year before and this is posing a headache for Daimler-Chrysler, which agreed to acquire 34% of the Japanese automaker. This is a headache that Daimler-Chrysler can do without in light of its many other problems. Mitsubishi has further problems as police in Tokyo have launched an investigation into allegations that the company was criminally negligent in covering up defects. Mitsubishi declined to comment on the ongoing probe although investigators told the Japanese press they had evidence that serious car defects were secretly repaired at two of Mitsubishi technical centres by repairing or replacing car computers. Megumu Okubo, General Manager of Mitsubishi's car service department, said that the computers were not the problem; the problem was drivers mistakenly hitting the gas pedal instead of the brakes. Okubo indicated that there are two computers in the vehicles. One acts as a backup that takes over if the primary unit fails.

After Shigeo Toyoda's incident he asked Mitsubishi to inspect his car. The company said there was nothing wrong. So Toyoda went into action and created a website where Mitsubishi owners could report car problems. He received over 1000 complaints about Mitsubishi vehicles and passed the details to the police. However, winning a product liability lawsuit in Japan is not easy for consumers as judges often rule against the plaintiff. Further, it is tough taking on big business. Toyoda has received three visits from company executives who, he says, were rude and implied that he was liar. When Toyoda increased his online campaign, Mitsubishi filed a lawsuit in May 2000 demanding $5000 or the amount they said it cost them to examine Toyoda's car. In October, Toyoda filed a $20,000 damage counter-suit against Mitsubishi, alleging if he had hit and killed someone, he would have been imprisoned. Further, Kaibara the mechanic is feeling the heat. Mitsubishi sent a senior engineer to his dealership to try to convince the mechanic that the Diamante is trouble free. Kaibara is resolute and insists that the car problem is no mirage.*

Required

1. Discuss this case in depth according to quality issues considering the four elements in the concept of costs of quality and non-quality. What did Mitsubishi perhaps not do from a quality point of view? What should they have done? What is the current and future impact on Mitsubishi and its principal owner, Daimler-Chrysler, as a result of these quality-related problems? Why is the situation both a strategic and an operating issue?

2. What other issues in management and business seem apparent in this case?

3. In the case it states that: 'This is a headache that Daimler-Chrysler can do without in light of its many other problems.' What are the many other problems to which this sentence makes reference?

4. What do you think would have been different if had Mitsubishi been an American company?

5. Is there anything else you think is relevant in this case from a broad operations management point of view?

*Adapted from: 'A cover-up at Mitsubishi? As customer complaints rise, police probe the carmaker', Business Week, 9 October 2000, pp 32–33.

Case study 4.2 Wento Corp.

Situation

Nicholas Carrias was feeling happy as he drove to work along the San Diego Freeway. He had realized his dream and was now living in Santa Monica, California, not far from Los Angeles. He had been hired as quality assurance manager at Wento Corporation, a company in Van Nuys that made electric motors for the operation of automatic Venetian blinds, curtains, and light aluminium doors. Wento was a company of some 1750 people, and experiencing a period of rapid growth.

Nicholas was French. He was an engineer and had completed a masters degree at the Lyon Graduate School of Business in France. During this programme, he had completed a six-month training assignment, covering the certification ISO-9001 for Somfy, a company in Cluses, in the French Alps, which also makes motors for sunblinds. Somfy subsequently hired Nicholas as quality coordinator, a post he held for two years.

Somfy is well known for the high-quality products. Wento believed that in hiring Nicholas, they would be able to improve the quality of their motors. It wasn't the first time that Wento had received complaints from clients as sometimes the motors would cease operating for no apparent reason during operation.

Nicholas went into his office, dropped his briefcase, and hung up his coat. He had scheduled the whole of the day to finishing a report on a quality management seminar he had attended in San Francisco, and contacting vendors regarding motor specifications. As he sat down, the door flew open and in strode a red-faced Bill Bates, President of Wento.

'Nicholas, you have to sort out this quality problem. We have been having many complaints from clients about our new motor, reference DLW-1455. One incident was particularly embarrassing as the client was Disney Corporation. During the opening night of one of their presentations the curtains jammed half-open.

Michael Eisner was in the audience. He was really upset. I really don't know where the problem is, but in my opinion, those people in production aren't very good. I haven't seen the production line for some time, but Mike Burton, the production manager says his workers lack motivation. I'm putting the solution in your hands, Nicholas'.

With that Bill dashed out again, saying he would be gone for the rest of the week. Nicholas sighed. He decided he would have to visit the production line of model DLW-1455. He put on his jacket, and crossed the yard, passing the avocado and orange trees towards the building that housed production of motor DLW-1455. 'Boy, is it hot today,' he thought, even though it was still so early in the morning. It must be Santa Monica weather. He entered the front door. The temperature wasn't much different from that outside. He went over to Mike's office. He was in heated discussion with Sam Marchand, one of the superintendents on the line.

'Well we had no choice,' Sam was saying, 'The copper wiring sent to us from our supplier was the wrong diameter but we were able to work with it by modifying the connections somewhat. It wasn't easy but we met the requirements of the master schedule. The supplier of this copper wire is not very reliable. It is not the first time we have had material that is not according to specifications. And, what's more, when it does arrive, it's not always on the date promised.'

Nicholas went into Mike's office.

'Hi, Mike. I was talking to Bill this morning and he tells me there have been some difficulties with the production of model DLW-1455. I wonder if I might take a look around.'

Mike was fuming, obviously irritated by his conversation with Sam.

'Oh, Bill is a silly old fool. He's always complaining. There is nothing wrong here. Sure, once in a while we have to shut down the line because machines malfunction but we have always sufficient in-process inventory on hand to prevent a complete stoppage of the line. Yes, and it's true the components supplied by our suppliers are not always according to specifications. You know our specs are quite rigid. However, my operators are very smart; they are always able to fix the faulty units. We always meet our demand requirements.'

'Do you mind if I take a look around?' asked Nicholas.

'Well, you won't find anything wrong here. I'm not sure why they hired a manager of quality assurance. We can fix the problems ourselves,' Mike went on. 'Let me come with you.'

'No thanks, I would prefer to go alone,' said Nicholas.

Nicholas strolled down to the upstream part of the operation where the chassis were being drilled. He noticed that several chassis were sitting at the side of the drilling machine.

'What are these?,' he asked the operator.

'Oh, these are rejects,' he said.

'I've only been on the line for three days,' said the operator. 'I was transferred from the wiring section and I still have not mastered how to operate these drilling machines.'

'Can't your supervisor help?,' enquired Nicholas.

'Oh he's no use, besides he's off sick today. Well, that's what I've heard.'

The cost of non-quality must be high; I wonder how they are using statistical process control, thought Nicholas. He wandered further along to where the controller unit for the motor was being assembled. This was a six-step operation performed by women whose function was to wire, solder, and connect the appropriate joints. Between the third and fourth steps lay a pile of inventory. The fourth operator seemed harassed, trying to keep up with her operation. By contrast the fifth and sixth operators seemed to have no problem in performing their work.

'Is Jidoka an accepted practice here?,' Nicholas asked the last operator.

The woman had a weird look on her face as she stared at Nicholas. She was utterly confused, and wondered what the heck he was talking about. Nicholas explained the concept to her. He didn't think it was worth asking her about kaizen.

'What are these controller units in the red container?', asked Nicholas.

'Oh, those are pieces that need redoing. Julie, the operator at post number 1, put the front panel on upside down,' said the operator.

'Have you talked to R&D about poka yoke?,' enquired Nicholas.

"Oh! Those fellows think they are too educated for us. They, don't have much to do with this assembly line,' she added.

Nicholas continued on further to the R&D Department.

'Hi John, what are you doing?,' he asked the head of R&D.

'Oh, we are just working on modifying the specification for the cam shaft of model DLW-1455. We are not happy with the definitions and our suppliers for the raw materials are continually having problems meeting our requirements,' John said bluntly.

'Have you taken a look at applying the Taguchi concepts,' said Nicholas. 'That might help.'

Nicholas continued down the line to where the braking assemblies were being machined. On his way he passed Cindy Atkinson's office. She was responsible for planning and scheduling. He walked in. Cindy's office was a mess. On one corner of the desk was a computer terminal; any remaining space was covered with paper, order forms, and charts.

'Good morning, Cindy, you look as if you are busy,' said Nicholas cheerfully.

'Oh! I'm struggling with the company-wide planning of all our products. I've developed what I thought was a reasonable aggregate plan but our salespeople keep modifying their requirements. First it's up, then it's down. I don't know whether we are coming or going. Each morning I consult our MRP system I note some entries have been modified. Sometimes it's sales changes, but not always. These means that I have to keep modifying my written work orders to the operators.'

As he was talking, the phone rang. Cindy picked it up. The caller was speaking loudly. He recognized the high-pitched voice of Mike Burton. Cindy talked for a while, and then put the phone down.

'I have to dash,' said Cindy, 'our number three milling machine is down.' With that, she was gone.

Nicholas glanced at his watch. It was close to lunchtime. He felt he had seen enough for the morning so he set off at a steady pace to his office. He was glad to be away from the noise of the DLW-1455 production line.

Back in his office, Nicholas glanced at the half-finished quality management report sitting on his desk. The first thing he thought he would do for the problems with model DLW-1455 was to make an Ishikawa and Pareto analysis. Since he knew the Somfy Corporation well, he also wondered about benchmarking.

Required

How would you assess the quality situation at Wento from a total quality management point of view? What improvements would you suggest? (Note that some of the elements in consideration may be found in subsequent chapters.)

Selected further reading

CREECH, Bill (1995) *The 5 Pillars of TQM: How to Make Total Quality Management Work for You*, Plume Publishing.

GOETSCH, David L., DAVID, Stanley B. and DAVIS, Stanley (1999) *Quality Management: Introduction to Total Quality Management for Production, Processing, and Services*, 3rd edition, Prentice-Hall.

OAKLAND, John S. and PORTER, Les (2000) *Total Quality Management: Text and Cases* (Contemporary Business Series), Butterworth-Heinemann.

WALTON, Mary and DEMING, W. Edwards (1988) *Deming Management Method*, Perigee Publishing.

WEIMERSKIRCH, Arnold and GEORGE, Stephen (1998) *Total Quality Management: Strategies and Techniques Proven at Today's Most Successful Companies* (Portable MBA Series), 2nd edition, Wiley.

An extensive listing of further reading can be found on the website.

What's on the web?

Further learning resources are available to lecturers and students at www.supplychain-online.com, including the following which are specific to *Quality management*:

Resources	Subject
Chapter overview	Quality management
Application exercise: Cardoso	Frequency check sheet and Pareto analysis
Case study: The Heck Travel Agency	Quality management
More further reading	Quality management

5 An environmental balance

Chapter overview

- Environmental issues
- Sources of environmental damage
- Product lifecycle analysis
- Product packaging
- Transportation systems
- Cost–benefit analysis for environmental considerations
- Organizing for environmental management
- ISO–14000 certification series

Environmental issues

The business firm is a system that interacts with the external environment. Among the many concerns in this external environment is economic use of natural resources, and pollution. Since the operations and supply chain is a subsystem of the business firm, operations management must take into account the environment from an ecological point of view.

A strategic component

As with quality, environmental management issues are strategic. The decisions for a chemical firm to phase out the production of chlorofluorocarbons, for an airline company to invest in quieter and more fuel-efficient airplanes, or a paper company to eliminate chlorine-based bleaching, are long term, require significant capital investment, and must have full top management support. Like quality management, environmental issues have broad implications in operations. In the worst scenario, it may often be as a result of poor operations management that environmental accidents occur.

Drivers for an environmental balance

Besides the extreme case of industrial accidents, other reasons management needs to be concerned about the environment are that environmental controls in the European Union, the USA, and to a certain extent in

Japan are becoming stricter. There is pressure from a growing environmentally conscious public, often fortified by the activities and discoveries of environmental organizations such as Greenpeace, perhaps one of the most radical environmental groups. Further, many industry leaders believe good environmental management makes long-term economic sense. Companies that score well on environmental programmes can become a market leader. Many consumers equate sound environmental products and/or processes with quality. Finally, every operations manager is and every top manager is a consumer. All business people live in society. Thus from a moral, social and ethical point of view environmental issues must be on a manager's agenda.

Environment and the supply chain

Environmental issues impact the entire operations supply chain. They are a consideration in plant location, raw material purchases, product design, technologies employed, manufacturing processes, packaging, transportation, energy consumption, worker safety, marketing, sales, use, and final product disposal when it reaches the end of its life.

Population is the environmental trigger

Population growth (the UN estimates some 11 billion people by 2200) is the trigger of environmental matters since more consumers demand more goods and services and the production, use, and disposal of these leads to

Figure 5.1 The chain of environmental damage

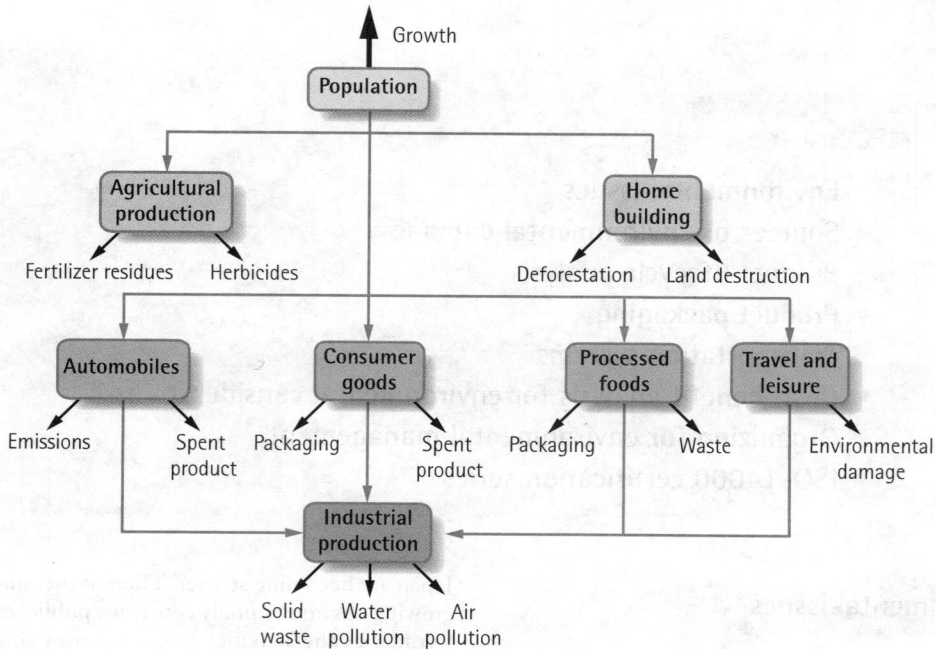

environmental damage as illustrated in Figure 5.1. It is true that businesses, particularly some industries such as oil refining, fertilizer production, papermaking, and chemicals, are directly responsible for most environmental damage. However, the blame should not be heaped entirely on firms as they provide goods and services at an economic price. Consumers are happy to use plastic wrapping, gasoline for automobiles, refrigerators, computer products, throw-away diapers, etc.

Financial implications

If companies suffer an environmental disaster, the damage both to the company's image, and in direct financial terms can be high. It can even lead to bankruptcy. Consider the following catastrophic operational situations.

Sandoz

On 1 November 1986 there was a fire at the Sandoz (Novartis after the 1996 merger with Ciba-Geigy) production site near Basel, Switzerland. Some 15,000 cubic metres of water used to contain the fire flowed into the Rhine, carrying with it over 1300 tons of agricultural chemicals, toxic insecticides, and mercury compounds.[1] Hundreds of fish died, including 220 tons of eels, and drinking water for Swiss, French, German,

and Dutch communities was contaminated. The public reacted by boycotting the company's products and safety threats were made to executives. The estimated cost to the company was SF 60 million ($50 million).[2]

Exxon Valdez

On the 24 March 1989 the oil tanker *Exxon Valdez* ran aground in the Prince William Sound, Alaska. Some 45,000 tons of oil discharged along 1700 kilometres of the coastline. Many species of fish and birds were destroyed. The fishing community suffered heavy losses. Again, people boycotted Exxon oil products, the stock price dropped, and the president and officers of Exxon were lambasted in the press by their reaction to the disaster. The cost to Exxon was over $1 billion.[3]

Three Mile Island

On 29 March 1979 the cooling system of Unit 2 of Metropolitan Edison's Three Mile Island nuclear power plant near Harrisburg, Pennsylvania, failed to operate. By mistake, the safety cooling system was shut off and the reactor temperature system rose to a dangerous level. There was a threat of a meltdown that could have released 100 tons of radiation into the atmosphere. All pregnant women and children were evacuated within an 8-kilometre radius. To relieve system pressure, 1.5 millions litres of lightly contaminated water was dumped in the Susquehanna River. Ten years later the cost of the accident was put at $973 million, seven times the estimate made immediately after the accident. The nuclear facility will never reopen.[4]

Johns-Manville Corporation

Johns-Manville Corporation, Denver, USA was the world's largest producer of asbestos products. Asbestos is a fibrous material, which is easily woven, does not burn, and is a poor conductor of heat. As a result, it was used extensively in insulation of buildings and ships, for floor and ceiling tiles, and for automotive brake linings. Subsequent research showed asbestos to be carcinogenic, and many consumers filed expensive lawsuits against the company. Even though it was financially healthy, Johns-Manville filed for Chapter 11 bankruptcy on 26 August 1982 because of the litigation. Liability was of the order of $2 billion. The company (under a different name) re-emerged from bankruptcy but Johns-Manville no longer exists.[5]

Global concern

Environmental concerns are not a local, regional, or even a country issue. They are global. Consider:

- Toxic chemicals from the Sandoz accident, spilled into the Rhine in Switzerland, and then poisoned the drinking water for German, French, and Dutch residents.
- Acid gases emitted by British power plants destroy the forests of Sweden.[6]
- The explosion in the Soviet Chernobyl nuclear power plant in 1986 spewed radiation over much of eastern, and western Europe, and was even detected in the USA.[7]

Sustainable development

Resources are limited. Sustainable development is the management of economic growth, avoiding irreparable damage to the environment. By balancing economic requirements with ecological concerns, people's needs can be satisfied without jeopardizing the prospects of future generations.[8] The concept of sustainable development is illustrated with the practice of deforestation.

Deforestation

Trees are an inventory of oxygen, and absorb carbon dioxide, a major greenhouse gas. Clear cutting, deforestation, or destroying large swathes of forests such as the Amazon rain forests destroys wildlife (more than 90% of the world's animals inhabit forests). Forests are a source of raw materials for many drugs.

Further, destruction of trees reduces the ability of land to absorb rain, causing flooding. Cutting down trees enhances soil erosion and in mountain areas, the natural barrier to avalanches is removed (avalanches are a continuing problem in the European Alps). The practice of most logging companies now, in recognition of sustainability, is to plant at least an amount of trees equivalent to that which have been cut down.

No coordinated strategy

There are some environmentalists who believe that there is no comprehensive or coordinated global environmental strategy and that policies and industrial operations and technological developments will lead to disaster as the elements in Table 5.1 illustrate.[9]

Sources of environmental damage

Environmental damage is air, water, and solid waste pollution and excess noise. The following summarizes the principal causes.

Air pollution

Contaminants, or excess chemicals in the air, which in humans lead to respiratory or other health problems, cause air pollution. On structures and equipment it leads to corrosion, and air pollution damages plant and animal life.

Acid rain

Fossil fuels, particularly oil and coal, produce sulphur dioxide and sulphur trioxide when burnt. These gases, dissolved in atmospheric moisture, constitute acid rain. Acid rain kills plants by attacking foliage and roots. In rivers, it destroys marine life. On building structures, acid rain corrodes metal and degrades stone and paint. Figure 5.2 shows the concentration region of acid rain compared to other well-known products.

Fog

When burned, coal is reduced to fly ash which when airborne, and mixed with moist air, produces fog. A notorious fog occurred in London, UK in 1950–51 when between 4000 and 5000 people died due to several foggy days as a result of coal combustion. This disaster led to tough clean air laws in Britain, which among others forbids the open burning of coal. Today, fog is a problem in such areas as eastern European countries, Turkey, and China.

Table 5.1 No coordinated strategy

Issue	Reality
World population exceeds the earth's capacity	Secular and religious policies often encourage population growth, and limit contraception. For some of these beliefs, more people translate into more power
Global warming will have devastating effects	The Kyoto Agreement in Japan sets greenhouse gas levels back to 1990 levels by the year 2010. Thus, there is no real reduction and no real change. In 2001 the USA refused to accept the Agreement
Overall efficiency of a car is 2% and it is a very wasteful means of transport	People prefer the convenience and status of cars, even though they guzzle fuel, cause congestion, accidents, local air pollution, waste materials, and contribute to global warming
Applying the Pareto principle, 20% of the world's population use 80% of global resources	People in developed countries strive for an ever improving lifestyle characterized by conspicuous consumption and self-indulgence. People in developing countries want only to emulate this apparently luxurious lifestyle
Third world debt increases, but financial aid decreases	At Rio de Janeiro rich countries agreed to meet UN target of 0.7% of GNP to go to developing countries. Currently, none of the G7 countries meet this target
Commercial high technology brings short-term profits for the few, and long-term problems for the many	Every day more than five new industrial chemicals are added to the estimated 150,000 already polluting the oceans. The natural gene pool is being polluted by genetic modifications, the implications of which are unpredictable and likely to be disastrous
Huge resources are used for armaments to be exported around the world so humans can destroy one another while also destroying the planet	More important than ethical foreign policies is short-term concern in the manufacturing countries that arms exports provide jobs and growth
Economic growth is seen as the measure of a country's success	Most of earth's resources are finite so economic growth must be finite. Yet economies continue to reduce the size of resource base by pollution, deforestation, over-fishing, climate change, etc.
Politicians do not have the courage to give a true inspirational lead to sustainability	Elected people are too concerned with short-term power, and popular image
Too few people in developed countries care enough to take action	The majority of people don't want to know, and are content to bury their head in the sand because the truth is unpleasant

Chlorofluorocarbons

Chlorofluorocarbons (CFCs) are inert, non-toxic, chlorine-based chemicals used in the manufacture of propellants for paint and deodorant in aerosol sprays, coolant in refrigerators, and air conditioners (Freon), cleaning fluids for electronic circuit boards, and plastic foam (Styrofoam) for packing cartons used for eggs, hamburgers, and electronic components. CFCs when expelled into the atmosphere react with ultraviolet light that breaks down CFCs into chlorine that subsequently attacks the ozone. The destruction of the ozone barrier in the stratosphere allows high concentrations of ultra-violet rays to reach the earth's surface resulting in increased incidence of skin cancer, glaucoma, cataracts, weakened immune systems, crop damage, and disrupting the reproduction of plankton that anchor the marine food chain. As a result of the Montreal Protocol in September 1988, amended in June 1990 and November 1992, the production and use of both CFCs and halons is being phased out.[10]

Halons

Halons are a group of chemicals containing bromine used in fire extinguishers. Bromine acts in a similar way to the chlorine of CFCs and attacks ozone. Although the production of halons is small compared to CFCs, bromine is considered more damaging to the ozone layer than an equivalent amount of chlorine from CFCs.

Figure 5.2 **Product acidity**

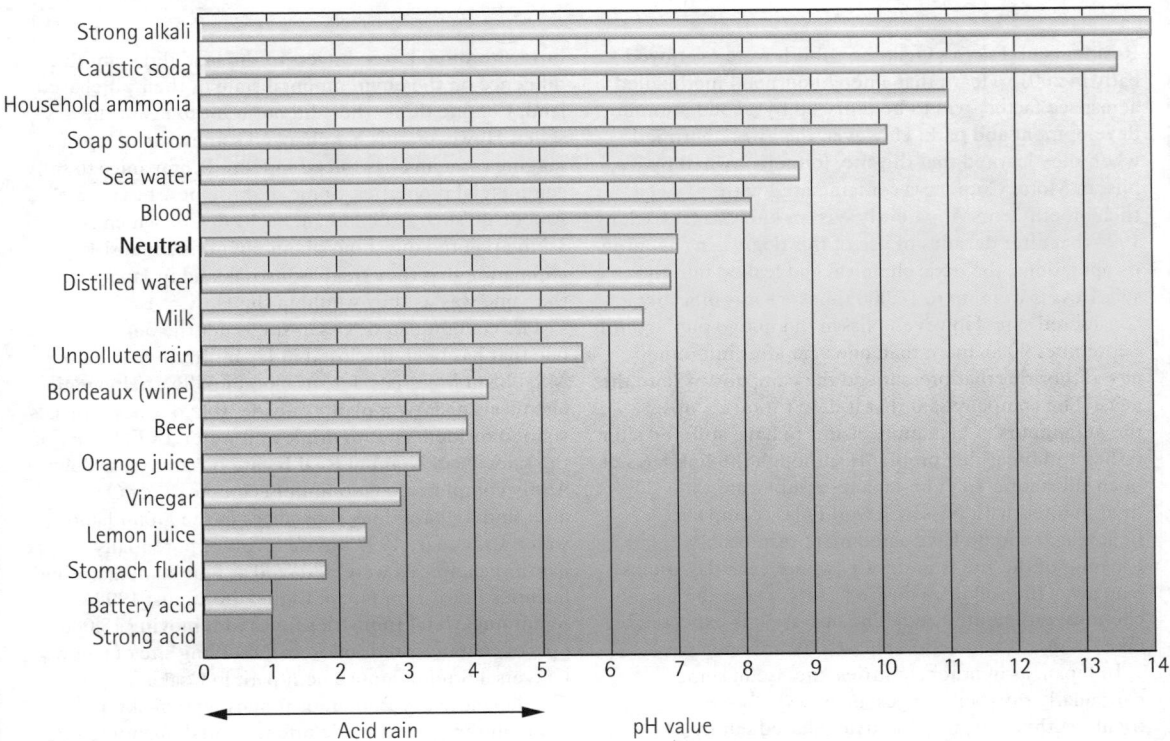

Acid rain

pH value

Smog

The action of sunlight on automobile exhausts and factory emissions, principally nitrous oxides, initiates a photochemical reaction to create smog of which ozone and NOX (nitrous oxides) are the main constituents. If an atmospheric inversion layer exists, and conditions are still, then this smog is trapped at ground level making respiration difficult. Los Angeles, Denver, Athens, Tokyo, Mexico City and Grenoble in France are all cities that have chronic smog problems. Besides the respiratory effects on humans, smog attacks rubber on car tyres, windshield wipers, and gasket joints.

Lead oxide

Lead oxide is an additive used to upgrade gasoline. Vaporized lead in the atmosphere from automobile exhausts is highly toxic and can damage the brain. Its use in the USA has been phased out and there are moves in the same direction in Europe. However, leaded gasoline is still used in Mexico, India, and other developing regions.

Carbon dioxide

Carbon dioxide is an odourless, colourless gas under normal conditions, and although not toxic, contributes to the *greenhouse effect*. Carbon dioxide is the product of the burning of all organic materials including fossil fuels such as oil, gas, coal, and wood. The theory of the greenhouse effect is that carbon dioxide and methane are trapped in the upper atmosphere and their presence prevents the escape of heat. This causes the temperature of the earth's surface to rise with a consequent impact on weather patterns and agriculture.

Radiation

Radiation is perhaps the most insidious of all pollutants. It is silent, odourless, and invisible. High exposure is fatal and even small doses can lead to cancer. Sources of radiation include nuclear power plants, nuclear weapons and associated manufacturing plants, nuclear testing sites, nuclear transportation systems such as submarines, aircraft carriers, and rockets. Hospitals use radioactive iodine and cobalt for medical treatment. Also, radon arises naturally from the decay of uranium.

Industry insight 5.1

Soil and ground water pollution in Japan

Residents of Tokyo's Ogikubo suburb were overjoyed early in 2001 to learn that a neighbourhood mothballed aerospace factory was to be replaced by a condominium development and park. However, they were horrified when they learned that the site, formerly owned by Nissan Motor Corp., was contaminated with trichloroethylene. Apparently Nissan knew as far back as 1994 that after decades of use of this degreasing agent in its operations, the toxic chemical had leaked into the soil. Levels were up to 16,000 times what is officially considered safe. However, Nissan did not go public until September 2000, more than one year after informing city authorities that pressurized the company to state the facts. The company said that it didn't want to 'upset the neighbours'. One family claims to have suffered skin rashes and breathing problems, although the link has not been substantiated. The Japanese public are disappointed with Nissan, a world-class company, believing it should have acted more responsibly. Cleanup of the site is underway where each day trucks haul away the soil to an onsite facility where the chemicals are neutralized. The operation is expected to take six months and cost at least $20 million.

In Japan, as in other countries, the use of some particularly toxic substances, including trichloroethylenes, was gradually phased out by the late 1980s. However, after years of mishandling, the chemicals had already seeped into the ground. Since there was little fear of liability, landowners paid little attention. Later, buyers of the land did scant due diligence on the environmental state of their purchased land. For one thing, they did not want to insult the seller. However, this has changed somewhat as Japan's sagging economy has forced indebted companies to sell commercial properties. Some of these new buyers are American, such as Goldman, Sachs & Co., which is asking pointed questions about environmental risk stipulating that they treat industrial land in Japan the same way as they would in the USA.

The contaminated Nissan site is not the only recent one that has been disclosed in Japan. In August 2000 Mitsubishi Materials detected potentially carcinogenic chemicals near twin plants outside Tokyo. Local officials warned residents not to drink well water. In February of the same year, Nomura Real Estate began to tear down a nearly completed condominium complex near Osaka after finding hazardous substances in the ground and water. In January 1999 unsafe levels of potentially harmful chemicals were detected at four manufacturing facilities in western Japan. Earlier, in August 1998, Sumitomo Metal Industries finished removing 15,000 tons of contaminated soil from a building site of a new Universal Studios amusement park in Osaka. The Japanese government is proposing to make soil pollution a punishable offence and demanding corporations to pay for the damage. Estimates put the cost of pollution damage in Japan at some $122 billion.

Adapted from: 'Digging up trouble', *Business Week*[11]

Water pollution

Water pollution is the discharge of toxic products, chemicals and other materials directly into rivers, lakes, and the sea. It also concerns them being dumped on land because the toxic products can percolate into water sources. The following gives some of the contaminants and Industry insight 5.1 illustrates a particular situation of ground water pollution in Japan.

Phosphates

Phosphates originate principally from detergents and their presence promotes the growth of algae. When algae bloom and spread, they deplete oxygen and block sunlight, killing fish and other marine life.

Trichloroethylenes

Trichloroethylenes are those chemicals used in dry cleaning and as degreasing agents in industry. They are toxic and if not disposed of properly find their way into the drinking water systems.

Heavy metals

Heavy metals include lead originating from batteries, soldering operations, and cans; chromium from stainless steel products, cement, rubber, and composition floor coverings; cadmium also from batteries; and mercury. Heavy metals are highly toxic and if dumped in waterways are consumed by fish thus poisoning the food chain. Perhaps the most notorious example of heavy metals poisoning is the Minamata Bay scandal in Japan in the 1960s. Mercury waste from a rubber and plastics maker was discharged into Minamata Bay. More than 5400 people who ate fish caught in the bay died, were crippled, or gave birth to deformed children.[12] A more recent contamination from heavy metals occurred in April 1998 when a reservoir in Spain owned by Boliden Ltd, a Canadian–Swedish mining company, containing lead, zinc, arsenic, cyanide, and other toxic materials collapsed. Nearly 5.5 cubic metres of waste escaped, contaminating farming land and a nature reserve, killing much wildlife.[13]

Sodium chlorate

Sodium chlorate is an oxidizing agent and bleach for making chlorine dioxide used in paper manufacture, ore processing, herbicides, defoliants, and pharmaceuticals.

Oil

Oil pollution originates from tanker or oilrig disasters, the illegal washing of oil containers at sea, and natural seepage.

Asbestos

Asbestos was used in the USA until the 1970s for pipe insulation, fireproofing, brake linings, roofing, and flooring. It is banned in the USA but is still used in Europe (although it is being phased out there) and elsewhere in the world.

Arsenic

Arsenic occurs naturally in small amounts in food and is found in wood preservatives, paints, and dyes. It is used in pesticides, and solvents employed in the electronics industry.

Ethylene oxide

Ethylene oxide is used for sterilizing hospital surgical equipment, in the manufacture of solvents, lubricants, and the sweetening of gasoline.

Vinyl chloride

Vinyl chloride is used in the manufacture of polyvinyl chloride for plastic, particularly beverage bottles, and in cigarette manufacture.

Benzene

Benzene is present naturally in some foods and occurs in gasoline, oil, solvents, and other petroleum-based products. It is found in cigarettes and is emitted in vehicle exhaust.

Solid waste pollution

Solid waste pollution in this context refers to the dumping of untreated commercial, consumer, or industrial waste directly on land. In this case, in addition to being an eyesore, the concern is that toxic products from this waste eventually percolate into water sources. Alternatively, solid waste might be dumped into waterways, which becomes a direct water pollution problem.

Human waste

This includes all untreated human waste, which is a great problem in large urban areas particularly in developing regions.

Domestic waste

Domestic waste is all packaging, newspapers, containers, etc. The quantity is enormous, as evidenced by the mountains that accumulate during a garbage collectors' strike.

Dioxins

Dioxins are a common family of chemicals compounds that have approximately 100 different structures. The most toxic is the chlorinated derivative 2, 3, 7, and 8 tetrachlorodibenzo-p-dioxin usually referred to as TCDD. This chemical is the by-product of many chemical operations including chlorine bleaching of wood pulp. This bleaching process leaves traces of the dioxin in paper used in such products as coffee filters, toilet tissues, tampons, tea bags, diapers, and kitchen towels. Dioxins are carcinogenic.

Farm waste

Farm waste is the solid waste from agricultural or animal farming and may be contaminated with fertilizers, herbicides, and insecticides.

Industrial waste

Industrial waste includes mine tailings from coal, copper, gold, and silver mining and waste from paper, and lumber mills.

Nuclear waste

A nuclear power plant uses rods of plutonium to generate heat. This in turn generates steam, which drives a power turbine. The plutonium, when spent, has to be stored and the only way to do this is in land repositories. Decay of the material to safe levels can take hundreds of years. Nuclear wastes from hospitals have to be treated in the same manner.

Noise pollution

Noise is a pollutant, which, in excess, can impair hearing, reduce employee productivity, and cause physical damage. Sound is measured in decibels and the addition of only ten decibels doubles the sound level. Experts indicate that about 85 decibels is the highest safe level for the uncovered human ears. In many urban areas, manufacturing plants are near to, or exceed those levels. Table 5.2 gives some qualitative examples for various decibel levels.

Natural pollution

Not all pollution is man made. Some atmospheric pollution occurs naturally. For example:

- Particles in the atmosphere come from dust, forest fires, and volcanoes.
- Plants decay and naturally give off chemicals.
- Sulphates from sea spray occur around coastal areas.
- Radiation comes from the sun.

Table 5.2 Decibel damage

Decibels	Audibility	Example
2		Breathing
10		Private office
20	Faint	Average living room
40	Moderate	Vacuum cleaner
60	Loud	Food blender
80	Very loud	Power lawnmower
100	Deafening	Rock music
120	Painful	Smoke alarm, home alarm
140	Structural damage	Jet taking off

- Radon arises from the natural decay of materials.
- Sulphur is emitted by volcanoes.
- Natural oil seepage occurs as, for example, off the coast of Santa Barbara, USA, which causes both air and water pollution.

Product lifecycle analysis

Because of the potential of environmental damage, one role of the operations manager is to consider a product lifecycle analysis (LCA). This is the evaluation of the life of a product from conception, through design, extraction of raw materials, purchasing, production, packaging, distribution, use, and eventual disposal at the end of the product's life. The objective of a lifecycle analysis is to minimize environmental damage, by paying attention to upstream activities, and to avoid downstream or the *end of pipe cleanup*, that is, the cleaning up after the product has caused environmental problems. Other terminology used is lifecycle assessment, or a cradle to grave approach, as illustrated in Figure 5.3. The following gives some illustrations.

Product conception

In the development of new products (see further in Chapter 6) considerations are to decide if the product is really needed. Does one really need electric

Figure 5.3 Lifecycle assessment

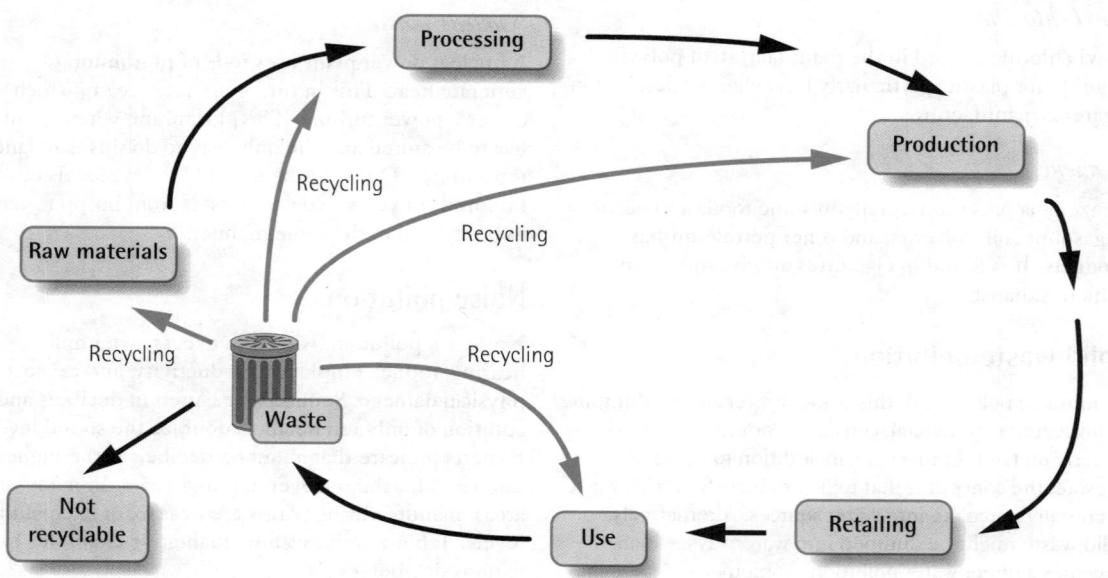

can openers, gasoline-driven leaf blowers, electric toothbrushes, potent herbicides, glues that also damage the skin, etc?

Product design

In product design attention should be paid to:

- Keeping the use and concentrations of toxic chemicals low. Polaroid in the late 1980s initiated a programme to reduce its use of toxic chemicals in the photographic industry.[14] Chemical companies have in place similar programmes related to the development of insecticides and herbicides.
- Developing new product formulations, which are non-toxic. Hydrogen peroxide instead of chlorine for bleaching; water-based rather than oil-based paints; lead-free paints; enriched gasoline rather than leaded gasoline.
- Using recycled materials such as paper in book publishing, plastic (PVC) in the construction industry, and metals in tool making.
- Not designing with materials, or components which are becoming extinct such as ivory, exotic woods, or animal skins.
- Designing products from renewable resources such as wood, or cellulose-based plastic rather than petroleum-based plastic.
- Using less material, and design a process to minimize waste.
- Designing to ease disposal, and recycle. Mobil Chemicals introduced biodegradeable trash bags to replace the previous non-biodegradeable products.[15] Further, standardized materials are often easier to recycle. McDonald's designed a paper wrapping for hamburgers to replace the polystyrene clamshell packing.[16]
- Designing to avoid the use of heavy metals.
- Designing products that minimize harm to environment, such as phosphate-free detergents, or electric automobiles to replace gasoline-driven ones for certain situations (e.g. baggage-handling trucks at airports, postal delivery trucks, certain utility vehicles).
- Designing products that minimize the consumption of energy when in use, such as automobiles, dishwashers, space heaters, and airplanes.
- Designing products that can be reused, rather than discarded, when finished.
- Using rigid reusable plastic containers, rather than disposable cardboard.
- Designing using biotechnological means rather than requiring herbicides such as for certain food products.

Purchasing

When purchasing from external suppliers, enact the following considerations:

- Using those that respect environmental issues. The environment is a factor for Hewlett-Packard when selecting suppliers (see Chapter 16).
- Using local suppliers, rather than imported materials to minimize transportation. For example, local lumber rather than that from the Far East, or chemicals produced in the country rather than from, say, the Middle East.

Operations

The operations side of firms is probably the biggest potential environmental threat.

Waste

- Use raw materials efficiently. For example, the paper industry, which once used only one half of a tree and threw away the other half, now uses 90%. It puts half of the rest back on the land as part of reforestation, and burns the final 5% to produce energy.[17]
- In process and manufacturing operations, reuse wastewater rather than dumping. Install catch basins to trap firewater, any scale, dirt, etc. which can be collected and removed in special process units.
- Collect and recycle solvents, and the solid material they contain. Motor vehicle manufacturers use cutting fluids or solvents to cool and lubricate the work piece in machinery operations. They have installed filter systems that remove all iron filings, and burr from the solvent rather than letting it be discharged. This steel waste is sent back to the foundry and the solvents are reused.[18] Refining and chemical companies use a system of traps to prevent leaking oil and chemicals from going to the sewer systems and this is also reused.

Energy

In the use of energy sources such as electricity, coal, gas, or oil:

- Use new energy-efficient and non-polluting equipment and machinery.
- Develop cogeneration systems (using low level heat) for electrical and thermal power.[19]
- Install energy efficient lighting and heating including automatic on/off devices.
- Automatic plant control usually uses less energy.

- Consider using cleaner fuels that don't contain polluting sulphur.
- Improve combustion by increasing amount of oxygen in the combustion process or adding preheat. When the temperature of the combustion cycle is increased fewer pollutants are formed.

Combustion gases

- Pass exhaust gases through mechanical equipment such as filters, screens, cyclones, electrostatic precipitators to catch the dust particles.
- Build tall chimneystacks – high enough to carry the pollutants away from urban areas and disperse them in the atmosphere. (But better, clean up the pollutants *before* they are emitted.)
- Use scrubbing systems where exhaust gases are passed through a stack and washed with water to remove acid gases.
- Use chemical treatment to reduce sulphuric gases to elemental sulphur.
- Use catalytic converters, of the type used in car exhausts, to reduce automobile pollution.

Testing

Do not test products on animals. This is particularly the case in health and beauty products such as hair sprays, perfume, and eyeliners.

Packaging

In packaging the product use:

- Just the amount necessary for protection. Reduced packaging reduces space thus less storage area is needed. Also, less packaging reduces transportation costs since more products can be carried in one truck.
- Use packaging that is recyclable, reusable plastic packaging or plastic containers, or packaging that is biodegradeable.

Transportation

In deciding on the transportation and distribution part of the operation:

- Plan and select in a manner to minimize environmental damage such as maximizing the capacity of transport vehicles and plan that a vehicle makes the return journey loaded.
- Use train transport rather than road transport where feasible.

Use

Educate consumers so that products, or services are used in the most environmentally acceptable manner. In addition:

- Car pooling is encouraged.
- Appliances where possible, such as dishwashers, dryers, and washing machines, are used in the evening or night when energy demand is lower. This then reduces demands for the construction of new power plants.
- Airplanes do not fly at night to/from urban areas.

Disposal

Manufacturers cooperate in the collection, recycling, and disposal of their products. Some recycling activities such as paper for newsprint, bottles for reuse or pulverizing for making tiles, aluminium cans for melting and reuse, are quite common.

Motor vehicles

Motor Vehicles represent a special case for disposal. More than eight million cars 'die' in the USA every year. Scrapyards have long made money crushing and recycling the steel, and other metals from junk cars, but this still leaves three million tons of rubber, glass, and plastic, which is not easy to reuse. To compound the problem, the proportion of iron and steel in cars has dropped by some 20% since 1977, whereas the proportion of plastics has risen some 36% in the same period as illustrated in Figure 5.4.[20]

There is pressure from governments (Germany is an example) to make automobile manufacturers responsible for the cradle to grave or lifecycle of vehicles.[21] This puts pressure on the producer to pay attention to feasibility of recycling automobile materials including not only metal parts but plastic components, tyres, batteries, glass, and paint:

- Car batteries are environmentally damaging as the lead and acid can leach into ground water supplies if the battery is simply dumped. Now, more than 80% of batteries are recycled for reuse or recycled into such products as beverage containers, and solar panels.
- Automotive glass generally winds up in landfills. The glass contains plastic to prevent it from shattering in an accident and this glass–plastic is difficult to recycle.
- Tyres pose a major difficulty in recycling. In the USA, about 240 million tyres are scrapped annually, with an estimated 85% ending up in landfills, although some uses are being developed, such as fuel in the cement

Figure 5.4 Automobile ingredients

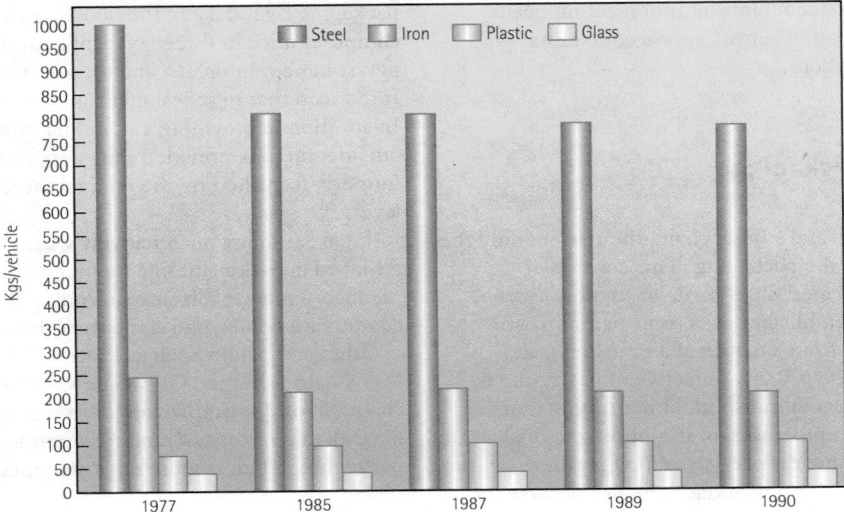

industry by Ciment Vicat, and Compagne Française des Ferrailles,[22] in France and in the manufacture of sandals and other light shoes such as by DejaShoes, Oregon, USA.[23]

- Oil is recyclable. In the spring of 1991 Exxon Company, USA, launched a pilot programme in Baton Rouge, Louisiana, and Richmond, Virginia, to collect and recycle used motor oil. They contracted with collection services in the two cities to pick up spent oil from service stations and recycle it into fuel for a variety of industrial uses.[24]

Advantages of a lifecycle analysis

In addition to minimizing the pollution impact of products and processes by which they are produced, companies can use lifecycle analysis to justify claims made in product advertising, and to avoid regulatory pressure from governmental agents. Further, lifecycle analysis has shown that some products, processes, or activities are more environmentally harmful, than the considered alternatives as the following illustrates.

Procter & Gamble

After performing a lifecycle analysis on babies' diapers, Procter & Gamble, together with Arthur D Little Consultants, concluded that the disposable varieties create less environmental impact on the environment than cloth diapers which require a lot of water, and energy, to clean them for reuse.[25]

Paper cartons

Non-refillable paper cartons have less impact than bottles. Bottles occupy more space, use more energy for transportation, and use a lot of water and energy for washing. Paper cartons in addition require less energy in refrigeration. Bottles when eventually disposed in a landfill take up more space than paper, and are not biodegradeable.

Assumptions of a lifecycle analysis

A lifecycle analysis depends on the initial assumptions:

- In the supply chain, over what distance are products transported? The conclusions may be different in a small country like Switzerland from, say, the USA.
- How many times will, say, a bottle be used? The environmental impact may be less if the answer is 200 times rather than, say, ten times.

BATNEEC principle

The BATNEEC principle (best available technology not entailing excessive cost) is similar to the lifecycle analysis except that it looks directly at cost. It is the response to the criterion, 'if the cost is affordable, and the product is more environmentally acceptable, then this would be the preferred technology'.[26] Some examples are as follows:

- Design a photocopier unit that uses solvent-free inks, and accepts paper that has been recycled. (More dust is produced from some recycled paper, however.)

- Develop fuel-efficient, and quieter engines for aircraft and road vehicles.
- Design roll-on deodorants, or pump-action beauty products, instead of aerosol sprays containing chlorofluorocarbons.

Product packaging

In the operations and supply chain, there is not only the product but also the packaging. This consists of cardboard, corrugated fibreboard, wood, polystyrene foam, glass, paper, blister packs (transparent plastic packaging made from a matrix of air pockets), and other plastics. The primary objective of packaging is to protect products in transport, either during transfer in the production processes, or in shipping to final consumers. In some cases, such as food products (ketchup, yoghurt, and breakfast cereals), detergents, and beauty products, the packaging and product are associated. It is a major element in the marketing mix as a medium for communicating product identity.[27]

Package redesign

Packing cannot be eliminated, but waste, and costs can be reduced by such changes as:

- Redesigning packing structure to eliminate one or more layers.
- Modifying production and/or product design of existing packing to reduce weight.
- Eliminating a packing type in favour of another more environmentally acceptable such as one that is biodegradable (paper, cardboard, and to a certain extent some plastics).

Digital equipment

Digital Equipment Corporation (DEC) of the USA estimated that it spends $54 million annually on packaging. This translates into 27,000 tons or 127,500 cubic metres of annual waste. DEC reduced packaging by redesign. Previously it would pack its computer mice in three layers of material – blister pack, polystyrene reinforcers, and then a cardboard box. It reduced that to redesigned single cardboard box. In addition to providing all product information on the outside, the box provided the strength and protection formerly furnished by the original three packing layers.[28]

Table 5.3 shows quantitatively what Digital Equipment achieved in packing design for four of its computer products – mouse, software (including documentation), computer modules, and computer cabinets.

Other companies such as Procter & Gamble, McDonald's, Burger King, Gateway (UK supermarket chain), and Migros (Switzerland's biggest retailer), have all taken steps to modify, monitor, or minimize packaging so that is more environmentally friendly.

Technology and package weight reduction

Over the years, industry has made significant progress through technological modifications such as redesign, reformulation, or manufacturing changes to reduce the unit weight of packing. As an illustration, from the 1950s to the early 1990s the weight of a milk bottle has been reduced some 40%, and a beer can some 80%.[29]

Pouch technology

Pouch technology is a means of reducing packaging weight while simultaneously maintaining strength. The idea originated in France several decades ago and is widely used in dry food packaging and has been adapted for liquid products. Here, a typical pouch of 3 mm includes a polyolefin seal layer, with polyester and nylon for the pouch construction. Weight and volume are reduced by 60 to 90%.[30]

Table 5.3 Digital Equipment's packing design achievements

Product	Product volume (cm³)	Package volume to product volume (before)	Package volume to product volume (after)	Reduction (%)
Mouse	216.96	8.62	0.94	89.1
Module	791.98	2.79	0.72	74.3
Software	181.90	15.17	1.79	88.2
Cabinet	900,472.00	0.36	0.25	31.0

Recycling ideas for packaging

The following are just some of the products that can be made from waste packaging:[31]

- Benches, and anti-noise walls from plastic packaging (Limburgse Vinyl Maatschappij, Belgium).
- Air flow deflectors from polyurethane plastic scrap (Dow Chemicals, and Mobay Corporation, USA).
- Pig pens from old plastic bottles (Reko BV, the Netherlands).
- Chipboard that can be turned into briefcases, wall clocks, and vases from drink cartons (Tetra Pak, a Swiss–Swedish packaging company).[32]

Transportation systems

The supply chain in operations includes transporting goods, or people, either by road, sea, air or pipeline for liquid products.

Road transportation

Road transport is particularly polluting and the current tax and charging system for road transportation does not take into account environmental damage. Transferring road haulage to rail helps but in many instances it is not cost effective, neither is it compatible with just-in-time operations (see Chapter 15). Convenient rail links are not always available, and outdated work practices in railroads make this transportation mode even more expensive. (See also Chapter 17.)

Pressure in Europe to pay more attention to transportation systems is coming from the European Union, which is advocating zero emissions from road vehicles. Initial proposals are asking that, by 2010, there is a 70% reduction in carbon monoxide, volatile organic compounds, particulate matter, and a 65% reduction in total NOX emissions.[33] Some considerations for reducing the environmental impact of transportation are now given. Further, Figure 5.5 gives comparative data for alternative fuel proposals.[34]

Unleaded gasoline

Lead-free gasoline, with the same octane rating as previously, is produced by modifying the cracking operations in oil refineries. The USA has been supplying lead-free gasoline since 1978. Most OECD countries have lead-free gasoline but it is still not in use in many emerging economies.

Gasoline fuel reformulation

Gasoline is a mixture of as many as 100 organic compounds obtained from the selective distillation of crude oil. Benzene, a major component, is carcinogenic and with other hydrocarbons is a contributor to ground-level ozone and photochemical smog. Oil companies (e.g. Arco, USA;[35] Neste Oy, Finland[36]) are experimenting with different types of less polluting gasoline.

Lean-burning gasoline engines

Lean-burning engines burn less fuel at lower temperatures and thus emit fewer oxides of nitrogen for

Figure 5.5 Storage volume and weight for fuels compared to gasoline

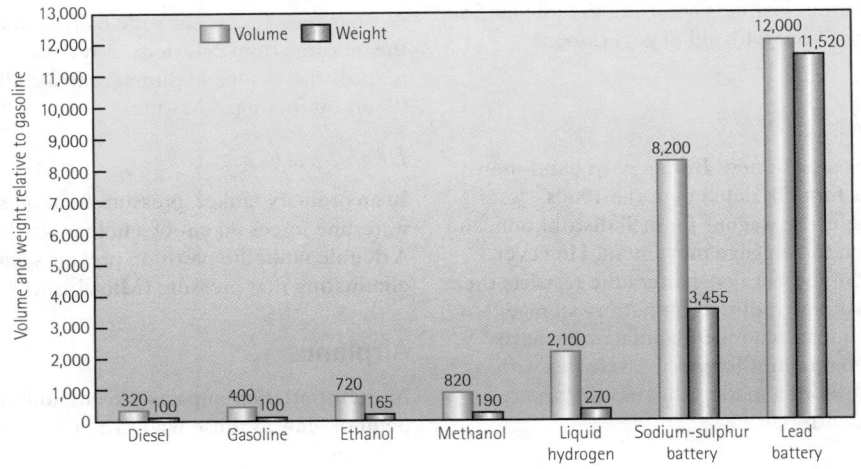

similar engine performance. Automobile firms have long been working on these developments.[37]

Catalytic converters for gasoline engines

Catalytic converters, containing platinum compounds or other materials, are fitted immediately upstream of the tail pipe of motor vehicles to minimize emissions of carbon monoxide, nitrous oxides, and unburned hydrocarbons. They have long been around in the USA and are becoming more common in OECD countries where non-leaded gasoline is used. (Lead in gasoline 'poisons' the catalyst making the converter unworkable.) The technology of catalytic converters is not new. However, one of their drawbacks is that they only work at 260°C. Unfortunately, the largest quantity of emissions from an automobile occur at startup, when the catalytic converter is cold. These pollutants are not trapped. Companies are currently investigating the use of electrically heated converters, which would make them immediately effective.

Methanol and ethanol

Methanol, made from natural gas or coal, or ethanol from corn, sugar cane, or maize do not contain all the hydrocarbon elements of gasoline and as such the associated emissions are less polluting. However, the engines are more expensive and the real cost of developing the fuel is considered higher than gasoline.[38]

Rape oil, or colza

Rape oil, or colza, is another liquid substitute fuel for diesel or gasoline that produces only marginally less power per litre than fossil fuel. Rape is a European herb similar to the mustard plant used as a forage crop for sheep and pigs. A strong impetus behind rape oil fuel is that with government-mandated cutbacks in farm production in Europe, farmers are using the idle land set aside to grow rape seed with aid of government support.[39]

Electric vehicles

Electric vehicles are not new. Britain used hand-drawn electric vehicles for milk delivery in the 1960s, California uses electric wagons for mail distribution, and airports use them for baggage movement. However, wider usage is limited because battery life restricts their range, and the volume required for battery storage. However, all major automobile manufacturers have development programmes for electric vehicles with an eye on the California market that has the severest environmental controls.[40]

Hydrogen-powered vehicles

Hydrogen-powered vehicles are an alternative to a cleaner form of transport, although they still face the following technology challenges:[41]

- On-board fuel storage volume is much greater than gasoline, even in liquid form.
- The safety aspect. Hydrogen burns very easily. Further, it is odourless and colourless and so is difficult to detect.
- There is a need to establish a viable hydrogen manufacturing and refuelling infrastructure.

Electronic regulation of traffic movements

Electronic regulation of traffic movements comprises a system in which a vehicle driver with computerized monitors can see in advance variables, such as road conditions, traffic tie-ups, and weather patterns and thus make appropriate journey modifications. Automatic guidance systems make travelling efficient by reducing unnecessary travel distance and time with the secondary effect of fuel economy, and reduced emissions. Many companies including Nissan, Hitachi, Renault, Philips, General Motors, Ford, Motorola, and Intel have electronic regulation development projects.[42] They were beginning to make an appearance in 2000, but are still expensive.

Oil tankers

Oil spills are a major concern in water pollution and some considerations in oil tanker design which might avoid problems are now summarized.[43]

Double hull

A double hull gives more strength. The *Exxon Valdez* might have spilled 60% less oil had it been double hulled.

Catamaran design

A catamaran design has wide ballast tanks that shield the oil cargo from collisions. A recessed tanker bottom reduces the chance of puncture in a collision (Shell International Marine).

Double tank

In an ordinary tanker, pressure from oil above the waterline forces oil out of a hole in the bottom. A double tank, the partition prevents leaks by eliminating that pressure (Mitsubishi).

Airplanes

Air transportation impacts the environment from a noise point of view as those who live in the flightpath of a major airport can testify. The noise problem is pushing manufacturers to build quieter airplanes. However, it is also putting pressure on authorities to ban, or reduce night flying and not to permit the construction of additional runways. Airlines, for their part, claim this is financially damaging to their business. In addition to noise, airline exhaust emissions in the upper atmosphere cause extensive pollution that is increasing rapidly with the growth of air travel. Air manufacturers for their part are also developing more fuel-efficient, and less polluting engines.

Cost–benefit analysis for environmental considerations

A cost–benefit analysis is an analytical tool for deciding whether expenditures for a certain project are greater or less than the financial benefits that would be obtained if the project were executed, or the operations were continued (see Chapter 23 for further considerations). A cost–benefit analysis is a useful tool where environmental situations are concerned since very often the battle is between those who think a project makes economic sense, and others who think it makes for poor environmental sense. The following illustrates the broad concept.

Steel mill

Suppose a decision is to be made concerning keeping a steel mill in operation. Elements to be considered in an environment-based cost–benefit analysis include the following.

Benefits

Over an operating period of, say, 10 years the sum of the following total benefits are calculated.

- Salaries paid to mill employees.
- Social benefits to paid to employees and families.
- Income generated by the firm's employees to the surrounding community (stores, real estate, service industries).
- Taxes paid by the firm and employees at the local and national level.
- Dividends to stockholders.

Over the same period the environmental 'costs' are calculated.

Direct environmental costs

- Installation of equipment to improve safety, and minimize pollution.

Indirect environmental costs

- Excess health costs as a result of unhealthy work environment.
- Deaths (employees or town residents) above normal levels because of the mill.
- Agricultural and plant damage from pollution.
- Property damage from pollution (sulphur, and acid rain).
- Lost income from tourism (unattractive area).
- Reduced quality of life in the town (unattractive living area).

Using the cost–benefit criteria, if the benefits outweigh the cost, that is, the ratio is less than one, then the programme should be continued.

Toll roads

Some countries, France, Italy, and soon Germany[44] for example, have an extensive motorway system controlled by tollbooths as a means of recuperating direct costs. Other countries, USA, and England, do not have tolls but pay for the network through various tax mechanisms. Motor vehicles entering a toll road (taking a ticket) and leaving (paying) are idling. In idle mode, oxides of carbon and hydrocarbon emissions increase by a factor of 2.5 compared to running at average speed. A cost–benefit analysis for using toll roads, taking environmental concerns into consideration, might be developed as follows.

Revenues

- These would be the total toll fees collected, which represent benefits to authorities.

Direct costs to build

- Construction cost of facilities including entrance and exit roads, and parking.
- Cost of land for construction (not including motorway).
- Salaries of all employees to build the facility.

Direct costs to operate

- Maintenance costs.
- Salaries of people to run the facility.

Annual accounted profit

This is basically the annual revenue less annual direct costs. In practice, the building costs would be depreciated over a certain time period yielding an annual depreciated cost. This would be added to the annual operating costs to give a total cost.

Environmental costs

- Cost associated with the driver's time lost approaching, waiting, and leaving toll entrance.
- Cost associated with driver's time lost approaching, waiting, and leaving toll exit.
- Pollution damage due to vehicle decelerating, idling, accelerating.
- Additional vehicle cost due to vehicle decelerating, idling, accelerating.
- Value put on environmental loss of land for booth and entrance/exit roads.
- 'Irritant' cost due to waiting.
- Costs associated with accidents on other roads as drivers refuse to use toll roads, as the direct cost to them is too high. (Motorways are safer than other highways.)

When the environmental cost is added into the profit equation, do the benefits outweigh the cost? That is, should the tollbooths be eliminated and financing be arrived at by other means such as taxation, as the case in Britain and the USA? It should be noted that there are efforts to reduce delays at the tollbooths (and thus vehicle emissions) by using *télépeage*. Vehicle owners can buy prepaid cards equipped with a computer chip and this is automatically read as the vehicle passes through the automatic tollgate.

Real-world operating decisions

Table 5.4 presents some company decisions where the environmental benefit obtained from a change in operations have outweighed the cost.[45,46]

Table 5.4 **Cost savings by changing the operating system**

Company	Change in the operating system
Arco	At its Channelview, Texas, propylene oxide plant, it installed a distillation process to recover spent benzene from liquid waste. The savings in using the recycled benzene largely offset the cost of the new distillation process
AT&T	It redesigned the circuit board cleaning process that resulted in an annual cost reduction of $3 million, and the elimination of using toxic chemicals
Dow Chemical	By reducing a toxic solvent used to make its Verdict herbicide, it saved about $3 million a year and reduced waste by 50%. At its Plaquemine facility near Baton Rouge, Louisiana, it spent $15 million on waste reduction projects in 1990 and saved $18 million in toxic waste and raw material cost. These projects are all part of its WRAP (Waste Reduction Always Pays) programme
Du Pont	At its Beaumont, Texas, plant it used to spew out 55,000 annual tons of waste. By adjusting production to use less of one raw material it was able to reduce the waste by two-thirds. Product yields increased and the cost savings were $1 million a year. At its Mobile, Alabama, plant that makes herbicides and insecticides it began to extract the solvents and titanium in the waste streams. The solvents were recycled and the titanium was shipped to its DeLisle, Mississippi, plant where it is used to make paint pigments. By this change in operation it was able to reduce emissions by some 20%
3M Company	At its pharmaceutical plant in California, it developed a water-based medicine tablet coating replacing a solvent-based product. The cost of the change was $60,000. However, this outweighed the need for pollution control equipment costing $180,000
Monsanto	At its nylon fibres plant in Pensacola, Florida, it has reduced its toxic air emissions by 90% since 1987 and saved millions of dollars in raw material cost. The plant is capturing a toxic solvent in a mineral bath before it escapes to the smokestack. Both the solvent and the mineral are recycled. At its Sauget, Illinois, plant it reduced its air and water emissions also by 90% by cooling the waste vapour and capturing the subsequent crystalline chemicals before they were emitted. By loading the chemical product directly into tank cars under sealed conditions they were able to reduce emissions even further
Procter & Gamble	At one of its units in Germany it introduced Lenor concentrated fabric softener in a small and flexible refill pouch. This reduced packaging waste by up to 85% with a corresponding cost saving to the company
Reynolds Metals	It replaced solvent-based inks with water-based products in packaging plants. This cut emissions by 65% and saved $30 million in production equipment
Xerox	It instituted reuse of packaging and pallets based on standardized designs. This saved up to $15 million annually and reduced waste by 10,000 tons

Criticisms of cost–benefit, and the EPA

The US Environmental Protection Agency (EPA) often uses a cost–benefit analysis in assessing industry performance using uniform standards for emissions. If environmental costs outweigh the benefits, action has to be taken. Some of the criticisms of this approach are as follows.

Evaluation

How does one reasonably assess the costs and benefits of clean air, water, health, and life?

Technology

Industries, such as steel, using different technologies are penalized. Those companies using older technology have to pay more to clean up effluent.

Small firms

Small companies cannot meet cost and have to close down. Alternatively, small companies cannot afford temporary closure of a facility to install pollution abatement equipment.

High expectations

Expectations are sometimes unreasonable. The automobile industry claims that levels for gasoline automobile in the Californian market are unobtainable. This has promoted the development of electric vehicles.

Sanctions

EPA regulations give no incentives for reducing pollution. All they do is provide sanctions. This is the *stick*, rather than the *carrot* approach.

Organizing for environmental management

Like total quality management (see Chapter 4) top management must give 100% support concerning environmental strategies, policies, and operations. Some of the strategic and associated operational elements to consider in organizing for environmental management include the following.

Worker safety

Employee safety is paramount. Are employees being exposed to toxic chemicals such as asbestos, sulphur compounds, mercury, or benzene derivatives? Multiple chemical exposure, which is the exposure to a combination of chemicals that can interact and have a more pronounced, or even perhaps a reduced toxicity effect, needs to be considered.

Organizational changes

The Valdez Principle, after the *Exxon Valdez* oil spill, calls on companies to make organizational changes and appoint an environmentalist to the corporate board, and also to conduct an annual public audit of the company's environmental progress.

Compensation

Include environmental improvements in the evaluation for an individual's salary. (Du Pont, USA, has made environmental criteria part of determining a manager's compensation.)

Internal cadre of environmentalists

An internal cadre of environmentalists includes having in place a crisis management team to respond to any emergencies. (See also Chapter 19.)

Research and development on environmental matters

In May 1987, after the Rhine disaster, Sandoz, set aside 10 million Swiss Francs for research and development related to the protection of the river.

Compensate for environmentally risky endeavours

Applied Energy Services, a power plant management firm, donated $2 million in 1988 for tree planting in Guatemala to compensate for a coal-fired plant it was building in Connecticut. The trees were intended to compensate for the carbon dioxide emissions from the coal facility that might contribute to global warming.

Overseas environmental practices

Ensure that environmental practices used in developing countries are the same as those used in your own country. The equation is:

$$\left\{ \begin{array}{l} \text{Environmental} \\ \text{practices overseas} \end{array} \right\} = \left\{ \begin{array}{l} \text{Environmental} \\ \text{practices at home} \end{array} \right\}$$

Gain environmental legitimacy and credibility

Give evidence to the public that your company is doing the maximum to preserve the environment. (The chief executive officer of Du Pont regularly delivers speeches on corporate environmentalism.)

Collaborate with environmentalists

Work with, and inform environmental groups when conducting an activity that will cause concern. Shell did not communicate properly on its proposed sinking of the Brent Spar Oilrig in 1995 or its drilling in the oil-rich Niger delta resulting in the abuse of the Ogoni people in this Nigerian region.[47]

Prevent confrontation with governmental agencies

Inform and collaborate with the appropriate agencies before potentially damaging activities are carried out. Comply early with regulations and take advantage of innovative compliance programmes.

Caterpillar Corporation

This US construction company defied a Federal warrant by blocking inspection of its factory in York, Pennsylvania, where it was suspected that cadmium or perhaps other substances were causing health hazards. Caterpillar was threatened with fines and the imprisonment of two of its plant managers.[48]

Financing and accounting of resources

- Recognize that environmental damage is a cost, and that true liability means also environmental costs.
- Demonstrate that anti-pollution programmes pay and show the overall impact of the pollution reduction programme.
- Gain the respect of the socially responsible investment community. As a corollary, a lending institution should consider environmental performance in assessing loans.

Provide the means

Provide the means to help consumers respect environmental practices. For example, hypermarkets and supermarkets have implemented recycling programmes to treat glass, plastic, paper, clothing, and by establishing collection areas in their parking lots. This is partly in recognition that, as a service operator, they are indirectly responsible for much of the pollution problems. Some supermarkets provide its customers with large plastic bags for a nominal cost. These bags can be exchanged at any time, at no charge, and the store takes the responsibility of recycling spent bags.

Human resources

- Recognize that there are individuals who are environmentally conscious and maybe there is pressure from those concerned about the company's image regarding environmental issues.
- Environmental performance and attitudes may be a consideration in attracting potential recruits.
- Work with employee unions, as they are interested in safety and environmental issues.

Trading pollution rights

Manufacturing companies pollute and it has to be recognized that a minimum is unavoidable. Trading pollution rights is the process of buying, or selling the right to pollute. This is a scheme proposed for minimizing the overall pollution level and works as follows:[49]

- Specific pollution limits would be set for each company by government agencies or the local environmental control office.
- Companies able to reduce their pollution level below the established limit would receive credits in the form of permits. Those permits could be sold to other firms.
- Companies wishing to expand, or who could not comply with established limits, would have to buy the necessary credits from other similar companies who have credits to sell.
- Thus, all companies would have a financial incentive to keep pollution levels to a minimum.

Develop and expand environmental cleanup services

Building on the expertise gained in cleaning up its own plants, Du Pont has formed a safety and environmental resources division to help industrial customers clean up their toxic wastes.

Procedures

Have in place effective operating procedures before an accident occurs. The following illustrates the necessity.

Three Mile Island

The Three Mile Island nuclear accident was in part the result of ineffective management communication procedures at Babcock and Wilcox (B&W) the firm that designed the plant. About 18 months before the accident, an engineer and a manager at B&W recommended changes in operator instructions at nuclear power plants designed by B&W. Had they been followed by the operators of Three Mile Island, the accident would not have happened. However, the instructions were never issued by B&W because poor management communication procedures obstructed timely decision making. In addition, B&W management had not established an appropriate communication environment and effective communication practices.[50] At the facility, even though a sophisticated information system existed, human and organizational factors limited effectiveness.[51]

Environmental audits

Carry out an environmental audit regularly. An environmental audit is a systematic, documented, periodic, and objective evaluation of how well an organization, its management, and equipment perform on environmental matters. An audit facilitates management control of environmental practices and assesses compliance with internal company policies and external government regulations. It helps avoid accidents, legal action, bad publicity, and even perhaps prison terms for employees.[52]

Steps and objectives

1. Define the scope – corporate, technical, design, and plant operation.
2. Establish legal and policy requirements – emission limits, waste inventories.
3. Review actual performance against standards and policies.
4. Highlight positive aspects and principal achievements of performance.
5. Identify inefficiencies and problems. This may lead to cost reductions.
6. Indicate priorities for improvement.
7. Develop a list of action items, responsibilities, means of improvements, and a schedule for achieving modifications.
8. Publish a statement of achievements, performance, and future strategy for internal and public access.
9. Use the statement to demonstrate to clients and the public the effectiveness of the company's environmental management system.

European union

The European Union is pushing for a proposal that would have companies:

- undertake periodic self-assessment audits of their performance
- have the self-assessments verified by an independent registered auditor
- produce a statement of performance which would be public information.

Public affairs

Don't appear insensitive to environmental issues. If a company gives the public an impression that it is insensitive to environmental matters, the company's products could end up being boycotted, which can impact profits, and the company image. Some illustrations follow.

Exxon

Exxon appeared insensitive to the *Valdez* incident, as their reaction was defensive, and antagonistic. In a survey after the accident, 41% Americans said they would consider boycotting the company. Even after *Valdez*, on 1 January 1990 a pipeline owned by Exxon fractured on Staten Island, New York, and leaked into the Arthur Kill, a narrow waterway separating New York City from New Jersey. Exxon faltered again, taking too long to announce its eagerness to set things right. It apparently could not understand what the combination of bad luck, arrogance, and ineptitude could do to its public image.[53]

Sinking of the Mont-Louis

On 25 August 1984 the French cargo boat, *Mont-Louis* collided with the British car ferry, *Olau Britannia*, about 20 km from Ostend, Belgium. The *Mont-Louis* sank in 15 metres of water with 30 containers of 450 tons of toxic uranium hexafluoride in its holds. The last container of the gas was not retrieved from the wreckage until 4 October 1984. The maritime company was slow to admit that nuclear material was in the holds of the sunken vessel. The ecological group Greenpeace gave the alert. This insensitivity angered the public greatly and, according to Greenpeace, was proof of the insecurity in the ways that toxic materials are transported by sea.[54]

Union Carbide

Union Carbide received high marks for its quick response to the Bhopal disaster. The accident occurred on 3 December 1984. The same Monday, the company dispatched a team of experts, medical supplies, respirators, oxygen, and a US doctor with an extensive knowledge of methyl isocyanate. Production of methyl isocyanate was immediately stopped at the company's other facility in Institute, West Virginia, USA. On Thursday 5 December Warren M Anderson, the then Chairman and Chief Executive Officer of Union Carbide, flew to the plant site.[55]

AT&T

Another eloquent approach to an accident (not directly the result of environmental damage) occurred when a malfunctioning computer program led to a huge disruption of AT&T long distance telephone services. An apology by the Chairman, Robert E Allen, appeared across the country the next day in the press.[56] (See also Chapter 19.)

Certification

Probably the most concrete evidence that a firm is organized for environmental management and is doing its best to respect regulations is to obtain ISO-14001 certification, described in the next section.

ISO-14000 Certification series

Background of the ISO-14000 series

From the 1960s environmental laws were enacted in the United States and European countries that were rather an 'end of the pipe' approach: that is, firms were required to clean up when the environmental damage was done. In the USA, there were many different local, state, and national laws governing the environment, and in Europe, laws varied from country to country. These independent standards and regulations placed an onerous burden on firms regarding tracking regulation, monitoring compliance, not to mention cost. Further, they were viewed as potential barriers to international trade, particularly the unfair trade advantages gained by the less environmentally regulated countries.

In response to the growing concern among industry, government, and the public about the environment and inconsistent practices, an international team of environmental experts was convened in 1993 under the auspices of the International Organization for Standardization (ISO) to develop a series of environmental standards. These became know as the ISO-14000 series for the environment and as of 2001 include ISO-14001, 1410–12, 1421–24, ISO-1431, and ISO-1441–44. The development and the motor behind ISO-14000 was strongly influenced by the British

Standard BS-7750 for the environment, the European Communities' Eco-Management and Audit Scheme (EMAS), Chemical Industry Responsible Care, the International Chamber of Commerce (ICC), the Global Environmental Management Institute (GEMI), Coalition for Environmentally Responsible Economies (CERES), and, particularly, the ISO-9000 Quality Standards (see Chapter 4). The ISO-14000 standards are an effort to level the playing field in terms of barriers to trade and competition and to ensure that organizations have a consistent environmental programme in place. They do not have the force of law but companies will have to be certified ISO-14000 series as a prerequisite for doing business in those countries that have adopted the standard.[57]

ISO-14001, Environmental management system specifications and guidance standard

This standard is at present the only one against which a company can be certified. It provides requirements for developing an environmental management system that can be certified by an external party, termed a registrar, as well as practical guidance on system design and implementation. The standard requires that a company have a system that allows business units, division, and plants to meet environmental goals without continuous oversight from a corporate environmental department. This means that in the company:

- A formal environmental policy and standards or specification are communicated and understood by all employees.
- Environmental measures, objectives, and goals are developed and tracked.
- Legal requirements and compliance are monitored.
- Appropriate training is developed and implemented.
- Adequate documentation exists, and is controllable.
- Emergency preparedness and response have been developed and implemented.

Like all the other standards, ISO-14001 is voluntary but certification is expected to lower liability insurance and borrowing costs. For example, one environmental insurance underwriter in the US reports up to 25% reduction in certain liability insurance premiums to firms with sound environmental management systems.[58] Other advantages include decreased regularity oversight, enhanced ability to compete in the global marketplace, in the USA and Europe a stronger position to compete on government procurement projects, and, perhaps most importantly, provide greater environmental efficiencies and substantial cost savings.

ISO-1410–12 Environmental auditing standard

This section describes the general principles of environmental auditing, procedures for conducting environmental audits, and the qualification criteria for environmental auditors. Companies have to ensure that they not only have a corporate-level audit programme, but also an audit programme at the business unit/division, and the plant level, which requires performing regular, periodic self-audit assessments.

ISO-1421–24 Environmental labelling standard

This section describes the general requirements for various environmental seal and other label programmes and deals with all environmental product claims regardless of the media used. Companies using environmental product advertising, or making environmental claims for products would have to do so according to ISO standards. The objective of this standard is to prevent false advertising or claims.

ISO-1431 Environmental performance evaluation standard

This requires a company to evaluate its environmental management system and the various operational systems that should be in place. Companies must develop measures and goals to assess environmental performance such as the percentage reduction in air emissions, hazardous waste generated, reduction in energy, water, and other natural resource consumption, and the reduction in fines and penalties.

ISO-1441–44 Life cycle assessment standard

This section describes the principles and guidelines used to determine a products impact on the environment from the design stage through disposal (cradle to grave). This implies that firms should implement design for the environment (DFE) initiatives including training and revised engineering processes to study how their products impact the environment. This addresses such issues as finding benign or less hazardous substitutes for hazardous materials, redesigning manufacturing processes to use less energy, water or other natural resources, redesigning products and packaging for ease of disassembly, for reuse, and/or to use less materials that end up in landfills, and redesigning processes to reduce or eliminate discharges and waste.

Relationship between ISO-14000 and ISO-9000

The ISO-14000 is a series of international standards providing guidelines and requirements for environmental management systems (EMS) and the ISO-9000 is a series of international standards providing guidelines and requirements for quality management systems (QMS). Both series of standards were developed by ISO in Geneva. There are seven elements common to both series:

- structure and responsibility
- training, awareness, and competence
- document control
- records
- corrective and preventive action
- internal audits
- management review.

These similarities allow for greater efficiency when conducted in an integrated manner and ease of implementation of ISO-14000 for those facilities with an existing ISO-9000 certification (which is very often the case).

Summary of key elements

- Environmental issues are part of an organization's strategy but are also important in operations and supply chain management. Pollution levels are a function of population growth.

- Drivers for an environmental balance include the threat of industrial accidents, regulatory pressure from governments, an environmentally conscious public prompted by environmental organizations, economic advantages, and simply the moral, social, and ethical responsibility.

- Environmental issues are a global concern and all organizations in their operations should consider the concept of sustainable development, which is striking a balance between economic growth and environmental issues.

- Air pollution includes acid rain, fog, ozone damage by chlorofluorocarbons, smog, gaseous lead oxide from automobile exhausts, carbon dioxide as a component of the greenhouse gases, and radiation from nuclear power plants.

- Water pollution is the discharge of toxic products including chemicals, heavy metals, and other materials into rivers, lakes, and the sea. There are also concerns about their being dumped on land because the toxic products can percolate into water sources.

- Solid waste pollution is the dumping of untreated commercial, consumer, or industrial waste directly on land. Besides being an eyesore the concern is that toxic products from this waste eventually percolates into water sources.

- Noise is a pollutant, which in excess can impair hearing, reduce employee productivity, and cause physical damage. Sound is measured in decibels and the addition of ten decibels doubles the sound level.

- A product lifecycle analysis permits evaluation of the environmental impact of a product from its conception to its disposal at the end of its useful life.

- The BATNEEC principle brings in the element of cost. The concept is to select the best available technology not entailing excessive cost.

- Packaging contributes to solid waste pollution, particularly relevant when packaging adds little value to the product. Package redesign, new technology, and recycling or reuse of the packaging, are ways in which to minimize the environmental impact.

- In operations, transportation in the supply chain contributes to environmental damage. Firms are investigating new technology as a way of reducing environmental damage with the electric vehicle key in certain areas of road transportation.

- A cost–benefit analysis is a quasi-quantitative means of assessing the benefits of a project or operation when there are environmental issues to consider. Using this approach, when the benefits exceed the cost, the programme should proceed.

- Organizing for environmental management means setting up all the programmes, plans, and resources necessary to avoid or minimize environmental problems. One key element is to have in place an environmental audit.

- The ISO-14000 standards are a set of procedures to enable organizations to have a consistent programme to ensure environmental problems do not occur. There are similarities between the ISO-9000 series for quality and the ISO-14000 series for the environment.

- ISO-14001 is the environmental standard by which a company is certified. It provides requirements for developing an environmental management system and practical guidance on system design and implementation.

Notes and references

1. 'After the fire: How Sandoz dragged its corporate image from smoking ruins and rebuilt it', *Tomorrow*, July 1993, pp 10–15

2. 'Le Rhin pollué par accident en Suisse', *Chronique du 20ème siècle*, Larousse, Paris, 1990, p. 1287

3. 'Despite big cleanup, many Alaskans feel damage left by oil', *Wall Street Journal Europe*, 5 September 1991

4. *Chronique du 20ème siècle*, Larousse, Paris, 1990, p. 1175

5. STEINER, George A. and STEINER, John F., 'Asbestos litigation bankrupts Manville: A case study', *Business, Government and Society. A Managerial Perspective*, Random House, London, 1988, 5th edition, p. 44

6. SAWYER, Jacqueline, 'Acid rain, and air pollution', *Worldwide fund for nature*, Switzerland, 1989

7. MEDVEDEV, Gregori and TAURIS I. B., *Truth about Chernobyl*, Basic Books, London, 1991

8. *ICC: The Brundtland Report, The Greening of Enterprise: Business leaders speak out on environmental issues*, International Chamber of Commerce, June 1990, pp 219–27

9. CAWSEY, David, 'Apocalypse now?', *EEE Bulletin (The bulletin of the University Enterprise Training Partnership in Environmental Engineering Education)*, 2/98, p. 4–5.

10. 'Phasing out CFCs: The Vienna Convention and its Montreal Protocol', *Climate Change Fact Sheet* 224. http://www.unep.ch/iucc/fs224.html

11. 'Digging up trouble: Japan finds a legacy of tainted soil, and cleanup costs will be steep', *Business Week*, 8 January 2001, pp 22–3

12. 'Japan's green tinge', *The Economist*, 2 February 1991, p. 50

13. 'Breaking the toxic chain: Spain tries to limit damage at European marvel', *International Herald Tribune*, 5 May 1998

14. 'Polaroid: Case study', *Management Institute for Environment and Business*, 1997

15. 'Mobil Chemical Corp.: Case study', *Management Institute for Environment and Business*, 1997

16. 'McDonald's environmental strategy: Case studies', *Management Institute for Environment and Business*, 1997

17. 'Both ends of the pipe: *The Economist* survey', *The Economist*, 6 September 1990, p. 15

18. Renault VI, Lyon, France, is an example

19. 'Technology update, alternate energy', Texaco Co. report

20. 'Automobile ingredients', *Wall Street Journal Europe*, 6 May 1991

21. 'Reporter question: Can car move? It's blocking the Buffet', *Wall Street Journal*, 11 September 1991

22. 'Valerco propose une solution globale', *Lyon Fig-Eco*, 18 February 1991

23. 'This walking shoe has one foot in the landfill', *Wall Street Journal Europe*, 6 August 1991

24. 'Exxon launches pilot programs to recycle used motor oil', *Exxon News*, September 1991, p. 1

25. 'Procter & Gamble: Case study', *Management Institute for Environment and Business*, 1997

26. *Waste Minimisation Guide*, Institution of Chemical Engineers, UK, 1992

27. *Le pack: Guide pratique du marketing de l'emballage produits de grande consommation*, BSN Emballage, CEP Communications, Paris, 1987

28. NIELSON, Larry J., 'Measurement techniques in packaging waste management', *Proceedings of Corporate Environmental Management*, Washington DC, 9–10 January 1991

29. *The Economist*, 13 April 1991

30. LEAVERSUCH, Robert D., 'Pouch packaging', *Modern Plastics*, vol. 69, issue 6, June 1992, pp 64–5

31. 'Bottled up: EC builds momentum for recycling plastics, but few are listening', *Wall Street Journal Europe*, 15 October 1991

32. 'Waging war on waste', *International Management*, November 1991, p. 67

33. WHITE, David, 'On the road to zero emissions', *The Chemical Engineer*, 25 July 1996, pp 34–41

34. *The Economist*, 13 October 1990

35. 'Gee, your car smells terrific', *Time*, 22 July 1991, p. 38

36. 'Auto-industry briefs, Neste Oy', *Wall Street Journal Europe*, 17/18 May 1991

37. '55 miles per gallon: How Honda did it', *Business Week*, 23 September 1991

38. 'GM to sell green line of cars that can burn methanol, or gasoline', *Wall Street Journal*, 7 November 1991

39. 'Growing green fuel may be alternative to set-aside', *Financial Times*, 15 September 1992

40. 'Renault and Peugeot plan to develop electric car', *Financial Times*, 29 July 1992

41. 'Hydrogen car moves on to the horizon', *Financial Times*, 8 July 1992, p. 9

42. 'A computer in every dashboard', *International Herald Tribune*, 7 October 1997

43. 'Tankers designed to limit leaks', *Fortune*, 16 July 1990

44. 'Berlin approves tolls for trucks', *International Herald Tribune*, 16 August 2001, p. 2

45. GUPTA, Mahesh C., 'Environmental management and its impact on the operations function', *International Journal of Operations and Production Management*, vol. 15, no 8, 1995, pp 34–51

46. 'Cleaning up: Chemical firms find that it pays to reduce pollution at its source. By altering processes to yield less waste, they make production more efficient. Dow reuses a toxic solvent', *Wall Street Journal Europe*, 12 July 1991

47. 'Can you be sure of Shell?', *The Chemical Engineer*, 22 May 1997, p. 11

48. 'Can Cat keep out the watchdogs?', *Business Week*, 6 May 1996, p. 33

49. 'Breathing easy: Want clearer skies? Just turn pollution into a commodity. US promotes the trading of emissions certificates in global-warming pact. Money going up the stacks', *Wall Street Journal Europe*, 3–4 October 1997

50. MATHES, J. C., 'Three Mile Island: The management communication role', *Engineering Management International* (Netherlands), vol. 3, issue 4, January 1986, pp 261–8

51. BURNS, Christopher, 'Three Mile Island: The information meltdown', *Information Management Review*, vol. 1, issue 1, Summer 1985, pp 19–25

52. 'Environmental training for the process industries', *Institution of Chemical Engineers*, Rugby, England, 1993

53. YAGODA, Ben, 'Cleaning up a dirty image', *Business Month*, volume 135, issue 4, April 1990

54. *Chronique du 20ème siècle*, Larousse, Paris, 1990, p. 1246

55. STEINER, George A. and STEINER, John F. (1988) *Business, Government and Society. A Managerial Perspective*, Random House, London, 5th edition, p. 311

56. 'The day that every phone seemed off the hook', *Business Week*, 29 January 1990, pp 23–4

57. Tropea, Lawrence C., Vice-President, 'An opinion … ISO-14000 – a corporate perspective', *Global Environmental Services*, AMP Inc., PO Box 3608, MS21-20, Harrisburg, Pennsylvania 17105-3608, 1996. Internet: wysiwyg://81/http://www.dep.state.pa.us/dep/deputate/pollprev/ISO14000/amp.htm

58. http://www.iso14000-saic.com/path.htm (updated 5 May 2000)

Review and discussion topics

1. Environmental practices
Consider operations with which you are familiar, such as the following, and suggest areas where you think environmental practices could be improved:
(a) university
(b) medical centre
(c) supermarket
(d) library
(e) firm where you may have done some training.

2. Environmental groups
Environmental groups, most notably Greenpeace, are sometimes very harsh when it comes to attacking the activities of firms. For example, Shell Oil was castigated for its original decision to dump its Brent Spar oil platform in the Atlantic and then later, in 1996, for its exploration activities in Nigeria, which were connected by the government's execution of Ken Saro-Wiwa, a political activist. Sometimes, the environmental groups' arguments are not too sound but they usually convince the public. Do you believe there is the right balance environment/business operation in Europe? Discuss, and justify.

3. Lifecycle analysis
Perform a product lifecycle analysis on the following products:
(a) the car you drive
(b) your household comestibles during an average month (include food and non-food items, associated packaging, and the way it is purchased)
(c) the computer you use.

4. Traffic reduction law
In January 1997 a bill to reduce traffic and encourage cycling, walking, and public transportation, passed its second reading in the House of Commons. It was hoped that it would become law by 1998. List all the elements for a cost–benefit analysis for this type of situation.

5. Economics and operations
Some people believe that there should be an outright ban on the production of chlorofluorocarbons, oil-based paints,

nuclear power, and the transportation of nuclear waste. In distribution, forced use of train transport instead of the truck is often advocated. This is because of the environmental issues, even though the alternatives may not be economical. What is your opinion? Take into consideration any other operations you consider 'marginal' in the environmental sense.

6. Services and the environment

It is often assumed that it is the manufacturing firm that is responsible for environmental management. What do you believe the following service firms might do to improve their environmental management. Consider the whole chain of activities:

(a) Lufthansa Airlines
(b) Hilton Hotels
(c) Tesco supermarket
(d) London Business School
(e) local government.

Case study 5.1 Imprim

Situation

Imprim is a printing company, established in 1957, based in Slough, England with an operating area of some 10,000 square metres. Its product range includes:

- newspapers
- magazines
- publicity brochures
- catalogues
- publicity packaging
- folding boxes
- calendars
- administration and sales documents
- labels
- accounting forms.

It has a diverse client base, in both the service sector and manufacturing and they are one of the leading printers for the pharmaceutical and cosmetic industry.[*]

Imprim is principally an offset printer, that is, it uses the printing technique where an aluminium plate is etched according to the client requirements. The image from this plate is then transferred to a rubber-blanketed cylinder mounted onto the printing machine. This cylinder rotates at high speed and transfers the design to the printing paper that is fed through the press. Imprim's equipment includes individual sheet printing:

- 4 offset printers which can print in five colours in a 71 × 102 cm format
- 1 offset printer in two colours with a 71 × 102 cm format
- 1 offset printer in one colour of format 45 × 64 cm.

All the offset printers are Heidelberg machines from Germany that have built-in sensors to determine the paper feed rate, detect the rate of ink flow, and to monitor the photo alignment. Imprim also has three rotating presses where paper from large bobbins is fed through the press at high speed. Rotating presses produce at a higher rate than the page-by-page presses but the print quality is usually inferior.

The operation at Imprim is in three basic steps.

Preparation of the plate

Preparation of the plate involves engraving images onto metal plates. This is a process that rejects silver, hydroquinine (an inhibitor in biological purifiers), chromium, copper, and lead. The composite metal offset plates, which are discarded after use, produce hydrochloric acid and zinc chloride during the photoengraving process. The image from the metal plate is then transferred to a composite rubber plate that is also discarded after the printing process.

Printing

Paper, either page by page, or from bobbins, is fed through the printing press. In colour printing pigments contain heavy metals such as titanium, iron, and copper; also inflammable solvents are used containing alcohol, acetone, and esters. Other additives employed contain cobalt and volatile organic compounds (VOCs). Drying of the printed paper is by ultraviolet light and this produces toxic fumes and ozone products. In the printing process, the first part of the printing process is a trial that is discarded.

Once a printing operation has been completed, the machines, especially the rollers must be cleaned with rapid drying solvents applied using cotton cloths.

Finishing

After the printing, depending on the product, the paper is cut to size and trimmed on large guillotines. For those products that need binding, this is performed on machines where a resin of glue is applied mixed with solvents. After these operations, the customer order is shipped out on wooden pallets.

Required

A print shop is a service function, and individually they are small. However, if one considers Europe alone, there are literally thousands of printing firms. Discuss what you think some of the environmental problems associated with printing are using the information given here and your own knowledge, as a consumer of printed products. What needs be done to minimize environmental problems in this type of service operation?

*Based on reports by Anne-Caroline Ulrich and Régis Laffont, masters students 1993/94 at the Lyon Graduate School of Business.

Case study 5.2 The business traveller

Situation

Fred Seidel is in his office in London Docklands preparing for a business presentation in Los Angeles. He rough draughts his slides on PowerPoint and prints some 30 transparencies to see how they look. He then spends a couple of hours going over them making modifications in red ink. When he is satisfied he goes back to his portable computer and makes the modification in his file marked 'LA meeting'. When done, he prints off a master copy on white paper and then asks his secretary to make 20 copies each, plus a transparency set.

The next morning Fred picks up the transparency package that his secretary has made for him, and tosses it into his briefcase He hops into his BMW en route for Heathrow Airport. Fred's flight leaves at midday and he arrives in good time to park, and have a coffee and sandwich in the executive lounge. On the flight, Fred is offered a lunch of salmon and avocado salad. He picks at the plate, but after the sandwich at the airport he is not hungry and so he leaves most of the food and settles in to go over his presentation. When the next meal is offered, two hours before landing, Fred is fast asleep.

At Los Angeles International Airport, Fred picks up a rental car and drives to his hotel, a Hilton, close to Santa Monica, a beach city some 30 minutes' drive from Los Angeles. On the way, as he has not eaten much on the plane, he stops at a McDonald's for a hamburger, French fries and coke.

By the time Fred gets to the hotel it is 8pm. He checks in and takes the elevator to his room on the second floor. The room is cold from the intensity of the air conditioning. Unable to open the window, as they are permanently fixed, he turns the air conditioning off, drops his bags, and goes down to the hotel lobby for a drink.

The next morning, after a shower, Fred goes down for the buffet breakfast. He leaves the hotel at 8.30am for his meeting in downtown Los Angeles. There are 15 people sitting at the conference table, and after giving each person a package of his transparencies, Fred gives a very well-received presentation. He is hosted for lunch at a restaurant at the nearby Bonaventure Hotel. After lunch, the team returns to the meeting room to go over some points on Fred's presentation, and the meeting winds up at about 4pm. Feeling pretty tired because of jet lag, Fred drives back to his hotel and takes a shower. Before dinner, he uses the hotel's copying machine and then drops some clothing off at the hotel cleaners. At the restaurant, he meets a colleague and they dine together. At noon the following day he has a flight scheduled for New York to make another presentation.

Required

The business traveller, and there are thousands of them, uses a host of services, from car rental agencies, airlines, restaurants, hotels, cleaning services, copying services, etc. What are some of the environmental issues that the operations of these services have to deal with? Where appropriate, consider their operations on a global perspective taking a lifecycle approach.

Selected further reading

ALLENBY, Braden R. and GRAEDEL, Thomas E. (1995) Industrial Ecology, Prentice-Hall.

JACKSON, Suzan L. (1997) The ISO 14001 Implementation Guide: Creating an Integrated Management System, Wiley.

KANHOLM, Jack (1998) ISO 14000 Requirements, 61 Requirements Checklist and Compliance Guide (AQA ISO 14000 Series), AQA Press.

KINSELLA, John, MCCULLY, Annette D. and BURNGASSER, David (illustrator) (1999) Handbook for Implementing an ISO 14001 Environmental Management System: A Practical Approach, EMCON Publishing.

SACHS, Wolfgang, LOSKE, Reinhard and LINZ, Manfred (1998) Greening the North: A Post-Industrial Blueprint for Ecology and Equity, Zed Books.

An extensive listing of further reading can be found on the website.

What's on the web?

Further learning resources are available to lecturers and students at www.supplychain-online.com, including the following which are specific to *An environmental balance*:

Resource	Subject
Chapter overview	An environmental balance
More further reading	An environmental balance

Part II

Design in operations management

Part II explains that the supply chain is a system and has to be designed so that it meets the strategic objectives of the firm. These key design elements for the supply chain system are developed in terms of design of the product, process design and the operations network, human resources in the system design, and design of the facility layout.

'The rung of a ladder was never meant to rest upon, but only to hold a man's foot long enough to enable him to put the other somewhat higher.'

Thomas H Huxley

Part II: Design in operations management

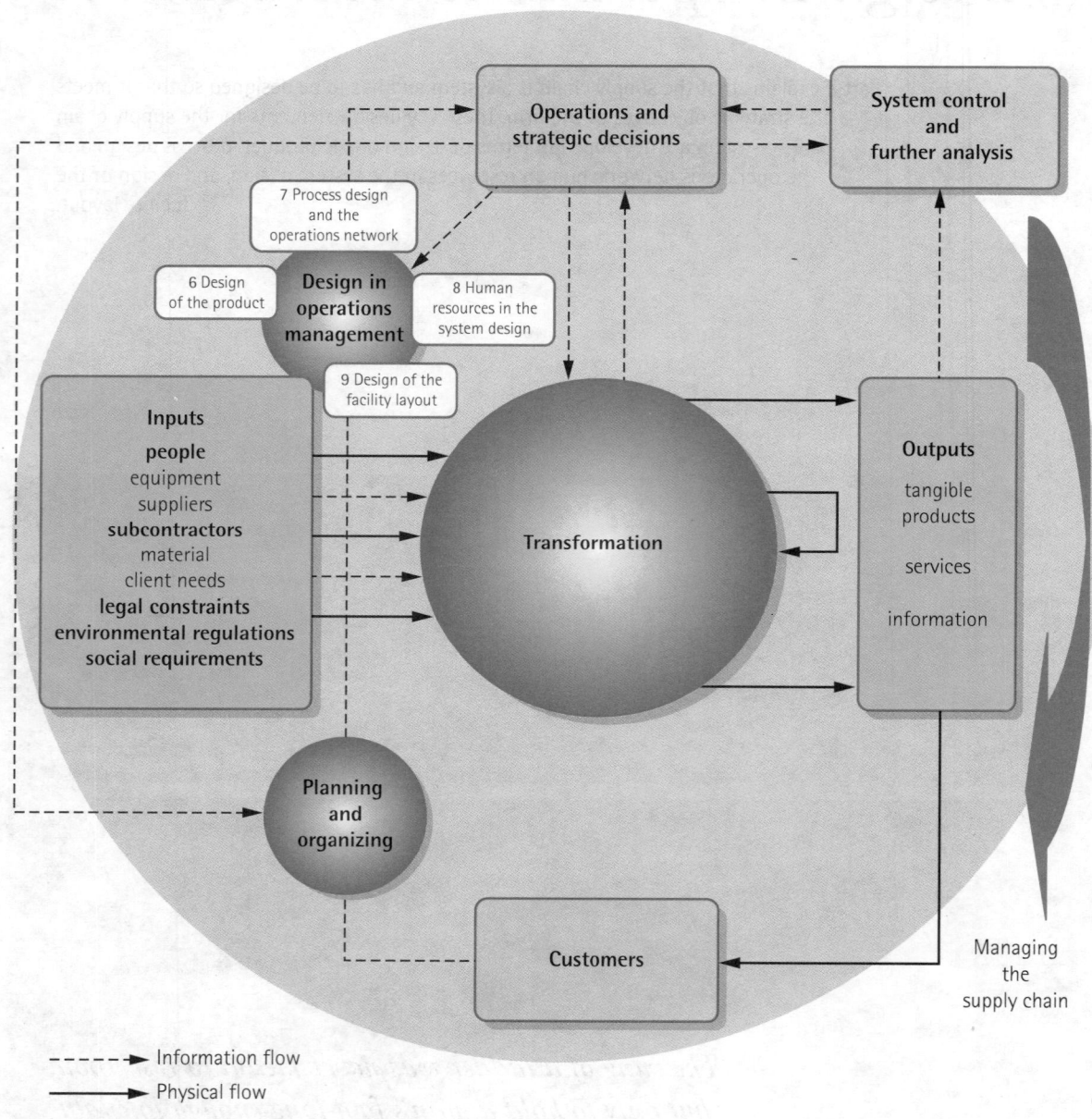

Operations and strategic decisions

System control and further analysis

7 Process design and the operations network

6 Design of the product

Design in operations management

8 Human resources in the system design

9 Design of the facility layout

Inputs

people
equipment
suppliers
subcontractors
material
client needs
legal constraints
environmental regulations
social requirements

Transformation

Outputs

tangible products

services

information

Planning and organizing

Customers

Managing the supply chain

- - - - → Information flow
———→ Physical flow

6 *Design of the product*

The product

The end product, when delivered, or made available to the customer represents the end of part, or the complete integrated supply chain. The product is the culmination of an operation, or perhaps a project, and is what the firm, or organization has been targeting to achieve. To arrive at this stage perhaps lengthy and complex supply chains have been involved. The product is designed to satisfy a certain need and normally is sold in a competitive environment and so the product's success is very much driven by market forces and must compete on cost, quality in the broad sense, and delivery time. Products can be services or tangible goods as the following illustrate.

Products from service organizations

Products in services may be those provided by financial institutions, travel companies, hotel chains, telecommunications firms, universities or other educational institutions, etc., and might include:

- a two-week vacation package in Tahiti
- a rail service between Paris and London
- the collection and disposal of garbage
- a university MBA programme
- a hotel room with breakfast and dinner included
- a phone card that provides worldwide telephone access
- a financial product offering banking, credit card service, and stock transactions
- legal advice on a corporate merger programme.

Service products may also be a combination of products from various organizations. As an illustration, a holiday firm might offer the two-week vacation package in Tahiti, including the round-trip airfare (subcontracted with the airline), accommodation (subcontracted with a hotel chain), and car rental (subcontracted with a car rental agency).

Products from manufacturing firms

Tangible manufactured products can be classified into industrial products, sometimes referred to as intermediate goods, which are sold to other companies in a business-to-business transaction. Alternatively, they may be consumer products that are purchased at retail stores by catalogue, or through a website. It is the consumer goods which are at the very end of the integrated supply chain, where, generally, industrial goods are the intermediate parts of an integrated supply chain.

Industrial products

An industrial product is a finished item, X, made at Company A and then purchased by Company B. At Company B the product may be used as is, or used in the assembly of another product, Y, that may then subsequently become a consumer product. Examples of industrial products are:

- sheet steel used in the manufacture of automobiles, washing machines, or steel cabinets or copper wire used in electrical appliances, transmission cables, or switchgear
- starter motors used in the assembly of motorbikes, trucks, or automobiles

- glass bottles used for wine, beer, and soft drinks
- extruded polypropylene used in the manufacture of plastic toys, container boxes, or automobile components
- flow meters used by power companies for measuring fluid flow
- airplanes purchased by airline companies
- oil drilling rigs purchased by firms such as EssoMobil, Texaco, Shell, or BP-Amoco.

In some cases, an industrial good never becomes a consumer good as would be the case for an airplane, a printing press, or a communications satellite.

Consumer products

Consumer products are those that arrive at the end of the supplier chain through a business-to-consumer transaction and would include, for example:

- automobiles purchased through a dealer
- washing machines, refrigerators, or other kitchen appliances purchased though an electrical goods store
- computers, printers, diskettes, paper, or related items
- yoghurt, chocolate bars, milk, and bread from a supermarket.

For economic purposes, consumer products are also further classified into durable goods such as automobiles, appliances and audio-visual products, and non-durable items, which include food and clothing.

Standard products

A standard product is one destined for the mass market and there is essentially no discernible difference between one product and the next. They can again be subdivided into manufactured and service products as follows.

Manufactured products

- Refrigerators, televisions, washing machines or other durable consumer goods
- a carton of milk, a roast chicken, a bottle of Heineken beer or other non-durable consumer goods
- a roll of sheet steel, a 25 kg sack of extruded polyethylene, 200 metres of a textile or other industrial products.

Services

To categorize service operations as standardized is difficult, as, by their very nature, they involve working directly with the clients who have their own particular needs. However, some almost standardized service products are:

- a hamburger sold at a McDonald's restaurant
- the train service between Brussels and London
- the service provided at a Formule 1 hotel
- an appendectomy at a medical centre (although there would be some differences according to the patient's physique and health).

Characteristics in relation to the operating environment

Standard manufactured products exhibit a high degree of uniformity. In general, the following are some characteristics of standard products relative to customized products:

- They exhibit a low unit cost.
- They are produced in high volumes or, conversely, a low cycle or production time.
- They use standardized methods in their production.
- They are produced without receiving specific customer orders.
- They are *produced to stock*, meaning that, from a planning point of view, a storage of goods is kept in inventory.
- Since they are produced to stock they are available *off the shelf* or essentially zero delivery time since the supplier maintains an inventory of these goods.

Services may not have the same characteristics, especially where inventory is not involved. However, they do, relative to customized products, have a low unit cost.

Customized products

Customized products are those that are specifically made to suit a certain customer's tastes, requirements, or needs as the following demonstrate.

Services

- In medical services, a face and nose change in plastic surgery.
- A training programme developed for a certain firm.
- The travel arrangements for the prime minister.
- The repair of an automobile.
- A firm's publicity brochure.

Manufactured products

- Durable consumer products would include say an architect-designed house or a sofa made to a special size with a special fabric.
- Non-durable consumer goods might be a custom-made suit or a wedding dress.

- Industrial products would include an auxiliary backup power system for a factory, a printing press, or a construction derrick.

Characteristics in relation to the operating environment

Since customized products are produced to specific customer specifications, then, relative to standardized products:

- They have a high unit cost.
- They are produced in low volumes and often have a high cycle time.
- The production is planned only when a specific customer order is received.
- They may use special production methods, or materials, in their manufacture.
- They necessitate a certain delivery, or lead time, between receipt of order and delivery of finished product to the client.
- The orders appear on the producer's books as backlog, as there is no inventory of the product.

(See also Chapter 12 for a detailed discussion on backlog.)

A project is a product

A project is also a 'product' but is special in the sense that it is unique, or one off and thus by this very definition it is a customized item. A project is not in the strict sense an operation since it is not continuous but in order to execute a project, many of the operations management functions come into play. Major projects can involve very lengthy and complex supply chains. The following gives some illustrations of projects (and for more detail see Chapter 18).

Construction project

A construction project is a tangible *product* designed according to certain specifications, for special needs, and under unique conditions. Examples would include:

- an oil refinery designed to process Arabian crude oil
- a dam over the Rhône River, France
- a factory to build BMW automobiles in the USA
- construction of the tunnel under the Channel between France and England
- construction of the TGV (train à grande vitesse) terminus in Lyon, France
- construction of Los Angeles Airport, California
- the development of the Docklands region in London.

Intangible projects

Intangible projects include:

- The installation of a complex computer network to handle all the supply chain activities, the billing, and sales activity of a firm.
- Modifying all the post office systems so that they can handle addresses with a numerical postal code.
- Changing all the computer codes in banking statements, credit cards, and loan payments so that they could accept the first two digits, 20 after the year 2000 rather than the earlier two digits of 19.
- All activities involved in introducing the euro into the 12 Eurozone countries in January 2002.

Study projects

A project may also be a specific activity, service, or study for an operation, carried out internally by the manufacturing firm or service organization concerned. There may not be always be a tangible product at the termination of this type of project and usually these types of projects are of short duration, and are not excessively expensive. For example:

- A project to study reducing the setup times and implementing SMED of a cutting machine (see also Chapter 15).
- A project to simplify the manufacture of a laser printer.
- A project to reduce the lead time (time from order to delivery) of a particular manufactured product.
- A project to study the best distribution network for a firm.

Product lifecycle

The product lifecycle is the analogy between a product's evolution and the human lifecycle, which includes development in the mother's womb, birth or introduction into the world, growth to the adult stage, maturity, and finally decline and death. The profile for these phases relating it to products is illustrated in Figure 6.1, and the characteristics are discussed in this section.

Development

All products go through a development period prior to commercialization, as illustrated by the curve in Figure 6.1. In this development phase, the product is undergoing conception, design, prototype tests, and

Figure 6.1 Product lifecycle in terms of revenues, costs, and profit

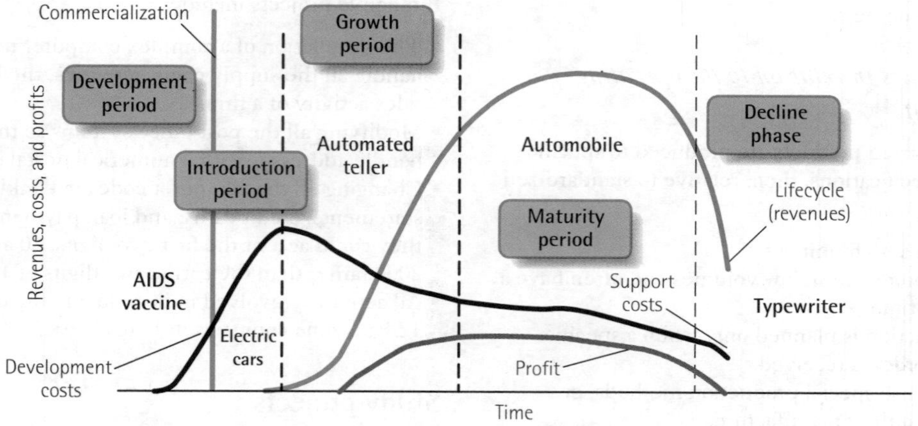

modifications prior to market launch. Principally, this phase would involve research and design personnel, although operations people would normally be involved to be sure that the product can be successfully manufactured. In this phase there are no revenues, only costs. The time for the development phase depends on the type of product. For example, searching for a successful AIDS vaccine is taking years, whereas the development of some computer programs may take just a matter of months. Further details of product development are presented in a later section.

Introduction

The introduction phase is where the consumer starts to see the product as it is commercialized and launched onto the market. From this point on, operations personnel are heavily involved in all the activities to produce the product for expected market demand. Initially, sales may be slow as customers get used to accepting the product or the time involved for the advertising efforts to reach the public. Revenues start to be generated at this stage, which offsets costs. The principal cost would now be production costs, support costs to market and distribute, and after-sales service. Some examples of products in the introduction phase might include electric cars, exotic vacations, video conferencing, direct electronic banking, website purchasing, and certain computer products.

Growth

The growth period is when the product is well accepted on the market, revenues are growing rapidly, and support costs decline somewhat as the product is somewhat self-marketing. At some point in the growth

period, total revenues will have offset the cumulated development costs, and the successful product will start to show an overall profit. Operations play a dominant role in this phase trying to keep production in pace with the customer demand. Examples of products in this period might be automated tellers, cruise vacations, compact discs, personal computers, bullet trains, snow surfing, and Formule 1-type hotels.

Maturity

The product in the maturity phase is where its existence is never given a second thought (although, for example, one might ask from time to time, 'How did we do without plastic bags?'). Products are the most numerous in this phase, the automobile, credit cards, fast food, airplane travel, and plastic automobile components. Profits continue to be generated here, although they are extremely affected by other competitive products in the marketplace. Operations is dominant in this phase but fluctuating demand may make planning somewhat complicated leading to lean production periods. Examples of products in the maturity phase include automobiles, radios, colour television, airline travel, and fast food services.

Decline and death

Decline and death is when the product reaches the end of its life and is eventually withdrawn. This may be because of technological innovations such as the following:

- 33 rpm records and tapes being replaced by compact discs and digital recordings
- the typewriter by the word processor

Industry insight 6.1

The Airbus A380

Airbus Industries of Toulouse, in France, is hoping to be the leader in the sales of commercial airplanes ahead of Boeing, USA. Until recently Boeing was the only manufacturer of jumbo jets, with its celebrated 747. Airbus now has firm orders for its new A380 that is due to enter into service in 2006. Although the A380 will be almost 50% larger than the Boeing 747-400, which carries up to 413 passengers, all the airlines that have placed orders for the A380 plan to operate it with only 525 to 550 seats in three classes. This will give passengers plenty of room to get up and walk around and allow space for lounges, cafeterias, baby-sitting space, a pub, a casino, bedrooms, showers, treadmills for the exercise enthusiasts, a duty-free store, and a business centre. These are the sort of amenities to be found on the *Queen Elizabeth II* cruise ship. Until now air travel obliges people to remain seated during the flight but the new Airbus 380 is hoping to encourage people to move around and using the plane like a flying 'holiday ship'. This would be a complete innovation in air travel.

Airbus is assembling a full-size mock-up of the cabin, which is a prototype to see how the interior of the plane would function. The first class section has a huge bar and lounge in front and vast Pullman seats that swivel 360° and can be turned into a bed, a cocooned entertainment centre, or an office. It is the kind of luxury currently found on only the most exclusive executive jets. The first impression from this mock-up is of entering a large ferry, not a plane. From a spacious entry area, a double staircase leads to the upper deck and in the cabin there is a cocktail bar under the staircase. The ability to move around will reduce the risk of deep vein thrombosis that is a concern on long haul flights. However, since the plane will have an operating range of some 8000 nautical miles (13,000 km) lasting some 18 hours there will be space for a small medical centre staffed by a qualified crewmember and linked to a doctor on the ground through satellite communications. With all the space and amenities, Airbus is hoping to put the fun back into flying and at the same time earn between $300,000 to $500,000 a day for the airplane operator.

Adapted from: 'A peek at the Airbus giant', *International Herald Tribune*[1]

- travellers' cheques by the international credit card
- the biplane by the single-wing airplane
- mechanical watches by quartz battery-driven watches
- the slide rule by mechanical calculators and then electronic calculators.

Economics, perhaps modified by technological innovations, may herald declines such as automatic teller machines (ATMs) replacing many teller-assisted bank cash withdrawals, transatlantic sea crossings by air travel, and hotel valet services such as porters opening car doors, carrying luggage, and maids turning down the bed at night have disappeared in all but the most expensive hotels. Governments might step in and ban a product such as asbestos, oil-based paints, leaded gasoline, chlorofluorocarbons, cotton nightdresses, and DDT. Finally, customers' fad changes might herald the decline, albeit temporarily, such was the case of the min-skirt in the 1960s and, more recently, alcohol-free beer.

In the decline phase, operations management activities essentially stop, although for manufactured products often an inventory of parts is maintained, usually for ten years, to service those products still in use. Not all products die or pass through the decline phase, but rest in the mature phase, perhaps as a result of continuous innovation and redesign through technological advancements or repackaging. One product which has been on the market for some 100 years is aspirin that is still one of the most widely sold over-the-counter drugs, whose base formula of acetyl salicylic acid has barely changed. Similarly, there is the automobile and the airplane (if dated from the first powered flight by the Wright Brothers in 1903). The innovation and redesign of one airplane is illustrated in Industry insight 6.1.

Technology in product design

Product design changes, new products, and the decline of existing ones have come about because of new technological innovations particularly the development of new materials and computer-aided design systems (CAD). Manufactured products have mushroomed because of the development of cheaper new materials, often which have characteristics superior to the materials they have replaced, coupled to the ease of design using CAD systems. Service industries have been able to grow often as a result of new products as, for example, fibre optic cables in telecommunications, inexpensive building materials for the hotel and resort industry, durable plastics and the computer chip for banking and credit cards. The following highlights some of the major new developments since the turn of the century and the appendix gives further information.

Petrochemicals

Petrochemicals are the basis for almost all plastics. The world's first petrochemical, isopropyl alcohol, was discovered by the French chemist, Pierre Berthelot, in 1855 and was first commercialized in 1920 by the Standard Oil Company of New Jersey (now ExxonMobil). It was originally used as an additive in gasoline which was particularly important as, in the 1920s, Henry Ford was introducing his Ford T, the first assembly line-built automobile. The commercialization of isopropyl alcohol led to the rapid growth of the petrochemical industry whose products are used in clothes, cars, televisions, videocassette recorders (VCRs), videotapes, surgical supplies, tyres, food packaging, and plastics. Isopropyl alcohol is also used in pharmaceuticals, cleaning fluids, printing inks, and thinners for paint and lacquers.[2]

Plastics

Plastic is a generic term for synthetic substances that are replacements for inorganic-based materials such as metals, ceramics, cement, and the like. Just about every product today contains some plastic component if they are not made entirely of plastic. Plastic development probably started around World War I, when the Germans, cut off from supplies of natural rubber, worked on the development of synthetic equivalents. In 1936 the firm of IG Farben presented the first synthetic rubber at the Berlin automobile show. About the same time Imperial Chemical Industries (ICI) of Britain developed the first polyethylene, or polythene, by the polymerization of ethylene. This material is widely used in packaging, moulded materials, pipes, electric wire insulation, metal coatings, upholstery etc. In 1938, Du Pont of the USA commercialized nylon, a polyamide discovered by W H Carothers. Parachutes used in World War II were one of the first nylon products made on a large scale, which is now used in all branches of the textile industry. In 1938 polystyrene was commercialized and used as insulation material in refrigerators and air conditioners, packaging, wall tiles, and food utensils. Silicones, used in rubber surface treatment for glass and textiles, first appeared in 1943. In 1957 polypropylene, used for automobile moulded parts, appliances, cordage, bottles, started to be developed in large quantities. Today the number of different plastics made from different chemical compounds is almost infinite.

Composites

Composites are alloyed materials that have properties superior to the individual constituents from which they are made. For example, fibreglass is made from a film of glass and a synthetic resin and it is more durable and does not shatter like the glass from which it is derived. A popular composite material is Kevlar, which is an aramide fibre development in 1965 by Du Pont and commercialized since 1972. Kevlar is very light, resists corrosion, does not burn, and can be easily machined. It is used in making the shells of electrical cables, protective clothing, sail boat hulls, and has significant use in the automobile, aeronautics, and aerospace industry. A perhaps unexpected and growing market for Kevlar is for bulletproof vests for police and other security personnel. This material has proved so strong in that it has not only saved the lives of police officers from bullets but also from being struck by a lighting bolt, from getting hit by shrapnel from a pipe bomb, and also from being run over by a Honda Accord automobile.[3]

Ceramic fibre composite materials play an important role in the electrical and electronics industry because of their insulating properties. Composite polymer materials are used in the automobile industry for bumpers, radiator grills, wheel hubs, and the hardware in the computer industry. Carbon fibre material is used in the sports industry notably for skis, tennis rackets, racing bike wheels, and golf clubs. New alloys of metals, for example aluminium–lithium, have been developed which are extremely light and are used in the space industry.

Computer-aided design

Computer-aided design (CAD) was developed in the 1970s and is universally used today. It is a special interactive graphic image system on computer terminals, which enables products, equipment, and processes to be designed, and modified, in three dimensions.

CAD provides designers with what word processors give to writers, that is, the freedom to make changes without having to remake the whole thing. The automobile, aeronautics, and engineering and construction industry makes extensive use of CAD. The use of CAD systems enables firms to make design changes quickly. It also enables designs to be sent to suppliers or clients over the Internet for their approval or modification without relying on blueprint drawings. All of this helps minimize errors and the time-to-market of new products.

Development of the product

Market growth

Technology changes rapidly, products die, and thus for firms to grow in terms of profit and/or market share their strategy includes continually developing, innovating and bringing out new products. Firms such as General Electric, Minnesota Mining and Manufacturing, Saatchi and Saatchi (advertising), Microsoft, and British Airways are continually introducing new products or services, which makes these firms leaders in their field. A classic example is General Electric, USA.

General Electric

General Electric (GE) of the USA is one of the most profitable companies and in terms of market capitalization, at $477.4 billion as of the end of 2000, it is also the world's biggest.[4] Its growth has been based principally on using new technology to develop new products.[5] The precursor of GE was created by Thomas Edison in 1878 after the creation of the electric light bulb. Some milestones in its product development can be seen in Table 6.1.

Today GE is the world leader in:[6]

- production of electric motors
- construction of locomotive engines and railway stock
- aircraft engines
- medical instruments in imagery and diagnostics
- turbine motors and nuclear and thermal power plants
- industrial control systems
- plastic products for various industrial sectors
- information network systems
- television through NBC and the CNBC news network
- credit leasing financial services.

Table 6.1 Milestones in the history of GE

1895	Building of the world's biggest steam locomotive weighing 90 tons
1905	Invention of the electric toaster
1915	Development of the refrigerator
1932	Development of the dishwasher
1942	Production of the aircraft engine for the war effort
1954	Conception of the first turbine motor for the airplane
1978	Building of the largest nuclear power station at Tokaï-Mura in Japan
1986	Development of television networking after acquiring RCA which included NBC
1987	Launch into medical imagery after an exchange with Thomson, France

General Electric is in second place for neon and incandescent lighting and kitchen appliances including washing machines, dishwashers, and refrigerators.

In order continually to grow in the market many companies have product development departments, and new product managers who follow a product from conception to commercialization. The stages in new product development are summarized in Figure 6.2, and reviewed in the following sections.

Generation of new product ideas

As illustrated in Figure 6.3 in order to start the process of developing new products, companies solicit opinions from various quarters.

Customers

Customers are an important source of new product ideas as they are the end users of the product. This is particularly the case for industrial customers, as they 'know what they want'. Very often for industrial products the customer is involved in the design and development such as in airplanes, electrical switchgear for the power plant industry, or plastic components for new automobile models.

Sales staff

Company salespeople are continually in contact with clients and as such often have good notions of what type of new products would sell well in the marketplace. Salespeople are motivated in this respect since if they can persuade their company to develop new products to satisfy their customers, then one of their main objectives has been met.

Competitors

Often a competitor introduces a new product on the market (a proactive strategy), and another firm introduces a similar product on the market at a later period (reactive strategy). For example, US automobile companies introduced compact cars onto the market, following the successful Japanese introduction, particularly by Nissan and Toyota, in the 1980s.

Top management

Top managers who have spent many years with the company, and also have many outside contacts, are another source of new product ideas.

Product development team

Product development teams have the role to develop new products. As a starting point they might use the

Figure 6.2 Steps and activities in product development

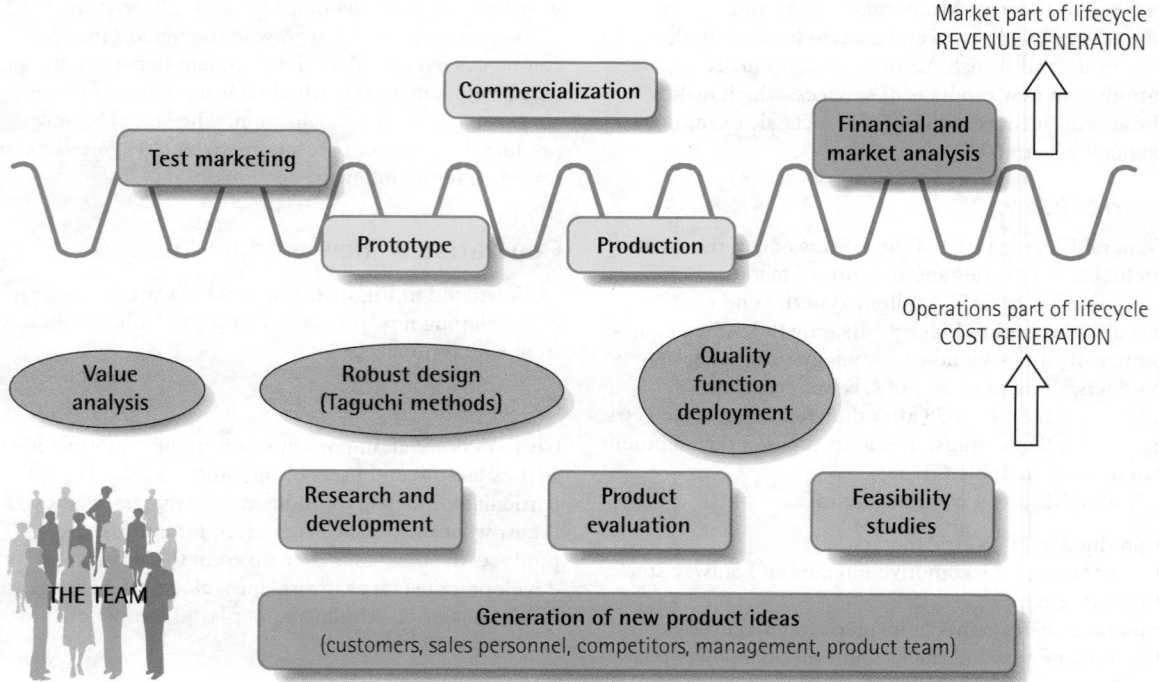

Market part of lifecycle
REVENUE GENERATION

Commercialization

Test marketing

Financial and
market analysis

Prototype

Production

Operations part of lifecycle
COST GENERATION

Value
analysis

Robust design
(Taguchi methods)

Quality
function
deployment

Research and
development

Product
evaluation

Feasibility
studies

THE TEAM

Generation of new product ideas
(customers, sales personnel, competitors, management, product team)

Figure 6.3 Generation of new product ideas

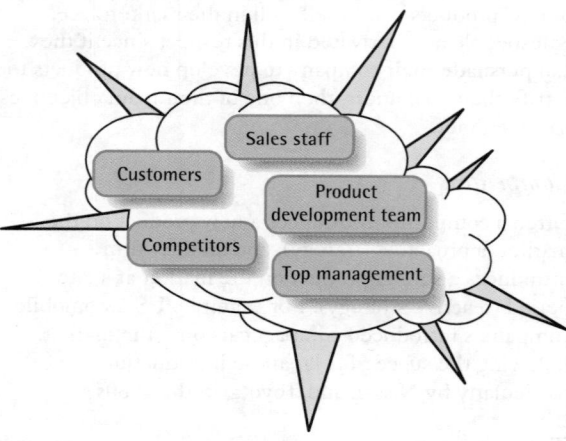

Sales staff

Customers

Product
development team

Competitors

Top management

technique of brainstorming for coming up with new ideas. Brainstorming is a process where a small group of people in the company, often from different departments, meets and without any inhibitions or preconceived notions, put forward their ideas for new products. In brainstorming:

• Participants should be free to express their thoughts, and should not criticize others.

• Members of the group should be encouraged to come up with as many ideas as possible. The logic being that the greater the number of ideas, the more likelihood that a workable one will be achieved.

• Members should feel free to build upon one another's ideas. It is often the combination of inputs, particularly when members are from diverse backgrounds, which lead to the development of a new product.

Research and development

Many companies have research and development departments which are continually testing new ideas or performing experimental work. Firms such as Du Pont have research departments that devote time to developing new concepts without at first necessarily having an immediate commercial objective. This comes later. The development and subsequent wide use of nylon, discussed earlier, is a classic example.

Product evaluation

The product evaluation step involves expanding on the new product ideas, and also eliminating those products which may not be viable in the long run, or do not fit the company's strategic objectives. A product evaluation

Figure 6.4 **Product evaluation matrix**

	Weighting importance	Product rating					Total	Maximum possible	%
		Poor 1	2	3	4	Excellent 5			
Potential sales revenues	8			X			24	40	60.00
Competitive products	8		X				16	40	40.00
Production costs	6				X		24	30	80.00
Product life	6					X	30	30	100.00
Time-to-market	5			X			15	25	60.00
Environmentally friendly	5			X			15	25	60.00
Patent possibilities	4					X	20	20	100.00
Raw material availability	3				X		12	15	80.00
Total							156	225	69.33

matrix is an analytical tool that can be used for such an evaluation (see Figure 6.4). In the matrix shown, a numerical weight is assigned to various selection criteria according to their importance. The criteria are now discussed.

Potential sales revenues

Companies are in business to make money. Thus in bringing out new products the revenue-generating possibilities is perhaps one of the most important criteria. Here it has been assigned the highest value.

Competitive products

Whether there are competitive products on the market is also an important criterion. If competitors exist it makes sales penetration more difficult, puts a constraint on gaining market share, and as such makes marketing costs higher. Burger King, of the UK, pulled out of the fast food market in Paris in 1997 since it said it could no longer compete with McDonald's and Quick (Belgium) restaurants which were in the same market sector.

Production costs

For a given market price, high production costs for the product will eat into profits and so is an important criterion. However, if the product is relatively unique and successful, a firm might be able to charge a high price to offset production costs, and to recoup development costs. This was the case with Texas Instruments when they brought out their new electronic calculator in the 1970s. At that time, there were no real competing products and so, initially, they were able to charge a very high price.

Product life

The product life has to be a consideration since if the life is short, there may not be time to generate sufficient

revenues to make the product financially attractive to the firm.

Time-to-market

The time-to-market represents the elapsed time from product conception to when it is available to the consumer. This is important if, for example, there are competing products on the market, since the first one to appear will have a greater possibility of obtaining a larger market share. Automobile companies are very conscious of this and the classic example is the small automobile introduced by the Japanese into the US market in the 1970s. Competitive US companies (General Motors, Ford, and Chrysler) were very slow in bringing out competing models and thus permanently lost market share.

Environmentally friendliness

Environmentally friendliness, discussed in more detail in Chapter 5, is the criterion that ensures the product will be accepted both according to government regulations and consumer acceptance. It might apply to herbicides, drugs, engines, or other products that might pollute, but also the safety element. Sears, a US retailer, withdrew a toy dart game from the market in the 1980s after a wrongly thrown dart injured a child.

Patent possibilities

Patent possibilities are a consideration when a new product is introduced, as a patent would give a certain amount of protection against competitive products. However, applying for a patent is expensive, and fighting a patent infringement can be costly. The textile/clothing industry is notorious for idea copying. Even though taking out a patent is possible, companies rarely do because of the expense, and also due to the short duration of clothing and fabric styles and fashions.

Raw material availability

This criterion is a consideration if the product uses raw materials or components that might one day be in short supply. With the globalization of markets this is not often a problem, although from time to time this might apply when suppliers of raw materials have badly planned their production capacity.

Once the criteria for product evaluation have been established, those involved in the product development, or other experts, would assign a score for each of the criteria. The weighted total score for each criterion is determined from which is calculated a total weighted average. In the matrix shown the total points possible are 225 of which the score is 156 or 69% of the maximum. To accept or reject a product would depend on the policy of the company. For example, a company might be prepared to go ahead with those products that score, say, 65% or more of the possible weighted average.

Feasibility studies

Feasibility studies in new product design examine the ease (or difficulty) of producing a product and its commercialization. It might include resolving such issues as:

- Are the necessary human resource skills available?
- Is there sufficient capacity in the present facility?
- Is there the financial capability to invest?
- Can the needed technology changes be incorporated?

Quality function deployment

Quality function deployment (QFD) is an analytical method introduced in Japan in 1966,[7] and used by such companies as Toyota, Matsushita Electronics, and Nippon Steel, to ascertain that a new product or service meets customer requirements. Its objective is to develop a design aimed at satisfying the consumer, and then translating these requirements into design targets used throughout the development and production stage of the product. Quality function deployment is sometimes referred to as the 'house of quality' because of its shape, or also as the 'voice of the customer', because of its purpose. The concept is now illustrated.

Electric weed trimmer

An electric weed trimmer is a gardening tool used for trimming weeds that are growing in places where a

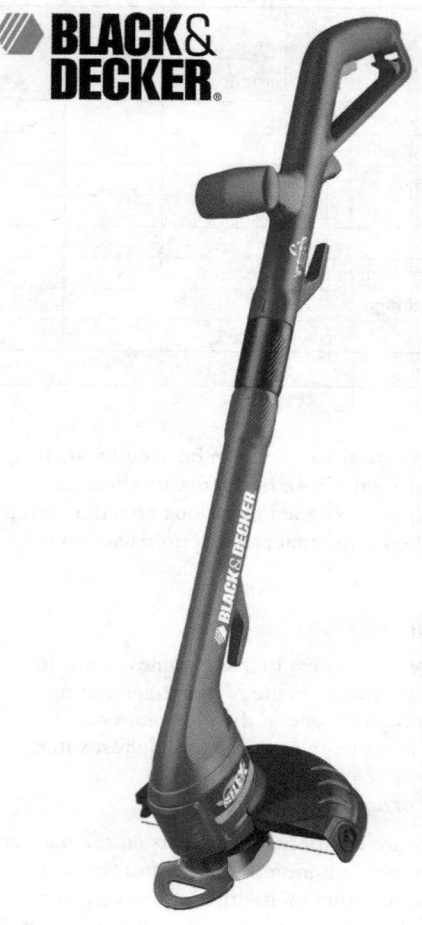

Figure 6.5 Black & Decker electric weed trimmer

lawnmower cannot be used. The weeds are trimmed by a plastic thread that spins at a high velocity and literally decapitates the weeds. There are several manufacturers; a model by Black & Decker is illustrated in Figure 6.5.[8]

A QFD diagram for this product is illustrated in Figure 6.6. The left-hand column is what the customer desires in the product according to a rating (comfortable to hold through to quiet operation). The information on the top line above the matrix is the firm's design proposals to meet the customer requirements. The degree of strength of these designs, with the customer wants, is then indicated in the body of the matrix. For example, there is a strong correlation between quiet operation and a sealed insulated motor. The roof of the house illustrates the relationship between each of the design capabilities of the firm. In this illustration, high-speed rotation has a medium

Figure 6.6 Quality function deployment for electric weed trimmer

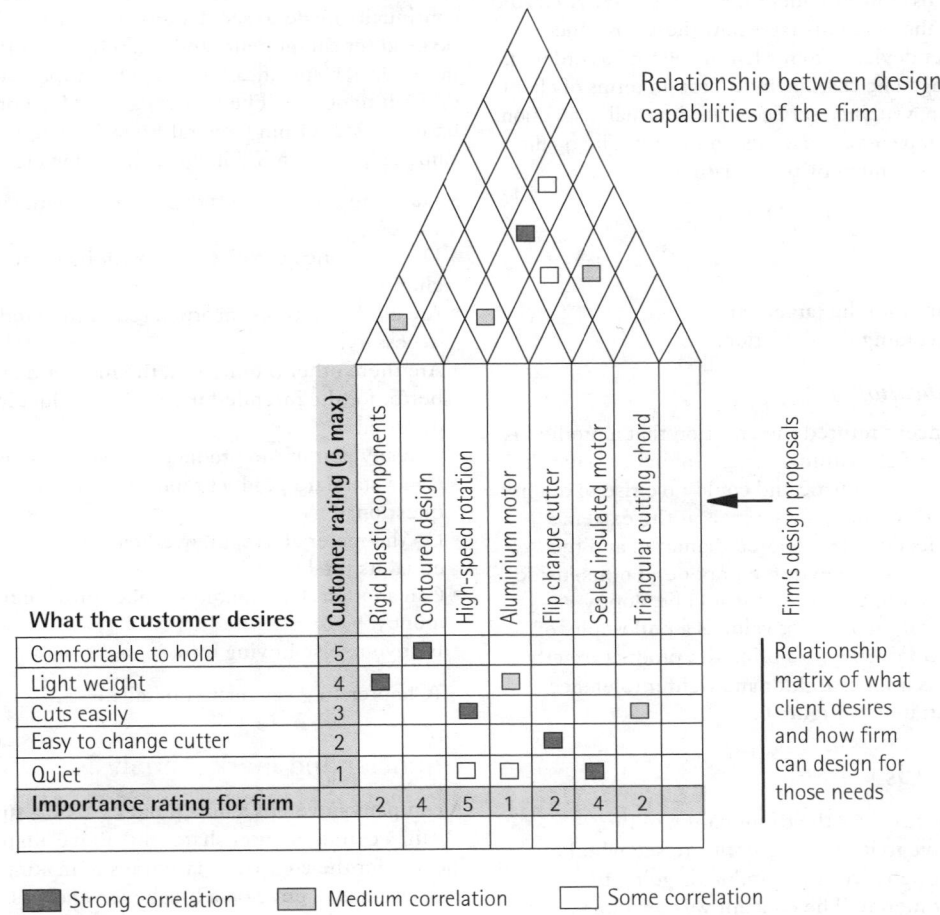

Relationship between design capabilities of the firm

Firm's design proposals

Relationship matrix of what client desires and how firm can design for those needs

What the customer desires	Customer rating (5 max)	Rigid plastic components	Contoured design	High-speed rotation	Aluminium motor	Flip change cutter	Sealed insulated motor	Triangular cutting chord
Comfortable to hold	5		■					
Light weight	4	■			■			
Cuts easily	3			■				■
Easy to change cutter	2					■		
Quiet	1			■	■		■	
Importance rating for firm		2	4	5	1	2	4	2

■ Strong correlation   ■ Medium correlation   ☐ Some correlation

correlation with aluminium motor, a strong correlation with a sealed insulated motor, and some correlation with the triangular cutting cord.

Robust design using Taguchi methods

As mentioned in Chapter 4, Taguchi methods are quality improvement techniques developed by Genichi Taguchi of Japan in the 1980s to improve product, and also process design, by attempting to make product designs production proof by building in tolerances for manufacturing variables known to be unavoidable. The argument is that missing the quality target in a consistent manner can be better than hitting it a few times with the rest being scattered all over the board. The following are the three basic concepts in the Taguchi methods.[9]

Quality robustness

Quality robustness suggests that products can be produced uniformly and consistently in a variety of different manufacturing conditions. The idea is to eliminate effects of adverse conditions, rather than removing their causes. This is often cheaper and more effective in producing a robust product. For example:

• Designing a product whose quality is not impaired by small changes in raw material quality, such as might be the case for clothing or paper.
• A product whose quality is not destroyed by small changes in process conditions, such as temperature, machines used, or operators employed, as, for example, in the case of chemicals or plastic products.

Quality loss function

The quality loss function identifies all the costs associated with poor quality and illustrates how these costs increase as the product deviates from what the client has ordered, or is expecting. The costs include 'cost' in terms of client dissatisfaction, warranty, service costs, internal inspection, repair, and scrap costs, and 'costs' to society. The quality loss function is defined by the equation:

$$L = D^2 \cdot C$$

where,
L is the loss
D is deviation from the target value
C is cost of avoiding the deviation.

Target specification

Taguchi's concept refuted the criterion that a product is acceptable if it falls within a certain tolerance. He felt that this was too simplistic and could give rise to quality problems. For example, if a screw is at the extreme lower end of its outside tolerated diameter, and the associated nut is at the extreme upper end of its inside tolerated diameter, then the fit would be sloppy. Target specification or target value is a philosophy of continuous improvement to bring the product exactly on target. This implies tighter and tighter tolerance limits as illustrated in Figure 6.7.

Value analysis

Value analysis involves the examination of the product relative to its proposed price to see whether the consumer perceives this product is going to give value for money. The concept was developed by

Larry D Miles at General Electric, USA, between 1939 and 1945. Under wartime conditions, studies were continually made to see if alternative materials could be used for components and assemblies as often those in the design specifications were too expensive or difficult to obtain. The following tests for a product, based on ideas from General Electric, with the idea of value analysis in mind include the following:

- Does the use of the product by the client contribute value?
- Does the price correlate well with its usefulness to the client?
- Are all the features incorporated in the product necessary?
- Are there other products on the market that are better for the intended use of the product in question?
- Can any part of the product be made at a lower cost?
- Can a standard product replace the product in question?
- Do the material, labour, overhead, and expected profit equal its total 'cost'?
- Can another dependable supplier provide it for less money?
- Is anyone else buying it for less?

  (Chapter 16 gives further details.)

Financial and market analysis

A company develops a new product to be a success, to obtain a certain market share, and above all, to generate income for the company. Two ways of making an evaluation is to develop a breakeven analysis, or a pro-forma income statement.

Breakeven analysis

The breakeven analysis determines what level of product units need to be sold in order that revenues are equal to total fixed and variable costs. Above this breakeven point, the company would make a profit (see also Chapter 16 for details of developing a breakeven analysis).

Pro-forma income statements

A pro-forma income statement is a financial model estimating the revenues, costs, and profit from the sale of the new product. A pro-forma income statement sometimes can be the deciding factor to go ahead for the new product. The costs are the easiest part to estimate. The most difficult is to estimate sales. The presentation of the Hershey Co. strategic options (in Chapter 2) is a type of pro-forma income statement.

Figure 6.7 Taguchi methods for quality: Target specification

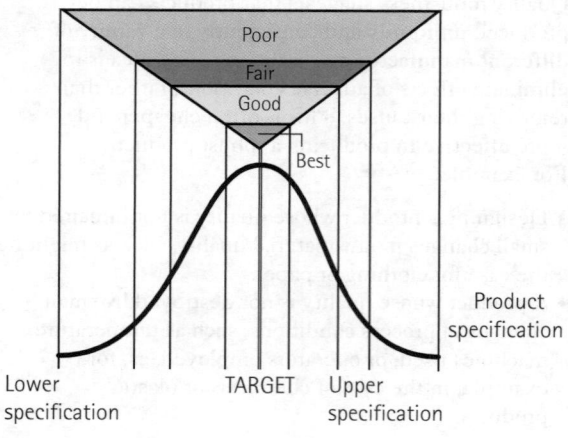

Prototype

A prototype of a new product is a smaller scale or perhaps even a full-scale version of the final product such as an automobile, a chemical plant, a turbine, a credit card, etc., incorporating all the features of the intended commercial product. The purpose of a prototype is to see if the product performs as expected and can be commercialized at an acceptable cost.

Test marketing

Test marketing involves introducing the product in a limited geographical market. The objective of test marketing is to have a sample programme which helps to minimize the risk of immediately commercializing a product nationwide. (Chapter 27 gives more information on sampling.)

Concurrent engineering

Concurrent engineering means having research and development personnel and design engineers work closely or in parallel, rather than in sequence, with production people to ensure a product can be easily, and cost effectively manufactured. This can avoid costly design changes at a later stage, and helps to reduce the length of the supply chain. Renault Automobile France believes that by bringing all its technicians under one roof, in order that they can work on a new design simultaneously, they can cut development time for its vehicles from 58 months to 38 months. This would reduce the cost of designing each model by up to €230 million or 20%.[10] This idea is illustrated in Figures 6.8 and 6.9, using average figures for automobile time-to-market.

Commercialization

Commercialization is the full-scale production of a product, or service onto the national or international market.

Product success

At the beginning stage of searching for new product ideas, many suggestions may be thrown out. However,

Figure 6.8 Sequential engineering

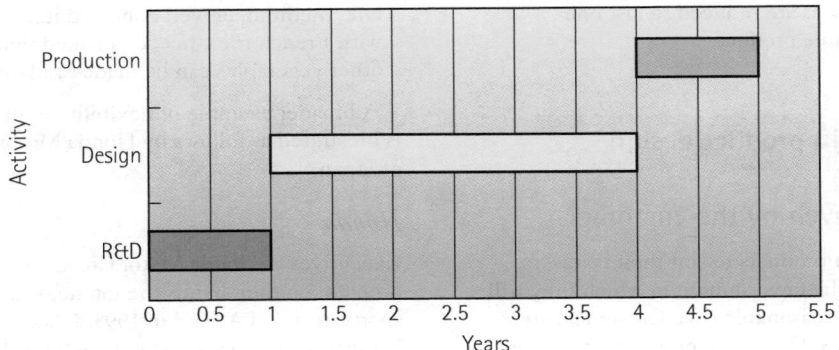

Figure 6.9 Concurrent engineering

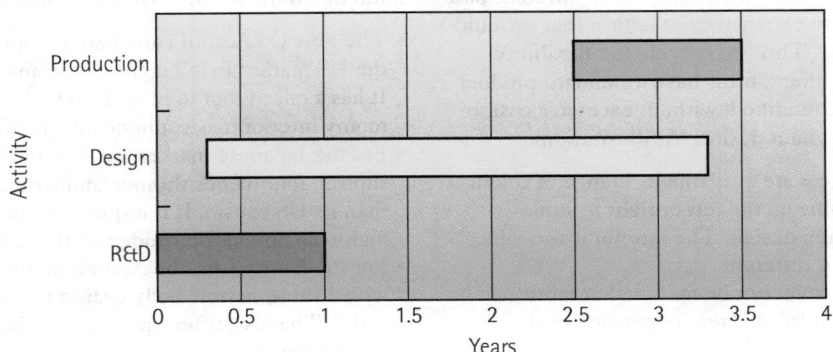

Figure 6.10 Product ideas and commercialization

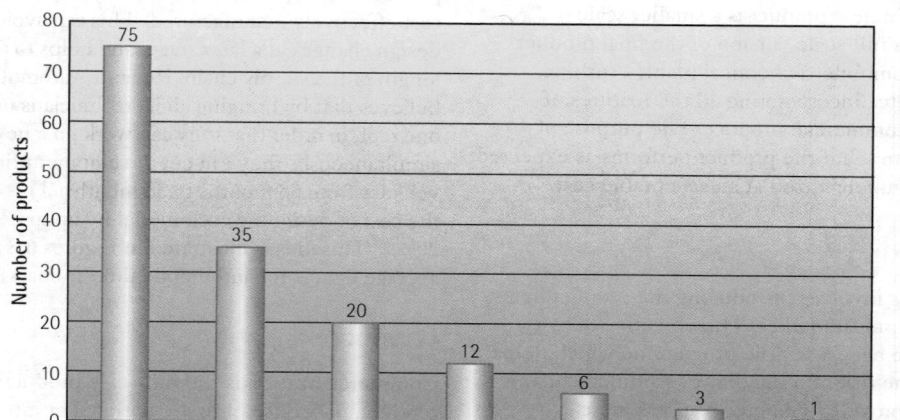

as these ideas are analyzed and studied in more detail, the 'successes' may be very limited. This process is illustrated in Figure 6.10. This illustrates that going through all the evaluation stages, the original 75 ideas are reduced to just one commercially viable product.

Flexibility in product design

Flexibility driven by the customer

Customers select products to suit their tastes, to be adaptable to the environment in which they will be used, and at a reasonable cost. Customers are different, and thus, for certain products firms need to build flexibility into the product design such that it will appeal to a broad range of clients. To develop a broad range of products, each with a completely different base design, would be so expensive to the firm that it would not be competitive. Thus, to provide the flexibility demanded by the client, firms have a standard product design that can be modified, without excessive cost, to offer what the customer desires. As illustrations:

• Kitchen appliances are available in a range of colours, with doors opening on the left or right to suit a customer's kitchen design. The interior is the same, but the outside is different.
• Colour tones of wood can be modified or fabric can be changed to give furniture a more personalized appearance.

• A package holiday can be modified to include certain stopovers or special attractions to satisfy client requirements.
• A steak dinner can be prepared with the meat being rare, medium, or well done and it might be served with French fries, rice, or a baked potato and various other vegetables can be made available.

A broader example of flexibility in product design is illustrated as follows by Honda Motor Company of Japan.[11]

Honda

Executives at Honda Motor Co. knew they had a problem on their hands the moment they launched the sporty, restyled Accord in 1993. It was too cramped for US drivers, but not stylish enough for the Japanese. The president, Nobuhiko Kawamoto, ordered a redesign of the vehicle, which cost tens of millions of dollars to build flexibility to suit customer tastes. As a result:

• The new US Accord launched in September 1997 for the US market is 189 inches long, and 70 inches wide. It has a raised roof to provide extra headroom and a roomy interior to accommodate a family.
• For the Japanese market the Accord is six inches shorter, four inches thinner, and with a lower roof than its US cousin. It is a sporty compact loaded with high-tech options demanded by the Japanese customers.
• For the Europeans, the Accord for 1998 is designed with a short, narrow body geared to the tiny streets and will have a stiffer, sportier ride the 'Old World' drivers prefer.

Figure 6.11 VAT classification in manufacturing

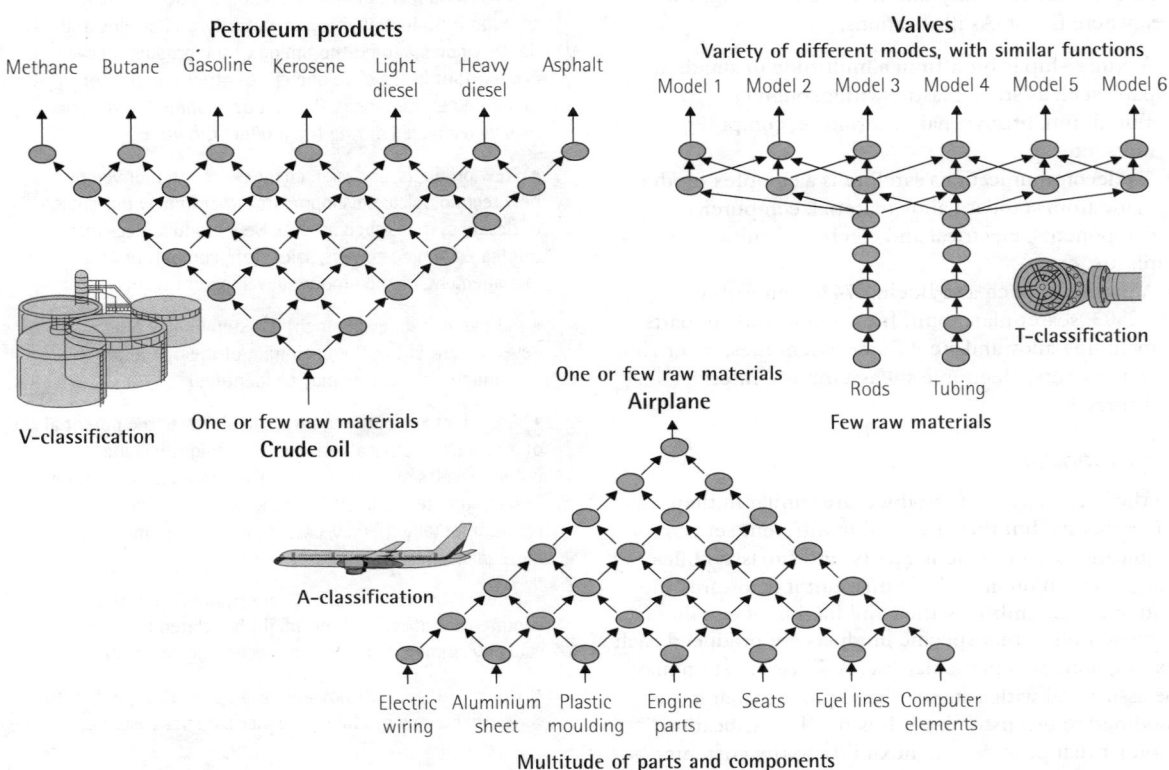

Flexibility dictated by the process

In manufacturing, flexibility in product design declines as one moves through the production process (process design is the subject of the next chapter). The implication of this to the operations manager is that one has to be sure of market requirements before finalizing the production plans or a producer may end up with finished goods for which there is limited market. This flexibility constraint can be illustrated by using a VAT classification which is grouping items according to the type of end product, and to a certain extent, by the manufacturing process employed as shown in Figure 6.11.[12]

V-classification

The V-classification is where from one, or a few raw materials, a variety of different end products can be produced. The base of the V represents the raw material, and the top the end products. At the start point there is almost infinite flexibility as to what products can be produced from the raw material but moving through

the production process, the degree of freedom of declines. The following are examples:

- Crude oil by simple distillation can be turned into propane, butane, gasoline, kerosene, fuel oil, diesel, asphalt, etc.
- Wood pulp can be turned into newsprint, paper of letter quality, book printing paper, cardboard, packaging, light building material, etc.
- Iron ore can be processed into sheet steel, wire, construction steel, nails, screws, stainless steel cutlery, etc.

A-classification

An A-classification is the opposite to the V in that from a multitude of raw materials, parts, and components (the bottom of the A) is made a single or a few products (the apex of the A). Very often for the A-classification the end product is either a project or a customized product. Many of the component parts used in building the product are standard items that have uses in many types of products. However, as soon as they move through the production process, they become a part of a subassembly, and their flexibility for use elsewhere is lost. As illustrations:

- A cruise ship is built from a multitude of standard parts such as steel, plastic, wiring, engines, aluminium, fittings, paint, furniture, computer units, etc.
- A telecommunications satellite is a complex product made from standard alloy material, computer components, electrical and electronic units, steel, plastic, etc.
- A jumbo jet such as a Boeing-747 or an Airbus-300 is a 250+ seater plane built from a multitude of parts including alloy and steel frame assemblies, jet engine components, electronic subassemblies, interior fittings, etc.

T-classification

In the T-classification, products are similar in their functionality, but they are used in different services or applications. Components, parts, and subassemblies may be common in each product but it is towards the end of the assembly by the combination of certain subassemblies, that specific products are produced each having their own particular use. A T-classification may be associated with a standardized product that is modified to be customized. It is the T-classification product that provides the flexibility to the customer discussed at the beginning of this section. Other than the household appliances already mentioned, T products would include:

- flow control valves for water, gas, and other fluids
- electronic measuring instruments in the chemicals industry
- computers where internal cards can be added to modify the characteristics.

Summary of key elements

- Manufactured products are either industrial goods for another firm, or consumer goods. Consumer items are further classified into durable or non-durable goods. Service firms usually (but not always) provide non-tangible items.

- Standard products are destined for the mass market as opposed to customized products that are according to particular customer specifications and as such they are usually more expensive than standard items. A project is also a product, but by definition is customized to certain specifications.

- Most products exhibit a lifecycle from development through introduction, growth maturity, and decline and death. Understanding the timing of the product lifecycle is important in the development of other products or modifying existing ones. Product development costs are usually recovered during the product growth period.

- New products, or design changes are often driven by new technological developments either in new materials, or design systems such as CAD. New product ideas may originate from customers, sales staff, competitors, top management, or the product development team.

- Research and development is a step in new product development but at the beginning of the operation no commercial venture may be identified.

- A product evaluation matrix can illustrate the potential of a new product. Evaluation criteria might include potential sales revenue, competitive products, production costs, estimated product life, time-to-market, being environmentally friendly, patent possibilities, and raw material availability.

- A feasibility study examines constraints for product commercialization, and this might be related to plant capacity, human, financial, and technological resources.

- Quality function deployment is an analytical method to verify that a new product or service satisfies customer requirements.

- Taguchi methods, or robust design, are techniques to ensure product designs are production proof by building in tolerances for variables known to be unavoidable.

- A value analysis evaluates a product to see if it provides value for money.

- A breakeven analysis indicates the point at which profits might be generated from a new product. A pro-forma income statement gives an estimate of future revenues and costs for the new product.

- A prototype is a small-, or equal, scale version of the final product that has the objective to test the viability of the commercial version.

- Test marketing involves testing the product in a limited market to minimize the risk of immediate introduction on a large scale. The success rate of new product ideas may be only a small percentage of the products originally conceived.

- Product flexibility to the customer means tailoring the product to suit certain customer tastes. The flexibility of raw material and component products usage is reduced as one moves through the production chain.

Notes and references

1. 'A peek at the Airbus giant: Could the A380 become tomorrow's cruise ship of the sky?', *International Herald Tribune*, 2 March 2001, p. 9
2. McGhie, Juliet A., 'Birth of an industry: Petrochemicals made an unheralded debut 75 years ago in New Jersey', *The Lamp*, Exxon Corporation Shareholders Services, vol 77, no 3, fall 1995
3. 'US armor makers have vested interest in survivors' stories: They say bulletproof attire fends of many dangers; Wounded buck stops here', *Wall Street Journal Europe*, 1–2 March 1996
4. 'The world's largest companies', *Financial Times*, 11 May 2001
5. '1878–1997: La saga d'une entreprise qui a fait l'Amérique', *L'Expansion*, 10–24 July 1997, p. 30
6. 'General Electric. Les secrets de la plus belle entreprise du monde', *L'Expansion*, 10–24 July 1997, pp 26–7
7. Akao, Yoji (ed.), *Quality Function Deployment: Integrating Customer Requirements into Product Design*, Productivity Press, Cambridge, Massachusetts, 1990
8. *Users' manual*, Black and Decker Products (with permission)
9. American Supplier Institute, *Taguchi Methods: Selected Papers on Methodology and Applications*, ASI Press, Dearborn, Michigan, 1988
10. *The Economist*, 27 May 1995
11. 'Can Honda build a world car?', *Business Week*, 8 September 1997, pp 38–44
12. Chase, Richard B. and Aquilano, Nicholas J., *Production and Operations Management: A Life Cycle Approach*, Irwin, London, 1989, 5th edition, p. 817

Review and discussion topics

1. Lifecycle of products
Describe some products which:
   (a) have disappeared from the marketplace (give reasons why you believe they have 'died')
   (b) are nearing the end of their useful life
   (c) have been repackaged so that their maturity has been extended
   (d) are in the development phase.

2. Technology
What role do you think technology will play in the future of the following types of product? What will be the impact to the provider of these products?
   (a) food
   (b) university degree programme
   (c) textiles and clothing
   (d) sports equipment.

3. Introduction of new products
The text quotes General Electric of the USA as an example of a company that has been very successful in developing new products. Can you name other companies, either manufacturing or services, which are leaders in product development?

4. Quality function deployment
Consider the following products:
   (a) the bus or train service you use to get to and from your work or school
   (b) the writing implement you use
   (c) the car you drive
   (d) the degree programme you are on
   (e) the meal that is served to you at lunchtime.
   For these products apply the concept of quality function deployment. First, identify what you expect from these products. Then, analyze them to see if, in the context in which they are made, they satisfy you as a customer, or user. If not, what modifications would you propose to the producer that would make them meet your needs more?

5. Value analysis
Identify five products that you use on a regular basis, either tangible goods or services, where you as a customer are satisfied that you are getting value for money. Then select another five products where you feel you are not getting value for money. Justify your reasoning.

6. Robust design
How would you apply the concept of 'robust design' to the following products? Describe the materials, processes, customers that play a part in the robust design process:
   (a) university degree programme
   (b) a pair of shoes
   (c) the vehicle you drive.

Case study 6.1 Four products

Situation
The following describes some of the history, growth, and current status of four products, two from service firms, and two tangible products.

Airline travels
The worldwide air transport boom continues. In 1995 the number of passengers carried by airlines increased by almost 5% to 2.2 billion with demand particularly strong in Europe which was up 6.8% to 644 million, and the Asia–Pacific region, up 7.6% to 358 million. Affordable prices, and the expansion in world trade are both boosting the airline business. Air travel is likely to grow by an annual 5 to 6% doubling in volume over the next 15 years or so, while cargo traffic should also increase at an above average rate. By far the strongest growth is

expected for the Asia–Pacific countries. Air transport is already contending with serious constraints especially in Europe, where roughly one in three flights there arrives late due to delays on the ground or in the air.[1]

Aspirin

On 10 August 1897 Felix Hoffman, a research chemist in the employ of a German dyestuffs company called Bayer, managed to acetylate the phenol group of a compound called salicylic acid, developing acetylsalicylic acid, better known as aspirin. Hoffman had developed the world's first truly synthetic drug, that is, not merely an artificial copy of a naturally occurring compound. Since the synthesis of aspirin, the product has gone from strength to strength. It was first marketed mainly as an anti-inflammatory, particularly for people suffering from rheumatism, but its popularity as a general purpose painkiller followed quickly. It has not suffered proscription, as happened to its near contemporary, heroin. Neither have more modern substances overtaken it. Paracetamol and ibuprofen may have nibbled at its share of the over-the-counter painkiller market, but aspirin still outsells them both. In Germany, for instance, half of the OTC market belongs to aspirin-based products and Bayer itself produces 11 billion tablets a year.[2]

Hamburger

The rise of the hamburger is a metaphor for the rise of America. It came ashore with immigrants from Hamburg, who had long since acquired the habit of eating raw ground beef, with onion juice, from nomadic Tatar tribes. Like the immigrants themselves, the hamburger evolved in the New World. It was cooked, it was sheathed in bread. Then, sometime around 1920, a bun replaced the sandwich bread. In 1948 Richard and Maurice McDonald opened the first fast burger joint. The food was prepared in advance and kept warm under infrared lamps. The pre-packaged hamburger, standard, efficient, cheap, fitted the mass American culture that emerged after the war.

Today, the average American eats three hamburgers a week, a collective effort that puts paid to 40 billion burgers annually. Despite cholesterol phobia, the number of hamburgers and cheeseburgers consumed in restaurants has jumped by nearly one-fifth since 1990. So far McDonald's has served 70 billion hamburgers, enough to reach to the moon and back 17 times over. The production of hamburgers has become as automated as Henry Ford's assembly line. McDonald's has opened restaurants in 103 countries, most recently in Tahiti and Cyprus. Like America, the hamburger has come to dominate the world. As with America, the question remains: Can the product last forever?[3]

Lladro

Lladros are the romantic porcelain figurines made by the company of the same name in Valencia, Spain. They have worldwide appeal because they deal with universal themes, based very often on the Victorian era and they captivate people with their delicacy and romanticism. King Juan Carlos of Spain often gives the statuettes as gifts when on official state visits. And Lyn Cole, a long-time collector from Queensland, Australia, professed in a recent letter to Lladro that she feels 'moved by the beauty' of each of her 45 Lladro pieces. In fact, she says, Lladro has become 'an important part of my life'. In 1996 Lladro's sales stood at 14.8 billion pesetas ($95.4 million) almost one-third of that coming from the USA. There are 9700 stores that sell the ceramic products worldwide. Lladro has its own distribution company in the USA and a joint distribution venture in Japan.

Lladro was founded in 1933 by three brothers. When the brothers were teenagers they worked on the family farm in eastern Spain during the day and studied painting and sculpture at a local school in the evening. Together they began to make their first ceramic figurines in the family backyard. Each figurine is made by hand from a series of clay moulds at Porcelain City, as the Valencia factory is known. The pieces are fired separately and then melded together by hand with a special porcelain-based liquid. Each piece is hand painted and fired once. The ceramic pieces range in price from about $30 for a Christmas bell to $25,000 for the carriage of Cinderella drawn by four horses. Limited editions that sold for $70 in 1985 now go for as much as $16,000.[4]

Required

Examine these four products using the concepts presented in the chapter. From a product point of view, how are they similar and how are they different? Look at their history, particularly the role of market forces on their growth rate. Where has technology played a role? Does technology have a future role? How would you apply the product lifecycle to these four products? What about future development and flexibility? Finally, what do you feel is the future for airline travel, the aspirin, the hamburger, and Lladro figurines? What events might modify sales either upward or downward?

[1] Commerzbank.

[2] 'An aspirin a day keeps the doctor at bay: The world's first blockbuster drug is a hundred years old this week', *The Economist*, 9 August 1997.

[3] 'As hamburgers go, so goes America?', *The Economist*, 23 August 1997.

[4] 'Lladro carves out global role for statuettes: Word "kitschy" doesn't deter the porcelain's collectors', *Wall Street Journal Europe*, 29 July 1997.

Selected further reading

CROSS, Nigel (2000) *Engineering Design Methods: Strategies for Product Design*, 3rd edition, Wiley.

MCGRATH, Michael (2000) *Product Strategy for High Technology Companies*, 2nd edition, McGraw-Hill.

OTTO, Kevin N. and WOOD, Kristen (2000) *Product Design*, Prentice-Hall.

ROY, Ranjit, K. (2001) *Design of Experiments Using the Taguchi Approach: 16 Steps to Product and Process Improvement*, Wiley-Interscience.

ULRICH, Karl T. and EPPINGER, Steven D. (1999) *Product Design and Development*, 2nd edition, McGraw-Hill.

An extensive listing of other further reading can be found on the website.

What's on the web?

Further learning resources are available to lecturers and students at www.supplychain-online.com, including the following which are specific to *Design of the product*:

Resource	Subject
Chapter overview	Design of the product
Case study: Typewriters and Smith Corona	Design of the product
More further reading	Design of the product

7   *Process design and the operations network*

Chapter overview

- Design of the process system
- Capacity of the process system
- Vertical integration
- Automation in process design
- Information technology in the process system
- Electronic commerce
- Artificial intelligence
- Operations network chart
- Business process reengineering

Design of the process system

The previous chapter was devoted to the design of the product. To produce and deliver the product as planned requires a well-organized process design system, complete with an integrated supply chain network to ensure that material and information flow and product transformation is smooth and efficient. There is a process system and operations network for both manufacturing and services as illustrated as follows.

Manufacturing

In manufacturing, the process system and the operations network is the supply chain whose complexity depends on such factors as the type of product, the volume produced, the size of the market, and the final consumers. As a minimum, the supply chain will include the delivery of the raw materials and components from suppliers and subcontractors, the manufacturing and assembly at one or several sites, and then product distribution either directly, or via warehouses, to the client. Specific considerations for design of the process network include the following. Most of them are covered in further detail elsewhere in the book.

Site location

Site considerations cover whether there is sufficient capacity to produce at an existing location or will it be more feasible to build a new facility. In this case will the facility be built domestically, or internationally? (See further Chapter 3.)

Make or buy

Make or buy is an economic decision concerning whether a firm will manufacture the subassemblies and finished product itself or will it purchase them from existing suppliers, or employ subcontractors to perform specific parts of the work. (See further Chapters 16 and 25 for the make and buy calculation method.)

Layout

The physical layout of the facility is very much a function of the type of product. If the production were expected to be small then perhaps a batch-type operation producing in small lots would be appropriate. For high volumes a continuous process would be a consideration. This would involve a more rigid layout. The continuous flow might be for, say, liquid pharmaceutical products, or an assembly line operation, for mechanical pieces. (Chapter 9 treats this in detail.)

Technology

What will be the extent of technology employed? Will the system be highly automated involving a high capital investment? If so what technological tools and machines will be employed? Alternatively, will there be significant manual input? (These elements are discussed further in this chapter.)

Information systems network

This covers all the network system for communicating between parties concerned. It would include the architecture for the computer links with purchasing, within the manufacturing site, and for distribution. (This is addressed later in this chapter.)

Distribution network

Issues to be resolved here include how the product would be delivered to the client. What storage areas will be necessary? What transportation systems will be the most economic? (See further Chapter 17.)

Services

Many of the elements in process design for manufacturing also apply to services. A particular difference with services is that the network is designed very much with the customer in mind. This is as opposed to manufacturing where the customer convenience really only takes consideration at the end of the chain. Some specific considerations in services are as follows.

Air travel

For a major airline company, as a minimum, the physical process system consists of terminals to handle flight arrivals and departures, passengers, baggage handling, ticketing, and restaurant services. Then there is the information systems network for flight planning, weather reporting, operations planning, airline control etc. Many airlines, such as British Airways, operate a hub and spoke system where Heathrow, London, is a 'hub' for arrivals and departures of almost all its flights. The 'spokes' extend worldwide into North America, Australia, Europe, Africa, and Asia covering some 165 destinations and handling over 36 million people.[1]

Rail travel

Rail companies have an elaborate network to service as best as possible the entire country and, in the case of Europe, internationally. In some cases, such as the SNCF in France, the network also has stations that interconnect with airports such as Paris, Charles De Gaulle, and Lyon. Similarly in Britain there are rail links to Heathrow and Gatwick airports. Again, in addition to the physical network there is also an information systems network for route planning, ticketing, etc.

Telecommunications

Companies such as BT (British Telecom), AT&T, USA or France Télécom, which provide telecommunications services worldwide, have complex system design including networks of fibre optic cables, satellites, undersea cables, relay points for the mobile phones and associated computer tie-ups.

Consulting firms

Consulting companies like McKinsey, Booz Allen Hamilton, and the Boston Consulting Group, provide international consulting services. Their system design principally involves the offices, computer systems, and the high-priced consultants. Virtual offices (dealt with in Chapter 9) may eventually replace physical ones.

Hotels

The system design includes location, room accommodation, restaurant service, and communications links for the clients.

Correlation product and process design

The product type defines very much the process design system. Hayes and Wheelright[2] developed a correlation for product and process design of which an adaptation is illustrated in Figure 7.1. The horizontal bar at the top gives the characteristics of products ranging from low volume, custom-designed products (Box A) going through very high volume standard products (Box D). The vertical bar on the left represents the process characteristics. At the top (Box 1) is functional layout or job shop, going through to completely continuous flow (Box 4). For these various categories the circles in the centre give examples of various product activities that fit these various categories. Flexibility, product volume, unit cost are the important elements of this correlation.

Flexibility

Products and process systems illustrated in Circle A-1 by the machine shop, consulting firm, hospital, and car repair are relatively flexible as to the type of products or services they can produce or handle. To a certain extent, by changing or modifying equipment, the service or product range can be quite large. Contrariwise, the oil refinery, polyethylene plant, electric power plant, and telecommunications network illustrated in Circle D-4 are inflexible as to the range of products they can produce. Once a refinery or chemical plant is in place, to change product type would involve significant reengineering and layout modification.

Figure 7.1 Correlation product and process design

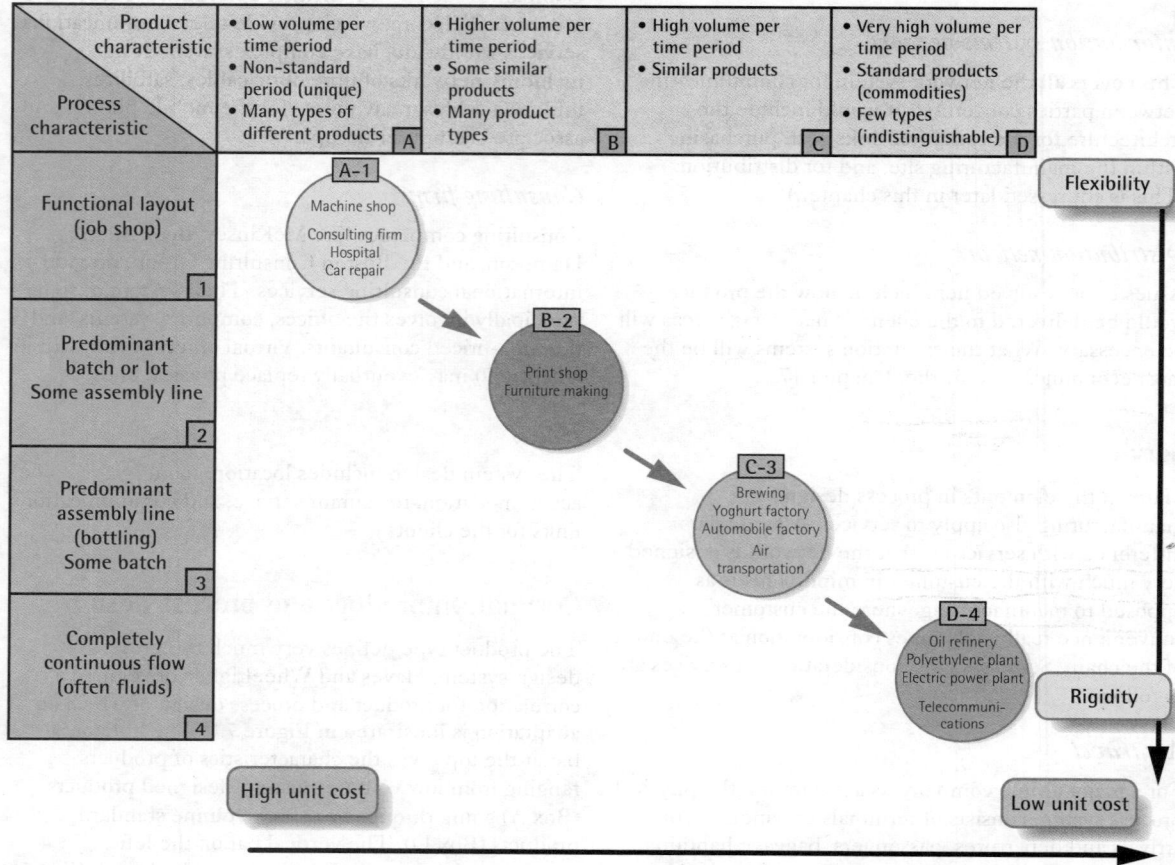

Process characteristic \ Product characteristic	• Low volume per time period • Non-standard period (unique) • Many types of different products A	• Higher volume per time period • Some similar products • Many product types B	• High volume per time period • Similar products C	• Very high volume per time period • Standard products (commodities) • Few types (indistinguishable) D
Functional layout (job shop) 1	A–1 Machine shop Consulting firm Hospital Car repair			
Predominant batch or lot Some assembly line 2		B–2 Print shop Furniture making		
Predominant assembly line (bottling) Some batch 3			C–3 Brewing Yoghurt factory Automobile factory Air transportation	
Completely continuous flow (often fluids) 4				D–4 Oil refinery Polyethylene plant Electric power plant Telecommuni-cations

Flexibility

Rigidity

High unit cost

Low unit cost

Product volume

Those products, or services, of the type illustrated in Circle A-1 are produced in much lower volume, or have a longer cycle time, than those type of products exhibited by the Circle D-4. To repair one car might take three hours, but a barrel of diesel oil can be produced in minutes.

Unit cost

Products and processes represented by Circle A-1 have relatively high unit cost due to the fact that they are unique products, and also the education level of the personnel employed is high. By way of contrast, those represented by Circle D-4 have a low unit cost. Compare the cost of a telephone call compared to that of a car repair!

Between the two extremes are given illustrations of other types of processes/products. The correlation is

perhaps easier to conceptualize with physical products, than with service-designed products.

Capacity of the process system

A consideration in the design of the process system is determining what capacity should be developed in order that the products can be made, or the services can be offered, in order to meet the demand of customers. Like many facets of operations management, capacity planning is market driven. System capacity involves a significant capital investment so that planning should be made carefully in order to optimize the utilization of financial resources with demand. Customers can be quickly lost if a firm's capacity is insufficient to meet demand. Alternatively, under-utilized capacity can be very costly to the firm.

Defining capacity

Capacity is defined as the maximum possible output, or use, from a system under normal design, or planned conditions, in a given time period. The effective capacity, or capacity utilization, expressed as a percentage, is given by the ratio:

$$\left\{\begin{array}{l}\text{Effective capacity, or}\\ \text{capacity utilization}\end{array}\right\} = \frac{\text{Actual capacity used}}{\text{Design capacity}}$$

The actual capacity used, under normal conditions, can only be less than the design capacity. When on average this percentage starts to arise above, say, about 90% then considerations should be given to adding additional capacity. If the capacity utilization hovers around 100% during certain time periods then on occasions there are almost certainly bottlenecks or queues occurring.

Services

The capacity of many service firms is dictated by the physical arrangement of a capital facility whose utilization varies seasonally, weekly, or even daily. Some illustrations are as follows.

Transportation

Transportation systems such as airplanes, trains, buses, ferry boats and the like have a fixed capacity according to the number of seats available. Capacity utilization is measured by the ratio of number of seats filled to the number of seats available. At certain times of the day, such as morning, and early evening, some transportation systems like inner city buses, and underground trains are filled to capacity with lines of people waiting. As transportation networks such as runways or rail tracks are fixed, transport firms are finding it difficult to increase capacity to accommodate this periodic demand. Some approaches are to use double-decker buses or trains on rail networks (as the French Paris–Lyon TGV line, for example) or to use river transport (on the Seine in Paris, the Thames in London, or the Hudson River in New York), to absorb some of the surface transportation. Similarly road networks, again particularly around large urban areas, have a capacity that is quickly saturated. The airline industry very often publishes its average seat capacity in annual reports, which is also considered a measure of efficiency.

Hotel industry

The capacity of the hotel industry is governed by the number of rooms available. Its capacity utilization is the number of rooms used to those available. This ratio is very dependent on the period as, for example, during

holiday time many hotels operate close to capacity. Similarly, in cities that accommodate the business traveller, hotels are usually heavily booked during the week but less at the weekend. The utilization of hotels for a country is often an indicator of the success of its travel industry.

Theatres, cinemas, restaurants

The capacity for theatres, cinemas, restaurants, or those services where clients are seated, as in transportation, is again limited to the number of places available. In restaurants, the capacity of the system has some flexibility as it depends both on the time a customer takes to eat, and the service time.

Hospitals

The major capacity limitation for hospitals is the number of beds available (on the assumption there is adequate medical staff). New hospital construction is expensive, and often paid by the state or the national government. Efforts to increase the capacity of hospitals is made by limiting stay, or where feasible, moving from overnight treatment to outpatient care. In OECD countries, where the average age is increasing, hospital demand is also increasing as a consequence.

Manufacturing

The capacity of manufacturing firms is measured by the product output. All manufacturing systems have a nominal, or design capacity, which is based not only on the size of the physical facility, but also the design throughput of the equipment and machines (taking into account the non-operating time for maintenance and cleaning), the processing time necessary for each of the value-added activities, the flow of the raw materials and components from suppliers, and all the labour necessary. Again, capacity design is market driven. This fact was brought home sharply to Boeing Aircraft Company which, in 1997, was caught offguard by the significant global customer demand in aircraft orders. It found its capacity too low due to insufficient labour and component parts and as a result was forced to freeze production of its 747 and 737 jetliners in October. This capacity-related problem had the additional impact of causing a drop in the price of Boeing's shares.[3]

Pharmaceutical manufacturing companies are spending millions of dollars to develop an effective AIDS vaccine in a market demand that is soaring astronomically in most countries of the world, and particularly in Africa. One firm, Merck & Co., brought out a new drug, Crixivan, that showed a lot of promise but at the beginning the company struggled with capacity in order to meet market demand. This interaction of market demand with capacity planning, together with new product development, system design, research and development, technology, prototype facilities, subcontractors, mass production, and competitive pressure are highlighted in Industry insight 7.1.

An AIDS drug but insufficient capacity

Merck & Co. spent more than $1 billion over the past decade to create Crixivan, one of the most promising drugs ever to be developed in the fight against AIDS. It has paid off. The drug won the fastest US federal approval in regulatory history, is helping to restore health and hope to thousands of patients, and is soon expected to bring Merck $500 million in annual revenue. After just seven months on the market, it outsold other similar new drugs. There was just one problem, however. It did not have sufficient capacity to meet demand. About 90,000 patients worldwide already used the drug but there was only enough supply for about 110,000. As a result, Merck has been in a race to increase production and avoid a public relations disaster – the prospect of running short of supply and having to turn away AIDS sufferers. How did one of the world's most powerful drug makers get into this predicament?

Merck created some of its own problems since, despite a worldwide abundance of production capacity, it chose to build its own plants rather than contract out the work to a supplier. Then, on learning that two rivals might beat it to market with similar therapies, Merck requested and got FDA approval of Crixivan, the most complex drug it had ever tried to mass produce, well before it had the necessary production capacity ready.

Competition to develop a new class of AIDS drugs began in 1989 when Merck published its discovery of the three-dimensional structure of the enzyme protease, a promising target for attacking the human immune efficiency virus that causes AIDS. Protease acts like scissors, cutting up a key HIV protein and enabling the virus to replicate itself. The new drugs, dubbed protease inhibitors, would mimic part of the protein's shape, creating a decoy to lure protease away from the real protein and prevent it from fulfilling its duties. By the early 1990s companies such as Merck, Roche Holding, Abbot Laboratories, Upjohn, Vertex Pharmaceuticals, and Agouron Pharmaceuticals had promising candidate drugs. Merck began testing Crixivan in humans in early 1993 and that summer, not even knowing whether the drug would work, scientists began to discuss how to mass produce their drug. Launching full-scale production of a new drug begins only after the drug is in advanced testing and has at least an 80% chance of success. The Crixivan effort, because of the AIDS crisis, and competitive pressures, began far earlier when the drug had only between a 5 and 10% success rate. The effort was further hampered by the huge quantities of Crixivan that would be needed, since each patient must take six 400-milligram pills each day, in combination with other AIDS drugs to achieve the desired effect of reducing HIV levels in the blood. To supply just 90,000 patients with Crixivan is the equivalent of producing enough Vasotec, Merck's hypertension drug, for more than 21 million people.

Merck pushed other projects aside, assigned 400 employees to the Crixivan programme, and found ways to produce small quantities of Crixivan while rushing to build two factories even before it knew exactly how the production lines would work. In late 1993 the team was using a prototype plant in Rahway, New Jersey, to produce batches of the drug. Each batch took four months to produce. Further, only 15% of the quantity of ingredients emerged in the desired shape of the complex Crixivan molecule. The team needed to reduce production time to one month and bring the yield rate up to 50%. It took extensive study work and it was not until November 1994 that the team had designed the complete Crixivan process. At this stage, Merck had to decide whether to subcontract the drug production or to build the grassroots facilities themselves. A competitor, Abbot Laboratories, who had by this time developed its own protease inhibitor, Norvir, had to make a similar decision. It subcontracted with firms in Japan, Italy, and France to produce 80% of the expected demand. Merck was not confident on giving the complex drug-making process to outsiders and relied only on Mitsui of Japan and DSM of the Netherlands to handle just seven of the total 15 steps required in the drug production – and the less complicated ones, to boot. Performing most of the work in-house would required a capital investment from Merck of several hundred million dollars to design and construct new production lines, even though Crixivan was not expected to go before regulators for another two years. It was a big gamble, given that Crixivan had shown promising results in fewer than a dozen patients who were taking it in combination with the older drug, AZT. However, recognizing the risk, in February 1995 Merck's board gave the go-ahead for the commercial production of Crixivan and frantic construction to build sufficient production capacity began at existing plants in Elkton, Virginia, and Albany, Georgia, a month later.

Even as Merck was rushing to increase production capacity, it was being lambasted by AIDS activists about dragging its feet in its production efforts for the drug. Further, by September 1995 competitors Abbot Laboratories and Hoffman-La Roche reported successful clinical trials on similar drugs for which they later received FDA approval. This put pressure on Merck to file its FDA application by January 1996 eight months earlier than planned and before its production lines were ready. The FDA accepted Merck's Crixivan in March 1996 but was concerned about the firm's capacity to supply sufficient quantities of the drug. If too many AIDS patients started taking the drug and then had to stop even for a short time because they were unable to get refills, their bodies risked developing a resistance to Crixivan. Merck assured the FDA it could produce enough Crixivan on its prototype line for up to 30,000 patients. In order to ensure a steady supply for these Merck funnelled most of its prescriptions to a single distributor, Stadtlanders Pharmacy in Pittsburgh, which could control the number of patients on the drug and bar new patients when demand matched supply. With this distribution policy they further encountered protests by activists saying they had created a monopoly that price gouged patients.

As Merck produced small quantities of the drug at maximum capacity at its prototype plant in New Jersey, construction proceeded at a frantic pace at its plants in Elkton and Albany. On 27 May 1996 they were ready for production and six weeks later, on 6 July, the last of the first batch's white capsules were in boxes ready for shipment. However, demand for the drug had begun to pick up after the benefits of protease inhibitors received wide press coverage following an international AIDS conference that same week. The Merck crew still had months of work ahead in order to bring the plants up to full production capacity and the unnerving question was: 'Would Merck be able to get the facilities up to full-scale production capacity before being overtaken by demand?'

Adapted from: 'Short supply: Success of AIDS drug brings new concern: Can Merck keep pace?', *Wall Street Journal Europe*[4]

Capacity under–utilization and flexibility

Many service systems are notoriously inefficient in the sense that the capacity utilization may be close to zero for long periods of the time. Schools and universities are often closed for up to three months during the year. Many hotel and holiday resorts are practically empty in the October to December period. Transportation systems may be severely under-utilized in the mid-morning and mid-afternoon periods, as are restaurants. Manufacturing facilities that provide seasonal products such as ski equipment, swim wear, winter clothing also have a fluctuating demand. Chapter 12 discusses some possibilities that both service systems and manufacturing facilities might adopt to smooth out and at the same time increase their overall capacity utilization.

Capacity planning methods

Capacity planning requirements can be determined by forecasting the market demand. Quantitative forecasting methods in this respect are covered in Chapter 10. Then Chapter 23 gives further planning approaches for deciding on capacity levels and the risks involved. Finally, Chapter 25 goes into marginal analysis, and the relationship with short-term and long-term capacity planning.

Vertical integration

Definition

Vertical integration in the operations network is the combination, under a single ownership, of two or more stages of production and/or distribution in the supply chain of entities that are normally separate. Firms resort to integration because they deal in large volumes, and believe it is more efficient, reliable, and economic to have control over suppliers and/or customers. Vertical integration might be backward or forward integration; alternatively the integration may be both backward and forward given the firm control over the entire supply chain.

Backward integration

Backward integration is when the firm owns some or all the activities upstream of its operation. This might be the raw materials, the suppliers of parts and components, and perhaps even the transportation equipment used to deliver the raw materials. As an example, in mid-1981 for $7.3 billion, Du Pont, the US-based diversified chemical company acquired Conoco, which had interests in oil, gas, and coal. The chairman of Du Pont stated that the merger would give the company: 'a captive hydrocarbon feedstock source which would reduce the exposure of the combined companies to fluctuations in the price of energy and hydrocarbons'. Dairy-producing firms represent a type of backward integration where, through cooperatives, the milk-treating, cheese-making, and packaging firms own the upstream dairy farms.

Forward integration

Forward integration is when the firm owns some or all of the activities downstream of a firm's operation. For the manufacturing firm of finished products this might include the distribution centres and retail outlets. For a manufacturer of raw materials or components this might be the ownership of the manufacturing and assembly operation of the finished product. As an illustration, in the 1970s Texas Instruments of the USA, a producer of integrated circuits and electronic components, integrated forward into calculators, watches, and other electronic products. Delivery firms such as UPS, or Federal Express own the delivery vehicles, and even airplanes so that they can completely control their schedules.

Complete integration

Complete integration is the control or ownership of the entire supply chain. Oil companies such as Chevron-Texaco, BP-Amoco, Shell, or ExxonMobil (Esso in Europe) are examples of an almost completely integrated firm. These firms first own and operate the

oil refinery that distils the crude oil into gasoline, aviation fuel, diesel and other products. They are backwardly integrated, owning the upstream production activities for the crude oil including the drilling platforms and pumping equipment that bring the oil to the surface. In addition, they own the pipelines for delivering the crude oil to port, and the oil tankers that transport the oil to the oil refinery. In some cases, they also own the crude oil although this has changed over the years with nationalization of oil fields by foreign governments. Oil companies are then forwardly integrated, owning the downstream marketing activities including the tanker trucks, or the tanker ships, which deliver the refined products to the distribution outlet, and in many cases, the gasoline retail outlets themselves. This arrangement is illustrated in Figure 7.2. In some cases, oil companies go further and own downstream the chemical plants which produce a range of products based on petroleum feedstock. Some US automobile manufacturing companies have a partially integrated network since they own the facility that manufactures the component parts, as well as dealer networks that sell the finished product.

Benefits of integration

Vertical integration can be of strategic importance to the operations manager as it might provide possibilities for cost reductions, low levels of inventory, and easier scheduling.[5]

Figure 7.2 Vertical integration: Operations network of an oil company (Photo: Corbis)

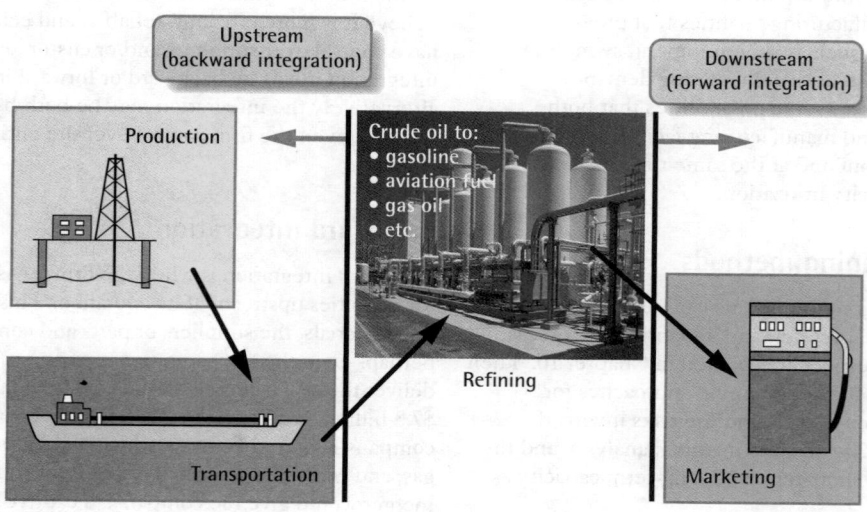

Transaction costs

Vertical integration can reduce the buying and selling costs that are incurred when two separate companies own two stages of production and perhaps the physical distribution. When integrated, the marketing activities such as sales, advertising, promotion, and market research can be considerably reduced.

Reliability of supplies

Vertical integration may be essential to assure a supply of critical raw materials. This fact was made very evident in the 1970s during the oil crisis when foreign owners of crude oil cut off supplies thus reducing the availability of gasoline supplies for automobile use in addition to sharply increasing product costs.[6] Michelin, the French tyre company, owns some rubber plantations in Asia that supply the raw material for its top of the line tyre products.

Captive customers

If a firm owns the downstream distribution centre and retail outlets then to a certain extent it is creating a captive client base such as the case for an automobile company which owns a dealership, or paint manufacture who owns a paint store.

Easier coordination

With vertical integration, coordination in the supply chain may be easier in terms of production and inventory scheduling between activities in the chain since the flows in the supply and distribution networks are known with some certainty.

Technology

Another argument is that with integration companies are better equipped to use innovative technologies because they participate in many of the production and distribution activities where changes in innovations are likely to occur. If a firm installs a certain type of ERP system, for example (see Chapter 13), then if the same system is installed throughout the integrated firm the linkage and control should be more reliable.

Entry barriers

The more vertically integrated a business, the greater the financial resources that are required for competitors to enter and compete in this market. Thus, vertically integrated companies have a certain monopoly, discouraging competitor entry. This fact is often used by regulatory agencies as an argument to break up companies or to refuse mergers of firms because of their perceived monopolistic powers. Two examples in 2000 were the merger of General Electric and Honeywell and Schneider and Legrand both of which were refused by the European Union.

Disadvantages of integration

Disadvantages of integration include increased capital requirements, unbalanced throughput, reduced flexibility, and loss of specialization as now discussed.

Capital requirements

If a firm integrates either backward, or forward, it needs to provide the capital that the newly acquired operation requires to be successfully integrated with the acquiring firm. In order for the combined firm to increase, or at least maintain its profitability, the operating cost savings of the newly integrated organization must be substantially greater than the capital investment required for the integration.

Unbalanced throughput

In combining the various stages of production, and/or distribution, the capacity of each unit must be matched in order that cost reduction and efficiencies are obtained such as avoiding inventory build-up. For example, an automobile constructor might acquire a component manufacturer which has a capacity greater than the acquiring firm. To balance the system would mean that the automobile firm would have to produce more automobiles, which may not be feasible because of market constraints.

Reduced flexibility

When companies integrate vertically they are accepting the work practices, and operating methods of the acquired firm. If market conditions, or technology changes, then the controlling firm may not be able to compete effectively in the marketplace. This has occurred in the steel and textile industries, when firms purchased steel or textile mills that operate with old technology. When markets changed, these sites became obsolete, were closed down, and charged as a write-off to the owner company.

Managerial style

Firms that acquire other firms sometime impose their management style on the acquired firm, which may not correspond with the market, or environment, in which the acquired firms operates. In the past, major producing companies such as paint firms, tyre producers, and oil companies have owned the retail outlets. These new owners, whose mentality is producing, have not always had the flexible and customer-oriented marketing capabilities for the outlets to remain competitive. Today, as is the case of some gasoline stations, oil companies have given up direct ownership and operate the retail outlet as a franchise. These franchise owners have maintained and increased their business by moving into food sales and other products for the automobile traveller.

Japanese firms and keiretsu

Japanese manufacturing firms such as Sony, Mitsubishi, and Nissan avoid direct vertical integration but have a middle of the road approach and control their supply chain by having a vast network of suppliers who provide many of the components used in the assembly of the finished product. These suppliers are not strictly independent but many are financially supported by the manufacturing firm and become part of a network coalition known as keiretsu. Members of the keiretsu are assured long-term relationships and as such are expected to be reliable partners providing technical expertise and continually quality products. With the poor business climate in Japan that started in the mid-1990s the keiretsu networks are coming under criticism as they tie up a lot of capital of the client company. As an illustration, when Renault acquired a large share of Nissan, Japan began to dismantle some of the 1300 companies in the Nissan keiretsu network for the very reason of tying up productive capital. This included selling its interests in Akebono Brake Industry, Fuji Heavy Industries, and Ikeda Bussan.[7]

Disintegration

After integrating their operations network vertically some firms are finding that the economic gains are not as expected and it is found cheaper to purchase components and raw materials directly from independent suppliers where they have more flexibility. These suppliers, having to fight for business, are sometimes able to produce at lower costs, better quality, and provide more reliable delivery than the integrated supplier. In the last case, the integrated supplier, knowing he has an assured customer, provides a lower than expected service.

This idea of disintegration is evident in the non-profit sector where local and state governments who used to control all the municipal services such as cleaning, maintenance, landscaping etc., find it cheaper and more efficient to subcontract out these services. On a larger scale, governments privatizing industry (British Rail, British Airways, BT, etc.) are finding that the privatized firm, cut off from the government's chain, is a more profitable entity.

Virtual companies

Having an integrated supply chain can be bureaucratic, reducing the flexibility for many firms especially with changing markets, new technology, and globalization. Virtual companies, also known as *hollow corporations* or *network companies*, are those that can be created or 'integrated' on demand to provide the services or network required. Virtual companies have flexible moving organizational boundaries that allow them to create a unique enterprise, providing services such as payroll, screening new hires, designing products, providing consulting services, manufacturing components, conducting tests, or distributing products. The relationship may be short term, true partners, or only collaborators, or simply able suppliers and subcontractors. The advantage of virtual companies include specialized management expertise, low capital investment, flexibility, speed and they can easily be disbanded when the service is no longer needed.[8]

Automation in process design

Automation in process design is the replacement of labour with machinery which are almost all computer controlled. Computers saw their beginning in the 1950s with machines, developed by IBM, Burroughs and others, housed in air-conditioned rooms. Today the use and application of computers has mushroomed to the control of equipment and machines, information exchange, printing, designing, material movement, financial transactions, etc. Even the 'experts' underestimated the dramatic growth and utilization of computer-based equipment, as illustrated in Figure 7.3. The range of automated equipment in manufacturing and services is vast and some examples are as follows.

Mechanical aids

Mechanical aids are not necessarily computer controlled but are often simple feed systems, which eliminates the operator performing the work. They result in more accurate operation, and very often reduce the risk of injury. Some examples are:

- feed attachments for punching and drilling machines
- centring and grasping devices for lathes
- strip feeders for stamping machines
- feeders that release precise quantities (either weight or volume) into containers.

Figure 7.3 Profound statement relating to computer technology

'I think there is a world market for maybe five computers!'
(Thomas Watson, Chairman of IBM, 1943)

'Computers in the future may weigh no more than one and a half tons!'
(the magazine, *Popular Mechanics*, forecasting the relentless march of science, 1949)

'I have travelled the length and breadth of this country, and talked with the best people, and I can assure you that data processing is a fad that won't last out the year!'
(editor in charge of business books for Prentice-Hall, 1957)

'But what is it good for?'
(engineer at the Advanced Computing Division of IBM commenting on the microchip, 1968)

'There is no reason anyone would want a computer in their home!'
(Ken Olson, Founder and Chairman, President of Digital Equipment Corporation, 1977)

'640 K ought to be enough for anybody!'
(Bill Gates, Cofounder, and Chair of Microsoft, 1981)

Numerically controlled machines

Numerically controlled machines are those that have control systems that read instructions and translate these instructions into machine operations. Machines are pre-programmed with computer commands to perform repeated cycle of operations that replace the manual changing of machine settings. They are available in such operations as turning on lathes, drilling, boring, and milling, assembly operations, printing, weaving, quality control such as found in sensing on a bottling line, etc.

Robots

Robots, machines performing human manipulations controlled by computers, were introduced in the 1970s. They are used extensively in the automobile industry, and the manufacture of electrical appliances such as television, radio, washing machines etc. Robots enable repetitive work like soldering to be performed more rapidly, and with precision. They are useful in dirty environments such as the paint spraying of automobile chassis or in dangerous zones such as in the nuclear and chemical industry. As a result of the incessant miniaturization of electronics, and micro-mechanics, there are even robot systems that can perform some kinds of brain and bone surgery.[9] One drawback of robots is their high capital cost and they are not always as flexible as humans even though they can work 24 hours a day. Further, sometimes there is resistance to their use from labour unions as they result in a loss of personnel. Figure 7.4 illustrates the stock of industrial robots in use. The clear leader is Japan which accounts for over half the units in the world.[10] However, companies in Europe are also investing heavily in robotic equipment as Industry insight 7.2 illustrates.

Computer–aided manufacturing

Computer-aided manufacturing systems (CAM) translate CAD information (discussed in Chapter 6) into instructions for automated production machinery. This machinery performs the necessary production operations on the products with a minimum of direct worker involvement.

Flexible manufacturing systems

Flexible manufacturing systems (FMS) are clusters of computer-controlled machines that produce a variety of products. Computers give instructions, robots handle materials, and machine settings are automatically changed by computer commands to produce the different products.

Figure 7.4 Robot units by country (yearend 2000)

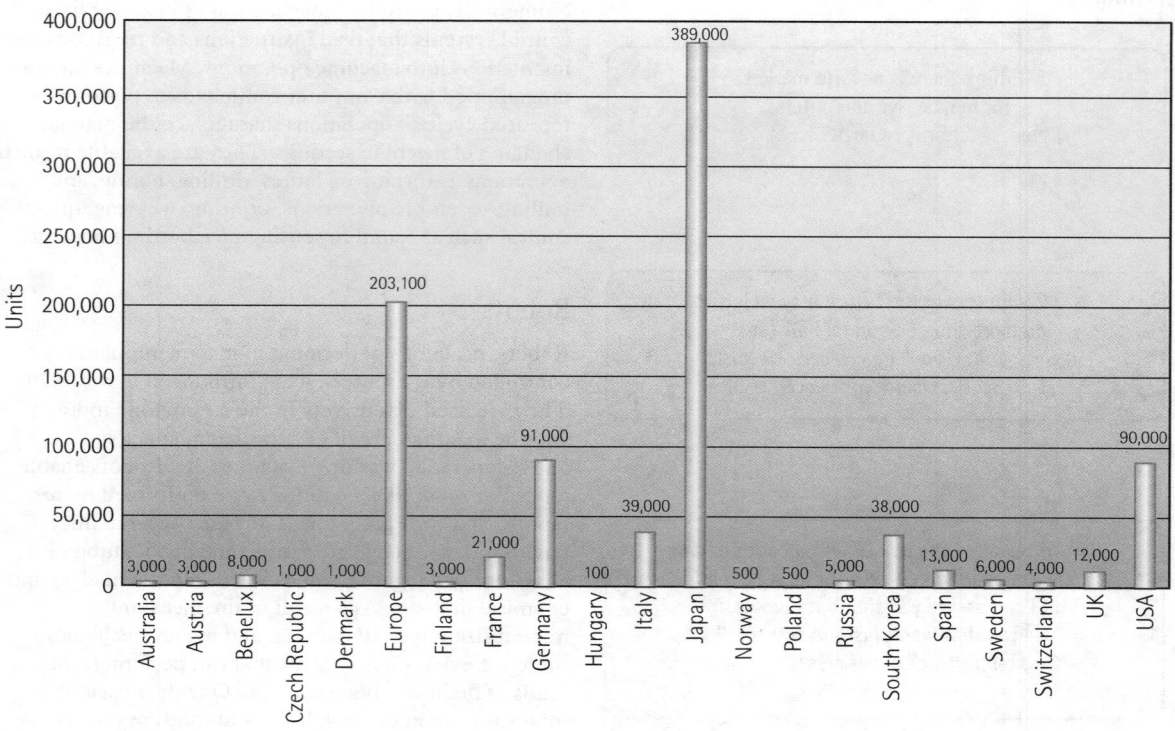

Robots are cheaper than human labour

Companies throughout Europe are investing heavily in automation, replacing people with machines. The European market for automated systems has grown more than 10% this year and shows no signs of letting up. The reason for the expansion is simply that it is cheaper to use robots than it is to use human labour. For example, in Germany, it costs an estimated $10 per hour to run a robot compared to between $30 and $37 an hour for a person. As a result, Asea Brown Boveri (ABB), one of the world's largest producers of robots, expects between $1.6 and $1.8 billion in sales in 1997 compared to $1.4 billion in 1996. This will be mostly in Europe where the market is bigger than it is in North America. Europe has twice as many robot units than the USA. (See the Figure 7.4.) A basic ABB robot arm designed to perform assembly work costs about $45,000 in 1995, half the $90,000 it cost in the late 1980s. With its worker-overregulated labour market European firms find it cheaper to buy robots than to hire people.

The growth in the automation market is something of a mixed blessing as high unemployment is already

wracking the European continent, especially since the boom is spilling out of heavy industry, automation's traditional base, into the job-rich heart of the service economy. However, since automation prices are dropping, the trend could spark a boom in productivity growth. Economists say, in fact, that the capital expenditure in automation is already a prime reason why western Europe has been able to remain competitive in the global marketplace despite its notoriously high labour costs. OECD data seem to underscore this observation, since labour productivity grew at an average annual rate of 2.2% in France and 1.1% in Germany between 1979 and 1996, compared with just 0.8% in the USA. Further, automation is one reason why Europe has been able to retain some of its sunset industries such as glass and china in France, paper and wood products in Scandinavia, and textiles in Italy, all of which rely heavily on specialized machines.

Consider Benetton's plants outside Treviso, Italy. They are tied up via computer links directly to the Italian retailer's sales outlets and to an automated warehouse that employs only 19 people to handle 30,000 boxes a day that contain precise orders for, say, blue sweaters and yellow slacks for direct shipment to stores. Without robots the warehouse would need some 400 people. The company says that when the 1992 recession hit, it either had to move production to the Far East, or invest massively in automation.

On the fourth floor of the opulent Breuninger department store in Stuttgart, Germany, is a massive robot arm that is able to fetch shoes from the stocking area. The salesperson has a hand-held computer with a bar code scanner that indicates what shoes are in stock and allows the robot to go and fetch the item. The robot has helped the store to double sales since it was introduced, partly because salesmen are no longer hidden in the stockroom looking for shoes and partly because the robot, in a new Plexiglas-enclosed storeroom, has become an attraction. In a store near Nuremberg, customers use a touch screen to buy whole cases of cola or beer from what may well be the world's largest drink machine. Germany's most prominent think tank for automation issues, the Fraunhofer Institut für Produktionstechnik und Automatisierung, or IPA, is developing a robotized system to clean the glass ceiling of Berlin's new train station. It previously developed systems that scrub Lufthansa jets, sort waste for recycling, and trim pork bellies. Most of these systems were designed for companies whose officers say automation is the only thing that has kept them from moving jobs abroad.

In France, the Formule 1 hotel chain is expanding its success around prefabricated buildings and hotels that are unattended at night. Guest check in via an automated teller machine. The showers and toilets clean automatically when a guest leaves the system. The Paris mass-transit authority, shut down by a strike in 1995, is building a new driverless subway line through the heart of the city. It will mimic similar lines in Lille and Lyon. In the Crédit Agricole branch on Boulevard Montmartre in Paris, the tellers' drawers don't contain any cash. All deposits and withdrawals pass through an array of seven specialized automated teller machines. This saves employees from the tedious job of counting and locking up money and reduces administrative costs by 12%. It allows the tellers to concentrate on more added-value activities such as selling stock funds, insurance, and credit.

Copenhagen Taxas, the Danish capital's largest taxi company is expanding its system that directs a million cabs a year to callers' addresses automatically. The address automatically pops up on a small screen in the nearest available cab. Also in Denmark, MD Foods Amba paid 12 million kroner ($1.8 million) for a two-robot system that stacks orders for seven dairy products on pallets for supermarket delivery. The firm has also ordered a new 17 million kroner ABB system that uses four robots to stack orders for 60 different types of creams, milks, and yoghurts received nightly from 800 supermarkets that are tied to the network electronically. The system enabled the firm to cut one-third of its total workforce. It should be noted that the gains from automation systems are not always immediate as the robots are complex units linked to a computer system and there is always a learning curve to respect.

Adapted from: 'Brave old world: European business uses more robots and fewer people', *Wall Street Journal Europe*[11]

Automatic guided vehicles

Automatic guided vehicles (AGVs) are computer-driven vehicles that transfer material and machinery from one work zone to another. They are used in the automobile, and heavy industries often for transferring engines from one zone to another.

Automated storage and retrieval systems

Automated storage and retrieval systems (AS&RS) are computer-controlled warehouses and storage systems. Here material and parts are automatically removed (picked) for shipping. Alternatively, components and raw materials are placed in the appropriate storage area after delivery. At the Leclerc supermarket/hypermarket, distribution centre in L'Isle d'Abeau, France, there is an automatic storage and retrieval system in a warehouse zone which contains 8054 pallets of food products, stored 14 metres high, in seven alleys and managed by just three operators.[12]

Computer–integrated manufacturing

Computer-integrated manufacturing (CIM) includes the entire system of production incorporating the latest in high-tech production technology.

Virtual systems

Virtual systems are non-physical representations of the 'real thing' most often represented by computer-based simulations. In the operating environment, they are very often an extension of computer-aided design. Two illustrations are given in Industry insight 7.3.

Virtual manufacturing

Virtual manufacturing is simulating the complete manufacture of a product before any physical operation starts. This is what Boeing did when it built the 777 aircraft. Engineers used data in digital form, which could be treated by other computer programs, and which could be copied and shared by designers in any location, and which, therefore, permitted collaboration on the same project. They used a system called CATIA, developed by Dassault Systèmes, a software company in France, to assemble an entire virtual 777. They were able to ensure that the hundreds of thousands of parts fitted, redesigning those that did not, before physically manufacturing the plane. As a result, when the first 777 was completed, it fitted together almost perfectly without additional machining modifications, which is sometimes the case in normal manufacturing.

... and virtual construction

Computer software systems such as DMAPS, also by Dassault, and others by Tecnomatix Technologies, of Herzlia in Israel, can simulate an entire manufacturing facility. Engineers can calculate the most efficient route for a spray-painting robot to take around a car body, work out how quickly parts must be supplied, look for bottlenecks, or even evaluate if a human worker's task is likely to give him backache. These simulations underscore many problems before construction of the manufacturing facility.

Adapted from: 'Manufacturing technology: The immaterial world', *The Economist*[13]

Information technology in the process system

Information technology in the broadest sense encompasses all the technological innovations to transmit information globally, visually, voice, or in written form on computer screens or downloaded onto paper, as illustrated in Figure 7.5. Some of these elements are discussed as follows and others are presented in Table 7.1.

The Internet

The Internet, or net as it is more commonly known, is a sophisticated international network of smaller networks as opposed to one big network. It was born in the 1960s in the USA out of a concern of the US military who were afraid that a nuclear attack would make their communication system ineffective. As a result of this, researchers connected up four small computers in a network between the University of California in Los Angeles, and Stanford University such that if one computer were out of action, the others were still able to function. That is, the intelligence of the system was not localized in one centralized super-computer but distributed throughout the network. Today information is sent through the network via telephone lines, fibre optic cables, radio waves, satellite, or undersea cables. Perhaps e-mail (electronic mail) is one of the most widely used functions on the Internet and Queen Elizabeth II sent her first e-mail in 1976.[14]

In order to use the Internet three essential elements are needed:

1. A personal computer with a minimum of 4 mega octets on the hard disk, and 4 mega octets of live memory.
2. A modem or 'black box', connecting the telephone line and computer enabling access to the Internet.
3. A subscription to an Internet service provider.

World Wide Web

The World Wide Web (the web, or WWW) is a set of standards on the Internet for storing, retrieving, formatting, and displaying information using a client/server architecture. The web employs graphical user interfaces for easy viewing and is based on hypertext mark-up language (HTML) that formats documents and links other documents and pictures in the same or remote computers. With these links, one is able to click on a key word, or icon, to be connected to information at another site, perhaps thousands of kilometres away. These sites are considered to be circulating in cyberspace, or space without any geographic boundaries. They are 'browsed' by net surfers or those people that use the Internet.

Web page

A web page is a block of information that can be called up across the World Wide Web. It is a way of organizing

Figure 7.5 A worldwide information network system

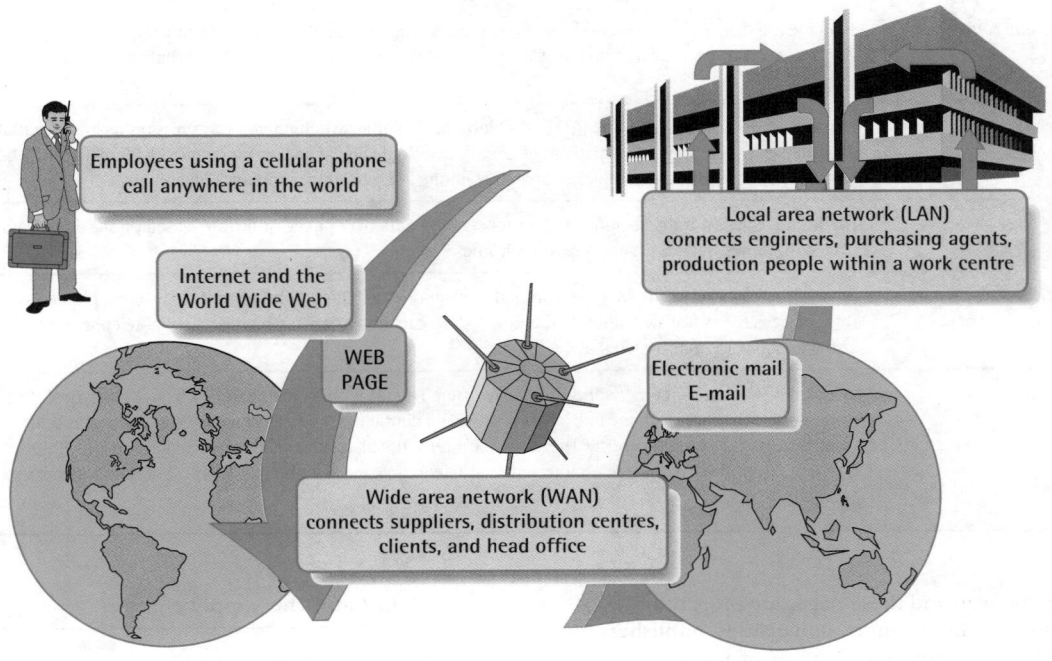

Table 7.1 Key terms in information technology

Client/server	The client/server setup is a method of computing in which one computer acts as a central repository for files and programs (server) that can be shared by a number of personal computers (clients) connected by a network. The client is the user in the system working from either a desktop or portable (laptop) computer, or even a mainframe such that he can retrieve data for analysis and reporting from the server. The server is usually a mainframe computer that stores data and also manages and controls access to shared databases. The client/server system replaces the previous mainframe centric arrangement
Local area network	A local area network (LAN) is a network within a building, or limited area, that links computers and peripheral devices permitting the sharing of information, programs, and equipment such as printers, or computer-controlled machines in a manufacturing environment. Most LAN systems connect within a 700-metre radius using their own communication channels
Ethernet	The ethernet is a set of local area network (LAN) standards that allows networking products from different vendors to communicate. It was introduced in the mid-1970s by Xerox, Digital Equipment, and Intel and is perhaps the most widely used LAN technology. Other ethernet systems include Appletalk by Apple Computer, Token Ring developed by IBM and Texas Instruments, and ARCnet from Datapoint
Wide area network	The wide area network (WAN) is an enterprise-wide communications network that allows signals to be transmitted from a LAN via public or private lines to other LANs in distant locations. A WAN may consist of a switched or dedicated line. The former is a telephone line that a user can access using his computer system where the information is switched to the appropriate destination. The dedicated line is one that is continuously available to the user. AT&T, MCI, France Télécom, Deutsche Télécom and BT (UK) are some of the carriers for WAN systems

(Continued)

Table 7.1 (Continued)

Bridge and router	A bridge is a device that links two local area networks together so that they can share data. A router, which is really a sophisticated bridge, is a device that connects local area networks that use different standards
Asynchronous transfer mode	The asynchronous transfer mode (ATM) is a high-speed digital switching and transmission technology that allows voice, video, and data signals to be sent over a single line at speeds ranging from 25 million to 1 billion bits per second (bps). For example, an analogue phone line transmits at about 2 million bps
Frame relay	The frame relay is a transmission standard for sending data over public or private leased phone lines. Data are placed in frames, each the same size, for relaying
Private branch exchange	Private branch exchange (PBX) is an automatic telephone switching arrangement for internal phone systems that replaces the office switchboard. The PBX system can store, transfer, hold, and redial telephone calls and also manage voice mail systems
Integrated services digital networks	Integrated services digital networks (ISDN) are offered by local phone companies which is a protocol that turns a standard copper phone link into a high-speed digital link that can send voice, data, image, and video information simultaneously. The system is international, having been developed in the late 1970s by the Consultative Committee on International Telegraphy and Telephony (CCITT) that represents over 150 countries

data on the web and these pages are prepared by individuals, manufacturers, universities, publishers, hospitals, restaurants, etc. as a way of advertising their activity. The home page is the text and graphical screen display that explains the organization and leads the user onto other web pages. All these pages constitute the website. Thousands of organizations use web pages on the Internet in their purchasing, sales and other activities to obtain better and faster service and to increase international reach.[15]

TCP/IP

TCP/IP (transmission control protocol/Internet protocol) is a common computer language of the Internet developed by Vinton Cerf and Robert Khan. It was launched in 1972 by the Defence Advanced Research Projects Agency (DARPA) of the USA to help researchers link up computers. In 1983 it becomes the standard for communicating between computers over the Internet. One of these protocols, FTP (file transfer protocol), allows users to log onto a remote computer, list the files on that computer, and download files from it.

Electronic data interchange

In its purest form electronic data interchange (EDI) is the transfer of structured data by agreed message standards from one computer at one site to another computer at a different location using transmission

Figure 7.6 EDI and the supply chain

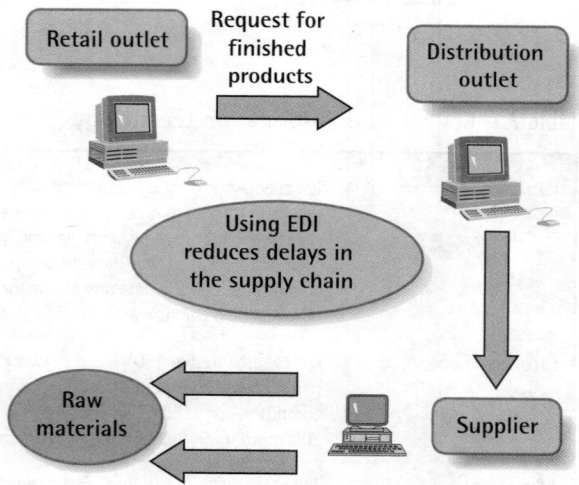

through the telephone or other network systems. Information sent using EDI might include customer orders, purchase requests, delivery orders, shipping instructions, invoices, manufacturing requests and the like. A simple scheme illustrating a supply chain where EDI is used is given in Figure 7.6. Electronic data interchange (EDI) replaces the paper documents that are exchanged between organizations, or in other words it is paperless trading. EDI has significant use both in manufacturing and the service sector permitting the more efficient management of operations.

Before EDI

Regular mail (or snail mail as it is sometimes derogatorily called) was the alternative before electronic communication. It could take an average of eight days for an order to get from a customer to a supplier where the activity involved:

- the customer writing out the order
- enclosing the order in an envelope
- putting the order in the mail
- mailman delivering the letter to the supplier
- supplier opening the envelope
- supplier logging in the order requirements.

With EDI

Using electronic data interchange, the time to communicate an order may be as little as a few minutes:

- The customer types in his order on his computer terminal.
- The order is transmitted electronically to the supplier's computer.
- The supplier does not have to record invoice details as these are already in his computer file.

Advantages of EDI

Some of the advantages of EDI include:

- Quicker response as there is real-time customer service.
- It eliminates paper and thus reduces costs.
- It is inexpensive in the fact there are fewer people involved in sending the message.
- There is better quality service as there are fewer administrative mistakes.
- The order status is always available so it is easy to track orders.
- The inventory management is more effective as there is quicker update of units in stock.
- It provides 'closeness' between customers or suppliers promoting more cooperation with the possibility of creating partnerships or alliances.

Drawbacks of EDI

Some of the drawbacks of EDI are that:

- Initial setup costs are high as these include purchase of computer hardware, software, cabling, and training of personnel.
- Users have to agree to message standards.

Table 7.2 Message standards in EDI

Customer's format	Supplier's format
Customer address	Product reference
Customer name	Price
Product reference	Supplier name
Price	Supplier address
Supplier address	Customer name
Supplier name	Customer address

- There may be a problem accepting EDI messages as legal documents.
- There is a reduction in human contact between parties concerned.

Message standards in EDI

Message standards have to be used with EDI in order that messages are sent in a format acceptable to the receiver. Table 7.2 indicates that the current message format of a customer does not correspond with the format of the supplier even though all the information is the same.

If only two firms are involved then they can agree to a data structure. However, in the automobile industry, companies such as Citroën, Ford, and Daimler-Chrysler have thousands of suppliers. In this case it is necessary to have an agreed standard. The Organization for Data Exchange by Telephone Transmission in Europe (ODETTE) is a group within the Society of Motor Manufacturers (SMMT) that created EDI message standards for the automobile industry. Another, created by the United Nations, is EDIFACT or Electronic Data Interchange for Administration, Commerce, and Trade.

Business use of information technology

The use of information technology is growing very rapidly. In a survey by the Management Centre Europe of 1055 senior managers, out of 15 business situations on the use of information technology, an aggregate of two-thirds of the responses were positive. These 15 areas of utilization, and the percent response are given in Figure 7.7.[16] Use of information technology is illustrated in Industry insight 7.4.

Figure 7.7 Business utilization of information technology

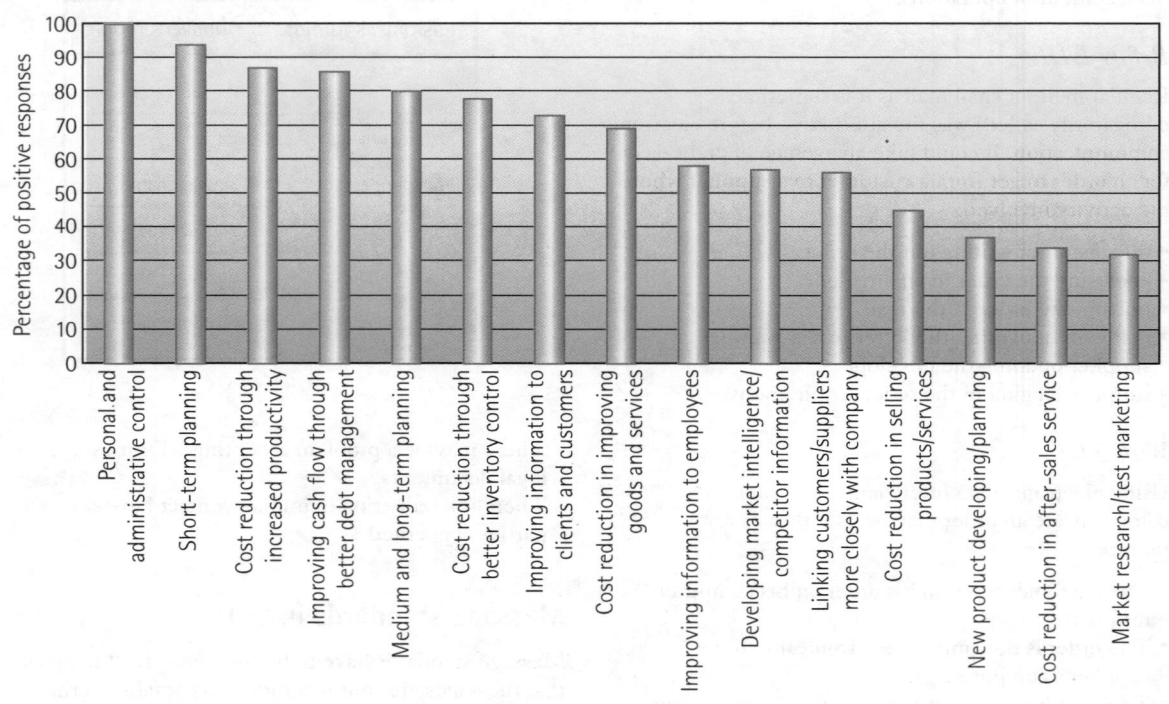

River Hills West Health Care Center

The River Hills West Health Care Center in Pewaukee, Wisconsin, has 245 residents. Each of the 245 residents receives multiple doses of up to 15 different medications a day. In the past, every time a doctor wrote a new order, it had to be transcribed by a secretary to a phone order, a pharmacy sheet, and several other patient forms. These all had to be checked by nurses, and then entered into a three-ring binder. Each month, nurses, and secretaries spent about 64 worker hours transferring records to new logbooks.

Now the routine has changed. Nurses write the first three letters of the drug's name on the screen of an electronic notepad called a CompuScriber. A list of choices appears on the screen, along with boxes to check off for doses and time of day. Once these items are entered, the network system sends the information to the River Hills network server. Records are instantly updated eliminating about five stages of paper work.

Adapted from: 'Kiss that old patient logbook goodbye',
Business Week[17]

Electronic commerce

Business transactions

The transaction in the supply chain might simply be business to business, or B2B, where one business firm supplies industrial goods to another firm. Alternatively, the transaction might be business to consumer, or B2C, where a business entity supplies finished goods to the final consumer. Electronic commerce facilitates these product transactions by allowing the buyer to communicate their requirements using the Internet, and it allows the seller to communicate product availability and specifications. In either case, electronic commerce plays a significant role including reducing both lead times and transfer costs and at the same time increasing the marketing potential for the firm. The following gives details of how electronic commerce functions in business-to-business and business-to-consumer links.

Figure 7.8 Business-to-business electronic commerce

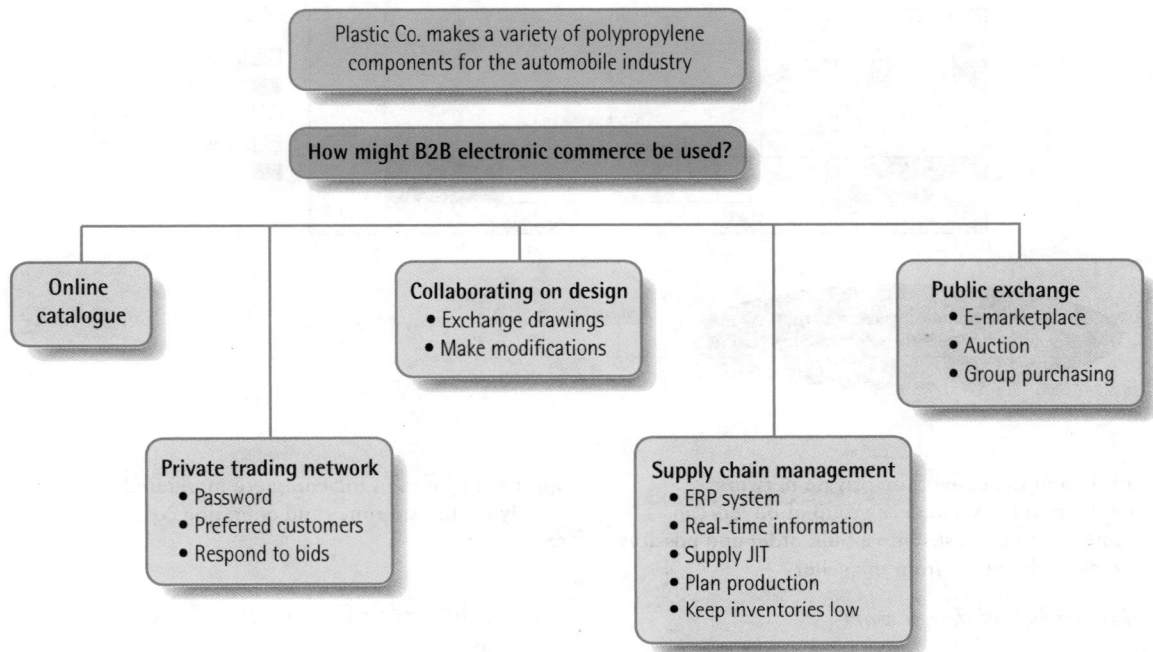

Business to business

Suppose a firm, Plastic Co. makes a variety of polyethylene, polypropylene and composite components and parts for the automobile industry – electrical casings, interior moulded fittings, etc. – the packaging industry – boxes, cases, bottles, etc. – and the household appliances industry – the outside covers of irons, toasters, coffee percolators, etc. Figure 7.8 summarizes the ways in which Plastic Co. might carry out electronic business-to-business transactions using the web and they are explained as follows.

An online catalogue

Here Plastic Co. has developed its own electronic website catalogue of all the products that it is able to supply. Prospective customers can browse the catalogue and see the entire product line. Orders can be place through the network in the same way in which you might buy a book through Amazon.com, for example.

Private trading network, or private exchange

In this case Plastic Co.'s catalogue is not open to everyone but is only accessible through a password,

known only to its preferred or largest customers. These customers can order directly online through Plastic Co.'s internal computer system and the customer is able to obtain online information as to when the order has been received by Plastic Co., when it is processed, when it has been shipped, and the expected delivery date.

Proposals with the private exchange

If Plastic Co. has a private exchange it can send proposals in response to bids put out by its customers for special purpose orders. In addition, if Plastic Co. has excess inventories of certain products, it can use the network to auction off this material.

Public exchange network

An alternative to the private exchange is that Plastic Co. can establish a public exchange network, or e-marketplace, where buyers and sellers are able to communicate in order to auction of their products, or respond to bids. On the upside this public exchange exposes Plastic Co. to a larger market where it might have a better chance of selling its products. However, on the downside, it might be forced to accept lower

Figure 7.9 Automobile industry: How lead times could be reduced

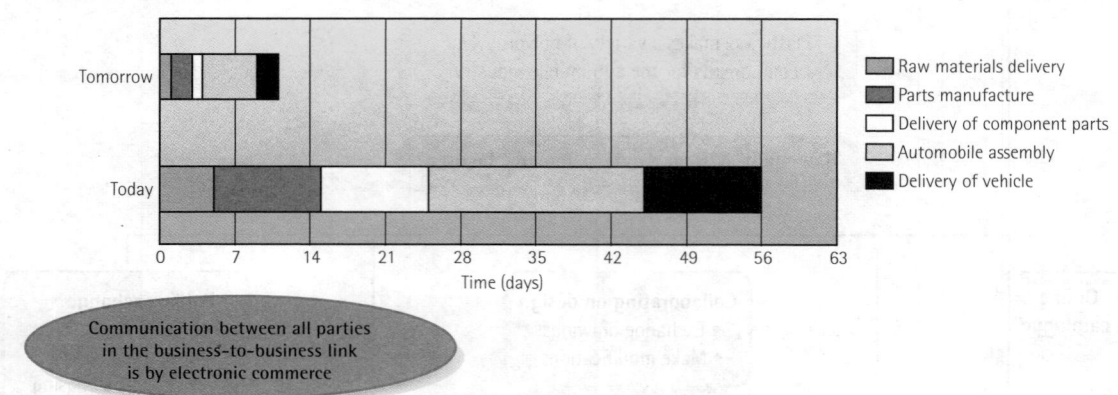

prices than in the case of the private network. Using the public exchange, a group of buyers can combine their purchases into a bulk order and possibly obtain price discounts from the seller.

Collaborating on design work

If Plastic Co. has a contract with, say, an automobile firm to design a new component destined for a new automobile model, then all the designs can be transmitted over the network. Both the client firm and Plastic Co. can review the designs and make appropriate modifications. This saves time, and reduces possible errors by faxing or mailing drawings each time a design change is made. Engineering and design firms use this approach when working with their subcontractors. (See Chapter 18.)

Supply chain management

Using either a private network or perhaps the public exchange, and if Plastic Co. has an ERP system (see Chapter 13) link with its customer, it will be able to manage its production schedules and inventory better. With the network and the ERP system, Plastic Co. has real-time information, on an hourly basis if needed, about its customers' needs, its utilization rate of components, current inventory, and future requirements. It can ship the products on a just-in-time basis (without first telephoning the customer) thus reducing the possibly of high inventories at the customer's site or, worse, a stockout. In addition, it can plan in advance an order to meet the customer's requirements exactly thus reducing the operating expense of inventory carrying costs. Upstream of Plastic Co. its suppliers can provide the same sort of service. If this management

approach is used in the complete integrated supply chain lead times and operating costs will be reduced.

Lead time reduction using electronic commerce

Using electronic commerce reduces the lead times in the business-to-business transactions as the parties to the transaction have real-time information on product specification requirements and need dates. In this way, suppliers can schedule production of component parts such that they are available just when their customers need them. Automobile companies, for example, which currently have about an eight-week lead time between when a customer places an order for a vehicle and the delivery date, are hoping they can reduce this to just 11 days, as illustrated in Figure 7.9.

Business to consumer for catalogue shopping

Suppose a buyer wishes to buy a clothing item using the Internet's World Wide Web. The procedure is illustrated in Figure 7.10 and explained as follows:

1. A customer browses the web to see the article she would like and then places the order electronically to the supplier.
2. The supplier electronically receives the order.
3. The supplier electronically checks to see if there is sufficient inventory in stock, and also the profile of the customer, regarding her credit rating.

Figure 7.10 Using the Internet in the supply chain (catalogue ordering)

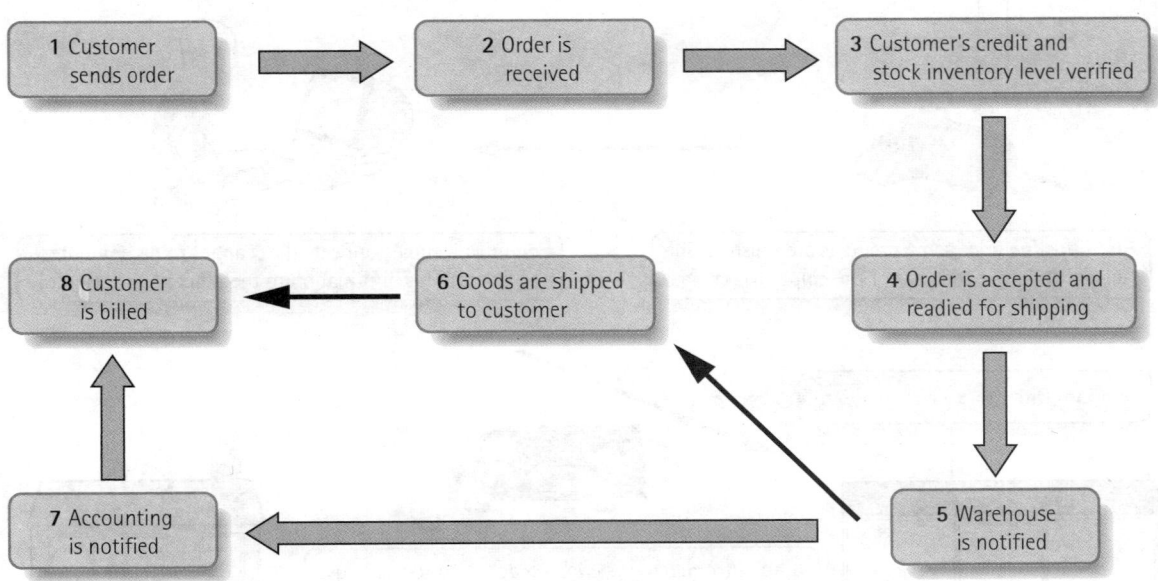

4. If the credit rating is good, the order is verified and accepted.
5. The necessary shipping instructions are sent to the warehouse where the article is in storage.
6. At the warehouse, the item is physically located, picked, packaged, and sent to the customer.
7. The accounting department is notified of the order.
8. The customer is electronically billed.

In this supply chain, all the transactions have been carried out by electronic interchange, with the only physical flow being the delivery of the item.
The lead time for this sort of purchasing can be in the order of five days. This is longer perhaps than the time taken to buy the article from a store but the advantage of the catalogue shopping is that the customer may have more product choice, lower prices, and does not have to put up with the hassle of going to the store.

Business to consumer for online grocery shopping

In the 1950s a common way to deliver grocery items to customers was that, during the week, the buyer would come into the grocery store with her order book listing the grocery items she would like. The assistant in the grocery store would select the items and pack them in a cardboard box. Later, the grocery boy would load a certain number of boxes, usually a maximum of five, onto a pedal cycle with a carrier at the front, and deliver the groceries. The delivery boy would decide the optimum route and receive cash payments for the groceries. Depending on delivery dates customers might wait one or perhaps two weeks for their order.[18] In 2000 a similar service is now available but all communication is performed electronically and delivery is by van.

The concept of shopping for groceries online is illustrated in Figure 7.11. It works as follows:

- Customer finds that some of the grocery items are getting low and so using her laser reader she clicks on the bar codes of the products she wishes to order.
- When the bar codes have been read, the scanner is inserted into the home computer and the order information is transferred electronically to the grocery store where it is received almost immediately.
- In the evening the order is delivered by van to the customer. Payment is made to the deliverer by credit card using his mobile card reader. The client has never set foot in the store.

The success of grocery shopping electronically is presented in Industry insight 7.5.

Figure 7.11 Electronic commerce and online grocery shopping

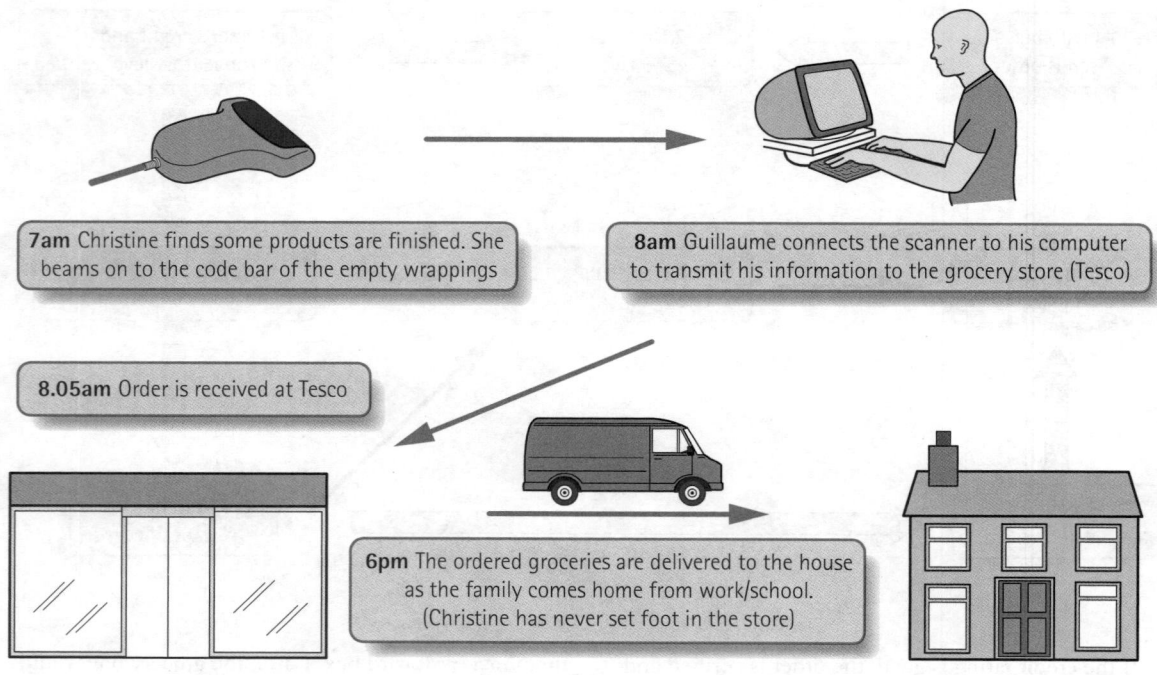

7am Christine finds some products are finished. She beams on to the code bar of the empty wrappings

8am Guillaume connects the scanner to his computer to transmit his information to the grocery store (Tesco)

8.05am Order is received at Tesco

6pm The ordered groceries are delivered to the house as the family comes home from work/school. (Christine has never set foot in the store)

Tesco, UK, and online grocery shopping

Industry insight 7.5

Tesco was assailed by analysts during the peak of the dot.com boom for its go-slow approach to selling groceries over the Internet. Now, Britain's N° 1 supermarket chain has watched one rival after another put up the white flag, and Tesco has assumed the mantle of the world's largest and most successful online grocer. Its gamble was to bet small such that in 1996, when the web was exploding and online groceries seemed a brilliant idea, Tesco plc invested just $58 million outfitting a single store in Osterley, England, to accept orders by phone, fax, and a simple website. The idea was to test whether customers would buy groceries without shopping in conventional supermarkets. Further, Tesco wanted to establish whether it made more sense to pick groceries off the current store shelves, or to build separate warehouses to fill online orders. By March 1998 the company had proved there was sufficient online demand and that picking from existing stores worked. It kept tweaking the process to get the economics right and by September 1999 it provided online service in 100 of its stores.

In the operations of its online sales, Tesco uses around 24 employees per store to pull products of the shelves and to deliver them by van to customers. At first the

process of picking products off the shelf was inefficient until Tesco came up with a better solution. Rather than having pickers traverse the entire store filling orders for individual customers, each supermarket is divide into six zones: groceries, produce (fruits and vegetables), bakery, chilled foods, frozen foods, and 'secure products' such as liquor and cigarettes. Each picker is equipped with a rolling cart and traverses a single zone retrieving products for six customers at a time. The rolling cart has a wireless touch-pad computer that plans the optimal route through the store and indicates to pickers what to retrieve, item by item. To save time and improve accuracy, each item is scanned at the moment it is picked and then customers' shipments are assembled in a back room and loaded into vans for delivery. Pickers average just 30 seconds per item and so a typical order of 64 items can be filled in 32 minutes, or a cost of about $8.50 including labour and depreciation. This is still high at some 7% of the average $123 order but the company saves as checkout clerks are not needed, and the fact that online orders tend to have gross margins of more than 30% against the average of 25%. This is because online shoppers are usually from a more affluent section of the community and purchase more profitable products such as organic vegetables, top-quality meat, and private label goods. Tesco.com typically fills two to three waves of orders a day and this allows customers to buy as late as midday and receive orders by 10 pm the same day. The online operation with the pickers in the store provides constant publicity for the web service helping to extend the Tesco name brand.

Tesco.com is like an electronic version of the 1950s' delivery boy, except there is a much steeper delivery charge of £5 ($7.25) per order. The chain now gets more than 70,000 online orders weekly and collects $27 million a year from these delivery charges alone which largely covers the cost of vans and drivers. Further, the fee encourages customers to place large orders in order to get their money's worth. The average purchase through Tesco.com is often three times a typical $35 supermarket transaction, which is a vital contributor to the online operations gross margin (see Table). In addition, charging the fee increases the probability that customers will be at home during the two-hour window

for delivery, since they have to pay again for redelivery. That is important to Tesco, since returning merchandise to the store and restocking it could destroy the margins.

By 2001 Tesco.com had handled more than 3.7 million orders a year, with half of its online customers coming from competitor's stores. It had expanded to 250 outlets or more than one-third of the chain's 690 British stores that enables it to deliver to 91% of Britain's population. The business generated revenues of more than $450 million in 2001 with a respectable estimated net operating margin from groceries of around 5% or more than $22 million. Although in 2000 the dot.com unit lost $13 million due to the cost of expanding into new business such as CDs and videos, it was profitable on groceries. The online operation gets free ads in Tesco's quarterly mailing to its 10 million affinity card holders and has linked its websites to store databases so customers can easily reorder products they have previously ordered on line or in a supermarket.

Table 7.3 compares shopping online with Tesco to standard shopping in a supermarket.

Table 7.3 Financial analysis of Tesco.com compared to a supermarket

	Tesco.com		Tesco supermarket	
	$	% of income	$	% of income
Average sale	123.25	94.44	34.80	100.00
Delivery fee	7.25	5.56	0.00	0.00
Total income	130.50	00.00	34.80	100.00
Cost of groceries	85.66	65.64	26.10	75.00
Checkout in store		0.00	0.87	2.50
Other store costs	15.16	11.62	4.28	12.30
Marketing/administration	5.67	4.34	1.60	4.60
Picking and delivery	17.80	13.64	0	0.00
Total costs	124.29	95.24	32.85	94.40
Net profit	6.21	4.76	1.95	5.60

Adapted from: 'Tesco bets small – and wins big', *Business Week*[19]

Artificial intelligence

Artificial intelligence is an aspect of information technology and is, broadly, the use of computers to mimic or copy aspects of human intelligence, such as learning languages, making decisions, and performing physical actions. Robots come under the definition of artificial intelligence where the robot is programmed to accomplish specific coordinated manual tasks. Three elements of artificial intelligence, which has application in the design

of processes, include expert systems, neural networks, and fuzzy logic, which are summarized as follows.

Expert systems

Expert systems are knowledge-based systems that emulate expert thinking, or human logic, to solve complex problems in a particular domain. The difficulty with expert systems is the design of the 'system' so that it corresponds to the human brain. This means detailed programming so that every possible cause of action is taken in consideration. Expert systems are computer-based iterations that are rule based which means they contain a predefined set of knowledge that is used for all decisions. The system uses the predefined rules to produce results by using inference rules, which are coded into the system. Depending on the kind of input, and rules used, expert systems can be used either as quantitative, or qualitative tools. A generic expert system will contain two main modules: the knowledge base, and the inference engine.

Knowledge base

The knowledge base contains knowledge of the system regarding the specific domain, or area, for which it is designed to solve problems, or make recommendations. For example, in the financial domain, the knowledge base will include specific rules that the system contains (decisions concerning shares, price levels, or margins for example).

Inference engine

The inference engine processes and combines facts related to the particular problem, case, and question, using that part of the knowledge base that is relevant. The selection of the appropriate data in the knowledge base is performed according to searching criteria.

Table 7.4 contains some examples of the process applications of expert systems.

Neural networks

Neural networks are computer hardware or software that attempt to copy the processing patterns of the biological brain. The brain has about 100 billion neurons and can operate at 100 hertz. This is slow by computer standards where an Intel 80486 chip operates at up to 100 megahertz, or millions of cycles per second. Neural networks have found application in the medical field (for pap smear tests that detect cervical cancer, for example), prediction of securities ratings, stock purchasing, inspection and flaws in steel plates, classification of welding defects, sound analysis, and identification parts in a production line.

Neural networks are different from expert systems, as here, the human simulation is based on rules where neural networks emulate the human brain and are modelled from experience.

Fuzzy logic

Computer systems basically rely on the exact binomial approach such as open or closed, on or off, yes or no, right or wrong. Human thinking is not so precise. For example, is 4 km a long way to walk, or not very far? Is 32°C hot, or

Table 7.4 Process applications of expert systems

Subject area	Activity
Chemical compounds	Formulation of data about unknown chemical compounds
Infectious diseases	Diagnosing infectious diseases and proposing appropriate treatment
Credit cards	Validating user credit card access by financial firms
Consulting	Diagnosis or troubleshooting operations for consulting firms
Lung diseases	Diagnosis and reporting the presence, and severity of lung diseases
Engineering	Providing information on structural designs of buildings
Molecular biology	Design and simulation of experiments in molecular biology and genetic experiments
Mathematics	Development of new mathematical concepts and their associated proofs
Space travel	Diagnosing and proposing solutions related to spacecraft anomalies
Playing chess!	IBM's Deep Blue computer won a chess tournament against the reigning world champion, Garry Kasparov, in May 1997

a comfortable temperature? Is 10 kg too much to carry, or manageable? The response is inexact, or fuzzy and depends on a person's judgment, their physical make-up, and external conditions. Fuzzy logic is a rule-based development in artificial intelligence that can be used to develop and solve certain problems. If the logic is expressed with some carefully defined impression, then fuzzy logic can be closer to the way people actually think than traditional if–then rules. As an example, Ford Motor Co. developed a fuzzy logic application that backs a simulated tractor–trailer into a parking space. The application uses the following three rules:

1. *If* the lorry is near jack-knifing, *then* reduce the steering angle.
2. *If* the lorry is far away from the dock, *then* steer toward the dock.
3. *If* the lorry is near the dock, *then* point the trailer directly at the dock.

Fuzzy logic is widely used in Japan in the design of home appliances such as refrigerators, vacuum cleaners, washers, dryers, rice cookers, and air conditioners.[20]

Operations network chart

A process operations network can be designed, or later analyzed, using an operations network chart (sometimes referred to as a process flow chart). If the process network has yet to be designed its purpose would be to see what might occur. If the network has already been designed then the chart could be used to find out what is going on and thence to establish ways of improving the process design.

Terms in the network chart

The heart of the flowchart lies in the five symbols to be seen in Figure 7.12. They are explained as follows.

Figure 7.12 Process flow chart pro-forma

Process Flow Chart													
Section									Operators				
Operation started													
Operation finished													
Summary		O □ D → Δ											
Total actual time													
Total expected time													
Difference													

Description	Operation	Inspection	Wait	Transfer	Store	Quantity	Time (a)	Frequency	Distance	Surface	Lot size	Observations
1	O	□	D	→	Δ							
2	O	□	D	→	Δ							
3	O	□	D	→	Δ							
4	O	□	D	→	Δ							
5	O	□	D	→	Δ							
6	O	□	D	→	Δ							
7	O	□	D	→	Δ							
8	O	□	D	→	Δ							
9	O	□	D	→	Δ							
10	O	□	D	→	Δ							
11	O	□	D	→	Δ							
12	O	□	D	→	Δ							
13	O	□	D	→	Δ							
14	O	□	D	→	Δ							
15	O	□	D	→	Δ							

(a) End of operation

Figure 7.13 Process flow chart: Transformer mounting

Process Flow Chart							
Section		Transformer mounting				Operators	
Operation started		Monday			08:15	Guillaume WALLER/Derek CUSIN	
Operation finished		Tuesday			17:48	Odette DUCREY/Cédric ACCARY	
Summary		O	□	D	→	Δ	
Total actual time	33:33	8:29	2:22	3:08	11:54	7:40	33:33
Total expected time	18:45	7:30	0:45	0:30	8:30	1:30	18:45
Difference	14:48	0:59	1:37	2:38	3:24	6:10	14:48

	Description	Operation	Inspection	Wait	Transfer	Store	Quantity	Time (a)	Frequency	Distance	Surface	Lot size	Observations
1	Component B-16	O	□	D	→	Δ	60	08:15			25.3		Storage area SA-25
2	Component B-16	O	□	D	→	Δ	60	08:45		5.5			By conveyor
3	Component B-16	O	□	D	→	Δ	60	09:48			9.0		Change of machine tools
4	Component B-16	O	□	D	→	Δ	60	14:52			6.1		Machining. Now ref C-18
5	Component C-18	O	□	D	→	Δ	58	16:12			5.7		Specifications checked
6	Component C-18	O	□	D	→	Δ	58	17:15			5.7		Trolleys not available
7	Component C-18	O	□	D	→	Δ	58	17:50		47.0			To adjacent work centre
8	Component C-18	O	□	D	→	Δ	58	18:52			10.3		No unloaders available
9	Component C-18	O	□	D	→	Δ	56	20:57			21.7		Assembly. Now ref DC-180
10	Component DC-180	O	□	D	→	Δ	56	21:59			9.3		Electric test for solder joints
11	Component DC-180	O	□	D	→	Δ	55	23:38		37.0			To storage area, SA-11
12	Component DC-180	O	□	D	→	Δ	55	07:18			56.8		In storage area, SA-11
13	Component DC-180	O	□	D	→	Δ	35	08:38		75.0			To packing zone
14	Component DC-180	O	□	D	→	Δ	35	09:58			34.0		Blister pack/wood boxes
15	Component DC-180	O	□	D	→	Δ	35	17:48					Shipped to client

(a) End of operation

O Operation

An operation is any activity that transforms an element from one form to another, adding value during the operation. In services, this might be recording information, performing a treatment, or making a transaction. In manufacturing, it would involve the transformation of a piece of inventory into something different as might occur in cutting, drilling, or assembly.

□ *Inspection*

Inspection is an activity where a controller, a production manager, or a client, for example, is inspecting the service or material for quality, to see if it is according to specification, or simply to see if the right number of units is present. No change is taking place, and thus no value is being added.

D *Waiting*

Waiting is simply that inventory or people are 'waiting' for someone to do something. This might be in a service centre, office, work centre, vehicle, on a machine, etc. No change is taking place and thus no value is being added.

→ *Transfer*

Transfer is when material, people, or documents are being moved from one area to another. This might be from:

- one work area to another
- a work area to storage
- storage to a client
- one office to another.

For materials, the transfer might take place by an operator carrying the units, on a moving belt, or in a truck. For services, such as a hospital, it might be the transfer of a patient from one treatment zone to another. In an airport, it could be the transfer from one terminal to another. In a design office it might be the transfer of written specifications from one building to another. Essentially, no change is taking place in the service operation or to the inventory material, and so it might be argued that no value is being added. However, in both manufacturing and services, the patient, document, baggage, or inventory is of no use unless it is at the right place. In which case, the fact of getting it to the right place can be considered to add value. A Philips television set, for example, is of no value to a client at the factory in Eindhoven. However, it would be of value if it were on sale in a store in Amsterdam.

Δ *Storing*

Storing is when material is physically housed in an area devoted to that very purpose. For a finished consumer product, this might be the storage area of a supermarket, it might a distribution centre, or it might be the warehouse for finished products at the production centre.

As shown in the figure for the five various activities, the quantity of units handled is entered, together with the time, frequency, distance, surface area involved, and the lot size.

Completed network chart

A network chart, which has been completed for an existing operation, is illustrated in Figure 7.13. It illustrates the activity of components coming from storage, and delivery to the final client. A line connects each activity so that the flow of material can be easily seen. The summary at the top of the chart gives the difference between actual times, and expected times. Any differences would give rise to further investigation. Some observations from this chart are:

- There is a significant difference between actual times (33 hours and 33 minutes) and expected times (18 hours 45 minutes).
- Non-value-added time including waiting, transfer, and storing is long. (25 hours 4 minutes (33:33 − 8:29). As a percentage the non-value-added activity is about 75%.)
- In two of the operation steps, fewer units leave than enter, suggesting, perhaps, that faulty parts are being used, or incorrect process work is being performed.

Business process reengineering

Definition

Business process reengineering (BPR) was an idea presented in 1990 by two Americans, James Champy and Michael Hammer. It is defined as the means by which an organization can achieve radical change in performance by the application of a variety of tools and techniques that focus on the business as a set of related customer-oriented core business processes rather than a set of organizational functions. Performance may be measured by such factors as cost, cycle time, service and quality. The primary objective of BPR is intended to boost competitiveness in the operations network through simpler, leaner, and more productive processes. It has been applied in labour and capital-intensive industries such as automobile production, telecommunications, pharmaceuticals and also in service sectors such as insurance and banking. Business process reengineering coins the phrase 'breaking the china', meaning that the firm is brave enough to ignore, or even destroy, the process design activities that went on before, and start all over again.[21]

Real-world illustration

The AT&T Power Systems in Dallas, Texas, produces custom switching power supplies in a very competitive market. The original process design process for each customer from proposal request to delivery of the finished product was identified as being made up of 42 different process activities including 12 scheduled meetings, as illustrated in Figure 7.14. A detailed analysis showed that the product could not continue to be competitive on costs and in addition the product was taking on average 53 days to be delivered to the customer.

The company completely revamped the process design processes creating multifunctional design teams and using standard designs where possible and still keeping the power supplies customized. By standardizing, the design teams were assured of parts availability in stock since the same components were required for other standard subassemblies. In the new processes design configuration, a number of the old activities were retained but assigned to a design cell,

Figure 7.14 Formal design process for custom switching power supplies (before)

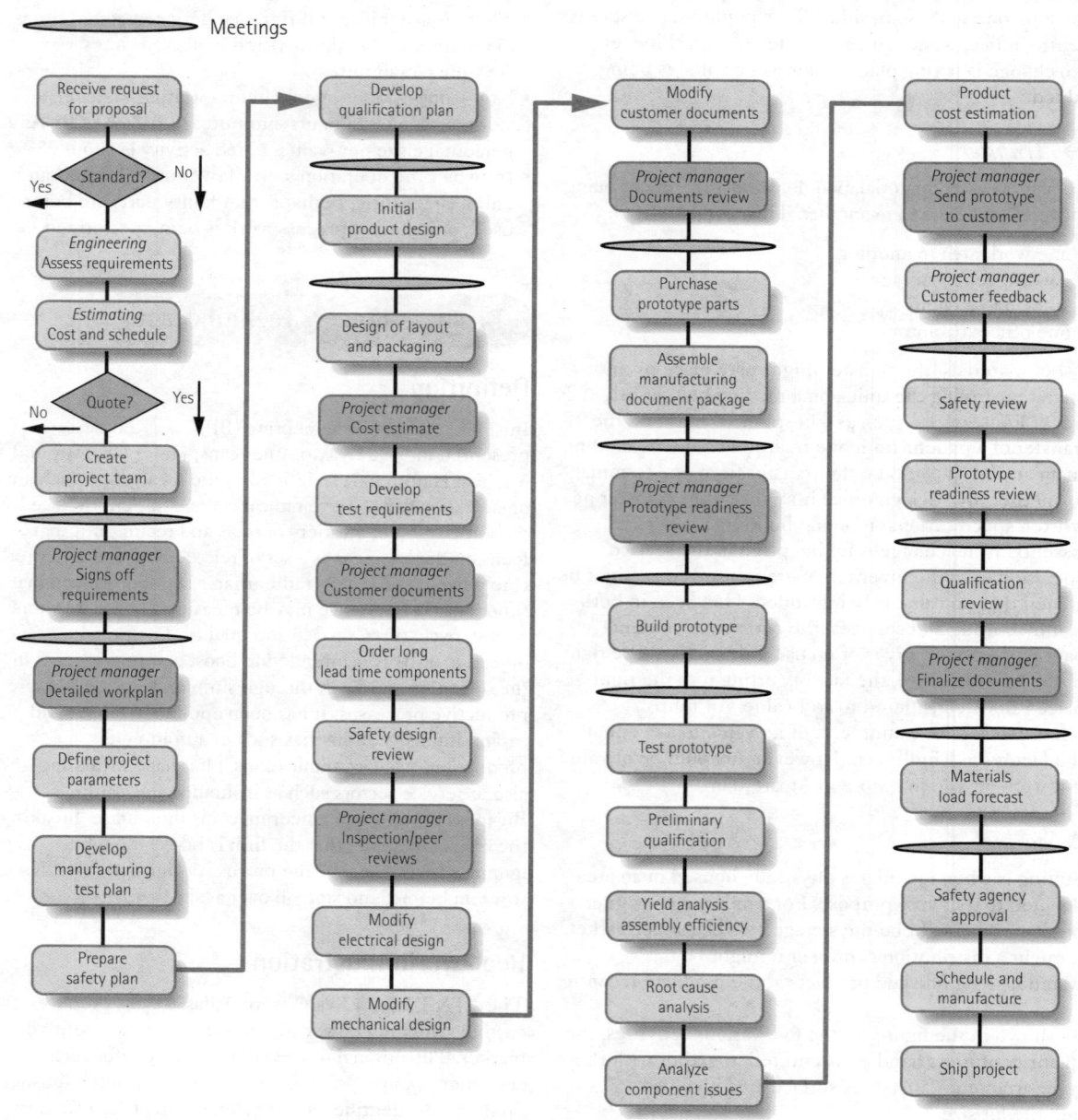

which is a dedicated group comprising electrical, mechanical, test, and quality engineers plus a model builder and the project manager who worked in close harmony to cut throughput time. Each team member was made responsible for his own work avoiding cross-checking, reviews, and formal meetings. As a result, 17 process design activities were eliminated, ten were combined into cell activity, leaving only 17 formal steps

and one meeting, as illustrated in Figure 7.15. As a result of this BPR delivery time was reduced to five days or a reduction of 90% over the original time.[22]

Does BPR always work?

In a study of more than 100 companies, Hall, Rosenthal, and Wade from Harvard, concluded that business

Figure 7.15 **Formal design process for custom switching power supplies (after)**

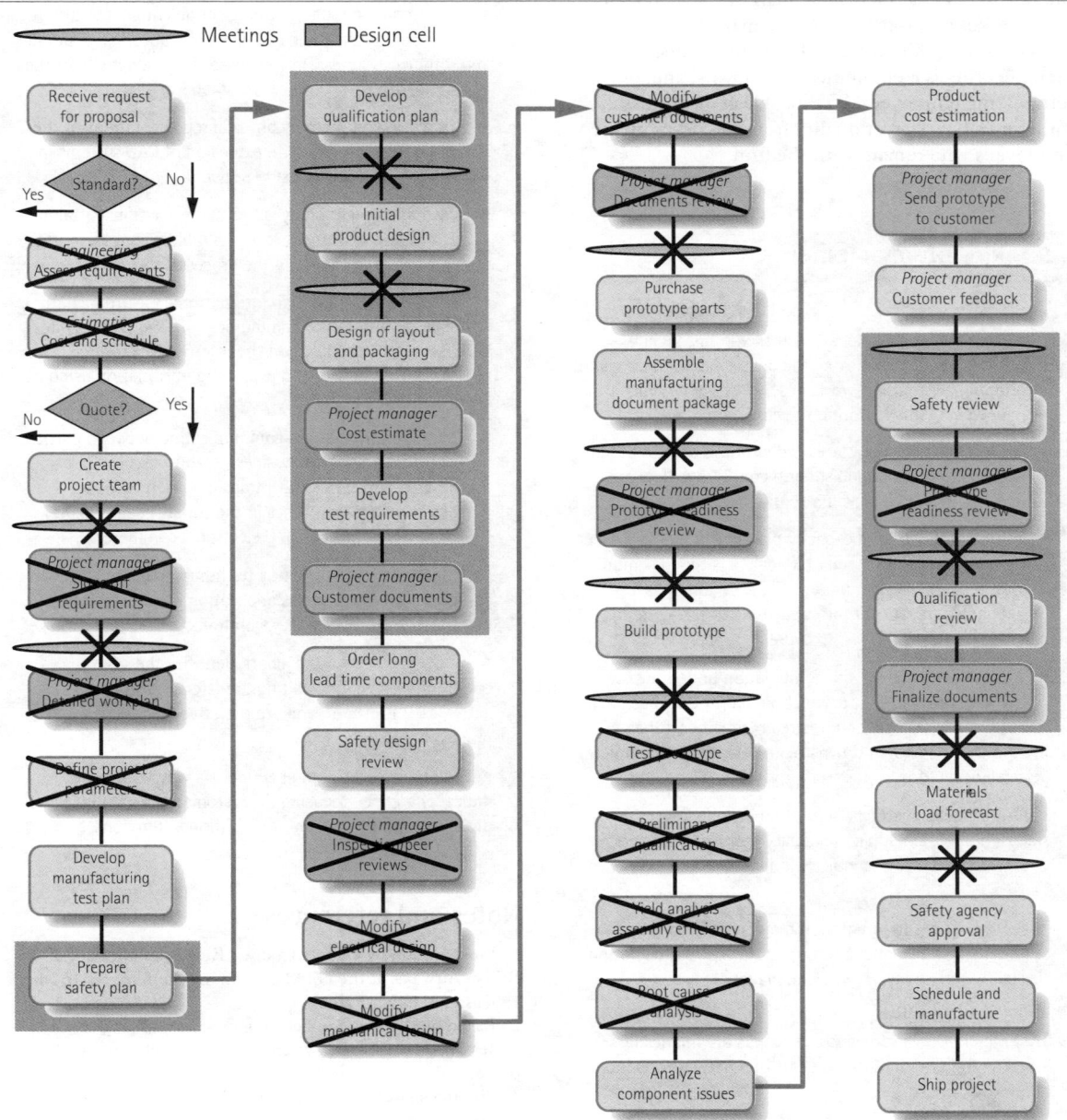

process reengineering is not always a success and they cite many instances where it fails to achieve real business impact. They clarify that business process reengineering is a 'top down' exercise and that even with sufficient breadth and depth, a reengineering project will fail without the full commitment of senior executives.[23] CSC Index, a consulting firm, surveyed 497 large companies in the United States, and another 124 in Europe, and found that reengineering is far from being a guarantee of corporate renewal. Fewer than half the firms aiming at increasing market share achieved their market and some failed abysmally.[24]

As Chapter 4 highlighted, for many, business process reengineering is a euphemism for downsizing, or terminating employees. The backlash of this has sometimes been lower quality from the de-motivated employees who remain with the firm.

Summary of key elements

- Design considerations of the process system in manufacturing include location, make or buy, facility layout, technology employed, the physical distribution, and information systems network. In services the network is developed very much around the customer.

- Product types can be correlated with the process design. Between extremes of a job shop to continuous flow are differences in flexibility, volume, and unit cost.

- In the process system capacity planning, which is market driven, is a key design element. Capacity is the maximum output, or use of system under normal conditions. Utilization is the ratio of the capacity used to the design capacity.

- Vertical integration is the combination under one owner of two or more stages of production and/or distribution. It can be backward, involving upstream activities, forward, involving ownership of downstream activities, or complete vertical integration.

- Advantages in vertical integration include lower transaction costs, supplier reliability, captive customers, easier coordination, technology innovation, and high entry barriers.

- Disadvantages to integration may include high capital requirements, unbalanced throughputs, reduced operating flexibility, and an incompatible managerial style.

- Japanese firms have vast quasi-integrated networks. They may not own suppliers but outlets are financially aided by the firm and become part of a network coalition known as keiretsu.

- There is a move among some organizations to disintegrate as the economic advantages and increased flexibility outweigh the advantages of vertical integration.

- A virtual company is a type of vertical integration that has no physical structure. It can be disbanded when the service offered is no longer needed.

- Automated equipment in process design includes numerically controlled machines, robots, computer-aided and/or integrated manufacturing, flexible manufacturing systems, automatic guided vehicles, and automated storage and retrieval systems. They increase the productivity of the operation, often at the expense of labour.

- Virtual systems are non-physical representations of the real thing. They are often an extension of CAD systems in simulating the process design network.

- Information technology is the electronic transmittal in visual, voice, or document form. Its rapidly increasing use vastly improves response in the process network.

- The Internet, or net, is an international electronic data interchange facilitating communication. The World Wide Web is a set of standards on the Internet for storing, retrieving, formatting, and displaying information using a client/server architecture.

- Electronic commerce is communicating between parties on the Internet either in business-to-business (B2B), or business-to-consumer (B2C) transactions. Its use can drastically reduce lead times in the supply chain. Online shopping is one form of B2C electronic commerce.

- Artificial intelligence emulates human logic to solve complex problems and has application in process design in manufacturing and service operations.

- An operations network chart identifies the operation, inspection, waiting, transfer, and storing activities. It is used to analyze the effectiveness of a process network.

- Business process reengineering is a way to achieve radical change by focusing on customer-oriented business processes, rather than on organizational functions.

Notes and references

1. Presentation by George Cooper, European Director of British Airways, at the G7 Management Conference, 16 May 1997, E. M. Lyon, France
2. Based on 'Link manufacturing process and product life cycles', *Harvard Business Review*, January–February, 1979, pp 133–40
3. 'Boeing shares drop on production crunch', *International Herald Tribune*, 4–5 October 1997

4. 'Short supply: Success of AIDS drug brings new concern: Can Merck keep pace? Company rushed Crixivan to market: Now it faces a production bottleneck. Watching the patient count', *Wall Street Journal Europe*, 5 November 1996

5. BUZZELL, Robert D., 'Is vertical integration profitable', *Harvard Business Review*, January–February 1983, 61 no 1, pp 92–102

6. TEECE, David J., *Vertical Integration in the Oil Industry*, Edward J. Mitchell (ed.), American Enterprise Institute, 1976, p. 105

7. 'Revival at Nissan is a sign of hope for Japan Inc.', *Wall Street Journal Europe*, 16 November 2000

8. HEIZER, Jay and RENDER, Barry, *Production and Operations Management*, 4th edition, Prentice Hall, p. 534.

9. 'Robot revolution', *National Geographic*, July 1997, pp 76–95

10. 'Economic and financial indicators', *The Economist*, 1 December 2001, p. 100

11. 'Brave old world: European business uses more robots and fewer people. Higher wages compel firms to invest in automation, even in the service sector. This "crocodile" eats jobs', *Wall Street Journal Europe*, 22 July 1997

12. Study project by the author, 1996

13. 'Manufacturing technology: The immaterial world', *The Economist*, 28 June 1997, pp 104–6

14. 'Evolution of the net', *Wall Street Journal Europe*, 12 October 1999, p. VIII

15. 'Europe Inc. starts to get wired: With US rivals outdistancing them, more companies join the information revolution', *Business Week*, 17 March 1997, p. 19

16. 'Business utilisation of information technology', *Wall Street Journal Europe*, 1/2 August 1997

17. 'Kiss that old patient logbook goodbye', Information Technology Annual Report, *Business Week* 26 June 1995

18. Author's experience. In the 1950s he was a grocery delivery boy for seven years delivering groceries on Tuesday and Thursday evening and Saturday morning for the Co-op in Watford, England

19. REINHARDT, Andy, 'Tesco bets small – and wins big', *Business Week*, e.biz, 1 October 2001, EB14–EB18

20. LAUDON, Kenneth C., and LAUDON, Jane P., *Management Information Systems: Organization and Technology*, Prentice Hall, 4th edition, New Jersey, USA, 1996, p. 668 (more in-depth study of artificial intelligence, and information technology)

21. 'Business process reengineering', *International Management*, May 1994, p. 43

22. JOHANSSON, Henry J., McHUGH, Patrick, PENDLEBURY, A. John and WHEELER III, William A., *Business Process Reengineering: Break Point Strategies for Market Dominance*, John Wiley & Sons, 1993, pp 65–79

23. HALL, Gene, ROSENTHAL, Jim and WADE, Judy, 'How to make re-engineering really work', *Harvard Business Review*, November–December 1993, pp 119–31

24. 'Reengineering reviewed: Reengineering is the fad of the hour, as many reengineered dole claimants know to their cost. But is it doing any good?', *The Economist*, 2 July 1994

Review and discussion topics

1. Process system design
Describe the process system design for the following:
  (a) a hospital
  (b) an educational facility
  (c) a restaurant
  (d) a theatrical presentation.

2. Vertical integration
Discuss the advantages and disadvantages of vertical integration for the following organizations. Consider all the elements in the integrated form:
  (a) backward integration for an automobile company
  (b) forward integration of a film producer with cinemas
  (c) complete integration for the steel industry from raw materials through refining to manufacturing of raw steel in sheet, wire, or other forms.

3. Automation in industry
Unions traditionally oppose automation in industry, be it services or manufacturing. What are their concerns? Do you believe they are justified? How would you communicate with union people and explain the issues?

4. The Internet
The Internet and the e-mail have greatly improved the system design, and simplified the circulation of information in business. However, there are those who believe that computer-based communicating has reduced personal contact, created misunderstandings, reduced the personal side of business, and created more stress. What is your opinion? Justify your response with examples.

5. Electronic commerce in business
The global economy is being dominated by electronic commerce. Automobile companies are linking up with Internet providers to improve purchasing of automobile components in their business-to-business links. Some, such as Ford Motor, have created their own portals. Supermarkets, including Tesco and Sainsbury's in the UK, have established separate units where customers can shop online given a powerful thrust to their business-to-consumer business. Dot.com companies have given the Nasdaq new importance. Silicon Valley in California has generated numerous new companies devoted to electronic commerce.

How do you see electronic commerce changing the way in which firms do business? How does it work? What is the impact on its operations and its financial performance? Be specific, using actual information from target companies.

6. Operations network chart
Develop a process flow chart for the:
  (a) postal service from the preparation of a package in London, to the delivery in a small village some 50 km from Rome

(b) the manufacture, distribution, and sales of ceramic gift items sold in a large department store

(c) gasoline sold at a gasoline service station, considering the flow from the raw crude oil to the finished product

(d) the manufacture of a custom-made suit from the raw textile to the shipment of the finished product.

Develop the flow chart according to the various steps in the procedure. Make your best judgment on the times involved.

7. Business process reengineering

What are some of the process activities in either business, or day-to-day living, that are, or have been, radically changed where you could say the concept of business process reengineering (BPR) has been applied even though during the transformation the concept of BPR was probably never used.

Case study 7.1 Airbus Industries

Situation

The aviation industry is facing the prospect that its recession, aggravated by the 11 September 2001 terrorist attacks, could drag on for years. In November 2001 domestic traffic for the main American carriers was down by more than one-fifth on the previous year. Transatlantic travel has collapsed by almost half for some carriers, such as American Airlines. The bad news has now gripped the two big aircraft makers: America's Boeing and Airbus, which is part of the European Defence and Space Company (EADS). Both manufacturers are lowering their delivery forecasts. The timing of this slump is particularly bad for Airbus, and its parent, EADS. Airbus will be building expensive prototypes of its 550-seater super-jumbo, the A380, by 2003. The €1 billion that this will cost to develop annually could mean that EADS makes next to no profit in 2003 and 2004 unless it postpones its A380 spending.

As if all this were not enough, there is concern at EADS's twin head offices in Paris and Munich that the company's odd management structure could leave it vulnerable in a crisis. As well as two head offices, the company has two chairmen, and two chief executives, one German and one French. On top of the cross-border tensions that such a setup inevitably creates, there is also friction between the bosses of Airbus and EADS, given that Airbus dominates the business, but is technically EADS's corporate daughter. However, even as a consortium of French, German, Spanish and British endeavours, Airbus did a formidable job of selling airplanes with more than 2500 produced since the first A300 rolled out of the main factory in Toulouse in 1972. In 2000 it delivered 39% of the big jets sold worldwide, up from 15% in 1990.

Airbus, with more than 44,000 employees and revenues of $17.2 billion in 2000, figures its profits can only grow as it slashes overhead and streamlines its process operations. Managers predict they can boost their bottom line by €350 million annually just through efficiencies gained by integrating. The production system supply chain that was originally designed to minimize financial risk, by spreading work among lots of partners, and to create jobs, not profit was a process network of more than a dozen facilities spread across Europe not set up in the name of efficiency. Instead, it was designed to build broad political support through what managers called 'passport politics'. Consider how Airbus built one of the A320 planes, serial N° 1398, for jetBlue Airways of New York in 2000–2001. The activity in November included that on the 14th the front fuselage was flown from St Nazaire, France to Toulouse; on the 16th the rear fuselage was flown from Hamburg to Toulouse; on the 22nd the tail was flown to Toulouse from Madrid and the wings from Broughton, Wales, both in separate gigantic transport planes. On the 28th the fin and rudder were flown from Hamburg to Toulouse. Assembly then began, and during the next 43 days workers fitted the pieces together, threading lengths of cable, fastening thousands of rivets, and testing dozens of computer systems onboard. Activity in January 2001 included, on the 4th the first flight of the plane in Toulouse; on the 9th a ferry flight took the plane to Hamburg; and then starting on the 10th workers spent the next 13 days filling it with seats, toilets and galleys; on the 23rd there was another ferry flight back to Toulouse; and on the 25th painting began in jetBlues blue and white colour scheme. The plane was handed to jetBlue on 8 February 2001.

Airbus has since made modifications to the assembly system used for jetBlue's A320 saying that they have saved up to 20% on the production of A321 using 'integrated final assembly'.

Required

This information gives just a part of the process design activity of Airbus Industries which is the main competitor of Boeing. Using this, plus further research into Airbus, discuss how you believe Airbus can cut costs, including using some of the concepts presented earlier in this chapter.

Selected further reading

BAUSBACHER, Ed and HUNT, Roger (1998) *Process Plant Layout and Piping Design*, Prentice-Hall PTR/Sun Microsystems Press.

FELDMANN, Clarence G. (1998) *The Practical Guide to Business Process Reengineering Using Idefo*, Dorset House Publishing.

HARRINGTON, H. James, ESSELING, Erik K. C. and NIMWEGEN Harm Van (1997) *Business Process Improvement Workbook: Documentation, Analysis, Design,* *and Management of Business Process Improvement*, McGraw-Hill.

JOHANSSON, Henry J., McHUGH, Patrick, PENDLEBURY, John, JOHANSSON, Hank and WHEELER, William A. (1993) *Business Process Reengineering: Breakpoint Strategies for Market Dominance*, Wiley.

SHARRATT, P. N. (1998) *Handbook of Batch Process Design*, Chapman & Hall.

An extensive listing of other further reading can be found on the website.

What's on the web?

Further learning resources are available to lecturers and students at www.supplychain-online.com, including the following which are specific to *Process design and the operations network*:

Resource	Subject
Chapter overview	Process design and the operations network
Industry insight: C F Braun & Co.	Vertical integration
Industry insight: AT&T	Vertical integration
Industry insight: Siemens Nixdorf	Information technology in the process system
Exam topics	Process design and the operations network
More further reading	Process design and the operations network

8 *Human resources in the system design*

Chapter overview

- The working environment
- Management theorists
- Job design
- Attitude towards employees
- Work measurement
- Learning and the experience curve
- People and change

The working environment

People

Another element in design in operations management is the human resources, or the people. In any part of the supply chain, people are the most important resource, but the most complex to manage. People can go on strike, leave the company, or, at the very least, perform their task well below their capacity. A machine, however, provided it is well maintained, will always produce at the design output and operate 24 hours a day if necessary. A motivated, well-trained, and loyal workforce can make the company a market leader, financially strong, and efficient. It is imperative to create and maintain a work environment in which people feel comfortable, at ease, enabling them to work in a team. Even with all the most up-to-date automated equipment and technology, a workforce lacking motivation, in a disagreeable work environment will impede the efficiency and profitability of the organization. An ineffective organization can disrupt the supply chain of which this organization is a part. The worst scenario is a breakdown in communications leading to a strike that can have a disastrous effect on revenues and customer relations as the following illustrations demonstrate.

Labour unrest in services

In late 1999 the pilots' union at American Airlines ordered a sickout (members do not turn up to work, pretending to be sick), protesting the acquisition of Reno Airlines by American. The issue to the union was the integration of Reno Airlines pilots onto the union's seniority list. The sickout, which lasted for nearly a week, forced American to cancel more than 6000 flights which the airline estimated cost the company nearly $250 million in lost revenue. The unions also lost. A US district judge in Dallas, Texas, ordered the work action to stop, but the union refused. The judge levied a fine of $45.5 million against the union, which was upheld by the US Supreme Court. This was one of the largest fines ever levied against a US labour union and the union claims the amount of the fine exceeds its assets.[1]

Labour unrest in manufacturing

Union members struck at a Renault engine plant in northern France in October 1991. The 22-day strike crippled Renault, forcing the company to close all but one of its French and Belgian car assembly plants for lack of engines and gearboxes. It cost Renault an estimated 1.4 billion French francs ($250 million) and wreaked havoc with profits at a company still recuperating from six years of heavy losses in the 1980s. What upset the union leaders most was not the money but the failure of Renault to build a new kind of labour system involving a leaner more cooperative one that would help state-owned Renault survive rising Japanese competition. As a comparison, Japanese carmakers in Britain have won virtual no-strike contracts from their unions.[2]

The past

At the end of the 19th century, and into the early 20th century, factory conditions in manufacturing were appalling. Working hours were long, children were employed, and management treatment of employees was harsh. This environment, together with the absence of any meaningful dialogue with management, was the breeding ground for unionization. Many writers including the following used the inhuman working conditions as a central theme in their books.

Charles Dickens

In his book *Hard Times*, published in 1854, Charles Dickens denounced capitalism and the way people were exploited.[3]

Emile Zola

In 1885 Emile Zola published his seminar work *Germinal* that addressed the harshness of working conditions in the coalmines and the brutal behaviour in a strike.

Upton Sinclair

The USA meat packing industry was the subject in Upton Sinclair's book, *The Jungle*, published in 1906. This work was concerned not only with working conditions but also the lack of health standards in the food processing industry.

The present

Today, in developed countries there is certainly better attention paid to people. However, there are still human resource issues that surface such as the following.

Equal pay for equal work

Women, who in many cases do the same work as men, do not receive the same pay as is illustrated in Figure 8.1.[4]

Sexual harassment

Sexual harassment incidents against women (and sometimes men) continually surface, especially in the USA. For example, a female employee of Mckinsey Co., one of the world's biggest consulting firms, filed a sexual harassment suit in 1996 alleging discrimination in job promotion.[5]

Race relations

In 2001 seven current and former employees of Microsoft Corp., the Redmond, Washington, software company sued the firm for $5 billion, alleging racial discrimination. The suit accused Microsoft of fostering a hostile work environment in which black employees were discriminated against in evaluations, promotions, and compensation and also for wrongful termination of African-American employees. Statistics showed that just 2.6% of Microsoft's some 22,000 employees and only 1.6% of its 5155 managers were black.[6]

Some years earlier, in late 1996, Texaco Corp. agreed to a hefty financial settlement, and dismissal of some of its management people, for poor treatment and racial slurs relating to some of its non-white employees.[7]

Sweatshops

In 1995 California officials freed 72 Thai immigrants from a sweatshop in El Monte, east of Los Angeles, who had been forced to work for up to 17 hours a day. They were held captive in a razor-wired compound and were paid between $0.60 and $1.60 an hour, at a time when the minimum wage was $4.25. Clothing made at this sweatshop was on sale at big retailers such as Montgomery Ward.[8] (Montgomery Ward filed for bankruptcy in 2001.)

Figure 8.1 Men's and women's weekly earnings

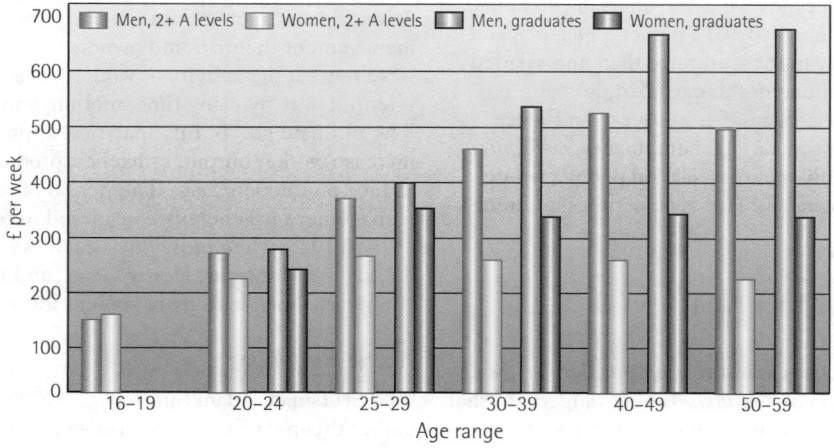

Child labour in Morocco

While ministers attend a conference in the state-owned arts and crafts centre in the medieval city of Fez, in a back room, five-year-old girls have their own manufacturing supply chain operation. They are huddled over a row of looms weaving carpets for tourists. The smallest of the girls stand on wooden boxes, some with their arms cut where the scissors have missed the wool. To keep the work on schedule, a seamstress beats time with a stick and raps knuckles when a child's attention slips. Parents receive about $10 a month for their daughters' ten-hour work days and they work long after the self-professed socialist ministers have left the conference in their limousines. As a result of their children's efforts, Morocco produces about 750,000 m² of carpet and their bargain prices attract the tourists who provide a significant proportion of the country's hard currency. A UNICEF programme to ensure that carpets carry childfree certificates was never applied to Morocco. The organization's Morocco director says that if it had been, the handcraft sector, the country's second-largest employer, would have been crippled. In the

manufacture of pottery, another collectors' item for tourists, young boys are used to collect the wood and fire the ovens.

Child labour in Morocco is not just in manufacturing and not always for the benefit of tourists. Hordes of shoeshiners with wooden footrests compete for clients at railways stations and cafés. Grocers hire children to stock their shelves during the night. The number of child maids in hotels and homes is estimated up to one million. A child maid costs one-third the price of an adult. Prostitution is rampant among children and the American State Department estimates that in Casablanca alone more than 10,000 child prostitutes ply their trade.

Morocco made education compulsory in 1963, but nearly 40 years later the government admits that some 2.5 million children are not in school. Some in the country feel that child labour is the lesser of two evils since in the current education system each year, 100,000 of the graduates are unable to find employment.

Adapted from: 'Children in the boiler-room', *The Economist*[9]

Overseas

In some emerging economies, and elsewhere overseas, there is much to be done to improve the treatment of factory employees as illustrated in Industry insight 8.1.

Salaried and non–salaried

Human resources, by the strict definition, means everyone from top management through to those who maintain the machines. However, very often when the term is used it applies to hourly paid employees rather than salaried people (those who received a monthly salary regardless of whether they work 160 hours or 240 hours). Salaried workers generally have a higher education, and have more flexibility in the workforce than non-salaried workers. In this section, for the most part, human resources refer to non-salaried employees. (In France there is a very strict separation of employees, *non-cadres* for hourly people and *cadres* for salaried people, whose treatment under the labour laws is sometimes different.)

Management theorists

In 1832 Charles Babbage, in his book entitled *On the Economy of Machinery and Manufacturers*,[10] suggested that an axiom on the division of labour is that wages for a job

should exactly match the skills required. If a job required only one skill, then only that skill should be recognized. However, if a job required several skills, then wages paid should be according to the highest skill level. Ever since then management theorists, industrialists, and researchers have tried to explain, modify, control, and improve the human resources in organizations. Two significant phases have been the scientific management and the human relations movements.

Scientific management

Scientific management was an early approach by management theorists and owners, whose objectives were to treat the activity of workers in a logical, scientific way by using time, motion, and methods study. The ultimate goal of this analytical approach was to increase worker output, efficiency, productivity, and to reduce production costs. The period of scientific management is generally considered to be from about 1875 to 1925, when individuals such as Frederick Taylor, the Gilbreths, Henry Gantt, and Henry Ford coupled science with management ideas.

Adam Smith

The Scotsman, Adam Smith (1723–1790), was a much earlier theorist in scientific management when among other ideas he suggested in his book, *The Wealth of Nations* in 1776, that labour specialization would reduce labour costs.[11] He based this idea on the following observations:

- Workers, by repeating their tasks, would increase their speed in that particular activity.
- If workers remained at the same task, then less time would be lost through job changing.
- Specialized tools could be developed for each task.

Frederick Taylor

Frederick Winslow Taylor of the USA (1856–1915) is the dominant theorist in scientific management. He rigorously examined the field of operations as a science, proposing to increase worker efficiency, and thus productivity, by job design.[12] His logic was that there was one best way to work and it was this way that should be developed and put into action. According to Taylor, all non-value-added activity should be eliminated. Taylor's work is illustrated by studies at Bethlehem Steel, in the period 1900–1910 where he modified the jobs of employees whose sole responsibility was the shovelling of materials. He made assumptions that this task could be reduced to a science by first presenting the following questions:

1. Will a good employee do more work a day with a shovelful of 5, 10, 15, 20, 30, or 40 pounds of material?
2. What kinds of shovel work best, and with which materials?
3. How quickly can a shovel be pushed into a pile of material and pulled out properly loaded?
4. How much time is required to swing a shovel backwards and then throw the load a given horizontal distance and a given height?

As Taylor began formulating answers to these questions he developed ways to increase the productivity and efficiency by matching shovel size with such factors as men, materials, height and distances materials were to be thrown. In three years of these experiments, he was able to:

- reduce number of persons shovelling from approximately 600 to 140
- increase the average number of tons moved per worker a day from 16 to 59
- increase the average earnings from $1.15 to $1.88 per worker a day
- reduce the average cost of shovelling from $0.072 to $0.033 per ton.

Frederick Taylor is considered the father of scientific management and it is his name that has been used to coin the concept of *Taylorism*, which is considered synonymous with rigidity, excessive organization, and inhumanity in the management of people. Taylorism is very much scorned today as a managerial approach, however, there are many work areas that have some foundations of Taylorism, such as the practice of just-in-time and use of ISO-9000 quality standards. (See Chapters 4 and 15.)

The Gilbreths

This husband and wife team, Frank (1868–1924) and Lillian Gilbreth (1878–1973) of the USA, analyzed operations management as a science in the period 1900–1910. Their primary research tool was motion studies in order to reduce a job to its most basic movements. This research was used to establish performance standards, and to eliminate unnecessary movements. Frank Gilbreth, himself an apprentice bricklayer, found that bricklayers could increase output by concentrating on some movements and eliminating others. His studies resulted in reducing the number of motions necessary to lay a brick by approximately 70%, which subsequently resulted in tripling bricklaying production.

Henry Ford

Henry Ford (1863–1947) was the founder of the Ford Motor Company in Detroit, USA. His engine assembly shop foreman, William C Klann, had visited slaughterhouses and had been impressed with how conveyers carried hogs and cattle through a disassembly process.[13] Based on this approach, Ford designed, and put into operation the first assembly line (1890–1930) for automobile production. This operations layout embodied elements of scientific management including standardized products, mass production, low unit cost, high volume, mechanized assembly lines, specialization of labour, and interchangeable parts. A typical product example was the Model T Ford only obtainable in black. With this scientific approach in the assembly line operation, production time of the Model T was reduced from 14 to under two hours, which resulted in a corresponding reduction in price from $850 to $265. In 1927, when production of the Model T ceased, over 15 million models had been sold. (See later in this chapter.)

Human relations

The human relations approach to management was altogether different from scientific management, as its basic objective was to treat those in the workforce with respect and dignity. The human relation period is considered to be from about 1925 to 1960. However, in many respects, the human relations approach to management is an ongoing process. Notable theorists on the human motivation side of work include Elton Mayo and his colleagues, Henry Gantt, Abraham Maslow, Frederick Herzberg, Douglas McGregor, and Peter Drucker.

Elton Mayo

In the period 1927–1932 Elton Mayo, together with F J Roethlisberger, and William J Dickson, examined the conditions of workers at the Hawthorne, Illinois, plant of Western Electric Co. Their original plan was to investigate the effect of lighting on productivity. They then went further and studied the human relationships of the workforce. They concluded that the human elements, the contact between workers, and the role played by individuals was more important to productivity than physical conditions such as the lighting. These experiments, often referred to as the Hawthorne Studies, were one of the earliest analyses of human relations in the work environment.[14]

Henry Gantt

Henry L Gantt of the USA (1861–1919) was interested in both the human and scientific approach to management. On the human side, his perception of company managers was that they were slavedrivers, forcing workers to do jobs, under poor conditions, in which they had little interest or desire to execute. Gantt believed it was totally wrong for a manager to present himself as a slavedriver. Further, when the manager requests workers to perform tasks, he should endeavour to motivate workers such that they feel it is in their best interest to perform the task. Further, the manager should be careful not to ask what is impossible, or unreasonable. Whereas Taylor had developed a wage system where everyone was paid the same rate, Gantt proposed that workers could earn a bonus as an incentive, in addition to the piece rate, if they produced beyond the daily production quota.[15] (Today, from a quality perspective, this is not appropriate, as workers will try to produce more at the expense of the quality of their work.)

Even though Gantt had a more human side than Taylor, he was still interested in increasing worker efficiency. His philosophy was that exact *scientific knowledge* of what could be done should always take precedence over the *opinion* of what should be done. He said that the best systems are those in which tasks are properly scheduled and this led to the development of the Gantt scheduling chart discussed in Chapter 14.

Figure 8.2 Basic needs according to Abraham Maslow

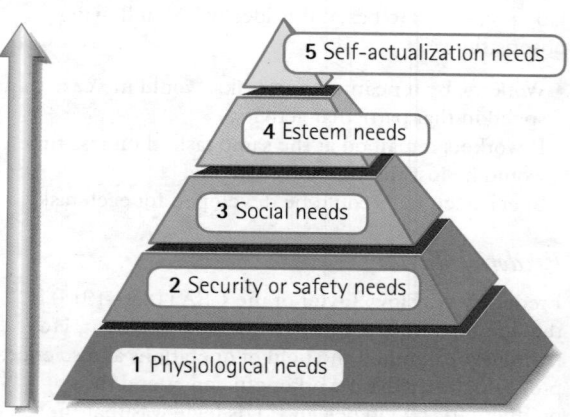

Table 8.1 Hierarchy of needs

Needs	Definition
1. Physiological	Normal body requirements such as food and water, rest, sex, and air. Until these needs are met, individual behaviour is aimed to satisfy them
2. Security or safety	Needs people feel to keep themselves free from physical harm, and economic ruin. Management can help in satisfying these needs with salaries, since with appropriate income employees can purchase food and accommodation
3. Social	These include the desire for love, and friendship, and reflect a person's desire to be accepted by others
4. Esteem	These are the desire for self-respect, and the giving of respect to others
5. Self-actualization	These ultimate needs are the desire to maximize a person's potential, for example, a company manager who has a strong desire to become president, or an employee wishing to start his own business

Abraham Maslow

Abraham H Maslow of the USA is best known for his 1943 publication, *A Theory of Human Motivation*, in which he theorized that people have five basic needs.[16] Using a pyramid approach moving from the base to the apex of the pyramid, as illustrated in Figure 8.2, he described these need levels according to Table 8.1.

Table 8.2 Factors impacting job satisfaction and dissatisfaction

Dissatisfaction: Hygiene or maintenance factors	Satisfaction: Motivating factors
Company policies	Opportunity for achievement
Administration policies	Opportunity for recognition
Level of supervision	The work itself
Relationship with supervisor	Level of responsibility
Relationship with peers	Possibilities of advancement
Relationship with subordinates	Opportunities for personal growth
Working conditions	Opportunities for learning new methods
Salary	Opportunities for working overseas

Maslow postulated that these needs are progressive. When Level 1 is satisfied, desires move upward until Level 5 is reached.

Frederick Herzberg

Frederick Herzberg concluded in his research on human motivation in the 1960s that there were two different variables that influenced people in an organization. They were hygiene, or maintenance factors which impacted job dissatisfaction, and motivating factors, which influenced job satisfaction. Hygiene factors relate to the work environment, and motivating factors are connected to the work itself.[17] Illustrations of these are presented in Table 8.2.

Douglas McGregor

Douglas McGregor developed a set of assumptions about people and said they were either of Theory X type, which usually had negative assumptions about people, and Theory Y which had positive ideas about people.[18] This theory could be used in a management environment where the implications were that Theory X managers were bad and Theory Y managers were good and the better leaders. These assumptions are illustrated in Table 8.3.

Peter Drucker

Peter Drucker has written extensively on employee motivation and the role of management in organizations.

Table 8.3 Theory X and Theory Y assumptions

Theory X assumptions (negative)	Theory Y assumptions (positive)
The average person has an inherent dislike for work and they will avoid it if possible	Physical and mental effort in work is as natural as play or rest
People must be coerced, controlled, directed and threatened with punishment in order to get them to put forth adequate work efforts	People will exercise self-direction and self-control in the objective of the organization Commitment to objectives is a function of rewards associated with achievement
People prefer to be directed, wish to avoid responsibility, and have little ambition	The average person learns, under proper conditions, both to accept and seek responsibility
The average person is interested only in security	The capacity to exercise a relatively high degree of imagination, ingenuity, and creativity, is common among people

He is responsible for establishing the idea of management by objectives in an organization, which has the following three basic characteristics:[19]

1. All individuals in an organization are assigned a set of objectives that they attempt to achieve during a reasonable time period. These objectives are established and agreed to mutually between the individual and the manager.
2. Performance reviews are conducted periodically to determine how close the individual is to achieving these objectives.
3. Rewards are given to individuals on the basis of how close they are to reaching their objectives.

Job design

Job design entails matching tasks or work activities with individuals or work groups. The ultimate objective is to increase the efficiency of an organization with the parallel goal of making working conditions more agreeable. As illustrated in Figure 8.3, for some situations job design may be progressive moving from specialization to empowerment. These concepts are illustrated as follows.

Figure 8.3 Job design

As skills increase, responsibility and job motivation will climb

Empowerment

Job enrichment

Job enlargement

Job rotation

Job specialization

Job specialization

Job specialization involves having people with certain skills who are dedicated to a certain activity in the operation. The following illustrates this for a manufacturing environment:

- Foundry workers responsible for pouring molten metal.
- Intricate soldering on computer circuit boards.
- Wiring electric control boards.
- Performing a certain assembly line job in automobile production.

As Frederick Taylor emphasized, job specialization should mean efficiency, because people are performing work they know how to do well. However, the repetitive nature of some jobs means they can be boring to the point that people become sloppy, quality suffers, and costs rise. Job specialization is contrary to some philosophy of human resource management although it is sometimes difficult to find workers who are completely flexible. A foundry work may not have the dexterity to work on the same company's assembly line, for example.

Job rotation

Job rotation moves beyond specialization where people who have the required skills can rotate (say on a weekly basis) from one job to another to get away from the job specialization rut. For example, assembly line workers involved in engine mounting may, the following week, be working on assembling dashboard components. Incorporating job rotation can help to reduce the monotonous aspects of the job.

Job rotation may not be desirable for everyone, even though the necessary skills are in place. The author once worked in a chocolate factory where there were several groups of women on the assembly line boxing the many different varieties of chocolate. It was suggested that these groups changed periodically both in their make-up and the location in which they worked. The women loudly rejected this idea. They felt comfortable remaining with their groups who they knew, and also in a job which required little additional thought.

Multi-skills and plant flexibility

Job rotation implies multi-skilled personnel. It is not only advantageous and motivating for the employee, but it also gives the employer the flexibility to adjust to client needs. If a customer increases the order requirement, modifies the product specifications, or speeds up the delivery date, a production manager needs to have the facility to reassign personnel accordingly. In a similar manner, when there are multi-skilled employees replacement when an employee is sick or on vacation is simplified. Of course, in order to have multi-skilled employees the company must provide the appropriate training which involves a cost and time away from the job of the employees in question.

Job enlargement

Job enlargement is to avoid an employee becoming trapped in job specialization by trying to improve the variety within a certain sphere of a person's ability, and interest. Enlargement would mean expanding the tasks involved in a job. For example, adding shaping and forming could enlarge a cutting operation. This would be horizontal expansion of the job.

Job enrichment

Job enrichment means expanding the job vertically by adding design and planning elements. For example, a purchasing secretary whose basic job is correspondence for group of purchasing people, could have the job enriched by planning the work assignments of the group, being an intermediate in customer contacts, and maybe helping in the evaluation of some proposals. That is, her job is enriched from being a secretary to becoming more of an assistant. This is certainly the situation today when many of the classic secretarial duties are decreasing as more and more people acquire their own personal computer.

Empowerment

Empowerment is an extension of job enrichment by adding complete employee trust, and responsibilities not originally associated with the job. In a sense, the employee manages his or her own activity. Consider the two following examples, one for a service industry and the other for manufacturing.

Services

Nordstrom, the US fashion retailer based in Seattle, Washington, believes in empowering its workers. Its *Employee Handbook* consists of a single sheet of paper urging people to set their goals high, stating the company's confidence in their ability to meet them, and spelling out a single corporate rule: 'Use your good judgment in all situations.' The employees respond by serving customers with an assiduousness that can extend to writing personal thank-you notes or pumping up flat tyres in the parking garage. Run at the top by a collective leadership of fourth-generation Nordstroms, the company devolves its merchandise buying to the local level, in contrast to most department stores, which buy centrally.[20]

Manufacturing

When Chrysler, the US-based automobile constructor, sets out to create a new model, or revamp an old one, it forms a team of about 700 people from engineering, design, manufacturing, marketing, and finance, including specialists of all kind, or as Chrysler labels them, 'a self-contained multidisciplinary group'. A vice-president acts as 'godfather' to the group, but leaders below that rank direct all the actual work. Top management meet with the group to sketch out a vision for the vehicle, and set aggressive goals for design, fuel economy, and cost. Management works out a contract with the team setting out objectives after which the group is empowered to take on complete responsibility.[21]

A personal experience in contrast to job empowerment happened in the 1960s when I was doing an internship in a manufacturing firm. While operating a drilling machine a side screw holding the chuck came loose and I was obligated to stop the machine. I asked my supervisor for a screwdriver as I said that I could easily fix the problem. 'No, you can't do that,' he said. It is against the work rules. I was told to complete a work order to have maintenance come and fix the problem. As a result, the drilling machine was down for nearly three hours.[22]

Special considerations in job design

No matter at what level an organization is regarding job design whether it be specialization or empowerment, the following are some other considerations which apply to all.

Women in the workforce

At the turn of the century men well high dominated the workforce, principally in manufacturing. Women's move into the factories began in World War I. When war broke out, women filled the role of men who were at the front and some remained when war ended. A similar situation occurred during World War II. Since the 1950s the proportion of women in the workforce has continued to rise, such that in Europe-15 in 1994 women represented 41.4% of the workforce. This was from a high of 48.7% in Sweden to a low of 34.0 in Spain.[23] Data are similar for the USA and Japan, and in all three regions the proportion of women working is increasing.

Thus, in job design the aptitudes and characteristics of women, compared to men, need to be considered. In assembly work involving activities like detailed soldering, mounting of subassemblies in motors, clocks, or computers, women are considered to have more dexterity than men. Work involving physical strength such as erecting scaffolding, building construction, etc. anatomically fits a man better. Although it is wrong to stereotype people in employment there are jobs whose design as such are better suited to women, and vice versa. Even though women are replacing men in many forms of employment, their wages or salaries are still less than men. The argument that women perform better than men in activities such as wiring, soldering, or other detailed work, is sometimes hiding the fact that the company can pay them lower wages which reduces their product costs.

Historically, in some service sectors such as nursing, secretarial, telephone operation, and flight attendance, only women were employed. When the commercial airline industry really took off in the 1950s and 1960s not only did the flight attendants have to be women but also they had to correspond to a certain physical make-up. Today there are many male flight attendants, nurses, secretaries, and telephone operators.

Ergonomics

Ergonomics pays attention to the equipment and machinery in job design by balancing the work of the employee with the machine or the task at hand, in order to minimize human effort and to make the work as comfortable as possible. For example:

- Renault VI, France, has designed its heavy vehicles (buses and trucks) so that assembly work on the roof of the bus can be performed at arm's length rather than the operator straining at connecting elements that lie above his head.
- Computer keyboards have been redesigned such that they are more comfortable to the operator.
- Cooking appliances in restaurant kitchens are where possible placed so that chefs do not have to do excessive bending. (Back and neck problems among restaurant kitchen staff are very common ailments.)

Basic skill level

In job design, even though an individual may be competent at performing the work, some basic skills may be lacking. For example, with globalization there is considerable movement of people whose language or other skills may not be sufficient. At the work centre level, operators may not speak the native language. Thus in the job design, operating instructions need to be translated, or be simple. It might be better to avoid figures and letters, but you can always use colours and

symbols. Cashiers at McDonald's, Burger King, and Quick use symbol cash registers that avoid the need for the cashiers to perform calculations. This avoids errors and speeds up the throughput of customers.

Flexible work schedules

All countries have a legal standard work schedule based a certain number of hours per week. In Britain and the USA it is 40 hours and in France it is 35 hours. It used to be that these times were spread out evenly across a five-day week. Now many firms have flexible work schedules (flexitime) to suit both employee and employer. For example, it might be ten hours for four days rather than eight hours for five. Alternatively, if the requirements are that an employee has to be present for eight hours a day the employee can start later and finish later, provided he is present during so-called core hours of the firm such as between 10am and 3pm. Alternatively, employees might work a 50-hour week during heavy customer demand, and 30 or fewer hours a week during slack demand. For many service firms, employees with modems and the Internet are able to work from their home, which gives them maximum flexibility regarding their working hours. It is very advantageous for both employer and employee to have work hour flexibility. However, for the firm, this flexibility requires close monitoring to ensure that neither productivity nor competitiveness is being compromised.

Attitude towards employees

All operations involve management, or senior people, dealing with lower level employees. The way these lower level people are treated and addressed can have a significant impact on the working relationships and motivation, which themselves have a direct bearing on the firm's productivity and cost. The following are some guidelines in the way people should be treated.

Communication

- Treat all people with respect, no matter their level in the organization. This includes the cleaners, janitors and other service personnel. In the communication do not demean a person's job.
- Communicate with, and listen to, the employees. Let them know the positive side as well of the negative side of the business. Good communication minimizes the effect of 'corridor talk' and false rumours.
- Compliment employees when they do good work.

- Let employees know when their work is not as expected but indicate mistakes in an objective, and not a threatening manner.
- Work any conflict through with people.
- Managers should often visit the work centre and talk directly with the workforce.
- Depend on people to do the job right and avoid 'breathing down their necks'.

Working environment

- Provide an atmosphere in which employees feel secure and confident.
- Provide an environment in which employees feel they are making a contribution to the progress of the firm.
- Create an atmosphere where there is trust and people are open with each other.
- Avoid special parking slots for those in senior positions.
- Keep workgroups as small as feasible so that individuals can contribute.
- Emphasize teamwork.
- Everyone respects the rules of the organization. Just because one is a manager is no reason to arrive late for a meeting, or to smoke in a non-smoking area.
- Avoid segregation of eating areas.
- Use a first-name basis for employees at all levels. Allow lower level employees to use first names for managers.
- Provide a physically clean, pleasant, and safe working environment.
- Provide appropriate work tools, storage areas, toilets, and washing facilities.

- Provide appropriate training for the employees so that they are well trained for their job. Help them if they have problems.

Company objectives

- Provide clear and commons goals for the workforce.
- Allow employees to share in the profits of the company.
- Provide opportunities for growth within the organization.
- Where possible, promote from within rather than bringing in people from outside.

Management style and decision making

Managers spend much of their time making decisions. There are two extremes to making a decision, as illustrated in Figure 8.4.

The best way

Before a decision is made, discuss all the elements with those people who will be involved when the final decision is made. This will make it easy to implement the decision when the time comes. That is, take a bottom up approach to decision making.

The worst way

Avoid the top down approach to decisions where management makes the decision and pushes the new plan onto the workforce. This will make it much more difficult to put the decision into effect, and will de-motivate the workforce. This sort of an approach may lead to a strike.

Figure 8.4 Ways of decision making

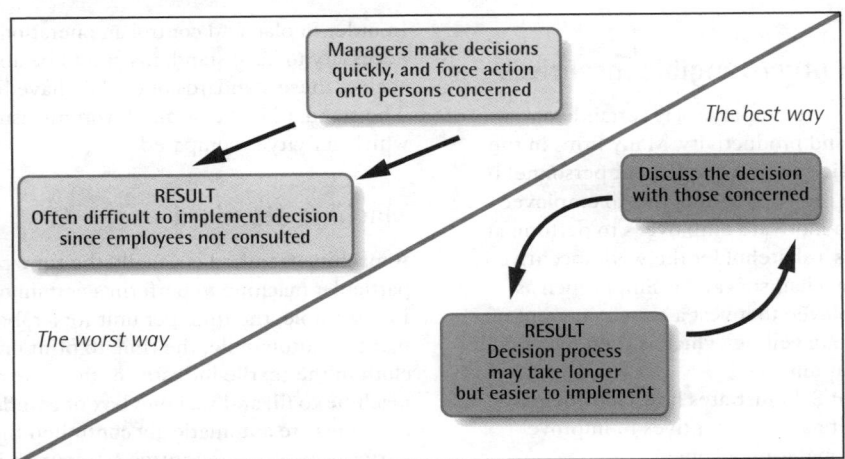

Net income is up and so is employee morale

Kevin Nguyen, a Continental Airlines flight attendant, was worried when he was called into the cockpit during a flight from Newark, New Jersey, to Las Vegas. He thought he had done something wrong. He believed that this fear was confirmed when one of the pilots said that Gordon Bethune, Continental's Chairman, was on the phone wanting to talk with him. It turned out that the Chairman wanted to tell Kevin that he had won a new Ford Explorer in a raffle held for workers with perfect attendance for the previous six months. Fred Miller, a veteran pilot, had a similar experience and won a Ford Explorer for, in his words, 'just coming to work like I was supposed to'. A week before the Explorer giveaway, Continental declared 22 January 2001 'Independence Day', and each of its 54,000 employees received $100 to mark the airline's purchase of a controlling stake held by Northwest. Three weeks later, on 14 February, Bethune and the president, Greg Brenneman, handed out more cheques based on a share of Continental's profits equal to about 4% of every worker's salary. In addition to all this, there are the countless company picnics, ice cream parties, barbecues, and turkey and fried chicken dinners that dot the calendar throughout the year.

The benefits to the employees are only a very small proportion of the company's costs but the good employee relationship generated thereby translates down to the bottom line. In 2000 Continental returned a profit for the sixth consecutive year and according to the government's statistics in 2000 Continental ranked first in on-time arrivals and departures. Further, it consistently scores high on customer satisfaction surveys by J D Powers and Associates, the California-based survey firm. This is a great turnaround since the times of the bitter labour strife under the helm of Chief Executive Frank Lorenzo in the 1980s and early 1990s. In this period, the airline filed twice for bankruptcy and it was felt the company was headed for oblivion. Continental now has the highest morale in the airline industry.

Every employee now receives at least $65 for each month that Continental ranks among the top three on-time airlines by the US Transportation Department, or completes at least 80% of its flights on schedule. This amount rises to $100 for every month that Continental ranks first in on-time schedules. Over the last six years the bonuses have totalled $157 million, or, according to the company, half of what it would have cost the airline in terms of hotel charges and other passenger compensation. Further, the 83 Ford sports-utility vehicles that Continental has given away since 1996 have saved the firm about $20 million by reducing the airline's rate of absenteeism. Then, the some three or four celebrations a year cost some $20 per employee but this is considered peanuts to the company's payroll. However, the celebration event sticks in the mind of the employee to foster loyalty to the firm.

Adapted from: 'At Continental, even the bottom line is looking up', *International Herald Tribune*[24]

The first approach will take longer to arrive at a final decision, but the long-term benefits will be more advantageous.

Financial and other tangible incentives

Financial incentive to employees is certainly one way of boosting morale and productivity. Many firms in the USA give the option to its management personnel to buy shares in the firm. Extending this to employees at all levels can help motivate employees to perform at their best since as a shareholder the work incentive is improved. The mechanism can be simple such as allowing the employee to invest a certain amount of salary up to a certain ceiling, which is then matched by the firm's contribution.

Industry insight 8.2 illustrates how Continental Airlines has used financial incentives to improve productivity and operating income.

Work measurement

In order to plan and control an operation effectively it is necessary to have standards and to be able to measure against these standards once they have been developed. The standard is the norm of work measurement against which activity is compared.

Machine standard

A machine standard is usually the time per unit for a particular machine to perform a certain operation. For example, the time per unit for a robot to spray paint an automobile, the time to print one metre of cloth in the textile industry, or the time per unit for a machine to fill and seal one box of cornflakes. Since machines are automatically controlled they can perform the same repetitive action with little variation from unit to unit. Thus, machine standards are relatively easy to define.

Labour standard

A labour standard is the time for a worker with the appropriate training to perform a certain well-defined activity under normal conditions. This might be the time for the preparation of a hamburger at a McDonald's restaurant, the time per unit to load a pallet of items on a truck, or the time per unit for a person to enter information into a computer database.

Labour standards are more difficult to establish than machine standards since skill levels, physical ability, and concentration levels vary between individuals. In addition to the standards one has to take into consideration rest periods, and the time of day. People may be faster in the morning, and slower at night. Two notable researchers on labour standards was L H C Tipitt of England who, in 1934, performed work-sampling studies to develop production standards and H B Maynard of the USA who, in 1948, developed time measurement methods.

Reasons for standards

Work standards have the concept of Taylorism buried in them but they are necessary for the following reasons.

Financial proposals

Business firms are in a competitive environment and often need to give financial estimates, or proposals for performing work for clients. For example, a client might required a proposal for the printing of 10,000 copies of a publicity brochure. In order to develop the financial estimate the following would be some of the elements:

- cost of paper required for 10,000 copies (Quantity * Unit cost of paper)
- cost of ink for 10,000 copies (Quantity * Unit cost of ink)
- preparation of printing plate (Labour standard * Cost/hour)
- machine cost for printing (Machine standard per unit * Cost per unit)
- operator cost (Labour standard * Unit cost).

Scheduling

For scheduling and planning purposes a firm needs to know the labour and machine standards in order to be able to assign work to people and machines in the most efficient manner.

Cost control

For cost control purposes a firm needs to know various standards for work in order that these costs can be accounted for and billed to the appropriate entity. For example, in the assembly of an automobile, the paint-spraying operation may be a cost centre for the production site. Using appropriate standards, these costs can be appropriately allocated to the complete production site.

Capacity planning

Knowing the various standards, a firm can plan for current and future capacity requirements. Then, if necessary, appropriate steps can be made, say, for subcontracting activity if it is found that current capacity is not sufficient.

Budgeting

With standards, a firm can develop operating and capital budgets.

Bonus incentive

If standards are established and employees exceed the standards as far as the work output is concerned, employees can earn a bonus. This might be appropriate in, say, a sales environment but probably not in a manufacturing centre. Employees who tried to exceed standards may go too fast and compromise on product quality. The emphasis should be to 'work to quality' and not 'work to quantity'.

Comparing different operations

With appropriate standards the cost of doing work according to different operating methods, or using different machines, can be compared.

Criticism of labour standards

The use of labour standards in industry is very controversial and is often a source of conflict between management and labour. Labour unions often complain that labour standards are set too high, meaning that their members are continually under stress. Management, however, criticize them and say they are set too low so that product costs are high compared to competitors. This is particularly a criticism between Europe and Asian countries, whose labour standards are lower.

Motion studies

A motion study (sometimes referred to as a time and motion study) is one way to analyze the time needed to perform a certain activity, develop this into appropriate standards, and then to translate this information into the output for a particular operation. To perform motion studies a job is broken down into its individual elements and the time taken to perform these tasks for a certain sample size are measured. This information is then used for designing the system.

The illustration of a simple time and motion study is illustrated by the time and activities involved in preparing a hamburger. The information collected and the computations are shown in Table 8.4.

Activities in the operation

The making of a hamburger is broken down into its individual elements. Here, there are eight. First, the operator takes the two halves of the toasted hamburger bun from the toaster, and replaces them with two fresh halves for the next hamburger. On the toasted bottom part of the bun she then spreads mayonnaise, places the cooked hamburger meat onto this and then garnishes the meat with a piece of lettuce, tomato, and an onion ring. The operator then spreads mayonnaise onto the top half of the toasted bun and then closes the hamburger with this second part of the bun. The final operation is wrapping the hamburger.

Sample size

Here the operation is timed for a sample of 15 hamburgers. In practice, using statistics, one would determine the correct sample size that is representative of the population within a certain confidence level, say, 95%.

Measurement

The operator times the activity on a continuous basis noting only the time at the end of each activity. For example, for the first hamburger the operation starts at 9.45am and the stopwatch is at zero. When the bun is taken from the toaster the reading is five seconds and this is also the activity time since the watch started at zero. The reading after a fresh bun has been put into the toaster is seven seconds. Thus the activity time for putting the bun in the toaster is two seconds (7 − 5). The time at the end of wrapping is 1:24 (1 minute 24 seconds) and the time at the end of closing the bun is 1:07. Thus the time to close the bun is 17 seconds (1:24 − 1:07). For the second hamburger, the reading after the toasted bun has been taken from the toaster is 1:37 and thus the time to do this activity is 13 seconds (1:37 − 1:24).

Cycle time

The cycle time is the total time for the eight activities, or the time to prepare one hamburger for a customer.

The cycle time for the 15 hamburgers is the last row on the principal table.

Average time

The average time for each activity and for the hamburger preparation are given in the column 'average time'. These values are simple: the total times divided by 15.

Rating factor

The rating factor (shown by the column of that name) is a performance number estimated according to whether the determined time is considered above or below a real average value. It is subjectively obtained number based on the observer's analysis. A value greater than 1.0 means that, in the evaluation of the observer, the worker performed at a rate faster than she or he would under normal conditions. The reverse applies for a value less than 1.0. These factors are not easy to assess. An operator who knows they are being timed may be faster than normal, hoping to impress the recorder or management. Alternatively, if the operator expects salaries and output are going to be based on these results, he may be slow during the study knowing that, in practice, he can exceed the rate and thus be considered a good employee. Thus, assigning of realistic rating factors is difficult.

Normal time

The normal time for each activity, given in the last column, is the product of the measured time and the rating factor. The normal cycle time for the preparation of a hamburger is the sum of all the normal activity times, which in this case is 1 minute 57 seconds.

Standard time

To the normal time is added allowance to arrive at the standard time. The allowance again is subjective and it is a factor to take into account stoppages, fatigue, or interruptions. In this illustration, an allowance of 20% is given. Thus the standard time is Normal time * 1.20. In one eight-hour day there are 480 minutes thus dividing the standard unit time into this gives the standard time a day. In this case, it is 205 hamburgers a day per operator (rounded down rather than up to be sure this figure is attainable).

Performing a motion study may at first seem straightforward but it needs complete cooperation from workers involved. In a factory or service environment people become very suspicious when they see management personnel arrive with a clipboard and a watch and might do everything they can to disrupt the experimental work.

Table 8.4 Preparation of a hamburger

Start time: 9:45:00	Finish time: 10:13:28	Date: 20 October	Operator: Cindy Burton	Recorder: John Saunders	Operation: Making a hamburger

Activity		Number of hamburger buns made															Average time	Rating factor	Normal Time
		1	2	3	4	5	6	7	8	9	10	11	12	13	14	15			
1. Remove toasted bun	Time	00:05	00:13	00:06	00:05	00:14	00:08	00:07	00:13	00:08	00:14	00:19	00:16	00:14	00:27	00:18	00:12	0.90	00:11
	Reading	00:05	01:37	03:05	04:54	07:01	08:27	10:35	12:08	13:55	15:51	17:58	19:47	21:39	24:19	26:32			
2. Bun in toaster	Time	00:02	00:10	00:12	00:13	00:11	00:21	00:07	00:09	00:13	00:17	00:14	00:14	00:12	00:15	00:18	00:13	1.10	00:14
	Reading	00:07	01:47	03:17	05:07	07:12	08:48	10:42	12:17	14:08	16:08	18:12	20:01	21:51	24:34	26:50			
3. Sauce on bottom	Time	00:04	00:05	00:07	00:18	00:16	00:17	00:19	00:12	00:14	00:17	00:10	00:14	00:12	00:23	00:22	00:14	0.95	00:13
	Reading	00:11	01:52	03:24	05:25	07:28	09:05	11:01	12:29	14:22	16:25	18:22	20:15	22:03	24:57	27:12			
4. Meat on bottom	Time	00:10	00:13	00:13	00:17	00:10	00:07	00:13	00:10	00:16	00:17	00:19	00:13	00:28	00:11	00:06	00:14	1.00	00:14
	Reading	00:21	02:05	03:37	05:42	07:38	09:12	11:14	12:39	14:38	16:42	18:41	20:28	22:31	25:08	27:18			
5. Garnish on meat (lettuce, tomato, onion)	Time	00:12	00:13	00:15	00:16	00:07	00:20	00:11	00:13	00:14	00:25	00:17	00:10	00:27	00:13	00:16	00:15	0.95	00:15
	Reading	00:33	02:18	03:52	05:58	07:45	09:32	11:25	12:52	14:52	17:07	18:58	20:38	22:58	25:21	27:34			
6. Sauce on top	Time	00:21	00:19	00:15	00:16	00:14	00:26	00:07	00:17	00:18	00:10	00:09	00:16	00:20	00:22	00:20	00:17	0.95	00:16
	Reading	00:54	02:37	04:07	06:14	07:59	09:58	11:32	13:09	15:10	17:17	19:07	20:54	23:18	25:43	27:54			
7. Close bun	Time	00:13	00:08	00:18	00:24	00:08	00:17	00:09	00:16	00:11	00:11	00:11	00:21	00:19	00:11	00:21	00:15	1.20	00:17
	Reading	01:07	02:45	04:25	06:38	08:07	10:15	11:41	13:25	15:21	17:28	19:18	21:15	23:37	25:54	28:15			
8. Wrap	Time	00:17	00:14	00:24	00:09	00:12	00:13	00:14	00:22	00:16	00:11	00:13	00:10	00:15	00:20	00:13	00:15	1.15	00:17
	Reading	01:24	02:59	04:49	06:47	08:19	10:28	11:55	13:47	15:37	17:39	19:31	21:25	23:52	26:14	28:28			
Cycle time		01:24	01:35	01:50	01:58	01:32	02:09	01:27	01:52	01:50	02:02	01:52	01:54	02:27	02:22	02:14	01:54	1.20	01:57

Standard time in seconds	0:01:57
Allowance over normal time	20%
Standard time, mins and secs	02:20
Time available in an 8-hour day, hours	8:00:00
Daily standard for preparation of hamburgers per operator	205.63

Chapter 25 gives more quantitative details about standards and the explanation of variance from standards.

Learning and the experience curve

When anybody starts something new, there is a learning process before she arrives at her optimum ability. In the lifecycle, we learn to walk, to talk, we learn to study, we learn in a professional environment. Some activities are harder to learn than others. Further, some individuals are quicker to learn than others. This learning concept impacts productivity, costs, and profit in all phases of the operations and supply chain.

New products

If a company develops a new product, or process, it takes time for engineers, operators, and/or maintenance personnel fully to understand the process and the design and thus to be efficient regarding all the activities involved. As such, the operating and/or product cost at the early stage are higher than at later periods.

New hires

New hires in a company that has already in place established programmes and procedures take time to become fully operational. Thus, the productivity or output of these new hires is initially less than employees already in the firm.

Manufacturing and services

Some processes show greater improvement over time, or a definite learning curve, than others. This is particularly the case where there are complex labour operations in a manufacturing process, for example, in automobile manufacture, aircraft assembly, or machine tool production. Service operations such as financial institutions, distribution firms, restaurants, hotels and the like do not exhibit the same trend and may, in fact, have a barely perceptible learning curve.

The curve

The experience or learning curve, sometimes called the *manufacturing progress function*, is a mathematical relationship between the cumulative production output and its cost, expressed either in financial terms, or in production time. Studies have indicated that, for certain activities, production costs will decline in the order of 10% to 30% with the doubling of the cumulated output, illustrating that it takes time fully to learn new processes or new ideas. The concept of the learning curve is based on the premise that the learning rate, as a percentage, is quite regular and its progression can be predicted. Research has shown that the more complex a system, the greater is the rate of learning. This learning can be illustrated by an exponential type curve, or a straight line, if a logarithmic scale is used.

Mathematical representation

A mathematical learning curve can be developed by the representation of production labour hours versus the quantity of products produced. The curve decreases exponentially showing that starting with a new production operation, as the number of units produced increases, the labour hours/unit decreases as operators becomes more familiar with the task. Learning curves are presented according to the learning rate such as 75%, 80%, 85%, or 80%. For example, an 80% learning curve means that the number of labour hours per unit to double the quantity produced goes down by 80%.

Exponential 80% learning curve

Assume that to manufacture a product for the first time takes 50 hours. Then, at an 80% learning rate, the time to produce the second unit would be 40 hours (50*80%). The time to produce the fourth unit would be 32 hours (40*80%). And the time to produce the eighth unit would be 25.6 hours (32*80%). Table 8.5 gives the progression and Figure 8.5 shows the relationship graphically.

The curve declines rapidly at first, and then evens out, declining very slowly as new units are produced. It is this almost horizontal level that conforms to the labour standard for the particular item of work as discussed in the previous section.

The mathematical relationship has the exponential form $T_n = T_1 * (n^b)$, where:

- T_n = labour hours/unit when n units are manufactured
- T_1 = labour hours to produce the first unit
- n = the unit number produced
- b = is a constant representing the slope of the curve.

Logarithmic analysis

The expression $T_n = T_1 * (n^b)$ can be converted to the logarithmic form to give the straight line relationship:

$$\log_e T_n = \log_e T_1 + b * \log_e n$$

Table 8.5 Exponential 80% learning curve

Units produced	1	2	4	8	16	32	64	128	256
Hours per unit	50.00	40.00	32.00	25.60	20.48	16.38	13.11	10.49	8.39

Figure 8.5 Exponential 80% learning curve

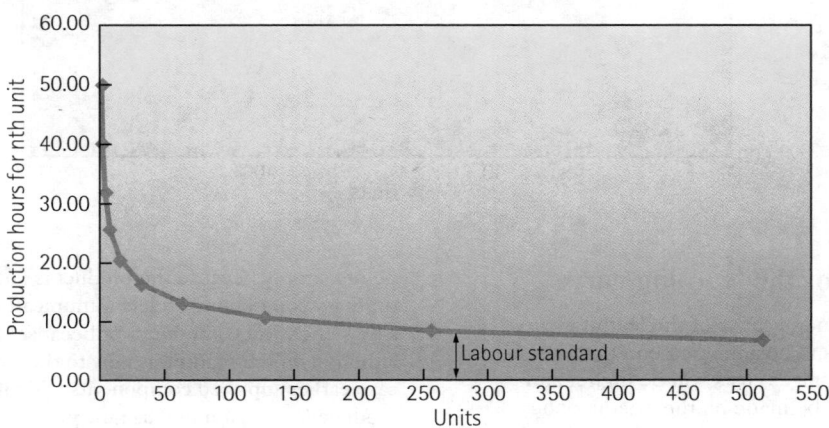

The slope of the straight line is b, and this can be rewritten as:

$$b = \frac{\log_e T_n - \log_e T_1}{\log_e n}$$

If L denotes the learning rate, the value of b can be determined by considering the time to produce the first unit, and also the time to produce the second unit. The time to produce the second unit is given by $T_1 * L$ (by definition of the learning process). Substituting this expression for T_n in the equation for b gives:

$$b = \frac{\log_e T_2 - \log_e T_1}{\log_e 2} = \frac{\log_e T_1 * L - \log_e T_1}{\log_e 2}$$
$$= \frac{\log_e T_1 + \log_e L - \log_e T_1}{\log_e 2} = \frac{\log_e L}{\log_e 2}$$

For an 80% learning rate, L = 0.80, and so:

$$b = \frac{\log_e L}{\log_e 2} = \frac{\log_e 0.80}{\log_e 2} = \frac{-0.2231}{+0.6931} = -0.3219$$

That is, a negative slop indicating that the time decreases as the number of units produced increases.

Alternatively, the value of b can be determined using the information from Table 8.5. If we consider, say, the production time for the first and 16th unit and

substituting these in the equation for the slope, b, then:

- Labour hours to produce the 16th unit is 20.48.
- Labour hours to produce the first unit is 50.00.
- Unit number produced is 16.

Then, in the equation for the slope b:

$$b = \frac{\log_e 20.48 - \log_e 50.00}{\log_e 16} = -0.3219$$

Substituting this value b in the exponential equation gives $T_n = T_1 . n^{-0.3219}$. From this, the labour hours for any unit number can be determined. For example, the labour hours required to produce the 25th unit would be calculated as follows:

$$T_{25} = 50 * 25^{-0.3219} = 17.74 \text{ labour hours}$$

Figure 8.6 is the alternative logarithmic graph of the 80% learning curve which is a straight line given by the equation:

$$\log_e T_n = \log_e T_1 - 0.3219 \log_e n$$

Similar calculations and the corresponding graphs can be made for other learning curves such as 70%, 75%, 80%, 85%, 90%, and the like.

Demonstrating the concept 8.1 illustrates the learning curve principle.

Figure 8.6 Logarithmic 80% learning curve

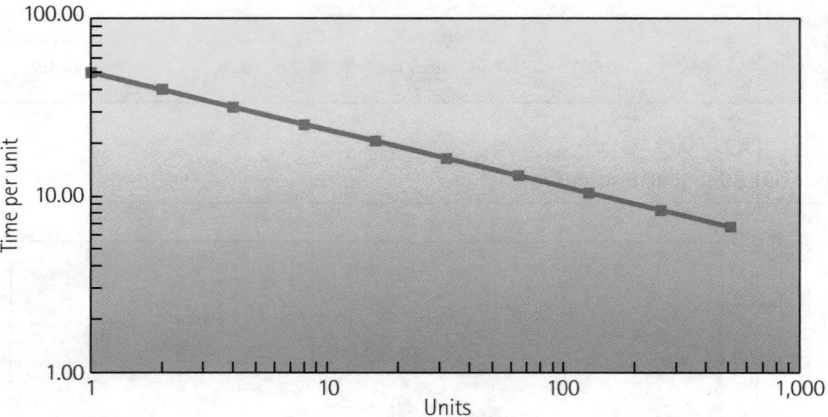

Implications of the learning curve

For costs to decline because of the learning curve concept there has to be an increase in production volume. In early stages costs will be higher and decisions need to be made on the pricing policy.

Producing a new product

The decision to be made at the early stage is to whether to demand a higher product price to compensate for higher unit costs, or to have an average cost and accept a lower margin at the beginning, which would rise with progression of the learning curve. The production costs of new airplanes are higher, and decline as the output increases.

Proposals

A company proposing a project, or a new order, for which it has little experience, may price it accordingly higher to take into account learning. This might make it uncompetitive with other firms. Or the company might be prepared to take a lower margin, or even a loss, in order to gain experience for future projects or sales. Pratt and Whitney and General Electric of the USA were prepared to take a loss to supply Singapore Airlines with engines for its new twin-engine Boeing-777s. This was a prestigious order, which would have given it learning experience for future orders for the 777 airplanes. Unfortunately for Pratt and Whitney and General Electric, the Singapore order went to Rolls-Royce.[25]

Purchasing

Assume a company approaches a potential supplier to provide a product of which the supplier has not furnished before simply because the product is entirely new (military components, telecommunications equipment, or a new chemical compound) or because the product, although on the market, is new to the supplier. In this case earlier supplied components will take longer to produce (and cost more) as new procedures and methods need to be employed. As more and more of the products are produced, the unit cost decreases. From a purchasing point of view it might mean that the client company pays more at the early stages of supply than it does later. That is, the client has to pay for the 'learning' process.

Real-world illustrations

In the past, the learning curve has demonstrated the following real situations.

Computer chip production

Figure 8.7 shows how the unit price per computer chip has reduced in the period 1978 through 1984. This experience process has had the result that the price of personal computers has decreased enormously.[26]

Price of a Model T Ford

The Model T Ford was the automobile introduced by Henry Ford in the early part of the 20th century. Figure 8.8 shows the learning curve at approximately an 85% slope.[27] The Ford Model T benefited from the experience curve for close to two decades. However, an inflexible devotion to the vehicle proved the company's downfall when the car became obsolete.[28]

Other US industry

Table 8.6 gives other real-world illustrations of the learning curve concept.[29]

Figure 8.7 70% experience curve for dynamic RAMs

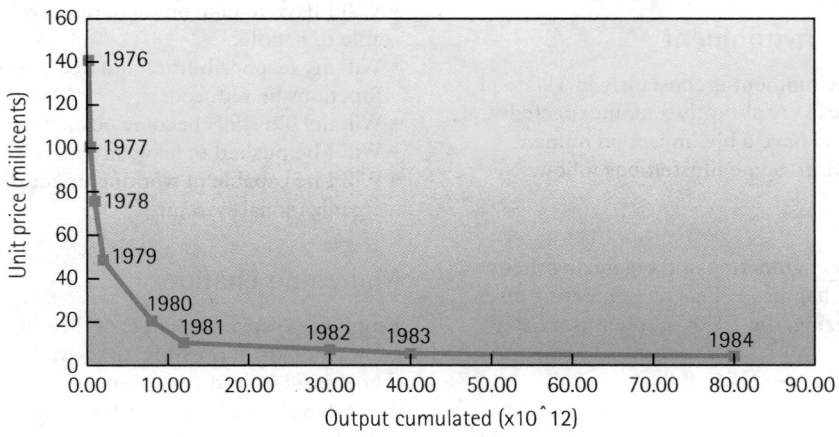

Figure 8.8 Price of a Model T Ford (1909–1923)

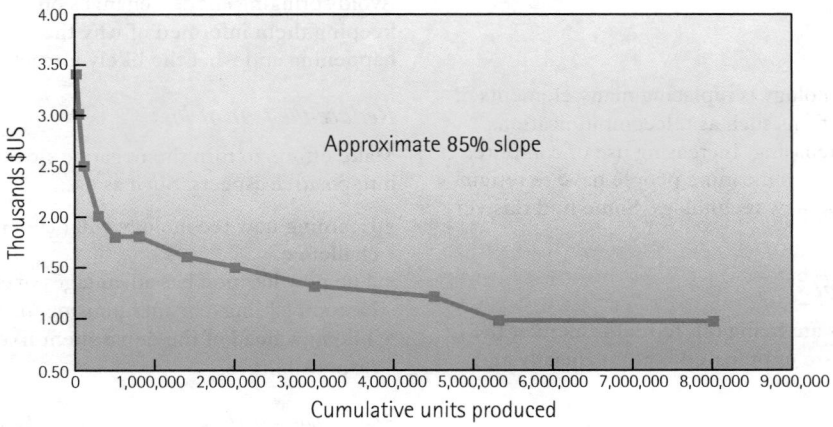

Table 8.6 Real-world illustrations of the learning curve concept

Operation	Parameter decreased	Cumulative	Rate (%)	Period
Aircraft assembly	Direct unit labour hours	Units produced	80	1925–1957
Equipment maintenance at GE	Average time to replace group of parts	Number of replacements	76	Around 1957
Oil refinery	Labour hours/barrel refined	Millions US barrels refined	84	1860–1962
Electric power generation	Mils per kW hour	Millions of kW hours	95	1910–1955
Steel production	Production hours/unit	Units produced	79	1920–1955
Integrated circuits	Average price/unit	Units produced	72	1964–1972
Hand calculator	Average factory selling price	Units produced	74	1975–1978
Disk memory drives	Average price per bit	Number of bits	76	1975–1978

People and change

The business environment

The business environment is constantly in a state of change sometimes very abruptly and unexpectedly. These changes can have a big impact on human resources in the firm. Some illustrations follow.

Reengineering

Companies are reengineering or reorganizing their operations (see Chapter 7). This reengineering often results in downsizing, the 1990s' euphemism for layoffs.

Relocating

Firms are moving facilities away from home countries to overseas low cost sites resulting in closures, or significant domestic staff reductions.

Technology

Information technology is replacing many elements of human labour in firms such as telecommunications, banking, and purchasing. Increasing use of computer systems in business is meaning people have to retrain in order to use the new technology. Some find this very difficult.

Early retirement

Loyal employees are being offered retirement at the age of 55. Many are unprepared both financially and physiologically.

Mergers and acquisitions

Companies are being merged, or acquired by others. The resulting new organization often means that there is duplication of positions so that these have to be trimmed.

Stress and change

Organizational changes have a physiological impact not only on the people who lose their employment, but also on those that remain. Stress situations may be prompted by concerns such as the following:

- Will I be the next to lose my job?
- Will I have to relocate to another area?
- Will I have more work, which means working more hours?
- Will I have to do more travelling and spend significant time away from my family?
- Will I have to take on more responsibilities than I am able to handle?
- Will my responsibilities and decision-making functions be reduced?
- Will my old skills become obsolete?
- Will I be pushed to leave my friends?
- Will I be capable of working under the new organizational system?

Managing change

Employees sensing change, or 'hearing it through the grapevine', try, if possible, to resist. During the period that change is 'in the air' motivation and productivity drops. Some considerations for managing people during this upheaval are as follows.

Eliminate surprise situations

Avoid springing sudden changes on the employees by keeping them informed of why the changes are happening and what the likely impacts are, etc.

Reduce the fear of loss

Make efforts to turn the negative sides of the change into positive aspects. Such as:

- Learning new technology will be an interesting challenge.
- The new location has advantages over the present location (skiing, cheaper housing, better schools, etc.).
- The new head of the department likes to delegate responsibilities.

Management should openly sell the change

Sometimes, non-management employees have difficulty grasping reasons for reorganizations making them very resistant. Management at all levels should demonstrate a positive attitude towards proposed changes in order to give encouragement to others. Middle management openly criticizing top management's decisions can only acerbate the company stress level.

Plant closure

Employees' sharp reaction to change was violently illustrated in March 1997 when Renault, France, which faced big losses for 1996, unveiled plans to shut down its plant in Vilvoorde, Belgium, in July 1997. This was part of a broad reorganization of its European production facilities,[30] as Industry insight 8.3 illustrates.

Vilvoorde, Belgium

Renault's Vilvoorde closure, home of Belgian Prime Minister Jean-Luc Dehaene, provoked outrage in Belgium and across Europe because it appeared that Renault, although majority owned by private investors since last summer when a further sale of shares dropped the government's stake to 46%, was sacrificing Belgian jobs to save French ones, and violating European Union rules on worker consultation. Angry employees occupied the plant, taking hostage some 4000 finished cars, and, in March, an estimated 70,000 union members from around Europe converged on Brussels to protest that European integration has failed to protect workers Last week, Belgium Renault employees blocked a Eurostar train to London and a TGV (express train) to Paris, claiming they were 'symbols of the Europe of capitalism'.

Adapted from: 'A road to nowhere?', *Time*[31]

Summary of key elements

- People are the key in any business function. The worst scenario in human relations is a breakdown in communication leading to a strike. This can have a disastrous effect on revenues, customer relations, and the working environment.

- Working conditions have evolved considerably in the 20th century but issues including equal pay for equal work, sexual harassment, race relations, and sweatshop work continue into the 21st century. Conditions in some emerging economies are still poor.

- The scientific management period, from about 1875 to 1925, treated work in a logical and scientific way. Frederick Taylor was the most prominent contributor in this area and his name coined the concept Taylorism.

- The human relations period from about 1925 to 1960 put a more human side to the management of people. Notables in this area include Elton Mayo, Henry Gantt, Abraham Maslow, Frederick Herzberg, Douglas McGregor, and Peter Drucker.

- Job design entails matching job tasks with individuals or work groups. An objective is to increase the organizational efficiency with the parallel goal of making working conditions more agreeable. Job design encompasses job specialization, job rotation, job enlargement, job enrichment, and empowerment. It must take into consideration women, ergonomics, skill levels, and work schedules.

- The correct attitude towards employees can have a positive effect on productivity and costs. Communication, a proper working environment, and clear company objectives are elements, which contribute to a smooth working environment.

- When management makes decisions involving personnel it is better to discuss these with the people involved, rather than pushing decisions onto the employees.

- Part of work measurement involves machine and labour standards. Standards are needed for proposal development, scheduling, cost control, capacity planning, budgeting, comparing different operating methods, and perhaps bonus schemes.

- A motion study (or time and motion) is used to develop labour standards. It involves breaking a work assignment into its various components and timing each to come up with a total cycle time. A standard time is then developed by also incorporating qualitative considerations.

- The learning curve is based on an exponential relationship illustrating that the time to perform an activity decreases as the number of units produced increases. An 80% learning curve means that as output doubles, the labour hours decline by 80%.

- The learning curve concept is a consideration in new product development, hiring new employees, proposal preparation, and purchasing.

- People in organizations are constantly under stress, brought about by such factors as reengineering, firms relocating, technological changes, forced early retirement, plant closures, and mergers and acquisitions.

- In managing change leaders should 'level' with employees by avoiding surprise situations, reducing the fear of loss, and openly selling the change to those concerned.

Notes and references

1. SWOBODA, Frank, 'Supreme Court lets fine stand against pilots', *International Herald Tribune*, 27 February 2001, p. 3

2. 'Challenge of the 1990s: Renault strike shows the need to transform relations with labour. To compete with Japanese, Europeans have to learn to co-operate in factories. Of disruptions and disasters', *Wall Street Journal Europe*, 19 November 1991

3. DICKENS, Charles, *Hard Times*, Signet Classic, New American Library, New York, 1961

4. 'The Dearing report' (published in *The Economist*, 4 October 1997, Universities Survey, p. 11)

5. *Business Week*, 9 December 1996

6. DREAZEN, Yochi, J., 'Black Microsoft workers allege bias', *International Herald Tribune*, 4 January 2001, p. 14

7. *Business Week*, 18 November 1996

8. 'Stamping out sweatshops: Dress code', *The Economist*, 19 April 1997, p. 54

9. 'Morocco: Children in the boiler-room', *The Economist*, 7 October 2000, p. 63

10. *On the Economy of Machinery and Manufacturers*, London, 1832

11. *An Inquiry in the Nature and Causes of the Wealth of Nations*, London, 1776

12. TAYLOR, Frederick W., *Principles of Scientific Management*, Harper and Brothers, New York, 1911

13. 'The line starts here, but whose idea was it?', *Wall Street Journal Europe*, 14 January 1999, p. 12

14. ROETHLISBERGER, F. J. and DICKSON W. J., *Management and the Worker*, Harvard University Press, 1939

15. CERTO, Samuel C., *Principles of Modern Management: Functions and Systems*, Allyn & Bacon, London, 4th edition, pp 36–8

16. MASLOW, Abraham H., 'A theory of human motivation', *Psychological Review*, 50, 1943, pp 370–96

17. HERZBERG, Frederick, MAUSNER, B. and SNYDERMAN, B.B., *The Motivation to Work*, John Wiley, New York, 1965

18. MCGREGOR Douglas, *The Human Side of Enterprise*, McGraw-Hill, New York, 1960

19. DRUCKER, Peter, SMIDDY, Harold and GREENWOOD, Ronald G., 'Management by objectives', *Academy of Management Review* 6, April 1981, p. 225

20. *The Economist*, 15 February 1997, p. 49

21. 'Empowerment that pays off. Chrysler gives power to its people, and the result is a string of hot cars and record earnings. But CEO Robert Eaton still isn't satisfied', *Fortune*, 20 March 1995, p. 95

22. Internship with British Oxygen Co. in North London, UK, 1962

23. 'Facts through figures', *Eurostat*, 1996

24. ZUCKERMAN, Laurence, 'At Continental, even the bottom line is looking up', *International Herald Tribune*, 28 February 2001, p. 2

25. 'Aircraft engines: Rolls-Royce flies high', *The Economist*, 28 June 1997, p. 79

26. GHEMAWAT, P., 'Building strategy on the experience curve', *Harvard Business Review*, March–April 1985, pp 143–9

27. ABERNATHY W. J. and WAYNE K., 'Limits of the learning curve', *Harvard Business Review*, September–October 1974, pp 109–19

28. 'Riding the experience curve', *Technology Review*, March–April 1976, pp 53–9

29. CUNNINGHAM, James A., 'Using the learning curve as a management tool', *IEEE Spectrum*, June 1980, p. 45

30. 'Renault to axe Belgian plant, take $421.1 million charge', *Wall Street Journal Europe*, 28 February/1 March 1997

31. 'A road to nowhere? Renault's troubles typify a European car-making industry where profits are low and problems high', *Time*, 7 April 1997

Review and discussion topics

1. Unemployment

In the USA and Britain, unemployment is about half that of France and Germany even though the skill levels and the potential market are pretty much the same. Discuss why this is so. What are the 'people' elements that help to explain these differences?

2. Child labour

In developing countries, child labour is often used in mining, the clothing industry, and assembly plants. Products produced are then sold to the West (Europe, Japan, and USA). Some people abhor this idea, and say that we should boycott all products, and firms that resort to child labour. Other people say that if the children were not used in the working environment, they would end up in prostitution where they would be worse off. What is your opinion? What can be done?

3. Price and the learning curve

Because of the concept of the learning curve, firms might price high at the early stages of the introduction of a product, and then lower the price later as the learning curve levels out. What are the dangers of applying this principle? What are some of the advantages?

4. International differences in the learning curve

A firm which has identical manufacturing facilities in two different countries may have different learning rates for the same work being performed. Give your reasons why this might be the case. What impact does this have on international firms that are looking for facilities overseas? Based on the information provided in Chapter 3, can you identify those regions that might have a faster learning rate?

5. Purchasing and the learning curve

What impact does the learning curve concept have on the relationship between the supplier and client? If there is a high rate of learning, how might this benefit the client? The supplier? Conversely, if there is a low rate of learning, how might this benefit the client? The supplier?

6. Services and the learning curve

Why is the impact of the learning curve not as marked in services as it is in manufacturing? What are some of the characteristics of a service organization that make the principle of the learning curve more complicated than in a manufacturing environment?

7. Time and motion study

You work for a unionized textile company in Europe whose business is struggling because of competition from overseas, and rising operating costs. Your boss has suggested that you organize a time and motion study of the activity on the manufacturing floor in order to understand exactly what is happening, and to see if the standards developed some time back are still meaningful.

How would you carry out a time and motion study in a manufacturing situation?

8. Workweek

In 2000 France implemented a 35-hour workweek. One of its aims was to reduce the level of unemployment by limiting the number of hours people work, thus obligating employers to hire additional labour. What are your comments on this idea? Look at the impact on both the firm and the human resources.

Demonstrating the concept 8.1 Turbines

Situation

The Saudi Arabia government is developing a desalination and energy complex in the country. For this project a certain number of special turbines are needed to operate in a region where there are frequent sandstorms. The Saudi government has a contract with a manufacturer in Sweden to manufacture the turbines. The first turbine built for the first phase of the project took the manufacture 18,000 labour hours to assemble. The Saudi government has an option to purchase 20 similar turbines.

The average labour rate for the manufacturing company is $32.00/hour. The cost of the product is calculated using this labour rate. Based on past experience, the company has a 75% learning rate. In addition, it expects to make a 40% margin on the selling price of these turbines to the Saudi government. This margin is calculated individually on each turbine, not averaged.

Required

1. Develop a learning curve for the turbine production in terms of labour hours up to a production of 20 turbines.
2. For five turbines, what is the:
   (a) average manufacturing time per unit
   (b) average cost/unit
   (c) average purchase price/unit that the Saudi government expects to pay when it benefits from the learning curve concept
   (d) total profit to the manufacturing company?
3. If the Saudi government exercised its option for all 20 units, then, what is:
   (a) average manufacturing time per unit
   (b) average cost/unit
   (c) average purchase price/unit that the Saudi government expects to pay when it benefits from the learning curve concept
   (d) total profit to the manufacturing company?

Solution

1. Table 8.7 gives the required data for the turbine manufacture, and Figure 8.9 shows the corresponding learning curve.

The slope of the curve b is calculated by the relationship:

$$b = \frac{\log_e L}{\log_e 2} = \frac{\log_e 0.75}{\log_e 2} = \frac{-0.2877}{+0.6931} = -0.4150$$

The manufacturing time/unit for each unit is calculated from the relationship:

$$T_n = T_1(n^b)$$

where T_1 is 18,000 hours, and T_n is for the nth unit.
Cost per unit is $32 * T_1(n^b)$.
Price per unit is $(32 * T_1(n^b))/(1 - 0.4)$ and 40% margin is assumed for each unit.

$$\text{Margin} = \frac{\text{Price} - \text{cost}}{\text{Price}}.$$

Total profit is

$$(\text{Price/unit} - \text{cost/unit}) * \text{N}^\circ \text{ of units.}$$

2. For five turbines (figures are rounded up to nearest whole number):
   (a) average manufacturing time per unit = 12,453 hours
   (b) average cost/unit = $398,486
   (c) average purchase price/unit that the Saudi government expects to pay when it benefits from the learning curve concept = $664,143
   (d) total profit to the manufacturing company = $1,328,287.
3. For 20 turbines (figures are rounded up to nearest whole number):
   (a) average manufacturing time per unit = 7945 hours
   (b) average cost/unit = $254,257
   (c) average purchase price/unit that the Saudi government expects to pay when it benefits from the learning curve concept = $423,761
   (d) total profit to the manufacturing company = $3,390,087.

Table 8.7 Turbine manufacturing data

Average labour rate, $/hr	32.00
Learning rate	75.00%
Profit margin	40.00%

Slope, b	−0.4150

$$\text{Margin} = \frac{\text{Price} - \text{Cost}}{\text{Price}}$$

Turbine N°	Time for this unit (hours)	Cost for this unit ($)	Price for this unit ($)	Profit for this unit ($)	Cumulated profit ($)	Cumulated price($)
1	18,000.00	576,000.00	960,000.00	384,000.00	384,000.00	960,000.00
2	13,500.00	432,000.00	720,000.00	288,000.00	672,000.00	1,680,000.00
3	11,409.04	365,089.44	608,482.40	243,392.96	915,392.96	2,288,482.40
4	10,125.00	324,000.00	540,000.00	216,000.00	1,131,392.96	2,828,482.40
5	9,229.41	295,340.99	492,234.98	196,893.99	1,328,286.95	3,320,717.38
6	8,556.78	273,817.08	456,361.80	182,544.72	1,510,831.67	3,777,079.18
7	8,026.48	256,847.36	428,078.93	171,231.57	1,682,063.24	4,205,158.11
8	7,593.75	243,000.00	405,000.00	162,000.00	1,844,063.24	4,610,158.11
9	7,231.46	231,406.77	385,677.95	154,271.18	1,998,334.42	4,995,836.06
10	6,922.05	221,505.74	369,176.23	147,670.49	2,146,004.92	5,365,012.29
11	6,653.58	212,914.61	354,857.69	141,943.07	2,287,947.99	5,719,869.98
12	6,417.59	205,362.81	342,271.35	136,908.54	2,424,856.53	6,062,141.33
13	6,207.89	198,652.58	331,087.64	132,435.06	2,557,291.59	6,393,228.97
14	6,019.86	192,635.52	321,059.20	128,423.68	2,685,715.27	6,714,288.17
15	5,849.93	187,197.70	311,996.17	124,798.47	2,810,513.73	7,026,284.33
16	5,695.31	182,250.00	303,750.00	121,500.00	2,932,013.73	7,330,034.33
17	5,553.80	177,721.53	296,202.55	118,481.02	3,050,494.75	7,626,236.88
18	5,423.60	173,555.08	289,258.46	115,703.38	3,166,198.14	7,915,495.34
19	5,303.25	169,703.89	282,839.81	113,135.92	3,279,334.06	8,198,335.15
20	5,191.54	166,129.30	276,882.17	110,752.87	3,390,086.93	8,475,217.33

Number of units	Average time/unit	Average cost/unit	Average price/unit	Average profit/unit	Total profit
5	12,452.69	398,486.09	664,143.48	265,657.39	1,328,286.95
20	7,945.52	254,256.52	423,760.87	169,504.35	3,390,086.93

Figure 8.9 Learning curve for turbine manufacture

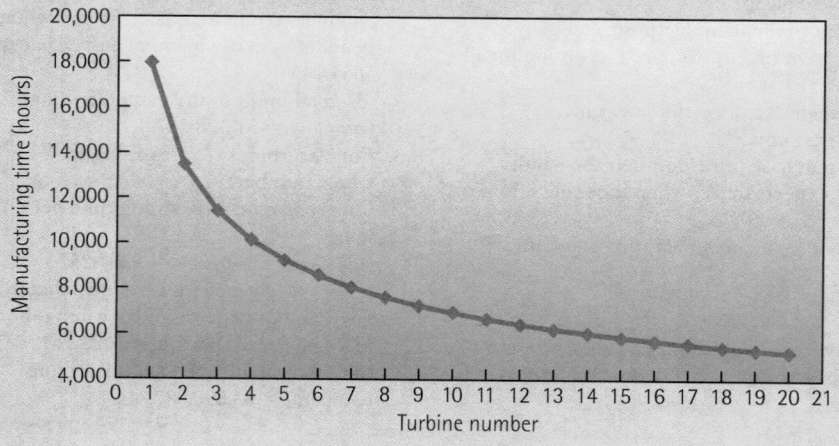

Application exercise 8.1 Engines

Situation

A certain airplane manufacturer has developed a new twin-engine airplane. In parallel with the work, it offered a contract with an engine manufacturer to build a commercial prototype of a new aircraft engine. This took 55,000 labour hours. The airline company, which is going to purchase this new plane, has an option on 25 planes.

The average labour rate for the engine manufacture, including the design engineers is $38.00/hour. The cost of the engine is calculated using this labour rate. Based on past experience, the engine company has an 80% learning rate. In addition, it expects to make a 25% margin on the sale of these engines to the airplane manufacturer. This margin is calculated individually on each engine, not averaged.

Required

1. Develop a learning curve for the engine production in terms of labour hours up to the maximum production expected if the airline company exercises its full option.
2. For 12 engines, what is the:
   (a) average manufacturing time per unit
   (b) average cost/unit
   (c) average purchase price/unit that the airplane manufacturer expects to pay if it benefits from the learning curve concept
   (d) total profit to the engine manufacturer?
3. If the airline company exercised its option for all 25 planes, what is:
   (a) average manufacturing time per unit
   (b) average cost/unit
   (c) average purchase price/unit that the aircraft manufacturer expects to pay if it benefits from the learning curve concept
   (d) total profit to the engine manufacturing company?

Case study 8.1 Lamson & Sessions Co.'s plastics factory

Situation
The following article illustrates a real-world situation in relationships with people.*

Life at the factory: Full Time, Part Time, Temp – All See the Job In a Different Light

Pay, Loyalty and Status Vary In Flexible Work Force In U.S., and Strains Show

Toolbox as emblem of power

By TIMOTHY AEPPEL

Staff Reporter

Bowling Green, Ohio –There isn't supposed to be a seniority system in Lamson & Sessions Co.'s plastics factory on the out-skirts of this college town. But don't try telling that to Robert Wendel.

His assignment today includes relieving co-workers at the various molding machines while they go to lunch. But as he tells one woman when he can cover for her, she snaps back that she decides when she eats. He rearranges his schedule.

"Did I mess up?" he asks, looking nervously at Dawnna DeVries, one of the plant's two full-time trainers and a sort of unofficial shepherdess for new hires.

Mrs. DeVries smiles and urges him to be tougher next time. "The one who wins around here is the one who doesn't back down," she says.

So much for workplace harmony.

Five groups of workers

Operating round the clock, the plant has five categories of workers, mostly women. It has about 90 full-time, permanent employees; approximately 40 of them stand in front of bus-size molding machines that thump out items such as the plastic boxes that hold the guts of light switches in walls. It also has 40 temporaries, who operate the machines, too. In addition, it has 70 independent contractors who work outside the facility. And it has people who work only in summer and others who work part time.

Such flexibility is becoming more common in some types of manufacturing in the U.S., especially in fast-growing, nonunion plants such as this. It helps a company in a cyclical business meet ebbs and flows of demand. It also appeals to single mothers and college students. Lamson & Sessions considers the Bowling

Green factory one of its best plants, even though such an arrangement complicates the dynamics of the work force and can generate conflicts.

Each group of workers views the job differently and feels varying degrees of loyalty. And even within a single group there are divisions, mainly among the full-time workers who have more invested in the job. Those who once held union jobs stick together in disputes over speeding up the molding machines. Those doing repetitive, tedious tasks clash with a small elite, the all-male technicians who change the molds and keep the machinery running.

Some Dissension

The Cleveland-based company strives to get all these people to mesh smoothly, but not always with complete success.

"We get a lot of people in here who act brain-dead," complains one permanent worker, Nancy Lein, tapping her forehead with a finger and referring to people standing at other machines less than seven meters away, doing the same work but employed as temporaries. "You got to keep that thing clear," Ms. Lein notes, pointing to a bin at the end of a conveyor belt at a nearby temp's machine. The bin is starting to overflow with parts.

Turnover among newcomers runs as high as 40% a month. As a result, workers such as Ms. Lein are constantly teaching new people tricks, such as picking up four parts in each hand simultaneously to examine them for faults. Turnover among permanent workers is under 1%.

The plant arrived at its present work-force structure through an often-bumpy evolution. When it opened in 1989, in the empty hulk of a former plastic-pipe plant, it had just one molding machine and 12 workers. It had no reason to call them permanent; employees were employees.

Several Advantages

After that, everyone who began working at the plant started out as a temporary despite having the same shifts and doing the same jobs. That system holds down costs because temps, as employees of an agency, don't get the same benefits or pay, and the managers can preview their skills before making a commitment to hire them. It also avoids layoffs of permanent workers when business slumps. But it sparks a classic us-vs.-them clash, of a kind usually dividing management and workers.

Involved most frequently in clashes are the temps. Although they make up half of the 80 operators, the core group that runs machines and packs boxes, and they work along-side the others, their pay is far lower. They get only $6.50 an hour, while permanent operators earn $8.60 to $11.19 an hour, plus benefits and a toolbox.

Toolboxes are emblems of power. When an operator wins permanent status, the company gives him or her a black plastic case stuffed with things such as Exacto knives and pliers. Many decorate the inside of the lids with pictures of their children and spouses, then prop them open on the edge of their workbenches so they can glance at them while working.

Moreover, permanent workers get something less tangible but more significant: They vote on which temps join their ranks. The system makes some sense. They work alongside the temps, see their work habits and attitudes and train them.

"That one over there's definitely going to make it, you can just tell," says Becky Clements, a 30-year-old permanent worker, pointing across the factory floor to a man holding a part up to the light and shaving off excess plastic with a knife.

Then she points down the corridor to a woman wearing a baseball cap and a dour expression. "That's the other extreme," she says. "She's got a bad attitude."

To do the job right, workers must learn a lot of tiny, repetitive tasks. Operators are assigned each day to one of 16 molding machines. The same machine may make different parts each day, depending on which mold is running in it.

"Most of the people in here aren't enjoying themselves; they're enduring," says Michelle Toney, a temp. Today, she is assembling cartons and pushing them to end of a conveyor belt, where parts plop directly into the boxes. When the boxes are filled, she drags them off and seals them for shipping. Unlike the woman next to her, Karen Diedrick, Mrs. Toney isn't hoping to graduate to a permanent slot; she is waiting for a job to open up at a unionized pudding factory nearby.

But Mrs. Diedrick wanted a permanent job, mainly for the extra money. She wanted it so badly that when she caught her hand in a bagging machine on one of her first days at work, she made a point of returning from the hospital to finish her shift. "Three hours in the emergency room," she says, holding up her hand to show a jagged scar. "The only tough part was working with my hand bandaged," adds the 34-year-old mother of two. Her dedication paid off: Last month, she became a permanent employee.

Futile Tactics

"Some people try to make it a popularity contest," comments Gary Keel, the plant's office manager. They offer to buy permanent workers coffee, for instance, or often volunteer for overtime. But Mr. Keel says such people seldom make it. "They're good at trying to be everybody's friend, but they can't make a part worth a damn, and the other people see that."

Plant managers acknowledge the difficulty of having so many temporaries, mainly because of rapid turnover. About half the temps leaving each month are told not to come back, because of poor attendance or inability to keep up with the work pace. In this area of Ohio, however, they can always go elsewhere: Local unemployment was only 4.7% in January.

The temps don't hurt product quality, says James Zechinati, the plant manager, because the work is double-checked.

But with less vested in the job, they sometimes create annoying glitches. Some newly hired temps have stalked out after a few hours or never come back after lunch. Others leave machines messy at the end of a shift or pocket expensive tools.

Temps themselves say they dislike the open-ended nature of their employment. They have no clear idea how long they may wait for a permanent slot to open up, and they may be nominated several times before making it – if at all. "You feel jerked around," says Lu Ann Welch, a 38-year-old permanent worker who spent 14 months as a temp before moving up.

Eva Harter, who recently found out that she is entering the promised land of permanent employment after five months as a temp, has bitter memories of her initiation. Shortly after starting as a temp, she was in the vending-machine room when a permanent worker – though once a temp herself – began talking loudly. "She went on and on about how temps make so many mistakes, they're dumb, the whole thing," the 56-year-old says. "She knew I was sitting there."

The Independent Contractors

Surprisingly, the issue of independent contractors, a source of much labor unrest elsewhere, stirs up less conflict. The plant started using them in 1995 to replace some bottom-rung employees who did tasks such as screwing together parts and putting them in bags.

One of the contractors is Carla Tiell, 26, the mother of two girls. She carts home boxes of parts, assembles them and brings them back a week later, earning about $100 for groceries. "I can do this at my own pace, while watching TV or between loads of laundry," she says. Because contractors aren't covered by the factory's insurance, she isn't allowed inside the plant but doesn't care and doesn't feel excluded.

Workers in the plant don't view contractors as interlopers, mainly because no one lost jobs to them. The people who did that work were promoted to better jobs as operators and ultimately earned more money. Because the plant is nonunion, there was no organized opposition to the change. And nepotism helps: Relatives of current workers get preference in obtaining outside assembly work.

Anyway, much of the friction occurs within the various groups. Permanent employees who need to go on part-time because of medical conditions often leave at midday, causing headaches for other permanent employees, who usually end up manning two machines for the rest of the shift. There is also a strong but largely unspoken division between those who support the notion of unionizing and those who don't. One pro-union worker, who resents the long work shifts and a program to speed up machines, keeps her anger to herself for fear of being fired or badmouthed by colleagues. "They would get rid of us and replace us," she says.

Another battle goes on between the operators, two-thirds of whom are women, and the crew of about 20 technicians, all men. (The plant once had two female technicians, but one left the company and the other switched to quality-control work because she wanted better hours.) The technicians, who change molds and keep the machines running smoothly, earn $11.59 to $12.70 a hour. They stride through the factory wearing head-phones to talk to each other – adding to the aura of an exclusive fraternity.

Tension With Technicians

Many women complain that the technicians go out of their way to make them feel stupid when they call for help when a machine breaks down. The women also believe that because many technicians never worked as operators, they have no idea how difficult the job actually is.

Suddenly, a bell goes off on the press Ms. Clements is operating. She tries unjamming it without success, then dials the intercom for help. When Erwin Szafraniec arrives, he sweeps past her without a word and fiddles with her press. He vanishes and comes back with more tools.

"Going to change the mold?" she asks.

"Yup," he says.

"Thanks for telling me," she replies, her voice thick with sarcasm.

However, Steve Holderman, another technician, says the operators sometimes ask for trouble by, for example, stuffing too many scraps of plastic into a grinder and jamming it. "Sure, I get frustrated and even swear sometimes," he says. "But I always look away so nobody can hear."

Plant managers say such tension is inevitable in any factory, especially when companies need different mixes of people to match changes in demand. Of course, management must be flexible itself in creating a flexible workplace.

About a year after the plant opened, it had 30 employees and was ready to go to a seven-day-a-week schedule. The company tried creating a separate, part-time class of workers just for weekends, assuming farmers' wives and college students would want the jobs. But the wives weren't interested and the students were too undependable, especially when they wanted to go to a big dance or had exams. So the disastrous experiment was dropped,

though the plant still hires a dozen or so college students in summer when demand for construction-related products soars.

"I forgot what I knew in college," says Mr. Keel, the office manager. "You party on the weekend. We're flexible, but even we couldn't deal with that."

Required

Discuss the situation presented in the terms of the product, the process, and the people. Using the concepts presented earlier in this chapter, discuss what you believe are improvements that could be made.

*Aeppel, Timothy, 'Life at the factory: Full time, part time, temp – all see the job in a different light', *Wall Street Journal Europe*, 19 March 1997.

Selected further reading

GIBSON, James L., IVANCEVICH, John M. and DONNELLY, James H. Jr (1999) *Organizations: Behavior, Structure, Processes*, 10th edition, McGraw-Hill Education.

MATHIS, Robert L. and JACKSON, John H. (1999) *Human Resource Management*, 9th edition South-Western Publishing.

MAYO, Andrew (2001) *The Human Value of the Enterprise: Valuing People as Assets – Monitoring, Measuring, Managing*, Nicholas Brealey Publishing.

NOE, Raymond A., HOLLENBECK, John R. and GERHART, Barry (1999) *Human Resource Management: Gaining a Competitive Advantage*, 3rd edition, McGraw-Hill.

PFAU, Bruce N. and KAY, Ira, T. (2001) *The Human Capital Edge: 21 People Management Practices Your Company Must Implement (Or Avoid) To Maximize Shareholder Value*, McGraw-Hill.

An extensive listing of other further reading can be found on the website.

What's on the web?

Further learning resources are available to lecturers and students at www.supplychain-online.com, including the following which are specific to *Human resources in the system design*:

Resource	Subject
Chapter overview	Human resources in the system design
Exam topics	Human resources in the system design
Application exercise: Chateau	Learning curve
Case exercise: Caterpillar	Human resources in the system design
More further reading	Human resources in the system design

9 Design of the facility layout

Chapter overview

- Defining facility layout
- Layout in manufacturing
- Retail facilities
- Restaurants
- Airports
- Engineering, consulting, or design office
- Methods for facility layout

Defining facility layout

Chapter 7 addressed the conceptual steps involved in designing the process for delivering tangible products, or services to a customer. This chapter details that part of the process design involving the physical layout, or arrangement, of all machines, equipment, and workstations used in the operating environment. For supply chain considerations, the design of the layout is important as a poorly organized facility can delay the flow of materials, or information, and thus impact timely delivery of the goods, or services to the client. Facility layout applies to both manufacturing and service firms as now discussed.

Manufacturing

A manufacturing site is established to transform raw materials, or components into finished goods destined for final consumers or industrial use. Here a facility layout would include the organization of:

- machines used in cutting, drilling, printing, packaging, filling, painting, etc.
- workstations for individuals, teams of operators, or robot-controlled systems
- storage areas for raw material, purchased components, packaging, and finished products
- offices for all the service-related functions such as purchasing, accounting, human resources, etc.

Service organization

Many service facilities offer direct client contact and so the facility layout is heavily influenced to provide maximum customer convenience. The layout depends very much on the service offered and might include:

- aisle and shelving arrangement in retail stores
- reception areas for clients in a bank, insurance, or accounting firm
- offices for personnel in consulting, engineering, purchasing, etc.
- repair bays in an automobile repair shop
- operating rooms, treatment areas, and patient beds in a medical centre
- loading and unloading docks for the transportation vehicles in a distribution centre
- storage zones for finished products in a wholesale or distribution operation.

Material and information flow

All firms, either manufacturing or services, contain flow streams of material, people, transfer equipment, and information. The global objective of any facility layout is efficiency such that it:

- uses a flow pattern that is the most cost effective
- optimizes utilization of space
- facilitates the installation of an information systems network
- conforms to health regulations
- respects safety rules

- takes into consideration the comfort and well-being of employees
- is the most agreeable for customers.

Facility access

Whatever the facility, it should offer easy access to transportation routes and adequate parking for utility vehicles and for customers and employees. One noticeable difference between Europe, Japan, and the United States is that, because in the US space is not so much at a premium, there is often an abundance of parking compared to the other geographical locations. In entering the facility there should be escalators and/or lifts if work or service areas are on several floors.

The cost of facility layout

The preparation and implementation of facility layout is costly, both in terms of labour, materials, and time. In addition, to reorganize an existing arrangement is doubly costly not only because of the direct cost of the reorganization itself but also because of the expense of curtailing operations during this changeover. For this reason, careful consideration has to be made in deciding on a facility layout as the arrangement is normally long lasting. Nonetheless, with changing markets, needs, or new technology, firms all modify layouts from time to time.

Site selection and layout

In locating a new facility, discussed in Chapter 3, the prospect of additional space for facility expansion, needs always to be taken into consideration.

Layout in manufacturing

Manufacturing steps

A manufacturing operation is a process network involving the movement of materials and, if optimized, value will be added at each step in the activity. Some steps would include:

- Raw materials, components and packaging are delivered at the manufacturing site.
- The material is unloaded, inspected for conformity, and placed into storage.
- Material is taken from storage as needed for the production process.
- In-process inventory on the shop floor is transferred from one work post to another.

- Finished products are taken from the last work post and put into a storage area.
- Finished goods are taken from storage and dispatched to the client.

Factors in the layout

The layout will depend on the type of production operation, the size of the organization, and the number of different components handled. Some considerations will include the following.

Types of material

- For solid materials, the volume, weight and fragility are important considerations. A firm might be dealing with iron castings, which are heavy but may crack on impact, glass or ceramic materials, which break easily, or plastic components, which are light but can be easily scored or punctured.
- Sterile zones might be required, such as in the production of pharmaceutical products, syringes, and other medical equipment.
- Refrigerated areas may be needed for food, vaccines, or other perishable items.
- Some products might be affected by humidity so dehumidified zones need to be incorporated.
- Computer components and nuclear-related products need areas that are free from dust and electrostatic charges.

Building construction

- The building used to house the facility should be such that walls, ceilings and floors have sufficient structural strength for machines and heavy equipment such as stamping presses, furnaces, robots, overhead cranes, etc.
- If the facility is in an earthquake zone, such as southern California, Japan, or Mexico, the building structure needs to take this into consideration.
- Insulation from noise and vibration should be such that activity in other areas will not be affected by noise.

Environmental and safety

For personnel working at the facility, environmental and safety regulations need to be respected:

- Noise levels should be kept to an acceptable level and lighting, heating, and air conditioning should be adequate.
- Flammable liquids such as petroleum products, cleaning fluids, or paints should be away from personnel in an appropriate area.

Figure 9.1 Functional layout in manufacturing

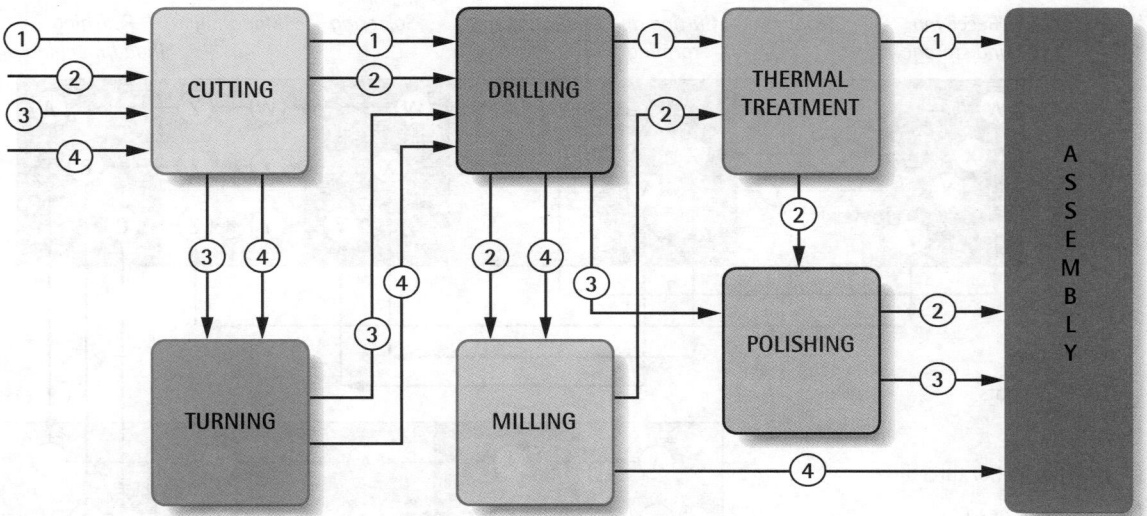

• Storage silos for fine solid materials such as grain, chemical products, or coal should be far away from personnel areas as they could explode under adverse conditions. (In Bordeaux, France, in 1997 a grain silo exploded and killed people in an office building located nearby.)

Working area

• The area should be conformable and agreeable for employees and customers who visit the site.
• There should be sufficient room to carry out necessary maintenance procedures. In a chemical plant, for example, maintenance people need to be able to clean out heat exchangers, change fluid pumps, or work on furnace equipment.
• There should be sufficient space for people and mobile equipment such as front-end loadings in distribution centres to negotiate around the area.

Meeting rooms

• Meeting rooms for operators to discuss improvements, quality aspects, etc. should be available near the production area.

Functional layout

A functional layout, also known as a job shop, batch or process layout, is where different types of products are subjected to different process operations such as cutting, welding, drilling, milling, cleaning, painting, heat treatment and the like, as illustrated in Figure 9.1.

Table 9.1 Families of material in a job shop

Reference number	Material
1	Copper units for electrical use
2	Aluminium units for impeller blades
3	Carbon steel flanges
4	Stainless steel cogwheels

If the company is a small business, and the volume of any one type of product is small, then this type of layout is perhaps the best arrangement. The facility is organized according to the process operation employed, rather than the products themselves, and materials may not pass directly through the facility. The work force is often specialized in a certain process operation and these people remain in the department concerned.

In the functional layout illustrated in Figure 9.1, the Numbers, 1, 2, 3, and 4 represent a group of different families of products, as shown for example in Table 9.1, which pass through the various process centres of the job shop.

With this layout there are waiting periods while operators are working on a particular reference group. For example, if in the cutting area, work is currently proceeding on reference group 1 then any components in groups 2 to 3 are waiting. A similar situation would occur in the other functional areas.

Figure 9.2 Process layout of a costume jewellery company

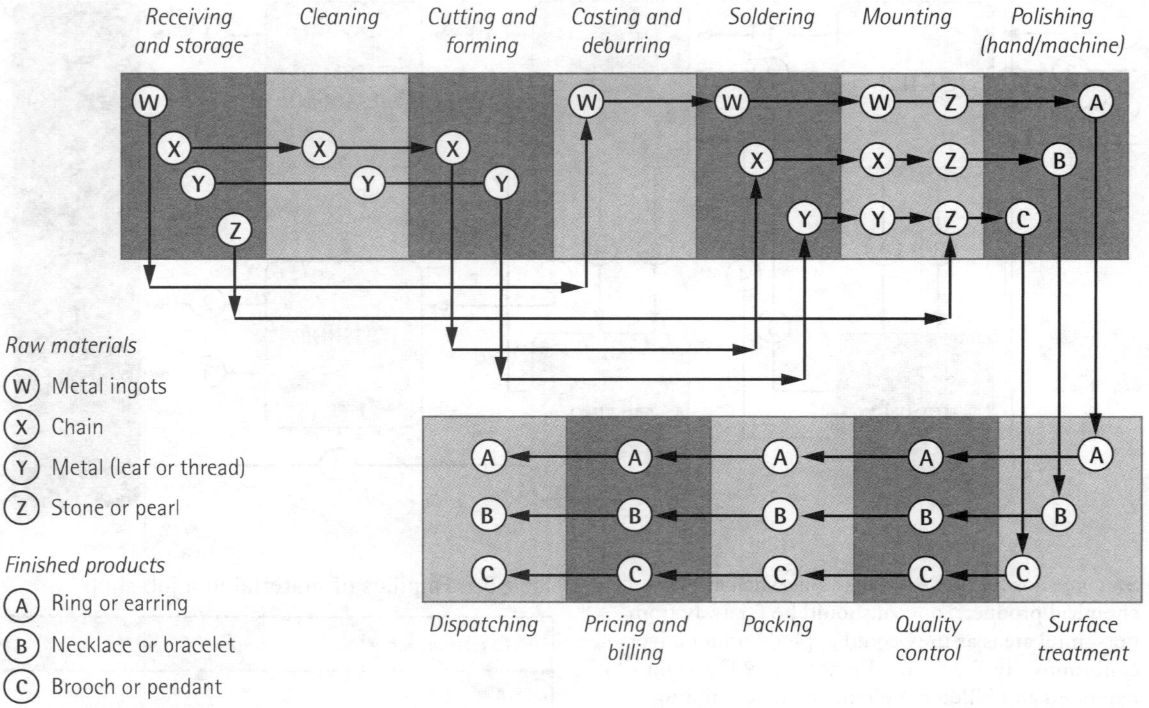

Jewellery manufacture

A functional layout for the manufacture of costume jewellery is shown in Figure 9.2. This is a family-owned business near Annecy, France, that employs about 50 people and exports its products worldwide. From the basic raw materials of chain, stones, and gold or silver for coating it makes several hundred different models of rings, earrings, necklaces, bracelets, pendants and brooches. The functional areas are receiving and storage of the raw materials, cleaning, cutting and forming, casting and deburring, soldering, mounting, hand and machine polishing, surface treatment, quality control, packing, and dispatching. In each of the functional areas people are specialized in the particular operation.[1]

Cellular layout

The inconvenience, and certain inefficiency, arising from the functional layout can be considerably minimized if the work centre is organized according to the product, rather than functional activity, as illustrated in Figure 9.3. In this scheme, the reference group illustrated in Figure 9.1 now flows directly from one process operation to another as equipment is dedicated

to a particular product line or cell. If the system is correctly balanced, there will be essentially no waiting time. In this arrangement, operators have to be multi-skilled so that they can work on any process operations and concentrate on the product flow. With cellular layout there is less movement of parts, waiting time is reduced, the volume of in-process inventory is reduced, and if properly designed, the productivity of the operation is increased. An alternative to the linear cellular layout is given in Figure 9.4. Here the concept is the same but the equipment is arranged in a rectangular form where the operators have to move less than would be the case of a straight line arrangement. This type of layout, together with a quantitative description is also presented in Chapter 15.

Cellular layout provides greater flexibility in manufacturing. However, compared to a functional layout, it involves a bigger capital investment in machinery, equipment, and often surface area. Further, it will only work if operators are multi-skilled, although, in any event, multi-skilled employees are often more motivated and have more utility to an organization since there is the flexibility to rotate operators according to production needs. Before an organization restructures its work centre into a cellular

Figure 9.3 Cellular manufacturing

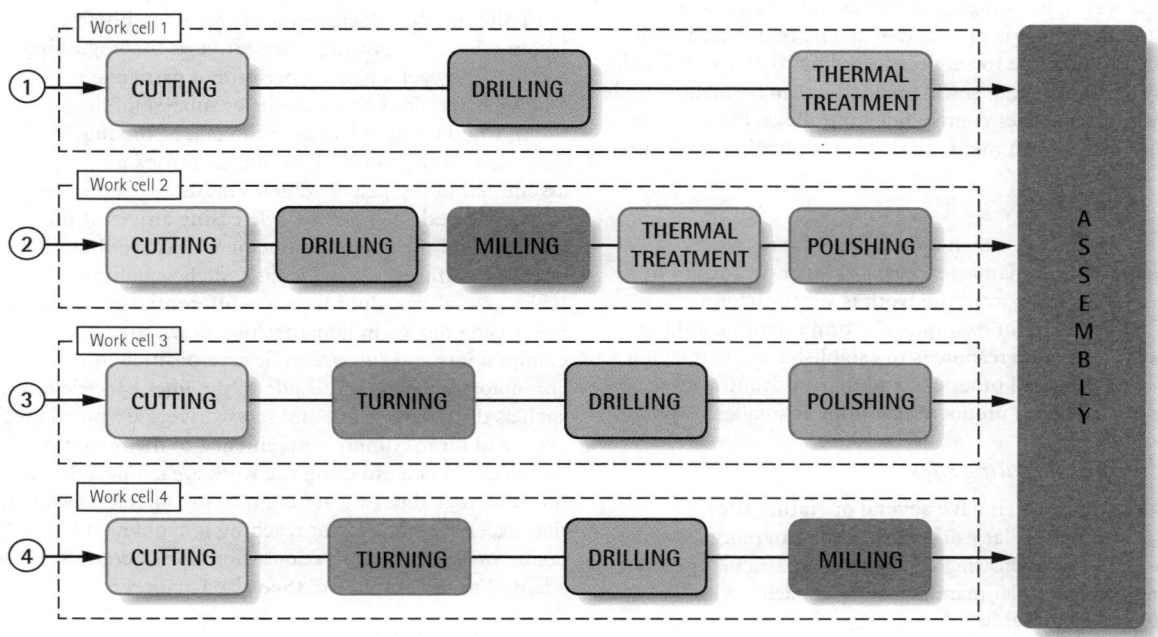

Figure 9.4 Cellular layout in a block or 'island'

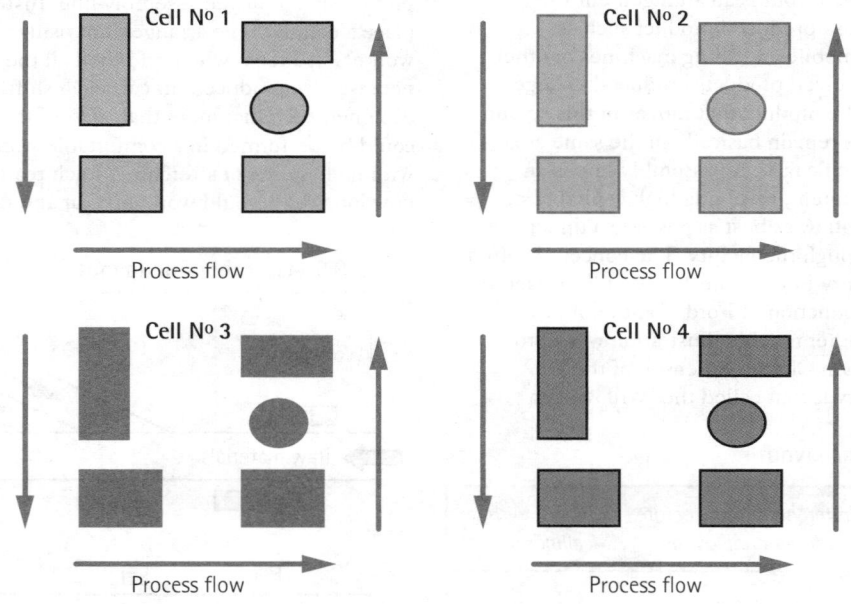

layout a financial analysis needs to be made to be sure the additional investment is justified and that there is a payback over a relatively short time, say, a maximum of three to five years. Further, it needs to be clear that there will be continued future work for the particular production operation concerned. If complete cellular reorganization is not feasible some alternatives to consider might be the following.

Mobile equipment

One way of minimizing the investment is to have equipment that is mobile that can be transferred from one product line to another according to demand. Small drilling, cutting, or sewing machines can be made mobile by mounting them onto wheeled trolleys. Large heavy, automated equipment, however, is difficult to relocate.

Subcontracting

For small firms, which do not have the necessary financial or human resources, a cellular organization can be used if part of the work is subcontracted (Chapter 16). For example, the firm might be able to use its available resources to establish a cellular layout for the principal products, and then subcontract out products whose production volume is smaller.

Multiple operating sites

Companies which have several operating sites, performing similar work, may be able to reorganize their facilities by dedicating each site to a particular product line using cellular manufacturing at each site, as illustrated in Table 9.2.

Assembly line layout

The assembly line layout is an arrangement to accommodate mass-produced product such as computers, automobiles, washing machines or other relatively standardized products produced in large quantities. It is the product that moves in this layout, and the operators remain basically in the same area, performing a specific task. An assembly line is an inflexible arrangement, involving high capital cost, and designed to allow as best as possible a direct material flow through the facility. The concept is often attributed to Henry Ford in the 1920s with his facility layout for the production of Ford T automobiles (Chapter 8). Another notable illustration was during World War II, when Charles Sorenson of the USA designed a facility layout called the 'Willow Run

Assembly Line', which was able to produce one B-24 Liberator bomber every hour.

Figure 9.5 shows schematically an assembly line layout where the raw materials arrive at the beginning of the line and each operator performs a particular task, adding as required components or subassemblies, before the finished product leaves at the end of the line. Assume that the finished product is a truck axle as assembled in the heavy vehicles industry (Caterpillar, Volvo, Mercedes). The raw axle casing arrives at the beginning of the assembly line on a conveyer belt. Each operator performs a specific task, such as bolting on brake assemblies, fluid lines, or differential units as the axle casing moves in linear fashion down the line. Components and subassemblies are positioned in chronological order at the side of the line. Electric tools such as drills, wrenches, and screwdrivers are positioned overhead for maximum convenience to the operators and to avoid encumbering the work area. The axles are positioned at about waist height to the operators such that excessive bending or reaching is avoided. That is, ergonomics is a consideration where the operation is adapted to the employee. (See also Chapter 8.)

Volvo experiment

In 1987 Volvo of Sweden embarked on an experiment to mass produce its Volvo Model 740 by not using its previously employed assembly line. Instead, it put in place a cellular-type arrangement using seven to ten workers in a team who performed all the assembly work necessary to produce four cars each shift. The cells were designed such that more than 80% of the assembly could be performed in a comfortable working position with no bending or stretching. Each team determined how long they would work on a car and take the

Table 9.2 Cellular layout

Site	Product references made before, using a functional layout	After, with a cellular layout
1	A, D, E, F, G, K	A, D, E
2	A, E, G, K, L, X	F, G, K
3	A, D, F, K, L, M	L, X, M

Figure 9.5 Assembly line layout

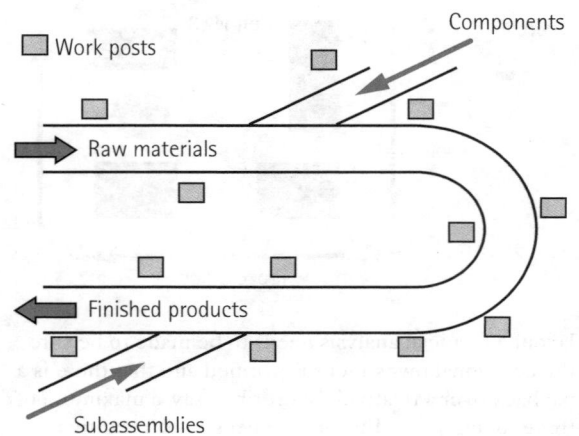

responsibility for fixing defects. Volvo's experiment was put in place to try to improve the monotonous work of the operators and reduce absenteeism and turnover, which in Volvo plants was around 20%, and 30% respectively. At the Uddevala plant, where this experiment was put in place, absenteeism was only 8% and morale was reported to be high.[2] Sony, of Japan, also changed from assembly line to cellular production for its camera units and found that output was 10% higher than in a conventional assembly line.[3]

Flexible manufacturing system

Flexible manufacturing implies a single assembly facility that can build a wide assortment of models and types of product on one assembly type layout. The traditional assembly line with the rigid conveyor system does not permit this and so in flexible manufacturing, the conveyor is replaced by automatic guided vehicles (AGVs), which transfer parts to various work areas according to specific computer commands. The concept of flexible manufacturing is illustrated in Industry insight 9.1.

Layout and throughput

In general terms, the differences between the three layouts, functional, cellular, and assembly line, can be illustrated by an exponential curve of the type shown in Figure 9.6. This curve correlates the layout with volume throughput, and product variation and Table 9.3 compares the two extreme cases for the assembly line and a functional layout. A cellular layout is intermediate between the two.

Flexible manufacturing at Nissan   Industry insight 9.1

Production people at the Nissan Motor plant at Kanda-Cho, Kyushu, the southernmost of Japan's five main islands, struggled to design a 'flexible manufacturing system' that could build a wide assortment of models and types of car at high speed on one assembly line. One of the biggest problems was the conveyor, which held every vehicle on a line hostage to the progress of the car that took the longest to build. The conveyor has now been replaced by a convey of 'intelligent motor-driven dollies', little yellow platforms that tote cars at variable speeds down the production line, sending out a stream of computer-controlled signals to manage both the workers and the robots on the production line. The objective of this new system is to give the plant the flexibility to handle production of five or six different vehicles on the same line according to customer needs. This is a big change from the mass production system where tools and conveyors are set to turn out 240,000 copies of the same basic car. Retooling of these systems for a new model can take up to ten months. However, reprogramming the robots in the flexible manufacturing system can be done in as little as three months.

Adapted from: 'Nissan takes the mass out of production to increase flexibility at its "dream factory" ', *Wall Street Journal Europe*[4]

Figure 9.6 Nature of layout configurations

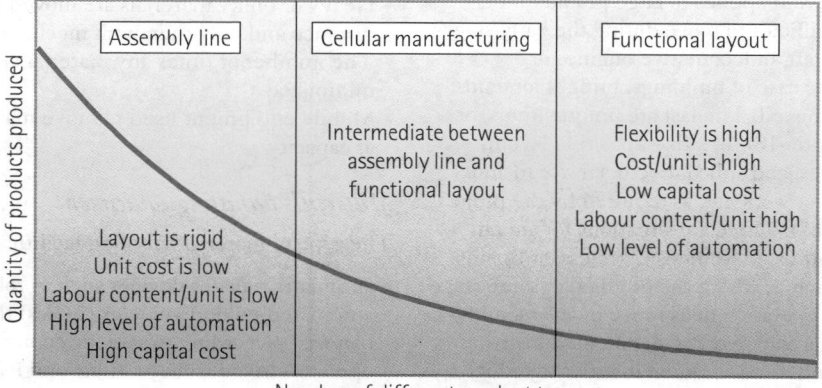

Quantity of products produced

| Assembly line | Cellular manufacturing | Functional layout |

Intermediate between assembly line and functional layout

Flexibility is high
Cost/unit is high
Low capital cost
Labour content/unit high
Low level of automation

Layout is rigid
Unit cost is low
Labour content/unit is low
High level of automation
High capital cost

Number of different product types

Table 9.3 Comparison of assembly line and functional layout

Assembly line	Functional layout
Unit throughput is high	Unit throughput is low
Capital cost for equipment is high	Capital cost for equipment not excessive
Layout is rigid	Flexibility with type of products handled
Labour employed is low	Labour employed is high
High proportion of automation	Low proportion of automation
Number of different products is low	Number of different products is high

Figure 9.7 Fixed position layout

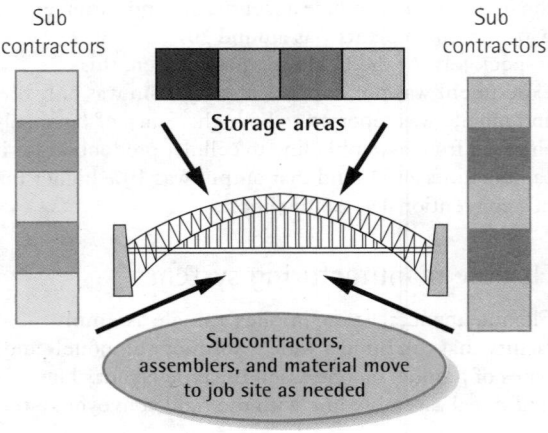

Fluid flow

Fluid flow layouts apply to continuous manufacturing operations such as oil refineries, chemical facilities, pharmaceutical plants and parts of some food operations such as in the production of beer, soft drinks, wine, milk, yoghurt, etc. The processing steps might include heating, distillation, catalytic transformation, cooling, mixing, or fermentation. This type of layout incorporates pipelines, reaction vessels, and heat exchangers and is often limited to a very narrow range of products. The layout is rigid, has a high capital investment, and, once in place, is difficult to change. The workforce is limited to a few personnel who manage the facility operations from a control room incorporating a sophisticated network of automatic process control systems.

Fixed position layouts

A fixed position layout applies to large product units which are either difficult to move during the early stages, such as ships, aircraft, or locomotive engines or, alternatively, in the case of buildings, bridges, or dams, simply *cannot* be moved. The last are unique items, or projects (see Chapter 18). In a fixed position layout, materials, machines, and subcontractors move to and from the product, or worksite, as required by the project plan (see Figure 9.7). There are situations for aircraft manufacture at Airbus, in Toulouse, France, or Boeing, in Seattle, Washington, where the product, at some stage of the production operation does move in an assembly-type operation on a conveyor arrangement. This is becoming more and more common in order to reduce production time as is discussed in Industry insight 15.1.

Movement of materials

Manufacturing involves a lot of handling and movement of materials. In the design of the facility layout best efforts should be made such that:

* Materials flow through the system in a linear flow pattern in order to minimize zigzagging and backtracking.
* The production processes are arranged to facilitate the direct flow of material.
* Work posts are positioned such that material movement is minimized.
* Storage areas are located near the usage area to minimize movement of operators.
* Equipment is positioned ergonomically such that operators working with material are at their normal standing or sitting level to avoid bending, stretching, and reaching.
* Heavy physical activity of lifting or carrying loads is avoided by using automatic systems, including robots.
* Heavy or bulky materials are moved the shortest distance and only then with mechanical equipment.
* The number of times any material is moved is minimized.
* Mobile equipment used to move material is operated at capacity.

Materials handling equipment

The type of material handling facilities include:

* automatic transfer devices such as robots and automated guided vehicles (AGVs) that move materials according to specific computer commands
* operator-driven trolleys, front-end loaders, or trucks (see Figure 9.8)

Figure 9.8 Equipment for material transfer

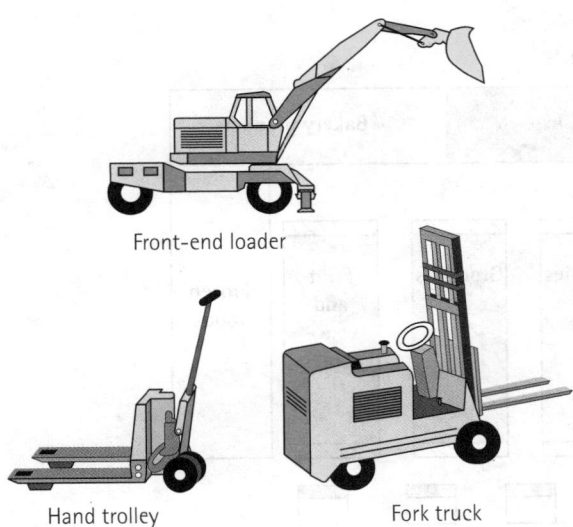

Front-end loader

Hand trolley

Fork truck

- overhead, or moveable operator-controlled cranes
- moving carpets, conveyors, belts, chains, or rotating carousels or turntables
- rigid plastic boxes, handcarts, pallets, tote boxes or wire bins
- elevators for moving from floor to floor, or to move from one storage platform to another.

Retail facilities

Retail facilities are service operations that offer products for sale directly to the consumer. They differ in terms of products they sell, surface area, location, sales service offered and product price. Some of the most common include the following.

Hypermarkets

A hypermarket, common in France and some other European countries, but less common in the USA, sells a diverse selection of products from food, clothing, automobile products, large electrical appliances such as refrigerators, washing machines, and small appliances like toasters, coffee percolators, razors, and other consumer goods. Harrods, in Knightsbridge, London, is a very special hypermarket that 'sells everything' (an elephant if you wish, apparently) although it may not always be on display.

Supermarkets

A supermarket sells principally food and drink items and other products related to the household, such as paper goods, cleaning fluids, and plastic items. Depending on the surface area the supermarket may also sell a limited amount of clothing, books, and toys.

Grocery stores

A grocery store, or superette has a small surface area and sells almost exclusively food and household products. They are common in villages and towns of Europe and some smaller towns in the United States.

Petrol station convenience stores

Petrol station convenience stores run by such oil firms as EssoMobil, BP-Amoco, and Total FinaElf sell travel-related items, including packaged food, automotive products, reading material, etc. This is now an important part of gasoline stations' business.

Specialty stores

Specialty stores are, in this instance, large stores that sell a specific ranges of items such as sporting goods, hi-tech equipment, or do-it-yourself items, etc.

Boutiques

Boutiques are also specialty stores but with a smaller surface area. They may sell clothing, perfume, or gift items.

Warehouse discount stores

Warehouse stores are those that sell a range of items at a discount if products are bought in bulk. There is often minimal display of the products. They are common in the USA and Canada but less so in Europe.

Department stores

A department store sells a wide range of goods including clothing, furniture, home appliances, garden equipment, travel goods, etc. Very often they have one or more restaurants in the facility such as Selfridges in England, or Galerie Lafayette in France.

Location of retail outlets

Very often large retail outlets such as a hypermarket, supermarket, department store, or specialty goods stores

Figure 9.9 Layout of a grocery store

- ■ Products purchased on impulse
- ▨ High margin products or promotional products

Dairy products		Cooked meats	Bakery products

Fresh meat	Cleaning paper products	Groceries	Groceries	Groceries	Fruit and vege- tables	Frozen foods
Fish						
Beer and wine						

Checkout counters

are located in out of town shopping malls. This is because land prices are lower and also locating different stores in the same location can increase customer frequentation. Shopping malls are very common in the United States and, to a certain extent, in some European countries although land availability and government restrictions on shopping malls in Europe restrict their numbers.

Objectives of a retail outlet

A retail outlet is a profit centre and its principal objective is to maximize sales. Stores, which belong to a chain, are very often benchmarked according to their sales volume during similar periods. One element in maximizing sales is the layout or physical location of the goods in the store. For example, many department stores will have men's items close to the entrance and often on the ground floor to make it easy for men to shop as, in general, it is not one of their preferred pastimes. For retail outlets selling food and related items the layout is principally a merchandising function where the location of products in the store, and their positioning on shelves, strongly influences their sale. The following are considerations.

Aisle arrangement

Figure 9.9 shows schematically the layout of a grocery store or supermarket. Some of the criteria for the aisle arrangement are:

- Frequently sold items such as milk, bread, and cheese are located at the end of the store. This obliges

Figure 9.10 Layout: Shelf positioning

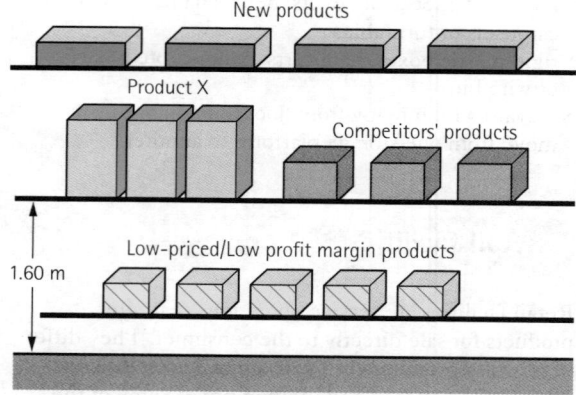

New products

Product X

Competitors' products

1.60 m

Low-priced/Low profit margin products

consumers to pass through the entire store, increasing the probability that other articles will be purchased on impulse as they pass other displayed items.
- Related products such as tea, coffee, and sugar are grouped together so that the purchase of one might help to trigger the purchase of another.
- High margin items such as beauty products, and pet foods are located in the most frequently used aisles, which are often the first and last in the store.
- Long continuous aisles are created, rather than short broken ones, which again forces customers to walk through the whole length of the store.
- Promotional goods or high margin items are located at the end of shelves where customers have a higher probability of seeing them.

Sainsbury's, UK

In 1949 Alan (Lord) Sainsbury returned to Britain from a voyage of discovery to the USA. Self-service he announced was the future. Sainsbury's was a chain of food shops where, in the practice of the time, the customer was discouraged from touching any goods until they had been requested from an assistant, approved of and, of course, paid for. Marble counters separated the customer from the assistant, in a white apron, who would expertly cut the cheese and shape the butter, wrap up the provisions in a flash, and, as a finale, tot up the bill of pounds, shillings and pence in an instant. There was a chair for anyone whose feet were killing them, and 'Would madam care for the goods to be sent to her home?' This was the service that the grandfather of Mr Alan, as he was known, had brought to perfection since the first Sainsbury's had been started in 1869.

Now here was Mr Alan with his wild proposals from America. He was listened to with close attention by other Sainsburys on the board and in management, among them a brother, uncles, nephews, sons and cousins. (Very much a family firm was, and indeed is, Sainsbury's.) He tried not to make his discovery sound like a traveller's tale, but understandably there was some concern. If people could pick up goods as they pleased, would they not walk out of the shop without paying? This had not, it seemed, happened in America. But America was not Britain, where food was still scarce and rationed. Still, let no one say that the firm was not progressive. Mr Alan was given permission to try out self-service at a shop in Croydon, an outer suburb of south London. If it were a flop, perhaps no one would notice.

The shop was an astonishing success. An envious competitor reckoned that it did better than any other shop of its size in the country. Thus, Britain began its shopping revolution. From then on counters were being ripped out and aisles were piled temptingly high. Sainsbury's was opening a new self-service shop every three weeks. The last of its counter shops closed in 1982. Although, Lord Sainsbury called himself a socialist he said: 'Profit is the first motive for a commercial business and it always must be so.' Sainsbury's has returned the compliment to America: it owns Shaw's, a chain of supermarkets strong in New England.

Adapted from: 'Obituary of Lord Sainsbury', *The Economist*[5]

- Disperse, in different locations, items that are purchased frequently such as wine, bread, milk, cheese, meat, and paper goods, as again, this obliges customers to traverse other departments.
- Place spontaneously purchased items such as chewing gum, candy, and magazines at the checkout.
- Position shelves to provide for impulse buying of articles.
- Change the store layout from time to time. This confuses customers who are obliged to 'search again' for products. During their search, they pass through aisles and make impulse purchases of other items.

Shelf layout and merchandising

Consider the shelf position as illustrated in Figure 9.10, which shows a particular product, X, whose sales one wishes to maximize over and above competing products:

- Position product X about 1.60 metres from the floor. This is where the consumer can best see the product.
- Position competing brands, which have a higher price, close to product X so that consumers can easily make the price comparison.
- Position products that have lower prices, or lower profit margins, near floor level where consumers are less likely to see them.

- Position new products on the upper shelves. People are more likely to look up than down.
- Make the face of product X large, with a bigger surface area, or of bright colours, so that it draws the attention of the customer.
- Design product X with an eye-catching design.

In addition to the customer-oriented layout aspects for retail outlets, aisles and shelves need to be positioned in the stores so that they can be easily restocked from the warehouse. Externally, parking zones need to be planned so that they provide easy access for customers, and there is adequate space for delivery vehicles. In Britain, Lord Sainsbury of the Sainsbury's stores pioneered the concept of the self-service food store or supermarket after a trip to the United States as Industry insight 9.2 illustrates.

Restaurants

Restaurants are service firms, which, in general, can be divided into three principal categories: full service, self-service, and fast food. The qualitative nature can be presented by an exponential-type curve, similar to that in manufacturing, as illustrated in Figure 9.11. The following are some relative characteristics of the three types.

Figure 9.11 Comparison of eating establishments

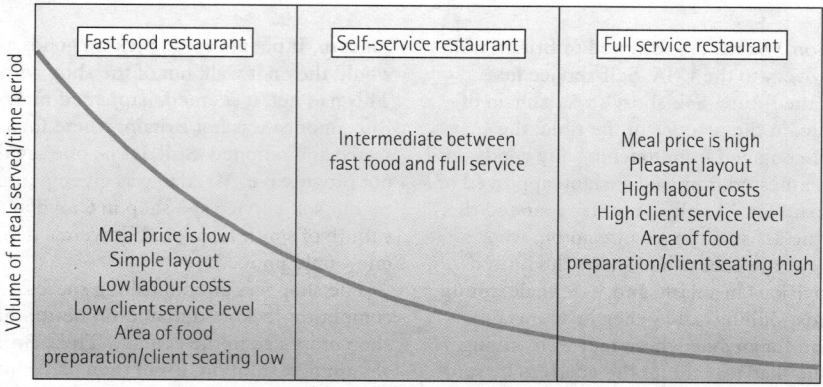

Different meal choices available

Full service restaurant

The full service restaurant provides a complete waiter or waitress service:

- The layout enables effective flow of servers between food preparation area, and clients.
- The layout and decor provides a pleasant eating and/or social environment.
- Total labour costs are high.
- Meal prices are high.
- Food preparation surface area relative to client area is high.
- Variety of meal choices is high and customized (a well done, medium, or rare steak, for example).
- Clients remain in place during serving of food and it is the servers who move.
- The cycle time for both service and food consumption is high.
- Some full service restaurants offer banquet possibilities.

Self–service restaurant

In the self-service restaurant, clients help themselves to the food. The restaurant operators clean up the tables after the meal:

- The layout provides efficient flow of clients past a food service area.
- The clients move during service of food and operators/servers remain in place.
- Total labour costs are average.
- Meal prices are medium.
- Food preparation surface area relative to client area is average.
- There is a limited variety of meal choice.

- Cycle time for both service and food consumption is average.

Fast food restaurant

A fast food restaurant is at the opposite end of the scale of a full service restaurant. Here, the principal objective is to provide fast customer service with a limited menu:

- The layout provides a seating area for customers, and a service counter. Often, there may be an outside eating area.
- Layout and decor is simple with inexpensive furnishings.
- Total labour costs are low.
- Meal prices are low.
- Food preparation surface area relative to client area is low.
- Variety of meal choice is small and the products are standardized.
- Operators remain in place during serving of food and the clients move.
- Clients clean up after the meal.
- Cycle time for service and food consumption is very low.

McDonald's

McDonald's, founded by the late Ray Kroc in the early 1960s, is the largest of the fast food restaurants chains, with franchise outlets worldwide. There is an enormous amount of standardization in McDonald's restaurants from the food, preparation time, restaurant decor, packaging, food preparation equipment, and uniforms worn by the operators. A floor plan for a small McDonald's is illustrated in Figure 9.12. The area is small but efficient so that employees do not have to

Figure 9.12 Layout of food preparation area for a small McDonald's

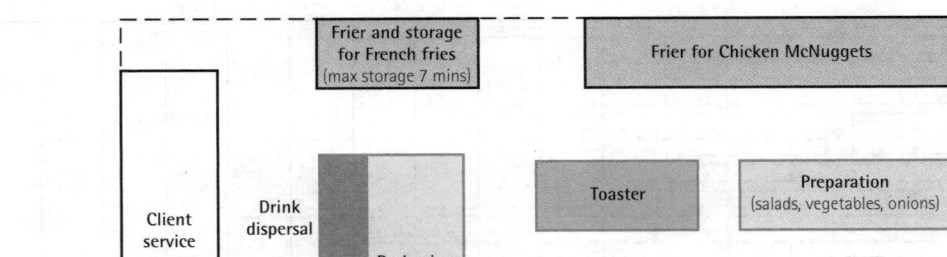

move distances. During peak periods, principally lunchtime, there is a team of three at the counter, one at the grill and fryer, and two jointly on the toaster and preparation of vegetables and onions and to do the packaging. The food preparation is closely programmed with some of the standards as follows:

- Toaster time for hamburger buns is slightly less than one minute to give it a sunny brown texture and slightly crusty.
- The hamburger 'assembly' operation is to lay out toasted bottom, spread mayonnaise, add grilled beef, top with lettuce and onions, close with toasted top, and package.
- Preparation time of a hamburger is 90 seconds.
- French fries must remain in storage for a maximum of only seven minutes.
- Prepared food that is packaged can only remain for a maximum of ten minutes in the prepared area. After that, it is discarded.

For those at the service counter their programmed instructions are to:

1. Welcome the customer with a smile.
2. Take the order.
3. Collect and prepare the order on a tray.
4. Present the order.
5. Take the payment.
6. Thank the client, and invite them to return.

In McDonald's, like other fast food chains, the cash register has icons of the item purchased, rather than numbers. This facilitates completing the bill for the food purchased, and minimizes errors. There are some differences in the food selection at the McDonald's outlets. For example, in the United States beer is not served but it is in France. In England, you cannot buy a salad but you can in France. There is a difference in price worldwide, as illustrated in Figure 9.13.[6] These data indicate that, on average, the Philippines is the least expensive whereas Switzerland is the most.

For all eating establishments kitchen appliances are positioned so that the staff do not have to do excessive bending, or stretching. Nonetheless, a common ailment with chefs is neck problems associated with bending over the cooking area.

Airports

Characteristics

An international airport is perhaps the single biggest service operation and supply chain whose layout is a complex system handling a vast number of clients and freight. The world's ten busiest airports according to passenger use in the period January to May 2001 are as shown in Table 9.4.[7]

The surface area of airports is enormous. Paris, Charles de Gaulle, covers 3113 hectares (1260 acres), and the world's biggest in surface area, King Khaled International in Riyadh, Saudi Arabia, covers 22,100 hectare (8950 acres). In 1990 there were 37,739 civil airports, of which 45% were in the USA, 6% in Europe, and with less than 1% in Japan.[8]

A distinguishing operating aspect of the airport is that the inside layout is concentrated very much on the conveyances of the clients (the passengers), whereas the outside layout is concerned very much on the operational aspects for arrival and departure of the aircraft.

Figure 9.13 Price of a Big Mac at McDonald's outlets worldwide

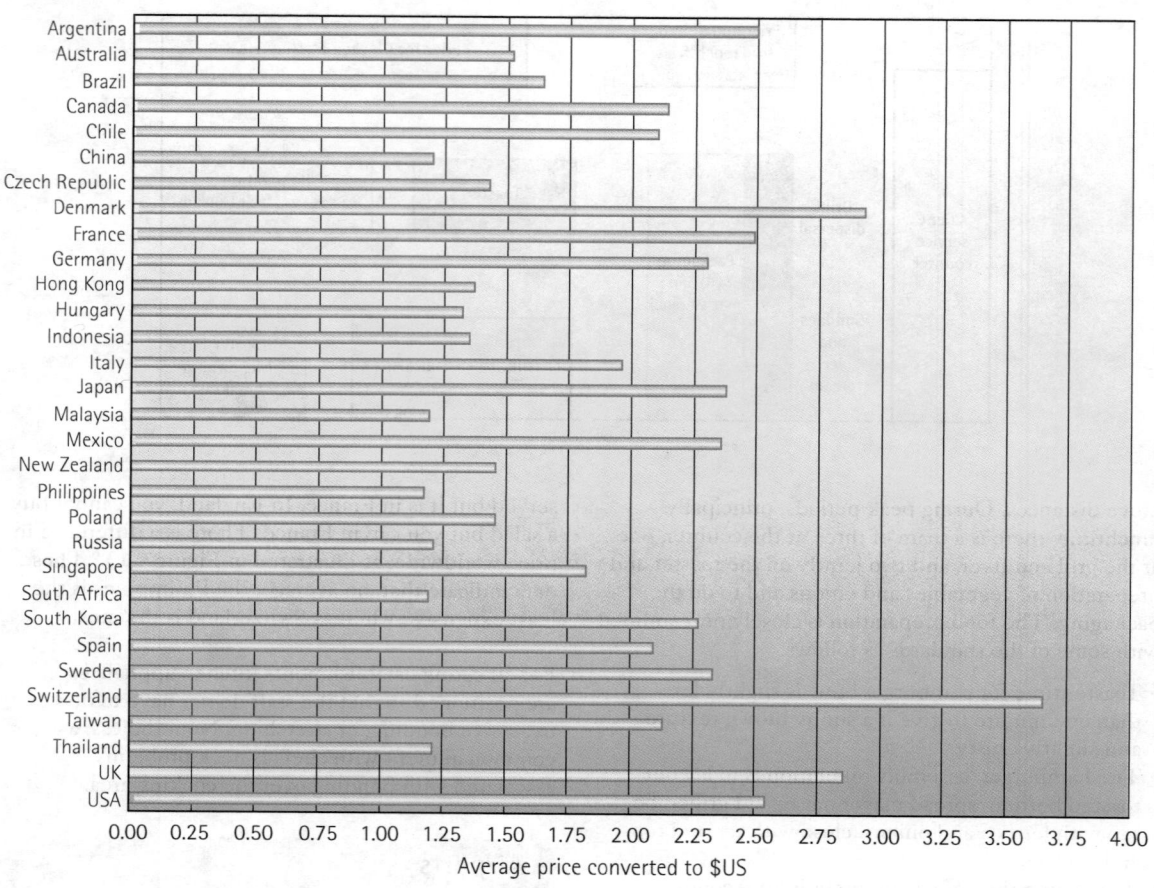

Average price converted to $US

Table 9.4 The world's ten busiest airports (2001)

Airport	Passengers (millions) Jan–May 2001
Atlanta, USA (ATL)	32.9
Chicago, O'Hare, USA (ORD)	27.6
Los Angeles, USA (LAX)	26.5
London, Heathrow, UK (LHR)	24.6
Dallas-Fort Worth, USA (DFW)	23.8
Tokyo, Japan (HND)	23.2
Paris, Charles de Gaulle, France (CDG)	19.7
Frankfurt, Germany (FRA)	19.4
Phoenix, USA (PHX)	15.7
Schipol, Amsterdam, the Netherlands (AMS)	15.6

Hub and spoke-type arrangement

Most major airports' physical layouts are designed in a hub and spoke-type arrangement whose basic form is illustrated in Figure 9.14. Each hub and spoke system constitutes a terminal and depending on the size of airport, there may be more than one terminal. London's Heathrow currently has four terminals, one each for international, European, domestic, and British Airways.

Hub

The hub houses the passenger services, which would include amenities for ticket sales, shops, restaurants, arrival and departure lounges, transfer equipment such as carousels and moving carpets for baggage, escalators and people movers for passengers, and security systems.

Spokes

The spokes outside are the arrival and departure gates for the airplanes. Inside, they provide the departure lounge for passengers and are connected to the hub by

Figure 9.14 **Hub and spoke system of an airport** (Photo: Corbis)

long corridors, which, in some cases, have moving carpets for the passengers.

Surrounding the airport terminals are the control towers, and runways which, in major airports, permit up to a combined 35–40 takeoffs and departures every hour. In addition, there are facilities for parking, and some airports, such as London, Heathrow, Paris, Charles de Gaulle, and Lyon, St Exupery, have rail connections to major European networks. (This physical layout of a hub and spoke is not to be confused with the 'hub and spoke' worldwide operations network presented in Chapter 1, where, for example, London might be a hub for spokes in South Africa, New York, and Argentina.)

Technology

An airport has some of the most up-to-date technological equipment. Apart from the airplanes themselves with their complex material construction and sophisticated controls, the airport has ground-to-air communication, computerized ticketing, complex flight scheduling systems, weather forecasting equipment, security networks, etc.

Environment

Environmental constraints are high for the development, and operation of an airport. The site itself swallows up a large surface area of land. Then, the noise of landing/takeoff of airplanes causes environmental concerns for neighbouring communities, plus the road networks leading to and from the facility add to road congestion.

Engineering, consulting, or design office

Every organization, be it a service or manufacturing business has offices. A pure service such as a bank, a consulting organization or the headquarters of a major organization consists of just offices. A manufacturing site also has office areas for the engineers, purchasing, accounting, etc.

Cellular offices

Historically, most corporate offices were cellular layout where office departments which had the most contact with one another were located in the proximity. Employees had their own individual enclosed area (the decor depending on position), with desk, telephone, and bookcase. An illustration follows.

Braun

In the 1970s and 1980s I worked with C F Braun & Co., an engineering and construction company in Los Angeles, California. It was called the 'campus'. The gardens were immaculate, with trees and plants from all over the world. Every employee had his own cellular carpeted office, with telephone, an upholstered desk chair, and two matching chairs for visitors. For those low on the totem pole, the desks were metal with a formica top. When a promotion came you were awarded a solid wooden desk and upholstered chairs of a more pleasing hue. Project and department managers graduated to a very sturdy wooden desk with more efficient storage areas. Vice-presidents had even more attractive wooden desks, and a bigger office area. Office layout, furniture, and location were status symbols.[9]

Open plan offices

The office concept has changed, as many companies such as Hewlett-Packard (computers), Unisabi (pet foods) Valéo (automobile components) have adopted open plan layouts where employees are totally exposed to their co-workers. Privacy is being replaced with productivity. Hierarchy is being replaced with teamwork and status is being replaced with mobility. To minimize interruptions, meeting rooms are available. Open plan layout has reduced cost in terms of space, increased ease of human contact, but, according to some, reduced efficiency because of the noise of telephones ringing, adjacent conversation, and passing footsteps.

After salaries, office space is the next biggest expense for many companies. As a result, some companies are trying to move away from the concept of the one-desk rule and are adopting the policy of 'hot desking' where desks are shared. However, unless jobs are very specific, and can be properly scheduled, desk sharing can be complicated. Besides, most people have their own files, documents, books and the like. A compromise to this is locker trolleys that can be wheeled to a free desk.[10]

Hoteling

Hoteling is an open plan office at its very extreme and is being adopted by sales- and service-based companies, such as IBM, AT&T, and major accounting and consulting firms. Private offices are eliminated in place of hotelling, which is a system to provide temporary space for employees when they are on-site. This saves money on rent and gets employees out spending more time with customers.[11] The following is how it works.

Reservation

An employee phones in advance, or makes contact with the aid of his personal computer to indicate the length of time he or she needs an office. A space is allocated, equipped with appropriate connections for telephone and computer. When the employee arrives, even after normal hours, he or she can access his space with the insertion of a magnetic card. Space is allocated in a first come, first served basis (so the first gets a better place).[12]

Layout

The office space is open plan, which allows for working alone, or in groups. Filing cabinets on wheels containing employee's documents and the like can be located where necessary. Coffee areas are available in which the employee can relax.

Closed offices

These are available for a limited time when an employee needs to work in isolation, or to have meetings with others. The number of these offices is limited to be sure that they are used to the maximum.

Conference rooms

These are available on reservation.

Office management

A concierge is present on the site full time to keep reservations straight, and to be sure things run smoothly.

Dilbert's viewpoint of hoteling

The only drawback to the cubicle-oriented office is that some employees develop a sense of 'home' in their little patch of real estate. Soon pride of ownership sets in, then self-esteem, and poof! – good-bye productivity. But thanks to the new concept of 'hoteling', this risk can be eliminated. Hoteling is a system by which cubicles are assigned to the employees as they show up each day. Nobody gets a permanent workspace, and therefore no unproductive homey feelings develop. Another advantage, hoteling eliminates all physical evidence of the employee's association with the company. This takes the fuss out of downsizing: the employee doesn't even have to clean out a desk. With hoteling, every employee has 'one foot out the door' at all times. Hoteling sends an important message to the employee: 'Your employment is temporary. Keep your photos of your ugly family in the trunk of your car so we don't have to look at them.'[13]

The home office

As companies try to reduce the cost of office space, and with the worsening of traffic bottlenecks, firms are more and more allowing certain classifications of people to work at home. This is feasible with the ease of telecommunications, fax, modem, electronic mail, and the Internet. In this case, the employee is now confronted with the layout design of an office in the home. When the house is large, perhaps a separate office is possible, however, it may be that part of the family living space has to double as the office. The two-dimensional template approach to the layout, discussed in the next section, can be a useful way of organizing the arrangement of the office and in addition the following other considerations are:[14]

- If the workspace is long and narrow, arrange the office furniture galley style with the desk in front and the storage area behind.
- If the workspace is small and square, make an L-shaped workstation with one part of the L for the computer, and the other for spreading paper.
- Keep books and documents that are used frequently close by, with others stored away.
- Make the most use of wall space by installing shelving.
- If the wood floor is stained a pale colour, or a neutral rug is chosen, and the furniture is a light coloured wood this gives the impression of space.
- Add a soft rug and relaxing chair in the corner of the workspace to create an oasis of calm.

Methods for facility layout

The following are some methods for developing a facility layout. They are considered heuristic methods in that they may not give the optimum solution, but there is certain logic to their development and the layout obtained is pragmatic.

Two-dimensional templates

With the two-dimensional template approach, first the room area, where equipment is to be located, is measured, and the surface area and shape are drawn to scale. Then, two-dimensional forms called templates are made of the plan view of the equipment, machines or furniture of the same scale as the floor plan. These cut-outs are then arranged as desired on the facility plan. The use of a two-dimensional template is a simple way of planning a layout for offices, small machinery areas, and at home where the floor plan already exists.

Load–distance analysis

Load–distance analysis is a method that can be employed in a manufacturing organization when material is being transferred from one location to another. The objective of the layout is to develop a plan when the sum of the product of the material movement and the distance is a minimum. Mathematically this is represented as:

$$\sum_{i=j}^{n} \sum_{j=1}^{n} Q_{ij} D_{ij}$$

where:

- n is the number of work centres or departments
- i, j are the individual departments
- Q is the quantity of material moved from department i to department j
- D is the distance between department i and department j.

The method of load–distance analysis is illustrated in Demonstrating the concept 9.1.

Contact–distance analysis

A contact–distance analysis is a layout method that might be employed in a service function when there is contact with various functional departments (accounting, purchasing, sales, etc.). The objective of this approach is to adopt a department layout where the product of the total number of physical contacts and distance travelled is a minimum. The logic is similar to the load–distance analysis except that material flow is not involved. This idea is illustrated in Demonstrating the concept 9.2.

Systematic layout planning

Systematic layout planning, developed in the early 1960s by Richard Muther, is a variation on the quantitative contact–distance approach, which allows qualitative inputs on the desirability of departments being closely located.[15] The approach first draws up a relationship table between departments in the firm regarding whether they should be located close or not. The criteria for being close might include:

- Constant communication is important.
- Departments share the same personnel, such as secretaries or assistants.
- The same equipment is used (photocopying machine, computer terminal, printer).
- Next sequence in the work flow.
- Perform very similar work.

The criteria for avoiding proximity might be:

- Unpleasant working conditions (printing inks, dyes, or cleaning fluids).
- Confidential information processed.
- Excessive noise.

From the relationship table is then developed a relationship diagram and subsequently the final layout. The procedure is illustrated in Demonstrating the concept 9.3.

Assembly line balancing

The assembly line balancing approach is the grouping of work teams in a manufacturing assembly line operation to maximize product throughput, and to minimize worker idle time. To balance the assembly line, the following information is necessary:

1. The tasks necessary to complete the finished product.
2. The time necessary to perform each task in the assembly line.
3. A division of the tasks among members of the workforce.
4. The production rate needed to meet client demand.
5. The cycle time, or elapsed time, products leave the line in order to maintain the required production rate.

6. The permitted way tasks can be combined to form a compatible workgroup. When this is established specific jobs are allocated. For example:
   - Tasks are grouped that use common materials in order to reduce the amount of material travel and the number of inventory storage locations.
   - Tasks are grouped according to safety requirements. (A welding operation would not be combined with one that uses cleaning fluids.)
   - Tasks are grouped that are adjacent to each other in the assembly sequence.
   - Tasks are grouped that have similar operating environments. Greasy or dirty tasks would not be combined with those requiring a clean room environment.
   - Tasks are grouped that use the same machines and equipment.
   - Tasks are grouped that require the same level of labour skill.

The line balancing procedure can be analyzed by two approaches.

Most tasks following

The operations performed first are those that have the longest number of operations that follow afterwards. However, precedence has to be taken into account, which means that an activity cannot be completed unless a pre-required activity has been completed.

Longest time to complete

The operations performed first are those that take the longest time to complete. Again, precedence has to be taken into account.

Demonstrating the concept 9.4 gives an illustration of the line balancing technique.

Computer aids in facility layout

When a facility is large and there are many constraints, manual design of a facility layout is complicated. As with any design approaches, there are many computer programs, such as those developed by IBM, General Electric, USA, Microsoft, and others available to assist in optimizing facility layouts according to needs.[16] A well-known program for facility layout is CRAFT (computerized relative allocation of facilities technique).[17] There also exists computer programs which will optimize the way retail shelves are stocked with the objective of maximizing sales.

Summary of key elements

- Facility layout is the arrangement of all physical resources used in operations.

- A good layout establishes cost-effective flow patterns, optimizes space utilization, facilitates installation of an information systems network, conforms to regulations, and takes into account the comfort and well-being of employees and customers.

- A functional, or job shop layout, is organized according to specific activities. Throughput is low, labour is specialized, and inventory often accumulates.

- In a cellular layout operators work as a team concentrating on the product as opposed to just the function. Employees are multi-skilled and more motivated.

- The constraint of capital investment in cellular layout may be overcome by using mobile equipment, subcontracting, or dedicated product lines at different sites.

- An assembly line layout in mass production is where the product moves through the facility with workers resting in the same area performing repeat operations.

- Companies, notably Volvo, have experimented with turning assembly lines into cellular manufacturing to boost employee motivation, and increase productivity.

- A flexible manufacturing system is where one facility can produce different products. Computer-controlled AGVs transfer material to respective work areas.

- The layout for a continuous fluid flow operation involves a series of transfer pipes, exchanges, and reaction vessels. It is completely automatically controlled.

- In fixed position layouts the product does not move and the operating functions, work teams, and storage areas are organized around the product.

- Materials handling equipment includes, robots, elevators, AGVs, trolleys, front-end loaders, trucks, cranes, moving conveyers, handcarts, and containers.

- The layout of a retail facility is a merchandising function where aisle arrangement, and shelf layout have an impact on the volume of products sold.

- Restaurants are full service, self-service, or fast food. Layout is concentrated on providing a pleasing customer environment with efficiency for the operators.

- Airports are hub and spoke arrangements to provide efficiency for airplane movements, passenger convenience, and ease of baggage handling.

- Open plan layouts are replacing cellular offices to reduce cost. Hotelling, the extreme of open plan layout, is where office space is reserved as needed.

- Two-dimensional scaled templates may be used in the layout of small surface areas.

- The load–distance layout method minimizes the total movement of products.

- The contact–distance layout method minimizes the total of the personnel contact.

- The systematic layout planning method takes into consideration the desirability of work centres or departments being close together.

- The line balancing method in assembly line layouts creates groups of work teams to maximize throughput and minimize idle time.

Notes and references

1. Information provided by the owner, Monsieur Trenel, 1995

2. 'Volvo's radical new plant: The death of the assembly line?', *Business Week*, 28 August 1989, p. 54

3. 'Back to the past: Some plants tear out long assembly lines, switch to craft work', *Wall Street Journal Europe*, 25 October 1994

4. 'Nissan takes the mass out of production to increase flexibility at its "dream factory" ', *Wall Street Journal Europe*, 10/11 July 1992

5. 'Obituary of Lord Sainsbury' (Lord Sainsbury died on 21 October 1998), *The Economist*, 7 November 1998, p. 118

6. 'Big Mac currencies', *The Economist*, 21 April 2001, p. 82

7. 'Airports of the future: 10 busiest airports', *International Herald Tribune*, 8/9 September 2001, p. 18

8. FRÉMY, Dominique and FRÉMY, Michèle, *Quid*, Editions Laffont, Paris, 1993, pp 1561–2

9. *Organisation for Engineering*, C. F. Braun & Co., Alhambra, California, 1969, p. 96

10. 'White-collar factories: Good office design can sound like a fancy indulgence or a marginal extra. But managers neglect it at their peril', *The Economist*, 25 November 1995, pp 95–6

11. 'The new work place: Walls are falling as the office of the future finally takes shape', *Business Week*, 6 May 1996, pp 56B-E–56H-E

12. 'Vie quotidienne des sans-bureau-fixe', *L'Expansion*, July 1996, p. 14

13. ADAMS, Scott, 'Dilbert's Management Handbook', *Fortune*, 13 May 1996, pp 53–4

14. AALUND, Dagmar, 'Home rules: Working from your house sounds tempting but it's tricky', *Wall Street Journal Europe*, 1–2 June 2001

15. MUTHER, Richard, *Systematic Layout Planning*, Cahners Publishing Company, Boston, USA, 1973

16. FRANCIS, R. L., McGINNIS, L. F. and WHITE, J. A., *Facility Layout and Location*, Prentice-Hall, London, 1992

17. BUFFA, E. S., ARMOUR, G. S. and VOLLMAN, T. E., 'Allocating facilities with CRAFT', *Harvard Business Review*, March/April 1964, pp 136–59

Review and discussion topics

1. Current facility layouts

Analyze the following layouts with which you are familiar:
- (a) university
- (b) grocery store
- (c) car repair operation
- (d) your house, or living accommodation.

Do you think the layout is efficient, and pleasing? If not, what changes would you propose? Justify your reasoning.

2. Cost and productivity

List and discuss all the elements in a poor facility layout that can reduce productivity in a manufacturing or service firm.

3. Technology

What impact do you believe technology will have in the future on the organization and layout of the following? Justify your arguments:
- (a) retail store
- (b) medical centre
- (c) distribution centre
- (d) automobile manufacturer
- (e) consulting company's office
- (f) hotels.

4. Floor plan of a house

You have purchased a piece of land of 2000 square metres big on which you plan to build a house. The liveable area of the house will be 200 square metres. You are married with two teenage children; you currently have two cars, and two large dogs. What are some of the considerations you think are important in arranging the floor plan of your house?

5. Assembly line layout

Discuss the positive and negative aspects of an assembly line layout. Consider the impact on investment, productivity, and human resources.

Demonstrating the concept 9.1　Guillaume Co.

Situation

The Guillaume Co. manufactures transformer units, which are sold to electricity companies throughout Europe. The company is considering relocating its plant from the centre of Grenoble, France, to a location outside the city. The company has nine operating departments, coded 1 to 9. Two possible L-shaped layouts for the new facility, Plan A and Plan B, indicating where the departments would be located are given in Figure 9.15. The company produces five basic products, whose reference numbers are L-32, B-41, N-65, P-25, and H-95. Each of these products is assembled differently and the operating departments that handles these products, together with the weekly production rate is given in Table 9.5. The sequence means, for example, considering product L-32, that the assembly operation starts at Department 1, moves to Department 3, then to Department 6, then

Department 8, and finally Department 9. The average distance in metres between departments, measured from the centre of the working area, is given in Table 9.6.

Required

Determine which layout would be the optimum for the Guillaume Co.

Solution

The solution is given in the Table 9.7:

- First, the total distance travelled for each product is calculated for Plan A, and Plan B.
- Next, the production quantity is multiplied by the distance to give the unit distance measurement. These values are summed for Plan A and Plan B.
- The smallest total unit distance would be the preferred plan. In this case it is Plan B.

Figure 9.15　Guillaume Co.: Floor plans

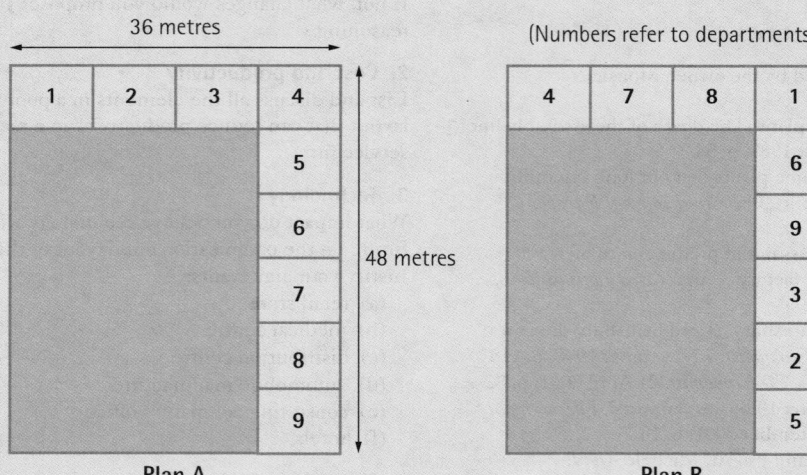

Plan A

Plan B

Table 9.5　Guillaume Co.: Weekly production rates

Reference	Sequence of assembly operation by department					Weekly production units
L-32	1	3	6	8	9	250
B-41	2	7	6	5	4	385
N-65	4	9	5	2	6	190
P-25	6	9	2			565
H-95	7	1	8	4		420

Table 9.6 Guillaume Co.: Average distance between departments

From	To	Distance Plan A	Distance Plan B	From	To	Distance Plan A	Distance Plan B
1	3	26.00	33.00	9	5	41.00	33.00
3	6	21.32	25.00	5	2	22.58	17.00
6	8	25.00	14.52	2	6	26.56	33.00
8	9	17.00	21.32	6	9	33.00	17.00
2	7	32.63	39.58	9	2	46.95	25.00
7	6	17.00	22.58	7	1	38.60	26.00
6	5	17.00	41.00	1	8	44.42	17.00
5	4	17.00	50.95	8	4	41.00	26.00
4	9	49.00	34.00				

Table 9.7 Guillaume Co.: Facility layout

Reference	Department operating sequence					Reference	Weekly production units
L-32	1	3	6	8	9	L-32	250
B-41	2	7	6	5	4	B-41	385
N-65	4	9	5	2	6	N-65	190
P-25	6	9	2			P-25	565
H-95	7	1	8	4		H-95	420

	From	To	Distance Plan A	Distance Plan B	Total Plan A	Total Plan B	Units*Distance A	Units*Distance B
L-32	1	3	26.00	33.00				
	3	6	21.32	25.00				
	6	8	25.00	14.52				
	8	9	17.00	21.32	89.32	93.84	22,329.00	23,459.20
B-41	2	7	32.63	39.58				
	7	6	17.00	22.58				
	6	5	17.00	41.00				
	5	4	17.00	50.95	83.63	154.12	32,197.49	59,335.28
N-65	4	9	49.00	34.00				
	9	5	41.00	33.00				
	5	2	22.58	17.00				
	2	6	26.56	33.00	139.14	117.00	26,437.08	22,230.00
P-25	6	9	33.00	17.00				
	9	2	46.95	25.00	79.95	42.00	45,170.63	23,730.00
H-95	7	1	38.60	26.00				
	1	8	44.42	17.00				
	8	4	41.00	26.00	124.02	69.00	52,090.10	28,980.00
Total							**178,224.30**	**157,734.48**

Demonstrating the concept 9.2 Justin Co.

Situation

The Justin Co. writes, and distributes, computer software for small companies in France, Belgium, and French-speaking Switzerland. The company has its headquarters in a small office block in the centre of Beaune, France. However, demand for its product has grown and it is planning to relocate to one floor of a large building in Dijon. The proposed office plan is given in Figure 9.16; and the average distances between each room, measured from centre to centre in metres is in

Table 9.8. Justin has six departments, which are listed in Table 9.9. Finally, Table 9.10 is the average number of contacts each week made by personnel in each department, based on past data. This is interpreted for example that Consulting and Design have 90 total contacts per week where either personnel go from Consulting to Design or vice versa.

Required

Optimize the layout keeping Administration in area A as this is closest to the entrance and is thus the most convenient place for receiving clients and suppliers.

Solution

A trial and error solution is made by locating the departments in each of the office spaces, but always keeping Consulting and Developing in adjacent offices since they have the maximum number of contacts. The distance is multiplied by the number of contacts and the total distance contact was calculated for each proposed layout. (The total is divided by 2 to nullify the double accounting.) The optimum solution is given in Table 9.11.

Figure 9.16 Justin Co.: Proposed office plan

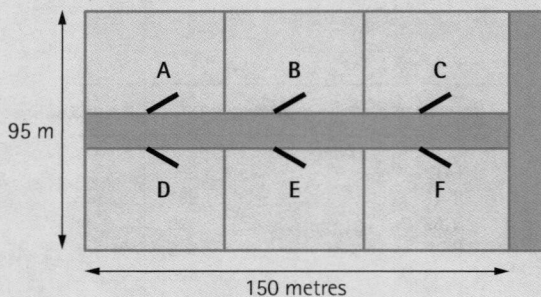

Table 9.8 Justin Co.: Average distance between rooms

	A	B	C	D	E	F
A		90	140	45	95	145
B			90	95	45	95
C				145	95	45
D					90	140
E						90
F						

Table 9.9 Justin Co.: Departments in the company

Code	
1	Development
2	Consulting
3	Design
4	R&D
5	Computing
6	Administration

Table 9.10 Justin Co.: Average number of weekly contacts

	Development	Consulting	Design	R&D	Computing	Administration
Development		90	25	23	11	18
Consulting			8	5	10	16
Design				10	25	7
R&D					4	2
Computing						3
Administration						

Table 9.11 Justin Co.: Office layout optimum solution

Distance			Distance in metres between each room			
	A	B	C	D	E	F
A	0	90	140	45	95	145
B	90	0	90	95	45	95
C	140	90	0	145	95	45
D	45	95	145	0	90	140
E	95	45	95	90	0	90
F	145	95	45	140	90	0

Contact	Average contacts/week between departments					
	Development	Consulting	Design	R&D	Computing	Administration
Development	0	90	25	23	11	18
Consulting	90	0	8	5	10	16
Design	25	8	0	10	25	7
R&D	23	5	10	0	4	2
Computing	11	10	25	4	0	3
Administration	18	16	7	2	3	0

Layout	A Administration	B Consulting	C Computing
	D R&D	E Development	F Design

		A	B	C	D	E	F
		Administration	Consulting	Computing	R&D	Development	Design
Distance							
A	Administration	0	90	140	45	95	145
B	Consulting	90	0	90	95	45	95
C	Computing	140	90	0	145	95	45
D	R&D	45	95	145	0	90	140
E	Development	95	45	95	90	0	90
F	Design	145	95	45	140	90	0
Contact							
A	Administration		16	3	2	18	7
B	Consulting	16		10	5	90	8
C	Computing	3	10		4	11	25
D	R&D	2	5	4		23	10
E	Development	18	90	11	23		25
F	Design	7	8	25	10	25	

(Continued)

Table 9.11 (Continued)

		A	B	C	D	E	F	
				*Contacts * Distance*				
	CONTACT	Administration	Consulting	Computing	R&D	Development	Design	Total
A	Administration	0	1440	420	90	1710	1015	**4675**
B	Consulting	1440	0	900	475	4050	760	**7625**
C	Computing	420	900	0	580	1045	1125	**4070**
D	R&D	90	475	580	0	2070	1400	**4615**
E	Development	1710	4050	1045	2070	0	2250	**11,125**
F	Design	1015	760	1125	1400	2250	0	**6550**
	Total	**4675**	**7625**	**4070**	**4615**	**11,125**	**6550**	**38,660**

(Divide by 2 to avoid double accounting)	**19,330**

Demonstrating the concept 9.3   Collins Co.

Situation

The Collins Co. is a small manufacturing firm that is planning to relocate its facilities to a new site. The principal functions of Collins include purchasing, storage of raw materials, machining, assembly, storage of finished products, maintenance, sales, accounting, loading of finished products for delivery, and unloading of raw materials.

The relationship between these departments is given in Figure 9.17. This is developed between departments, or work centres according to the necessity, or otherwise, of these being closely located. It is presented in a hierarchy form using categories such as 'essential' to 'avoid', giving each one a code. The meaning of the codes is as shown in Table 9.12.

Solution

From Figure 9.17 is developed a relationship diagram as illustrated in Figure 9.18. This is a block diagram of the departments with the closeness relationship connecting

Figure 9.17 Collins Co.: Relationship table in systematic layout planning

	Purchasing	Storage RM	Machining	Assembly	Storage FP	Maintenance	Sales	Accounting	Loading	Unloading
Purchasing		I	A	A	N	A	E	V	N	N
Storage RM	I		V	I	A	N	N	N	A	E
Machining	A	V		E	N	V	A	A	N	N
Assembly	A	I	E		E	V	A	A	N	N
Storage FP	N	A	N	E		N	I	N	E	A
Maintenance	A	N	V	V	N		A	A	I	I
Sales	E	N	A	A	I	A		V	I	N
Accounting	V	N	A	A	N	A	V		N	N
Loading	N	A	N	N	E	I	I	N		A
Unloading	N	E	N	N	A	I	N	N	A	

E = Essential
V = Very important
I = Important
N = Not important
A = Avoid

a block by a line of a different colour or thickness. (Only the essential, very important, and avoid are shown on this diagram.)

By trial and error a layout is identified by respecting the closeness criteria. The layout is then positioned in the total space available for the facility, as illustrated in Figure 9.19. As a result of all the combinations, it may not always be possible to respect every relationship to the letter and some adjustments may need to be made. For this example, the criterion was to avoid putting Sales, Purchasing and Accounting offices next to the production areas. A complete separation was not possible and separating the offices from the production area by a wide corridor was the method used to accommodate the requirement.

Figure 9.19 Collins Co.: Systematic layout planning (2)

Purchasing	Storage RM		Unloading
Accounting	Mainten-ance	Machining	
		Assembly	Loading
Sales	Storage FP		

Table 9.12 Collins Co.: Hierarchy codes

Closeness relationship	Code
Essential	E
Very important	V
Important	I
Not important	N
Avoid	A

Figure 9.18 Collins Co.: Systematic layout planning (1)

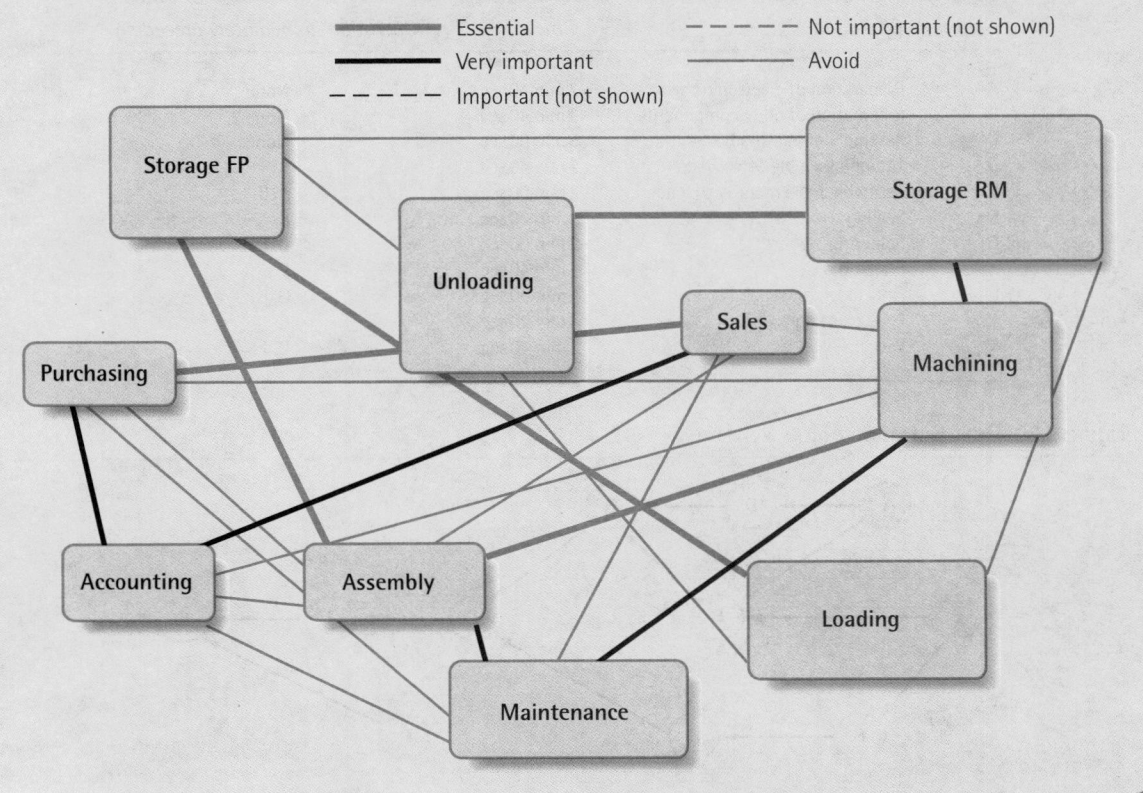

——— Essential	– – – – Not important (not shown)
——— Very important	——— Avoid
– – – – Important (not shown)	

Demonstrating the concept 9.4   Dorf Company

Situation

The Dorf Company is a small manufacturing concern in Belgium that assembles high-quality walking and talking dolls. All raw materials, and components are imported from Hong Kong. The current facility layout is rather haphazard, and the company is having difficulty arriving at its output objective of 50 dolls a day. This target is based on the market demand within Europe. The Production Manager, Michael Dorf, is considering modifying the facility layout in order to increase the production level to the desired objective. The assembly consists of 11 operations, which, together with the estimated time for completion, are given in Table 9.13. The company works eight hours per day, five days per week.

Required

Determine the optimum assembly line arrangement showing a flow scheme with workstations, and calculate the theoretical efficiency.

Use two approaches:

1. Perform those operations that have the longest number of operations that need to be completed afterwards (most tasks following method). Precedence has to be taken into account. For example, sewing [F] cannot be performed until the body component operation [B] has been performed.
2. Perform those operations that take the longest to complete (longest task method). Precedence has to be taken into account.

Solution

Figure 9.20 illustrates the layout with the precedence relationship.

1. The longest task calculations are given in Table 9.14. Here the number of workgroups is five and the layout has an efficiency of about 71%.
2. The most task following calculations are given in Table 9.15. Here the number of workgroups is four with an efficiency of about 89%.

Table 9.13 Dorf Company: Assembly operations and completion times

Step	Operation	Time	Operation immediately preceding
A	Preparation of electronic parts	2 min 40 sec	None
B	Preparation of body components	3 min 40 sec	None
C	Assembly of packing boxes	5 min 00 sec	None
D	Tuning/assembly of voice box	2 min 40 sec	A
E	Assembly movement with limbs	2 min 00 sec	A, B
F	Sewing	2 min 20 sec	B
G	Soldering	3 min 00 sec	D, E
H	Pressing	4 min 40 sec	F
I	Final assembly	1 min 00 sec	G, H
J	Final painting	4 min 20 sec	I
K	Packing	2 min 40 sec	C, J

Figure 9.20 Dorf Company: Flow scheme

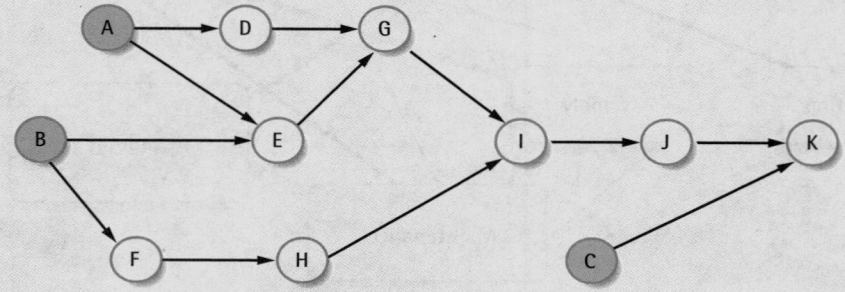

- The cycle time is determined based on the required production rate. The cycle time is given by the time available divided by the customer demand rate. The cycle time is the rate at which a finished product will come off the assembly line.
- Cycle time is 576 seconds.

Most tasks following method:

- elapsed time for doll assembly = 2304 seconds
- actual time used = 2040 seconds
- dead time = 264 seconds
- efficiency is 88.54%.

Four workstations are required, as shown in Table 9.16. Figure 9.21 shows the 'most tasks following' scenario in diagrammatic form.

Longest task method:

- elapsed time for doll assembly = 2880 seconds
- actual time used = 2040 seconds
- dead time = 840 seconds
- efficiency is 70.83%.

Five workstations are required, as shown in Table 9.17. Figure 9.22 shows the 'longest task' scenario in diagrammatic form.

Table 9.14 Dorf Company: Longest task

Information		Source or calculation
Production rate, units/day	50	Given
Hours per day	8.00	Given
Cycle time, secs/unit	576.00	Secs per day/production rate
Theoretical work groups	3.54	Operating time/cycle time

Task	Operating time (secs)	Task	Longest time (secs)
A	160	C	300
B	220	H	280
C	300	J	260
D	160	B	220
E	120	G	180
F	140	A	160
G	180	D	160
H	280	K	160
I	60	F	140
J	260	E	120
K	160	I	60
Total	**2040**	**Total**	**2040**

Grouping according to longest task

Task	Operating time (secs)	Time left (a)	Dead time	Group
C	300	276.00		
B	220	56.00	56.00	1
A	160	416.00		
D	160	256.00		
F	140	116.00	116.00	2
H	280	296.00		
E	120	176.00	176.00	3
G	180	396.00		
I	60	336.00		
J	260	76.00	76.00	4
K	160	416.00	416	5
Total			**840**	

(a) Calculation method given in Table 9.15.

Number of work stations required	5
Operating time per doll, secs	2040
Elapsed time per doll, secs	2880 (Operating time + dead time)
Efficiency (operating time/elapsed time)	70.83%

Table 9.15 Dorf Company: Most tasks following

Information		Source or calculation
Production rate, units/day	50	Given
Hours per day	8.00	Given
Cycle time, secs/unit	576.00	Secs per day/production rate
Theoretical workgroups	3.54	Operating time/cycle time

Task	Operating time (secs)	Number of tasks following	Task	Longest time (secs)
A	160	6	C	300
B	220	7	H	280
C	300	1	J	260
D	160	4	B	220
E	120	4	G	180
F	140	4	A	160
G	180	3	D	160
H	280	3	K	160
I	60	2	F	140
J	260	1	E	120
K	160	0	I	60
Total	**2040**		**Total**	**2040**

Grouping according to most tasks following

Task	Tasks following	Time	Time left (b)	Dead time	Group	(b) Calculation
B	7	220	356			576 − 220 = 356
A	6	160	196			356 − 160 = 196
D	4	160	36	36	1	196 − 160 = 36
F (c)	4	140	436			576 − 140 = 436
E	4	120	316			436 − 120 = 316
H (d)	3	280	36	36	2	316 − 280 = 36
G	3	180	396			576 − 180 = 396
I	2	60	336			396 − 60 = 336
J	1	260	76	76	3	336 − 260 = 76
C	1	300	276			576 − 300 = 276
K	0	160	116	116	4	276 − 160 = 116
Total				**264**		

(c) Place F before E because of the longest time.
(d) Place H before G because of the longest time.

Number of workstations required	4
Operating time per doll, secs	2040
Elapsed time per doll, secs	2304 (Operating time + dead time)
Efficiency (operating time/elapsed time)	88.54%

Table 9.16 Dorf Company: Workstations in 'most tasks following' method

Workstation	Task
1	B, A, D
2	F, E, H
3	G, I, J
4	C, K

Table 9.17 Dorf Company: Workstations in 'longest task' method

Workstation	Task
1	C, B
2	A, D, F
3	H, E
4	G, I, J
5	K

Figure 9.21 Dorf Company: Flow scheme: Most tasks following

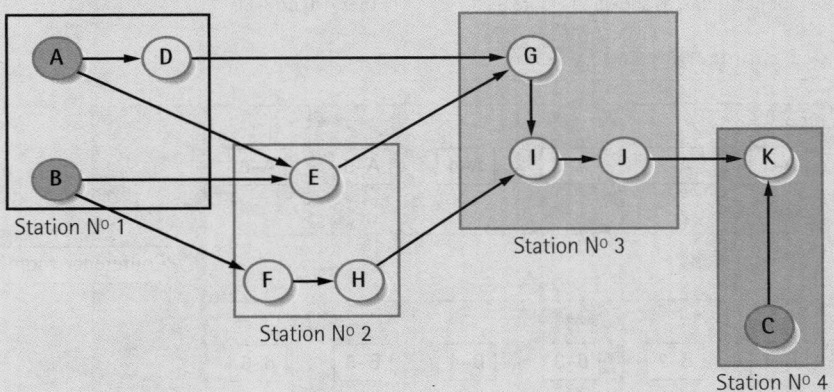

Figure 9.22 Dorf Company: Longest task

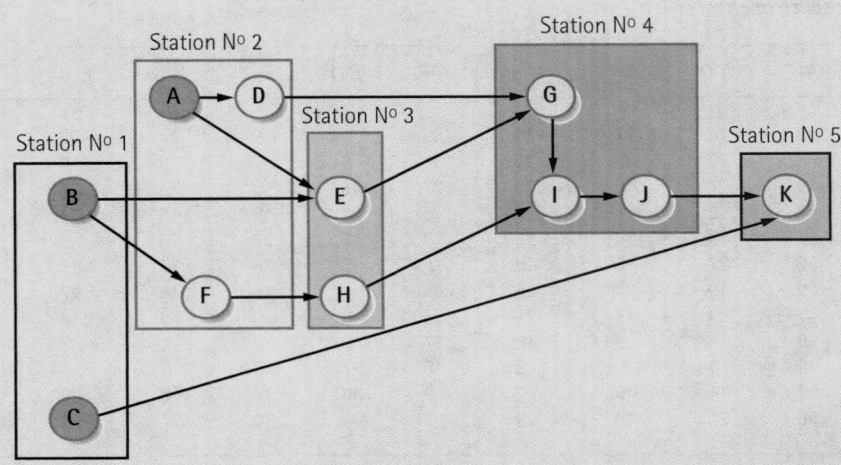

Application exercise 9.1 Baird Engineering Co.

Situation

The Baird Engineering Co. has been awarded a design and engineering contract. The project team, to be led by a project manager, will consist of people from the following departments:

- Accounting
- Chemical Engineering
- Civil Engineering
- Design Engineering
- Mechanical Engineering
- Piping Engineering
- Plant Modelling
- Process Engineering
- Purchasing
- Scheduling

In addition, there will be customer representatives working with the project team.

The complete project team will work in an open plan office space, with soundproof partitions, as shown in Figure 9.23.

The length of each office space is 9 metres, and the distance between each space is given in Table 9.18. In addition, based on experience with past projects, the average contacts per week between functional groups are given in Table 9.19.

Required

Optimize the layout of the office space by considering the contacts and the distance between partitions. Assume that distances travelled to opposite spaces are the same. For example, a person in space A-1, would have the same distance to go to space A-4 or space B-4.

As the project manager organizes many reunions, he will have a space next to the conference room (either A-6 or B-6).

Figure 9.23 Baird Engineering Co.: Office layout

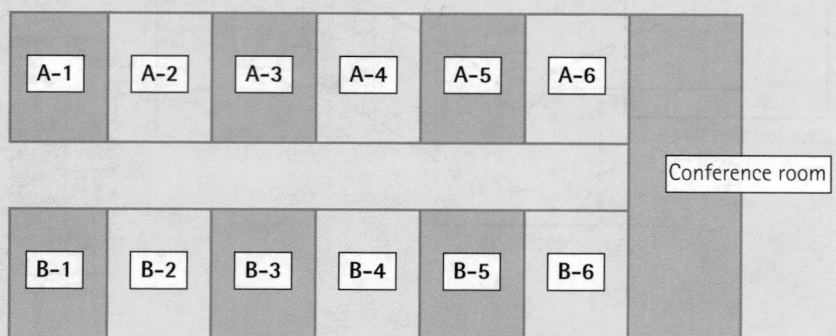

Table 9.18 Baird Engineering Co.: Distance between each office spaces

Length of office space (metres) = 9

	A-1	A-2	A-3	A-4	A-5	A-6	B-1	B-2	B-3	B-4	B-5	B-6
A-1		9	18	27	36	45		9	18	27	36	45
A-2	9		9	18	27	36	9		9	18	27	36
A-3	18	9		9	18	27	18	9		9	18	27
A-4	27	18	9		9	18	27	18	9		9	18
A-5	36	27	18	9		9	36	27	18	9		9
A-6	45	36	27	18	9		45	36	27	18	9	
B-1		9	18	27	36	45		9	18	27	36	45
B-2	9		9	18	27	36	9		9	18	27	36
B-3	18	9		9	18	27	18	9		9	18	27
B-4	27	18	9		9	18	27	18	9		9	18
B-5	36	27	18	9		9	36	27	18	9		9
B-6	45	36	27	18	9		45	36	27	18	9	

Table 9.19 Baird Engineering Co.: Average contacts a week between departments

	Purchasing	Accounting	Scheduling	Civil Eng	Process	Design	Customer	Modelling	Piping	Project Mn	Mechnical	Chemical	Total
Purchasing		12	24	8	2	1	15	1	1	25	8	8	105
Accounting	12		8	5	2	16	8	5	17	21	2	7	103
Scheduling	24	8		7	8	14	9	2	12	15	7	3	109
Civil eng	8	5	7		10	14	5	12	19	12	15	15	122
Process	2	2	8	10		12	6	5	8	6	21	23	103
Design	1	16	14	14	12		6	18	22	21	25	15	164
Customer	15	8	9	5	6	6		2	5	32	5	7	100
Modelling	1	5	2	12	5	18	2		22	9	18	6	100
Piping	1	17	12	19	8	22	5	22		10	15	8	139
Project mn	25	21	15	12	6	21	32	9	10		12	8	171
Mechanical	8	2	7	15	21	25	5	18	15	12		27	155
Chemical	8	7	3	15	23	15	7	6	8	8	27		127
Total	105	103	109	122	103	164	100	100	139	171	155	127	1498

Totals are given for checking purposes

Application exercise 9.2 Dawson

Situation

An engineering and construction company has been awarded a contract to perform the process design, engineering, and construction of a chemical facility in the Middle East. The key personnel on this project will be the project manager, design engineers, process engineers, purchasing, model shop, estimaters, and scheduling. In addition, the client will be resident on site. The facility available for the project is given in Figure 9.24.

As for all projects, finishing on schedule, and within budget is critical, thus the project manager needs always to be kept informed of the situation. Further, although it is important for the client and project manager to be in contact, it is not desirable to have the client involved in the day-to-day activity of the work as this will impede

Figure 9.24 Dawson: Facility availability

R-1	R-2	R-3	R-4
R-5	R-6	R-7	R-8

Table 9.20 Dawson: Interdepartmental relationships

Department code		1	2	3	4	5	6	7	8
		PM	DE	PE	PU	MS	ES	SC	CL
Project manager (PM)	1		C	D	C	D	A	A	A
Design engineers (DE)	2	C		A	B	B	A	D	E
Process engineers (PE)	3	D	A		E	E	D	C	F
Purchasing (PU)	4	C	B	E		E	C	B	F
Model shop (MS)	5	D	B	E	E		D	D	E
Estimators (ES)	6	A	A	D	C	D		C	E
Scheduling (SC)	7	A	D	C	B	D	C		C
Clients (Cl)	8	A	E	F	F	E	E	C	

Table 9.21 Dawson: Interdepartmental relationship criteria

Code	A	B	C	D	E	F
	Critical	Very important	Necessary	Desirable	Unimportant	Not desirable

progress. The desired relationships for office departments is given in Table 9.20 and Table 9.21 gives the criteria.

Required

Using the concept of systematic layout planning, decide on an appropriate room arrangement for the project team.

Application exercise 9.3 Milky Candy Co.

Situation

The Milky Candy Co. produces all types of chocolate candy that is boxed before being sent to the retail outlets.

After the chocolate has been poured, the candy production goes through all types of operation from adding fillings, shaping, decorating, coating and the like, before being put into boxes, wrapped, and put into cartons. This production/ assembly operation operates for 5 days/ week, 8 hours/day. Each week there is a demand for 3000 boxes of the chocolates.

Production/packaging consists of 13 operations. These, together with the estimated time for completion, are given in Table 9.22.

Required

1. Draw the process flow sheet taking precedence relationships into account.
2. What is the theoretical number of grouping?
3. What would the workstation groupings and the operation efficiency be using the most tasks following heuristic rule?
4. What would the workstation groupings and the operation efficiency be using the longest task heuristic rule?

Table 9.22 Milky Candy Co.: Production/packaging operations

Operation	Time (sec)	Operation immediately preceding
1	6	—
2	8	1
3	9	2
4	11	2
5	12	2
6	14	3, 4, 5
7	9	1
8	5	7
9	12	7, 8
10	8	9
11	9	6
12	12	10, 11
13	9	12

5. How would the assembly line arrangement change if the weekly demand doubled?

Case study 9.1 Intermark

Situation
Intermark, a food retailer, is planning a new distribution centre close to London, for its private label and brand-named products. Its function will be to receive the products in bulk quantities, put them into storage, and then distribute products according to requirements of the retail stores. The principal products it handles are classified into ten groupings, as shown in Table 9.23.

The proposed warehouse storage zones with the linear distance between each are given in Table 9.24.

There are three proposals for using the storage area, as Table 9.25 demonstrates.

Table 9.23 Intermark: Principal product classification

Dry goods	Vegetables, rice, sugar, cereals, etc.
Health/beauty products	Deodorants, dental products, soap, etc.
Paper goods	Towels, toilet paper, serviettes, plates
Frozen foods	Meats, pre-cooked meals
Non-alcoholic beverages	Cola, orange, water
Canned goods	Preserves, vegetables, fruit
Alcoholic beverages	Wine, beer, and spirits
Animal-related products	Dry/moist food for cats and dogs, miscellaneous
Household	Cups, plates, cutlery, brooms, mops, etc.
Soaps/detergents	Washing powders

Table 9.24 Intermark: Proposed warehouse storage zones

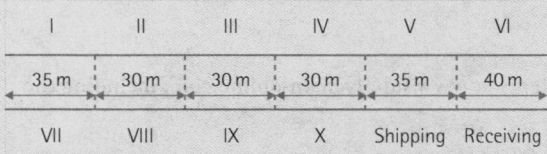

I	II	III	IV	V	VI
35 m	30 m	30 m	30 m	35 m	40 m
VII	VIII	IX	X	Shipping	Receiving

Table 9.25 Intermark: Proposals for storage area use

Zone	1st proposal	2nd proposal	3rd proposal
I	Dry goods	Frozen foods	Non-alcoholic beverages
II	Health and beauty products	Canned goods	Household
III	Paper goods	Health and beauty products	Dry goods
IV	Frozen foods	Paper goods	Health and beauty products
V	Non-alcoholic beverages	Non-alcoholic beverages	Animal-related products
VI	Canned goods	Alcoholic beverages	Frozen foods
VII	Alcoholic beverages	Animal-related products	Alcoholic beverages
VIII	Animal-related products	Dry goods	Soaps/detergents
IX	Household	Household	Canned goods
X	Soaps/detergents	Soaps/detergents	Paper goods

All products received go into storage and remain there from four to 14 days. The rotation depends on the items. Non-alcoholic beverages are faster moving than household products. When the retail outlets receive orders, the products are taken from storage (picking) to the shipping area where they are dispatched to the retail outlet. Based on historical data, Table 9.26 shows the average monthly number of journeys made by trolley handlers from reception to storage, and from storage to shipping. Numbers are always low for the receiving part since products arrive in bulk, whereas for shipping, products demanded are always of smaller quantities.

In order to calculate the distance travelled by a handler the following formulae are used:

Receiving to storage = 0.5 * (Length of receiving dock)
+ (Sum of lengths of other storage zones traversed)
+ 0.5 * (Length of storage zone used)

Storage to shipping = 0.5 * (Length of storage zone used)
+ (Sum of lengths of other storage zones traversed)
+ 0.5 * (Length of storage zone used)

For example, distances for the first proposal:

- Dry goods

Receiving to storage = 0.5 * 40 + (35 + 30 + 30 + 30)
+ 0.5 * 35 = 162.50 m

Storage to shipping = 0.5 * 35 + (30 + 30 + 30)
+ 0.5 * 35 = 125.00 m

- Non-alcoholic beverages

Receiving to storage = 0.5 * 40 + 0.5 * 35 = 37.50 m

Storage to shipping = 0.5 * 35 = 17.50 m

Table 9.26 Intermark: Average monthly number of trolley handler journeys

	Average movements in one month	
	Receiving to storage	Storage to shipping
Dry goods	270	1,230
Health/beauty products	40	850
Paper goods	120	630
Frozen foods	300	1,000
Non-alcoholic beverages	650	2,100
Canned goods	250	1,800
Alcoholic beverages	120	980
Animal-related products	230	1,645
Household	175	1,775
Soaps/detergents	80	1,270

Required

1. Based on using the load–distance analysis for layout, which of the three proposals should be chosen?

2. What are any other considerations in the facility layout of a distribution centre such as described here?

Selected further reading

ALMANZA, Barbara A., KOTSCHEVAR, Lendal H. and TERRELL, Margaret E. (1999) *Foodservice Planning: Layout, Design, and Equipment*, 4th edition, Prentice-Hall.

BAUSBACHER, Ed and HUNT, Roger (1998) *Process Plant Layout and Piping Design*, Prentice-Hall PTR/Sun Microsystems Press.

FRANCIS, Richard L., MCGINNIS, Leon F. Jr and WHITE, John A. (1998) *Facility Layout and Location: An Analytical Approach*, 2nd edition, Prentice-Hall.

PHILLIPS, Edward (1997) *Manufacturing Plant Layout: Fundamentals and Fine Points of Optimum Facility Design*, Society of Manufacturing Engineers.

TEICHOLZ, Eric (2001) *Facility Design and Management Handbook*, McGraw-Hill.

An extensive listing of other further reading can be found on the website.

What's on the web?

Further learning resources are available to lecturers and students at www.supplychain-online.com, including the following which are specific to *Design of the facility layout*:

Resource	Subject
Chapter overview	Design of the facility layout
Application exercise: Chic	Systematic layout planning
Application exercise: Dorf II	Line balancing
Application exercise: Template	Two-dimensional templates
More further reading	Design of the facility layout

Part III

Planning and organizing

Part III covers the core functions of the operations and supply chain including forecasting – the trigger in the supply chain – inventory management, operations and capacity planning, material requirements and enterprise resource planning, operations scheduling, lean production and just-in-time, purchasing and subcontracting, managing the integrated supply chain, and project management.

'Don't be afraid to take a big step when one is indicated.
You can't cross a chasm in two small jumps.'

David Lloyd George

Part III: Planning and organizing

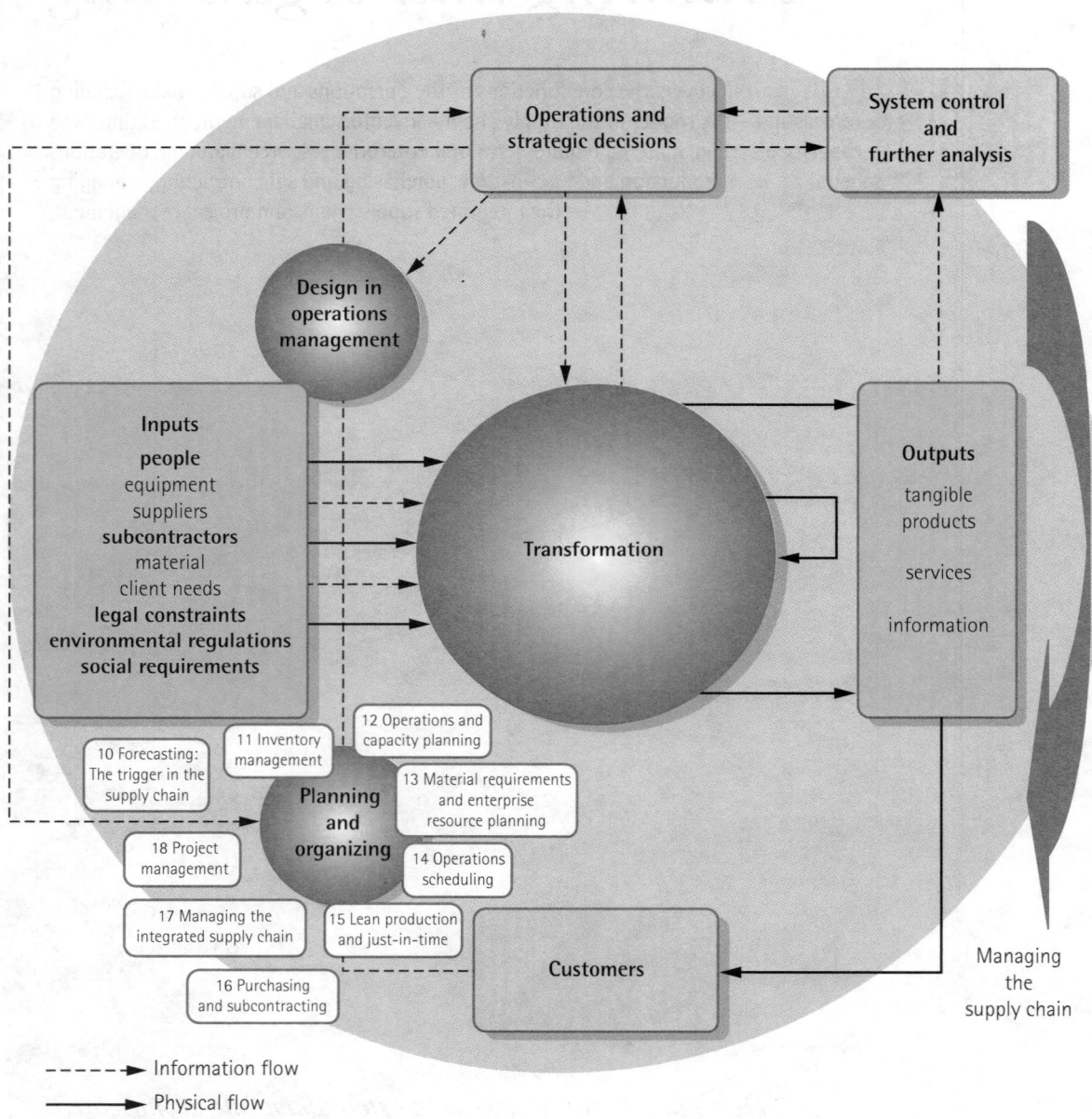

----→ Information flow
───→ Physical flow

10 Forecasting: The trigger in the supply chain

Critical nature of forecasting

Forecasting in operations

Forecasting, or estimating the demand for finished goods or services is the starting point for all operating activities. It is the trigger that sets the supply chain in motion including the preparation of:

- capital budgets for plant and equipment and shorter term operating budgets
- production plans
- short-term operating cash requirements
- personnel needs either full time, part time, or perhaps on a contract basis
- capacity levels of equipment, machines, and buildings
- purchase requirements of raw materials, components, and services
- plans for subcontractor requirements
- transportation requirements for raw materials, finished goods, and/or personnel.

Forecasting risks

Forecasting product, customer demand or other activity is probably one of the most inexact functions in management. One has to understand and evaluate the external environment where there is considerable uncertainty, including the market, clients, and changing technology. Sloppy forecasting of client needs by the marketing department often is the reason for poor production planning and as a result contributes to friction between marketing and production personnel. In forecasting demand, one might be optimistic, or making an estimate of demand higher than actually occurs. Alternatively, the forecast can be pessimistic, or estimating a demand lower than actually occurs. In either case, there are risks and associated costs as the following illustrate.

Optimistic forecast

A computer company estimates that it will sell 5 million units in one particular year. In reality, it only sells 3.5 million. The impact that might result is:

- There is unnecessary inventory of finished goods and raw materials together with associated high storage costs and capital tied up in the inventory.
- Part of the inventory becomes obsolescent. Thus, the cost of the product is lost.
- Plant capacity is used unnecessarily.
- The company is forced later to sell the products at a marked down price, possibly below its marginal cost.

Pessimistic forecast

A computer company estimates that it will sell 5 million units in one particular year. It, in fact, receives orders for 6.5 million. The effect that might result is:

- Stockouts occur resulting in lost orders, which translate directly into lost profit and perhaps permanently lost customers as the competition picks up these lost orders.
- The production line is stopped due to insufficient raw materials, which were ordered on the basis of 5 rather than 6.5 million orders.
- There are excessive costs from subcontracting, overtime, part-time labour as a result of trying to make up for the lost orders.

A situation like this happened in the computer industry in 1995. In January, analysts predicted that 1995 personal computer unit sales growth would slow to 15% from 20% in 1994. In fact sales increased, expecting to rise as much as 30% as consumers demanded more powerful machines to play the many new games or to connect or 'surf' the Internet. As a result, companies such as Hewlett-Packard, Apple, and Acer America Corp., fell short of components such as memory chips, CD-ROM drives, and monitors, causing them to lose millions of dollars in sales and giving them a backlog of orders. Compaq Computer, however, had built up $2 million in inventory and was largely able to satisfy its clients.[1]

Uncertainty

On balance, it is probably better to be optimistic with a forecast, rather than pessimistic, such that one can provide a high client service level. If one is pessimistic,

in the long term, continual stockout situations can cause clients to turn elsewhere for their products and internally, repeated stockouts can be costly, and employees can become de-motivated.

Time horizons in forecasting

Forecasts, or estimates can be made over any time horizon. However, normally the shorter the period being considered the more accurate is the forecast since one is more certain of the variables involved. Illustrations of forecast elements in three time horizons would include the following.

Short range

A short-range forecast is one for a time span of a few weeks up to say about three months. It would include forecasting such items as:

- purchase transactions
- cash requirements
- work schedules
- workforce levels
- job assignments
- production levels.

Medium range

A medium-range forecast is one that covers about three months up to one year. In this case, it would include such items as:

- sales plans
- production plans
- capacity plans
- operating cash budgets
- management levels
- subcontractor needs.

Long range

A long-range forecast is of about one to five years and would include:

- capital expansion plans
- new investment
- new product development
- facility location
- research and development programmes
- strategic plans
- implementing new technology
- acquisitions.

Variations of the time horizon

The category in which a type of forecast is placed very much depends on the type of industry, and the country in which it is located. For example:

- It is easy to increase, or decrease workforce levels in the USA and thus this element would be in a short-range horizon. However, in countries like

Holland, France, and Germany, where the social laws are stricter than in the USA it is more difficult to change workforce levels and so this would be in a medium-term horizon.

- A chemical company's time horizon is longer than for, say, a company that produces computer programs. Thus, time horizons for activities such as purchasing, production, or investment may be quite different.

Economic indicators in forecasting

There are indicators in the economy that can be used to describe past, current, or future macroeconomic conditions. The US government, for example, compiles leading, coincident, and lagging indicators.[2]

Leading indicators

A leading indicator is one that reaches a high, or a low, before a peak or a valley in related economic activity, as illustrated in Figure 10.1. For this reason, leading indicators can be important tools in forecasting as for example.

Construction contracts

A surge in new construction contracts awarded for industrial, commercial, or residential facilities are a forecast of future needs for building materials such as lumber, cement, steel and also for electrical fittings, plumbing, and furniture and for construction labour.

Plant and equipment

An increase in new contracts and orders for plant and equipment will forecast new demand for machines, tools, steel, fittings, etc., and also perhaps an indicator of the growth of inventory levels.

Business incorporation

New businesses incorporated and failed, or the net change in business population, gives a forecast, or reduction of employment levels.

Capital appropriation

Newly approved capital appropriation will be a forecast of additional building and construction.

Inventory levels

A decrease in inventories is often a forecast of new manufacturing activity to replenish the decline in stocks. If inventories are increasing, and sales are sluggish, this would be a forecast of a decline in manufacturing activity.

Manufacturing or service orders

New manufacturing orders, or new service demands, would be a forecast of hiring new personnel and an

Figure 10.1 **Leading economic indicators**

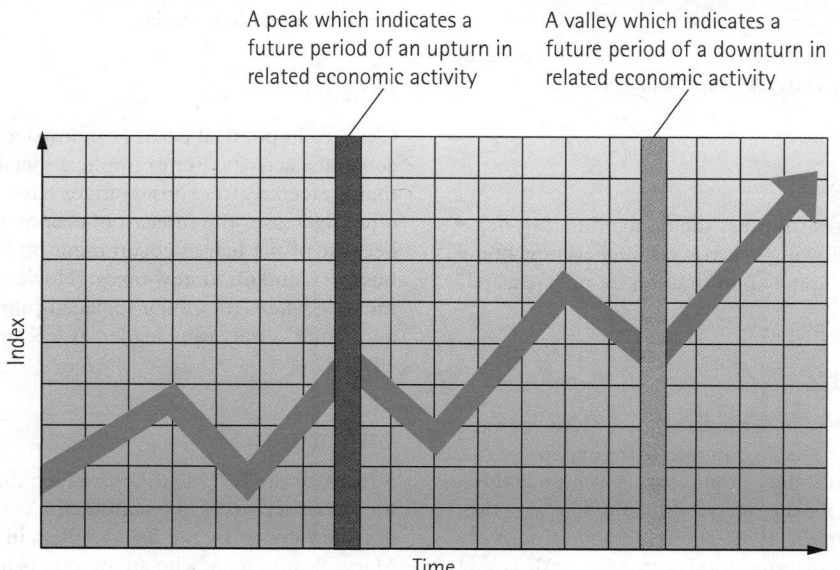

A peak which indicates a future period of an upturn in related economic activity

A valley which indicates a future period of a downturn in related economic activity

Index

Time

increase in demand of raw materials in the case of manufacturing.

Coincident indicators

A coincident, or simultaneous indicator is one that is in harmony with the associated economic activity. Coincident indicators have little use in forecasting since they are only indicating what is in fact now happening. Examples would include:

- gross national product (GNP), which indicates the current economic health of a country
- unemployment rate which indicates the current employment climate
- retail store sales, which are a record of what has been currently sold
- index of industrial production, which is an indicator of current production activity.

Lagging indicators

A lagging indicator is one that reaches its high, or low, after the economic activity has occurred. Here again, lagging indicators have little use in forecasting since they are only indicating what has already happened. Examples would include:

- labour cost per unit of production
- commercial and industrial loans
- book value of inventories.

Macroeconomic factors

Macroeconomic conditions can enormously impact the forecast of future activity. Some examples include the following.

Interest rates

High interest rates suppress the demand for big-ticket items where borrowing is involved, such as new homes, automobiles, or capital appropriation for new research programmes.

Exchange rates

A strong currency of a particular country reduces exports from that country since goods are more expensive to the buyer. Further, it reduces tourism receipts since it is more expensive for the overseas visitor. This was the case for Britain in the 1999 where the pound was very strong compared to euro-based currencies and, as such,

US travellers, for example, found Britain an expensive destination compared to, say, France. However, a strong currency increases the capital flow into that country since international investors have a higher confidence level in it.

Unemployment level

High unemployment reduces consumer purchases of items that can be deferred, such as new automobiles, eating out in restaurants, or taking expensive vacations.

Demographic trends

An increasingly elderly population forecasts the need for medical equipment and medical-related services and retirement homes. However, for the able-bodied it increases the forecast for travel and package holidays.

Government regulations

Government laws, or the hint of new laws, can impact forecasts:

- Tax law changes in the USA concerning retirement plans gave rise to a forecast increase in money available for investment.
- Laws related to smoking have reduced the forecast for the demand for cigarettes in the USA and some European countries. In California, which has one of the strictest non-smoking laws, it has reduced the forecast incidence of cancer.
- Regulations about the combustible nature of materials (clothing and furniture) have increased the demand of non-flammable material.

Political climate

Changes in political parties can impact the forecast of economic activity. For example, a socialist government that is elected after conservatives have been in power often decreases the forecast of economic activity because of the fear of government interference in business, and often new taxes. (However, this was not the case when Tony Blair replaced John Major, the outgoing Conservative leader, as UK Prime Minister in 1997.)

Labour unrest

Strikes, or the fear of strikes, reduce the forecast of industrial activity. For example, the continued threat of labour unrest by the dockworkers in the port of Marseilles, France, who are members of the CGT

(Confederation Générale du Travail) has reduced the forecast of business at the port but has increased the forecast of business at nearby Toulon, and also at the port of Genoa in Italy.

Elasticity of demand

To some extent, forecasting product demand is a function of the product price. The higher the price of the product, the less the product is demanded. However, there is a varying degree in the change in the demand, which is a function of the 'elasticity' of the product.

Inelastic product

A product is considered to be inelastic if the quantity demanded does not change dramatically with price changes. For example, the demand for products such as bread, table wine, milk, rail tickets, computer paper, or gasoline does not change a great deal with price:

- If the price increases, people would still buy in about the same amounts. These are relatively basic products, where there is really little substitute.
- If the price decreases, the amount consumed would not increase much either as there is a limit to how much of these products can be consumed. The quantity demanded is effectively saturated for a given population.

Elastic product

A product is considered to be elastic if the quantity demanded by customers changes significantly with price changes. The demand for products such as four-wheel drive recreational vehicles, champagne, holidays at the Club Meditérranée, a vacation home, and silk clothing changes considerably with price changes:

- If the price increases, people would defer purchase of these products because there are substitutes, or, for the moment, they can live without them.
- If the price decreases, the amount demanded increases as they become more affordable. These are types of luxury item, which are now within price range of a large population. An example would be the sale of personal computers in the early 1990s.

Elastic products are usually expensive items for which there might be substitutes, or they are not critical to a person's basic need.

Figure 10.2 shows a simple relationship between price and quantity for inelastic, and elastic products.

Figure 10.2 Elasticity of demand

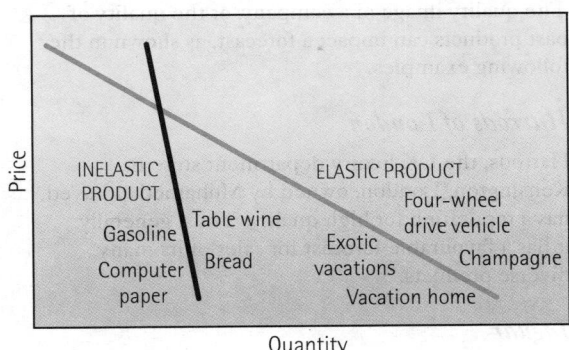

The phenomenon is important in long-range planning for both manufacturing and service organizations.

Microeconomic factors

Within a specific industrial sector, there are factors, one might call microfactors, concerning the organization, or the product, that can impact a forecast. The following illustrates.

Competition

A company's forecast of future sales depends very much on the extent of the competition.

IBM

When IBM introduces any new personal computer products onto the market it has to fight with competitors such as Hewlett-Packard/Compaq and Dell.

Texas Instruments

When Texas Instruments introduced its new scientific calculator in the early 1970s there was very little competition. As such, it cornered the market and was optimistic about future sales.

Boeing

When the demand for commercial aircraft is high, Boeing, in Seattle, Washington can be optimistic about forecast sales. However, it does have to battle with its major competitor, Airbus Industries of France, which, in 2000, announced its plans to build the 550-seater plane, the A-380, which will have almost twice the capacity of Boeing's 747.[3]

Reputation for quality

The quality image of a company, or the quality of past products can impact a forecast, as shown in the following examples.

Harrods of London

Harrods, the UK luxury department store in Kensington, London, owned by Mohamed al Fayed, has a reputation for high quality. Thus, generally it has a favourable forecast for sales of its many diverse products.

Jaguar

The automobiles produced by Jaguar in the early 1980s had a terrible reputation for quality. As a result, the forecast of increased sales was quite poor. Now, under the present ownership of Ford, USA, quality has improved somewhat.[4]

Firestone Tires

In the middle of 2000 Firestone Tires (owned by the Japanese Company, Bridgestone) had an enormous recall on its tyres used in Ford Motor Co.'s Explorer sports-utility vehicle. The recall was a result of many automobile deaths linked to faulty Firestone tyres. The result has been a loss in confidence of Firestone and a forecast of poor sales. To a certain extent the forecast of Ford's sales has also suffered.[5]

Price

Price levels always impact the forecast for future products. As a general rule, the lower the price the higher the sales. However, products shouldn't be priced so low that consumers consider that they are of inferior quality.

Market saturation

In the product lifecycle (see Chapter 6), after commercialization new products go through introduction, growth, maturity, and eventual decline. A successful new product exhibits its most rapid demand in the growth stage where the rate only slows down as market saturation approaches. However, one difficulty is to forecast at what point the market will become saturated. This concept is illustrated by mobile telephones where the Finnish company Nokia, often considered the bellwether of mobile phones, forecast its sales would be 140 million handsets for 2000 but in fact it sold only 128 million units. Further, the total number of units sold in 2000 was 405 million whereas the forecast was 420 million handsets. The principal reason was cited as market saturation in the European and Asian markets. As a result of this poor forecast Nokia shares fell 8.7% to €41, the share price of rival Ericsson of Sweden fell 4.3% to €11.17 and the share price of Vodafone, the UK-based mobile phone operator fell 3.4% to €3.47.[6]

Design

Knowing that a product is well designed enhances forecast of sales even though, on first appearance, the good design is not visible.

Volkswagen

The Volkswagen Beetle had, right from its introduction in the mid-1930s, a reputation for quality. During good times for the sales of all automobiles the sales forecast of the Beetle was very favourable. This was the case even though its style was not revolutionary. The same was true for Saab and Volvo automobiles from Sweden.

Heidelberg printing presses

Heidelberg printing presses from Germany are known for good design. Demand for their products is good in their particular market niche.

Delivery times

Manufacturers, suppliers, service industries, which have a reputation for being reliable in delivery are more likely to have favourable forecasts compared to those who are not considered reliable.

Disasters

Companies that experience an unexpected disaster with one of their products can expect difficulties in the future.

McDonnell-Douglas

In 1979 a DC-10 manufactured by McDonnell-Douglas crashed in Chicago because of a problem with the engine mounting. From that day on the company had difficulty competing in the commercial airline market. Now Boeing, Chicago, has swallowed it. (See Chapter 19.)

Ford Motor

Ford Motor, USA, used to manufacture a small automobile called the Pinto. In the early 1970s two people were killed when another motorist ran into the back of their Ford Pinto and it caught fire. The accident was blamed on poor shielding for the gasoline tank. Forecast sales of the vehicle began to fall and eventually Ford ceased manufacture of the Pinto.

Qualitative forecasting

Qualitative, or judgmental forecasting is based on assumptions, or intuitive estimates of those in the firm familiar with the market. This might include sales personnel, purchasing representatives, or management people who all have close contact with the client. The accuracy of a qualitative approach depends on the good judgment, honesty, and philosophy of the individuals concerned. Some considerations in qualitative forecasting are now discussed.

Get to know the customer

Is the contact and trust in the client good? Qualitative estimates can be improved by working closely with the client. If the client can be encouraged firmly to determine his future needs, both parties win:

- The client can be assured of obtaining his order, on time, and perhaps at an attractive price.
- The supplier can better plan his production needs.

If the producer/supplier has several clients, perhaps with some overseas, a close association with all clients may not be possible. However, working closely with as many as possible helps to minimize the uncertainty, and corresponding risk.

Producing to demand

In terms of avoiding unnecessary inventory, producing to demand, which is setting up the production plan after the client has given his order, is less risky than producing to stock or making standardized products. However, firms producing to order need to be very flexible with their operations and to have low lead times in order to be competitive.

Sales bonus

The sales forecast might be skewed if the nature of the forecast impacts the remuneration of the individual making the forecast. Consider a company that offers a bonus to salespeople who exceed their sales quota. For example:

- A bonus of 5% is given above a certain base sales estimate.

- This base sales quota is established according to forecasts of expected sales. However, it is usually the salespeople who have been involved in estimating expected sales since it is part of their job.
- Thus, sales personnel may be pessimistic in making a forecast because the lower the sales requirement, the easier it will be to obtain their base salary. In addition, the higher will be their bonus when the base sale is exceeded.

Understand the market

Markets can change rapidly, and completely modify the demand of products. The sales of a product which has been performing well in the past may start to decline rapidly because of a change in fad, desire of consumers, or other events.

Hamburgers

McDonald's underestimated the impact of the health food movement in the USA in the 1970s. This fad drastically reduced the demand for beef, thus reducing the demand for hamburgers and pushed McDonald's to develop other products such as chicken nuggets and even salads with fish products.

Automobiles

The US 'Big Three' automobile producers, General Motors, Chrysler (now Daimler-Chrysler) and Ford, grossly underestimated the US demand for small automobiles in the USA in the late 1970s. This opened the door to Toyota, Nissan, and others from Asian countries, which sharply ate into the market of the Big Three.

Calculators

Manufactures of slide rules such as Faber Castell, in Germany, underestimated the speed with which pocket calculators, initially introduced by Texas Instruments, would capture the market in the 1970s.

Tennis

The enthusiasm for tennis has waned for no real explanation. Thus, the market demand for tennis rackets, clothing, strings, and products associated with the sport have declined.

Beef

The outbreak of bovine spongiform encephalopathy or 'mad cow disease' in Britain in 1996 devastated the cattle industry and the demand for beef. This then later surfaced in other European countries including

Figure 10.3 Top management opinion

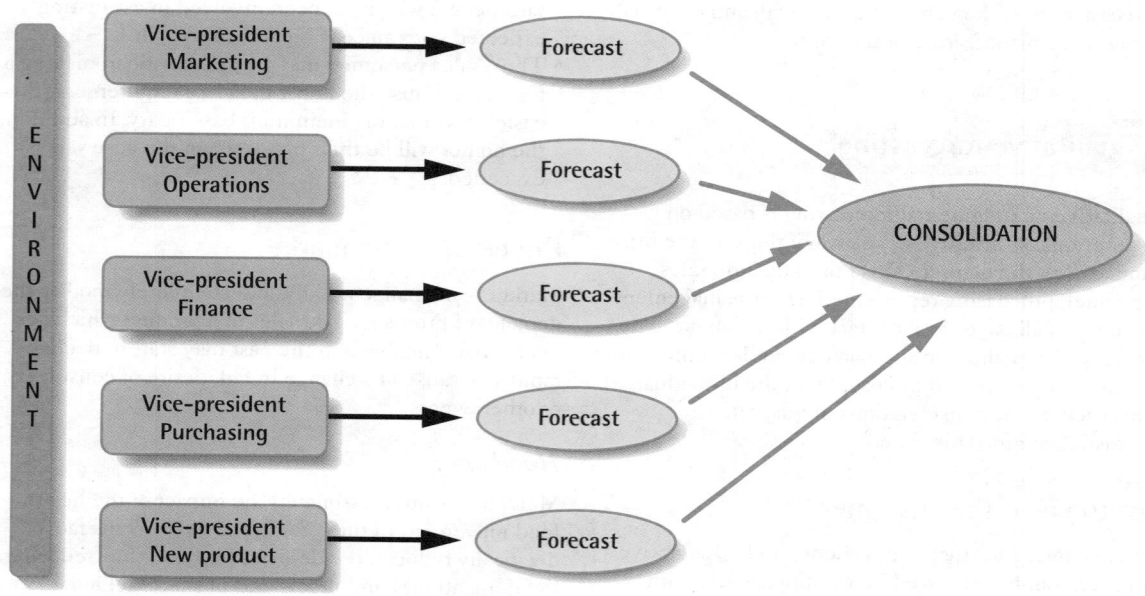

Switzerland, France, and Germany, and completely depressed the European demand for beef products.[7]

Opinions of top management

Executives, senior managers, and other business leaders have a prime interest in the business climate. They are responsible to their shareholders, and need to respond to their employees regarding the outlook for employment conditions. They also are concerned to know at what level to increase, or decrease, capital expenditures. Since these executives are often in contact with other business leaders, or government representatives, they are in a good position to make general forecast of future sales. In this respect, Figure 10.3 illustrates the process of consolidation when vice-presidents of various operating divisions have been in contact with the external environment.

Dun & Bradstreet of the USA make regular quarterly surveys of business confidence based on opinions of top management. An example is shown in Figure 10.4, which gives the sales expectations of world businesspeople for four consecutive quarters, starting from the first quarter of 2000.[8] The data present the net percent of businesspeople who expect higher sales (those expecting higher sales, less those expecting lower sales). According to these data the world index is less positive in that, in the fourth quarter,

only 48% of respondents expect sales to rise than expect them to decline. This is down from 53% in the third quarter and 58% in the second quarter. The decline in the third quarter was concentrated in east Asian countries such as Australia and New Zealand. In the fourth quarter business confidence stabilized in those regions but has declined in Canada, the USA, and, for the most part, in Europe, where France and Britain are less optimistic.

The salesforce composite

The salesforce composite is a specific judgmental forecast where opinions are solicited from line sales personnel at the regional level. The regional sales forecasts are then compiled at headquarters. This approach is illustrated in Figure 10.5, which shows how a company with headquarters in New York would gather sales data from its country branches in USA, England, and Germany. The country branches have themselves collected data from their regional offices within the country concerned. Using the opinion of the salesforce for compiling a forecast for future sales is:

- good in that line sales are in touch with customers
- misleading if used for salary/bonus system
- may be difficult to break down on a product-by-product basis, since product models may be different for different countries.

Figure 10.4 Sales expectation by quarter (2000)

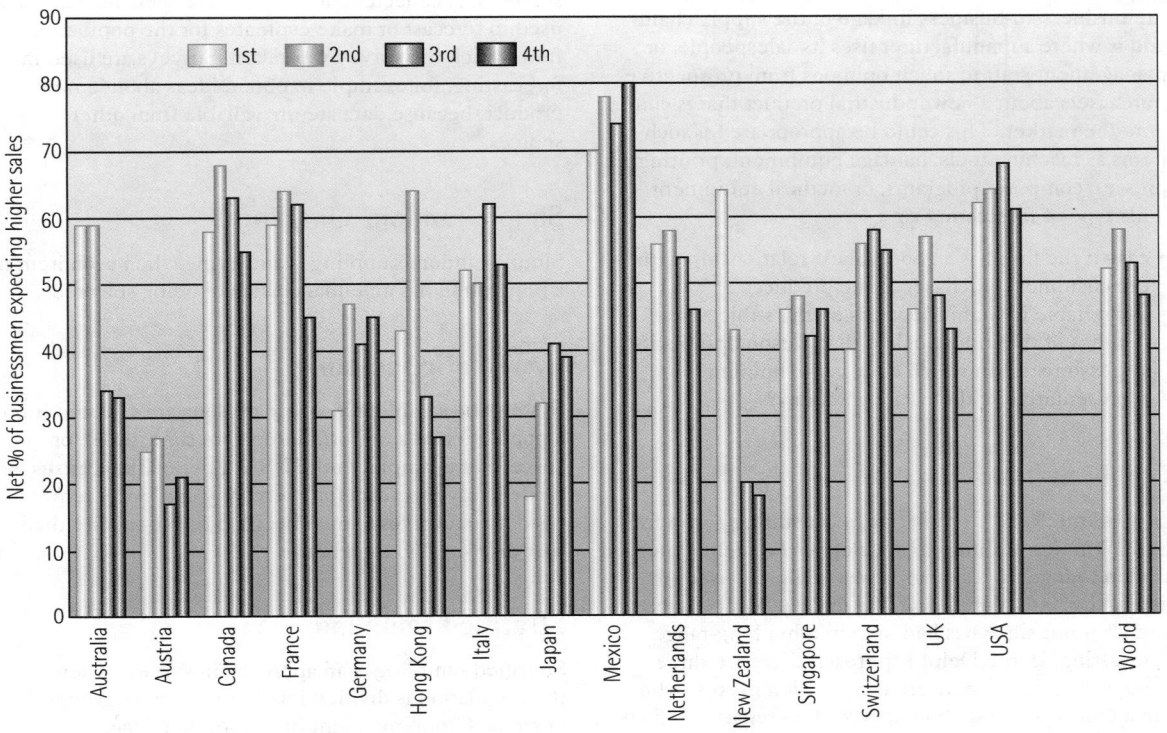

Figure 10.5 Salesforce composite

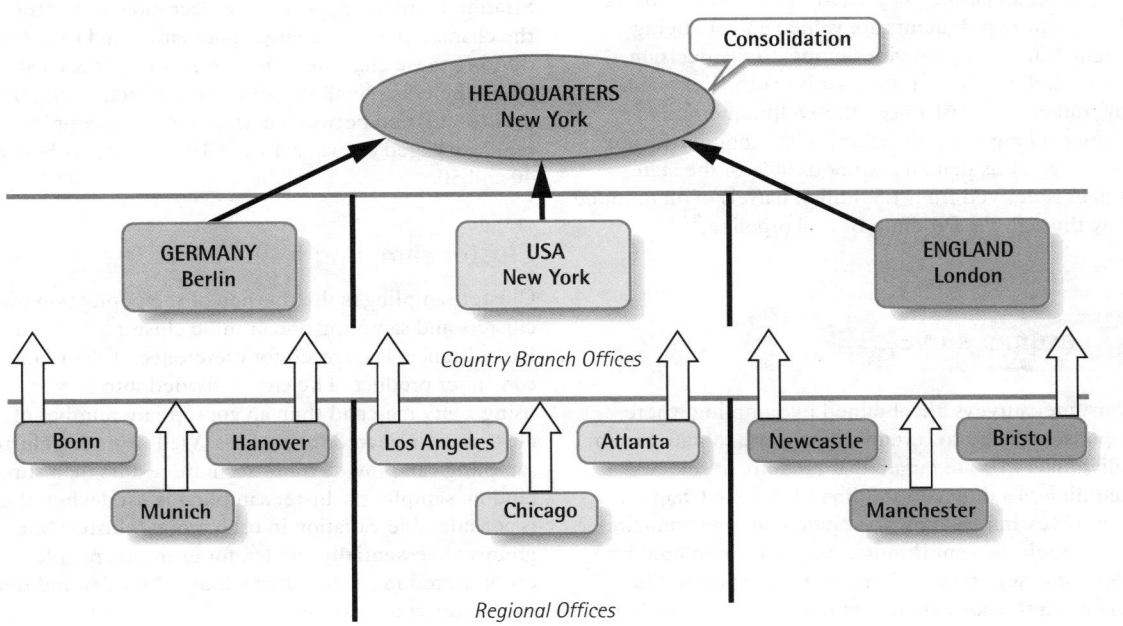

Buyers' expectations

Buyers' expectations is a forecasting approach in the business-to-business linkage of the supply chain and is where a manufacturer uses its salespeople, or management staff to solicit opinions from prospective purchasers about a new industrial product that is coming onto the market. This could be appropriate for such items as machine tools, haulage equipment, printing presses, computer programs, or medical equipment. This type of forecasting is:

- easy if the firm has a good honest relationship with the customer (purchaser of the product)
- not reliable in that it depends on the subjective feelings of the individual. Is that person optimistic, or pessimistic? In which case, is the opinion representative of the entire company?

Delphi method

In 1948 the Rand Corporation, a consulting group from Santa Monica, California, developed the Delphi method for long-range forecasting. It was originally used to assess the potential impact of a nuclear bomb attack on the USA but since has had uses in other long-range forecasting. In the Delphi approach there are three groups involved. There are the decision makers who are a group of five to ten experts who prepare the final forecast. There are staff people who assist the decision makers by developing, diffusing, collecting and summarizing a set of questionnaires. The third group is the respondents, the people, often located in different places, whose judgments are valued and are being sought. This group provides inputs to the decision makers before the final forecast is made. The state government of Alaska used the Delphi method to develop a long-range forecast for its economic future. The reason was that an enormous 90% of the state budget is derived from 1.5 million barrels of oil pumped daily through the Prudhoe Bay oil pipeline.[9]

Consumer surveys

Consumer surveys are obtained by sampling where responses related to certain subjects are solicited from individuals who are targeted at random, or selected according to a defined sampling plan. (See Chapter 27.) The survey information is prepared on questionnaires, which might be sent through the mail, completed by telephone, sent by electronic mail, or requested in person. In the last case this may be either going door to door, or soliciting the information in areas frequented by potential consumers such as shopping malls. The survey data collected, or sampled, are then analyzed and used to forecast or make estimates for the population from which the survey was taken. Surveys are used in forecasting, for example to obtain ideas about a new product, because data are unavailable from other sources.[10]

Simple random sampling

Simple random sampling is surveying when each item in a population has an equal chance of being selected.

Systematic sampling

Systematic sampling is where persons are selected from a population at a uniform interval in time, order, or space. For example, in the USA, a population census is made every ten years for everybody and every tenth residence receives a more detailed questionnaire than that delivered to each house.

Stratified sampling

Stratified sampling is an approach in surveys where the population is divided into homogeneous groups or strata. Grouping might be according to age. For example, people in the 40 to 50 age group may have a different preference for a specific automobile (sports car, for example) than those in, say, the 25 to 35 age group. Stratified sampling is used to reflect more accurately the characteristics of a target population and to avoid diluting these characteristics erroneously. It is used when there is a small variation within each group, but a wide variation between each group, for example, teenagers aged between 13 and 19 and parents between 40 and 50.

Cluster sampling

Cluster sampling is the division of the population into clusters and sampling one or more clusters. Assume Paris, France, is targeted for preference of a certain consumer product. The city is divided into clusters using a city map and then an appropriate number of clusters are selected for analysis. Well-designed cluster sampling can provide more accurate results than simple random sampling. Cluster sampling is used when there is considerable variation in each group (cluster) but groups are essentially similar, for example, people encountered in a shopping mall on a Monday and those encountered on a Tuesday.

Accuracy of consumer surveys

A well-designed sample survey can give reasonably accurate predictions of the requirements, desires, or needs of a population. The accuracy lies in the phrase 'well designed'. For example, in the US presidential elections in November 1948 the two candidates were Harry Truman, the Democratic incumbent, and Governor Dewey of New York, the Republican candidate. The *Chicago Tribune* was 'so sure' of the election outcome from the surveys that the headlines in their daily paper read, 'Dewey elected president'. Harry Truman won![11]

Cost of surveys

Consumer surveys are expensive. There is the cost of designing the questionnaire such that it is able to solicit the correct response. There is the operating side of collecting the data, and then the subsequent analysis. Outside consulting firms specialized in surveying are often used by business.

Survey response

Soliciting information from consumers is difficult: 'Everyone is too busy'. Postal surveys have a very low response and their use has declined. People who do respond may not be representative in the sample. Telephone surveys give a higher return because voice contact has been obtained. However, again the sample obtained may not be representative as those contacted may be the unemployed, retirees, or non-working people; others are not available. Electronic mail surveys give a reasonable response, as it is very quick to send the survey back. However, the questionnaire only reaches those who have e-mail. Person-to-person contact gives a much higher response for consumer surveys since a relatively large proportion of people will accept being questioned.

Time series data in forecasting

Definition

A time series is historical or past data that have been collected over a regular period of time, representing a certain activity. A time series might be used to illustrate the movement of such variables as sales revenues, cash flow, number of defective products manufactured, industrial accidents, shipments of raw materials, gross national product, consumer price index, stock price, wage rates, etc. Economic indicators, discussed in the previous section, are a form of time series data.[12]

A time series analysis is usually presented in graphical form with the time variable plotted on the x axis, the *abscissa*, or horizontal axis, and the variable of interest on the y axis the *ordinate*, or vertical axis. As an illustration, Figure 10.6 gives a time series analysis of the sale of granular fertilizer, in thousand tons, sold by a small chemical company over the last four years. (NPK are the chemical symbols for nitrogen, phosphorus, and potassium, the principal active ingredients in fertilizer.)

Components of a time series

Depending on the data being analyzed, components in the time series might indicate a trend, seasonal variation, cyclical pattern, irregular occurrence, or random variations.

Figure 10.6 Sales of NPK fertilizer

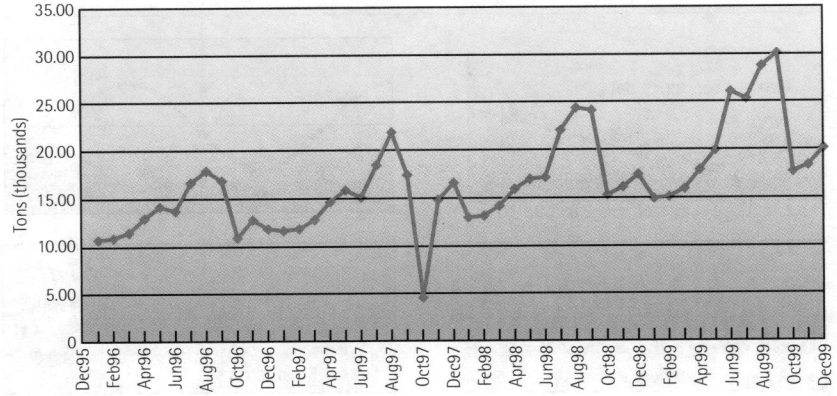

Trend

A trend in a time series can be either increasing or decreasing. Illustrations include:

- a steady increase in the consumer price index
- an increase in population
- an increase in annual salaries of top US executives
- an increase in product sales
- a decrease in the amount of alcohol consumed
- an increase in the unemployment rate in Europe in the early 1990s
- an increase in the average age of the population in Japan
- a decrease in sales of cigarettes in the United States
- a decrease in the fertility rate of western women.

Seasonal variation

Seasonal variations in the time series are changes that occur as a result of seasonal impacts. For example:

- swimsuit sales are higher in the spring and summer
- gasoline consumption is higher in the summer
- ski sales are higher in the autumn in the northern hemisphere
- beer sales are higher in the summer
- flu-related medicine consumption is higher in the winter
- school textbooks, pens, and paper are higher in the autumn.

Business cycle

Analyzing long-term business activities indicates that there is a cyclical activity, which seems to occur about every seven years. (Although there are indications in the 1990s that this may be changing.) This cycle is an increasing wave-like pattern, which can be demonstrated by financial stock market indicators such as the US Dow Jones Industrial Average, the UK *Financial Times* FT index, or France's CAC 40. The indices are somewhat unpredictable but there is evidence of repeat peaks and valleys, of business activities that have an effect on employment levels, capital investment, and company profits.

Irregular occurrences

Irregular occurrences are unpredictable such as:

- Severe weather like the rain-caused flooding in the USA in 1993 in the UK in 2000/2001 that disrupted industry, transportation, and agriculture.
- Labour problems such as the 1984 UK miners' strike which reduced economic output.
- Civil unrest such as the conflict in Northern Ireland that reduced investment in that region. Or the war in former Yugoslavia, which reduced tourism in that area but increased tourism in Spain and other Mediterranean Basin countries.

Random variations

Random variations are those for which there seems to be no accountable reason and would include whatever is remaining after all other variations have been taken into account.

Figure 10.7 illustrates actual time series data, and then shows the trend, seasonal, business cycle, and random variation components.

Components of interest for forecasting

The components of principal interest in forecasting, and which occur in similar cycle periods, are trends, seasonal variation, and random variations. Irregular occurrences are not included since, although of interest, they can

Figure 10.7 Ten-year time series data and components

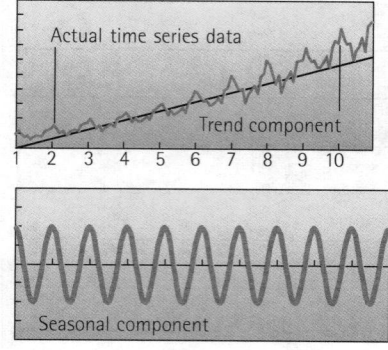

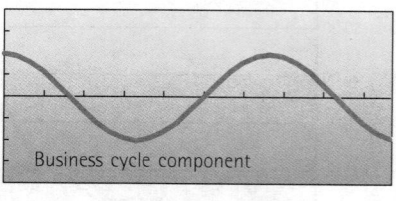

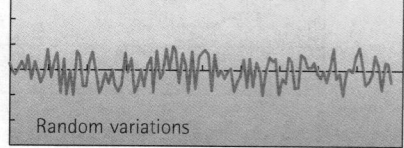

usually be easily identified. For example, in production, irregular occurrences might be effects due to operators' absences, equipment failures, or stockouts of raw materials. In sales it might be due to a very strong promotional activity or unusual weather conditions, such as a severe winter causing increasing sales of heating oil. Neither are business cycle variations incorporated into the time series analysis because such analyses are long term relative to most forecast periods encountered in the operating environment.

Forecasting models

Time series model

In Chapter 1, the concept of modelling was introduced as a useful management tool. In forecasting mathematical models are developed, which are premised on the assumption that past events are a reasonable predictor of future activity. For example, a model of revenues assumes that the historical sale's environment is representative of the future sale's climate. If factors like advertising, competitor behaviour, product design, technology, or needs of customers have changed, the developed model may not be representative of the future. Time series data that have shown a trend in the past may not always be reliable for future forecasting. Table 10.1 gives some products that were showing a steady growth but whose growth has either levelled out or is declining.

Further, Industry insight 10.1 demonstrates clearly a time series data model and explains what is happening to nullify the forecast model.

Two models of interest to illustrate sales are a multiplication and an additive model.

Table 10.1 Time series data and products' fortunes

Item	Reason
Oil prices in the 1990s compared to the 1970s	Producer country stability
Demand for large cars in the USA in the 1970s compared to the 2000s	Rising gasoline prices and the market success of Japanese small cars
Demand for glass today compared to two decades ago	Technology has helped to replace glass in packaging and also processes allow less glass for the same product function
Demand for beef today compared to two decades ago	Concern over cholesterol and the mad cow scare in Europe
Demand for typewriters today compared to the 1970s	Technology has replaced the typewriter with the word processor
Demand for cigarettes in the USA today compared to the 1950s	Government campaigns on the health risk of cigarettes has reduced consumption

Computer sales

In technology, the bellwether for growth was the personal computer. With Microsoft supplying operating systems, and Intel the computer chips, the major personal computer manufacturers, Hewlett-Packard, IBM, Dell, Gateway, NEC and Compaq believed they could have a reasonable forecast of next year's sales as Figure 10.8 illustrates.

However, this time series analysis for forecasting beyond 2000 is no longer valid. For the first time in 15 years worldwide personal computer sales are forecast to decline from the previous year. Industry puts the forecast 2001 level at 127 million units compared to 129 million in 2000. Whereas if the data from Figure 10.8 were modelled using a six-power polynomial, giving an almost perfect coefficient of determination, the forecast would be some 156 million units. The personal computer industry is sputtering, and in recent months

the five biggest PC makers have laid off thousands of employees and taken charges totalling $2.1 billion. Even Dell, the industry's darling, is signalling that for the first time in its 17-year history annual revenue will fall in 2001. There had been some hope that Europe would buoy the demand since only about one-third of European households have PCs compared with more than a half in the US. However, the market in Europe has also come to a shuddering halt. Although there have been PC slumps before, evidence is mounting that the situation is not a cyclical downturn. Back-to-school sales, a reliable barometer of Christmas home PC sales, are down. Further, companies are upgrading less frequently.

It is forecasted that the 15% a year gain in shipments that made the PC hardware and software industry one of the biggest generators of corporate and personal wealth

Figure 10.8 Worldwide shipment of personal computers

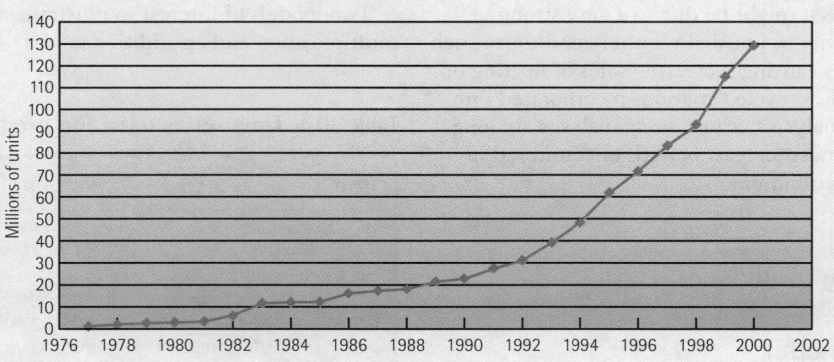

through much of the 1990s may never return. It seems that the industry's recent spotty record of producing innovations that appeal to buyers is at least partly to blame. PC makers, squeezed by price wars, have slashed spending on product research, leaving much of the important technology development to Microsoft Corp. and Intel Corp. After selling more than 800 million units since 1980 the personal computer industry has taken on attributes of other big mature industries. Like cars, televisions, and other home appliances PCs may be evolving into a product that owners keep unchanged for a relatively long time and replace only when the machine they have cannot handle a popular new use, such as managing digital music files.

Adapted from: 'Time to reboot: PC makers say farewell to 15-year boom', *Wall Street Journal Europe*[13]

Multiplication model

This is when the sales, or demand of a product, are a function of the product of several variables:

$$Y = T_f * S_f * C_f * R_f$$

Additive model

This is when the sales, or demand of a product, are a function of the addition of several variables:

$$Y = T_f + S_f + C_f + R_f$$

In both models:

- Y is the sales or other activity
- T_f is the trend over time on the assumption no external events are intervening
- S_f is a factor due to seasonal variations in the sales
- C_f is a factor which modifies the sales according to the business cycle
- R_f is a factor due to random occurrences.

Patterns in time series data

To establish whether a time series data is appropriate for developing a forecast model the data are plotted to see how they have changed over time, and to see if a pattern exists. For example, in Figure 10.6, a pattern appears to exist from which the following observations can be made:

- The quantity of fertilizer sold shows an increasing trend.
- For any given year, the sale of fertilizer peaks during the third quarter, or the months of July, August, and September, and falls in about the end of the fourth quarter and the first quarter. Thus, sales are seasonal.
- Something happened in October 1997 when the sale dropped dramatically. In researching records, it was noted that there was a fire in the plant during that period which cut down all activity for two weeks. This was an irregular occurrence.

Thus, data for fertilizer sales can be used to develop a relatively reliable forecast model.

Decomposing data

At first light, it might not be evident that past data can be developed into an appropriate forecasting model. As an illustration, Figure 10.9 shows the monthly sales in US dollars, over the last four years, of office filing cabinets manufactured by a producer in Texas. Initial

Figure 10.9 Sales of filing cabinets: All design types

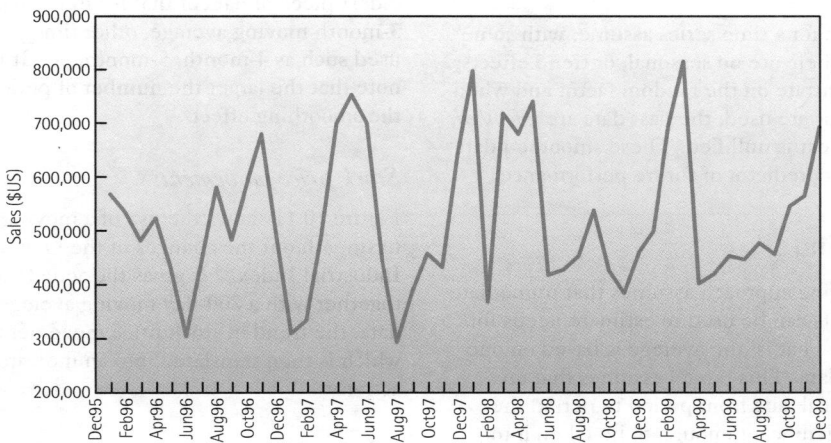

Figure 10.10 Sales of filing cabinets: According to design model

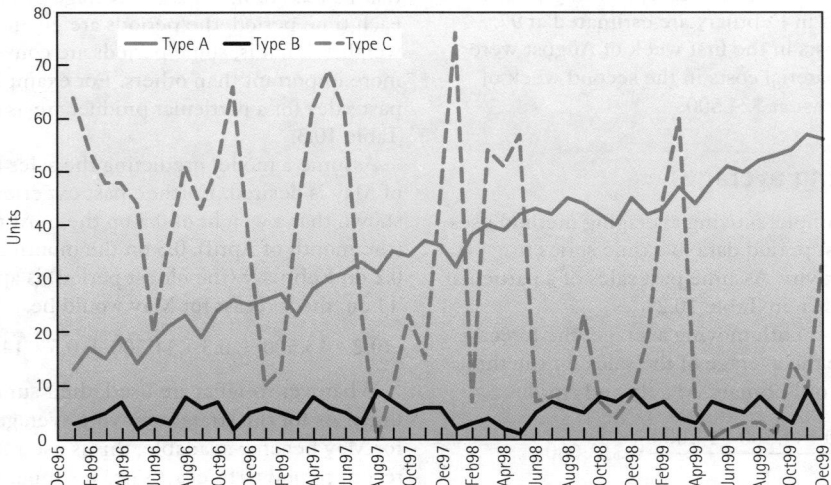

observations are that sales appear to be erratic and that it is difficult to discern a pattern.

A further study of the data is made, this time presenting the information in terms of units, rather than using financial figures. In addition, sales are broken down into three design types as shown in Figure 10.10. This time for two of the three models there appears to be a discernible pattern:

- Unit sales of design Type A are showing a steady increase.
- Unit sales of design Type B remain reasonably steady (not rising over ten units a month).

- It is design Type C which does not exhibit any pronounced pattern.

Thus, by decomposing the data, different forecasting models might be applied. Averaging or exponential models perhaps would be appropriate for designs B and C, and a linear regression model for design A. Even though the movement of Type C is wild there is more reliability for the other two types and thus by breaking down the data, the overall forecasting estimate to the firm can be improved, or the risk reduced, than if all the data had been taken together.

Average forecasting models

Averaging models for a time series assume, with some exceptions, that there are no seasonal, or trend effects. They only concentrate on the random factor and when averaging methods are used, the past data are *smoothed*, or the random effect is nullified. These smoothed data are then used as a predictor of future performance.

Naive averaging

The naive averaging approach assumes that immediate last period's results can be used to estimate needs for the next periods. That is, the average is based on one piece of sample data. This model assumes that on examining historical data from period to period the changes are not significant enough to be taken into consideration. As an illustration:

- Cash used in July was $17,500. Cash needs in August are estimated at $17,500.
- Personnel in Work zone A-101 were 97 in January. Personnel needs in February are estimated at 97.
- Raw material costs in the first week of August were $24,500. Raw material costs in the second week of August are forecast at $24,500.

Straight moving averages

The straight, or simple, moving averaging method uses the average of past period data in a time series to forecast future activity. Assume past sales of a particular product are as shown in Table 10.2.

Then using a 3-month moving average, the forecast for May would be the average of the sales for the three previous periods, or February, March, and April:

$$\frac{13,500 + 11,500 + 14,000}{3} = \$13,000$$

When the actual sales results for May become available, the forecast for June is then calculated by

Table 10.2 Past sales of a product: Straight moving average

January	$10,000
February	$13,500
March	$11,500
April	$14,000

using the average of the sales for March, April, and May. That is, one moves forward one period dropping the oldest piece of data or that for February. Instead of a 3-month moving average, other time periods can be used such as 4-month, 5-month, etc. It is important to note that the larger the number of periods, the greater the smoothing effect.

Stock price movements

Figure 10.11 shows the use of a moving average to smooth out the changes of the Dow Jones Industrial Index.[14] It gives the actual data for 1994 together with a 200-day moving average. From these data, the trend in stock price movements is illustrated which is then translated into an indicator of economic activity.

Weighted moving averages

The weighted moving average model is similar to the simple moving average approach except that instead of the straight average of the data for each time period, the periods are given different weights. That is, some periods are considered more important than others. For example, assume past sales for a particular product are as shown in Table 10.3.

Assume a model predicting the sales for the month of May is desired. Further, past experience has shown that a weight of 0.5 on the most recent period (the month of April), 0.3 on the month of March, and 0.2 on February (the oldest period) is appropriate. Then, the forecast for May would be:

$$(0.2 * 13,500 + 0.3 * 11,500 + 0.5 * 14,000) = \$13,150$$

Whatever weights are used, their sum *must* equal unity. As for the straight moving average, when the data for May become available, this is used for the most recent period to forecast sales for June. The data for February are then dropped.

Considerations in the averaging models

In using straight, or weighted moving averages in forecasting, increases and decreases are balanced, thus smoothing the forecast. In theory, the number of periods used can range from two up to the number of data points in the series. In the extreme case, if all data points were considered in the forecast, then the resulting model would be just the mean value for all the data. Caution has to be exercised, as the forecast is unreliable if a large number of periods are used and there is a trend.

Figure 10.11 Dow Jones Industrial Average

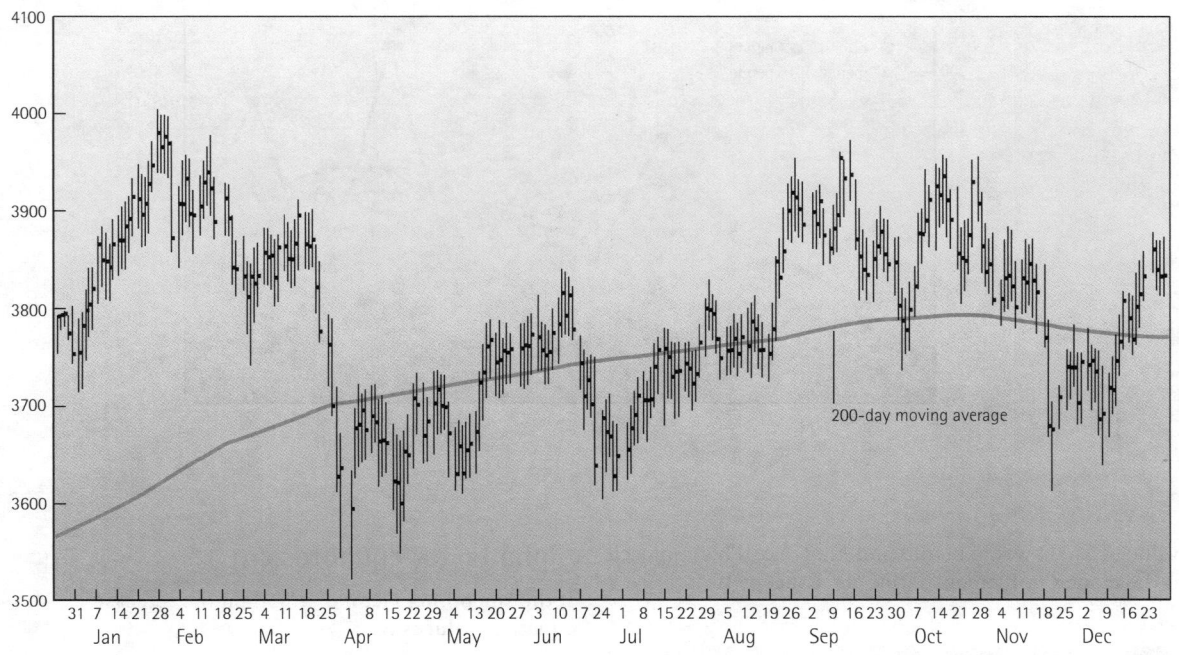

Table 10.3 Past sales of a product: Weighted moving average

January	$10,000
February	$13,500
March	$11,500
April	$14,000

The greater the number of periods, the greater the smoothing, or dampening effect, as illustrated in Figure 10.12, which shows actual data in a time series analysis, together with forecast model for two, four, and six periods. The smoothing effect is greater for six periods than it is for two periods. Also of interest is that all the models do not react immediately to changing patterns with the forecast lagging the actual data.

Model accuracy

When a forecasting model is developed by whatever method, it is important to know how well the model represents reality or how well the forecast compares to actual data. If there are wide discrepancies, then the model used is not appropriate, and another should be considered. It is rare that a forecast model will give perfectly accurate predictions all the time but a good model should give good indications of reality. One simple way of testing the averaging model is by using the concept of the mean absolute deviation, or MAD as now presented. Other methods for testing model accuracy are discussed in more detail towards the end of this chapter.

Mean absolute deviation

The mean absolute deviation is derived from the absolute deviation, which is the absolute value (the positive value) of the forecast error. The forecast error is the difference between the actual value, Y, and the forecast value $\hat{Y}$, in the same time period:

$$\text{Absolute deviation} = |(Y - \hat{Y})|$$

The mean absolute deviation then is the sum of each period absolute deviation divided by the number of data points, or periods in the series:

$$\text{Mean absolute deviation (MAD)} = \frac{\sum |(Y - \hat{Y})|}{n}$$

For each model that is developed, the mean absolute deviation is calculated, and the model with the lowest

Figure 10.12 Moving average forecasting

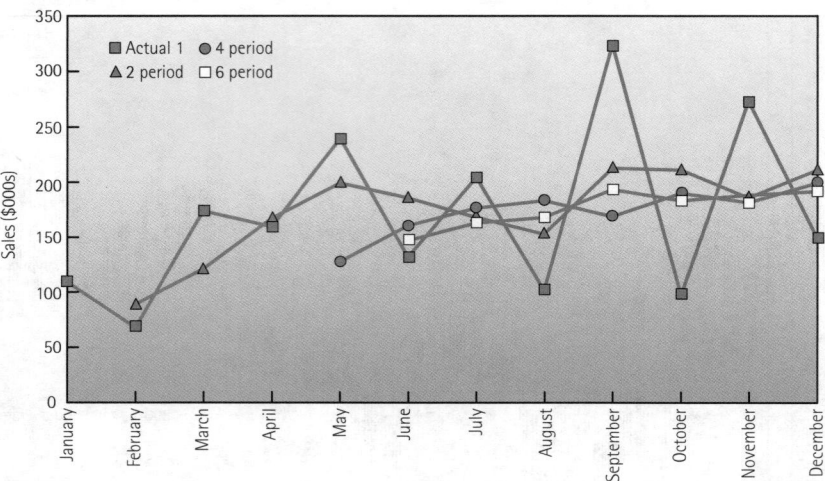

value of MAD would be the preferred one. This approach is developed in Demonstrating the concept 10.1.

Exponential smoothing

Exponential model

Exponential smoothing is somewhat similar to the moving averaging methods for forecasting but it eliminates some of the computational calculations.[15] The method develops a model using a single weighting, or smoothing factor, called alpha (α), which can take on a value greater than 0 but less than 1, to forecast the next period's activity. The mathematical model is:

$$F_{n+1} = F_n + \alpha(A_n - F_n)$$

or this can be rewritten:

$$F_{n+1} = \alpha A_n + (1 - \alpha)F_n$$

where:

- F_{n+1} is the forecast for next period
- F_n is the forecast for the current period
- α is the assigned alpha factor or smoothing constant
- A_n is the actual data for the current period.

For example, assume an automobile dealer predicted the sale of 23,000 vehicles for March in his region. The actual sales were 22,150. Using an α factor of 0.40 the forecast vehicle sales for April would be:

$$F_{April} = 23,000 + 0.40(22,150 - 23,000)$$
$$= 22,660 \text{ vehicles}$$

Alpha factor equal to zero

If the smoothing factor $\alpha = 0$, then the forecast equation reduces to:

$$F_{n+1} = F_n + 0(A_n - F_n) = F_n$$

This is the same as saying the new forecast is equal to the previous forecast which implies that there is no change in the data.

Alpha factor equal to unity

If the smoothing factor $\alpha = 1$, then the forecast equation reduces to:

$$F_{n+1} = F_n + 1(A_n - F_n) = A_n$$

This implies that the new forecast is equal to the previous actual data, which is the same as the naive averaging approach to forecasting.

Considerations in using exponential smoothing

- In exponential smoothing, the smaller the value of α, the greater the smoothing, or dampening effect, since a smaller portion of the actual data appears in the forecast. This is illustrated in Figure 10.13, where the actual data, and the model data for alpha values of 0.10, 0.50, and 0.90 are shown.
- Like the previously discussed straight, and weighted moving averaging methods, the forecast values in exponential smoothing lag the actual data. This is also illustrated in Figure 10.13.

Figure 10.13 Exponential smoothing: Effect of the value of alpha

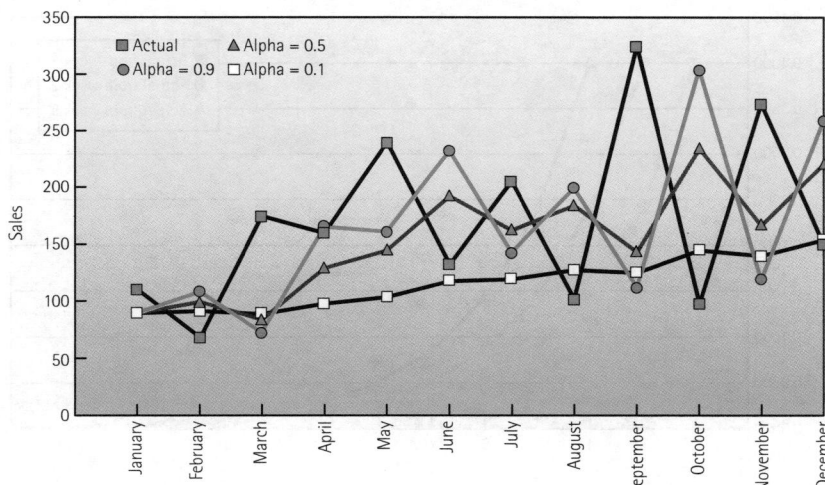

- The exponential smoothing method can only predict one period in advance.
- One needs an estimate of the first period forecast in order to develop the complete time series model. One way of estimating the first period's forecast is to take, say, arithmetic average of the actual data for the first three periods. Alternatively, the actual value for the first period is taken as the forecast value for the first period.

Model accuracy

The accuracy of the model developed by exponential smoothing can be determined in the same manner as the averaging methods using the criteria of the mean average deviation. This is illustrated in Demonstrating the concept 10.2.

Exponential profile

The reason why this forecasting approach is called exponential smoothing is illustrated as follows for an alpha factor of 0.4.

As indicated, the general equation for exponential smoothing is:

$$F_{n+1} = F_n + \alpha(A_n - F_n)$$

Profile periods

Second period The second period forecast is given by:

$$F_2 = F_1 + \alpha(A_1 - F_1) = F_1 + \alpha A_1 - \alpha F_1$$
$$= (1 - \alpha)F_1 + \alpha A_1$$

Thus, for the second period, the contribution of A_1 to the forecast is αA_1. With an alpha value of 0.4, the forecast data contain 0.4 of the actual data from Week 1.

Third period The third period forecast is given by:

$$F_3 = F_2 + \alpha(A_2 - F_2) = F_2 + \alpha A_2 - \alpha F_2$$
$$= (1 - \alpha)F_2 + \alpha A_2$$

Substituting the value of F_2 from the second period forecast in the equation for F_3 gives:

$$F_3 = (1 - \alpha)[(1 - \alpha)F_1 + \alpha A_1]) + \alpha A_2$$
$$= (1 - \alpha)^2 F_1 + \alpha(1 - \alpha)A_1 + \alpha A_2$$

Thus, here the contribution of A_1 to the forecast is $\alpha(1 - \alpha)A_1$ and for an alpha value of 0.4 the forecast data contain 0.24 of the actual data from Week 1 calculated from:

$$\alpha(1 - \alpha) = 0.4(1 - 0.4) = 0.24$$

Fourth period The fourth period forecast is given by:

$$F_4 = F_3 + \alpha(A_3 - F_3) = F_3 + \alpha A_3 - \alpha F_3$$
$$= (1 - \alpha)F_3 + \alpha A_3$$

Substituting the value of F_3 in the equation for F_4:

$$F_4 = (1 - \alpha)\,F_3 + \alpha A_3$$
$$= (1 - \alpha)\,[(1 - \alpha)^2 F_1 + \alpha(1 - \alpha)A_1 + \alpha A_2] + \alpha A_3$$

or:

$$F_4 = (1 - \alpha)^3\,F_1 + \alpha(1 - \alpha)^2 A_1 + \alpha(1 - \alpha)\,A_2 + \alpha A_3$$

Thus, for the fourth period the contribution of A_1 to the forecast is $\alpha(1 - \alpha)^2\,A_1$ and for an alpha factor of 0.4

Figure 10.14 Exponential smoothing: Fraction of actual data in forecast

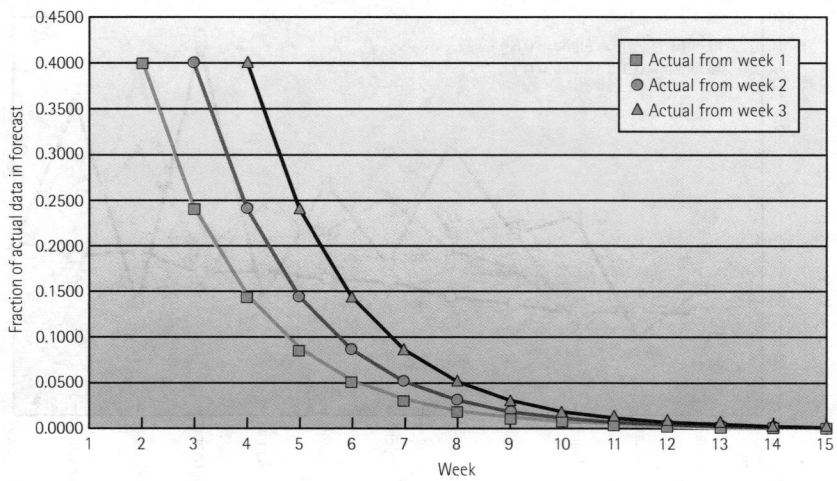

the forecast data contain 0.144 of the actual data from Week 1 as calculated from the relationship:

$$\alpha(1 - \alpha)^2 = 0.4(1 - 0.4)(1 - 0.4) = 0.144$$

The progression is similar for subsequent weeks in the forecast time horizon. For the nth period, the contribution of A_1 to the forecast is $\alpha(1 - \alpha)^{n-2}$, illustrating that the inclusion of the actual data for the first period, A_1, decreases exponentially with the increase in time.

This exponential decline of the forecast data is illustrated in Figure 10.14, supported from the data in Table 10.4.

Actual data from Week 2 and Week 3 follow the same exponentially decline as illustrated, except that there is a lag of one period in the fraction of data included.

Trend adjustment in exponential smoothing

Like the simple and weighting moving average methods, the simple exponential smoothing method smoothes out data, and there is a time lag in the forecast relative to the actual data. If there is a trend in the data the forecast will be additionally inexact. A modified version of exponential smoothing is with a trend adjustment factor. One model that is used is:[16]

$$FT_{n+1} = F_{n+1} + T_{n+1}$$

where:

- FT_{n+1} is the forecast for next period taking into account the trend adjustment

Table 10.4 Exponential decline of the forecast data

Week	Fraction of actual data from week 1 in forecast	Fraction of actual data from week 2 in forecast	Fraction of actual data from week 3 in forecast
1			
2	0.4000		
3	0.2400	0.4000	
4	0.1440	0.2400	0.4000
5	0.0864	0.1440	0.2400
6	0.0518	0.0864	0.1440
7	0.0311	0.0518	0.0864
8	0.0187	0.0311	0.0518
9	0.0112	0.0187	0.0311
10	0.0067	0.0112	0.0187
11	0.0040	0.0067	0.0112
12	0.0024	0.0040	0.0067
13	0.0015	0.0024	0.0040
14	0.0009	0.0015	0.0024
15	0.0005	0.0009	0.0015

- F_{n+1} is the forecast for the next period using simple exponential smoothing $= \alpha A_n + (1 - \alpha)F_n$
- T_{n+1} is the exponentially smoothed trend factor for the next period.

The exponentially smoothed trend factor is given by the relationship:

$$T_{n+1} = \beta(F_{n+1} - F_n) + (1 - \beta)T_n$$

where:

- β is a smoothing constant for the trend
- T_n is the exponentially smoothed trend factor for the current period.

As for the α value, factor β takes on a value between 0 and 1 but not equal to these values.

Demonstrating the concept 10.3 illustrates the trend adjustment in exponential smoothing using this method.

Simple linear regression in a time series

Simple linear regression in a time series is a useful tool for modelling when there is an increasing or a decreasing trend in the given data. The analytical procedure involves the development of a linear relationship between a dependent variable of interest such as sales revenues, profits, units sold, etc., and the time period, or the independent variable. Time is always independent since even if there is an earthquake, a fire, or a business goes bankrupt, tomorrow will arrive and be another time period, independent of any event.

Objective

The objective in simple linear regression is to develop a linear relationship of the general form:

$$\hat{Y} = a + bX$$

where:

- a is a constant, and the intercept on the y axis
- b is a constant, and the slope of the line
- X is the time, or the independent variable
- $\hat{Y}$ is the predicted, or forecast value of the dependent variable.

When this equation is developed, knowing a value of the independent variable, X, the value of the dependent variable, $\hat{Y}$ can be estimated. This would give a forecast, or estimate, for the corresponding value of X.

Least squares method

The method of least squares determines the best straight line for the given data, Y, by minimizing the error between the estimated points from the calculated line, and the actual observed points used to draw the line. Using the least squares method, the values of a and b are given by the following relationships. The variable n is the number of data points:

$$a = \frac{\sum X^2 \sum Y - \sum X \sum XY}{n \sum X^2 - \left(\sum X\right)^2} \quad \text{(i)}$$

$$b = \frac{n \sum XY - \sum X \sum Y}{n \sum X^2 - \left(\sum X\right)^2} \quad \text{(ii)}$$

Alternatively, a and b can be calculated from the relationships below using the linear equation of the line:

$$a = \overline{Y} - b\overline{X} \quad \text{(iii)}$$

$$b = \frac{\sum XY - n\overline{XY}}{\sum X^2 - n(\overline{X})^2} \quad \text{(iv)}$$

where $\overline{X}$ is the mean of the X values, and $\overline{Y}$ is the mean of the Y values.

Derivation of the linear equation

To illustrate the derivation, and use of the linear equation Table 10.5 gives the data for the filing cabinets, design type A, presented earlier in Figure 10.10. In the columns the values X represent the coded time period such that 1 is January 1996, 2 is February 1996, 3 is March 1996, etc., right up to 48 which is December 1999. The values Y are the actual number of units sold. The other columns and cells gives the values necessary for determining statistical values for the terms in the method of least squares.

Using either equation (i) or (iii) gives a = 14.3661 and either equation (ii) and (iv) gives b = 0.8541. Then, inserting these values in the standard regression function we get the following equation:

$$\hat{Y} = 14.3661 + 0.8541X$$

This then is the mathematical model that represents the sale of the filing cabinets. This regression function is shown plotted with the actual sales data in Figure 10.15. Note that the developed regression equation is a good representation of the real values. As a test, substitution of the value 48 in the equation (December 1999) gives a value of Y as follows:

$$\hat{Y} = 14.3661 + 0.8541 * 48 = 55.3631 \text{ or } 55 \text{ units}$$

Table 10.5 Sale of filing cabinets according to design

Date	X	Y	X²	X*Y	Y²
January 96	1	13	1	13	169
February 96	2	17	4	34	289
March 96	3	15	9	45	225
April 96	4	19	16	76	361
May 96	5	14	25	70	196
June 96	6	18	36	108	324
July 96	7	21	49	147	441
August 96	8	23	64	184	529
September 96	9	19	81	171	361
October 96	10	24	100	240	576
November 96	11	26	121	286	676
December 96	12	25	144	300	625
January 97	13	26	169	338	676
February 97	14	27	196	378	729
March 97	15	23	225	345	529
April 97	16	28	256	448	784
May 97	17	30	289	510	900
June 97	18	31	324	558	961
July 97	19	33	361	627	1,089
August 97	20	31	400	620	961
September 97	21	35	441	735	1,225
October 97	22	34	484	748	1,156
November 97	23	37	529	851	1,369
December 97	24	36	576	864	1,296
January 98	25	32	625	800	1,024
February 98	26	38	676	988	1,444
March 98	27	40	729	1,080	1,600
April 98	28	39	784	1,092	1,521
May 98	29	42	841	1,218	1,764

(Continued)

Table 10.5 (Continued)

Date	X	Y	X²	X*Y	Y²
June 98	30	43	900	1,290	1,849
July 98	31	42	961	1,302	1,764
August 98	32	45	1,024	1,440	2,025
September 98	33	44	1,089	1,452	1,936
October 98	34	42	1,156	1,428	1,764
November 98	35	40	1,225	1,400	1,600
December 98	36	45	1,296	1,620	2,025
January 99	37	42	1,369	1,554	1,764
February 99	38	43	1,444	1,634	1,849
March 99	39	47	1,521	1,833	2,209
April 99	40	44	1,600	1,760	1,936
May 99	41	48	1,681	1,968	2,304
June 99	42	51	1,764	2,142	2,601
July 99	43	50	1,849	2,150	2,500
August 99	44	52	1,936	2,288	2,704
September 99	45	53	2,025	2,385	2,809
October 99	46	54	2,116	2,484	2,916
November 99	47	57	2,209	2,679	3,249
December 99	48	56	2,304	2,688	3,136
Total	1,176	1,694	38,024	49,371	66,740

Variable	n	$(\Sigma X)^2$	$\bar{X}$	$\bar{Y}$	$(\Sigma Y)^2$
Value	48	1,382,976	24.5000	35.2917	2,869,636

This compares well with the value of 56 units from the data in Table 10.5.

Using the model

Once the regression model has been developed, it can be used to forecast future sales. For example, suppose one is interested to know the sales in June 2000. The coded value for June 2000 is 54 and this is the value X.

Figure 10.15 Sales of filing cabinets: Design type A with regression line

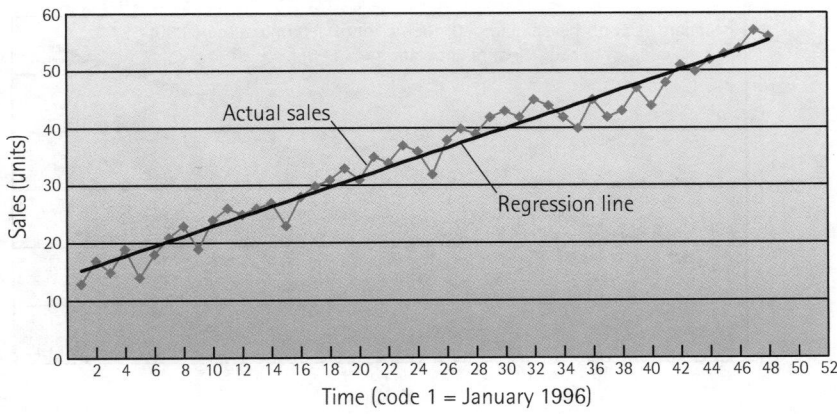

Substituting this value of 54 in the regression equation gives a forecast value of:

$$\hat{Y} = 14.3661 + 0.8541 * 54 = 60.4877 \text{ or } 61 \text{ units}$$

Standard error of the estimate

The standard error of the estimate measures the amount of variability, or scatter, around a regression line. The regression equation is established such that the vertical distance between the observed values, Y, and the predicted values, Y, balance out when all the values above and below the line are considered. Or mathematically:

$$\sum(Y - \hat{Y}) = 0$$

The standard error of the estimate, for n data points, is given by the relationship:

$$S_{Y/X} = \sqrt{\frac{\sum(Y - \hat{Y})^2}{n-2}}$$

This can be rewritten by using the identity:

$$\sum(Y - \hat{Y})^2 = \sum Y^2 - a\left(\sum Y\right) - b\left(\sum XY\right)$$

giving:

$$S_{Y/X} = \sqrt{\frac{\sum(Y - \hat{Y})^2}{n-2}} = \sqrt{\frac{\sum Y^2 - a\left(\sum Y\right) - b\left(\sum XY\right)}{n-2}}$$

Substituting the appropriate values from the data for the filing cabinets into the standard error of the estimate equation gives a value:

$$S_{Y/X} = 2.2634$$

The standard error of the estimate written $S_{Y/X}$ or S_e has the same units as the dependent variable, Y, and in this case is unit sales. The standard error of the estimate is analogous to the standard deviation used for example in sampling (see Chapters 20 and 27). In this latter case, the standard deviation measures variability around the mean (for example) whereas the standard error of the estimate measures variability around the regression line. One difference is that in the standard deviation for a sample of size n the value $(n - 1)$ is used in the denominator, whereas in the regression analysis $(n - 2)$ is used. This is because two degrees of freedom are lost, since two statistics, a and b, are used in the standard error equation in order to compute the standard error. Like the standard deviation, the closer the value of the standard error is to zero, the better the linear regression model fits the observed data. This concept is illustrated in Figures 10.16, 10.17, and 10.18. In the first two where there is a perfect fit, the standard error of the estimate is zero, and in the third it is 13.86.

Certainty and confidence limits

Assume that the question is asked: 'What is the 90% confidence limit for a predicted unit sales of file cabinets in June 2000?' The confidence interval is given by the relationship:

$$\hat{Y} \pm z.s_e \quad \text{or} \quad \hat{Y} \pm t.s_e$$

for small sample sizes.
  For the file cabinet relationship:

- n, the sample size is 48. Since it is greater than 30, z rather than t tables are used
- degrees of freedom are 46 (although degrees of freedom are only necessary for t tables)

Figure 10.16 Linear regression line with perfect positive fit

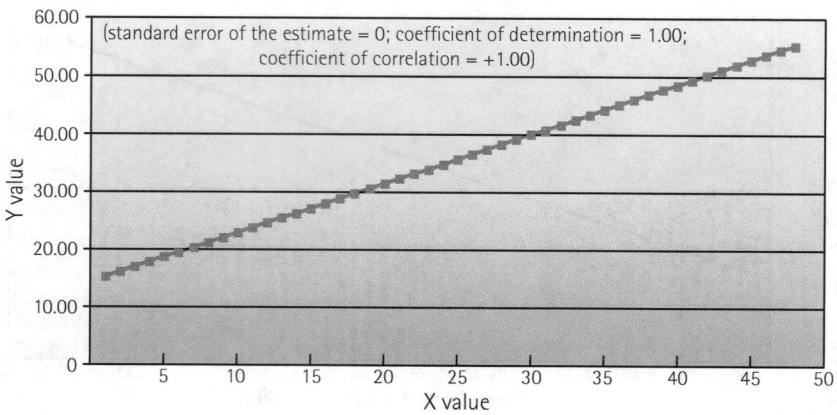

Figure 10.17 Linear regression line with perfect negative fit

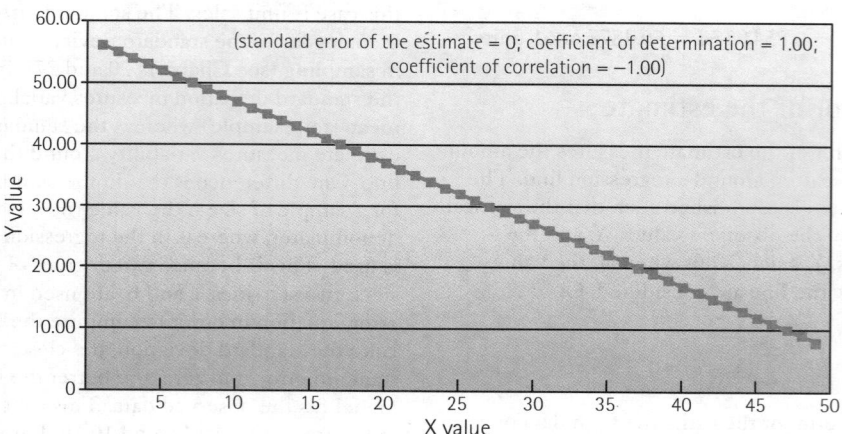

Figure 10.18 Linear regression line with no fit

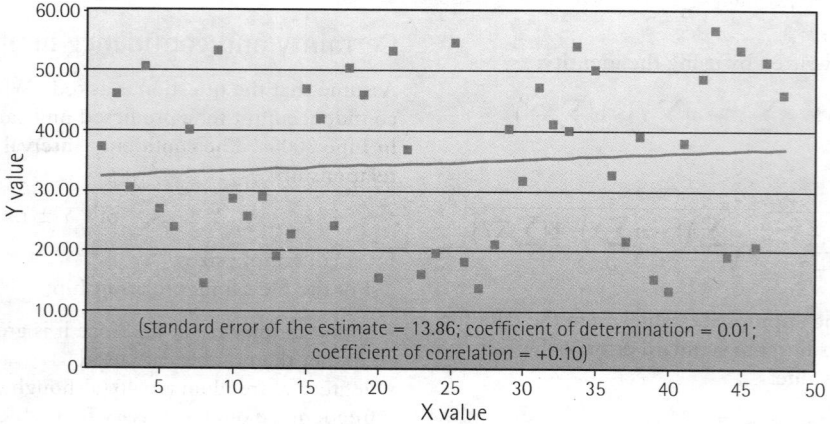

- z = 1.6449
- standard error = 2.2642
- z * standard error = 1.6449 * 2.2642 = 3.7244
- upper limit = 60.4877 + 3.7244 = 64.2121
- lower limit = 60.4877 − 3.7244 = 56.7633.

Thus, the response to the question would be that the forecast, or estimate, of unit sales in June 2000 is 60 units and there is a 90% confidence that the unit sales will lie between 57 and 64 units (rounding).

Coefficient of determination

In regression analysis the coefficient of determination, r^2, measures the variation in the dependent variable, Y, which is explained by the fitted simple regression equation. It is a measure of the strength of the relationship between the dependent and independent value. The value of r^2 is calculated from the ratio of the explained variation, to the total variation as follows:

$$r^2 = \frac{\text{Explained variation}}{\text{Total variation}}$$
$$= \frac{\text{Sum of squares due to regression}}{\text{Total sum of squares}}$$
$$= \frac{SSR}{SST} = \frac{\sum (\hat{Y} - \bar{Y})^2}{\sum (Y - \bar{Y})^2} \qquad \text{(i)}$$

where:

$$\text{Total variation} = \text{Explained variation} + \text{Unexplained variation}$$

Reorganizing:

$$\text{Explained variation} = \text{Total variation} - \text{Unexplained variation}$$

Then the coefficient of determination can also be written:

$$r^2 = \frac{\text{Total variation} - \text{Unexplained variation}}{\text{Total variation}}$$
$$= 1 - \frac{\text{Unexplained variation}}{\text{Total variation}} \qquad \text{(ii)}$$

The concept of explained and unexplained variation is illustrated in Figure 10.19. This shows a portion of the data for the sale in units of file cabinets design Type A from a coded time period 23 to 30. In addition to the actual data and the regression line also shown is the average value of Y or Y bar, $\bar{Y}$. If one considers the time period 27 then the following are the coordinates at this data point for the three curves:

the coordinates on the actual data curves are (X_{27}, Y_{27})

the coordinates on the regression curve are $(X_{27}, \hat{Y}_{27})$

the coordinates on the average curve for Y are $(X_{27}, \bar{Y}_{27})$.

Further:

the total variation from the mean at this point is $(Y_{27} - \bar{Y}_{27})$

the unexplained variation is $(Y_{27} - \hat{Y}_{27})$

the explained variation, or accounted for by the regression line is $(\hat{Y}_{27} - \bar{Y}_{27})$.

These variations are illustrated in Figure 10.19.

Figure 10.19 **Measure of variation in a regression line**

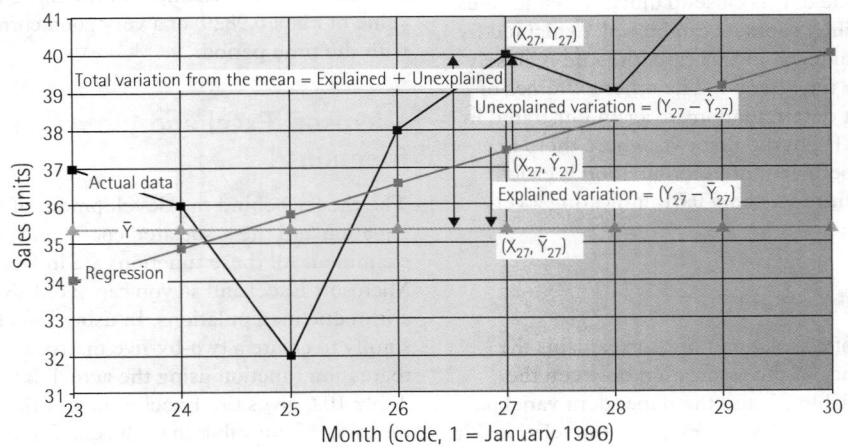

Table 10.6 Microsoft Excel and regression functions

	Column 1	Explanation	Column 2	Explanation
Row 1	b	Slope due to variable (X)	a	Intercept on y axis
Row 2	se_b	Standard error for slope (b)	se_a	Standard error for intercept a
Row 3	r^2	Coefficient of determination	S_e	Standard error of estimate
Row 4	F	F-ratio for analysis of variance	df	Degrees of freedom (n − 2)
Row 5	SS_{reg}	Sum of squares due to regression (explained variation)	SS_{resid}	Sum of squares of residual (unexplained variation)

Going further from equations (i) and (ii) the coefficient of determination can be defined as:

$$r^2 = 1 - \frac{\text{Error sum of squares}}{\text{Total variation}} = 1 - \frac{\text{SSE}}{\text{SST}}$$

$$= 1 - \frac{\sum(Y - \hat{Y})^2}{\sum(Y - \overline{Y})^2} \qquad \text{(iii)}$$

Using the summation rules (see Chapter 27), the coefficient of determination can be rewritten:

$$r^2 = \frac{a\left(\sum Y\right) + b\left(\sum XY\right) - \left(\left(\sum Y\right)^2 / n\right)}{\sum Y^2 - \left(\left(\sum Y\right)^2 / n\right)} \qquad \text{(iv)}$$

For the filing cabinet situation, substituting the calculated values from Table 10.5 into equation (iv) gives a value of the coefficient of determination of 0.9661. The coefficient of determination is always positive and the closer the value of r^2 is to unity, the more the value of Y is explained by the regression model containing the independent variable X. In this example, the value of r^2 is close to unity, which implies that the sale of filing cabinets can be well explained by the regression model or, in this case, the sale is closely explained by the time period. The other extremes of the coefficient of determination are again illustrated in Figure 10.16–10.18. In the first two, where there is a perfect fit, the coefficient of determination is exactly 1.00, and in the third it is only 0.01, indicating a very poor fit.

Coefficient of correlation

The coefficient of correlation r or $\pm\sqrt{r^2}$ explains the relative importance of the association between the independent variable, X, and the dependent variable, Y, or another measure of the strength of the relationship

Table 10.7 Matrix for the filing cabinet example

b	0.8541	a	14.3661
se_b	0.0236	se_a	0.6640
r^2	0.9661	S_e	2.2642
F	1310.7826	df	46
SS_{reg}	6720.0851	SS_{resid}	235.8316

between the two variables. The coefficient of correlation can take a value between ±1 and has the same sign as the slope of the curve. A value of −1 indicates a perfect negative relationship (Y decreases as X increases). A value of +1 indicates a perfect positive relationship (Y increases as X increases). Zero, or a very low value, would mean there is no relationship between X and Y. The coefficient of correlation is again illustrated in Figures 10.16–10.18. In the first curve r = +1.00, in the second r = −1.00, and in the third +0.10, or a poor correlation. In the example of the filing cabinets, the value of r is +0.9829, or a very good correlation of sales with the time period.

Microsoft Excel and the regression functions

The theory behind the development of the regression equation and the associated coefficients has so far been examined. All these functions are in fact built into Microsoft Excel and so you can avoid all of the arithmetic manipulations. In using Excel you need simply to create a two-by-five matrix and insert the regression function using the actual data points. Table 10.6 gives the Excel format of the matrix and the meaning of the value in each cell. Table 10.7 is the corresponding matrix for the filing cabinet example. In addition, from the graph of actual data, the regression line, the equation, and the coefficient of determination can be directly determined.

Causal forecasting and linear regression

Causal relationships

Causal forecasting is when sales or other activity, are related, or *caused*, by some other event. For example:

* The forecast sale of compact discs (CDs) increases as the sale of CD players increases.
* There is a reduced demand for dairy products as a result of a correlation with cholesterol (present in dairy products), and heart ailments.
* The demand for smaller automobiles increases as the price of gasoline rises.
* There is an increase in the use of public transport as city congestion increases.
* There is an increase in the incidence of skin cancer with increased exposure to the sun.
* The revenues for Microsoft increase as the sale of personal computers manufactured by say, Compaq, Dell, and IBM increases. This is because Microsoft Windows is the operating system for most personal computers and so, for every computer sold, there is a Windows system and more often than not, a Windows office package is sold (containing Word, Excel, PowerPoint, etc.).

Although time is not a direct correlating factor some causal events do occur over a changing time period.

Scatter diagram

A scatter diagram is a two-dimensional graph showing the x and y coordinates of various observations. The lines between successive data points may not be shown but the diagram appears simply as a series of data points or dots. The purpose of the scatter diagram is to examine visually if there appears to be a relationship, or pattern, between the two sets of data. If so, perhaps it can it be used for forecasting, or estimating, future activity. In a scatter diagram the variable believed to be dependent on another observation is plotted on the y axis and the other independent variable is plotted on the x axis. The objective is to see if there is a causal effect of the independent variable on the dependent variable. The approach is similar to the time series analysis, except that in the time series the dependent variable is time.

Figure 10.20 is a scatter diagram for the number of equivalent personnel days absent every month and the number of defective units discovered that same month for an assembly operation. The number of defective components is plotted on the y axis, and the employees absent a week plotted on the x axis. The purpose is to see if there is a relationship, or dependency, on defective units, and operator absenteeism. From the graph, it does appear so, in that the number of defective units increases with absenteeism. In this case, the question posed is: 'Is the rate of absenteeism a cause of product defects?'

Figure 10.20 **Absenteeism and defective components: Scatter diagram**

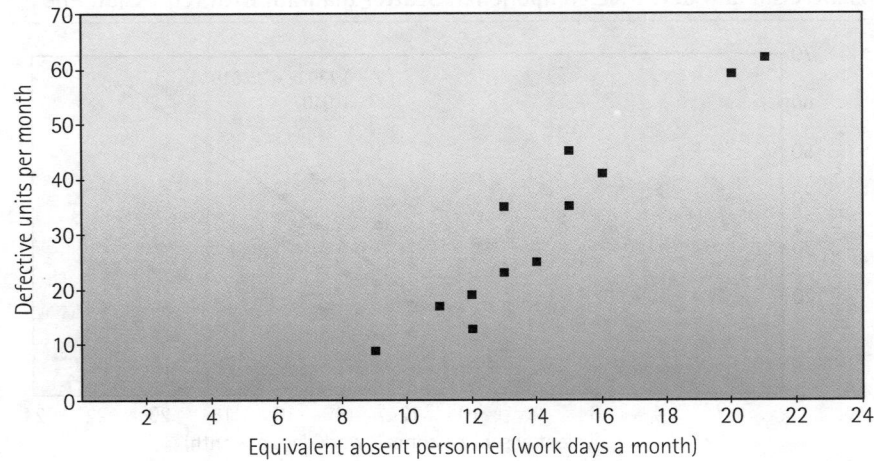

Linear regression equation

The data in Table 10.8 are those from which Figure 10.20 was developed.

Table 10.8 Linear regression

Employees absent (days) X	Defective products (units) Y	Employees absent (days) X	Defective products (units) Y
15	45	12	13
13	35	16	41
12	19	14	25
11	17	20	59
13	23	21	62
9	9	15	35

Table 10.9 Results using Microsoft Excel

b	4.7393	a	−35.6182
se_b	0.4692	se_a	6.8677
r^2	0.9107	s_e	5.4364
F	102.0287	df	10
SS_{reg}	3,015.3748	SS_{resid}	295.5419

In calculating absenteeism, two people absent for four days and one person absent for 3 days would be considered 11 days. As for a time series, the objective is to develop a linear equation of the form:

$$\hat{Y} = a + bX$$

where:

- X is absenteeism and the independent variable
- $\hat{Y}$ is the predicted value of the number of defective components
- a is a constant and the intercept on the y axis
- b is a constant, and the slope of the curve.

Using the regression function in Microsoft Excel gives statistical data as shown in Table 10.9.

Substituting the values for a and b gives the following regression equation:

$$\hat{Y} = a + bX = -35.6182 + 4.7393X$$

This regression line is plotted in Figure 10.21. Again, the line is such that the vertical distance between the observed Y value, and the predicted value, $\hat{Y}$ from the regression equation balance out. In other words, the Y values above the regression line, cancel out the Y values below the line.

Prediction

As in the time series analysis, once the causal regression equation has been determined, it can be used to predict other values of $\hat{Y}$, given the corresponding value of X. For example, if 18 employees are absent, the estimate of defective parts can be calculated from the regression equation:

$$\hat{Y} = a + bX = -35.6182 + 4.7393X$$

Figure 10.21 Absenteeism and defective components: Scatter diagram with regression line

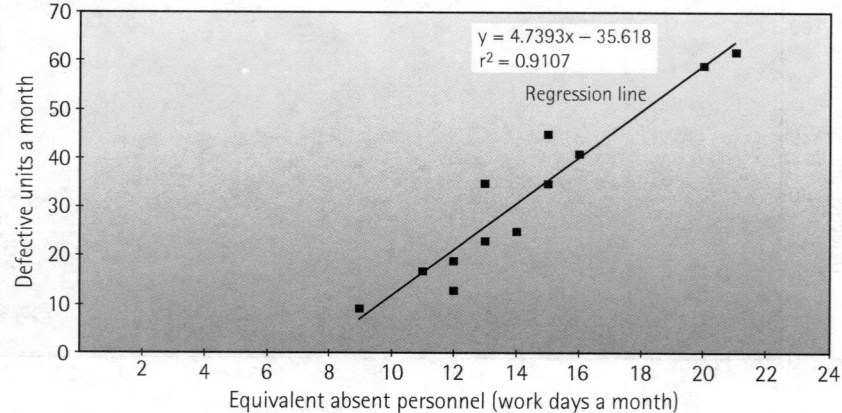

where:

- X = 18
- $\hat{Y} = a + bX = -35.6182 + 4.7393 * 18$
- $\hat{Y} = 49.6892$ (or an estimate of about 50 parts).

One must be careful in using the regression equation, for extrapolating beyond the data values given for X, because values for X to give $\hat{Y}$ may not be valid in this range.

Certainty and confidence limits

Assume the question is asked: 'What is the 90% confidence limit for a predicted number of defective parts?' The confidence interval is given by the relationship:

$$\hat{Y} \pm z.s_e \text{ or } \hat{Y} \pm t.s_e$$

for small sample sizes.

For the operator absenteeism relationship:

- n, the sample size is 12 and since it is less than 30, t rather than z tables are used
- degrees of freedom are 10 (here the degrees of freedom are needed for calculation)
- t = 1.8125
- standard error = 5.4364
- t * standard error = 5.4364 * 1.8125 = 9.8534
- upper limit = 49.6892 + 9.8534 = 59,54245 (say 60)
- lower limit = 49.6892 − 9.8534 = 39,8356 (say 40).

Thus, the response to the question would be that the forecast estimate of defective parts is 50 and there is a 90% confidence that the defective parts will lie between 60 and 40.

Coefficient of determination

From Excel the coefficient of determination, r^2, is 0.9107 as shown on the curve. This can be interpreted by saying that 91.07% of the product defects are explained by the simple linear regression equation based on absenteeism. Thus, one can say that there is a strong linear relationship between product defects and absenteeism.

Coefficient of correlation

The coefficient of correlation, r, is 0.9543 or again there is a strong linear relationship between product defects and absenteeism. Here, the idea of correlation is perhaps more understandable than for a time series as here one is saying there is a correlation between one

clearly measurable variable, quality, and another clearly measurable variable, absenteeism. Correlation with time is looser as many variables change with time.

Seasonal effects and forecasting

In the previous example for filing cabinets there was no apparent seasonal effect on the sales. For certain products, the activity is seasonal, such as in the northern hemisphere the demand for snow ski equipment is higher in the late autumn and winter months or the demand for swimwear is higher in the spring and summer months. The seasonal impact has already been shown with the sale of NPK fertilizer presented earlier in the chapter.

Seasonal models

In the section on modelling, a time series was represented as a function of a trend, a seasonal factor, a factor according to the business cycle, and random occurrences and illustrated by a multiplication and additive model. To use these models to determine seasonal effects we can ignore the business cycle factor on the basis that its time span is much longer than the normal forecasting period. Further, averaging forecasting methods, if there is no seasonal effect, can be used to treat the random effect. In this case, the multiplication and additive models can be reduced, respectively, to the following simpler forms:

$$Y = T_f * S_f$$

$$Y = T_f + S_f$$

where:

- Y is the observed, or actual values (sales for example)
- T_f is the sales trend over time on the assumption no external events are intervening
- S_f is a factor due to seasonal variations.

The objective of a seasonal analysis is to isolate the trend and the seasonal effect in order to forecast future sales.

Calculation procedure

The following is the calculation procedure to take into account the seasonal effects in a time series:

1. The raw data are plotted to see if there is a trend and a seasonal effect. The latter will be apparent if there are peaks and valleys at regular seasonal periods.

2. A centred moving average is determined around the time period in consideration. The centred moving average covers the six months prior to the quarter in question, and the six months after. In this way, by taking the average over one year the seasonal effect is smoothed.

   As an illustration, suppose one is considering the centred moving average around the summer. The middle of the quarter will be mid-summer, or 15 August. Six months before this period will include the first half of summer, all of spring, and one half of winter. Six months after will include the last half of summer, the autumn, and one half of the winter in the following year. The calculation is given by:

   $$\left[\frac{0.5 * Winter(n) + Spring(n) + Summer(n) + Autumn(n) + 0.5 * Winter(n+1)}{4} \right]$$

   where n is the data for a given year and (n + 1) is the data for the following year. Note that the seasons are broken up on a calendar quarter basis or 1 January to 31 March, 1 April to 30 June, 1 July to 30 September and 1 October to 31 December, rather than the seasonal equinoxes (about 21 March and 23 September), and the seasonal solstices (about 22 June and 22 December).

3. Divide actual sales by the centred moving average for each quarter. This is the specific seasonal index, SI, for each quarter.

4. Determine an average seasonal index, SI, for each of the four seasonal quarters. For example if four years are being considered, the average seasonal index for the summer would be the average of all the calculated SIs for the summer or:

   $$\left[\frac{(SI \ Year \ 1 + SI \ Year \ 2 + SI \ Year \ 3 + SI \ Year \ 4)}{4} \text{ for each summer} \right]$$

5. Remove the seasonal effect from the actual sales. In the multiplication model, this is by dividing the actual sales, Y, by the corresponding index for that quarter. This procedure is arrived at from the rewritten model:

   $$T_f = \frac{Y}{S_f}$$

   In the case of the additive model this would be arrived at from the rewritten expression:

   $$T_f = Y - S_f$$

6. Perform a regression analysis on the deseasonalized sales using, if necessary, a code value corresponding to the quarter. (In Excel the date is a numerical value and can be used in the calculation.) Determine the value of the intercept, a, and the slope, b.

7. Forecast deseasonalized sales for the next four quarters using the linear regression equation of the form:

   $$\hat{Y} = a + bX$$

8. Determine the forecast seasonalized sales from the regression forecast data. For the multiplication model this is given by the expression:

   $$\hat{Y} = T_f \times S_f$$

   For the additive model this is given by the expression:

   $$\hat{Y} = T_f + S_f$$

The procedure is illustrated for the multiplication model in Demonstrating the concept 10.4.

Empirical approach

Another method to take into account seasonal variations is an empirical approach by making a judgmental analysis on the available information. For example, assume that sales data for two successive years, Year 1, and Year 2, are available on a monthly basis. If there is a seasonal variation then the following is an empirical approach used to make a forecast:

1. Determine the difference in sales between similar months for Year 1, and Year 2.
2. Calculate average monthly difference for the complete 12 months.
3. Add the average difference between Year 1 and Year 2, to each month on Year 2 to obtain a forecast for Year 3.

Multiple regression forecasting

The limit of simple linear regression is that only one independent variable is considered whereas in the business world forecasts are very often a function of many variables. Multiple regression is a way to overcome this constraint as more than one independent variable is considered in the forecasting model, or regression equation. For example, it may be determined that the sales of a particular product are a function of independent variables such as the advertising expenditure, the number of salespeople, the number of sales contacts, the number of sales offices, the number of competing products, etc. That is, forecast sales are a function of many independent variables.

Two independent variables

If it is believed that sales are a function of two independent variables such as advertising expenditures, and the size of the salesforce, then perhaps a multiple regression equation model could be developed to describe the movement of sales. The regression equation would take the general form:

$$\hat{Y} = a + b_1 X_1 + b_2 X_2$$

where:

- a is a constant and the intercept on the y axis
- X_1 and X_2 are the independent variables (here, the number of sales persons and advertising budget)
- b_1 and b_2 are constants and slopes of the line corresponding to X_1 and X_2
- $\hat{Y}$ is the forecast value given by the best straight line for the actual data.

With two independent variables the data can be represented graphically on a three-dimensional axis, as illustrated in Figure 10.22.

To calculate the best straight line the least squares method can again be used. This locates the plane that minimizes the sum of the squares of the errors or the distance from the actual data points around the plane to the corresponding points on the plane. Using the actual data, the following three equations can be used to calculate the values of the constants:

$$\sum Y = na + b_1 \sum X_1 + b_2 \sum X_2$$
$$\sum X_1 Y = a \sum X_1 + b_1 \sum X_1^2 + b_2 \sum X_1 X_2$$
$$\sum X_2 Y = a \sum X_2 + b_1 \sum X_1 X_2 + b_2 \sum X_2^2$$

In the first equation, n is the number of data points. These three equations can be solved to determine the values of the intercept on the y axis, a, and the values of

the slopes b_1 and b_2. The use of multiple regression using two variables is illustrated by the first part of Demonstrating the concept 10.5 using the Microsoft Excel functions.

Multiple independent variables

The regression model may contain multiple independent variables. In this case the following would represent the regression equation:

$$\hat{Y} = a + b_1 X_1 + b_2 X_2 \ldots b_k X_k$$

where k would take the value of the number of independent variables being considered. The greater the number of independent variables the more complex the model, and perhaps the more uncertain the predicted value.

Microsoft Excel and multiple regression

As for simple linear regression, multiple regression functions can be solved using a computer program such as 'Linear regression' in Microsoft Excel. In Excel, when the y data, and the x matrix are entered into the regression function, the various statistical data are computed according to Table 10.10.

Table 10.10 Linear regression computations

b_k Slope due to variable, X_k	b_{k-1} Slope due to to variable, X_{k-1}	b_2 Slope due to variable, X_2	b_1 Slope due to variable, X_1	a intercept on Y axis
se_k standard error for slope, b_k	se_{k-1} standard error for slope, b_{k-1}	se_2 standard error for slope, b_2	se_1 standard error for slope, b_1	se_a standard error for intercept a
r^2 coefficient of determination	S_e standard error of estimate			
F ratio	df degrees of freedom			
SS_{reg} sum of squares due to regression (explained variation)	SS_{resid} sum of squares of residual (unexplained variation)			

Figure 10.22 Multiple regression plane (two independent variables)

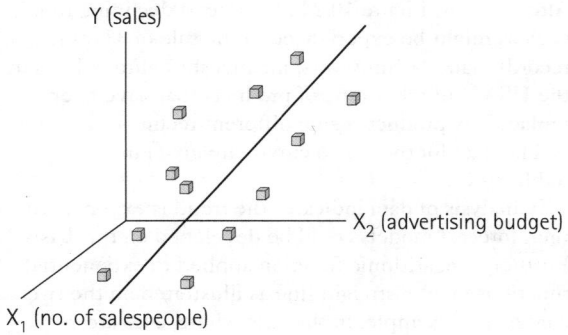

Y (sales)

X_2 (advertising budget)

X_1 (no. of salespeople)

Standard error of the estimate

The standard error of the estimate s_e (also known as the root mean square error, or mse) measures the degree of dispersion around the multiple regression plane. The value is given by:

$$s_e = \sqrt{\frac{\sum(Y - \hat{Y})^2}{n - k - 1}}$$

where:

- Y = an actual value of the dependent variable
- $\hat{Y}$ = estimated value of dependent variable predicted from the regression equation
- n = number of data points in the sample
- k = number of independent variables.

The denominator $(n - k - 1)$ is the number of degrees of freedom. For example, in a situation where there are ten data points for simple linear regression:

$n = 10 \quad k = 1 \quad$ degrees of freedom is $10 - 1 - 1 = 8$

Where there are three independent variables, then:

$n = 10 \quad k = 3 \quad$ degrees of freedom is $10 - 3 - 1 = 6$

Again, the smaller the value of the standard error of the estimate, the better the fit of the regression equation.

Confidence intervals

The confidence intervals of the predicted value for small samples are:

$$\hat{Y} \pm t \times s_e$$

Coefficient of multiple determination

The coefficient of multiple determination, r^2, measures the strength of the relationship among the independent variables. It is that fraction that represents the proportion of the total variation of Y that is 'explained' by the regression plane.

The use of multiple regression using two and three variables with the determination of the standard error of estimate, confidence intervals, and the coefficient of determination is illustrated by Demonstrating the concept 10.5.

Non–linear regression

Linear and multiple forecasting regression models assume that the forecast changes linearly, or at a constant amount according to the slope, with the change in the dependent variable. There are many situations when this is not the case, and the increases are a non-linear, or curvilinear function of the independent variable. For example:

- The rapid increase in demand of electronic calculators in the 1980s after they were first introduced by Texas Instruments.
- The rapid increase in demand for personal computers in the late 1980s and 1990s.
- The sharp decline in the demand for 33 rpm records in the early 1990s after the introduction of the compact disc.
- The rapid increase in the sale of portable phones in Europe in the 1990s.
- The increase in people contaminated with HIV in the 1980s and 1990s, particularly on the African continent.
- The propagation of viruses on the Internet such as the *I love you* virus, sent from the Philippines in 2000.

The curvilinear function can be a complex relationship between the dependent and the independent variables. Some basic forms include an exponential function, polynomial where the independent variable takes on integer values or non-integer values.

Exponential change

An exponential change moves according the general function $Y = ae^{bx}$ where a and b are constants (see further Chapter 27). Some illustrations follow.

Sales increasing

A curvilinear function may be exponential of a similar form to a learning curve (see section on learning curves in Chapter 8). Figure 10.23 shows an exponential relationship for an increase in sales of over a 12-month period. This is a progression that might explain the sale of computers, electronic calculators, or portable (mobile) telephones mentioned earlier.

Sales decreasing

Alternatively, Figure 10.24 illustrates a declining trend such as might be experienced in the sale of 33 rpm records, hand lawnmowers, manual shift automobiles in the USA, and other type of products that have been replaced by products using different technology.

The data for these two curves are given in Table 10.11.

If analysis of data indicates the trend is exponential then forecast models could be developed on this basis. Further, a logarithmic function applied to exponential functions gives a straight line as illustrated on the two curves. For example, in the case where sales are

Figure 10.23 Curvilinear increase in sales

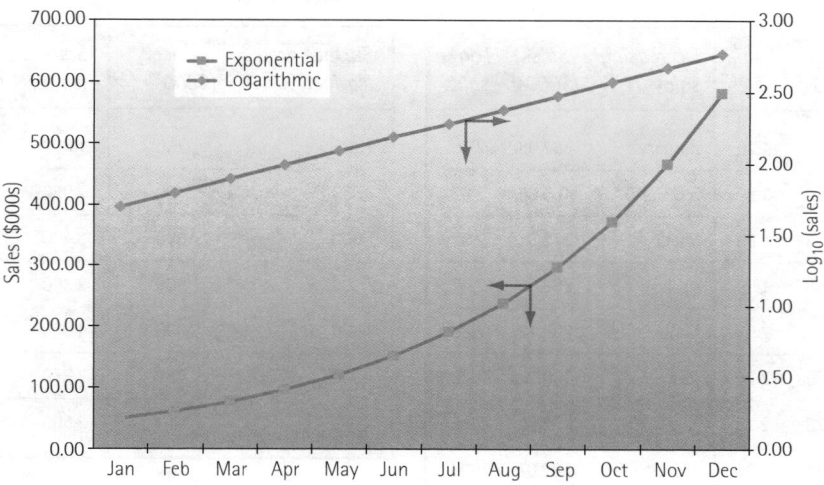

Figure 10.24 Curvilinear decrease in sales

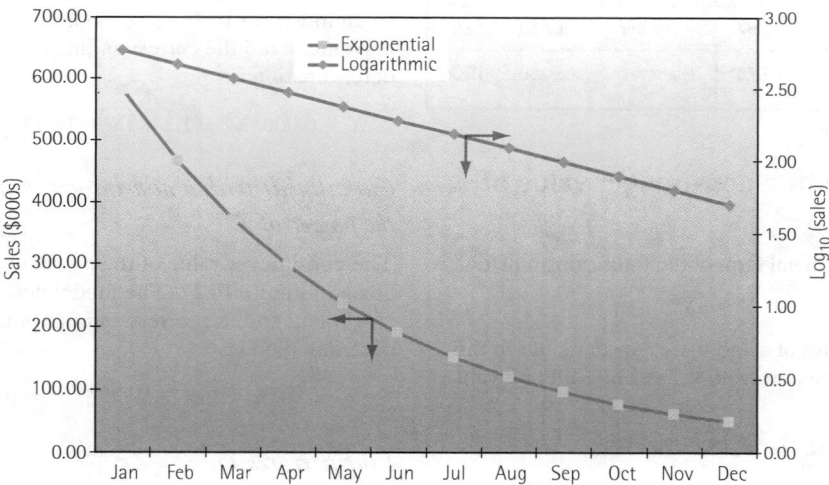

increasing, then the logarithmic value for sales in February is given by:

$$\log_{10}(62.50) = 1.80$$

Thus, if actual sales are monitored, and the model indicates that the trend is exponential, a logarithmic function can be developed. This function extrapolated can then be used to estimate future sales.

Polynomial

A polynomial function with integer values of X takes the general form:

$$Y = a + bX + cX^2 + dX^3 + \cdots + kX^n$$

where a, b, c, d, ..., k are constants. X is the independent variable such as time in a time series analysis, or another variable in the case of causal analysis. Y is the dependent variable such as sales. A two-power polynomial would have the form:

$$Y = a + bX + cX^2$$

The more the powers of x generally the closer the coefficient of determination is to zero, or the better the model.

Table 10.11 Sales data: Sales increasing and sales decreasing

Increasing sales	Sales ($000s)	Log$_{10}$ sales	Decreasing sales	Sales ($000s)	Log$_{10}$ sales
January	50.00	1.70	January	582.08	2.76
February	62.50	1.80	February	465.66	2.67
March	78.13	1.89	March	372.53	2.57
April	97.66	1.99	April	298.02	2.47
May	122.07	2.09	May	238.42	2.38
June	152.59	2.18	June	190.73	2.28
July	190.73	2.28	July	152.59	2.18
August	238.42	2.38	August	122.07	2.09
September	298.02	2.47	September	97.66	1.99
October	372.53	2.57	October	78.13	1.89
November	465.66	2.67	November	62.50	1.80
December	582.08	2.76	December	50.00	1.70

Table 10.12 Causal relationship between house price and surface area

Surface area (sq feet) X	Price ($000s) Y	Surface area (sq feet) X	Price ($000s) Y
900	250	1,000	680
1,550	400	950	175
1,600	590	3,100	2,800
2,200	900	2,300	1,100
3,200	2,100	4,000	5,200
1,820	750	3,750	3,550
1,710	684	3,500	3,750

Curvilinear with a non-integer value of the power of X

In this case, the general form of the forecasting equation is:

$$Y = aX^b$$

Again, the values of a and b are constants but in this relationship, b, the power of X, has a non-integer value.

Comparison of forecast models

The following compares forecast models that might be obtained from exponential changes, polynomial, and curvilinear with non-integer values of X. These results are then compared to the linear regression approach using the coefficient of determination as the basis for comparison.

Table 10.12 gives collected data on the causal relationship between house prices, and the surface area in a certain community.

Exponential

The exponential form is given in Figure 10.25. The model describing this movement, and the corresponding coefficient of determination is:

$$Y = 125.32e^{0.009X} \quad r^2 = 0.9202$$

Polynomial

A polynomial form where x has a power of 2 and 1 is given in Figure 10.26. The model describing this movement and the corresponding coefficient of determination is:

$$Y = 0.0005X^2 + 1.2499X + 11,094.2 \quad r^2 = 0.9628$$

Curvilinear with a non-integer value of the power of X

The non-integer value of the power of x form is given in Figure 10.27. The model describing this movement and the corresponding coefficient of determination is:

$$Y = 0.0005X^{1.9099} \quad r^2 = 0.8899$$

Linear regression

As a comparison, the linear regression form is given in Figure 10.28. The model describing this movement and the corresponding coefficient of determination is:

$$Y = 1.376X - 1.466 \quad r^2 = 0.8715$$

In summary, for this situation, the polynomial function is the best model as the coefficient of determination is closest to unity. (Note that the polynomial graphs, which are generated from Excel, use the form $Y = aX^2 + bX + c$, whereas in discussion here the general form $Y = a + bX + cX^2$ is used. However, knowing where the coefficient applies, the result is the same.)

Figure 10.25 House prices: Exponential curve

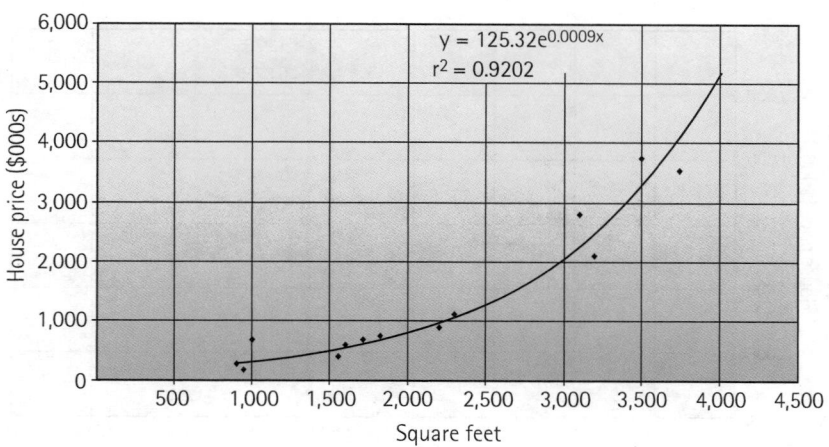

Figure 10.26 House prices: Polynomial

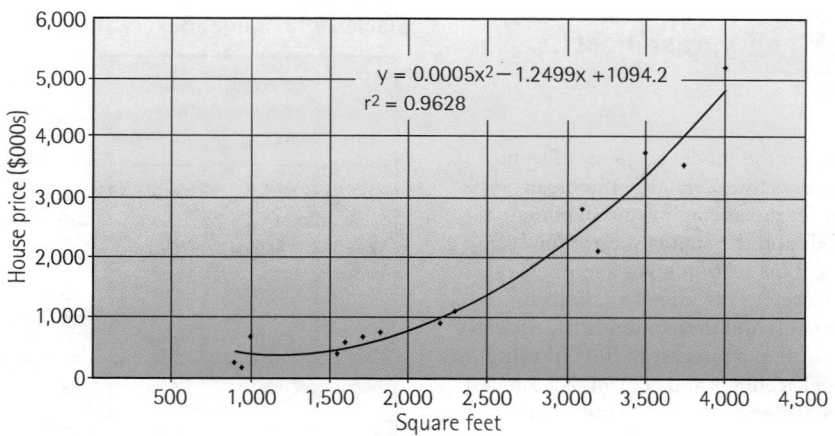

Figure 10.27 House prices: Non–integer values of the power of X

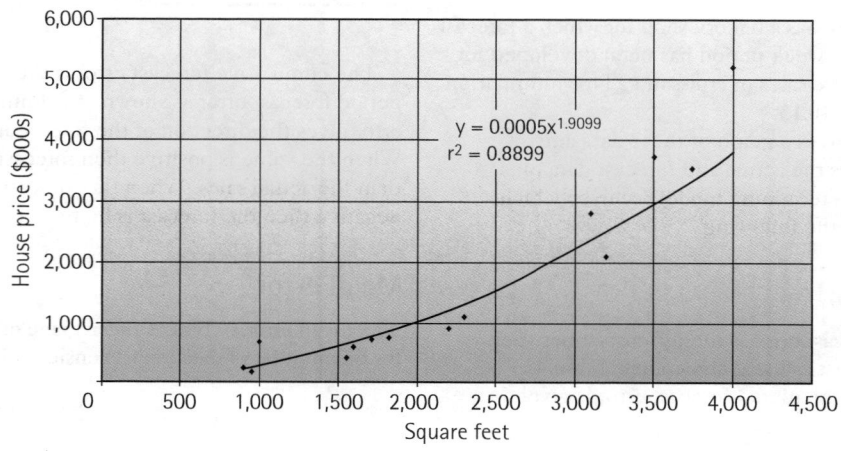

Figure 10.28 House prices: Linear regression

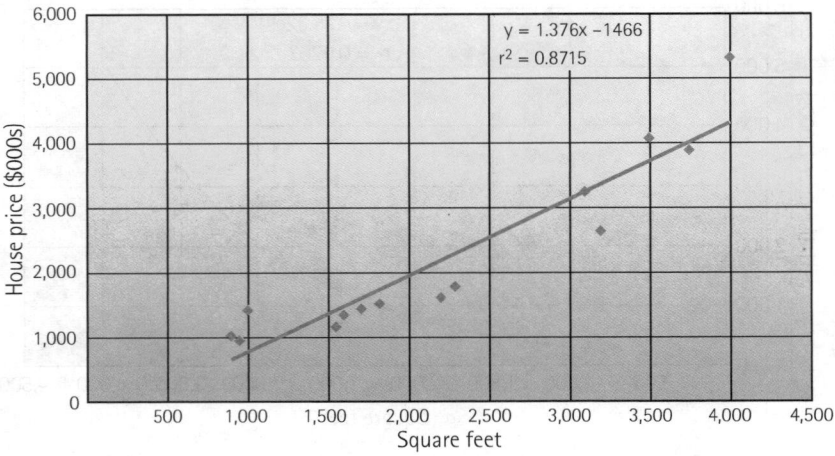

Accuracy of the forecast model

Introduction

Earlier in this chapter the model accuracy of some
of the models was presented, notably the mean
average deviation for the averaging and exponential
smoothing methods and the standard error for
regression models. This section gives a more
comprehensive treatment of various methods for
testing forecast models and then extends the accuracy
concept to the control of a forecast in the following
section. The model accuracy and control of a forecast
is illustrated by considering the following situation
for a bakery.

Scenario

The Ringe family has a bakery shop for which a forecast
model over a two-week period has been developed for
determining future sales of croissants. This information
is given in Table 10.13.

Figure 10.29 gives a graph of these data and
Table 10.14 gives the actual and forecast data plus
procedures for determining model accuracy which
are explained in the following.

Forecast error

The period forecast error is the difference between
actual and forecast sales, as shown in column 4.
Mathematically the period forecast error is given by:

$$\text{Forecast error} = (Y - \hat{Y})$$

Table 10.13 Ringe: Bakery shop forecast model

Day	Forecast sales (000s)	Actual sales (000s)	Day	Forecast sales (000s)	Actual sales (000s)
1	510	480	8	440	410
2	460	520	9	470	590
3	620	690	10	380	425
4	510	410	11	250	300
5	540	480	12	320	350
6	370	350	13	480	440
7	460	390	14	485	465

The cumulative forecast error is the sum of each
period forecast error as shown in column 5. The forecast
error gives the direction of the forecasting model.
When the value is positive then forecast sales are lower
than the actual sales. When the forecast error is
negative then the forecast is higher than actual sales.

Mean error

The mean error, or bias, is the average of the forecast error
for the number of data points considered. The equation is:

$$\text{Mean error} = \frac{\sum(Y - \hat{Y})}{n}$$

Figure 10.29 Ringe: Sales of croissants

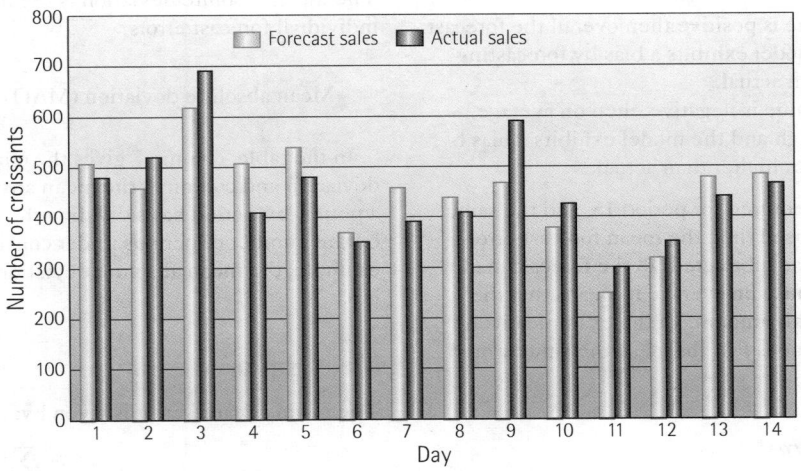

Table 10.14 Ringe: Sale of croissants

[1]	[2]	[3]	[4]	[5]	[6]	[7]	[8]	[9]	[10]	[11]
Day	Forecast (000s)	Actual (000s)	Forecast error	Cumulative forecast error	Absolute deviation	Cumulative absolute deviation	Mean absolute deviation	Tracking signal (N° of MADs)	Squared error	Mean percentage error
[1]	[2]	[3]	[3] − [2]	Cum [4]	Abs [4]	Cum [6]	[7]/[1]	[5]/[8]	[4]²	[4]/[3]
1	510	480	−30	−30	30	30	30.00	−1.00	900	−6.25%
2	460	520	60	30	60	90	45.00	0.67	3,600	11.54%
3	620	690	70	100	70	160	53.33	1.88	4,900	10.14%
4	510	410	−100	0	100	260	65.00	0.00	10,000	−24.39%
5	540	480	−60	−60	60	320	64.00	−0.94	3,600	−12.50%
6	370	350	−20	−80	20	340	56.67	−1.41	400	−5.71%
7	460	390	−70	−150	70	410	58.57	−2.56	4,900	−17.95%
8	440	410	−30	−180	30	440	55.00	−3.27	900	−7.32%
9	470	590	120	−60	120	560	62.22	−0.96	14,400	20.34%
10	380	425	45	−15	45	605	60.50	−0.25	2,025	10.59%
11	250	300	50	35	50	655	59.55	0.59	2,500	16.67%
12	320	350	30	65	30	685	57.08	1.14	900	8.57%
13	480	440	−40	25	40	725	55.77	0.45	1,600	−9.09%
14	485	465	−20	5	20	745	53.21	0.09	400	−4.30%
Total	6,295	6,300	5.00		745				−5.58	51,025	−9.66%
Mean	449.64	450.00	0.36		53.21				−0.40	3,645	−0.69%
Sq root										60.37	

The calculated data are given in the last cell at the bottom of column 4:

- If the mean value is positive then overall the forecast is low and the model exhibits a bias by forecasting values lower than actual.
- If the average value is negative, then on average, the forecast is high and the model exhibits a bias by forecasting values higher than actual.

If a forecast is required for period 15, and the same forecast model is used then the mean forecast error should be added (or subtracted) to the forecast made for period 15, because on average it means that the forecast is off by this amount. In the example given here the mean value is less than 1 so the value would not change.

Mean error is zero

If the mean error is approximately 0 for large samples, then the forecasting model may be considered accurate over the long range. However, a danger in this analysis is that mistakes in over-forecasting are offset by under-forecasting. In this example, if only the first four periods are considered, the forecast errors are -30, $+60$, $+70$, and -100 giving a mean value of 0. It might be concluded that the forecast model is good. In fact, individual forecasts exhibit a wide margin with the actual data.

If the mean error is zero then individual under- and over-forecasting may not be a great problem if the time periods are relatively short, and the product under consideration can be held in inventory, and used in subsequent periods, for example, standard products like compact discs, dry food, or clothing for example. The principal operating problem in this case is that there will be stocking costs, or at the worst, stockouts. However, if the inventory items are perishable food items, such as in this illustration for croissants, then high forecasts period by period will result in overproduction and thus waste, as the product cannot be put into storage. Costs will thus be higher than desirable.

Absolute deviation

The absolute deviation, or the absolute error, which has already been presented earlier, is the absolute value, or the positive value, of the forecast error:

$$\text{Absolute deviation} = |(Y - \hat{Y})|$$

Mean absolute deviation

The mean absolute deviation is the mean of all of the individual forecast errors:

$$\text{Mean absolute deviation (MAD)} = \frac{\sum |(Y - \hat{Y})|}{n}$$

In the table, column 7 gives the cumulative absolute deviation and column 8 the mean absolute deviation on a period-by-period basis dividing the cumulative data by the number of periods under consideration. In this example, the mean absolute deviation for the 14 days is 53.21.

Mean squared error

The mean squared error is given by:

$$\text{Mean squared error} = \frac{\sum (Y - \hat{Y})^2}{n}$$

The forecast error for each period, as given in column 4, is squared, and this removes the negative sign as shown in column 10. The mean of this is the mean squared error.

Standard error

The standard error is the square root of the mean squared error as given by the equation, and for this example, as shown in the last cell of column 10, is 60.37:

$$\text{Standard error} = \sqrt{\frac{\sum (Y - \hat{Y})^2}{n}}$$

The standard error is referred to as the consistency of the forecast. It is analogous to the population standard deviation presented in Chapter 27:

$$\text{Population standard deviation } \sigma_x = \sqrt{\sigma_x^2}$$
$$= \sqrt{\frac{\sum (X - \mu_x)^2}{N}}$$

Note that, in a rigorous statistical analysis, for samples from a population, as presented in the section on regression analysis, the standard error, also called the standard error of the estimate, is given by:

$$\text{Standard error} = \sqrt{\frac{\sum (Y - \hat{Y})^2}{n - 2}}$$

This compares to the sample standard deviation, or:

$$s = \sqrt{\frac{\sum (x - \bar{x})^2}{(n-1)}}$$

However, when the value of n is large, the difference between using n, or $n - 2$ in the standard error equation is small.

Comparing mean average deviation and standard error

If the errors that occur in a forecast can be considered normally distributed, then the relation between the mean absolute deviation and the standard deviation is:

$$\begin{bmatrix} \text{One standard error} \\ \text{(one standard deviation)} \end{bmatrix} = \sqrt{\frac{\pi}{2}} \times \text{MAD}$$

One standard error is equal to approximately 1.2533 of the mean absolute deviation, or conversely, 1 MAD = 0.80 standard deviations.

In the example given here:

Mean absolute deviation = 53.21   Standard error = 60.37

Using the mathematical relationship between mean absolute deviation and standard error, the standard error would be 1.2533*53.21 or 66.69, a difference of about 9% from the calculated value.

Percentage error

The percentage error is the forecast error divided by the actual sales for the corresponding period. Or, mathematically:

$$\text{Percentage error} = \frac{(Y - \hat{Y})}{Y} \times 100$$

The data are given in column 11 for each period, and the mean percentage error is calculated for the 14 pieces of data and is determined from the following relationship:

$$\text{Mean percentage error} = \frac{\left(\sum (Y - \hat{Y}) / (Y) \right)}{n}$$

Which error method?

Table 10.15 summarizes the errors from this illustration for the four approaches.

Table 10.15 Ringe: Errors displayed using the four methods

Method	Value for Ringe
Bias	0.36
Standard error (SE)	60.37
Mean absolute deviation (MAD)	53.21
Mean percentage error (MPE)	−0.69

The standard error, compared to the other methods, puts a greater emphasis on large individual errors since it squares the individual errors. Thus, if one is more concerned about minimizing large errors, the standard error might be used. If all errors have equivalent importance, then the other methods are appropriate.

Often, as already presented, the mean average deviation is commonly used to test the forecast models in the averaging and exponential methods and in regression analysis the standard error is used.

Control of a forecast

Once a forecast model is developed it should indicate if the actual demand is following the forecast. If not, why not? Perhaps the model being used is not appropriate. Control charts, similar to those used in quality control (see Chapter 20), using a tracking signal, can be used to monitor the forecast.

Tracking signal

The tracking signal indicates how well the forecast is predicting the actual data. The tracking signal, at a time period T, is given by:

$$\frac{\text{Cumulative forecast error (period T)}}{\text{Mean average deviation (period T)}} = \frac{\sum (Y - \hat{Y})}{\sum |(Y - \hat{Y})|/n}$$

In the Ringe example from the previous section:

- Cumulative forecast error is given in column 5.
- Mean absolute deviation day by day is given in column 8.
- Tracking signal is column 9 (column 5/column 8).

Figure 10.30 Ringe: Tracking signal

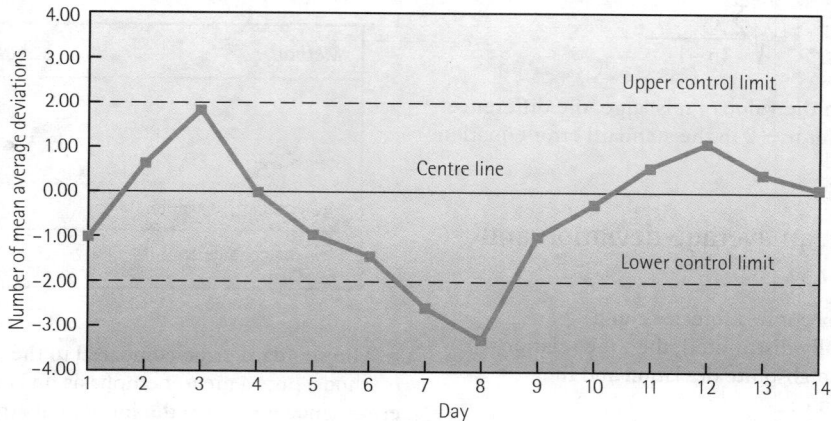

The tracking signal may be positive or negative, and it indicates how many mean average deviations the cumulative forecast error deviates from the actual value at any particular time period. If the tracking signal hovers around zero, then it means that the actual values are corresponding well to the forecast. If the tracking signal errs on the positive side then it means the forecast is predicting low (it is pessimistic). If the tracking signal errs on the negative side then it means the forecast is predicting high (it is optimistic). It is to be accepted that a forecast is just that, a forecast, and that there will be differences between the actual and estimated values. The question is how much deviation can be accepted before it is concluded that the forecast model is not valid. It is for this reason, control charts are useful.

Control charts

A control chart, which are treated in detail in Chapter 20, contains:

1. a centre line, CL, which is the target value of zero
2. an upper control limit, UCL
3. a lower control limit, LCL.

Figure 10.30 illustrates the movement of the tracking signal with control limits set at plus and minus two mean average deviations. This control chart illustrates that after the fourth day the tracking signal starts decreasing (forecasts are continually higher than actual sales) and that in periods 7 and 8, the lower control limit is exceeded.

Control limits

Control limits should be established such that:

- They are not so wide that large errors between the forecast and actual data are continually overlooked.

Table 10.16 Relationship between MAD, standard deviation and percentage of data

MAD	Std dev	% data
±1	±0.7979	57.2%
±2	±1.5958	89.4%
±3	±2.3937	98.2%

Std dev	MAD	% data
±1	±1.2533	68.26%
±2	±2.5066	95.44%
±3	±3.7599	99.72%

- They are not so narrow that limits are exceeded at a small difference between the forecast and actual data, which results in continuing doubt over the validity of the forecast model being used. It has to be accepted that there will always be differences.

Table 10.16 gives the relationship between the value of the mean average deviation, MAD, the standard error, and the percentage of data falling within the corresponding range.

For example, if control limits are set at ±2 MADs then about 89% of the data will be contained within the control limits assuming that the data can be considered to follow a normal distribution. Alternatively, with control limits of ±2.5 MADs (about ±2 standard deviations), then about 95% of the data will be contained within the data assuming a normal distribution.

Considerations in forecasting

The following are some elements to consider when developing a forecast model.

Time horizons

Managers would usually like a forecast to extend as far into the future as possible. Too long a period makes selection and development of a model complex because of the inability of methods to accommodate different time spans. The longer the time period, the more costly the development of the model. One possibility is to develop a model for different time periods, say short, medium, and long term, recognizing that the shorter time span model will probably be able to provide the most accurate information.

Collected data

Quantitative forecast models use collected data to estimate future outcomes. In collecting data it is better to have detailed, rather than aggregate information, as the latter might camouflage situations. This principle was illustrated in the sale of filing cabinets where the detailed data in terms of units sold were shown to be more useful than the aggregate data in terms of revenues generated. In addition to the distortion caused by aggregating design types, revenues as a variable can be distorted by market events such as price increases or exchange rates if exporting is involved. It is better to aggregate data after the forecast model has been developed, rather than before.

Coefficient of variation

When past data are collected for the purpose of making a forecast the coefficient of variation, the ratio of the standard deviation to the mean (σ/μ) of the data is an indicator of how reliable would be a forecast model. For example, consider the data in Table 10.17.

For Product A, the coefficient of variation is relatively low meaning that the dispersion of the data relative to their mean is small. In this case, a model such as exponential smoothing should be quite reliable. Contrariwise, for Product B the coefficient of variation is greater than one, or the sample standard deviation is

Table 10.17 Coefficient of variation

Period	Product A	Product B
January	1,100	800
February	1,024	40
March	1,080	564
April	1,257	12
May	1,320	16
June	1,425	456
July	1,370	56
August	1,502	12
September	1,254	954
σ (as a sample)	164.02	377.58
μ	1,259.11	323.33
Coefficient of variation, σ/μ	0.13	1.17

greater than the mean. Here, an exponential forecast, for example, would not be reliable. In situations like this, perhaps there is a seasonal activity of the product and this should be taken into account in the selected forecast model. In using the coefficient of variation as a guide, care should be taken as if there is a trend in the data this will, of course, impact the coefficient. As already discussed in this chapter, plotting the data on a scatter diagram would be a visual indicator of how good past data are for forecasting purposes.

Market changes

Market changes should be anticipated in forecasting. For example, in the past, steel requirements might be correlated with the forecast sale of automobiles. However, as illustrated in Chapter 5, plastic and composite materials are rapidly replacing steel, so this factor would distort the forecast demand for steel if the old forecasting approach were used. Alternatively, more and more uses are being found for plastics, so this element would need to be incorporated into a forecast for the demand for plastics. These types of event may not affect short-term planning but certainly are important in long-range forecasting when capital appropriation for plant and equipment is a consideration.

Models are dynamic

A forecast model must be a dynamic working tool with the flexibility to be updated, or modified as soon as new data become available that might impact the outcome of the forecast. For example, an economic model for the German economy had to be modified with the fall of the Berlin Wall in 1989 and the fusion of the two Germanys. Similarly, current models for the European economy are being be modified to take into account the impact of the euro as the single currency.

Model accuracy

All managers want an accurate model. The accuracy of the model, whether it is estimated at 10, 20 or say 50% can only be within a range bounded by the error in the collected data. Further, accuracy must be judged in light of control a firm has over resources and external events. Besides accuracy, also of interest in a forecast is when turning points in situations might be expected, such as a marked increase (or decrease) in sales so that the firm can take advantage of the opportunities, or be prepared for the threats.

Curvilinear or exponential models

One should exercise caution in using curvilinear functions, where the predicted value of Y changes rapidly with X. Even though the actual collected data may exhibit a curvilinear relationship, an exponential growth often cannot be sustained in the future perhaps because of economic or demographic reasons. In the house example presented in the section on curvilinear functions, a surface area of 10,000 sq feet forecasts a house sale price of $63.59 million! ($0.0005 * 10,000 * 10,000 - 1.2499 * 10,000 + 1,094.2$). Or, a continuing exponential model for the growth of portable telephones would forecast many more telephones sold than the population can absorb. (See the comment about Nokia at the beginning of this chapter and Application exercise 10.6 at the end of this chapter.) In the classic lifecycle curve in marketing, the growth period for successful new products very often follows a curvilinear, or sometimes more precisely an exponential growth model but this is unlikely to be sustained as the product moves into the mature stage.

Selecting the best model

It is difficult to give hard and fast rules to select the best forecasting model. The activity may be a trial and error process selecting a model and testing it against actual data or opinions. If a quantitative forecast model is used

there needs to be consideration of subjective input, and vice versa. Models can be complex. In the 1980s, in a marketing function in the USA, I worked on developing a forecast model for world crude oil prices. This model was needed to estimate financial returns from future oil exploration, drilling and refinery and chemical plant operation. The basis for forecasting was a combined multiple regression and curvilinear model incorporating variables in the US economy such as changes in the GNP, interest rates, energy consumption patterns, chemical production and forecast use, demographic changes, taxation, capital expenditure, seasonal effects, and also country political risk. Throughout the development, the model was tested against known situations.

A series of forecast models have been developed by a group of political scientists who study the US elections. These models use combined factors such as public opinions in the preceding summer, the strength of the economy, and the public's assessment of its economic well-being. The models have been used in all the US elections since 1948 and have proved highly accurate.[17]

Commercial forecasting tools and the supply chain

As was indicated earlier in this chapter, forecasting is the trigger that sets in motion all the activities in the supply chain. Today there are many commercial forecasting programs on the market that are an integral part of the application programs for supply chain management (see Chapters 13 and 17). Some of the better known commercial tools are given in Table 10.18.[18]

Table 10.18 Commercial forecasting tools

Supply chain applications program	Name of corresponding forecasting module
SAP	APO
Oracle	Demand management
PeopleSoft	Demand management
J D Edwards[19]	Demand management
Intentia	Moves
MAPICS	XA forecast
IFS	Demand planning

For the most part these programs tools are able to consider a vast range of different forecasting models and are able handle an infinite statistical database. Further, they employ the concept of datamining[20] where they have the capability automatically to select the best mathematical forecast model from the given input data. This capability is extremely useful as it helps to minimize risk in the decision process. Datamining is a standard in the well-known statistical standalone forecasting package of SPSS.[21]

Microsoft Excel for forecasting

In this chapter developing forecasting models was presented using Microsoft Excel and, particularly, functions such as regression were presented. There is alternative method to using Excel and that is by using 'Analysis tools' found in the Tools menu. These analysis tools include built-in methods for developing forecasting models for moving averages, exponential smoothing and regression. For the moving averages and exponential smoothing they avoid the development of the appropriate equation, as this is part of the tool. Whether to use these, or to develop the models oneself (very quickly done) is really a matter for personal preference.

Summary of key elements

- Forecasting, or estimating the demand for finished goods or services, is the trigger for all operating activities in the supply chain.

- Forecasting is not an exact science. An optimistic forecast can result in higher than normal inventories, increased storage costs, and plant capacity used unnecessarily. A pessimistic forecast may result in lost orders, lost clients, and/or idle production.

- Time horizons in forecasting might be short (up to about three months), medium (three months to one year), or long range (one to five years).

- Leading economic indicators, useful in forecasting, include new contracts, purchase orders, inventory levels, capital appropriation, and business incorporation.

- Forecasts are influenced by macroeconomic factors such as interest rates, exchange rates, employment levels, demographics, government regulations, and political climate.

- The demand for elastic products, usually high priced for which there are substitutes, changes sharply with price. The demand for inelastic products does not.

- Microeconomic factors for a firm, such as level of competition, reputation for quality, price, market saturation, design, delivery time, and accidents, can impact the sales forecast.

- Knowing the customer and markets are important qualitative aspects of forecasting.

- Forecasts developed by sales personnel when their bonuses are a factor run the risk being distorted.

- Forecasts based on the opinions of top management consolidate judgments of future activity from senior members of the organization.

- The salesforce composite is a consolidated judgmental forecast from the salesforce.

- Buyers' expectations in forecasting solicit opinions from prospective purchases of industrial products often making it a business-to-business relationship.

- The Delphi method of forecasting, developed by the Rand Corporation in California, is a long-range forecast developed from the judgment of experts.

- Consumer surveys to forecast product demand are expensive to implement and survey design needs to be such that they are representative of the population.

- A time series is historical or past data that may exhibit a trend, seasonal variation, irregular occurrences, a business cycle component, and random variations.

- In quantitative forecasting methods, the first step is to develop a mathematical model that is the best representation of the actual data.

- The naive averaging method of forecast assumes that the immediate last period's results can be used to estimate needs for the next period.

- Straight moving averaging models use the simple average of time periods. Weighted moving average models apply different weights on the time periods.

- Exponential smoothing models use an α factor such that $1 > \alpha > 0$. A trend-adjusted exponential smoothing model can improve the reliability of the exponential forecast model.

- Simple linear regression, useful in forecasting, is the development of a linear equation model which takes the general form: $\hat{Y} = a + bX$.

- In regression analysis, the coefficient of determination, r^2, or the coefficient of correlation, r, measure the strength of the relationship between X and Y. Numerically, the closer these values are to unity, the better is the model.

- Causal forecasting is when sales, or other activity, is caused or dependent on another variable. This relationship can be analyzed by using a linear regression equation.

- Many products exhibit a seasonal effect on sales. The seasonal effect can be taken into account by determining a seasonal index and applying this to the actual data.

- Multiple regression models can be used in forecasting where the dependent value such as sales is a function of two or more independent variables such as advertising budgets, sales offices, and the number of sales personnel.

- Non-linear regression forecasting, when the dependent variable is a curvilinear function of an independent variable, might be exponential or take some other polynomial form.

- The mean average deviation, the forecast error, the mean error, or the mean squared error can test the accuracy of forecast models.

- A control chart, plotting a tracking signal given by the ratio of the cumulative forecast error to the mean absolute deviation, can be used to monitor the accuracy of the forecast.

- Important considerations in a forecast model are the time horizon, accuracy of collected data, market changes, model flexibility, and model accuracy. Caution should be exercised when considering curvilinear models as they usually have a limited time horizon.

- There are many forecasting tools integrated into commercial applications programs for supply chain management. Many employ the concept of datamining where the best forecasting model is automatically selected from the given data.

Notes and references

1. 'PC makers aren't complaining, but … with demand booming, components are scarce', *Business Week*, 19 June 1995, p. 33
2. BYRNS, R.T. and STONE, G.W., *Economics: 'NBER Classification System'*, Scott, Foresman & Co., Glenview, Illinois, 1987, 3rd edition, p. 146
3. JAMES, Barry, 'Airbus super-jumbo faces trade storm', *International Herald Tribune*, 20 December 2000, p. 1
4. 'Have you driven a Jag lately? Ford bags the carmaker as GM backs away', *Newsweek*, 13 November 1989, p. 49
5. 'Quality control was lacking at Firestone: Bridgestone to implement new standards, Chief pledges', *International Herald Tribune*, 12 September 2000, p. 11
6. PRINGLE, David and HARRIS, Edward, 'Nokia says sales of mobile phones missed forecast', *Wall Street Journal Europe*, 10 January 2001, pp 1 and 20
7. COHEN, Roger, 'Two German ministers quit amid mad cow uproar', *International Herald Tribune*, 10 January 2001, p. 1
8. Dun & Bradstreet (published in *The Economist*, 25 November 2000)
9. HEIZER, Jay and RENDER, Barry, *Production and Operations Management*, Prentice-Hall, London, 4th edition, 1996, pp 161–2
10. ALRECK, Pamela L. and SETTLE, Robert B., *The Survey Research Handbook*, Dow Jones Irwin, New York, 1985
11. *Chicago Daily Tribune*, 3 November 1948
12. BOX G. E. and JENKINS G., *Time Series Analysis: Forecasting and Control*, Holden Day, San Francisco, 1970
13. McWILLIAMS, Gary, 'Time to reboot: PC makers say farewell to 15-year boom', *Wall Street Journal Europe*, 24/25 August 2001, pp 1 and 7
14. *Wall Street Journal Europe*, 9 January 1995
15. GARDNER E. S., 'Exponential smoothing: The state of the art', *Journal of Forecasting*, 4 March 1985
16. RUSSELL, Roberta S. and TAYLOR, Bernard W., '*Operations Management*', Prentice-Hall, London, 3rd edition, 2000, p. 465
17. 'Mathematically, Gore is a winner', *International Herald Tribune*, 1 September 2000
18. '36 progiciels de prévisions de vente' (36 computer packages for forecasting), *Stratégie Logistique*, France, N° 32, December 2000, supplement
19. J.D. Edwards home page: http://www.jdedwards.com/
20. 'Clementime, data mining made easy', http://www.datamining.com.sg/clementime/index.html, as an example
21. SPSS home page: http://www.spss.com/

Review and discussion questions

1. Forecast risks
In the long term, is it better to be optimistic, or pessimistic, in a forecast? Are the risks fewer for some firms than for others? Justify your reasoning.

2. Sales remuneration
Some companies give a bonus to sales staff according to the level of sales they make. The argument is that this motivates the salespeople. Other firms don't agree with giving a bonus because they argue that selling is a team effort and involves others in the company. What do you believe? Are there some products when a sales bonus is appropriate, and others when it is not?

3. Demographics
Illustrate situations where demographic changes have modified the forecast of the sales of goods and services.

4. Consumer surveys
At some stage, you have probably been confronted with responding to a survey, even maybe as an evaluation by a professor for a teaching programme. What do you think are the dangers of surveying? What are the advantages?

5. International

What are some of the international changes that have an impact on the sales of goods and services?

6. Causal factors

What are some of the causal factors which impact the forecast of the following? Consider both in the increasing and decreasing sense:

   (a) PVC piping
   (b) private education
   (c) skiing vacations
   (d) marriage
   (e) utilization of public transport
   (f) automobiles
   (g) pharmaceutical products
   (h) fish for consumption
   (i) golf clubs
   (j) increase in environmental laws
   (k) urban growth
   (l) alcohol consumption.

7. Multiple regression

What are the criticisms of using multiple regression models in forecasting? In what areas do you think multiple regression models are the most appropriate?

8. Forecast errors

Regardless of the type of forecast you are making, what are some of the factors that lead to errors in the analysis?

9. Non-linear regression

Give some other illustrations when the sales, activity, or progression of some events has followed, or will probably follow, a curvilinear change, either in a negative or positive sense.

Demonstrating the concept 10.1   Lube oil (1)

Situation

The Ipras Oil Refinery in Turkey has a processing unit for making lubricating oil (called lube oil in the business). Even though the production of lubricating oil requires a high capital investment, the profit margin from this product is higher than normal straight run products such as gasoline, and diesel fuel. The production manager in the lube oil plant needs to develop a simple forecasting model for estimating its blending requirements. Lubricating oil, unlike other refinery products, is not very seasonal. Table 10.19 gives the actual lubricating oil blended in a particular year.

Required

1. Develop a three-month simple moving average forecasting model.
2. Develop a three-month weighted moving average using a factor of 0.6 for the most recent period, 0.2 for the next period, and 0.2 for the oldest period.
3. Using the concept of the mean absolute deviation, which model is preferred?
4. Use the preferred model to forecast the lube oil requirements for the following January.
5. Plot the actual data, and the two forecasting models.

Solution

The solution for this exercise is given in Table 10.20.

1. The simple moving average data are given in column 3 of the table.

Table 10.19 Lubricating oil production

Month	Actual oil used (000s litres)
January	10,000
February	12,000
March	13,000
April	16,000
May	19,000
June	17,000
July	11,000
August	22,000
September	31,000
October	18,000
November	16,000
December	14,000

2. The weighted moving average data are given in column 5 of the table.
3. The weighted moving average has the lowest MAD and so this is the preferred model.
4. The forecast requirements for the next January are 15,200 litres.
5. The data are given in Figure 10.31.

Table 10.20 Lube oil (1): Averaging methods

		Weights	0.20	0.20	0.60
		Total	1.00		

1	2	3	4	5	6
		Simple moving average		Weighted moving average	
Month	Actual oil used (1000 litres)	Model	Absolute deviation from actual	Model	Absolute deviation from actual
January	10,000				
February	12,000				
March	13,000				
April	16,000	11,666.67	4,333.33	12,200.00	3,800.00
May	19,000	13,666.67	5,333.33	14,600.00	4,400.00
June	17,000	16,000.00	1,000.00	17,200.00	200.00
July	11,000	17,333.33	6,333.33	17,200.00	6,200.00
August	22,000	15,666.67	6,333.33	13,800.00	8,200.00
September	31,000	16,666.67	14,333.33	18,800.00	12,200.00
October	18,000	21,333.33	3,333.33	25,200.00	7,200.00
November	16,000	23,666.67	7,666.67	21,400.00	5,400.00
December	14,000	21,666.67	7,666.67	19,400.00	5,400.00
January forecast		**16,000.00**		**15,200.00**	
Mean average deviation (MAD)			6,259.26		5,888.89

Figure 10.31 Lube oil (1): Averaging methods

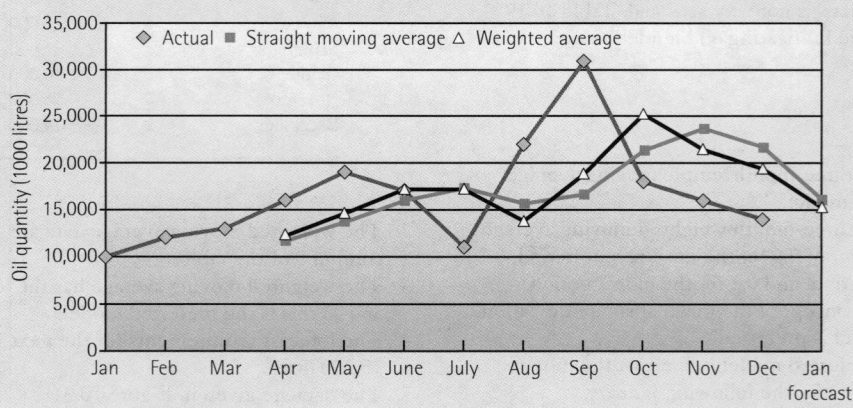

Demonstrating the concept 10.2   Lube oil (2)

Situation

The situation is the same as presented in Lube oil (1).

Required

1. Develop an exponential smoothing forecast model using an alpha factor of 0.1. Use the linear average of the first three months in order to start the development of the model.
2. Develop an exponential smoothing forecast model using an alpha factor of 0.5.
3. Using the concept of the mean absolute deviation, which model is preferred?
4. Use the preferred model to forecast the lube oil requirements for the following January.
5. Plot the actual data, and the two models.

Solution

The two models are given in Table 10.21.

1. The model for an alpha factor of 0.1 is given in column 3.
2. The model for an alpha factor of 0.5 is given in column 5.
3. The exponential smoothing model for an alpha factor of 0.1 has the lowest MAD, so this is the preferred model.
4. The forecast for January is 15,682,70 litres.
5. The plotted data are shown in Figure 10.32.

Table 10.21   Lube oil: Exponential smoothing

1	2	3	4	5	6
		Exponential smoothing		*Exponential smoothing*	
Month	*Actual oil used (1000 litres)*	*Model alpha 0.10*	*Absolute deviation from actual*	*Model alpha 0.50*	*Absolute deviation from actual*
January	10,000	11,666.67	1,666.67	11,666.67	1,666.67
February	12,000	11,500.00	500.00	10,833.33	1,166.67
March	13,000	11,550.00	1,450.00	11,416.67	1,583.33
April	16,000	11,695.00	4,305.00	12,208.33	3,791.67
May	19,000	12,125.50	6,874.50	14,104.17	4,895.83
June	17,000	12,812.95	4,187.05	16,552.08	447.92
July	11,000	13,231.66	2,231.66	16,776.04	5,776.04
August	22,000	13,008.49	8,991.51	13,888.02	8,111.98
September	31,000	13,907.64	17,092.36	17,944.01	13,055.99
October	18,000	15,616.88	2,383.12	24,472.01	6,472.01
November	16,000	15,855.19	144.81	21,236.00	5,236.00
December	14,000	15,869.67	1,869.67	18,618.00	4,618.00
January forecast		**15,682.70**		**16,309.00**	
Mean average deviation (MAD)			4,308.03		4,735.18

Figure 10.32 Lube oil (2): Exponential smoothing

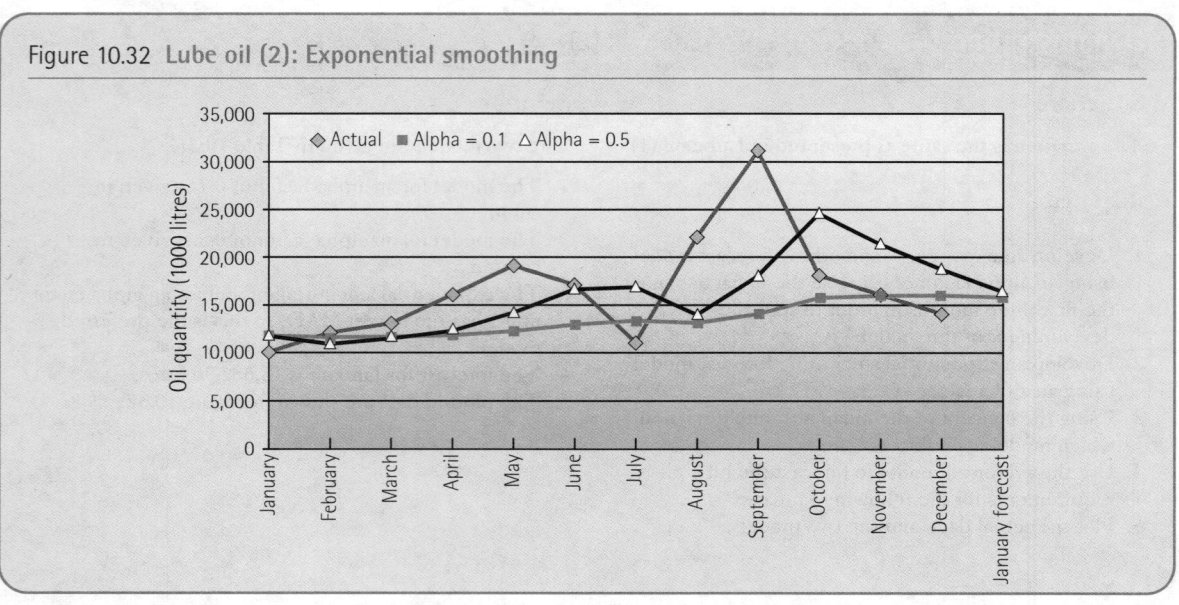

Demonstrating the concept 10.3 Restaurant

Situation

Close to a small city a new industrial park has been developed and more firms are moving into the park. As a result the demand for restaurant services has been increasing. Table 10.22 displays data from existing restaurants in the area, indicating restaurant customers for the past 12 months.

Required

Develop an exponential trend-adjusted forecast model and determine a forecast for the following January. Compare the forecast trend model to a simple exponential smoothing model. Use an α factor of 0.70 and a β factor of 0.30. Assume that the initial forecast estimate for January is equal to actual demand (a naive estimate) and that the initial trend factor is 0. This assumption is not unreasonable since the actual data period is relatively long (12 periods) and so when one arrives at the required forecast period (period 13) a reasonable trend factor should have been obtained.

Solution

The solution for this exercise is given in Table 10.23 and Figure 10.33.

Table 10.22 Restaurant customer numbers

Month	Customers
January	2,500
February	2,550
March	2,750
April	3,010
May	3,250
June	3,200
July	3,400
August	3,480
September	3,500
October	3,650
November	3,600
December	3,710

The January forecast with the trend adjustment is 3750 customers (rounded) and 3677 customers (rounded) without the trend. After about period 7, the exponential model with the trend adjustment follows well the movement of the actual data.

Table 10.23 Restaurants: Forecasting results

$$F_1 = 2500.00 \quad \alpha = 0.70 \quad \beta = 0.30 \quad T_1 = 0$$

Month	Code	Actual demand	Exp forecast (no trend)	Trend factor	Exp forecast (trend)	MAD (no trend)	MAD (trend)
January	1	2,500.00	2,500.00	0.00	2,500.00	0.00	0.00
February	2	2,550.00	2,500.00	0.00	2,500.00	50.00	50.00
March	3	2,750.00	2,535.00	10.50	2,545.50	215.00	204.50
April	4	3,010.00	2,685.50	52.50	2,738.00	324.50	272.00
May	5	3,250.00	2,912.65	104.90	3,017.55	337.35	232.46
June	6	3,200.00	3,148.80	144.27	3,293.07	51.20	93.07
July	7	3,400.00	3,184.64	111.74	3,296.38	215.36	103.62
August	8	3,480.00	3,335.39	123.45	3,458.84	144.61	21.16
September	9	3,500.00	3,436.62	116.78	3,553.40	63.38	53.40
October	10	3,650.00	3,480.99	95.06	3,576.04	169.01	73.96
November	11	3,600.00	3,599.30	102.03	3,701.33	0.70	101.33
December	12	3,710.00	3,599.79	71.57	3,671.36	110.21	38.64
January	13		3,676.94	73.24	3,750.18		
					Average	140.11	103.68

Figure 10.33 Restaurants: Exponential smoothing with and without a trend adjustment

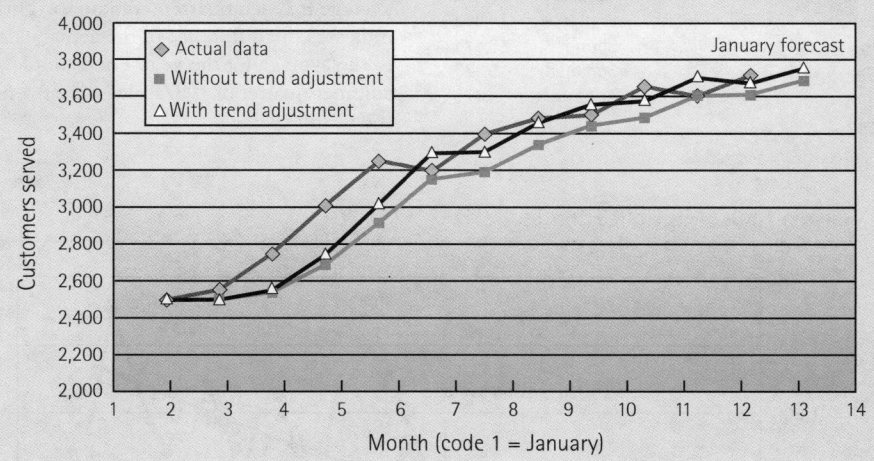

Demonstrating the concept 10.4 Garden tools

Situation

The Mersey Store in Arkansas in America is a distributor of garden tools. Table 10.24 shows the sales by quarter since 1993. All data are in $000s.

Required

1. Show graphically that the sales for Mersey are seasonal.

Table 10.24 Sales by quarter since 1993

Year	Quarter	Sales	Year	Quarter	Sales
1993	Winter	11,302	1997	Winter	13,184
	Spring	12,177		Spring	14,146
	Summer	13,218		Summer	14,966
	Autumn	11,948		Autumn	13,665
1994	Winter	11,886	1998	Winter	13,781
	Spring	12,198		Spring	14,636
	Summer	13,294		Summer	15,142
	Autumn	11,785		Autumn	13,415
1995	Winter	11,875	1999	Winter	14,327
	Spring	12,584		Spring	15,251
	Summer	13,332		Summer	15,082
	Autumn	12,354		Autumn	14,002
1996	Winter	12,658	2000	Winter	14,862
	Spring	13,350		Spring	15,474
	Summer	14,358		Summer	15,325
	Autumn	13,276		Autumn	14,425

2. Using the multiplication model, predict sales by quarter for 2001. Show graphically the moving average, de-seasonalized sales, regression line, and forecast.

Solution

1. The graphical data are given in Figure 10.34 and Table 10.25 gives the computed data. This information is explained by the following.
   • The actual data show there is a seasonal variation as there are peaks and troughs in the movement of sales. In addition, there is a trend as sales are increasing with time.
2. A centred moving average is calculated around each time period. For example, for the summer 1993 quarter, the centred moving average is:

$$\frac{\left[\begin{array}{c} 0.5*11,302+12,177+13,218 \\ +11,948+0.5*11,886 \end{array}\right]}{4}=12,234.32$$

The centred moving average for each quarter is calculated in a similar manner (column 5 of Table 10.25).
   • The actual sales are divided by the moving average for each quarter (column 6). This ratio indicates the difference of the actual data compared to the average for the year. For example, in the summer quarter of 1987, sales were 8% higher than the yearly average.

Figure 10.34 Garden tools: Multiplication model

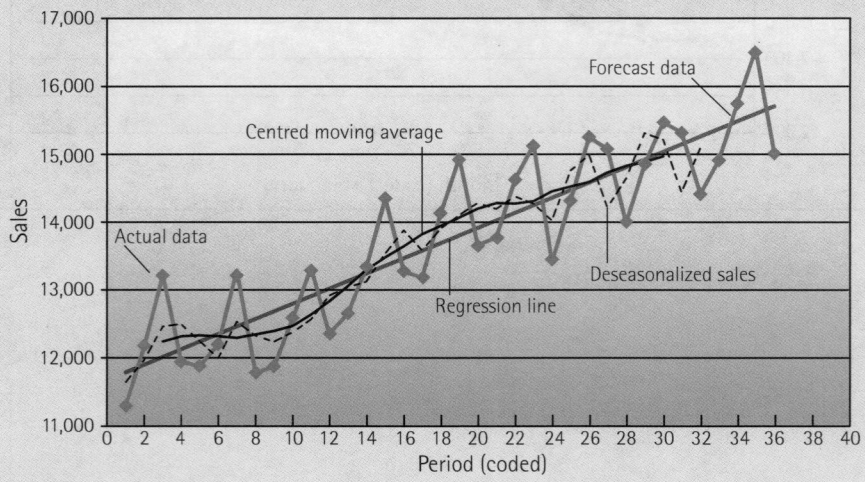

Table 10.25 Multiplication model

1	2	3	4	5	6	7	8	9
Year	Quarter	Period	Actual sales	Centred moving average	Sales/ mvg avg	Seasonal index	Sales/index deseasonalized	Regression line (predicted)
1993	Winter	1	11,302			0.9709	11,640.18	11,784.48
	Spring	2	12,177			1.02	11,966.15	11,896.40
	Summer	3	13,218	12,234.32	1.08	1.06	12,455.36	12,008.31
	Autumn	4	11,948	12,309.91	0.97	0.96	12,489.33	12,120.23
1994	Winter	5	11,886	12,321.98	0.96	0.97	12,241.60	12,232.14
	Spring	6	12,198	12,311.03	0.99	1.02	11,986.58	12,344.06
	Summer	7	13,294	12,289.25	1.08	1.06	12,526.71	12,455.98
	Autumn	8	11,785	12,336.14	0.96	0.96	12,318.62	12,567.89
1995	Winter	9	11,875	12,389.23	0.96	0.97	12,230.33	12,679.81
	Spring	10	12,584	12,465.18	1.01	1.02	12,366.00	12,791.72
	Summer	11	13,332	12,634.20	1.06	1.06	12,563.09	12,903.64
	Autumn	12	12,354	12,827.87	0.96	0.96	12,913.39	13,015.56
1996	Winter	13	12,658	13,051.86	0.97	0.97	13,036.90	13,127.47
	Spring	14	13,350	13,295.31	1.00	1.02	13,118.99	13,239.39
	Summer	15	14,358	13,476.26	1.07	1.06	13,529.58	13,351.30
	Autumn	16	13,276	13,641.47	0.97	0.96	13,877.03	13,463.22
1997	Winter	17	13,184	13,816.94	0.95	0.97	13,578.32	13,575.14
	Spring	18	14,146	13,941.55	1.01	1.02	13,901.17	13,687.05
	Summer	19	14,966	14,064.81	1.06	1.06	14,102.34	13,798.97
	Autumn	20	13,665	14,200.68	0.96	0.96	14,283.72	13,910.88
1998	Winter	21	13,781	14,283.96	0.96	0.97	14,193.16	14,022.80
	Spring	22	14,636	14,274.74	1.03	1.02	14,382.73	14,134.72
	Summer	23	15,142	14,311.80	1.06	1.06	14,268.35	14,246.63
	Autumn	24	13,415	14,456.96	0.93	0.96	14,022.43	14,358.55
1999	Winter	25	14,327	14,526.27	0.99	0.97	14,755.99	14,470.46
	Spring	26	15,251	14,592.10	1.05	1.02	14,986.88	14,582.38
	Summer	27	15,082	14,732.30	1.02	1.06	14,211.49	14,694.30
	Autumn	28	14,002	14,826.97	0.94	0.96	14,636.01	14,806.21
2000	Winter	29	14,862	14,885.23	1.00	0.97	15,306.59	14,918.13
	Spring	30	15,474	14,968.52	1.03	1.02	15,205.77	15,030.04
	Summer	31	15,325			1.06	14,440.79	15,141.96
	Autumn	32	14,425			0.96	15,078.16	15,253.88
2001	**Winter**	**33**	**14,919**			**0.97**		**15,365.79**
	Spring	**34**	**15,750**			**1.02**		**15,477.71**
	Summer	**35**	**16,544**			**1.06**		**15,589.62**
	Autumn	**36**	**15,021**			**0.96**		**15,701.54**

	Indices	Winter	0.97
		Spring	1.02
		Summer	1.06
		Autumn	0.96

Regression

Slope	111.916	11,672.56	Intercept on Y axis
	6.0389127	114.1818	
Coefficient of determination	0.9196685	315.414	Standard error of estimate
	343.45261	30	
	34,168,719	2,984,579	

- The average seasonal index for each quarter is determined. This is the average of the ratio, sales/moving average for like quarters. For example, the seasonal index for the summer quarter is the average of the ratios for summer 1993 through summer 2000 (average of 1.08 + 1.08 + 1.06 + 1.07 + 1.06 + 1.06 + 1.02 or 1.06). Column 7 gives the average seasonal index for each quarter.
- The seasonal effect from the actual sales is removed by dividing the actual sales by the corresponding index for that quarter (column 8).
- A regression analysis on the de-seasonalized sales is determined using a code value (column 3) corresponding to the quarter. This gives a value of:

  11,672   a, or intercept on the y-axis
  111.92   b, slope of linear regression line

Thus the linear regression equation describing the de-seasonalized sales is

$$\hat{Y} = 11{,}672 + 111.92X$$

- The de-seasonalized sales for the next four quarters are made using the regression equation. These data are given in the shaded area at the bottom of column 9.
- The forecast seasonalized sales are calculated from the regression forecast data calculated in 9. The seasonal sales is the (predicted sales × seasonal index). This information is given in the shaded area at the bottom of column 4, and shown as the last four pieces of data for periods 33 through 36.

Demonstrating the concept 10.5   Catalogue sales

Situation

The Chelsea Company is a distributor of a vast range of consumer products ranging from televisions, and kitchen utensils, through to audiovisual equipment. The company publishes a catalogue of its products, which is a key to its sales. Customer contact is either direct or by telephone. The Chelsea Company wants to see if there is any relationship between sales revenues, advertising budget, sales staff, and client contact, made either direct or by telephone. Historical data available on a monthly basis are shown in Table 10.26.

Required

Develop forecast models for two and three independent variables.

Two independent variables

1. Develop a two independent variable multiple regression model for the sales volume as a function of the advertising budget, and the number of salespeople.
2. Does the relationship appear strong? Quantify.
3. Assume for a particular month it is proposed to allocate a budget of $US 4000 and to use 30 salespeople, then what would be an estimate of the sales for that month?
4. What are the 90% confidence intervals?

Three independent variables

1. Develop a three independent variable multiple regression model for the sales volume as a function

Table 10.26   **Monthly historical data**

Sales $US	Advertising budget	Sales persons	N° of sales contacts
72,120	7,200	42	27,500
47,000	4,712	21	18,412
57,000	5,512	28	22,478
51,000	4,985	22	20,554
31,540	3,000	22	15,487
58,750	6,245	32	18,724
61,580	6,352	35	22,845
59,450	5,847	35	23,448
57,450	4,897	28	22,045
26,500	3,000	16	9,998

of the advertising budget, the number of salespeople, and the number of sales contacts made.

2. Does the relationship appear strong? Quantify.
3. Assume for a particular month it is proposed to allocate a budget of $US 4000 and to use 30 salespeople, with a target to make 21,000 sales contacts, then what would be an estimate of the sales for that month?
4. What are the 90% confidence intervals?

Solution

The solution for this problem is given in Table 10.27. The upper part of the table gives the regression constants for two variables, and the lower part gives the regression constants for three variables. The format of

Table 10.27 Forecasting multiple regression for catalogue sales

Two independent variables

Sales	Advertising budget (X_1)	Salespeople (X_2)		Salespeople	Advertising budget	Y intercept A
72,120	7,200	42		**204.022057**	**8.75514814**	**1,198.0886**
47,000	4,712	21		369.053843	2.14710352	4,966.22781
57,000	5,512	28		0.94134474	3,825.6676	#N/A
51,000	4,985	22		56.1706958	7	#N/A
31,540	3,000	22		1,644,198,562	102,450,128	#N/A
58,750	6,245	32		#N/A	#N/A	#N/A
61,580	6,352	35		#N/A	#N/A	#N/A
59,450	5,847	35		#N/A	#N/A	#N/A
57,450	4,897	28		#N/A	#N/A	#N/A
26,500	3,000	16		#N/A	#N/A	#N/A

Sales	Advertising budget (X_1)	Salespeople (X_2)	t	t*std err	Upper	Lower
42,339	**4,000**	**30**	**1.8946**	**7,248.11**	**49,587**	**35,091**

Three independent variables

Sales	Advertising budget (X_1)	Salespeople (X_2)	Sales contacts (X_3)	Sales contacts	Salespeople	Advertising budget	Y intercept A
72,120	7,200	42	27,500	**1.24942875**	**−99.875716**	6.52760037	−3,909.68902
47,000	4,712	21	18,412	0.33417288	**233.080602**	1.40362324	3,241.52987
57,000	5,512	28	22,478	0.98238505	2,264.47648	#N/A	#N/A
51,000	4,985	22	20,554	111.539945	6	#N/A	#N/A
31,540	3,000	22	15,487	1,715,881,568	30,767,122.3	#N/A	#N/A
58,750	6,245	32	18,724	#N/A	#N/A	#N/A	#N/A
61,580	6,352	35	22,845	#N/A	#N/A	#N/A	#N/A
59,450	5,847	35	23,448	#N/A	#N/A	#N/A	#N/A
57,450	4,897	28	22,045	#N/A	#N/A	#N/A	#N/A
26,500	3,000	16	9,998	#N/A	#N/A	#N/A	#N/A

Sales	Advertising budget (X_1)	Salespeople (X_2)	Sales contacts (X_3)	t	t*std err	Upper	Lower
45,442	**4,000**	**30**	**21,000**	**1.9432**	**4,400.33**	**49,843**	**41,042**

(Case 1   Y = 1,198.089 + 8.76 * (Ad budget) + 204.02 * (Salespeople)
Case 2   Y = 3,909.69 + 6.53 * (Ad budget) − 99.88 * (Salespeople) + 1.25 * (Sales contacts))

the table is according to the Microsoft Excel regression function.

Two independent variables
1. The regression equation is:

$$\hat{Y} = 1198.09 + 8.76 * \text{Ad. budget} + 204.02 * \text{N}^\circ \text{ salespeople}$$

2. A test for the strength of the relationship is the coefficient of multiple regression. In this case, for two independent variables, the coefficient of multiple determination is 0.9413. This means that 94.13% of sales are explained by the advertising budget, and the number of salespeople.
3. Inserting the corresponding values in the regression equation gives an estimate of sales of $42,339.

4. Here, for two independent variables, are 90% confidence levels:

- Sample size is 10
- Standard error is 3825.67
- Upper limit is 49,587
- Degrees of freedom are 7
- t is 1.8946
- Lower limit is 35,091

This can be translated as saying that the estimated sales with an advertising budget of $4000 and 30 salespeople is 42,339 and one is 90% certain that sales will lie in the range of $49,587 and $35,091.

Three independent variables

1. The regression equation is:

$$\hat{Y} = -3909.69 + 6.53 * \text{Ad.budget} - 99.88 * N^o \text{ salespeople} + 1.25 * N^o \text{ sales contact}$$

2. A test for the strength of the relationship is the coefficient of multiple regression. In this case, for three independent variables, the coefficient of multiple determination is 0.9824. This means that 98.24% of sales are explained by the advertising budget, the number of salespeople, and the number of sales contacts.

3. Inserting the corresponding values in the regression equation gives an estimate of sales of $45,442.

4. Here for three independent variables are the 90% confidence levels:

- Sample size is 10
- Standard error is 2264.48
- Upper limit is 49,843
- Degrees of freedom are 6
- t is 1.9432
- Lower limit is 41,042

This can be translated as saying that the estimated sales with an advertising budget of $4000, 30 salespeople, and 21,000 sales contacts is $45,442 and one is 90% certain that sales will lie in the range of $49,843 and $41,042.

Application exercise 10.1 Consulting

Situation

A consulting company which has a major activity related to the installation and integration of systems software for enterprise resource planning wishes to see if there is any correlation between the profits generated in this sector and several variables related to its practice. These are, for this particular sector of the work, the average number of consultants on projects, their average experience, and the percentage of time that the consultant spends away from his office. (This means the consultant is either travelling, or working at the client's facility.)

Table 10.28 shows historical data available on a quarterly basis.

Table 10.28 **Quarterly available historical data**

Profits ($US)	Years' experience	Number of consultants	Time away from office (%)
4,501,000	15	27	55
3,241,000	6	45	27
8,745,100	18	112	75
6,984,210	23	80	62
3,421,800	8	35	55
5,845,600	10	98	57
6,854,200	8	80	75
3,589,500	5	30	49
9,542,300	21	120	82
5,689,250	10	54	62

Required

Two independent variables

1. Develop a two independent variable multiple regression model for profits as a function of the years' experience and the number of consultants on the projects.
2. Does the relationship appear strong? Quantify your answer.
3. What would be an estimate of profits for a particular quarter if the average experience of consultants on projects were 15, and the average number 50?
4. What are the 90% confidence intervals?

Three independent variables

1. Develop a three independent variable multiple regression model for profits as a function of the years' experience, the number of consultants on the projects, and the time spent away from the office.
2. Does the relationship appear strong? Quantify your answer.
3. What would be an estimate of profits for a particular quarter if the average experience of consultants on projects were 15, the average number 50, and the percentage of time away from the office 60%?
4. What are the 90% confidence intervals?

Application exercise 10.2 Crude oil

Situation

Table 10.29 gives the average price of crude oil at the end of the week from the New York Mercantile Exchange.*

Required

1. Plot the data on a scatter diagram.
2. Develop the linear regression equation that best describes these data.
3. Is the linear equation a good forecasting tool for forecasting the future value of crude oil? What quantitative piece of data justifies your response?

4. What is a forecast value for the price of crude at the end of October?
5. Develop a trend-adjusted exponential smoothing model to forecast future oil prices using an α factor of 0.8, a trend factor, β, of 0.4, an initial trend value of zero, and the forecast value for the first period equal to the actual data.
6. Using the exponential model, what is the forecast for crude oil prices at the end of October 2000?
7. What are your comments about using the regression, or exponential models for forecasting crude oil prices, particularly on a long-term basis?

*'Tapping the oil reserve: A short-term solution', *International Herald Tribune*, 23/24 September 2000, p. 9.

Table 10.29 New York Mercantile Exchange crude oil prices

Month	Week or code	$/bbl	Month	Week or code	$/bbl	Month	Week or code	$/bbl
Apr 1999	1	16.00	Oct 1999	25	25.00	Apr 2000	49	25.60
	2	17.20		26	20.80		50	25.00
	3	16.60		27	20.56		51	25.60
	4	18.40		28	22.12		52	25.84
May	5	19.60	Nov	29	21.40	May	53	26.20
	6	18.40		30	24.40		54	26.08
	7	17.92		31	25.60		55	26.56
	8	17.56		32	26.80		56	26.80
Jun	9	17.20	Dec	33	27.40	Jun	57	29.80
	10	18.40		34	26.80		58	30.16
	11	19.60		35	25.00		59	30.64
	12	19.00		36	26.80		60	31.36
Jul	13	19.60	Jan 2000	37	25.60	Jul	61	31.60
	14	20.08		38	24.40		62	29.20
	15	20.56		39	28.60		63	30.40
	16	20.68		40	28.00		64	27.76
Aug	17	20.80	February	41	27.40	Aug	65	28.00
	18	20.56		42	26.80		66	29.20
	19	23.20		43	28.00		67	30.40
	20	20.80		44	29.80		68	31.00
Sep 1999	21	22.00	March 2000	45	31.00	Sep 2000	69	31.60
	22	24.40		46	30.64		70	31.36
	23	26.80		47	31.60		71	32.80
	24	25.60		48	28.60		72	35.20

Application exercise 10.3 Euro

Situation

Table 10.30 gives the value of the euro, compared to the $US, since its introduction. These data are given at the end of each week.*

Required

1. Plot the data on a scatter diagram.
2. Develop the linear regression equation that best describes these data.

Table 10.30 Value of the euro compared to the US dollar

End of week	Value ($US)	End of week	Value ($US)	End of week	Value ($US)	End of week	Value ($US)
07 Jan 99	1.18	13 May 99	1.06	16 Sep 99	1.04	20 Jan 00	1.01
14 Jan 99	1.17	20 May 99	1.04	23 Sep 99	1.05	27 Jan 00	0.99
21 Jan 99	1.16	27 May 99	1.04	30 Sep 99	1.04	03 Jan 00	0.97
28 Jan 99	1.14	03 Jun 99	1.04	07 Oct 99	1.07	10 Jan 00	0.98
04 Feb 99	1.13	10 Jun 99	1.03	14 Oct 99	1.06	17 Feb 00	0.98
11 Feb 99	1.13	17 Jun 99	1.03	21 Oct 99	1.08	24 Feb 00	0.98
18 Feb 99	1.12	24 Jun 99	1.03	28 Oct 99	1.08	02 Mar 00	0.97
25 Feb 99	1.10	01 Jul 99	1.01	04 Nov 99	1.02	09 Mar 00	0.97
04 Mar 99	1.08	08 Jul 99	1.03	11 Nov 99	1.04	16 Mar 00	0.96
11 Mar 99	1.09	15 Jul 99	1.07	18 Nov 99	1.03	23 Mar 00	0.95
18 Mar 99	1.09	22 Jul 99	1.07	25 Nov 99	1.02	30 Mar 00	0.96
25 Mar 99	1.07	29 Jul 99	1.07	02 Dec 99	1.02	06 Apr 00	0.95
01 Apr 99	1.08	05 Aug 99	1.07	09 Dec 99	1.03	13 Apr 00	0.94
08 Apr 99	1.06	12 Aug 99	1.06	16 Dec 99	1.01	20 Apr 00	0.93
15 Apr 99	1.06	19 Aug 99	1.06	23 Dec 99	1.02	27 Apr 00	0.92
22 Apr 99	1.06	26 Aug 99	1.04	30 Dec 99	1.02		
29 Apr 99	1.07	02 Sep 99	1.06	06 Jan 00	1.03		
06 May 99	1.07	09 Sep 99	1.05	13 Jan 00	1.01		

3. Is the linear equation a good forecasting tool for forecasting the future value of the euro? What quantitative piece of data justifies your response?

4. Using the regression information, what is the monthly change (every four weeks) of the value of the euro?

5. On a calendar year basis (52 weeks) what is an estimate of the value of the euro in one year from 27 April 2000 (the last piece of data provided).

6. On a calendar year basis (52 weeks) what is an estimate of the value of the euro in 7½ years from 27 April 2000 (the last piece of data provided).

7. What are your comments about the forecast data obtained in questions 5 and 6?

*'ECB faces a policy bind: Help the Euro or save face?', *Wall Street Journal Europe*, 27 April 2000, p. 1.

Application exercise 10.4 GardenLand

Situation

GardenLand is a family-owned retail garden shop in Henley, England. Besides supplying individuals, it also sells fertilizer to the local cricket and tennis clubs. One of its products is potassium nitrate, which is sold in 25-kilogram bags as a lawn fertilizer. GardenLand obtains its supplies from a Rhodia subsidiary in East Anglia. Purchases of the fertilizer are made quarterly, as there is a large discount on potassium nitrate purchased in bulk. GardenLand has limited storage space, and each year it likes to forecast its needs for the coming year on a quarterly basis.

Table 10.31 gives the actual sales of potassium nitrate in kilograms, for the years 1997 through 1999.

Required

1. Establish that the sales of potassium nitrate are seasonal throughout the year.

Table 10.31 GardenLand: Sales of potassium nitrate (1997–1999)

Quarter	1st	2nd	3rd	4th
1997	5,400	7,500	8,400	5,500
1998	6,000	8,200	9,300	6,300
1999	6,700	9,100	10,500	6,700

2. Determine appropriate seasonal indexes, and make a forecast of sales for the first, second, third, and fourth quarters in 2000.

Application exercise 10.5 Houses

Situation

San Marino is a reasonably affluent area in the northeast of Los Angeles in California. A study was made to see if there were a relationship between home prices and surface area of the house. Surface area of the land was not included. Table 10.32 gives a sample of 14 houses together with their market price in $000s.

Required

1. Plot a scatter diagram to demonstrate whether or not there is a relationship between surface area and house prices.
2. Develop a linear estimating equation for these data.
3. Show the linear regression line on the scatter diagram.
4. How would you interpret the slope of the regression line?
5. What coefficient demonstrates the strength of the relationship, and what is its value?
6. If a homeowner with a property of 1600 square feet were considering putting his home on the market, what would be a reasonable estimate of the market price?
7. Develop a 90% confidence interval for the price of a house that has a surface area of 1600 square feet.
8. What is the predicted market price for a house of 800 square feet? What are your comments about this value?
9. In addition to the regression line, develop the following addition regression curves. Based on the coefficient of determination, which seems to be the best forecasting model

Table 10.32 Sample houses and their market price

Area (ft^2)	Price ($000s)
900	250
1,550	400
1,600	590
2,200	900
3,200	2,100
1,820	750
1,710	684
1,000	680
950	175
3,100	2,800
2,300	1,100
4,000	5,200
3,750	3,550
3,500	3,750

(include in your comparison the linear regression model just developed)?

(a) a curvilinear regression with a non-integer value of x of the form $y = ax^b$
(b) an exponential curve of the form $y = ae^{bx}$
(c) a polynomial function of the form $y = ax^2 + bx + c$.

10. From question 9 forecast house prices for 1600, 2000, 4000 and 10,000 square feet. What are your comments and observations?

Application exercise 10.6 International telephone calls

Situation

Table 10.33 gives the worldwide international telephone calls in terms of international call minutes in billions (no. calls* duration in minutes). These data are from both fixed telephone lines and cellular phones.*

Required

These historical data are to be used for forecasting capital investment by such companies as France Télécom, AT&T, MCI/Sprint, and BT.

1. Plot the data on a scatter diagram.
2. Develop the linear regression equation that best describes these data. Is the linear equation a good forecasting tool for telecommunications companies? What quantitative piece of data justifies your response?
3. What is the forecast for international calls in 2005?

Table 10.33 Number and duration of international phone calls

Year	International call minutes (billions)
1990	34
1991	38
1992	43
1993	48
1994	55
1995	62
1996	72
1997	83
1998	93
1999	106

4. What is the forecast for international calls in 2050? What are you comments regarding forecasting to the year 2050?

5. Does a second-degree polynomial regression line have a better fit for these data? If so, why?

6. What would be the forecast for international calls in 2050 using this new polynomial relationship?

7. What are your comments using the polynomial function to forecast to the year 2050?

*'International calls', *The Economist*, 4 December 1999, p. 128 (based on data from TeleGeography consultancy).

Application exercise 10.7 Marino Co.

Situation

The Marino Co. in Ventura County, southern California, sells swimming pool equipment. The sales for swimming pool motors in southern California over the last 13 months is given in Table 10.34.

Required

1. Develop a forecasting model using a three-month simple moving average. Plot this model together with the original data. What is an estimate of demand for motors for next February?

2. Using a three-month weighted moving average, estimate the demand for swimming pool motors for next February. Use 1, 2, and 3 for the weights, with 3 being the weight for the most recent period, and 1 the weight for oldest period. Plot the model together with the original data.

3. Using the criteria of the mean average deviation, which of the methods would seem the most appropriate?

Table 10.34 Marino Co.: Sales of swimming pool motors

January	11,000
February	14,000
March	16,000
April	10,000
May	15,000
June	17,000
July	11,000
August	14,000
September	17,000
October	12,000
November	14,000
December	16,000
January	11,000

Application exercise 10.8 Personal computers

Situation

Table 10.35 gives the sales by units of personal computers in a certain part of England.

Required

1. Plot a scatter diagram of the total sales and develop a linear regression line for these data.

2. From the same, or other scatter diagram of the total sales, develop a polynomial (second-degree regression equation) for these data. Show the regression line for these data.

3. For the range of data given, which is the best forecasting equation? Justify your reasoning by a quantitative measurement.

4. From the linear regression equation, forecast the sale of personal computers at December 1998.

5. From the second-degree regression equation, forecast the sale of personal computers at December 1998.

Table 10.35 Sales of personal computers by unit

	Total (1000 units)		Total (1000 units)
Jan 97	7,500	Jan 98	18,563
Feb 97	8,625	Feb 98	20,944
Mar 97	9,375	Mar 98	23,063
Apr 97	10,125	Apr 98	23,719
May 97	10,875	May 98	24,375
Jun 97	11,625	Jul 98	25,688
Jul 97	12,375	Jul 98	27,188
Aug 97	13,313	Aug 98	28,875
Sep 97	14,250	Sep 98	30,750
Oct 97	14,813		
Nov 97	16,125		
Dec 97	17,250		

6. What do you believe is the better forecast between 4 and 5? Justify your reasoning.
7. From the linear equation, forecast the sales of personal computers at December 2003.
8. From the second-degree equation, forecast the sales of personal computers at December 2003.

9. From the forecasts developed in questions 7 and 8, which do you think is better? Justify your reasoning.
10. In marketing, there is the concept of the 'product lifecycle'. Where in the product lifecycle would you think these data belong? Because of this positioning, why should you exercise caution in your forecasting?

Application exercise 10.9 Stationery

Situation

A company's records for stationery supplies in pounds sterling are as shown in Table 10.36.

Required

1. Develop an appropriate linear regression equation for these data.

2. What can you say about the reliability of the model you have created? Justify your reasoning.
3. What would be the forecast of sales for June 2001, December 2001, and June 2002? Which would be the most reliable?

Table 10.36 Stationery sales

Month	£000s	Month	£000s	Month	£000s	Month	£000s
Jan 1997	13	Jan 1998	26	Jan 1999	32	Jan 2000	42
Feb 1997	17	Feb 1998	27	Feb 1999	38	Feb 2000	43
Mar 1997	15	Mar 1998	23	Mar 1999	40	Mar 2000	47
Apr 1997	19	Apr 1998	28	Apr 1999	39	Apr 2000	44
May 1997	14	May 1998	30	May 1999	42	May 2000	48
Jun 1997	18	Jun 1998	31	Jun 1999	43	Jun 2000	51
Jul 1997	21	Jul 1998	33	Jul 1999	42	Jul 2000	50
Aug 1997	23	Aug 1998	31	Aug 1999	45	Aug 2000	52
Sep 1997	19	Sep 1998	35	Sep 1999	44	Sep 2000	53
Oct 1997	24	Oct 1998	34	Oct 1999	42	Oct 2000	54
Nov 1997	26	Nov 1998	37	Nov 1999	40	Nov 2000	57
Dec 1997	25	Dec 1998	36	Dec 1999	45	Dec 2000	56

Case study 10.1 Wine sales

Situation
The Manzio family owns a small premium winery in the Florence area of Italy. The volume of wine in thousand litres sold during 1998, 1999, and 2000 is given in Table 10.37.

Required
Based on this information, the owner is interested in developing a forecast model to estimate future sales.

Part I
Using the full 36-month data, develop forecasting models using a 3-month, 4-month, and 6-month moving average. What is the best model? Using this, what is an estimate of January 2001 wine sales?

Part II
Can you improve on the 3-month moving average model if you use weighting factors of 0.4, 0.3, and 0.3, where 0.4 is for the most recent period,

Table 10.37 Wine sales in thousands of litres (1998–2000)

	1998	1999	2000
January	530	535	578
February	436	477	507
March	522	530	562
April	448	482	533
May	422	498	516
June	499	563	580
July	478	488	537
August	400	428	440
September	444	430	511
October	486	486	480
November	437	502	499
December	501	547	542

Table 10.38 Hotel and guesthouse bookings and wine sales

	1998	1999	2000
January	28,700	29,800	30,800
February	23,200	25,200	28,000
March	29,000	28,000	31,000
April	23,500	26,000	28,400
May	21,900	25,000	27,500
June	25,300	31,000	32,000
July	26,000	25,550	31,000
August	20,100	23,200	22,000
September	22,300	24,100	26,000
October	25,100	25,100	27,000
November	22,600	27,000	28,000
December	27,000	31,900	30,200

and 0.3 for the oldest period? Justify your response.

Part III

Using the full 36-month data, develop forecasting models using the exponential smoothing method with alpha values of 0.1, 0.3, and 0.5, and using 500,000 litres for the starting point of the model. What is the best model? Using this, what is an estimate of January 2001 wine sales?

Part IV

1. Is a regression analysis appropriate for forecasting if the independent variable is the time period? Plot a scatter diagram to justify your response.
2. What conclusions would you draw from calculating the coefficient of determination?
3. If regression is appropriate, use the regression equation, to determine the best estimate of January 2001 sales.

The Manzio family noted that most of their wine sales were to tourists, or people who normally lived outside the wine growing area. Many of these people stayed in the numerous hotels and guesthouses around Florence. Through a market survey of hotel accommodation, data were compiled of the number of persons booked into hotels, and guesthouses during equivalent periods of wine sales as shown in Table 10.38.

4. Does there appear to be a reasonable relationship between hotel occupancy and wine sales? Explain your analysis with the aid of a scatter diagram, and a regression curve.
5. What conclusions would you draw from ascertaining the coefficient of determination?
6. According to the tourist board, hotel bookings for January 2001 are 31,000, and 25,000 for February 2001. Using this information, what is your best estimate of wine sales for these months using the regression equation?
7. Discuss the variables, and other environmental factors, which play a role in forecasting this type of product. Include macro- and microeconomic factors.

Selected further reading

BROCKWELL, Peter J. and DAVIS, Richard A. (2002) *Introduction to Time Series and Forecasting*, 2nd edition, Springer Verlag.

CROSBY, John V. (2000) *Cycles, Trends and Turning Points: Practical Marketing and Sales Forecasting Technique*, McGraw-Hill.

MENTZER, John T. and BIENSTOCK, Carol C. (1998) *Sales Forecasting Management: Understanding the Techniques, Systems, and Management of the Sales Forecasting Process*, Sage Publications.

PANKRATZ, Alan (1991) *Forecasting with Dynamic Regression Models*, Wiley-Interscience.

WALLACE, Thomas F. and STAHL, Robert A. (2002) *Sales Forecasting: A New Approach*, T. F. Wallace & Company.

An extensive listing of other further reading can be found on the website.

What's on the web?

Further learning resources are available to lecturers and students at www.supplychain-online.com, including the following which are specific to *Forecasting: The trigger in the supply chain*:

Resource	Subject
Chapter overview	Forecasting: The trigger in the supply chain
Detailed chapter summary	Forecasting: The trigger in the supply chain
Exam topics	Forecasting: The trigger in the supply chain
Application exercise: British Gas	Seasonal effects
Application exercise: Exxon Corporation	Time series regression
Application exercise: Garden tools (2)	Seasonal forecasting
Application exercise: Housing starts	Regression
Application exercise: Parkas	Seasonal effects
Application exercise: Peanuts	Averaging and exponential smoothing
Application exercise: Railway ridership	Casual regression
Application exercise: Smoking	Casual regression
Application exercise: Stationery	Regression
Application exercise: Telephones	Linear and polynomial regression
Application exercise: Tube passengers	Casual regression
More further reading	Forecasting: The trigger in the supply chain

(Note: Text and software packages sometimes vary with the use of lower and upper case of r, x, and y. However, the meaning is generally the same.)

11 *Inventory management*

Inventory and the supply chain

In the supply chain one of the key variables which has to be managed is inventory. The inventory includes a vast spectrum of material that is being transferred, stored, consumed, produced, packaged, or sold in one way or another during a firm's normal course of business. Inventory has a financial value, which for accounting purposes is considered a short-term asset, and also represents part of the working capital of the firm. Thus, one goal in operations is to keep the level of inventory in the supply chain to as low as possible thus freeing up funds for other purposes. Another goal is to move the inventory, in its continually changing form, as quickly as possible through the supply chain, for delivery to the final client, in order to realize the gains in the value added. The other principal financial commitment of firms is capital goods or long-term assets which are shown on a balance sheets as a depreciated item. These may include machines, equipment, vehicles, and buildings used for operating the business including transforming, delivering, and storing the inventory. Capital goods are not consumed in the same way as inventory and may have a practical life of many years.

Every business, be it services or manufacturing, handles, consumes, or moves inventory of some sort or another and good inventory management is a critical part of the operations. Some types of material, which come under the global concept of inventory, are as follows.

Services

- Restaurants have inventory of raw food, in-process inventory of the food being cooked, and the finished meal itself. In addition there is wine, bread, sauces and everything else that goes with preparing a meal.
- Retail outlets have finished goods inventory that is waiting to be purchased by customers.
- Offices such as law firms, or consulting companies, have consumable supplies of inventory such as paper, pencils, computer diskettes, and the like.
- Distribution companies, or logistics firms, which provide storage and transport might have inventory of finished goods such as clothing, household or office equipment. Alternatively, the inventory might be raw material such as cocoa beans, animal carcasses, or paper pulp or it might be industrial goods destined for another firm such as engine parts, plastic moulds, or cut lumber for construction. Very often, the distribution firms do not own the inventory but is either owned by the supplier, or the client to whom the inventory is destined.
- Express delivery firms such as FedEx, UPS, or Deutsche Post (the owner of Danzas; it is also a majority stakeholder in DHL) process and deliver large quantities of inventory in the form of large or small packages.
- Pharmacies, and particular hospitals, hold a large inventory of often very expensive pharmaceutical products.
- Computer software companies such as Microsoft have an 'inventory' of intellectual property or the computer programs.

Figure 11.1 Inventory types

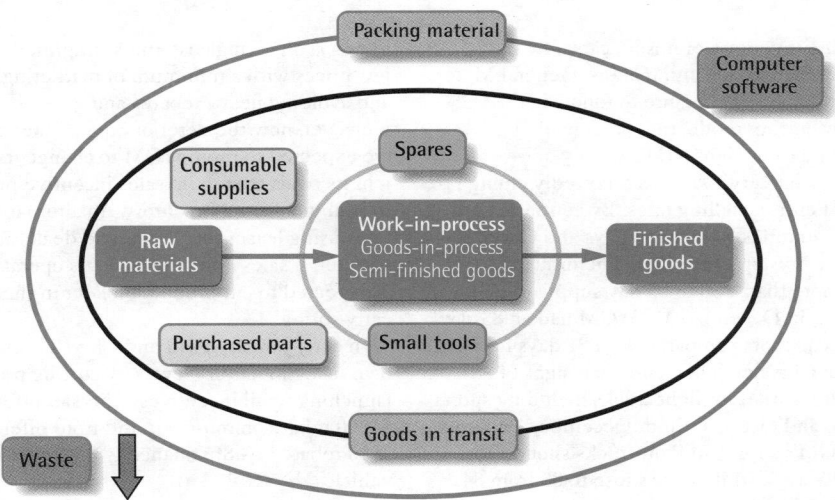

Manufacturing

Inventory is what production in the manufacturing sector is concerned about with its global supply chain being the purchasing, transformation, transfer, storing, and packaging of pieces, parts, and subassemblies. As illustrated in Figure 11.1, inventory associated with manufacturing includes the following.

Raw materials

Raw materials are the starting elements for any production process. In its lowest level form, raw material in the process industries may include iron ore, lumber, crude oil, wheat, water, paper pulp, etc. For some firms, raw materials may be purchased parts, intermediate chemicals, or subassemblies as for them this is the start point of their operation.

Purchased parts

Purchased parts, or components, are products that have been made by Company B and are used by Company A in their production operation or a business-to-business transaction in this part of the supply chain. Such items may include engine parts, tyres, and lights used by automobile companies, for example.

Work-in-process

Work-in-process, goods-in-process, or semi-finished goods are the pieces that are moving though the production operation. At each stage, the pieces are being modified and value is being added. All inventories between raw materials and finished goods constitute

work in process. The acronym for this type of inventory is WIP (work-in-process).

Finished goods

Finished goods are the products that have reached the end of the production line within a certain manufacturing organization. However, they may not necessarily be the finished goods that are used by the final consumer. Automobiles from Ford, televisions from Thomson, or computers from Dell are finished products whose next destination, after the distributor, is the customer. These are consumer goods and give business-to-consumer transactions in this part of the supply chain. However, starter motors for automobiles made by Valéo, meters for gas pipelines made by Schlumberger, or polypropylene for plastic products, made by Exxon Chemicals, are all finished goods destined for another firm. These are industrial goods in a business-to-business transaction and for the next downstream firm are purchased parts. Industry insight 11.1 illustrates how high finished goods can impact a firm's strategy.

Goods in transit

Goods in transit are products that are being transferred from one location to another. They could refer to raw material such as, crude oil being shipped from the Middle East to an oil refinery in Southampton, England, vanadium metal being shipped from South Africa to a tool firm in Germany, or, say, lumber from Norway being shipped to a construction firm in Spain. Goods in transit might be finished consumer items such as Volkswagen

Industry insight 11.1

High inventories result in a change of strategy

With its growing inventory of unsold cars now the highest of the US big three automakers, General Motors Corp. is under mounting pressure to follow its competitors by cutting production or launching aggressive rebate campaigns. GM's supply of cars on dealer lots on 31 January 1996 was reportedly enough to last 106 days at current selling rates. By contrast, Ford Motor Co.'s inventories stood at 83 days and Chrysler (now Daimler-Chrysler) at 97 days. The industry considers no more than a 60 to 65 day supply to be ideal. A month earlier, in December 1995, GM had an 83-day of supply on dealer lots compared with 81 days for Ford and 91 days for Chrysler. There are even signs of weakness in the market for light trucks including sports-utility vehicles and pickups. From December 1995 to January 1996 GM's supply of light trucks shot up to 87 days from 65 days, while Ford's rose to 88 from 84, and Chrysler's to 72 from 59 days.

Its rising inventories put GM in a bind as it pursues a new marketing strategy it calls 'value pricing'. The focus of this is on giving customers simplified and relatively low prices with a minimum of marketing gimmicks and avoiding heavy rebates and incentives. However, now the deteriorating market conditions are expected to prompt GM to change its strategy and join its rivals to step up sales incentive programmes to trim its bloated inventory. An alternative is to boost sales using leasing subsidies and dealer incentives. Further, if sales don't improve, its operations strategy is expected to cut production later in the winter or early spring.

In early January Ford and Chrysler responded to their own rising inventory levels by cutting production and launching retail incentives. Chrysler offered a minimum $1000 rebate on most cars and Ford offered a choice of $600 rebate or 4.8% financing on almost all its light vehicles.

Adapted from: 'GM faces lots of troubles as its car inventories grow', *Wall Street Journal*[1]

---

automobiles assembled in Mexico being shipped to consumers in Europe, clothing made in Hong Kong being shipped to consumers in France, or televisions made in Japan being shipped to consumers in the USA. Alternatively, goods in transit might be industrial goods for another firm.

Spare parts

Spare parts are inventory items that are kept in store for repair purposes. Piston rods, cogwheels, or springs would be spare parts kept for machinery. Wheels, chains, or brake blocks would be spare parts kept by a retailer for customers desiring to repair their bicycles. Spare parts are a special form of finished goods.

Small tools

Small tools are items that are used in a manufacturing or construction organization and are considered inventory because they are used up, maybe lost or perhaps stolen during the normal operation of the firm. Wrenches, screwdrivers, drills, work gloves, and overalls would be considered small tools in these industries. All manufacturing companies have tools as an inventory, as do construction companies. Typically, a construction company, in making a proposal for a building a process unit such as a refinery, or chemical plant would consider in the estimated project cost a figure between 2 and 5% to cover the cost of small tools.

Consumable supplies

Oil and cleaning fluids would be considered consumable supplies. In addition, as in a service company, there would also be office-type material such as pens, paper, files, envelopes, computer diskettes, etc.

Packaging

Packaging covers all the material used to protect finished goods, or to display items for marketing purposes. Cardboard boxes, corrugated paper, rubber sheeting is packing material for protection. The fancy, and often expensive, perfume bottles are also packing but their shape, and the associated wrapping, is also a marketing aid. Packaging represents finished goods to the producer of the packing material and to users such as Procter & Gamble, Hewlett-Packard, and Unilever, packing is a special inventory item.

Waste products

Waste products covers all the discarded products from a business and may in some instances have value (albeit a small amount). For example:

- Scrap metal from a firm making sheet steel, rod, girders and other metal products. The scrap can be sent back to a foundry for reprocessing.
- Scrap meat from a food processing factory that can be sold as animal feed.

- Wood scraps and sawdust from a lumber company that can be reprocessed into chipboard for furniture manufacture.

A special waste that represents a cost (and danger) is radioactive material principally from nuclear power plants. If it cannot be reprocessed this inventory has to be stored in repositories for many years. It essentially has no value.

Financial impact of good inventory management

Good inventory management in any part of the supply chain can improve the profitability of the firm and may even improve sales. Consider the situation shown in Table 11.1 for a small firm manufacturing and selling clothing items. In the column entitled Base case, the firm has annual sales of $50 million with the cost of goods sold, or the inventory, of $38 million. Taking into account other costs, the return on sales is 10%.

Reduce cost of goods sold

With good inventory management, by, say, keeping lower inventories of raw materials, in-process inventory,

and finished goods the firm is able to reduce the cost of goods sold by 4%. In doing this, the return on sales is now 13.04%.

Reduce general and administrative expenses

The fact that the inventory is lower, and turns over more quickly the inventory carrying cost is reduced which reduces the general and administrative expenses by 2%. Taking this additional factor into consideration increases the return on sales to 13.16%.

Increase customer service level

With good inventory management of finished goods, the firm is able to offer a better service level to its customers, resulting in fewer stockouts. In this case, the sales increase by an average of 3.25%. (The cost of goods sold increases accordingly.) The percentage return on sales is now 13.60%. When all these factors are taken into consideration, the increase in net income from the base case is over 40%.

Dependency of inventory

All inventories can be broadly divided into two groupings according to dependency on other items.

Table 11.1 Financial impact of good inventory management

| | Base case | Improved inventory management | | |
		Case 1	Case 2	Case 3
Income statement				
Sales	50,000,000	50,000,000	50,000,000	51,625,000
Cost of goods sold	38,000,000	36,480,000	36,480,000	37,665,600
Gross profit	12,000,000	13,520,000	13,520,000	13,959,400
General and administration expenses	3,000,000	3,000,000	2,940,000	2,940,000
Marketing expenses	4,000,000	4,000,000	4,000,000	4,000,000
Net income before taxes	5,000,000	6,520,000	6,580,000	7,019,400
Return on sales	10.00%	13.04%	13.16%	13.60%
By good inventory management				
Case 1: Cost of goods sold reduced by	4.00%			
Case 2: Carrying costs reduced by	2.00%			
Case 3: Sales increased by	3.25%	(because of better customer service level)		
Increase in net income	40.39%			

Independent demand inventory

Independent inventory is those items that are not dependent on other parts. This means that they are the ultimate finished product destined for the final consumer such as automobiles, cans of beer, washing machines, etc. Their demand depends solely on the requirements and demand of the consumer. Managing these inventory items requires forecast information of consumer needs and as such their movement is essentially the responsibility of the sales or marketing department.

Dependent demand inventory

Dependent inventory includes items that are usually assemblies or parts used in the manufacture of the final consumer product. For example, in the manufacture of a bicycle as illustrated in Figure 11.2, there is one frame, one saddle, one pair of handlebars, and two wheels. For each wheel there are 36 spokes (depending on the model) one tyre, 24 bearings etc. Except for components used for spare parts, the quantity of inventory of these components depends on the demand for the finished product. As these inventory items have a dependency, they can be effectively managed using a material requirements planning system (see Chapter 13).

Inventories and the economy

Inventories anywhere in the supply chain be they raw materials, manufactured goods, wholesale or retail goods are an indicator of economic changes as Industry insight 11.2 illustrates.

Figure 11.2 Product structure for a bicycle

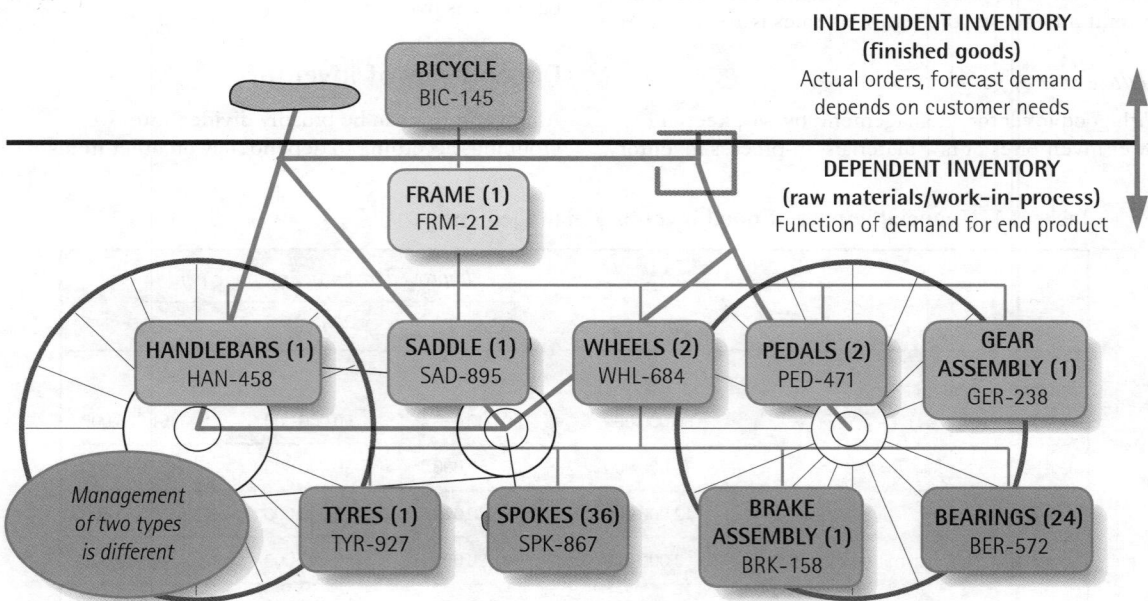

INDEPENDENT INVENTORY
(finished goods)
Actual orders, forecast demand
depends on customer needs

DEPENDENT INVENTORY
(raw materials/work-in-process)
Function of demand for end product

BICYCLE
BIC-145

FRAME (1)
FRM-212

HANDLEBARS (1)
HAN-458

SADDLE (1)
SAD-895

WHEELS (2)
WHL-684

PEDALS (2)
PED-471

GEAR
ASSEMBLY (1)
GER-238

*Management
of two types
is different*

TYRES (1)
TYR-927

SPOKES (36)
SPK-867

BRAKE
ASSEMBLY (1)
BRK-158

BEARINGS (24)
BER-572

Inventories as a measure of the health of the economy

Industry insight 11.2

According to data from the US Department of Commerce, inventories of goods held by US wholesalers grew by a modest 0.3% in October 2000. Though this figure is less than the 1% growth experienced in some earlier months it did give additional weight to the economists' thesis that the US economy is slowing. The October data also showed that the inventory-to-sales ratio, a measure of how long it would take to deplete inventories at the current sales pace, held at 1.3 months or the same is in September 2000 and close to the 1.29 months of a year ago. Further, sales in October remained flat at about $251 billion or virtually unchanged from the previous month. This suggests that even a modest increase in inventories could be a problem if, for example, sales continue to remain flat or even decline, but firms continue to increase inventories, then this could portend cutbacks in production and economic growth. Other October data, indicating an economic slowdown, showed that factory inventories rose 0.6% in October, inventories of non-durables, or manufactured items designed to last less than three years, also rose

0.6% up from 0.4% in September. The increase was led by gains in paper products, drugs, alcohol, and miscellaneous non-durables. Inventories of durables grew at a slower 0.2% led by a 2.7% increase in the electrical equipment category.

Adapted from: 'US inventories indicate a slowdown in the economy', *Wall Street Journal Europe*[2]

Reasons for holding inventory

Inventory has a value, so keeping a store of goods costs money. However, as summarized in Figure 11.3, and discussed in the following sections, there are many valid reasons why firms keep in storage a certain amount of inventory and often more than is required for the next immediate period.

Finished goods held by a distributor or retailer

Retailers (Marks & Spencer, UK; Safeway, UK; Carrefour, France; Wal-Mart, USA; Macys, USA) or wholesale distributors to retail outlets always have a certain amount of inventory on hand for reasons such as the following.

Figure 11.3 **Reasons for holding inventory**

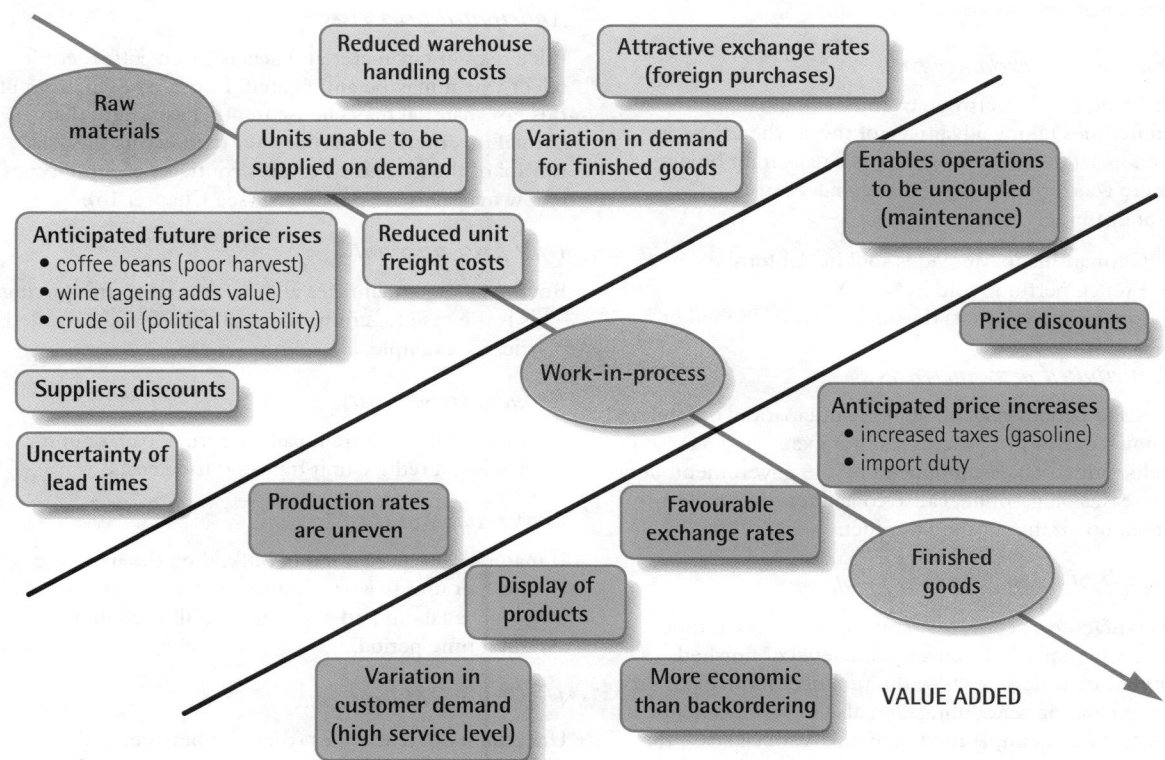

Variation in customer demand

Customers' demands vary from period to period and as it is not always easy to forecast their needs, extra supplies are kept in order to try to always satisfy the client (i.e. provide a high level of service). In addition, it is often more economical to hold inventory rather than place emergency orders for clients. Further, backordering of standard products may be unacceptable to the customer, as they will purchase elsewhere and the retailer would thus lose a sale and the resulting revenue.

Display of products

Holding inventory allows display of products to aid the sale. In some cases, displayed products may be unable to be sold after they have been used for display purposes. At least they are sold at a marked-down price. For example, clothing pinned to mannequins is difficult to sell as the pinning destroys the fabric, and sunlight in the window fades the material.

Price discounts

If finished products are purchased in bulk, discounts are often available. Thus, it is more economical to take advantage of lower unit prices, and store what is not immediately necessary.

Favourable exchange rates

Exchange rates between countries fluctuate and sometimes taking advantage of these when they are beneficial to the buying party is a reason for buying more goods than is immediately necessary.
For example:

- German-made Mercedes sold in California
- French perfume sold in New York
- Japanese televisions destined for the US market.

Anticipated price increases

Finished goods may be held in anticipation, or forehand knowledge of price increases. For example, increase in value added taxes announced by the government, or tax increases on gasoline, cause consumers, or retailers to stock up on the finished product.

Finished goods held by a producer

Manufacturing concerns strive to work just in time (see Chapter 15). Even so, some level of finished inventory is held to allow the producer more flexibility in production scheduling, and also to supply clients when there is unplanned demand. A special case for holding finished goods inventory is the following.

Milk

Candia, France, a Sodiaal subsidiary, has a 'quarantine' of four days on the finished product milk that it has pasteurized and put into cartons. This four-day holding period is to allow the quality control laboratory to perform required tests to be sure it is fit for consumption. The inventory is stored on pallets stacked 27 metres high in warehouses that have automatic placement and withdrawal systems.[3]

Raw materials

Raw materials are held in inventory by manufacturing companies for reasons such as the following.

Immediate delivery is not feasible

Supplies of crude oil, iron ore, coal cannot be supplied always immediately on demand and so the producer needs a certain level of inventory to permit reasonable production planning.

Variation in the demand for finished goods

If the demand for finished goods varies then this snowballs back along the production supply chain, and creates a variation in demand for the raw materials.

Anticipated price rises

Price rises of raw materials such as green coffee, crude oil, or wheat may be anticipated. In this case, the user of this raw material may choose to purchase larger than normal inventories. Often, rather than taking physical control of the inventory, futures contracts of these types of raw materials are purchased (see Chapter 16).

Unit price discount

Buying in large quantities allows favourable unit pricing. This is the case for crude oil, steel, fabric, and extruded plastic, for example.

Reduced freight costs

Buying in bulk (one trainload, one truckload, or one shipload) can reduce unit transportation costs.

Lower warehouse costs

If materials are purchased in bulk, then the handling charges per unit in a warehouse, or storage zone may be lower since labour and machines are all used in one assigned time period.

Uncertainty of lead times

Uncertainty of lead times (the time between ordering and delivery) because of political instability, strikes,

Figure 11.4 Material flow of work-in-process

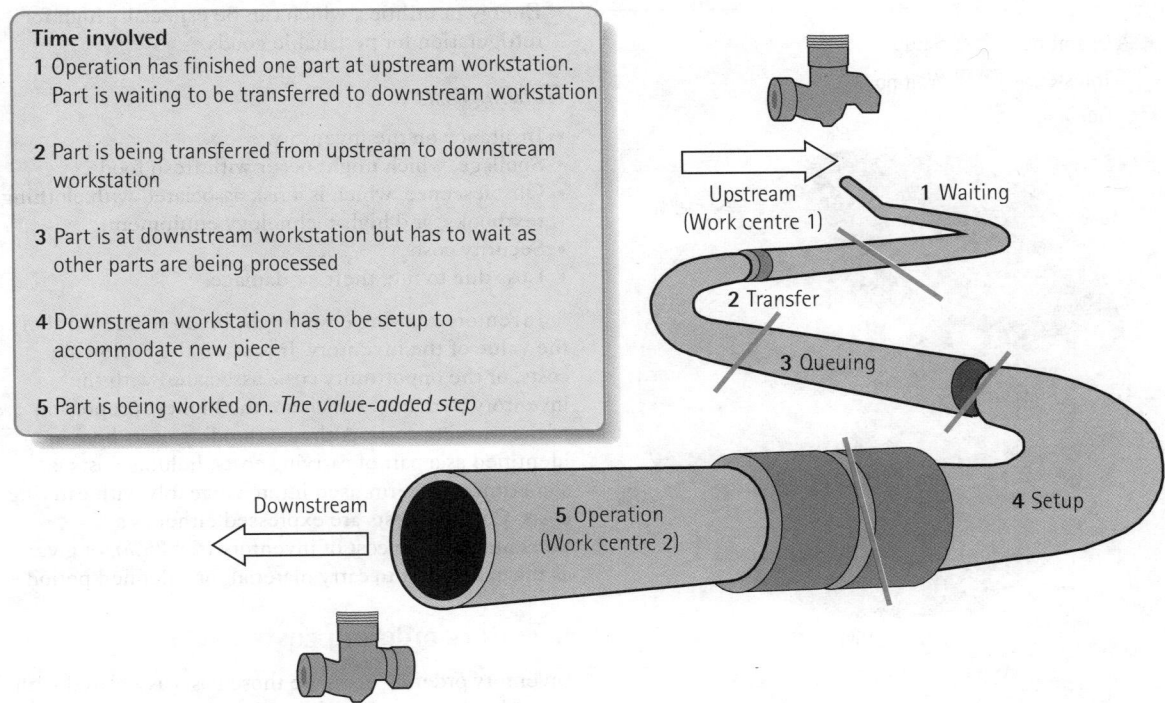

Time involved

1 Operation has finished one part at upstream workstation. Part is waiting to be transferred to downstream workstation

2 Part is being transferred from upstream to downstream workstation

3 Part is at downstream workstation but has to wait as other parts are being processed

4 Downstream workstation has to be setup to accommodate new piece

5 Part is being worked on. *The value-added step*

Upstream (Work centre 1)

1 Waiting

2 Transfer

3 Queuing

4 Setup

Downstream

5 Operation (Work centre 2)

---

weather, or tight supply situations may result in holding higher than normal inventory.

Work-in-process inventory

Work-in-process inventory arises principally because of waiting or delays of one type or another in the production 'pipeline'. This pipeline scheme is illustrated in Figure 11.4, which shows a flange connection used in fluid flow operation. Consider two work centres:

- Upstream, Work centre 1, where the left side of the flange is completed.
- Downstream, Work centre 2, where the right side of the flange is completed.

The pipeline can be considered broken into five zones:

1. Work centre 1 where the left side is finished, and the semi-finished flange is waiting to be transferred to Work centre 2.
2. The semi-finished flange is being transferred to Work centre 2.
3. At Work centre 2 there are other jobs being worked on, as the system is unbalanced. Thus, there is

queuing time for this particular flange. Queuing is also waiting but it means waiting for a specific activity. (Waiting for a bus to arrive would be another example.)

4. Setup time. At Work centre 2 the machines have to be adjusted to the specifications required by the flange in question.
5. Setup is finished, and the last stage is the time taken to do the operation. This is the only value-added step.

Actual delay times vary according to firm and industry, and the operation being carried out. However, to illustrate the point, Figure 11.5 gives a relative magnitude of the various zones where inventory is being held. Of importance, is that about only 5% of the total time, is value being added to the inventory. For 95% of the holding time, no value is being added.

Production managers' argument for keeping work-in-process inventory is that production rates are uneven, and uncoupling of operations can be achieved to give more flexibility. The counterargument for this is that the production rate should be balanced to allow for smooth flow throughout the operation.

Figure 11.5 Proportion of time spent by work-in-process inventory

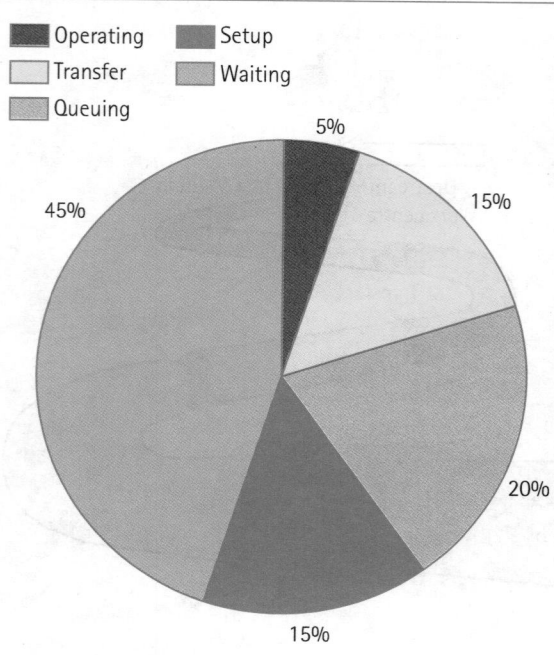

- Operating
- Transfer
- Queuing
- Setup
- Waiting

5%
15%
20%
15%
45%

Costs associated with inventory management

Three categories of cost in inventory management include carrying costs, ordering costs, and stockout costs.

Inventory carrying costs

Inventory carrying costs are those costs associated with keeping inventory in a storage area.

Investment in the inventory

- Borrowing costs associated with obtaining the funds to purchase the inventory.
- Opportunity costs, or financial returns that could be realized from investments other than using the cash to purchase the inventory.

Warehousing

- Property taxes on the facility.
- Rental, or purchase of the facility, which thus incurs a depreciation charge.

- Insurance on the warehouse facility for fire or other hazard.
- Energy or utilities, which can be especially high for refrigeration for perishable goods.

Holding costs

- Insurance on the inventory.
- Spoilage, which might occur with fresh foods.
- Obsolescence, which is a risk associated with clothing, textbooks, and high-technology equipment.
- Security costs.
- Loss due to fire, theft, or damage.

Inventory carrying costs might be up to one-third of the value of the inventory. It is often the borrowing costs, or the opportunity costs associated with the inventory purchase, which are the highest proportion of the carrying costs. Although holding costs here are identified as a part of carrying costs, holding costs is sometimes the term used interchangeably with carrying costs. Carrying costs are expressed either as a percentage of the cost of inventory (say 25%), or given as the actual cost to carry material for a defined period.

Inventory ordering costs

Inventory ordering costs are those costs associated with procuring the inventory. They are expressed as cost per order and do not include the purchase cost of materials. The inventory might be acquired externally, or internally.

Externally obtained inventory

Inventory might be purchased from an external sources such as the purchase of sheet steel for a manufacturing plant, packaging material, or textiles for a clothing manufacturer. In this case, the ordering costs would include:

- Salary of purchasing staff or those persons involved in proposal analysis, preparing and sending order.
- Accounting staff involved in paying for purchased goods.
- Communication costs including postage, telephone, fax, electronic mail, or Internet connection, or costs for developing a website.
- Expediting the goods if they don't arrive as planned.
- Warehouse costs associated with receiving, handling, separating lots, classifying, and inspection.

As the use of the Internet with websites becomes more the accepted practice in procuring material from suppliers it is expected that purchasing costs will decline.

Internally obtained inventory

The inventory might be produced by the same company. For example, Work centre B orders some engine assemblies from Work centre A. Both are cost centres and Work centre A would charge Work centre B for ordering the inventory in addition to the price of the inventory itself. This cost would be considered all, or part of the transfer cost and would include:

- preparation of production orders
- scheduling of the labour force
- preparation of materials and tools
- setup of machines and work posts in order to produce the required order.

In most instances, these various inventory ordering costs are associated with the salary, or wages of operating personnel.

Inventory stockout costs

Inventory stockout costs are those costs associated with having insufficient inventory to satisfy client demand. These costs may be related to the finished product, which is sold to clients, or to a production system, which uses the inventory in their operation. When placing orders to replenish inventory when it is getting low there are two extremes – ordering small quantities or ordering large quantities. Smaller quantities result in average lower inventory levels but since stockouts usually occur during lead time (the time between order and delivery), the likelihood of stockouts is increased when smaller orders are placed. Further, with small orders, more inventory cycles per year are needed (more inventory ordering). By way of contrast, placing large orders reduces the risk of a stockout but increases the average level of inventory, and thus the carrying cost. Stockout costs are hard to quantify directly and would not appear on an income statement. However, these 'costs' would include the following for finished goods and the production system.

Finished goods

- Lost profit of customer orders that cannot be filled.
- Loss of clients who go elsewhere for the products.
- Additional costs to satisfy order, such as subcontracting, overtime, or direct purchase from another source.
- If the customer accepts backlogging, additional costs can result from extra paperwork, special handling of orders, and expediting.
- Additional transportation costs to finally satisfy the demand.

Production system

- Shutdown costs due to insufficient raw materials.
- Machines under-utilized.
- Labour underemployed.
- Reduced employee morale which can lead to a decline in productivity.
- Expediting necessary articles.
- Startup costs such as the preparation of orders, and preparing machines when the inventory finally arrives.

Quantifying the value of a stockout

To quantify how much inventory to carry a company needs to determine the expected cost, or how much money it would lose if a stockout does occur. This is not easy to determine but might be estimated as follows using historical data and weighting the information. Assume that when a product is out of stock:

- 55% of the time, this results in preparing a backorder for the client. Backordering reduces the profit margin by $5.00.
- 25% of the time, this results in a lost sale for the product. This means a $50.00 loss in profit margin.
- 20% of the time, this results in a lost customer. This means a $500.00 loss.

Thus, the expected loss is:

$$0.55 * \$5.00 + 0.25 * \$50 + 0.20 * \$500 = \$115.25$$

This amount represents the average value of incurring a stockout. Thus, a company should carry additional inventory to avoid stockouts providing that on the average the cost of carrying this additional stock, does not exceed $115.25 per unit. (See Chapter 23 which gives more detail on this concept.)

Safety stocks

In selling, in production, or in purchasing operations there is uncertainty:

- Customers may increase an order.
- There may be a strike.
- Machinery might break down.
- Suppliers might be unable to deliver when promised.

To attempt to avoid stockouts resulting from these uncertainties, organizations might keep a safety stock 'just in case'. This safety stock is dead inventory. It provides a safeguard, but adds to inventory carrying costs.

Value added to inventory

As raw material and components move through the supply chain they are modified in one way or another (sheet steel is cut, drilled, shaped, and dipped). These operations add value to the material. As a result of adding value, finished goods is the inventory that represents the highest value to the firm. At the end of the production line, the maximum amount of value has been added. Thus, from a purely financial consideration it is less expensive to hold raw materials in stock, which have a lower value, than finished goods, which have a higher value. In addition, as explained in Chapter 17, as one moves through the production or supply pipeline, flexibility with the inventory is lost.

Ordering decisions for independent demand inventory

Inventory control

In inventory management control the most critical concern is not to run out of stock, such that customers are lost, or that a production line is shut down. However, at the same time it is important not to have so much inventory that carrying costs are excessive or that the inventory is wasted, such as may be the case for

perishable foods and products which quickly become obsolete. Two principal decisions to be made in ordering finished goods, or independent inventory are:

1. The quantity of goods to order. These units may come from an outside supplier or from a production department within the same organization. In either case, the amount depends on the expected future consumption and the amount of inventory that is already in stock.
2. When, or at what date, to place the order. This decision would be a function of the supplier lead time, or the time between when the order is placed and when the order is received and also the expected consumption of the inventory during this lead time.

Two possible approaches to ordering inventory are in fixed order quantities or fixed lot sizes, or ordering in fixed time periods.

Ordering in fixed order quantities

In ordering inventory in fixed lot sizes, as illustrated in Figure 11.6, purchase orders are placed for the same quantity of material in each inventory cycle (period between successive inventory ordering activities). The order quantity, Q, is constant and it is assumed this quantity is delivered in one single lot. When this inventory arrives, the level in storage increases to around a pre-established maximum level. As inventory

Figure 11.6 **Inventory movements using a fixed order quantity**

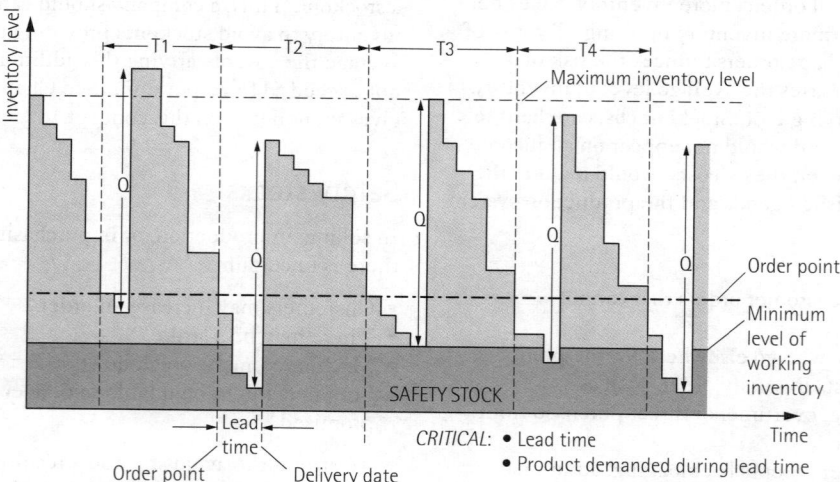

Order quantities are the same
Time between making each order is not necessarily the same
Lead times are not necessarily the same
T1, T2, T3, and T4 are not equal

Figure 11.7 Two-bin inventory system

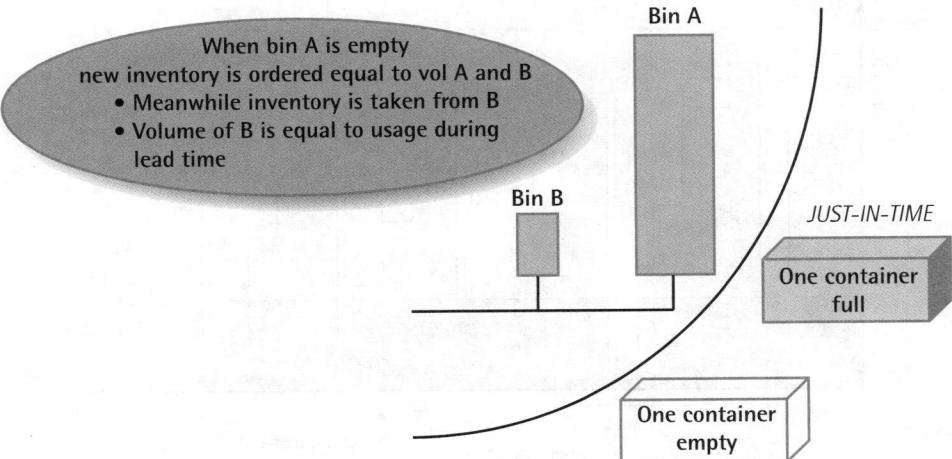

When bin A is empty
new inventory is ordered equal to vol A and B
• Meanwhile inventory is taken from B
• Volume of B is equal to usage during
  lead time

Bin A

Bin B

JUST-IN-TIME

One container
full

One container
empty

is taken out of storage for use, or sale, the level falls until it reaches a critical level, or the order point. At this level, another order is placed. The level of this order point is determined by estimating the expected usage of inventory during lead time, plus perhaps a safety stock. During this lead time, as illustrated, inventory is still being consumed and may or may not eat into the safety stock. At worst, a stockout may occur.

Two-bin system

A two-bin system is a special form of a fixed ordering system, which can be used for bulk products such as fertilizer, cattle feed, cement, chemical materials, fuel oil, propane, etc. Inventory of material is kept in two silos, or holding tanks A and B as shown in Figure 11.7. A is much larger than B and is the principal receptacle from which material is normally withdrawn. If the inventory is solid, then at the bottom of bin A might be a pre-printed requisition for another order of material. As the material is withdrawn and the container empties the requisition form falls through the exit nozzle. This requisition is then sent to purchase another lot of material. In the meantime, while the new order is waiting to be delivered, material is used out of container B. The container B is sized to hold enough material to last until the next inventory replenishment, which would be equivalent to the demand during lead time plus perhaps a safety stock. If the inventory is a liquid such as fuel oil, a level gauge fitted with an alarm system, will indicate when container A is empty and that a new order needs to be placed.

Just-in-time production (see Chapter 15) is often implemented using a type of two-bin system. At a

work post, an operator uses components based on the principle: 'One container empty and one container full'. At the work post there is always one container (bin) full of component parts, and one container (bin) from which pieces are being used. When this latter container is empty, the operator goes to inventory storage replaces it with a full container. Meanwhile production work continues using the container that was originally full. (Most machines run automatically and do not need the presence of an operator 100% of the time.)

Ordering at fixed time periods

Here, as illustrated in Figure 11.8, purchase orders are placed at preset time intervals. At these time intervals, the existing inventory level is measured and orders are placed to bring inventory levels back to some predetermined level. Thus, order quantities may be unequal but order intervals are equal. Small grocers or retailers might use this type of system where say inventory levels are measured at the end of the week, and the required order quantities are placed for delivery the following week.

For the provider of the inventory using a fixed time period system there is uncertainty between the ordering times since customer demand might be unusually high and result in a stockout. This uncertainty usually means that the level of safety stock needs to be higher than in an equivalent operation using a fixed order quantity system. In the fixed order period there is no direct internal control and the risk is external related to the fickleness of customers. However, in a fixed order quantity system the control point is internal and is the lower inventory level which is a trigger for a new order.

Figure 11.8 Inventory movements using a fixed order time period

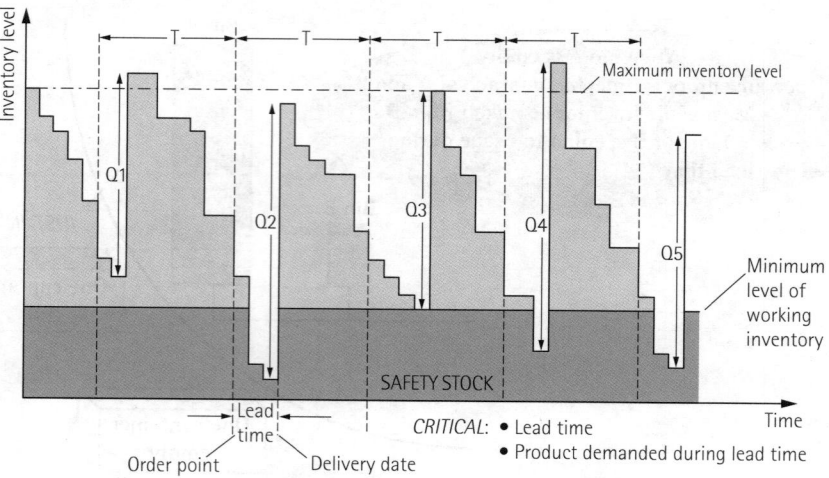

Time between making orders is the same
Order quantities are not necessarily the same
Lead times are not necessarily the same
Q1, Q2, Q3, Q4, and Q5 are not equal

Butcher's shop

To illustrate the fixed order period system: When a student, the author worked for five years in a cooperative butcher's shop in Watford, England. Every Friday afternoon he would work in the cold storage area counting the sides of beef, lamb, pork, the number of chickens, and turkeys. He gave to the butcher this inventory list who then called the slaughterhouse on Saturday morning to make an order for meat to bring his inventory up to a predetermined level. This order was delivered from the slaughterhouse on Monday morning. On occasions, the butcher would have a stockout of beef, for example, on a Thursday as the English weather had turned unusually cold and people were cooking more steak and kidney pie. So the butcher had to call the slaughterhouse and have a special order delivered mid-week.

Bar codes

The commonly used bar code is a way of uniquely identifying a product, including the price and the reference number plus other characteristics depending on needs. The code is a series of wide and narrow strips, or bars, stamped onto the product label. Symbols, letters, and numbers are used to identify the product, which can be read by a laser scanner. This system greatly improves the management, and ordering of inventory at the retail level and also in production

systems. When a customer, or user, takes a product the item is scanned, recorded, and with the firm's information system the item is automatically deducted from inventory. Thus management always has a continuous real-time accounting of inventory levels.

Inventory levels and order quantities

An objective in inventory management is to keep inventory-related costs to a minimum. The quantity ordered in each cycle can impact the average inventory level and thus the investment in this inventory. Consider a situation where there is a certain daily demand of inventory and to support this demand there are two inventory ordering choices:

1. Every five days a fixed quantity of 100 units of inventory are delivered or an average quantity of 20 units/day.
2. Every day, a fixed quantity of 20 units of inventory are ordered or an average quantity of 20 units/day, the same as in the first situation.

The movement of inventory for these two situations is illustrated graphically in Figures 11.9 and 11.10. In the case of the larger order, the average inventory level is over 50% higher, which results in higher carrying costs, but reduces the risk of a stockout. However, ordering costs would be lower, so there would be a trade-off between large or small orders. This analysis has considered no safety stocks. If safety stocks were held

Figure 11.9 Large inventory quantities delivered less frequently

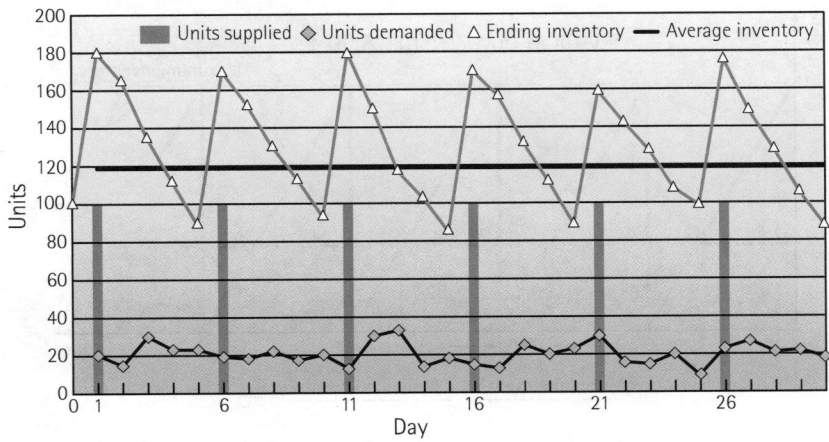

Figure 11.10 Small inventory quantities delivered more frequently

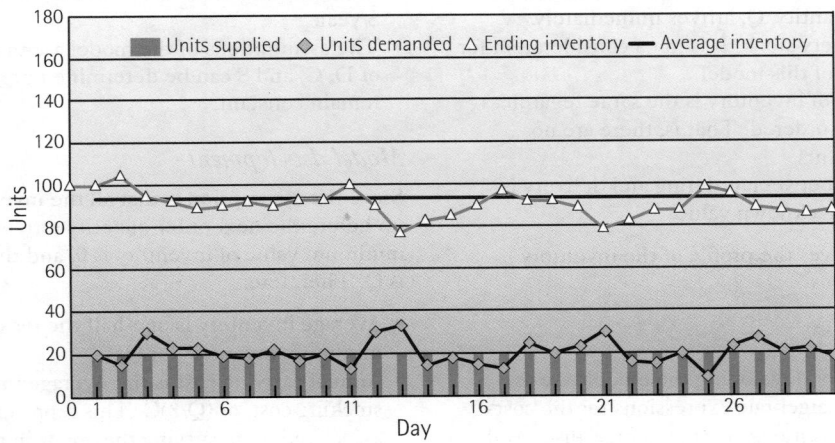

this would additionally increase the carrying cost. This concept is further discussed in the following section.

Economic order quantity models

Inventory models have been developed to determine an economic order quantity for independent inventory.[4] The economic order quantity, EOQ, is the optimum amount of material to order that has the least overall inventory-related cost taking into account, carrying costs, ordering costs, and stockout costs. If large quantities of material are ordered at any one time, rather than small quantities, then the inventory ordering costs per unit, and the probability of stockout will be low.

However, inventory carrying costs will be high. Thus, there is an inventory-related cost that tends to decrease (ordering cost and stockout cost), and one that tends to increase (carrying cost). The total inventory-related cost is the sum of the carrying costs, and the ordering costs and the economic ordering cost is when this total cost has a minimum value.

Model I: Basic EOQ

In developing the basic EOQ model the assumptions for ordering and using inventory are as follows.

- Inventory of quantity Q is delivered in one lot according to an ordering schedule.
- Delivered inventory is used at a uniform rate, or linearly.

Figure 11.11 Inventory profile for the basic EOQ model

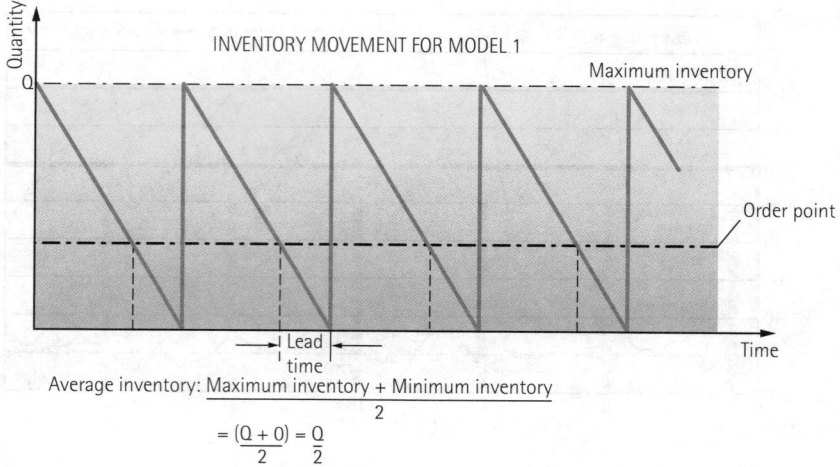

Average inventory: $\dfrac{\text{Maximum inventory} + \text{Minimum inventory}}{2}$

$= \dfrac{(Q + 0)}{2} = \dfrac{Q}{2}$

- When the last item of inventory has been consumed a new lot of quantity, Q, arrives immediately.
- There is no safety stock. It is not a consideration for the conditions of this model.
- The unit price of inventory is the same regardless of the quantity ordered. That is, there are no quantity discounts.
- The lead time between ordering and delivery is constant, and is a known value.

Figure 11.11 gives the profile of the inventory movement.

Terms

The terms used for developing the models are as follows. They are algebraic expressions for the costs associated with inventory management as discussed in the previous section:

- D is the annual demand by the client for inventory in units/year. However, the time period could be weeks, months, or some other period.
- Q is the quantity of material ordered each time a requisition is made and is measured in units/ purchase order.
- C is the cost of carrying one unit in inventory for one year, $/unit/year when one year is the time period in consideration. This value of C may be a given financial amount such as $10/unit/year or may be expressed as a percentage of the unit purchase price of the material, such as 25% * P where P is the unit price. This is important when there are price discounts, as C will change with the unit price.
- S is the average cost of placing a purchase order, $/order.

- TSC is the total annual inventory stocking cost, $/year.
- The assumptions of the model are that the values of D, C, and S can be determined precisely, and remain constant.

Model development

Since the assumption is that all the inventory is used up before the next order quantity arrives then the minimum value of inventory is 0, and the maximum is Q. Therefore:

- Average inventory is one-half the maximum and minimum inventory, or Q/2.
- Annual carrying cost is the Average inventory * Unit stocking cost, or (Q/2)C. This represents the total cost associated with carrying the goods in the warehouse or distribution centre.
- Number of orders made per year is the annual consumption/order quantity, or D/Q. For example, if the annual consumption is 250,000 units per year and the order quantity is 10,000 units, then the number of orders is 250,000/10,000 = 25.
- Annual ordering cost is the Number of orders * Ordering cost, or (D/Q)S. This represents the total cost associated with procuring the inventory.
- Total costs associated with inventory handling is the sum of the carrying and stocking costs, or:

$$\text{TSC} = \dfrac{Q}{2}C + \dfrac{D}{Q}S$$

This equation indicates that the total annual carrying costs are increasing with the value of Q, whereas the total annual ordering costs are decreasing as the value of Q increases. Thus the total costs are a minimum when the total carrying costs, and purchasing costs are equal, or:

$$\frac{QC}{2} = \frac{DS}{Q}$$

Reorganizing and making Q the subject:

$$Q = EOQ = \sqrt{\frac{2DS}{C}}$$

This is the economic order quantity or the quantity to purchase to make inventory-related costs a minimum.

Alternatively, this result can be arrived at by using calculus and differentiating the cost equation with respect to Q:

$$\frac{\delta(TSC)}{dQ} = \frac{C}{2} - \frac{D \cdot S}{Q^2}$$

This value will have a minimum when:

$$\frac{\delta(TSC)}{dQ} = 0$$

or:

$$\frac{C}{2} - \frac{DS}{Q^2} = 0$$

Solving this equation for Q:

$$Q^2 = \frac{2DS}{C}$$

$$Q = EOQ = \sqrt{\frac{2DS}{C}}$$

That is, the same as before.

Figure 11.12 shows the graphical relationship between inventory carrying costs, inventory ordering costs, and total costs. The inventory carrying costs increase linearly with the quantity Q, the ordering costs decline with Q, and the total costs exhibit a minimum. These curves are obtained by calculating the various costs for different inventory quantities.

Range of economic order quantity

In calculating the value of the EOQ, although there is mathematically only one precise value, there is a range of order quantities around the EOQ for which the total stocking costs do not change significantly. This is illustrated in Figure 11.13. In this figure, the mathematically calculated EOQ is 3536 units giving a total stocking cost of $35,355. However, if an order quantity of 2800 units were used (almost 21% smaller than the EOQ value) then the total stocking costs would be $36,321 or only 2.7% greater than the EOQ total stocking cost. Alternatively, if the order quantity were 4400 units (almost 25% greater than the EOQ value) the total stocking would be $36,205 or only 2.4% greater than the EOQ total stocking cost. This illustrates that

Figure 11.12 **EOQ model: Cost curves**

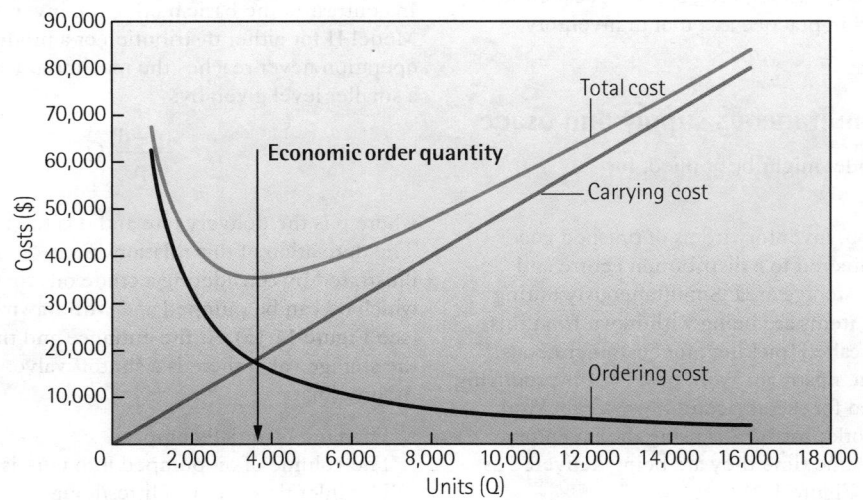

Figure 11.13 EOQ Model I: Range is large for small change in total cost

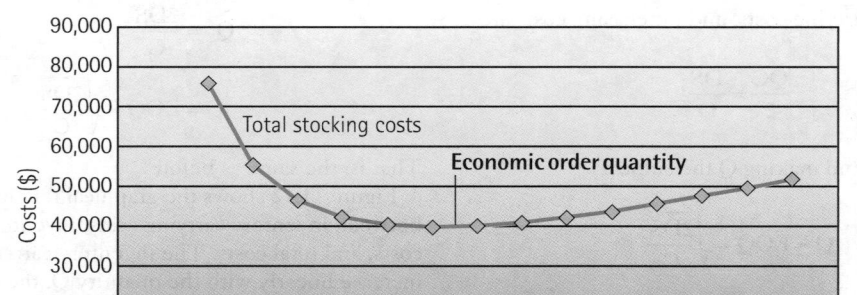

Figure 11.14 EOQ Model II: Inventory usage at adjacent workstations

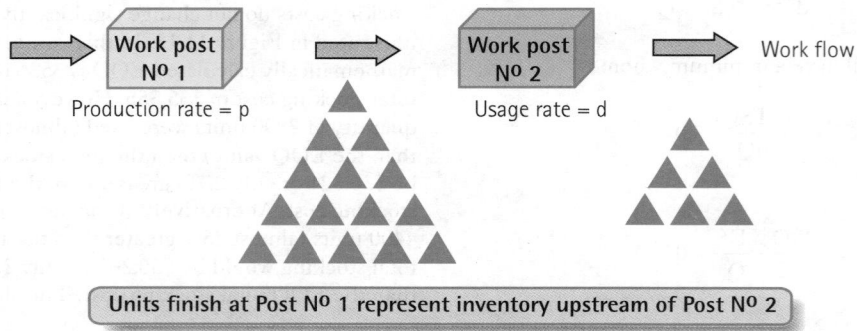

an economic order quantity for a practical application is flexible. Further, although the model is academic, it can be applied in practice as a tool in inventory management.

Model II: Simultaneous supply and usage

This type of model might be applied, for example, when:

1. In distribution, inventory items of finished goods are being delivered to a distribution centre and placed in the storage area. Simultaneously during this delivery, items are being withdrawn from this storage area, called 'picking', for customer needs.
2. In production, upstream Work post N° 1 is producing units destined for the adjacent downstream Work post N° 2. Work post N° 2 is using the inventory items at the same time they are being delivered as illustrated in Figure 11.14.

Maximum inventory

In contrast to the basic model, the inventory level in Model II for either distribution or a production operation never reaches the maximum value of Q but at a smaller level given by:

$$\frac{(p-d)}{p}Q$$

where p is the delivery rate and d is the usage rate. The derivation of this relationship is illustrated by considering a crude oil storage tank into which oil can be pumped and withdrawn (see Figure 11.15). At the entrance and the exit of the storage valve there is a shutoff valve. Assume that:

• The tank is initially empty.
• The volume of oil pumped into tank is Q litres.
• The inlet flow rate is p litres/hour.

Figure 11.15 Inventory build-up for gradual delivery and usage

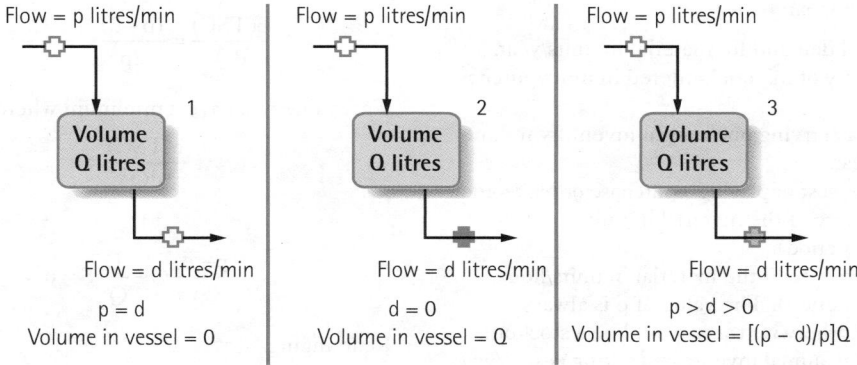

Figure 11.16 Inventory profile for Model II

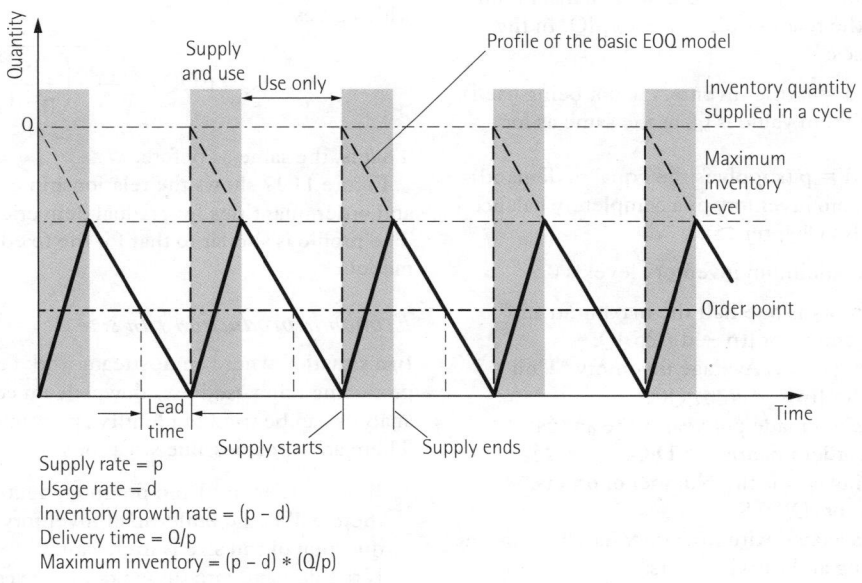

Supply rate = p
Usage rate = d
Inventory growth rate = (p − d)
Delivery time = Q/p
Maximum inventory = (p − d) * (Q/p)

- The outlet flow rate is d litres/hour.
- The volume of tank is Q litres.

There are three feasible situations:

1. The outlet valve is closed so there is no oil leaving and thus d = 0. The volume of oil in the vessel when pumping stops is Q litres.
2. The outlet valve is open and the outlet flow is considered equal to the inlet flow or d = p. The volume of oil in the vessel when pumping stops is 0 litres.
3. The outlet valve is partially open and here the outlet flow, d, is considered less than the inlet flow, p,

such that:
- build-up rate of crude oil is (p − d) litres/hour
- time crude flows into tank is Q/p hours
- maximum oil level is [(p − d)/p]Q.

Distribution

Here inventory is being delivered and used at the same time and the profile for this model is given in Figure 11.16. The shaded area is when there is both delivery and usage, and the non-shaded area for usage only. The figure also shows the profile if there was immediate delivery and now usage, or EOQ Model I.

The assumptions for Model II are essentially the same as for Model I except that terms supply rate, p, and demand rate, d, appear:

- D is the annual demand for material in units/year.
- Q is the quantity of material ordered in units/purchase order.
- C is the cost of carrying one unit in inventory for one year, $/unit/year.
- S is the average cost of placing a purchase order, $/order.
- d is the usage rate of the material in units/hour (or other time period).
- p is the delivery rate of the material in units/hour (or other time period). The value of p is always greater than d otherwise there would be a stockout.
- TSC is the total annual inventory stocking cost, $/year.
- Values of D, C, p, d, are known and are constant.

The inventory level never reaches the maximum value of Q, the quantity delivered, but at a maximum value given by the relationship $[(p - d)/p]Q$. In the two extreme cases:

- The value of d = 0 (the inventory is not being used), then the maximum value is Q, or the same as for Model I.
- The value of d = p (supply is the equal to demand), then there is zero inventory or a completely balanced system (see also Chapter 15).

As before, the minimum inventory level is 0:

- Average inventory is one-half the maximum and minimum inventory, or $[(p - d)/(2p)]Q$.
- Annual carrying cost is Average inventory * Unit stocking cost, or $[(p - d)/(2p)]QC$.
- Number of orders made per year is the annual consumption/order quantity, or D/Q.
- Annual ordering cost is the Number of orders * Ordering cost, or (D/Q) S.
- Total costs associated with inventory handling are the sum of ordering and carrying costs:

$$TSC = \frac{(p-d)}{2p}QC + \frac{D}{Q}S$$

Again, one cost is increasing with Q, and the other is decreasing with Q. Thus, total costs are a minimum when the annual ordering costs are equal to the annual carrying costs, or:

$$\frac{(p-d)}{2p}QC = \frac{D}{Q}S$$

Making Q the subject gives the following relationship for the economic order quantity:

$$Q = \sqrt{\frac{2DS}{C}\left(\frac{p}{p-d}\right)}$$

Alternatively, this can be arrived at by differentiating with respect to Q:

$$\frac{\delta(TSC)}{dQ} = \frac{(p-d)}{2p}C - \frac{D}{Q^2}S$$

This value will have a minimum when:

$$\frac{\delta(TSC)}{dQ} = 0$$

or:

$$\frac{(p-d)}{2p}C - \frac{D}{Q^2}S = 0$$

Rearranging:

$$Q^2 = \frac{2DS}{C}\left(\frac{p}{p-d}\right)$$

which gives:

$$Q = EOQ = \sqrt{\frac{2DS}{C}\left(\frac{p}{p-d}\right)}$$

That is, the same as before.

Figure 11.17 shows the relationship between the costs and order quantities for gradual deliveries and usage. The profile is similar to that for the fixed order quantity model.

Economic production run size

In a situation where an upstream work centre is producing units used by a downstream centre, the EOQ analysis can be used to identify an optimum run size. There are three possible situations:

1. If usage (demand) and production rate are equal there will be no build-up of inventory and the question of run size is irrelevant.
2. If the demand rate (usage rate) d, exceeds supply rate, p, then there will be a stockout.
3. If production, p, exceeds demand, d, then the EOQ analysis can be applied.
   - As long as production occurs, inventory continues to build.
   - It will be at a maximum when production ceases.
   - Demand occurs over the entire cycle. When inventory is exhausted, then production will begin again.
   - Since the firm makes the product itself the ordering or purchasing costs are now the machine setup costs and other associated preparation activities.
   - Setup costs are considered independent of run (lot) size.

Figure 11.17 EOQ Model II: Cost curves

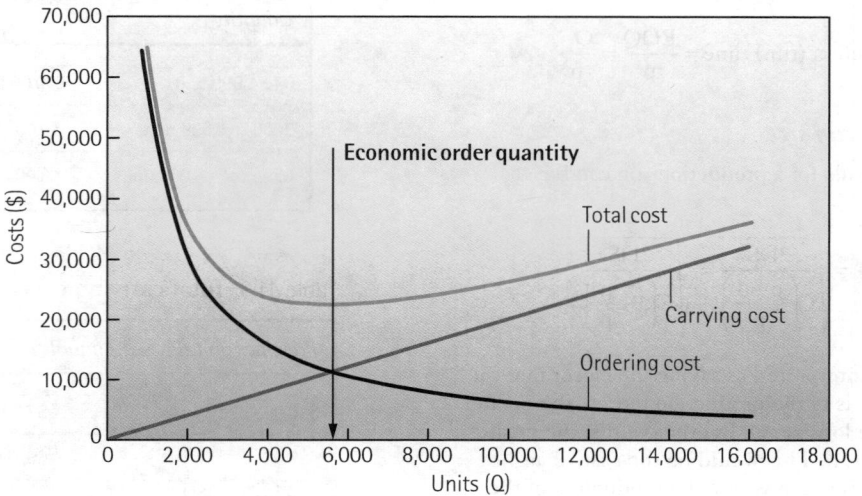

Figure 11.18 Economic production run size with Model II

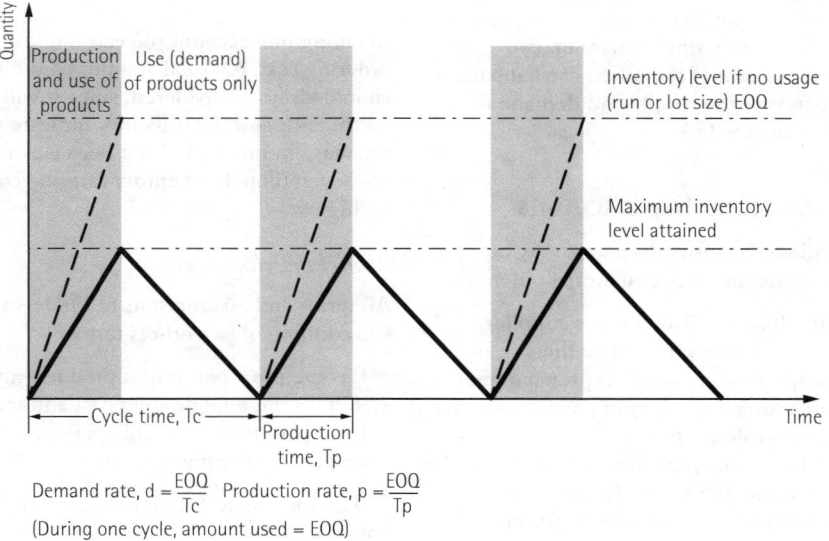

This profile, similar to that for distribution, is illustrated in Figure 11.18. The total setup and carrying costs are given by the relationship:

$$TSC = \frac{(p-d)}{2p}QC + \frac{D}{Q}S$$

And TSC is a minimum when Q, the lot size, is the economic order quantity:

$$Q = EOQ = \sqrt{\frac{2DS}{C}\left(\frac{p}{p-d}\right)}$$

Figure 11.17 presented a similar profile for a production operation. The difference is that one is for ordering outside, or a purchase cost, and the other is for ordering inside, or setup and other preparation costs. The cycle time or the time between starting one production run and the start of the next is a function of the run (lot) size, and the demand or usage rate, that is:

$$Cycle\ time = \frac{EOQ}{d} = \frac{Q_E}{D}$$

The production run time is a function of the run (lot) size and the production rate:

$$\text{Production (run) time} = \frac{EOQ}{p} = \frac{Q_E}{p}$$

Balancing the run size

This EOQ formula for a production run can be rewritten as:

$$Q = \sqrt{\frac{2DS}{C\left(\frac{p-d}{p}\right)}} = \sqrt{\frac{2DS}{C\left(1-\frac{d}{p}\right)}}$$

This can be interpreted as saying the closer that the demand rate, d, is to the production rate, p, the greater the value of the lot size, Q. In other words, the greater the production run. This would be the case of an assembly line operation where the production of the upstream work post is equal to the usage (demand) of the downstream work post. Both posts are in balance. In an assembly operation when p is greater than d, inventory starts building up. When d becomes greater than p, stockouts occur. In a similar manner, two workstations, one upstream of the other, use kanbans to achieve the balance of the supply and demand of components. (See Chapter 15.)

EOQ models with quantity discounts

In inventory situations, quantity discounts may be possible the greater the quantity of material ordered:

- In purchasing products from an outside supplier, quantity discounts are offered because there is an economy in transportation, and order preparation. For example, in purchasing a quantity of goods a supplier may offer the price scale as shown in Table 11.2.
- Similarly, in a production operation, the greater the lot size, or production run, the lower the unit cost because the number of setups would be fewer.

In situations when the carrying cost, C, is a percentage of the unit price, then the total annual carrying costs will change with price. As an illustration, using the unit cost prices just given and assuming an order quantity, Q, of 10,000 units and the carrying costs as 15% of the unit price, Table 11.3 gives the corresponding total carrying costs calculated by $(Q/2)*15\%*P$.

Of course, with 10,000 units ordered one would only pay $8.00 a unit according to the price scale but the purpose of the calculation is to show how the carrying costs decrease with a decrease in unit price. In summary, when there are quantity discount situations, in addition

Table 11.2 **Quantity discounts**

Quantity	Price
0 to 2,999 units	$10.00 a unit
3000 to 5,999 units	$9.00 a unit
More than 6,000 units	$8.00 a unit

Table 11.3 **Total carrying costs**

Price per unit (P)	Annual carrying cost
$10.00	$7,500
$9.00	$6,750
$8.00	$6,000

to taking into account the carrying cost, and the ordering cost, the total amount paid for the inventory should also be considered, since it will vary depending on the unit cost. Results may indicate that there is a savings in buying in bulk because of the lower unit cost even though inventory carrying costs will be higher.

Model development

All terms and assumptions of Models I and II apply with the addition of two others terms:

- P is the price per unit of product (inventory) in $/unit.
- TPC is the total product cost and includes the total price paid for the inventory, the total carrying costs, and the total ordering costs.

The total price paid for the material is the price times annual demand or $P*D$, where P is now a variable. Thus for either Model I or Model II:

$$TPC = TSC + DP$$

The economic order quantity is now when the total product costs given by the sum of the total inventory stocking costs plus total price paid is a minimum.

Model I-A

Here the delivery is immediate and so:

$$TPC = \frac{Q}{2}C + \frac{D}{Q}S + DP$$

Model II-A (either distribution or production)

Here there is continuous supply and usage and so:

$$\text{TPC} = \frac{Q}{2}\left(\frac{p-d}{p}\right)C + \frac{D}{Q}S + DP$$

Calculation procedure

1. The model EOQ is computed using each of the sales prices using either Model I or Model II depending on whether the consideration is instantaneous delivery or supply and usage at the same time. The vale of C, the carrying cost, is usually a function of sales price, or C = f(P). Thus, for example, if the carrying cost is 20% of sales price then the EOQ will change as P changes.

2. The feasible EOQ from step 1 is determined. That is that value of the EOQ that lies in the quantity range for the given price level. In some cases, it may not make sense to purchase the quantity, Q, calculated at the unit price given. In other cases, it may not be possible, according to the supplier's criteria, to purchase the quantity Q at the given unit price.

3. The total annual product cost, TPC, is computed for each feasible EOQ. In addition, values of TPC are calculated for purchase quantities, which may not arrive at from the EOQ relationship, but at which level a new lower unit price is possible according to the supplier's criteria. There will be different TPC curves for each price level (see Demonstrating the concept 11.1).

4. The order quantity with the lowest total annual product cost, TPC, is now the economic order quantity. This value may have no relationship to the EOQ calculated from the models.

EOQ inventory models and management

The EOQ theory illustrates that no matter what the situation, for every material held in inventory, there is an optimal order quantity where total costs are a minimum:

- Although the models are academic in their development they are a reasonable attempt to present the inventory situation in organizations.
- Because of assumptions made they are not a panacea for inventory management.
- However, in modelling inventory movement, it forces management closely to examine carrying costs, ordering costs, and stockout costs associated with inventory.

The use of these inventory models is illustrated in Demonstrating the concept 11.1.

Order points and service levels

In addition to knowing how much inventory to order, also required is the order point, or the date at which to place the purchase order for a new quantity of inventory. This quantity would normally be when the level of inventory currently being used has fallen to a certain minimum level as illustrated in Figure 11.6. This order point is based on the lead time (the time between placing the order, and receiving shipment) and the estimated amount of inventory that is going to be consumed, or demanded during this lead time period. For example, while a grocery store is waiting for a new shipment of cornflakes, there are still customers purchasing cornflakes. The value of this demand is critical. If it were higher than expected, there would be the risk of stockouts. Thus, a decision is how much cushion, or safety stock should be held? If the demand were low, inventory levels would be high giving high carrying costs.

Demand during lead time

The demand during lead time (DDLT) is derived from two components. One is the supplier's lead time and the other is the customer's demand.

Supplier's lead time

Suppliers may be extremely reliable and always deliver when promised. In this case, the lead time will not be a variable and the demand during lead time is an estimate of customer requirements during this known lead time period. However, there may be times when the weather is bad which delays delivery or at the supplier's facility machines break down or operators are absent which increase the time to complete the order. For these cases, the lead time is longer than planned, and so considerations should be given to having a safety stock on hand to cover these unexpected situations.

Customer's demand

Customers are not always predictable such that their daily demand for material varies. Alternatively, there may be external occurrences which changes demand such as a sudden hot spell increases the demand for beer, or an unseasonably wet period increases the demand for umbrellas. Thus, determining safety stock levels may not be straightforward.

Order point

The order point, OP, or the level of the present inventory at which a new order is placed is given by the sum of the expected, or average, demand during lead time, EDDLT, plus a safety stock, SS, or:

$$OP = EDDLT + SS$$

Increasing the safety stock for a material reduces the probability, and the cost of a stockout during lead time but it has the disadvantage of increasing carrying costs. The expected demand during lead time, EDDLT, can be estimated by using average values according to the following relationship:

$$EDDLT = \begin{bmatrix} \text{Average inventory} \\ \text{used per day} \end{bmatrix} * \begin{bmatrix} \text{Average supplier} \\ \text{lead time} \end{bmatrix}$$
$$= \bar{d} * \overline{LT}$$

Customer service levels

The customer service level in inventory situations is that proportion of orders that can be completed by using existing inventories of finished goods. In the case of production, it is that proportion of production department orders that can be filled by using existing raw materials inventories. Thus in this part of the supply chain, the customer might be the end user of the finished product, a downstream work centre, or a factory in the next town. In any event, the reason for keeping inventories is to satisfy this downstream customer taking into consideration uncertainties of the operation, be it a manufacturing or a service firm. If inventories are too low, stockouts could occur. A stockout situation is particularly critical during the lead time and if the customer is not satisfied there will be repercussions on the business (see Figure 11.19).[5]

Figure 11.19 **Customer service: The hard facts**

One unhappy customer will tell at least *nine* others

It takes *five* times as much effort, time and money to attract a new customer than it does to keep an existing one

96% of dissatisfied customers never complain *but* 90% of them will never return

Source: US Government Office of Consumer Affairs

Service levels are given as a percentage, say, 95%. A 95% service level means that on average, 95% of customers' orders are filled out of current inventory. The other 5% of customers' orders will not be filled from current inventory, and a stockout is experienced. These other 5% of orders will have to be filled at a later date. Or, in a worse situation, the client goes elsewhere to obtain this missing 5% of orders.

Stockout risk

Since there is a cost associated with holding inventory, or a safety stock, the risk of a stockout, must be traded off against the cost of carrying inventory. The objective is to carry the optimum level of inventory. The more inventory that is carried then the lower the probability or risk of a stockout. However, the greater the holding cost. The more the variability in either customer demand, or supplier lead time, then the greater the amount of safety stock required to achieve an established service level. The stockout risk is the complement of the service level or:

$$\text{Stockout risk} = 100 - \text{Percent service level}$$

Payoff tables for order point

Payoff tables might be used to optimize between carrying too little and carrying too much safety stock. In payoff situations there are two cost-related terms.

Long cost

The long cost is considered the cost of stocking one unit that is not demanded during lead time. That is, the unit is in inventory but there is no customer demand. This cost is usually associated with carrying costs, the cost of special handling, and other expenses involved in carrying a unit from one period to another.

Short cost

The short cost is the cost of not stocking a unit that is demanded during lead time. That is, there is a customer demand but that unit is not in inventory. This cost is ordinarily associated with stockouts such as lost revenue, or special handling and expediting to satisfy the customer.

Demonstrating the concept 11.2 illustrates the use of payoff tables for order points.

Distribution of demand during lead time

If historical data for an operating system exist, then frequency distribution curves can be developed for the inventory quantity demanded during the lead time.

Then, using this frequency distribution safety stock inventory levels during lead times can be estimated. The frequency distribution might be a continuous distribution (say, in the case of gasoline demanded from a service station), or a discrete distribution (say, in the case of boxes of chocolates demanded in a supermarket). However, whatever the situation, the inventory demand might be approximated by a normal distribution as shown in Figure 11.20. (Chapter 27 gives more on frequency distributions and the normal distribution.)

The average point in the curve is the most likely occurring quantity of inventory demanded and is the expected demand during lead time (EDDLT). It implies that 50% of the time, the inventory demanded is less than average or EDDLT, and 50% of the time it is more than average. The second situation is the more critical and thus to avoid stockouts, a cushion, or safety stock, needs to be held. As an illustration, a safety stock of 45% of the EDDLT as shown would give a service level of 95%. If this were an acceptable service level, then this would be the order point at which a new order is placed. As a corollary, the probability of a stockout is to the right of the order point or this case is 5%. If statistical data are available for the operating system then from:

$$\text{Order point} = \text{EDDLT} + \text{SS}$$

and replacing SS by $z * \sigma_{DDLT}$ gives:

$$\text{Order point} = \text{EDDLT} + z * \sigma_{DDLT}$$

Here σ_{DDLT} is the standard deviation of the demand during lead time or a measure of how the demand during lead time is distributed about the mean, or the EDDLT. The value z is the number of standard deviations the demand is from the mean.

Variable lead times and variable demand

When there is a variation in both the customer demand, d, and the supplier lead time, LT, and there are historical data for these two variables, the expected demand during lead time is given by the product of the average inventory demanded and the average lead time, or:

$$\text{EDDLT} = \bar{d} * \overline{LT}$$

Thus the order point is given by the relationship:

$$\text{Order point} = \bar{d} * \overline{LT} + z * \sigma_{DDLT}$$

The standard deviation of the demand during lead time can be rewritten as:

$$\sigma_{DDLT} = \sqrt{\overline{LT}\sigma_d^2 + \bar{d}\,\sigma_{LT}^2}$$

where σ_d and σ_{LT} are the standard deviation of the daily demand and the lead time respectively. Thus, the order point is given by:

$$\text{Order point} = \bar{d} * \overline{LT} + z * \sqrt{\overline{LT}(\sigma_d)^2 + \bar{d}(\sigma_{LT})^2}$$

Known lead times and variable demand

If it is difficult to obtain demand during lead time data then demand-per-day data might be used. In this case a constant lead time would be assumed. Supplier lead times are often more controllable than the variable nature of independent customer daily demand. In this case, the frequency distribution curve is the daily customer demand of inventory. The expected demand

Figure 11.20 Inventory demanded during lead time

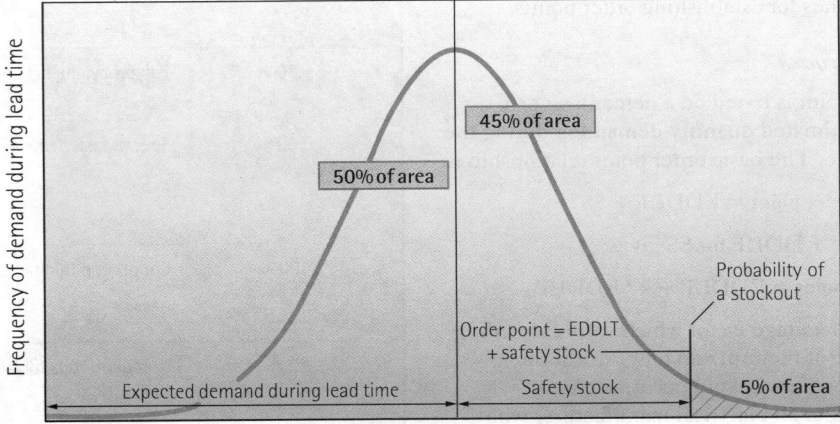

during lead time, EDDLT is now given by the constant lead time, LT, multiplied by the average daily demand, $\bar{d}$, or:

$$EDDLT = LT * \bar{d}$$

Also:

$$\sigma_{DDLT} = \sqrt{LT(\sigma_d)^2}$$

In this case, the order point is given by:

$$\text{Order point} = \overline{LT} \cdot \bar{d} + z \cdot \sqrt{LT(\sigma_d)^2}$$

Known demand and variable lead time

The other situation is when the average daily customer demand is reasonably constant (say, for example, in production which operates at a steady rate) but the supplier lead time is a variable. In this case, the frequency distribution curve is the supplier lead time for delivery of the inventory. The expected demand during lead time, EDDLT is now given by the constant demand, d, multiplied by the average lead time or:

$$EDDLT = \overline{LT} * d$$

Also

$$\sigma_{DDLT} = \sqrt{d(\sigma_{LT})^2}$$

In this case, the order point is given by:

$$\text{Order point} = \overline{LT} \cdot d + z \cdot \sqrt{d(\sigma_{LT})^2}$$

Arbitrary methods for order points

If reliable statistical data are not available for lead times and inventory demands then the following are two arbitrary approaches for establishing order points.

Percentage approach

Here the order point is based on a percentage or a fraction of the estimated quantity demanded during the supplier lead time. The basic order point relationship is:

$$\text{Order point} = EDDLT + SS$$

Substituting $k * EDDLT$ for SS gives:

$$\text{Order point} = EDDLT + k * EDDLT$$

Here, k is a percentage factor which varies according to the experience of the firm and how critical the situation would be if a stockout occurred. As an illustration, consider an electrical manufacturer who uses six classes of components that have been attributed

a value for k according to how severe the situation would be if a stockout occurred (see Table 11.4).

Assume that the expected demand during lead time for items in class 3 is 700 kilograms. Then the order point is given by:

$$\text{Order point} = 700 + 700 * 20\% = 840\,\text{kg}$$
and the safety stock is 140 kg

Classifications such as these would be custom designed for a firm's inventory system and uniformly applied to most materials in finished goods and raw material inventories.

Square root method

Here the safety stock is calculated as the square root of the expected demand during lead time. The basic order point relationship is:

$$\text{Order point} = EDDLT + SS$$

Substituting $\sqrt{EDDLT}$ for SS gives:

$$\text{Order point} = EDDLT + \sqrt{EDDLT}$$

As an illustration, suppose the EDDLT were 5, 25, 200, or 1000 units, then, using the square root method, Table 11.5 gives the corresponding safety stock, SS, the order point, OP, and the ratio of the safety stock to the EDDLT.

Table 11.4 **Stockout situation**

Class	Factor (k)	Material	Reasoning
1	5%	Packaging	Not essential Many suppliers
2	10%	Cleaning fluids	Essential Many suppliers
3	20%	Polypropylene	Essential Limited suppliers
4	50%	Special fasteners	Critical Few suppliers with required specifications
5	100%	Copper for lining	Extremely critical Limited sources at quality level
6	200%	Vanadium rods for tooling	Extremely critical Single source overseas

Table 11.5 Corresponding safety stocks

EDDLT	SS	OP	SS/EDDLT (%)
5	2.236	7	44.7
25	5.000	30	20.0
200	14.142	214	7.1
1,000	31.623	1,032	3.2

This method gives safety stock levels that are large relative to EDDLT when EDDLT is small. However, safety stocks are relatively small when EDDLT is large.

Demonstrating the concept 11.3 illustrates developing order points using normal distribution, and arbitrary methods.

Safety stocks, EOQ, and electronic linkup

Safety stocks are kept because of uncertainty. As more and more firms in the supply chain are being linked up electronically (discussed in the last section of this chapter) the level of uncertainty is reduced, thus firms in all parts of the supply chain need to hold a lower level, or perhaps zero safety stock.

Safety stocks have little effect on the economic order quantity, EOQ, in a fixed order quantity inventory system. However, the total annual stocking costs would change because:

- There would be increased annual carrying costs as safety stocks are dead stocks.
- There would be lower annual stockout costs holding a safety stock. In the economic models, the basic EOQ does not have a calculation for stockout costs. They exist, but are difficult to estimate.

Fixed order period systems

Situation

In a fixed order period system the objective is to select an optimal time period between which new orders are placed. There are two extreme situations.

Frequent orders

In this situation, orders are made very frequently and would involve high ordering costs and more frequent handling for placing the material in storage. However, it would reduce the probability of stockouts.

Less frequent orders

In this situation, ordering materials less frequently which would reduce total ordering costs, but might increase the risk of stockouts.

Model III: Economic order period

As in the models for economic ordering quantity, a mathematical model can be developed to arrive at an optimum time period for ordering materials. The model balances carrying costs against ordering costs to give an optimum time interval.

Assumptions

The assumptions are similar to economic order quantity models presented earlier:

- D is the annual demand for material (units/year).
- Q is the quantity of material ordered (units/purchase order).
- C is the cost of carrying one unit in inventory for one year ($/unit/year).
- S is the average cost of placing a purchase order ($/order).
- T is the time between orders (fraction of a year).
- TSC is the total annual stocking cost ($/year).

For these assumptions:

- Values of D, C, and S can be determined precisely, and remain constant.
- No safety stock is used.
- Lead time (time between placing an order and receipt) is known, and is constant.
- Orders are received at once in a single lot.
- Material is entirely used up by the time the next order arrives.
- There are no stockout costs.
- There are no quantity discounts.

Development

- If orders are made once a year, then average inventory is $0.5 * D$.
- If orders are made every six months, then average inventory is $0.25 * D$.
- If orders are made every three months, then average inventory is $0.125 * D$.
- Thus, the average inventory is Annual demand $* 0.5$ (time between orders) or $(T/2)D$.
- Annual carrying cost is the Average inventory $*$ Carrying cost or $DTC/2$.
- Orders per year is the reciprocal of the order period or $1/T$.

- Annual ordering cost is the order cost times the number of orders per year or S/T.

Total annual stocking costs = Annual ordering costs + Annual carrying costs:

$$TSC = \frac{S}{T} + \frac{DTC}{2}$$

The ordering costs decrease with T and stocking costs increase with T. The total annual stocking costs will be a minimum when these costs are equal, or:

$$\frac{S}{T} = \frac{DTC}{2}$$

Rearranging gives:

$$T = \sqrt{\frac{2S}{DC}}$$

Alternatively, using calculus and differentiating with respect to the variable T:

$$\frac{\delta(TSC)}{DT} = -\frac{S}{T^2} + \frac{DC}{2}$$

The minimum value is when the derivative:

$$\frac{\partial(TSC)}{DT} = 0$$

or:

$$\frac{S}{-T^2} + \frac{DC}{2} = 0$$

which gives:

$$T = \sqrt{\frac{2S}{DC}}$$

That is, the same as before.

Order quantity

When the time between orders has been established the next target is to determine the order quantity. This is calculated by the following relationship:

Order quantity = Max. inventory target − inventory level + EDDLT

Requirements for good inventory management

The roots of good inventory management lie in knowing the customers, and understanding their requirements, so that more accurate forecasts can be prepared. Once an accurate forecast is established production planning can be better organized. This is a function of demand management as discussed in Chapter 12. Another step is then to work closely with suppliers and aid them to improve, and respect delivery times so that no 'insurance' stocks need be held. With a well-organized supply chain, just-in-time and kanban systems can be put in place, which further helps to eliminate excessive inventory.

With regard to the inventory itself, managers should be aware of all the costs that make up inventory carrying costs, ordering costs from purchases made outside plus setup or other transfer costs when orders are made within the firm, and the impact of stockout costs on the operation. As already mentioned, with the use of electronic commerce the purchasing costs, when procuring from outside, are declining (see Chapter 16). In addition, the implementation of a classification system for inventory aids management is now discussed.

Classification of inventory

In a warehouse, or storage area of a manufacturing or a service organization supplying finished goods inventory, there are often numerous inventory items comprising perhaps hundreds of different reference numbers. Good inventory management means to use, or turn over, this inventory as frequently as possible. Decisions to be made also include how to classify this inventory according to that which is the most important to that which is considered the least important. Often, when one observes a large quantity of a particular material an inclination is to more closely manage these items because they are the 'most visible'. However, these may not be the items that contribute to the highest investment. One way of organizing and managing inventory is to use an ABC classification.

ABC inventory management

An ABC classification developed by H Ford Dickey of the USA in 1951 is a type of Pareto analysis. This analysis applies the 80/20 rule and in the case of inventory, observations have shown that approximately 80% of the quantity of inventory represents 20% of the cost. Conversely, 20% of the quantity contributes to 80% of the cost as illustrated in Figure 11.21. Here there are three classes A, B, and C. In Class A, about 20% of the quantity of inventory contributes to about 80% of the cost. Considering Class B and Class C together, about 80% of the quantity of inventory contributes to only about 20% of the cost. Class A would be considered the most important inventory to management, Class C the least important, and Class B an intermediary level.

Figure 11.21 ABC analysis as a histogram

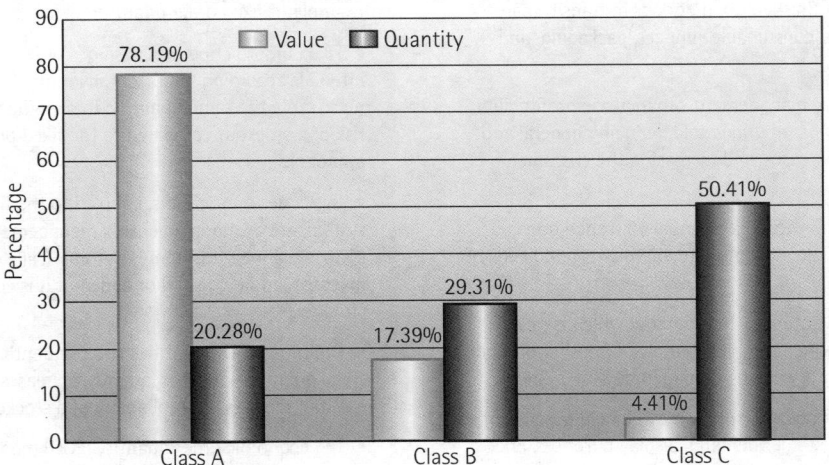

Demonstrating the concept 11.4 illustrates the development of an ABC analysis for classifying inventory.

Electronic commerce and inventory

If a firm in a business-to-business relationship has direct Internet connections with its component suppliers then, in this part of the supply chain, both the supplier and the client firm can better manage inventory and even reduce the level. For example, when the supplier is linked up electronically with the client firm it can establish immediately the level of components needed by its client and ship them as necessary. Thus, the supplier needs to keep less safety stock of this inventory in anticipation of unexpected client demands since the supplier has real-time information on the client's requirements. Further, with this information, the supplier can better manage its production schedules, which in itself will aid the supplier to keep its level of inventory in raw material, work-in-process, and finished goods to a minimum level. Downstream of the supplier, the client firm can keep fewer inventories of components in stock, knowing that its supplier will furnish whatever material is needed in a timely manner without telephone or fax requests from the client. A similar situation applies downstream at the retail level. As an illustration, Nestlé, the Swiss-based food company, in the past when it offered promotions on its products, had to make rough estimates of customer demand which made production planning and inventory management difficult. Now, using electronic linkups with its retail partners it has real-time information on its client needs and can adjust production levels

accordingly. Sainsbury and Tesco of Britain, for example, send Nestlé daily sales reports and demand forecasts over the web to Nestlé headquarters in Vevey, Switzerland. In addition, Nestlé managers at Vevey can check product inventory levels on the supermarket's computer systems.[6]

The customer and the risks

Good inventory management means providing the optimum service level to the customer but at the same time keeping associated inventory costs to a minimum. Inventory carrying costs can be estimated but it is difficult to measure the cost of a stockout. If there is a stockout, the customer might at least accept to have the product put on backorder. However, it might be that an individual sale is lost or, if the customer is so inconvenienced, he might be permanently lost. At the very worst, the customer talks to colleagues about the poor service and a whole slew of customers are lost. If in doubt, always organize to satisfy the customer, which means keeping inventory 'just-in-case'. This policy of carrying extra inventory is probably less of a risk than a stockout.

Summary of key elements

- Inventory is goods consumed during the normal course of business, accounted for as a short-term asset. All firms either manufacturing and services use some sort of inventory.

• Inventory includes raw materials, purchased parts, work-in-process, finished goods, goods in transit, spare parts, small tools, consumable supplies, packaging, and waste material.

• Good inventory management can increase profitability by reducing the cost of goods sold, reducing general and administrative expenses, and increasing the customer service level.

• Independent inventory is essentially finished goods whose demand depends on the requirements and needs of the customer.

• Dependent inventory is that material which is raw material, a component or subassembly of another product. Dependent inventory can be managed by MRP systems.

• High finished goods inventory may be held because of uncertainty in customer demand, display purposes, price discounts, favourable exchange rates, or anticipated price increases.

• High levels of raw materials may be held because immediate delivery on demand is not feasible, variations in the demand for finished goods, anticipated prices rises, unit price discounts, lower warehouse costs, and uncertainty of lead times.

• Work-in-process inventory arises because of waiting, transfer, queuing, setup and operating times. The last is the only value-added activity, and may be small relative to the other times.

• Inventory carrying and holding costs include investment in the inventory, warehousing, insurance, spoilage, obsolescence, and security costs. Ordering costs are external purchase costs, or internal setup and other transfer costs. Stockout costs cover lost customers, lost orders, and the shutdown of a production system in the case of non-delivery of raw materials.

• The cost of a stockout can be estimated by weighting estimated costs resulting from backordering, lost sales, and a lost customer.

• Safety stocks are dead stocks, held for uncertainty, and add to carrying costs.

• Due to the added value as one moves through the supply chain, holding a stock of raw material is less costly than holding finished goods inventory.

• In inventory control there are two basic issues. The quantity of inventory to order taking into account current inventory, and when to order the inventory considering supplier lead times.

• Fixed order quantity purchasing is ordering the same quantity each time an order is placed, but not necessarily in the same time interval. A two-bin system is a special example of fixed order quantity.

• Fixed order period purchasing is ordering in similar time intervals according to current inventory levels but not necessarily the same quantity. This method has a higher risk of a stockout compared to the fixed order quantity approach.

• Bar codes on products, coupled to the firm's information system, are an aid in inventory management. When the bar code is scanned this item is automatically deducted from inventory (if being sold) or added (if it is coming into storage).

• Ordering large quantities less frequently, as opposed to small quantities more frequently, increases the carrying cost but reduces the probability of a stockout.

• The economic order quantity (EOQ) models give the optimum order quantity to minimize the total inventory costs by balancing ordering costs with carrying costs. When there are unit price discounts the amount paid for inventory is taken into consideration and this will also change the carrying cost.

• The EOQ models are robust in the sense that a large change in the EOQ value may not change significantly the total inventory-related costs.

• The quantity demanded during lead time for inventory is a function of the customer's demand and the supplier's lead time.

• The expected demand during lead time (EDDLT) is the average inventory used per day * average supplier lead time. The order point for inventory (OP) is a function of the EDDLT and the safety stock (SS), and is given by the relationship OP = EDDLT + SS.

• A service level of 95% means that 95% of the time customers' orders can be filled out of current inventory. It also implies that the risk of a stockout is 5%.

• In payoff tables for inventory calculation, the long cost is associated with carrying too much inventory and the short cost is associated with stockouts.

• If a normal distribution can represent the quantity of inventory demanded during lead time, then the order point can be determined using the normal distribution relationships.

• The percentage approach for order point determination applies a factor k to the EDDLT according to the critical nature of the material and its ease of supply. The order point is given by OP = EDDLT + k * EDDLT.

• The square root method approach for order point determination considers that the safety stock is the

square root of the expected demand during lead time. The order point is given by the relationship
$$OP = EDDLT + \sqrt{(EDDLT)}.$$

- The fixed order period model gives the optimum time period between placing orders.

- ABC inventory classification is based on the 80/20 Pareto rule where small levels of certain inventory contribute to the highest value, and the highest levels of certain inventory contribute to the smallest value.

- With electronic commerce, firms in a business-to-business or business-to-consumer linkage can keep fewer inventories as they have real-time information of downstream requirements.

Notes and references

1. 'GM faces lots of troubles as its car inventories grow', *Wall Street Journal Europe*, 15 February 1996
2. 'US inventories indicate a slowdown in the economy: Rise of 0.3% suggest wholesalers are cutting orders from factories', *Wall Street Journal Europe*, 12 December 2000, p. 2
3. Visit to Sodiaal, Vienne, France, 7 April 1997
4. PLOSSL, G. W. and WIGHT, O.W., *Production and Inventory Control*, Prentice-Hall, Englewood Cliffs, New Jersey, 1967
5. US Government of Consumer Affairs
6. ECHIKSON, William, 'Nestlé: An elephant dances. The Net promises to make the lumbering giant one nimble operation', *Business Week*, 11 December 2000, p. EB 19

Review and discussion topics

1. Production and inventory
The Block Company manufactures fuel injection systems for airplanes. One particular assembly, Code AMB-1487, made from aluminium, passes through a drilling process where seven holes of three different dimensions are drilled into the unit. The next operation is polishing. During these two operations a significant quantity of in-process inventory is generated.
(a) Why might there be a high level of in-process inventory?
(b) Why is a high inventory level cause for concern?
(c) Suggest ways in which in-process inventory might be minimized.

2. Changing inventory levels
Sometimes in the press there is talk of inventories of finished goods that are increasing, or decreasing. Discuss the impact of changing inventories on industrial activity.

3. Higher than normal inventories
Discuss the reasons why, when, and in what circumstances, inventories may be higher than normal for a:
(a) food distribution firm
(b) automobile component parts manufacturer in Germany, or France
(c) gasoline station
(d) candy factory
(e) stationery store, or the stationery department of a departmental store.

4. Inventory management costs
For the following situations, discuss how, in practice, could you determine inventory-carrying costs, inventory-ordering costs, and inventory stockout costs:
(a) a retail store
(b) a production centre.

5. In-process inventory
What can be done to reduce the level of in-process inventories in a production operation?

Demonstrating the concept 11.1 Arbrelle

Situation

Arbrelle is a service organization that packages and distributes automobile components and accessories to retail outlets. The automobile components arrive from the manufacturer in bulk at Arbrelle where they are sorted, packaged automatically in display boxes, ticketed with a bar code, and then put into shipping cartons.

One product of particular interest is a security lock, reference SL-200. The estimated consumption (demand from the retail outlet) of this product is 10,000 units per year. The base price for purchasing the security lock from the manufacturer is €28.40. If more than 1000 units are purchased, there is a discount of 2.5% per unit on the base price. If more than 3000 units are purchased, there is a discount of 5% per unit of the base price. Ordering costs from the manufacturer are estimated at €190.00 per order.

Arbrelle works 250 days per year and the inventory storage cost for the security lock is estimated at 35% of purchase price from the manufacturer.

Required

Calculate the following information using the concept of the inventory models. Note that, to perform the calculations you should use the exact mathematical values, rather than rounding to whole numbers. In this way the differences in the cost values will be more clearly seen. In practice, of course, lot sizes or order quantities would be made in whole numbers.

1. If the security lock is purchased at the base price, and the units are delivered in one lot, determine the economic ordering quantity using the EOQ Model I.
2. If the security lock is purchased at the base price, and the units are delivered at a rate of 100 units per day from the manufacturer, determine the economic ordering quantity using the gradual usage and delivery model EOQ II. Assume that the packaging (usage rate) of the model is the average of the annual demand.
3. Determine the annual savings in inventory-related costs between the gradual usage and delivery model (question 2) and the basic model (question 1).
4. If the price discounts are taken into consideration, determine the economic order quantity using the base Model I-A. Illustrate graphically the total product cost curves indicating the EOQ quantity.
5. Determine the annual savings in inventory-related costs between using the basic model with no price discounts (question 1) and the basic model, using price discounts (question 4).
6. If the price discounts are taken into consideration, determine the economic order quantity using the gradual delivery usage model with the same delivery rate of 100 units per day. Illustrate graphically the total product cost curves indicating the EOQ quantity.
7. Determine the annual savings in inventory-related costs between using the gradual delivery usage model with no price discounts (question 2) and the gradual delivery usage model, using price discounts (question 6).

Solution

Table 11.6 gives the solutions for this exercise. The given data are inserted into the appropriate formula.

Single lot (Model I and Model I-A)

$$TSC = \frac{Q}{2}C + \frac{D}{Q}S$$

$$Q = EOQ = \sqrt{\frac{2DS}{C}}$$

$$TPC = \frac{Q}{2}C + \frac{D}{Q}S + DP$$

Simultaneous supply and usage (Model II and Model II-A)

$$TSC = \frac{(p-d)}{2p}QC + \frac{D}{Q}S$$

$$Q = EOQ = \sqrt{\frac{2DS}{C}\left(\frac{p}{p-d}\right)}$$

$$TPC = \frac{Q}{2}\left(\frac{p-d}{p}\right)C + \frac{D}{Q}S + DP$$

1. The given data are entered into the EOQ formula to give a value of 618.30 (say 618 units).
2. The average usage rate is given by the annual demand divided by the effective days a year or a value of 40 units/day.
   The given data are entered into the EOQ formula to give a value of 798.22 (say 798 units).
3. This is the difference between the total stocking costs for the two situations and the value is $1385.30. (Since the purchase price is the same, a similar value will be obtained using the TPC values.)
4. With the price discounts given the price levels are:
   * €28.40 as the basic price
   * €27.69 as the first discount price
   * €26.98 as the second discount price.
   The EOQ is calculated for each price level. The value of the EOQ changes since the value of C also changes, as it is a function of the unit price. Only the first EOQ value is feasible. EOQ levels for the other two do not fit with the quantity range. The total product cost, TPC, is determined for the valid EOQ figure. In this case there is only one.
   Since the supplier offers discounts above a certain level, the TPC can be determined for these quantity breaks or 1000 and 3000 units even though they don't fit the EOQ model. The 'EOQ' value is the quantity that gives the lowest TPC. In this case a purchase quantity of 1000 units. The TPC cost curves for these three price levels and various values of Q is illustrated in Figure 11.22.
5. This is the difference between the TPC for the two situations at the corresponding price level.
6. The EOQ is calculated for each price level. The value changes because the value of C changes, as it is a function of the price. Only the first EOQ value is feasible. EOQ levels for the other two do not fit with the quantity range. The total product cost, TPC, is determined for the valid EOQ figure.

Table 11.6 Arbrelle: Calculation sheet

	From	To		Comments
Question 1				
Base price, P (€)			28.40	
Stocking cost as a percent of price			35.00%	
Annual demand, D (units)			10,000	
Ordering cost, S (€/unit)			190.00	
EOQ			**618.30**	
TSC (€)			6,145.89	
TPC (€)			290,145.89	
Question 2				
Delivery rate, p (units/day)			100	
Working days/year			250	
Usage rate, d (units/day)			40.00	
(p − d)/p			0.60	
EOQ			**798.22**	
TSC (€)			4,760.59	
TPC (€)			288,760.59	
Question 3				
TSC(1) − TSC(2), €			**1,385.30**	
Question 4				
Price, P1 (€)	1	999	28.40	
Price, P2 (€)	1,000	2,999	27.69	
Price, P3 (€)	3,000	greater	26.98	
EOQ@P1			618.30	Only feasible
EOQ@P2			626.18	Not possible
EOQ@P3			634.36	Not possible
TPC@price P1 and EOQ-1 (€)			290,145.89	Possible
TPC@price P2 and EOQ-2 (€)			282,968.58	Not valid
TPC@price P3 and EOQ-3 (€)			275,790.28	Not valid
TPC@price P2 and supplier minimum			283,645.75	Possible best
TPC@price P3 and supplier minimum			284,597.83	Possible
Question 5				
TSP(1) − TSP(4)			6,500.14	
Question 6				
Price, P1 (€)	1	999	28.40	
Price, P2 (€)	1,000	2,999	27.69	
Price, P3 (€)	3,000	greater	26.98	
EOQ@P1			798.22	Only feasible
EOQ@P2			808.39	Not possible
EOQ@P3			818.96	Not possible
TPC@price P1 and EOQ-1 (€)			288,760.59	Possible
TPC@price P2 and EOQ-2 (€)			281,600.70	Not valid
TPC@price P3 and EOQ-3 (€)			274,440.05	Not valid
TPC@price P2 and supplier minimum			281,707.45	Possible
TPC@price P3 and supplier minimum			278,932.03	Possible best
Question 7				
TPC(2) − TPC(6), €			9,828.55	

Since the supplier offers discounts above a certain level, the TPC can be determined for these quantity breaks (1000 and 3000) even though they don't fit the EOQ model. The 'EOQ' value is the quantity that gives the lowest TPC. In this case a purchase quantity of 3000 units. The TPC cost curves for these three price levels and various values of Q is illustrated in Figure 11.23.

7. This is the difference between the TPC for the two situations at the corresponding price level.

Figure 11.22 Arbrelle: Total product cost with instantaneous delivery (Model I–A)

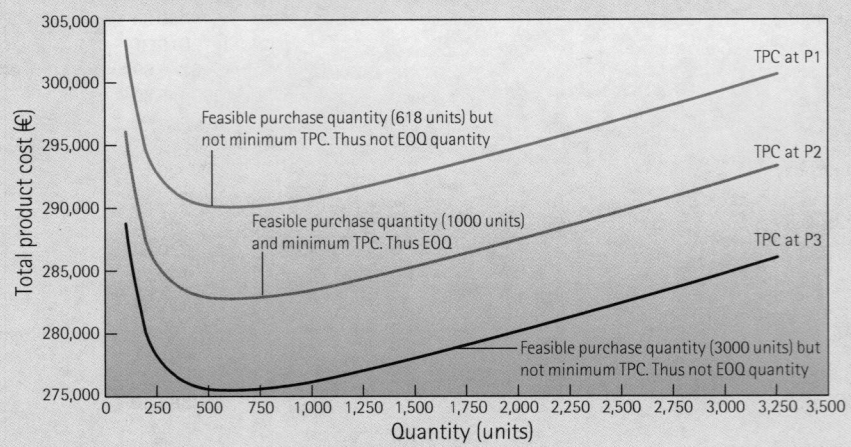

Figure 11.23 Arbrelle: Total product cost with gradual delivery and usage (Model II–A)

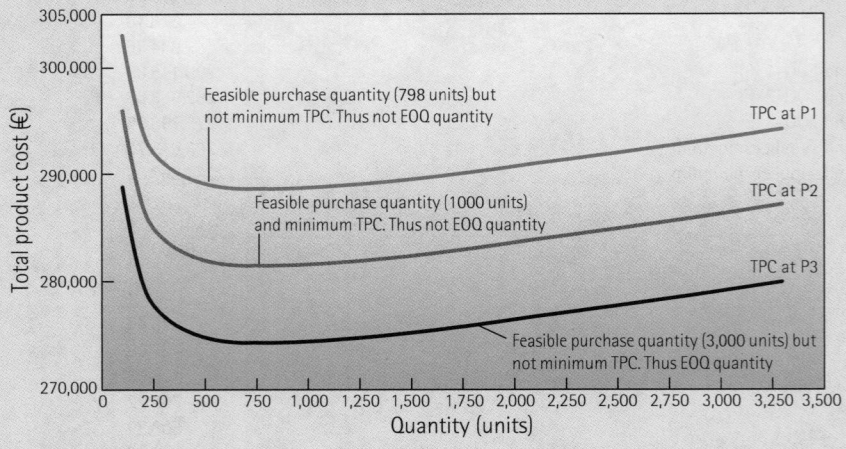

Situation

The raw material for producing ground coffee is green coffee. A producer, who purchases the green coffee from a local distributor, makes an estimate of the number of pallets of green coffee used per day over an 80-day period and also an estimate of the long and short costs. This information is as shown in Table 11.7.

Required

Determine the optimum number of pallets of green coffee to purchase in order to minimize the cost.

Table 11.7 Pallet demand and long and short costs

Pallets demanded	Days this level occurred
20	15
40	20
60	12
80	10
100	23
Total days	80

Long cost per pallet, $30
Short cost per pallet, $70

Solution

Table 11.8 shows the basic data, and the calculation for optimizing the number of pallets to purchase.

- The number of pallets demanded, and the days this level was demanded is converted into a frequency distribution by dividing the days occurred by the total number of days (column 1, Table 11.8) (see also Chapter 27).
- A payoff table is constructed showing the pallets demanded, the pallets to order, and the frequency of occurrence (Table 11.8).
- In each cell, the cost is developed using the long, and short cost. For example: 80 pallets are demanded and 40 pallets are stocked. Then the cost is (80 − 40) * $70 = $2800.00.
  20 pallets are demanded and 80 pallets are stocked. Then the cost is (80 − 20) * $30 = $1800.00
- The expected cost is given by the sum of the probabilities * individual cost or $1130.00.
- The cost is a minimum when 80 pallets are ordered.

Table 11.8 Coffee: Payoff tables

1

Pallets demanded	Days this level occurred	Frequency (%)
20	15	18.75
40	20	25.00
60	12	15.00
80	10	12.50
100	23	28.75
Total	80	100.00

Long cost, per pallet, $30
Short cost per pallet, $70

2

Order point no. of pallets	Pallets demanded					Expected cost ($)
	20	40	60	80	100	
20	0.00	1,400.00	2,800.00	4,200.00	5,600.00	2,905.00
40	600.00	0.00	1,400.00	2,800.00	4,200.00	1,880.00
60	1,200.00	600.00	0.00	1,400.00	2,800.00	1,355.00
80	1,800.00	1,200.00	600.00	0.00	1,400.00	1,130.00
100	2,400.00	1,800.00	1,200.00	600.00	0.00	1,155.00
Probability (%)	18.75	25.00	15.00	12.50	28.75	100.00

Minimum expected cost   1,130.00
Pallets to carry   80

Demonstrating the concept 11.3   Miko

Situation

The Miko company uses polypropylene pellets in 50kg sacks in its moulding machines for making plastic toy components. Based on past data, and supplier delivery time of the polypropylene pellets, the excepted usage during lead time (EDDLT) of 50kg sacks of the polypropylene pellets is 450 sacks. The usage is based on the customer demand for toy products.

Required

1. If the usage for polypropylene pellets can be considered normally distributed with a standard deviation of the demand of 35 sacks, determine the level of safety stock for the pellets, and the corresponding level of inventory at which Miko should place orders. Assume a client service level of 98%.
2. Using the arbitrary method of percentage of expected demand during lead time, with a factor k of 20%, determine the level of safety stock for the pellets, and the corresponding level of inventory at which Miko should place orders.
3. Using the arbitrary method, square root of expected demand during lead time, determine the level of safety stock for the pellets, and the corresponding level of inventory at which Miko should place orders.

Solution

The solution is given in Table 11.9. The method of using k factors gives the greatest security in terms of safety stock, whereas the square root method gives the least.

Table 11.9 Miko: Calculation sheet

Question 1	
EDDLT	450
Standard deviation	35
Service level (%)	98.00
z	2.0537
Safety stock = std dev*z	71.88
Safety stock (rounded)	**72**
Order point = EDDLT + SS	**522**
Question 2	
EDDLT	450
Safety stock policy (value k) (%)	20
Safety stock, k*EDDLT	**90**
Order point = EDDLT + SS	**540**
Question 3	
EDDLT	450
Safety stock = $\sqrt{(EDDLT)}$	**21**
Order point = EDDLT + SS	**471**

Demonstrating the concept 11.4   EDF: An ABC analysis

Situation

EDF is an electricity supply company and one of its branches provides repair, modification, and emergency services. For this purpose, in its large warehouse it keeps spares such as tyres for emergency trucks, copper cable, insulating joints, steel bars, lubricating oil, plastic tubing, switches, electric contacts, etc. Alarmed about the financial investment in the inventory, the regional manager asked for an analysis of the material used. The controller, with the help of the warehouse superintendent, compiled the data, presented as Table 11.10.

Required

Develop an ABC analysis of the given inventory items. Show the information graphically. Which items would go into the classifications of A, B, and C?

Solution

The ABC analysis is given in Table 11.11 and has been calculated as follows:

- Column 3 gives the cumulative percentage of the number of different types of products.
- Column 5 gives the percentage of the quantity of units of products used to the total.
- Column 6 gives the cumulative percentage of the quantity of units used.
- Column 8 gives the total cost of the units used (Unit cost * Quantity used).
- Column 9 is the total cost as a percentage of the total.
- Column 10 is the annual cost of each product reference as a cumulative percentage of the total cost.
- Column 11 gives a classification of the product references into an ABC analysis according to the annual cost of the particular products used. The cut-off point is not rigid. For example, item M-7895 may have gone into the A classification rather than the

Table 11.10 EDF: Basic data

Product reference	Units used a year	Cost $/unit
D-6698	3,200	0.55
D-9865	1,600	0.15
F-4589	800	9.16
F-4598	1,500	3.44
F-5892	3,200	2.20
G-5698	4,000	0.45
H-4562	800	0.75
K-8592	1,225	2.48
M-7895	400	30.50
M-8594	300	10.56
N-8591	850	2.54
Q-8594	800	9.00
S-1485	700	3.16
S-4985	2,400	0.10
T-7852	1,200	2.60
U-6821	1,500	28.80
W-4561	1,600	7.40
X-5986	2,500	0.42
Z-5642	1,100	19.20
Z-9876	775	56.00

B classification as shown. What is important is a logical classification.

Two curves showing the ABC analysis are illustrated:

- Figure 11.24 is the cumulative curve for the percentage number of different products. Here, 15% of the 20 different products are included in the A category, 40% in the B category and 45% in the C category.
- Figure 11.25 is the cumulative curve for the percentage quantity of products. Here about 11% of the 30,450 units are included in the A category, 28% in B and 61% in the C category.

The type of presentation used depends on the user. What is important is the annual cost of the inventory used and both curves gives this information and show the same product references in the three ABC categories.

Table 11.11 EDF: Inventory analysis

1	2	3	4	5	6	7	8	9	10	11
N° of different products	Product reference	Cumulative no. of different products (%)	Units used a year	Percent quantity (%)	Quantity cumulative (%)	Cost $/unit	Total cost	Cost (%)	Cost cumulative (%)	Class
0		0.00	0	0	0	0.00	0	0	0	
1	Z-9876	5.00	775	2.55	2.55	56.00	43,400.00	24.40	24.40	A
2	U-6821	10.00	1,500	4.93	7.47	28.80	43,200.00	24.29	48.69	A
3	Z-5642	15.00	1,100	3.61	11.08	19.20	21,120.00	11.87	60.56	A
4	M-7895	20.00	400	1.31	12.40	30.50	12,200.00	6.86	67.42	B
5	W-4561	25.00	1,600	5.25	17.65	7.40	11,840.00	6.66	74.07	B
6	F-4589	30.00	800	2.63	20.28	9.16	7,328.00	4.12	78.19	B
7	Q-8594	35.00	800	2.63	22.91	9.00	7,200.00	4.05	82.24	B
8	F-5892	40.00	3,200	10.51	33.42	2.20	7,040.00	3.96	86.20	B
9	F-4598	45.00	1,500	4.93	38.34	3.44	5,160.00	2.90	89.10	B
10	M-8594	50.00	300	0.99	39.33	10.56	3,168.00	1.78	90.88	B
11	T-7852	55.00	1,200	3.94	43.27	2.60	3,120.00	1.75	92.64	C
12	K-8592	60.00	1,225	4.02	47.29	2.48	3,038.00	1.71	94.34	C
13	S-1485	65.00	700	2.30	49.59	3.16	2,212.00	1.24	95.59	C
14	N-8591	70.00	850	2.79	52.38	2.54	2,159.00	1.21	96.80	C
15	G-5698	75.00	4,000	13.14	65.52	0.45	1,800.00	1.01	97.81	C
16	D-6698	80.00	3,200	10.51	76.03	0.55	1,760.00	0.99	98.80	C
17	X-5986	85.00	2,500	8.21	84.24	0.42	1,050.00	0.59	99.39	C
18	H-4562	90.00	800	2.63	86.86	0.75	600.00	0.34	99.73	C
19	D-9865	95.00	1,600	5.25	92.12	0.15	240.00	0.13	99.87	C
20	S-4985	100.00	2,400	7.88	100.00	0.10	240.00	0.13	100.00	C
	Total		30,450	100.00			177,875	100.00		

Figure 11.24 ABC analysis: EDF (value against number of different products)

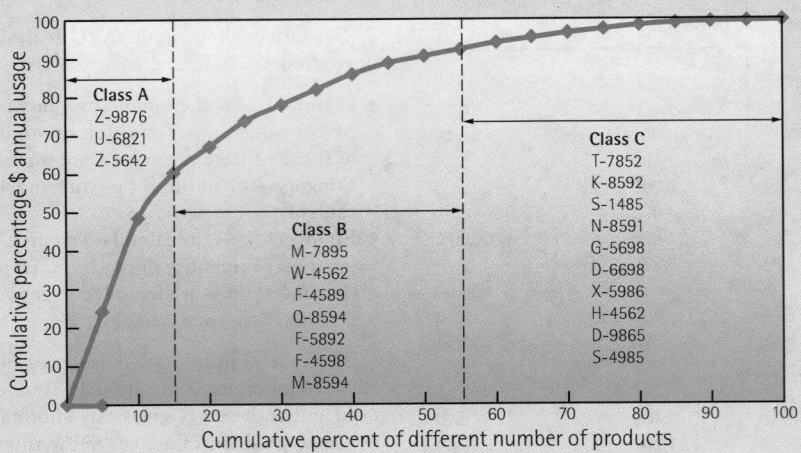

Figure 11.25 ABC analysis: EDF (value against quantity of products used)

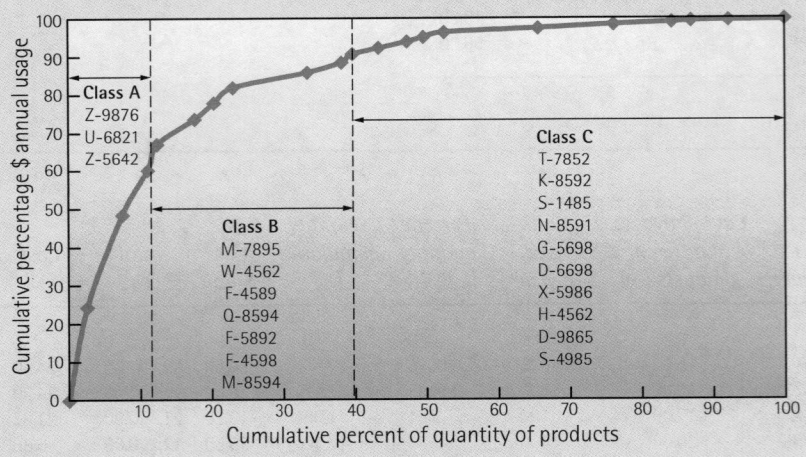

Application exercise 11.1 Cakes

Situation

A bakery calculates that, on average, the marginal profit for the sale of a Black Forest gateau is $1.50, and the marginal loss is $2.50. The average demand a day, based on past sales is given in Table 11.12.

Required

Using marginal analysis, how many cakes a day should the bakery make first thing in the morning to optimize the inventory situation?

Table 11.12 Average daily demand for Black Forest gateaux

Demand (units)	0	1	2	3	4	5	6	7	8	9	10
Probability of this demand	0.02	0.04	0.06	0.10	0.15	0.15	0.25	0.10	0.05	0.05	0.03

Application exercise 11.2   Cassis Co.

Situation

The Cassis Co., located on the shores of Lake Michigan, is a manufacturer of automobile engines. Table 11.13 gives historical data of typical annual usage of component parts for one of its six-cylinder engines. The cost of the finished engine has been increasing by about 5% a year. This is principally due to approximately the same increase in cost of the component parts.

Required

1. Examine the inventory usage data using the concept of the ABC analysis. Show the results graphically.
2. What is a reasonable grouping in categories A, B, and C? What part numbers are in category A?

Table 11.13   Cassis Co.: Cost of a finished engine

Part Nº	Annual quantity	Unit cost, $	Part Nº	Annual quantity	Unit cost, $
111D	32,000	1.00	334U	8,000	24.00
128H	50,000	0.50	352S	13,000	19.20
196G	7,490	22.40	391J	2,200	51.60
205Y	3,000	270.00	421A	4,500	9.60
216U	3,060	12.80	432S	4,890	7.60
217J	3,500	122.40	436S	75,000	0.25
228G	840	98.40	452F	3,800	13.50
235D	64,000	1.80	462R	4,000	16.80
249E	14,000	6.30	463H	3,000	132.00
258L	2,200	62.40	478L	27,140	1.20
261K	20,000	1.20	521I	3,000	13.80
272J	5,000	9.00	532Q	1,200	144.00
324H	22,000	1.50	610B	30,000	5.10
333C	2,280	15.40			

Application exercise 11.3   Flour

Situation

Boulanger is a medium sized baker. Based on past data, and supplier delivery time the expected usage during lead time (EDDLT) of flour is 7000 kg.

Required

1. If the usage for flour can be considered normally distributed with a standard deviation of the demand of 100 kg, determine the level of safety stock Boulanger should keep for the flour. What is the corresponding level of inventory at which Boulanger should place orders? Assume a client service level of 99.5%.
2. Using the arbitrary method of percentage of expected demand during lead time, with a factor k of 15%, determine the level of safety stock for the flour, and the corresponding level of inventory at which Boulanger should place orders.
3. Using the arbitrary method, square root of expected demand during lead time, determine the level of safety stock for the flour, and the corresponding level of inventory at which Boulanger should place orders.

Application exercise 11.4 Paper

Situation

A company purchases cartons of paper, which are then sold for photographic and printing purposes. It has looked at usage of paper for the last month in terms of boxes sold. This information is contained in Table 11.14.

Further, it estimates the long and short costs for stocking the inventory of paper as follows:

- long cost per carton, $5.00
- short cost per carton, $12.00.

Required

Determine the optimum number of cartons of paper to purchase in order to minimize the cost.

Table 11.14 Paper usage interms of boxes sold

Cartons demanded	15	35	45	55	70	100
Days occurred	1	2	9	4	8	6

Application exercise 11.5 Sparky Co.

Situation

The Sparky Co. is a service organization that distributes electric components through a local distribution centre.

Henry Wohler, the Purchasing Manager, is meeting with Agnes Mira, his assistant. The object of the discussion is to establish a stocking policy for certain products that are stored, and distributed from the warehouse in Portsmouth. There are three principal products at the warehouse, which can be classified according to an ABC analysis.

Transformer (Part N° TRA-100)
This is considered a Class A product as it represents about 20% of the quantity of inventory in stock, and about 75% of the total value. The basic cost of the transformer to Sparky is £59.80. Annual demand is estimated at 105,000 units a year and the ordering cost is £400.00 an order.

Armature winding (Part N° INT-137)
This is considered a Class B product as it represents about 30% of the quantity of inventory in stock, and about 20% of the total value. The basic cost of the armature winding to Sparky is £27.60. Annual demand is estimated at 15,000 units a year and the ordering cost is estimated at £200.00 an order.

Switches (Part N° BOU-1455)
This is considered a Class C product as it represents about 50% of the quantity of inventory in stock, and about 5% of the total value. The basic cost of the switches to Sparky is £15.00. Annual demand is estimated at 6500 units a year and ordering cost at £80.00 an order.

The Sparky Co. works 250 days a year and the inventory storage cost for all products is estimated at 35% of product cost.

Required

1. If transformers were delivered in fixed lots to Sparky, how many transformers would be ordered under the basic economic order quantity conditions?
2. If transformers were delivered to the warehouse at an average rate of 450 units/day what would be the new economic order quantity?
3. What is the savings in annual cost between questions 1 and 2?
4. If armature windings were delivered in fixed lots to Sparky, how many would be ordered under the basic economic order quantity conditions?
5. If armature windings were delivered to the warehouse at an average rate of 150 units/day what would be the economic order quantity?
6. What is the savings in annual cost between questions 4 and 5?
7. The supplier of the transformer indicates he is able to offer discounts as shown in Table 11.15.

Under these conditions, what is the optimal ordering quantity assuming instantaneous delivery in fixed lots, and

Table 11.15 Sparky Co.: Transformer discounts

Order quantity	Unit cost
1 to 999	£59.80
1,000 to 3,999	£59.40
4,000+	£59.20

assuming that the other information in question 1 remains unchanged.

8. For the transformer, what is the difference in total costs between the situation when price discounts are offered (question 7), and the case when there are no price discounts using the basic model (question 1)?

9. If the transformers were delivered at the average rate of 450 units a day, using the price discount situation, what would be the economic order quantity?

10. What are the costs savings between questions 9 and 2?

11. The supplier of the armature windings indicates he is able offer discounts as shown in Table 11.16.

Under these conditions, what is now the optimal ordering quantity on the basis that armature windings are delivered instantaneously in fixed lots?

Table 11.16 Sparky Co.: Armature winding discounts

Order quantity	Unit cost
1 to 999	£27.60
1,000 to 1,999	£27.40
2,000+	£27.28

12. For the armature windings, what is the difference in total costs between the situation when price discounts are offered (question 11), and the case when there are no price discounts (question 4)?

13. What is the economic order quantity for the switches?

14. What are your criticisms of using these types of model to manage inventory?

Case study 11.1 Fortnex

Situation

Fortnex is a subsidiary of a French Company in the Czech Republic that assembles small household appliances, including coffee makers, toasters, and food mixers. These products are sold principally in the European Union and some eastern European countries. About 65% of the components used in the assembly operation are purchased from suppliers in lots, and this leads to a considerable amount of raw material inventory in the work centre. In addition, the layout, scheduling, line balancing, and the fact that assembly is performed in lot sizes of 150 units, engenders a certain amount of in-process inventory.

The parent company of Fortnex has been concerned about the rising product cost of the finished products, which has led to reduced profit margins. (Household appliances are very competitive and increasing prices is not a viable option.) One of the demands of the parent company has been to review the inventory management practices of Fortnex. Two areas which Fortnex is currently investigating are economic order quantity purchasing, and ABC analysis.

Purchasing EOQ

At present the company purchases copper wire for a certain appliance under economic order quantities based on the information given in Table 11.17.

The supplier of copper wire is proposing a discount of 5% if Fortnex purchases in lot sizes of 1000kg, rather than the calculated EOQ.

ABC analysis

For a particular series of referenced products, the number of units used a year, and the unit cost are as shown in Table 11.18.

Table 11.17 Fortnex: Purchasing EOQ

Annual demand for copper wire, kg	12,000
Price per kg, $	2.45
Order cost, $/order	10.00
Carrying cost, % of price	20.00

Table 11.18 Fortnex: Number of units and unit cost

Product reference	Units a year	Unit cost ($)
B7894	700	1.10
C1289	875	0.36
G235	50	20.40
G458	250	8.40
Q4587	110	25.00
Z5892	375	2.40

Required

1. Discuss some of the requirements that would help to improve inventory management in this assembly situation. Consider all the elements in the supply chain from purchasing, assembly, to storage and distribution of the finished product.

2. In the case of the purchase of the copper wire should Fortnex take advantage of the price discount? Use calculations to justify your response.

3. What would the impact on the company be if it were to set up activities under a just-in-time operation?

4. In the referenced inventory items indicated, to which of the two should Fortnex give the maximum management attention? To which should the least be given?

Selected further reading

BERNARD, Paul (1999) *Integrated Inventory Management* (Oliver Wight Manufacturing Series), Wiley.

DONATH, Bob, MAZEL, Joe and DUBIN, Cindy (2002) *The Ioma Handbook of Logistics and Inventory Management*, Wiley.

SILVER, Edward, A., PYKE, David, F., PETERSON, Rein and MILTENBURG, G. John (1998) *Inventory Management and Production Planning and Scheduling*, 3rd edition, Wiley.

VIALE, J. David and CARRIGAN, Christopher (1997) *Basics of Inventory Management: From Warehouse to Distribution Center* (Fifty Minute Series), Crisp Publications.

WILD, Tony (1998) *Best Practice in Inventory Management*, Wiley.

An extensive listing of other further reading can be found on the website.

What's on the web?

Further learning resources are available to lecturers and students at www.supplychain-online.com, including the following which are specific to *Inventory management*:

Resource	Subject
Chapter overview	Inventory management
Detailed chapter summary	Inventory management
Demonstrating the concept: Maps	Fixed order period systems
Application exercise: Arbrelle II	Economic order quantity models
Application exercise: Bricks	Fixed order period systems
Application exercise: Stanford	ABC analysis
Case study: Transpack	Inventory management
More further reading	Inventory management

12 Operations and capacity planning

Chapter overview

- **Defining planning**
- **Aggregate planning and capacity**
- **Capacity adjustment to meet demand**
- **Modifying demand to accommodate capacities**
- **Aggregate planning choices in manufacturing**
- **Aggregate planning in services**
- **Master production schedule**

Defining planning

Planning are all those activities required to meet desired objectives. In business, the planning process generally has its roots in the strategic, or long-range plan that is then broken down into a more detailed operating plan. As discussed in the Chapter 2, a strategic plan has a time horizon, nominally of about five years, although it may be longer or shorter depending on the industry. Contrariwise, the horizon of the operations plan is about one year although for some firms it might be up to 18 months. The objective of the operating plan is to enumerate in detail all the activities necessary in order to produce end products, or to provide required services for the customer in a timely manner.

Operations plan

An operations plan itself may be further broken down into a short-term, and a medium-term plan as illustrated in Figure 12.1.

Short range

A short-range plan would cover less than three months, maybe one week, or even one day and the activities might include:

- scheduling production programmes
- establishing work assignments
- organizing deliveries of raw materials

- organizing shipments of finished goods
- hiring or termination of employees, in countries such as the USA. In the US management model, minimal social laws don't impede changing workforce levels: 'US firms can fire, so they hire. Japanese and German firms can't fire, so they don't hire,' says C Fred Bergsten, Director of the Institute for International Economics.[1]

Figure 12.1 Operations planning horizon

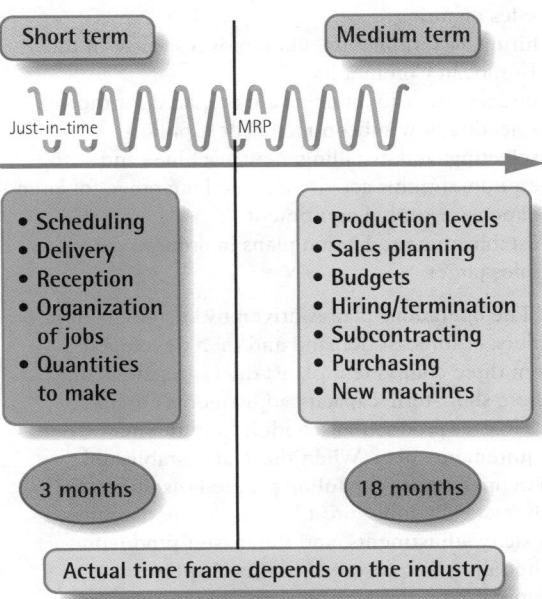

Figure 12.2 Planning stages in operations

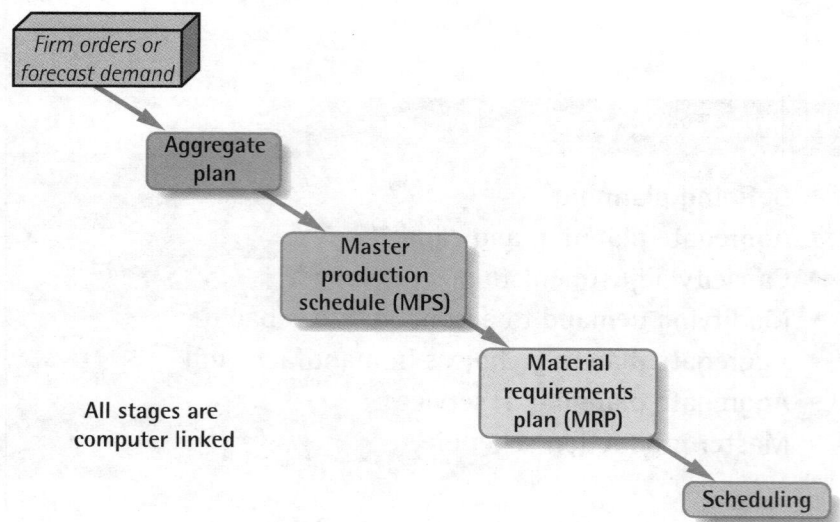

All stages are
computer linked

The utilization of just-in-time management methods lies within the short-range period, as indicated in Figure 12.1. (The concept of just-in-time is discussed in detail in Chapter 15.)

Medium range

A medium-range plan would cover the period beyond three months to about 12 or 18 months and some of the activities would include the following:

* sales planning
* hiring, or termination, of employees (most of the European Community)
* budgets (usually budgets are prepared for the year)
* selecting new subcontractors or suppliers
* selecting, and installing, new machines and equipment; this activity may be long range for large expensive capital equipment
* establishing production plans in order to meet a sales target.

The operations plan is driven by customers' firm orders, or forecast demand and then developed from three component plans: the aggregate plan, where short-term capacity adjustments are made, the master production schedule, and the material requirements plan. When these are established, then operations scheduling proceeds as illustrated schematically in Figure 12.2. Aggregate planning, capacity adjustments, and the master production scheduling are presented in this chapter. Material requirements planning and operations

scheduling are reviewed in the two subsequent chapters.

The operations plan (encompassing the aggregate plan), the master production schedule, and the material requirements plan are integrated, most often by computer integrated systems, and changing any one variable will change other variables and options in the plan. Further, like the strategic plan, the operations plan is dynamic and often in a state of flux because of variations in the external environment, or customer requirements. As such, those responsible for planning must be reactive particularly to the customer, or, as Tom Peters and Robert Waterman bluntly state in their book, *In Search of Excellence: Lessons from America's Best Run Companies:*[2]

In too many companies, the customer has become a bloody nuisance, whose unpredictable behaviour damages carefully made strategic plans, whose activities mess up computer operations, and who stubbornly insist that purchased products should work!!

The supply chain and planning

Evidently, rigorous attention to operations planning is critical for the smooth functioning of the supply chain. Poor scheduling in the reception of raw materials, in production programmes, or in the delivery of finished goods can all lead to delays and dissatisfied customers. Similarly, poor planning requirements for labour, machines, or subcontractors can diminish capacity availability meaning products cannot be produced and delivered when promised.

Aggregate planning and capacity

Formulating an aggregate plan

The aggregate plan is the combination of all the resources of the firm such as the people, machines, inventory available, etc., into a global or general operating programme. The starting point for the aggregate plan is the development of an estimate of future needs of end products. This estimate, which is essentially derived from marketing, may be firm orders from clients, anticipated orders that are 'promised' but not yet booked, or pure forecasts. When this estimate is established, all the end products are totalled or aggregated into a demand for the production facility. For production to convert this into capacity requirements the aggregate demand is translated into resource requirements of material quantities, labour hours and machine hours using appropriate standards. (Labour standards were presented in Chapter 8.)

The conversion of an aggregate demand into production units is relatively straightforward for a company who produces just one product, closely allied products, products that are reasonably homogeneous, or products that use few component parts. For example:

- cement factory
- coalmine
- shoe manufacturer
- oil refinery
- polyvinyl chloride plant
- ski company.

However, for facilities that produce a diverse set of products such as furniture, medical instruments, or household appliances, the development of an aggregate plan is more complex. This concept of converting demand quantities into production factors is illustrated in Demonstrating the concept 12.1. In this example, the capacity of the facility in terms of labour hours is illustrated and compared to the actual capacity required, or the load demanded. In the same way, required machine hours and raw material needs would be determined using machine standards and raw material standards per unit of product.

Capacity utilization and efficiency

Aggregate planning in the manufacturing or service sector involves deciding on how resources will be used to cost effectively meet the forecast or the actual client demand within the constraints of the capacity of the facility. In the operating environment the capacity of the facility is a function of some of the following elements:

- existing labour force within the company
- machines and equipment already in the facility
- raw materials and components that need to be purchased
- outside labour services including subcontracting.

The efficiency of the aggregate plan is expressed by the relationship:

$$\text{Efficiency} = \frac{\text{Actual output}}{\text{Facility capacity}}$$

A company strives to operate at maximum efficiency such that output is matched with capacity. Ideally, a firm would like to have a plan that is repetitive and can be effected at a steady rhythm, such as producing similar quantities of materials each week, using the same machines, and using a level labour force. All this would make organizing simple. However, client requirements are rarely constant and there may be peaks of high demand, and troughs of low demand. Thus, a well-conceived aggregate plan should provide for orderly production to accommodate the high and low demands but at the same time keeping resources such as machines, work teams, and existing building facilities operating close to capacity avoiding overloading and excessive under-loading or permitting resources to be idle.

Capacity adjustment to meet demand

The capacity of an organization is governed by the physical space (buildings and land) the labour force, financial resources, materials, and machines. In the short-term operating environment, physical space is not normally variable and plant expansion is considered long-term capacity planning. (Long-term capacity planning is referred to in Chapters 3 and 25.) Capacity adjustments in this chapter refer to short-term capacity changes or those that can be made within the framework of the operations plan. The following are some of the possibilities to make capacity adjustments to accommodate demand increases, or decreases, without modifying the size of the physical plant.

Hiring and termination of the permanent workforce

The needs of the labour force are determined by using labour standards or the ratios that indicate how much

Figure 12.3 Employer statutory termination notice requirement

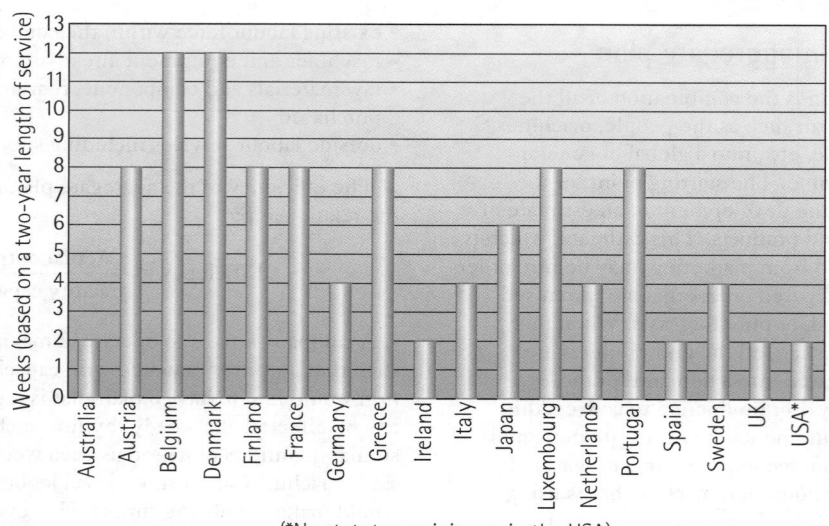

(*No statutory minimum in the USA)

time is needed to complete a certain task, or to make certain units. Then, the product of the labour standards and the number of units would be a measure of the number of people needed and the firm would hire, or terminate accordingly. If the firm were in a hiring mode then in the short term it assumes that there is sufficient space and sufficient machines in the current facility. In adding labour, the operations manager should take into consideration the changes in marginal costs. (See Chapter 25 for further details.) The costs involved in hiring include advertising, perhaps the use of outside hiring agencies, interviewing, and initial training. Further, new hires are not immediately as productive as current employees because of the learning curve process and so at first they are more costly in their production output than the more experienced employees. (See Chapter 8, in the section on learning curves.)

If it were indicated that the firm needed to reduce the level of the permanent work the firm's flexibility may be limited by union contracts, or government regulations. For terminating employees' statutory notice periods internationally vary widely from a high of 12 weeks in Belgium and Denmark to a low of two weeks in the UK, Ireland, and Australia as shown in Figure 12.3.[3] The shorter the required period, the more flexible the labour market is, giving the firm greater ease in its operating plan to respond to changing market conditions. In the USA there is no statutory termination notice period although as shown in the figure, two weeks is usually given. This is one reason why the

USA has greater flexibility in its operations planning and helps to explain the dominant strength of its economy. In terminating employees, direct costs would include severance benefits. In addition, when a firm terminates a portion of the workforce, it leaves uncertainty with the employees remaining and this can have a downward impact on productivity with a corresponding increase in cost. This is a continuing problem in turbulent economic times. Relative to most countries in Europe and Japan, the USA is very quick to resort to layoffs when the economy turns down. (A colleague of the author, who was the chief engineer for a firm in the USA, was terminated for economic reasons after over 25 years of service. He received the notice at 8am and was asked to leave the office by midday the same day. This seemingly rather brutal procedure was to avoid having a disgruntled employee in the firm who might demoralize those employees remaining, plus the person did not have the time to make photocopies of confidential material. The employee did, however, leave the firm with a substantial financial severance package.) However, as Industry insight 12.1 illustrates, termination of members of a loyal workforce may not always be the best long-term strategy for the firm.

Overtime

The current labour force can be put on overtime. This can be cost effective in the short term but, in the long term, productivity can be impacted if overtime is used for long periods. Further, labour contracts or

Termination of employment may not be the best solution

Industry insight 12.1

After the 11 September 2001 New York catastrophe many firms, particularly airlines, announced employee terminations, or layoffs, as they forecast difficult times ahead. However, even as competitors announced job cuts of 20%, Southwest Airlines of the USA considered employee layoffs as a last resort. In its 30 years of existence, even during jet fuel price increases, recession, and the 1991 Gulf War, the firm has never terminated a single employee for economic reasons. Rather than do that the firm looks for other cost-cutting measures such as reducing growth strategies, delaying new airplane deliveries, or cutting back on expansion or renovation programmes. Southwest is a member of the tiny fraternity of contrary companies that considers downsizing as unthinkable. What many of these different companies have in common is that have solid balance sheets and are not battered by the vagaries of economic changes especially those in which technology plays a role. It is not altruism at work. Arguments in support of non-downsizing are as follows.

Massive layoffs can backfire if one takes into account the following:

- severance and rehiring costs
- potential lawsuits from aggrieved workers
- loss of institutional memory and trust in management
- lack of qualified employees when the economy rebounds
- survivors who are risk averse, paranoid, and political.

Contrariwise, companies that avoid downsizing say they get:

- a fiercely loyal, more productive workforce
- higher customer satisfaction
- readiness to snap back with the economy
- a recruiting edge
- employees who are not afraid to innovate, knowing their jobs are safe.

Some economists say the USA has used layoffs too capriciously and that this approach should be the last place to look, rather than the first.

Adapted from: 'Where layoffs are a last resort',
Business Week[5]

government regulations may limit the amount of overtime that can be performed.

Part-time workers

Part-time employees have a contract or agreement with the company that they work something less than the full workweek. For example, three days instead of five or just in the morning. However, they are still part of the permanent labour force. There is some flexibility with part-time employees in that in times of high demand, they can be asked to work more hours and since they are experienced they would be more productive than say temporary workers. As Figure 12.4, illustrates the Netherlands has the highest proportion of part-time workers with an estimated 32%. In the USA some 13% of workers are part time, 23% in the United Kingdom and 23% in Japan. Large portions of part-time workers are women the highest of which is Luxembourg with 90% followed by Austria with 88% and Germany with 85%. Part-time workers by this definition are those working under 30 hours per week.[4]

Temporary workers

Temporary workers are those hired on an 'as needed' basis. This policy can be cost effective during peak demands. Retail stores and the post office use temporary labour during the Christmas season and vacation resorts use temporary labour during the peak summer or winter periods in ski resorts. Manufacturing companies use temporary labour for tasks that are not particularly specialized in heavy demand periods. In the secretarial field the Kelly Agency is well known as a supplier of temporary secretaries. In the US economy the temporary employee is becoming a prominant factor as illustrated by the article Industry insight 12.2.

An extra shift

If a company is operating at one or two shifts per day, a third shift can be added. This will take time to implement in the sense of finding, and training, the appropriate labour and negotiating required union agreements. As a result of these initial costs, the company needs to be certain that this third shift can be kept operational for a period of time to make it economical. This would be probably for a minimum period of, say, three months but, of course, it depends on the product, and the type of work. Experience has shown that the third shift (usually at night) is less productive than the day shift.

Figure 12.4 Employees working part time (part-time = less than 30 hours a week)

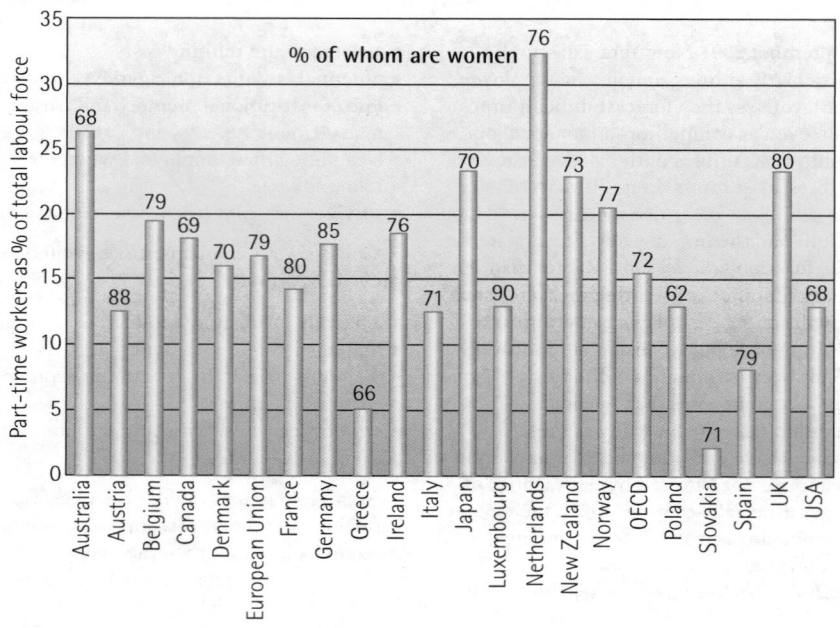

The temporary employee

On any given day, more Americans owe their jobs to temporary help outfits than are working in automobile or aircraft factories. About 10% of the job growth in the 1990s was in temp agencies or twice as much as in the 1980s. Manpower Inc. boasts of being America's largest employer. Temp agencies grew rapidly in the USA after state courts in the late 1970s and 1980s limited employers' ability to fire permanent workers. Temps were easier to fire than permanent workers and so employers hired more of them. By 1996, according to one survey, 50% of all employers and 75% of all manufacturing firms were using temporary agencies. Today more than 3.3 million workers are on temp firm placements, mostly in clerical or light manufacturing jobs.

The temp boom is a huge change in the way the economy works and is one reason the USA has pushed down the unemployment rate without increasing inflation. The temp agencies market their services making it easy for employers with openings and unemployed workers to find one another. When the slots are filled with sorely needed temps, the employers do not have to raise wages for existing workers. One economist says that employers tinker with wages in much the same way airlines tinker with

ticket prices to fill airplanes. Agencies help some workers get jobs they wouldn't get otherwise, often screening and auditioning workers to save the employers time. In some states more than 20% of the people leaving welfare for work spend time in a temp agency placement. When there was a tight labour market temp agencies could place anyone who wanted to work. At that time employers had the mirror test, 'Do they breathe?' Some temp agencies often offer a quick free way to brush up on computer skills, although this isn't altruistic because then the temp firm can charge higher fees to the employer for this 'trained' employee.

Hospitals use temp agency nurses because they say they are unable to fill vacancies. However, one hospital argues that the reason for their being unable to hire nurses is that the hospital wages for permanent nurses is lower than what temps can earn. A large North Carolina hospital hires as many permanent nurses as it can at $25.76 an hour in wages and benefits. It then fills vacancies by paying $40 for temps of which the nurse receives between $28 and $32 with few benefits. The winners in this situation are those who pay the hospital bills. The losers are the $26 an hour nurses who might otherwise make more money if the nursing shortage forced hospitals to bid up wages across the board.

In manufacturing the scenario is the reverse. A Midwestern auto plants plant pays $15.67 an hour for permanent workers and $10.88 for temps of which $7.50 goes to the workers. The company cannot hired experienced workers at the higher wage and takes its chance on unproven workers because they are cheap and failures can be fired easily. If it were not for the temps the company would be forced to raise wages to lure good workers from other firms. The losers here are again the permanent workers whose wages are kept low. Some temps may be winners since if they are successful they may land themselves a job they would not get otherwise.

Adapted from: 'U.S. temp workers have lasting effect on labour market', *Wall Street Journal Europe*[6]

Weekend work

Another possibility for increasing output is to work at weekends. This again depends on union contracts, and government regulations. Some stores in Europe at present are not allowed to open on Sundays (France and Germany, for example) even though it is felt there is a customer demand.

Machines

Machine capacity is limited by the fact that machines can only operate 24 hours a day. Additional machine output requires purchasing new machines, leasing, or subcontracting and these alternatives often require a long lead time. Planning, purchasing and installing, expensive equipment such as robots, printing presses, and bottling lines, plus the training of operators, would normally not be feasible in the timeframe of the operating plan period. However, smaller mobile machines can be moved in and out of the operating area to modify capacity.

Purchased materials

Supplies of raw materials, or parts can be adjusted up and down relatively easily if the supplier is well known, the product is unsophisticated (screws, sheet metal, or plastic mouldings) and the supplier is close at hand. However, for more sophisticated items, computer chips, vanadium, or carbon fibre, there may not be the same flexibility. When new sources of supply are developed there might be additional costs payable to the new supplier.

Subcontractors

Subcontracting, or outsourcing work, provides flexibility to the client company in terms of capacity and often the subcontractor can perform the work more cheaply than can the client firm. This is the principal reason subcontractors are used, although at first a make or buy analysis would be appropriate to see which is the most cost-effective approach. (See Chapter 16.) Using subcontractors, the client company might lose some control over the product quality and delivery date of required items. In addition, it may be required to share company technical know-how, which could be later used by the subcontractor to establish itself as a competitor to the client company. These concerns can be improved by careful selection, long-term relationships, and creating a climate of confidence between the client company and the subcontractor. The Japanese have a strong subcontractor relationship through their keiretsu network (see Chapter 7). Subcontracting is now a major strategy of most firms with automobile companies outsourcing between 60 and 80% of their activity in terms of product cost. Industry insight 12.3 underscores the importance of subcontracting.

Adjusting inventory levels

In manufacturing or warehouse/distribution when demand is slack, inventories are allowed to increase by continuing production at some pre-established level. These can be used to satisfy demand at a future period. This approach has to be balanced against the cost of carrying the inventory. (See Chapter 11.)

Demands on backorder or backlog

Backordering means booking the customer's order, and indicating that delivery will be made at some future date. On the company's books the orders then become backlog, either noted in unit quantity, labour hours, or financial terms. Backordering may be appropriate for custom-made products. However, clients may not accept backordering for standard items, which to the supplier firm could result in lost orders, and/or permanently, lost customers.

The concept of backlog is commonly used in service companies such as engineering and construction firms and shipbuilding (see Industry insight 12.3) or manufacturing firms such as the aircraft industry. For these companies, the end product is a unique project destined for a specific client. Work only commences when the company has received a contract from the

Shipbuilding at Chantiers de l'Atlantique

Chantiers de l'Atlantique near St Nazaire on the French Atlantic coast is a subsidiary of the French conglomerate Alstom SA. It is a sprawling shipyard, birthplace of the legendary *Normandie* and served as a submarine base for the Germans in World War II. For years the shipyard had a very thin backlog and the workforce was shrinking. No more. Under the 49-year-old Executive Patrick Boissier, who took over the helm in 1997, business is booming and with it changes in production planning and organization. The company has firm orders for 16 boats, or 40% of the world market share, and this has increased its backlog, and the profit picture now looks very bright. The orders have been boosted by the demand in cruise vacations and one of the latest orders for Chantiers de l'Atlantique was from the Los Angeles-based Princess Cruises who committed to buy two 89,000-ton luxury liners.

New workers are filling the shipyard at a rate of 200 a month and the demand is so strong that 40 women have enrolled in welding classes – a task formerly dominated by men. The new strategy of Chantiers de l'Atlantique is to rely on hundreds of subcontractors that handle everything from outfitting marble-lined spas, building the ornate walnut woodwork, laying the plumbing, painting, and installing all the electrical equipment including the wiring. Chantiers de l'Atlantique's role in the shipbuilding is the design, building the hull, and systems integration. The strategy of outsourcing at the shipyard mirrors the trend of the automobile industry where the specialized subcontractors can do the work more efficiently and at a lower cost. Today the subcontractors are responsible for 75% of the value of the ship compared to about 66% a few years ago. In 2000 as production increases, it is expected that subcontracted workers will increase to 8000 from the current 3000 whereas the number of Alstom employees will remain constant at 4000. The heavy reliance on subcontractors does have an unexpected human relation problem. These people, who work shoulder to shoulder with the Alstom employees, may earn up to 60% more than Alstom people plus they have advantages like profit sharing that averaged some $1300 per employee in 1999 and performance premiums which may add $220 to an employee's pay check a month. These differences do create some stress in the work teams.

The sudden burst of building activity has the shipyard, suppliers, and subcontractors searching frantically for qualified personnel. In addition Chantiers de l'Atlantique is replacing its aging (retirement age) employees at over 500 a year. With so much manual labour going into the building of a boat, Patrick Boissier and his team have changed many of the work practices. Originally workers wasted nearly an hour each day just moving around the boatyard that measures some two kilometres across. A fleet of 50 buses transported them from the front gate to their jobs each morning, hauled everyone back for lunch in a common mess hall manned by 80 table servers and then returned them to the front gate at the end of the day. Although they were paid for a 39-hour week only about 30 hours were actually productive. Now, the central canteen has been replaced by several smaller ones located around the yard to minimize transit time. Also, workers are allowed to drive straight to their worksite rather than park at the front gate. Further, for the first time there are two shifts at the yard to use the capacity of the expensive industrial equipment better. Work efficiency is critical to the success of the shipyard. The penalty clause for not completing a boat on time can be a crippling $1 million a day since boat owners have geared up marketing and booking to coincide exactly with the delivery date. (See Chapter 18 for more on penalty clauses.)

Adapted from: 'All hands on deck', *Wall Street Journal Europe*[8]

customer, and often with upfront financial payments. The backlog may be recorded as the number of hours on the books to complete contracted work, or the work is converted into revenues, based on the average rate for the hours on backlog, or recorded as the number of units which remain to be produced. As an example, in April 2001 the backlog of airplane orders for Boeing aircraft company numbered around 1600, which helped Boeing to remain financially strong even though other firms were weakening during an economic downturn.[7] Changes in backlog indicate the growth, or contraction of the firm. As an illustration, Figure 12.5 gives backlog data from the annual report for this major engineering and construction firm based in Los Angeles, California.

The backlog indicated represents construction projects such as oil refineries, chemical plants, office buildings, airports, and engineering work not necessarily involving construction.[9,10,11]

Backlog as a planning tool

The amount of backlog that a firm has on its order books is a very important leading indicator for planning purposes for the firm as highlighted in the following. (Leading indicators in a macroeconomic sense are discussed in Chapter 10.)

• Budgeting where an increase in backlog would be an indicator of increased financial needs. The fact that

Figure 12.5 Backlog: Fluor Construction

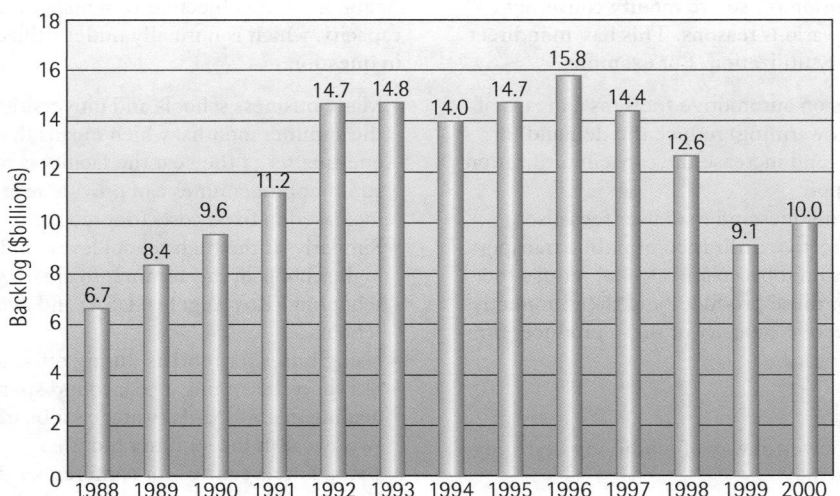

a firm has a high backlog should make borrowing needs from the bank easier. Also, a high backlog will usually push up the stock price increasing the firm's capital value improving credit ratings and making borrowing less expensive.

- Human resource needs would increase with an increase in backlog. Where specific skills are required, these human resources may take time to hire, particularly in a competitive environment.
- Procurement activity would eventually increase with increase in backlog and this may involve searching out new suppliers and new subcontractors.
- Work for new clients may decline with an increase in backlog as the firm's capacity to perform new work will decline. Also, prospective new clients would be wary of a firm with a high backlog, as they may perceive problems in getting their work completed on schedule.

Modifying demand to accommodate capacities

Another aggregate planning approach is to attempt to modify the demand at the customer level in order to impact capacity utilization or consumption patterns. This might be because surplus capacity exists in the firm, or governments wish, for various reasons, to modify demand. Modifying customer demand is not as easy to implement as production capacity changes, as it involves external environment and customer habits that are hard

to control. Further, the success of adjusting the demand is, to a certain extent, a function of whether the product is elastic, or inelastic (see Chapter 10). Some approaches to modifying the external demand include the following.

Reduction in product price

A reduction in product price is common in the service sector when fixed capacity exists. The objective of the price reduction is to increase demand during slack periods to soak up some of the unused capacity during these slack periods. If customers can be encouraged to switch from normally heavy demand periods to these slack periods, new capacity investment can be avoided. Examples include:

- Lower airline, train, or ferryboat fares during off peak periods.
- Cheaper electricity between 10.30pm and 6.30am, the case in France.
- Lower telephone rates between midday and 2pm or at nights and weekends.
- Lower cinema prices mid-afternoon or before 5pm
- Restaurants before midday for lunch or before 5pm for dinner.
- Lower vacation package prices during off-season periods.
- Lower toll road fees in off-peak hours.

In manufacturing or distribution firms, lowering prices such as sales or special promotions is also a way of reducing cumulated inventories.

Taxation and fees

Government taxation is used to modify consumer consumption for various reasons. This has an indirect impact on capacity utilization. For example:

- Increased taxes on automotive fuels (as a means of reducing global warming) reduce the demand for these products, and increase the capacity utilization of public transport.
- Increased parking fees and road user fees also increase the effective utilization of public transport.
- Increased taxes on tobacco and alcohol reduce the consumption of these products, and then indirectly reduce the effective capacity of these producer firms.

Advertising

Advertising is a powerful way of modifying demand such as the following:

- Health warnings on cigarettes reduce the demand.
- Sales advertising increases demand of end of line items. For example, for high-tech goods such as computers, when a more rapid computer chip comes onto the market, aggressive sales or promotions try to reduce the inventory of those machines with the old chip.
- In Europe in 2001 there was aggressive advertising to encourage the eating of beef as demand had plummeted because of the 'mad cow crisis'.

Again, by modifying the demand the capacity utilization of the producer firm is changed.

Cash payments

Cash payments by firms, or governments can modify demand as, for example:

- The European Union gives cash grants to farmers not to produce certain crops, or to rear certain livestock in order to avoid excess production. This doesn't change demand, but it does reduce the effective capacity.
- In France in 1994/1995 the government of Balladur, and then later Juppé, offered cash incentives to encourage the purchase of new cars as an effort to increase the output in the automobile industry. This artificial distortion had the desired impact during the grant period, but a slump in the car market occurred when the car payments ceased.
- Firms themselves such as makers of kitchen appliances, and car producers, sometimes offer cash grants, or rebates, to enhance the sale of their products.

Creating a new demand

Again, here the objective is to make use of a fixed capacity, which is normally under-utilized in the period in question:

- Many business schools and universities are closed in the summer months, which means that for maybe up to one-quarter of the year the facility is not used. Creating summer programmes can provide revenue without any increased in fixed costs (depreciation on the building).
- Similarly, at the high school level, adding teaching in high schools in the summer to create year-round schooling (Los Angeles, USA) and avoid building new schools.
- Using buses for tourists during off-peak period.
- Ski shops becoming a year-round sports supplier by dealing in surfboards (water), sailboards, and swimwear in the summer months.
- Using hotels centres for conferences during the day.
- Using holiday centres for seminars during off-peak holiday seasons, such as is done by Club Méditeranée.

Club Méditerranée

Although still famous for its image of sun and fun, nowadays Club Méditerranée SA increasingly spells commerce. On the French Riviera, near Nice, people from Ista, a French computer distributor, are getting an update on new IBM computer products, another meeting room is jammed with people from Babolat, a Lyon-based manufacturer of tennis equipment, while other business groups include Belgium's floor tile company, Inter Carrelages, and German representatives from the Epson computer company. Rooms are equipped with telephones that accommodate computer modems, and fax machines are also available.[12]

Aggregate planning choices in manufacturing

The choices of planning in a production operation include level production, synchronizing the production with the aggregate demand, or a hybrid of level and synchronized production.

Level production

Level production is when a plan is prepared such that the production rate is uniform over time. This is a preferred planning approach due to the following:

- Hiring, termination, and overtime of labour are minimized.

- Supervision is simplified, as the operation is smoother.
- Resource planning is less complicated.
- Scrap rates are lower because there are few production rate changes.
- Quality is usually higher due to the smoother production rate.
- Scheduling of maintenance programmes is simplified.
- Labour and material costs are reduced as the number of startups and shutdowns are minimized.

Seasonal demand

When product demand is seasonal, such as for skis, summer clothing, fertilizer, etc., a level production plan may be established based on the estimated total demand for a certain period (the whole year, for example) and then averaging this amount on a weekly, or monthly basis to create a level production plan. In these situations there will be sharp inventory changes. When demand is low, inventory builds up and with it the associated inventory carrying cost. When the demand is high, inventory levels are drawn down and this might be a critical period with the risk of stockouts. This situation is illustrated in Figure 12.6. Here the total requirements for the year are 21,000 units and this is broken down to a level production of 1750 units a month. There are periods in the winter months when demand is low which results in a build-up of inventory. In the summer months the demand increases which puts the inventory level very low in August and September. If the demand were more than estimated, the firm would be in a stockout situation.

Produce-to-stock

Produce-to-stock operations would be the case for standard products such as processed foods, plastic materials, kitchen appliances, etc. Although the demand for the products may not be seasonal there is a certain fluctuation of demand. Using level production the finished goods inventories buffer differences between the demand and production from period to period. Again, when demand is high, inventory is drawn down and when demand is low, the inventory builds up. Thus during slack demand a level production plan results in higher inventories with the associated high carrying costs. The buffering action of inventory for a produce-to-stock situation is illustrated in Demonstrating the concept 12.2.

Produce-to-order

When goods are produced-to-order for customized items, finished goods cannot be used as an inventory buffer since production doesn't begin until customer orders are received. This might be the case for furniture where there is a large choice of upholstery available, tailor-made clothing, or computer equipment for specific customer requirements. In this case, when a level capacity aggregate plan is used, it is the backlog of customer orders that buffer the difference between level production capacity, and variable demand. The buffering action of backlog for a produce-to-order situation is illustrated in Demonstrating the concept 12.2.

Figure 12.6 Level production and seasonal demand

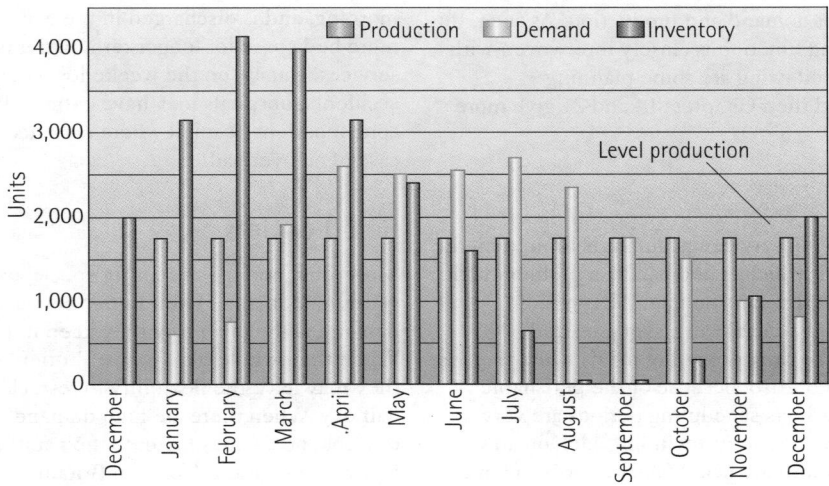

Synchronized capacity with aggregate demand

Synchronized capacity with aggregate demand is the production of just the amount required to satisfy demand for any given time period. In this case, the finished goods inventory is almost non-existent and so inventory carrying costs are low. However, synchronizing capacity with demand is not easy to operate as labour, machine, and material requirements change frequently, which, apart from making planning difficult, increases production costs. Further, many firms do not have the flexibility to adjust labour needs up and down. The just-in-time method for production, discussed in Chapter 15, is an approach whose goal is to synchronize capacity with aggregate demand.

Hybrid of level and synchronized production

A hybrid of a level and synchronized production plan would be where a firm establishes a base level production plan. Then, swings in customer demand, either up, or down would be handle by using temporary labour, overtime as necessary to accommodate customer needs.

Demonstrating the concept 12.3 illustrates the development of an aggregate plan using some of the variables discussed.

Aggregate planning in services

The difference between many aggregate-planning options for service firms and manufacturing is that in services, there is little, or no inventory to act as a buffer between customer demand and production. As such, the aggregate-planning function is closely interwoven with scheduling. The following are some planning considerations and then Chapters 14 and 21 give more on the subject.

Restaurants

The capacity of a full service restaurant is limited by the seating availability, which is not usually a problem with a fast food or self-service restaurant. All types of restaurants generally operate in a synchronized production mode by only preparing meals when there is a customer demand. Also, because of the perishable nature of their products scheduling periods are very short. The fast food industry, including McDonald's, Burger King, or Kentucky Fried Chicken, which have

relatively standardized products, often keep a small amount of finished products in anticipation of customer demand although for most of these the inventory is held for a maximum of about seven minutes. Self-service restaurants prepare some of the food in advance so that it is on display when customers are in the service line. Full service restaurants prepare a lot of the food on demand except in the case of vegetables and desserts.

Consulting, accounting, and design firms

Consulting and design firms have fixed capacity and this is the staff. The work by its very nature is customized and so they work in a synchronized production mode starting work when a contract is signed and putting other work on backlog when demand is higher than production capacity. Very often a firm's ability to start work immediately is a strong factor in being awarded a contract. These firms' flexibility with high demand is working overtime and weekends when here there is usually no regulations governing the amount of overtime these persons can perform. Also, with the use of the Internet and e-mail it is feasible to work 'any hour of the day'. When demand is low in these firms, employees spend their 'non-revenue' producing time by prospecting for new work, or updating their various standards.

Hospitals and medical services

Hospitals for in-patient care have a fixed capacity limited by the number of beds available. Hospital outpatient care and doctors' offices are capacity limited by staff availability. Using appointment schedules smoothes production and demand. Where feasible, hospitals are turning more and more to outpatient care for small surgical procedures (the patient comes in the morning, and is discharged in the evening) to provide more bed space for longer term patients. For emergency services, usually on the weekends when there are more accidents, hospitals may have extra staff, or have correspondent hospital where patients can be sent in the case of an overload.

Retail outlets

Most retail outlets, except for special orders, provide the goods on demand. Their buffer between supply and demand is the inventory they keep in their storage area. When their wholesaler, or distribution depot is close they may have the flexibility to restock within a half day. When there are high demands in the evenings, or weekends, stores increase their staff loading. Some retail outlets, Tesco in Britain is an example, are experimenting with using the Internet to permit customers to place orders, and then have the products delivered. When this approach becomes popular, it will enable smoother planning for the retail outlet.[13] (See also Industry insight 7.5.)

Travel industry

Airline companies and railways use planning schedules to increase capacity during periods of high demand in the mornings or evening (although this has its limitations in airports, with the availability of landing slots, and airplanes). Similarly with railways there are capacity limitations with the rolling stock and track availability. In periods of high demand, customers have the flexibility to switch from one airline company to another, use a different route, or take a later train. Further, in Europe one has the flexibility to switch from plane to train, or vice versa.

Master production schedule

Definition

The master production schedule, MPS, is a key planning tool, with a time horizon usually in weeks, or, depending on the firm, maybe months. The MPS indicates what quantity of end items need to be completed and in what time period. These end items might be:

* Finished products or consumer goods, to be shipped directly to the client (business to consumer).
* Finished products to be placed in inventory.
* Intermediate goods, or industrial products, to be dispatched to another firm (business to business).
* Intermediate goods to be transferred to another section of the same firm.

The master production schedule is the pilot for all work centres, and, as shown in Figure 12.2, it is the bridge between the aggregate plan and the material requirements plan. In many instances, the MPS is a computer-driven tool linked to other modules of the planning function. The MPS, which should be prepared in collaboration with the managers of production, sales, and perhaps finance, is established considering the firm's capacity constraints, the demands of clients, and financial capability. The objectives of the MPS are to develop a schedule of end items to be completed, when promised, so that client delivery dates are respected. It should also avoid overloading, or under-loading of the production facility so that the system is optimized.

Rough–cut capacity plan

The master production schedule is developed from firm, or expected customer orders, forecasts, inventory status reports, and production capacity information. The most urgent orders are placed in the first available open slot of the MPS and as all the orders are slotted, a rough-cut capacity plan emerges which shows the load of the production work centre in relationship to the available capacity. The load might equal the capacity, may be under-loaded, or it may be overloaded. As an illustration, Table 12.1 shows demand data for a manufacturing firm.

These data show the scheduled units to be finished each week, in a time horizon of 13 weeks, according to whether they are committed (that is there is a firm order), expected (not a firm order but pretty definite), and forecast based on sales estimates. The tabular data are shown transposed into an MPS bar chart (Figure 12.7). This shows the capacity of the facility, fixed by machine and labour availability, as 240 units each week.

Under-loading

Under-loading is the situation where, in the initial MPS, not enough production has been scheduled so that the facility is not fully loaded. In Figure 12.7, the facility is under-loaded in weeks 2, 6, 9, 10, 12, and 13.

Table 12.1 Demand data for a manufacturing firm

Week	1	2	3	4	5	6	7	8	9	10	11	12	13
Committed	220	180	160	45									
Planned			105	230	240	190	275	190	150	100	30	10	
Forecast								80	60	115	230	170	140
Total	220	180	265	275	240	190	275	270	210	215	260	180	140

Figure 12.7 Master production schedule: Rough cut

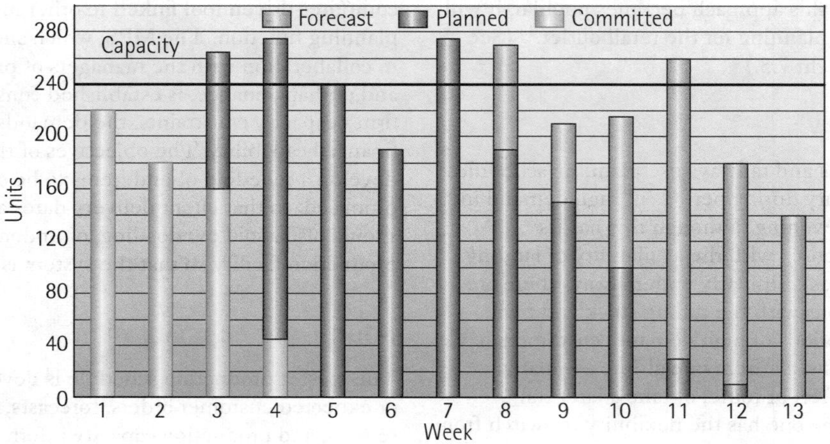

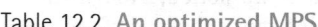

Table 12.2 An optimized MPS

Week	1	2	3	4	5	6	7	8	9	10	11	12	13
Committed	240	240	125										
Planned			115	240	240	240	240	155	150	100	30	10	
Forecast								85	90	140	210	230	40
Total	240	240	240	240	240	240	240	240	240	240	240	240	40

Overloading

Overloading is where too much production capacity has been scheduled. In Figure 12.7, this is the case for weeks 3, 4, 7, 8, and 11.

Balancing the master production schedules

The purpose of the rough-cut capacity plan is to see where adjustments can be made to balance the MPS. For the situation given, production units have been shifted from one time period to another to balance the load with capacity to thus create an optimized MPS as shown in Table 12.2 and illustrated in the new MPS (Figure 12.8). This shows the total units for each category have not changed but the system is completely balanced and the excess capacity is left for period 13.

This final MPS is shown broken down into four time zones, or fences, which firms might do according to the rigidity of the planning programme.

Frozen

The frozen period here is shown for the first two weeks, which is the schedule for all committed units. The implication is that definite plans have been made in terms of using staff, machines, and materials, and any changes during this time frame would seriously disrupt operations. As such, modifications in this period are usually prohibited because it would be costly to reverse plans. Changes would only be made under extraordinary circumstances and only then, with authorization from the highest level, such as the vice-president in charge of manufacturing.

Fixed

This second stage of the MPS, shown here covers weeks 3 through 5, is the programme for the remaining committed and some planned units. This timeframe is considered pretty rigid, though less so than the first two weeks. Plans may be modified in this section, but only under exceptional circumstances and they would be resisted as much as possible.

Figure 12.8 Master production schedule: Balanced

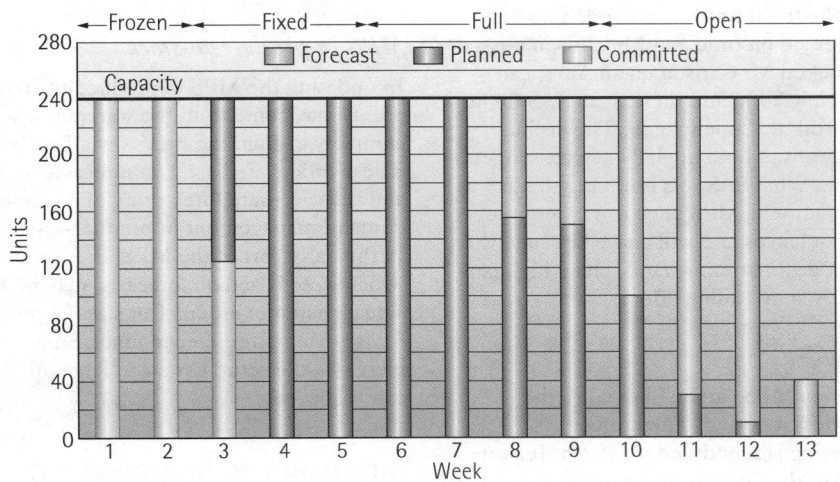

Full

This is the third stage of the MPS shown here covering weeks 6 through 9 for planned and forecast units. Here all the available production capacity has been allocated but changes might be made with not excessive increase in production costs. However, any effect on customer satisfaction is uncertain at this point.

Open

This is the fourth stage of the MPS shown here covering weeks 10 through 13. Not all production capacity has been allocated in period 13 and this is where any new orders would be slotted.

Rigidity of the MPS

It may be felt that a firm is being very inflexible if it adopts the time fence approach to planning and is not accommodating last-minute changes for the customer. This is true, in that the schedule once established is not flexible in the early periods. However, this drives home that it is important that for effective supply chain management, production, sales, and finance should be closely involved in the preparation of the master production schedule and they all make the commitment to support it once an agreement has been reached. Any last minute changes in the MPS represents a cost to the firm of which production will probably bear the brunt, but in reality sales, and finance belong to the same organization so unnecessary costs are also their problem. The following are real-world illustrations related to rigorous planning

which underscore the criteria of frozen, fixed, full, and open in the MPS.

Paint company

A small paint company prepared cans of paint of various colours for retail outlets. The company had three processing vessels that it used to mix the various paints. It would set its MPS covering a two-week period. There were occasions when, in the middle of mixing, it received an urgent order from its biggest client for an order of paint. In these cases often it would stop the preparation in process, discard the paint, clean the vessel, and restart the mixing operation for its major client. That is, it would interrupt its MPS in the first part of the time fence, rather than allocating new orders to the end. It was costly! The firm eventually went out of business.[14]

Scandinavian Airways

Airline companies often illustrate the quality of their service by the percent of on-time arrival, and departures. In the 1980s, Scandinavian Airways (SAS) had an advertisement on the radio touting the punctuality of its service. The tone of the advert, went something like this.

There was a daily scheduled flight on a Boeing-747 that left Los Angles around midday direct for Copenhagen. A certain David Carlson, president of a prestigious Swedish company, used this particular flight every week. One day, Mr Carlson called from his car phone while on the Santa Monica Freeway (the route that connects downtown LA with the airport) to say that he was going to be late. He didn't say in as many words, but the fact that he called the airline was an implicit request to delay the flight until he arrived. The SAS flight left as scheduled on time and Mr Carlson missed the flight. SAS booked Mr Carlson on an American Airlines flight to New York, and then on an SAS flight direct from New York to Copenhagen. The airline company did not want to hold up 450 or so passengers for just one person. What SAS was implying that it was not prepared to modify its MPS once it was put into action. A plane that leaves late will arrive late, and then be late for its next destination. That is, changing plans would have a costly snowballing effect.

Business meetings

The timeframe of an MPS can be likened to the conduct of a business meeting. The project management meeting is scheduled for 11 am. It starts at 11 a.m. with 19 of the 20 invited in attendance. Then, 15 minutes late, a senior executive enters. The project manager stops, and repeats the events of the last 15 minutes so that the executive does not miss anything. That is, the project manager 'modifies his MPS' at the last minute. There is a significant cost related to the time wasted of those who arrived at the meeting on time!

Updating of the MPS

The master production schedule is a dynamic (moving) tool and usually updated weekly. When one week is finished, this week is deleted from the front end, and a week is added to the end. The demands for the whole MPS are then re-estimated, taken into account changes, and if necessary the MPS is rebalanced. Data in the later part of the schedule are not as accurate as those in the early weeks, which is usually dominated by firm customers' orders whereas the later weeks are dominated by forecasts.

MPS in produce-to-order

In a produce-to-order firm, it is the customer's specific orders that dominate demand management in the MPS. Scheduling in the MPS comes from backlog and product forecasts may never be used. In updating the MPS, orders in backlog are assigned open production slots and the lot size (number of products to produce on an order) is usually determined by the customer requirements. If a customer orders 1000 desks for example, ordinarily 1000 of these desks will be produced on an order. This approach to lot sizing is called lot for lot (Chapter 13 gives more information on lot sizing). Since produce-to-order firms have many product

designs, the number of product references that have to be placed in the MPS may be large.

MPS in produce-to-stock

In updating the MPS in produce-to-stock firms product orders may come from the warehouse within the company or from the firm's own distribution centre. These orders are based on forecasts of future demand and thus accurate forecasting plays an important part in demand management in produce-to-stock situations. In the early part of the MPS, these warehouse orders, which were based on forecasts, may be backed up by actual customer orders. Lot sizes in produce-to-stock firms are a matter of economics. Small size lots increases the setup costs and large lot sizes increases carrying costs.

MPS planning horizon and the supply chain

The planning horizon for the master production schedule can be upwards from a few weeks to months. It depends on the industry but the horizon should be at least equal to the longest cumulative end item lead time. The cumulative end item lead time is based on the supply chain length and is the amount of time to obtain materials from suppliers, produce all parts and components, assemble items, packing, ready them for shipment, and then delivery to customers. It is the end item with the greatest cumulative lead time in the supply chain that determines the span of the planning horizon, although in practice, planning horizons are usually greater than this minimum.

Demand management and the MPS

Even with the best of tools and the most reliable of information there may not always be an optimum fit between the actual demand of end products and the capacity as indicated by the master production schedule. This is where the function of demand management, often the role of the scheduler who develops the MPS, is important. The scheduler must work closely with commercial people interpreting forecast, promised orders, branch requirements, interplant orders, spares, etc., to ensure the accuracy of the timing and quantity of orders slotted into the MPS. Demand management (or sometimes demand forecasting) also covers the decisions to take when sales are slow, or inventories are rising, to perhaps reduce prices. In this case, this part of demand management would usually originate from salespeople.

Summary of key elements

- An operations plan may have a time span of up to 18 months, depending on the firm. The operations plan is driven by customers' orders or forecasts and comprises an aggregate plan, a master production schedule (MPS), and a material requirements plan (MRP).

- The aggregate plan is developed by converting the needs of end products into production resource requirements using labour, machine, and material standards.

- Aggregate planning involves deciding how to select the most efficient mix of labour, machines, raw materials, and outside labour services.

- Short-term capacity can be modified by hiring or termination of employees, overtime, part-time or temporary workers, another shift, weekend work, using mobile machines, adjusting inventory levels, backorders, or by using subcontractors.

- Backordering is usually a concept for custom products. When a client makes an order this is a backorder to the client and represents backlog on the firm's order books.

- Product demand can be modified, impacting capacity utilization, by price changes, taxation and fees, advertising, cash payments, and creating a new demand.

- Level production is when the production rate is uniform over time. This mode is the easiest to plan, and probably the most cost effective in manufacturing.

- Seasonal demand can be accommodated using level production. Inventory is built up in periods of slack demand, and drawn down during periods of high demand.

- Level production is appropriate for produce to stock as inventory can be built up or drawn down. The inventory acts as a buffer between demand and production.

- Produce-to-order firms normally do not keep an inventory of products. It is the backlog of the company that acts as the buffer between demand and production.

- Synchronized capacity with aggregate demand is producing only what is required. It is hard to plan as it means constantly changing the level of production resources.

- A hybrid of level and synchronized production is a base-level production programme and accommodating changes by using temporary labour or overtime as needed.

- In aggregate planning in services there is usually no inventory to act as a buffer. Appointment schedules might be used to level out demand requirements.

- The master production schedule indicates the quantity and timing of end products. It is the bridge between the aggregate plan, and the material requirements plan.

- The rough-cut capacity plan indicates the extent of under-loading, and overloading in production. A balanced MPS will optimize the production system.

- A well-developed MPS with frozen, fixed, full, and open time fences will help to avoid unnecessary production costs.

- The MPS is a dynamic tool updated weekly. In produce-to-order firms it is the backlog used to make the updates in the MPS and in produce-to-stock firms it is the forecast.

- The MPS planning horizon should be at least equal to the greatest cumulative total lead time in the supply chain from raw materials through to product delivery.

- Demand management is the correct interpretation regarding the timing and quantity of orders slotted into the MPS. It may also involve price adjustments when sales are slow or the inventory of finished goods is increasing.

Notes and references

1. 'Dynamic model: US economy shows foreign nations ways to grow much faster. Denver may offer Europe, Japan lesson in the value of flexible capital, labour', *Wall Street Journal Europe*, 20/21 June 1997
2. PETERS, Thomas J. and WATERMAN, Robert H. *In Search of Excellence: Lessons from America's Best Run Companies*, Harper & Row, New York, 1982
3. 'Economic and financial indicators', *The Economist*, 5 January 2002, p. 84
4. 'Economic and financial indicators: Part-time workers', *The Economist*, 28 July 2001
5. CONLIN, Michelle, 'Where layoffs are a last resort: Treating them as unthinkable can have big benefits', *Business Week*, 8 October 2001, p. 49
6. WESSEL, David, 'US temp workers have lasting effect on labour market', *Wall Street Journal Europe*, 2/3 February 2001, p. 2
7. 'Plane sales triple Boeing profit', *International Herald Tribune*, 21–22 April 2001, p. 9
8. WOODRUFF, David, 'All hands on deck: A French shipbuilder thrives as it kicks the subsidy habit. The storied Chantiers yard remakes itself to catch US Cruise-ship wave. Farming out the woodwork', *Wall Street Journal Europe*, 2 February 2000, p. 1
9. Fluor Corporation, Annual Report, 1995
10. Fluor Corporation, Annual Report, 1999
11. Fluor Corporation, Annual Report, 2000
12. 'Swinging singles grow up: Club Med mixes work and play: French resort company displays a more mature image', *Wall Street Journal Europe*, 3–4 May 1996
13. 'No lines at Britain's first on-line grocery', *Wall Street Journal*, 25/26 July 1997
14. Based on the author's work in the Los Angeles Basin in the 1980s

Review and discussion topics

1. Planning horizons
An integrated oil company such as Chevron Texaco, BP Amoco, or Shell might be involved with the following:
- (a) searching for new oil fields
- (b) drilling for oil
- (c) building an oil refinery
- (d) refining the oil
- (e) delivering the oil from a domestic refinery to gasoline stations in the same country
- (f) the gasoline station with a retail store that sells food items, maps, books, compact discs, maps, and other automobile accessories. The owners are responsible for purchasing these sale items.

What might be an estimated time horizon for each of these activities? Which would fit into the long-, medium-, and short-range plan? Discuss.

2. Part-time workers
In both Europe, and the USA the number of part-time workers compared to those in full-time employment is increasing. Discuss some of the reasons for this situation.

3. Adding a third shift
Adding a third shift at night is an option in aggregate planning to increase capacity. However, experience has shown that quality of work, and productivity on this shift is less than during day work. What do you think are some of the reasons for this?

4. Taxation
Governments in Europe believe that one way to reduce the demand of gasoline (and thus environmental pollution) is to increase taxes. What are some of the fallacies of this economic policy? What is its impact?

5. Time fences
The time fences (frozen, fixed, full, and open) in a master production schedule make sense from an internal planning point of view. Discuss the constraints these time fences would have on the operation of a:
- (a) medical centre
- (b) small business serving big clients
- (c) consulting firm performing projects for big industrial firms
- (d) farm that produces agricultural products and rears animals.

6. Produce to stock/produce to order
In developing a master production schedule what are the advantages and disadvantages of produce to stock and produce to order?

7. Technology
What impact does new technology have on operations planning? Consider information technology, new products, and processes.

Demonstrating the concept 12.1   Attaché case

Situation

A small company in the Czech Republic makes leather attaché cases that it exports worldwide. Much of the work is performed by hand. Table 12.3 shows that, at the start of a planning period, the production manager had the following demand in units, for four of its major models, over an eight-week planning period.

Table 12.3 Demand in units

Week	Product A	B	C	D
1	110	440	325	180
2	170	450	300	185
3	100	480	410	180
4	150	470	385	175
5	140	410	510	145
6	90	390	345	190
7	80	385	325	185
8	120	425	320	270

From its labour standards, the company needs labour hours per unit, to produce the four different products, as shown in Table 12.4.

Required

1. Develop workforce loading data for the four products. Show the results graphically.
2. If the company has a permanent workforce of 80, who work 40 hours a week, illustrate the labour loading for the company.

Solution

1. The units demanded are multiplied by the unit labour hours and totalled for the whole production centre. For example, for product A in week 1 the

Table 12.4 Labour hours required

Product	A	B	C	D
Labour hours	3.25	2.05	4.28	3.85

units demanded are 110 and this multiplied by 3.25 gives 357.50 labour hours. The data for the four products are given in Table 12.5 and plotted in Figure 12.9.

Table 12.5 Aggregate plan for attaché cases

Week	Product (units)					Product	Labour (hours/unit)
	A	B	C	D			
1	110	440	325	180		A	3.25
2	170	450	300	185		B	2.05
3	100	480	410	180		C	4.28
4	150	470	385	175		D	3.85
5	140	410	510	145			
6	90	390	345	190			
7	80	385	325	185			
8	120	425	320	270			

Week	Product (labour hours)				Labour hours required	People required	Labour hours available	Difference Req. − Avail
	A	B	C	D				
0								
1	357.50	902.00	1,391.00	693.00	3,343.50	83.59	3,200.00	143.50
2	552.50	922.50	1,284.00	712.25	3,471.25	86.78	3,200.00	271.25
3	325.00	984.00	1,754.80	693.00	3,756.80	93.92	3,200.00	556.80
4	487.50	963.50	1,647.80	673.75	3,772.55	94.31	3,200.00	572.55
5	455.00	840.50	2,182.80	558.25	4,036.55	100.91	3,200.00	836.55
6	292.50	799.50	1,476.60	731.50	3,300.10	82.50	3,200.00	100.10
7	260.00	789.25	1,391.00	712.25	3,152.50	78.81	3,200.00	−47.50
8	390.00	871.25	1,369.60	1,039.50	3,670.35	91.76	3,200.00	470.35
Total	3,120.00	7,072.50	12,497.60	5,813.50	28,503.60		25,600.00	2,903.60

Figure 12.9 Attaché cases: Aggregate plan for four products

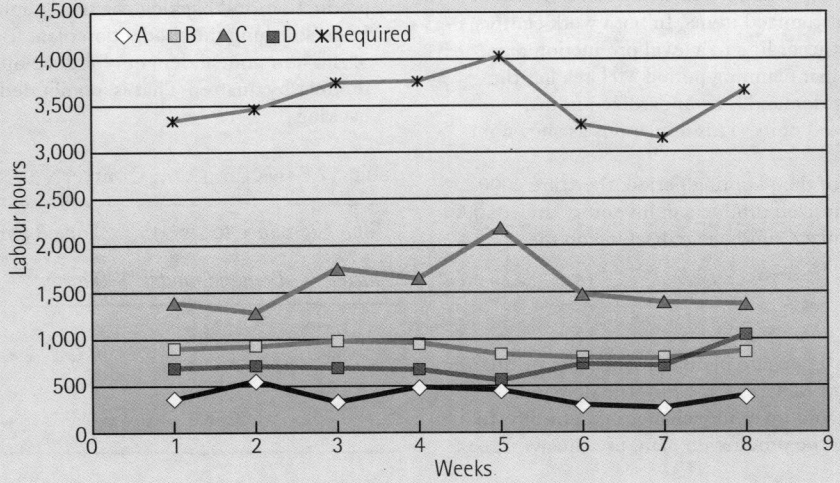

2. A labour force of 80 people represents 80 * 40 or 3200 hours per week. Thus, comparing this figure with the total column, except for week 7, there will be insufficient capacity to satisfy demand. Over the eight-week planning horizon there is a deficit of 2903.60 labour hours or the equivalent of about nine people each week (2903.60/(40 * 8)). The company will have to adjust short-term capacity by using overtime, part-time labour, or subcontracting some of the work. Figure 12.10 illustrates the charge for the company.

Figure 12.10 Attaché cases: Aggregate loading for labour

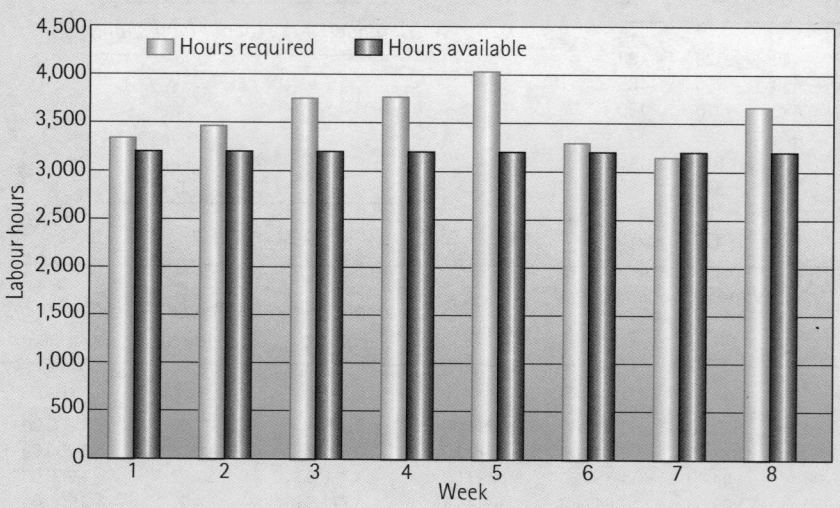

Demonstrating the concept 12.2 McCrea Co.

Situation

The McCrea Co., outside Edinburgh in Scotland, has a manufacturing operation for making office furniture. There are two work centres, Zone A, which is dedicated to producing standardized items, and Zone B, which is reserved for customized items. In both work centres, McCrea works according to a level production plan. For one particular planning period McCrea has the same quarterly demand for standardized items, as for customized units. This demand is as shown in Table 12.6.

At the start of the planning period, there are 4000 units of standardized products in inventory, and 10,000 units of customized products in backlog on the company's books.

Required

1. Develop an aggregate planning schedule, by quarter, for Zone A of McCrea Co. Show the demand, production, and inventory changes graphically. In establishing the production plan, use the average of the new annual demand for developing the product by quarter. That is, do not deduct the initial inventory.

2. Develop an aggregate planning schedule, by quarter, for Zone B of McCrea Co. Show the demand, production, and backlog changes graphically. In establishing the production plan, use the average of the new annual demand for developing the product by quarter. That is, do not deduct the initial backlog.

Table 12.6 McCrea Co.: Quarterly demand

Zone A (produce to stock)		Zone B (produce to order)	
Quarter	Demand (units)	Quarter	Demand (units)
1	30,000	1	30,000
2	40,000	2	40,000
3	50,000	3	50,000
4	35,000	4	35,000

Solution

1. The quarterly demand is totalled to give the annual demand of 155,000 units. This amount, divided by four, gives the quarterly production level. Excess inventory over demand is added to inventory. A shortfall of demand over production is taken from inventory. The demand, production level, and inventory levels per quarter are given in Table 12.7.

   The movement of material is illustrated in Figure 12.11.

2. The quarterly demand is totalled to give the annual demand of 155,000 units. This amount is divided by four to give the quarterly production level. Orders received are added to backlog.

This backlog is worked off according to the level production amount. The demand, production level, and backlog per quarter are given in Table 12.8.

The movement of material is illustrated in Figure 12.12.

In summary, the profiles for inventory and backlog changes are reversed. For a produce-to-stock situation, when the demand is higher than the production level, the inventory is reduced whereas for a produce-to-order situation, when the demand is higher than the production level, the backlog increases. The reverse is true when the demand is less than the production level (see Table 12.9).

Table 12.7 McCrea Co.: Demand, production level, and inventory per quarter

Quarter	Demand (units)	Production (units)	Inventory (units)
			4,000
1	30,000	38,750	12,750
2	40,000	38,750	11,500
3	50,000	38,750	250
4	35,000	38,750	4,000
Total	155,000	155,000	

Table 12.8 McCrea Co.: Demand, production level, and backlog per quarter

Quarter	Demand (units)	Production (units)	Backlog (units)
			10,000
1	30,000	38,750	1,250
2	40,000	38,750	2,500
3	50,000	38,750	13,750
4	35,000	38,750	10,000
Total	155,000	155,000	

Figure 12.11 McCrea Co.: Zone A: Produce to stock

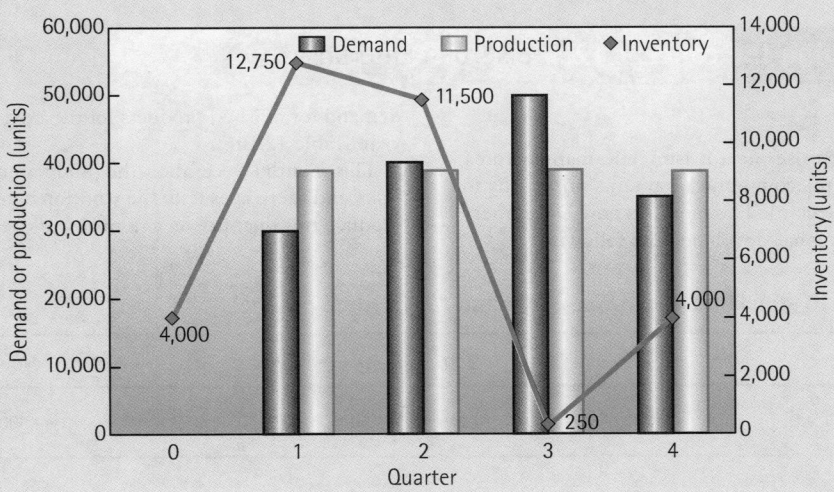

Figure 12.12 McCrea Co.: Zone B: Produce to order

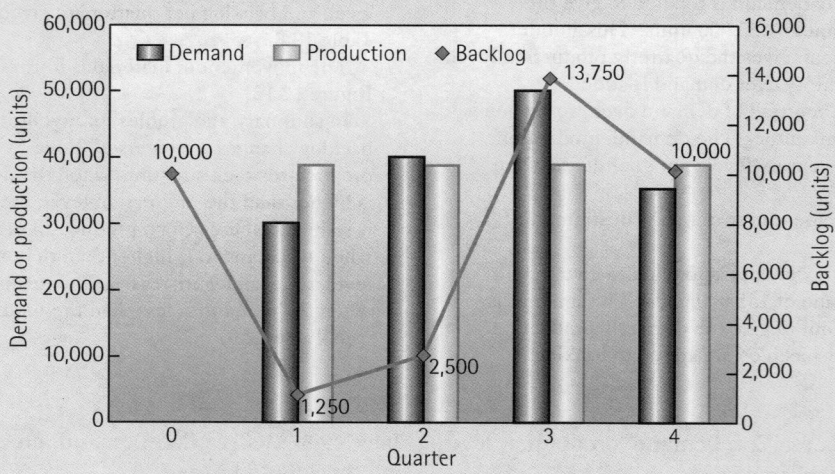

Table 12.9 McCrea Co.: Zone A (produce to stock); Zone B (produce to order)

	Zone A: Produce to stock				Zone B: Produce to order		
Quarter	Demand (units)	Production (units)	Ending inventory (units)	Quarter	Demand (units)	Production (units)	Ending backlog (units)
0			4,000	0			10,000
1	30,000	38,750	12,750	1	30,000	38,750	1,250
2	40,000	38,750	11,500	2	40,000	38,750	2,500
3	50,000	38,750	250	3	50,000	38,750	13,750
4	35,000	38,750	4,000	4	35,000	38,750	10,000
Total	155,000	155,000		Total	155,000	155,000	

Demonstrating the concept 12.3 Blackbird Enterprises

Situation

Blackbird Enterprises near Bristol, UK, manufactures and assembles telecommunication units principally for BT (British Telecom). The month is now December and the company has developed the following demand for finished products for the next calendar year (Table 12.10).

This month (December) the production level is 1800 units and there is exactly the workforce necessary to produce this quantity on a normal workweek basis,

Table 12.10 Blackbird Enterprises: Demand for finished products

Jan	Feb	Mar	Apr	May	Jun	Jul	Aug	Sep	Oct	Nov	Dec
2,700	3,500	4,700	1,800	1,500	3,245	4,250	3,875	2,975	1,875	2,500	1,100

without the recourse to overtime, or subcontracting. The ending inventory for December has been calculated as 250 units. Other operating data for the company are given in Table 12.11.

Required

Develop two aggregate plans, A and B as follows, and indicate which is the preferred plan on the basis of the given costs. In developing the plans round staff levels up to the nearest whole number. If necessary, assume that the labour force will work to its maximum capacity. Take into account the inventory at the beginning of the plan period, and determine the average inventory level based on linear usage between the beginning and end of the period.

Plan A

A synchronized aggregate plan where employees are hired or terminated as needed in order to produce exactly the amount required for that month. Use up the inventory at the beginning of the period. Overtime is not an option in this plan.

Plan B

Produce internally at a monthly rate equal to the minimum quantity demanded for the year using only normal work hours. Subcontract out production for the rest of the units. Make workforce adjustments in January, and record the appropriate charges for that month. Overtime is not an option in this plan.

Solution

The production variables used to calculate the two plans are shown in Table 12.12.

Plan A

This is shown in Table 12.13:

- Production level in units is the amount demanded less the amount in inventory at the beginning of the period.
- Labour hours is the production level times labour hours/unit.
- Staff level is labour hours divided by hours in the month (160). If there is a fraction, numbers are rounded up to the nearer whole number.
- Actual production in units is the staff (rounded up to the nearer whole number) times hours in the month, divided by labour hours per unit. Normally, this is the same as the production level in units except where the staff level has been rounded up. (That is, the production level is slightly higher.)
- Hiring is that amount to make up the deficit. Termination is when there is an excess of labour.

Plan B

This is developed with the same logic as Plan A and is given in Table 12.14.

From the two plans, A would be the preferred plan based on the total cost. However, in some straits, costs such as those presented may not be the only criterion for adopting a plan. Other conditions would include staff availability, productivity, etc.

Table 12.11 Blackbird Enterprises: Operating data

Ending December inventory, units	250
Stockout costs, £/unit	35.00
Holding cost, £/unit/week	2.50
Hiring cost/employee, £	350.00
Termination cost/employee	275.00
Labour cost, £/hour	8.00
Overtime cost, £/hour	12.00
Subcontracting cost, £/unit	35.00
Labour hours/unit	3.20
Production December	1,800
Workweek, hours	40
Maximum overtime/week, hours	10
Weeks/month	4

Table 12.12 Blackbird Enterprises: Production variables

Ending December inventory, units	250
Stockout costs, £/unit	35.00
Holding cost, £/unit/week	2.50
Hiring cost/employee, £	350.00
Termination cost/employee	275.00
Labour cost, £/hour	8.00
Overtime cost, £/hour	12.00
Subcontracting, cost £/unit	35.00
Labour hours/unit	3.20
Production December	1,800
Workweek, hours	40
Max overtime/week, hours	10
Weeks/month	4
Units/month/person (normal hours)	50.00
Units/month/person (overtime hours)	12.50

Table 12.13 Blackbird Enterprises: Plan A – synchronized production

Sales demand

Month	Dec	Jan	Feb	Mar	Apr	May	Jun	Jul	Aug	Sep	Oct	Nov	Dec	Total
Demand		2,700	3,500	4,700	1,800	1,500	3,245	4,250	3,875	2,975	1,875	2,500	1,100	34,020

Aggregate production plan

Month	Dec	Jan	Feb	Mar	Apr	May	Jun	Jul	Aug	Sep	Oct	Nov	Dec	Total
Demand		2,700	3,500	4,700	1,800	1,500	3,245	4,250	3,875	2,975	1,875	2,500	1,100	34,020
Labour														
Units to produce	1,800	2,450	3,500	4,700	1,800	1,500	3,245	4,245	3,870	2,945	1,870	2,470	1,070	33,665
Labour hours	5,760	7,840	11,200	15,040	5,760	4,800	10,384	13,584	12,384	9,424	5,984	7,904	3,424	107,728
Staff	36.00	49.00	70.00	94.00	36.00	30.00	64.90	84.90	77.40	58.90	37.40	49.40	21.40	673
Staff (rounded)	36	49	70	94	36	30	65	85	78	59	38	50	22	676
Actual production	1,800	2,450	3,500	4,700	1,800	1,500	3,250	4,250	3,900	2,950	1,900	2,500	1,100	33,800
Hiring	36	13	21	24	0	0	35	20	0	0	0	12	0	125
Termination	0	0	0	0	58	6	0	0	7	19	21	0	28	139
Inventory														
Beginning	250	250	0	0	0	0	0	5	5	30	5	30	30	
Ending	250	0	0	0	0	0	5	5	30	5	30	30	30	
Average	125.00	125.00	0.00	0.00	0.00	0.00	2.50	5.00	17.50	17.50	17.50	30.00	30.00	
Stockouts	0	0	0	0	0	0	0	0	0	0	0	0	0	
Costs														
Production		62,720	89,600	120,320	46,080	38,400	83,200	108,800	99,840	75,520	48,640	64,000	28,160	865,280
Hiring		4,550	7,350	8,400	0	0	12,250	7,000	0	0	0	4,200	0	43,750
Termination		0	0	0	15,950	1,650	0	0	1,925	5,225	5,775	0	7,700	38,225
Carrying		1,250	0	0	0	0	25	50	175	175	175	300	300	2,450
Stockouts		0	0	0	0	0	0	0	0	0	0	0	0	0
Total		68,520	96,950	128,720	62,030	40,050	95,475	115,850	101,940	80,920	54,590	68,500	36,160	949,705

Table 12.14 Blackbird Enterprises: Plan B – production at minimum demanded

Sales demand

Month	Dec	Jan	Feb	Mar	Apr	May	Jun	Jul	Aug	Sep	Oct	Nov	Dec	Total
Demand	0	2,700	3,500	4,700	1,800	1,500	3,245	4,250	3,875	2,975	1,875	2,500	1,100	**34,020**

Aggregate production plan

Month	Dec	Jan	Feb	Mar	Apr	May	Jun	Jul	Aug	Sep	Oct	Nov	Dec	Total
Demand	0	2,700	3,500	4,700	1,800	1,500	3,245	4,250	3,875	2,975	1,875	2,500	1,100	**34,020**
Production														
Units to produce	1,800	1,100	1,100	1,100	1,100	1,100	1,100	1,100	1,100	1,100	1,100	1,100	1,100	13,200
Labour hours	5,760	3,520	3,520	3,520	3,520	3,520	3,520	3,520	3,520	3,520	3,520	3,520	3,520	42,240
Staff	36.00	22.00	22.00	22.00	22.00	22.00	22.00	22.00	22.00	22.00	22.00	22.00	22.00	264
Staff (rounded)	36	22	22	22	22	22	22	22	22	22	22	22	22	264
Actual production		1,100	1,100	1,100	1,100	1,100	1,100	1,100	1,100	1,100	1,100	1,100	1,100	13,200
Hiring		0	0	0	0	0	0	0	0	0	0	0	0	0
Termination	14	0	0	0	0	0	0	0	0	0	0	0	0	14
Subcontract		1,350	2,400	3,600	700	400	2,145	3,150	2,775	1,875	775	1,400	0	20,570
Inventory														
Beginning	250	250	0	0	0	0	0	0	0	0	0	0	0	
Ending	0	0	0	0	0	0	0	0	0	0	0	0	0	
Average	125.00	125.00	0.00	0.00	0.00	0.00	0.00	0.00	0.00	0.00	0.00	0.00	0.00	
Stockouts	0	0	0	0	0	0	0	0	0	0	0	0	0	
Costs														
Production		28,160	28,160	28,160	28,160	28,160	28,160	28,160	28,160	28,160	28,160	28,160	28,160	337,920
Hiring		0	0	0	0	0	0	0	0	0	0	0	0	0
Termination		3,850	0	0	0	0	0	0	0	0	0	0	0	3,850
Subcontracting		47,250	84,000	126,000	24,500	14,000	75,075	110,250	97,125	65,625	27,125	49,000	0	719,950
Carrying		1,250	0	0	0	0	0	0	0	0	0	0	0	1,250
Stockouts		0	0	0	0	0	0	0	0	0	0	0	0	0
Total		80,510	112,160	154,160	52,660	42,160	103,235	138,410	125,285	93,785	55,285	77,160	28,160	**1,062,970**

Application exercise 12.1 Blackbird Enterprises

Situation

The situation for Blackbird Enterprises is the same as given in Demonstrating the concept 12.3.

Required

Develop two aggregate plans as follows to satisfy the client demand. Indicate which is the preferred plan on the basis of the given costs. In developing the plans round staff levels up to nearest whole number and assume labour works to its maximum capacity. Take into account the inventory at the beginning of the plan period and use the linear average of the beginning and ending inventory in order to determine the carrying costs. Compare these plans with the ones developed in Demonstrating the concept 12.3

Plan C

Produce at a monthly rate equal to the average quantity demanded for the year. Make workforce adjustments in January, and record the appropriate charges that month. Use inventory movements as a buffer between supply and demand. Neither overtime nor sub-contracting is an option in this plan.

Plan D

Establish a base level using normal hours to produce at a monthly rate equal to the unit production level of the previous December. To meet additional demands, use overtime up to the maximum permitted for this base rate. If this is insufficient, subcontract out the rest of the requirements.

Application exercise 12.2 Dresses

Situation

The clothing store One Day Elsewhere has established the next eight-week demand requirements for a certain model of ladies' dresses. The data in units of dresses are shown in Table 12.15.

The production standards for this model of dress are shown in Table 12.16

Required

1. Develop separate curves showing the aggregate loading for the production centre in terms of material needs, machine time, labour and costs.
2. What is the average cost of this line of dresses over the eight-week planning horizon?
3. If the firm expects to make a gross margin of 80% over the price of the dresses, what is the average price that the firm will charge?

Table 12.15 Eight-week demand requirements in ladies' dresses

Week	1	2	3	4	5	6	7	8
Dress size								
Small	2,500	2,800	3,200	3,700	4,100	3,800	3,200	2,100
Medium	3,200	3,500	4,100	4,950	5,200	4,900	4,000	3,200
Large	2,300	2,700	3,000	3,200	3,500	3,200	2,900	1,900
Extra large	1,900	2,100	2,300	2,700	3,000	2,500	2,100	1,500

Table 12.16 Production standards for model of dress

Standards	Material m^2	Machine time min/dress	Labour min/dress
Small	3.05	7.50	3.90
Medium	4.15	8.50	4.80
Large	4.92	9.50	6.10
Extra large	5.10	10.50	7.80
Labour cost, $/hr	17.85		
Material cost, $/m^2	1.75		
Machine cost, $/hr	150		

Application exercise 12.3 Gabriel Job Shop

Situation

The Gabriel Job Shop in Watford, England, manufactures pumps and cooling units for oil refineries, chemical plants, oilfield processing units, other types of chemical plants and food processing units. The company's products are either domestic orders for facilities in the United Kingdom, inter-company orders to Gabriel's subsidiaries in France and Spain (for European clients), or export orders to countries outside the European Community. Table 12.17 gives the demand requirements for the next 12 weeks, which includes firm orders for domestic, export, and inter-company clients and a forecast demand developed by the company's marketing department.

Gabriel develops its master production plan on a weekly planning schedule, using a time horizon of 12 weeks. The company has an operating programme of producing the pump assemblies in lot sizes of 100, and cooling units in lot sizes of 75. In addition, it has a policy of keeping a safety stock of a minimum of 20 units for the pump assembly, and 15 units for the cooling unit. The initial inventory at the beginning of the planning cycle is 80 units for the pump assembly, and 50 units for the cooling unit.

Required

Develop a separate master production schedule for Gabriel for the two products.

Table 12.17 Gabriel Job Shop: Demand requirements

| | Pump assembly | | | | | Cooling unit | | | |
Week	Domestic orders (units)	Export orders (units)	Inter-company orders (units)	Forecast orders (units)	Week	Domestic orders (units)	Export orders (units)	Inter-company orders (units)	Forecast orders (units)
1	30	10	8	1	1	30	0	17	0
2	28	7	0	0	2	30	0	0	5
3	34	15	20	20	3	10	30	0	15
4	19	0	20	15	4	20	20	0	15
5	24	4	0	45	5	10	10	20	20
6	5	0	0	50	6	10	20	0	20
7	2	0	0	55	7	0	0	5	20
8	0	0	0	50	8	5	15	15	15
9	10	0	0	50	9	0	0	20	15
10	0	0	0	40	10	0	0	30	15
11	0	0	0	40	11	0	0	15	15
12	0	55	0	40	12	0	0	0	15

Application exercise 12.4 Kayak manufacture

Situation

A small family-owned business in Kajaani, central Finland, makes handmade Kayaks. One of its models, 'Acirema', is sold exclusively through a distributor in the USA. For this reason, all the production costs are denominated in dollars. The production manager is developing her aggregate plan for the coming year. Through her US distributor, she has obtained a forecast demand for the next year as 2570 units broken down on a monthly basis as shown in Table 12.18.

The demand is seasonal. Activity is heaviest in February, March, and April to meet the summer season.

In addition, September, October, and November are relatively heavy to meet the holiday season. The workshop currently has 20 full-time people, each of whom can produce ten kayaks a month at a cost of $600 a unit. Inventory-carrying costs are $50.00 a unit a month. Backlog costs are $100.00 a unit a month. At the start of the planning period in January the inventory level of kayaks is 0. From the forecast demand, it can be seen there will be a shortfall of 170 units. (Annual demand is 2570 units: maximum capacity is 12 months * 10 units/month * 20 workers = 2400 units.)

Table 12.18 Forecast demand for kayak units

Month	Forecast demand (units)	Month	Forecast demand (units)
January	190	July	160
February	230	August	160
March	260	September	220
April	280	October	250
May	210	November	260
June	170	December	180

Required

Develop the following three aggregate plans, and select the least expensive.

1. **Plan A.** Hiring two additional people to commence working in January. One would be only on a temporary basis working through May. Hiring costs are $1000 per employee, and termination costs are $750 per employee.
2. **Plan B.** Hiring only one worker full time, at an additional cost of $1000. Any shortfalls are made up using subcontracting at $700 a unit. Maximum subcontracting allowed is 20 units a month.
3. **Plan C.** No new workers are hired. Any shortfalls are made up using only subcontracting. Maximum subcontracting allowed is 20 units a month.

Since there is plenty of competent labour in the area, a new hire will have the same productive output as the current employees. That is, there is no learning curve consideration.

Application exercise 12.5 Trenel

Situation

The Trenel company, at St Bonnet, east of Lyon in France, manufactures fireplaces. The key component of the product is the hearth, manufactured in cast iron with a glass window. The hearth is made in a foundry, and the window is assembled by hand. For one of its models, 'Radiant 700', the company has firm orders for the first quarter of the year, and a forecast demand for the remainder of this year. The number of these units is shown in Table 12.19.

Stocking costs for 'Radiant 700' are estimated at €9.00 a unit a month. If an order is put on backorder there is a cost of €19.00 a unit a month due to additional paperwork and an estimated amount for loss of potential customers. The production cost is €200.00 a unit. In addition, to increase the production level from one month to another, there is a cost of €17.00 a unit. For a decrease in production, there is a cost of €15.00 a unit. These costs are due to machine adjustments, and reorganizing the workshop. The company changes its production levels only at the beginning of a month.

For planning purposes, assuming a cyclical operation, assume that the demand in January of the following year is 190 units and the demand in December of the previous year was 180 units and this was also the production level for this month. The inventory at the end of December of the previous year was 0.

Required

1. Normally, the production manager operates the manufacture of the fireplaces with a level production plan

Table 12.19 Trenel: Firm and forecast demand

January	190	July	160
February	230	August	160
March	260	September	220
April	280	October	250
May	210	November	270
June	170	December	180

such that monthly production is an average quantity for the yearly demand. Adjusting inventory levels, or using backorders is the buffer between the demand and the production. On this basis, what is an estimate of the annual production cost?

2. A consultant has suggested operating the factory by synchronizing production with demand to avoid accumulation of inventory. On this basis, what would be an estimate of the annual production costs? Besides just the cost, what are the disadvantages of operating a factory under these conditions?

3. Is there a less expensive aggregate plan using a combination of synchronized and level production on the basis that production is in lots of multiples of 5? That is for example, 180, 185 or 190, units but not 181, 186, 192. (Chapter 24 may be helpful for this part.)

For each of the three production plans, show graphically the demand and production amounts monthly. This would be a planning schedule.

Application exercise 12.6 Veatch Co.

Situation

Veatch Co. is a manufacturer of light aircraft components in the Toulouse region of France. The company always prepares a nine-month aggregate plan to decide the optimum way to determine requirements for planning purposes, although this is modified when the demand requirements change. The estimated demand for a particular unit for the period January through September is given in Table 12.20. The current workforce is based on the production level in the previous December.

Operating data are given in Table 12.21.

Required

Develop the following aggregate plans.

1. **Plan A.** Vary the workforce level to meet exactly the demand requirements. There is no subcontracting. In January make use of the beginning inventory to reduce production requirements.
2. **Plan B.** Produce at a constant rate of 2000 units per month. Subcontract to meet a 100% service level every month.
3. **Plan C.** Produce at a constant rate equal to the average demand for the planning period. Subcontract to meet a 100% service level every month.

Table 12.20 Veatch Co.: Estimated demand for a product

Jan	Feb	Mar	Apr	May	Jun	Jul	Aug	Sep
1,785	1,850	2,100	1,975	2,300	2,550	2,100	1,750	1,500

Table 12.21 Veatch Co.: Operating data

Initial inventory, units	400
Stockout costs, $/unit	125
Carrying cost, $/unit/month	30
Hiring cost per unit	70
Termination cost per unit	85
Subcontract cost, $/unit	85
Production units the previous December	1,500
In-house production cost, $/unit	75

4. **Plan D.** Produce at a constant rate equal to the minimum quantity demanded for the year. Subcontract to meet a 100% service level every month.

Based purely on costs, which is the preferred plan? What other non-financial considerations might be taken into account?

Application exercise 12.7 Whirl

Situation

The Whirl company in Hamburg in Germany makes microwave ovens for sale in Europe. The forecast sales data for one particular model in France, Britain, Scandinavia, Italy, and German (domestic market) are as shown in Table 12.22.

The holding cost for finished units is estimated at €4.50 a unit and there are 1500 units in inventory at the start of the planning period.

Required

1. Develop a master production schedule for Whirl on the basis that the company produces in lot sizes of 2500 units, and that it has a policy of keeping a safety stock of 250 units. What is the impact on holding cost and setup times? Show the MPS on a bar chart.
2. Develop a master production schedule for Whirl on the basis that the company produces in lot sizes of

Table 12.22 Whirl: Forecast sales data

Week	1	2	3	4	5	6	7	8	9	10
France	350	450	240	650	780	560	240	430	220	380
Britain	120	220	175	210	300	420	225	250	185	325
Scandinavia	80	45	85	95	125	140	220	145	75	50
Italy	45	75	85	125	45	0	95	125	150	220
Domestic	520	55	560	650	725	625	550	450	250	780

2000 units, and that it has a policy of keeping no safety stock. What is the impact on holding cost and setup times? Show the MPS on the same bar chart as for question 1.
3. What do you believe would be the best policy for the company? Justify your reasoning.

Case study 12.1 Schultz Co.

Situation

Schultz Co. in Graz, Austria, is a small company of 50 people which manufactures control systems. The company was created in 1971 by three engineers who perfected a simple security device adaptable to private homes, hotels, banks, and other businesses. The product was very successful and sold well in Austria, Switzerland, and Germany. In the early 1980s Schultz received a large capital infusion from a private investor and a local bank, which enabled it to enlarge its manufacturing site in Graz. The expansion was necessary as a result of increased demand for the security systems and the addition of two new products, one for space heating and the other for restaurants. In parallel with that expansion, Schultz hired some very competent computer specialists and four commercial people to expand its market beyond its former territory.

All the products manufactured by Schultz are very high tech and the technology employed is constantly being updated. The security devices operate by electronic sensing into a small central computer that can activate alarms, flashing lights, messages to the local police station or other central areas, and firmly lock doors and windows. The space heating systems, for gas or electric appliances, use somewhat similar control and programming devices which switch on or off according to needs. In addition, a simple control card together with peripheries controls the raising or lowering of sunblinds according to ambient temperatures. The other product programmes cooking/baking units for restaurants.

Schultz's business is growing very fast. With Austria's entry into the European Union, it now has markets in all 15 member countries. In addition, thanks to some clever marketing, and flexible systems, it has penetrated the North American market where, among other things, the increase in the crime rate has provided a profitable niche. Demand for their products are somewhat seasonal – a higher demand in the spring months for security devices (businesses and homes are sometimes closed during the summer period) and the space heating and restaurant control products are more in demand during the winter period.

Schultz is currently pretty integrated regarding the manufacturing and assembly of the units. Schultz makes all the electronic components, sensing units, frames, cases, computing cards and connecting devices. It is these parts that were developed by the company and they are strategic to the finished product. Almost the only parts that Schultz purchases are various screws and fixation pieces, and some plastic mouldings. The company has several patents on the various units they have developed but some of these patents are beginning to expire. Competitors are being more and more dominant, particularly in Britain, which has more ease in penetrating the North American market.

With the expansion of the product demand Schultz is considering changing its policy towards manufacturing and assembly. All 50 employees are currently full time. However, labour costs in Austria are very high and the company is toying with the idea of subcontracting about 25% of its operation to a small firm in India that is very competent in the high-technology field. The alternative to this is to further expand the facility in Austria and increase employment levels.

Required

Schultz Co. needs to establish a new planning policy regarding anticipated growth. Discuss the advantages, and disadvantages, of the long-term and medium to short-term planning options.

Selected further reading

BRANDIMARTE, Paolo and VILLA, A. (1999) *Modeling Manufacturing Systems: From Aggregate Planning to Real-Time Control*, Springer Verlag.

CHOPRA, Sunil and MEINDL, Peter (2000) *Supply Chain Management: Strategy Planning and Operations*, Prentice-Hall.

LING, Richard C. and GODDARD, Walter E. (1995) *Orchestrating Success: Improve Control of the Business with Sales and Operations Planning*, Wiley.

ST. JOHN, Ralph E. (1999) *Material and Capacity Requirements Planning: Certification Review Course*, Amer Production & Inventory Control Society.

WALLACE, Thomas F. (1999) *Sales and Operations Planning – The How-To Handbook*, T. F. Wallace & Co.

An extensive listing of other further reading can be found on the website.

What's on the web?

Further learning resources are available to lecturers and students at www.supplychain-online.com, including the following which are specific to *Operations and capacity planning*:

Resource	Subject
Chapter overview	Operations and capacity planning
Industry insight: Sleepless in Seattle	Aggregate planning and capacity
Exam topics	Operations and capacity planning
Application exercise: Gabriel Job Shop	Master production schedule
More further reading	Operations and capacity planning

13 *Material requirements and enterprise resource planning*

Chapter overview

- Material requirements planning
- Lot sizing in production planning
- Manufacturing resource planning
- Enterprise resource planning

Material requirements planning

Overview

The concept of material requirements planning (MRP) was developed and refined by Joseph Orlicky, at IBM, and Oliver Wight, a consultant, in the 1960s and 1970s.[1] It is a mathematical planning tool, driven by the master production schedule, for determining the needs of dependent components such as raw materials, parts, subassemblies, or modules principally in a manufacturing but also a warehousing/distribution environment. Knowing the current inventory levels and the bill of materials that go into a particular product, then specifically the MRP indicates:

- The types of material, and the quantity that has to be purchased from outside, taking into account current inventory levels.
- The types of material that need to be manufactured internally, and in what quantity, taking into account current inventory levels.
- At what time to place these orders, either by purchasing outside, or for manufacturing inside, taking into account the lead times for materials.

With the introduction and explosive growth of computers, the concept and use of material requirements planning has considerable evolved making it a key planning tool in firms. Companies may have their own in-house developed system or purchased a system from one of the many commercial packages that are available usually as a module within an enterprise resource planning system (ERP).

As a planning tool, the MRP provides precise control to operations personnel regarding the amounts and timing of deliveries of materials necessary to produce end items indicated by the master production schedule. This control helps to avoid inventory stockouts, minimize excessive levels of inventory, and to optimize the utilization of labour and machines. The MRP system is a major planning tool for supply chain management linking the purchasing and manufacturing activities or the materials management function. When the MRP is coupled to a distribution requirements planning system (see Chapter 17), the combination serves to manage the supply chain as a complete integrated activity. The original material requirements planning is often referred to as MRP I to distinguish it from the later manufacturing resource planning, MRP II (presented in the next section).

Role of the master production schedule

As discussed in Chapter 12, the master production schedule indicates the quantity of finished goods and the time period that they are needed. This information then provides a basis for establishing component needs for the end product thus making the MPS the driving wheel for the MRP. In a good management system, when early periods of the MPS are considered frozen, this gives the operations department confidence that it can depend on this information for accurate planning purposes. Later periods in the MPS are not so definite (they are classed progressively as fixed, full, and open) so there is less certainty in this information. However, the MPS is dynamic such that early periods are dropped once the operation is completed.

Product structure or bill of materials

The product structure, or bill of materials, is a diagram, engineering drawing, or a listing of all materials, and quantities required to produce one unit of finished product, or end item. Every product in a work centre would have its own product structure. As an illustration, Figure 13.1 shows an engineering diagram, or product structure, of all the components that go into making one of Bosch's products.[2]

A product structure is often exhibited in a hierarchical relationship showing components and

Figure 13.1 Bosch electric hand drill

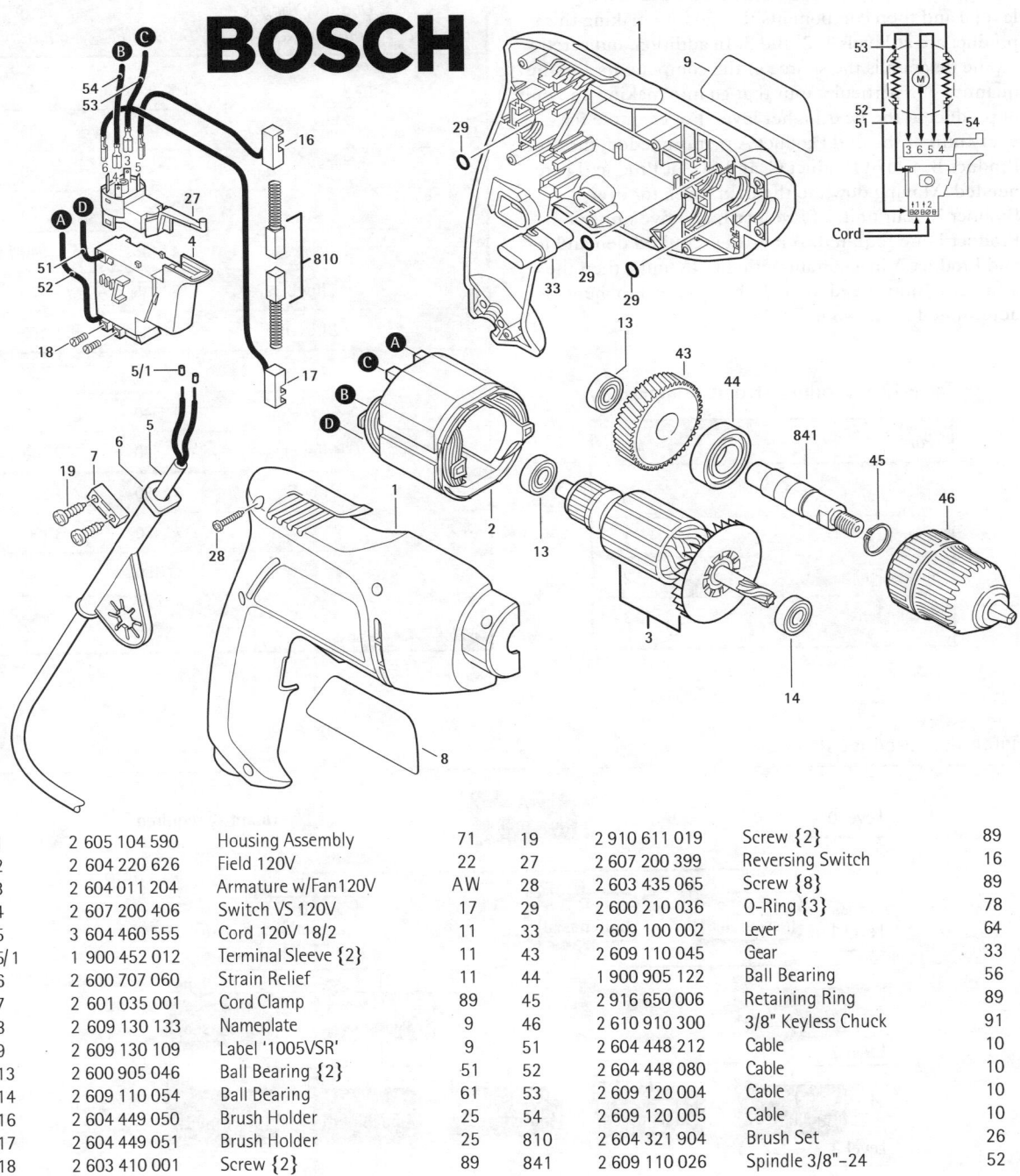

1	2 605 104 590	Housing Assembly	71	19	2 910 611 019	Screw {2}	89
2	2 604 220 626	Field 120V	22	27	2 607 200 399	Reversing Switch	16
3	2 604 011 204	Armature w/Fan120V	AW	28	2 603 435 065	Screw {8}	89
4	2 607 200 406	Switch VS 120V	17	29	2 600 210 036	O-Ring {3}	78
5	3 604 460 555	Cord 120V 18/2	11	33	2 609 100 002	Lever	64
5/1	1 900 452 012	Terminal Sleeve {2}	11	43	2 609 110 045	Gear	33
6	2 600 707 060	Strain Relief	11	44	1 900 905 122	Ball Bearing	56
7	2 601 035 001	Cord Clamp	89	45	2 916 650 006	Retaining Ring	89
8	2 609 130 133	Nameplate	9	46	2 610 910 300	3/8" Keyless Chuck	91
9	2 609 130 109	Label '1005VSR'	9	51	2 604 448 212	Cable	10
13	2 600 905 046	Ball Bearing {2}	51	52	2 604 448 080	Cable	10
14	2 609 110 054	Ball Bearing	61	53	2 609 120 004	Cable	10
16	2 604 449 050	Brush Holder	25	54	2 609 120 005	Cable	10
17	2 604 449 051	Brush Holder	25	810	2 604 321 904	Brush Set	26
18	2 603 410 001	Screw {2}	89	841	2 609 110 026	Spindle 3/8"-24	52

materials at various levels. The end product would be at the highest level, denoted level 0 or 1, and then components that go into making the end product are at lower levels as Table 13.1 demonstrates.

A product structure in a hierarchy form is illustrated in Figure 13.2, where end Product A is indicated at a level 0 and then components that go into making this product are at levels 1, 2, and 3. In addition, indicated on the diagram is the source of the components and the quantity of a particular unit that go into making one unit of product at the next higher level. For example for every unit of the end Product A that is needed, three of Product B, two of Product C, and five of Product D are needed. Moving down to the next level, for every Product B, four units of Product E and five units of Product F are required. If now the required demand for end Product A in a certain period is 45 units, then the number of units needed of all the other components is determined as shown in Table 13.2.

Rather than a hierarchical form, a product structure may also be presented in an indented form. For example, the hierarchical product structure of

Table 13.1 **Product structure hierarchy**

Part	Level
Finished product	0
Assemblies	1
Subassemblies	2
Raw materials	3

Table 13.2 **Product structure and demand**

Product	Quantity for one unit at next level	Derivation	Total quantity
A		Client demand	45
B	3	3*45	135
C	2	2*45	90
D	5	5*45	225
E	4	4*135	540
F	5 (for B)	5*135	675
F (a)	2 (for D)	2*225	450
G	2	2*225	450
H	4	4*540	2,160
J	4 (for E)	4*540	2,160
J (b)	5 (for G)	5*450	2,250
K	7	7*450	3,150
L	1	1*450	450

(a) Total F = 1,125 units
(b) Total J = 4,410 units

Figure 13.2 **Product structure**

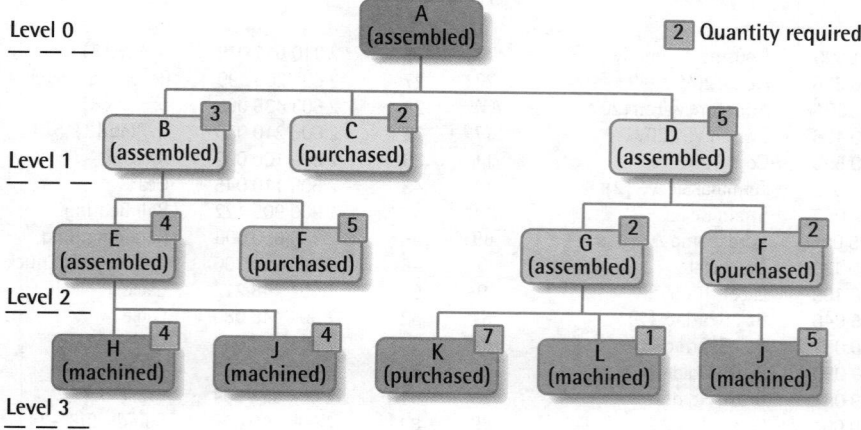

Figure 13.2 may be presented as follows where the indentation corresponds to the next level:

Product A
   Product B (3)
      Product E (4)
         Product H (4)
         Product J (4)
      Product F (5)
   Product C (2)
   Product D (5)
      Product G (2)
         Product K (7)
         Product L (1)
         Product J (5)
      Product F (2)

Inventory records file

The inventory file is a complete record of the quantity of each material held in inventory. A detailed file would show transactions, receipts, disbursements, scrapped materials, planned orders, order releases, projections of delivery dates, quantities of each materials to order, and when to place orders. Also, within the inventory file would be the lead times, or the time required to produce a production lot in-house, or to receive a lot purchased from a supplier. To take into account the lead time, a requirement in one time period will necessitate the release of the order in some earlier period according to the established delay or lead time.

Output of the MRP

When the data from the master production schedule, the inventory records file, are fed into the MRP programme, then for the given product structure, the MRP will generate the output requirements. These would include outside purchasing needs and production requirements for those materials produced internally. The input/output relationship is illustrated in Figure 13.3. The MRP is interrelated to all these elements so any errors in one can snowball throughout the system. This framework represents the original concept of materials requirements planning, or MRP-I. This was an open system with no feedback loop between inputs and outputs.

Terms in materials requirement planning

The use of a materials requirements plan is widespread. However, because there are many commercial products on the market the terminology used is different although the meanings are similar. The following are some generally accepted terms.

Gross requirements

Gross requirements are the total quantity of material needed to satisfy demand in a time period. Units already in inventory may satisfy some of the gross requirements.

On-hand inventory

On-hand inventory is material that is in the storage area at a particular time period. Although this on-hand inventory is in storage it may not always be available for a particular production operation as the firm may have a policy of keeping a certain amount for safety stock and some may have been allocated for other purposes. The on-hand inventory might also include scheduled receipts, which are planned to arrive at the time period when the on-hand inventory is noted.

Allocated inventory

Allocated inventory is material that is in storage, but that is destined for purposes other than the material requirements plan being developed. Other purposes might include spare parts or another designated production operation.

Safety stock

Safety stock is inventory that is not normally available for the operation in question. In this case the material

Figure 13.3 Needs and output of a material requirements plan

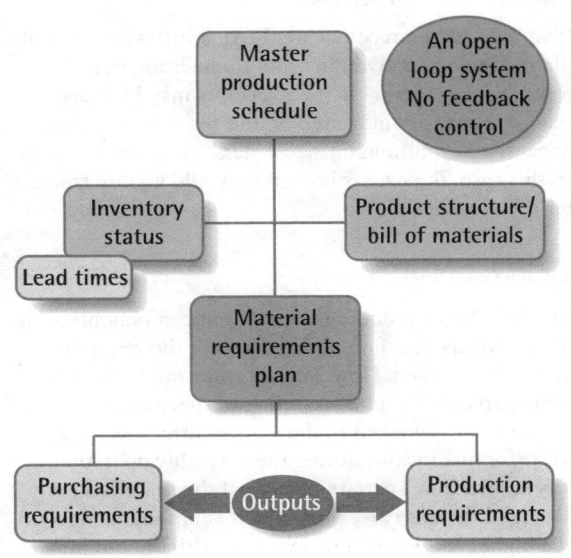

that can be used for the MRP programme would be determined from the following relationship:

$$\begin{bmatrix} \text{Inventory} \\ \text{for the MRP} \end{bmatrix} = \begin{bmatrix} \text{Inventory} \\ \text{on hand} \end{bmatrix} - \begin{bmatrix} \text{Inventory} \\ \text{allocated} \end{bmatrix} - \begin{bmatrix} \text{Safety} \\ \text{stock} \end{bmatrix}$$

Scheduled receipts

Scheduled receipts are the inventory quantities that are expected to be received from suppliers at a defined time period as a result of orders already placed such as through open orders. Scheduled receipts may be assumed to be available for use in the time period in that they arrive. However, if there were time need for inspection and putting them into storage, then they would be available at a later period. Scheduled receipts are not the same as planned ordered receipts.

Net requirements

Net requirements are the quantities of material needed to meet the scheduled demand and are calculated as follows:

$$\text{Net requirements} = \begin{bmatrix} \text{Gross} \\ \text{requirements} \end{bmatrix} - \begin{bmatrix} \text{Inventory} \\ \text{available} \end{bmatrix}$$

Planned ordered releases

Planned ordered releases are the quantities of units that must be planned to be released in a certain time period, so that they are available to meet planned ordered receipts at a future date. The time difference between planned ordered releases, and planned ordered receipts is the lead time.

Planned ordered receipts

Planned ordered receipts are the quantities of material planned to be received in order to meet the net requirements. Planned order receipts may be greater than the quantity indicated by the net requirements because of minimum lot size orders, for example. In this case, the excess inventory would go into storage for use at a later period.

Yield rate

Ideally, when a product is made from components and raw materials, it is hoped that 100% of the required materials are used. However, this may not be the case as some parts may not be according to specification, they may be damaged in the work centre, there may be waste, or historically, during the assembly operation, it is known that a certain portion of the materials are damaged. In this case, the yield of components needed at a higher level would be less than actually put into

operation at the lower level. The yield rate is the percentage of starting material that actually ends up in the product considering the proportion that does not conform to requirements and as such is unusable.

The yield rate needs to be known when calculating lot sizes since if material is lost during an operation, actual order quantity needs to be greater than net requirements. The actual order quantity, Q, is thus given by the relationship:

$$Q = \frac{\text{Net requirements}}{100 - \text{Percentage wasted}}$$

where (100 − Percentage wasted) is the yield rate.

For example, if net requirements of a subassembly unit in a lot-for-lot ordering system is 800 units, and estimated loss is 4%, then actual quantity to be ordered is (converting the percentages to proportions):

$$Q = \frac{800}{1.00 = 0.04} = 834 \text{ units (rounding up)}$$

The development of a material requirements plan, illustrating the concepts discussed, is given in Demonstrating the concept 13.1.

Lot sizing in production planning

In operations planning in manufacturing, warehousing/distribution, or purchasing, decisions need to be made about how much material, or what size of lots, to prepare. Lot sizing is an important part of MRP planning and depending on the size, ordering components in the MRP by lots results in a pattern of periods of high inventory when material arrives, interrupted by longer periods of low inventory as the material is being consumed. The following are considerations related to lot sizing.

Units produced to order

In units produced to order the products are only made when a customer order has been received. Thus, if feasible with the resources available, the lot size is equal to size of the order. For example, a furniture maker receives an order for 45 oak filing cabinets. The order quantity made is thus 45.

Units produced to stock

In units produced to stock the product is standard and the size of the lot is based on the economic size that is feasible, and the expected sale of the product.

Large lot sizes

If large lots are produced at any one period, then the:

- cost of machine setup per unit is less
- carrying costs are higher. Further, carrying costs for finished goods are higher than for raw materials because of the value-added activity.

Small lot sizes

If smaller lots are prepared (Chapter 15) then there will be:

- higher setup costs per unit
- lower carrying costs
- a reduced risk of obsolescence.

Size of a production run

Manufactured products may be produced on individual machines or a complete production line. Although products might be similar in nature and function, distinct differences might exist, for example:

- In a plastic moulding plant, blue plastic washbasins are produced followed by the production of red washbasins.
- In a printing operation, the printing machine first runs off the *TV Guide*, this is then followed by the *Sunday Review*.
- In the textile industry, a roll of white cotton cloth is printed in a red tartan design. The printing of synthetic fabric of a blue country design then follows this operation.

In each case, after each identifiable product has been produced, machines need to be shut down, cleaned, readjusted, or retooled, in order to be adapted to the next product. During this changeover time, there is 'lost' production and a certain amount of inventory, downstream of the machine in question, has to be kept in order to keep production moving. The longer the setup time, the greater the amount of this inventory needed. If setup costs are high (usually determined by the number of labour hours involved) production managers may decide on long production runs to minimize these changeover costs, even though product demand is less than the lot size (production run).

Production costs

In a production operation assume the following conditions exist:

- Variable costs are $15.00 a unit and include the labour, materials, and associated overhead. This cost does not change with the quantity of units produced.

Table 13.3 Operation costs

Lot size (units)	Total variable cost ($)	Setup cost ($/setup)	Total cost ($)	Average cost ($/unit)
5	75	275	350	70.00
10	150	275	425	42.50
15	225	275	500	33.33
30	450	275	725	24.17
50	750	275	1,025	20.50
100	1,500	275	1,775	17.75
175	2,625	275	2,900	16.57
200	3,000	275	3,275	16.38
250	3,750	275	4,025	16.10
350	5,250	275	5,525	15.79
450	6,750	275	7,025	15.61
500	7,500	275	7,775	15.55

- The setup cost is estimated at $275.00 and is considered fixed regardless of the quantity of pieces manufactured. This cost would include principally labour but possibly also new machine tools, new moulds, cleaning fluids, etc.

Then, for lot sizes ranging from 5 to 500 units, Table 13.3 gives the various costs for the operation. The total variable cost is the Variable cost per unit * Lot size; the setup cost is a fixed amount; the total cost is the sum of the variable and setup cost; and the average production cost per unit is the total cost divided by the lot size.

This information is shown graphically in Figure 13.4. This curve illustrates that the unit cost drops sharply at first, then evens out. Thus, given these data, for standardized products, or those produced for stock, there is a clear argument for large production runs. However, for non-standardized products, such as made to order, setting a production run exactly equal to the demand is more economical. If more are produced than demanded by a particular client, there is no guarantee that the excess would be sold. One of the reasons why custom products are more expensive is that a producer cannot take advantage of large production runs and so the high setup costs are passed on to the customer.

This curve also illustrates that for small lot sizes, the setup cost is a high proportion of total cost.

Figure 13.4 Unit production and lot sizes

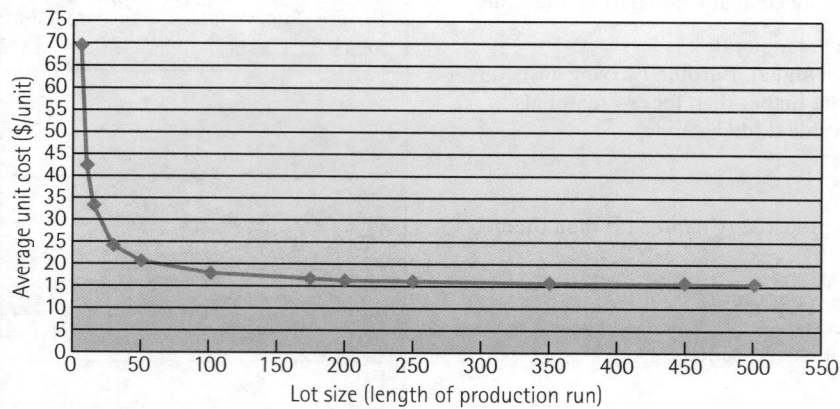

It underscores why companies strive to reduce setup times (and hence cost) so that they have more flexibility in their operation and are not always constrained to produce in large lot sizes. This is the basis of SMED (single minute exchange of die) that is presented in more detail in Chapter 15.

Lot sizes of purchased materials

When raw materials, components, or parts are purchased from an external source, then the quantity (lot size) might depend on price discounts available at certain quantity levels as the following examples demonstrate.

Supplier price discounts

A company may require 4000 units of an article. The unit purchase price is $2.50 a unit. However, the supplier offers a 10% discount on quantities over 5000 units, or at a unit cost of £2.25/unit. Since the purchaser anticipates using the extra 1000 units at some future date, he takes advantage of the price discount. The supplier is able to offer these discounts because his total costs, a function of his setup costs, are lower. (See also Chapter 11.)

Transportation costs

Purchasing in large lots may provide lower unit costs because of lower transportation costs. If a client purchases a truckload of goods, rather than, say, half-truck loads, his unit price shipping cost is usually less. The same criterion applies to shipping goods by train where unit costs for a whole trainload, such as automobiles, bottled water, or chemical products, is less than if only a portion of the trainload was used.

Methods for calculating an optimum lot size

Methods for calculating the optimum lot size generally depend on balancing the setup costs with holding costs. Thus, for lot-sizing calculation methods to be appropriate, it is necessary that these costs are known with some reliability. The following are some quantitative methods for determining lot size.[3]

Lot for lot

In the lot-for-lot (LFL) approach, the lot size manufactured, or purchased is equal to the net requirements at that particular time. Using this method minimizes inventory holding costs and avoids the risk of obsolescence. However, it means that setup costs are incurred for each operation. Also, if the lot sizes vary greatly from period to period, it makes planning more complicated.

Economic ordering quantity

Economic order quantity (EOQ) models, already presented in Chapter 11, might be used for optimizing the lot size. This approach assumes that the demand is reasonably stable from period to period (which may not be the case) and also using the basic models, price discounts are not taken into account.

Period order quantity method

In the period order quantity (POQ) method a certain quantity of material or parts is produced at a regular period, say every week, or every ten days. In this way, planning is somewhat simplified since setup requirements for the installation is known with regularity.

Part-period balancing

The part-period balancing (PPB) approach, like the economic order quantity method, balances the setup costs with holding costs with the exception that it is dynamic in that it reflects requirements for future demand requirements.

Demonstrating the concept 13.2 illustrates these four methods for calculating lot size.

Manufacturing resource planning

Evolution

MRP-I was an important planning tool in the 1970s. As an isolated unit it applied to a relatively small part of the manufacturing function and at the time had the disadvantage that as an open system there were no feedback loops between inputs and outputs. In the 1980s and early 1990s the basic MRP-I system evolved into the so-called MRP-II system or manufacturing resource planning (or, for some firms, material resource planning) which took into account upstream and downstream elements of the business firm. From the MRP-II system was developed the business applications software systems, which for the completely tuned system are able to manage a company's entire business either at one site, several sites in the same country, or sites internationally. These business applications software systems are referred to as business resource planning (BRP), or enterprise resource planning (ERP) systems and are presented in the next section.[4]

Structure

The structure of the manufacturing system is illustrated in Figure 13.5. Here the original material requirements plan, MRP-I, is still present but early upstream of this is the business plan which feeds the sales plan, the production plan and then the master production schedule. The material requirements plan then feeds the capacity plan, purchasing activities and, ultimately, all the shop floor planning and control operations. Unlike the early MRP-I, the MRP-II has feedback loops which allows automatic adjustment of the other modules should the capacity of a downstream module be insufficient for upstream requirements. For example, if the master production schedule is unable to produce the required output either in quantity or at the required time period then a feedback loop could adjust the sales plan. Of course, if the adjustment would not provide the required customer service level, then other considerations would have to be reviewed. With the feedback, the whole system is a closed loop, which gives the opportunity to fine-tune the complete operation.[5]

Performance

The MRP-II system requires that every employee, the operator, analyst, quality inspector, sales person, purchasing agents, planning staff, and even

Figure 13.5 Manufacturing resource planning (MRP II)

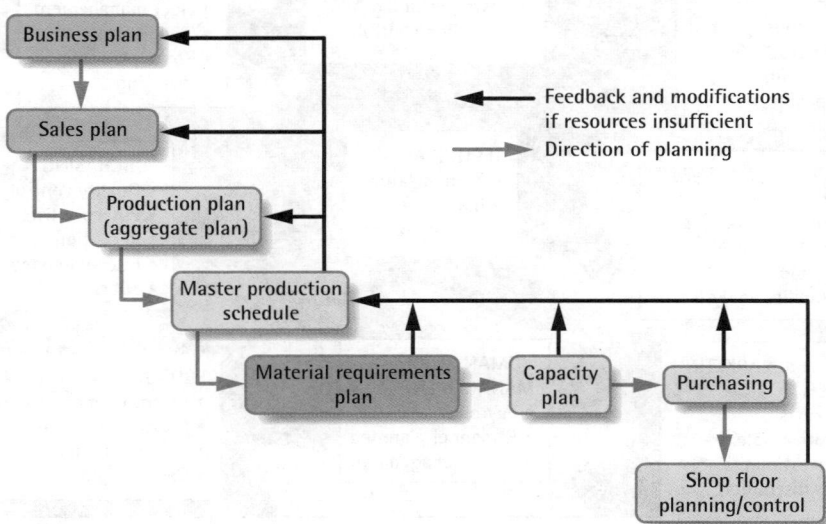

accounting, be thoroughly and strictly disciplined about entering current data into the system. Managers can calculate the requirement of every part or subassembly week by week, and track in advance possible delays or material shortages. People in inventory control can then plan the release dates and meet promised deliveries. At the business level, the MRP-II verifies the marketing and production plans to determine the availability of resources. Then, by combining the business plan with production goals it considers what is in inventory, the time it takes for vendors to deliver, cash flow, and dates the product can be delivered to the customer.[6]

Enterprise resource planning

Basic structure

An enterprise resource planning system, ERP, is a computer-based tool that integrates all the business operations of the firm such as sales, finance, human resources, manufacturing, and distribution with the objective of providing the optimum company-wide efficiency. The core of the ERP system is a single comprehensive database which both collects data from, and routes data to, modular functional components that support all the firm's worldwide activities. Figure 13.6 illustrates some of the modules that are available in an ERP system. When data are entered into one module appropriate modifications are made throughout the system. Say, for example, a sales agent in Los Angeles, USA, who works for an electronics company in Scandinavia, receives a new order for a quantity of mobile telephones. The agent, with his laptop computer taps into the firm's ERP system and enters into the sale's module the customer's order. This module provides a contract specifying the product, the delivery date, and the price in both euros and dollars. Through the linkage in the ERP system the order is entered into production planning for the division in Singapore plus all the purchasing needs are updated and the optimum route planning is made between Singapore and Los Angeles. When the order is received the ERP systems prints out the customer invoice in Scandinavia that is then mailed or sent electronically to the customer.

Figure 13.6 Modular arrangement of enterprise resource planning systems

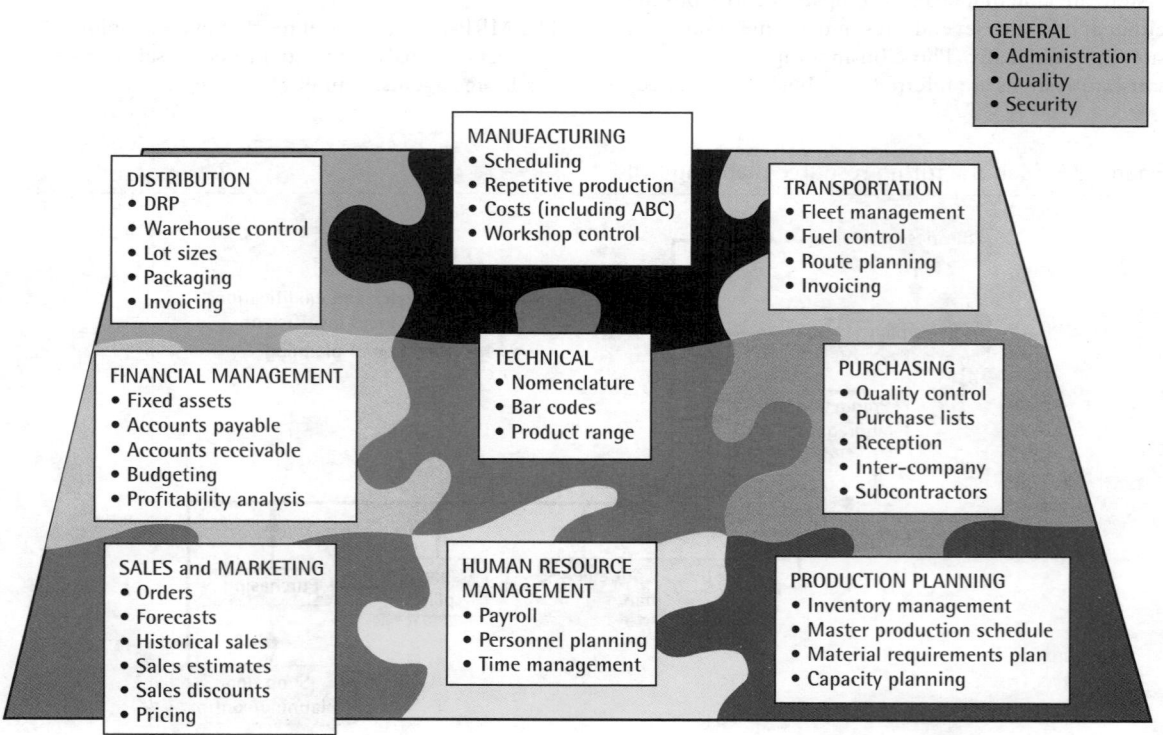

Commercial systems

There are numerous vendors of ERP systems offering client/server applications some of which are given in Table 13.4.[7] There are four companies that dominate the market and as of 2001 by far the biggest was SAP (Systems Applications and Products) of Walldorf, Germany[8] with its R/3 product, with some one-third of the market, followed by Oracle and then J D Edwards and PeopleSoft.

Modules in the ERP can be either stand-alone products, or can be combined with other modules to give a complete integrated system and are usually able to operate on Microsoft, UNIX, or IBM AS/400 systems. Commercial products are different in their application. They might apply to the process industries such as refining and chemicals, assembly operation such as electronics or automobiles, the foods industry where menus replace the product structure for assembled products, or services such as retail, healthcare, and financial firms. Some modules might be available with one company, and not with another. Support service may be better then another and, commercial terms are probably different. The main modules of the SAP R/3 system are illustrated in Table 13.5.

Within these main modules are sub-modules that provide for specific functions. As an example in the materials management (MM) the sub-modules include: stock database; stock management; stock valuation; purchasing; and invoice control. Further, Figure 13.7 gives an example of some of the functions supported by their specific supply chain module.[9]

Considerations in installing an ERP system

The number of firms installing ERP systems continues to grow (as evidence, SAP's revenue was €6.3 billion in 2000, up 23% from the previous year). Some of the advantages of having an ERP system are indicated as follows:

- Throughout the firm, both domestically and internationally, it demands consistent operating practices across all units. This standardization improves the quality of all activities.
- Since the firm is completely integrated it reduces costs by eliminating duplicate operations.
- There is direct access for all concerned to real-time operating information.
- The flow of all data is streamlined.
- Productivity of the firm is enhanced.

However, since ERP systems have been available, installing and using them has not always been plain sailing. There have been horror stories about failed projects from FoxMeyer Drug, saying that its system helped to drive it into bankruptcy; Dell Computer found that its system would not fit its new decentralized management model; Dow Chemical spent seven years and close to $7 billion implementing a mainframe enterprise system and then decided to start over again with a client–server version.[10] Thus, although implementation of an enterprise system may, strategically, be a wise business move, a rash decision must not be made. Some questions to be considered are as follows:

1. Why am I installing this system? Is it to have full integration of my system and ultimately to increase efficiency, lower costs, and provide better quality?
2. Is it compatible with existing systems within the corporation? Or do I have to modify my operation to suit the ERP system? This is a common concern with firms that have found that they have had to modify

Table 13.4 **Commercial ERP systems**

Acacia	Marcam
Baan	MK Group
Dataworks	Oracle
IFS	PeopleSoft
Infinium Software	Platinum Software
Intentia	QAD
JBA	Ross
JD Edwards	SAP
Lawson	SSA
MAPICS	Symix

Table 13.5 **Main modules of SAP R/3 system**

Sales and distribution (SD)	Quality management (QM)
Materials management (MM)	Plant maintenance (PM)
Production planning (PP)	Human resources (HR)
Financial accounting (FI)	Project system (PS)
Controlling (CO)	Workflow (WF)
Fixed assets management (AM)	Industry solutions (IS)

Figure 13.7 SAP R/3 logistics module

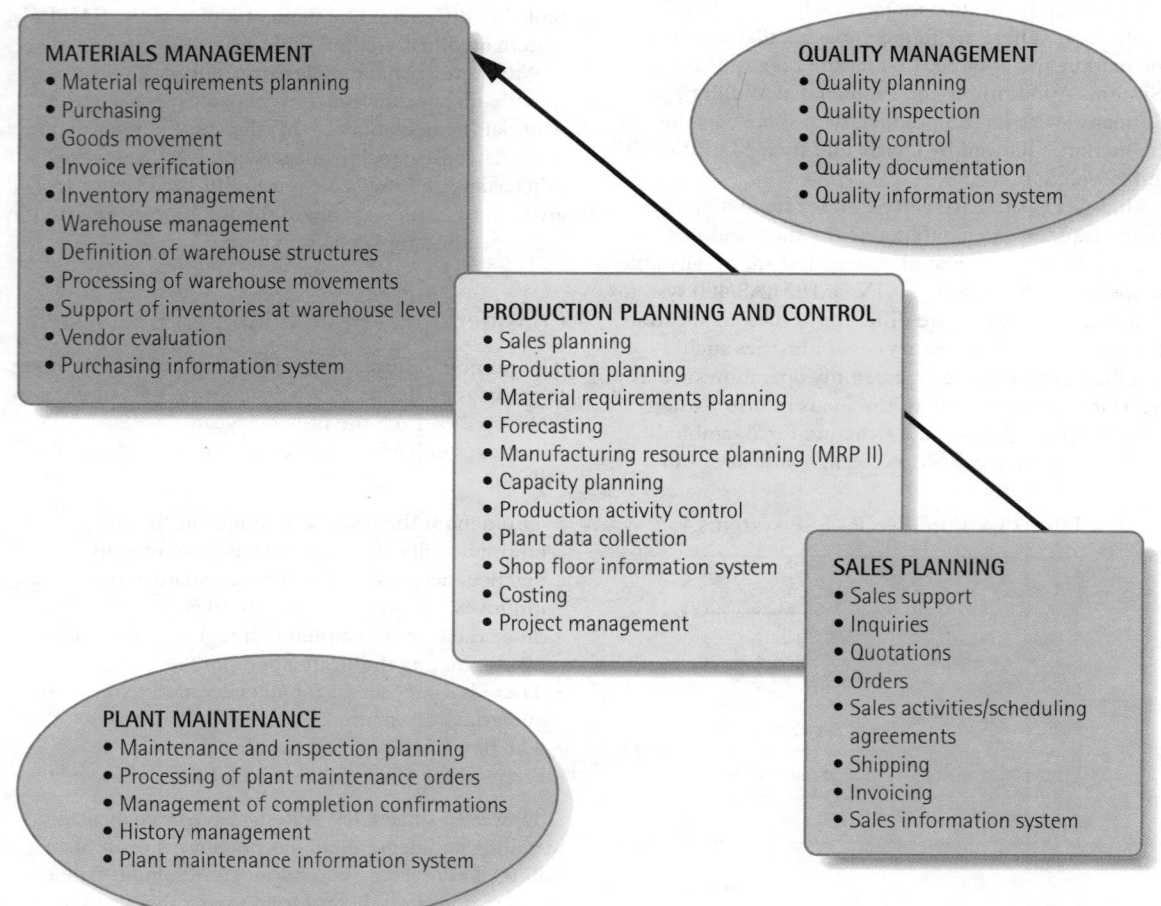

MATERIALS MANAGEMENT
- Material requirements planning
- Purchasing
- Goods movement
- Invoice verification
- Inventory management
- Warehouse management
- Definition of warehouse structures
- Processing of warehouse movements
- Support of inventories at warehouse level
- Vendor evaluation
- Purchasing information system

QUALITY MANAGEMENT
- Quality planning
- Quality inspection
- Quality control
- Quality documentation
- Quality information system

PRODUCTION PLANNING AND CONTROL
- Sales planning
- Production planning
- Material requirements planning
- Forecasting
- Manufacturing resource planning (MRP II)
- Capacity planning
- Production activity control
- Plant data collection
- Shop floor information system
- Costing
- Project management

SALES PLANNING
- Sales support
- Inquiries
- Quotations
- Orders
- Sales activities/scheduling agreements
- Shipping
- Invoicing
- Sales information system

PLANT MAINTENANCE
- Maintenance and inspection planning
- Processing of plant maintenance orders
- Management of completion confirmations
- History management
- Plant maintenance information system

their business practices to suit the ERP, rather than the reverse.

3. How much does it cost to purchase? ERP systems are very expensive, running perhaps into thousands of dollars and thus may take a big chunk of the firm's budget. The high cost may make the payback period unattractive.

4. How many of my people will I need for the installation? Many firms have found that they have had to take their line personnel out of action for many months in order to install the system. This has increased operating costs and reduced output and productivity during this period.

5. What is the time for installation? Can my operation withstand the interruptions during the time the ERP system is installed?

6. When considering specific vendors there are also considerations such as: What installation service can I expect from the supplier? How much training is provided with the package? Is all the system modular such that I can add other modules later?

An enterprise resource planning system imposes its own logic on a firm's strategy and organization and it forces the company towards full integration even when a certain amount of segmentation might be more appropriate. Also, within the firm it imposes generic processes when customized processes might be more profitable. Thus, if a company rushes to implement an ERP system the goal of integration could turn into a disaster.

Summary of key elements

- A material requirements plan determines needs of dependent components taking into account lead times. MRP-I is an open system with no feedback loop.

- The inputs for the material requirements plan come from the master production schedule, the product structure, and the inventory records file.

- Gross requirement is the amount needed to satisfy demand in a certain period.

- On-hand inventory is the amount of inventory in storage. Allocated inventory is material for other purposes such as spare parts. Safety stock is inventory not normally available for the MRP. Inventory for the MRP is inventory on-hand less allocated inventory and safety stock.

- Scheduled receipts is inventory expected to be received from suppliers at a defined time period as a result of orders already placed such as through open orders.

- Net requirements are the quantity of material needed to meet the scheduled demand. It is the gross requirements less the inventory available.

- Planned ordered release is the quantity to be released in a time period, to satisfy planned ordered receipts at a future date. The time difference is the lead time.

- A planned ordered receipt is to satisfy net requirements although lot size limitations may result in planned ordered receipts being greater than net requirements.

- The yield rate is the percentage of starting material that actually ends up in the product. It takes into account the proportion of unusable non-conforming material.

- With large lots, unit setup costs are less but carrying costs are high. Finished goods carrying costs are higher than for raw materials because of the value added.

- If lots are small then unit setup costs are high but inventory-carrying costs are lower, and there is a reduced risk of obsolescence.

- With high setup costs, large lot sizes are more economical. However, this constraint underscores the drive to reduce setup times to give more plant flexibility.

- Firms may purchase in large lots to take advantage of supplier discounts, or reduced unit transport costs.

- The lot-for-lot (LFL) method for lot sizing calls for lots equal to the net requirements. This minimizes carrying costs and avoids the risk of obsolescence.

- The economic order quantity (EOQ) method for lot sizing balances setup costs with carrying costs.

- In the period order quantity (POQ) method for lot sizing a certain quantity of material or parts is produced at a regular period.

- The part-period balancing (PPB) method for lot sizing balances setup costs with holding costs, but takes into consideration requirements for future periods.

- MRP-II is an expansion of MRP-I and is a closed loop system to manage a firm's supply chain by integrating business, marketing, and production plans.

- An ERP system integrates all the business operations of the firm such as sales, finance, human resources, manufacturing, and distribution to provide optimum efficiency.

Notes and references

1. ORLICKY, Joseph, *Material Requirements Planning*, McGraw-Hill, New York 1975
2. Robert Bosch handdrill (with permission, 14 November 1997)
3. HEIZER, Jay and RENDER, Barry, *Production and Operations Management*, Prentice-Hall, 4th edition, London, pp 662–6
4. WALDRON, David, 'What follows MRP II? Enterprise resource planning', *Professional Engineering*, vol 5, issue 5, May 1992, pp 22–3
5. GROUSSAUD, Gabrielle, 'La méthode MRP II clé de voûte d'une GPAO' (The method MRP-II key to the method of production assisted by computer), *L'informatique professionnelle*, N° 119, December 1993
6. JOHNSON, Alcia, 'MRP? MRPH? OPT? CIM? FMS? JIT? Is any system letter-perfect?', *Management Review*, vol 75, issue 9, September 1986, pp 22–7
7. 'ERP monde: SAP, leader incontesté' (ERP worldwide: SAP is the uncontested leader) *Logistiques Magazine*, N° 134, January/February 1999, p. 62
8. Headquarters, SAP Aktiengesellschaft, PO Box 1461, D-69190 Waldorf, Germany
9. SAP-logistics module. http://www.sap.com
10. DAVENPORT, Thomas H., 'Putting the enterprise into the enterprise system', *Harvard Business Review*, July–August 1998, p. 122

Review and discussion topics

1. Product structure
Prepare a product structure for:
    (a) a dining room chair
    (b) a briefcase or attaché case
    (c) skis (one ski of a pair)
    (d) a bed
    (e) the lock on a door (both sections)
    (f) a portable computer
    (g) a trolley basket used in a supermarket
    (h) major sections of an airplane
    (i) an electric guitar.

2. Safety stock
Discuss the advantages and disadvantages of keeping safety stock.

3. Yield rate
If a firm is using the concept of yield rate, what does this imply? What suggestions might you propose?

4. Lot sizing
Discuss the reasons why firms might produce in large or small lots. What are the advantages and disadvantages of these two modes of operation? Consider the type of product that are being produced.

5. ERP systems

The installation of enterprise resource planning systems is a fast growing business. What advantages are there for a firm's having in place an ERP system such as supplied by J D Edwards, Oracle, or SAP? What impact does it have on the personnel? What might be some of the disadvantages?

Demonstrating the concept 13.1 Farley Co.

Situation

Farley Co., a small private company near Amsterdam, Holland, makes specialized bicycles for sale throughout Europe. The company principally performs assembly of the bicycles from components purchased in Nottingham, England, though it does have a machine shop where it produces the frames and handlebars. Much of this work is hand crafted. Details of the product (simplified) are given in Figures 13.8 and 13.9.

Farley receives an order for 2700 bicycles of identical models from a French distributor. Of these, 900 are to be ready in the 6th week, and 1800 are to be ready in the 10th week. Inventory data for all of the components are given in Table 13.6. The explanation for this information is as follows.

Figure 13.8 Farley Co.: Bicycle assembly

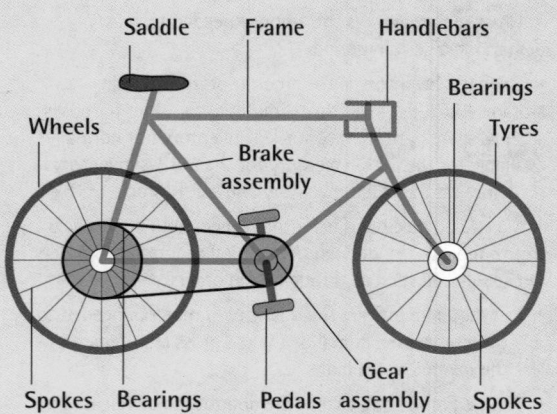

Figure 13.9 Farley Co.: Product structure for a bicycle

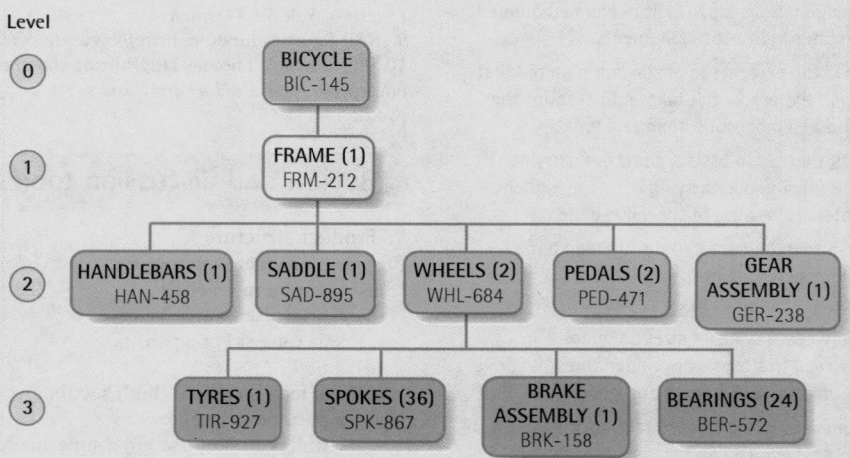

Description, reference, quantity in product, and level
This information is identical to the structure information given in the figure.

Source
This indicates the origin of the components. Those units that are assembled, or machined, are performed in-house by Farley. All the purchased parts are from outside suppliers.

Lead time
This is the elapsed time between ordering a part (either externally or internally) and its receipt ready for use in the work centre.

Minimum lot size
In this case, this applies to the purchased tyres, spokes, and bearings and is the minimum lot ordered based on economic criteria.

Table 13.6 Farley Co.: Bill of materials and inventory records file

Description	Reference	Quantity in product	Level	Source	Lead time (weeks)	Minimum lot size	Safety stock	Inventory allocated	Inventory level week 1	Scheduled receipts Quantity	Scheduled receipts Week
Bicycle	BIC-145		0	Assembled	1		0	0	0		
Frame	FRM-212	1	1	Machined	1		0	0	5		
Handlebars	HAN-458	1	2	Machined	1		0	0	20		
Saddle	SAD-895	1	2	Purchased	2		0	0	0		
Wheels	WHL-684	2	2	Assembled	1		0	30	60		
Pedals	PED-471	2	2	Assembled	1		20	10	70		
Gear assembly	GER-238	1	2	Purchased	3		0	0	0		
Tyres	TIR-927	1	3	Purchased	2	2,000	100	0	120	4,000	1
Spokes	SPK-867	36	3	Purchased	2	60,000	1,750	19,000	1,900	60,000	1
Brake assembly	BRK-158	1	3	Purchased	2		0	20	80		
Bearings	BER-572	24	3	Purchased	2	50,000	15,000	1,500	1,250	50,000	1

No minimum lot size indicates that policy is lot for lot

Safety stock
For some components, Farley keeps a safety stock in the firm for use in emergency situations to supply key customers. This safety stock is not available for use for other planning purposes.

Inventory allocated
This is the inventory allocated for spare parts for identified clients. It is not available for normal planning purposes.

Inventory level, week 1
This is the total inventory in stock. Farley always records total amounts as this information is used by the Finance Department for determining inventory investments.

Scheduled receipts
These are items that are delivered periodically on a blanket order basis. They are those items that are held in safety stock to satisfy rush orders for clients. The information shown is the scheduled receipts which are due to be delivered in week 1. They are available for use in that week and are available for the MRP.

Required

Develop a weekly period material requirements plan for Farley based on the information given. Use Table 13.7 for the development of the MRP.

Solution

The material requirements plan is given in Table 13.8. The explanation of four of the schedules is as follows.

Bicycle, BIC-145

- Gross requirements in week 6 are 900, and 1800 in week 10 as demanded by the client.

Table 13.7 MRP development grid

Description	Ref	Quantity		Week 1	2	3	4	5	6	7	8	9	10
			Gross requirements										
			Scheduled receipts										
			Inventory available										
			Net requirements										
			Planned ordered receipts										
			Planned ordered releases										

Table 13.8 Farley Co.: Material requirements plan

Description	Reference	Quan		1	2	3	4	5	6	7	8	9	10
										Week			
Bicycle	BIC-145	0	Gross requirements	0	0	0	0	0	900	0	0	0	1,800
			Scheduled receipts	0	0	0	0	0	0	0	0	0	0
			Inventory available	0	0	0	0	0	0	0	0	0	0
			Net requirements	0	0	0	0	0	900	0	0	0	1,800
			Planned ordered receipts	0	0	0	0	0	900	0	0	0	1,800
			Planned ordered releases	0	0	0	0	900	0	0	0	1,800	0
Frame	FRM-212	1	Gross requirements	0	0	0	0	900	0	0	0	1,800	0
			Scheduled receipts	0	0	0	0	0	0	0	0	0	0
			Inventory available	5	5	5	5	5	0	0	0	0	0
			Net requirements	0	0	0	0	895	0	0	0	1,800	0
			Planned ordered receipts	0	0	0	0	895	0	0	0	1,800	0
			Planned ordered releases	0	0	0	895	0	0	0	1,800	0	0
Handlebars	HAN-458	1	Gross requirements	0	0	0	895	0	0	0	1,800	0	0
			Scheduled receipts	0	0	0	0	0	0	0	0	0	0
			Inventory available	20	20	20	20	0	0	0	0	0	0
			Net requirements	0	0	0	875	0	0	0	1,800	0	0
			Planned ordered receipts	0	0	0	875	0	0	0	1,800	0	0
			Planned ordered releases	0	0	875	0	0	0	1,800	0	0	0
Saddle	SAD-895	1	Gross requirements	0	0	0	895	0	0	0	1,800	0	0
			Scheduled receipts	0	0	0	0	0	0	0	0	0	0
			Inventory available	0	0	0	0	0	0	0	0	0	0
			Net requirements	0	0	0	895	0	0	0	1,800	0	0
			Planned ordered receipts	0	0	0	895	0	0	0	1,800	0	0
			Planned ordered releases	0	895	0	0	0	1,800	0	0	0	0
Wheels	WHL-684	2	Gross requirements	0	0	0	1,790	0	0	0	3,600	0	0
			Scheduled receipts	0	0	0	0	0	0	0	0	0	0
			Inventory available	30	30	30	30	0	0	0	0	0	0
			Net requirements	0	0	0	1,760	0	0	0	3,600	0	0
			Planned ordered receipts	0	0	0	1,760	0	0	0	3,600	0	0
			Planned ordered releases	0	0	1,760	0	0	0	3,600	0	0	0
Pedals	PED-471	2	Gross requirements	0	0	0	1,790	0	0	0	3,600	0	0
			Scheduled receipts	0	0	0	0	0	0	0	0	0	0
			Inventory available	40	40	40	40	0	0	0	0	0	0
			Net requirements	0	0	0	1,750	0	0	0	3,600	0	0
			Planned ordered receipts	0	0	0	1,750	0	0	0	3,600	0	0
			Planned ordered releases	0	0	1,750	0	0	0	3,600	0	0	0
Gear assembly	GER-238	1	Gross requirements	0	0	0	895	0	0	0	1,800	0	0
			Scheduled receipts	0	0	0	0	0	0	0	0	0	0
			Inventory available	0	0	0	0	0	0	0	0	0	0
			Net requirements	0	0	0	895	0	0	0	1,800	0	0
			Planned ordered receipts	0	0	0	895	0	0	0	1,800	0	0
			Planned ordered releases	895	0	0	0	1,800	0	0	0	0	0
Tyres	TIR-927	1	Gross requirements	0	0	1,760	0	0	0	3,600	0	0	0
			Scheduled receipts	4,000	0	0	0	0	0	0	0	0	0
			Inventory available	20	4,020	4,020	2,260	2,260	2,260	2,260	660	660	660
			Net requirements	0	0	0	0	0	0	1,340	0	0	0
			Planned ordered receipts	0	0	0	0	0	0	2,000	0	0	0
			Planned ordered releases	0	0	0	0	2,000	0	0	0	0	0
Spokes	SPK-867	36	Gross requirements	0	0	63,360	0	0	0	129,600	0	0	0
			Scheduled receipts	60,000	0	0	0	0	0	0	0	0	0
			Inventory available	−18,850	41,150	41,150	37,790	37,790	37,790	37,790	0	0	0
			Net requirements	0	0	22,210	0	0	0	91,810	0	0	0
			Planned ordered receipts	0	0	60,000	0	0	0	91,810	0	0	0
			Planned ordered releases	60,000	0	0	0	91,810	0	0	0	0	0

(Continued)

Table 13.8 (Continued)

Description	Reference	Quan		Week 1	2	3	4	5	6	7	8	9	10
Brake assembly	BRK-158	1	Gross requirements	0	0	1760	0	0	0	3,600	0	0	0
			Scheduled receipts	0	0	0	0	0	0	0	0	0	0
			Inventory available	60	60	60	0	0	0	0	0	0	0
			Net requirements	0	0	1,700	0	0	0	3,600	0	0	0
			Planned ordered receipts	0	0	1,700	0	0	0	3,600	0	0	0
			Planned ordered releases	1,700	0	0	0	3,600	0	0	0	0	0
Bearings	BER-572	24	Gross requirements	0	0	42,240	0	0	0	86,400	0	0	0
			Scheduled receipts	50,000	0	0	0	0	0	0	0	0	0
			Inventory available	−15,250	34,750	34,750	42,510	42,510	42,510	42,510	6,110	6,110	6,110
			Net requirements	0	0	7,490	0	0	0	43,890	0	0	0
			Planned ordered receipts	0	0	50,000	0	0	0	50,000	0	0	0
			Planned ordered releases	50,000	0	0	0	50,000	0	0	0	0	0

- There is no on-hand inventory. Thus, net requirements for both weeks are 900 and 1800 respectively.
- Planned order receipts are 900 in week 6, and 1800 in week 10, equal to net requirements since there is no minimum lot size.
- There is a one-week lead time and so planned ordered releases are 900 in week 5, and 1800 in week 9.

Frame, FRM-212
- Gross requirements in week 5 are 900, and 1800 in week 9 as the frame requirements depend on the bike (one frame for each bike). It is the period, and the quantity of the planned ordered releases for the bike which drive the frame requirements.
- There are five units of inventory onhand and so net requirements in week 5 are 895 (900 − 5). Net requirements in week 9 equal gross requirements (no inventory on hand).
- Planned order receipts are 895 in week 5, and 1800 in week 9, equal to net requirements since there is no minimum lot size.
- There is a one-week lead time and so planned ordered releases are 895 in week 4, and 1800 in week 8.

Wheels, WHL-684
- Gross requirements in week 4 are 1790, and 3600 in week 8 as the wheel requirements depend on the frame (two wheels for each frame). It is the period, and the quantity of the planned ordered releases for the frame which drive the wheel requirements.
- There are 60 units of inventory on hand and of this, 30 have been allocated. Thus inventory available is 30 (60 − 30). Thus, net requirements in week 4 are 1760 (1790 − 30). Net requirements in week 8 equals gross requirements (no inventory on hand).

- Planned order receipts are 1760 in week 4, and 3600 in week 7, equal to net requirements since there is no minimum lot size.
- There is a one-week lead time and so planned ordered releases are 1760 in week 3, and 3600 in week 7.

Bearings, BER–572
- Gross requirements in week 3 are 42,240 and 86,400 in week 7 as the bearing requirements depend on the wheel (24 bearings for each wheel). It is the period, and the quantity of the planned ordered releases for the wheel which drive the bearing requirements.
- There are 1250 units of on-hand inventory, 1500 have already been allocated, and there is a safety stock requirement of 15,000. Thus, inventory 'available' in week 1 is −15,250 (1250 − 1500 − 15,000). However, in week 1 there are 50,000 bearings of scheduled receipts to arrive. Thus, for use in week 3 (when they are required) is 34,750 (50,000 − 15,250).
- Net requirements in week 3 are 7490 (42,240 − 34,750).
- Planned order receipts are 50,000 in week 3 as this is the minimum lot size requirement even though only 7490 units are required.
- Carried over to inventory in week 4 are 42,510 units of inventory (50,000 − 7490), and this appears in the inventory file until week 7 when it is needed.
- Net requirement in week 7 is 43,890 (86,400 − 42,510).
- There is a two-week lead time, so that in week 1 there are 50,000 units of planned ordered releases and 50,000 units in week 5.
- There are 6110 units of inventory carried over to week 8 and beyond (50,000 − 43,890).

The logic for the other schedules is the same.

Demonstrating the concept 13.2 Benoit Co.

Situation

The Benoit Co. outside Lille, France, makes a variety of plastic moulded components used in the automobile industry. The components are made in a variety of colours and before a new production run is started, the presses have to be cleaned, the appropriate type mould has to be installed, and the equipment has to be pre-heated. Data indicate that the setup time (order cost) for producing a new lot is €96.00. Carrying costs for the finished products is estimated at 0.01 €/unit/week and there is no initial inventory. Carrying costs for raw materials are not taken into consideration. For the next ten weeks the gross requirements for the end product are as shown in Table 13.9.

Required

1. Develop a plan for lot sizing using the lot for lot criterion. Determine the carrying costs, ordering costs, and the total plan concept using this method.
2. Develop a plan for lot sizing using the criterion of economic order quantity. Determine the carrying costs, ordering costs, and the total plan concept using this method.
3. Develop a plan for lot sizing using the criterion of periodic order quantity. Determine the carrying costs, ordering costs, and the total plan concept using this method.
4. Develop a plan for lot sizing using the criterion of part-period balancing. Determine the carrying

Table 13.9 Benoit Co.: Gross requirements for end product

		Week								
	1	2	3	4	5	6	7	8	9	10
Gross requirements	340	310	350	220	150	0	280	330	180	220

costs, ordering costs, and the total plan concept using this method.
5. Which is the preferred plan?

Solution

1. Table 13.10 gives the planning schedule for this criterion. Production lots are made each week according to the gross requirements. Each time a production is made, a setup, or ordering cost is incurred.
2. Table 13.11 gives the planning schedule for this criterion:
   - Each time the inventory level falls below the economic order quantity, a production equal to the EOQ is made.
   - Average inventory is the mean of the beginning and ending inventory.
   - Carrying cost is the sum of the average inventory times the inventory carrying cost.
   - Ordering cost is the number of setups made during the planning period times the setup cost.

Table 13.10 Benoit Co.: Lot for lot

Order cost, €/order	96.00
Carrying cost, €/unit/week	0.10
Lead time, weeks	0
Beginning inventory on hand	0

				Week							
	1	2	3	4	5	6	7	8	9	10	Total
Gross requirements	340	310	350	220	150	0	280	330	180	220	2,380
Beginning inventory	0	0	0	0	0	0	0	0	0	0	
Production lots	340	310	350	220	150	0	280	330	180	220	2,380
Ending inventory	0	0	0	0	0	0	0	0	0	0	0
Average inventory	0.00	0.00	0.00	0.00	0.00	0.00	0.00	0.00	0.00	0.00	
Carrying cost, €	0										
Number of orders made	9										
Ordering costs, €	864.00										
Total costs, €	864.00										

Table 13.11 Benoit Co.: Economic order quantity

Order cost, €/order	96.00		Demand during planning period (D)	2,380
Carrying cost, €/unit/week	0.10	$EOQ = \sqrt{\dfrac{2DS}{C}}$	Carrying cost in plan period (FF)	1.00
Lead time, weeks	0		EOQ	675.99
Beginning inventory on hand	0		EOQ (rounded)	676.00

					Week						
	1	2	3	4	5	6	7	8	9	10	Total
Gross requirements	340	310	350	220	150	0	280	330	180	220	**2,380**
Beginning inventory	0	336	26	352	132	658	658	378	48	544	
Production lots	676	0	676	0	676	0	0	0	676	0	**2,704**
Ending inventory	336	26	352	132	658	658	378	48	544	324	
Average inventory	168.00	181.00	189.00	242.00	395.00	658.00	518.00	213.00	296.00	434.00	
Carrying cost, €	329.40										
Number of orders made	4										
Ordering costs, €	384.00										
Total costs, €	713.40										

Table 13.12 Benoit Co.: Periodic order quantity

Order cost, €/order	96.00	Demand during planning period (D)	2,380
Carrying cost, €/unit/week	0.10	Carrying cost in plan period (FF)	1.00
Lead time, weeks	0	EOQ	675.99
Beginning inventory on hand	0	EOQ (rounded)	676.00

Orders during planning period (D/EOQ)	3.52		
Period order quantity is:		$EOQ = \sqrt{\dfrac{2DS}{C}}$	
Weeks in planning period/orders	2.84		
POQ (rounded)	3.00		

					Week						
	1	2	3	4	5	6	7	8	9	10	Total
Gross requirements	340	310	350	220	150	0	280	330	180	220	**2,380**
Beginning inventory	0	660	350	0	150	0	0	510	180	0	
Production lots	1,000	0	0	370	0	0	790	0	0	220	**2,380**
Ending inventory	660	350	0	150	0	0	510	180	0	0	
Average inventory	330.00	505.00	175.00	75.00	75.00	0.00	255.00	345.00	90.00	0.00	
Carrying cost, €	185.00										
Number of orders made	4										
Ordering costs, €	384.00										
Total costs, €	569.00										

3. Table 13.12 gives the planning schedule for this criterion:
   - The economic order quantity is calculated as before.
   - The orders made during the planning period are calculated by the total requirements in the planning period divided by the EOQ.
   - Periodic order quantity is the weeks in the planning period divided by the number of orders.
   - This number is rounded.
   - Thus for each POQ a production lot is made to equal the demand for that period.
4. Table 13.13 gives the planning schedule for this criterion:
   - The economic part period, EPP, is calculated as the ratio order costs divided by carrying costs. This value

means that the number of units held in inventory for one week would have a carrying cost equal to the ordering cost. Thus, the concept is to find the cumulative part-period that corresponds to the EPP.
   - First, a lot size equivalent to the gross requirements of period 1 is calculated. In this case, the excess units produced is 0. The period (weeks) this number of units is carried is also 0. Thus, the cumulative part-period is 0.
   - Next, a lot size equal to the first two weeks is assumed to be produced in week 1. In this case the excess units produced is the requirements for the second week. This amount is carried for one week. Thus, the part-period (quantity * time) is calculated.

Table 13.13 Benoit Co.: Part-period balancing

Order cost, €/order	96.00	Economic part period (EPP) is:	
Carrying cost, €/unit/week	0.10	Order costs/carrying costs	960.00
Lead time, weeks	0		
Beginning inventory on hand	0		

| Periods combined | Lot size (trial) | Excess units | | Part-period | Cum part period |
		Quantity	Periods carried		
1	340	0	0	0	0
1 and 2	650	310	1	310	310
1, 2 and 3	1,000	350	2	700	1,010 (Closest to economic part-period)
4	220	0	0	0	0
4 and 5	370	150	1	150	150
4, 5 and 6	370	0	2	0	150
4, 5, 6 and 7	650	280	3	840	990 (Closest to economic part-period)
8	330	0	0	0	0
8 and 9	510	180	1	180	180
8, 9 and 10	730	220	2	440	620 (No following period)

| | Week | | | | | | | | | | |
	1	2	3	4	5	6	7	8	9	10	Total
Gross requirements	340	310	350	220	150	0	280	330	180	220	2,380
Beginning inventory	0	660	350	0	430	280	280	0	400	220	
Production lots	1,000	0	0	650	0	0	0	730	0	0	2,380
Ending inventory	660	350	0	430	280	280	0	400	220	0	
Average inventory	330.00	505.00	175.00	215.00	355.00	280.00	140.00	200.00	310.00	110.00	
Carrying cost, €	262.00										
Number of orders made	3										
Ordering costs, €	288.00										
Total costs, €	550.00										

- Next, a lot size equal to the requirements for weeks 1, 2, and 3 is assumed. The excess units over and above weeks 1 and 2 are the requirements for the third week. This amount is carried for two weeks. The part-period is the quantity * periods carried. A cumulative amount is then calculated. This figure of 1010 is close to the EPP of 960 and so a lot size equal to the requirements of the first three weeks is made.
- The steps are repeated for the subsequent weeks, each time stopping when a cumulative part-period is found which is closest to the EPP.

Table 13.14 Benoit Co.: Total costs

Lot for lot	€864.00
Economic order quantity	€713.40
Periodic order quantity	€569.00
Part-period balancing	€550.00

- The planning schedule for lot sizes is then developed as the other cases.
5. In summary the total costs are as shown in Table 13.14.

Thus, the part-period balancing approach gives the lowest overall cost.

Application exercise 13.1　Belecom

Situation

The Belecom company in Montpellier, France, manufactures car telephones. One product, Model J-610, comprises two subassemblies F-956, two assemblies N-458, and one purchased component X-459. Each assembly N-458 is manufactured from three subassemblies P-891, and two components G-587.

Each subassembly P-891 is made from three components M-897, two components J-953, and three components D-896.

Table 13.15, gives the inventory records file including lead times for the final product and all its components.

Table 13.16 gives the master production schedule for the finished product for a six-week planning horizon.

Table 13.15 Belecom: Inventory records file

Reference number	Minimum lot size	Lead time (weeks)	Quantity in stock (week 1)	Safety stock	Stock already assigned	Scheduled receipts in week 1
J-610	500	1	300	200	50	100
F-956	700	1	250	100	0	3,000
N-458	4,000	1	1,000	200	0	3,000
X-459	1,500	1	500	100	300	1,500
P-891	25,000	1	800	50	0	20,000
G-587	18,000	1	1,000	40	120	13,000
M-897	250	2	1,500	100	40	80,000
J-953	50,000	2	400	120	75	60,000
D-896	85,000	1	800	400	55	80,000

Table 13.16 Belecom: Master production schedule

Reference		Week					
		1	2	3	4	5	6
J-610	Gross requirements	0	1,500	2,250	1,750	4,000	5,000

Required

As director of production, prepare a material requirements plan for the finished product J-610 and all its components.

Application exercise 13.2 The Bewdley Company

Situation

The Bewdley Company in Shropshire, England, makes automobile components for Ford Motor Co. Two major products are steering wheel assemblies. There are two models of the steering wheels, A-0137 and H-1455 and the indented product structure for the two products is shown in Figure 13.10. In this product structure there is a one-for-one basis for component requirements. The inventory records file is given in Table 13.17.

Gross requirements are given in Table 13.18.

Required

1. Using this given information, develop a material requirements plan for the two finished products, and all the components.
2. Redo the material requirements plan assuming the following:
   - Assembly from level 2 to level 1 the yield rate is 92%.
   - Assembly from level 1 to level 0 the yield rate is 96%.

Figure 13.10 The Bewdley Co.: Product structure

A-0137	H-1455
B-1365	J-8954
D-1865	E-4789
E-4789	F-0265
C-1258	K-6957
F-0265	E-4789
G-1285	F-0265
	C-1258
	F-0265
	G-1285

Table 13.17 The Bewdley Co.: Inventory records file

Reference number	Minimum lot size	Lead time (weeks)	Inventory on hand
A-0137	0	1	10
B-1365	0	2	100
C-1258	50	2	50
D-1865	0	1	50
E-4789	0	1	600
F-0265	200	2	1,500
G-1285	0	1	75
H-1455	0	1	45
J-8954	300	3	100
K-6957	0	3	100

Table 13.18 The Bewdley Co.: Gross requirements

						Week						
	1	2	3	4	5	6	7	8	9	10	11	12
A-0137	0	0	0	0	0	200	150	200	250	50	50	150
H-1455	0	0	0	0	300	250	150	50	100	200	50	100

Application exercise 13.3 Burton Co.

Situation

Burton Co. in England produces subassembly motor units for refrigerators, which are shipped to various clients. One particular subassembly, reference CAT-1892, is made on special equipment. Past data indicate that the setup time (order cost) for producing a new lot of the subassembly units is a high £3000 as a result of special adjustments to the equipment. Carrying costs for the finished products is estimated at £1.75/unit/week. Carrying costs for raw materials are not taken into consideration.

For the next ten weeks the gross requirements for the end product are as shown in Table 13.19.

Initial inventory is 1750 units.

Required

1. Develop a plan for lot sizing using the lot-for-lot method. Determine the carrying costs, ordering costs, and the total plan concept using this method.
2. Develop a plan for lot sizing using the economic order quantity method. Determine the carrying costs, ordering costs, and the total plan concept using this method.

3. Develop a plan for lot sizing using the periodic order quantity method. Determine the carrying costs, ordering costs, and the total plan concept using this method.

4. Develop a plan for lot sizing using the part-period balancing method. Determine the carrying costs, ordering costs, and the total plan concept using this method.
5. Which is the preferred plan?

Table 13.19 Burton Co.: Gross requirements for the end product

	Week									
	1	2	3	4	5	6	7	8	9	10
Gross requirements	1,100	1,570	1,550	1,750	1,050	1,250	1,180	450	1,150	1,250

Application exercise 13.4 Table lamp

Situation

The BTO Lamp Company is a firm making all types of lighting product for retail outlets such as BHV, IKEA, and Habitat. At one particular period it has ten-week demand for two of its projects, a blue table lamp (Product 1) and an orange table lamp (Product 2) as shown in Table 13.20.

The product structure for these two products (shown in Figures 13.11 and 13.12) makes it clear that, in all cases, there is a one-for-one requirement for each product at the next level. For example, if we consider the blue table lamp, for each finished product, one unit of Component 61 is needed for

Product 1, one unit of Component 32 is needed for Component 61, etc. The lead time for all components, which are assembled in-house, is one week. The effective lead times for the raw materials, which are purchased from outside, are according to Table 13.21.

The inventory on hand at the beginning of week 1 and for use in this operation is according to Table 13.22.

Required

Develop a material requirements plan covering the assembly of these two finished products.

Table 13.20 Ten-week demand for table lamps

	Week									
Gross requirements	1	2	3	4	5	6	7	8	9	10
Product 1	3,200	4,280	4,730	4,590	4,300	4,440	4,210	3,540	3,460	3,170
Product 2	795	875	855	745	675	595	505	625	865	945

Table 13.21 Effective lead times for raw materials for table lamps

Purchased product	83	93	04	14
Lead time (weeks)	3	4	2	2

Table 13.22 Inventory on hand and for use

Product	1	2	61	71	32	42	52	83	93	04	14
Inventory	4,500	800	6,000	900	5,000	1,000	7,000	10,100	2345	20,000	8,000

Figure 13.10 Structure for blue table lamp (Product 1)

Figure 13.11 Structure for orange table lamp (Product 2)

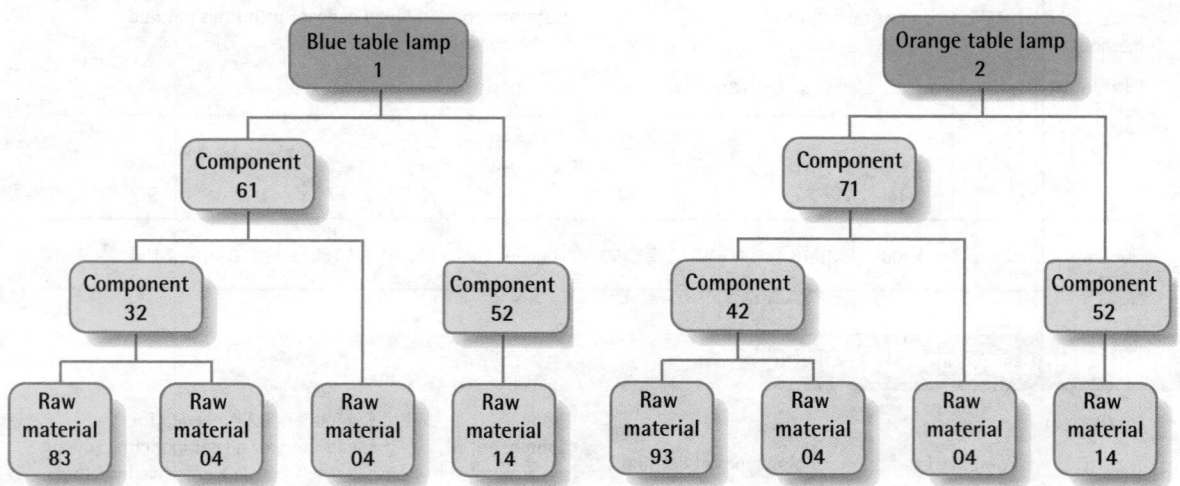

Selected further reading

HOSSAIN, Liaquat, PATRICK, John D. and RASHID, Mohammad A. (2002) *Enterprise Resource Planning: Global Opportunities and Challenges*, Idea Group Publishing.

O'LEARY, Daniel E. (2000) *Enterprise Resource Planning Systems: Systems, Life Cycle, Electronic Commerce, and Risk*, Cambridge University Press.

ORLICKY, Joseph and PLOSSL, George W. (1994) *Orlicky's Material Requirements Planning*, 2nd edition, McGraw-Hill.

PTAK, Carol A. (1996) *MRP and Beyond: A Toolbox for Integrating People and Systems*, McGraw-Hill.

WALLACE, Thomas F. and KREMZAR, Michael H. (2001) *ERP: Making It Happen: The Implementers' Guide to Success with Enterprise Resource Planning*, 3rd edition, Wiley.

An extensive listing of other further reading can be found on the website.

What's on the web?

Further learning resources are available to lecturers and students at www.supplychain-online.com, including the following which are specific to *Material requirements and enterprise resource planning*:

Resource	Subject
Chapter overview	Material requirements and enterprise resource planning
Demonstrating the concept: Plastic Products Co. (1)	Material requirements planning
Application exercise: Plastic Products Co. (2)	Material requirements planning
Application exercise: Sprinkler	Material requirements planning
More further reading	Material requirements and enterprise resource planning

14 Operations scheduling

The scheduling activity

Scheduling is the function that involves the preparation of a timetable for work that needs doing in order to meet client need dates, or for activities to achieve some desired objective. In the supply chain, effective management of the scheduling activity is important to avoid bottlenecks, to optimize the utilization of equipment, labour, and machines, and at the same time to ensure the smooth flow of goods or services to customers. Operations scheduling covers those activities that are normally repetitive in nature and have a relatively short-term timeframe of hours, days, weeks, or perhaps a few months. Illustrations for certain industries are given in the following.

Print shop

This might include scheduling the following activities to publish a sales catalogue:

1. Making the film.
2. Mounting.
3. Preparation of the plates.
4. Printing.
5. Binding.
6. Trimming.
7. Packaging.
8. Shipping.

Foundry

This might include scheduling the following activities to make a bronze impeller blade for a boat:

1. Making the sand mould.
2. Pouring liquid metal into the mould.
3. Cooling of the mould.
4. Separation of casting from mould.
5. Removing burrs and joints.
6. Cleaning and polishing the casting.

Chocolate manufacture

This might include scheduling the following activities to produce an order of milk chocolate bars:

1. Roasting cocoa beans.
2. Making cocoa paste.
3. Adding milk.
4. Crushing.
5. Moulding.
6. Cooling.
7. De-moulding.
8. Wrapping.
9. Packaging.
10. Delivery.

Railway company

This might include scheduling the following activities for the use of rolling stock:

1. Departure and arrival timetables.
2. Equipment (buffet car, 1st and 2nd class).
3. Personnel (drivers and ticket controller).
4. Food/drink for restaurant and bar.
5. Cleaning.
6. Maintenance.

Business school

This might include scheduling the following activities for the preparation and delivery of classes:

1. Programme.
2. Instructors.
3. Classrooms to be used.
4. Teaching material (computer, TV).
5. Exam schedule.
6. Marking exams.

Medical facility

This might include scheduling the following activities for the effective treatment of patients:

1. Consultations.
2. Timetable for surgical procedures.
3. Use of beds.
4. Staff requirements – nurses and doctors.
5. Delivery of medical supplies.
6. Rehabilitation treatment.

Food distribution centre

This might include scheduling the following activities to meet the needs of retail outlets:

1. Warehouse personnel.
2. Reception dates of bulk products.
3. Storage areas to be used.
4. Preparation of client pallets (picking).
5. Organizing delivery vehicles.
6. Drivers necessary.

In contrast to operations scheduling, which is short term, is project scheduling which is long term, involving the development of a timetable for a unique activity where the project completion timeframe may be several years. This type of scheduling is presented in more detail in Chapter 18.

The Gantt chart

The engineer Henry L Gantt of the USA (1861–1919), developed the Gantt (now commonly known as a bar) chart in 1916. Its purpose is to provide managers with an easily understood summary of what work is scheduled for certain time periods, how much of the scheduled work is completed according to plan, and what operating function performed the work.

An example of a Gantt chart for a printing operation is given in Figure 14.1. This chart is explained in the following sections.

Figure 14.1 Gantt chart for a printing operation

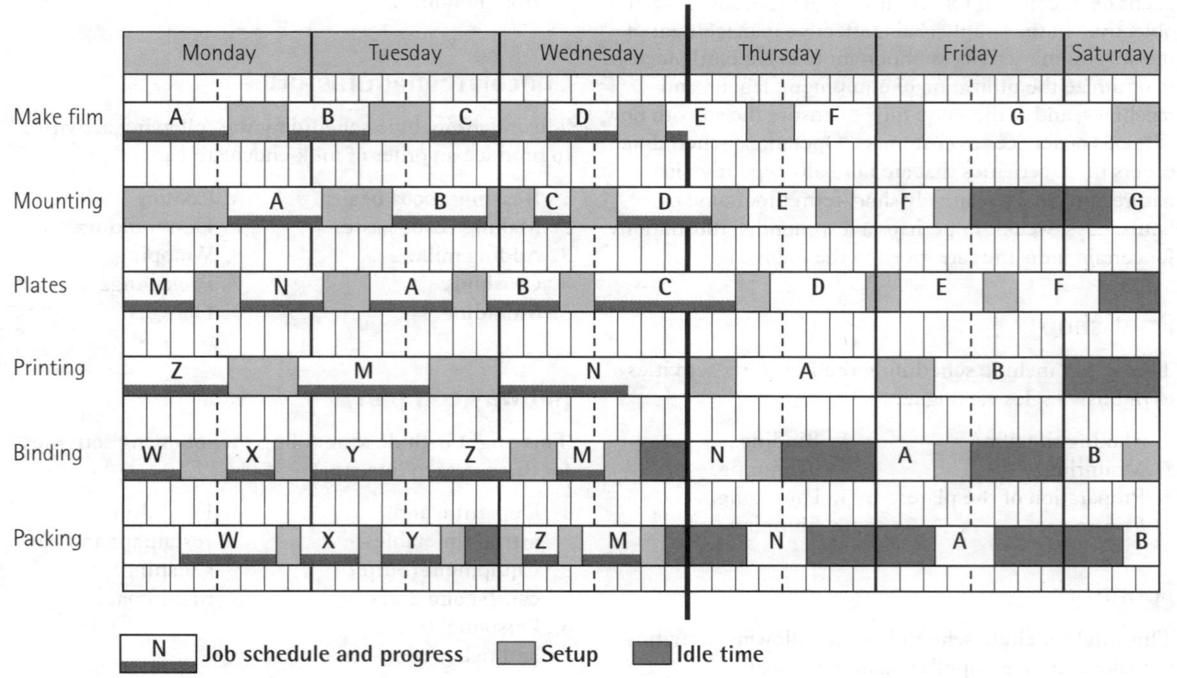

Activities in a printing operation

The activities to be performed are on the left side of the chart:

- Making a film.
- Mounting the film.
- Preparation of the final plates.
- Printing on an offset printing machine.
- Binding the printed documents.
- Packing finished product to deliver to the client.

Time

The timeframe is given on the top of the chart:

- A week's work is Monday through Saturday morning.
- Each day is broken down into hours from 8am to 5pm. Production stops for lunch between midday and 1pm. (This time is not shown.)

Jobs

The job references are shown on the bars:

- There are seven jobs, A, B, C, D, E, F, and G which start this particular week.
- There are six jobs, M, N, W, X, Y, Z which were started in a previous period.

Planned schedule

- The non-shaded horizontal bars give the start and finish for a particular activity for a certain job.
- The light shaded area is the setup time required to adjust the machine and to do all that is necessary to prepare for the next job.
- The dark shaded area is the idle time when no activity is planned.

All this information would have been prepared prior to the start of the week, for example, Friday evening, or early Monday morning. As the actual time proceeds, the status of the activity, for each job, is marked on the Gantt chart by the thick black horizontal line on the bottom of the bar.

Update to operations manager

Suppose the time period is now Thursday 8am. The Gantt chart illustrates the status as shown in Table 14.1.

Using a Gantt chart, an operations or production manager can see if resources can be modified to ensure that activities are kept on schedule. In this example, printing is behind schedule which then risks delaying the following jobs A and B. If this happens, this will

Table 14.1 Update to operations manager Gantt chart

Activity	Status
Making a film	Job E is on schedule
Mounting the film	Job D is ahead of schedule. This job is finished although it was not scheduled to be finished until 09h00 Thursday morning
Preparation of the final plates	Job C is ahead of schedule. This job is finished although it was scheduled to be finished at 10h00 Thursday morning
Printing on an offset printing machine	Job N is behind schedule. This job was scheduled to be finished by Wednesday at 17h00. It is 2½ hours behind schedule
Binding the printed documents	Activity is on schedule. Binding of product N is ready to begin
Packing finished product	Activity is on schedule. At the present time there is no activity

have repercussions in the downstream operations of binding and packing putting jobs A and B behind schedule.

Advantages of the Gantt chart

With the Gantt chart the following questions can be asked:

- Since mounting and preparation of plates is ahead of schedule, can personnel from here assist in printing?
- There is idle time in packing. Can people here be used in printing?
- Can the printing time for A and B be reduced to avoid delays?
- Can the setup time in printing between jobs N and A be reduced to avoid delays in printing?

The Gantt chart is a useful tool to help a production manager monitor the activities of a production operation. In addition, in presenting activities according to a timescale, a manager can see if operation improvements can be made. In the example here, the chart shows that setup times are long in comparison to operating time. There is considerable idle time in binding, and packaging. Perhaps scheduling can be reorganized to avoid this situation. In order to have the flexibility to transfer personnel from one operation to another, the workforce must be multi-skilled. Hence the importance of training in order to be able to meet client needs, or to have flexibility when operations do not proceed according to plan.

Order sequencing

Resources such as labour, machines, and time are limited in any production or service operation. Order sequencing is to decide in which sequence to process jobs or people that are waiting upstream. These might involve:

- machining operations in a manufacturing concern
- assembling machined parts
- trucks waiting to depart to deliver goods to clients
- packaging of finished goods
- serving a customer at a service centre such as a retail store, bank, insurance firm, or restaurant.

One particular operating sequence might be more acceptable than another in terms of overall costs. Some sequencing rules include the following, which are illustrated for a situation when there is only one processing centre.

First come, first served

First come, first served (FCFS) means that the next job to be processed is the one that arrived first in the waiting line. This would be a fairness approach, particularly if one were dealing with people. In inventory management it is synonymous with FIFO (first in, first out) meaning the first piece of inventory to arrive at a storage area is the first to be used.

Earliest due date

The earliest due date (EDD) means that the next job to be processed is the one that has the earliest (closest) date when the finished job is promised to the client. This criterion is important to avoid not irritating, and perhaps losing, the customer. As an illustration, assume that the following five jobs, with the due date in hours to the customer are waiting to be processed (see Table 14.2). The date is now zero.

Then, using the EDD criteria, the processing sequence would be B-D-A-C-E. This assumes that there is no constraint with the processing time, which is a consideration in the least slack time method given later.

Table 14.2 EDD schedule

Jobs	A	B	C	D	E
Due date to client	8	3	12	7	13

Table 14.3 SPT schedule

Jobs	A	B	C	D	E
Processing time (hr)	7	8	39	16	9

Shortest processing time

The shortest processing (SPT) time means the next job to be processed is the one taking the least time necessary to complete. The philosophy here is to get the smallest jobs over quickly which gives a psychological impression that one is being more productive. The problem with this approach is that large jobs, which might be more urgent, get pushed behind. As an illustration, assume that a company that works 40 hours a week has the jobs given in Table 14.3 to be processed.

If it is now first thing Monday morning, then using the shortest processing time, and assuming no client constraints, for the coming week jobs A, B, D, and E will be processed for a total of 40 hours. Thus, at the end of the week one can say that 80% of the work has been accomplished (four jobs divided by a total of five).

Longest processing time

The longest processing (LPT) time means that the next job is the one that has the longest processing time. The logic here is to get the biggest jobs over with first. Consider the same illustration that was presented for the shortest processing time (now see Table 14.4).

Using the longest processing time criteria, job C would be performed first. At the end of the week one could say that 20% of the work has been completed (one job divided by five). In practice if jobs have long processing times it is often better to try and break them down into two or more smaller ones. Scheduling works best when one is dealing with jobs that require roughly equal processing time, or resource requirements.

Table 14.4 LPT schedule

Jobs	A	B	C	D	E
Processing time (hr)	7	8	39	16	9

Table 14.5 LST schedule

Jobs	A	B	C	D	E
Due date to client	9	8	20	22	16
Processing time	1	7	4	3	7
Stack time	8	1	16	19	9

Table 14.6 Order sequence using LST criteria

Jobs	B	A	E	C	D
Due date to client	8	9	16	20	22
Processing Time	7	1	7	4	3
Slack Time	1	8	9	16	19

Last arrived, first processed

The last arrived, first processed (LAFP) means that the next job to be processed is the one that arrived last. This is probably illogical, and is sloppy management, but it means that the last job that is put on the top of the pile is then processed first.

Least slack time

The least slack time (LST) means that the next job is the one that has the least amount of slack time. The slack time, sometimes referred to as the float time, is the difference between the date or time when the job is promised, and the processing time to complete that job. This is illustrated in Table 14.5 using the same criteria for the jobs under the earliest due date, except that now in addition, the processing time is given. All figures are in hours.

Using the least slack time criteria, the order sequence would be as in Table 14.6.

Further, in using these criteria for the data given, no job is late as the (due date − finish date) is positive or zero for all jobs as illustrated in Table 14.7.

Table 14.7 Order sequence and job status using LST criteria

Jobs in order sequence	B	A	E	C	D
Due date to client	8	9	16	20	22
Processing time	7	1	7	4	3
Slack time	1	8	9	16	19
Start	0	7	8	15	19
Finish	7	8	15	19	22
Due date − finish date	1	1	1	1	0

Table 14.8 Status change following due date change

Jobs in order sequence	B	A	E	C	D
Due date to client	8	3	16	20	22
Processing time	7	1	7	4	3
Slack time	1	2	9	16	19
Start	0	7	8	15	19
Finish	7	8	15	19	22
Due date − finish date	1	−5	1	1	0

However, care should be taken in using this approach. Say, for example, the due date for job A is after 3 and not 9 hours. In this case job A would be late as the (due date − finish date) is −5 as indicated in Table 14.8.

If sequencing of jobs A and B were reversed no jobs would be late and the best sequence would be in accordance with the client due date (see Table 14.9).

Critical ratio

The critical ratio (CR) means that the next job to be processed is the one that has the lowest critical ratio, which is defined as follows:

$$\text{Critical ratio} = \frac{\text{Time to the due date}}{\text{Process time}}$$

If the critical ratio is less than unity, it means that the job will be finished after the promised delivery date. In this case, effort should be made to utilize other resources such as overtime, part-time labour, etc., to reduce the overall processing time, in order that the critical ratio is

Table 14.9 **Best sequence according to client due date**

Jobs in order sequence	A	B	E	C	D
Due date to client	3	8	16	20	22
Processing time	1	7	7	4	3
Slack time	2	1	9	16	19
Start	0	1	8	15	19
Finish	1	8	15	19	22
Due date − finish date	2	0	1	1	0

above unity. In this way the client will be satisfied. There are two ways of considering the critical ratio:

1. Set the schedule according to the calculated critical ratio for each job at the start of the operation taking all jobs into consideration before the work starts.
2. Use a dynamic critical ratio that changes after each job is processed since the remaining processing time will decrease after successive jobs are processed.

These two approaches are illustrated in Demonstrating the concept 14.1.

Least changeover cost

The least changeover cost means the next job is one that involves least machine changeover, or setup time. That is, try to minimize the cost of changeover by treating those jobs that have similar machine settings. For example, a machine shop is currently processing rectangular mouldings in red plastic. The jobs waiting upstream are rectangular mouldings in blue plastic, and a cylindrical moulding in red plastic. It may be more cost effective to produce the red cylinder moulding next since this will avoid cleaning the machine (a procedure which would be necessary were the blue moulding the next job processed).

Non-quantifiable sequencing rules

Other sequencing rules, which are normally not planned, but nevertheless exist in real life, include the following.

Client who shouts the loudest

Sometimes in the real world clients who are very persistent and put verbal pressure on their suppliers

in order to get preferential treatment for their job are successful in having their work processed early.

Best client

Sequencing rules may be adopted to satisfy those clients who pay the highest price, have the highest margin, or purchase in large quantities. Thus, the best go first.

Emergency situations

In the medical profession, patients who have a life-threatening situation are treated first. Also, when emergency supplies are needed such as medical products, raw materials because of a plant shutdown, and food after an earthquake for example, schedules might be completely revamped.

Criteria for comparing sequencing rules

If processing times and delivery dates are known with some certainty, then the following criteria might be used to compare sequencing rules.

Average flow time

The average flow time is the average amount of time each job stays in the work centre. It is calculated by the total flow time (the total time each job stays in the work centre including processing time, and non-active time calculated from the start of the first job) divided by the number of jobs being handled. In a sense, average flow time represents the 'average inventory' of jobs.

Average number of jobs in the work centre

The average number of jobs in the work centre is the total flow time (the total time each job stays in the work centre from the start of the first job) divided by the total production time.

Number of jobs late

The number of jobs late is the number of jobs that are not completed according to the date promised to the client.

Average jobs late

The average jobs late is the number of jobs that were finished after the promised due date, divided by the total number of jobs processed in the work centre.

Number of days late

The number of days late is the total number of days that jobs are delivered after the date promised to the client.

Average days late

The average days late are the total days late divided by the number of jobs processed.

Changeover cost

The changeover cost is the total cost of making all of the machine changeovers for a group of jobs.

Preferred sequence method

There is not necessarily one optimal method, as it really depends on the circumstances but the following are some considerations.

Respecting delivery dates

An important management criterion in the supply chain is to satisfy the client. Thus, those sequencing rules which respect delivery dates, or at least minimize delays, would be the best. These sequencing rules include the critical ratio, earliest due date, and the least slack time.

First come, first served

The first come, first served rule does give customers a sense of satisfaction, and is fair when dealing with people. However, from a planning or cost point of view it is not necessarily optimal.

Shortest processing time

Using this means that at the beginning, more jobs will be completed which gives some psychological satisfaction of achievement. The disadvantage is that long-duration jobs may be continuously pushed back in the schedule in favour of the short-duration jobs.

Longest processing time

This provides the satisfaction of getting 'the worst out of the way'. However, it certainly may not be optimum.

Changeover costs

The least changeover or setup cost is an important criterion to take into consideration, providing that in applying this rule, client jobs are not delayed. Under ordinary circumstances, jobs that require similar machine setups should follow each other at a work centre. However, to minimize changeover costs, efforts should be made to implement a SMED system (see Chapter 15).

Demonstrating the concept 14.1 illustrates the use of some of the sequencing rules for various operating times and delivery dates.

Johnson's rule

Johnson's rule is a scheduling technique developed by S M Johnson of the USA in 1954 for job shop scheduling. It is used when several jobs need to be processed successively through two work centres. With more than two work centres the method is more complex but if certain criteria apply, it can be developed for three centres.[1]

Two work centres

The method establishes the best processing sequence, which will be the same for both centres, and which optimizes the use of resources and minimizes the total processing time. Type of work centres might include the following:

- Forged components that must first pass through a drilling operation, before going to milling.
- A book-binding operation where books must first pass through binding before going to trimming.
- Finished products, which must pass through inspection before going to packing.
- A medical centre where a doctor must see patients before they pass onto the x-ray department.

In applying Johnson's rule to these situations, the assumption is that there is only one resource available at each work centre such as one drilling machine, one milling machine, one binding unit, one trimmer, one inspector, one packer, one doctor, one specialist, for example.

Procedure

Assume there are two processing areas, Work centre 1, and Work centre 2. There are six jobs to be processed, A, B, C, D, E, and F:

1. Select the shortest processing time for all the operations for all jobs in both work centres. Assume the shortest processing time is for job D.
2. If the shortest processing time occurs at Work centre 1, then schedule job D first at Work centre 1 and job D would also be first at Work centre 2.

If the shortest processing time occurs at Work centre 2, then schedule job D last at Work centre 1 and also last at Work centre 2.

3. Eliminate further consideration of job D.
4. Select the shortest processing time for jobs remaining. Repeat steps 2 to 3 assigning a schedule either from the front (Work centre 1) or the back (Work centre 2) until all jobs have been allocated a schedule position.
5. If a tie for the shortest processing time occurs in different work centres, there is no problem in determining the job sequence. However, if a tie occurs in the same work centre, the competing two job sequences need to be evaluated by comparing cumulative processing times. The lowest cumulative processing time would be the recommended sequence.
6. Johnson's rule is based on the assumption that the optimum sequence is the same in Work centres 1 and 2. This implies that work cannot be carried out simultaneously on the same job in both work centres.

The use of Johnson's rule for two work centres is illustrated in Demonstrating the concept 14.2.

Three work centres

Three work centres would include an extension of the operations just given:

- Forged components that must pass through cutting, drilling, and finally milling.
- A book-binding operation where books pass through printing and binding before going to trimming.
- Finished products, which pass through polishing and inspection before going to packing.
- A medical centre where patients see a doctor, pass onto x-ray, and then consult a specialist.

Johnson's rule can be applied if either of the following two criteria applies:

1. The smallest time at the first processing operation is at least as great as the largest duration on the second processing operation.
2. The smallest duration on the third processing operation is at least as great as the largest duration on the second operation.

Procedure

To apply Johnson's rule to three work centres, for calculation purposes (see Table 14.10), the three centres are reduced to two by combining the times of each job in the Work centre 1 and 2 to give (in the lower half of

Table 14.10 Applying Johnson's rule to three work centres

Job	Work centre 1 Time (hours)	Work centre 2 Time (hours)	Work centre 3 Time (hours)
A	X_1	X_2	X_3
B	Y_1	Y_2	Y_3
C	Z_1	Z_2	Z_3

Job	Work centre [1/2] Time (hours)	Work centre [2/3] Time (hours)
A	$X_1 + X_2$	$X_2 + X_3$
B	$Y_1 + Y_2$	$Y_2 + Y_3$
C	$Z_1 + Z_2$	$Z_2 + Z_3$

the table) a Work centre [1/2] and combining the times of each job in the Work centre 2 and 3 to give a Work centre [2/3].

Then Johnson's rule is applied treating the situation as two workstations.

Assignment method of job allocation

Criteria

The assignment method of job allocation is a way of assigning tasks when there are several possibilities as, for example:

- There are several jobs waiting to be processed that can be assigned to one of various work centres.
- There are drilling jobs waiting to be processed that can be assigned to one of several numerically controlled drilling machines.
- There are many engineers in a design department who can be assigned to one of several design projects.
- There are several salespersons who can be assigned to one of several sales territories.

Objective

The objective of the assignment method is either to minimize the cost, or to maximize the profit, depending on the situation being considered. In the assignment method for job allocation the assumption is that the job can be correctly processed in any work centre. In the assignment method for personnel, the assumption is that each individual is multi-skilled and can perform any of the tasks (design or sales function) to which they would be assigned. Further, it is assumed that there are n assignments, which need to be assigned to n work centres.

Demonstrating the concept 14.3 illustrates the situation where the linear programming tool 'Solver' of Excel has been used to optimize the solution.

Run-out method of scheduling

Description

The run-out method of scheduling is a way of scheduling:

- Standard products as opposed to those that are custom made to order.
- Products that go into inventory awaiting delivery to clients, although it does not try to optimize inventory storage costs.
- When there is limited production capacity such that each product is produced in a batch quantity on the same assembly line, or the same processing unit (see Figure 14.2).

Figure 14.2 Run-out method of scheduling (Photo: Edward Rozzo. Copyright © 2002 Corbis)

The run-out method assumes that the product demand rate can be reasonably well estimated. There are two approaches:

1. products produced in fixed inventory quantities
2. aggregate run-out time method.

Products produced in fixed quantities

This approach assumes that products are produced in fixed inventory quantities either determined as a result of equipment limitations, customer requirements, or economic lot size. Run-out means determining which of the product's stock would be depleted first (run-out of stock) if production were stopped. In which case, it is this product, which is scheduled next for production. The run-out of stock is given by the relationship:

$$\text{Run-out time for Product X} = \frac{\text{Current inventory of Product X}}{\text{Customer demand for Product X}}$$

In order to apply the method for a series of products, there must be sufficient inventory available of each product to satisfy customer demand, while production of the other products is in operation.

Demonstrating the concept 14.4 illustrates the application of the run-out method when there are fixed inventory quantities.

Aggregate run-out time

The aggregate run-out time approach assumes that lot sizes are not fixed, but can be varied according to requirements. It considers all the products together, as an aggregate, and determines the aggregate time that all products will be depleted. A schedule is then developed in consideration of this time. The key steps involve:

- determining the equivalent processing time in current inventory
- determining the equivalent processing time in product demand.

Then:

$$\text{Aggregate run-out time (ART)}$$
$$= \frac{\text{Total equivalent processing hours available}}{\text{Total equivalent processing hours required}}$$
$$= \frac{\left[\begin{array}{c}\text{Equivalent processing} \\ \text{time in aggregate} \\ \text{inventory}\end{array}\right] + \left[\begin{array}{c}\text{Processing time in} \\ \text{processing period}\end{array}\right]}{\text{Processing time need by client demand}}$$

The processing time in the processing period could be say, 40 hours, or the workweek for the production operation. Demonstrating the concept 14.4 illustrates this use of the aggregate run-out time method.

Line of balance technique

The line of balance technique is a useful scheduling tool when there is a fixed quantity of a customized product which is to be delivered to a client over a period of time. The purpose of the technique is to check at various reporting periods, if the various operations in producing the final product are on schedule. That is, is the actual operation in balance with the scheduled operation. Elements of the line of balance technique include the following.

Delivery schedule

The delivery schedule includes the timing when the units of product are scheduled to be delivered to the client. A point delivery schedule is converted to a cumulative delivery schedule to serve as a control tool.

Assembly/lead time chart

This is a diagram illustrating the various activities in the assembly of the product together with the lead times. On the assembly chart are various control points indicated by a circle, square, or other symbol, showing the start or finish of an activity. These control points are analogous to the activity start or finish points in a network diagram, which is discussed more fully in Chapter 18.

Progress at a given time

Inventory levels are indicated on a histogram showing the status at any given point so that the production manager can ascertain progress.

Demonstrating the concept 14.5 illustrates the line of balance technique.

Personnel scheduling

Scheduling in services

Personnel scheduling is a planning activity in all organizations. Service operations, such as the airline industry, a full service restaurant, highway tollbooths, government offices, and supermarket checkouts, are by their very nature heavily people oriented, and scheduling is a major activity. In manufacturing firms, besides the functions that deal with tangible goods, there are support services involving personnel scheduling such as the employee restaurant, the medical centre, customer billing, computer services, or the printing department. Since the operation of a service function is labour intensive, one challenge is to optimize labour costs. However, that is not to say that service industries, with heavy capital investment such as airlines, leisure cruises, and hotels should not have a first priority to maximize facility utilization. In the service function the demand often varies according to the time of day, time during the week, or season of the year. Further, unlike manufacturing there is no buffer of inventory to smooth out fluctuations. Some scheduling possibilities for personnel include the following.

First come, first served

Using the first come, first served scheduling sequence relies on waiting lines to buffer the difference between demand and the system capacity (see Chapter 21). From a scheduling point of view, this will permit a uniform system capacity from period to period as might be the case in a supermarket, tollbooth, or a doctor's waiting room (a profession that is notorious for putting a high value on doctors' time and a low value on patients' time). This type of scheduling, often used, is advantageous to the operation of the service because it facilitates planning and costs can easily be predetermined. However, it might be unacceptable to the client if they have to wait. In a competitive situation, such as a supermarket, clients may choose to go elsewhere.

Appointment schedules

Appointment schedules to level demand would be the case in the medical profession when patients who want to visit a doctor, dentist, or other specialist make an appointment for a certain time period to satisfy the capacity of the service such as the number of doctors, or dentists available, although even scheduling does not always avoid the waiting line situation since it is not always possible to know the service time required.

Priority system

A priority system in scheduling might be applied to emergency medical care, or large orders for a good client.

Adjusting capacity

To further satisfy the needs of clients, and to avoid excessive capacity when not needed, companies strive to adjust schedules to balance the system. This often means putting more personnel in the system when demand is high, and vice versa. If part-time personnel can work alongside full-time personnel, this helps to avoid idle time:

- On the toll roads in France, there are more tollbooths open during holidays, weekends, and other heavily used periods.
- Cashiers in a hyper- or supermarket are more numerous in the lunch period, and early evening when demand is heavy.
- Hospitals schedule more emergency medical staff on Friday and Saturday evenings when demand is heavy as there are more drunks, fights, and other 'accidents'.
- In countries where stores and distribution centres are closed on Sundays there are more truck drivers on a Monday morning to supply inventory demand, which has been run down from the weekend.
- Many US banks use part-time tellers during peak hours, although this is declining with ATMs, and automatic deposit systems.

Emergency services

For emergency services such as fire departments for a city or community, or for an oil refinery complex, ambulance crews, police, and similar services provide a 24-hour full-crew coverage. During low demand periods if the crews are multi-skilled they can perform other tasks such as maintenance, office work, cleaning, etc. During peak demand, off-duty personnel, services from other communities, or even other countries might be called in. This might be the case of forest fires, earthquakes, rail disasters, or similar emergencies.

Demonstrating the concept 14.6 illustrates the development of a personnel scheduling using Excel Solver.

Computer-based advanced planning and scheduling systems (APS)

Shortcomings of ERP/MRP systems

Many firms in business-to-business relationships in the supply chain are using website transactions in order to respond better and faster to their clients' needs, which can change frequently. The major weaknesses of the MRP-based systems include:[2]

- MRP assume that lead times are known constants and do not vary with flow and work load (see also the section on scheduling and constraints in Chapter 22).
- The system requires fixed processes or routings, ignoring alternative processes that could be used.
- The sequencing logic prioritizes orders only by period or date when other options such as minimum setup times or load smoothing are perhaps preferred.

- All work is loaded under assumption of infinite capacity when in reality, working capacity is always constrained by the resources available, although if this occurs, the feedback loop of the MRP system is brought into play.
- The process of schedule regeneration takes considerable time to calculate, review and then process the recommended actions. As a result, many firms are only able to generate their material requirements on a monthly basis. This is insufficient as client demands often require firms to implement daily changes in supply chain requirements.

Basis of APS systems

Artificial intelligence (see Chapter 7) has to a certain extent enabled the development of APS systems. The scheduling solutions are based on mathematical formulae, or algorithms that crunch data entered into the APS model going through numerous iterations of production schedules, adjusting to accommodate the constraints each time, until they produce an optimal schedule for meeting delivery dates while also making the most efficient use of all resources. The relevant constraints may include the availability of machines, raw materials, components, labour, tools, moulds, plus energy requirements, setup times, earliest possible start times and client due dates. Full scheduling can be performed in a matter of seconds by simply selecting certain menu items. The iterations can be performed quickly because unlike MRP they do not rely on databases to store and locate the data they use to perform calculations. Instead, they keep the most current information about availability and movement of resources in memory thus avoiding repetitive read-and-write transactions to and from a database.

APS systems in the business–to–business supply chain

APS systems coupled to the web in business-to-business transactions can reduce the cycle time and cost of administration as the APS can formulate rapidly the precise time and date that direct materials and items are required for use. A supplier can consult the client's requirement and if all the resources such as capacity and material are available the APS system will schedule the order in real time. This information can then directly be communicated to the client with the exact delivery date and time confirmed. This open connection is the normal way for B2B to be undertaken whether it is for internal clients/suppliers on the intranet or external clients/suppliers on the Internet. APS makes it possible to update schedules daily or continuously which translates into shorter lead times in the supply chain, reduced inventory, and faster customer response. Constantly updating scheduling runs, or reducing their cycle time, ensures that the updated schedules are correct. If schedules are developed using information that is, say, a week old it may add a week to the process. The longer the scheduling cycle time the greater the chance of producing the wrong item, in the wrong quantity and at the wrong date.

Summary of key elements

• Scheduling involves the preparation of a timetable for work that needs doing to meet client need dates, or for activities to meet some desired objective.

• A Gantt chart (also known as a bar chart) is a tool that indicates work scheduled for certain time periods, how much is completed according to plan, and who performed the work. Using a Gantt chart, an operations or production manager can see if resources can be modified to ensure that activities are kept on schedule.

• Order sequencing is used to decide the optimum order for processing jobs or people. Sequencing rules include: first come, first served; earliest due date; shortest processing time; longest processing time; last arrived, first processed; least slack time; critical ratio; and least changeover cost where setups are involved.

• An important criterion is client satisfaction, thus, those sequencing rules which respect delivery dates, or at least minimize delays such as critical ratio, earliest due date, and least slack time are often the most appropriate.

• Johnson's rule is a scheduling method when several jobs need to be processed successively through two work centres. If certain criteria apply, it can be adapted to three work centres.

• The assignment scheduling method is to assign personnel or jobs to certain activities, or work posts, to minimize the cost, or to maximize the profit.

• The run-out method of scheduling determines which product to process next to avoid running out of stock. There are two approaches: one considering fixed inventory quantities, the other the aggregate run-out time.

• The line of balance technique is a scheduling tool when there is a fixed quantity of a customized product to be delivered over a period of time. The technique checks at various reporting periods, if operations producing the final product are on schedule or, if the actual operation is in 'balance' with the scheduled operation.

• Scheduling possibilities for personnel include first come, first served, appointment schedules, a priority system, adjusting capacity, or using emergency services.

• Advanced planning scheduling systems are based on artificial intelligence and can produce in real-time optimum schedules taking into account all the resource constraints. Coupled to the web they can increase customer reliability in B2B supply chain transactions.

Notes and references

1. JOHNSON, S. M., 'Optimal and three-stage production schedules with set-up times included', *Naval Research Logistics Quarterly*, 1954, pp 61–8
2. FERRAR, Andy, 'Advanced planning and scheduling in the online world – APS and B2B', *Control*, The Institute of Operations Management, UK, May 2001, pp 7–9

Review and discussion topics

1. Gantt chart
Prepare a Gantt scheduling chart for your activities for the forthcoming month. Indicate on the schedule those that are:
  (a) value-added activities
  (b) non-value-added activities (but necessary, eating, sleeping, etc.)
  (c) idle time.
  After the Gantt chart has been prepared, analyze it and see if any improvements can be made to increase the proportion of value-added activities.

2. Information technology
Discuss how information technology has improved scheduling in both service and manufacturing industries.

3. Unplanned occurrences
What are some of the unplanned occurrences that can upset the scheduling for the following operations?
  (a) airline transportation, such as British Airways or American Airlines
  (b) automobile construction, such as Ford Motor or Renault
  (c) a hotel such as the Hilton Hotel or Motel 6
  (d) storage and distribution
  (e) pharmaceutical production such as Aventis or Bayer
  (f) a major hospital.

4. Supply chain
Discuss the repercussions in the integrated supply chain of poor scheduling for firms such as the following. Consider both the operating firm, and the clients:
  (a) Benetton (clothing)
  (b) Boeing (aircraft manufacturer)
  (c) Arcelor (steel products)
  (d) Nestlé (food products).

5. Layout and scheduling
Discuss the impact of facility layout and site selection on operations scheduling. Give illustrations for both manufacturing and service firms.

Demonstrating the concept 14.1 Carver

Situation

Carver and Son operate a small print shop in the Chico area of northern California, where they have an offset printer to perform work for customers. By scheduling the personnel, they are able to operate the print shop 7 days a week at 8 hours a day. The eight hours is for printing jobs. Setup time for change-over of jobs is performed on overtime, either in the evening, or early morning. Orders received are put on backlog until current scheduled work has been completed. At February 24 (day 55), jobs waiting to be processed are shown in Table 14.11.

Required

1. Develop the schedule using a first come, first served sequencing rule.
2. Develop the schedule using the method of critical ratio established at the start before any jobs are processed.
3. Develop the schedule using the method of a dynamic critical ratio that is modified each time a job is processed.

For all cases, prepare a Gantt chart for these two rules and determine:

- total elapsed flow time (time to process all jobs from day 55)

Table 14.11 Carver: Job processing waiting times

Job	A	B	C	D	E	F
Process time	9	11	8	12	7	5
Date received	39	42	47	48	37	55
Date due	71	81	75	98	86	108

- average flow time/job, or average completion time/job (total flow time/number of jobs in system)
- average jobs in system (total flow time/total processing time)
- number of jobs late
- average days late (total days late/total number of jobs).

Solution

With a seven-day work schedule, and the assumption that there are no vacation days, there is sufficient time to process all the jobs by the end of the last due date:

- Total processing time necessary: $(9 + 11 + 8 + 12 + 7 + 5) = 52$ days
- Processing time available: $(108 - 55 + 1) = 54$ days

First come, first served

Here the jobs are processed according to the date they are received. This sequence is given in Table 14.12 and Figure 14.3. The explanation of the terms is as shown in Table 14.13.

For this sequencing rule there are three jobs late with a total of 20 days late for the three jobs giving an average lateness for the six jobs job processed of 3.33 days per job.

Critical ratio (developed and fixed before any jobs are processed)

The critical ratio is given by:

$$\text{Critical ratio} = \frac{\text{Time to the due date}}{\text{Process time}}$$

- For Job A, this is $(71 - 55)/9 = 1.78$.
- For Job B, this is $(81 - 55)/11 = 2.36$.
- Etc.

Figure 14.3 Gantt chart for Carver: First come, first served

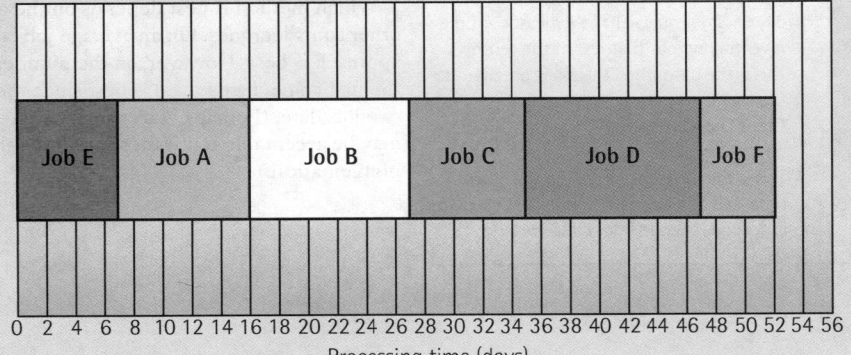

Table 14.12 Carver: First come first served

Today's date			55					
First come first served								
Job		E	A	B	C	D	F	Total
Process time		7	9	11	8	12	5	52
Date received		37	39	42	47	48	55	0
Date due		86	71	81	75	98	108	0
Flow time (time in centre)*		7	16	27	35	47	52	184
Date finished		62	71	82	90	102	107	0
Days late		0	0	1	15	4	0	20

*After the schedule has been developed, not from when the order has been received.

FCFS

Number of jobs processed	6	
Total flow time	184	
Average flow time	30.67	(Total flow time)/ (Number of jobs processed)
Average jobs in system	3.54	(Total flow time)/ (Total process time)
Number of jobs late	3	
Average number of jobs late	0.5	(Number of jobs late)/ (Number of jobs processed)
Number of days late	20	
Average days late	3.33	(Number of days late)/ (Number of jobs processed)

Table 14.13 Explanation of terms in Table 14.12

Process time	This is the time needed to complete each of the six jobs
Flow time	This represents the time that the jobs rest in the centre, based on the start date of day 55. It is equivalent to a measure of the *inventory* of jobs that rest at the centre
Due date	This is the date when the job is promised to the client
Date finished	This is the start date of the job plus the processing time
Days late	This is the difference between the date promised and the date finished. If the value is positive, then the days late are zero

Here the sequence is given in Table 14.14. The explanation for the terms is the same as for the first come, first served method. The Gantt chart is in Figure 14.4. For this sequencing rule there are two jobs late, with a total of 24 days late for the three jobs giving an average lateness for the six jobs job processed of 4.00 days per job.

Critical ratio (calculated after each job is processed)
The critical ratio is, once again, given by:

$$\text{Critical ratio} = \frac{\text{Time to the due date}}{\text{Process time}}$$

The critical ratios are calculated first for all the jobs and the one with the lowest critical ratio is put first. In this case it is still Job A, with a critical ratio of 1.78. Now A will take nine hours to process and so this will bring the new start date up to 64 (55 + 9). So the critical ratios are recalculated for the remaining jobs. For example:

- For Job B, this is (81 − 64)/11 = 1.55.
- For Job C, this is (75 − 64)/8 = 1.38.
- Etc.

Thus the next job to be scheduled is the one with the lowest critical ratio. In this case, it is Job C. Now when C is processed it will bring the new start date up to 72 (55 + 9 + 8). Thus the new critical ratios are calculated for the remaining jobs. For example:

- For Job E, this is (86 − 72)/7 = 2.00.

Again, from the jobs remaining, the next to be processed is the one with the lowest critical ratio. The process is repeated until the sequence for all the jobs has been established. Here, the sequence is given in Table 14.15. The Gantt chart is in Figure 14.5. For this sequencing rule, there are three jobs late with a total of ten days late for the three jobs giving an average lateness for the six jobs job processed of 1.67 days per job.

Which method is best depends on the customer and other considerations. On an average job lateness, the last approach is best. However, on the number of jobs late, the first come, first served is best since there are just two jobs late. (Perhaps two customers receiving late jobs may be acceptable but if there are three that could be problematical.)

Table 14.14 Carver: Critical ratio (established before jobs are processed)

Today's date   55
Critical ratio (non-dynamic)

Job	A	B	C	D	E	F	Total
Process time	9	11	8	12	7	5	52
Date received	39	42	47	48	37	55	
Date due	71	81	75	98	86	108	
Critical ratio	1.78	2.36	2.50	3.58	4.43	10.60	
Flow time (time in centre)*	9	20	28	40	47	52	196
Date finished	64	75	83	95	102	107	
Days late	0	0	8	0	16	0	24

*After the schedule has been developed, not from when the order has been received

	CR	
Number of jobs processed	6	
Total flow time	196	
Average flow time	32.67	(Total flow time)/(Number of jobs processed)
Average jobs in system	3.77	(Total flow time)/(Total process time)
Number of jobs late	2	
Average number of jobs late	0.33	(Number of jobs late)/(Number of jobs processed)
Number of days late	24	
Average days late	4.00	(Number of days late)/(Number of jobs processed)

Figure 14.4 Gantt chart for Carver: Critical ratio established before jobs are processed

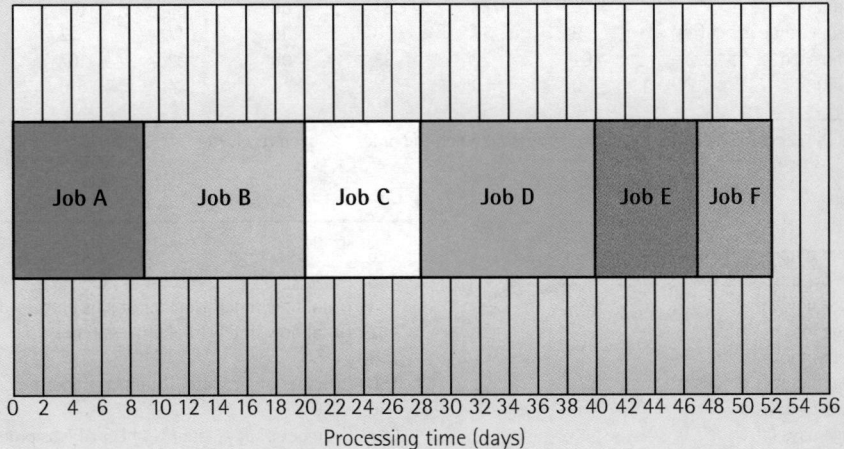

Processing time (days)

Table 14.15 Carver: Dynamic critical ratio

Today's date (start date)   55
Critical ratio (dynamic)

Job	A	B	C	D	E	F	
Process time	9	11	8	12	7	5	
Date received	39	42	47	48	37	55	
Date due	71	81	75	98	86	108	
Critical ratio (1)	1.78	2.36	2.50	3.58	4.43	10.60	
Sequence (1)	A	B	C	D	E	F	
Remaining		B	C	D	E	F	
New start date		64	64	64	64	64	
Critical ratio (2)		1.55	1.38	2.83	3.14	8.80	
Sequence (2)		C	B	D	E	F	
Remaining			B	D	E	F	
New start date			72	72	72	72	
Process time			11	12	7	5	
Date due			81	98	86	108	
Critical ratio (3)			0.82	2.17	2.00	7.20	
Sequence (3)			B	E	D	F	
Remaining				E	D	F	
New start date				83	83	83	
Process time				7	12	5	
Date due				86	98	108	
Critical ratio (4)				0.43	1.25	5.00	
Sequence (4)				E	D	F	
Remaining					D	F	
New start date					90	90	
Process time					12	5	
Date due					98	108	
Critical ratio (4)					0.67	3.60	
Sequence (5)					D	F	
Actual sequence	A	C	B	E	D	F	Total
Process time	9	8	11	7	12	5	52
Date due	71	75	81	86	98	108	
Flow time (time in centre)*	9	17	28	35	47	52	188
Date finished	64	72	83	90	102	107	
Days late	0	0	2	4	4	0	10

*After the schedule has been developed, not from when the order has been received

	CR	
Number of jobs processed	6	
Total flow time	188	
Average flow time	31.33	(Total flow time)/(Number of jobs processed)
Average jobs in system	3.62	(Total flow time)/(Total process time)
Number of jobs late	3	
Average number of jobs late	0.50	(Number of jobs late)/(Number of jobs processed)
Number of days late	10	
Average days late	1.67	(Number of days late)/(Number of jobs processed)

Figure 14.5 Gantt chart for Carver: Dynamic critical ratio

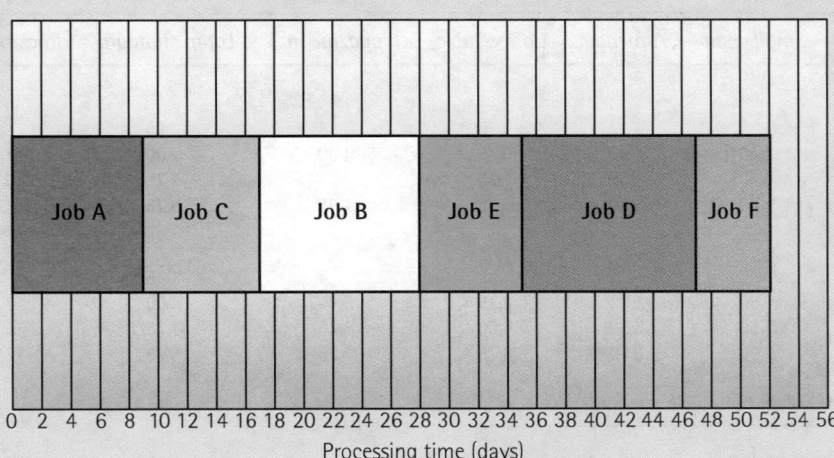

Demonstrating the concept 14.2   Kneier Company

Situation

The Kneier Company is a small family firm that manufactures customized items of wood furniture. Raw lumber arrives at the factory where it is cut to length, turned, and shaped according to customer specifications in work centre 1. From work centre 1 jobs pass to work centre 2, where the components are assembled and finished. Assembly involves mounting the components either using tongue and groove joints or gluing. Finishing is the final sanding, polishing, and/or varnishing. The staff is limited, and work crews can work on only one job at a time. On one particular Monday morning, six jobs were waiting to be processed (see Table 14.16). They were all for the same client and were to be delivered together.

Required

1. Using the first come, first served sequencing rule, develop a planning schedule for work centres 1 and 2. After what elapsed time can the client expect the total six jobs to be completed? Present the schedule on a Gantt chart.
2. Using Johnson's sequencing rule, develop a planning schedule for work centres 1 and 2. After what elapsed time can the client expect the total six jobs to be completed? Present the schedule on a Gantt chart.

3. Compare the schedule under first come, first served with that of Johnson's Rule.

Table 14.16 Kneier Company: Job processing list

Item	Order of arrival	Work centre 1 Job time (hours)	Work centre 2 Job time (hours)
Small chair	1	1.50	0.50
Armchair	2	4.00	1.00
Coffee table	3	0.75	2.25
Magazine rack	4	1.00	3.00
Lamp standard	5	2.00	4.00
Rocking chair	6	1.80	2.20

Solution

1. Table 14.17 gives the calculation procedure for this schedule and Figure 14.6 gives the Gantt chart.

Using this scheduling rule all the jobs will be finished after 17.95 hours. There are three idle periods in the operation. There is a time of 1.50 hours in work centre 2 before the first job, the small chair, can start. Also in work centre 2 there is a time of 3.50 hours, since the second job, the

Table 14.17 Kneier Company: First come, first served

Job	Small chair	Armchair	Coffee table	Magazine rack	Lamp standard	Rocking chair	Total
Work centre 1							
Order of arrival	1	2	3	4	5	6	
Process time, hr	1.50	4.00	0.75	1.00	2.00	1.80	**11.05**
Start time, hr	0.00	1.50	5.50	6.25	7.25	9.25	
Finish time, hr	1.50	5.50	6.25	7.25	9.25	11.05	
Work centre 2							
Order of arrival	1	2	3	4	5	6	
Process time, hr	0.50	1.00	2.25	3.00	4.00	2.20	**12.95**
Start time, hr	1.50	5.50	6.50	8.75	11.75	15.75	
Finish time, hr	2.00	6.50	8.75	11.75	15.75	17.95	

Summary or process and idle times

Work centre	1	2	Total
Idle time	0	1.50	**1.50**
Small chair	1.50	0.50	**2.00**
Idle time	0.00	3.50	**3.50**
Armchair	4.00	1.00	**5.00**
Coffee table	0.75	2.25	**3.00**
Magazine rack	1.00	3.00	**4.00**
Lamp standard	2.00	4.00	**6.00**
Rocking chair	1.80	2.20	**4.00**
Idle time	6.90	0	**6.90**
Elapsed time	17.95	17.95	
Total idle time	6.90	5.00	**11.90**

Figure 14.6 Bar chart for Kneier Company: First come, first served

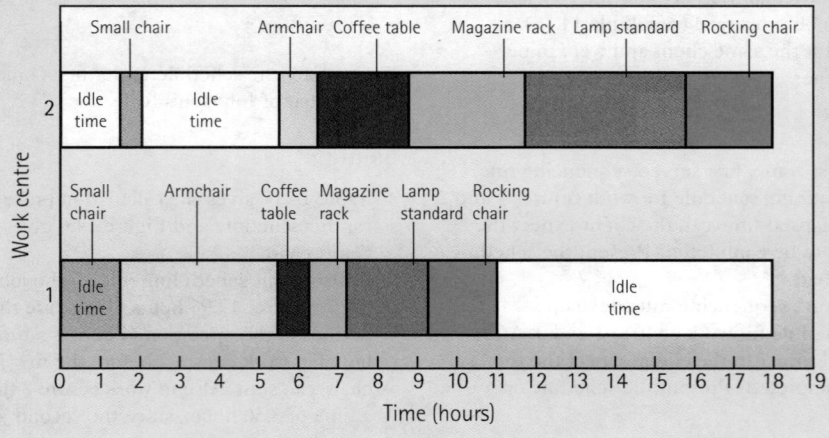

Table 14.18   Kneier Company: Johnson's rule

Job	Coffee table	Magazine rack	Rocking chair	Lamp standard	Armchair	Small chair	Total
Work centre 1							
Order of arrival	3	4	6	5	2	1	
Order with Johnson	1	2	3	4	5	6	
Process time, hr	0.75	1.00	1.80	2.00	4.00	1.50	11.05
Start time, hr	0.00	0.75	1.75	3.55	5.55	9.55	
Finish time, hr	0.75	1.75	3.55	5.55	9.55	11.05	
Work centre 2							
Order of arrival	3	4	6	5	2	1	
Order with Johnson	1	2	3	4	5	6	
Process time, hr	2.25	3.00	2.20	4.00	1.00	0.50	12.95
Start time, hr	0.75	3.00	6.00	8.20	12.20	13.20	
Finish time, hr	3.00	6.00	8.20	12.20	13.20	13.70	

Summary or process and idle times

Work centre	1	2	Total
Idle time	0.00	0.75	**0.75**
Coffee table	0.75	2.25	**3.00**
Idle time	0.00	0.00	**0.00**
Magazine rack	1.00	3.00	**4.00**
Rocking chair	1.80	2.20	**4.00**
Lamp standard	2.00	4.00	**6.00**
Armchair	4.00	1.00	**5.00**
Small chair	1.50	0.50	**2.00**
Idle time	2.65	0.00	**2.65**
Elapsed time	13.70	13.70	
Total idle time	2.65	0.75	**3.40**

armchair, has not been finished in work centre 1. Finally, there is an idle time of 6.90 hours in work centre 1 until the jobs are finished in work centre 2. This is a total idle time of 11.90 hours in both work centres.

2. Table 14.18 gives the calculation procedure for this schedule and Figure 14.7 gives the Gantt chart. The order of processing is arrived at as follows:
• The smallest processing time out of all of the times is 0.50 hours for the small chair. Since this time occurs in work centre 2 this job is scheduled last.
• The next smallest processing time out of all of the jobs remaining is 0.75 hours for the coffee table. Since this time occurs in work centre 1 this job is scheduled first.
• The next smallest processing time out of all of the jobs remaining is 1.00 hour for the magazine

rack in Work centre 1 or 1.00 hour for the armchair in Work centre 2. Since the times occur in different work centres there is no conflict. The magazine rack will follow the coffee table and the armchair will immediately precede the small chair.
• The next smallest processing time out of all of the jobs remaining is 1.80 hours for the rocking chair. Since this time occurs in Work centre 1 this job is scheduled after the magazine rack.
• The job remaining is the lamp standard and this is scheduled after the rocking chair and before the armchair.

Using this scheduling rule all the jobs will be finished after 13.70 hours. There are two idle periods in the operation. There is a time of 0.75 hours in work centre 2 before the first job, the coffee table, can start. In Work centre 1, there is an idle time of

Figure 14.7 Bar chart for Kneier Company: Johnson's rule

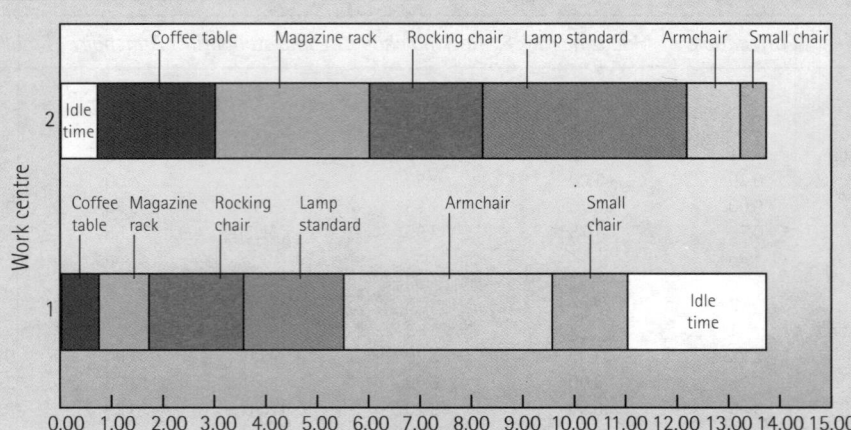

2.65 hours before all the jobs are finished in work centre 2. This is a total idle time of 3.40 hours in both work centres.

3. If the two rules are compared, using Johnson's rule means that total elapsed time has been reduced from 17.95 hours to 13.70 hours or almost 24% (23.68%):
   • Idle time in work centre 1 has been reduced from 6.90 hours to 2.65 hours, or almost 62% (61.59%).
   • Idle time in work centre 2 has been reduced from 5.00 hours to 0.75 hours, or 85%.

• Total idle time for the whole operation has been reduced from 11.90 hours to 3.40 hours, or about 71% (71.43%).

Johnson's rule takes into account processing times for all jobs and has the objective of minimizing idle times at both centres. In practice, with proper planning, the idle time at the end of Work centre 1 for both schemes can be allocated to work on other assignments.

Demonstrating the concept 14.3 Biodecta

Situation

The Biodecta company in Birmingham, England, performs research and development on genetic recombination. The Manager of the Research Division, Jacques Enorme, has identified five biotechnology programmes for the forthcoming year. These are:

• the improvement of the production of wheat
• the modification of the growth of tomatoes
• a new blood-testing technique

• a biodegradable plastic
• a perfume made from the sweat of pigs.

There are five teams at the centre managed by John Jordan, Sally Stock, Mandy Mooner, Brian Brains, and Lucia Label. Each of the five teams is relatively polyvalent, such they are able to work on any of the five projects. The manager has estimated costs, in thousands of pounds, for the first phase for each research project, according to which team carries out the work (see Table 14.19).

Table 14.19 Biodecta: Research project costs (base data)

Project	Wheat	Tomatoes	Blood	Plastic	Perfume
Team					
Jordan	624	1440	228	468	828
Stock	588	1428	252	456	876
Mooner	780	1380	216	444	804
Brains	660	1404	264	480	828
Label	600	1464	240	432	816

Required

Considering only the costs given in the table, what would be the optimum way to schedule these projects? What is the corresponding minimum cost?

Solution

Optimum way to schedule these projects: Table 14.20 gives two possible solutions for this project.

Alternative N° 1
- Sally Stock would be assigned to the improvement of the production of wheat.
- Mandy Mooner would be assigned to the modification of the growth of tomatoes.
- John Jordan would be assigned to the new blood-testing technique.
- Lucia Label would be assigned to the biodegradable plastic.
- Brian Brains would be assigned to the perfume made from the sweat of pigs.

The total (minimum cost) for the five projects is £3,456,000.

Alternative N° 2
- Sally Stock would be assigned to the improvement of the production of wheat.
- Brian Brains would be assigned to the modification of the growth of tomatoes.
- John Jordan would be assigned to the new blood-testing technique.
- Lucia Label would be assigned to the biodegradable plastic.
- Mandy Mooner would be assigned to the perfume made from the sweat of pigs.

The total (minimum cost) for the five projects is £3,456,000.

Setting up framework

The framework for the two alternatives is set up in the following way:

- The upper table (rows 1 to 8) gives the setup for the job assignments. The variables to be solved are in the matrix [B-2] ... [F-6]. Before starting the simulation these values are given a value of 0.
- The centre table (rows 11 to 18) gives the matrix for the job costs established for the problem.
- The bottom tables (rows 21 to 28 for Alternative 1) and (rows 31 to 38 for Alternative 2) gives the allocation of job assignments.
- The objective is to minimize the cost. In Solver, the value in Cell [G-28] for Alternative 1, and Cell [G-38] for Alternative 2 is set to be a minimum.
- For Alternative 1, Cell [G-28] contains the formula [B-28] + [C-28] + [D-28] + [E-28] + [F-28].
- For Alternative 1, Cell [B-28] contains the formula [B-2]*[B-12] + [B-3]*[B-13] + [B-4]*[B-14] + [B-5]*[B-15] + [B-6]*[B-16].
- For Alternative 1, Cells [C-28], [D-28], [E-28], and [F-28] contain the similar formula to [B-28] for the corresponding column.

The constraints for the problem are that the defined variables have a value:

- greater or equal to 0
- less than or equal to 1
- that comprises whole numbers.

This effectively means that they take on the value of either 1 or 0.

- Cell [B-8] is given the constraint that it is equal to 1. This cell contains the formula (sum of column Cells [B-2] through [B-6]). The constraint and formula is similar for Cells [C-8] through [F-8].
- Cell [G-2] is given the formula (sum of Cells [B-2], [C-2], [D-2], [E-2], and [F-2]).
- Cells [G-3] through [G-6] are assigned similar formulae.

Thus the setup arrangement for Solver is binomial. When 1 appears in a variable cell, it means that the corresponding job has been assigned. When 0 appears, it indicates that no job has been assigned.

Table 14.20 Biodecta: Job assignments using Excel Solver

	A	B	C	D	E	F	G
1		Wheat	Tomatoes	Blood	Plastic	Perfume	Total
2	Jordon	0	0	1	0	0	1
3	Stock	1	0	0	0	0	1
4	Mooner	0	1	0	0	0	1
5	Brains	0	0	0	0	1	1
6	Label	0	0	0	1	0	1
7							
8	Total	1	1	1	1	1	5
9							
10	Cost (minimum is shown for alternative 1)						
11		Wheat	Tomatoes	Blood	Plastic	Perfume	Total
12	Jordon	624	1,440	228	468	828	
13	Stock	588	1,428	252	456	876	
14	Mooner	780	1,380	216	444	804	
15	Brains	660	1,404	264	480	828	
16	Label	600	1,464	240	432	816	
17							
18	Cost	588	1,380	228	432	828	3,456
19							
20	Assignment (alternative 1)						
21		Wheat	Tomatoes	Blood	Plastic	Perfume	Total
22	Jordon	0	0	228	0	0	
23	Stock	588	0	0	0	0	
24	Mooner	0	1,380	0	0	0	
25	Brains	0	0	0	0	828	
26	Label	0	0	0	432	0	
27							
28	Cost	588	1,380	228	432	828	3,456
29							
30	Assignment (alternative 2)						
31		Wheat	Tomatoes	Blood	Plastic	Perfume	Total
32	Jordon	0	0	228	0	0	
33	Stock	588	0	0	0	0	
34	Mooner	0	0	0	0	804	
35	Brains	0	1,404	0	0	0	
36	Label	0	0	0	432	0	
37							
38	Cost	588	1,404	228	432	804	3,456

Demonstrating the concept 14.4 Toubon Co.

Situation

The Toubon Co., just outside Namur in Belgium, is a family-owned operation that makes its own named brand chocolate bars. The company has a steady business but has limited production capacity. Toubon's most popular chocolate bars are milk, black, brandy filled, nut, and cherry filled and these can only be manufactured on one production line. Producing the bars basically involves mixing the chocolate, adding the ingredients, moulding, cooling, wrapping, and packaging. On one particular Friday evening the operating data for the five varieties of chocolate bars are as shown in Table 14.21.

- Run size was the number of 100-gram bars of chocolate produced each time the equipment was set up. Differences were generally due to the limitations of the equipment available for the various chocolate recipes.
- Production time was the time from mixing to final wrapping of the bars.
- Demand per week in units, or number of 100-gram bars, was the estimated demand from the work centre to the various distribution centres in Belgium.
- Current inventory was the quantity of wrapped 100-gram chocolate bars in final product storage at the Toubon production centre.

Required

1. Using the run-out method for fixed lot sizes, develop a production schedule for the next nine production runs. Show the production schedule on a Gantt chart. Assume weekly demand is based on 40 hours a week, but also assume a continuous production programme.
2. Using an aggregate run-out time method (lot sizes are not fixed) develop a production schedule for the

next five weeks. Show the production schedule on a Gantt chart. Assume 40 hours of production time a week.

Solution

1. Production schedule using the run-out method for fixed lot sizes: solution is given in Table 14.22 and the Gantt chart is in Figure 14.8. These are developed as follows:
   - The run-out time is calculated for each type of chocolate bar using the ratio:

$$\text{Run-out time (hours)} = \frac{\text{Current inventory}}{\text{Demand per week}/40}$$

   - Production is scheduled first for that product which has the least run-out time. For the first production load this is the nut chocolate [Cell (F-7)]. Here the run-out time is given by:

$$(11{,}000/6000) * 40 = 73.33 \text{ hours}$$

(multiply by 40 since demand is in weeks).
   - Production time is 25.00 hours. During production of nut chocolate, inventory is being used according to the demand rate for all of the products. For example, for milk chocolate, in 25 hours 6250 units are taken out of inventory for the customer (10,000/40) * 25. Thus the inventory remaining is 30,000 − 6250 = 23,750 units (Cell [E-17]). For the nut chocolate, the inventory demand by customers in 25 hours is 3750 units (6000/40) * 25. However, during this period a quantity of 15,000 units is produced. Thus the inventory remaining after production is 11,000 − 3750 + 15,000 = 22,250 (Cell [E-20]). The final inventory at the end of the first production run for all five products is given in Cells [E-17] through [E-21].
   - The run-out calculation is then repeated after the first production load. In this case, it is the brandy-filled chocolate that must be scheduled for the second production load (Cell [F-19]).
   - The planning schedule is thus developed each time making the run-out test after a production run.

The five-week planning schedule is giving in the cell matrix [A-121]··[C-129] and illustrated as a Gantt chart in the figure.

2. Using an aggregate run-out time method: solution is given in Table 14.23 and Figure 14.9. These are developed as follows:
   - The first section of the table entitled start, and schedule for the first week gives the initial

Table 14.21 Toubon Co.: Operating data for five chocolate bars

	Run or lot size (units)	Production time (hours)	Weekly demand (units)	Current inventory (units)
Milk	24,000	30.00	10,000	30,000
Black	20,000	18.00	8,000	19,000
Brandy filled	18,000	24.00	4,000	9,000
Nut	15,000	25.00	6,000	11,000
Cherry filled	17,500	21.00	3,200	7,500

Table 14.22 Toubon Co.: Products produced in fixed inventory quantity

	A	B	C	D	E	F
1	**Start**	Run size	Production time (hours)	Weekly demand (units)	Current inventory (units)	Run-out time (hours)
2						
3						
4	Milk	24,000	30.00	10,000	30,000	120.00
5	Dark	20,000	18.00	8,000	19,000	95.00
6	Brandy filled	18,000	24.00	4,000	9,000	90.00
7	Nut	15,000	25.00	6,000	11,000	73.33
8	Cherry filled	17,500	21.00	3,200	7,500	93.75
9						
10	Min run-out time	73.33				
11	Schedule	**Nut**	1st production run			
12	Production time	25.00				
13						
14	**1st production load**		Inventory remaining (units)	New production (units)	Total inventory (units)	Run-out time (hours)
15						
16						
17	Milk		23,750	0	23,750	95.00
18	Dark		14,000	0	14,000	70.00
19	Brandy filled		6,500	0	6,500	65.00
20	Nut		7,250	15,000	22,250	148.33
21	Cherry filled		5,500	0	5,500	68.75
22						
23	Min run-out time	65.00				
24	Schedule	**Brandy filled**	2nd production run			
25	Production time	24.00				
26						
27	**2nd production load**		Inventory remaining (units)	New production (units)	Total inventory (units)	Run-out time (hours)
28						
29						
30	Milk		17,750	0	17,750	71.00
31	Dark		9,200	0	9,200	46.00
32	Brandy filled		4,100	18,000	22,100	221.00
33	Nut		18,650	0	18,650	124.33
34	Cherry filled		3,580	0	3,580	44.75
35						
36	Min run-out time	44.75				
37	Schedule	**Cherry filled**	3rd production run			
38	Production time	21.00				
39						

(Continued)

Table 14.22 (Continued)

	A	B	C	D	E	F
40	**3rd production load**		Inventory remaining (units)	New production (units)	Total inventory (units)	Run-out time (hours)
41						
42						
43	Milk		12,500	0	12,500	50.00
44	Dark		5,000	0	5,000	25.00
45	Brandy filled		20,000	0	20,000	200.00
46	Nut		15,500	0	15,500	103.33
47	Cherry filled		1,900	17,500	19,400	242.50
48						
49	Min run-out time	25.00				
50	Schedule	**Dark**	4th production run			
51	Production time	18.00				
52						
53	**4th production load**		Inventory remaining (units)	New production (units)	Total inventory (units)	Run-out time (hours)
54						
55						
56	Milk		8,000	0	8,000	32.00
57	Dark		1,400	20,000	21,400	107.00
58	Brandy filled		18,200	0	18,200	182.00
59	Nut		12,800	0	12,800	85.33
60	Cherry filled		17,960	0	17,960	224.50
61						
62	Min run-out time	32.00				
63	Schedule	**Milk**	5th production run			
64	Production time	30.00				
65						
66	**5th production load**		Inventory remaining (units)	New production (units)	Total inventory (units)	Run-out time (hours)
67						
68						
69	Milk		500	24,000	24,500	98.00
70	Dark		15,400	0	15,400	77.00
71	Brandy filled		15,200	0	15,200	152.00
72	Nut		8,300	0	8,300	55.33
73	Cherry filled		15,560	0	15,560	194.50
74						
75	Min run-out time	55.33				
76	Schedule	**Nut**	6th production run			
77	Production time	25.00				
78						

(Continued)

Table 14.22 (Continued)

	A	B	C	D	E	F
79	**6th production load**		Inventory remaining (units)	New production (units)	Total inventory (units)	Run-out time (hours)
80						
81						
82	Milk		18,250	0	18,250	73.00
83	Dark		10,400	0	10,400	52.00
84	Brandy filled		12,700	0	12,700	127.00
85	Nut		4,550	15,000	19,550	130.33
86	Cherry filled		13,560	0	13,560	169.50
87						
88	Min run-out time	52.00				
89	Schedule	**Dark**	7th production run			
90	Production time	18.00				
91						
92						
93	**7th production load**	.	Inventory remaining (units)	New production (units)	Total inventory (units)	Run-out time (hours)
94						
95						
96	Milk		13,750	0	13,750	55.00
97	Dark		6,800	20,000	26,800	134.00
98	Brandy filled		10,900	0	10,900	109.00
99	Nut		16,850	0	16,850	112.33
100	Cherry filled		12,120	0	12,120	151.50
101						
102	Min run-out time	55.00				
103	Schedule	**Milk**	8th production run			
104	Production time	30.00				
105						
106	**8th production load**		Inventory remaining (units)	New production (units)	Total inventory (units)	Run-out time (hours)
107						
108						
109	Milk		6,250	24,000	30,250	121.00
110	Dark		20,800	0	20,800	104.00
111	Brandy filled		7,900	0	7,900	79.00
112	Nut		12,350	0	12,350	82.33
113	Cherry filled		9,720	0	9,720	121.50
114						
115	Min run-out time	79.00				
116	Schedule	**Brandy filled**	9th production run			
117	Production time	24.00				
118						

(Continued)

Table 14.22 (Continued)

	A	B	C	D	E	F
119	Product	Time (hours)	Time (weeks)			
120						
121	Nut	25	0.63			
122	Brandy filled	24	0.60			
123	Cherry filled	21	0.53			
124	Dark	18	0.45			
125	Milk	30	0.75			
126	Nut	25	0.63			
127	Dark	18	0.45			
128	Milk	30	0.75			
129	Brandy filled	24	0.60			
130						
131	**Total**	**215**	**5.38**			

Figure 14.8 Toubon Co.: Run-out method: Production in fixed inventory quantities

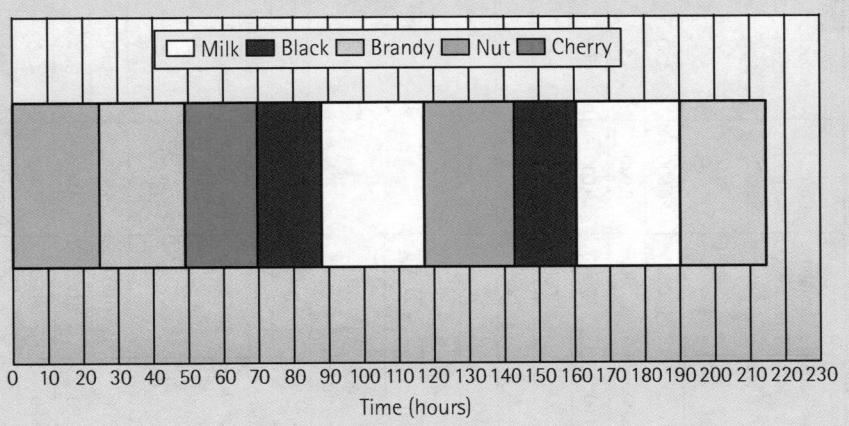

Time (hours)

data and the development of the aggregate run-out time.

• Columns B, run size, and C, production time for lot, are not considered in this scheduling method, but are used to calculate column F, production time per unit is given as follows:

$$\text{Production time per unit, secs} = \frac{\left[\begin{array}{c}\text{Production time}\\\text{for lot}\end{array}\right]}{\text{Run size}}$$

For example, the production time per unit for milk chocolate is 4.5 sec (30 * 60 * 60/24000) (Cell [F-6]).

• Equivalent production time in inventory (column G) is the amount of processing time represented by the inventory and is given by the product (current inventory * production time per unit). For example the 30,000 units of inventory for milk chocolate is equivalent to 37.5 hours [(30,000 * 4.5/60 * 60)] (Cell [G-6]).

Table 14.23 Toubon Co.: Aggregate run-out time scheduling

Start, and schedule for 1st week

	A	B	C	D	E	F	G	H	I	J	K
1	Product	Run size (units) [not used]	Production time for lot (hours)	Demand per week (units)	Current inventory (units)	Production time/unit (secs)	Equivalent production time in inventory (hours)	Equivalent production time in weekly demand (hours/week)	Gross requirements (units)	Net requirements (units)	Production hours needed for net requirements
2											
3											
4											
5											
6	Milk	24,000	30.00	10,000	30,000	4.50	37.50	12.50	34,453.78	4,453.78	5.57
7	Dark	20,000	18.00	8,000	19,000	3.24	17.10	7.20	27,563.03	8,563.03	7.71
8	Brandy filled	18,000	24.00	4,000	9,000	4.80	12.00	5.33	13,781.51	4,781.51	6.38
9	Nut	15,000	25.00	6,000	11,000	6.00	18.33	10.00	20,672.27	9,672.27	16.12
10	Cherry filled	17,500	21.00	3,200	7,500	4.32	9.00	3.84	11,025.21	3,525.21	4.23
11	**Total**						93.93	38.87			40.00
12											
13	Aggregate run-out time (ART) (weeks)		3.4454								
14											

After one week, and schedule for 2nd week

	A	B	C	D	E	F	G	H	I	J	K
15											
16	Product	Run size (units) [not used]	Production time for lot (hours)	Demand per week (units)	Current inventory (units)	Production time/unit (secs)	Equivalent production time in inventory (hours)	Equivalent production time in weekly demand (hours/week)	Gross demand (units)	Net requirements (units)	Production hours needed
17											
18											
19											
20											
21											
22	Milk	24,000	30.00	10,000	24,454	4.50	30.57	12.50	34,743.61	10,289.83	12.86
23	Dark	20,000	18.00	8,000	19,563	3.24	17.61	7.20	27,794.89	8,231.86	7.41
24	Brandy filled	18,000	24.00	4,000	9,782	4.80	13.04	5.33	13,897.44	4,115.93	5.49
25	Nut	15,000	25.00	6,000	14,672	6.00	24.45	10.00	20,846.17	6,173.90	10.29
26	Cherry filled	17,500	21.00	3,200	7,825	4.32	9.39	3.84	11,117.96	3,292.75	3.95
27	**Total**						95.06	38.87			40.00
28											

29	Aggregate run-out time (ART) (weeks)	3.4744

31 After two weeks, and schedule for 3rd week

	A	B	C	D	E	F	G	H	I	J	K
32	Product	Run size (units) [not used]	Production time for lot (hours)	Demand per week (units)	Current inventory (units)	Production time/unit (secs)	Equivalent production time in inventory (hours)	Equivalent production time in weekly demand (hours/week)	Gross demand (units)	Net requirements (units)	Production hours needed
38	Milk	24,000	30.00	10,000	24,744	4.50	30.93	12.50	35,033.44	10,289.83	12.86
39	Dark	20,000	18.00	8,000	19,795	3.24	17.82	7.20	28,026.75	8,231.86	7.41
40	Brandy filled	18,000	24.00	4,000	9,897	4.80	13.20	5.33	14,013.38	4,115.93	5.49
41	Nut	15,000	25.00	6,000	14,846	6.00	24.74	10.00	21,020.07	6,173.90	10.29
42	Cherry filled	17,500	21.00	3,200	7,918	4.32	9.50	3.84	11,210.70	3,292.75	3.95
43	Total						96.19	38.87			40.00

45	Aggregate run-out time (ART) (weeks)	3.5033

47 After three weeks, and schedule for 4th week

	A	B	C	D	E	F	G	H	I	J	K
48	Product	Run size (units) [not used]	Production time for lot (hours)	Demand per week (units)	Current inventory (units)	Production time/unit (secs)	Equivalent production time in inventory (hours)	Equivalent production time in weekly demand (hours/week)	Gross demand (units)	Net requirements (units)	Production hours needed
54	Milk	24,000	30.00	10,000	25,033	4.50	31.29	12.50	35,323.27	10,289.83	12.86
55	Dark	20,000	18.00	8,000	20,027	3.24	18.02	7.20	28,258.62	8,231.86	7.41
56	Brandy filled	18,000	24.00	4,000	10,013	4.80	13.35	5.33	14,129.31	4,115.93	5.49
57	Nut	15,000	25.00	6,000	15,020	6.00	25.03	10.00	21,193.96	6,173.90	10.29
58	Cherry filled	17,500	21.00	3,200	8,011	4.32	9.61	3.84	11,303.45	3,292.75	3.95
59	Total						97.31	38.87			40.00

(Continued)

Table 14.23 (Continued)

61	Aggregate run-out time (ART) (weeks)						3.5323			
62										
63	**After four weeks, and schedule for 5th week**									

	A	B	C	D	E	F	G	H	I	J	K
64	Product	Run size (units) [not used]	Production time for lot (hours)	Demand per week (units)	Current inventory (units)	Production time/unit (secs)	Equivalent production time in inventory (hours)	Equivalent production time in weekly demand (hours/week)	Gross requirements (units)	Net requirements (units)	Production hours needed
70	Milk	24,000	30.00	10,000	25,323	4.50	31.65	12.50	35,613.10	10,289.83	12.86
71	Dark	20,000	18.00	8,000	20,259	3.24	18.23	7.20	28,490.48	8,231.86	7.41
72	Brandy filled	18,000	24.00	4,000	10,129	4.80	13.51	5.33	14,245.24	4,115.93	5.49
73	Nut	15,000	25.00	6,000	15,194	6.00	25.32	10.00	21,367.86	6,173.90	10.29
74	Cherry filled	17,500	21.00	3,200	8,103	4.32	9.72	3.84	11,396.19	3,292.75	3.95
75	**Total**						98.44	38.87			40.00

76										
77	Aggregate run-out time (ART) (weeks)						3.5613			

Schedule summary: Production hours used

	Week 1	Week 2	Week 3	Week 4	Week 5
Milk	5.57	12.86	12.86	12.86	12.86
Dark	7.71	7.41	7.41	7.41	7.41
Brandy filled	6.38	5.49	5.49	5.49	5.49
Nut	16.12	10.29	10.29	10.29	10.29
Cherry filled	4.23	3.95	3.95	3.95	3.95
Total	40.00	40.00	40.00	40.00	40.00

> Figure 14.9 Gantt chart for Toubon Co.: Aggregate run–out time scheduling

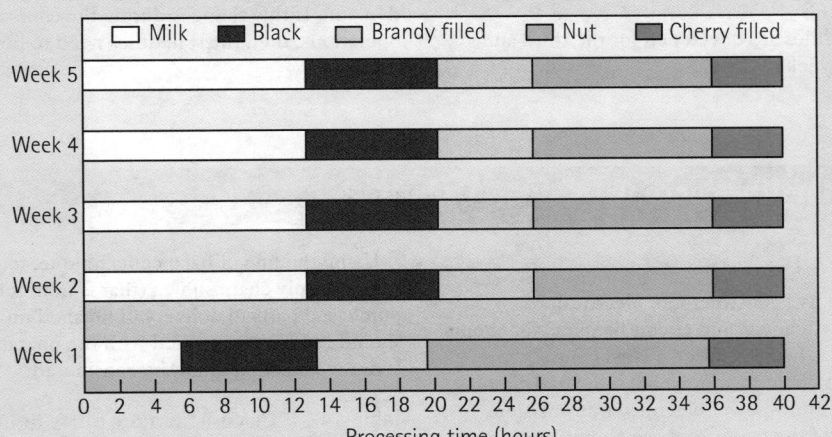

- The equivalent production in inventory is calculated for each product and then totalled (Cell [G-11]).
- Equivalent production time in weekly demand (column H) is the amount of processing time represented by the weekly demand. This is calculated by (weekly demand * production time per unit). For example, for the milk chocolate this is 12.50 hours [(10,000 * 4.5/60 * 60)] (Cell [H-6]). This is calculated for each product and then totalled (Cell [H-11]).
- Aggregate run-out time, ART, in weeks is calculated from the following relationship:

$$\frac{[\text{Equivalent processing time in aggregate inventory}]+}{\text{Equivalent processing time needed by client demand}}$$

where the processing time is 40 hours for the week. For example, ART for the first week is 3.4454 weeks [(93.93 + 40)/(38.87)] (Cell [D-13]).

- The aggregate run-out time means that if chocolate production is left operating for one week (40 hours), then the current inventory, plus the inventory produced during one week, will be depleted in 3.4454 weeks.
- Lot sizes are then determined based on the aggregate run-out time.
- Gross requirements, column I, for each product during the aggregate run-out time of 3.4454 weeks are then calculated by:
  Gross requirements = Demand per week * ART.
  For example, for the milk chocolate, the gross

requirements = 10,000 * 3.4454 = 34,453.78 units (Cell [I-6]).
- Net requirements are Gross requirements − Current inventory. For the milk chocolate, this is 34,453.78 − 30,000 = 4453.78 units (Cell [J-6]).
- Production hours needed is given by Net requirements * Production time/unit. For the milk chocolate, this is (4453.78 * 4.50)/(60 * 60) = 5.57 hours (Cell [K-6]).
- Total production hours needed (Cell [K-11]) are the hours available during the production (processing) period (40 hours in this case). These represent the amount of time processing must be spent on each type of product during the week. This is given in the Gantt chart for week 1.

The second section of the table entitled 'After one week', and schedule for the second week gives the development for the second week:

- Current inventory is now the gross requirements from the previous week less the demand for that same week. For example, for the milk chocolate this is 24,454 units (34,454 − 10,000) (cell [E-22]) (numbers are rounded). The current inventory is calculated in the same manner for the other products (Cells [E-22] to [E-26]).
- Thus, since the current inventory level has changed, there is a new value for the equivalent production time in inventory (Cell [G-27]). Using this gives us a new value for ART of 3.4744 weeks (Cell [D-29]).

- With the new ART new net requirements are determined and thence a new schedule (Cells [K-22] through [K-26]).
- Similar schedules are developed for the third and subsequent weeks.

A five-week schedule plan has been developed assuming no changes in the weekly demand. If this changes during the course of operations, then the schedules need to be adjusted accordingly.

Demonstrating the concept 14.5   Circuit breakers

Situation

The Neider Co. is a constructor of electrical transformers, switchgear, and circuit breakers for clients worldwide. It has been awarded a large contract to a Southeast Asian client to supply 200 industrial circuit breakers for medium-power electrical transmission. A large portion of the work for these circuit breakers is subcontracted with some major machining work performed by Neider. Other activities for Neider are to test some key components before final assembly, and final test. The elapsed time for the activity for Neider is eight weeks. This includes a two-week delivery schedule from France to the client. Figure 14.10 gives the control points, and the lead time for Neider.

The client has contracted with Neider to deliver the units according to the schedule in Table 14.24.

Required

Neider is at week 12 of the schedule. Table 14.25 shows the status of the units at the 15 control points of the assembly schedule. The lead time in weeks is taken from Figure 14.10 and the units are either finished or semi-finished products.

Using the line of balance technique, for the portion of the supply chain shown (that is from receipt of purchased parts to delivery of finished units on site) should Neider be satisfied with the operation? If not what action might be considered?

Table 14.24 Circuit breaker units delivery schedule

Week	Units delivered on site	Week	Units delivered on site
1		14	9
2		15	10
3		16	11
4	1	17	11
5	2	18	11
6	2	19	12
7	3	20	12
8	4	21	12
9	5	22	13
10	6	23	13
11	6	24	14
12	7	25	14
13	8	26	14

Figure 14.10 Assembly/lead time chart for circuit breakers

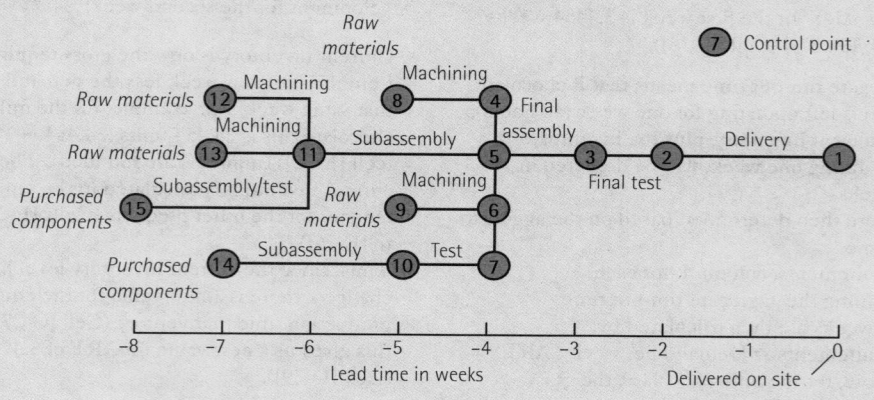

Table 14.25 Status of control points

Control point	1	2	3	4	5	6	7	8	9	10	11	12	13	14	15
Lead time	0	2	3	4	4	4	4	5	5	5	6	7	7	7	8
Units	36	55	67	72	70	76	78	82	80	79	90	100	108	110	120

Table 14.26 Client's required schedule for circuit breakers

Week	1	2	3	4	5	6	7	8	9	10	11	12	13	14	15	16	17	18	19	20	21	22	23	24	25	26
Units in this week				1	2	2	3	4	5	6	6	7	8	9	10	11	11	11	12	12	12	13	13	14	14	14
Cumulative units	0	0	0	1	3	5	8	12	17	23	29	36	44	53	63	74	85	96	108	120	132	145	158	172	186	200

Figure 14.11 Circuit breakers: Required delivery schedule

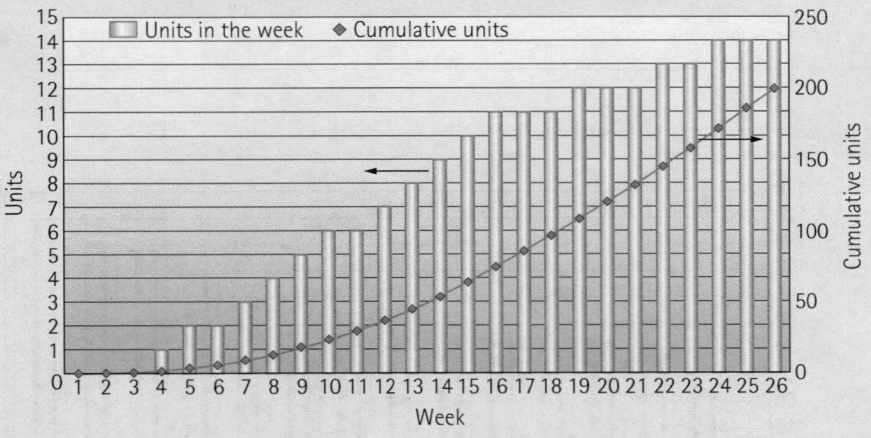

Solution

- In the line of balance technique, the weekly delivery schedule is converted into a cumulative delivery schedule. These data are given in Table 14.26, and shown graphically in Figure 14.11.
- For week 12, Table 14.27 gives the actual units either finished as at control points 1, 2, and 3, or semi-finished units at control points 4 through 15. Also shown in this table are the scheduled units or semi-finished units, which must be in inventory at each control point according to the client's requirements. The difference between the scheduled units at the site and the actual units on the site is also given. Figure 14.12 shows the information graphically. The situation at the control points is as follows.

Control point N° 1

At week 12, the cumulative units that should be at the site are 36. Actual units on site are 36. Thus, as far as finished products are concerned, delivery is on schedule, or there is a line of balance as illustrated by the two bars on the histogram for Control point N° 1.

Control point N° 2

This is the end of the final test. After this point there is a two-week delivery time. Thus, the quantity of units, which must be at Control point N° 2 at week 12, must be that quantity of units given on the cumulative delivery schedule two weeks ahead of week 12, or week 14. This is because when two weeks have elapsed, these units will arrive at the delivery site at week 14. From the cumulative delivery schedule this number

Table 14.27 Control situation for circuit breakers

Current week   12

Control point	Activity	Lead time (weeks)	Equivalent time (weeks)	Actual units	Scheduled units	Scheduled – actual units	Status
1	At client's site	0	12	36	36	0	On schedule
2	End of final test	2	14	55	53	−2	Ahead of schedule
3	End of final assembly	3	15	67	63	−4	Ahead of schedule
4	End of machining	4	16	72	74	2	Behind schedule
5	End of test	4	16	70	74	4	Behind schedule
6	End of machining	4	16	76	74	−2	Ahead of schedule
7	End of test	4	16	78	74	−4	Ahead of schedule
8	Start of machining	5	17	82	85	3	Behind schedule
9	Start of machining	5	17	80	85	5	Behind schedule
10	End of subassembly	5	17	79	85	6	Behind schedule
11	Start of subassembly	6	18	90	96	6	Behind schedule
12	Start of machining	7	19	100	108	8	Behind schedule
13	Start of machining	7	19	108	108	0	On schedule
14	Start of subassembly	7	19	110	108	−2	Ahead of schedule
15	Start of subassembly/test	8	20	120	120	0	On schedule

Figure 14.12 Circuit breakers: Line of balance delivery schedule

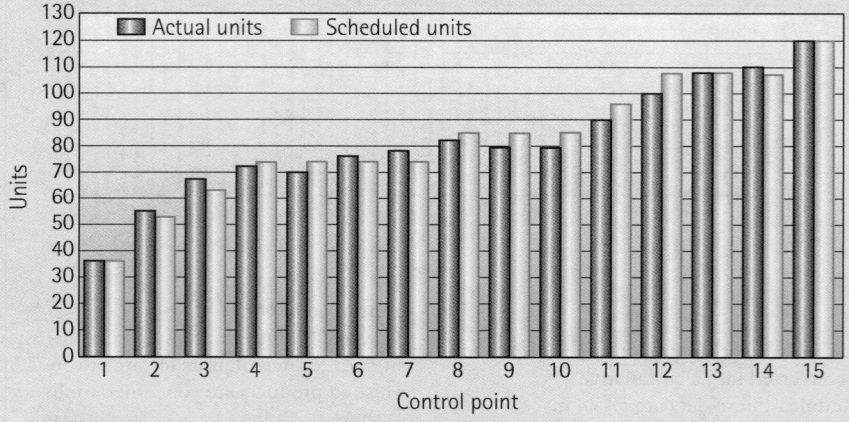

should be 53 units. Actual units are 55 either from the table or the figure (the difference between the two is −2 units). There is no line of balance. Production is ahead of schedule at this point so there is unnecessary inventory and unnecessary inventory storage costs.

Control point N° 3
This is the end of the final assembly. After this point there is a three-week period before the units must be at the site. Thus, the quantity of units, which must be at Control

point N° 3 at week 12, must be that quantity of units given on the cumulative delivery schedule three weeks ahead of week 12, or week 15. This is because when three weeks have elapsed these units will arrive at the delivery site at week 15. From, the cumulative delivery schedule this number should be 63 units. Actual units are 67 either from the table or figure (a difference of −4 units). Thus, production is ahead of schedule at this point so there is unnecessary inventory and unnecessary inventory storage costs. There is no line of balance.

Control point Nº 4

This is the end of machining. After this point there is a four-week period before the units must be at the site. Thus, the quantity of units, which must be at Control point Nº 4 at week 12, must be that quantity of units given on the cumulative delivery schedule four weeks ahead of week 12, or week 16. From the cumulative delivery schedule this number should be 74 units. Actual units are 72 (a difference of +2) Thus, production is behind schedule at this point. There is no line of balance.

The status at all the other control points in interpreted in the same manner. A summary of all is given in Table 14.26.

The production manager needs to pay attention to those control points where production is behind schedule perhaps considering the following approaches:

- Transfer resources from those activities that are behind schedule, to those which are ahead of schedule.
- Use overtime.
- Use additional labour.

It is important now to make attempts to 'balance the line' in order not to break the supply chain and fall behind with deliveries.

Demonstrating the concept 14.6 Moopick

Situation

The Moopick company operates a chain of restaurants that serve the motorways in Switzerland. On one of its outlets near Zurich it needs to determine staffing needs per week. Based on historical data of occupancy at the restaurant, it knows that the scheduled personnel needed are as shown in Table 14.28.

According to regulations, it has to give each employee two consecutive days off during the week. And its entire staff are permanent such that on any one day, the staff are either working, or on their day off.

Required

Develop a planning schedule showing the staffing for Moopick in a week.

Solution

Table 14.29 gives a planning schedule for Moopick that has been developed using Excel Solver and Figure 14.13 is a bar chart illustrating minimum staff scheduled, and actual staff scheduled. This information is developed as follows:

- Cells [A-3] through [A-9] are the possible combinations of days off for employees.

Table 14.28 Moopick: Scheduled personnel requirements

	Mon	Tue	Wed	Thu	Fri	Sat	Sun
Total required	23	17	13	14	15	22	24

- In each row 3 through 9 are the working days for the employee. A value of 1 indicates the employee works. A value of 0 indicates the employee has a day off.
- Cells [C-13] through [I-13] in row 11 are the required staff set by Moopick.
- The objective is to have the minimum staff. Cell [B-11] is the objective function whose value is set to a minimum.
- The formula in Cell [B-11] is the sum of Cells [B-3] through [B-9] in column B.
- Variables in the solution are Cells [B-3] through [B-9] in column B.

Constraints in the system are:

- Cells [B-3] through [B-9] in column B are greater than 0.
- Cells [B-3] through [B-9] in column B are integer numbers.
- Cells [C-11] through [I-11] in row 11 are greater than or equal to Cells [C-13] through [I-13] of row 13.
- Formula in Cell [C-11] is [B-3] * [C-3] + [B-4] * [C-4] + [B-5] * [C-5] + [B-6] * [C-6] + [B-7] * [C-7] + [B-8] * [C-8] + [B-9] * [C-9].
- Formula in Cell [D-11] is [B-3] * [D-3] + [B-4] * [D-4] + [B-5] * [D-5] + [B-6] * [D-6] + [B-7] * [D-7] + [B-8] * [D-8] + [B-9] * [D-9].
- Formula in Cell [E-11] is [B-3] * [E-3] + [B-4] * [E-4] + [B-5] * [E-5] + [B-6] * [E-6] + [B-7] * [E-7] + [B-8] * [E-8] + [B-9] * [E-9].
- Formula in Cell [F-11] is [B-3] * [F-3] + [B-4] * [F-4] + [B-5] * [F-5] + [B-6] * [F-6] + [B-7] * [F-7] + [B-8] * [F-8] + [B-9] * [F-9].

Table 14.29 Moopick: Planning schedule

	A	B	C	D	E	F	G	H	I
1			Day working						
2	Time off	Staff off	Mon	Tue	Wed	Thu	Fri	Sat	Sun
3	Monday, Tuesday	2	0	0	1	1	1	1	1
4	Tuesday, Wednesday	7	1	0	0	1	1	1	1
5	Wednesday, Thursday	4	1	1	0	0	1	1	1
6	Thursday, Friday	8	1	1	1	0	0	1	1
7	Friday, Saturday	3	1	1	1	1	0	0	1
8	Saturday, Sunday	1	1	1	1	1	1	0	0
9	Sunday, Monday	1	0	1	1	1	1	1	0
10									
11	Total scheduled	26	23	17	15	14	15	22	24
12									
13	Total required		23	17	13	14	15	22	24
14									
15	Total paid staff		26	26	26	26	26	26	26

Figure 14.13 Moopick: Staff scheduling

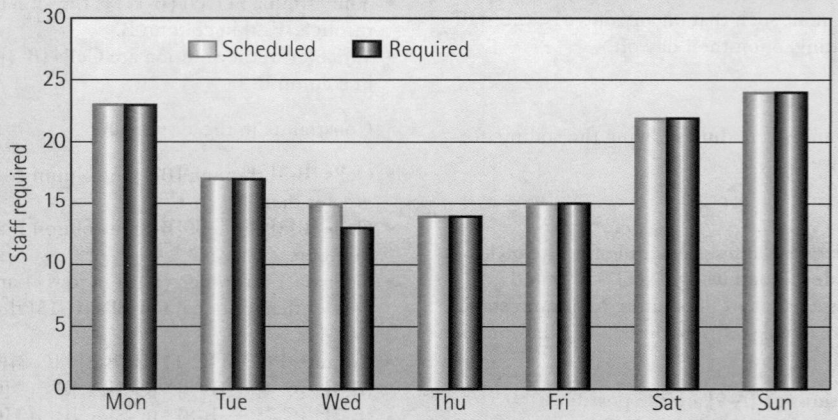

- Formula in Cell [G-11] is [B-3] * [G-3] + [B-4] * [G-4] + [B-5] * [G-5] + [B-6] * [G-6] + [B-7] * [G-7] + [B-8] * [G-8] + [B-9] * [G-9].
- Formula in Cell [H-11] is [B-3] * [H-3] + [B-4] * [H-4] + [B-5] * [H-5] + [B-6] * [H-6] + [B-7] * [H-7] + [B-8] * [H-8] + [B-9] * [H-9].
- Formula in Cell [I-11] is [B-3] * [I-3] + [B-4] * [I-4] + [B-5] * [I-5] + [B-6] * [I-6] + [B-7] * [I-7] + [B-8] * [I-8] + [B-9] * [I-9].
- Cells [C-15] through [I-15] in row 15 show that on any day there are 26 staff members on the payroll. This includes those in the restaurant, and those on their day off.

Application exercise 14.1   Carver

Situation

The Carver print shop, and the scheduling conditions, is the same as presented in Demonstrating the concept 14.1.

Required

1. For the following sequencing rules:
   (a) earliest due date
   (b) shortest processing time
   (c) longest processing time
   (d) last arrived, first processed
   (e) least slack time

determine:
   • total elapsed flow time (time to process all jobs from day 55)
   • average flow time/job, or average completion time/job (total flow time/number of jobs in system)
   • average jobs in system (total flow time/total processing time)
   • number of jobs late
   • average days late (total days late/total number of jobs).
     Illustrate each sequence on a Gantt, or bar chart.
2. What is the preferred sequencing rule for this situation including the first come, first served and the critical ratio presented in Demonstrating the concept 14.1?

Application exercise 14.2   Kiln

Situation

Annie Sabatier runs a gift shop in the south of France. In addition, she has a single pottery kiln in which she bakes pottery items for her many clients in the area. When she runs the kiln, she separates items into lots according to the client. The time needed for baking is a function of the clay, and the glazing employed. Generally each client always uses the same type of clay and glazing compound, although these materials vary from client to client. Annie Sabatier only runs the kiln eight hours a day, five days a week. There is an automatic shutoff of the kiln for any lots that take more than eight hours to bake.

On one particular Monday morning, Annie Sabatier has the following six lots waiting to be baked (see Table 14.30). This

Table 14.30   Kiln processing times

Job lot	A	B	C	D	E	F
Process time (hours)	7	3	4	5	6	8
Order received	1	2	3	4	5	6
Time due	16	8	8	32	24	24

information gives the processing time for the lot, the order it was received, and the time required by the client (eight hours corresponds to Tuesday at 8am, 16 at Wednesday at 8am, 24 hours to Thursday, 32 to Friday and 40 to Saturday each at 8am).

Required

1. For the following sequencing rules:
   (a) first come, first served
   (b) earliest due date
   (c) shortest processing time
   (d) longest processing time
   (e) last arrived, first processed
   (f) least slack time
   (g) critical ratio
determine
   • total elapsed flow time (time to process all jobs from time 0)
   • average flow time/job, or average completion time/job
   • average jobs in system
   • number of jobs late
   • average hours late.
     Illustrate each sequence on a Gantt, or bar chart.
2. What is the preferred sequencing rule for this situation?

Application exercise 14.3   Neoservice

Situation

Neoservice* is a company in France which designs, manufactures, and assembles food trolleys of the type used in hotels and restaurants for displaying desserts, in businesses for delivering tea (principally the British market), and also external use for ice cream.

The products are handcrafted out of wood. In the workshop there are two work centres 1 and 2. The first is for the preparation of the wood and varnishing, and the second is assembly and finishing. The time taken to perform these various activities is given in Table 14.31 for the six principal models produced by the company. In addition, the order of arrival for the order is indicated.

Table 14.31 Neoservice: Activity times of product models

Model	Paris	Tahiti	Savoie	Pose P	Loire	Glace
Order of arrival	1	2	3	4	5	6
Work centre N° 1						
Total time N° 1 (min)	306	345	322	330	303	371
Work centre N° 2						
Total time N° 2 (min)	294	309	306	288	352	371

Required

1. Develop the schedule according to the arrival time, that is, first come, first served, for Work centre N° 1 and Work centre N° 2. Determine the total time for each operation, the total elapsed time to finish the six products including both work centres. Present the sequence on a Gantt chart, showing operating times, and dead times.
2. Repeat the scheduling procedure using Johnson's rule for Work centre N° 1 and Work centre N° 2. Determine the total time for each operation, the total elapsed time to finish the six products including both work centres. Present the sequence on a Gantt chart showing operating times, and dead times. What is the percentage of time saved?

*Based on a study by Benoit Stos and Sidney Grünbergy, students at ESC Lyon, France, 1997.

Application exercise 14.4 Software

Situation

Software is a computer products company based in Palo Alto, California, which plans to establish European sales offices specifically in France, Germany, Norway, Benelux, Italy, and Spain. There will be a sales manager at each of these branches. Software performed a market survey for each of these countries, and then asked its prospective managers to make an estimate of the first year's annual sales revenues it might generate, based on the market survey, their particular knowledge of the country, language ability, and sales experience.

The estimated first year sales revenue in $000s, for each of the six countries, estimated by each of the six prospective managers, Julia, Andy, Fred, John, Alice, and Joan is given in Table 14.32.

Table 14.32 Software: First year sales revenue

	France	Germany	Norway	Benelux	Italy	Spain
Julia	700	700	925	1,025	1,200	425
Andy	900	850	450	1,010	950	525
Fred	500	900	525	950	875	946
John	800	1,000	945	525	950	850
Alice	625	750	825	850	850	650
Joan	525	955	675	590	725	725

The first year fixed costs for these branches in $000s is shown in Table 14.33.

And, the annual salaries in $000s for the six managers is shown in Table 14.34.

Required

1. Using the assignment method, which would be the optimum way to schedule the assignments for these sales personnel if the objective were to maximize profit?

Table 14.33 Software: First year fixed costs

	France	Germany	Norway	Benelux	Italy	Spain
Cost	250.00	200.00	350.00	200.00	100.00	150.00

Table 14.34 Software: Managers' annual salary

Manager	Julia	Andy	Fred	John	Alice	Joan
Salary	120	80	75	60	110	90

2. Software is somewhat uncertain of the success of this venture. If the annual operating costs for each site were estimated as the sum of the fixed cost, and the annual salary of the sales managers, what would be the best way to schedule the location of the sales personnel if the criterion was to minimize cost?

3. Which assignment schedule would you propose based on the information given? (See also Chapter 23.)

Application exercise 14.5 Supermarket

Situation

A supermarket store is open from 8am until 10pm six days a week. Based on historical data, it knows that the scheduled cashiers needed at the store on Mondays through Fridays are as shown in Table 14.35. (Saturday is different as it is pretty busy throughout the day.)

   The cashiers work eight hours a day and to accommodate this, the store gives its cashiers three consecutive two-hourly periods off during the day. All its cashiers are permanent employees, such that on any one day, the staff are either working, or they are off.

Required

Develop a planning schedule showing the cashier requirements for Monday through Friday.

Table 14.35 Scheduled cashiers needed at a supermarket

Time period	8am to 10am	10am to Midday	Midday to 2pm	2pm to 4pm	4pm to 6pm	6pm to 8pm	8pm to 10pm
Total required	12	20	30	18	25	35	16

Application exercise 14.6 Stamping Inc.

Situation

Stamping Inc. is a firm that makes metal frame assemblies destined for the electricity, automobile, and construction industry. One of its stamping presses is dedicated to the production of five frame assemblies A-654, B-498, C-325, D-785, E-458. Because of the setup time involved for the stamping press, Stamping makes the assemblies in lot sizes. This information, together with the production time, customer demand a week, and the current inventory at the beginning of the week is given in Table 14.36.

Table 14.36 Stamping Inc.: Lots sizes, production time, demand, and inventory

	Run size (units)	Production time (hours)	Weekly demand (units)	Current inventory (units)
A-654	800	12	350	200
B-498	600	8	200	160
C-325	250	15	125	240
D-785	750	20	180	230
E-458	250	10	200	100

Required

1. Using the run-out method for fixed lot sizes, develop a production schedule for the next five weeks. Show the production schedule on a Gantt chart. Assume 40 hours of production time a week.

2. Using an aggregate run-out time method (lot sizes are not fixed) develop a production schedule for the next five weeks. Show the production schedule on a Gantt chart. Assume 40 hours of production time a week.

Case study 14.1 Speedy

Situation

Speedy is a small hardware and repair store in the centre of town that, in addition to selling hardware items, does various odd jobs such as making keys, cutting dog tags, stitching shoes, picture framing, and printing visiting cards. The store is open six days a week, Monday to Saturday, from 8am to midday and 2 to 6pm. During the lunch period the store is closed and no work is performed. There are three people employed in the store, Bill, John, and Sarah. Bill and John both work 40 hours a week and Sarah is part time, working 16 hours a week according to the schedule shown in Table 14.37.

Bill and John are multi-skilled and alternate their weekly activity. During one week, John will be in the back area working on jobs that have accrued from the previous week, and Bill will be in the store serving customers and taking in repair work either to be executed the following week, or, alternatively, if he has the time Bill will do the job on the spot. In the following week the roles will be reversed, Bill will be working in the back and John will serve in the store. Bill will always do repair work on Monday and John will always do repair work on Saturday. Sarah always serves customers hardware items and/or takes in repair work.

Speedy's policy on repair work is to estimate the processing time to the nearest half-hour according to the policy in Table 14.38. For examples, keys are always assessed to take 0.50 hours, dog tags 1.00 hour, etc.

The processing time includes collecting the required materials from their small stock at the back of the store, adjusting the equipment that is used, and writing out the invoice.

The customer is given a collection day and time for the following week. The date and time are partly a function of the client's needs and also a rough estimate of when Speedy thinks the work can be completed. One policy that Speedy has is that work has to be collected at the end of the morning at midday or at the end of the afternoon at 6pm to minimize disruption in the store.

On one particular Saturday afternoon jobs had been logged in according to the order they were received, an estimate of the processing time, and the date they were promised to the client (see Table 14.39). For example, Monday morning would be hour 4, Monday afternoon would be hour 8 and Tuesday morning hour 12, etc. At the present time when either Bill or John process the work they do it on a first come, first served basis.

Required

Evaluate the present scheduling method used by Speedy. What are your comments? Do you think it could be improved to increase the customer service level? What other considerations should Speedy consider in order to maximize efficiency and improve customer service level? Justify your response with appropriate charts and quantitative indicators.

Table 14.37   Speedy: Work schedule

Monday	Tuesday	Wednesday	Thursday	Friday	Saturday
Bill	Bill	Bill	Bill	Bill	Sarah
Sarah	John	John	John	John	John

Table 14.38   Speedy: Repair work processing times

Item	Key	Dog tags	Shoes	Visiting cards	Framing
Code	K	D	S	C	P
Time (hour)	0.50	1.00	1.50	2.00 or 2.50	≥3.00

Table 14.39   Speedy: Jobs to be processed

Job	Order received	Process time/hours	Date due	Job	Order received	Process time/hours	Date due
S-1	1	1.50	Monday morning	D-4	14	1.00	Friday afternoon
C-1	2	2.50	Monday morning	C-7	15	2.00	Friday morning
D-1	3	1.00	Monday evening	C-8	16	2.00	Saturday morning
P-1	4	3.00	Monday evening	K-2	17	0.50	Thursday morning
C-2	5	2.50	Wednesday morning	S-2	18	1.50	Thursday afternoon
K-1	6	0.50	Tuesday morning	C-9	19	2.00	Wednesday afternoon
C-3	7	2.00	Thursday morning	C-10	20	2.00	Saturday afternoon
P-2	8	3.00	Tuesday afternoon	C-11	21	2.00	Saturday afternoon
D-2	9	1.00	Thursday afternoon	C-12	22	2.00	Friday morning
C-4	10	2.00	Tuesday morning	P-3	23	3.50	Saturday afternoon
C-5	11	2.00	Wednesday morning	P-4	24	3.00	Friday afternoon
C-6	12	2.00	Wednesday afternoon	S-3	25	1.50	Saturday afternoon
D-3	13	1.00	Tuesday afternoon	D-5	26	1.00	Saturday morning

Selected further reading

Ashby, James R. and Uzsoy, Reha, 'Scheduling and order release in a single-stage production system', *Journal of Manufacturing Systems*, vol. 14, issue 4, 1995, pp 290–306.

Bassett, Glenn and Todd, Robert, 'The SPT priority sequence rule', *International Journal of Operations and Production Management*, vol. 14, issue 12, 1994, pp 70–8.

Cheng, T. C. E., 'Due-date assignment and single machine scheduling with compressible processing times', *International Journal of Production Economics*, vol. 43, issues 2 and 3, 1 June 1996, pp 107–13.

Kimms, Alf (2001) *Mathematical Programming and Financial Objectives for Scheduling Products* (International Series in Operations Research and Management Science, Volume 38), Kluwer Academic Publishers.

Metters, Richard and Vargus, Vicente, 'A comparison of production scheduling policies on costs, service levels, and schedule changes', *Production and Operations Management*, vol. 17, no. 3, 1999, pp 76–91.

An extensive listing of other further reading can be found on the website.

What's on the web?

Further learning resources are available to lecturers and students at www.supplychain-online.com, including the following which are specific to *Operations scheduling*:

Resource	Subject
Chapter overview	Operations scheduling
Demonsrating the concept: Serre Co.	Johnson's rule
Application exercise: Frost	Johnson's rule (three work stations)
More further reading	Operations scheduling

15 Lean production and just-in-time

Chapter overview

- Concepts
- Analysis of a traditional push system
- Analysis of a just-in-time pull system
- Balancing production under just-in-time
- Kanban
- Inventories in lean production
- Machine setup times, and single minute exchange of die
- Overall equipment effectiveness
- The five S rules
- The five and 'six' zeros
- Quality
- Just-in-time in services
- Risks in lean manufacturing

Concepts

Lean production

Lean production has its roots in the Toyota Automobile Co. of Japan where waste was to be avoided at all cost: The waste in time caused by having to repair faulty products, the waste of investment in keeping high inventories, and the waste of having idle workers. Lean production involves having a highly disciplined approach to engineering and manufacturing and some of the elements include the following:

- Develop a coherent manufacturing schedule involving sales and don't modify it at the last minute.
- Minimize unnecessary workspace without jeopardizing safety and security.
- Use where appropriate low-cost flexible machines rather than expensive robots.
- Produce in small batches rather than in large lot sizes.
- Consider the organization in terms of a supply chain of value streams that extends from suppliers of raw materials, through transformation, to the final client.

- Organize workers in teams and have everybody in the organization conscious of their work.
- Produce products of perfect quality and have continuous quality improvement as a goal.
- Organize the operation by product, or cellular manufacturing, rather than a functional layout (see Chapter 9).
- Operate the facility in a just-in-time mode.
- Suppliers are part of the team and should be included in activities and decisions related to manufacturing and assembly.
- Eliminate all non-value-added activities.

Industry insight 15.1 illustrates the importance of lean manufacturing in order for firms to be cost effective and competitive.

Just-in-time

A key element of lean production is just-in-time (JIT) conceived by the late Taiichi Ohno, the former president of Toyota Motor Co. of Japan in the 1980s. Other Japanese manufacturing and service companies later perfected JIT, and it is now a philosophy adopted by firms worldwide. The Japanese manufacturing success

Lean manufacturing at Boeing Aircraft Company

At the vast Boeing assembly plant for 737s at Renton, Washington, the doctrine of lean manufacturing is now very much the rule. This includes reducing waste, shrinking factory floor space, and eliminating unnecessary inventories. No longer do mechanics have to walk long distances to obtain parts, or go in the opposite direction to collect blueprint drawings and tools. Previously these non-value-added activities could absorb two hours of a mechanic's day. Now all the parts are delivered in kits in 'point-of-use carts' and the drawings and tools are just where they are needed, as mechanics are able to call for them through a two-way radio system.

Boeing is retooling some its most complex manufacturing practices including putting in place moving assembly lines for its planes that it hopes will reduce production time by 50%. In addition, the company is using more standard designs, requiring fewer parts for assemblies and a tighter integration with suppliers including just-in-time delivery and allowing the suppliers to spend time on the assembly line working with Boeing mechanics to determine more efficient ways to install parts. Further, suppliers are able to see in real time the level of inventories of parts through the Boeing website and when they are at the preset minimum the supplier immediately restocks the appropriate pieces. Another innovation is that paralleling the main assembly line at Renton are more than 30 feeder lines where components are pre-assembled in order to save time in the final assembly. For example, it used to take mechanics 42 hours to install the 204 parts of the mixer bay assembly, the unit that circulates and filters the cabin air. With these new feeder lines, assembling the parts in modules of just 14 units, the time has been cut to 16 hours, reducing flow time by 62%.

Implementing these new lean procedures at Boeing is not easy for a workforce that has many entrenched ideas. Managers assigned to implement the programme use a nine-point lean guideline entitled,

'Tactics to improve operational efficiency', and hold frequent meeting on the new procedures, asking for volunteers to work on the moving assembly lines and requesting feedback. One concern among the workforce is the impending staff cuts. For five decades building Boeing's plane was a blend of engineering design and creative craftsmanship on the part of the skilled line workers. The new procedures now standardize much of the work effort reducing the individual contribution. When the final assembly line is reduced from 18 to 11 days, and then the current three assembly lines for the 737s are streamlined to two moving lines in 2002 the labour force is starting to equate 'lean' with 'layoffs'.

The Seattle conglomerate is counting on its lean philosophy to restore its tarnished reputation in manufacturing which is disappointing compared to its competitor, Airbus Industries of France whose plane designs are just years old compared to decades for Boeing. In 1997 Boeing brutally understood how critical to its strategy was its manufacturing operations. Then a demand for new planes increased and the company tried to double production almost overnight. A problem with part supplies and a shortage of workers forced it to shut down the 747 and 737 assembly lines. As a result some customers turned to Airbus and Boeing's commercial airplane division lost $1.6 billion even though it sold a record $24.5 billions' worth of airplanes. However, now, with some of the new lean procedures in place, Boeing reported a first-quarter 2001 operating margin of 10% for the first time in a decade. When all the lean procedures are working smoothly Boeing's long-term goal is to reduce by half the average order-to-delivery time for a plane to six months. This it hopes will make it a formidable competitor to Airbus Industries once more.

Adapted from: 'Boeing goes lean. It's revamping factories to gain an edge against Airbus', *Business Week*[1]

with increased productivity, low product cost, and often superior quality products can very much be attributed to just-in-time manufacturing methods. JIT means:

- Producing that quantity of units that is needed, no more, and no less.
- Producing them at the date, and time required, not before, and not after.
- A supplier delivers the exact quantity demanded, at the scheduled time and date.

Any deviation from these requirements means that either resources are being unnecessarily wasted, or that

client's needs are not being respected. There is really no technological sophistication with JIT. It is simply an acronym for being efficient, organized, rigorous, the ability to be flexible, with an ultimate objective of satisfying the client, respecting delivery times, having the specified quality, and producing at minimum cost.

Requirements

For just-in-time to work effectively, stable and level production schedules are desirable. Ideally, the same products are produced in the same sequence, in the same quantities, and in similar time periods as for example each week. Just-in-time works best with smaller and more focused work centres, as these small, specialized centres are easier to manage. The method requires reduced lot sizes, a reduction in inventory levels, and the communication between work posts using kanbans, or cards.

Enforced problem solving

The just-in-time mode of operation presents a system of enforced problem solving. There are no safety factors because:

- Every item of material is expected to meet quality standards.
- Every component and part must arrive at the right place, at the right time.
- Every worker is required to work productively.
- Every machine must function without breakdowns.

That is not to say that just-in-time is easy, or does not have other problems. In the words of an official of Renault VI, France, a manufacturer of trucks, buses, and other heavy vehicles:[2]

We have put in place a system of just-in-time in all our work areas including, the foundry, pressing and stamping, machining, and assembly. We have succeeded in reducing inventory. We have reduced costs. We have increased our competitiveness. We have improved product quality. And, we have increased the stress level of our operators!!

MRP 'push' and just–in–time 'pull'

Analogies are often made between just-in-time being a flexible pull system, and MRP being a rigid push system. As discussed in Chapter 13, MRP is driven by the master production schedule which is based not only on firm orders but also forecasts so that when the planning system is set in motion some products are being pushed through the pipeline (see Figure 15.1).

Pull system

Just-in-time is a pull system because it is the client's order that triggers a demand. This demand *pulls* the required product through the supply chain from distribution, manufacturing, back to purchasing. As an illustration, in European automobile manufacturing, at any given time (Citroën's automobile facility at Aulnay-sous-Bois, France, is one example) sequentially, on the same assembly line, are semi-finished vehicles of various colours, of different models, some with

Figure 15.1 MRP (push) and JIT (pull) systems

steering wheels on the right (for England), and some with steering wheels on the left. Each one of these is being pulled through the production line by a specific customer order placed through a dealer.[3]

Push system

The strict *push* concept is where products are manufactured, pushed through the supply chain where it is then it is up to the sales personnel to find clients. For example, in 1977, I purchased a sports car in Los Angeles. I wanted white, with black interior and certain options. I was unable to order in advance and had to visit various car dealers in the area to see if the model I wanted was available. At each dealership, salespersons tried to convince me to purchase another colour/design offering each time an 'attractive' price. They were 'pushing' their products onto a prospective client. Now, as the previous paragraph has illustrated, in Europe, if one purchases an automobile, one is able to give the exact specifications to a dealer (colour, interior fittings, options, etc.) and this order is transmitted to the manufacturer. In about four to six weeks (depending on production levels) the required vehicle is ready.

That is not to say that automobile manufacturers are entirely producing on the 'pull' system. In the USA, Longo Toyota in El Monte, California, the world's biggest car dealer, 'pushes' their products onto the clients. At this dealership there is an enormous parking lot where clients can purchase a vehicle on the spot to suit their requirements. The dealership is open 364 days per year (December 25 is the exception), from 7 in the morning until 10 at night. In 1995 21,000 vehicles were sold.[4]

Analogy of push and pull

An analogy of the *pull and push system* can be demonstrated in the way two different cultures purchase and consume a staple commodity: Bread.

The Americans

There are few individual bakeries in the USA and bread is usually purchased in supermarkets. The most popular bread is sliced containing food preservatives that give it a relatively long life of 7 to 14 days if kept in a freezer. The following is the purchase and consumption process:

- As in MRP, a shopper estimates household bread consumption between two successive trips to the supermarket. This quantity, plus a safety stock, is purchased and stored in the freezer. At the time of the purchase, inventory is high and then, as in the MRP system, declines during the consumption period until the next purchase.
- Bread consumption is unplanned and erratic. (Unlike in France and some other European countries, it is not eaten with every meal.) Thus, inventory decline is not predictable.
- More loaves are purchased at the next shopping cycle according to the inventory remaining in the freezer.

This can be likened to a push system. Inventory of bread stored in the freezer is *pushed* to the user, as consumption is desired. The cycle time is long, up to two weeks, and the turnover of bread is low.

The French

The French usually only eat fresh bread and very often it is the baguette, which is only fresh for the day. Bread is usually purchased at the local bakery, fresh, every day. (A baker starts work at 4am) The purchase and consumption process is as follows:

- A baguette (one or several according to that day's estimated needs) is purchased in the morning. At this point, after the purchase, inventory level is at a maximum.
- Bread is consumed with most meals, and always with cheese.
- The inventory of bread at night, after the last meal, is zero, or near zero.
- In the morning, the bread container is empty, or that remaining is hard as baguettes contain few preservatives. Thus, another, or several baguettes are purchased.
- The cycle is repeated.

This is a pull system. Zero fresh bread inventory in the morning and the day's requirement for bread 'pulls' another baguette through the household pipeline. The cycle time is short (one day). A given unit of bread remains at most one day in inventory. Thus, inventory turnover is high.

The supply chain and integration of MRP and JIT

Although it might at first seem that MRP, or the MRP module of the ERP, and JIT are incompatible since they function differently, and have different time horizons (JIT operates in a much shorter timeframe than MRP) the two systems can be effectively combined to give an integrated planning tool for the entire supply chain. As an illustration, a major manufacturing company in Europe, which produces a wide range of consumer products, operates as follows:

- The manufacturing site obtains the sales forecast for Europe for about the next 18 months and this becomes the company-wide sales plan.
- This sales plan is broken down into an aggregate plan covering a three-month period.
- The aggregate plan is reduced to a master production schedule and a MRP system covering a six-week time horizon.
- The MRP is the driver for the daily just-in-time operation using kanbans in the manufacturing centres.

Analysis of a traditional push system

Consider a simple production operation with three work posts and one operator at each work post as illustrated in Figure 15.2.

Capacity

In this traditional push system, each operator works at his own rhythm disregarding what is going on upstream, or downstream. The following is the capacity of each work post.

Work post N° 1

- Capacity of this work post is one unit can be produced every 20 seconds or 180 units per hour $(60*60/20)$.
- Operator makes a lot of five units before they are transferred or 'pushed' to post N° 2.
- Under normal operation the hourly production is 36 lots $(180/5)$.

Work post N° 2

- Capacity of this work post is one unit can be produced every 25 seconds or 144 units per hour $(60*60/25)$.

Figure 15.2 Traditional approach in production

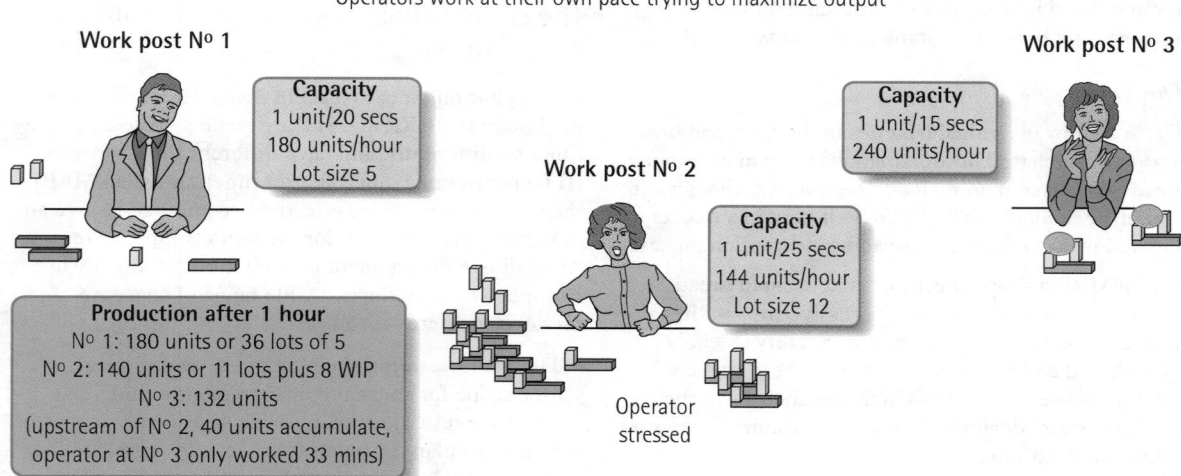

Operators work at their own pace trying to maximize output

Work post № 1

Capacity
1 unit/20 secs
180 units/hour
Lot size 5

Work post № 2

Capacity
1 unit/25 secs
144 units/hour
Lot size 12

Work post № 3

Capacity
1 unit/15 secs
240 units/hour

Production after 1 hour
№ 1: 180 units or 36 lots of 5
№ 2: 140 units or 11 lots plus 8 WIP
№ 3: 132 units
(upstream of № 2, 40 units accumulate,
operator at № 3 only worked 33 mins)

Operator
stressed

- Operator makes a lot of 12 units before they are transferred or 'pushed' to post № 3.
- Under normal operation the hourly production is 12 lots (144/12).

Work post № 3

- Capacity of this work post is one unit can be produced every 15 seconds or 240 units per hour (60 * 60/15).

Actual production

The following would be the actual production situation after the first hour of operation on the assumption there was no in-process inventory at the start of the operation. The transfer time is not taken into consideration in the calculation.

Work post № 1

- 180 units have been produced, or 36 lots of 5 units per lot.
- These units have been passed along to Work post № 2.
- The first lot of units reaches post № 2 after 100 seconds which is the time to produce the first lot (5 * 20).

Work post № 2

- Operator has to wait 100 seconds before receiving the first lot of units from post № 1. Thus, the effective operating time in one hour is 3500 seconds (60 * 60 − 100).

- Operator produces 140 units (3500/25). This represents 11 complete lots (11 * 12 = 132) which are passed onto post № 3. The remaining eight units (140 − 132) remain downstream at post № 2 until a lot is completed.
- The first lot of units reaches post № 3 after a total of 400 seconds have elapsed from the start of the operation. This is 100 seconds for the delay between post № 1 and post № 2 and 300 seconds for the time for post № 2 to finish the first lot (25 * 12).
- Upstream of the operator are 40 units (180 − 140). The presence of this accumulated inventory stresses the operator.

Work post № 3

- Effective operating time in one hour is 3200 seconds (60 * 60 − 400).
- Operator starts on the first unit after 400 seconds and finishes these after 580 seconds have elapsed (400 + 180).
- Since the second lot from post № 2 is not finished until 700 seconds have elapsed, the operator has to wait 120 seconds (700 − 580).
- As a result of having to wait for lots to arrive from post № 2, post № 3 completes only 11 of the lots from post № 2 or 132 units (12 * 11).

The situation of the actual production is shown in Table 15.1.

Table 15.1 Analysis of a traditional production operation

| Work post | Capacity | | Lot size units | No. of lots | Units finished after 1 hour | WIP after 1 hour | Upstream inventory after 1 hour | Lots finished after 1 hour |
	units/sec	units/hour						
1	20	180	5	36	180		0	36
2	25	144	12	12	140	8	40	11.67
3	15	240			132	0	0	

Work post number 1			
Lot No.	Start time	Time to produce lot	Finish time
1	0	100	100
2	100	100	200
3	200	100	300
4	300	100	400
5	400	100	500
6	500	100	600
7	600	100	700
8	700	100	800
9	800	100	900
10	900	100	1,000
11	1,000	100	1,100
12	1,100	100	1,200
13	1,200	100	1,300
14	1,300	100	1,400
15	1,400	100	1,500
16	1,500	100	1,600
17	1,600	100	1,700
18	1,700	100	1,800
19	1,800	100	1,900
20	1,900	100	2,000
21	2,000	100	2,100
22	2,100	100	2,200
23	2,200	100	2,300
			(Continued)

Table 15.1 (Continued)

	Work post number 1		
Lot No.	Start time	Time to produce	Finish time
24	2,300	100	2,400
25	2,400	100	2,500
26	2,500	100	2,600
27	2,600	100	2,700
28	2,700	100	2,800
29	2,800	100	2,900
30	2,900	100	3,000
31	3,000	100	3,100
32	3,100	100	3,200
33	3,200	100	3,300
34	3,300	100	3,400
35	3,400	100	3,500
36	3,500	100	3,600

	Work post number 2		
Lot No.	Start time	Idle time before starting	Production time for lot	Finish time
1	100	100	300	400
2	400	0	300	700
3	700	0	300	1,000
4	1,000	0	300	1,300
5	1,300	0	300	1,600
6	1,600	0	300	1,900
7	1,900	0	300	2,200
8	2,200	0	300	2,500
9	2,500	0	300	2,800
10	2,800	0	300	3,100
11	3,100	0	300	3,400
12	3,400	0	300	3,700

	Work post number 3			
Lot No.	Start time	Idle time before starting	Production time for lot	Finish time
1	400	400	180	580
2	700	120	180	880
3	1,000	120	180	1,180
4	1,300	120	180	1,480
5	1,600	120	180	1,780
6	1,900	120	180	2,080
7	2,200	120	180	2,380
8	2,500	120	180	2,680
9	2,800	120	180	2,980
10	3,100	120	180	3,280
11	3,400	120	180	3,580
12	3,700	120	180	3,880

Flow times

Consider now that the operation has been running for one hour with the accumulation of units as illustrated in the previous section. Now a new unit, Piece A, arrives upstream of post N° 1. The following gives the elapsed time when this piece has been finished at all three work centres and is illustrated in Figure 15.3. The clock on this diagram is referenced here by [Clock N°]. Again, the transfer time is not taken into consideration in the calculation.

Work post N° 1

- Piece A arrives at time 0 [Clock 1] which is one hour after the system has been running.
- It takes 20 seconds to work on Piece A [Clock 2].
- Operator then makes four more units (lot sizes of five units) before sending these to post N° 2. Thus, operator at post N° 2 must wait 100 seconds (5 * 20) or 1 min 40 sec before he receives Piece A [Clock 3].

Figure 15.3 Flow time in traditional approach in production

Work post N° 2

- At the start of this second hour there already are 40 units waiting upstream of post N° 2.
- In the 100 seconds that operator at post N° 1 is working on the lot containing Piece A, the operator at post N° 2 completes four of the 40 units (100/25). These four units make up a lot from the eight units from the previous hour and are sent to post N° 3.
- This leaves 36 units of inventory from the first hour upstream at post N° 2.
- Operator needs another 900 seconds (36 * 25) or 15 min to complete the remaining 36 units upstream.
- Thus the operator at post N° 2 cannot work on Piece A until 1000 seconds (100 + 900) or 16 min 40 sec have elapsed [Clock 4].
- Operator at post N° 2 takes 25 seconds to work on Piece A. He then makes another 11 to complete a lot of 12 units before passing them to post N° 3.
- Thus, Piece A rests at post N° 2 for an additional 300 seconds (12 * 25) before being sent to post N° 3.
- Work post N° 3 receives Piece A when 1300 seconds or 21 min 40 sec have elapsed [Clock 5].

Work post N° 3

- It takes operator at post N° 3, 15 seconds to work on Piece A.
- Thus, elapsed time for Piece A to be finished is 1315 seconds or 21 min 55 sec [Clock 6].

Value added

Thus, in this production operation the waiting time for Piece A is 1255 seconds (1315 − 20 − 25 − 15) or 20 min 55 sec. This is equivalent to 95.44% of the elapsed flow time. Alternatively, the actual operating time where value is being added is one minute (20 + 25 + 15 sec) or just 4.56% of the total elapsed time. This underscores the inefficiency of waiting time or non-value-added activity as presented in Figure 11.5.

In addition to the non-value-added analysis of this operation could be a high cost of non-quality. For example, assuming Piece A on leaving post N° 3 was inspected for quality and was found to be off-specification. What is more, Piece A originated from a lot that was poor. Thus, it would take almost 21 minutes to discover this (20 min 55 sec) and all the pieces following Piece A would be of poor quality. This would represent a significant cost of non-quality to the operation.

Reasons for low productivity in traditional production

This illustration gives quantitative inefficiencies in a traditional approach to production. Other qualitative occurrences to take into consideration are in Table 15.2.

Table 15.2 Reasons for low productivity in traditional production

Criteria	Reasons/outcome
Operators poorly trained	Do not fully understand task
Poor product design	Complex manipulations for operators
Workstations unbalanced	Rate upstream greater than downstream creating bottlenecks
Operators stressed	Inventory build-up upstream creates 'panic'
Communication	Poor communication creates unbalance
Learning curve	Time needed to assimilate task
Idle time	Operators not fully occupied, demotivated
Layout not optimized	Wasted space and units have to be transferred in lots
Lack of teamwork	Each operator has to deal with his own problems

Analysis of a just–in–time pull system

In this just-in-time situation there are the same three work posts with the capacities as presented in the previous section. However, units are sent to the next work post on a unit basis rather than in lots. Furthermore, the upstream operator does not produce a unit if there is a unit already waiting upstream of the next workstation (see Figure 15.4).

Actual production

The following would be the actual production situation after the first hour of operation on the assumption there is no in-process inventory at the start of the operation. The transfer time is not taken into consideration in the calculation.

Work post N° 1

- It takes the operator 20 seconds to work on the first unit, which is sent onto post N° 2 and the operator here immediately takes this unit to work on.
- There is no inventory waiting upstream of post N° 2 (the operator at post N° 2 is working on the first unit)

Figure 15.4 Just-in-time approach in production

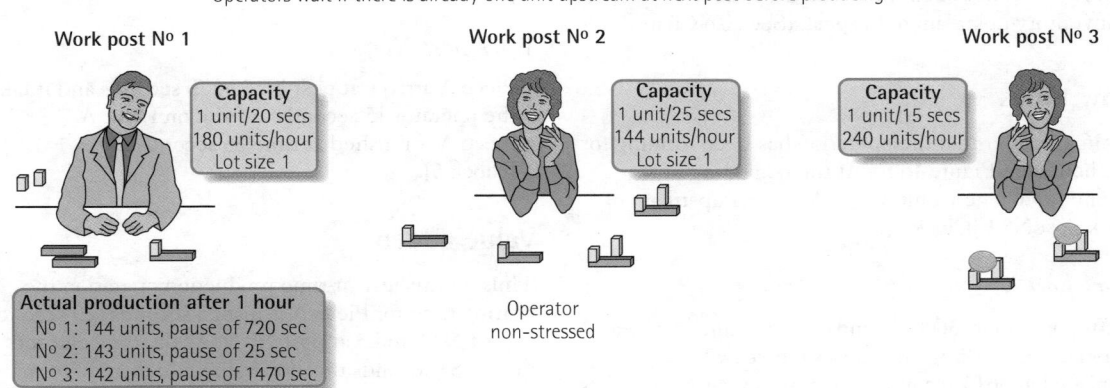

Operators wait if there is already one unit upstream at next post before producing

Work post Nº 1

Capacity
1 unit/20 secs
180 units/hour
Lot size 1

Work post Nº 2

Capacity
1 unit/25 secs
144 units/hour
Lot size 1

Work post Nº 3

Capacity
1 unit/15 secs
240 units/hour

Actual production after 1 hour
Nº 1: 144 units, pause of 720 sec
Nº 2: 143 units, pause of 25 sec
Nº 3: 142 units, pause of 1470 sec

Operator
non-stressed

and so the operator at post Nº 1 starts on the second unit and finishes it after 40 seconds (20 + 20).

- The second unit is passed onto post Nº 2 after 40 seconds have elapsed.
- At post Nº 2 there is WIP (the first unit being worked on) which will be finished after 45 seconds (20 + 25) plus the second unit waiting upstream. Thus, the operator at post Nº 1 waits 5 seconds (45 − 40).
- At 45 seconds the operator at post Nº 2 starts on the second unit. Thus, operator at post Nº 1 starts working on the third unit.
- At this rhythm the operator starts on the 144th unit at 3570 seconds (143 * 20 + 142 * 5) since there is no pause before starting second unit and the first unit starts at time 0.
- The 144th unit is finished at 3590 seconds (3570 + 20).
- The 145th unit is started at 3595 seconds but is not finished until 3615 seconds (3595 + 20) or after the first hour has elapsed.
- In the first hour 144 units have been produced with a total production time of 2880 seconds (144 * 20) and non-productive time in the first hour of 720 seconds (3600 − 2880).

Work post Nº 2

- Operator has to wait 20 seconds before receiving the first unit from post Nº 1.
- Operator works on the first unit which he finishes at 45 seconds (20 + 25).
- At 45 seconds he starts on the second unit, which he finishes at 70 seconds (45 + 25).
- At this rhythm the operator starts on the 143rd unit at 3570 seconds (142 * 25 + 20).
- The 143rd unit is finished at 3595 seconds (3570 + 25).

- The 144th unit is started at 3595 seconds, but is not finished until 3620 seconds (3595 + 25) or after the first hour has elapsed.
- In the first hour 143 units have been produced with a total production time of 3575 seconds (143 * 25) and non-productive time in the first hour of 25 seconds (3600 − 2575).

Work post Nº 3

- Operator has to wait 45 seconds before receiving the first unit from post Nº 2 (20 + 25).
- Operator works on the first unit which he finishes at 60 seconds (45 + 15).
- At 60 seconds the operator at post Nº 2 is still working on the second unit thus the operator at post Nº 3 must wait 10 seconds (70 − 60).
- At 70 seconds the operator at post Nº 3 starts working on the second unit which he finishes at 85 seconds (70 + 15).
- At this rhythm the operator starts on the 142nd unit at 3570 seconds (141 * 15 + 45 + 141 * 10).
- The 142nd unit is finished at 3585 seconds (3570 + 15).
- The 143rd unit is started at 3595 seconds (3585 + 10), but is not finished until 3610 seconds (3595 + 15) or after the first hour has elapsed.
- In the first hour 142 units have been produced with a total production time of 2130 seconds (143 * 25) and non-productive time in the first hour of 1470 seconds (3600 − 2130).

Thus in summary, within the one hour there are 142 units completed at post Nº 3 ready for the client as opposed to 132 units in the traditional approach to production or an increase of 6%. Although production of

Work post Nº 1 has been reduced in-process inventory has been virtually eliminated, and the operator at Work post Nº 2 has not been intimidated by the accumulation of inventory upstream of his post. (See also Chapter 22.)

Flow times

Again, consider that the operation has been running for one hour (see Figure 15.5). At the beginning of the second hour, a new unit, Piece A, arrives upstream of Work post Nº 1 [Clock 1].

Work post Nº 1

- After one hour (3600 seconds) or now time zero the operator is working on the 145th piece which is finished at 3615 seconds. Then he waits for 5 seconds as there is a unit upstream of post Nº 2.
- Operator starts working on Piece A at 3620 seconds or 20 seconds if 3600 is time 0 [Clock 2].
- Thus, there is a delay of 20 seconds (3620 − 3600) for Piece A.
- It takes 20 seconds to work on Piece A which is finished at 40 seconds (20 + 20) and sent to post Nº 2 [Clock 3].

Work post Nº 2

- When Piece A arrives at post Nº 2 at 40 seconds the operator is working on the 145th unit which is not finished until 45 seconds.
- Thus there is a delay of 5 seconds for Piece A (45 − 40).

- Operator starts working on Piece A at 45 seconds and is finished at 70 seconds (45 + 25) and sent to post Nº 3 [Clock 4].

Work post Nº 3

- Piece A arrives at post Nº 3 at 70 seconds and it takes the operator 15 seconds to work on Piece A.
- Piece A is finished at time 85 seconds (70 + 15) [Clock 5].

Value added

Thus, in this just-in-time production operation the waiting time for Piece A is just 25 seconds (20 seconds at post Nº 1 and 5 at post Nº 2). As the total elapsed time is 85 seconds this non-value-added activity is 29.41%. The value-added activity is now 70.59%. This would rise to 92.31% if Piece A arrived at 1 min 20 sec at post Nº 1 avoiding any waiting time.

Balancing production under just-in-time

Cycle time

Cycle time is the rate at which units are being produced on a production, or assembly line. To be efficient, and to avoid building up unnecessary inventory, the cycle time should be equivalent to the client's demand rate.

Figure 15.5 Flow time in just–in–time approach in production

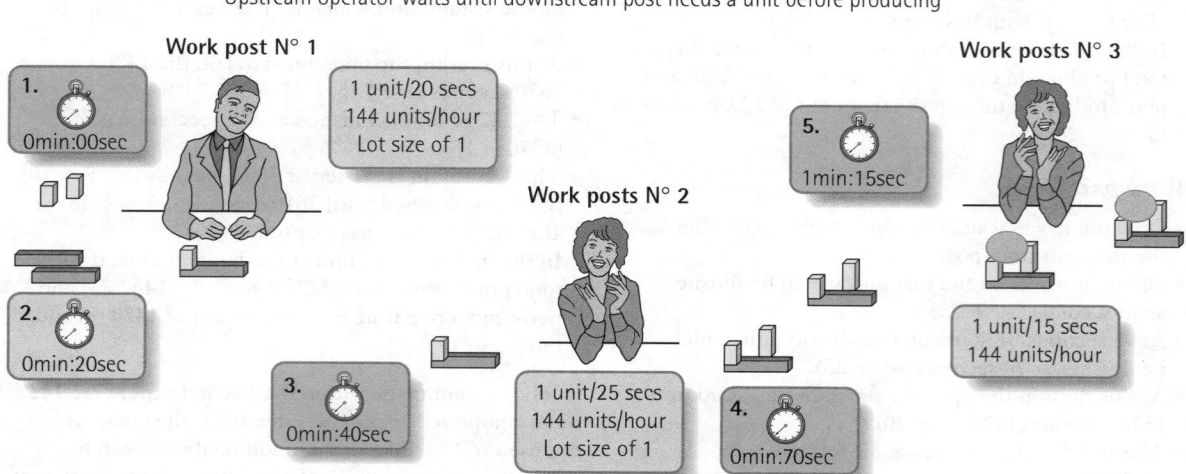

Figure 15.6 Flexibility in just-in-time with multi-skilled operators

Cycle time analogous to 'Takt' time

An analogy of the cycle time is *Takt* time. *Takt* is a German word meaning rhythm where an orchestra plays slowly or quickly according to the requirements of the conductor. In production, the conductor is the client. Thus, the production team should be working at the same rhythm, or cycle time, demanded by the client. Consider the following based on the three work posts.

Situation no 1

The client demands 4320 units per day. Assume there are three shifts to produce a product with three operators per shift (see Figure 15.6):

- Each shift works 8 hours/day. Thus, total production time is 86,400 seconds (8 * 3600 * 3).
- Cycle time, or rate at which units must be produced, is 20 seconds (86,400/4320).
- Post N° 1 needs 20 seconds to produce one unit, or at the client cycle (*Takt*) time.
- Currently post N° 2 requires 25 sec/unit, and post N° 3 requires 15 sec/unit with 10 seconds pause.
- If operators at posts N° 2 and 3 are multi-skilled such that can do either task, then combined time per unit for posts N° 2 and 3 is 40 seconds (25 + 15).
- Operator at post N° 2 performs task for post N° 2 then continues on same unit for task originally performed at post N° 3.
- Line is balanced and operators work at the same rhythm (*Takt* time) as client demands.

Situation no 2

Client demand drops to 2880 units per day from the original 4320 units per day. Assume again there are three shifts (see Figure 15.7):

- Each shift works 8 hours/day. Thus, total production time available is 86,400 seconds.
- Cycle time (rate at which units must be produced) is 30 seconds (86,400/2880).
- If operators are completely multi-skilled (they can perform the tasks originally performed at the three work posts), then each operator takes 60 seconds to complete a piece (20 + 25 + 15).
- Thus, only two operators per shift are needed to meet the client's demand, or *Takt* time. Each operator produces 480 units (8 * 3600/60) or 960 units/shift. This is a total of 2880 units a day for three shifts (3 * 960).
- The third operator can be redeployed elsewhere.

If this arrangement were adopted, then, to minimize the movement of the operator, the machines should be positioned around this person, or a cellular arrangement. If necessary, in order to make appropriate adjustments, equipment, or machines, can be removed and redeployed elsewhere. Having them on trolley-type arrangements can facilitate the movement of machines. (See Chapter 9.) This cellular, or 'block' layout, in addition to reducing the distance the operator would have to walk would also minimize the surface area required for the operation. Both would increase productivity and significantly if the gain in surface area can be used for additional production.

Kanban

Definition

Kanbans are the heart of just-in-time production. Kanban is a Japanese word meaning card and these cards are the means of communicating within, to, and from a work

Figure 15.7 Just-in-time operation: Two completely multi-skilled operators

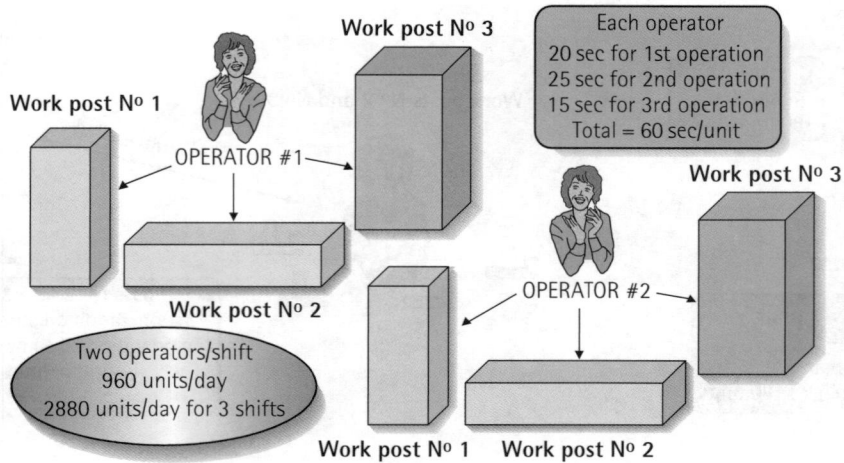

Work post Nº 3

Work post Nº 1

Each operator
20 sec for 1st operation
25 sec for 2nd operation
15 sec for 3rd operation
Total = 60 sec/unit

OPERATOR #1

Work post Nº 3

Work post Nº 2

OPERATOR #2

Two operators/shift
960 units/day
2880 units/day for 3 shifts

Work post Nº 1   Work post Nº 2

centre. Kanbans effectively replace all written work orders, move tickets, and routing sheets. No parts can be moved, produced, or used without an appropriate kanban. Parts, and components are transferred from one work area to another in rigid plastic containers. These containers are just large enough to hold a small, and fixed quantity of units of the same component reference. Different parts are not put into the same container.

Kanban forms

The physical form of kanbans depends on the organization, and the particular work centre within that organization. They may be magnetic strips which can be affixed to a board adjacent to a work post, they may be cards which are put into the containers containing the products, or the containers themselves may be the kanban. Hewlett-Packard, Valéo, and Renault VI of France all use a combination of these types of kanban.

Written on the kanban is information concerning the part. This will include the reference number, storage areas, and associated work centres. Figure 15.8 illustrates the type of information that would be found on two types of kanban, the withdrawal kanban, and the production kanban.

Production kanban

Figure 15.9 illustrates the use of kanbans with one type of card, the production kanban.

- An operator at the downstream Work post Nº 2 has an empty container, containing a production kanban, K_p.

Figure 15.8 Information contained on kanbans

WITHDRAWAL KANBAN

Part number	1455-137
Container capacity	75
Downstream Work post	T-36
Downstream inventory location	A-100
Upstream Work post	T-35
Upstream inventory location	A-99

PRODUCTION KANBAN

Work post	T-35
Part number to produce	1455-137
Container capacity	75
Inventory location	A-99
Raw materials	
Part number	1455-164
Inventory location	A-90
Part number	1732-83
Inventory location	A-74
Part number	170582
Inventory location	A-14

The fact that the container is empty is the authorization to the operator to obtain additional components.

- The operator goes either to the storage area containing the parts (if a dedicated storage area exists) or to the

Figure 15.9 Kanban system (one card)

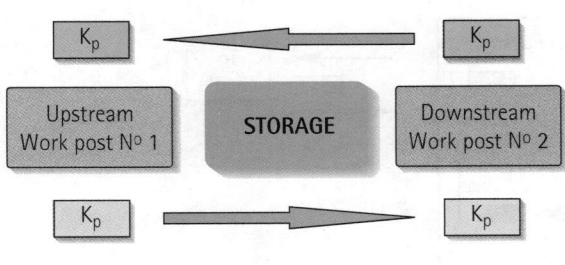

upstream Work post N° 1 where the needed parts are being machined.

- The operator exchanges the empty container for a full container containing the required parts in which there is also a K_p kanban.
- The production kanban that was contained in the empty container is posted at the upstream work centre. This is the authorization for the upstream Work post N° 1 to produce another container of parts.
- The operator returns to Work post N° 2 to continue production.

Production and withdrawal kanban

Figure 15.10 illustrates the use of kanbans with two type of cards, the production kanban, and the withdrawal kanban.

- An operator at the downstream Work post N° 2 has an empty container, containing a withdrawal kanban, K_w. The fact that the container is empty is the authorization to the operator to obtain additional components.
- The operator goes to the storage area containing the parts. He takes a full container of parts, which also contains a production kanban, K_p. The operator replaces the K_p kanban with the K_w kanban that was in the empty container.

Figure 15.10 Kanban system (two cards)

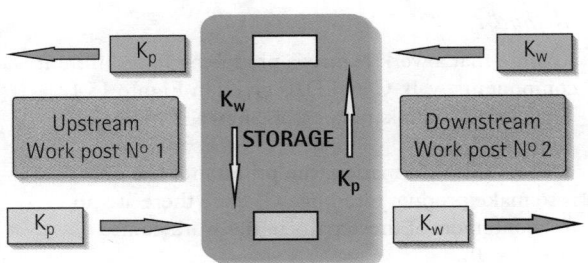

- The K_p card is posted at Work post N° 1. This is in the instruction for personnel at Work post N° 1 to produce a container of parts.
- The operator returns to Work post N° 2 and continues producing.

With the two-card system the withdrawal cards circulate around the downstream Work post N° 2, and the production cards circulate around the upstream Work post N° 1. If additional inventory of a product is needed such as for example another work post requires the same parts, it would be sufficient to have more K_p cards in circulation than K_w cards.

With either type of card system some industries operate on the principle of 'one container full, one empty'. That is to say, at the downstream work post there are two containers for a product with the same reference number. When one of the containers is empty, the operator goes to collect a new container of parts. In the meantime, the machine is working from the full container (if the machine has an automatic feeder, then the operator can leave the work post while the machine is producing).

Kanbans outside the work centre

The principle of using kanbans can be extended to the supplier, and the client as illustrated in Figure 15.11.

- From the supplier, full containers of component parts are delivered to the work centre. With a good working relationship with the client, the supplier can deliver the component parts directly to the storage area of the work centre without passing by a reception area, or quality control.
- Empty containers, with kanbans, are removed by the suppliers, which are the instructions to the suppliers to provide additional parts. This is the communication, or information flow.
- In the work centre, the components are cards flow through the four work areas (Machining-1, Machining-2, Assembly, and Packaging).
- The finished products are delivered to the client's delivery vehicles in the kanban containers. Empty containers that are returned are the instructions to the work centre to provide more finished components.

Kanbans and bar codes

Although the kanban system dates back to the 1980s it is still in wide use today. Probably the major change is that for most industries the kanbans are written in bar code form. When containers arrive at a centre, the bar codes are controlled by a laser reader that automatically records them into the systems database.

Figure 15.11 Kanbans between supplier, work centre, and client

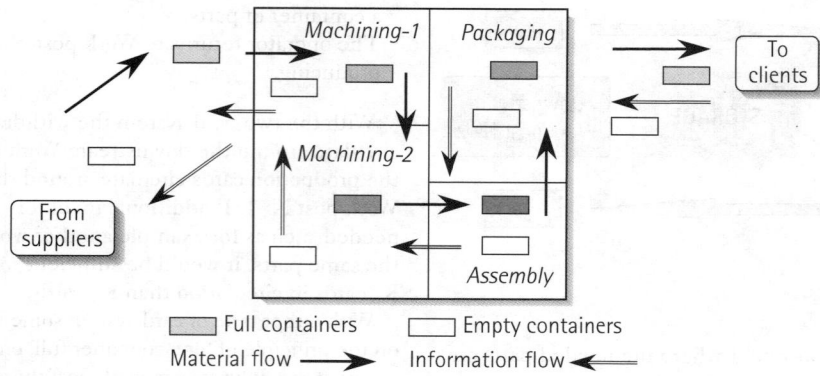

Full containers   Empty containers
Material flow ⟶   Information flow ⟵

Similarly when containers leave the operating centre the bar codes are scanned by the laser reader that then deducts the items in the container from the system.

Determining the number of kanbans

The number of kanbans to put into circulation might be determined by calculation or empirically.

Calculation

The number of kanbans might be determined from the formula:

$$N = \frac{R * T * (1 + X)}{C}$$

where, and for example:

- R is the rate of utilization of components, say 750 units/hour
- T is the delay in receiving a container and would include the production time, transfer time, and waiting time, say 45 minutes or 0.75 hour
- C is the capacity of the container in units, say 50 units
- X is a variation which takes into account demand or other randomness in the operation, say 6%.

Thus:

$$N = \frac{R * T * (1 + X)}{C} = \frac{750 * (45/60) * (1 + 0.06)4}{50}$$
$$= 11.925 \text{ or say 12 kanbans}$$

In this calculation as both the randomness in the operation and the delay are reduced then the number of kanbans can be reduced. This is the direction of just-in-time to approach a continuous flow process with minimum delays.

Empirical

It is the number of kanbans in circulation that determines the amount of products that can be produced, used, or transferred. One way of deciding on the number of kanbans is first to make a rough estimate of the number necessary by analyzing operating rates and utilization at all of the work posts involved. This number is put into circulation. Afterwards, the movement of inventory is analyzed. If there is two much inventory of a particular product reference then the number of kanbans is gradually reduced in order to obtain a smooth flow. If stockout situations start to occur for a particular reference, then the number of kanbans is increased. (See also Tadaaki Fukukawa, 'The determination of the optimal number of kanbans in a just-in-time production system'.[5])

Priority work when using kanbans

Whenever there are kanbans posted at a work post it means that somewhere in the system there are empty containers of parts. When several products are being produced at a work post, a question always arises which reference should be made next, or what is the priority. The following gives three methods.

Method 1

Assume that a work centre is producing four different components A, B, C and D as given in Figure 15.12. The status of the kanbans is as shown in Table 15.3.

From this information, the priority for the operator is to make product reference C, since there are no full containers of these parts in the work centre (4 − 4 = 0).

Figure 15.12 Priority board for using kanbans: Method 1

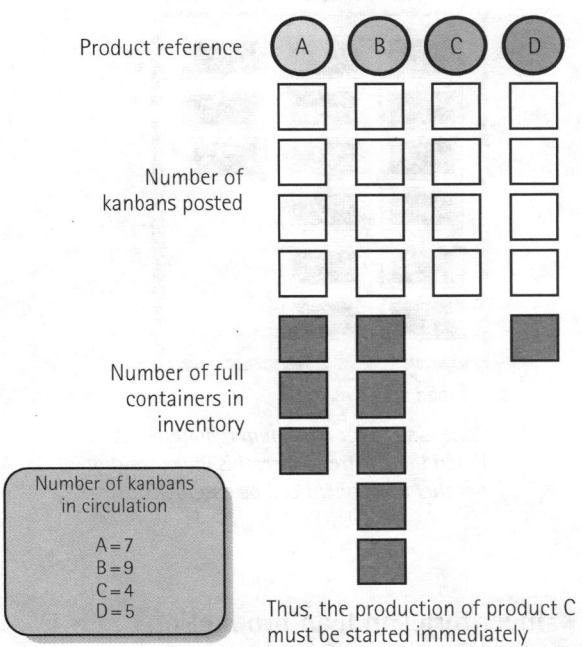

Product reference

Number of kanbans posted

Number of full containers in inventory

Number of kanbans in circulation

A = 7
B = 9
C = 4
D = 5

Thus, the production of product C must be started immediately

Table 15.3 Kanban status in work centre producing four components

Product reference	A	B	C	D
Kanbans in circulation	7	9	4	5
Number of kanbans posted	4	4	4	4
Number of full containers in work centre	3	5	0	1

Method 2

Another approach, used by a manufacturer of automobile components, is illustrated in Figure 15.13. For the particular workstation shown there are four components being produced of reference numbers 586-769, 186-354, 186-527, and 184-892. Each reference has an area where the kanbans are posted. Above each posting area the zone is marked green (far left), orange (centre), and red (far right). If there are kanbans posted in the red zone this means that these products have a high priority of being produced. If they are in the green zone then this is a low priority. For the situation illustrated the status is as shown in Table 15.4.

Figure 15.13 Priority board for using kanbans: Method 2

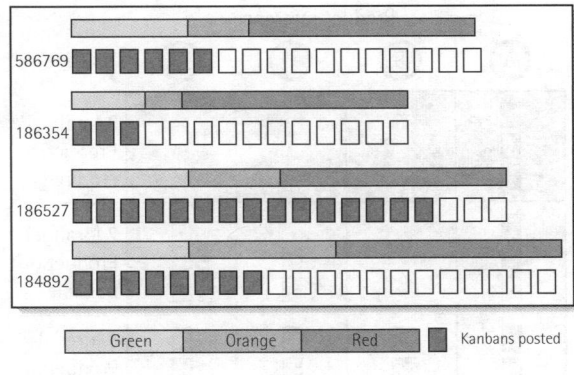

| Green | Orange | Red | ■ Kanbans posted |

Table 15.4 Kanban status in automobile component manufacture

Reference	586769	186354	186527	184892
Zone present	Orange	Green	Red	Orange
Status	Required soon	None required	Urgent	Required soon

Thus the next component to be produced would be N° 186527. As components are being used in the work centre the kanbans would be returned to this display board. Thus, the kanbans now in the orange zone would move to the red zone, and so these components would have a high priority for production.

Method 3

This approach is used by a manufacturer of a variety of consumer products as illustrated in Figure 15.14. Like Method 2 there are three zones (see Table 15.5).

- If there are kanbans posted in Zone 3 (as is the case for product reference A) then production is necessary immediately.
- If there are no kanbans posted in Zones 2 or 3 (as is the case for product reference B) then production is stopped. (The absence of kanbans means that in the work area there are containers of product reference B.)
- For product references C and D production is possible and would depend on the resources available.

Figure 15.14 **Priority board for using kanbans: Method 3**

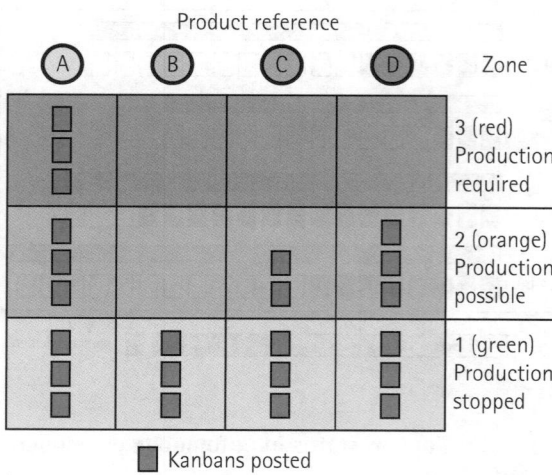

Product reference

A   B   C   D   Zone

3 (red)
Production
required

2 (orange)
Production
possible

1 (green)
Production
stopped

◼ Kanbans posted

Figure 15.15 **Kanban zones for large objects**

Reference GDHW 10

Taped area

*Zone is sized for maximum requirements
When there is free space, this indicates that
another component can be assembled*

Table 15.5 **Kanban status for variety of consumer products**

Zone	Situation
1	Production stopped
2	Production possible
3	Production required

Kanban zones for large objects

When large components are being handled such as automobile engines, pumps, or furniture items, the card system can be replaced by kanban zones marked out on the work centre floor as illustrated in Figure 15.15. Here the zone is a rectangle marked out by a yellow tape. This zone contains the maximum number of components. When the zone is not completely filled, this is the authorization for operators immediately upstream of this storage area to produce another component. When the zone is full, no production is necessary.

An alternative organization for the kanban zones is to colour code them in green, orange, and red, similar to the display board. When the red zone is uncovered this means that production requirements take a high priority. The reverse would be when the green zone is uncovered.

Inventories in lean production

In lean manufacturing the ideal situation is to have zero inventory thus keeping waste of resources to a minimum. In practice, this is probably impossible because it would mean that the entire purchasing, production, and distribution function are finely tuned. However, it is desirable to have the minimum amount of inventory to keep costs low, and at the same time maintaining a smooth production operation.

High inventories

If there is a high level of raw material, in-process and/or finished goods inventories, then it may not be immediately critical if:

- suppliers are late delivering the raw materials
- orders are modified either by the customer or by the production department
- material is off-specification and cannot be used
- product designs are changed at the last minute
- machine setup times are long necessitating high inventories to account for the downtime
- production orders change often
- a machine malfunctions as it is poorly maintained

Figure 15.16 Inventory is analogous to rocks in a river (1)

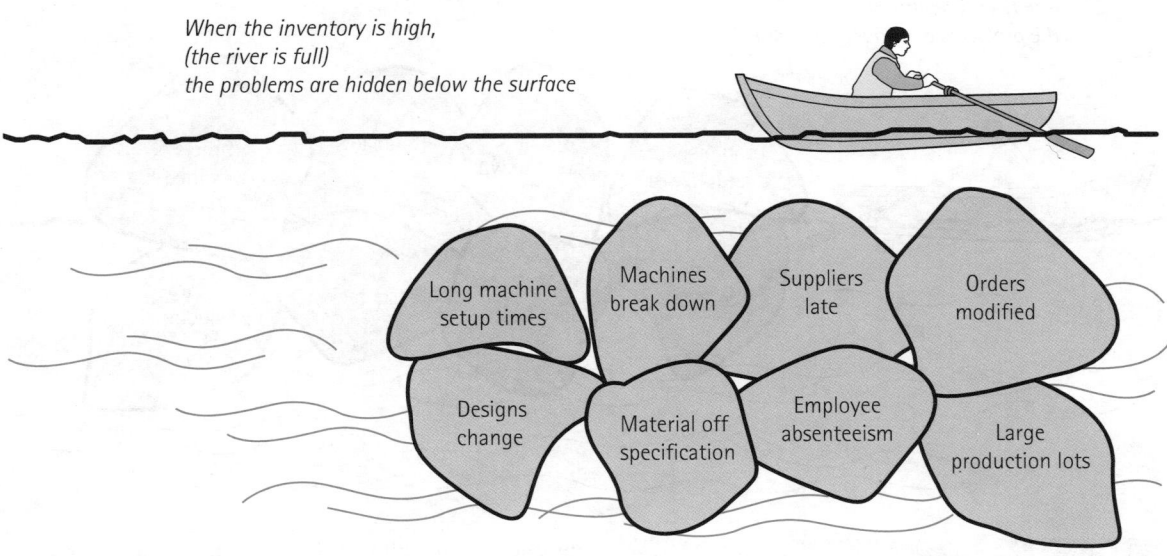

When the inventory is high,
(the river is full)
the problems are hidden below the surface

- Long machine setup times
- Machines break down
- Suppliers late
- Orders modified
- Designs change
- Material off specification
- Employee absenteeism
- Large production lots

- scrap rates are high because of poor operation
- production lots are large
- information flow to work posts is slow and incomplete
- employees are often absent
- work pauses are long.

A high level of inventory of raw materials, components, and finished products in the form of 'safety stock' is a buffer against these uncertainties. However, all this 'safety stock' represents a large financial investment, which can be put to better use elsewhere.

Low inventories

A part of the just-in-time philosophy is to keep minimum inventories. To do this, scrupulous attention has to be paid to all aspects of operations including:

- Reduce machine setup times.
- Eliminate last-minute design changes.
- Preventive maintenance of all equipment and machines.
- Motivation of workforce to reduce absenteeism.
- Reduce lot sizes.
- A close working relationship with sales and operations to minimize last-minute order changes.

- Working with suppliers so that they respect delivery schedules. If not engage other suppliers. (It is a competitive world!)
- Enforce attention to quality to avoid off-specification material.

If attention is not paid to these aspects, and inventory is reduced, then problems will occur preventing production to meet client demands.

Analogy

The high inventory situation can be compared to the situation of rocks at the bottom of a river. In the spring, when the river is running high, there is no problem to the oarsman out for his daily row (Figure 15.16). However, in the autumn, when the river level has fallen to a low level the rocks become closer to the surface, or are even exposed. In this case, the situation becomes critical and dangerous to river users (Figure 15.17). This is analogous to the firm. When the operation is running at a relatively steady state and there are high inventories operating problems may not be immediately critical. However, if the customers' demand increases rapidly inventory will drop and the firm's operating problems will be exposed so that it is unable to meet demand.

Figure 15.17 Inventory is analogous to rocks in a river (2)

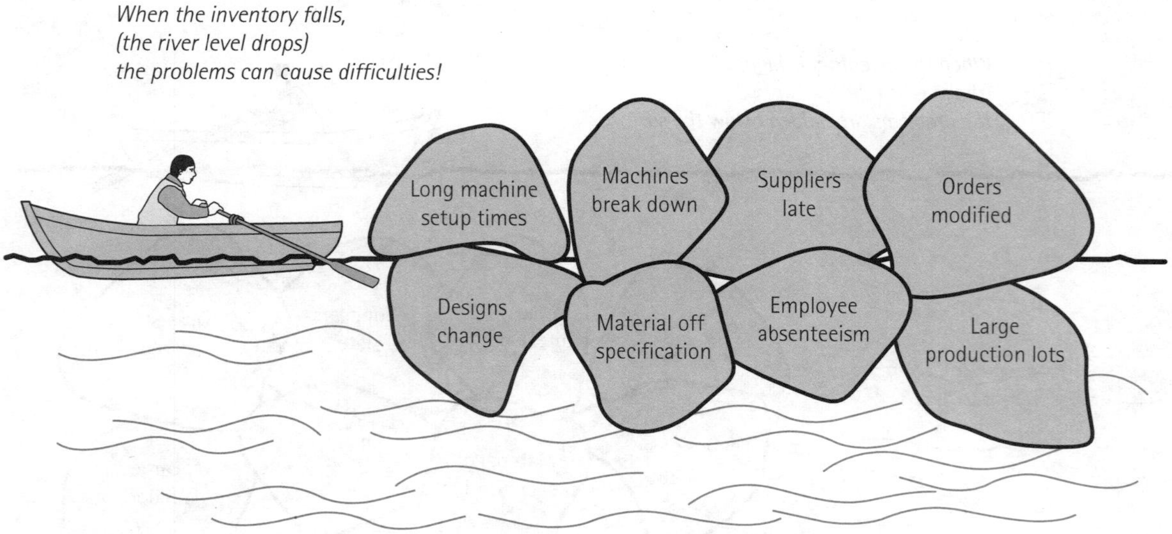

When the inventory falls,
(the river level drops)
the problems can cause difficulties!

Machine setup times, and single minute exchange of die

Producing in lots

A machine setup involves all the activities to prepare for a production run. This might involve heating up feed lines such as the case for plastic moulding, changing the machine die in order to accommodate a different unit format, or cleaning the equipment before a different product is made. Very often, the reason why units are produced in lots is because these setup times, a non-value-added activity, are long. The setup times translate into an operating cost because of the salaries or wages that have to be made to the operators to perform these setup tasks. As a result, the logic is that more products should be produced in one batch or lot in order to reduce the unit setup costs (setup cost/units per lot). Operating with large lots has the effect of increasing inventory levels. The following gives two illustrations.

Pharmaceutical industry

Many pharmaceutical products are made by batch processes. For example, for a certain antiseptic cream, the sold active ingredient is dissolved in a mixing vessel water to give an aqueous solution. This solution is then transferred to another stainless steel mixing vessel where lanolin or other grease materials are added in order to make a cream formula (creams are better absorbed by the skin). This resulting batch is then unloaded to the filling area where the cream is filled into tubes. Assume that the next production run for the two vessels is a mosquito cream whose formula is quite different from the previous antiseptic cream. In this case, the two vessels and the inlet and outlet lines have to be completely steam cleaned before the next production run can be made. This cleaning is the setup time and may take between two and four hours depending on the operation. In order that the filling line has continuous feed, an upstream inventory of semi-finished goods of any of the products made in the mixing vessel has to be maintained.

Injection moulding in the plastics industry

Consider the plastic crates that are used for transporting merchandising. These are produced in large injection moulds. The master mould, from which the plastic item is produced is often steel, quite heavy, and has to be bolted onto the injection machine. The setup in this instance includes the changing of the mould for different formats. Further, if the colour of the object changes, then the feed lines have to be thoroughly cleaned so that the previous colour does not contaminate the colour about to be used. A particular problem arises in making yellow objects after red. It is very difficult to remove 100% of the red and so the first yellow items that are produced contain red speckles and have to be scrapped. Again, in order not to interrupt the flow during the setup operation, an inventory of units has to be maintained at least sufficient to ensure continuous operation during the machine downtime.

Implementation of SMED

Just-in-time systems concentrate on reducing the setup times on machines in order that it is more economic to produce in small lot sizes. The principle of analyzing the system is known as single minute exchange of die, or SMED. The principle evolved from the work of Shigeo Shingo, of Toyota Motor Co. in Japan in the 1980s who spent some 19 years rigorously analyzing the setup procedures related to automobile manufacture.[6] An ultimate objective was to change a machine tool in under ten minutes and thus the expression, *single minute exchange of die*. The idea comes from Formula 1 motor racing where the rapid pit change of wheels, oil, filters, etc., can enormously enhance the chance of a driver winning a race.

To effect SMED procedures, the logic is to establish the distinction between:

* an external setup that occurs when the machine is running and producing units
* an internal setup when the machine is stopped in order to make the necessary adjustments.

To maximize throughput, the setup procedures should be performed where possible while a machine is running, or an *external setup*. That is, the activity is being performed in parallel with actual production time. Only those setup procedures which cannot be performed unless the machine is stopped, or an *internal setup*, should be carried out at this time. For example, the transfer of machine tools, moulds, or dies to the storage area should only be performed while a machine is running. The actual changing of a die, or a mould, can normally only be performed while the machine is stopped. If preheating of a machine is necessary, perhaps this can be performed while a machine is operating. In general setup times can be reduced by:

* Locating required inventory, and machine tools closer to the operating area.
* Standardizing the setup functions of machines.
* Improving the procedures for tool preparation.
* Eliminating unnecessary machine adjustments.
* Synchronizing operator jobs.
* Automating setup procedures, using computer control, although this should only be implemented if overall it is less costly than manual adjustments.

Figure 15.18 gives an example of the impact on the total operating time when a system SMED is implemented. The setup time has been reduced from 2.5 hours to 8 minutes. This allows the total production time for producing four products, A, B, C, and D to be

Figure 15.18 Single minute exchange of die (SMED)

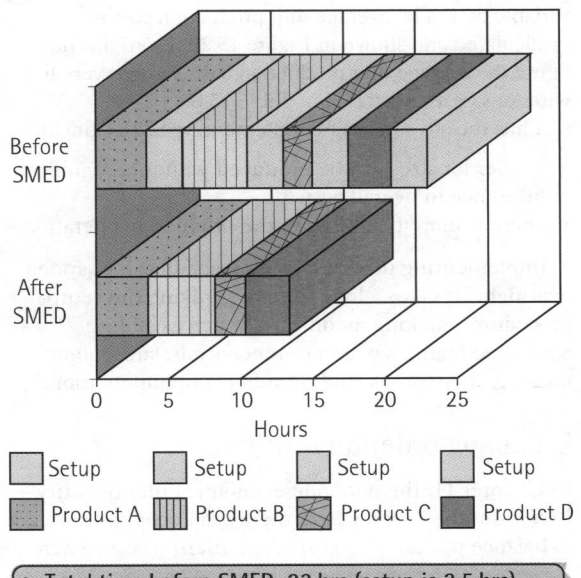

| Setup | Setup | Setup | Setup |
| Product A | Product B | Product C | Product D |

* Total time before SMED 23 hrs (setup is 2.5 hrs)
* Total time after SMED, 13 hr 32 min (setup is 8 min)
* Reduction of 41%

Table 15.6 SMED and setup times: Presses

Company	Setup time (before)	Setup time (after)	Reduction factor
Arakawa Auto Body Industries	1 hr 40 min	7 min 46 sec	13
Matsushita Electric	2 hr 10 min	7 min 25 sec	18
Sharp Electric	1 hr 20 min	5 min 45 sec	14
I Metals	50 min	2 min 48 sec	18
Toyota Manufacturing	4 hr 0 min	4 min 18 sec	56

reduced from 23 hours to 13 hours 32 minutes, or some 41%. The reduction in setup time translates into a reduction in cost and a gain in productivity of resources. Tables 15.6 and 15.7 give some industry examples.[7]

Average unit production cost

In Chapter 11, the average unit production cost was shown when the setup cost was $275.00/unit and the unit variable cost was $15/unit. This curve is repeated in Figure 15.19.

Assume that with the implementation of SMED the setup cost is reduced to $2.75/unit keeping the same $15/unit variable cost. The average unit production cost is recalculated and shown in Figure 15.20. From this new figure the average unit production cost changes very little with lot size as illustrated in Table 15.8.

Thus the advantages in implementing SMED include:

- Smaller lot sizes can be produced without a significant difference in overall cost.
- There is more flexibility in the production operation.

Implementing the SMED approach doesn't happen overnight. It takes a long time of studying the setup procedures, making modification such as adding automatic features or computer controls, subsequent training of operators, and then final implementation.

Economic order quantity

In Chapter 11, the notion of economic order quantity, EOQ, was discussed where there is an economic lot size to balance the carrying costs and ordering costs where

Table 15.7 SMED and setup times: Plastic forming machines

Company	Setup time (before)	Setup time (after)	Reduction factor
M Manufacturing	6 hr 40 min	7 min 36 sec	53
N Rubber	2 hr 0 min	4 min 18 sec	28
N Chemicals	40 min	3 min 45 sec	11
D Plastics	50 min	2 min 26 sec	19
Y Synthetics	40 min	2 min 48 sec	14

Figure 15.19 Lot size and average unit cost (before SMED)

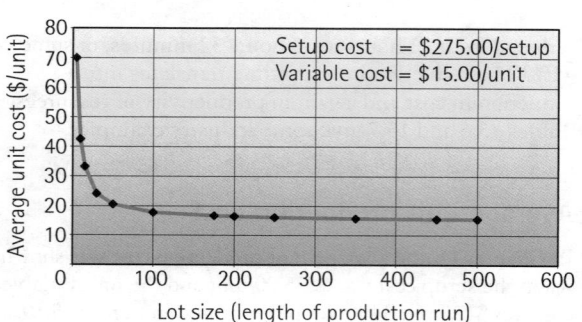

the ordering costs would be equivalent to setup costs for an internal company operation. Figure 15.21 shows the EOQ curve where there is a balance between the ordering costs and carrying costs such that the total costs are a minimum. In this case it occurs when the number of units is 3536.

Applying SMED

Applying the SMED principle to reduce the setup time, and thus reducing the ordering costs, has the effect of

Figure 15.20 Lot size and average unit cost (after SMED)

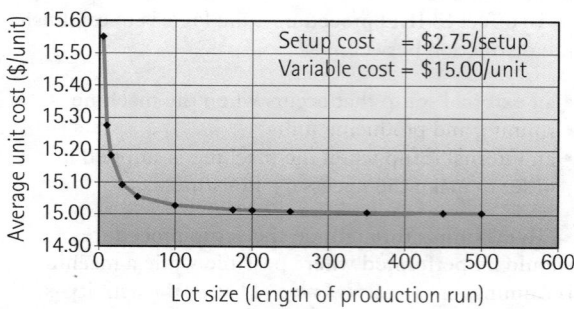

Table 15.8 SMED and production costs

	Lot size (units)		
	5	500	Change (%)
Cost after SMED ($/unit)	15.55	15.01	3.47
Cost before SMED ($/unit)	70.00	15.55	77.78

Figure 15.21 EOQ: Carrying and ordering costs (ordering = $125.00/order)

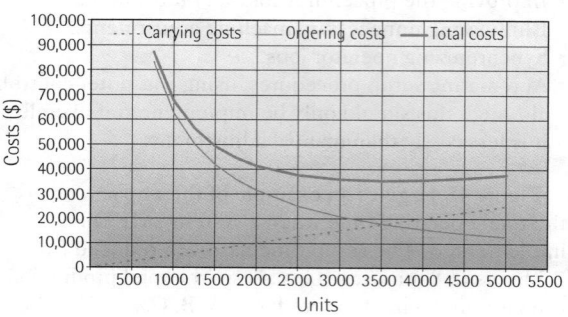

decreasing the number of units to balance ordering costs and carrying costs. This is illustrated in Figure 15.22 where the ordering costs have been reduced by a factor of 10. In this case the EOQ quantity is now 1118 units.

Going further by decreasing the ordering cost by yet another factor of 10 to $1.25/order (Figure 15.23) results in an EOQ quantity of 354 units.

Thus, in applying the SMED principle, the economic production lot size approaches zero as the setup costs approach zero, which has the impact of nullifying the importance of EOQ with a real just-in-time operation. An alternative in a just-in-time operation, and still applying the EOQ concept, is to accept a small value for the EOQ and then to determine what ordering costs (the setup costs and indirectly the setup time), would be needed in order to produce small lot sizes.

Overall equipment effectiveness

Principle

When an operator in a production operation is assigned to a production operation such as running a lathe, cutting, or drilling machine, the just-in-time philosophy requires that the time spent should be maximized to working on the part in question, or adding value. If a large proportion of time is occupied by non-value activities, then productivity is low. An analysis of machine utilization, or work post, can be performed by determining the overall equipment effectiveness. Figure 15.24 illustrates the overall equipment effectiveness analysis and the terms are discussed as follows.

Open time

The open time is the total time a day, say eight hours, that an operator has available to work on a machine. This would be a theoretical, or open time of 100%.

Operator pause

Operator pauses include the time that an operator stops for coffee, to go to the bathroom, or just to 'chat'. In the example given, the time for breaks in any one day is considered to be 5 minutes every hour, or 40 minutes in the 8-hour day. This reduces the effective time to 92% of open time.

Machine breakdown

Machine breakdown is the time when a machine stops running, or has to be shut down because of unforeseen mechanical problems. In this case 35 minutes has been assumed. This reduces effective time to 84% of the open time.

Figure 15.22 EOQ: Carrying and ordering costs (ordering = $12.50/order)

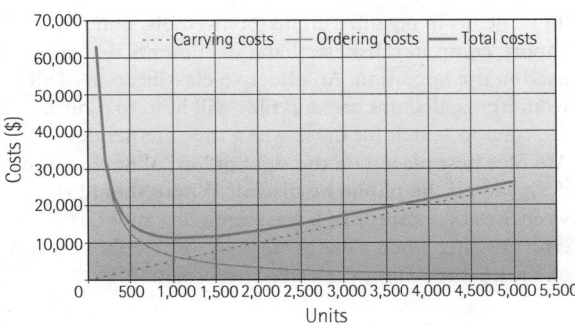

Figure 15.23 EOQ: Carrying and ordering costs (ordering = $1.25/order)

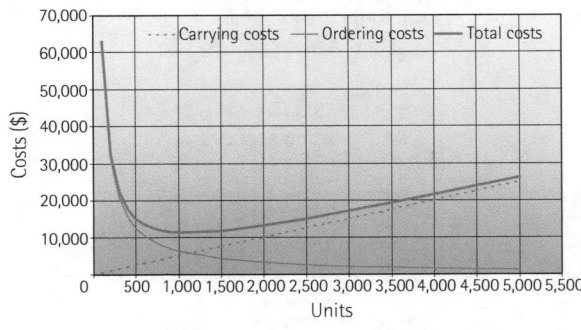

Figure 15.24 Overall equipment effectiveness

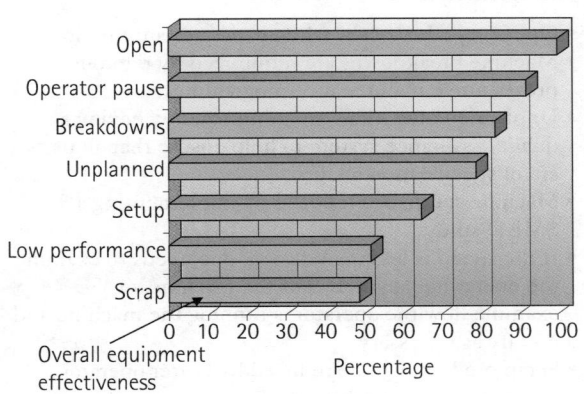

Unplanned interruptions

Unplanned interruptions represent the time lost because, say, the part jams up the machine, or the machine has to be modified in order to accept the piece because it is too large, or too small. Here, 24 minutes has been assumed which drops the effective time of the machine to 79%.

Machine setup

Machine setup is the time taken to readjust the machine so that it can work on a different product. Here, 70 minutes has been assumed which drops the machine effectiveness to 65% of the open time.

Low performance

Low performance is that the machine throughput is less than design. This might be because the machine has been badly maintained and is not running correctly, or the operator is not correctly trained for running the machine. Here, 62 minutes has been assumed which drops the effective operating time to 52%.

Scrap products

Scrap products represent the time spent on producing parts that are not according to specification and have to be scrapped. Here, 12 minutes has been assumed which has reduced the effective time to 49%. This final figure is then the overall equipment effectiveness.

Thus, unless careful attention is paid to the operation of a machine the effective usefulness can drop rapidly. If this is the case, in-process inventory needs to be maintained upstream of each machine or workstation to take into account these operating inefficiencies.

Improving machine effectiveness

Considerations that can bring the overall equipment effectiveness closer to 100% are:

- Operators take breaks when machines are running.
- Machine breakdowns are minimized by rigorous preventative maintenance programmes.
- Unplanned operations are minimized by having a quality assurance system to help ensure that all parts are of specification quality.
- Machine setups are reduced by implementing a SMED study.
- If the speed is less than design, one needs to examine the operating parameters of the machine, or examine how the operator is running the machine and modify as necessary.
- Scrap products can be reduced by better operator training, improving quality procedures upstream of the machine in question, or assuring suppliers provide materials always of specification quality.

The five S rules

Lean production incorporating just-in-time implies being rigorous, organized, and efficient. The Japanese have five expressions for this (see Figure 15.25).

Seiro (remove)

Here the philosophy is to remove from the work area any unneeded work tools, materials, equipment, or paperwork. The idea being is that if you don't need it, don't have it cluttering the operating area because it might get in the way and slow down your activity. This applies equally to an operator in a production centre, as to person working in an office. In the latter case if you receive clients in your office, a cluttered desk gives the impression that you are a sloppy worker. In the 1970s and the 1980s I worked for an engineering services company. We had instructions to have only one design sheet on our desk at any one time. If there were any more then it was considered we were 'not organized'.

Seiton (organize)

This means to organize all materials, tools, pencils, papers, computer diskettes, and documents that are used in the operation. An effective classification of all work items, documents, and files will help to reduce the time to search for these when they are needed. Are files best placed on the right or left? Where on the desk should the phone be placed? Where should the wrenches be located? In a service environment, it is embarrassing when a client stops by, or telephones, and one is unable to find the correct information.

Figure 15.25 The five S rules

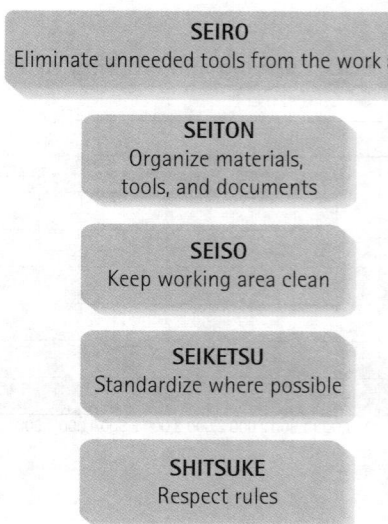

Seiso (keep clean)

If in a manufacturing environment, keeping the working area clean, is appropriate from a health and safety point of view. If machines are being used this means removing excess oil, dirt, water etc. In the food industry it goes without saying that the work environment should be kept clean. In the office, keep desks clean and computer equipment free of grease. A clean working area not only looks better but also it aids in doing quality work (at least psychologically) and gives a good impression to clients, co-workers, or supervisors who might stop by the office.

Seiketsu (standardize)

Where possible standardize operations and activities so that whoever is at the work centre, the job in hand is performed in the same manner, and with the same materials. Standards should be set for how a job is to be performed, how a design is to be executed, when machines should be cleaned or overhauled, or where material should be filed, etc. When standards have been established, they should be made visible and easily accessible to all those concerned in the organization. Setting standards for the operations is one of the criteria for ISO-9000 quality standards, which are discussed in Chapter 4.

Shitsuke (respect the rules)

Organizations, firms, and society function through teamwork and cooperation, which involves respecting rules. Specific rules might apply to procedures for machine cleaning or adjustments, or materials to use. Or, there might be general rules related to safety, arriving or leaving at the correct time, smoking only in the designated areas, etc. Respecting rules avoids stressful situations among teams and enhances efficiency.

The five and 'six' zeros

For a perfect, ideal operation there are five zeros (and by corollary) a sixth, as illustrated in Figure 15.26.

Zero breakdowns

Zero breakdowns means that all equipment, tools, and machines are in perfect running order during production. To achieve this, there has to be a regular schedule of preventive maintenance. A printing press, a numerically controlled drilling machine, or an air compressor that malfunctions during production will result in unnecessary costs, delays, and probably irritated clients.

Zero defects

Zero defects implies that all raw materials, component parts, and finished products are faultless. This means that suppliers respect all specifications and quality control before delivering their products to the client. Plant operators upstream verify the quality of their work before passing it along to the downstream post. The key is 'quality at the source'.

Zero delays

Zero delays implies that all delivery dates are respected. A supplier delivers his components when promised, an operator finishes his work when scheduled, and a manager completes his report on time. To achieve this, schedules that are prepared must be realistic, and all those implicated in the work must be aware, and agree to the planning.

Zero inventory

Zero inventory is that stocks of raw material, in-process parts, and finished goods are zero. In practice this is impossible and probably not desirable. However, the philosophy is to keep stocks to as near zero as feasible to keep the operation functioning smoothly. Unnecessary inventory means idle investments, space used unnecessarily, and risk of obsolescence. Of course less than zero inventory is more of a problem since this implies stockouts and production shutdowns, and/or dissatisfied or lost clients.

Zero paper

The use of kanbans as a method of communication reduces paper orders and instructions. Paper instructions can be misinterpreted (especially if badly written). Also, it has to be recognized that some persons in a

Figure 15.26 The five (and even six) zeros

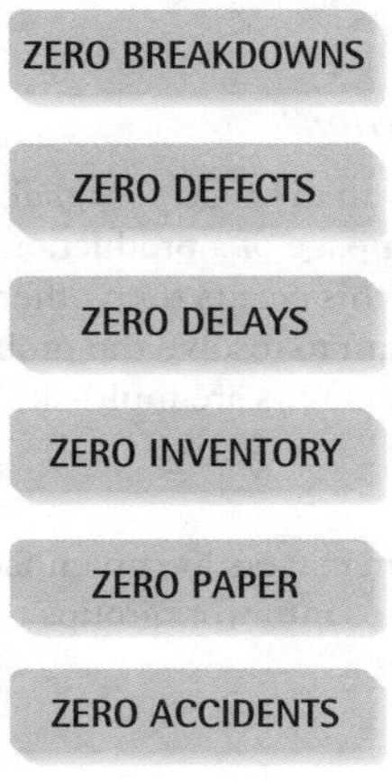

ZERO BREAKDOWNS

ZERO DEFECTS

ZERO DELAYS

ZERO INVENTORY

ZERO PAPER

ZERO ACCIDENTS

production centre may not have a good command of the working language and thus unable to correctly interpret instructions. Electronic data interchange and other computer transfers also reduces the paper flow. Again, for the moment it is hard to envisage a real 'zero paper' world. However, again the requirement is to minimize the quantity employed.

'Zero accidents'

Zero accidents is the corollary of a well-managed operation. Machines properly serviced and protected, the workplace well organized and clean, the necessary training, and the required protective clothing should be available to keep accidents at zero. In addition to the most important human aspect, accidents result in delays, cost, and company image.

All these 'zero' concepts can be attained with good management, the correct training, and appropriate control systems in place.

Quality

Lean production enforces adherence to quality work at all levels. (See also Chapter 4.) The following summarizes some of the quality elements and the role in lean production.

Quality at the source

Quality at the source means putting all employees in the driver's seat as far as the responsibility of the quality of their work.

Control station

Every operator is also a quality control station. In addition for machining, assembling, or other task, the worker is responsible for inspecting his own work, identifying any defects, reworking them, and correcting any cause of defects.

Stopping production

Each worker is given the right to signal, by pressing an alarm bell, the stoppage of a production line if a problem is encountered. If this occurs then other workers on the chain work as a team to resolve the problem. This implies that the operators are multi-skilled.

Work groups

Workers and line managers are given facilities to organize themselves into workgroups to analyze

problems, or to discuss production improvements. These work groups are informal, and kept small (seven to nine people). For example in the motor assembly area of Renault VI in Lyon, France, there are eating areas positioned very close to the assembly line. Experience has shown that workers feel more comfortable discussing work on the spot, rather than being taken away to another location. Also, time is not wasted in looking for a meeting place. These workgroups are also known as quality circles in Japanese manufacturing organizations.

Inventories

With a reduction in inventories, there is no safety margin. If there are stoppages due to machine problems or defective components production has to stop until the problem has been fixed. For example, if components are defective because of a machine fault, the fact that there are low inventories means that only a few parts are affected and the cost involved is small. Since production is stopped until the problem is corrected, attention then is on solving the quality problem, so that it will not be repeated.

Well-trained employees

In just in time, similar type products are produced every day. With well-trained employees, job assignments are well understood, workers are familiar with their task, and this aids in improving product quality. Again, multi-skilled employees improve the flexibility of the organization and the motivation of the individual.

Purchasing

In just-in-time, companies strive to have a small number of suppliers, and supplier networks, which can be relied on to deliver parts of perfect quality, or *quality at the source*. As illustrated in Figure 15.10, suppliers use the replacement principle of kanban in which small, standard size containers are used to deliver supplies frequently to customers and giving them the authority to delivery components directly to production line without going through inspection. (See Chapter 16.)

Automated equipment

Using automated equipment, and robots goes a long way in helping to manufacture parts of superior quality. Automated machines produce a consistent output in such areas as soldering, painting, and stamping, although robots may not always be the answer as they lack the flexibility of the individual and there is a high investment cost.

Preventive maintenance

To avoid production interruptions, intensive preventive maintenance programmes are in place to adjust machines and equipment before they break down. Machines constantly in adjustment produce parts that are within quality standards. (See also Chapter 19.)

Statistical quality control

The use of statistical quality control techniques (see Chapter 20) are used to monitor the quality of parts produced at each workstation. Further, easy to understand charts and graphs are used to communicate progress to workers and managers.

Just-in-time in services

Toyota's just-in-time approach was originally conceived for a manufacturing organization. However, since JIT is strongly focused on organization, processes, and repetitive activities service firms can operate very much in a just-in-time mode. The following are some illustrations.

Fast food restaurants

Fast food outlets like McDonald's, Burger King, or Quick restaurants operate with many just-in-time characteristics. Here there are standard products, low inventories of finished goods, and repetitive processes in the food preparation (fries, hamburgers, coffee, etc.) and the way it is served (tray on the counter, ask for order, ring up the order, place the food on the tray, and take the money). There is rigorous organization and design of the food preparation facility (see Chapter 9) and even the cash registers with their icons, rather than numbers, speed up the efficiency of serving the client. Further, the addition of a drive-in service means clients can be served 'just-when-needed'. Some fast food firms are considering they will go further with their just-in-time service by installing computer-monitored machines to make the fries, robots to prepare drinks, and computer systems to 'sense' traffic so orders can be prepared in advance and perform an analysis of how many employees are needed on any particular day.[8]

Delivery services

Delivery services such as Federal Express, UPS, and Deutsche Post offer a just-in-time approach for collecting and dispatching packages providing almost worldwide next-day deliveries. These services of course came about when government-run postal services were unable, or unwilling to provide reliability of their services.

Transportation

Many modern transportation systems are designed to offer almost immediate or continuous service analogous to just-in-time. Concerning the equipment, for example, on the bullet trains in Japan or France, which travel at 300 km/hr, a service can be offered every 3 or 4 minutes. (The distance separating the trains is a minimum of seven kilometres and they need three kilometres to stop from the maximum speed.) Metro or underground rail offers services every minute. Even international airports can allow up to about 40 planes every hour landing or taking off on the same runway. At the airports there is careful synchronization and planning between connecting flights, baggage handling, and passenger changes.

Entertainment

In the entertainment field, theme parks (Disneyland being a prime example) operate using the criteria of lean production certainly when it comes to the five S terms. The attraction parks are clean, staff has standard procedures, preventive maintenance of equipment is well planned, and attractions are synchronized to permit the maximum number of clients to visit during the day.

News emissions

Television stations offering news programmes such as CNN, BBC World News, or Euronews (based in Ecully, France) operate on a just-in-time operation where the presentations provide immediate 'just-happened events'. In fact CNN is credited being better than the US government in providing up-to-date information.

Risks in lean manufacturing

Lean manufacturing involves rigorous organizing, a disciplined workforce, few suppliers, and minimum inventories. That is, no fat. This involves risks, which can be very costly when there are unplanned occurrences such as in Industry insights 15.2 and 15.3. Both concern the Toyota Company, the originator of both lean manufacturing and just-in-time!

Industry insight 15.2

An earthquake ...

At 5.46am on 17 January 1995 an earthquake of 7.2 on the Richter scale shook the Kansai region of Japan for 20 seconds, with an epicentre between the port of Kobe and the island of Awaji. It resulted in the deaths of 6300 people, destroyed 100,000 buildings, and severely damaged another 100,000. The Toyota plant was not itself affected but two of its suppliers near Kobe, which provide car radios and brake callipers suffered serious damage and had to shut down production. Since Toyota was working rigidly with its just-in-time programme having parts delivered just when needed, the loss of these two plants forced Toyota to close all 12 of its Japanese assembly plants. The earthquake affected not only Toyota but hundreds of other companies both in Japan and overseas which depend on parts and components from firms located in the Kansai region, an area that accounts for some 12.2% of Japan's industrial production. As a Toyota official remarked: 'The JIT system runs very smoothly but we are unable to build into it an act of God like an earthquake. This is a problem, but we will fix it.'

Adapted from: 'Not quite in time', *Business Week*[9]

Industry insight 15.3

... then a fire

In February 1997 there was a major fire at the Aisin Seika plant in Kariya, Japan which makes master cylinders that pump hydraulic fluid for brakes and clutches and also proportioning valves that regulate hydraulic fluid in brake lines. The fire destroyed a major part of the plant and was shut down. Over 80% of these component parts are supplied to Toyota Automobile in Japan and the snowball effect was that production of 16,200 automobiles a day at 29 of Toyota's Japanese assembly plants was shut down for several days. This stoppage came at a critical time for Toyota, whose Japanese plants were striving to keep pace with brisk domestic sales and strong US demand for popular exports as the RAV4, Lexus, and 4-Runner sports-utility models. Taking into account the approximate 30,000 yen ($2470) average profit Toyota makes on an average car, the shutdown was estimated at about 4.9 billion yen a day ($40.4 million).

The fact that one supplier could paralyze a complete automobile firm illustrates the vulnerability to the just-in-time method of production and also the weakness of the *keiretsu* network system where companies still depend on affiliates for much of their sourcing. Aisin Seika is about 28% owned by Toyota and another Toyota affiliate, Toyota Automatic Loom Works. In the past, Toyota had used two suppliers for these particular automobile components but because of strict cost control measures this was reduced to just one supplier, the Aisin Seika plant in the central part of the country.

Adapted from: 'Fire at parts supplier's factory forces Toyota to shut down production in Japan', *Wall Street Journal Europe*[10]

Summary of key elements

• Eliminating waste is an objective in lean production, for example, the waste of time in repairing faulty products, in the investment of high inventories, and of having idle workers.

• Just-in-time (JIT) is producing or delivering exactly the quantity of units demanded, at the correct date, and at the right place. It is a system of enforced problem solving with no safety factors. All material meets quality standards, every worker is productive, and machines function correctly.

• Just-in-time is a pull system where client orders pull material through the supply chain. This is the opposite of the system in which producers push material through the pipeline.

• JIT and MRP systems can be effectively integrated in an operating environment.

• Insufficient training, poor product design, unbalanced workstations, poor communication, idle time, and poor job design are reasons for low productivity.

• Designing a system under a just-in-time mode can enormously increase efficiency in terms of the value-added time.

• If operators are multi-skilled, then changes in customer demands can be accommodated by balancing the system with cellular-type arrangements.

• A kanban is a card used for communicating between work centres. Modifying the number of kanbans in circulation can change the volume of products produced.

- In kanban systems, colour-coded priority boards can be used to indicate which units should be the next in production.

- For large objects, kanban zones can be marked out on the floor of a work centre.

- SMED is a study to reduce setup times, which ultimately will reduce unit production costs. To implement SMED, distinctions must be made between external setups when the machine is running, and internal setups when the machine is stopped.

- If the SMED principle is applied this has the effect of nullifying the impact of the economic order quantity in production situations.

- The overall equipment effectiveness involves an analysis of machines, or work posts, to increase the value-added time of an operation. It analyzes breakdowns, operator pauses, non-quality of materials, setup times, etc.

- Adopting the five S rules, *seiro* (remove), *seiton* (organize), *seiso* (keep clean), *seiketsu* (standardize), and *shitsuke* (respect rules), aids operation efficiency.

- The five zeros in JIT are zero breakdowns; zero defects; zero delays; zero inventory; zero paper; which, if practised, give the sixth corollary of zero accidents.

- Quality in lean production pertains to quality at the source, reduced inventories, trained employees, few suppliers, automated equipment, preventive maintenance, and using statistical quality control.

- Just-in-time can apply to services in which there are repetitive operations and standard products such as in fast food outlets, delivery services, transportation, theme park attractions, and news delivery.

- Unplanned occurrences such as fire, earthquake, strike, etc., can be very costly for a firm operating in a just-in-time mode since there is no 'fat'.

Notes and references

1. HOLMES, Stanley, 'Boeing goes lean. It's revamping factories to gain an edge against Airbus', *Business Week*, 11 June 2001, p. 60EU2
2. Renault official at Vennisseux, France, March 1995
3. Operations visit to the Citroën facility at Aulney sous Bois, France, 6 December 1993, organized by Marc Gourisse and Monsieur Da Silva of Design Development
4. 'La plus grande concession du monde, la concession Toyota d'El Monte, près de Los Angeles, écoule 5000 voitures de plus par an que les 110 concessionnaires Toyota éparpillés dans toute la France!' (The world's biggest car dealer, Toyota at El Monte near Los Angeles, sells 5000 more automobiles per year than all the 110 car dealers throughout all of France!), *L'auto journal*, no 447, 26 September 1996, p. 118
5. FUKUKAWA, Tadaaki and HONG, Sung-Chan, 'The determination of the optimal number of kanbans in a just-in-time production system', *Computers and Industrial Engineering*, vol. 24, issue 4, October 1993, pp 551–9
6. SHINGO, Shigeo, *A revolution in manufacturing: The SMED system*, Productivity Press, Cambridge, Massachusetts, 1983
7. SHINGO, Shigeo, *A revolution in manufacturing: The SMED system*, Productivity Press, Cambridge, Massachusetts, 1983, pp 114–15
8. 'McDonald's robot: Fries. With. That?', *International Herald Tribune*, 13 November 1997, p. 12
9. 'Not quite in time: When he was dreaming up Toyota Motor Corporation's famous "Just in Time" inventory system, Taiichi Ohno never factored in 7.2 on the Richter scale', *Newsweek*, 30 January 1995, p. 26
10. REITMAN, Valerie, 'Fire at parts supplier's factory forces Toyota to shut down production in Japan', *Wall Street Journal Europe*, 4 February 1997

Review and discussion topics

1. Environmental concerns
In a manufacturing firm, what are some of the positive aspects of just-in-time where the environmental impact is considered? What are some of the negative aspects? Consider the complete supply chain from purchasing, manufacturing, to product distribution. (Refer also to Chapter 5.)

2. Human impact
A company has had very sloppy management practices with loose planning and organization. After a change of ownership and an injection of capital investment, lean manufacturing and just-in-time procedures are put into practice. Discuss what you believe might be the positive and the adverse effects on the employees.

3. Overall equipment effectiveness
Analyze the following activities and apply the principle of overall equipment effectiveness. How efficient are you? Could you make any improvements, or are you convinced that you are 100% efficient?
  (a) Studying
  (b) working at your job
  (c) gardening
  (d) looking after a child.

4. SMED
Analyze the activities of the following individuals. Apply the SMED principle. Are there any improvements you could propose?
  (a) A co-worker (or member of your group)
  (b) your spouse
  (c) your roommate.

5. Five S words
Now analyze the following activities. Do you practise the elements presented in the five S words? If not, what improvements do you believe could be made?
  (a) Studying
  (b) working at your job

(c) gardening

(d) looking after a child.

6. Quality at the source

One of the elements of lean production is quality at the source. Consider the following operations with which you are familiar:

(a) university or business school

(b) supermarket or hypermarket

(c) government office (mayor's office, immigration, tax office, etc.).

Do you consider that quality at the source is practised? If not, what improvements might you propose?

7. Uncertainty in just-in-time

In any activity there is always uncertainty and risk (see Chapter 23).

(a) Examine a manufacturing operation, and look at some of the possible risks, and the outcome when just-in-time is practised.

(b) Repeat by looking at a service organization.

Application exercise 15.1   Assembly

Situation

An automobile company has an assembly operation for the components of the gearbox. The company uses kanbans for the operation and operating details for one part of the assembly operation are shown in Table 15.9.

Table 15.9 Operating details for assembly operation

Rate of utilization of components (hours)	350
Production time/unit (min)	2.75
Delivery time of a container (min)	2
Capacity of the container (units)	60
Variation in the demand rate (%)	3

Required

1. Using the calculation procedure, determine how many kanbans would be needed for this operation.

2. The layout of the operation is changed, such that it takes 20 minutes for delivery of the container from the storage area. In this case, now calculate the number of kanbans required.

3. Assume that the variation in demand rate increases to 25%, and all the other conditions of question 2 remain the same, how many kanbans would be required?

Application exercise 15.2   Lathe

Situation

A company in Latvia makes drive shaft assemblies for propeller motors used on boats. The principal equipment used for this operation is a 1950s lathe machine that is adjusted by hand. The setup data, and other information for a typical annual demand of 20,000 units are given in Table 15.10.

Table 15.10 Lathe setup data and annual demand

Annual demand (D) (units)	20,000
Carrying cost ($/month)	4
Setup time (min)	125
Persons needed for setup	2
Average wage cost ($/hr)	10.50

The company is having financial difficulties and is under consideration for purchase by a British firm which is planning to inject new capital into the firm, including putting in automated controlled machines.

Required

1. Under the old operation, what would be the economic lot size to balance carrying costs, with setup costs (ordering costs)? Illustrate the ordering costs, carrying costs, and total costs on an economic lot size curve highlighting the minimum value of total costs (the EOQ quantity).

2. With the proposed new equipment the personnel to perform the setup could be reduced to one. What would have to be the setup time if the economic lot size required were 20 units? Illustrate the new costs (ordering costs, carrying costs, and total costs) on an economic lot size curve that would show the economic lot size as 20 units.

Application exercise 15.3 Press Co.

Situation

Press Co. is engaged in making rigid plastic storage containers from PVC in a variety of colours. The production operation basically involves injecting the heated plastic into a mould housed in a hydraulic press. After cooling, the item is ejected, rough edges are cleaned, and metal brackets are attached. Press makes the containers in lot sizes in multiples of 20 (20, 40, 60, etc.).

Table 15.11 shows the initial operating data for making the containers. The variable unit cost includes the plastic material, and operating labour.

Table 15.11 Press Co.: Initial operating data

Variable unit cost ($/unit)	4.00
Setup cost ($/setup)	150.00

Production costs can be estimated as the sum of the setup cost and the variable unit labour cost.

Required

1. Develop an average unit product cost curve for the operation from lot sizes ranging from 20 to 400.
2. At what lot size does the average unit cost drop below 10% more of the variable unit cost?
3. After what lot size does the change in average unit cost from one lot size to another fall below 1%?
4. Press implements a SMED operation, which reduces the setup cost by a factor of 20. Redo the average cost curve again using lot sizes from 20 to 400 in multiples of 20.
5. After SMED, at what lot size does the average unit cost drop below 10% of the variable unit cost?
6. After SMED, after what lot size does the change in average unit cost from one lot size to another drop below 1%?
7. What is the impact on the firm on its pricing policy, and/or its margin if it implements a SMED programme?
(Chapter 25 may be helpful for this exercise.)

Case study 15.1 Fabrix

Situation

Fabrix is a manufacturer of medical instruments in Idaho, USA. The company was started by the Fabrix family in 1938 and had been very innovative in the types of instrument that it put onto the market. The employees were very faithful to the company and many had been with the firm all their working life. The average age was 46. In 1996 the family was approached by a large German competitor that wanted to purchase the Fabrix facility. Since the Fabrix family had no children who were willing to continue the business, the family sold in January 1997. The acquiring company agreed to keep the Fabrix name, but no guarantee was to given regarding the employment situation of the present personnel.

Fabrix had been reasonably profitable in early years, but as little new investment had been made since the 1970s, profit margins had declined, primarily due to increasing operating costs. In addition, new products developed by the company did not have the same performance as some competitor products.

At the time of the purchase, the physical facilities of Fabrix included two manufacturing/assembly buildings, called ABO-1 and ABB-2, plus a small building, ABX-3, for management personnel, accounting, purchasing, and a sales meeting room. There were five key products manufactured and assembled by Fabrix, called Models A, B, C, D, and E. The first four were machined and assembled in building ABO-1. The layout of the production operation showing the process flow of these four models is illustrated in Figure 15.27. All the models pass through final assembly to test, before packaging. Building ABB-2 was similar in surface area to ABO-1 and contained the machining and component assembly of the fifth product line, Model E. Final assembly, test and packaging for Model E was carried out in building ABO-1 (flow line indicated on diagram). In addition, building ABB-2 was used for rework of defective units, and also for the storage of some obsolete components. In both the manufacturing buildings there was a considerable quantity of inventory items.

After the purchase, an audit team from the acquiring company analyzed the details of Fabrix's operation with the objective of incorporating lean manufacturing and injecting whatever investment necessary to achieve these goals.

Required

1. What are your comments on the Fabrix's operation as it is currently presented?
2. What are some changes you might propose for the Fabrix's operation to incorporate the idea of lean manufacturing?
3. Within your analysis, where would you propose to incorporate some of the logic of optimized production technology? (See Chapter 22.)

Figure 15.27 Fabrix: Layout (building ABO-1)

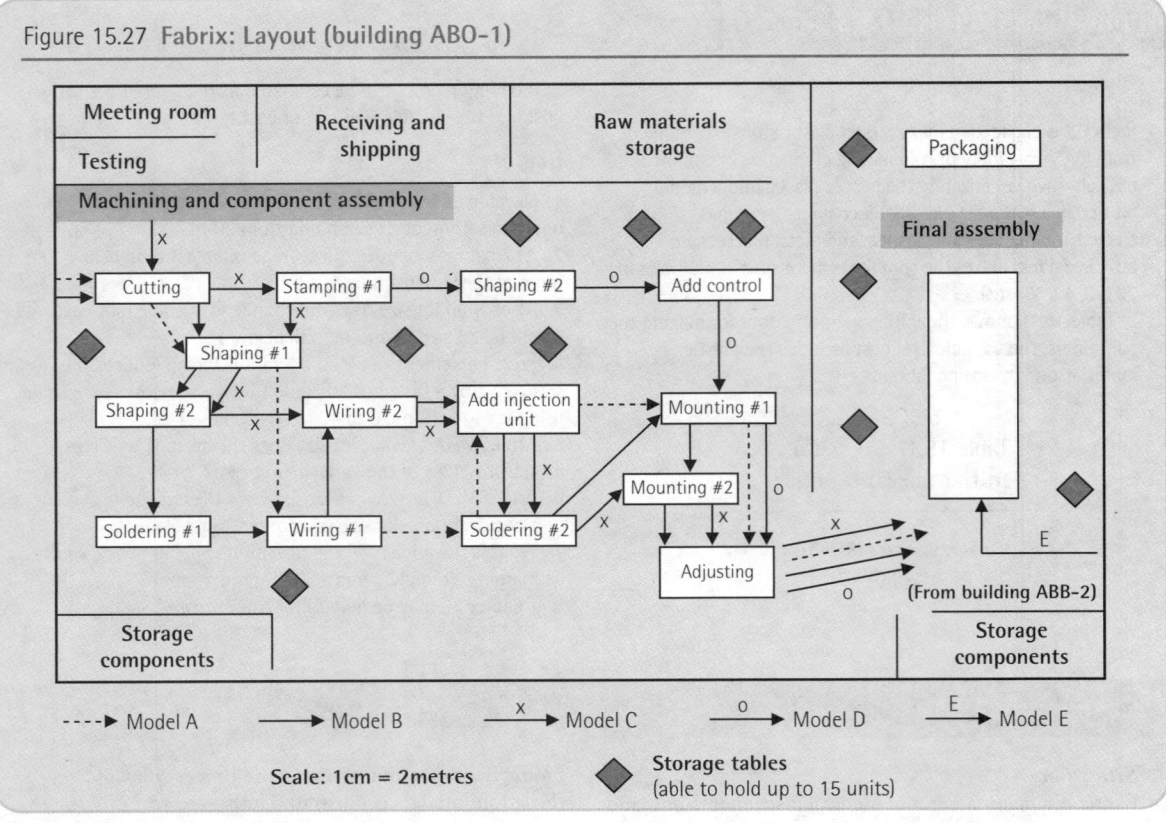

Selected further reading

DELBRIDGE, Rick (1998) *Life on the Line in Contemporary Manufacturing: The Workplace Experience of Lean Production and the 'Japanese' Model*, Oxford University Press.

KOCHAN, Thomas A. and LANSBURY, Russell D., 'Lean production and changing employment relations in the international auto industry', *Economic and Industrial Democracy*, vol. 18, issue 4, November 1997, pp 597–620.

LEE, Choong Y., 'JIT adoption by small manufacturers in Korea', *Journal of Small Business Management*, vol. 35, issue 3, July 1997, pp 98–107.

NILSSON, Tommy, 'Lean production and white-collar work: The case of Sweden', *Economic and Industrial Democracy*, vol. 17, issue 3, August 1996, pp 447–72.

WOMAK, James, JONES, Daniel and ROOS, Daniel (1991) *The Machine That Changed the World: The Story of Lean Production*, HarperCollins.

An extensive listing of other further reading can be found on the website.

What's on the web?

Further learning resources are available to lecturers and students at www.supplychain-online.com, including the following which are specific to *Lean production and just-in-time*:

Resource	Subject
Chapter overview	Lean production and just-in-time
More further reading	Lean production and just-in-time

16 Purchasing and subcontracting

The purchasing activity

Purchasing is the buying of materials or services from an outside source and thus involves the transfer of goods from one distinct entity to another. The purchasing activity is the upstream part of the supply chain and is set in motion by the client's demand for finished goods at the downstream end. A client's requirement is negotiated with marketing, this establishes the basis for operating plans and then production decides what needs to be purchased. In order to ensure an unbroken supply chain, purchasing, marketing, and production must work in a team to ensure delivery dates are met.

Purchased products might include those shown in Table 16.1.

Magnitude of purchasing operations

Purchasing represents a significant part of a company's business. Food firms (Danône, Nestlé), appliance manufacturers (Whirlpool, Maytag), and automobile constructors (GM, Toyota) report that between 60 and 80% of their manufacturing costs are for purchased materials. In 1994 Ford Motor Company spent $50 billion on purchased parts and services. Jose Ignacio Lopez, the former head of purchasing at General Motors, before he defected to Volkswagen in 1993, reportedly saved the company an estimated $1 billion

Table 16.1 **Purchased products**

Purchased product	Examples
Raw materials	Crude oil, green coffee beans, sheet steel, paper pulp
Parts	Nuts and bolts, plastic tubing, impeller blades
Subassemblies	Computer frames, electrical armature windings, truck axles
Assemblies	Pumps, compressors, automobile lights
Machinery and equipment	Printing press, computers, numerically controlled drilling machines
Packaging	Cardboard, bottles, aluminium cans, plastic tops
Office supplies	Paper clips, pencils, paper, printing cartridges, diskettes
Services	Restaurant, payroll, medical, rental of vehicles, rental of buildings, travel services personnel, temporary staff
Finished goods	Clothing, sports equipment, household appliances
Subcontractor services	Electrical installations, building extension, painting

Chrysler and its purchasing budget

Chrysler, the US arm of the German automobile company Daimler-Chrysler, is to cut its $40 billion a year components purchasing budget by 15%, or $6 billion, in the first stage of a radical restructuring. The loss-making firm told its suppliers on 7 December 2000 that it would reduce prices paid for materials and services by 5% from 1 January 2001 and seek a further 10% cut over the next two years.

After meeting suppliers at Chrysler's Michigan headquarters, Dieter Zetsche, Chrysler's President, said that the company is in a difficult business situation, and that the only way to initiate change effectively is by working together. Chrysler had been seeking annual cost cuts of 3% from its suppliers and this new move signals a tougher approach from the firm which lost $514 billion in the third quarter 2000 and is expected to report a significant deficit for the last quarter. This cost squeeze on suppliers, coupled with automobile production cuts and a softening US automobile market, prompted profit warnings from suppliers including

Visteon, Dana, TRW, Lear Group, and Delphi, the world's largest automobile component supplier.

Under Chrysler's plan, suppliers will be expected to cut prices by 5% in January 2001 and then deliver additional savings through 2002. The reductions apply to technology, common parts, and redesign of existing components for all car models, as well as Jeeps, minivans and light trucks. In the second phase, Chrysler plans to send specialists to suppliers to explore further ways of cost reductions. More than 150 suppliers, over 75% of the annual component purchasing, are expected to cooperate in the scheme in its first year. This purchasing plan of Chrysler coincides with further temporary plant closures where unit sales fell by 5% in November 2000. Of Chrysler's 12 North American facilities, two were idle the first week of December and five are due to stop production the week beginning 18 December 2000.

Adapted from: 'Chrysler to slash supplier costs by $6 billion', *Financial Times*[1]

Figure 16.1 Purchasing managers' index

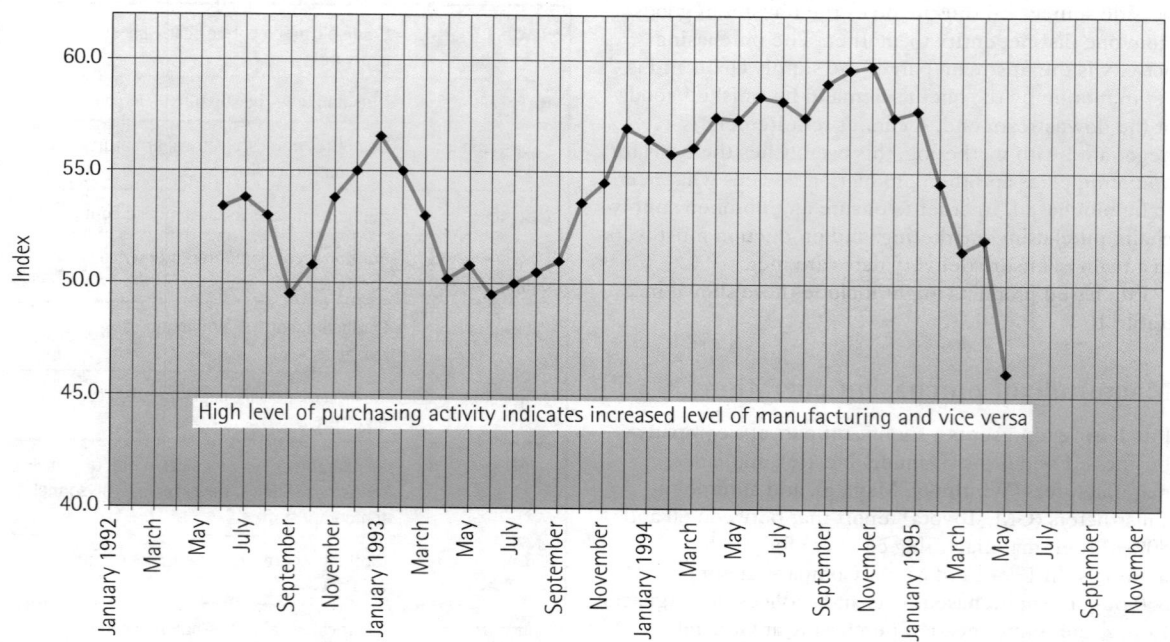

High level of purchasing activity indicates increased level of manufacturing and vice versa

on purchased materials. The magnitude of the supply chain purchasing function is illustrated by Industry insight 16.1.

Purchasing function

It is the purchasing department's responsibility to maintain a database of available suppliers, covering such aspects as the types of products offered, quality, price, and delivery times. It is purchasing which normally make the ultimate buying decisions, although not without prior consultation and recommendations from other departments such as research and development, manufacturing, marketing, finance, engineering, etc.

Purchasing managers' index

The purchasing activity is the early part of the material movement in the supply chain and is directly tied to manufacturing operations. A high level of purchasing signals an increase in manufacturing, and vice versa. In the USA, the National Association of Purchasing Management compiles a monthly index that measures factory activity as illustrated in Figure 16.1.[2] This index means that a value above 50% indicates an expansion of activity in US production centres, while a reading below 50% measures a decline. The higher (or lower) the reading, the greater is the pace of expansion (or contraction). In Europe, Reuters publishes a similar purchasing managers' index, which measures activity in the Eurozone manufacturing sector. This is compiled from a survey of 1500 manufacturing companies in Germany, France, Italy, Spain, and Ireland, which account for approximately 82% of the Eurozone's manufacturing activity. As an illustration, the index was 57.4 in December 1999 the ninth consecutive month that the index was above 50.[3]

Purchasing is international

For most companies, purchasing is an international operation. Raw materials may be purchased from abroad because those are the only sources, such as coffee from Brazil and the Ivory Coast, oil from Kuwait and Saudi Arabia, or uranium from the USA and Russia. Alternatively, raw materials are purchased internationally because they are less expensive or better quality. This might apply to textiles, computer chips, or steel, for example.

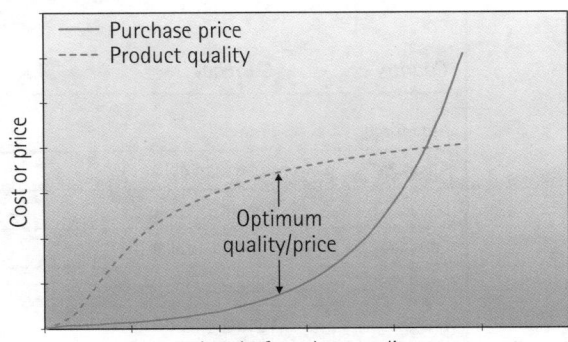

Figure 16.2 Sourcing: Optimize quality/price ratio

Sourcing

Sourcing is the activity of searching worldwide for a supplier (a source) of raw materials, or products, which present the best value according to the quality/price ratio as illustrated by Figure 16.2. Companies might operate their own sourcing activity, although, since covering the globe requires tremendous resources of personnel, contacts, money, and time, firms are apt to use services specialized in sourcing. For example, major European retailers use the services of sourcing agents based in Hong Kong. There is considerable risk in using sourcing as qualities may not conform to specifications, and price levels may change as a result of fluctuating exchange rates.

Exchange rates

Table 16.2 shows how exchange rates have changed in a 12-month period between 2001 and 2000.[4] These fluctuations can have a big impact on the price of materials purchased internationally in different periods. Consider, for example, the following.

Downside risk

In the downside risk, a purchasing firm in the USA loses between one period and a later period as the value of the currency, in the country in which the supplier is located, increases relative to the US dollar:

- A US company purchases 10,000 computer assemblies from Mexico in July 2000 at a unit price of 90 Mexican pesos (local currency). The total price paid is 900,000 pesos or $US 94,538 (900,000/9.52).
- If the company purchased the same quantity of assemblies in 2001, at the same unit price of 90 pesos, then the cost would be $US 99,228 (900,000/9.07), an increase in $4,690.

Table 16.2 Exchange rates in currency units per $US for selected countries

Country	Currency	Currency units to per $US 04 July 2001	04 July 2000	Percent change*
Argentina	Peso (P)	1.00	1.00	0.00
Australia	Australian dollar (A$)	1.93	1.69	−14.20
Brazil	Real (R)	2.39	1.80	−32.78
Canada	Canadian dollar (C$)	1.51	1.49	−1.34
Chile	Chilean peso (peso)	640.00	536.00	−19.40
China	Yuan	8.28	8.28	0.00
Columbia	Columbian peso (peso)	2,304.00	2,169.00	−6.22
Czech Republic	Koruna (Kc)	39.90	37.30	−6.97
Egypt	Egyptian pound (£E)	3.93	3.49	−12.61
Eurozone	Euro (€)	1.18	1.05	−12.38
Hong Kong	Hong Kong dollar (HK$)	7.80	7.80	0.00
Hungary	Forint (Ft)	285.00	272.00	−4.78
India	Indian rupee (Rs)	47.10	44.70	−5.37
Indonesia	Rupiah (Rp)	11,365.00	9,375.00	−21.23
Israel	New shekel (NIS)	4.18	4.08	−2.45
Japan	Yen (¥)	124.00	107.00	−15.89
Malaysia	Malaysian dollar (ringgit)	3.80	3.80	0.00
Mexico	Mexican peso (PS)	9.07	9.52	4.73
Peru	Nuevo sol (new sol)	3.52	3.49	−0.86
Philippines	Philippine peso (P)	53.00	43.80	−21.00
Poland	Zloty (Zl)	4.00	4.32	7.41
Russia	Rouble (Rb)	29.20	28.00	−4.29
Singapore	Singapore dollar (S$)	1.82	1.74	−4.60
South Africa	Rand (R)	8.08	6.78	−19.17
South Korea	Won (W)	1,296.00	1,117.00	−16.03
Sweden	Swedish krona (Skr)	10.89	8.80	−23.75
Switzerland	Swiss franc (SFr)	1.80	1.62	−11.11
Taiwan	Taiwan dollar (T$)	34.40	30.80	−11.69
Thailand	Baht (Bt)	45.50	39.60	−14.90
Turkey	Turkish lira (L)	1,276,000.00	620,215.00	−105.74
United Kingdom	Pound (£)	0.71	0.66	−7.58
Venezuela	Bolivar (Bs)	719.00	683.00	−5.27

*Based on the local currency to buy $1 (when the value has increased in this period the change is shown as negative to indicate that the currency has weakened).

Upside risk

In the upside risk, a purchasing firm in the USA gains between one period and a later period as the value of the currency, in the country in which the supplier is located, decreases relative to the US dollar:

- A US company purchases 50,000 metres of textile from Turkey in July 2000 at a price per metre of 400,000 Turkish lira (local currency). The total price paid is 20 billion Turkish lira or $US 32,247 (20,000,000,000/620,215).
- If the company purchased the same quantity of textiles in 2001, at the same unit price of 400,000 Turkish lira, then the cost would be $US 15,674 (20,000,000,000/1,276,000), or a decrease of $16,573.

Forward buying

If a company which does its accounts in US dollars believes that prices are rising, such as illustrated by the downside risk, then it might purchase in large quantities to lock in the favourable price. This is sometimes referred to as forward buying and in this case the purchasing company would incur the associated stocking costs.

Hand-to-mouth buying

Alternatively, if the company believes that prices are falling such as illustrated by the upside risk, then it would purchase just that quantity of material needed. This is sometimes referred to as hand-to-mouth buying and is a sort of just-in-time purchasing.

Degree of risk

If a company is buying regularly from a purchaser in another country, then the degree of risk taken by either the buyer or the seller is not necessarily cut and dry according to the current exchange rates but could be negotiated between the two parties. If parties believe their currency exchange rates are fluctuating rapidly they may establish a maximum future price (if they are the purchaser) or a minimum price (if they are the supplier) in order to minimize the risk.

Hedging

Hedging is the purchase, or sale, of a futures contract of a specific commodity to offset the purchase, or sale, of a cash commodity. Hedging is to offset the risk incurred in fluctuating commodity markets or to guarantee a source of raw materials.

Table 16.3 **Commodity market price fluctuations**

Product	Price (December 2001)	Price (December 2002)	Difference (%)
Cotton, $/lb	0.3425	0.4050	+18.25
Copper, $/lb	0.6370	0.6700	+5.18
Corn, $/bushel	2.1150	2.6275	+24.23
Coffee, $US//lb	0.4565	0.5450	+19.39

Commodities

Commodities may be raw materials for food companies such as, livestock (cattle and hogs), or agriculture products like corn, soybeans, wheat, cotton, orange juice, coffee, sugar, and cocoa. Commodities may be metals for the electrical, electronic, jewellery, and photographic industries such as gold, copper, and silver. Alternatively they may be liquid products for the refinery, and chemical industry, such as crude oil and refined petroleum products. Commodity market prices can fluctuate widely as illustrated in Table 16.3, using information taken from the futures market.[5]

Hedging is like an insurance policy. An insurance policy protects against loss by paying a cash sum at the end of a predetermined period, or as the result of a certain loss. The premium represents the cost of receiving the cash payment in return.

Buying hedge

A buying hedge protects against price fluctuations when a fixed price sale is made now, for delivery at a future date. Consider the transaction of crude oil as a commodity:

- An oil producer in June sells 20,000 barrels of crude at $19.00/bbl or a total of $380,000, on the spot (cash) market. He buys on the futures market 20,000 bbl of January crude at $20.50/bbl or a total of $410,000.
- In November of the same year he buys 20,000 bbl of crude at $20.30/bbl, or a total of $406,000 on the spot market. He sells on the futures market 20,000 barrels of January crude at $21.75/bbl or a total of $435,000.
- Loss on spot market is $1.30/bbl (20.30 − 19.00) or a total $26,000 (1.30 * 20,000). Gain on futures market is $1.25/bbl (21.75 − 20.50) or a total of $25,000 (1.25 * 20,000). Net loss is $0.05/bbl or $1000.

If trading were just done on the spot (cash) market then the trader would have lost $26,000. However, by also trading on the futures market, losses are reduced.

Selling hedge

A selling hedge is used to protect the value of inventory in a market whose prices are declining. Consider:

- An oil refiner in June owns 20,000 barrels of crude at $20.50/bbl (total value $410,000). He sells on the futures market 20,000 bbl of January crude at $21.50/bbl, or a total of $430,000.
- In November he refines, 'sells', 20,000 bbl of crude at $19.00/bbl (total value $380,000). He buys on the futures market 20,000 barrels of January crude at $20.05/bbl (total value $401,000).
- Loss on refined oil is $1.50/bbl (total value $30,000). Gain on futures market is $1.45/bbl (total value $29,000). Net loss is $1000.

Without trading on the futures market, the refiner would have lost $30,000.

Completely knocked down

Completely knocked down (CKD) is the term used for companies that export their products (sell to purchasers) in a disassembled, or kit form. Renault, France, operates part of its business in this manner where automobiles parts, or subassemblies, are exported to such countries as Turkey, Morocco, Argentina, Columbia, Venezuela, and Thailand 'completely knocked down'. CKD purchasing usually means that:

- The product can be purchased at a lower price.
- Shipping costs are less because the product can be packaged more precisely (less wasted space).
- Customs duties are less, as there is often a lower tariff on components than on finished goods.

The CKD approach to selling may often be the requirement of the buying country, as they want to use local labour in the assembly of the finished goods. That is, they will not, in fact, permit the importation of the finished product. Weighing against the CKD approach is the time and labour necessary in unpacking and assembly of the products. In addition, the expertise of those assembling in the country of purchase may not be equivalent to those who manufactured the product. Thus, product quality could suffer.

Barriers to international purchasing

In addition to the financial risk, other barriers to international purchasing include the following.

Language

Negotiating prices and specifications of products in another language is difficult if the purchasing agent is not fluent. English is more and more the language of transaction, although, if the purchaser is unable to converse correctly he/she may not get the best deal. In Europe purchasing personnel are often trilingual or more.

Culture

Performing transactions in India, Taiwan, or Columbia is not the same as it is in Germany, the USA, or Britain. If the latter are the buyer countries, patience has to be used, as negotiating is not always as blunt and straightforward as it is in Anglo-Saxon regions.

Customs duty

Duty or taxes payable on imported goods can sharply increase prices if there are no reciprocal trade agreements, although, with the North American Free Trade Agreement (NAFTA) between Canada, the USA, and Mexico and the existence of the European Union (EU) duties are on their way to be eliminated for many trading partners.

Quotas

Countries sometimes have quotas on the amount of products that can be imported into a country which have the objective of protecting their home markets.

Specifications and norms

Design specifications and codes differ across the globe. There are specifications in the British measuring system, and others in metric. Electric wiring and electrical codes are different. Paper size is different. Building specifications are not the same. Environmental regulations covering car emissions are very strict in California, much less in other areas. The list is enormous. The International Standards Organization, ISO, is making inroads into standardizing the multitude of specifications. (See Chapter 4 on ISO-9000, and Chapter 5 on ISO-14000.)

Local laws

Laws in foreign countries vary enormously. The relatively clearly stated laws in Europe or the USA make it somewhat easy for firms to do business in these regions. However, in Asia, the Middle East, and South America local laws are more complicated. Thus, if there is a contract problem with a purchase such as, for example, regarding quality, quantity, or delivery times, in countries where litigation is onerous, obtaining an equitable solution may be time consuming, and costly. Thus, the advantage obtained in price, may be completely lost because of legal problems. Some companies refuse to do business with certain countries because they perceive the legal risk to be too high.

Political risk

Having supply contracts with countries that are politically unstable (see Figure 3.9) can pose a risk of a cut off of supplies if war or civil strive breaks out. South Africa (under apartheid), Iran, Nigeria, Iraq, Cuba have in the past presented problems of this nature.

Organization of purchasing departments

For organizations that have several manufacturing sites, the purchasing activity might be completely centralized or decentralized. This would present the two extreme cases. Alternatively, the firm may practise a hybrid of the two approaches. The following explains the various policies.

Centralized purchasing

Centralized purchasing means that all purchased items for every division are centralized through one department, or operating site. This gives the following advantages:

* Buying in larger quantities usually means it is possible to obtain more attractive prices from suppliers.
* Purchasing in large quantities often means the supplier is more attentive to the order (more clout with the supplier).
* Permits a standardization of purchased products and thus guarantees a constant quality throughout the organization. This is especially important where food products are concerned (Nestlé, Switzerland; Danône, France; General Mills, USA).
* Larger purchasing departments, as a result of ordering for many manufacturing sites, means that a company can afford greater staff specialization. For example, there could be a group concentrating on piping, one in valves, one in steel, etc. This can lead to greater purchasing competence, and lower material cost.
* Combining small orders reduces, administrative costs, the time taken to negotiate orders, billing time, customs procedures where appropriate, and thus overall cost.
* Relation with the suppliers is simplified since there are fewer interlocutors.
* Reduction of transportation costs because orders are shipped in larger quantities.

Decentralized purchasing

With decentralized purchasing it means that every division within the organization makes its own purchasing decisions. This has the following advantages:

* There is a much quicker response than using a centralized operation (less bureaucratic).
* Transportation costs might be lower if the supplier is located close to the division making the purchase.
* Sometimes local purchasing is more responsive to the needs of the particular operation. For example, the requirements for, say, wheat in a division of a food company located in France may not be the same for a division located in Britain because of differences in consumer tastes.
* Reduces inventory costs since divisions only purchase the quantity needed. (In centralized purchasing larger quantities are purchased.)
* The risk is reduced in buying in smaller quantities. For example, consider a food company with six operating companies which purchases a large quantity of sugar from Cuba for all the operating companies. If the exchange rate suddenly changes, or there is a problem with quality or delivery dates, the risk to the purchasing company can be high. However, if all the operating companies have a decentralized purchasing policy and individually purchase their required quantities of sugar from Europe, Australia, South Africa, Brazil, Mexico, and Cuba, the risk arising from currency exchange, quality, or delivery is minimized.

Hybrid of purchasing functions

A mixed purchasing organization (hybrid of centralized and decentralized) may be established depending on the items to be purchased:

* Small or rush orders, or those specific to a site needs are purchased locally (decentralized).
* High cost capital equipment, high volume material, standardized products which are used for several operating companies, goods with a high technical content, or those purchased overseas are purchased by the head office (centralized).

Organization chart

The type of organization chart for a purchasing department depends on the size of the organization, the activity of the firm, and whether the company is decentralized or centralized. The basic structure is given in Figure 16.3. There is a purchasing vice-president who reports to the president (for large companies, where purchased products represent a significant proportion of a company's activity). Below the vice-president are purchasing managers who are responsible for particular products. Reporting to these

Figure 16.3 Organization chart for a purchasing department

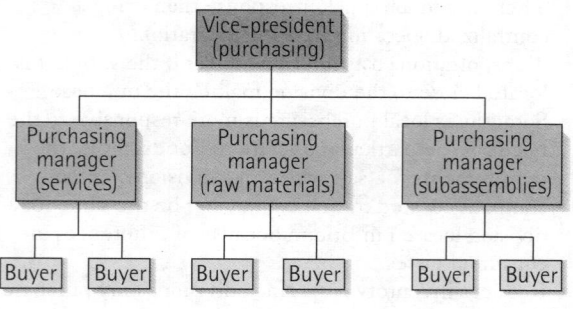

Table 16.4 Purchasing activity organization

Industrial electrical equipment	Ship construction firm
Services	Hull construction material
Raw materials	Interior fittings and air conditioning
Mechanical components	Energy (propulsion) and lubricating fluids
Electrical components	Paint, subcontracting, and customs
Electronic components	Safety equipment and office material
Other industrial components	Quality control of suppliers
Insulation material	Receiving and quality control of all supplies

managers are buyers. It is the buyers who have the direct contact with the supplier organization. Table 16.4 illustrates how two European firms organize their purchasing activities. Both have seven departments.

Some companies, particularly in a centralized organization where products are purchased in large quantities, the buyers might be few, or non-existent. In this case, purchasing is done directly by negotiation with the purchasing manager.

Buying

Buying is performed by the buyers in the purchasing departments. These buyers usually are specialized according to a commodity such as copper, steel, valves, livestock, etc. This specialization allows buyers to become experts at purchasing their particularly commodity. In addition, the quality of the buyers is enhanced if they are knowledgeable in the following areas.

Company

A buyer should have a good understanding of their own company including manufacturing process, products, sales and other company policies. They should be cost and value conscious so they can negotiate the best contract terms for their company.

Price structure of purchased product

The buyer should know the market and the going price of the commodity available. This includes being aware of the cost structure of the purchased product. For example, assuming a buyer for a food company purchases steel cans from a supplier that is used for canning fruits and vegetables. The buyer should know in the price of the purchased product, an estimate of how much the supplier includes for material cost, labour, and profit margin. Understanding this breakdown, the buyer will be better able to negotiate a price.

Price structure of end product

In addition to the purchased product, the buyer should be aware of the cost structure of the finished products sold by their company. Again, consider a can of vegetables for which the buyer purchases the steel cans. The buyer should know what proportion in the cost price of the finished product (a can of vegetables) constitutes the can. If the proportion is low then the buyer should exercise less effort, and less time, in his negotiations for the purchase than if the proportion is high.

Laws

Be knowledgeable of the laws that govern their areas of responsibility such as contract law, misrepresentation and fraud, infringement of patent rights, damage claims against suppliers, and shipping regulations. This also includes legislation governing security of transport, product labelling, product safety, and specific regulations regarding, say, pharmaceuticals, or foods.

Human relations

Buyers should feel comfortable and behave diplomatically when interviewing salespeople who call on them daily and they must to be able to schedule their time well so salespeople do not use excessive time. They should be good at dealing with people, including negotiating internally with their own company, as well as externally with the supplier company. Further, senior buyers should be able to manage and lead a team of buyers when it comes to particular projects, or when negotiating multiple contracts.

Companies often only permit their buyers to remain, say, for two years on a particular purchasing activity. Longer than this it is felt the buyers become too familiar with the supplier and thus may lose their objectivity for their employer company.

Ethics in purchasing and buying

Questionable practices

Salespersons deluge buyers with free lunches, gifts, travel offers, etc., which can easily open the door to unethical situations. The buyers may feel obligated to salespersons who have given them gifts and as such may not act in the best interest of their own firm. The question to ask is at what point is the gift giving too much? Some companies limit the annual gift to no more than $25, or no single gift exceeding $25. The author, when working on government projects in the USA, was unable to even buy a hamburger for a representative! Although an exception, Industry insight 16.2 illustrates how far unethical practices in buying might go.

Without going as far as the article discusses, some questionable, unethical, or illegal buying practices are as follows:

- Taking advantage of obvious clerical, or computational errors in quotations.

Kickbacks in the retail industry

Among retailers, Jim Locklear was known as a first-rate house wares buyer with an eye for fashion and a knack for negotiating low prices. After ten years at a Dallas retail chain, then owned by Federated Department Stores, he joined Allied Stores, Jordan Marsh chain in Boston in 1987 at an annual salary of $96,000. However, he became homesick for his native Texas and after only three months at Jordan Marsh he joined J.C. Penney in late 1987. His position was as a buyer of house wares at a base salary of $56,000, or a $40,000 pay cut when at Jordan Marsh. At that time of joining Penney, Locklear was 38, with a pile of problems. He had four children from four marriages, child support payments of $900 a month, a half million dollar house that would soon go into foreclosure, and four years of probation remaining on a charge of indecency with a minor, a charge to which he had pleaded guilty.

As a buyer, Locklear controlled the spending of millions of dollars a year and in 1988 he started peddling that influence. He admits that he sold crucial information to some suppliers' and manufacturers' representatives such as the amount of their competitors' bids, or to others he sold the promise of large orders. In exchange for his favours, some vendors gave Locklear cash, others wrote cheques to front companies that he set up. Over the years he supplemented his salary with as much as $1.5 million in bribes and kickbacks. After just a little over a year at J.C. Penney, a cutlery supplier of the firm blew the whistle indicating that Locklear was taking kickbacks. Further, in an internal J.C. Penney memo, an assistant buyer said he was suspicious of Locklear's choice of suppliers. In May 1989 Penney, unknown to Locklear, hired an outside firm to investigate their employer. Although this firm uncovered Locklear's financial problems, they were unable to establish any proof of bribery. One reason that Locklear may still have seemed trustworthy was his sparkling performance. In theory, a buyer influenced by kickbacks would perform poorly, compared with one seeking solely to satisfy customer demand. However during Locklear's tenure Penney's annual sale of tabletop merchandise at one point rose to $45 million from $25 million. In the three years 1989, 1990, and 1991, Penney named Locklear one of its buyers of the year. Locklear didn't just buy fast selling goods he also created new lines. Suppliers loved him as he could spot a new trend, jump on it quickly, and thus be the first in the market.

In July 1992 an anonymous letter informed a Penney official of a special relationship between Locklear and Charles A Briggs, a Dallas manufacturers' representative from whom Locklear later admitted to taking $200,000 in bribes and kickbacks. Penney subsequently launched a second private investigation and uncovered Locklear's front companies. As a result, he was fired. Apparently, it would not have taken a genius to figure out that Mr. Locklear was living beyond his means. He had a lifetime membership in a country club, spent vacations at resorts, had a luxury car, and securities accounts. In his confession to Federal authorities, Locklear admitted accepting and soliciting bribes and kickbacks almost from the beginning of his time with Penney. He sold information on competitors' bids to an appliance manufacturer in New Jersey for at least $39,000 over a four-year period. He received $10,000 in cash from Westly Forge, a cutlery maker in Norfolk, Virginia, that represented a percentage of every cutlery set that Westly sold to Penney. In all Locklear took $161,000 from an independent sales representative for Westly

Forge. To obtain kickbacks from manufacturers' representatives, Locklear threatened to take their business away and award it to competitors. For some small appliance manufacturers, lining Locklear's pockets became a matter of survival as they admitted that he threatened to pull their line from J.C. Penney, which would have put the firm out of business. One particular representative said that he didn't go to Penney because it was his word against Locklear, the Penney buyer of the year. Another firm, Taylor and Ng, who made wok and coffee makers, said their independent sales representatives paid $100,000 in commissions and advertising money to a company that, unbeknown to them, was owned by Locklear.

Neither Penney nor the Federal court had sympathy for suppliers' and manufacturers' representatives who knowingly gave kickbacks to Locklear. They say plenty of other vendors turned him down and faced no retribution from him while still managing to sell to Penney. Locklear faced up to five years in prison and a maximum fine of twice his financial gain, or twice the loss to Penney, whichever was the greater. He also owed

Penney a portion of a $789,000 judgment that the company obtained in its civil suit against him.

Unlike kickbacks to government buyers, retail bribery hurts customers, not taxpayers but because customers can shop around not much fuss is made. However, estimates put the cost at millions of dollars a year. Wal-Mart stores thinks the amount is so significant that it has a very strict conflict of interest policy to the point that buyers cannot even accept a cup of coffee from vendors. For Wal-Mart, this policy is black and white and goes a long way in explaining why their prices are so low. Harrods of London takes a very hard view of accepting any gifts to the point that receiving anything is forbidden. The chief buyer at Harrods regularly reminds its staff not to accept personal gifts, vouchers, trips, services, or entertainment. The store's conflict of interest regulation also forbids buyers and their families from investing in supplier companies or doing outside work for them without written approval from Harrods.

Adapted from: 'Deals on the side: How a Penney buyer made up to $1.5 million on vendor's kickbacks',
Wall Street Journal Europe[6]

- Fixing prices.
- Collusion among bidders for a project or for an order.
- Playing favourites among suppliers in awarding orders.
- Failing to respect personal obligations such as a firm makes a verbal obligation but then reneges on this obligation later.
- Upgrading product samples, with the intention of supplying lower grade products.
- Reciprocity, which is purposely buying products from a company because that company buys your product. The philosophy of 'you scratch my back and I'll scratch yours'. This occurs not infrequently and is often ignored as far as being unethical.
- Providing information regarding the completion. For example, assume that three primary Contractors A, B, and C, are in competition, bidding on a project for Client T. Since the project will require subcontractors, Firm A solicits quotations from Subcontractors X, Y, and Z in order to develop a proposal. It so happens that primary Contractors B and C also solicit quotations from Subcontractors X, Y, and Z. During proposal discussions between the primary contractors and the subcontractors, the subcontractors either knowingly or unknowingly provide information about the other primary contractors.

In an attempt to minimize these types of problem, the USA over the years has put in place the following laws governing the purchasing and buying activity.

Sherman Act

The Sherman Act of 1890 prohibits:

- price fixing among competitors
- group boycott by competitors or agreeing not to buy from a supplier
- allocation of customers or markets
- agreement between a manufacturer and customers that they will not buy competitor's products.

Clayton Act

The Clayton Act of 1914 extended coverage under the earlier Sherman Act and covers:

- Price discrimination or charging different prices to different buyers for identical articles.
- Tying clauses requiring the purchase of another item, with the purchase of the desired item.
- Exclusive dealing meaning prohibiting buyers from carrying products of other manufacturers.
- Full-line forcing or requiring buyers to buy the entire seller offering, and not just selected items.

US Federal Trade Commission Act

The Federal Trade Commission Act of 1914 gave the Federal Trade Commission (FTC) the power to pursue companies that engage in unfair competition or deceptive practices. In the USA, all proposed corporate mergers must withstand the FTC test of unfair competition.

Robinson–Patman Act

The Robinson-Patman Act is the 1936 Amendment to the Clayton Act and governs conditions under which it is lawful to charge different prices to different buyers and includes the following:

- Quantity discounts for large orders.
- Lower prices on the end-of-season products (sale items).
- Goods which are in danger of deteriorating.
- Private label brands, as opposed to named items.
- Charging the same prices as competitors prices in good faith for example with the slogan 'we will not be undersold'.

Foreign Corrupt Practices Act

The US Foreign Corrupt Practices Act of 1997 makes it illegal to bribe foreign clients in order to obtain contracts. This law was enacted after Lockheed, the US aerospace company, was found guilty in 1976 of bribing government officials in Europe, Japan, and Latin America to purchase its military equipment.[7] Prince Bernhard of the Netherlands was accused of having received $100,000. Further, Tanaka of Japan, Strauss of Germany, and the Italian Andreotti were also mixed up in the scandal.[8] The Lockheed Corporation bribery of Japanese government officials brought down both Tokyo's government and the Netherlands' royal family.

Some European rules

Compared to the USA, rules in Europe are less rigid and are not always consistent. For example, the German law regarding ethics are somewhat contradictory. It is illegal to demand and accept kickbacks, but it is essentially legal to pay them. German companies are allowed to deduct such payments from their tax bills as a business expense. The law has been modified since 1996, which says the payments are taxable as soon as they become the subject of a criminal complaint.[9] Prosecutors can open an investigation involving public officials on the basis of an anonymous tip, but they are prohibited from probing private sector kickbacks unless someone lodges a formal complaint. Prosecution of public sector corruption is given a high priority and can result in stiff penalties. However, private sector corruption is considered a problem companies should solve themselves. Penalties, which are rare to begin with, often amount to a slap on the wrist. In early 1996, the Opel (Germany) unit of GM launched an internal investigation into charges that an official at its Bochum plant took bribes of 3 million marks ($2 million) from its supplier, Pagid AG, an Essen-based company that makes brake linings in exchange for orders.[10] In France, the regulations governing payments to foreign governments to ensure contracts *pots-de-vins* are very fluid. Companies who make such payments may deduct the amount from taxes under the rubric of 'commercial expenses for export purposes'. The company has to justify the amount paid and it should not be excessive compared to the profits reported.[11]

With the growth of the European Union (EU), it appears that unethical practices are being brought more into line with those of the United States as Industry insight 16.3 illustrates. EU antitrust rules, like those in

---

Europe clamps down on price fixing

Industry insight 16.3

The European Commission fined six companies a total of €57.53 million for fixing prices on sodium gluconate, a chemical used in a wide range of cleaning processes for metal and glass such as washing bottles, cleaning utensils, and in treating various surfaces. During the period of illegal activity from 1987 until June 1995 the European market for the product was valued at €18 million a year. Six companies together accounted for most of the world's sodium gluconate production, allowing them to fix prices and carve up markets among themselves. The biggest fines went to Jungbunzlauer AG of Switzerland (€20.40 million), Roquette Frères SA of France (€10.80 million), and Archer Daniels Midland

(ADM) of the USA (€10.13 million). Three co-conspirators, Akzo Nobel NV and Avebe BA of the Netherlands, and Fujisawa Pharmaceutical Co. of Japan received smaller fines of €9.00 million, €3.60 million, and €3.60 million respectively.

The Commission made extensive use of discretionary authority under European Union rules. This authority rewarded whistleblowers, who therefore played a key role in unearthing price-fixing cartels, and at the same time punished companies for any aggravating circumstances. Jungbunzlauer's fine was increased by 50% because the Commission determined that it was the ringleader of the cartel. Fujisawa was given an 80%

reduction in its fine because it was the first company to come forward with decisive evidence in the case. Fujisawa could have received total amnesty from fines, but it only came forward with evidence against its co-conspirators after the Commission had already become aware of the cartel, and sent the companies concerned a letter seeking information. ADM, along with Roquette, received a 40% reduction in its fine in view of the value of its cooperation once the Commission's investigation got underway.

Global price fixing affects every consumer. It raises the price of gasoline, vitamins, and soft drinks, makes it more expensive for patrons and museums to buy painting and sculptures at auctions, and increases the price of dynamite and ammonium nitrate used in the coal and metal mining industries. In the past, investigators have uncovered a 17-year conspiracy among American, German and Japanese makers of sorbates, a preservative used in foods ranging from cheese to baked goods that affected more than $1 billion in sales in the United States alone. The investigators also exposed a cartel involving major American, Belgian, and Dutch marine construction companies that build and move huge offshore oil and gas drilling platforms in places such as the North Sea and the Gulf

of Mexico. The conspirators fixed contracts in an industry with annual sales of $1 billion, and their collusion ultimately contributed to higher prices at the gasoline pumps. A graphite cartel involving firms from France, Germany, Japan, and the United States was unravelled after a steel maker complained to investigators about the lack of competition. Graphite is used for making the rods for heating scrap metal into steel and the price rose by more than 60% in the period 1993 to 1997.

The highest profile price-fixing case heading for trial in New York involves A Alfred Taubman, the former Chairman of the auction house Sotherby and Sir Anthony Tennant, his counterpart at Christies. However, in this situation Europe, or more specifically Britain, is not being cooperative because Sir Anthony has vowed to remain in Britain, from which he cannot be extradited. London does not impose criminal liability on an executive engaged in price fixing. In the case, the two men are alleged to have conspired to fix commission fees charged to more than 130,000 customers over six years. The trial began in autumn 2001.

Adapted from: 'EU Commission fines six companies in cartel case', *Wall Street Journal Europe*,[12] and 'Europeans help turn heat up on cartels', *International Herald Tribune*[13]

the USA, cover all activities on local markets, not just local companies.

Suppliers

Supplier selection

Suppliers, often called vendors, are those companies that furnish goods and services to buyer operations. Good management and control of suppliers is necessary in order to keep production costs at the appropriate level and thus selecting the appropriate supplier is important. Some criteria for the selection of an appropriate supplier are presented in Table 16.5.

Global cost structure

For some companies it is not just sufficient to negotiate strictly on price, but also to understand how a particular product will perform in a manufacturing operation, which might have consequences on the global cost structure of the end product. For example, paper for a printing operation may be purchased at a low price. However, if it continually tears during the printing operation, causing several shutdowns, what is gained in a low price of the raw material is lost during the

processing operation. Alternatively, raw meat purchased for a food company may be a low price, but during processing there is a high loss because of fat in the meat. In this case it might be advantageous to purchase precooked meat. Even though it costs more, there is less loss during processing.

Checklist for supplier selection

Companies often use checklists, with weighting criteria, in order to evaluate suppliers. The criteria are graded (very good to very poor, for example), and the criteria themselves are weighted according to their importance to the buying company. A sample evaluation checklist can be found in Table 16.6.

This rating sheet evaluates both the product, and the supplier company. The evaluation criteria for the product cover quality through warranty conditions and the evaluation criteria for the supplier cover technical capability through environmental awareness. The buyer firm assigns an importance factor to the various criteria from 1 to 5, arranged in descending order of importance. The criteria themselves have a quantitative rating of 5 (excellent) to 1 (very poor). The last column is the product, Weighting * Importance factor. For example, if a supplier has a product whose quality (factor = 5) is judged fair (weighting = 3), then the score would be 15 (5 * 3). If a supplier whose management competence

Table 16.5 **Criteria for supplier selection**

Criterion	Includes
Product price	Unit price; price for large quantities; other discounts available
Quality of material	Does supplier have quality certification such as ISO-9000, or is it certified by the buying company?
Reliability	Supplier's history of meeting delivery dates
After-sales service	Services such as replacement of defective parts, instructions on equipment use, repairs, or update of products
Supplier location	This can impact delivery time, transportation costs, and response time for rush or replacement orders. Where feasible, firms might choose to buy locally to create goodwill, improve the buying company's image, or to improve the local economy. With the same logic, firms may choose to purchase in the country in which they operate, rather than overseas
Inventory availability	Does the supplier always have sufficient supplies available?
Supplier flexibility	Willingness to respond to changes in demand, design, or order quantities
Financial stability	How long has it been in business, profit and debt levels? Is the supplier a going concern, or one that will be around in the years to come?
Technical capability	Capacity of the supplier in research and development. Does the supplier have facilities continually to develop and improve products?
Product range	Ability to supply a wide range of products. For example, if a food company needs to purchase food additives it would be better to find a supplier who can supply a wide range of additives rather than the food company having to negotiate with several different suppliers. Having a single, or a few suppliers, is less costly

Table 16.6 **Supplier rating sheet**

	Excellent 5	Good 4	Fair 3	Poor 2	Very poor 1	Factor Max = 5	Weighting * factor
PRODUCT							
Quality						5	
Price						4	
Delivery reliability (time)						3	
Delivery reliability (conditions)						2	
Warranty conditions						1	
Total						**15**	
SUPPLIER							
Technical capability						5	
Financial strength						5	
Quality certification						4	
Flexibility with buyer						4	
Profit consistency						3	
Labour relations (unionized)						3	
Capacity available						3	
Management competence						3	
Knowledgeable sales staff						3	
After-sales service						3	
Location relative to buyer						2	
Human rights (emerging economies)						1	
Environmental awareness						1	
Total						**40**	
Total product and supplier						55	

The *Weighting* header spans the Excellent, Good, Fair, Poor, and Very poor columns.

were being evaluated (factor = 3) and was given a rating good (weighting = 4), then the score would be 12 (3 * 4). The use of a supplier checklist is illustrated in Demonstrating the concept 16.1.

Figure 16.4 Reducing the number of suppliers

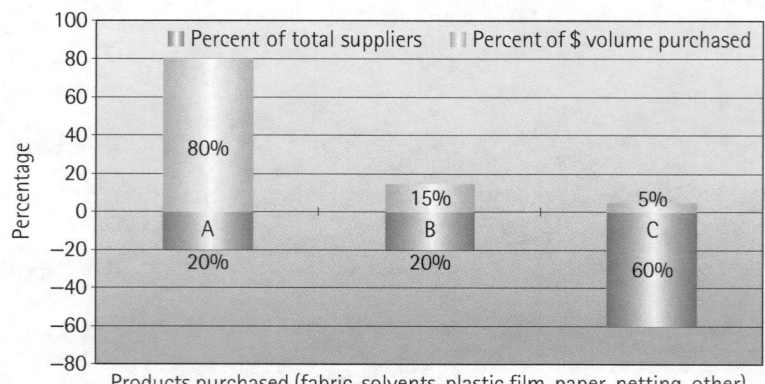

Suppliers before

Suppliers after

REDUCING
NUMBER OF SUPPLIERS

• Reduces administrative costs
• Improves response
• Facilitates management
• Reduces number of buyers

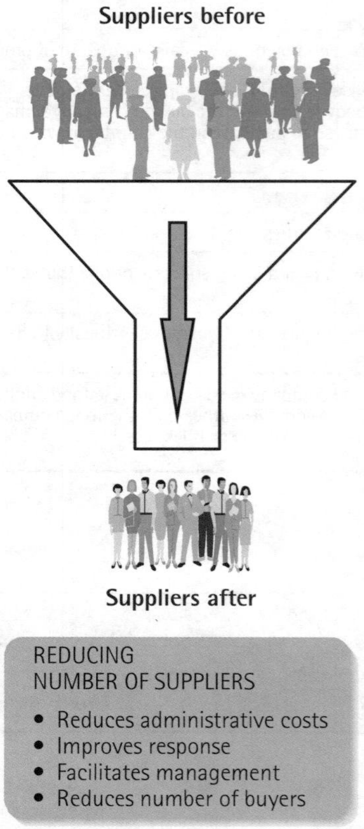

Number of suppliers

Well-established companies over the years build up large databases of suppliers that either they use frequently, or hardly at all. In order to reduce cost, companies make attempts from time to time to reduce the number of suppliers that are used by the organization as conceptualized in Figure 16.4. The reasons for this is that, with fewer suppliers:

• Administrative costs are lower.
• When a supplier knows that it is one of a few suppliers, and furnishes a large proportion of product to a purchasing company, then the purchaser can exercise more power over the supplier regarding contract terms.
• Facilities management of the purchasing function.
• Enables a buyer company to reduce its number of purchasing staff.

ABC analysis of suppliers

If one wants to reduce the number of suppliers, a question to ask is who to keep? Who to let go? A first approach might be to make an ABC analysis of the suppliers according to the monetary volume purchased, and the number of suppliers. As an illustration, the division of a textile company near Lyon, France, which purchased a wide range of fabrics, solvents, plastic film, paper, netting, and other material had 110 suppliers in its database. In performing an ABC analysis it established that almost 80% of the monetary volume purchased was from 20% of the total suppliers whereas 60% of the total suppliers only furnished 5% of the monetary value of the supplied material as illustrated in Figure 16.5.[14] Thus, a first step in reducing the number of suppliers after an ABC analysis has been carried out is

Figure 16.5 ABC analysis for supplier evaluation

Percentage

Percent of total suppliers   Percent of $ volume purchased

80%
A
20%

15%
B
20%

5%
C
60%

Products purchased (fabric, solvents, plastic film, paper, netting, other)

to start elimination in category C moving through B, and eventually category A. Rating sheets are also used to evaluate the best suppliers.

Standardizing supplied products

Another way to reduce the supplier costs is to standardize the components that go into making finished products. This was the thrust of Ford Motor, USA, in 1995 which set a goal to hold its overall costs at 1995 levels through the end of the decade, and to this effect asked its 250 biggest suppliers worldwide to join in a 'collaborative effort' to cut costs of parts 5% a year from 1996 through 1999.[15] The major thrust of this cost-cutting effort was to reduce complexity by reducing the number of alternative components used on vehicles as for example:

- reducing the number of types of car horn from 30 to 3
- reducing the number of types of battery from 40 to 14
- reducing the number of types of steering wheel from 50 to 11
- using a single material on colour on trunk carpeting in all vehicles instead of the present half dozen materials and colours. This was expected to reduce costs by 7%.

Steps in the purchasing process

The procedure for securing a purchased item or service differs from company to company, and the monetary volume of the purchase. Nevertheless, the general procedure used for say a quantity of mechanical components is illustrated in Figure 16.6. The following details the steps.

Purchase requisition

A purchase, or material requisition, is issued by production and sent to purchasing. This document is a request to buy an item and this requisition would include:

- Identification of the item to be purchased.
- Quantity to be purchased.
- Delivery date or schedule when it is needed.
- Account to which purchase order is to be charged.
- Delivery location.

Request for quotation

Purchasing, with the aid of production, prepares a request for quotation (RFQ) which is a document defining the item for prospective suppliers. This RFQ would include:

- Description of the item to be purchased.
- Detailed specification such as the materials to be used, composition, operating temperatures of the material, etc.
- Diagram of the item showing dimensions.

Out-for-bidding

The RFQ would be sent out to several vendors, or suppliers for quotations, which would include price and delivery time, if this is not specified by the buying company. This is competitive bidding and very often firms would select three suppliers for quotations. Depending on the size of the order, purchasing personnel may go out and visit the prospective suppliers.

Figure 16.6 The purchasing process

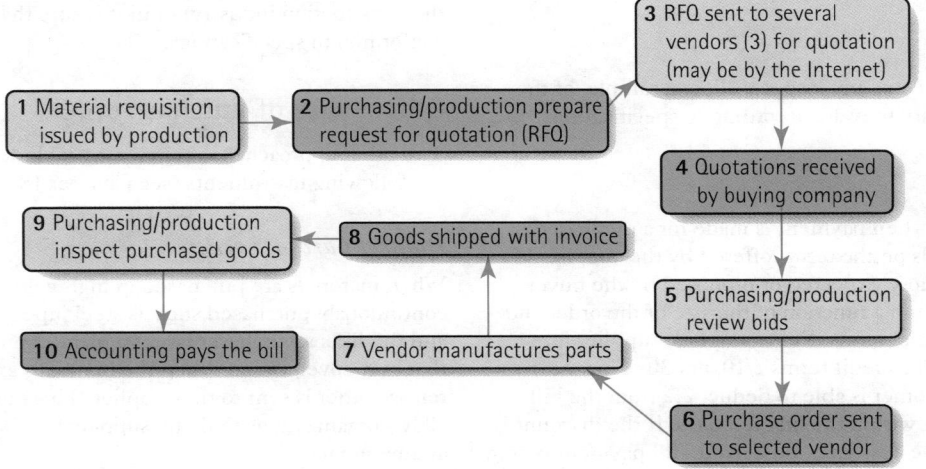

Reception of quotations

Proposals are sent from the prospective suppliers to the buying company. Suppliers may deliver their quotation personally to the buying company in order to explain in detail their quotation and be able to directly answer any questions. However, the buying company might insist that first the quotation is first delivered by mail before any meetings with the supplier are conducted.

Vendor selection

Purchasing, with the aid of production, and say perhaps R&D, or other technical departments would review the proposal documents from the vendors (suppliers). Then, purchasing, and maybe production personnel might visit the vendors to review the proposal in more detail. The best supplier would be selected based on such criteria as, price (or global cost), delivery time, quality, availability of spares, after-sales service, and the like as detailed in Table 16.6.

Purchase order

The purchasing department sends out a purchase order to the selected vendor that may include the terms and conditions for payment from the client firm to the supplier.

Supplier manufactures

The selected vendor sets in motion the production of the required components.

Shipping

Goods are shipped to the buyer with invoice.

Inspection

The buying company inspects all, or a sample, of the goods to verify they are according to specifications.

Payment

The timing when payment is made for a purchased item depends on the terms offered by the supplier of the goods, those expected or proposed by the buyer. These are often a function of the size of the order and agreed financial terms. For example, a supplier firm might offer the credit terms 2/10, net 30. This means that the customer is able to deduct 2% from the bill when paying within the first ten days. If the discount is not taken, the customer must make full payment within 30 days. Not taking the discount can be costly as illustrated:

Assume that the bill for a purchase order is £100.00 with the terms 2/10, net 30. This means the supplier can pay £98.00 up to the 10th day, or £100.00 at 30 days. If the cash discount is not taken, it means having the use of £98.00 for 20 days, at a £2.00 fee. This is equivalent to an annual cost of 36.72% as now calculated.

Cost of not taking cash discount:

$$\frac{\text{Discount (\%)}}{(100-\text{discount})} * \frac{360}{(\text{Final due date}-\text{Discount period})}$$

The cost of not taking the cash discount is:

$$\frac{2}{(100-2)} * \frac{360}{(30-10)} = \frac{2}{98} * \frac{360}{20}$$

Or 2.04% * 18 = 36.72%.

At this high rate it would be better to take the discount, and borrow money elsewhere.

There may be no credit terms offered and the buyer pays for goods after, say, 60 days' receipt of invoice. In the food industry in France, payment terms are 30 days for perishable food, and 20 days for live animals and fresh meat.

Large purchased items

For large items it may be that the buyer gives money upfront to the supplier before his production starts. Alternatively, progress payments might be made. For example:

- 10% of the cost is paid before fabrication starts
- 50% is paid halfway
- 85% is paid on completion.

The buyer retains a holdback of say 15% (common in the construction industry) until it is sure that the item(s) conform(s) to specifications.

Other types of purchase order

Two other approaches to purchasing include the use of the following instruments (see Chapter 18).

Blanket purchase order

When materials are purchased in high volume and are continuously purchased such as steel pipe, fittings, glass, and the like, a purchaser issues a blanket purchase order that may cover a year. When the materials are needed, a release order is sent to the supplier. This procedure allows organizations to tie up suppliers for long-term arrangements.

Open purchase orders

For small purchases, or consumable supplies, like, paper, pencils, work gloves, these are often purchased from the petty cash of the department using open purchase orders.

Purchasing and the Internet

The Internet is becoming more important as a medium for purchasing in that it is much quicker, minimizes the paperwork, and hence is less costly. Consider the following illustration for a hotel chain that wants to purchases a quantity of bathroom towels from a known supplier.

Purchasing procedure before the Internet

- Bill, the Operations Manager, wishes to replace the bathroom towels for the hotels in his region and writes an internal order to Purchasing.
- Sarah, in Purchasing, completes a requisition form.
- Fred, Sarah's manager, approves the requisition form.
- Jennifer, the assistant prepares the purchase order.
- Jill, the secretary, faxes the purchase order to the supplier.
- John, in Operations, checks the incoming goods.
- Ann, in Accounting, receives the invoice from the supplier.
- Accounting pays the invoice.

Purchasing procedure using the Internet

- Bill, the Operations Manager, wishes to replace the bathroom towels for the hotels in his region. He sends an internal e-mail to Purchasing giving his requirements.
- Sarah, in Purchasing, puts the specification for the towels on its website. The supplier has access to this information.
- John, in Operations, checks the incoming goods.
- Accounting pays the invoice through the Internet.

Value analysis

Introduction

Companies continually examine ways to reduce purchasing costs and value analysis, or value engineering, has this ultimate objective. It is a study of the function of purchased materials to see if, without impairing use or performance, specifications can be modified in order to reduce cost. Larry D Miles of General Electric developed the concept of value analysis during World War II. Under wartime conditions, studies were continually made to see if alternative materials could be used for components and assemblies, as those specified were either expensive or difficult to obtain. (See also Chapter 6.)

Function of the product

Value analysis attacks two aspects of a product:

- Use function, or the ability of the product to perform according to specifications.
- Aesthetic function or the appearance or style of the product.

Value analysis is easier to apply to industrial products, as the client is principally interested in the product performing correctly, rather than its appearance. Consumer products (foods, household appliances, automobiles) are often purchased according to their appearance where the aesthetic function is a marketing tool. Even though changing the aesthetic function might dramatically lower the cost, it might also markedly reduce the sale. (Who would buy Chanel perfume in a simple plastic bottle?)

Considerations for a value analysis

Purchasing people would work alongside technical personnel in carrying out a value analysis. Points to be considered, as illustrated in Figure 16.7, might include:

- Could a cheaper part or material be used? (Plastic instead of metal.)
- Can the component be eliminated without impairing the operation of the assembled unit? (Replacing the corner window in automobiles with a single window.)
- Is the function necessary? (Does one need seven different cycles on a washing machine?)
- Could the function of two or more parts or components be performed by a single part at a lower cost? (One flexible tube in a vacuum cleaner, instead of several steel tubes that have to be 'sleeved' together.)
- Is the cost of the part in line with its function? (Would carbon steel be suitable in place of more expensive stainless steel?)
- Can the part be simplified?
- Could product specifications be relaxed so that parts can be produced at lower cost?
- Could standard parts be substituted for custom-made parts? (A standard automobile injection system to serve many types of engines.)

Figure 16.7 Value analysis

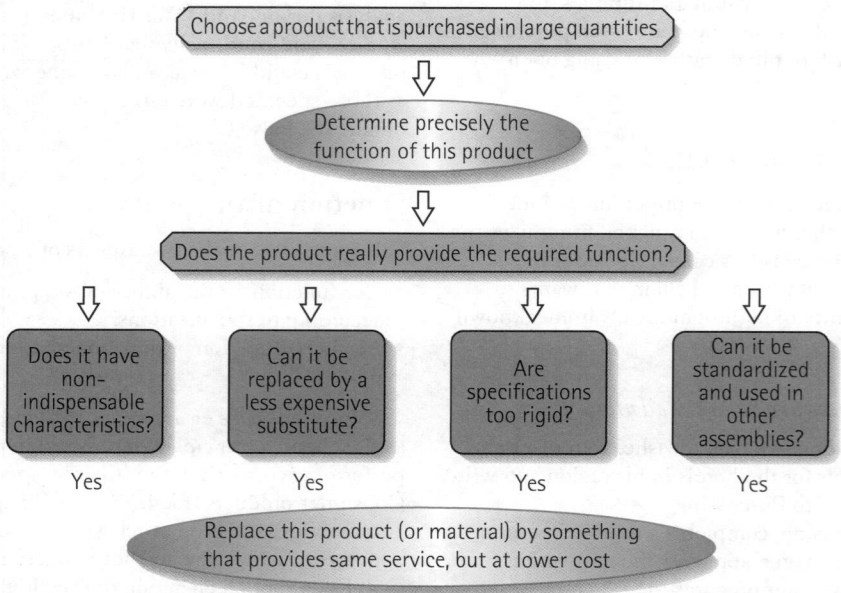

Costs decline: Profits increase!

- Can the weight be reduced by redesign, or using different materials? This would reduce not only production costs, but also transportation costs.
- Can the packaging volume be reduced at the same time giving the same protection of the item?

Steps in carrying out a value analysis

Conducting a value analysis would proceed as follows:

1. Establish the objectives. The ultimate objective is to reduce the cost of the purchased product.
2. Constitute a multidiscipline team from marketing, sales, production, cost control, suppliers, and purchasing. These would be the team leaders.
3. Analyze the production process of the supplying company. This would include decoupling the cost price at each step of the production process.
4. Analyze, phase by phase, the use of the product at the purchaser's company.
5. Decompose and analyze the various characteristics of the purchased product, applying a weighting coefficient to each according to their importance. Characteristics would include physical attributes such as size, shape, and form, chemical composition, use, taste (in the case of food), and preparation.
6. Brainstorming, which would be a creative session to explore all alternative possibilities with the team not having any preconceived ideas.

7. Sort the ideas and establish the cost of each.
8. Selection of the best alternative.
9. Develop a plan for implementing the change.

Technology changes

With new technological developments there has been a significant increase in the purchase of plastic and composite components to replace metal, glass, and wood. Plastic and composites are cheaper, lighter, more corrosive resistant, and often easier to mould and shape. As we saw in Figure 5.4, plastic use has increased to the detriment of steel. A typical product example is the automobile gasoline filler cap. Today it is most often made of one piece of moulded plastic. In the 1960s it was made of chromium plated steel head, a metal shaft, with a steel spring cap, and rubber gaskets.

In the packaging field, plastic has replaced glass for liquids, particularly for soft drinks and water. Even where glass has not been replaced there has been a significant improvement in the technology to reduce the unit weight. For example, glass is still used for wine, milk, beer and other food products but the weight of glass is now some 50% of the weight in similar products used in 1940.

As technology is constantly changing companies need periodically to make a value analysis for their manufactured and purchased products. Every year is a timeframe often used by many firms.

Just-in-time purchasing

If a company is operating under a just-in-time (JIT) mode (see Chapter 15) then JIT must apply to purchasing. Essential elements of purchasing, in order for just-in-time to be effective, are as follows.

Long-term relationships

Firms develop a network of long-term contracts with a few suppliers rather than short-term contracts with many suppliers. The Japanese call these *subcontractor networks*, and refer to suppliers as *co-producers*. Having few suppliers keeps ordering costs low and the networks build trust between buying and supplying firms as well as providing dependable supplies of raw material and parts. Repeat business is awarded to the same suppliers with competitive business normally limited to new parts. A buying firm continually evaluates the suppliers so it keeps competitive and any vertical integration with the supplier is avoided. The suppliers are encouraged by the buying company to also operate under just-in-time and to extend just-in-time methods to their own suppliers.

Proximity

To manage just-in-time purchasing better, companies might have a policy that suppliers must be located near the buying firm's factory such that they can deliver small orders throughout the production day thus lead times are shorter and more reliable. Parts, in exact quantities, are delivered in small standard-size containers with a minimum of paperwork. This keeps inventories low. However, for some companies proximity may not be a requirement. In this case, the company would analyze the risk in having a *distant* supplier and develop an appropriate inventory policy.

Quality

Since suppliers have a long-term relationship with the buying firms, and because parts are delivered in small lots, quality of purchased materials tends to be high. The buying firm should work closely with the supplier to improve quality and should impose just the necessary product specifications. Further, the suppliers should be encouraged to use statistical process control rather than inspection of lots and to use company-owned, or contract transport, rather than common carriers to permit easy control of the material.

Risk

Companies need to analyze the risk involved in implementing a just-in-time policy. For example, if just-in-time is in place what would be the outcome on production if purchased parts are late as a result of accidents, strikes, or supplier equipment malfunctions? This was a severe problem after the US government curtailed transportation movements following the New York attacks on 11 September 2001.[16]

Responsibility

In just-in-time it must be clear who is responsible for initiating the delivery of the purchased product – the production centre, or the buyer. Without clear delineation of responsibility, the supply chain can be broken.

Suppliers on the shop floor

Some firms are going even further with just-in-time purchasing by having their suppliers physically located in the firm's facility rather than having them located nearby in their own plant. This has its advantages in that decision making is quick, inventories are kept low, but as we have already seen, there are concerns of confidentiality and conflict of interest.

Subcontracting

Suppliers as subcontractors

The line differentiating a supplier and a subcontractor is not always evident to organizations. Generally, a subcontractor is a third party which produces a customized product, or provides a service, for a firm and there is a specific contract detailing the work, the delivery date, and price, between the two parties. For example, Rolls-Royce is a subcontractor to Airbus for an Airbus-300 aircraft engine. A supplier, by way of contrast, often supplies standard products to firms and there may be no contract, just a purchase requisition. For example, Gilbert, a European supplier of office material provides standard diskettes, paper, and office supplies to Airbus and many other firms. In the service field, very often companies have a subcontractor on their site to operate a restaurant, printing, and perhaps travel services. There would be a contract for these service which might be reviewed, and renewed or not, say, every five years.

Employing subcontractors can be considered a purchasing function since one is purchasing the services of a third party. Selection of the right subcontractor is important in manufacturing as poor quality subcontracted work can have a negative client perception on the quality of the final assembled product.

Evaluating subcontractors

Firms use check sheets to evaluate subcontractors, similar to those for suppliers. Table 16.7 gives the example of the criteria in a check sheet used by Hewlett-Packard where the subcontractor evaluation is made jointly by engineers and those in purchasing.[17] The environment criterion is a factor that is becoming more important for firms in subcontractor selection as the certification ISO-14001 is becoming a requirement for firms. (See also Chapter 5.)

Proportion of work performed by subcontractors

Judgments are often made saying that a subcontractor, or supplier, to a client should limit to 20% the proportion of his business to any one entity.
The reason being that more than this figure means the subcontractor, or supplier, becomes too dependent on one client, in which case the buyer can put pressure on the subcontractor to reduce his price if he wants to retain the buyer's business. Further, if the client goes out of business, then the subcontractor will be in a difficult situation.

Table 16.7 **Hewlett-Packard subcontractor evaluation criteria**

Criteria	Definition
T Technology	Ability of the subcontractor to provide the necessary technical expertise
Q Quality	The level of the quality of the work performed
R Responsiveness	Is the subcontractor a viable concern in the long term?
D Delivery	Ability of the subcontractor to accept, and respect delivery dates
C Cost	Cost, or the price of the services performed
E Environment	Verification that the subcontractor respects environmental regulations, uses non-toxic materials where possible, and that products are recyclable

However, each industry should be looked at individually before percentage values are criticized. In many cases, performing considerably more than 20% of one's business with the same client may not be unreasonable as, for example:

- A client (buyer) who has developed a good long-term relationship with a subcontractor will not let this subcontractor go so easily.
- Assume a subcontractor has 80% of its business with one client, and the supplied product is strategically important to the client. In this case, the client would be more willing to work closely with the subcontractor and provide assistance such as evaluating production methods to ensure that subcontractor quality is maintained. A client would not be prepared to do this if its subcontractor provides component parts to other companies, some of which may be competitors of the client.
- A subcontractor who is aligned with a reputable client, such as a food producer to Marks & Spencer may be happy to have a high proportion of his business, perhaps close to 100%, with the client. This particular client has a strong reputation for quality, and provides attractive profit margins to the subcontractor.

In summary, a supplier should carefully analyze the potential risk in its association with the client regarding the volume of work it contracts to provide.

Subcontractor–client partnerships

Historically, US and European companies have kept their suppliers and subcontractors at arm's length. Relationships have often been adversary and some clichés often used include:

Give them only the information you need to know.

Be careful, they will tell the competition.

Don't trust them.

Now the climate has considerably changed. Japan has for a long time had close contacts with suppliers and subcontractors with its keiretsu network. European and US companies are also finding that close supplier relationships are cost-effective, lead to innovative ideas, and decrease supply time as the following two examples illustrate.[18]

Ford Motor Co.

When this US automobile manufacturer built a paint-finishing plant in Oakville, Canada, it developed an alliance with Asea Brown Boveri, rather than going through the normal bidding process. ABB's effort reduced the cost to 75% of the expected amount, and correspondingly cut short the completion time.

Outsourcing to Flextronics

Flextronics, officially based in Singapore, but with top executives in San José, California, is one of the world's largest electronics manufacturing services (EMS) companies. Rivals include Solectron, Celestica, Jabil, and SCI Systems. This industry designs and assembles personal computers, telephones, and other electronic devices, conceived by the likes of Nokia, Compaq, and Cisco and then outsourced to EMS firms to produce and assemble the physical product. Flextronics has 150 factories with more than 70,000 employees in 27 countries including China, Brazil, Hungary, and Mexico. Some of these facilities have been purchased from firms such as Siemens, Bosch, and Ericsson. As a result, Flextronics now has teams of industrial, mechanical, and chip engineers scattered around the world. A Flextronics-made cell phone may comprise radio frequency components designed in Norway, custom chips created in Israel, circuit boards crafted in India, factory tooling developed in Italy, and mechanical engineering from Taiwan and Colorado.

One of Flextronics' newest facilities is on a 125-acre industrial park in Guadalajara, Mexico, where 4000 workers turn out thousands of Ericsson cell phones, 3Com Palm Pilots, Compaq circuit boards, and Cisco routers, each day. In addition, one line churns out web TV set-top boxes, which connect television with the net for Philips, in the Netherlands, while an adjacent line makes the same product for Sony, a Philip's competitor. Flextronics not only manufactures all the brand name hardware assembled on the site but also handles all the distribution and logistics services for the final products. The firm also offers after-sales service and helps design new products thus being entrusted with the intellectual property of the designer firm. The hallmark of EMS firms such as Flextronics is flexibility. They can rapidly change from assembling one product to another as the market changes, meaning that they are always operating at close to maximum capacity. Manufacturing times drop from more than a week to less than a day, which radically shortens the entire supply chain. To provide this flexibility and shorter lead times many of the component suppliers to Flextronics are located close to the assembly facilities.

Adapted from: 'Have factory, will travel', *The Economist*,[19] 'The barons of outsourcing', *Business Week*,[20] and 'Flextronics rides big wave', *International Herald Tribune*[21]

Marks & Spencer

By creating an alliance with a knitwear supplier, this British retailer was able to reduce delivery from 14 weeks to a few days.

Outsourcing

Outsourcing is really another term for subcontracting, although in a global context it means giving to the outsourced supplier, perhaps overseas, a significant portion of the work including responsibility for the product design, planning, production and even logistics management. That is, outsourcing goes another step further than the subcontractor–partnership relationship discussed in the previous section. An important outsourcing activity is by EMS companies (electronics manufacturing services) as illustrated by Industry insight 16.4.

Although these forms of strategic alliance have their benefits, it is not to say that all companies are creating such cosy relationships with their suppliers or subcontractors. In Germany, for example, there is a tendency for the reverse approach where Volkswagen and Opel have agreed to dismiss fewer workers in return for greater flexibility on wages and working practices which is resulting in less subcontracting as the retained workers have to be given something to do. Instead of 'outsourcing' (subcontracting) these companies are 'insourcing' (doing the work themselves). Insourcing tasks for Opel include the development of plastic parts and Volkswagen has restarted the production of power steering systems and axles.[22]

Make or buy

One decision for a manufacturing firm is whether to completely make all the components of a product in-house, or to purchase some assemblies, or subassemblies from outside. It might be that the company's production department can make parts for less cost, better quality, faster delivery, than from suppliers. Alternatively in some cases it might be more cost effective to purchase the components from outside, if reliable suppliers are available.

Criteria for making

Some of the detailed reasons for making a product within the firm might include:

- It is cheaper to manufacture within the company rather than to purchase outside.

- The confidence in the suppliers for delivery time, quality, and price is low.
- There is better quality control which is not able to obtain from suppliers.
- There is excess capacity in work centres and making in-house will contribute to fixed costs.
- The particular part is strategic to the company which is concerned about divulging technology and know-how to outsiders as this may impair competitiveness.
- Purchasing would involve layoffs within the organization, which would have a negative impact on the labour force.
- There is concern about supplier collusion (even though illegal) regarding price, specifications, delivery of product, and a firm's business.
- Purchasing the product would involve eliminating specialized know-how meaning that in the long run the firm would lose its competitiveness.
- Excessive time is needed to find a supplier, work with him, and make initial tests, in order to obtain the desired product.
- There is a concern about legal problems if the supplied part does not meet specifications. (In the USA legal ramifications can affect the whole supply chain even if a company did not make the part, but used a purchased part in an assembly.)

Criteria for buying

The criteria for purchasing (some of which are obviously the antithesis of the criteria for making) are as follows:

- It is overall less expensive to purchase outside than to make within the company.
- There is a high confidence in the reliability of the suppliers.
- Unable to produce in-house because patent rights protect the product.
- There is insufficient machine and labour capacity in-house to manufacture.
- To make would mean adding additional capacity in terms of labour, machine, and surface area and the long-term needs of this additional capacity are uncertain.
- By purchasing, the investment in inventory is reduced and the firm's policy is to have the supplier hold inventory until it is needed (just-in-time for the firm).
- There will be more flexibility with the production operation when demand requirements are unclear. Flexibility increases if there are several suitable suppliers.
- The supplies of raw materials to make necessary part are not readily available.
- Purchasing enhances company's cash position enabling it to enact other strategies, such as

Table 16.8 Simple breakeven analysis

Units are purchased	
• Price per unit (no price discounts)	$20.00
Units are made	
• Variable cost per unit (materials, labour)	$15.00
• Fixed cost (machines, buildings, overhead)	$20,000
Level of units required is x	
• Production cost for x units is sum of fixed and variable cost	20,000 + 15x
• Purchase cost for x units	20x

acquisitions, capital improvements, and increase dividend payments.
- Product is relatively simple and producing within the company would add very little value to the operation.

Breakeven analysis

A quantitative method for deciding whether to make, or buy, is to use a breakeven analysis. This approach determines at what quantity of units the total cost to purchase is equal to the cost of producing, or the breakeven quantity. The logic being that below this breakeven value it is cheaper to purchase and above it is cheaper to produce. Table 16.8 gives a simple illustration. (See Chapter 25 for further details.)

There is a breakeven point when total production costs equals total purchase costs:

$$20x = 20,000 + 15x$$
$$5x = 20,000$$
$$x = 4000$$

That is, the breakeven point is at 4000 units. Thus, based strictly on this quantitative analysis the decision would be to purchase when fewer than 4000 units are needed and produce when more than 4000 units are needed. If only variable costs were considered then, in this situation, it is always cheaper to produce than to buy, with a difference of $5 per unit. However, this is not the case when fixed costs are added and it is only at 4000 units that the total difference between purchase price and production cost that fixed costs are absorbed. Figure 16.8 shows how the cost curve picture changes according to the number of units required.

The analysis has to be treated with caution, since, if a firm has already in place some fixed capacity which is available for production, yet it purchases from outside, there is no contribution to the cost of this fixed capacity. (See also Chapter 25.) And, of course, a breakeven situation only occurs if variable costs per unit are less than the purchase price per unit.

Figure 16.8 Breakeven point

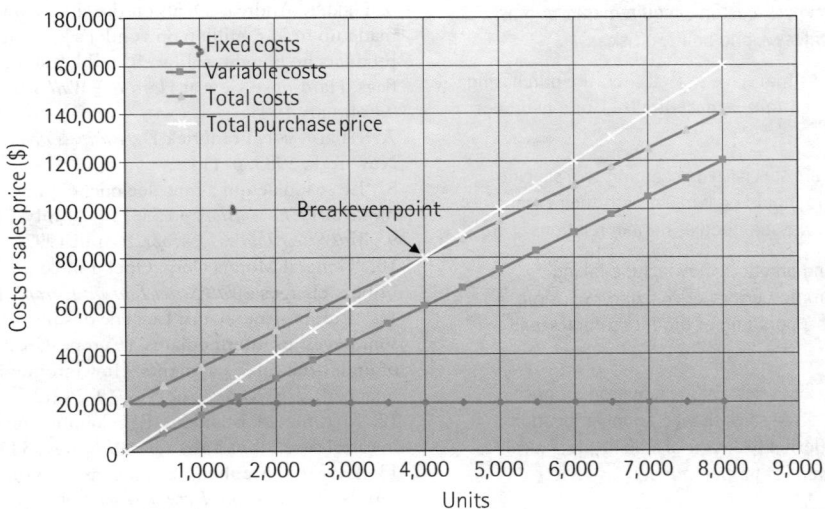

New product

Assume a company is considering introducing a new product onto the market and a make and buy analysis indicates that making is the least expensive. However, this may not be the best strategy because the new product may not succeed. If the company has invested in new production equipment, it can be costly. A better strategy might be:

• Initially to buy (even though the price is higher, there is less long-term financial risk).
• See if the product is successful in the marketplace.
• If successful make the necessary investment to be able to make.

This was the type of strategy of a major European food company which wanted to introduce a new food product onto the market. Its approach was:

• It negotiated a contract with a company in England to supply the purchased products over two years.
• In the contract, the supplier company furnished the product for two years. And, for two years after that, it had the option exclusively to supply the client company.
• After it was proven the product was a success, the food company invested in the necessary equipment to make the product itself.

The danger with this type of strategy is that a supplier company, at the end of the contractual period, could become a competitor.

Summary of key elements

• Purchasing is the buying of materials or services from an outside source. Upwards of 60% of the cost of goods in manufactured products can come from purchases.

• Purchased products include raw materials, parts, subassemblies, machinery, equipment, packaging, supplies, finished goods, and subcontractor services.

• A purchasing manager's index is directly related to manufacturing. An index above 50% indicates an increase of manufacturing, below means a decline.

• Sourcing is the activity of searching worldwide for a supplier (a source) of raw materials, or products, which present the best value of quality to price.

• Fluctuating exchange rates are a risk in international purchasing. Forward buying for increasing prices, or hand-to-mouth buying for declining prices, can offset risk.

• Hedging is the purchase, or sale, of a futures contract of a commodity to offset the purchase, or sale, of a cash commodity. It is used to offset the risk occurring in fluctuating commodity markets or to guarantee a source of raw materials.

• Completely knocked down (CKD) is the term used for companies that export their products (sell to purchasers) in a disassembled, or kit form.

- Barriers to international purchasing include language and cultural differences, customs requirements, quotas, specifications, local laws, and political risk.

- For organizations that have several sites, the purchasing activity might be centralized, decentralized, or a hybrid of the two.

- Buyers usually are specialized according to a specific commodity. Buyers should be familiar with their company, price structures, laws, and good at human relations.

- Unethical buying practices may include taking advantage of quotation errors, price fixing, collusion, playing favourites, upgrading of product samples, and reciprocity.

- Criteria for supplier selection include product price, quality, reliability, after-sales service, supplier location, inventory policy, flexibility, financial stability, technical capability, and extent of product range.

- With few suppliers, administrative costs are lower, a purchaser has more clout with suppliers, and purchasing staff can be reduced.

- The steps in purchasing are purchase requisition, request for quotation, out for bidding, reception of quotations, supplier selection, purchase order, supplier produces, shipping, inspection, and final payment.

- Value analysis is a study of the function of purchased materials to see, without impairing performance, how specifications can be modified in order to reduce cost.

- If a firm operates under just-in-time, then purchasing is just-in-time. Having a competent physically close network of suppliers aids JIT purchasing.

- Subcontractor selection is a purchasing function as it involves the purchasing of services of a third party. Selection can be aided by using weighted checklists. Outsourcing is subcontracting where the outsourced firm has a significant responsibility in the work.

- Manufacturing firms make decisions whether to buy or make products. A financial breakeven analysis between the two choices is useful in this context.

Notes and references

1. Burt, Tim and Tait, Nikki, 'Chrysler to slash supplier costs by $6 billion: Carmaker launches overhaul with initial 15% cut in components budget', *Financial Times*, 8 December 2000, p. 21
2. 'Latest data in US signal slowdown in manufacturing', *Wall Street Journal Europe*, 2–3 June 1995
3. 'Purchasing managers index reaches a peak, signalling euro-zone growth', *Wall Street Journal Europe*, 4 January 2000
4. 'Economic and financial indicators', *The Economist*, 7 July 2001, pp 107–8

5. 'Futures prices', *Wall Street Journal Europe*, Money & Markets section, 5/6 October 2001, p. 19
6. Gerlin, Andrea, 'Deals on the side: How a Penney buyer made up to $1.5 million on vendor's kickbacks. But the products he bought, sold well, and US store ignored some red flags. Hard-nose view at Harrods', *Wall Street Journal Europe*, 9 February 1995
7. Sturdivant, Frederick D., *Business and Society*, Irwin, New York, 1985, p. 114
8. 'Le scandale qui a tout déclenché' (The scandal which broke all) *L'Expansion*, no 553, 10–24 July 1997, p. 44
9. *Wall Street Journal Europe*, 9 April 1997
10. 'General Motors Corp: Opel unit confirms official is facing bribery charges', *Wall Street Journal Europe*, 1–2 March 1996
11. 'Europe-Etats-Unis: Le choc des pots-de-vin: Comment sont payés les intermédiares' (Europe-USA: The shock of under-the-table payments. How intermediaries are financed), *L'Expansion*, no 553, 10–24 July 1997, p. 44
12. Mitchener, Brandon, 'EU Commission fines six companies in cartel case', *Wall Street Journal Europe*, 3 October 2001
13. Labaton, Stephen, 'Europeans help turn heat up on cartels', *International Herald Tribune*, 4 June 2001
14. Study at the Groupe ESC Lyon, 1993
15. 'Ford says goal is to keep costs at 1995 levels', *Wall Street Journal Europe*, 10 May 1995
16. Haddad, Charles, 'How UPS delivered through the disaster: Decisions before and during the attack helped it cope', *Business Week*, 1 October 2001, p. 58
17. Bleakley, Fred R., 'Strange bedfellows: Some companies let suppliers work on site and even place orders', *Wall Street Journal Europe*, 16 January 1995
18. 'Holding the hand that feeds: More and more companies are forming cosy partnerships with their suppliers. Such relationsips can be risky', *The Economist*, 9 September 1995, p. 71
19. 'Have factory, will travel', *The Economist*, 12 February 2000, pp 65–6
20. Engardio, Pete, 'The barons of outsourcing', *Business Week*, 28 August 2000, pp 98–9
21. Markoff, John, 'Flextronics rides big wave: Assembling high-tech gadgets proves fruitful', *International Herald Tribune*, 16 February 2000, p. 13
22. 'DIY in Germany', *The Economist*, 2 March 1996

Review and discussion topics

1. Suppliers versus subcontractors

Close-It Company has a patent on automatic garage door openers. It performs a limited amount of manufacturing but about 80% of its activity is the assembly of the units from components. The door openers and unit assembly include:

  (a) screws, bolts, springs, and other fasteners
  (b) a complex control mechanism to a specification written by Close-It
  (c) a timer
  (d) standard plastic covers
  (e) cardboard cartons for packaging of the assembled product.

All these components are obtained from outside sources. Which of these parts do you believe might be obtained from suppliers, and which would be subcontracted? Justify your reasoning. Discuss the difference between a supplier and a subcontractor.

2. Value analysis

Examine:

(a) the car you drive
(b) the bus you take
(c) the bicycle you use
(d) the books you use.

Could you apply value analysis to these products? Discuss, explain, and justify.

3. Make and buy

A make and buy analysis is strictly a comparison between costs. What other considerations should be taken into account (not necessarily quantitative aspects). Consider both a manufacturing and a service organization.

4. International purchasing

More and more developed nations (the USA, Europe, and Japan) are purchasing raw materials, and services in developing countries. Firms' owners think this is the only way to stay competitive. Employees, and often governments (particularly in Europe) don't always agree. Discuss the merits of purchasing from overseas.

5. Just-in-time purchasing

Japan has no trouble in applying just-in-time purchasing. Europe, however, has difficulty in applying the same concepts. Why do you think this is so? Do you feel that some European countries are better than others?

6. Purchasing through the Internet

More and more companies are using the Internet for their purchasing activity. Using real industry examples, discuss what you believe are the advantages and disadvantages of this approach.

Demonstrating the concept 16.1 Stainless steel

Situation

The Purchasing Department at the Chirac plant in Colmar France is looking for a new supplier of stainless steel tubing, sheet, and wire. There are three suppliers being considered:

- Sheffield, England
- Karlsruhe, Germany
- Mulhouse, France.

The Purchasing Department has evaluated the proposals from the three locations and completed checklists for each supplier. These are given in Tables 16.9, 16.10, and 16.11.

Table 16.9 Supplier rating sheet: Sheffield, England

	Excellent 5	Good 4	Fair 3	Poor 2	Terrible 1	Factor Max = 5	Score Wt * factor
			Weighting				
PRODUCT							
Quality	X					5	
Price (high price = low score)				X		4	
Delivery reliability (time)		X				3	
Delivery reliability (conditions)	X					2	
Warranty conditions			X			1	
Total						15	
SUPPLIER							
Technical capability		X				5	
Financial strength		X				5	
Quality certification		X				4	
Flexibility with buyer			X			4	
Profit consistency		X				3	
Labour relations (unionized)		X				3	
Capacity available				X		3	
Management competence	X					3	
Knowledgeable sales staff		X				3	
After-sales service			X			3	

(Continued)

Table 16.9 (Continued)

	Excellent 5	Good 4	Fair 3	Poor 2	Terrible 1	Factor Max = 5	Score Wt * factor
			Weighting				
Location relative to buyer			X			2	
Environmental awareness	X					1	
Total						**39**	
Total product and supplier						54	

Weighted score

PRODUCT

	Excellent 5	Good 4	Fair 3	Poor 2	Terrible 1	Factor Max = 5	Score Wt * factor
Quality	X					5	25
Price (high price = low score)				X		4	8
Delivery reliability (time)		X				3	12
Delivery reliability (conditions)	X					2	10
Warranty conditions			X			1	3
Total						**15**	**58**

SUPPLIER

	Excellent 5	Good 4	Fair 3	Poor 2	Terrible 1	Factor Max = 5	Score Wt * factor
Technical capability		X				5	20
Financial strength		X				5	20
Quality certification		X				4	16
Flexibility with buyer			X			4	12
Profit consistency		X				3	12
Labour relations (unionized)		X				3	12
Capacity available				X		3	6
Management competence	X					3	15
Knowledgeable sales staff		X				3	12
After-sales service			X			3	9
Location relative to buyer			X			2	6
Environmental awareness	X					1	5
Total						**39**	**145**
Total product and supplier						54	203

Table 16.10 Supplier rating sheet: Karlsruhe, Germany

	Excellent 5	Good 4	Fair 3	Poor 2	Terrible 1	Factor Max = 5	Score Wt * factor
			Weighting				
PRODUCT							
Quality		X				5	
Price (high price = low score)	X					4	
Delivery reliability (time)			X			3	
Delivery reliability (conditions)		X				2	
Warranty conditions			X			1	
Total						**15**	
SUPPLIER							
Technical capability				X		5	
Financial strength		X				5	
Quality certification				X		4	
Flexibility with buyer				X		4	

(Continued)

Table 16.10 (Continued)

	Weighting					Factor	Score
	Excellent 5	Good 4	Fair 3	Poor 2	Terrible 1	Max = 5	Wt * factor
Profit consistency		X				3	
Labour relations (unionized)		X				3	
Capacity available			X			3	
Management competence	X					3	
Knowledgeable sales staff		X				3	
After-sales service				X		3	
Location relative to buyer				X		2	
Environmental awareness		X				1	
Total						**39**	
Total product and supplier						**54**	

Weighted score

PRODUCT

	Excellent 5	Good 4	Fair 3	Poor 2	Terrible 1	Max = 5	Wt * factor
Quality		X				5	20
Price (high price = low score)	X					4	20
Delivery reliability (time)			X			3	9
Delivery reliability (conditions)		X				2	8
Warranty conditions			X			1	3
Total						**15**	**60**

SUPPLIER

	Excellent 5	Good 4	Fair 3	Poor 2	Terrible 1	Max = 5	Wt * factor
Technical capability				X		5	10
Financial strength		X				5	20
Quality certification				X		4	8
Flexibility with buyer				X		4	8
Profit consistency		X				3	12
Labour relations (unionized)		X				3	12
Capacity available			X			3	9
Management competence	X					3	15
Knowledgeable sales staff		X				3	12
After-sales service				X		3	6
Location relative to buyer				X		2	4
Environmental awareness		X				1	4
Total						**39**	**120**
Total product and supplier						**54**	**180**

Table 16.11 Supplier rating sheet: Mulhouse, France

	Weighting					Factor	Score
	Excellent 5	Good 4	Fair 3	Poor 2	Terrible 1	Max = 5	Wt * factor
PRODUCT							
Quality		X				5	
Price (high price = low score)			X			4	
Delivery reliability (time)			X			3	
Delivery reliability (conditions)		X				2	
Warranty conditions		X				1	
Total						**15**	

(Continued)

Table 16.11 (Continued)

	Excellent 5	Good 4	Fair 3	Poor 2	Terrible 1	Factor Max = 5	Score Wt * factor
			Weighting				
SUPPLIER							
Technical capability				X		5	
Financial strength			X			5	
Quality certification				X		4	
Flexibility with buyer				X		4	
Profit consistency			X			3	
Labour relations (unionized)					X	3	
Capacity available			X			3	
Management competence		X				3	
Knowledgeable sales staff		X				3	
After-sales service				X		3	
Location relative to buyer	X					2	
Environmental awareness					X	1	
Total						39	
Total product and supplier						54	
Weighted score							
PRODUCT							
Quality		X				5	20
Price (high price = low score)			X			4	12
Delivery reliability (time)			X			3	9
Delivery reliability (conditions)		X				2	8
Warranty conditions		X				1	4
Total						15	53
SUPPLIER							
Technical capability				X		5	10
Financial strength			X			5	15
Quality certification				X		4	8
Flexibility with buyer				X		4	8
Profit consistency			X			3	9
Labour relations (unionized)					X	3	3
Capacity available			X			3	9
Management competence		X				3	12
Knowledgeable sales staff		X				3	12
After-sales service				X		3	6
Location relative to buyer	X					2	10
Environmental awareness					X	1	1
Total						39	103
Total product and supplier						54	156

Required

Based on these ratings, which is the preferred supplier?

Solution

The completed rating sheets are given in the second matrix for each location. The overall score for product and supplier are:

- Sheffield, England   203
- Karlsruhe, Germany   180
- Mulhouse, France   156

Thus, based on these evaluations, Sheffield would be the preferred supplier.

Application exercise 16.1   Chips

Situation

The purchasing department at a computer manufacturer in California is evaluating the suppliers of computer chips. There are three suppliers being considered in different locations:

- USA
- Japan
- Hong Kong.

The purchasing department has evaluated the proposals from the three locations and completed checklists for each supplier. These are given in Tables 16.12, 16.13, and 16.14.

Table 16.12 **Supplier rating sheet: USA**

	Weighting					
	Excellent 5	Good 4	Fair 3	Poor 2	Terrible 1	Factor Max = 5
PRODUCT						
Quality		X				5
Price (high price = low score)				X		4
Delivery reliability (time)		X				3
Delivery reliability (conditions)	X					2
Warranty conditions		X				1
SUPPLIER						
Technical capability			X			5
Financial strength	X					5
Quality certification		X				4
Flexibility with buyer			X			4
Profit consistency	X					3
Labour relations (unionized)					X	3
Capacity available				X		3
Management competence		X				3
Knowledgeable sales staff			X			3
After-sales service			X			3
Location relative to buyer	X					2
Environmental awareness			X			1

Table 16.13 **Supplier rating sheet: Japan**

	Weighting					
	Excellent 5	Good 4	Fair 3	Poor 2	Terrible 1	Factor Max = 5
PRODUCT						
Quality	X					5
Price (high price = low score)				X		4
Delivery reliability (time)	X					3
Delivery reliability (conditions)	X					2
Warranty conditions		X				1
SUPPLIER						
Technical capability		X				5
Financial strength	X					5
Quality certification		X				4
Flexibility with buyer				X		4
Profit consistency			X			3
Labour relations (unionized)	X					3

(Continued)

Table 16.13 (Continued)

	Excellent 5	Good 4	Fair 3	Poor 2	Terrible 1	Factor Max = 5
						Weighting
Capacity available				X		3
Management competence	X					3
Knowledgeable sales staff			X			3
After-sales service				X		3
Location relative to buyer			X			2
Environmental awareness				X		1

Table 16.14 Supplier rating sheet: Hong Kong

	Excellent 5	Good 4	Fair 3	Poor 2	Terrible 1	Factor Max = 5
						Weighting
PRODUCT						
Quality		X				5
Price (high price = low score)	X			X		4
Delivery reliability (time)			X			3
Delivery reliability (conditions)		X				2
Warranty conditions			X			1
SUPPLIER						
Technical capability				X		5
Financial strength		X				5
Quality certification				X		4
Flexibility with buyer				X		4
Profit consistency		X				3
Labour relations (unionized)		X				3
Capacity available			X			3
Management competence	X					3
Knowledgeable sales staff		X				3
After-sales service				X		3
Location relative to buyer				X		2
Environmental awareness		X				1

Required

Based on these ratings, which is the preferred supplier?

Application exercise 16.2 Timing

Situation

A company requires 14,000 timing units for its electrical circuit breakers and wishes to make a decision whether to purchase the timing units, or to manufacture them internally. The timing unit is essentially made from a stainless steel rod, springs, and steel caps and if made would be produced in Work Centre A. When finished, the timing unit would then be sent to Work Centre B where it will be incorporated into the final circuit breaker. Table 16.15 shows the essential operating data.

Table 16.15 Essential operating data for timing units

	Units	Value
Variable labour costs		
Labour rate	£/hour	6.00
Employer social charge	%	12.00%

(Continued)

Table 16.15 (Continued)

	Units	Value
Variable material costs		
Stainless steel rod	£metre	0.75
Steel caps	£/unit	0.15
Springs	£/unit	0.05
Variable overhead, Centre A		
Energy cost for work centre	£/shift	35.00
Work centre supervision	£/shift	175.00
Tool centre charges	£/shift	95.00
Warehousing	% material cost	0.95%
Cutting/lubricating fluids	£/finished unit	0.15
Other	£/unit	0.10
Allocated fixed overhead, A	£	7,500.00
Purchase information		
Purchase price	£/unit	6.00
Quantity required	Unit	14,000

(Continued)

Table 16.15 (Continued)

	Units	Value
Design information		
Stainless steel rod	Metres/unit	0.35
Steel caps	Number/unit	6
Springs	Number/unit	20
Production, Work centre A		
Operators	Number/unit	3
Production rate	Units/hr	30

Required

1. Based on the quantity required, should the company make or buy?

2. Is there any quantity level at which the make or buy decision might change? Show your analysis on cost curves for making, and buying.

3. What other considerations need to be taken into account in this type of decision?

Case study 16.1   Lockheed*

Situation

On Friday 26 October 2001 Lockheed Martin, the largest defence contractor in the USA, emerged the winner after a heated five-year battle with Boeing Co., to build the joint strike fighter (JSF), a highly agile, radar-evading aircraft intended to serve as the workhorse for the US Air Force, Navy, and Marines. The potential value of the contract was $200 billion (€224.23 billion) for a programme to last through to 2040. The first test planes are expected to be delivered in 2005 and the first operational planes to be delivered in 2008. The current plan calls for the United States to buy 2852 planes, which includes 1763 for the Air Force, 609 for the Marines and 480 for the Navy. The British, who have already pledged $2 billion toward JSF development, initially planned to purchase about 150 of the planes including 90 for the Royal Air Force and 60 for the Royal Navy. Another 3000 planes are expected to be sold to international customers.

The initial JSF contract provided about $19 billion to the Lockheed consortium that includes Northrop Corp. and BAE Systems of Britain as its biggest partners. Another $4 billion contract went to Pratt and Whitney, the unit of United Technologies, to produce the attack aircraft's engine. The first part of the contract, to build an initial 22 aircraft, was expected to create more than 5000 jobs for Lockheed and its biggest teammates. Lockheed already had the contract for the current F-22 Raptor Air Force Fighter, which saw its first flight in 1997, and which is set to enter the fleet in 2005, with production scheduled to end in 2013. The JSF project, together with the F-22, puts Lockheed in line to control the venerable market for high-performance jets. The JSF plane is expected to be the last manned fighter jet ever to be built and is destined to replace the air force's A-10 attack plane and F-16 Falcon fighter, as well as the early versions of the navy's F/A-18 Hornets and the marine corp.'s Harrier aircraft.

For Britain's BAE Systems plc, Lockheed Martin consortium's victory crowns two years of acquisitions and restructuring that have turned the former British Aerospace firm from an also-ran military supplier, into the world's second-largest defence contractor, and a leader in the fast growing area of electronic warfare. Two of its recent acquisitions have been from Lockheed itself that could increase its original 12% stake in the JSF project to nearly 15%. BAE already does around 20% of its business in the USA and the JSF work should boost that further. For the consortium, BAE brings a spectrum of technologies ranging from aerospace equipment to cutting-edge manufacturing. As the British government has been involved in the JSF project from early on, and with its $2 billion financial commitment, BAE will not simply be a supplier of UK JSFs, which is the role it has played in previous transatlantic projects. Instead, with facilities in both the UK and the USA, BAE will be a fully fledged participant in the programme producing big chunks of every plane, such as the rear fuselage, fuel and life support systems and electronic warfare components. This programme is expected to net British companies more than $34 billion of work and create more than 8000 jobs at BAE alone. This special relationship between Britain and the USA means that, for example, an American pilot will be able to land with equal ease on a British or an American-made aircraft carrier.

Final assembly of the aircraft will be at Lockheed's plant in Fort Worth, Texas, with assembly of major parts in El Segundo, California, and Britain. In addition, there will be some 40 major subcontractors in the United States including in California, Florida, Texas, Illinois, and many of the East Coast states. This, in turn, will spore the involvement of numerous suppliers and other subcontractors. Other British companies involved include Smiths Aerospace, that supplies electronics, electrical and mechanical systems to Lockheed Martin, and Rolls-Royce for the engine and vertical takeoff capability of the warplane. Smiths Aerospace predicted it would earn more than $10 million from the new project, and Rolls-Royce is expected to earn $1 billion in development work. Apart from Britain, other European countries expected to participate in the project include Denmark, Italy, the Netherlands, Norway, and Turkey. Although Boeing lost the award, its St Louis, Missouri-based military operations are expected to participate as a subcontractor in some of the programme.

Required

1. Why will the purchasing function of Lockheed be such a key operational and strategic element in this programme?

2. Why would the learning curve concept play an important role in the purchasing, and other operational activities of Lockheed? (See also Chapter 8, the section entitled 'Learning and the experience curve'.)

3. What are some of the policies that Lockheed should have towards suppliers? What are some of the tools that might be used in analysis? What are some of the key elements in the analysis of suppliers?

4. What are some of the considerations Lockheed might use regarding inventory management related to purchased components? Where would just-in-time purchasing play a role? How does this programme differ from other non-government contracts?

*Adapted from the following:

SQUEO, Anne Marie and MICHAELS, Daniel, 'Lockheed Martin's recovery takes wing with huge jet deal', *Wall Street Journal Europe*, 29 October 2001.

JAMES, Barry, 'Lockheed fighter award also cheered in Britain', *International Herald Tribune*, 29 October 2001.

HOLSEN, Laura M., 'Rising star keeps Lockheed aloft: Former test pilot helped clinch contract for the Joint Strike Fighter', *International Herald Tribune*, 2 November 2001, p. 13.

Selected further reading

BARNETT, Howard, HIBBERT, Reg, CURTISS, Andy and SCOLTHORPE-PIKE, Max, 'The Japanese system of subcontracting', *Purchasing and Supply Management*, December 1995, pp 22–6.

CAVINATO, Joseph L. and KAUFFMAN, Ralph G. (1999) *The Purchasing Handbook: A Guide for the Purchasing and Supply Professional*, 6th edition, McGraw-Hill.

CRUZ, Clarissa, 'Global economy pushes purchasing offshore', *Purchasing*, vol. 122, issue 6, 17 April 1997, pp 20–1.

DOBLER, Donald W., BURT, David N. and LEE, Lamar (1995) *Purchasing and Supply Management*, 6th edition, McGraw-Hill.

POOLER, Victor H. and POOLER, David (1997) *Purchasing and Supply Management – Creating the Vision*, Kluwer Academic Publishers.

An extensive listing of other further reading can be found on the website.

What's on the web?

Further learning resources are available to lecturers and students at www.supplychain-online.com, including the following which are specific to *Purchasing and subcontracting*:

Resource	Subject
Chapter overview	Purchasing and subcontracting
Industry insight: Just-in-time (2)	Just-in-time purchasing
Industry insight: Suppliers help develop new products	Subcontracting
Demonstrating the concept: Pistons	Make or buy
Application exercise: Comfort	Breakeven analysis
More further reading	Purchasing and subcontracting

17 Managing the integrated supply chain

The supply chain

The concept of the supply, or logistics, chain has already been introduced in Chapters 1 and 7, as being the integrated process operations network in place to provide tangible goods or services to a client. In manufacturing, this supply chain is the linkage for the physical movement of all materials from suppliers and subcontractors, through transformation, then as finished goods for the customer. In service concerns such as retail stores or a delivery service like UPS or Federal Express, the supply chain is distribution where the start point is the finished product that has to be delivered to the client in a timely manner. For a pure service operation, such as a financial services firm, or consulting operation, the supply chain is principally the information flow. However, whatever organization is concerned, in the supply chain there is always an information flow back from the customer to the provider of the service.

Activities in supply chain management

Management of the supply chain involves rigorous attention to quality, cost, and lead or delivery times. It implies teamwork, cooperation, and effective coordination throughout the entire organization. Some key management activities, many of which have already been presented in earlier chapters, include the following.

- Site selection as to where best to locate a facility to achieve the most rapid response. This includes not only the manufacturer's facility but also the supplier's factory, service centres, offices, warehouse, and distribution centres. This chapter covers the distribution centre but see also Chapter 3.
- Forecasting the demands for customers, which is the activity that sets into motion planning and the material flow in the supply chain. (Chapter 10.)
- Development of an operations plan that corresponds to the sales needs. This includes all the integrated activities such as development of the master production schedule, the material requirements plan, and the operations schedule. (Chapters 12, 13 and 14.)
- Management of raw materials inventories, work-in-process, and finished goods such that there is sufficient not to have stockout situations, but not too much so that costs are unnecessarily high. This activity will almost certainly involve just-in-time management practices. (Chapters 11 and 15.)
- Layout of the facility so that material goods can flow smoothly through the system be it a storage area, manufacturing, or a retail outlet. (Chapter 9.)
- Purchasing and subcontracting to ensure that the right materials, of the expected quality and specifications, are delivered at the right location on the specified date. (Chapter 16.)
- Distribution requirements planning, route planning, and transportation for finished products, which is covered in this chapter.

Figure 17.1 The supply chain

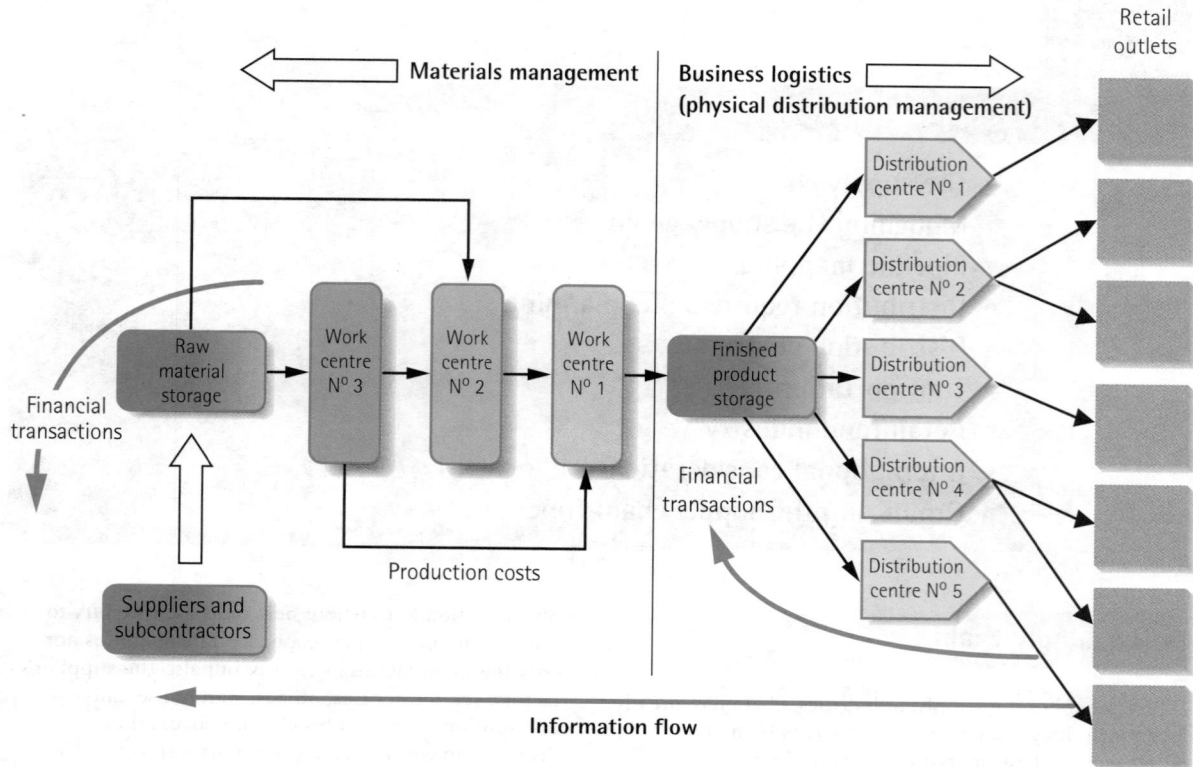

An integrated supply chain

The concept of an integrated supply chain is illustrated in Figure 17.1. (This is similar to the flow scheme already presented in Chapter 1 (Figure 1.1).) Raw material, or parts from suppliers and subcontractors, are delivered and stored in a raw materials warehouse at the production centre. From here, material is withdrawn as needed by the production centre that in this illustration is comprised of three work centres.

Work centre Nº 3

Here the raw materials are transformed into subassemblies that are sent through the chain to Work centre Nº 2. Work centre Nº 3 also prepares semi-finished goods that are sent to Work centre Nº 1.

Work centre Nº 2

Work centre Nº 2 transforms its raw materials from storage, plus the subassemblies received from Work centre Nº 3, into semi-finished goods that are passed onto Work centre Nº 1.

Work centre Nº 1

Work centre Nº 1 produces the finished products from the semi-finished goods it receives from Work centre Nº 2 and Work centre Nº 3. Finished goods from here are put into finished product storage.

From storage, the finished goods are delivered to the distribution centres (here five are shown) by some form of transportation. This may be by truck, as illustrated, but it could be by rail and later by ship or air, depending on the location. From the distribution centre the products are then sent to the client, which may, in the case of consumer goods, be simply retail outlets. All this activity represents the physical flow of material. In the reverse sense, as illustrated, is the information flow from the client going way back to the suppliers.

Financial flows

Associated with the physical movement of material from purchasing through transformation to distribution, and the information flow in the reverse sense, there are also financial transactions covering all the integrated supply chain. Upstream, at the purchasing end there is the payment for goods and services to the supplier. In transformation, or manufacturing, there are all the costs associated with the activity, including payment of salaries to employees. Then, at the client end, there is payment for the finished products. Depending on the information networks in place, these transactions may be effected electronically. Thus, an important part of managing the supply chain is to optimize all these associated costs.

Lead times

To satisfy the customer, products need to be delivered according to schedule. The operations manager, or logistics manager, needs to be sure the supply chain is not broken. Further, lead times, or the time to complete an activity, are critical to planning customer needs. For example, assume in Table 17.1, that the following are lead times, or duration for various activities.

The minimum lead time from ordering raw materials to delivery of a specific order to the distribution centre is the cumulative time of each activity or eight weeks. Any delays in any activity will of course add to the total lead time and result in finished goods being delivered late. The World Wide Web can reduce the supply chain lead time by permitting direct purchasing, delivery, and invoicing of goods. (See Chapter 7.)

Supply chain in two parts

From a management viewpoint, organizations sometimes consider the supply chain as two distinct activities: Materials management and physical distribution management, rather than a complete integrated network, as was illustrated in Figure 17.1.

Materials management

Materials management is the upstream part of the chain. It covers purchasing of raw materials, components, and packaging, their storage, and the production or transformation phases including internal transfer within the work centre. A material requirements plan probably coupled to the ERP system (as already discussed in Chapter 13), might effectively manage this phase.

Physical distribution management

Physical distribution management, sometimes called business logistics, is the downstream portion of the chain and covers the storage and inventory control of the finished products, order processing, distribution planning, order picking (removal from the storage centre) transportation of the finished products to the distribution centres, and then to wholesalers, and retailers. This part of the chain can be managed by a

Table 17.1 Lead times for various activities

Activity	Lead time or duration
Delivery of raw materials	4 weeks
Reception, control, and storage of raw materials	3 days
Production in Work centre N° 3	1 week
Production in Work centre N° 2	1 week
Production in Work centre N° 1	4 days
Control, storage of finished goods	4 days
Delivery of finished goods to distribution centre	3 days
Total lead time	**8 weeks**

distribution requirements plan. For retail outlets this may be the only logistics phase since their activity involves transporting the finished products from the warehouses and distributing them to stores for final sale. Many firms outsource the physical distribution management function of their organization.

Even though the supply chain may be two parts, belonging to separate organizations, many kilometres apart, maybe in different countries, for effective management, the supply chain has to be considered as an integrated network since a problem in one part can impact the other, and vice versa.

Distribution network

The distribution network in the supply chain covers the complete delivery zone for the finished products and an illustration is shown in Figure 17.2. Here we see the production centre at Namur, Belgium, and five distribution centres at Ettelbruck in Luxembourg, Arnhem in the Netherlands, Metz in France, Hof in Germany and St Gallen in Switzerland. The distribution centres might be:

• Wholesalers from where the product goes further to retailers.
• A holding centre or distribution platform for component parts manufactured by a supplier where the client draws on these component parts as needed. For example, Valéo, a manufacturer of automobile parts for companies such as Renault, General Motors, or Citroën, manages large distribution centres located close to the client. Valéo owns this inventory until such time as they are withdrawn by the client.

Figure 17.2 **Distribution network in Europe**

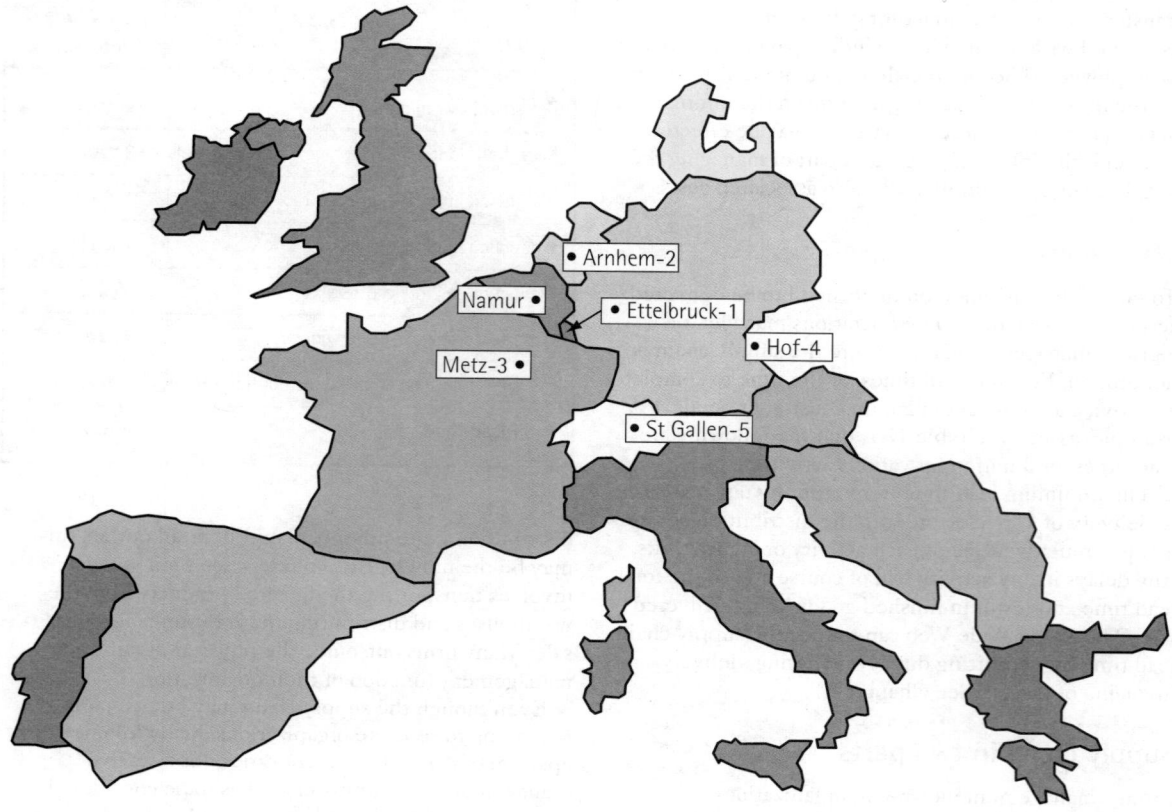

Considerations in planning the supply chain

The client's demand triggers an order, which triggers production, which triggers purchasing of those components and materials that are not made in-house. All along the supply chain are planning factors that need to be considered to avoid missing the client delivery date. Table 17.2 lists some of the elements that need to be taken into account. (This table is converted into a check sheet in Chapter 26.)

Supply chain management is critical

Supply chain management is a critical activity to serve the customer. Consider Producer A of washing machines whose products are sold through specialized chains and hypermarkets. The simplified activities and events of one particular top-loading model, reference BB-40, is illustrated in Figure 17.3:

- Producer A subcontracts out the manufacture of the tumbler section, article T-489, of model BB-40.

- The supplier of the sheet steel for the tumbler delivers a bad lot to the subcontractor.
- The subcontractor has insufficient safety stock of this particular steel and so tumbler production stops until a new supply of steel is received.
- The interrupted supplies of the tumbler to Producer A delays the final assembly of washing machine, BB-40.
- A retailer temporarily runs out of stock of model BB-40.
- A retail customer wishes to purchase a washing machine, model BB-40, but it is not in stock.
- An efficient salesperson convinces the customer to purchase a washing machine manufactured by Whirlpool, a competitor of Producer A. Thus, Producer A has lost a sale, and the associated revenue.

Global operations

Multinational firms producing, say, automobiles, airplanes, or computers have multiple players and the

Table 17.2 Considerations in planning the supply chain

Considerations in purchasing

Have lead times for raw materials, component parts, and packaging been considered in client delivery dates?

If there are several purchased components, have their delivery dates been considered in scheduling production?

Have times for unloading, controlling, and storage of raw materials been taken into account in the planning?

Are payments for raw materials being delayed to as late as possible?

Have timing and amount been taken into consideration in production costs?

Are the delivered quantities of raw materials and component parts appropriate for a just-in-time operation?

Is the number of suppliers kept to a bare minimum to avoid unnecessary management activity from the purchasing staff?

Are all suppliers quality certified (ISO-9000) or other certification such as ISO-14000 as required by your organization?

Is the quality of received goods always perfect and according to specifications?

Considerations in production

Is the labour sufficient in each work centre to meet production requirements?

Are finished goods made to order, or made to stock? Producing to order simplifies the production forecast

Have setup times between each product been considered in planning?

Is labour multi-skilled such that it can be transferred between assembly posts or different sites?

Is hiring necessary to meet planned production level?

Have inventory storage costs been considered in production costs?

Is production capacity sufficient?

If normal capacity is tight, what overtime possibilities exist?

Are production quantities made as an economic batch, or just-in-time?

Is there an integrated planning system for production?

Are there frequent machine changeovers to satisfy important clients?

(Continued)

Table 17.2 (Continued)

Is the production cycle time as short as possible?

Can the production operation respond quickly to change in customer requirements?

Is the facility layout optimum for the production operation?

If products are perishable, is the production cycle time optimum to permit a satisfactory shelf life of the end products?

Has optimum use been made of subcontracting?

Are customer complaints of your produced products close to zero?

Considerations in distribution

Is the delivery by company-owned transport?

Has consideration been given to subcontracting delivery?

Is the truck weight sufficient?

Is the truck volume sufficient?

Have loading and unloading time been taken into consideration in planning?

Is there sufficient transportation?

Is the capacity of the distribution centre sufficient?

Has consideration been given to subcontracting the warehouse activity?

If activity is seasonal, are there periods when additional warehouse capacity is needed?

Considerations in forecasting

Are the sales forecasts consistent with actual demand?

Are the sales forecasts based on past data?

Are the sales forecasts timely, such that the production operation can respond accordingly?

Is the forecasting model sufficiently responsive to actual customer needs, especially when changes occur?

logistics chain can be very complex. Raw materials may come from any of the five continents and the subassemblies may originate in Mexico, Ireland, Singapore, and elsewhere. The final product is then assembled in the USA before being exported to Europe. If something goes wrong, such as a shipment of plastic components goes missing in Hong Kong, causing a factory to stop work in Detroit, and so the

Figure 17.3 Supply chain management is critical

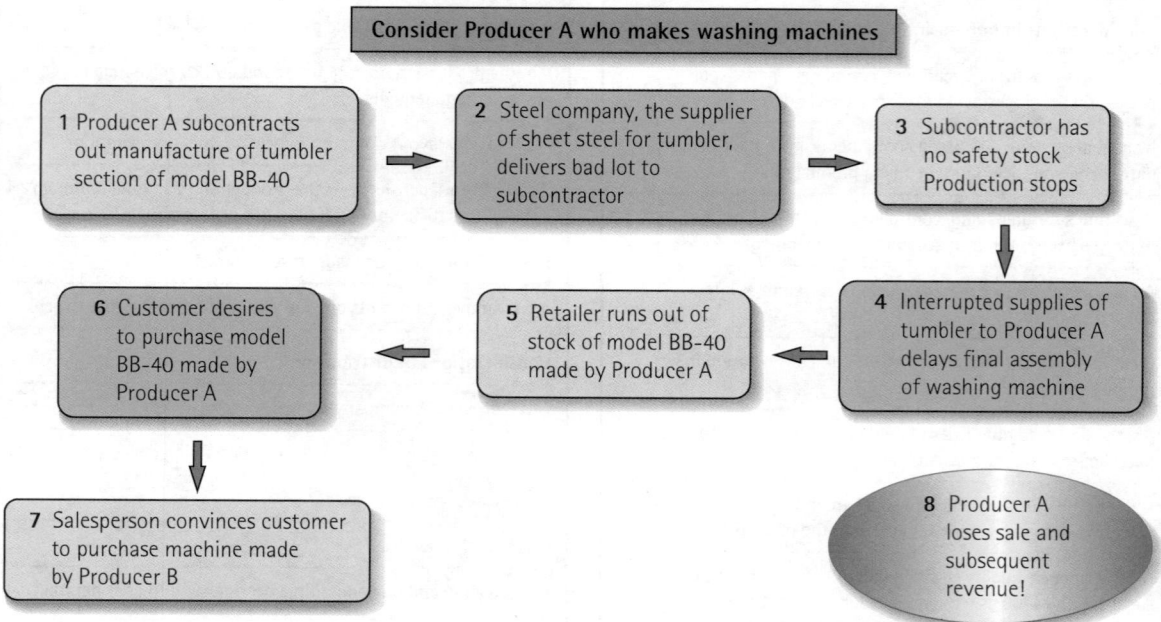

Consider Producer A who makes washing machines

1 Producer A subcontracts out manufacture of tumbler section of model BB-40

2 Steel company, the supplier of sheet steel for tumbler, delivers bad lot to subcontractor

3 Subcontractor has no safety stock Production stops

4 Interrupted supplies of tumbler to Producer A delays final assembly of washing machine

5 Retailer runs out of stock of model BB-40 made by Producer A

6 Customer desires to purchase model BB-40 made by Producer A

7 Salesperson convinces customer to purchase machine made by Producer B

8 Producer A loses sale and subsequent revenue!

client in Paris does not get his order, this can bring a company to its knees. These types of concern, and the others summarized now, are reasons that are driving firms to improve the management of their supply chain:

- Increasing pressure from overseas manufacturing competitors.
- Manufacturing sites that are geographically very dispersed and often situated in low cost labour countries such as in Asia, and Central and South America.
- Cut-throat marketing channels such as independent dealers that push down prices of final goods.
- Maturing of world economies increasing demand for locally made products.
- Increasing pressure from clients to provide quick and reliable delivery of finished products.

Modelling the supply chain

If a supply chain is broken down into smaller elements or modelled, understanding, and thus management, can be significantly improved. The concept is illustrated as follows.

Value-added cells

The various operating stages in the supply chain can be represented by a simple model of a material transformation processing cell where value is added to the upstream component to produce something of a higher value at the downstream end. At each processing cell there is a supply, and a demand and this model applies at any level as illustrated in Figure 17.4.[1]

Manufacturing

In automobile assembly this could be the paint spraying of the chassis. The supply is the bare steel chassis, the transformation is the painting and the demand is the downstream work centre.

Warehousing

In a warehouse, products arrive in bulk on a truck or train and are unloaded and stored. This is the supply. Clients trigger the demand and smaller units are withdrawn by the picking operation and dispatched. This is the transformation.

Packaging

In the packaging of beer or soft drinks into cases the separate cans of the beverage are the supply. The packaging process of putting a ring of plastic over six

Figure 17.4 Modelling the supply chain

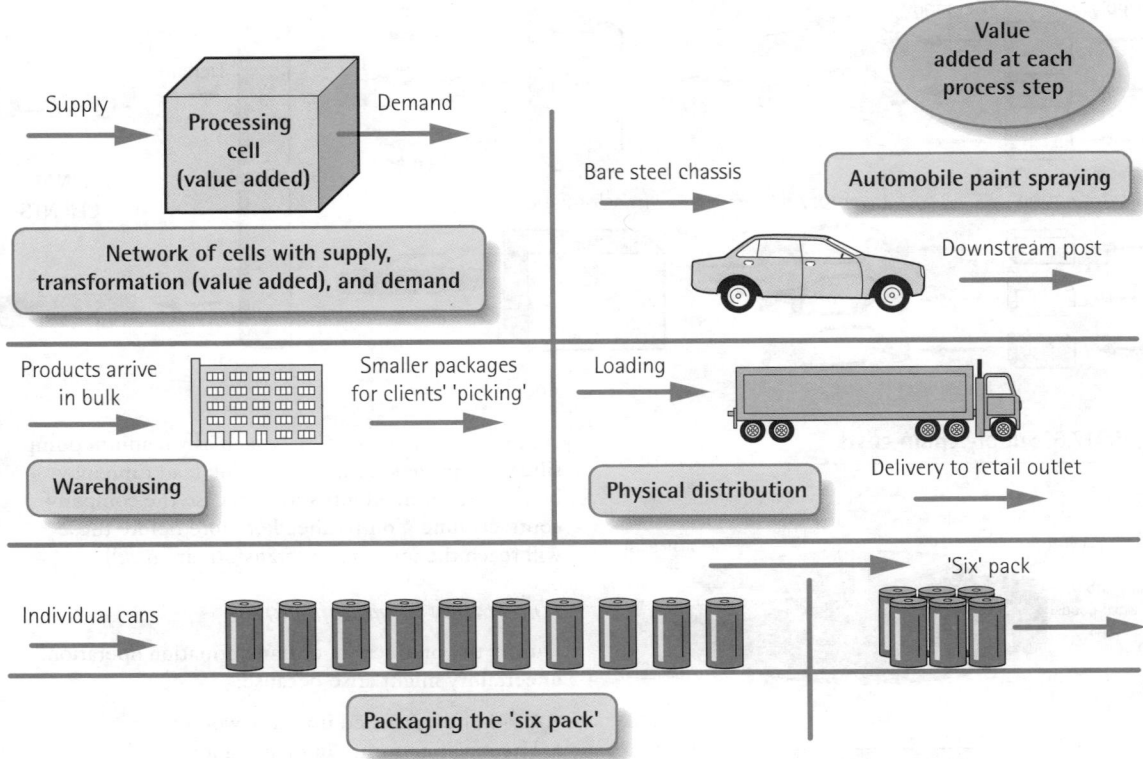

cans would be the transformation. The demand would be the pallet waiting to stack the six packs.

Distribution

The distribution of a product from a warehouse to a retail outlet is considered a value-added step. Even though the product's characteristics do not change, the fact that a customer is able to find the product in the store adds value in the eyes of the customer. It has no value to the customer if it is sitting in a warehouse some 150 km away! As a value-added cell, the supply is loading the product onto a truck and the demand is the retail outlet. The value-added step is represented by the cost of the service activity or the physical distribution.

An integrated supply chain thus can be considered a network of material-processing cells as illustrated in Figure 17.5. The supplier may be a third party supplying purchased parts, a subcontractor, or an internal unit in the manufacturing organization. The downstream demand may be the next work centre, or the final client.

Supply chain costs

Supply chain costs are high and so the greater the value added in each processing cell, the more efficient the supply chain. Figure 17.6 gives a breakdown of the supply chain costs according to the various steps from supply of raw materials, to delivery of finished goods.[2] Studies indicate that, on average, of the total supply chain costs, upstream activity accounts for about 29%, transformation 7%, and downstream cost 64%. The biggest logistics cost is the transportation of the finished goods (32%), which varies, of course, depending on the form of transportation. For example, in Japan in 1993, the cost per ton of transportation from Tokyo to Kyushu, a distance of some 1200 km, was 12,000 yen ($100) for sea and 150,000 yen ($1250) for air.[3]

Inventory in the supply chain

In the supply chain model, uncertainty exists which is one reason why inventory, or safety stock is kept both upstream and downstream of the cells. A critical decision of the logistics chain is to decide how much

Figure 17.5 Supply chain in a production operation

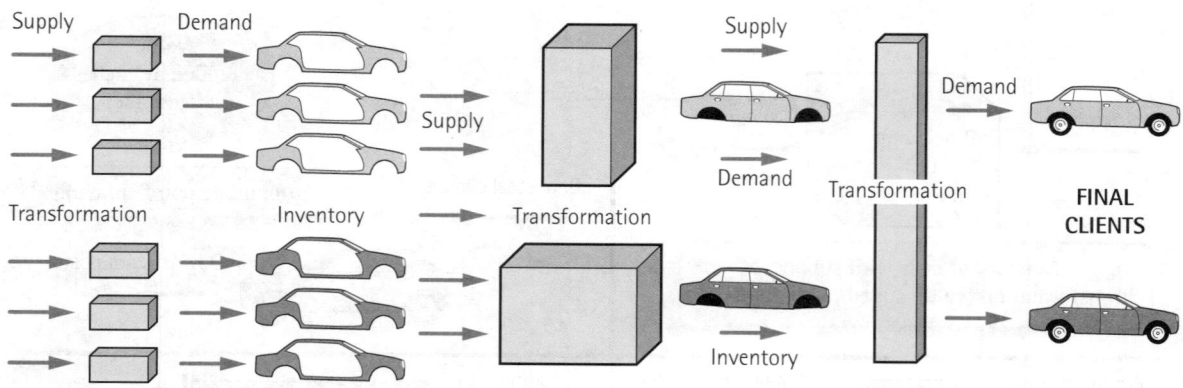

Figure 17.6 Supply chain costs

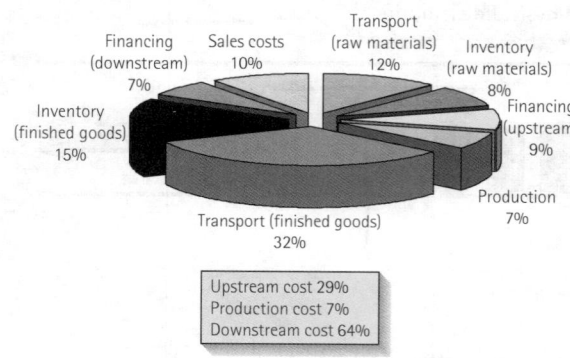

Upstream cost 29%
Production cost 7%
Downstream cost 64%

raw materials, work-in-process, or finished goods inventory to hold. Even companies using just-in-time approaches to operations management carry some inventory or, alternatively, their suppliers hold the inventory. With this inventory comes associated cost. This inventory is insurance against uncertainty that might arise for several reasons.

Uncertainty of the on-time delivery of suppliers

- The supplier quotes a delivery date, but he is late.
- There was a truck drivers' strike.
- The packaging equipment broke down.
- Two of the machine operators were sick.
- A ferryboat sank.
- One of the suppliers was late in delivering the assembly screws.

The more unsure one is of the on-time delivery of the supplier, the more safety stock is held. Long lead times also add to uncertainty. If companies purchase complex

components or raw materials such as vanadium pumps, silicon chips, or special pistons, the lead time may be long, say nine months. In this case the company contracts nine months ahead or more before these will reach the input to the transformation cell.

Uncertainty in manufacturing

During the production, or transformation operation, uncertainty might arise because:

- Another project tied up a key worker.
- The machine went out of alignment.
- One of the operators was injured on the shop floor.
- The subcontractors' components were not up to specification.

The more variable, or more uncertain the operation, the more inventory is held. The more unreliable the process operation, or the more lax the preventive maintenance, the more safety stock held.

Uncertainty of the client's real needs

- The client changes his mind at the last minute.
- The demand forecast was too low.
- 'Our clients are fickle.'
- The customer's customer cancelled his order.

The more fickle the customer, or the more uncertainty in the forecasting technique, the larger the inventory of finished products, so that the customer can be satisfied from completing orders as needed. This type of situation brings rise to the concept of agile manufacturing where the firm should have the agility (flexibility) to respond to customers whose orders change frequently.

To manage inventory better, firms need to audit performance to see what is happening with inventory movement, with the objective of making improvements. Better control of the uncertainties is critical as all inventory is safety stock to cover the uncertain world! (See Chapter 26.)

Pipeline mapping

A pipeline map is an analytical tool used to monitor inventory movements, and operating activity as an aid in supply chain management. The pipeline map is a linear flow scheme of the supply chain highlighting each operation by the processing time and also holding time that material stays in the supply chain. The object of the pipeline map is clearly to expose all the activity times and when this has been done, improvements can be proposed to minimize these times, and thus improve throughput and reduce lead times.[4] The concept and development of a pipeline map applies to any type of organization and here it is illustrated by the analysis of a small European foundry.

Process description of a foundry

The foundry makes a wide variety of non-ferrous alloyed products such as rings, bearings, flange bearings, nuts, gears, impellers, pumps, valve bodies and slide bars for the automobile industry, chemical industry, and other manufacturing firms. The alloys include tin–bronze, lead–bronze, aluminium bronze, electrolytic and chrome copper, lead and its alloys, white metal, cuprous–nickel, and other aluminium alloys. Foundry customers include Valéo, Alstom, Pont-à-Mousson, Péchiney, Renault VI, Mobil Oil, and Rhodia.

Processing steps

The simplified processing scheme is given in Figure 17.7 and the steps are detailed as follows:

1. Using the customer's blueprint design, a subcontractor makes a premould casing in wood to serve as the sand mould for the alloy product. It takes two half sections of a mould to make one complete unit.

Figure 17.7 Processing steps in a foundry

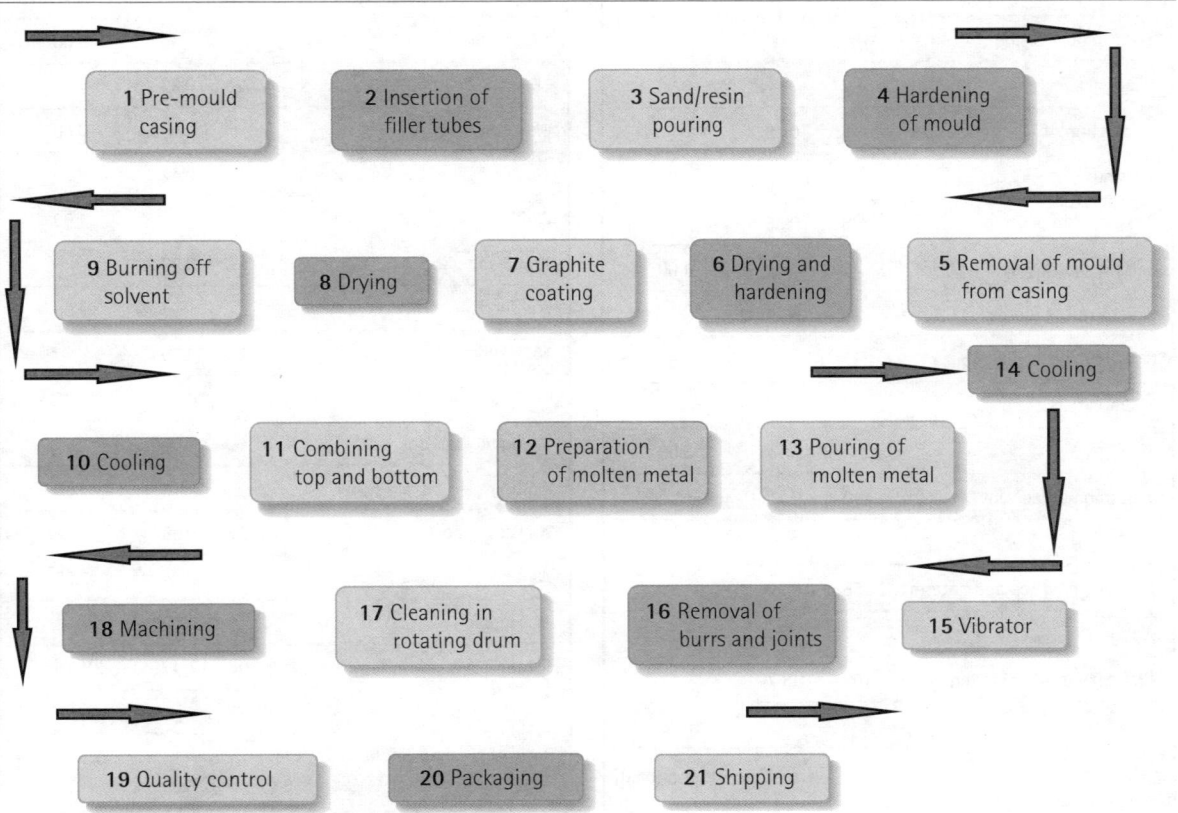

2. At the foundry, filler tubes of asbestos (this product is being replaced) are embedded in the mould to allow for the pouring of the metal.
3. A mixture of sand (15% new and 85% recycled) and resin is poured into the premould casing to form a compact mould for pouring the metal.
4. The mould is left so that the resin/sand mixture dries and hardens to take the exact form of the product.
5. The sand mould is removed from the wooden casing.
6. Mould, free of the casing, is further allowed to dry and harden.
7. The mould is coated with a graphite and alcohol solvent mixture to smooth the surface of the sand.

8. The mould is left to dry allowing the excess solvent to evaporate.
9. The mould is ignited which burns off the alcohol solvent leaving a smooth surface around the mould. This will give a smooth finished to the metal product.
10. The mould is left to cool.
11. Two sections of the mould are united (bottom and top make a complete mould). The joint is sealed with a sand resin mixture similar to that used for preparation of the mould.
12. Preparation of the molten metal.
13. Molten metal is poured into mould.
14. Mould is allowed to cool.

Table 17.3 Processing and waiting times in a foundry

Operation	Process time Mins	Process time Hours	Waiting time upstream of operation (hours)
Waiting			6.25
1. Pre-mould casing	180	3.00	
Waiting			0.50
2. Insertion of filler tubes	45	0.75	
Waiting			0.25
3. Sand/resin pouring	35	0.58	
4. Hardening of mould			1.00
5. Removal of mould	15	0.25	
6. Drying and hardening			0.50
7. Graphite coating	25	0.42	
8. Drying			3.00
9. Burning off solvent	10	0.17	
10. Cooling			4.00
11. Combining top and bottom	55	0.92	
Waiting			1.25
12. Preparation of molten metal	100	1.67	
Waiting			0.75
			(Continued)

Table 17.3 (Continued)

Operation	Process time Mins	Process time Hours	Waiting time upstream of operation (hours)
13. Pouring of metal	5	0.08	
14. Cooling			5.00
15. Vibrator	20	0.33	
Waiting			0.50
16. Removal of burrs and joints	25	0.42	
Waiting			1.00
17. Cleaning in rotating drum	18	0.30	
Waiting			2.50
18. Machining	180	3.00	
Waiting			0.75
19. Quality control	60	1.00	
Waiting			1.50
20. Packaging	35	0.58	
Waiting			3.00
21. Shipping		4.00	
Total	808	13.47	28.75
Pipeline volume (hours)	42.22		
Ratio of pipeline height to volume	68.10%		

15. Mould is dumped onto a vibrator where the mould is broken, and the sand falls off. The sand from the mould is sent to a regenerating vessel where fines are removed. Regenerated sand is reused.

16. Burrs and moulding joints are cut from the metal product.

17. Forged pieces are cleaned in a rotating drum akin to a washing machine, which contains small metal beads which rough polishes the surface.

18. Machining: The machine shop contains numerical controlled machines and operations include drilling, turning, and polishing.

19. Quality control for dimension, surface finish, and inspection of any irregularities in the metal.

20. Packaging: This involves wrapping the products in bubble packing for protection and then boxing in cardboard cartons.

21. Shipping: This involves preparing the shipping documents and contacting the shipping agent.

Pipeline map

The activity times for the various foundry operations are given in Table 17.3. From this is developed the pipeline map, as given in Figure 17.8. Here, the vertical bars represent the time when the product is waiting before and after a particular process operation. This may include cooling periods, or just 'waiting'. The horizontal lines represent the time for each processing step.

Pipeline length

The pipeline length is the sum of all the horizontal lines and is equivalent to the total processing time. These are the value-added activities. Theoretically, it would represent the absolute minimum lead time in the supply chain in order to respond to a new customer demand assuming that in-process inventory were not available for this order. In practice some time would have to be added for the air-cooling and air-drying activities. However, these could be reduced by cooling and drying in exchangers.

Pipeline height

The pipeline height is the sum of all the vertical bars and is representative of all the waiting times, or principally non-value-added activities. Again some of

Figure 17.8 Pipeline map for foundry

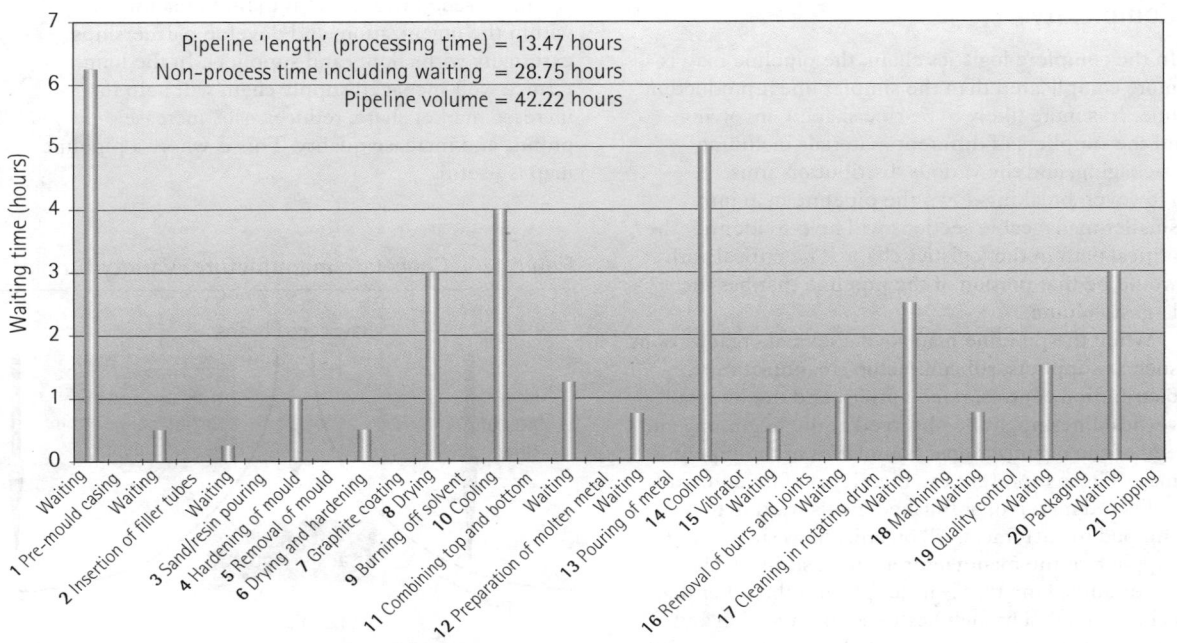

Pipeline 'length' (processing time) = 13.47 hours
Non-process time including waiting = 28.75 hours
Pipeline volume = 42.22 hours

Activity (processing times not to scale)

the drying and cooling times have to be considered part of the processing step.

Pipeline volume

The pipeline volume is the sum of all the vertical and horizontal lines and is equivalent to the time required to 'drain' the complete supply chain at the current throughput.

Ratio of pipeline height to pipeline volume

This ratio is a measure of the efficiency of the operation as it is the same as non-value-added activities to total activities. In this case the value of 68% is high.

An objective of a pipeline map is to identify where either the vertical or horizontal lines can be reduced. If such reductions are possible then inventory costs can be lowered and also customer response time can be improved. Often, if the horizontal lines, representing the process time, can be reduced then the vertical lines, representing the inventory holding time, can also be reduced. For example, if a production manager were able to pull a product through four hours quicker, then he would be inclined to hold a correspondingly smaller inventory. In addition, reducing setup times would help in reducing the vertical lines or the waiting time.

Complexity

In the complete logistics chain, the pipeline map is more complicated than the simpler linear production line. It is more likely to be tree shaped, involving all the suppliers of different materials including packaging, and the various distribution arms. However, breaking down the pipeline map into smaller manageable sections will help to identify the critical path in the logistics chain. The critical path would be that portion of the pipeline that has the largest volume.

When the pipeline map covers several organizations such as suppliers, subcontractors, manufacturers, distribution centres, retail outlets, and the like, tall vertical lines might be observed at the beginning and end of the organizational boundaries of the pipeline map. These represent the high level of inventory of delivered material, or finished goods waiting to be shipped to customers. All organizations such as the supplier, or the manufacturer, are ensuring against uncertainty. One that is in supply and the other that is in demand. Through better communication and sharing of information, it should be possible to reduce the length, or even eliminate at least one of the

vertical lines. This is what has come about with electronic procurement and distribution where upstream and downstream partners have real-time information of their customers needs.

Usefulness of a pipeline map

Using a pipeline map will help to uncover potential problems as:

- Inventory in unmanaged areas.
- Disjointed flows as a result of uncoupled production processes.
- Employees not having the same objective because of different performance measures, conflicting strategies, or a poor organization.
- Interface difficulties with players such as sloppy suppliers, manufacturing over producing for fear of stockouts, or sales over forecasting for fear of not having enough products for clients.
- Integrated operating problems such as lack of management support, suppliers unreliable, quality of raw materials is sometimes low, poor communication throughout the supply chain, poor customer forecasts, data unreliable, motivation levels low, etc.

The client is king! An optimized supply chain is customer focused, always meeting internal and customer schedules. It helps to build teamwork within the organization, and develop partnerships externally with clients and suppliers. In the long term, a well-managed supply chain will help to increase market share, reduce costs, increase profits, and increase quality. This is where a pipeline map is useful.

Figure 17.9 Chocolate manufacture: Variety funnel

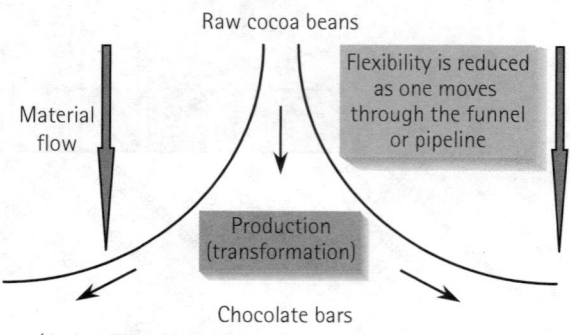

Raw cocoa beans

Material flow

Flexibility is reduced as one moves through the funnel or pipeline

Production (transformation)

Chocolate bars
(dark, milk, + almonds, + cherries, + orange, + rum, + whisky, + rice, + nougat, + peanuts, ...)

Variety funnel

A variety funnel can be developed and used in conjunction with the pipeline map. The variety funnel shows the reduction of flexibility with materials as the operation moves through the supply chain or pipeline. A variety funnel for chocolate manufacture is illustrated in Figure 17.9. This shows that as one moves through the pipeline, or processes (adding milk to the chocolate mix, putting in the almonds, etc.) or increases the added value, there is less flexibility with components, or in this case ingredients, the further one moves downstream. (Once a mixture contains milk and almonds it can be moulded into nothing else but milk chocolate bars with almonds.) The same idea occurs with the assembly of computers, and the textile industry. In the latter case, some firms will make clothing of white stock and then die them at the last minute according to the colour demands of the client. The variety funnel has similarities to the VAT analyses presented in Chapter 6.

Distribution requirements planning

Distribution requirements planning (DRP) is the planning process in the supply chain to help ensure that finished goods destined for a client reach the right location, at the right date, and in the right quantity. The supply chain covering the DRP may be from the manufacturer through the various distribution centres, to the retailer, or it might just be from the distribution centres to the retailers in a service firm like a large grocery store moving finished goods from the distribution centre to the retail stores.

Integrated distribution requirements plan

A complex and more complete DRP would be a module within the ERP system (see Chapter 13) where the DRP is interconnected with the master production schedule, and the material requirements plan of the production organization, as shown schematically in Figure 17.10. Here a production centre is located in Lyon, France. There are two distribution centres, one in Strasbourg, and the other in Toulouse. Retail outlets are in Brussels, Belgium, and Amsterdam, that are served by the distribution centre in Strasbourg. Then there are retail outlets in Bordeaux, and Madrid, served by the distribution in Toulouse. Physical flow is from the production centre, to the distribution centres and finally the retail outlets. The flow of information, by electronic data interchanged if the network is established, is from the retail outlets to the distribution centres, and then from the distribution centres to the production centre. The production centre in Lyon, with the required client information, then develops its master production schedule, and thence the material requirements plan based on the real-time information it receives from the business logistics network. The distribution requirements plan might be a pull or a push system.

Pull system

A pull system is the most common type of planning approach and for many it is the only distribution

---

Figure 17.10 Integrated distribution and manufacturing

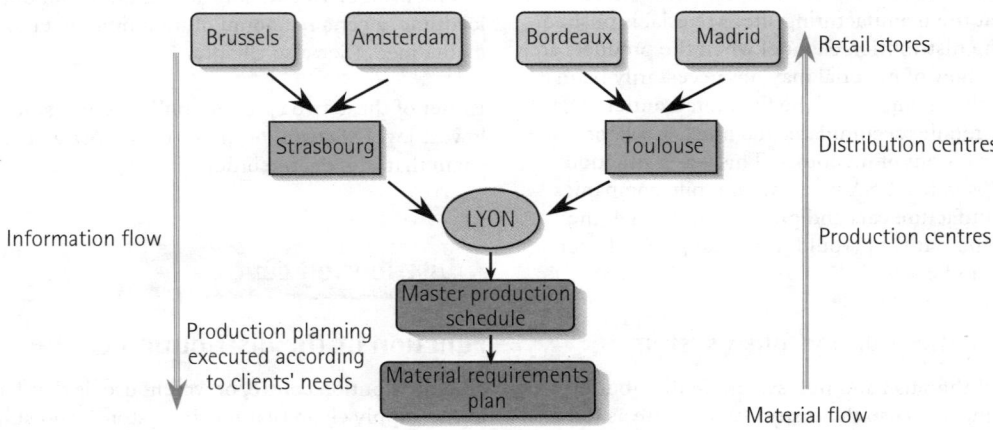

requirements plan. A pull system is when the outlet at the lowest level, or end, of the distribution network, usually the retailer, initiates the order. The retailer 'pulls' the products through the distribution, or supply chain network. The retailer has its own ordering policy and the supplier only makes a delivery when a specific order has been made.

Client demands

The only independent demand is from the retail outlets. The other demands are dependent demands. This is analogous to the MRP system. In MRP, the independent demand is the finished product. The dependent demands are the components that go into making the finished product.

Master production schedule

The demand from each of the retail outlets imposes a master production schedule (MPS) on the manufacturer that may not be optimum. The manufacturer loses some control of his planning process and has to be flexible to accommodate customer demands. In some instance the pull system may impose an MPS on the manufacturer that is not feasible, as, for example, insufficient resources are available. If a just-in-time system is in place the manufacturer will perhaps have more flexibility.

The development of the pull system DRP is shown in Demonstrating the concept 17.1.

Push system

In the push system, the supplier at the beginning of the network, usually the manufacturer produces the finished products according to his master production schedule (MPS). This MPS would have been established according to estimates of clients' demands and then modified to suit the company's resources available at the manufacturing site. Material is pushed through the distribution channel when the products are ready. The flow of material may not necessarily be in harmony with the needs of the final retail outlet. As a result, the retailer accumulates too much stock, or worse, he runs out of inventory. This was a situation in the 1970s in the USA when automobile companies would manufacture cars and push them through the supply chain, but they would just end up on a dealer's lot waiting to be sold.

Hybrid of the pull and push system

A hybrid of the push and pull system in distribution requirements is to use the distribution centre as the

inventory buffer. In the scheme presented, Lyon develops its master production schedule to suit its own resources. Finished products are then 'pushed' out to the distribution centres at Strasbourg and Toulouse. The retail outlets at Brussels, Amsterdam, Bordeaux, and Madrid, 'pull' their product requirements as needed from the corresponding distribution centre. It is the distribution centres that are the buffer and incur corresponding storing costs. To avoid stockouts (assuming the gross amount produced by Lyon is sufficient), then either Lyon increases its distribution to Strasbourg and reduces it to Toulouse, or vice versa. Alternatively, Strasbourg and Toulouse have the possibility of exchanging inventory as needed.

Alternative to distribution requirements planning

Some simple alternatives to a distribution requirements plan network might be the following.

Base stock system

A base stock system is where an organization maintains a base, or minimum stock of a certain product. The ordering policy is that each time an item is sold, an order is placed for a new item. This type of ordering, a sell one, buy one approach, is a form of just-in-time. It might be an approach used for large items, or for retail outlets that have limited space for inventory such as refrigerators or other large household appliances.

Reorder point system

In a reorder point system, or replenishment system, the inventory policy of the outlet is to maintain a certain level, which is considered full stock. When the inventory level falls to some predetermined low level the inventory is replenished. To take into account demand during the leadtime, a certain amount of minimum inventory is maintained. (See also Chapter 11.)

Either of these two cases are pull systems, since it is the lowest level of chain, or the furthest upstream in the chain that triggers the order.

Distribution centre

Function of the distribution centre

The distribution centre, or warehouse, is that facility in the supply chain that receives, stores, and ships end

Figure 17.11 Activity in a distribution centre or warehouse

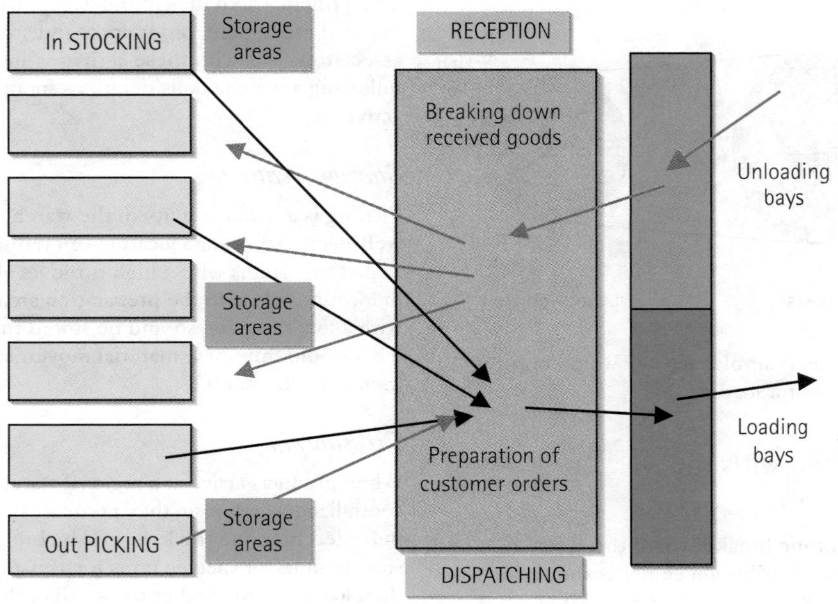

products to clients. These end products might be finished goods destined to final clients such as household furniture, food, or sports equipment or intermediate products for another business firm such as automobile parts destined for Ford, Renault, and Daimler-Chrysler. Figure 17.11 shows a typical layout, described as follows.

Reception

Here goods arrive by truck to the unloading bays where they are unloaded by forklift truck (see the illustration in Chapter 9) in the reception area. The goods might be stacked on pallets, or they might be bulk items packed in cartons. In the reception area, the items are controlled for quality and the quantity is verified. They are then entered into the warehouse inventory database either by manual recording or by laser scanning the bar code affixed to the items. If the distribution centre has a rail spur then items may also arrive by train and there would be an equivalent reception area close to the rail siding.

Stocking

From the reception area, product items according to their type are taken by forklift truck and placed in the storage areas. For sophisticated warehouses, the

exact placement of the items in the storage area is automatically indicated by the information system. For some warehouses automatic cranes would load the items on the high storage platforms that may be some 18 metres high. In some cases there may be complete automatic storage and retrieval systems.

Picking

Picking is the taking of items from the storage area according to a specific customer order. These orders are then assembled on pallets in the dispatching area where they are controlled to verify they are correct, and labelled with a bar code identifying the customers, type of goods, destination, etc. Depending on the type of products, the complete pallet might be encircled in a transparent plastic wrapping. From the preparation area, the pallets are transferred by forklift truck to the loading bays.

Dispatching

From the dispatching area the pallets are taken by forklift and loaded onto trucks waiting in the loading bay. Again, there would be a control to ensure that the correct pallets are loaded onto the designated trucks. The role of the handlers at this point would also be to ensure that the loading is optimal to maximize the usage

Figure 17.12 Breakdown of costs in a distribution centre

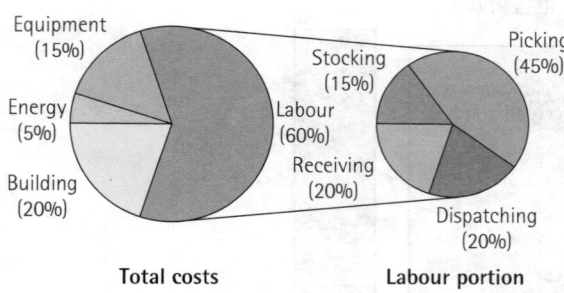

Equipment (15%)
Stocking (15%)
Picking (45%)
Energy (5%)
Labour (60%)
Building (20%)
Receiving (20%)
Dispatching (20%)

Total costs   **Labour portion**

of the truck volume. A similar activity would occur if there were rail spurs for loading.

Costs associated with the distribution centre

An order of magnitude breakdown of the costs associated with the distribution centre is shown in Figure 17.12. The major costs are the building structure itself, the equipment used for transferring the products, energy and the labour. The building and equipment would be essentially fixed costs depreciated over, perhaps, ten years for the building, and five years for the equipment. If either the buildings or equipment were leased then there would be rental charges instead of depreciation. Energy, which is heating, lighting, and perhaps refrigeration, may be considered a fixed cost, as it does not change very much with the movement of materials within the warehouse. (Note: Actual costs will depend on the type of centre.)

Labour is the principal expense in the warehouse and represents some 60% of the costs of the centre. It is a variable cost and covers normal wages, overtime, and the entire obligatory social charges and applies to the permanent labour force and the part-time and occasional labour. Within the labour costs the highest would be the picking activity since this is the most meticulous of all the material movements involving time for collecting the items and organizing them for dispatching. This is where layout of the facility and optimum location of the inventory items is important. For example, assume a handler is able to pick 100 items an hour but because of non-optimum location in picking items the handler has to make an extra five steps. These five steps are about three metres and then in one hour he moves an extra 300 metres (100 * 3) which could amount to say 60 km a year (300 * 2000 hours).

Efficient management of the warehouse

The principal activities in the warehouse involve material movement, order entry and storage and the associated costs with these activities are high. The following are some considerations for optimizing the activities.

Storage location

Picking is a major activity in the warehouse and so well-managed storage location can reduce the time in picking. Items with a high turnover should be stored in locations close to the preparation area and others with a low turnover, should be stored further away. This would minimize material movement times. (See also Chapter 9.)

Crossdocking

When products arrive at a regional warehouse from a centralized warehouse, they normally have to be unloaded from the truck, logged in, broken down into smaller units, or specific units for a customer's need, and then loaded onto another truck. All of these operations take time, involve labour, and increase inventory holding time. To minimize this, a policy of crossdocking may be employed. When goods arrive every effort is made that they just 'cross the docks'. This principle is to avoid opening large containers, logging in, and breaking down packages into smaller units. Instead, the units are directly relocated to their corresponding dispatching truck.

Computer control

Some warehouses have a computer control system that manages the arrival of the products from the warehouse, and the preparation of the orders for individual retail stores. For the preparation of the order, the computer software produces the required label indicating, quantity, and the location of where each article can be found in the warehouse. Most software is able to present the labels in both alphanumeric and bar code form. Once the articles have been retrieved from the picking area the label is affixed to the customer order and is thus ready for shipping. The computer labels are a form of kanban cards with the same objective in a manufacturing operation to reduce written or verbal instructions and to smooth material flow.

ABC analysis of inventory items

An ABC analysis of the inventory items, similar to that described in Chapter 11, can be used to classify those items which have a high turnover (Items A) compared to those which have a lower turnover (Items C). The results of this analysis will help in positioning the storage area. Items A would be close to the dispatching area and Items C further away with those in Category B intermediately located. Those which have a very high turnover of, say, less than a day can be targeted for crossdocking.

Benchmarking

To compare and challenge the productivity within a distribution network some companies develop an internal benchmarking policy. Some elements compared in benchmarking are:

- stocking costs per type of product per square metre of storage area
- number of packages prepared per unit of time
- number of trucks loaded, and unloaded a day.

Chapter 26 presents more on benchmarking.

Packaging and palletization

Packaging is not part of the product, is usually trashed, and as such adds little product value in the eyes of the customer. However packaging is a necessity to protect the product from damage, particularly in the warehouse environment with the unloading, stocking, picking and loading activities. However, the volume of packaging used is an important consideration because besides the direct costs of the packing material there are the shipping costs that can be attributed particularly to the volume and perhaps the weight of the packaging being moved. As an illustration, firms that handle furniture items, even in kit form such as IKEA, may have a net product volume of as little as 40%. This means that of the gross volume of the item being moved, only 40% can be attributed to the product, which is eventually sold to a customer and thus represents the added-value portion of the transaction.

Most items when they are loaded or unloaded at the distribution centre are on pallets. Again packaging should be designed that it fits perfectly onto a pallet such as not to waste space, which is important when a truck is loaded. One way of keeping packaging-related costs reasonable is to standardize, or modularize the packaging so that individual packs fit onto a standard pallet. Figure 17.13 illustrates this in the case of canned goods or beverages. Here individual packs of standard sizes will fit onto a basic module. The basic module can be arranged several ways on the pallets without wasting any space.

Figure 17.13 Modular system for packaging

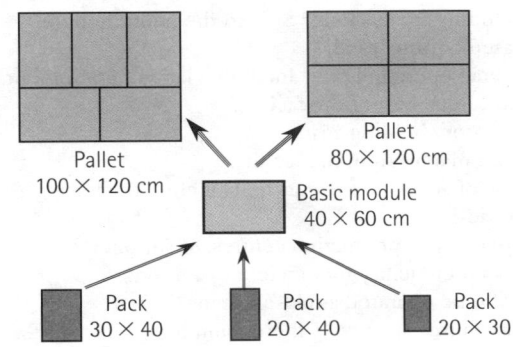

Computer-aided packing simulations are available which optimize the packing of components onto standard containers.

To further keep costs low it is best, if feasible, to put the pallets into containers at the distribution centre and not to unload the container until it has reached its final destination. Containerization is such that, if necessary, the packed goods can be loaded into a truck, offloaded and then loaded onto a train, and then loaded directly onto a cargo ship without unpacking the unit. Further, this minimizing product handling from supplier to customer reduces the quantity of packaging needed. (See also Chapter 16, the section on CKD, and Chapter 5, which discusses packaging from an environmental point of view.)

Considerations in selecting a distribution centre

The following are some considerations in establishing or selecting a distribution centre or warehouse:

- First, is the distribution centre really needed? Minimizing the number of distribution centres may reduce costs.
- Would it be more cost effective to subcontract (outsource) the physical distribution rather than operate it yourself? This is the direction that many firms are moving which explains the rapid growth of distribution companies.
- How close is the facility located to final clients? Is the site in an optimum location? (See Chapter 3.)
- What about security, particularly as regards theft?

- What handling equipment will be necessary? What would be the costs to fully automate the facility including the packing? Should the equipment be leased or purchased?
- Overall operating costs including labour, equipment, and capital cost of the facility.
- Inventory holding cost.
- Profit margin from the facility.
- Ease of access to the centre. Is it close to major arteries?
- Proximity to production centres, or suppliers?
- Layout of facility for efficient operation.
- Will it be operated at close to capacity?
- Maximum capacity. Is there room for expansion?

Transportation

In the supply chain, raw materials or finished goods from a work centre have to be transported to their next destination. This may be another manufacturer, an industrial user, a distribution centre, a retail outlet, or the final client. Further, this next destination may be local, national, or international. Transportation is a key element in the supply chain. Since even if products are produced according to schedule, are of acceptable quality, and at the right price, if the correct transportation is not available resulting in late delivery and/or arrive damaged, the client will at the least be irritated or at the worst may not accept the goods.

Selection criteria

The criteria of selection for transportation include:

- Does a network exist? Can the delivery routes be easily optimized?
- Distance to be travelled.
- Speed with which products can be delivered to the client. Will they arrive on time?
- Volume limitations on the transportation mode.
- Weight limitations on the transportation mode.
- Security, and safety of the products during shipment.
- Regulations which govern shipping regulations (some toxic products may not be allowed to be shipped by truck, for example).
- What are the costs including per kilometre, hourly, and overtime costs?
- Unloading times.

Transportation types

The type of transport used by a firm depends on the product such as its size, weight, and composition and also the point of departure and the point of arrival. Exhaustively, the transport possibilities are by air, inland waterways, pipeline, rail, road, and sea. Table 17.4 summarizes these transportation systems, indicating their advantages and disadvantages. In many instances, transport of goods is multimodal such as truck, rail and truck, or truck, plane, truck, etc.

Transportation in the USA

As Figure 17.14[5] illustrates, road transportation is far the most dominant mode of transport in the USA with some 74% in terms of tonnage. Road haulage is the most flexible in that goods can be loaded at their original starting point and offloaded at their final destination without any intermediate unloading and loading. For the other modes of transport, usually three stages are required. For example, even if rail is the principal transport method a truck has to deliver the goods to the rail loading centre and a truck has to deliver the goods from the rail point of arrival to their final destination as the majority of firms do not have rail spurs. As a result this usually makes road transportation the cheapest method of transport. Railroads, pipelines, and waterways are the USA's backbone for moving bulk commodities like coal, iron ore, and grain accounting for the remainder of the one-quarter of the total tonnage. The pipeline figures include all products that can be transported in slurry form but do not include petroleum products. Within the USA, air transport in terms of tonnage is very small (some 0.04%) but in terms of value it amounts to some 4%. Air transport is used for perishable products such as cut flowers and distribution firms like UPS, FedEx and the US Postal Service make extensive use of air transportation.

Transportation in the European Union

In the European Union, although road transport is the principal mode with some 44% in terms of tonnage, sea transportation between member countries is almost equally important with some 41% (see Figure 17.15).[6] A high proportion of this sea freight is concentrated in the ports of Rotterdam, Antwerp, Marseille, Hamburg, Le Havre, and London. As in the USA, the use of rail transportation as a percentage has fallen some 6% in the period 1970–1998 while truck transport has increased to 35% and sea

Table 17.4 Transportation means

Advantages	Disadvantages
Air	
Fast	High cost
Useful for perishable products, or those required urgently such as medical supplies	Three journeys necessary: Factory to airport, airport to airport, airport to delivery location
Useful for inaccessible locations in, say, Africa, central Australia, Central America	Limit to size of products that can be transported
Inland waterways	
Relatively inexpensive	Limited to where there is an inland waterway network
Useful for bulk products, e.g. coal	Usually three journeys necessary: Factory to dock, port to port, port to delivery location
Environmentally friendly	Slow
Pipeline	
Relatively low cost	Only suitable for products in liquid, or gaseous form, e.g. petroleum and chemical products, and coal in the form of slurry
Continuous flow	Only feasible where pipeline exists
Can cross any terrain	
Rail	
Piggybacking (using loading and offloading direct to trucks)	Often three journeys necessary if factory supplier does not have a rail spur: Factory to station, station to station, station to delivery location
Containerization possible (liquids, gas, automobiles)	Limited to at least one wagon load, or even one train load, thus not effective for just-in-time operation
Reasonably fast	
Good for bulk products, e.g. coal, chemicals, steel	
Relatively low cost for long journeys	
	(Continued)

Table 17.4 (Continued)

Advantages	Disadvantages
Road	
Relatively low cost	Weather conditions can affect delivery times
Cheaper than train over short distances	Affected by labour unrest
Accessibility. Only a single journey necessary: Supply site to demand location	Circulation difficult on some routes due to traffic conditions
Flexibility regarding size, and time for departure	
Sea	
Only economic means for some country-to-country deliveries	Usually three journeys necessary: Factory to dock, port to port, port to delivery location
Containerization possible	Only feasible where port exists
Useful for bulk products	
Usually no size limitations for products	
Inexpensive relative to air transport	

transport has increased to 27%. Industry insight 17.1 goes some way towards explaining the problem with rail transport in Europe. The transport infrastructure of Germany and France is the most extensive as both countries have the longest rail networks and the most kilometres of motorways. The river Rhine, navigable for 1000 km, is the backbone of Europe's inland waterway network. Major canals link it to the Meuse, the Scheldt, the Elbe, and since 1992, to the Danube. However, France and the Netherlands have one of the longest inland waterway networks, although this is principally used for pleasure purposes. Airfreight within the European Union is extremely small in terms of tonnage, although again it is used for small package movement by UPS and FedEx and also Deutsche Post (Germany) and La Poste (France).

International transportation

Internationally, sea transport is the dominant mode in terms of tonnage where, for example, major ports of

Figure 17.14 Breakdown of freight transport in the USA by tonnage (1997)

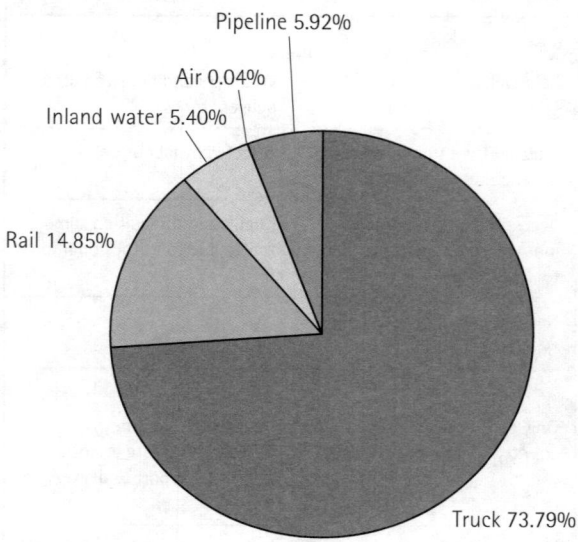

Pipeline 5.92%

Air 0.04%

Inland water 5.40%

Rail 14.85%

Truck 73.79%

Figure 17.15 Breakdown of freight transport in the European Union by tonnage (1998)

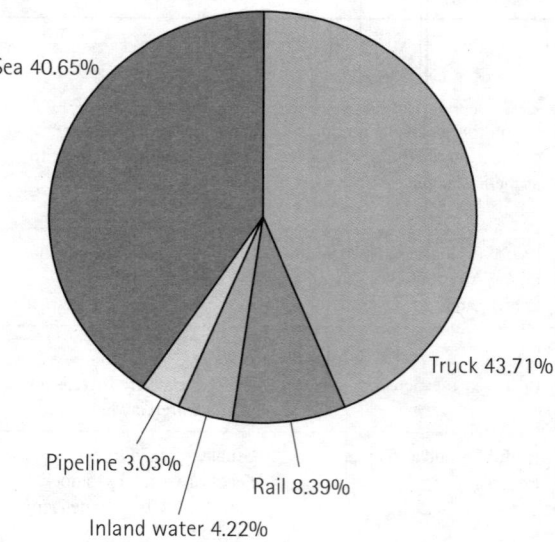

Sea 40.65%

Truck 43.71%

Pipeline 3.03%

Rail 8.39%

Inland water 4.22%

Rail freight in Europe

Industry insight 17.1

Rail freight is unified Europe's biggest and costly exception. Across the region, borders have all but disappeared with the advent of high-speed passenger trains, highways without customs posts, and a single currency. Europe's state-owned phone monopolies, electricity utilities, airlines, and other national franchises have all been pried open to competition, but rail freight remains a patchwork of protected, antiquated national networks. No two European countries use the same signalling system or electric current for their trains. As a result trains from Denmark to Germany must change locomotives and drivers. Trains in France and Britain run on the left side of dual-track lines, while those in the rest of Europe run on the right. As France and Spain use two different gauges of track, trains crossing their shared border must stop to let each carriage be lifted so that its wheels can be changed. Railway operators' computers aren't compatible so that documentation regarding

shipping often has to be replicated between one country and another.

European shippers say that they have tried to use rail freight but it is clear that road is much more efficient. IKEA, with a large distribution centre at St Quentin Fallavier near Lyon, France, is a prime example. Its transport manager says that trucks undercut rail price by some 20% and, further, they are able to guarantee deliveries of a container load of furniture in eight hours compared to 48 hours by train. Furthermore, a rail strike in France steered IKEA away from using rail freight. The result is that European roads are heavily clogged with traffic, air pollution is getting worse, and there have been fatal truck accidents in the French–Italian Mont Blanc and the Swiss St Gothard tunnels.

Adapted from: 'Changing trains: Freight rail system shows Europe is still as far apart as ever', *Wall Street Journal Europe*[7]

Rotterdam, Los Angeles, and Kobe, near Osaka in Japan, play a significant role in the import and export of international goods. The big container ships that carry most of the world's long-haul manufactured exports by weight travel at 23 knots (26.5 miles an hour) at best, and barely 17 knots in heavy weather. Airfreight offers speed for the 40% of the world's trade by value

that travels in cargo flights or in the holds of passenger aircraft but it costs ten times more than sea transport. This is fine for flying tiny microchips into Europe or the United States from Asia, other high valued products, perishable goods, emergency items, but too expensive for bulky goods. Thus cargoes of cars, car parts, tractors, cookers, and washing machines still travel at about the speed of a running man. It takes a ship full of parts a week or more to cross the Atlantic and around three weeks to go from Asia to Europe. In effect, this ties up working capital in floating stock. Containerization, where goods are prepacked in containers that can be offloaded from a truck or train and directly loaded onto a ship, has greatly helped to reduce transportation times. A new boat design, as illustrated by Industry insight 17.2, hopes to reduce shipping times even more.

Notwithstanding all the arguments against air transportation Industry insight 17.3 illustrates that there are exceptions in using air transportation for bulky items.

Trucking costs

On a European basis, a breakdown of the costs, as a percentage, for using road transport is given in Figure 17.16. The wages/costs for the driver are about 41% of the cost followed by 21% for the total fuel cost of which there is a high proportion for taxes.[8] In the United States fuel costs are lower as are the imposed taxes and thus fuel has a lower overall percentage in the total cost, although, on average, the distances travelled per journey by trucks in the USA is some two to three higher than in Europe. As in Europe, the costs associated with the driver represent the highest expense.

Like all capital assets, trucks are only earning money when they are moving and thus trucking companies try to have 24-hour day utilization. This is not easy to manage, as it requires having two drivers all the time in the cabin. Besides the cost of having to pay two drivers, trucking companies say it is difficult to constitute a 'team' of two drivers. By the very nature of their work, truck drivers are an independent bunch. The alternative is to have the second (or even third and

---

Revolutionary container ships
Industry insight 17.2

Ever since the Vikings built their longships it has been accepted that the way to move quickly across the water is to have long thin boats. This is because the faster a ship travels, the more water it drags along with it. Not only does this drag consume considerable energy it also causes high-speed vessels to squat low in the water pulled down behind the 'captive wave' at the bow. Propellers vibrate at high speeds, causing shocks that can break hulls. Hydrofoils that lift the hull out of water, and use water jets, are fine for passenger ferries, but not for big heavy container ships.

Firms are increasingly seeking faster and flexible supply chains in international transportation and FastShip Atlantic is a design company that believes it has a solution to the current sluggishness of cargo ships. Their container ship looks like a giant speedboat that would carry about 1400 containers, compared to up to 7000 for conventional container ships, and would run at speeds of up to 38 knots in all weathers. To achieve such a performance, the boats will rely not on their enormous

Rolls-Royce-designed jet engines, or on being long and thin, but on a revolutionary design allowing the vessel to slice through the waves and float above the ocean's drag. This design includes a sharp bow that cuts through waves up to 40 feet high, and a concave hull bottom which creates a wave at the stern which prevents the vessel squatting too low in the water. The stern wave lifts the vessel enabling it to plane along the water. The result is a tubby vessel that is stable and fast in rough seas.

FastShip has another idea to speed up its service, and that is to use a roll-on, roll-off system to transfer containers between trains and ships. This is much faster than cranes and the company claims it reduces turnaround time in port from 16 to six hours. It hopes that companies will be attracted to a service that offers seven-day, door-to-door delivery for half the price of airfreight delivery of four to six days.

Adapted from: 'Fast container ships: How to shrink the world', *The Economist*[9]

The mighty Antonov is only way to fly your locomotive
Industry insight 17.3

How do you get a 21 metre long diesel locomotive or a 77-ton Pepsi Cola bottling line across the Atlantic quickly?

By Antonov, obviously.
For $250,000 a load – about $11,000 a flying hour – you can hire an Antonov 124, one of the biggest planes aloft.

It comes with everything – a score of chain-smoking, sleep-deprived Russians, jet engines prone to burning out, and a cargo bay big enough to haul almost anything almost anywhere.

A yacht to California, 230 ostriches to England, oil rigs to Azerbaijan, helicopters (five at a time) to Somalia, and a 200-year-old, 19 metre cactus to Spain. All these things have flown Antonov.

Peace dividend

The mighty Antonov 124 was designed to carry 165 tons of Soviet ammunition, trucks and tanks into battle, and it is now available to consumers – an odd peace dividend of the former Cold War.

Federal Express and Flying Tiger aren't sweating this competition, however. The Antonov is an inefficient fuel guzzler, and a primitive one at that. It uses about 900 gallons (3420 litres) of jet fuel just to taxi onto a runway.

Consider what happened recently when a flight bound for the Mexican city of Guadalajara carrying eight semi-trailers full of new Pepsi bottling equipment stopped in Shannon, Ireland, for refueling after just a three-hour hop from Italy: the Russian navigator pulled out a slide rule to help calculate the next, transAtlantic, leg. An exhausted pilot napped. And Anatoly, a technician, climbed a ladder to tighten three screws that help hold a Russian jet engine on the right wing.

Clearly, these planes have few advantages apart from their size. Too crude and costly to compete with western air freighters for the bulk of air cargo, they work the fringes of world trade in outsized stuff.

Antonovs can handle loads too big to be flown by any other means, and there is enough of that sort of business to keep two east-west joint ventures flying as many as ten Antonovs in round the world, round the clock marathon service for western clients. Air Foyle Ltd of Luton, England, operates with the Antonov Design Bureau of Kiev, Ukraine. HeavyLift of Stansted, England, works with Volga-Dnepr Airlines of Ulyanovsk, Russia.

On the Air Foyle/Antonov Design Bureau flight to Guadalajara, the 124 carries 19 crewmen. Most of them apparently have less to do with *flying* the plane than with tending to its many needs – checking vital signs, and making slightly unnerving repairs. In the cockpit, four engineers operate the radio, navigate and monitor the engines and the hydraulics. There are two pilots.

Design flaw

The engines are a problem. 'Our domestic-manufactured engines are not so good,' concedes Vladimir M Sudorgin, a flight manager for the design bureau. Some have been scrapped after just 1000 hours' use. Jet engines manufactured in the west typically last 8000 to 10,000 hours before major maintenance is required.

Not much about being a passenger on this particular cargo plane is comforting. There are no magazines and no movies. Everyone smokes, no one wears seat belts. Carry-on bags are not stowed beneath the seat in front of you. Cartons of mineral water, spare parts and the crew's luggage litter the floor of the flight deck. But then, these planes, like the US military's C5, were designed for tanks, not tourists.

Adapted from: 'The mighty Antonov is only way to fly your locomotive', *Wall Street Journal Europe*[10]

Figure 17.16 Breakdown of costs for a 38-ton vehicle

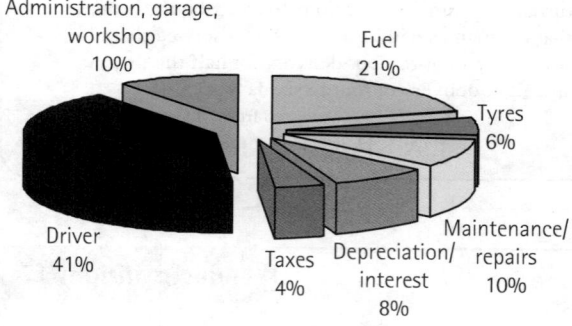

Administration, garage, workshop 10%

Fuel 21%

Tyres 6%

Maintenance/ repairs 10%

Depreciation/ interest 8%

Taxes 4%

Driver 41%

fourth drivers) to be strategically located on the truck route, say, lodged at a hotel, which, of course, adds to the cost. Even when a truck is working, it may not be

moving since it can be stuck in traffic or waiting during loading or unloading. Traffic congestion resulting in lost time is a worldwide problem with delays occurring around all major cities and is very difficult to manage. Delays might be minimized by rerouting avoiding known congestion sites or by scheduling arrival and departure times that do not coincide with rush hour traffic. Resulting traffic delays have a snowball effect in that a truck arriving late at a delivery site misses the schedule for loading/unloading and may have to wait longer than planned as the necessary handlers, or stockers are not available. Global positioning systems, for locating the trucks, do help to offset potential problems.

Significant savings can be obtained in transportation costs by optimizing route planning and linear programming is the heart of many of the many commercial software packages available. Linear programming (described in Chapter 23) formulates the

Swedish truckers launch website

Cargo traffic on Europe's roads is increasing by nearly 5% a year, and it is expected that by 2010 there will be some 52 million tons of truck cargo, up from 32 million tons in 2000. Further, it is expected that 30% of all trucks on the road in Europe are running with no payload. These empty trucks harm the environment and keep shipping prices higher than necessary. Two Swedish truckers, Patrick Nordin and Thomas Nilsson, founded Delego.com in 2000, a logistical business-to-business website and wireless web portal that offers shippers up to 40% discount on deliveries by electronically rerouting trucks with unused space to do extra work. Delego is a frontrunner in what analysts expect to become a thriving online transportation market. Web-based transportation and supply chain services are estimated to generate $150 billion in annual revenue in the USA alone.

Nilsson, a cheerful man with a ruddy face and a goatee, was a truck driver for 16 years during which time he experienced driving thousand of kilometres with near empty containers. Together with Nordin, his tall, spiky-haired partner, they first thought of creating a web-based logistics company during the summer of 1999 on a trip from Sweden to Frankfurt. On the ferry from Denmark to Germany, the duo ran into a colleague on his way to Ghent in Belgium, whose truck was also only half-full. Over a few beers at the ferry's bar, the three men complained about how much time they were wasting by making much the same trip with two trucks, considering both trucks left from Stockholm to head south in a near straight line. If only one fully loaded truck could stop in both places, they mused, everyone would be better off.

On their return to Sweden, Patrick Nordin and Thomas Nilsson seriously worked on their idea and initially adopted the name Emptyexpress.com, which they later changed to Delego.com from the Latin word meaning transport. With the promise of financing, the two dropped their truck driving jobs and sold their five-truck transportation fleet to focus on the new project. Arthur Andersen Consulting helped them shape their business plan; they received firm financing from the Swedish venture capital company, Speedventures, and signed on a Harvard MBA as chief financial officer.

How does Delego.com work? Trucking companies and shippers enter coordinates and facts on their truck fleet and potential load. When a transport company has an empty truck en route, the company can communicate the destination of the truck using the web, an Internet-enabled phone, or by calling a Delego call centre. Delego then provides an instant estimate on whether the truck can pick up additional cargo somewhere and how much it will bring in revenues. Delego has been received well in its home market of Sweden, and ABC Carrier Association, a group of transport companies in the Stockholm area agreed to sign up with Delego as did Svealands AB, a distribution centre in Stockholm. Recently, on route E20 outside the Swedish capital, Thomas Nilson punched in a few commands on his Internet-enabled phone. After a loud beep indicated his message had been received, he turned to the two scruffy truckers beside him saying that they could pick up an extra load on the way to their next destination. This spared the truckers a 160 km trip with just three pallets in their rig plus bringing in some extra money.

Adapted from: 'Two truckers pull a lot of freight on the Internet', *Wall Street Journal Europe*[11]

---

least cost plan for the distribution of goods from multiple origins to multiple destinations during a particular planning period, say, for example, daily, weekly, or monthly.

The Internet and transportation

It was not so long ago, that, because of national rules, in Europe trucks delivering goods from one country to another were not allowed to load goods from that country. This rule has now changed somewhat and in order to optimize truck usage Internet-based websites are springing up where companies can contact haulers to see if truck space is available. A pioneer in this area is Delego.com whose activity is discussed in Industry insight 17.4. (Not all countries have dropped their protectionist climate as, for example, in Germany some state governments protect local trucking companies, prohibiting out-of-state operators from picking up certain cargo even if their containers are empty.)

Retail food industry

Product variety

The retail food industry, as for example, Albertson in the USA, Casino in France, Tesco in the UK, poses a special challenge in the supply chain in that food products, and especially fresh foods have to be moved rapidly through the network. In the case of fresh food, which includes fruits and vegetables and meat and fish, there is no value-added process operation as found in manufacturing, instead the 'value added' step is getting the products, of the right size, of the correct brand, to the desired place, at the expected date – and fresh. In addition to the fresh foods, there are the dry goods such as rice, beans and sugar, canned foods, beverages, paper goods, etc. Some products are standard and others are very specialized. Some are from local suppliers, some are national and others come from foreign suppliers. Proper management of inventories, especially for fresh food stocks, which have a short life, and the logistics chain, is the key to success of the organization.

Distribution

The logistics for retail food companies represents a significant cost, estimated up to 25% of sales. The industry attempts to operate in a just-in-time mode keeping inventory levels to a minimum and the use of transportation is optimized. In delivery of items from the warehouse to the retail centre there are essentially two extremes of delivery. One is that trucks might serve

only a single store delivering a variety of different products so that a driver has only to drive to one urban area, park and unload. The alternative would be one truck serving many stores with the same product. In this latter case there is a lot of dead time as the truck has to negotiate traffic at several locations, park, and unload. The larger the number of delivery sites, the greater is the amount of non-added-value time due to delays as Table 17.5 illustrates.[12]

In addition to the lost time with the delays, as the truck is moving through its 'supply chain' it is becoming progressively empty and thus productivity as measured by truck capacity utilization is low.

Supply chain for fresh foods

The scheme for the supply chain for fresh food is illustrated in Figure 17.17, where the challenge is to have the products available to the consumer within a window of 24 hours from the supplier. The cycle is illustrated as follows:

- Assume that at 7am on Monday a retail store of a certain supermarket chain communicates by computer network its requirements to the head office.
- The head office aggregates similar orders from other of its stores and relays this to the supplier at 7.30am on Monday. At the same time, the retailer's warehouse order is notified of the arrival of a pending order.
- The order is shipped from the producer (supplier) between 10.30am and 2.30pm on Monday.
- The order is received at the producer's warehouse between 2.30 and 6.30pm on Monday.

Table 17.5 Delay = non-added-value time

Number of delivery sites	One	Two	Three
Delay time over planned schedule, min	30	90	210

Figure 17.17 **Supply chain for fresh food**

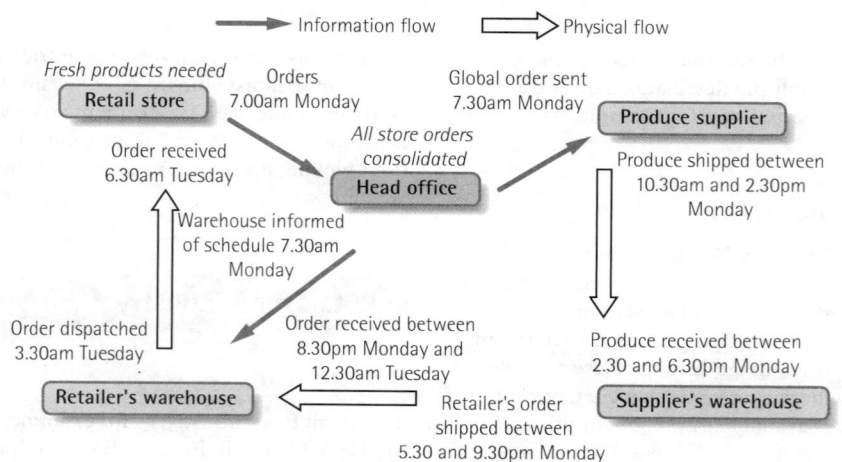

- The order is broken down according to the retailer's requirement and shipped from the supplier's warehouse between 5.30 and 9.30pm on Monday.
- The order is received at the retailer's warehouse between 8.30pm on Monday and 12.3am on Tuesday.
- Order is dispatched at 3.30am on Tuesday and is received by 6.30am Tuesday.

Times depend on location of the various sites, loading and unloading times, and travel times. However, the object is to ensure that the store receives the produce the next day it is ordered. For fresh food, attention is made to using local producers, and conveniently located warehouses in order that the 24-hour window can easily be respected.

Dry and canned foods

The principle is the same as for fresh foods, although the objective here is to have the products delivered within two weeks of the order. In this case it means that the retail outlet has to keep in stock a minimum of two weeks' demand.

Combining warehouse

For some food retailers, fresh produce, dried and canned goods have been treated separately as their handling, storage, and inspection requirements are quite different. This results in a duplication of loading, shipping, and unloading. To avoid this duplication a concept is to combine fresh food and dry unit warehouses. In the industry some call this the 'pump'.

International considerations

The supply chain of many organizations is international. A manufacturing firm in Germany might import raw materials from China, and export finished goods to the United States. And this firm might have a second manufacturing facility in, say, Nigeria. As soon as international boundaries are crossed, the nature and management of the supply chain activity becomes more complex.[13] The following are some considerations.

Trade restrictions

Many countries are parties to the World Trade Organization (WTO, formerly GATT, the General Agreement on Tariffs and Trade) that has an objective to break down trade barriers between nations and facilitate the movement of goods. However, as the following illustrates, there still exist many anomalies in trade, or foreign government policies that can severely add to the costs involved in the supply chain.

Tariffs

Tariffs are charges applied by foreign governments to products imported into that country with a primary purpose to protect local activity. When tariffs are added to the price one must charge to cover all costs to earn a profit, they may or can make a product non-competitive with similar, locally made products.

Subsidies to local firms

In this case, subsidies are financial inputs by governments to national industries. Subsidized firms can afford to earn less in their home markets. This means that even if real costs are similar, or higher than imported goods, they can price below imported products. Alternatively, on foreign markets subsidized firms can price lower than local firms who are not subsidized making it difficult for these non-subsidized firms to compete. This is an ongoing problem in agriculture.

Subsidies to foreign firms

In this case, the subsidies are financial inducements to the foreign firm to relocate in that country with objectives such as the foreign firm will provide needed employment (discussed in detail in Chapter 3). In this situation, the foreign firm benefits and may decide initially to price lower in order to create a market.

Product standards

Governments mandate product standards and other rules relating to safety, health, and the environment. Many of these are legitimate as governments have the right and obligation to ensure that imported products do not harm their citizens. However, such requirements have the effect of excluding imports. The US Federal Drug Administration (FDA) makes it very hard for foreign firms to import drugs or pharmaceutical products. Europe, likewise, is not open about importing genetically altered vegetables from overseas.

Patents and copyright

Firms take out patents and copyright on their product, which is a valuable asset. However, if governments, through neglect or lack of enforcement, make it easy for nationals to infringe on property protection, then competitiveness is lost. This has been the case with clothing, music recordings, and high-tech products from Asian countries.

Investment restrictions

Investment restrictions in a foreign country can range from the outright prohibition of foreign involvement in a specific industry to severe limitation on what a foreigner can do with the money earned within that country.

Shipping regulations

When a company's supply chain extends beyond national boundaries then there are shipping regulations with corresponding documents which have to be submitted to authorities in the country concerned either before or during shipment of goods. Even with the most sophisticated supply chain network in place, without the correct documentation, raw materials for a production operation or finished goods for a client can be held up at national borders creating a bigger delay than ever expected in the supply chain put in place. Many companies are familiar with the cry, 'Our products have

arrived in the country but they are being held at the docks'. Common export and import documents required in international shipping are given in Table 17.6.[14] Table 17.7 gives a listing of the most common terms related to international transportation.

Trading partners

The international supply chain is made simpler when countries that are physically close create trading partnerships that liberalize trade barriers and permit faster movement of goods across their frontiers. It also makes goods cheaper by eliminating all tariffs and quotas. The leading trading groups are now examined.

European Union

As of 2001 there are the 15 countries in the European Union (EU): Austria, Belgium, Denmark, Finland, France, Germany, Great Britain, Greece, Ireland, Italy, Luxembourg, Netherlands, Portugal, Spain and

Table 17.6 Common export and import documents

Export document	Description
Ocean bill of lading	This is a receipt for the cargo and a contract between a shipper and the ocean carrier. It may also be used as an instrument of ownership, which can be bought, sold or traded while the goods are in transit
Dock receipt	This is used to transfer accountability between domestic and international carriers at the ocean terminal. It is the document prepared by the shipper or forwarder, which the ocean carrier signs and returns to the delivering inland carrier, acknowledging receipt of the cargo
Delivery instructions	This provides specific information to the inland carrier concerning the arrangement made by the forwarder to deliver the merchandise to a particular pier or steamship line
Export declaration	Required to control exports and acts as a source document for export statistics and includes complete particulars of the shipment
Letter of credit	This is a financial document issued by a bank at the request of the consignee guaranteeing payment to the shipper of the cargo
Consular invoice	This is used to control and identify goods shipped to a country. It is usually prepared on special forms and may require legalization by the country's consul
Commercial invoice	This is a bill for the goods from the seller to the buyer. It is often used by governments to determine the true value of goods for the assessment of customs duties and is used to prepare consular documents
Certificate of origin	This is a document to assure the buying country precisely in which country the goods were produced. A recognized chamber of commerce usually performs the certification of the origin of the merchandise
Insurance certificate	This assures the consignee that insurance is provided to cover loss or damage to the cargo while in transit
Transmittal letter	This is a list of the particulars of the shipment and a record of the documents being transmitted, together with instructions for disposition of documents. Any special instructions are also included

(Continued)

Table 17.6 (Continued)

Import document	Description
Arrival notice	This is sent by the carrier and informs the customer the estimated arrival date of the vessel and gives information regarding the nature of the goods
Customs entry	A form required by countries of entering goods into that country. It provides information about the goods, their origin, estimated customs duties
Carriers certificate and release order	A document to advise customs of the details of the shipment, its ownership, port of loading, etc. This document is certification of the owner or consignee of the cargo
Delivery order	The consignee, or his customs broker, issues this to the ocean carrier as authority to release the cargo to the inland carrier. It includes all data necessary to ascertain that the cargo may be released
Freight release	This is evidence that the freight charges for the cargo have been paid
Customs invoice	A document usually prepared by the exporter or forwarder and used by customs to determine the value of the shipment

Table 17.7 Terms in international transport

Ex works	Here the seller's only responsibility is to make the goods available at his premises. It is the buyer who bears the full cost and is involved in moving the goods from the seller's location to their final destination
Ex ship	Here the seller makes the goods available to the buyer to the destination named in the sales contract. It is the seller who bears the full cost and risk of getting the goods to that point
Ex quay	Here the seller makes the goods available to the buyer on the quay at the destination named in the sales contract. Again, it is the seller who bears the full cost and risk of getting the goods to that point
FOB	This is an acronym for 'free on board', meaning that goods are placed on board a ship by the seller at a port of shipment named in the sales contract. The risk of loss or damage to the goods is transferred from the seller to the buyer when the goods pass the ship's rail
FOR/FOT	These are free on rail, and free on truck, with the same obligations as FOB
Free carrier	This term meets the requirements of multimodal transport such as containers, or 'roll on roll off' traffic by trailers and lorries and is based on the same main principle as FOB and the seller's obligation are fulfilled when the goods are delivered to the carrier as the named point
FOB airport	This is similar as the ordinary FOB term but applies to goods sent by air
FAS	This term means free alongside ship. Under this arrangement, the seller's obligation are fulfilled when the goods have been placed alongside the ship on in lighters (barges used for loading or unloading). In this case the buyer bears all costs and risks of loading damage after this activity has been fulfilled. Unlike FOB, FAS means that it is the buyer's responsibility to clear the goods for exship
C&F	This term means cost and freight and it is the seller who must pay the costs and freight necessary to bring the goods to the next destination. However, the risk is transferred from the seller to the buyer when the goods pass the ship's rail in the port of shipment
Delivered at frontier	This means that the seller's obligations are fulfilled when the goods have arrived at the frontier, but before the customer's borders in the country named in the sales contract

(Continued)

Table 17.7 (Continued)

CIF	This is cost, insurance, and freight. It is C&F but with the addition that the seller has to buy marine insurance against the risk of loss or damage to the goods during transport
OCP	This means that the seller pays freight and transport to a named destination. It is equivalent to C&F but is appropriate for modes of transport other than ships
CIP	This term is OCP but with the addition that the seller also buys transport insurance. Again it is equivalent to CIF but is appropriate to modes of transport other than ships
Delivered duty paid	This term, followed by words naming the buyer's premises, is the maximum obligation a seller can accept. The seller takes all risk and expenses in delivering the goods.

Sweden, although other countries in the former eastern Europe have also made application for membership. Within the European Union, the lead time for the movement of goods is considerably shortened as much of the paperwork, and customs inspections have been eliminated. The introduction of a common currency, the euro, in January 2002, should further facilitate the movement of goods.

North American Free Trade Association

The North American Free Trade Association, or NAFTA, is the trade association between the USA, Canada, and Mexico.

Association of South East Asian Nations

The Association of South East Asian Nations (ASEAN) includes the trading partners of Brunei, Burma, Indonesia, Laos, Malaysia, the Philippines, Singapore, Thailand, and Vietnam, with a combined population of 500 million people.

Southern African Development Community

The Southern African Development Community (SADC) includes the trading countries of Angola, Botswana, the Democratic Republic of the Congo, Lesotho, Mauritius, Mozambique, Namibia, Seychelles, South Africa, Swaziland, Tanzania, Zambia, and Zimbabwe.

Organizing the supply chain function

Functional organization

How a firm is functionally organized to handle the supply chain linkage very much depends on the firm. The activity will always exist but it may not be specifically defined as illustrated in Figure 17.18. Here the vice-president, or manager, is responsible for all the functions related to the manufacturing operation itself, including production and design, plus functions that are somewhat peripheral to manufacturing such as shipping, purchasing, subcontractor liaison, and inventory control of both raw materials and finished goods.

An alternative organization is to split the manufacturing responsibility into two functions, production, and logistics with a manager for each as illustrated in Figure 17.19. The production manager now is concerned with all of the production aspects proper. The logistics manager is involved with those functions that encircle the manufacturing. In addition, the order compilation, which is assembling all customer orders, has been removed from the finance function and put under the control of the logistics manager. This new organization now has an individual whose primary concern is managing all the flow of materials from the beginning of the supply chain to customer delivery. The production manager is involved with all the activities of transformation and capacity planning. Since the logistics manager and the production manager both report to the vice-president of manufacturing this should make for a smooth flowing organization. If a more stronger logistics control was needed, an alternative organization could be to create a vice-president of logistics reporting directly to the president. Another illustration where the logistics function is clearly identified is given in Figure 17.20 for a European brewery.

Specific activities of the logistics manager

Some of the specific activities of the logistics manager and what that person would do in collaboration with other departments in the organization are now described.

Physical distribution

• Selection of the transportation means such as road or rail. In many cases it would involve selecting the subcontractor to do the transportation.

Figure 17.18 Organization chart: No logistics function

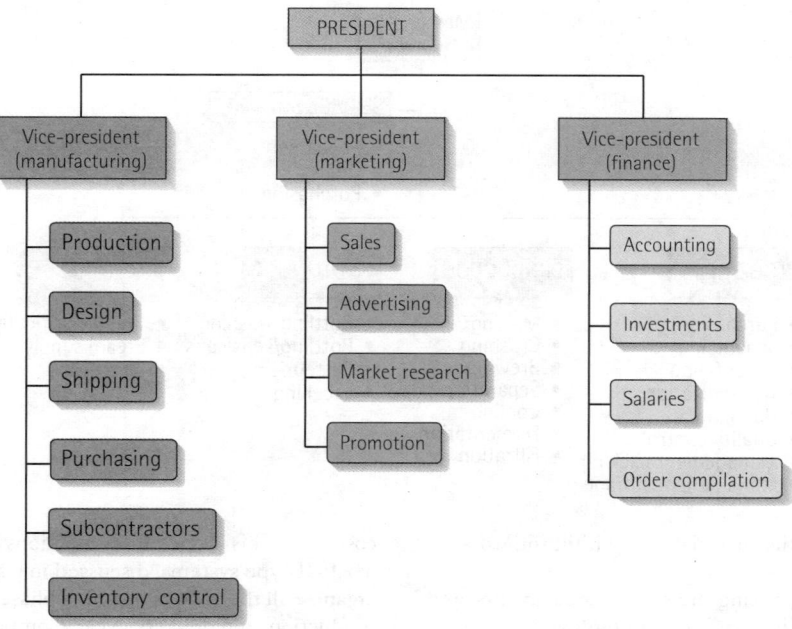

Figure 17.19 Organization chart: With logistics function

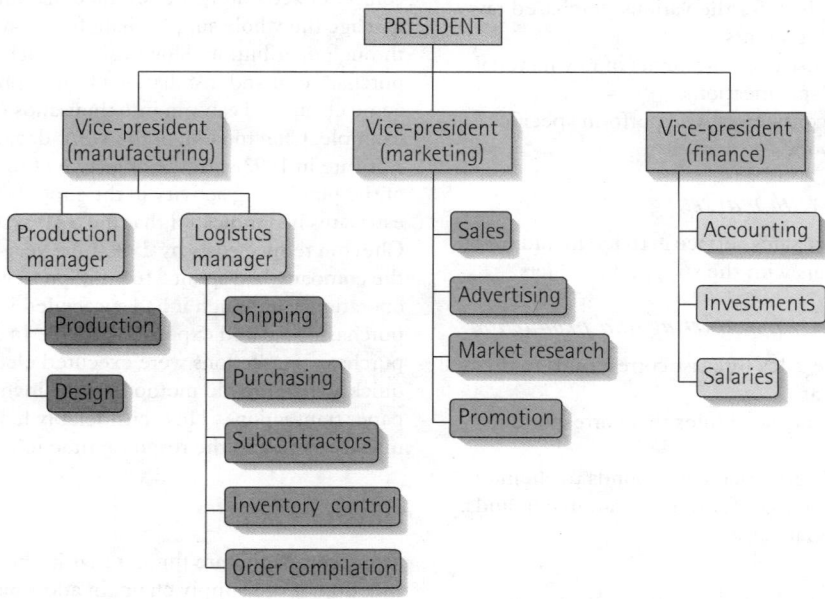

- Schedule the transportation, both incoming and outgoing.
- Organization and planning activities of the distribution centres.

In collaboration with production

- Establishing the production levels to meet sales requirements.

Figure 17.20 Logistics function in a brewery

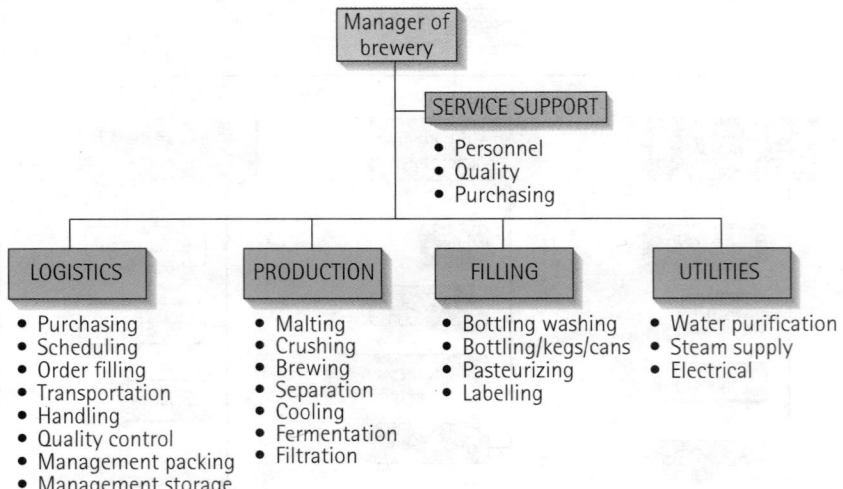

- Optimization of the material flow within the work centre.
- Planning and organizing the storage area layouts, and the type of handling equipment employed.

In collaboration with production and purchasing

- Selection of suppliers for the various purchased raw materials and components.
- Establishing quantity requirements of raw material, price levels, and specifications.
- Selection of subcontractors who perform specific sections of the work.

In collaboration with marketing

- Organize the after-sales service activity, including resolving problems with the supplied products.

In collaboration with marketing and production

- Verifying that the sales forecast corresponds to the real needs of the client.
- Developing delivery schedules that correspond to clients' due dates.
- Developing packaging that corresponds to clients' needs, physical strength for transportation demands, and at an appropriate cost.

Computerized network integration

Accurate scheduling and planning is one of the key elements in managing the supply chain in order to ensure the smooth flow of materials from purchasing, through manufacturing, to the client and at the same time keep costs low. This is one of the functions of integrated MRP-II-type systems, discussed in Chapter 13, to organize all the various planning phases of the purchasing, production, and delivery cycle. Companies such as SAP, Oracle, J D Edwards and PeopleSoft, in collaboration with major consulting firms, are booming with their computerized enterprise resource planning tools that manage the whole supply chain function from production through distribution. However, although effective, the purchase cost and installation of these products doesn't come cheap and can run into thousands of dollars. For example, Chevron Oil, of the USA, decided to use SAP's software in 1992 with the objective of reducing the cost of the purchasing activity in the supply chain. Internal estimates had indicated that the SAP system could help Chevron reduce costs by 25%. Five years later, by 1997, the company had spent $160 million to get SAP operational, although it had succeeded in cutting purchasing-related expenses by 15%. In addition, purchase transactions were executed electronically more quickly than the old method, which involved a lot of paper transactions. This considerably helped to improve management and the response time in the supply chain.[15]

Outsourcing

Many companies are finding that in the distribution function of the supply chain, in addition to standard practices as, negotiating long-term transportation contracts, increasing useful capacity of trucks, or subcontracting use of trucks on a return journey is to subcontract the complete distribution function as Industry insight 17.5 illustrates.

The growth of outsourcing logistics

Until recently most manufacturers handled both incoming and, outgoing logistics themselves and, in the case of giants like General Motors of the USA, assigning whole departments to the process. Now, thanks to deregulation of the US trucking industry, efforts to capitalize on Europe's single market, and in an effort to cut costs, more and more manufacturing firms are outsourcing various portions of their logistics activities. Logistics outsourcing has become a $20 billion a year industry in Europe, and a $50 billion activity in the USA.

Europe's logistics boom started in the late 1980s, driven by the 1992 single market programme and also the British food and retail industries started outsourcing their logistics activities to break the logjam of labour unions, a practice that spilled over onto the Continent. During the 1990s, a pan-European wave of corporate restructuring and cost cutting as well as the EU's effort to abolish national restrictions on intra-European transport, added to the momentum, as did multinationals setting up centralized distribution and warehousing facilities for the entire continent. Now, half of the 800 largest USA and Japanese companies have established European distribution centres. To a certain extent Europe is ahead of the USA because US trucking has been restrained by restrictions on interstate transport. Further, Europe has had to move quickly as it needs to provide a variety of products to suit national preferences; computers sold in Germany, France, or the UK all require different keyboard layouts; the format of electrical plugs and sockets is different in almost every European country; and automobile components have to suit continental Europe's left-hand and Britain's right-hand driving. As such, it has been necessary to cut costs by centralizing logistics. Large shipping and storage companies in Europe include Royal Nedlloyd Group NV and Pakhoed Holding NV of the Netherlands, Swiss-based Kuehn & Nagel AG, and Bilspedition AB of Sweden. The Netherlands, with Rotterdam the world's largest harbour, is the largest centre in Europe for logistics services with some 50% of the European Union's market. The rest is dominated by Belgium and Germany, with other member countries playing a minor role.

US rethinking on logistics management started in the auto industry in the early 1980s when Detroit began to adopt the Japanese just-in-time inventory management philosophy. The industry was able to save money by reducing factory and warehouse inventories of parts to the minimum just necessary to keep a steady flow of production. The biggest trucking companies in the USA include Ryder System, Roadway Services, and Schneider National, which are able to handle the transport of the entire manufacturing supply chain from raw materials to finished goods for many of the Fortune 500 manufacturers. In August 1995 Roadway, based in Hudson, Ohio, spun off its unionized trucking business to focus on its young logistics division. Then in 1993 Hewlett-Packard (HP) transferred its inbound raw materials warehousing activity in Vancouver, Washington, to Roadway logistics. The warehouse operates 24 hours a day, seven days a week. Only 140 Roadway employees took over from some 250 HP employees, who now coordinate the delivery of parts to the warehouse and manage storage. When an order comes from HP's nearby printing manufacturing plant, Roadway fills a container, loads it onto a truck, and delivers it just in time for assembly. After the containers are emptied by HP employees, Roadway picks them up, takes them back to the warehouse and prepares for the next trip. HP says the arrangement has cut warehouse operating costs about 10% while freeing its own employees to work on the printer business. The savings reflect Roadway's expertise, developed over years in the trucking business, in moving goods from point A to point B, in time and in the correct order.

Labour unions are fighting the outsourcing movement, as the flipside of subcontracting is jobs, especially when the move is perceived as a way to break unions and lower wages. When Chrysler considered outsourcing the transportation operations of its Kokomo, Indiana, transmission plant some years ago, the United Auto Workers union refused to step aside.

Adapted from: 'Driving force: In today's economy there is big money to be in logistics', *Wall Street Journal Europe*[16]

Challenges for the logistics manager

Thus, the job of a logistics manager is very broad and crosses many functional lines with challenges to establish the best equilibrium between:

- the sales forecast
- the delivery schedules for purchased parts, materials, and finished goods
- the production schedules and operating plans
- the inventory levels of raw materials, in-process materials, and finished goods
- the flexibility of the production centre.

That is to say, find the best compromise between cost and service, at all times satisfying the client.

Definition of the logistics manager

The supply chain takes its origin from logistics management, which has its roots in wartime. The following gives a 'real' definition of the logistics manager, or the logician:[17]

> Logicians are bitter people. They are very much in demand during wartime, but are quickly forgotten in peacetime. They are faced with the difficult task of serving people who are pursuing their dreams. They are present in wartime, because war requires reality. They disappear in peacetime because peace permits all sorts of frivolity. These people who pursue dreams and who have need of logicians in wartime, but ignore them in peacetime, are the army generals. The generals belong to the titled class. They shine with pride and exude power. Like the Olympic gods, they feed on ambrosia and drink nectar. In peacetime they behave magnificently. On a map, they can invade an empire with a simple majestic gesture are able to trace the access routes, scale the gorges, and crush all obstacles with their hand.
>
> In times of war, they move more cautiously. Each general has, in fact, a logician who follows him like his shadow. He knows that at any time the logician can lean over and whisper to him, 'No, that's not possible'. The generals are afraid of the logicians in wartime and they try to forget them in peacetime. Generals are accompanied by operational staff officers (tactical and strategic). The logicians scorn the tacticians and the strategists. The strategists and the tacticians ignore the logicians just up to the moment when they themselves become generals, which is often the case.
>
> It sometimes happens that a logician is promoted to a general. In this case he must identify with the hated class of generals. He is followed by a cortege of strategists and tacticians, who he detests. And, on his back is a logician, whom he fears. That is why the logicians who make it to generals get stomach ulcers and are not able to drink the nectar!

Summary of key elements

- In manufacturing, the supply chain is the network of the flow of goods from suppliers through transformation to distribution of finished products. In the reverse direction is the information flow. The supply chain for a pure service firm is principally information flow.

- In the supply chain there are also financial flows which include payment to the supplier for goods and services, operating costs in transformation, and payment for the finished products.

- Lead times include delivery of raw materials, operating times, distribution times of finished goods, and waiting or non-value idle time. The World Wide Web can reduce the supply chain lead time by permitting direct purchasing, delivery, and invoicing of goods.

- The supply chain may be in two parts. Materials management, or the flow of materials from suppliers through to the finished product, and physical distribution management, or the distribution of the finished product to the client.

- A supply chain can be modelled into a series of value-added cells with an input and output. An objective is to have cells that maximize the value-added content.

- Inventory is held in the supply chain because of uncertainty related to suppliers, manufacturing operations, and the clients' real needs.

- A pipeline map is a series of horizontal lines (pipeline length) representing processing steps and vertical bars (pipeline height) representing waiting periods. Pipeline volume is the sum of the two and is an indicator of the firm's flexibility.

- A variety funnel shows the reduced flexibility as one moves through the pipeline.

- Distribution requirements planning (DRP) is a tool in the supply chain to ensure that the specified finished goods arrive as planned. A pull system DRP is when the client triggers the orders. A push system is when the supplier triggers the movement of goods.

- The major activities in a distribution centre are reception, stocking, picking, and dispatching, with the most labour intensive and thus the most costly being picking.

- Management of a distribution centre can be improved by optimizing storage location, using crossdocking, computer control, ABC analysis, and benchmarking with similar facilities.

- Modularized packing and using standard pallets can reduce supply chain costs particularly in the distribution centre.

- Factors to consider in selecting a distribution centre include location relative to clients and suppliers, capacity, layout, handling equipment, and ease of access.

- Criteria for selecting a mode of transport include network availability, distance, speed, volume and weight restrictions, security, regulations, and overall costs. Both in the USA and Europe the truck is the dominant form of transport.

- The retail fresh food industry has a supply chain network that in many cases permits the delivery of fresh foods in a cycle time of under 24 hours.

- International considerations in the supply chain include the host country's policies on tariffs, subsidies, product standards, patents and copyrights, and investment. In addition, shipping regulations and document needs are part of the international considerations.

- Having in place a defined logistics function can improve a firm's performance. Further, outsourcing of the distribution function can reduce costs and is becoming standard practice.

Notes and references

1. Davis, Tom, 'Effective supply chain management', *Sloan Management Review*, summer 1993, pp 335–46
2. *L'Usine Nouvelle*, France, 24 February 1994
3. Palenet Corporation, Japan (subsidiary of Mitsubishi) 1993 (report by Christine Daval, ESC)
4. Scott, Charles and Westbrook, Roy, 'New strategic tools for supply chain management: Supply chain effectiveness can be enhanced by the strategic tools described in the article – the pipeline map, and the supplier relationship grid', *International Journal of Physical Distribution and Logistics Management*, vol 21, no 1, 1991, pp 23–33
5. Commodity Flow Survey, US Census Bureau, 1997, Economic Census, 9 December 1999, http://www.bts.gov/cfs/desc.html
6. EU Transport in Figures, 2000, European Commission, Luxembourg
7. 'Changing trains: Freight-rail system shows Europe is still as far apart as ever', *Wall Street Journal Europe*, 29 March 1999, pp. 1 and 2
8. Abbati, Carlo degil, *Transport and European Integration*, European Perspectives Series, Brussels, 1986
9. 'Fast container ships: How to shrink the world', *The Economist*, 4 August 2001, pp 51–2
10. Lavin, Douglas, 'The mighty Antonov is only way to fly your locomotive: Soviet military relic carries anything; Despite quirks, behemoth does the job', *Wall Street Journal Europe*, 30–31 December 1994
11. 'Two truckers pull a lot of freight on the Internet: Frustrated by logistics, Swedish duo builds a site', *Wall Street Journal Europe*, 11 May 2000
12. Study at E. M. Lyon, 1996
13. Gattorna J. L. and Walters, D. W., 'International supply chain management: Issues and implications', *Managing the Supply Chain, A Strategic Perspective*, Macmillan, London, 1996, pp 239–48
14. The Port Authority of New York and New Jersey, Port Service Improvement Committee, One World Trade Center, New York
15. 'The best software business Bill Gates doesn't own', *Fortune*, 29 December 1997, pp 68–72
16. Bignes, Jon and du Bois, Martin, 'Driving force: In today's economy there is big money to be made in logistics. Trucking firms lead way in creating an industry that's bringing in billions. Rotterdam acts as magnet', *Wall Street Journal Europe*, 12 September 1995
17. By an anonymous office of the Pentagon
18. Ball, Deborah, 'Italian inspections find violations rife in meat plant: search for mad-cow disease turns up plenty of hygiene problems', *Wall Street Journal Europe*, 1 February 2001, p. 2

Review and discussion topics

1. Pipeline map
Develop a pipeline map for the supply chain for:
    (a) the growing, cutting, and delivery of lumber to a pulp mill
    (b) the sale of sugar from the refining to its consumption in a household
    (c) the production of cotton T-shirts from raw materials to final sale
    (d) the publishing of a book from delivery of final manuscript to when the product appears on the bookshelves.
    Indicate on the map which are process steps and which waiting times. Although you may not be able to put in quantitative numbers, indicate on the map your estimation of relative values.

2. Transportation in Europe
In Europe, road networks are heavily congested, particularly around major cities. What do you believe might be some of the solutions to easing the distribution problems? Look at some of the advantages from both an economic and an environmental point of view.

3. Site selection and the supply chain
Discuss the relationship between site selection (Chapter 3), consumer needs, and the supply chain. What developments do you see in emerging markets such as China and what will be the impact on regions such as the USA, and Europe?

4. Comparison of the supply chain
Compare the differences between the supply chain network within the USA, Europe, and Japan. Identify the reasons.

5. Food supply chain
Since the late 1980s in Europe there has been considerable concern over the quality of its food. In 1986 20 people died in Italy after being poisoned by drinking wine tainted with methane. In 1998, also in Italy, arsenic was found in several panettoni, the sweet bread that is very popular at Christmas. In 1999 Belgian authorities discovered cancer-causing dioxin in eggs, meat, poultry,

and dairy products, allegedly originating from spent motor oil. In the same year the Belgian government banned Coca-Cola after many people fell ill after drinking the beverage. According to Coca-Cola this was due to poor-quality carbon dioxide that had been used to carbonate the drinks. Also in 1999 France came under attack from the European Parliament for using sewage sludge in animal feed. In 2001 mad cow disease is the major food concern. Bovine spongiform encephalopathy (BSE), as it is correctly known, has been traced to feeding animals meal made from diseased ground-up animal body parts. It was first disclosed in Britain

in 1996 and, to date, 83 people are known to have died after contracting the human form of BSE, known as Creutzfeld-Jakob disease (CJD), having eaten tainted beef. The problem has now spread to many other European countries.[18]

As a result of these food concerns, the European Parliament is asking for a complete accounting of the food supply chain from its original source to final consumption, and disposal of waste. Present, in the form of a process flow sheet, the food supply chain, identifying the activities and the associated potential problems of contamination.

Demonstrating the concept 17.1   Chianti

Situation

A small winery in Milan, Italy produces, among its many products, Chianti. This is bottled in one-litre green bottles with a colourful cork, and the traditional Italian raffia around the bottle. The winery has two distribution centres, one in Zurich, Switzerland, and one in Torino, Italy. The centre in Zurich supplies three retail outlets in Baden, Zug, and St Gallen. The centre in Torino supplies retail outlets in Como, Piancenzo, and Bergamo. The network for the system is shown in Figure 17.21.

The average quantity of wine demanded (sold) by each retail outlet, the current inventory on hand, at the

quantity ordered from the distribution centre each time an order is made, is given in Tables 17.8 and 17.9. All the data are in cases of wine. Delivery time from the distribution centre to the retail outlet is one week.

Weekly demand
This is the average amount sold a week based on past data. The weekly forecast could be different if the retailer had a more sophisticated planning model.

Inventory on hand
Inventory on hand is the quantity of cases of wine in the store available for sale.

Figure 17.21 Distribution network: Milan winery and its outlets

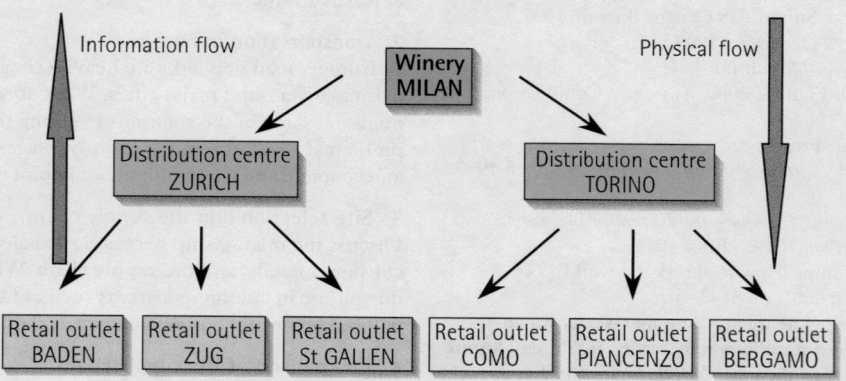

Table 17.8 Wine distribution centre, Switzerland

Retail outlet	Weekly demand	Inventory on hand	Order quantity
Baden	8	12	15
Zug	9	14	20
St Gallen	12	19	15

Table 17.9 Wine distribution centre, Italy

Retail outlet	Weekly demand	Inventory on hand	Order quantity
Como	15	18	25
Piancenzo	18	21	35
Bergamo	22	32	30

Order quantity

This is the amount of cases ordered by the retail outlet according to its purchasing policy. This would be an economic quantity based on the inventory carrying costs, space available, and transportation costs.

Similar data for the distribution centres are given in Table 17.10 which shows the current inventory on hand, and the quantity ordered by each distribution centre from the winery each time an order is made. All the data are in cases of wine. Delivery time from the winery to the distribution centre is one week.

Inventory on hand

This is the quantity of cases of wine in the distribution centre available to be shipped to the retail outlets.

Order quantity

This is the amount of cases ordered by the distribution centre according to its ordering policy. This would be an economic quantity based on the inventory storing cost, space available, and transportation costs.

Finally, Table 17.11 gives the inventory on hand at the winery, and the production lot each time an order is made. The production lot represents the cases of wine bottled and packaged. Normally, the wine is stored in bulk in large fermenting-type vessels and only bottled when needed. It takes one week to bottle and package the wine.

Inventory on hand

This is the quantity of cases of wine in the winery available to be dispatched to the distribution centres.

Production lot

This is the quantity of cases that the winery prepares each time for shipping to the distribution centres. The Chianti is stored in large container vessels and is only bottled, and packed when needed by the distribution centres.

Required

1. Develop a 'pull' distribution requirements plan, over an eight-week period, using the weekly demand from each retail outlet as the independent demand, which pulls the product through the network.
2. Calculate the average inventory each week at the six retail outlets.

Solution

1. The distribution requirements plan, preceded by the initial data, is illustrated in Table 17.12. The DRP plan was generated automatically from the initial data using Microsoft Excel. Each retail outlet only generates a demand when the inventory level is insufficient to satisfy the demand. All inventory data are for the end of the week. For example, consider the Baden retail outlet.

Baden retail outlet

- In week 1 there is sufficient inventory on hand of 12 cases to satisfy the demand of eight cases for that week.
- Inventory level at the end of week 1 drops to four cases given by (12 − 8).
- The four cases at end of week 1 will be insufficient to supply the demand for week 2, and so an order is made in week 1 of 15 cases according to policy. This quantity arrives in week 2.
- At end of week 2 there are 11 cases of wine on hand (15 + 4 − 8).
- The movement of inventory continues in the same manner for the eight-week planning schedule.
- At week 8 ending inventory is 8 (15 + 1 − 8) so there is sufficient for the 9th week on the assumption that the demand requirements are the same.
- For the planned ordered cells, a logic function (*if clause*) is used to generate the value. For example for Baden, week 1, the test is:
  − If the inventory on hand at the end of week 1 is less than the demand, then order the required amount (15 cases), if not the value is 0.

Zurich distribution centre

All the planned orders for the three retail outlets in Switzerland are totalled to give the demand required from the corresponding distribution centre. For example:

- The total demand for the Switzerland retail outlets at week 1 is 50 cases (15 + 20 + 15). This in the gross requirements for week 1 for Zurich.
- At the start of week 1 there are 65 cases, at the end there are 15 cases (65 − 50).

Table 17.10 Distribution centres with inventory on hand and quantity

Distribution centre	Inventory on hand	Order quantity
Zurich, Switzerland	65	50
Torino, Italy	105	70

Table 17.11 Milan winery inventory on hand and production lot

	Inventory on hand	Production lot
Milan	80	160

Table 17.12 Pull system for Chianti supply and distribution

Supplied from distribution centre at Zurich			
	Weekly demand	Inventory on hand	Order quantity
Baden	8	12	15
Zug	9	14	20
St Gallen	12	19	15

Delivery time from Zurich to retail outlet is one week

Supplied from distribution centre at Torino			
	Weekly demand	Inventory on hand	Order quantity
Como	15	18	25
Piancenzo	18	21	35
Bergamo	22	32	30

Delivery time from Torino to retail outlet is one week

Supplied from Milan winery		
	Inventory on hand	Order quantity
Zurich	65	50
Torino	105	70

Delivery time from Milan to distribution centre is one week

Milan winery		
	Inventory on hand	Production lot
Milan	80	160

Retail stores, Switzerland

					Week					
	0	1	2	3	4	5	6	7	8	9
Baden (Inventory on hand is as of end of period)										
Gross requirements		8	8	8	8	8	8	8	8	8
Inventory on hand	12	4	11	3	10	2	9	1	8	0
Planned receipts		0	15	0	15	0	15	0	15	0
Planned orders	0	15	0	15	0	15	0	15	0	15
Zug (Inventory on hand is as of end of period)										
Gross requirements		9	9	9	9	9	9	9	9	9
Inventory on hand	14	5	16	7	18	9	0	11	2	13
Planned receipts		0	20	0	20	0	0	20	0	20
Planned orders	0	20	0	20	0	0	20	0	20	0
St Gallen (Inventory on hand is as of end of period)										
Gross requirements		12	12	12	12	12	12	12	12	12
Inventory on hand	19	7	10	13	1	4	7	10	13	1
Planned receipts		0	15	15	0	15	15	15	15	0
Planned orders	0	15	15	0	15	15	15	15	0	15

(Continued)

Table 17.12 (Continued)

Retail stores, Italy

		Week								
	0	1	2	3	4	5	6	7	8	9

Como (Inventory on hand is as of end of period)

	0	1	2	3	4	5	6	7	8	9
Gross requirements		15	15	15	15	15	15	15	15	15
Inventory on hand	18	3	13	23	8	18	3	13	23	8
Planned receipts		0	25	25	0	25	0	25	25	0
Planned orders	0	25	25	0	25	0	25	25	0	25

Piancenzo (Inventory on hand is as of end of period)

	0	1	2	3	4	5	6	7	8	9
Gross requirements		18	18	18	18	18	18	18	18	18
Inventory on hand	21	3	20	2	19	1	18	0	17	34
Planned receipts		0	35	0	35	0	35	0	35	35
Planned orders	0	35	0	35	0	35	0	35	35	0

Bergamo (Inventory on hand is as of end of period)

	0	1	2	3	4	5	6	7	8	9
Gross requirements		22	22	22	22	22	22	22	22	22
Inventory on hand	32	10	18	26	4	12	20	28	6	14
Planned receipts		0	30	30	0	30	30	30	0	30
Planned orders	0	30	30	0	30	30	30	0	30	30

Distribution centres

		Week								
	0	1	2	3	4	5	6	7	8	9

Zurich (Inventory on hand is as of end of period)

	0	1	2	3	4	5	6	7	8	9
Gross requirements	0	50	15	35	15	30	35	30	20	30
Inventory on hand	65	15	0	15	0	20	35	5	35	5
Planned receipts		0	0	50	0	50	50	0	50	0
Planned orders	0	0	50	0	50	50	0	50	0	30

Zurich routing to

	0	1	2	3	4	5	6	7	8	9
Baden	0	15	0	15	0	15	0	15	0	15
Zug	0	20	0	20	0	0	20	0	20	0
St Gallen	0	15	15	0	15	15	15	15	0	15
Total	0	50	15	35	15	30	35	30	20	30

(Continued)

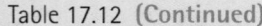

Table 17.12 (Continued)

		Week								
	0	1	2	3	4	5	6	7	8	9
Torino (Inventory on hand is as of end of period)										
Gross requirements	0	90	55	35	55	65	55	60	65	55
Inventory on hand	105	15	30	65	10	15	30	40	45	60
Planned receipts		0	70	70	0	70	70	70	70	70
Planned orders	0	70	70	0	70	70	70	70	70	0
Torino routing to										
Como	0	25	25	0	25	0	25	25	0	25
Piancenzo	0	35	0	35	0	35	0	35	35	0
Bergamo	0	30	30	0	30	30	30	0	30	30
Total	**0**	**90**	**55**	**35**	**55**	**65**	**55**	**60**	**65**	**55**

Manufacturing site

		Week								
	0	1	2	3	4	5	6	7	8	9
Milan (Inventory on hand is as of end of period)										
Gross requirements	0	70	120	0	120	120	70	120	70	30
Inventory on hand	80	10	50	50	90	130	60	100	30	0
Bottled/ready		0	160	0	160	160	0	160	0	0
Planned production	0	160	0	160	160	0	160	0	0	0
Actual shipping from Milan to										
Zurich	0	0	50	0	50	50	0	50	0	
Torono	0	70	70	0	70	70	70	70	70	
Total	**0**	**70**	**120**	**0**	**120**	**120**	**70**	**120**	**70**	

Average inventory at retail levels, week [n + (n + 1)]/2

Baden	8.00	7.50	7.00	6.50	6.00	5.50	5.00	4.50
Zug	9.50	10.50	11.50	12.50	13.50	4.50	5.50	6.50
St Gallen	13.00	8.50	11.50	7.00	2.50	5.50	8.50	11.50
Como	10.50	8.00	18.00	15.50	13.00	10.50	8.00	18.00
Piancenzo	12.00	11.50	11.00	10.50	10.00	9.50	9.00	8.50
Bergamo	21.00	14.00	22.00	15.00	8.00	16.00	24.00	17.00

Italy retail outlet and distribution centre

The same calculation is made for all the retail outlets, and the distribution centre in Italy:

- In Torino, at the start of week 1, there are 105 cases, at the end there are 15 cases (105 − 90). The 90 cases is the total ordered by the retail outlets in Italy at the end of week 1. These will arrive in week 2 as planned receipts.

Milan winery

- The gross requirements for Milan at week 1 are 70 cases. This is triggered by the planned orders from the distribution centres at week 1 (0 + 70).
- The gross requirements for Milan at week 2 are 120 cases. This is triggered by the planned orders from the distribution centres at week 1 (50 + 70).

Plan period

- The distribution resource plans are generated for the eight-week period. It is assumed that the demand for the 9th week is the same is for the 8th so that in some cases a planned order is triggered.

2. The average inventory for each retail site is shown in Table 17.12. It is based on the average of the inventory at the end of one week and the inventory at the end of the following week.

Comments

- The only independent demand is from the retail outlets. The other demands are dependent demands on these quantities. This is analogous to the MRP system. Here, the independent demand is the finished product. The dependent demands are the components that go into making the finished product.
- The demand from each of the retail outlets imposes a master production schedule (MPS) on the manufacturer, which may not be optimum. The manufacturer loses some control of his planning process and has to be flexible to accommodate customer demand. In some instances, the pull system may impose a MPS on the manufacturer that is not feasible.
- All the retail outlets hold a certain amount of stock, but there is never a stockout situation.

Application exercise 17.1 Chianti (2)

Situation

In Demonstrating the concept 17.1, the forecast demand by cases of wine for each retail centre is now as follows (see Table 17.13). Further, the inventory on hand at the beginning of the plan period is 130 cases at the Torino distribution centre and 125 cases at the Milan winery. All the other information from the worked example remains the same.

Required

Develop a new distribution requirements plan for the Chianti situation. In addition, determine the average inventory held for each retail centre.

Table 17.13 **Forecast demand for Chianti**

				We	ek				
	1	2	3	4	5	6	7	8	9
Baden	8	10	12	7	9	5	4	12	10
Zug	9	8	7	12	12	13	12	8	12
St Gallen	12	15	12	13	14	15	10	8	12
Como	15	17	20	14	12	5	6	12	8
Piancenzo	18	20	22	25	18	17	19	17	14
Bergamo	22	25	25	14	22	28	26	21	19

Application exercise 17.2 Cupboard

Situation

A furniture manufacturer in Copenhagen makes a wide range of Scandinavian-type modular furniture that it sells throughout Europe. One popular product is a cupboard whose design is such that one model type can be assembled in three different ways. For one of its supply networks, the company has distribution centres near Paris in France, and Frankfurt in Germany. The distribution centre in Paris supplies large retail outlets in Nantes,

Marseille, and Geneva while the distribution centre in Frankfurt supplies retail outlets in Dresden, Hamburg, and Essen. Based on past data, the forecast demand for each of the six retail outlets, for the next nine weeks is given in Table 17.14.

Whenever an order is required, each retail outlet makes fixed order quantities from the corresponding distribution centre. These amounts, and the current inventory levels at the start of week 1, are given in Table 17.15.

Table 17.14 Forecast demand for cupboards

					Week				
	1	2	3	4	5	6	7	8	9
Nantes	10	6	12	14	16	10	20	22	25
Marseille	14	18	17	25	30	19	15	25	18
Geneva	10	6	14	25	32	17	18	18	22
Dresden	8	14	15	22	23	22	25	14	25
Hamburg	10	12	14	25	23	32	18	17	18
Essen	16	9	28	18	28	24	12	15	14

Table 17.15 Fixed order quantities and current inventory levels

Site	Inventory on hand	Order quantity
Nantes	12	25
Marseille	14	30
Geneva	19	25
Dresden	18	30
Hamburg	21	35
Essen	32	25

Table 17.16 Distribution centre fixed order quantities and current inventory levels

Site	Inventory on hand	Order quantity
Paris	80	65
Frankfurt	110	70

The distribution centre makes fixed order quantities from the producer. These amounts, and the current inventory levels at the start of week 1 are given in Table 17.16.

Finally, the producer in Copenhagen assembles the cupboards in fixed lot sizes of 150 units. Inventory on hand at start of week 1 is 80. Delivery time from the producer to the distribution centre, and from the distribution centre to the retail outlet is one week. This takes into account the actual transportation time, and the time for unloading and putting the inventory in storage. Similarly, the production lead time in Copenhagen is one week.

Required

Develop a 'pull' distribution requirements plan for the next eight weeks, using the weekly demand from each retail outlet as the independent demand, which pulls the product through the distribution network.

Case study 17.1 Cisco Systems

Situation

Cisco Systems was started by two Stanford computer scientists in 1984 and became publicly traded in 1990. Its principal product is the router, or the combination of hardware and software that controls the TCP/IP networks (transmission control protocol/Internet protocol) that make up the Internet and the corporate intranet systems. With the tremendous growth of the Internet technologies, the demand for Cisco's products mushroomed and by 1997 it ranked among the top five companies in the USA in terms of return on revenues and return on assets. Only Intel and Microsoft have equalled this achievement.

In the early 1990s Cisco was using a UNIX-based computer software package to support functional areas such as finance, manufacturing, and customer order entry systems. The firm was growing into a $5 billion plus business and the existing software didn't provide the necessary degree of reliability. In January 1994 there was a major failure of the software system, and Cisco was essentially shut down for a couple of days. This was

the trigger that launched management into the decision to install an ERP (enterprise resource planning system). The company contacted several vendors and eventually selected the Oracle system, principally as it was very manufacturing oriented and the system was flexible. Incorporating the ERP system was a $15 million project and involved 100 team members of Cisco from a cross-section of the firm plus consultants from KPMG and experts from Oracle. When Cisco first cut over to the Oracle system in January 1995 results were disappointing. Business performance plummeted as users attempted to deal with a new system that, on average, went down nearly once a day. However, over the course of the next three months Cisco and the Oracle vendors stabilized and added capacity to the ERP system. It is now living up to its promises and improving the company's performance and saving it money.[1]

In 2000 Cisco added power to its ERP system by electronic business-to-business networking with its suppliers. With its dedicated extranet it now had connections to 32 manufacturing plants. These suppliers are not owned by Cisco in any form of vertical integration but they are independent firms that have submitted to the rigorous Cisco certification process to ensure that they meet the required quality and other standards demanded by the client. Using the network, the suppliers are easily able to respond with a component price, delivery time, and a record of their recent performance on reliability and quality. Cisco's supply system is significant in that it uses a form of electronic market to set prices. The electronic exchange of information between buyers and sellers is very rapidly changing the nature of Cisco's integrated supply chain.[2]

Cisco is not the only firm using the Internet to revolutionize its supply chain in its business-to-business and business-to-consumer relationships. Automobile firms such as GE, Ford and Daimler-Chrysler of the USA and Renault and Peugeot of France are developing websites to display their requirements for components and outsourcing of services. They expect that, eventually, some 80% of suppliers and services will be procured through the web. Downstream, the automobile firms have business-to-consumer electronic linkages where they expect to sell a large chunk of their sports-utility vehicles, automobiles and light trucks though the web. A consumer, with his or her 'specification' of an automobile, can tap onto the Internet and see what is available. For less expensive products, retail firms such as Tesco and Sainsbury's of the UK or Wal-Mart in the USA have themselves developed electronic business-to-consumer linkups modifying their supply chain and increasing revenues.

Required
This case highlights two technologies that have come to prominence in the last decade, ERP systems and the Internet. Both of these have tremendously modified the way in which firms operate. The case uses phrases such as improving the company's performance and saving it money, and rapidly changing the nature of the supply chain. Discuss in depth the functions of ERP systems and the Internet in manufacturing and service firms and review broadly how and why they are improving the performance of business. Address financial considerations, human resources, and international impact, quality, operating, strategic and other aspects you consider are important. If you are able, use real examples to illustrate your response. You might wish to consider ERP and the Internet as separate technologies first and then how, as integrated systems, they are improving performance.

[1] Extracted from the case 9-699-022 'Cisco Systems, Inc: Implementing ERP', *Harvard Business School*, 1998.
[2] E-management survey', *The Economist*, 11 November 2000, p. 24.

Selected further reading

CHOPRA, Sunil and MEINDL, Peter (2000) *Supply Chain Management: Strategy, Planning and Operations*, Prentice-Hall.

CHRISTOPHER, Martin (1999) *Logistics and Supply Chain Management: Strategies for Reducing Cost and Improving Service*, 2nd edition, Prentice-Hall.

EMMETT, Stuart, 'How to improve your freight transport and warehouse operations', *Control*, The Institute of Operations Management, November 2001, pp 8–12.

GOVIL, Manish and PROTH, Jean-Marie (2001) *Supply Chain Design and Management*, Academic Press.

STUART, F. Ian, 'Supply-chain strategy: Organizational influence through supplier alliances', *British Journal of Management*, vol. 8, issue 3, September 1997, pp 223–36.

An extensive listing of other further reading can be found on the website.

What's on the web?

Further learning resources are available to lecturers and students at www.supplychain-online.com, including the following which are specific to *Managing the integrated supply chain*:

Resource	Subject
Chapter overview	Managing the integrated supply chain
Exam topics	Managing the integrated supply chain
Application exercise: Chianti (3)	Distribution requirements planning
More further reading	Managing the integrated supply chain

18 *Project management*

Chapter overview

- **A project and project management**
- **Contracts in a project**
- **Phases of a project**
- **Project organization**
- **Scheduling and controlling**
- **Network diagrams**
- **Accelerating (crashing) a project**

A project and project management

A project is an item of work that is unique, for which there is a budget, and which has a start and a finish date. Project management then involves the planning, scheduling, budgeting, and control of this work using an integrated team of workers and specialists. A project can be of any size, may be external or internal to an existing organization. The following sections illustrate.

Complex projects with unknown elements

Complex projects with unknown elements are those construction projects which are very large in terms of financial investment, running into maybe billions of dollars, and are complicated because they involve many untested design elements. The time horizon for their completion may be many years. Examples include:

- The tunnel under the Channel between France and England. This was the most significant international transport project since the Panama Canal. This project, completed in December 1993, established an important physical supply chain between the two countries. (See Industry insight 18.1.)
- The Aswan Dam on the river Nile in Egypt, built to provide hydroelectric power to the country, to alleviate flooding, and to provide irrigation in the Nile valley. This project, which was completed in July 1970, cost over $5 billion, and was in part financed by the then Soviet Union. It employed some 40,000 people, including 5000 Russians.[1,2]

- The construction of the US–Alaskan pipeline which was completed in June 1977. This project involved the laying of a 1.20 metre diameter pipeline stretching 1280 km from the Prudhoe Bay oilfields in the north of the state to the port of Valdez in the south, from where the crude oil could be shipped by tanker to oil refineries in California. During the pipeline construction workers had to endure temperature of −60°C in the winter and up to 40°C in the summer. The project involved the utilization of 320 tractors, 250 bulldozers, 600 trucks, and 650 welding stations set up along the route.[3]
- The Three Gorges dam project on the Yangtze River in China. This mega-dollar hydroelectric project, still underway in 2001, will create a reservoir some 400 miles long, submerge 150,000 acres of land, 1500 factories, 160 towns, and 16 archaeological sites and require the resettlement of 1.3 million people. It is designed to generate over 18,000 megawatts of power, help flood management, and improve navigation on the Yangtze.[4]

Large projects with standard elements

Large projects with standard elements are those with a timeframe of, perhaps, 18 months to five years, cost thousands of dollars, and which, in part, duplicate design and construction that has been performed before. They might include:

- an oil refinery, say, for Exxon in France
- an industrial automobile complex, say, for BMW in the USA

- a housing estate for 30 homes
- the construction of the section of a motorway – another part of the physical supply chain.

Intermediate projects

Intermediate projects, perhaps of an internal nature, lasting only a matter of months, and costing hundreds to a few thousand dollars might include:

- installing a new offset print machine
- installing an enterprise resource planning system (see Chapter 13)
- implementing a cellular layout in a factory (see Chapter 9)
- landscaping around an office building.

Small projects

Small projects would be those activities lasting a few weeks, or even a few days, and which are of relatively low cost. They might include for example:

- installing cabling in an office for Internet connections
- painting an existing home
- a small consulting or marketing study
- a SMED application at a work post (see Chapter 15).

Elements of a project

All projects, whether internal, or external, large or small, have common elements, as shown in Table 18.1.

Turnkey project

A turnkey project is one which starts from zero to proceed to a finished 'product'. The concept of turnkey is that when the project is finished *one turns a key to set the facility in operation*. The General Motors Saturn plant in the USA was a turnkey project as it was built on a previously virgin site. Another name for turnkey is grassroots, meaning the plant is built on the *roots of the grass in the field*. As opposed to a turnkey project is the expansion, or the extension of an existing facility.

Projects, operations, and the supply chain

The difference between a project and operations is that a project starts and finishes whereas operations are ongoing or continuous. Project management is treated here in a text on operations management with an emphasis on the supply chain because of the following relationship project/operations.

Table 18.1 Common elements in different projects

Objective	There is a well-defined objective, which is achieved by accomplishing a series of activities
Plan	There is a detailed work plan with corresponding dates of all the milestones in the project
Schedule	A project has a start date (it is 'kicked off') and a stipulated finish date. To a client these dates are critical, since between the start and the finish date costs are incurred. Then, for many projects, revenue is generated after the finish date. Thus, a late project can delay the generation of revenues
Team	A project is made up of a cohesive team, led by the project manager, all with the same objective. The team is disbanded for the particular project once the work is completed
Budget	All projects have a financial budget attributed to the project. One of the responsibilities of the project manager is to complete the project within budget

A project is the start of operations

A project is often the start of operations. The project to build the General Motors Saturn plant in the USA was the starting point for the operation to build new models of automobiles. The building of a dam is the start of an operation to supply electricity to a surrounding community. The building of a new hospital is to improve the operations of medical services to a defined region.

A project has similar functions to operations

Within a project, once it gets underway, there are operations, or many of the activities and functions that are similar, if not identical, to those performed in operations management. There are scheduling activities, management of inventory during the various phases of the projects, human resource management, productivity considerations, quality control, just-in-time planning, purchasing, etc.

A project team is composed of operators

In the composition of a project team are often operating related personnel who have familiarity with the type of project in question such as engineers, purchasing personnel, planners, cost accountants and schedulers.

Project team members become operators

When a project is terminated, persons who have been involved in a project, often become part of the operating team because of their familiarity with the programme from its embryonic stage.

There are projects in the operations management environment

From time to time, within any operating environment, there are projects to be executed which might include:

- In a supermarket, the project may be changing the layout of the aisles and shelving to improve product sales.
- In manufacturing, it may be the installation of a new robot to improve productivity and quality.
- In a consulting office, the project may be the threading all the cables necessary for Internet connections.
- In an education centre, the project may be the construction of a new amphitheatre to accommodate increased student admissions.

New products involve projects

Firms are continually developing new products that are used in the operations environment and this involves a project. For example, assembly lines have such automatic functions as bottle filling, soldering, or packaging, which use automatic controllers or automats. The development of the product, or the automat, is a project involving evaluating market needs (the manufacturing firm who uses the automat), product conception and design, design of the process to produce the product, testing and commercialization. Group Schneider (Square D in the USA or Télémécanique in Europe) is heavily involved in this type of project/product work.[5]

A physical unit in the supply chain was once a project

A completed project might be any of the physical facilities in a supply chain. For example, consider the supply chain for computers. A project at the start of the supply chain may be the plant for making computer chips that are used in the computers. The project might be the transformation facility where the computers are assembled. The project might be the distribution centre for storing and the delivery area for supplying the computers to the retail outlet. Finally, the project might be the retail store that sells the computers.

The Eurotunnel project

Industry insight 18.1

For almost 200 years engineers had dreamed of building a tunnel under the English Channel to link France with England. In 1802 the French engineer Albert Mathieu presented the first project but this was abandoned because of the British fear that a tunnel would weaken national defence. After World War II and the beginning of the formation of a united Europe, a Channel tunnel became a serious proposition. The first real digging of the tunnel began in 1974, in a project essentially financed by the governments of the two countries. However, after some 560 metres had been dug on the English side, the British Labour government cancelled the project in January 1975 for economic reasons, as cost estimates had risen by 200%. In 1981, with the Conservatives in power under Margaret Thatcher, the idea of building the tunnel was revised. In January 1986 the British and French governments awarded the Channel tunnel project to a joint British–French consortium called the Transmanche-Link (TML). On the British side this consortium consisted of five construction companies and two banks (Balfour Beatty Construction, Costain UK, Tarmac Construction, Taylor Woodrow Construction, George Wimpey International, National Westminster Bank, and Midland Bank), and on the French side five construction firms and three banks (Bouygues, Dumez, Société Auxiliaire d'Entreprises, Société Générale d'Entreprises Sainrapt et Brice, Spie Batignolles, Banque Nationale de Paris, Crédit Lyonnais, and Banque Indosuez). The project was to build a tunnel complex drilling from both countries, meeting in the middle under the Channel.

Although work on the tunnel started in 1986 to link Cheriton near Folkestone, England, to Coquelles, France, the real work, or the tunnel-boring work started on 15 December 1987 by eleven tunnel-boring machines (TBMs), six on the British side, and five on the French. On the UK side these drilling machines, which cost on average £7 million ($10 million) and weighing 1350 tons were lowered in pieces down a shaft of 110 m deep and 10 m in diameter and assembled in a specially built erection chamber. On the French side, the TBMs were launched from an open access shaft 75 m deep and 55 m in diameter. After the tunnelling work was completed, several of the TBMs were left buried in the ground and concreted over, as the expense of lifting and storing them was considered too high. The drilling work included two parallel rail tunnels each of almost 50 km in length and 7.6 m in diameter and a middle service tunnel of the same length but a smaller diameter of 4.8 m. Some 38 km of the tunnel is under the Channel, which at the deepest point is 130 m below sea level. At every 375 m along the length of the tunnel there are security link passages of 3.3 m diameter which link the rail tunnels to the service tunnel. Also, at one- and two-third points the rail tunnels enter submarine caverns constructed to allow trains to cross from one rail tunnel to another to permit maintenance on one or the other tunnels. These caverns are each 164 m long by 21 m wide and 15 m high and are the largest ever to be excavated under the sea. (These caverns were used much earlier than anticipated when a fire in the tunnel put one of the running tunnels out of action for several months in 1998.)

On the British side, the tunnel was drilled through homogeneous chalk marl and water-bearing folded strata on the French side. This latter rock formation caused drilling difficulties and subsequent project delays. Excavated material from each side of the tunnels amounted to some 4.3 million m^3. The tunnels were lined with 800,000 pre-cast concrete segments put in place by the TBMs as they moved forward in the drilling operation. These concrete segments each weighed between one and nine tons and fitted together to make a ring. The UK segments were made at a special casting yard at the Isle of Grain in Kent from high-quality granite aggregate which was delivered by ship from a special quarry near Fort William in Scotland. There is an equivalent of 450 km of fluid pipes in the tunnel supported by over 100,000 fixing brackets and over 950 km of overhead power cables to supply electricity for the trains. The power consumption for the trains is in excess of 160 MW or the equivalent of the consumption of electricity, at peak times, of a town of 0.25 million people. In addition, there are 20,000 light fittings in the tunnel and 1300 km of electrical cable to distribute power underground.

The Channel Tunnel project was also the construction of a terminal at Folkestone, UK, and one in Coquelles, France. Each terminal includes four multi-span over-bridges 350 m long to allow rapid loading and unloading of road vehicles from the shuttle trains. In addition, there are 17 other bridges in England and 11 in France related to the terminal and its infrastructure plus 115,000 m^3 of block-paved surfacing for platforms, ramps, carparks, and walking areas.

The Channel Tunnel project was completed in December 1993. The tunnels stretch 50 km from terminal to terminal and the final total cost including the terminals, rolling stock etc. was some £7.2 billion ($10.3 billion). The construction cost of the tunnel itself was £2.7 billion ($3.9 billion). At the peak of construction there were some 15,000 employees and costs were exceeding £4 million ($5.7 million) a day. The train shuttle service, which carries cars and heavy vehicles, has a departure every 15 minutes at peak times from each terminal with a minimum departure of one an hour at other times. In addition to the shuttle, Eurostar is a 140 kph passenger rail service using the tunnel to link Paris with London.

The Channel Tunnel was not only unique because of its design, construction, logistics, and material movement but also because of the unprecedented scale of financing the project. As part of the project's acceptance, there was to be no government financing. At the early part of the project, in September 1986 an initial equity of £46 million ($66 million) was subscribed by the Transmanche partners. This was increased by a £206 million ($294 million) private institutional placement in October. In May 1987 the European Investment Bank agreed to lend £1 billion ($1.4 billion) for the project. In early November 1987 a syndicated bank loan and letter of credit facility was arranged for funds totalling £5 billion ($7 billion) and later that same month a public share offer raised a further £700 million ($1 billion) from investors in France, Britain, and a few other countries. In May 1990 a further £300 million ($430 million) loan was obtained from the European Investment Bank and in October that same year Eurotunnel signed an agreement for a £1.8 billion ($2.6 billion) additional bank credit facilities. In December 1990 a rights issue raised a further £566 million ($808 million) and later in November 1991 Eurotunnel signed a long-term loan facility for £200 million ($286 million) with the European Coal and Steel Community.

The Channel Tunnel was a success in that a tremendous engineering feat had been achieved overcoming some enormous physical hurdles. However, financially the project was not so successful. The financing and subsequent refinancing of the loans even after the opening of the tunnel has put the project heavily in to debt. Any income from the tunnel operators, the joint British–French company, Eurotunnnel SA, has gone towards repayment of this debt. In 2001 it was operating at a loss. In 2000 the company posted an operating loss of £173 million ($158.4 million) which compared to an operating loss of £193.6 million ($177.3 million).[6] The channel tunnel operation will remain in private hands until 2052 when it reverts to the control of the French and British governments.

Adapted from: *Eurotunnel: The Illustrated Journey,*[7] and *Eurostar*[8]

Contracts in a project

Types of contract

For external projects, involving several parties, most projects are backed up by some form of a written contract which contains all the terms and conditions of the work including the schedule and financial payments. Contracts can take many forms depending on the work involved and the requirements, or demands, of both the contractor and the client. The financial terms could be fixed price, a guaranteed maximum with an incentive clause, or cost plus. In all of these contracts there may be a penalty clause and a holdback provision. The type of contract executed between the client and contractor of the services depends very much on the market conditions at the time the agreement is signed. If the demand for contractor services is high, as was the case in the 1970s, then the contractor may be able to sell a contract that is financially more attractive to his firm. However, if the market for services is poor, as was the case in 2000, then the financial conditions are more attractive for the client. When the demand for services is low, competition is very tough and the contractor may bid for the work at, or even below cost, such that little or no net income is generated. The strategy behind this approach is to avoid having to terminate key employees, but to retain them on the payroll in anticipation for the next forecast upswing in market demand. (Chapter 10 discusses some of the economic factors related to forecasting market demand.)

The next sections describe types of contract, the penalty clause and the holdback provision using a scenario where a Contractor A performs a project for a Client B.

Fixed price or lump sum contract

In a fixed price, or lump sum contract, Contractor A agrees to do the work for a fixed sum of money for Client B. In this case, the work must be well defined so that the contractor's allowance for risk, which may be his only profit potential, is reasonable and fair to both parties. For large projects, the fixed price may include the total project costs of engineering, purchasing, labour, material, and construction costs. Small engineering design, or consulting work is often performed under a fixed price contract as the work is usually of relatively short duration, can be well defined, and thus presents a low risk. Here the fixed price would cover all labour and material costs, plus an allowance for profit. With a fixed price contract, the budget level is critical to Contractor A because if things go poorly, and the budget is exceeded, this will eat into his profit margin and may even result in a financial loss. If things go well, then Contractor A stands to gain. When projects are of a long duration, poorly defined or with uncertainties, contractors resist offering terms under a fixed price contract because of the risk.

Guaranteed maximum with an incentive clause

A guaranteed maximum contract, with an incentive clause, is one that has a guaranteed maximum price to the client but if the project is completed in less than this amount then both the client and the contractor share in any cost savings. This might for example be according to an 80/20 or 75/25% client/contractor split. As an illustration, Contractor A has a contract with Client B for a project at a guaranteed maximum price of $45,000,000. In the agreement there is an incentive clause for an 80/20 savings on any under-runs based on the guaranteed maximum. Assume the project is subsequently completed for $43,000,000, or an under-run of $2,000,000. Thus, Contractor A receives $43,400,000 for the project, or $400,000 more than the actual price (20% * $2,000,000) and Client B saves $1,600,000 (80% * $2,000,000) from the guaranteed maximum. This is a win–win situation for both parties where both had an incentive to do everything to complete the work for a lower amount. However, if the guaranteed maximum is exceeded, then it is Contractor A who absorbs the difference.

Guaranteed maximum contracts are used when the project scope cannot initially be well defined. This might be, for example, when the project is a commercial plant whose design is being scaled up from a pilot plant design. Trying to establish a fixed price under these circumstances is difficult and would involve too great a risk for both the client and the contractor. The guaranteed maximum contract provides the client with a cost ceiling, yet an under-run potential to encourage both the client and contractor to define the work early in the project, and then, most importantly, not to keep changing the scope during the engineering and design phase. Changes during the engineering and design phase are the worst situation a contractor has to deal with because it destroys the efficient flow of information through the organization. Design changes in the construction of the Sydney Opera House in Australia were one of the reasons the building cost some $58 million (US) up from an original estimate of $7 million.[9]

Cost plus contract

A cost plus contract is basically when Contractor A contracts to do the work for Client B at Contractor A's cost plus a specified percentage amount above cost to cover overhead and profit. This would be for large projects, and when the time period is long such that material and labour costs may be changing, giving cause to greater risk. For a cost plus contract, over-budget is perhaps more financially onerous to the client. However, over-budget can impair client–contractor relationships obliging the contractor perhaps to take part of the financial loss.

Penalty clause

The purpose of the penalty clause in the contract is to put pressure on Contractor A to ensure that the work is finished according to the time schedule. The penalty clause stipulates that if Contractor A is unable to meet the contractual finish date, then Contractor A is obliged to pay a financial penalty to Client B. For example, suppose Client B contracts with Contractor A to build an office block for which tenants have already agreed to lease the facility. If the building were late in its completion, then the owner (Client B) would lose rental fees in addition perhaps having to pay unplanned interest on borrowed capital used to finance the project. The objective of the penalty clause is to offset these revenue losses and interest payments because of delays from the agreed date.

Holdback provision

The holdback provision is a clause to provide a guarantee that the project is completed according to the specified quality levels and performs according to expectations as expressed in the contract. The holdback provision is usually a financial amount equal to a percentage of the project cost, or a fixed sum of money. For large projects a holdback provision would be typically 5 to 10% of the project cost and about 15% for small projects. Client B holds this subsequent financial amount back until he has checked out and is satisfied that the completed project meets expectations. Normally, the Client B has a time limit of, perhaps, 90 days, when he must reply in writing, to the Contractor A, to 'sign off' completely on the project, that is to say that he is completely satisfied. In which case, he is obligated to pay the holdback amount to Contractor A. If not, the Client B indicates in writing the areas of non-conformity, which then have to be resolved by Contractor A. When all the conditions are satisfied, the holdback amount is eventually paid to Contractor A.

Phases of a project

Work packages

Some projects, very often because of their magnitude, are released in phases, or work packages. Projects for the US or European government, or other government agencies, are very often awarded in phases. The following are some reasons.

Project modification

A phased project, gives the client (the government agency) an opportunity to make modifications, or even cancel the project should market conditions change. For example, in the late 1970s when oil prices started to rise to around $30 per barrel because of cut-backs from Middle East suppliers, many energy projects were awarded in the USA and Canada to produce oil from tar sands, and gas from coal. However, when the crisis ended, oil prices dropped and most of these projects were cancelled. Some were only in the engineering stage, but some were in construction. In June 1997, in France, the newly elected socialist government cancelled the construction of the Rhine–Rhône canal, a project that had been approved by the previous right-wing government.

Level the workload

If one contractor is given one phase of the project and another phase is given to a different contractor this shares out the workload among companies. This approach is a strong consideration in government contracts as the government is interest in maintaining equitable employment levels.

Ethics

Splitting the work of a large project between several parties helps to keep all the work 'above board'. That is, unethical practices particularly in purchasing should be eliminated or at least minimized. (See Chapter 16.)

Splitting a project into phases adds to the cost and the completion time of the project since it involves coordination between different organizations, which is more onerous than if only one outfit were involved.

Proposal stage

The proposal stage, or pre-project, is where a proposal is made to the client describing how the supplier firm (engineering and construction company, for example) proposes to perform the project. Some of the key elements in the project proposal would include:

- the estimated cost or budget for the project
- the schedule of the activities or a realistic estimate of when the project will be completed
- details such as resumes and letters of recommendations of the key persons who will be working on the project, including at least the project manager, senior engineers and procurement personnel
- a draft contract for the project that would include things such as a payment schedule and a penalty clause if the project were not completed according to schedule, and budget.

Design and conception

Once the project is awarded, the first phase is the design and the conception of the project. This would involve preliminary designs and estimates, and development of the overall project schedule, which at this point would then be considered quite definite.

Detailed design

This second phase of the project might be for, say, in the case of a plant construction project, the detailed design including flow diagrams, piping and instrument diagrams, site planning, facility layout, detailed cost estimates, labour requirements, etc. The detailed design is performed using three-dimensional computer displays, which can be provided to the client at the end of the project.

Construction

If a project involves a completed structure then construction is the final phase when all of the design work is translated into building the facility. It is at this phase of the project when the site is prepared, all purchased equipment arrives, and there is a heavy concentration of field craftsmen (electricians, mechanical personnel, riggers, etc.). The early part of the construction phase, such as site preparation, may be carried out in parallel with design work.

Mechanical completion, startup and handover phase

Mechanical completion is when the project or the facility is finally finished. This is immediately followed by the startup, test run, or acceptance phase. In the case of a chemical plant or a manufacturing facility the test run is when all the machines and equipment are put

into operation and before the client accepts the facility he would verify that the design, operation, product specifications, throughput, noise level, appearance, etc., are all according to the specifications detailed in the contract. From the author's own experience, this last phase can be a very stressful time between the contractor and client. The contractor believes he has provided the maximum and the client wants the maximum. But very often the maximum of the client's expectations does not exactly equal the maximum of the contractor's believed best efforts.

Project organization

A project team is made up from appropriate personnel in the supplier firm who have experience on that type of project work such as an oil refinery, a chemicals plant, a food processing facility, a nuclear power plant, a road bridge, a sky scraper, etc. On projects where the client firm and the supplier are from different organizations, such as for example, an engineering and construction firm building a brewery for Heineken in the Netherlands, then the client (Heineken) might want to approve the key personnel proposed to work on his project.

Consider, for example, a major construction project such as a dam, office complex, chemical plant, automobile assembly facility, then key members of the team would include the following, as illustrated in Figure 18.1.

Project manager

The project manager is the key individual in the project. This person is the direct contact with the client, the interface between the client and top manager of his own organization, and responsible for managing the financial budget, controlling the project schedule, and ultimately responsible for the quality of the work. Depending on the size of the work, the project manager may be the contact with the subcontractors. This lead position of the project manager, with many cross-functional contacts, gives the person very high visibility within the organization and often commands an attractive salary. Although all this is accompanied with a certain amount of stress since there is a heavy burden of responsibility.

Engineers

The engineers whether their discipline is chemical, mechanical, structural or civil usually form the nucleus

Figure 18.1 Organization chart for an engineering and construction project

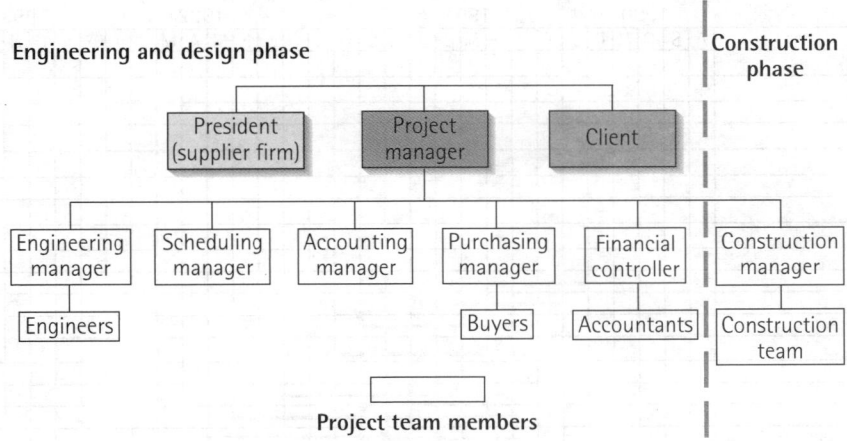

of a project organization. It is these persons who perform the preliminary and detailed design, and later might work with field construction personnel to see the project is being built according to design specifications.

Scheduler

The scheduler is the person who monitors the day-to-day progress of the work. It is this individual who communicates with the project manager when the schedule falls behind or is ahead of plan. If it is behind schedule then it is the project manager's responsibility to decide what can be done to bring the project back on schedule. Or, if the project is ahead of schedule how can resources be efficiently utilized.

Purchasing personnel

Purchasing personnel are those that handle all the purchasing of raw materials, equipment, and of other services such as transport, restaurant facilities, and the like. The purchasing people are the main contact with the suppliers and are responsible for assuring that material, equipment, and services arrive according to the schedule and conform to the quality specification. (See also Chapter 16.)

Controller

The controller is the person responsible for all the financial management of the project. This will include the payment of bills for supplied material, contacting clients for invoice payments, managing day-to-day

disbursement of cash, and the payment of salaries and wages to those people working on the project.

Construction manager

The construction manager is responsible for the project once it reaches the activity in the field. Depending on the project, this might be in such harsh climates as Alaska, the Middle East, or South America. Construction managers are chosen for their international experience, their ability to manage and handle people, and their adaptation in often harsh conditions. The construction manager may be responsible for managing over 10,000 field craftsmen on a single project.

Scheduling and controlling

Once a project is defined, the principal task of the project team is to complete the project, within schedule, within budget, and according to design specifications. To monitor these activities, the project team reports on-time progress, project costs, and quality of the work to the project manager. The project manager, at his discretion, will then pass this information onto the client. The following are some scheduling tools that might be used.

Gantt charts

Horizontal bar charts are an application of Gantt charts (see also Chapter 14). As an illustration, Figure 18.2 gives a Gantt chart for a project that lasts some three years.

Figure 18.2 Gantt schedule for a high-density polyethylene plant

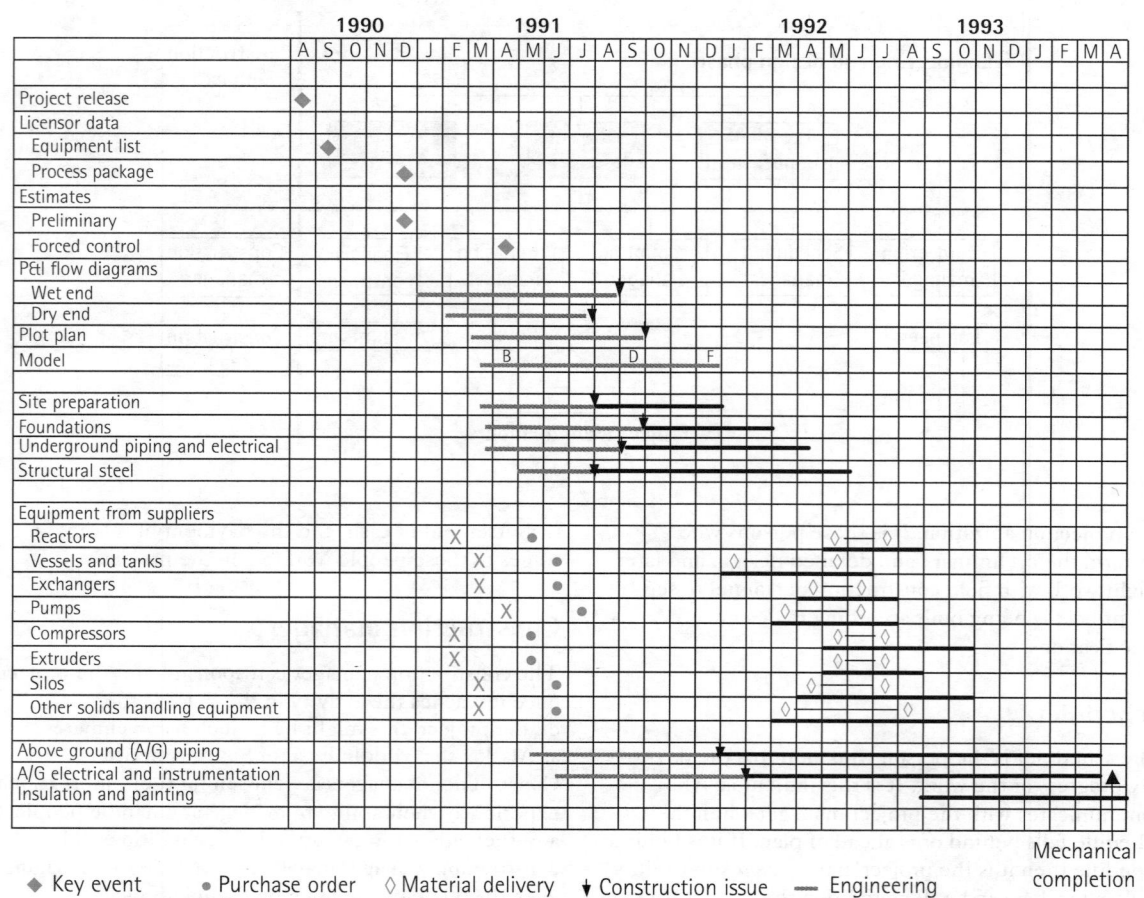

◆ Key event   ● Purchase order   ◇ Material delivery   ▼ Construction issue   — Engineering
— Construction   B Block model   D Design issue   F Final model review   X Request for quotation

Legend

The Gantt chart shows the timeframe of each activity illustrated by a horizontal bar. The legend is explained by Table 18.2.

Advantages of a Gantt chart

The advantages of a Gantt chart for a project is that it is:

- easy and not expensive to prepare
- easy to understand
- easy to modify, especially when computerized. For most large projects, firms have computerized Gantt-type charts. When one activity time is changed, this automatically adjusts associated activities.

Disadvantages of a Gantt chart

On complex projects, Gantt charts can become unwieldy and the charts may not indicate the relationship between the project activities.

Table 18.2 Explanation of terms in Gantt chart (2)

Key event	Start or end of phase; also known as a milestone
Purchase order	When a purchase order is made
Material delivery	When material must be delivered to the field or construction site
Construction issue	Construction activity of a phase
Engineering	Timeframe for engineering and/or design work
Construction	Timeframe for the construction work
Block model	Model ready for design

Figure 18.3 Monthly project expenditures

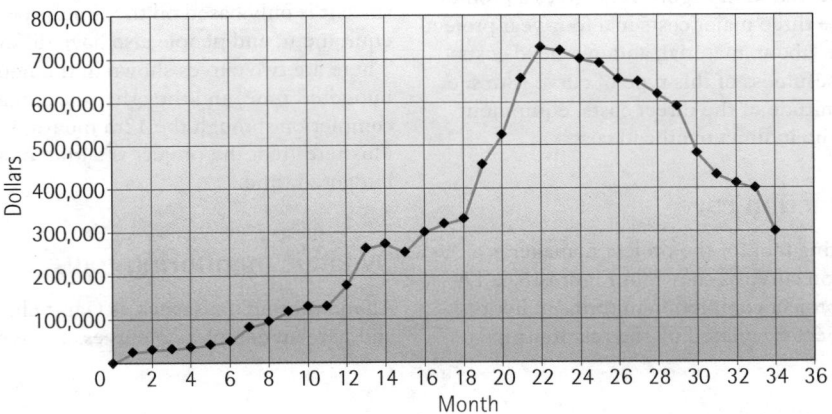

Figure 18.4 Cumulative project expenditures

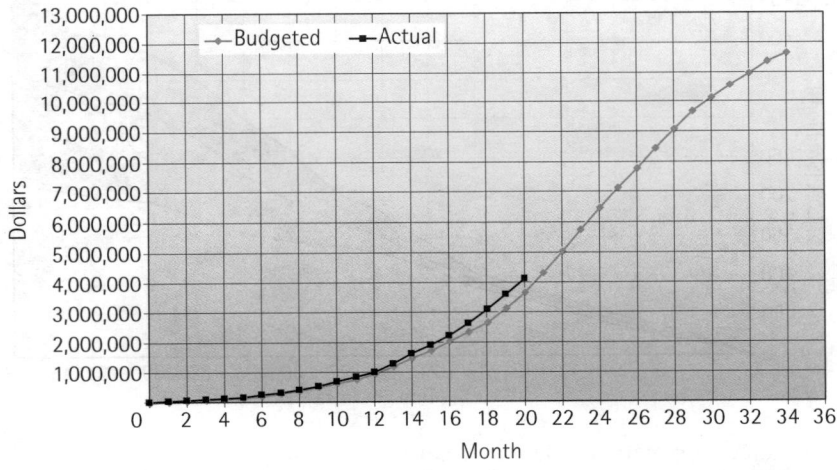

Project cost curves

Project cost curves are used for monitoring the expenditures of a project. The following three forms might be used.

Monthly budget curve

The monthly budget curve plots the planned expenditures for a project, as illustrated in Figure 18.3, which gives the budgeted monthly costs associated with the turnkey high-density polyethylene plant whose Gantt chart was presented earlier. This curve illustrates that at the early engineering phase of the project, costs rise relatively slowly. The principal costs here are salaries of the design engineers. As the project moves into the construction phase, cost starts to rise more rapidly as earth-moving work is started, heavy vehicles are purchased or rented, material equipment purchases

arrive, and there are the salaries of the numerous construction workers, and craftpeople in the field. At some point the monthly expenditures peak and then start to fall as the project approaches completion. Towards the end of the project, costs are more associated with personnel such as painters, and the startup crews.

Cumulative project cost curve

A project manager's responsibility is to see that expenditures are in control and for this purpose a cumulative project cost curve might be used as illustrated in Figure 18.4, which shows the budgeted cumulative cost curve, and also the actual costs incurred. A plot of the actual, expenditures, against budget is a clear way to see if the project is running according to schedule. Shown here, after the 20th week it is clear that the work is running above budget.

Project cost distribution

This curve, as illustrated in Figure 18.5, gives a profile of the cumulative three major costs in a four-year project showing how the labour, material, and overhead costs build up. The usefulness of this type of curve is to see the relative magnitude of the direct costs, equipment and labour, and the indirect overhead costs.

Percent completion curve

Another monitoring tool for the project manager is a project completion curve as shown in Figure 18.6. This curve gives the project completion in terms of hours spent on the project calculated by the relationship

(Number of people * Hours per month). This representation of the project is independent of the costs since it is only based on the time expended, there is no equipment, and people also have different salary rates. There are two curves shown in the figure, one for the budgeted time, and the other the actual percentage completion through the 12th month. Here the curve illustrates that the project is taking more than the budgeted time.

Dynamic monitoring tools

All monitoring tools, such as Gantt charts, cost curves, and percent completion curves, are dynamic in that they

Figure 18.5 Cost breakdown for a project

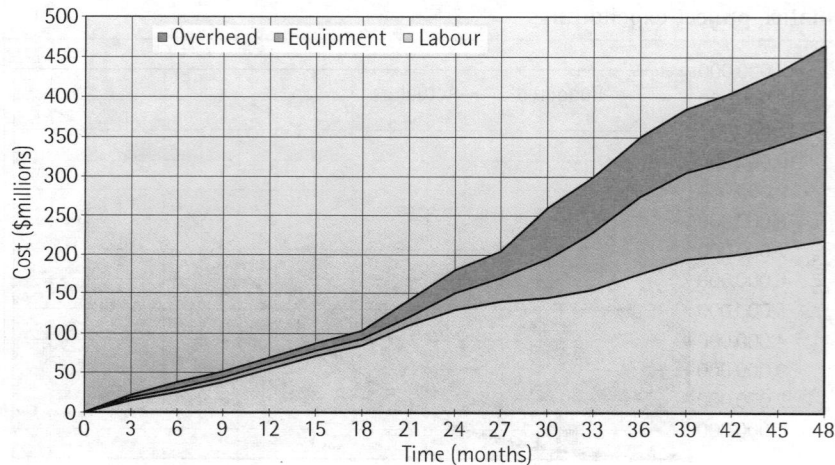

Figure 18.6 Percent project completion in terms of hours

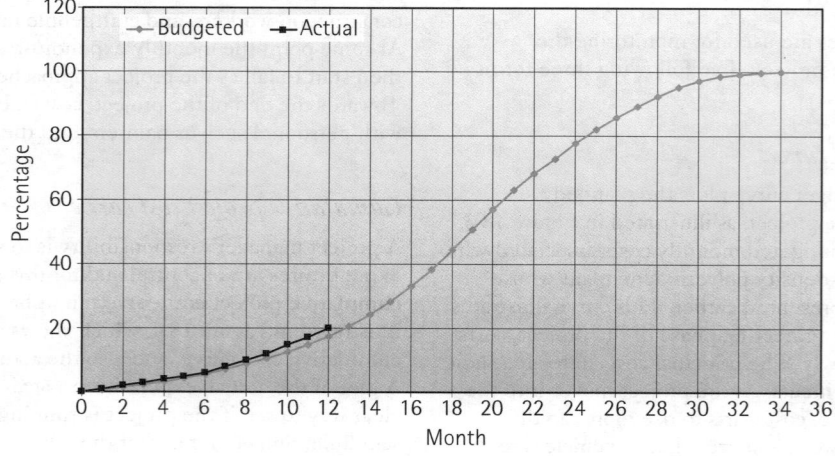

are modified according to changes in the project as work progresses. There may be modifications due to unforeseen circumstances, such as delays, bad weather, industrial disputes, etc. I was involved on a project when one of the barges delivering equipment for an ammonia plant sank! One of the reasons for the delay in the building of the Channel Tunnel was that the soil turned out to be much rockier than expected and this increased drilling, and thus overall construction time.

Network diagrams

Description

A network diagram is a flow sheet, which clearly indicates sequentially the various activities in a project and the estimated time involved to complete each activity. They are useful for projects, which have many activities and where on time completion is a key criterion. Network diagrams are dynamic computer-based systems that can be continually updated as a project proceeds and provide information such as:

- The date when the project should be finished.
- When each individual part, or activities, of the project is scheduled to start and finish.
- Which steps of the project are critical and must be completed on time in order that the overall project is not behind schedule.

- Where it might be possible to shift resources from non-critical sections of the project to more critical parts, or those that must be finished on time, without affecting the overall completion date of the project.
- From among the many sections of the project, where should management concentrate most of its effort in order that the budget and schedule are respected?

Terms in network diagrams

A network diagram is made up of arrows and nodes. There are two ways of presenting a project, one with the activity shown by an arrow, and the other with the activity represented by the node. Here the convention of the activity on the arrow is used and the following are key terms in such a network diagram. The terms are also illustrated in Figure 18.7.

Activity

An activity is a well-defined task in a project. It requires a certain time to complete and absorbs a portion of the project's financial budget. For example, in the construction of a building, the pouring of the foundations may be considered a specific activity. In the network diagram, an arrow represents an activity where the head of the arrow indicates the finish of the activity and the butt the start of the activity. The length of the arrow does not have to be related to the time duration of the activity.

Figure 18.7 Terms in a network diagram

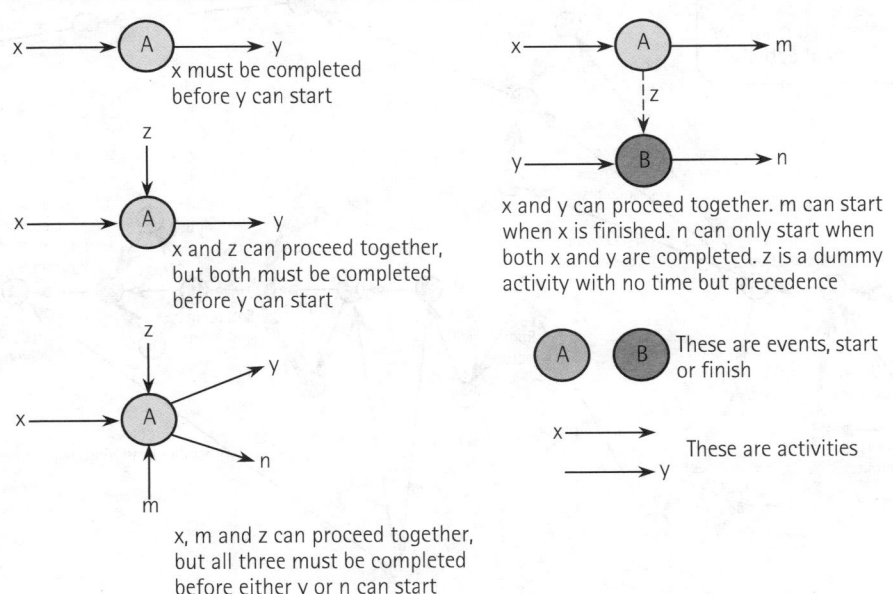

Beginning and ending activities in a project

A network diagram is constructed in a logical sequence, showing the beginning activities on the left of the flow scheme to the ending activities on the right-hand side. In describing the project, the sequence of the activities is defined indicating those that are an immediate predecessor of another activity. As such, in constructing the network diagram, the starting activities in the project would be those that have no preceding activities and the ending activities would be those that do not precede any other activities.

Event

An event is represented by a circle or node and occurs at the start or finish of an activity. The event has no time. An activity cannot start from a node until all the activities leading into that node have been completed.

Dummy activity

A dummy activity is a fictitious activity, which is included in a network diagram to indicate a precedence relationship. There is no time involved.

Path

A path is the route taken passing though several activities to arrive at a specific activity, or the end of the project.

Critical path

The critical path is the longest path in the network diagram.

Independence

An activity has only one path. It is assumed that the duration time of a path in an activity is independent of the duration time of another activity.

Completion

A project is not finished until all paths in the project have been completed. This means not just the critical path but also all other paths in the network diagram.

Network diagram for a house construction

Figure 18.8 illustrates in general the various activities in the design and construction of a house. Each activity is

Figure 18.8 Network diagram for the construction of a house

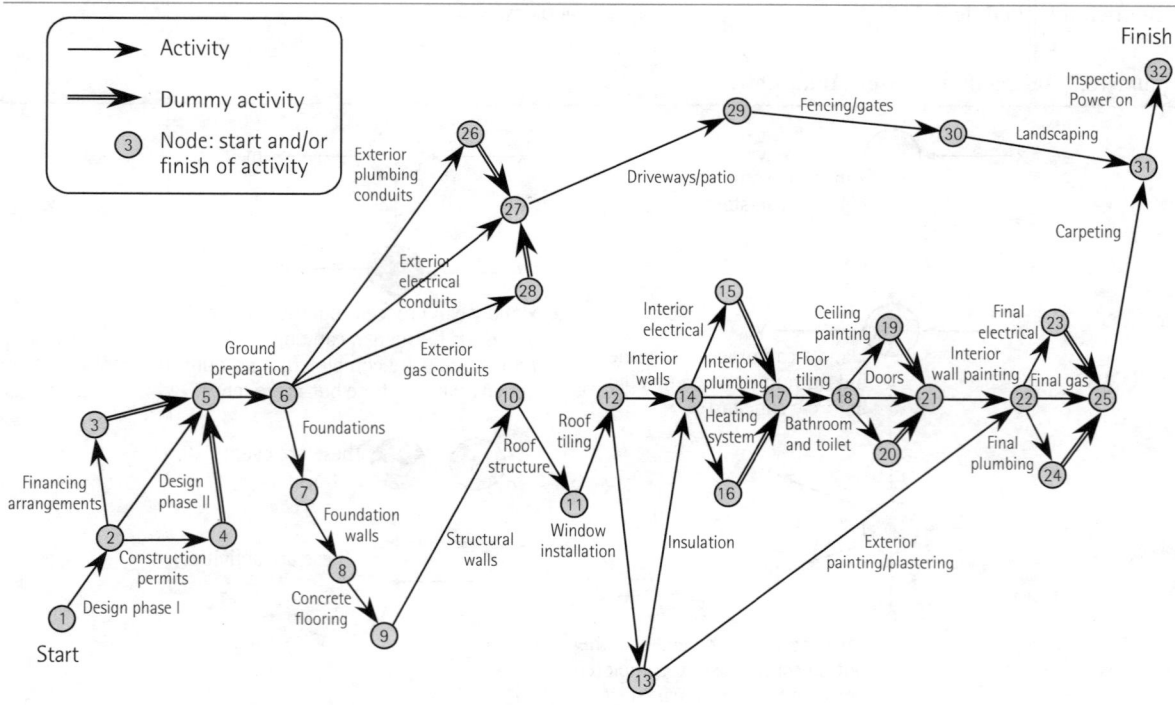

shown on the arrow, and the beginning and ending of activities are indicated on nodes 1 to 32. Dummy activities are also shown.

Critical path method

The critical path method (CPM) is a network diagram approach developed in 1957 by J E Kelly of Remington Rand and M R Walker of Du Pont to help schedule maintenance projects in chemical plants. It is useful for projects that have many activities and where on-time completion is imperative. CPM methods are dynamic systems that are continually updated as the project proceeds. The method uses single time estimates which are considered to be certain, or *deterministic*.[10]

Procedure in the CPM method

The following give the steps involved in using the CPM method.

1. In a sequential order, draw the network diagram indicating the beginning and ending events on a node, and the activities by an arrow. This gives a global overview of the complete project. By convention, the project starts on the left, and finishes on the right.
2. Show on the arrows the time duration (T) of each activity.
3. Starting from the left-hand side of the diagram for the first activities in the project, show as time zero the earliest start time (ES) for the activity on the butt of the arrow. Calculate the earliest finish time (EF) for these activities which is given by the earliest start time plus the activity duration (EF = ES + T). Show this time on the head of the arrow.
4. Continue the procedure in step 3 for the entire network, using as the earliest start time for a following activity the earliest finish time for an immediate preceding activity. For the last activities in the project, the largest of the earliest finish time will be the earliest time that the project can be completed. It is also the latest time that the project can be finished.
5. Starting now from the right-hand side, or at the end of the project, and using the latest finish time (LF) determine the latest start time (LS) for each activity by deducting the duration of the activity (LS = LF − T).
6. Continue the procedure in step 5 until the start of the project is reached and all the latest start times have been determined.
7. For each activity, determine the difference between the latest finish time and the earliest finish time.

This will give the slack time for each activity. Alternatively, the slack can be calculated from the difference between the latest start and the earliest start time.
8. Where an activity has a slack time of zero, then this is an activity on the critical path.
9. The critical path for the project is the one where all the activities have a slack time of zero.

Demonstrating the concept 18.1 illustrates the principle of the critical path method.

Program evaluation and review technique

The program evaluation and review technique (PERT) was developed in 1958 jointly by Lockheed Aircraft, the US Navy Special projects office, and the consulting firm of Booz, Allen, & Hamilton. It was specifically directed at planning and controlling the Polaris missile programme which was a project involving 250 prime or major contractors and over 900 subcontractors.[11]

PERT is similar to the CPM method regarding functions, network diagrams, internal calculations, and resulting project management reports. One exception is that it considers the uncertainty of the duration of activities by incorporating different time estimates and this leads to probability situations. The time estimates for activities are developed from people who are familiar with the type of project work and can take on one of three values, a, m, and b, as illustrated in Table 18.3.

Beta probability distribution

A beta probability distribution as illustrated in Figure 18.9 is commonly used in PERT. Unlike a

Table 18.3 Time estimate values

Time	Explanation
a	This is the optimistic time, or when things go very well. For example, all equipment is delivered on time, there are no quality problems, and the weather is good so that there are no construction delays
b	This is the pessimistic time, or worst conditions when many things go wrong. For example, suppliers are late, unexpected repairs and corrections have to be made, and bad weather delays the construction fieldwork
m	This is the most likely time, or the consensus of the best estimate under 'average' project operating conditions

normal distribution for example, the beta distribution has the properties that all the data are entirely contained within a finite interval. (There will always be a finite optimistic time and a finite pessimistic time.) The beta distribution has no predetermined shape, such as the bell shape of the normal curve, and takes the shape or is skewed, according to the time estimates. The mean duration time, t, and the variance of the distribution, σ^2, can be approximated from the optimistic, the pessimistic, and the most likely time estimates as shown in the following. (See also Chapter 27.)

Mean or expected time, t, for an activity is given by:

$$t = \frac{a + 4m + b}{6}$$

Variance is given by the relationship:

$$\sigma^2 = \left[\frac{(b-a)}{6}\right]^2 = \frac{(b-a)^2}{36}$$

The standard deviation for the activity is the square root of the variance or:

$$\sigma = \sqrt{\sigma^2} = \left[\frac{(b-a)}{6}\right]$$

The magnitude of the variance reflects the degree of uncertainty associated with the time of an activity. An activity with a variance of 20 would have more uncertainty with respect to its actual duration, than one with a variation of 5. The standard deviation of each activity's time is estimated as one-sixth of the difference between the pessimistic and optimistic times. This is analogous to all the area under a normal distribution, which lies within ±3 standard deviations of the mean, or a range of six standard deviations. (See Chapter 27.)

The standard deviation, or variance, can be computed for each path by summing the individual variances, or

standard deviations for each activity path. This enables project managers, or schedulers to make probabilistic estimates of the project completion times. For example:

- The probability a project will be completed with 15 months of start is 92%.
- The probability that project will take longer than 18 months is 3%.

These statements are based on assumption that the path duration is a random variable that is normally distributed around the expected path time. This is true for large samples, and can be considered approximately true for smaller samples.

Demonstrating the concept 18.2 illustrates the use of the PERT method. (Since this example uses the principle of probabilities, Chapter 27 may be helpful.)

Advantages of network diagrams

Using network diagrams has the following advantages:

- They force a project manager to organize, and quantify, available information, and to recognize where and what additional information is needed.
- They provide a visual display of the project, and its associated activities.
- They identify activities that should be closely watched because of the potential for delaying the project.
- They identify activities that have slack time and so can be delayed without affecting the project completion time. This identification gives the possibility of reallocating resources in order to optimize costs.

Limitations of network diagrams

There are limitations, and caution should be exercised when using network diagrams:

- They are time consuming, and, therefore, costly. However, this is usually outweighed by their advantage since their cost is a small proportion of the project cost.
- The established precedence relationships may not be correct and this could upset the project schedule.
- The time estimates are sometimes difficult to estimate, although similar past projects are useful in helping in this respect.
- The probabilistic capabilities of PERT are open to criticism. It is difficult enough to make one good time estimate for each activity as in CPM and making three accurate time estimates in PERT, each with a different meaning, is even more complicated. For this reason PERT is more costly than CPM both in direct financial terms of dollars and the management effort.

Figure 18.9 Beta distribution for a PERT diagram

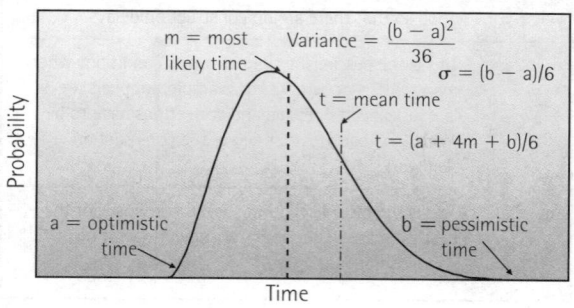

Computerized systems

Today, the network diagram systems are computerized and there are many packages for CPM and PERT methods on the market by such firms as Microsoft, Primavera, and IBM.

Accelerating (crashing) a project

Concept

Many projects have the habit of running behind schedule for a variety of reasons – suppliers are late, employees are sick, the weather is bad, etc. As such in order to bring the project back on schedule, project managers may be required, to accelerate, or 'crash', the project. Acceleration means to reduce the duration of the project, which means also additional costs. Project managers would particularly consider this option if the project were in danger of running over schedule when there was a penalty clause in the contract. Another situation could be that the project is on schedule but for some reason the client would like to have it finished sooner. Some of the options that are available to accelerate a project include the following:

- Putting existing personnel on overtime, including weekends and night.
- Hiring additional personnel.
- Subcontracting out some portions of the project.
- Expediting materials if this is a reason for the delay.
- Renting more heavy equipment such as cranes, front-end loaders, trucks etc.

The principle of crashing is illustrated in Figure 18.10. In this illustration a particular project has a normal duration of ten weeks for a total cost of $300,000. The project can be reduced to duration of three weeks and the cost would be now $1,000,000. Thus, for a reduction in time of seven weeks the cost has increased by $700,000. The illustration here shows a linear reduction, which may not necessarily be the case.

Network diagrams and crashing

In a project that has several activities that can be crashed or accelerated, the following are the general rules to adopt:

1. Crash only critical activities in the network.
2. Do not crash non-critical activities, as this will not reduce the project's overall duration. (This is a similar concept to not increasing the capacity of a non-bottleneck work post in an operation, as discussed in Chapter 27.)
3. Start by crashing activities with the lowest crashing cost per unit of time and continue until the desired project duration is achieved.
4. When parallel critical paths exist, each of the parallel paths must be reduced, since compressing only one of the paths will not reduce the overall project duration.

To crash a project successfully, one examines the network, not its activities, and compares normal costs with crash costs for each activity. The objective is to find those activities on the critical path where time can be cut substantially with minimum expenditures. The objective is the greatest time reduction for the least increase in project cost.

Demonstrating the concept 18.3 illustrates the principle of crashing a project.

Figure 18.10 **Principle of accelerating (crashing) a project**

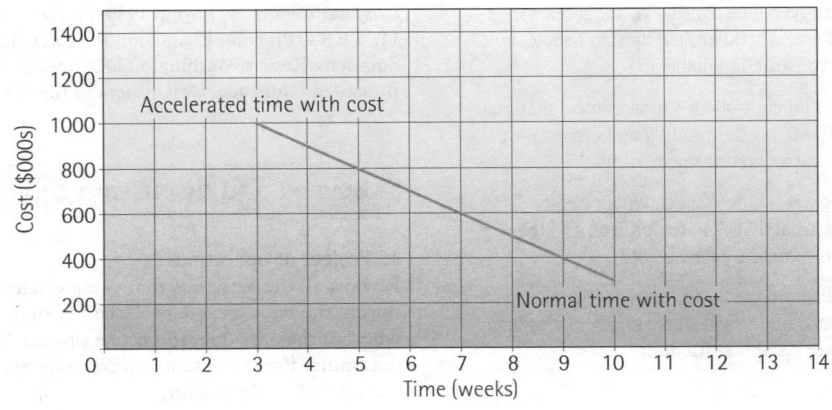

Summary of key elements

• A project is a unique item of work. Project management is the planning, scheduling, budgeting, and control of this work using an integrated team.

• A project might be classified as complex with unknown elements; large with standard elements; intermediate; or small. These generally will decrease in cost and completion time.

• Elements of a project include a well-defined objective, a plan, a schedule giving a start and finish date, a dedicated project team, and a financial budget.

• A turnkey, or grassroots, project is completely new, and constructed on a virgin site.

• Projects, operations, and the supply chain are related. A project is often the start of operations. Project activities are similar to operating functions. A project team may be composed of operating personnel. When a project is terminated, some of the project team may become operators. There are projects encountered in the operations environment. New products involve projects. A physical unit in the supply chain was once a project.

• Contracts in a project might be some form of a fixed price or lump sum contract, a guaranteed maximum contract with an incentive clause, or a cost-plus contract. All contracts might contain a penalty clause, and a holdback provision.

• Projects, particularly when government entities are involved, are awarded in phases, or work packages. This permits modifications if market conditions should change, levels the workload among firms, and may help to avoid unethical practices.

• The stages of a project move from proposal, design and conception, detailed design, construction, and mechanical completion, through to start-up or hand-over phase.

• A project organization is composed of a project manager, who has overall responsibility, and a team perhaps of engineers, schedulers, purchasing people, a controller, and a construction manager.

• For scheduling and controlling a project tools that may be used include Gantt charts, monthly and project cost curves, and percent completion curves.

• A network diagram is a flow sheet, which clearly indicates the various activities in the project, and the estimated time to complete each activity.

• In a network diagram the critical path is the longest path in the network, and this is where a project manager should concentrate his or her attention.

• The critical path method (CPM) in network diagrams uses single time estimates for activities. Under this criterion it is a deterministic method.

• The programme evaluation and review technique (PERT) method in network diagrams uses optimistic, pessimistic, and most likely time estimates based on a beta distribution. As such the PERT method is probabilistic.

• Crashing a project involves using additional resources such as overtime, subcontracting, expediting, and hiring additional personnel to reduce the time duration of a project.

Notes and references

1. 'Le barrage d'Assouan menace les temples de Nubie' (The Aswan Dam threatens the Nubian temples), *Chronique du vingtième siècle*, Larousse, Paris, 1990, p. 970

2. 'Le barrage d'Assouan est terminé' (The Aswan Dam is finished), *Chronique du vingtième siècle*, Larousse, Paris, 1990, p. 1063

3. 'Un pipeline en Alaska' (A pipeline in Alaska), *Médiathèque: Cent ans d'histoire contemporaine – Les années 70* (100 years of contemporary history – the 1970s), Société Générale d'Edition et de Diffusion (SGED), Paris, France, 1998. (From the original version, Bertelssmann, Germany), p. 160

4. Ex-Im Bank, http://www.exim.gov/3gorges.html, 5 June 1996

5. Based on a study project by the author with the Groupe Schneider, Dijon, France, February–June 2001

6. 'Eurotunnel posts a narrower loss', *International Herald Tribune*, 20 February 2001, p. 16

7. WILSON, Jeremy and SPICK, Jerome, *Eurotunnel: The Illustrated Journey*, Harper Collins, London, 1994

8. PIELOW, Simon, *Eurostar*, Ian Allan Publishing, Shepperton, England, 1997

9. 'After 25 years, Sydney embraces Jorn Utzon', *International Herald Tribune*, 28 September 2000

10. KELLY, James E. and WALKER, Morgan R., 'Critical path planning and scheduling', *Proceedings of the Eastern Joint Computer Conference*, Boston 1959, pp 160–73

11. PERT, Program Evaluation Research Task, Phase I Summary Report, Washington DC, Special Projects Office, Bureau of Ordnance, Department of the Navy

Review and discussion topics

1. Project or operations?
Review all the activities that you are scheduled to do during the next six months. Classify them according to whether they are operations or a project. Justify your reasoning. For those that you consider are projects, develop a Gantt scheduling chart.

2. Project proposal

Consider that you are developing a client proposal for the following projects. Indicate the major sections and the type of information that you would include in the proposal. What would be some of the important elements in the contract? What financial terms might you propose?

(a) A marketing study concerning the construction of a polyethylene plant in the Middle East

(b) the construction of a new motorway linking two major cities

(c) the design and construction of a nuclear repository in Greenland for nuclear waste from nuclear warheads originating in the USA and the former USSR (a consideration by the government in Greenland).

3. Network diagrams

A network diagram is a series of nodes (events) connected by arrows (activities). Develop a network diagram of your planned, or desired, strategy for your life. This should include your strategy for both your personal and professional endeavours. What are some of the risks and uncertainties involved?

4. Project manager

Discuss what you believe should be some of the important criteria for the selection of a project manager for the following types of project. Consider some of the elements that would be included in the project:

(a) the construction of an automobile facility in China

(b) a marketing study for the development and introduction of a new pharmaceutical product for the European market

(c) a European-government sponsored project for environmental improvement in the European Union.

5. Technology and project management

Discuss areas in which you think technology is able to improve the function of project management. Consider the activity from a global perspective, including all functions managed by the project manager.

6. Project acceleration or crashing

This chapter deals with ways in which a project's duration can be reduced (accelerated or crashed). Discuss the impact of the various possibilities on a project and their implications for the project supply chain.

Demonstrating the concept 18.1 Enviroteck Co.

Situation

The Enviroteck Co. wishes to construct a pilot plant north of Sitges, Spain, for the treatment of domestic waste. The activities for this project are as shown in Table 18.4.

Required

1. Identify the critical path. What is the minimum time to complete this project?
2. How can several activities be managed if personnel were limited?

Solution

1. Network diagram and activity times
   • The network diagram is completed respecting the precedence for each activity and the duration times for each activity is indicated on this network diagram. This information is shown in Figure 18.11.

Table 18.4 Enviroteck Co.: Domestic waste treatment activities

	Activity	Duration (weeks)	Activity immediately preceding
A	Equipment delivery	6	None
B	Site preparation	10	None
C	Development of control systems	14	A
D	Equipment assembly	8	A
E	Underground connections	6	B
F	Process connections	18	B
G	Training of operating team	10	C
H	Delivery and preparation of raw materials	12	F
I	Installation and equipment checkout	6	D, E

Figure 18.11 Enviroteck Co.: Network with activities and duration

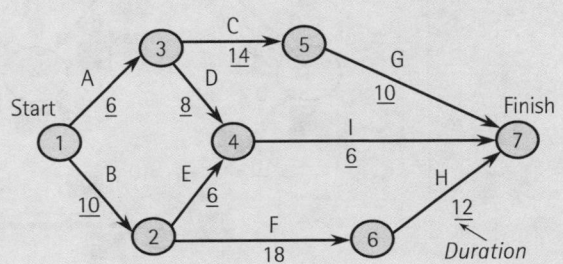

This network diagram and the activity duration times are used to calculate the earliest start and finish times, the latest start and finish times, and the slack times. The calculation is shown on the Excel spreadsheet in Table 18.5 and then illustrated in Figure 18.12. The explanation is as follows.

Earliest times
• The earliest start time and the earliest finish time are determined for each activity. It is assumed that the earliest start time for the beginning of the project is 0. The earliest finish time is given by the sum of the earliest start time and the activity duration.

Table 18.5 Enviroteck Co.: Network data

		Duration (weeks)	Activity immediately preceding	Earliest start date	Earliest finish date	Latest start date	Latest finish date	Slack time (weeks)
A	Equipment delivery	6	None	0	6	10	16	10
B	Site preparation	10	None	0	10	0	10	0
C	Development of control systems	14	A	6	20	16	30	10
D	Equipment assembly	8	A	6	14	26	34	20
E	Underground connections	6	B	10	16	28	34	18
F	Process connections	18	B	10	28	10	28	0
G	Training of operating team	10	C	20	30	30	40	10
H	Delivery and preparation of raw materials	12	F	28	40	28	40	0
I	Installation and equipment checkout	6	D, E	16	22	34	40	18

Critical path	B-F-H
Project completion time	40 weeks
Total slack time	**86 weeks**

Figure 18.12 Enviroteck Co.: Network with activities, duration, start, and finish times

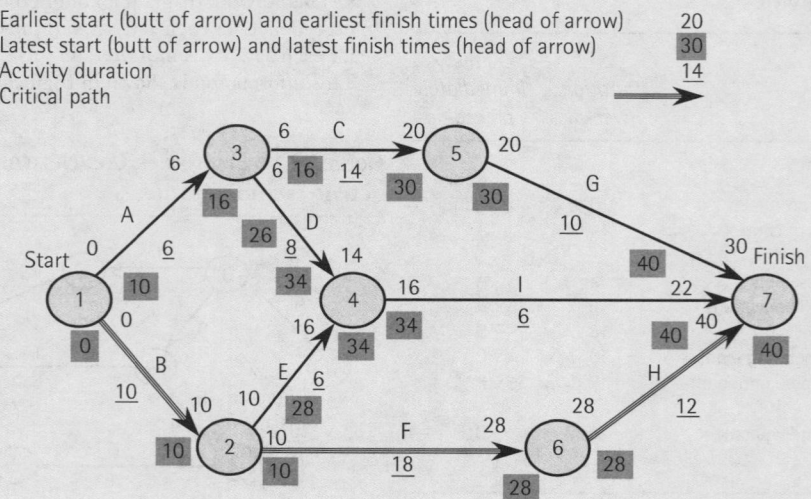

For example, the earliest start time for A is 0, and thus the earliest finish for A is $0 + 6 = 6$ weeks.
• For activity C, the earliest start time is equal to the earliest finish time for A, or 6 weeks. Thus the earliest finish time for activity C is $6 + 14 = 20$ weeks.
• In the case where there is more than one activity arriving at a node, the activity leaving that node cannot start until all the entering activities have been completed. This is the case at node 4. Activity I cannot start until both activities D and E have been completed. D finishes after 14 weeks and E finishes after 16 weeks. Thus I cannot start until 16 weeks have elapsed.
• In proceeding with the calculation through the whole network, the earliest finish time for the complete project is 40 weeks, determined by activity H. However, the earliest finish times for activity G is 30 weeks and 22 weeks for activity I.

Latest times

• Since the project cannot finish until activity H has been completed, the latest finish date for both activities I and G can also be 40 weeks as there is no urgency to have them finished before H.
• Starting with 40 weeks, determine the latest start for each activity. This is given by the latest finish time less the duration.

• For activity G, the latest start is $40 - 10 = 30$ weeks (compared to 20 for the earliest start).
• For activity I, the latest start is $40 - 6 = 34$ weeks (compared to 16 for the earliest start).
• For activity H, the latest start is $40 - 12 = 28$ weeks, the same as the earliest start.
• The latest finish for both activities D and E is 34 weeks, or the same as the latest start for I.

Slack times

• Determine the slack time for each activity. This is either the difference between the earliest start and the latest start, or the difference between the earliest finish, and the latest finish.
• Those activities with a zero slack time are on the critical path. In this case activities B, F, and H.
   The critical path for the project is thus site preparation (B), process connections (F), and delivery and preparations of raw materials (H).
2. The project manager can evaluate those non-critical activities where there is slack time (equipment delivery, development of control systems, equipment assembly, underground connections, training of operating team, and installation and equipment checkout) to see if resources from these such as personnel or money can be utilized on the critical path activities to ensure that this path is not delayed.

Demonstrating the concept 18.2 Biltmore

Situation

The Biltmore company wants to build a deluxe hotel in Igls, Austria, ready for the ski season. The project manager, together with the project team, have identified the principal activities for the construction together with time estimates, in weeks, based on pessimistic, optimistic, and mean times. This is given in Table 18.6. The pessimistic times are principally due to bad weather that might be encountered. Further, Biltmore is going to use a subcontractor for the construction of the parking, and there will be a severe penalty if construction is not completed on the

Table 18.6 Biltmore: Principal activities for hotel construction

	Activity	Immediate predecessor	Optimistic time (a)	Realistic time (m)	Pessimistic time (b)
A	Access road	None	15	20	25
B	Foundations	None	8	10	12
C	Landscaping/pool	A	25	30	40
D	Parking structure	B	15	15	15
E	Hotel structure	B	22	25	27
F	Interior/exterior – hotel	E	15	20	22
G	Interior/exterior – parking	D	20	20	22

date promised. This is why the optimistic, realistic, and pessimistic are the same.

Required

1. Analyze the project and determine the critical path, the critical time for each activity, and the total time for completing the project.
2. What is the probability that the project will take more than 57 weeks to complete?

Solution

1. • The network diagram is given in Figure 18.13.
   • The mean time for each activity is calculated from the optimistic, pessimistic, and realistic time using the relationship:

$$t = \frac{a + 4m + b}{6}$$

These values are given in Table 18.7.
   • Using the mean times, the earliest start date, earliest finish date, latest start date, and latest finish

date are calculated in the same manner as for Enviroteck. The data are shown in Table 18.8.
   • The slack time is determined from the difference between the latest and earliest start date, or the latest and earliest finish date. This information is given in Table 18.8. There is no slack time on the path B-E-F and this is then the critical path.
   • Figure 18.14 gives the completed network information. A period of 54.33 weeks is the project completion date, based on the information given.

2. • The completion time was calculated based on the mean times for each activity. For each of these activities, a pessimistic time was given and it is these data that lead to a probability situation.
   • The variation for each activity is given in Table 18.7. It is calculated from the relationship:

$$\sigma^2 = \left[\frac{(b-a)}{6}\right]^2 = \frac{(b-a)^2}{36}$$

• The sum of the variation for each of the three paths from start to finish of the project is obtained by summing the individual variances for each activity. This is given in Table 18.9.
   • The standard deviation of each of the three-summed variance is determined by taking the square root. This is given in Table 18.9.
   • The z value, or the number of standard deviations from the mean, is calculated from the relationship:

$$z = \frac{x - \mu}{\sigma}$$

Here, the value of x is 57 weeks, μ is the mean time obtained by summing the mean time for each activity on the path, and σ is the calculated standard deviation (see also Chapter 27). The probabilities are

Figure 18.13 Biltmore: Network diagram with activity times

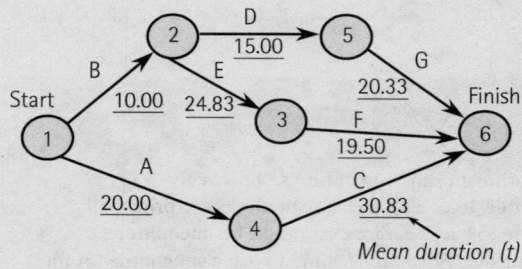

Mean duration (t)

Table 18.7 Biltmore: Activity time data

		Immediate predecessor	Optimistic time, a (weeks)	Realistic time, m (weeks)	Pessimistic time, b (weeks)	Mean time, t (weeks)	Variance (weeks)²	Standard deviation (weeks)
A	Access road	None	15	20	25	20.00	2.78	1.67
B	Foundations	None	8	10	12	10.00	0.44	0.67
C	Landscaping/pool	A	25	30	40	30.83	6.25	2.50
D	Parking structure	B	15	15	15	15.00	0.00	0.00
E	Hotel structure	B	22	25	27	24.83	0.69	0.83
F	Interior/exterior – hotel	E	15	20	22	19.50	1.36	1.17
G	Interior/exterior – parking	D	20	20	22	20.33	0.11	0.33

Table 18.8 Biltmore: Start and finish dates

		Duration (weeks)	Immediate predecessor	Earliest start (weeks)	Earliest finish (weeks)	Latest start (weeks)	Latest finish (weeks)	Slack time (weeks)
A	Access road	20.00	None	0.00	20.00	3.50	23.50	3.50
B	Foundations	10.00	None	0.00	10.00	0.00	10.00	0.00
C	Landscaping/pool	30.83	A	20.00	50.83	23.50	54.33	3.50
D	Parking structure	15.00	B	10.00	25.00	19.00	34.00	9.00
E	Hotel structure	24.83	B	10.00	34.83	10.00	34.83	0.00
F	Interior/exterior – hotel	19.50	E	34.83	54.33	34.83	54.33	0.00
G	Interior/exterior – parking	20.33	D	25.00	45.33	34.00	54.33	9.00

Critical path   B-E-F
Project completion time   54.33 weeks
Total slack time   **25.00 weeks**

Figure 18.14 Biltmore: Network diagram with critical path

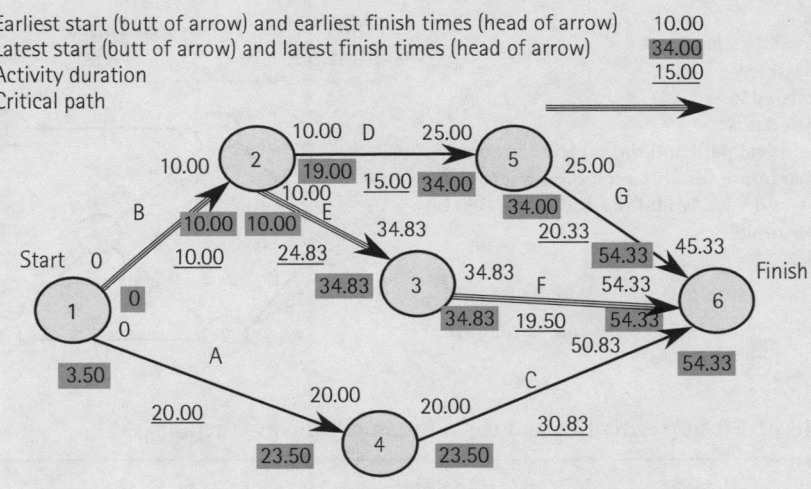

Table 18.9 Biltmore: Probabilities

	Variance	σ	z	P (finish)	P (not)
Project completion time, weeks	54.33				
Limit of completion data, weeks	57.00				
Total time on path B-D-G (mean value)	45.33	0.5556	0.7454	15.6525	100.00%	0.00%
Total time on path A-C (mean value)	50.83	9.0278	3.0046	2.0524	97.99%	2.01%
Total time on path B-E-F (mean value)	54.33	2.5000	1.5811	1.6865	95.42%	4.58%
Combined probabilities					93.50%	6.50%

determined from the normal probability distribution in Excel using the calculated value of z. The values are given in Table 18.9.
• The probability of being finished within 57 weeks is determined for each path. For path B-D-G there is no uncertainty but for A-C there is a probability of 97.99% being finished, and for path B-E-F a probability of 95.42%.

• Since all probabilities need to be considered, the joint probability of being completed within 57 weeks is the product of the three probabilities 1.00 * 0.9799 * 0.9542 = 0.9350, or 93.50%.
• Thus the probability of the project running over the 57 weeks is 100% less 93.50 or 6.50%. All this is shown in Table 18.9.

Demonstrating the concept 18.3   Gibson

Situation

The activities, duration, schedule and cost data for the construction of a section of an oilrig are given in Table 18.10.

Required

1. Develop the network for this project.
2. What are the:
    (a) earliest possible start dates
    (b) latest start dates
    (c) earliest finish dates
    (d) latest finish dates?
3. What are the critical path and the project duration?
4. What is the maximum feasible time the project can be reduced by and what would the additional cost be to arrive at this time?

Solution

1. This is given in Figure 18.15 taking into account the precedence relationship.

2. • These are given in Table 18.11 using the same criteria as for Demonstrating the concepts 18.1 (Enviroteck).
    • Figure 18.16 shows the activity times, latest and earliest start times and the latest and earliest finish times.

Figure 18.15 Gibson: Network with activities and duration

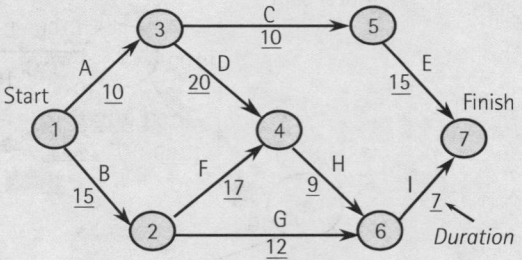

Table 18.10 Gibson: Activities and costs for an oilrig construction

Activity	Activity immediately preceding	Normal duration (weeks)	Accelerated duration (weeks)	Activity immediately preceding	Normal cost ($000s)	Accelerated cost ($000s)
A	None	10	9	None	1100	1500
B	None	15	13	None	2000	2500
C	A	10	6	A	900	2000
D	A	20	18	A	2500	3000
E	C	15	10	C	2000	3500
F	B	17	15	B	2000	3000
G	B	12	10	B	1500	2500
H	D, F	9	8	D, F	1200	1800
I	G, H	7	6	G, H	1000	1500

Table 18.11 Gibson: Initial network data

Activity	Normal duration (weeks)	Accelerated duration (weeks)	Activity immediately preceding	Normal cost ($000s)	Accelerated cost ($000s)	Cost to reduce ($000s/week)	Earliest start date	Earliest finish date	Latest start date	Latest finish date	Slack time (weeks)
A	10	9	None	1,100	1,500	400	0	10	2	12	2
B	15	13	None	2,000	2,500	250	0	15	0	15	0
C	10	6	A	900	2,000	275	10	20	23	33	13
D	20	18	A	2,500	3,000	250	10	30	12	32	2
E	15	10	C	2,000	3,500	300	20	35	33	48	13
F	17	15	B	2,000	3,000	500	15	32	15	32	0
G	12	10	B	1,500	2,500	500	15	27	29	41	14
H	9	8	D, F	1,200	1,800	600	32	41	32	41	0
I	7	6	G, H	1,000	1,500	500	41	48	41	48	0

Critical path   B-F-H-I
Project completion time   48 weeks
Total slack time   44 weeks

Figure 18.16 Gibson: Network with activities, duration, start, and finish times

Earliest start (butt of arrow) and earliest finish times (head ofarrow)   20
Latest start (butt of arrow) and latest finish times (head of arrow)   48
Activity duration   10
Critical path

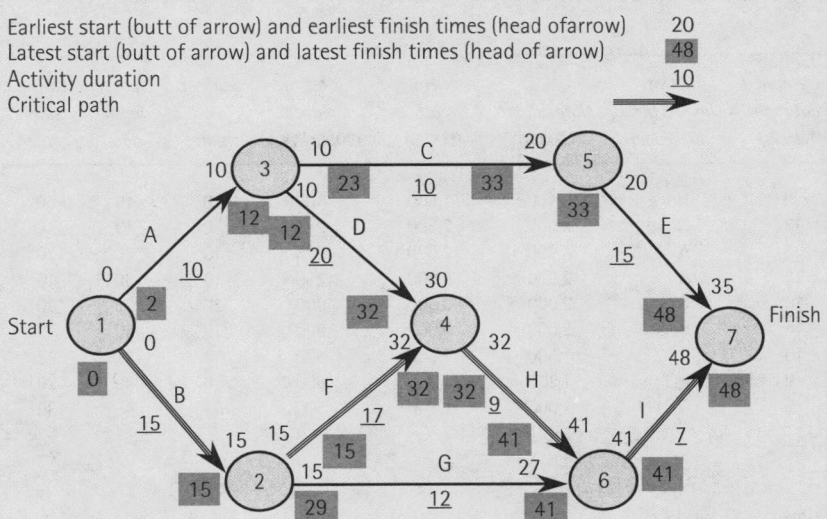

3. The critical path is where there is no slack time. This is the path B-F-H-I.
4. Convert the accelerated costs into a common base or accelerated cost to reduce per week by using the ratio:

$$\frac{(\text{Accelerated cost} - \text{Normal cost})}{(\text{Normal duration} - \text{Accelerated duration})}$$

• This is given in Table 18.11.

• Start by crashing on the critical path, and selecting that activity that is the least costly to reduce. In this case, reduce B from 15 to 13 weeks for an additional cost of $500,000 (see Table 18.12).
• Reducing the time of B now puts A on the critical path. So there are two critical paths for the project, B-F-H-I, and A-D-H-I.

Table 18.12 Gibson: Network data with project acceleration 1st: Reducing activity B from 15 to 13 weeks

	Revised duration (weeks)	Accelerated duration (weeks)	Activity immediately preceding	Normal cost ($000s)	Accelerated cost ($000s)	Cost to reduce ($000s/week)	Earliest start date	Earliest finish date	Latest start date	Latest finish date	Slack time (weeks)
A	10	9	None	1,100	1,500	400	0	10	0	10	0
B	13	13	None	2,000	2,500	250	0	13	0	13	0
C	10	6	A	900	2,000	275	10	20	21	31	11
D	20	18	A	2,500	3,000	250	10	30	10	30	0
E	15	10	C	2,000	3,500	300	20	35	31	46	11
F	17	15	B	2,000	3,000	500	13	30	13	30	0
G	12	10	B	1,500	2,500	500	13	25	27	39	14
H	9	8	D, F	1,200	1,800	600	30	39	30	39	0
I	7	6	G, H	1,000	1,500	500	39	46	39	46	0

Additional cost, $000s	500
Two critical paths	B-F-H-I A-D-H-I
Project completion time	46 weeks
Total slack time	**36 weeks**

Table 18.13 Gibson: Network data with project acceleration 2nd: Reducing activity I from 7 to 6 weeks

	Revised duration (weeks)	Accelerated duration (weeks)	Activity immediately preceding	Normal cost ($000s)	Accelerated cost ($000s)	Cost to reduce ($000s/week)	Earliest start date	Earliest finish date	Latest start date	Latest finish date	Slack time (weeks)
A	10	9	None	1,100	1,500	400	0	10	0	10	0
B	13	13	None	2,000	2,500	250	0	13	0	13	0
C	10	6	A	900	2,000	275	10	20	20	30	10
D	20	18	A	2,500	3,000	250	10	30	10	30	0
E	15	10	C	2,000	3,500	300	20	35	30	45	10
F	17	15	B	2,000	3,000	500	13	30	13	30	0
G	12	10	B	1,500	2,500	500	13	25	27	39	14
H	9	8	D, F	1,200	1,800	600	30	39	30	39	0
I	6	6	G, H	1,000	1,500	500	39	45	39	45	0

Additional cost, $000s	500
Two critical paths	B-F-H-I A-D-H-I
Project completion time	45 weeks
Total slack time	**34 weeks**

- Reduce activity I from 7 to 6 weeks, for a total cost of $500,000 (see Table 18.13). There are still two critical paths.
- Reduce activity F from 17 to 15 weeks, for a total cost of $1,000,000. Project critical path is now only A-D-H-I (see Table 18.14).
- Reduce activity H from 9 to 8 weeks, for a total cost of $600,000. Project critical path is still A-D-H-I (see Table 18.15).
- Reduce activity D from 20 to 18 weeks, for a total cost of $500,000. Project critical paths are now A-D-H-I and B-F-H-I (see Table 18.16). This is the furthest one can go. This is illustrated in Figure 18.17.
- Thus the overall project schedule has been reduced by six weeks, from 48 weeks, to 42 weeks. The additional cost for accelerating the project is $3,100,000.

Table 18.14 Gibson: Network data with project acceleration 3rd: Reducing activity F from 17 to 15 weeks

	Revised duration (weeks)	Accelerated duration (weeks)	Activity immediately preceding	Normal cost ($000s)	Accelerated cost ($000s)	Cost to reduce ($000s/week)	Earliest start date	Earliest finish date	Latest start date	Latest finish date	Slack time (weeks)
A	10	9	None	1,100	1,500	400	0	10	0	10	0
B	13	13	None	2,000	2,500	250	0	13	2	15	2
C	10	6	A	900	2,000	275	10	20	20	30	10
D	20	18	A	2,500	3,000	250	10	30	10	30	0
E	15	10	C	2,000	3,500	300	20	35	30	45	10
F	15	15	B	2,000	3,000	500	13	28	15	30	2
G	12	10	B	1,500	2,500	500	13	25	27	39	14
H	9	8	D, F	1,200	1,800	600	30	39	30	39	0
I	6	6	G, H	1,000	1,500	500	39	45	39	45	0

Additional cost, $000s   1000

One critical path   A-D-H-I
Project completion time   45 weeks
Total slack time   **38 weeks**

Table 18.15 Gibson: Network data with project acceleration 4th: Reducing activity H from 9 to 8 weeks

	Revised duration (weeks)	Accelerated duration (weeks)	Activity immediately preceding	Normal cost ($000s)	Accelerated cost ($000s)	Cost to reduce ($000s/week)	Earliest start date	Earliest finish date	Latest start date	Latest finish date	Slack time (weeks)
A	10	9	None	1,100	1,500	400	0	10	0	10	0
B	13	13	None	2,000	2,500	250	0	13	2	15	2
C	10	6	A	900	2,000	275	10	20	19	29	9
D	20	18	A	2,500	3,000	250	10	30	10	30	0
E	15	10	C	2,000	3,500	300	20	35	29	44	9
F	15	15	B	2,000	3,000	500	13	28	15	30	2
G	12	10	B	1,500	2,500	500	13	25	26	38	13
H	8	8	D, F	1,200	1,800	600	30	38	30	38	0
I	6	6	G, H	1,000	1,500	500	38	44	38	44	0

Additional cost, $000s   600

One critical path   A-D-H-I
Project completion time   44 weeks
Total slack time   **35 weeks**

Table 18.16 Gibson: Network data with project acceleration 5th: Reducing activity D from 20 to 18 weeks

	Revised duration (weeks)	Accelerated duration (weeks)	Activity immediately preceding	Normal cost ($000s)	Accelerated cost ($000s)	Cost to reduce ($000s/week)	Earliest start date	Earliest finish date	Latest start date	Latest finish date	Slack time (weeks)
A	10	9	None	1,100	1,500	400	0	10	0	10	0
B	13	13	None	2,000	2,500	250	0	13	0	13	0
C	10	6	A	900	2,000	275	10	20	17	27	7
D	18	18	A	2,500	3,000	250	10	28	10	28	0
E	15	10	C	2,000	3,500	300	20	35	27	42	7
F	15	15	B	2,000	3,000	500	13	28	13	28	0
G	12	10	B	1,500	2,500	500	13	25	24	36	11
H	8	8	D, F	1,200	1,800	600	28	36	28	36	0
I	6	6	G, H	1,000	1,500	500	36	42	36	42	0

Additional cost, $000s   500

Total additional cost   3100
One critical path   A-D-H-I   B-F-H-I
Project completion time   42 weeks
Total slack time   **25 weeks**

Figure 18.17 Gibson: Network with activities after reducing schedule

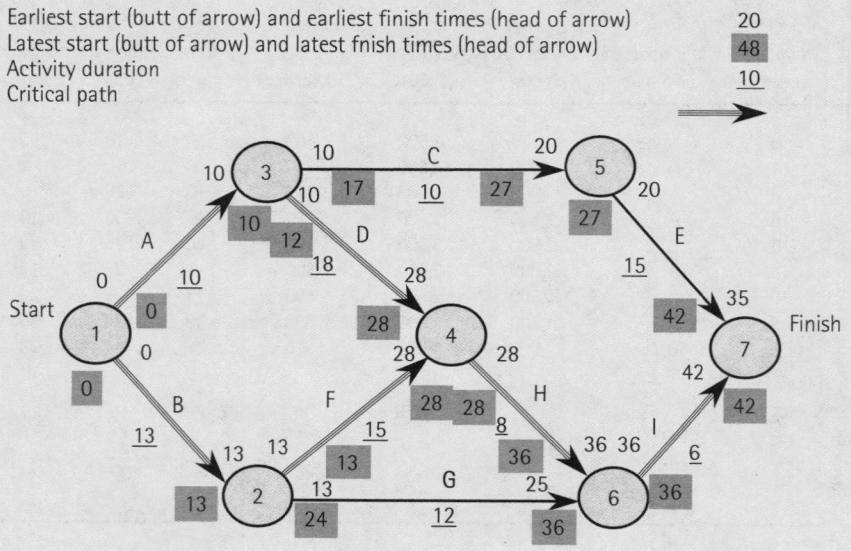

Earliest start (butt of arrow) and earliest finish times (head of arrow)   20
Latest start (butt of arrow) and latest fnish times (head of arrow)   48
Activity duration   10
Critical path

Application exercise 18.1   Euston

Situation

The schedule and cost data for the construction of a commercial shopping centre are given in Table 18.17. This information gives the 15 activities, the activities that immediately precede, and the normal duration for each activity in a month. The cost data include the direct cost to reduce the duration of the activity for one, two, or three months. In addition, the indirect costs for this construction work are estimated at $4000 a month.

Required

1. Develop the network scheme for this project.
2. What is the critical path?
3. The client would like to cut six months off the completion time for the project. What would be the additional direct costs required to achieve this?
4. What is the optimal time for reducing this project if all the given costs are taken into consideration? Justify your answer with a graph showing the movement of costs.

Table 18.17   Euston: Construction schedule and cost data

Activity	Immediate predecessor	Normal duration (months)	Crash cost for first month ($)	Crash cost for second month ($)	Crash cost for third month ($)
A	None	5	1,800	2,200	No
B	None	4	1,200	2,400	2,600
C	None	3	1,000	1,500	2,500
D	A	8	2,400	2,500	2,500
E	B	12	No	No	No
F	C	12	800	1,300	No
G	D	7	3,000	3,000	3,500
H	E	5	4,000	4,000	4,000
I	B	6	300	1,000	1,200
J	F	9	500	1,200	No
K	G	4	1,500	2,000	No
L	I	9	200	700	1,000
M	J	8	1,400	1,500	No
N	K, H	11	3,000	3,300	3,600
P	L, M	1	2,600	No	No

Application exercise 18.2   Harbour

Situation

A coastal town on the Mediterranean has signed up a project to build a new yacht harbour. The assigned project team has developed a schedule based on a PERT network diagram approach (see Table 18.18).

Required

1. Develop the network scheme for this project.
2. What is the critical path?

3. Since there is a heavy penalty clause on this project, the project manager wants to know what the probability of completion on schedule will be. Develop a curve showing the probability of completing the project in two years (104 weeks) to two years four months (120 weeks) in intervals of one week.
4. Would you be prepared to sign a contract saying the project can be completed in two years? If not, what completion date would you be confident to give to the client?

Table 18.18 Harbour construction schedule

	Immediate predecessor	Optimistic time (weeks)	Realistic time (weeks)	Pessimistic time (weeks)
A	None	17	20	25
B	None	43	55	64
C	None	62	68	75
D	A	13	15	27
E	D	22	25	35
F	E, B	18	20	28
G	D	17	20	31
H	G	19	22	26
J	G	14	17	21
K	G	20	37	62
L	C, F, H	12	14	25
M	J	18	25	41

Application exercise 18.3 Layout

Situation

A company is considering changing the layout of its manufacturing facility in order that it can better incorporate lean production and just-in-time into its operation. Table 18.19 shows the activities, and the times in weeks in order that this reorganization can be made.

Required

1. Develop the network scheme for this project.
2. What is the critical path?
3. What is the total slack time?
4. What would happen if the duration of activity E were reduced by 50%?

Table 18.19 Reorganizational activities

Activity	Immediate predecessor	Normal duration (weeks)
A	None	6
B	A	4
C	None	5
D	C	3
E	B	8
F	B	4
G	B	10
H	D, E	9

Case study 18.1 Sana

Situation

Sana is a subcontractor to Boeing, for engineering projects related to its military aircraft projects. The relevant activities, duration, and total cost for the activities for the construction of a section of a military transport airplane are given in Table 18.20.

Required

As project manager, develop the following for this project:

1. the network diagram for the complete project
2. the earliest start and finish, and the latest start and finish for each activity

3. the critical path for the project
4. the cumulative project completion curve by month using the earliest start and the latest start information, illustrating on the curve each month what activities have been completed. Assume that activities are completed on a linear basis. For example, after one month, one-third of activity A would have been completed
5. Develop the cumulative cost curves for the project based on:
   (a) commencing an activity on the earliest date possible
   (b) commencing an activity at the latest time possible.

Use a time period of a month, and assume that expenditure a month is linear with time. For example, for activity A, the duration is three months, and the total cost is $1,200,000. Thus, the cost a month is $400,000.

6. Sana has a $100 million line of credit with a bank to finance this construction activity. The interest rate is 9%, compounded daily. Using electronic data interchange, cash is borrowed on the first day of each month, for that month's activity. The total amount of the funds borrowed is repaid to the bank one year after project completion. For the purpose of calculations, assume a 30-day month, thus one year is equivalent to 360 days, then determine:

   (a) total cost of the project (direct cost plus interest costs), starting each activity on the earliest date possible

   (b) total cost of the project (direct cost plus interest costs), starting each activity on the latest date possible.

7. What are your conclusions about this project?

Table 18.20 Sana: Activities and costs for construction of a military transport airplane section

Activity	Duration (months)	Immediate predecessor	Total cost ($000s)
A	3	None	1,200
B	2	None	8,000
C	1	A	1,600
D	4	A	800
E	5	D	3,000
F	2	B, C	4,000
G	1	B, C	3,000
H	3	E, F	720
I	4	G	9,600

Selected further reading

KERZNER, Harold (2000) *Project Management: A Systems Approach to Planning, Scheduling, and Controlling*, 7th edition, Wiley.

MACLEOD, Kenneth R. and PETERSEN, Paul F., 'Estimating the trade-off between resource allocation and probability of on-time completion in project management', *Project Management Journal*, vol. 27, issue 1, March 1996, pp 26–33.

MAYLOR, Harvey (1999) *Project Management*, 2nd edition, Prentice-Hall.

PROJECT MANAGEMENT INSTITUTE (2001) *A Guide to the Project Management Body of Knowledge*, 2000 Edition, Project Management Institute.

SHTUB, Avraham, BARD, Jonathan F. and GLOBERSON, Shlomo (1994) *Project Management: Engineering, Technology, and Implementation*, Prentice-Hall.

An extensive listing of other further reading can be found on the website.

What's on the web?

Further learning resources are available to lecturers and students at www.supplychain-online.com, including the following which are specific to *Project management*:

Resource	Subject
Chapter overview	Project management
Application exercise: Biltmore (2)	PERT analysis
Application exercise: Enviroteck (2)	Critical path network (CPM)
More further reading	Project management

System control and further analysis

Part IV acknowledges that operations are both quantitative and qualitative, and although earlier chapters have presented some quantitative approaches, the purpose of this part is to go into more analytical depth. Reliability and maintenance, statistical quality control, waiting lines, decision making and risk, linear programming, financial analysis, auditing the operations and supply chain are all discussed before Chapter 27 'closes the loop' on this integrated operations management textbook with a supply chain approach.

'Quality is never an accident; it is always the result of high intention, sincere effort, intelligent direction and skillful execution; it represents the wise choice of many alternatives'

Willa A Foster

Part IV: System control and further analysis

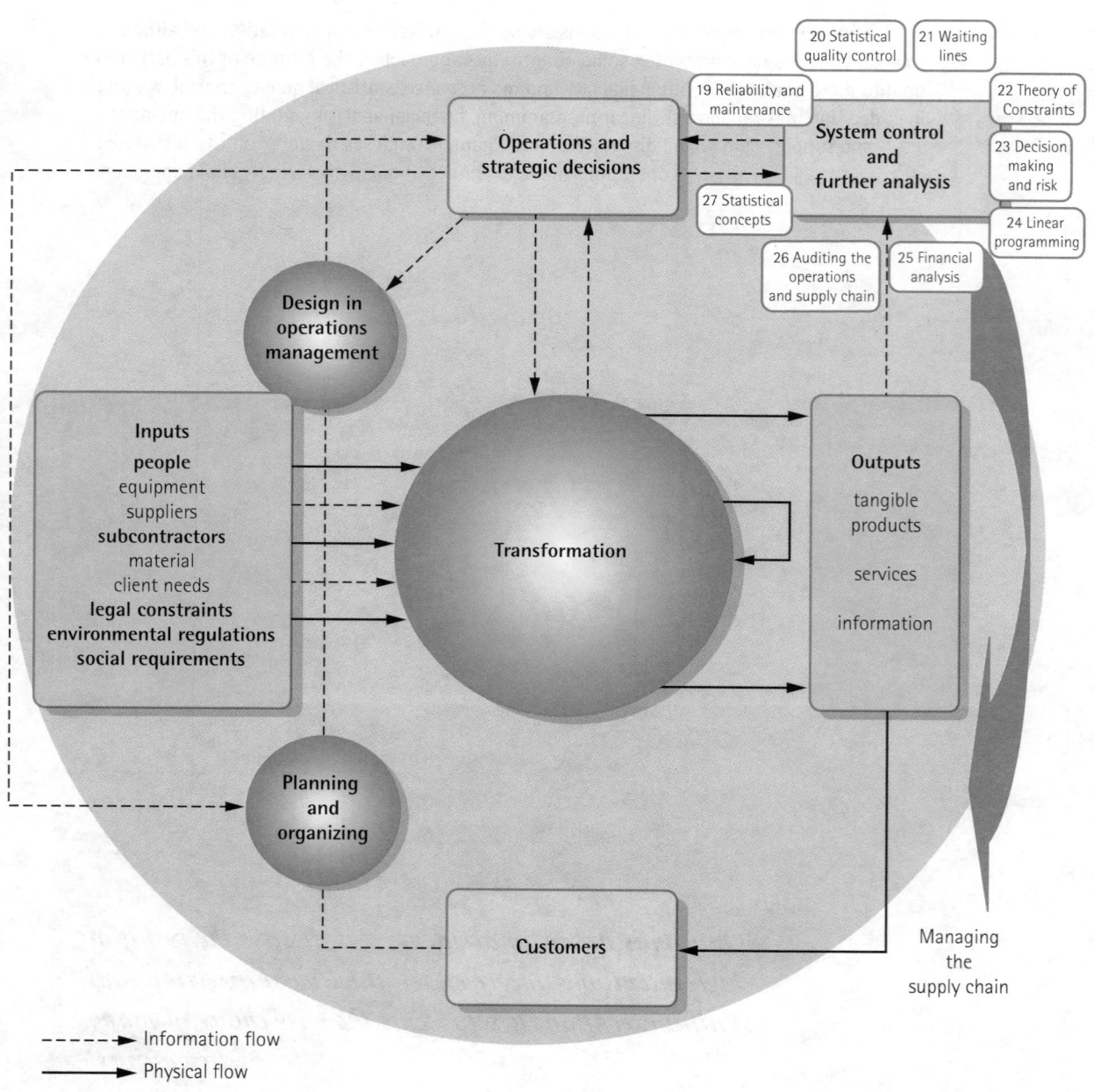

20 Statistical quality control

21 Waiting lines

19 Reliability and maintenance

System control and further analysis

22 Theory of Constraints

23 Decision making and risk

27 Statistical concepts

24 Linear programming

Operations and strategic decisions

26 Auditing the operations and supply chain

25 Financial analysis

Design in operations management

Inputs

people
equipment
suppliers
subcontractors
material
client needs
legal constraints
environmental regulations
social requirements

Transformation

Outputs

tangible products

services

information

Planning and organizing

Customers

Managing the supply chain

- - - ➤ Information flow
——➤ Physical flow

19 Reliability and maintenance

Chapter overview

- Reliability
- Failure mode, effect, and criticality analysis
- Maintenance
- Recovery from a failure

Reliability

The supply chain is a complex network of suppliers, manufacturers and distributors whose ultimate objective is to provide goods and services to the client in a timely manner. The reliability of this supply chain depends on all the people in the network, plus the reliability of all the equipment employed including transportation vehicles, sophisticated machines and computer-based information systems. The reliability of this equipment depends very much on their design, maintenance, and subsequent repairs.

Reliability is the confidence one has in a product, process, service, work team, or individual, to operate under prescribed conditions without failure or stopping, in order to produce the required output to meet client needs or to perform according to the defined specifications. Reliability might be applied to aspects as to whether the trucks delivering raw materials arrive on time, whether the suppliers produce quality components, whether the operators turn up for work, or whether the packing machines operate without

breaking down. Reliability has a chain effect. If there is a malfunction upstream in the supply chain, delivery of finished goods downstream will be impacted. Alternatively, even if the upstream part of the supply chain is perfectly reliable, a downstream malfunction will retard delivery of the finished goods. Unreliable systems resulting in a failure can have diverse consequences ranging from customer inconvenience, lost revenue, delayed production, poor quality, or, at the worst, tragedy.

Poor product design

As discussed in Chapter 6, all tangible goods and services go through a design phase before they are finally commercialized into what is expected to be a reliable product. This design phase involves engineering checks, measurements, and perhaps the development of a prototype. A poorly conceived and designed product, as Industry insight 19.1 illustrates, can prove unreliable, have embarrassing results for the company image, and be costly.

Industry insight 19.1

Daimler–Benz

In November 1997 the new Mercedes A-class small car, produced by Daimler-Benz, won the satirical 'Golden Steering Wheel' award as 'car' of the year from a German tabloid newspaper. The problem was that the car failed the so-called Elk test where a vehicle is subjected to two sharp turns at 65 km an hour, intended to mimic a driver attempting to evade a collision

with wildlife that has wandered onto the highway. This incident was a monumental embarrassment to Daimler-Benz, which had spent DM 2.5 billion developing the vehicle. After the episode occurred Daimler promised to fit different tyres on the vehicle, blaming the problem on those originally supplied by Goodyear (much to *that* company's indignation). It also said it would recall cars and fit for free an optional bit of drive control electronics to improve handling. However, as other motoring journals repeated the test, and came up with the same results, more orders dried up. On 11 November, after about 2% of the A-class's 100,000 orders had been cancelled, Daimler admitted that the car was unsafe in extreme conditions. The firm proposed a new chassis design that would lower the body, improve stability of the axles, and require tyres that hold the road better. The cost of the redesign was estimated at DM 300 million ($175 million).

One month later, in December 1997, Daimler-Benz suffered a further embarrassment when it was forced to suspend the sale to the public of its two-seater Smart car (dubbed the 'Swatchmobile' because Daimler's 19% joint venture partner is the Swiss-based Société Suisse de Microélectronique et d'Horlogerie SA which makes the trendy Swatch wristwatches). The reason for the suspension was again that the car flipped over in the Elk test. A subsequent quality audit of the vehicle discovered technical flaws, some related to suppliers' parts, only three months ahead of the March 1998 introduction date. The Daimler Chief Executive, Juergen Schrempp, demanded a six-month delay until October 1998 to give engineers time to widen the car's wheelbase, shift the vehicle's weight closer to the ground, and retool the production line to upgrade some 5000 parts. The delay with the Smart car was estimated to cost Daimler DM 300 million ($169.1 million).

(In November 1998 Daimler-Benz AG (now Daimler-Chrysler) bought out its partner in this automobile project, Société Suisse de Microélectronique et d'Horlogerie, SMH, by paying an estimated $70 million for the 19% of stake of SMH it didn't already own.[1])

Adapted from: 'Car safety: Mercedes bends', *The Economist*;[2]
'Daimler hits brakes on second flawed model', *International Herald Tribune*;[3] 'Daimler's Swatchmobile faces delays', *Wall Street Journal Europe*.[4]

Figure 19.1 Reliability: Series and parallel systems

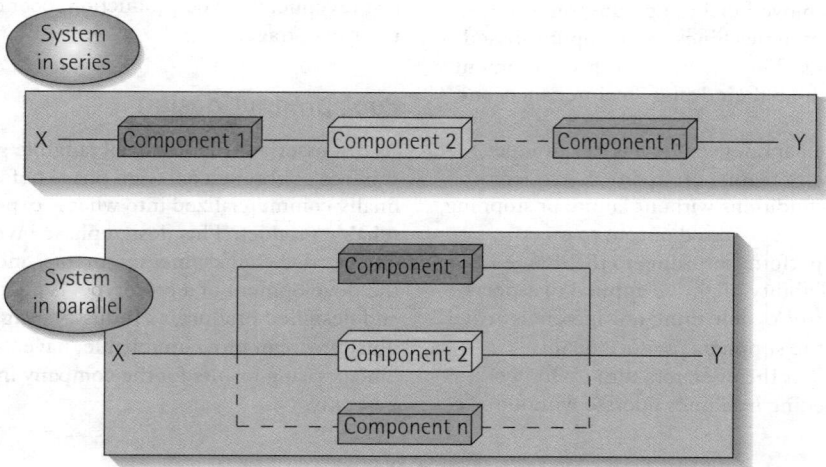

Components and reliability in a series system

The more components in a product, or process, the more complex the system, and thus the greater the risk of failure, or unreliability. Consider a product built up in a series arrangement, as illustrated in the upper scheme in Figure 19.1.

This is a basic structure, which contains n components where n can take on any integer value.

In the series arrangement, the relationship between the overall system reliability, R_s, and the number of interacting parts, n, or components is a joint probability relationship (see Chapter 27 for information on joint probability) that can be expressed by the following relationship:

$$R_S = R_1 * R_2 * R_3 * R_4 * \cdots R_n$$

Here R_1, R_2, R_3, etc., represent the reliability of the individual components. The relationship assumes that

Figure 19.2 Series system reliability according to number of components

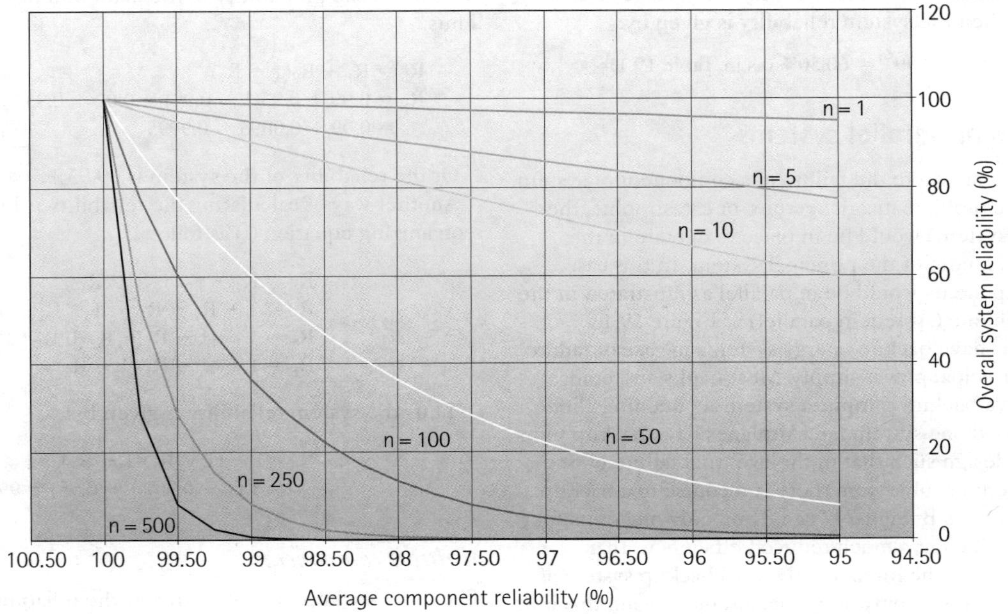

each component is independent of the others and that the reliability of one does not depend on the reliability of the others. However, the complete system does depend on all the components functioning, i.e. they are *inter*dependent, so that if one component fails, the system fails. For example, in an electric food mixer, there is a switch, a cutting blade, and an electric circuit. Each one is an independent unit, but if any one fails, the food mixer will not work.

The reliability, or the value of R, is expressed as a percentage, such as 99%. This means that a component will perform as specified 99% of the time, or it will fail 1% of the time (100 − 99).

Two components

Consider the system between point X and Y in the figure with two components R_1, with a reliability of 99%, and R_2 with a reliability of 95%. The system reliability is given as follows:

$$R_S = R_1 * R_2 = 0.99 \times 0.95 = 0.9405 \text{ or } 94.05\%$$

Multiple components

Since R is always less than 1.00 (nothing is 100% reliable all the time) the reliability of the system in a series arrangement decreases with the number of components. This concept is illustrated in Figure 19.2.

Table 19.1 Average component reliability

Number of components	1	5	10	50	100	250	500
System reliability (%)	99.00	95.10	90.44	60.50	36.60	8.11	0.66

Here, the various curves show the rapid decline in the system reliability as the number of components increase from 1 to 500 for various average component reliability. For example, as illustrated in Table 19.1, for an average component reliability of 99% the system reliability drops from 99% to less than 1% as the number of components increases from one to 500. Conversely, this means that the system would be working less than 1% of the time in this worst case.

Equal reliability

In a situation where there are similar components of quantity, n, which can be considered to have the same reliability, then the system reliability would be given by the relationship:

$$R_S = R^n$$

For example, if there are 50 components in a series system where each component has an average reliability of 99%, then the system reliability is given by:

$$R_S = 0.99^{50} = 60.50\% \text{ (as in Table 19.1)}$$

Backup or parallel systems

In situations where the failure of a component or system would be problematic, dangerous, or catastrophic, then backup systems would be in place to operate in the eventual failure of the principal system. In this case, the components would be in parallel as illustrated in the lower scheme (system in parallel) of Figure 19.1. Hospitals have backup energy systems in case of failure of the principal power supply. Most banks and other firms have backup computer systems containing client data should one system fail. Airplanes have backup units in their design such that in the eventual failure of one component or subsystem there is recourse to a backup. For example a Boeing-747 can fly on only one of its four engines, albeit at a much reduced efficiency. To a certain extent the human body has a backup system as it can function with only one lung, although again this is at a reduced efficiency. When backup systems are in place this implies redundancy since the backup units are not normally operational. A real example of not having a backup system, and the consequences, is illustrated in Industry insight 19.2.

Two components in a parallel system

As an example, consider from Figure 19.1 a generating system between point X and Y with the principal generator, R_1, having a reliability of 99% and R_2, the backup generator, having a reliability of 95%. The system reliability, R_S, is given by the relationship:

$$\begin{bmatrix} \text{Probably} \\ \text{of main} \\ \text{component } (R_1) \\ \text{working} \end{bmatrix} + \begin{bmatrix} \text{Probability} \\ \text{of backup} \\ \text{component } (R_2) \\ \text{working} \end{bmatrix} * \begin{bmatrix} \text{Probability} \\ \text{of needing} \\ \text{backup unit} \end{bmatrix}$$

where the probability of needing the backup unit is $(1 - R_1)$ or the probability of the main unit not working. Thus:

$$R_S = R_1 + R_2(1 - R_1) \tag{i}$$
$$R_S = 0.99 + 0.95(1 - 0.99) = 0.99 + 0.95 * 0.01$$
$$= 0.99 + 0.0095 = 0.9995$$

Or the reliability of the system is 99.95%.
Another way of calculating the reliability is by reorganizing equation (i) as follows:

$$R_S = R_1 + R_2 - R_2 * R_1$$
$$R_S = 1 + R_1 + R_2 - R_2 * R_1 - 1$$
$$R_S = 1 - (1 - R_1 - R_2 + R_2 * R_1)$$
$$R_S = 1 - (1 - R_1)(1 - R_2)$$

Thus the system reliability is given by:

$$R_S = 1 - (1 - R_1)(1 - R_2)$$
$$= 1 (1 - 0.99)(1 - 0.95) = 99.95\%$$

Multiple components

The more backup units, the greater the reliability of the system. The system reliability can be calculated from the relationship:

$$R_S = 1 - (1 - R_1)(1 - R_2)(1 - R_3)(1 - R_4) \cdots (1 - R_n)$$

where $R_1, R_2 \cdots R_n$ represent the reliability of the individual components.

This relationship is illustrated in Figure 19.3. Here the curves give the reliability with no backups to three backup components (four components in total). Of course, ideally, one would always want close to 100% reliability, however, with greater reliability, the greater is the cost. For many years, the US Federal Aviation Administration had a requirement that all airplanes flying over water for a duration of one hour or longer should have three engines, in case of failure of one. Airline manufacturers complained and said this was an unnecessary expense because of the reliability of

---

the engines. It is only recently that the FAA has permitted commercial airlines with two engines to make transatlantic flights. However, as Industry insight 19.3 illustrates, perhaps having three engines is necessary.

Equal reliability

When the backup components of quantity, n, have the same reliability, then the system reliability would be given by the relationship:

$$R_S = 1 - (1 - R)^n$$

Failure rate

The failure rate is a measure of the reliability of products. It might be determined by the number of failures among the total number of products tested and then expressed as a percentage according to the following ratio:

$$\text{Failure rate}(\%) = \frac{\text{Number of products which failed}}{\text{Total number of products tested}}$$

Alternatively, the failure rate might be expressed as the number of failures during a specified period of

Figure 19.3 System reliability of a parallel backup system

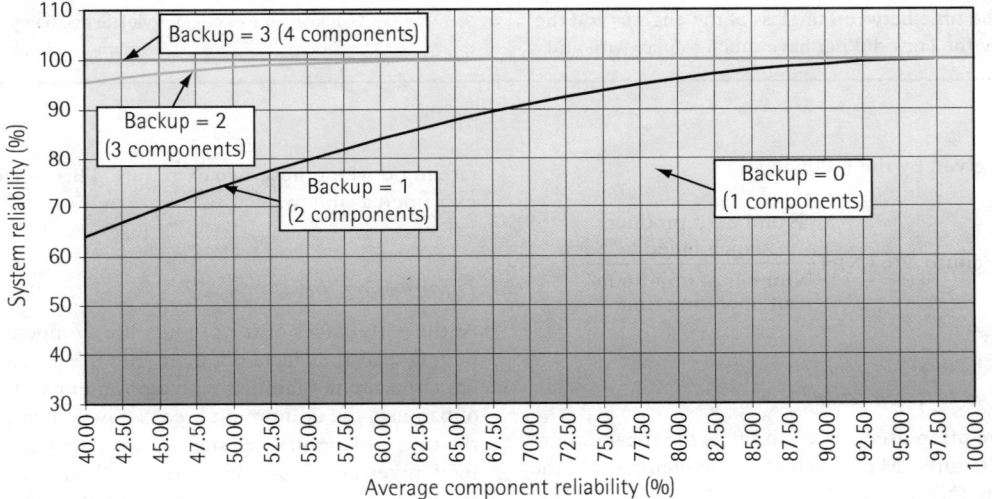

Failsafe devices that didn't work

Air Transat flight 236 was on its way from Toronto to Lisbon overnight on 23–24 August 2001 with 291 passengers and a crew of 13. The airplane belonged to Air Transat of Canada and was an Airbus A330-200 with two Rolls-Royce engines. At 5.25am on 24 August, with the airplane at 39,000 feet and nearly 200 miles from the nearest landing site, the pilots were warned that they had a fuel shortage and an emergency was declared. At 6.13am the fuel-starved right engine failed completely and the pilot, Robert Piche, took the plane down to 32,000 feet. Normally, an Airbus can fly safely on one

engine, but at 6.26am the left engine shut down as well, apparently, also out of fuel. The pilot and the co-pilot then manoeuvred the 200-ton plane into a glide hoping to reach the Azores, 98 miles away, but if necessary they were prepared to ditch the plane into the sea. The passengers, who by now were starting to panic, were instructed to put on lifevests.

The co-pilot, Mr DeJager, said that with virtually no precedent, the crew was flying as if in a simulator, making instant decisions as problems arose. He said that a small propeller activated under the wings helped give the plane minimum hydraulics to maintain flight control. From the cockpit, with the public address shut down since there was no power (it is the engines that supply the airplane's power) the co-pilot shouted instructions to the cabin crew that were then relayed to the passengers. The pilot focused on keeping the plane aloft and on course balancing speed and altitude with the help of the traffic controllers. At 6.46am the airplane hit the ground hard at Lajes, a Portuguese airbase on Terceira Island, at a speed the crew estimated at nearly 300 miles an hour. Almost all the tyres were blown out on impact after the antilock brakes on the wheels were lost. In less than two minutes after the landing emergency chutes had deployed and all the passengers and crew were evacuated. There were no serious injuries and the terrifying experience ended for the 304 people on board.

In the time between the loss of the engines and the landing the crew did not have much to play with and

there would not have been a second chance to make the landing. Both Airbus Industries and Rolls-Royce said that what happened over the Atlantic should never have occurred because of failsafe systems built into their equipment. Investigators indicated that a maintenance error led to a fuel leak in the right engine. At the moment of the crisis the two engines were like conjoined twins, mutually vulnerable. Whatever the reason whether it was bad design, mechanical flaw, or human error, the situation violated a cardinal rule of aviation of the requirements of having backups for all critical systems. The resulting double engine failure has long been considered so unlikely that many airlines do not even teach their pilot to fly a big jet as a glider, which is what this crew ended up doing.

Adapted from: 'Accelerating toward-near disaster', and 'Linkage of two engines violate aviation principle', *International Herald Tribune*[6]

time and given by the following ratio:

$$\text{Failure rate (N)} = \frac{\text{Number of products which failed}}{\text{Number of unit hours of operating time}}$$

Mean time between failures

A measure often used for reliability is the mean time between failures, MTBF, which is the reciprocal of the failure rate (N):

$$\text{MTBF} = \frac{1}{\text{Failure rate (N)}}$$
$$= \frac{\text{Operating time for units}}{\text{Number of products which failed}}$$

The principle of these measurements of failure rate is illustrated in Demonstrating the concept 19.1.

Lifetime failure rate

All products and processes fail at some point in their lifetime. The failure rate profile, illustrated by the bathtub curve in Figure 19.4 (somewhat analogous to the human profile) shows that there are high rates both at the early or infant stage and the old or wear out stage towards the end of the product's life. There is a relatively low, or what is considered the normal, failure

rate in between these two extremes. This concept is explained as follows.

Infant mortality

At the early stages of the product life, components may be fragile as they have not been 'run in', or conversely, operators are not familiar with equipment and because of bad use, the equipment breaks down. This is often the case with appliances such as washing machines, food mixers, or power lawn mowers. Some companies might 'run in' or 'burn in' a product before it is released onto the market to ensure that all the teething startup problems have been overcome. For other products, such as in the case of automobiles, the requirement is that an operator does not run it above a certain speed for say the first 3000 km, after which it has to be serviced. To cover the possibility of failure in the early days of a product's life, certain firms provide a 90-day warranty for their products. The term infant mortality is used because obviously young children are fragile at this point in their life.

Normal failure

Once a product has been used for a certain period, it is normally quite robust if it is well designed for the appropriate service, and with the correct preventive maintenance will last throughout its expected lifetime. During this period the failure rate is pretty constant and

Figure 19.4 Product lifetime failure rate

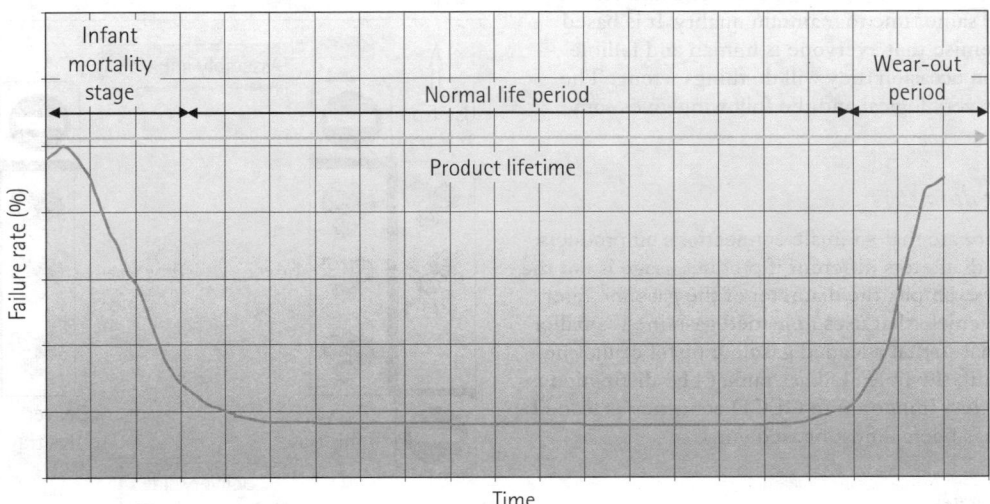

low. Again, the analogy is to the human body, which is pretty robust, although from time to time, 'breakdowns' do occur either through some random occurrence (illness), or improper use (accidents).

Wear out failure

Towards the end of the life of a product or process, the failure rate starts to increase rapidly again as parts become used or worn and eventually fail. Again, this is the analogy of the human body.

Responsibility and the supply chain

Reliability in the supply chain depends on all team members 'pulling their weight' such that the work in hand is completed according to schedule, budget, and at the required quality or specification level. Failure in one phase impacts other elements of the chain. With tangible products, responsibility starts with the design engineers who conceive the product and develop the final design. Purchasing personnel have the responsibility to verify the quality of the purchased materials used in the assembly of the product. Suppliers and subcontractors have the responsibility of delivering parts on time. Operating personnel have the responsibility to verify that products are manufactured according to the established specifications. Further, once a product is in service, maintenance personnel have the responsibility to verify that proper maintenance work is carried out.

The millennium bug

Probably one of the most expensive, and far reaching, reliability problems to occur was the so-called 'millennium bug' which was the responsibility of computer design engineers and programmers who, back in the 1960s, in order to save computer memory, used only two digits instead of four, to represent a year (69 for 1969 for example). As a result, the digits 00 would be expected to be read as the year 1900, and not the then approaching year 2000. As a consequence, there was a concern that when 1 January 2000 arrived, public services such as hospitals, police, and government could be disrupted and airports, nuclear power plants, and industrial concerns might be uncontrollable. In addition, the accounts in financial services such as banks, stock exchanges, and insurance firms would be destroyed. Depending on who was right, the worldwide cost to fix this design problem was estimated to be up to $600 billion.[7] As it turned out, there was minimal damage to systems but vast sums of money were spent to 'avoid' the problem plus numerous people had to work between 31 December 1999 and 1 January 2000 just in case of a problem.

Poka yoke

Poka yoke, from *poka* meaning inadvertent errors and *yokeru* meaning to prevent, which has already been referred to in Chapter 4, is an approach to increase reliability. It is an idea originally conceived by Shigeo

Shingo of Japan to make a product, process, service, or environment, mistake-proof in order to avoid errors, and at the same time to maintain quality. It is based on the premise that everyone is human and fallible and that on occasion they will do things wrong. The concept is very logical and the following gives some examples.

Different diameters

When there are male–female connections on products, make the diameters different if product usage is not the same. For example, the diameter of the gasoline filler hole in a vehicle that uses unleaded gasoline is smaller than normal so that a leaded gasoline pistol cannot be inserted into the unleaded gas tank. (The distinction is becoming less important in OECD countries as leaded gasoline has been almost phased out.)

Guide notches

Install guide notches, which match in only one sense, on components that are to be joined together in order to avoid an erroneous assembly. For example, incorporating appropriate guide notches on automobile headlights so that they cannot be installed upside down.

Alternative fittings

In the electrical industry, for example, provide different type plug fittings to ensure that a 120-volt appliance cannot be connected to a 240-volt outlet.

Reverse door openings

In restaurants, the entrance/exit doors in restaurants open in the opposite direction so that waiters exiting the kitchen with a tray of food don't collide with a waiter entering with a tray of dirty dishes. Some years ago, car doors opened from the front with the hinge at the rear so that if the door opened accidentally while in motion, it could be torn off in the wind. The door positioning is now reversed.

Geometric shape

When covers are made for containers, they should be round and not square. Square covers can fall through the hole since the length of the side of a square is less than the diagonal. Square manhole covers would fall through the hole into the sewer!!

Assembly operations

* In the assembly of products that have different fittings, for example, automobile axles, keep

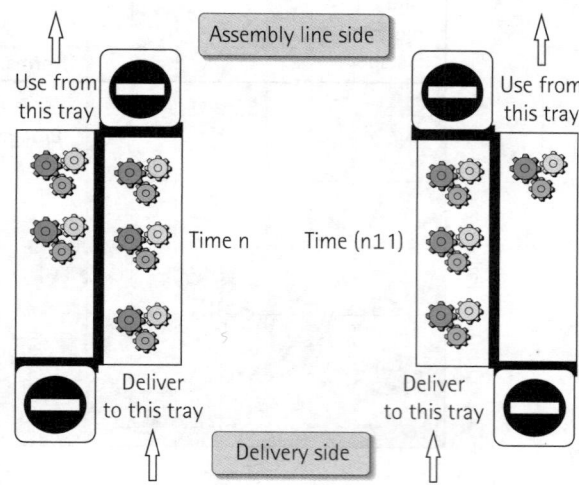

Figure 19.5 Ensuring components are used on a FIFO basis

components destined for the right side in green containers, and those for the left in red containers.

* To ensure first in, first out usage of components, when there are two delivery conveyers, have a system which alternately blocks off one while the other is in use as illustrated in Figure 19.5.[8] Here, during time, n, components are delivered to the right-hand conveyer, but are used (withdrawn) from the left-hand conveyer. When the left conveyor is empty, time (n + 1), an arm is swung over so that components can be taken from the right conveyer. This automatically blocks the right side and opens the left for delivery of components.

Failure mode, effect, and criticality analysis

A failure mode, effect and criticality analysis, FMECA, is the detailed study of a product design, manufacturing operation, or distribution network to determine which features are critical to various modes of failure. The concept was developed in the USA in the 1950s particularly to increase the reliability for military equipment, in aviation, and also by NASA (the North American Space Agency) for its space programmes. The FMECA analysis appeared in Europe in the 1970s in the electronics industry, and it is now common practice in automobile firms. Using FMECA involves input from other functional areas including marketing, design, purchasing, production, operations, finance etc.

Elements in the FMECA analysis

The three principal study areas in a detailed FMECA analysis are failure mode, failure effect, and failure criticality. These studies may be applied at any stage of conception, design, development, production, or final use. However, since the objective of FMECA is to prevent failure, the study is most often applied at the design stage. Perhaps a more rigorous FMECA analysis might have avoided the disastrous explosion and loss of the seven astronauts in the Challenger launch on 28 January 1986.[9]

Failure mode analysis

The failure mode is analyzing the operation of the product, or the process to see what are the most likely modes where failure would occur. This would include describing the conditions, the components involved, the time elements, location, etc.

Failure effect analysis

The failure effect is the study of the potential failures to ascertain the likely impact on the performance of the whole product, the process, or service, and/or related elements.

Failure criticality analysis

Failure criticality is the examination of the potential failures of the product, process, or service to determine how critical the failure would be. The criticality might range from customer irritation, a lowering of performance, shutdown of an operating plant, a safety problem, an environmental hazard, or a catastrophic occurrence.

Procedural steps in the FMECA analysis

The step-by-step procedures in FMECA depend to a certain extent on what service, or product, is being examined, but the following are the key phases:

1. In the product, or the process, identify all the components, and assemblies that are part of the operating system.
2. Make an exhaustive listing of all the possible failure modes of each component in the system.

Table 19.2 Rating for automobile hydraulic braking system

Value	1	2	3	4	5	6	7	8	9	10
P		X								
S									X	
D					X					

3. Establish the effects that each mode of failure would have on the product, process, or service.
4. Make a list of all the possible causes of each failure mode.
5. Assign a numerical value to each occurrence for each of the following criteria:
   - P, the probability of each failure mode occurring.
   - S, the seriousness, or the criticality, of the failure.
   - D, the difficulty of detecting the failure before the product or service is used by the client.

   For example, a scale of 1 to 10 can be used with 1 being low or easy, and 10 high. As an illustration, Table 19.2 shows the rating for an automobile hydraulic braking system.

6. For each possible failure mode, determine the value of the product $P * S * D$ which is considered the criticality index, or the risk priority number, RPN. Using Table 19.2, the maximum value of RPN, which would have the highest priority, is $10 * 10 * 10$ or 1000 and the minimum value, with a low priority, is $1 * 1 * 1 = 1$. For example, the value of RPN for the automobile brake situation given in step 5 is $2 * 9 * 5 = 90$. This index represents the relative priority of each mode in the failure prevention study.
7. Determine the corrective action necessary to avoid the failure in question, and also which department or function would be responsible for the corrective action.
8. Rank the RPN for the whole product or process such that the necessary corrective action can be taken in light of the resources available.

Real–world pharmaceutical application

Table 19.3 gives a selection of some of the elements considered in the preparation of an over-the-counter drug.[10]

Table 19.3 FMECA analysis for the pharmaceutical preparation of a gel for the treatment of insect bites

Component or process	Failure mode	Cause	Failure effect	Detection	P	S	D	RPN
Purified water for dissolving ingredients	Presence of ozone in the mixing vessel	Poor treatment of feed water	Products would be oxidized	Presence of ozone activates alarm	2	6	3	36
Purified water for dissolving ingredients	Microbiological contamination	Water treatment system malfunctioning	Contamination of final product	Quality inspection at treatment facility	1	7	6	42
Active ingredient	Quantity of product insufficient	Loss during transfer in the feed pipe	Concentration too low	Detected by an operator	2	4	6	48
Active ingredient	Not according to specification	Poor mixing of powder upstream	Final production not conforming	Quality control inspection	3	8	2	48
Sodium hydroxide solution	Microbiological contamination	Using dirty utensils	Product toxic	Quality control inspection	2	7	2	28
Sodium hydroxide solution	Concentration too high	Solid ingredients incorrectly weighed	Lot would have to be rejected	Quality control inspection	2	4	1	8
Mixing all components	Mixture non-homogeneous	Agitation temperature too low	Gelatin formation would be impaired	Detected by the temperature controller	3	2	1	6
Mixing all components	Foam appears on the final solution	Agitation too strong	Gelatin formation would be impaired	Visual inspection	4	7	2	56
Formation of gelatine	Gel non-homogeneous	Machine incorrectly adjusted	Product non-conforming. Lot would be rejected	Final quality control inspection	2	6	3	36
Transfer of gel to filler	Microbiological contamination	Transfer pipes not clean	Lot would be rejected	Inspection prior to filling	3	8	3	72
Filling 30 ml tubes	Tubes incorrectly sealed	Caps of poor quality	Lot to be dumped	Quality control inspection				
Filling 30 ml tubes	Volume too little	Filling machine incorrectly adjusted	Product quantity non-conforming	Quality control inspection	2	6	3	36

It should be noted that in the FMECA analysis, since the value of RPM is the product of three values, the effect of a high value of the seriousness of a failure, S, could be reduced by a low value of D, the difficulty of detecting the failure. In practice, if the value of S is high, then the value of D should be low.

Maintenance

Maintenance covers all those operations such as monitoring, inspecting, adjusting, repairing, and/or doing whatever is necessary to put or keep a machine, facility, a piece of equipment, or transportation vehicle in proper working order. A maintenance programme may consist of just emergency maintenance, simple preventive maintenance, or more sophisticated well-managed preventive maintenance-type programmes such as total productive maintenance (TPM) or reliability-centred maintenance (RCM).

Poor maintenance

An example of poor maintenance is illustrated in Industry insight 19.4 that resulted in both tragedy and horrendous financial cost.

Emergency maintenance

Emergency maintenance, or run-to-breakdown maintenance, is repairing machines or equipment after a failure has occurred. Obviously, this is not an ideal way of keeping equipment operating but is very often the policy with home users of appliances such as washing machines, televisions, dishwashers and other appliances where the owner waits until the machine breaks down before calling a repairer. Light bulbs are commonly only replaced when they go out. This policy usually creates no safety hazard and is more usually an inconvenience to the user. However, when emergency maintenance occurs in operating equipment, the system capacity is reduced, workers are idle and this causes direct labour costs to rise. Costs increase because of the necessity of calling in emergency maintenance crews and urgently

American Airlines and the DC-10

Industry insight 19.4

In Chicago, USA, on 25 May 1979 everything happened so quickly. The only remains of American Airlines flight N110AA, a McDonnell Douglas DC-10 that assured the liaison Chicago–Los Angeles, was the burnt wreckage scattered in a field. Just 31 seconds after takeoff from O'Hare airport, the engine broke away from the wing, the airplane reared, rolled to one side and the end of its left wing hit the ground. The plane was immediately transformed into a fireball. The 279 passengers and crew were burnt to death, as well as two people on the ground. The subsequent inquiry oriented towards a mechanical failure caused by the rupture of one of the bolts, which secured the engine to the aircraft wing. The maintenance procedures had not verified this anomaly.

On 6 June 1979 the US Federal Aviation Authority (FAA) withdrew the flightworthy certificate from the 270 DC-10s in service of which 58 belonged to European airline companies. This grounding, resulted in flight cancellations worldwide (including the author's flight to Europe for his wedding!), and millions of dollars in lost revenues. In addition, American Airlines and McDonnell Douglas were subjected to costly lawsuits from the terrible loss of life from the USA's worst commercial airline accident.

The European airlines were angered at the FAA's grounding decision and acted alone. At a meeting on 12 June in Strasbourg, France, they adopted their own revised aircraft maintenance programme. And, on 18 June, in Zurich, Switzerland, they voted to permit the flying of their DC-10s in spite of the FAA ruling. However, the FAA refused to allow these European planes to fly over US territory and the 138 USA-registered planes remained grounded. It was only after intense pressure from airlines and further research that the FAA in Oklahoma rescinded the DC-10 grounding on 13 July 1979.

(The long-term outcome of this failure and the poor maintenance programme was the complete loss in passenger confidence in the DC-10 jumbo jet (in favour of Boeing's 747). McDonnell Douglas Corp.'s market share of commercial aircraft sales tumbled, and it finally stopped production of the DC-10 and essentially pulled out of commercial aircraft manufacture. This episode was the catalyst resulting in McDonnell Douglas being swallowed by its competitor Boeing in July 1997.[11])

Adapted from: 'A DC-10 loses an engine on takeoff',[12] and 'Flying for the DC-10s is authorized'[13]

acquiring the necessary spare parts. Further, client service level drops because units cannot be produced according to the master production schedule meaning that orders cannot be delivered when promised.

Preventive maintenance

Preventive maintenance is the work activity that has been programmed on a regular basis to inspect a system, to uncover potential problems, and to make whatever repairs are necessary to ensure that the system does not fail during normal operation. Studies have indicated that if good preventive maintenance management practices are applied, and integrated with other operations activities, cost reductions of 35% or more are possible.[14]

Level of preventive maintenance

Maintenance is a cost and to a customer really adds no value to a product. The costs include the salaries of the people performing the maintenance, inventories kept for the maintenance procedures such as spares for machines, and the lost time when equipment is down for repairs. The frequency of maintenance must be balanced with the cost if a failure should occur. The breakdown of a piece of equipment upstream of a production line can be costly if it means the shutdown of the whole plant. Besides, the cost of lost production, there will be idle employees during the period the maintenance is performed. In some instances, it might be less costly to run a machine until it breaks down, and then to perform the necessary emergency repairs. The relationship between the maintenance costs and the cost of failures is illustrated in Figure 19.6. This curve illustrates that there is an optimum level when preventive maintenance programmes should be carried out. The exact level depends on the systems in question

Figure 19.6 Frequency of maintenance and associated costs

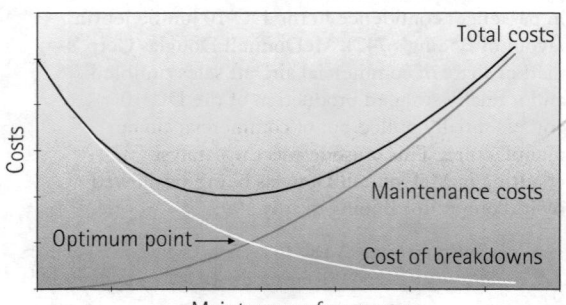

and the mean time between failures as discussed in the previous section.

An illustration of the costs associated with preventive maintenance programmes is developed in Demonstrating the concept 19.2.

Total productive maintenance

Total productive maintenance (TPM) is a well-defined and organized maintenance programme developed in Japan, which places a high value on teamwork, consensus building, and continuous improvement, or kaizen. As the name suggests, TPM implies a gain in productivity. Specific actions, according to Ron Moore of the RM group, Knoxville, Tennessee, require the following.[15]

Restoring equipment to a like new condition

This implies that the technology, instrumentation, software and standards are available to ascertain this like-new condition.

Having operators involved in the maintenance of the equipment

However, it has to be recognized that at times operators need to be able to call on specialists for complex problems to help the operator in the diagnosis to restore the equipment to like-new equipment. It also calls for operators to work with purchasing, engineering, and maintenance to modify procurement standards to assure maximum reliability in future equipment.

Improving maintenance efficiency and effectiveness

This requires that the maintenance staff is able to accurately determine the condition of the equipment so that specific needs can be determined. For example Ron Moore's experience was that 10% to 20% of maintenance work required rework, which indicated that there was clearly an opportunity to improve maintenance efficiency and effectiveness.

Training the labour force to improve on their job skills

Technology is constantly changing, thus operators and maintenance personnel need continuous training that includes for the integration of operations, engineering, purchasing and maintenance practices. This training also calls for people trained in communication skills, teamwork, performance metrics, and cross-functional relationships.

Equipment management and maintenance prevention

Equipment is managed through standards for reliability at purchase, or overhaul, during storage, installation, operation and maintenance and then in a continuous cycle feeding the design process for reliability improvement. Maintenance prevention is accomplished by doing those things that increase equipment life, maximize maintenance intervals, avoid unnecessary preventive maintenance, and constantly seek to improve reliability.

Effective use of preventive and predictive maintenance technology

The best preventive maintenance procedures are those that simply do not schedule preventive maintenance. Rather, they are those that, typically, use a computerized maintenance management system to provide for machine histories, failure frequencies, Pareto analyses, stores and parts histories, and interface to purchasing, resource loading, and maintenance planning, and scheduling.

The philosophy in TPM is that if equipment is in good condition and making what it is designed to make, most problems arise from human error. In which case, firms should aim to employ equipment that is easy to use correctly, but difficult to use incorrectly. Under this approach, TPM thus focuses on improving reliability of the complete manufacturing system, reducing uncertainty within the supply chain, reducing lead times, and increasing customer service level. All this is without increasing the level of inventory.[16]

Reliability-centred maintenance

Reliability-centred maintenance (RCM) refers to a scheduled maintenance programme designed to realize the inherent reliability of the capabilities of equipment. It originated in the air transport industry in 1974 and by its emphasis on reliability, interest in its application soon spread to other areas. It focuses on establishing what exactly is meant by the right maintenance rather than just very frequent complete overhaul of equipment. It determines what must be done to ensure that any physical asset continues to fulfil its present operating context ensuring that equipment and systems work as designed with minimal problems.[17] RCM focuses on function, not equipment, and its ultimate benefit are to drive down corrective maintenance costs and to reduce costs associated with outages and downtime.[18]

In a system there are the following three types of possible failure:

1. functional failures that would be observed or evident to the crew operating the system
2. potential failures which would be uncovered by the maintenance crews
3. hidden failure of redundant systems that would only be observed under test conditions.

In order to avert these types of failure there are the following four scheduled maintenance tasks in RCM:

1. On condition inspection of items to find and correct any potential failures.
2. Rework at, or before, some specified age limit.
3. Discard at, or before, some specified life limit.
4. Failure-finding inspections of hidden function items to correct functional failures.

The procedure can be undertaken by using a yes/no decision diagram called the RCMII decision diagram that guides the analyst through the dominant failure modes towards one or more appropriate scheduled maintenance tasks.[19]

As an illustration, the Madawaska paper mill in Maine, USA, implemented RCM and defined the following goals for the programme:

- Reducing scheduled maintenance from 2% to 1.5%.
- Reducing unscheduled maintenance from 2% to 1.5%.
- Achieving a total mill efficiency improvement of 1.5%.

For Madawaska, the change to RCM required maintenance departments to adopt the principles of planning and anticipation, in place of policies based on fix it and forget it. It also obliged maintenance to forge new relationships with engineering and production personnel.[20]

Another illustration of the advantages of RCM is from the Huddersfield, UK, plant of Zeneca (now Astrazeneca), a bioscience company. This firm implemented RCM, at a cost of £11,000 on a 20-year-old ice manufacturing plant that was critical to the site, as this plant supported a range of other facilities. With RCM in place in 1995 the firm was able to reduce downtime by 1500 hours, which translated into a savings of £1.5 million.[21]

It should be noted that reliability-centred maintenance concepts support and enhance the basic tenets of the total productive maintenance philosophy.

Recovery from a failure

For all that is said about reliability and maintenance, even with the best programmes in place, in the best of organizations, failures do occur either through poor product design, poor operation, poor maintenance or just plain bad luck. In this event, a firm should have in place programmes, or systems, in order to recover from the failure. The following are some considerations.

Product redesign

When products are commercialized it is assumed that their design is appropriate for the service for which they are intended. However this is not always the case. Ford Motor Co. commercialized the Pinto in the 1970s, which proved to have insufficient heat shielding on the gasoline tank. After several accidents it was withdrawn from service. Bridgestone/Firestone had blowouts on its tyres fitted to Ford automobiles in 1999 and 2000. This resulted in Ford cancelling the long-standing contract between Ford and Bridgestone (see Industry insight 4.2). As a contrast, Industry insight 19.5 illustrates where firms are working on a redesign to bring a product back into service.

Just-in-time

The just-in-time philosophy of operations (Chapter 15) has built in the sense of rapid recovery from failure. In just-in-time, operators are trained to be polyvalent such that when equipment breaks down, or there is a problem on the production line, operators, as a team,

---

Concorde

The idea of the Concorde supersonic airplane was conceived in 1956 by a group of British aircraft and engine manufacturers, and government officials. In the early 1960s serious discussions with the British and French took place and the specifications for an Anglo-French supersonic plane, which could fly at Mach 2.2, were published. Construction of the plane was awarded to the British Aircraft Corporation and Aerospatiale of France who were responsible for the airframe and Rolls-Royce (Britain) and SNECMA (France) for the Olympus 593 jet engines. In June 1963 Pan Am of the USA signed options to buy six of the airplanes and by May 1967 sales options reached a total of 74 aircraft from 16 airlines. The British and the French worked in parallel developing prototypes and commercial units with the governments of both countries investing heavily in the project.

Concorde was put into service in 1976, first with transatlantic services between Washington DC and London and Paris. Later services were from the European capitals and New York. Only British Airways and Air France had the airplane as all the other companies cancelled their options. These cancellations were strongly influenced by a December 1975 decision by the US House of Representatives which voted 199 to 198 to put a six-month ban on Concorde's landing in the USA. In 1979 the British and French governments announced that no more Concordes would be built. Britain had seven of the aircraft and France six.

On Tuesday 25 July 2000, 14 years after being in service, the first fatal accident involving Concorde occurred when an Air France plane crashed 60 seconds after takeoff when a tyre blowout ruptured a fuel tank. This started a sequence of events that caused a fire which eventually lead to the failure of the two port engines. The aircraft crashed into a hotel killing all 100 passengers, nine crewmembers plus four people in the hotel. The cause of the accident was attributed to a hard metal strip of titanium found on the Paris Charles de Gaulle airport runway, which apparently ruptured the tyre. This metal strip came from a poorly executed repair to a Continental Airlines McDonnell Douglas DC-10 thrust reverser. As a result of the accident, Concorde's certificate of airworthiness was suspended.

Concorde was never a success commercially. However, the airplane is very prestigious to both the British and the French government and British Airways and Air France wanted the plane back into service. Although Concorde is noisy and polluting, and perceived as a plaything for the superrich, there was also a strong following among clients who wanted Concorde back in the air. Thus, in order to recover from this crisis, EADS (formerly Aerospatiale) and BAE Systems (formerly British Aerospace) proposed a redesign of the underside of the plane which included a floating, flexible Kevlar sheet in the fuel tanks which, if fuel started to escape rapidly from the wing underside, would block the hole to limit the flow to a rate which would not cause danger. In addition, Michelin redesigned a more durable tyre for Concorde to minimize the risk of blowout. Concorde resumed commercial service in November 2001.

Adapted from: 'Poor repair to DC-10 was cause of Concorde crash', *Flight International*,[22] and the Concorde website[23]

provide the necessary help to bring the system back to its normal operation in order to minimize downtime. This is a far cry from the time when all operations were strongly unionized and organized by function. As an illustration, the author was a drilling operator in a manufacturing firm in the 1960s. One morning, a screw came loose from the drill machine and the machine shut off. The author could have fixed the problem in a few minutes easily but was unable to do because of union rules. Instead, he had to fill in a work order for a maintenance man to come and fix the problem. The result was that the assembly operation was down for two hours.[24]

Subcontractor/supplier network

Having in place in reliable subcontractor or supplier network can be extremely helpful in an organization in that if something goes wrong, such as a machine fails, a truck breaks down, or raw materials do not conform, then a firm has outside contacts to call on in case of emergency situations. Industry insight 19.6 illustrates a situation from Japan whose strong supplier relationship, or keiretsu, made the difference in the recovery from a failure resulting in a disastrous fire.

Crisis management

Crisis management is a function in place by major corporations and often governments to respond and to recover from a failure very often on a large scale. Chemical firms have crisis management teams in place to recover from failures resulting from industrial accidents such as fires, or other occurrences which result in plant shutdown or environmental disasters (see Chapter 5). Alternatively, governments and some firms might have in place crisis management teams to respond to natural disasters or economic downturn as is illustrated, for example, in the Industry insight 19.7.

In crisis management the ultimate objective is to reduce the impact of the failure or a crisis. Activities included in crisis management would involve:

- Undertaking a risk evaluation analysis to identify what might be possible occurrences.
- Developing appropriate action plans and strategic plans in order to respond to the failure.
- Developing failure information systems in order to record and report the occurrences.

Toyota's recovery — Industry insight 19.6

No one knows what caused the fire that destroyed Aisin Seiki Co.'s Factory Nº 1 in the morning of Saturday 1 February 1997. The fire incinerated the main source of a crucial brake valve that Toyota buys from Aisin and uses in most of its cars. Most Toyota plants kept only a four-hour supply of the $5 valve and without it Toyota had to shut down its 20 auto plants in Japan, which built 14,000 cars a day. Some experts thought Toyota wouldn't recover for weeks. But just five days after the fire, Toyota's car factories started up again. The secret lay in Toyota's close-knit family of parts suppliers which rushed to the rescue. Within hours they had begun taking blueprints for the valve, improvising tooling systems, and setting up makeshift production lines. By the following Thursday, the 36 suppliers, aided by more than 150 other subcontractors, had nearly 50 separate lines producing small batches of the brake valve. In one case, a sewing machine maker that had never made car parts spent about 500 manhours refitting a milling machine to make just 40 valves a day.

Adapted from: 'To the rescue: Toyota's recovery from factory fire shows firm's clout', *Wall Street Journal Europe*[25]

Heathrow Airport — Industry insight 19.7

Authorities at Heathrow International Airport London had a crisis on Friday 12 December 1997 after a roof fire closed the airport's busiest passenger Terminal 1 for half the day severely restricting operations and forcing flight cancellations for tens of thousands of passengers. Fortunately, the fire occurred in the early morning and helped to avoid a replay of the tragic fire that swept through Dusseldorf International Airport in 1996, killing 17 people and causing damage totalling $55 million. Heathrow learnt some lessons from the German fire and credited the rapid control of the blaze to the $1.65 million new investment in fire detection, alarms, other safety systems, and their crisis management team.

Adapted from: 'London scurries to restore flights', *International Herald Tribune*[26]

• If appropriate, putting in place teams to respond to pressure groups and to respond to the public, and to the media.

Like the Heathrow Airport incident, the ultimate effectiveness of crisis management can be measured from the speed with which the organization recovers, the degree to which it recovers, the extent of the operational and organizational improvement added during the recovery, and the amount of crisis resistance added since the failure arose.[27]

Summary of key elements

• Failure of equipment will have diverse consequences ranging from customer inconvenience, lost revenue, delayed production, poor quality, and perhaps even tragedy.

• Reliability is the confidence one has in a product, process, service, work team, or individual to operate under prescribed and expected conditions.

• A product assembled in a series arrangement of components $R_1, R_2, \cdots, R_n$ has a system reliability, R_S, given by $R_S = R_1 * R_2 * R_3 * R_4 \cdots R_n$.

• If a failure would be problematic, backup systems operate in the eventual failure of the principal system. Here, components $R_1, R_2, \cdots, R_n$ are connected in a parallel giving a system reliability

$R_S = 1 - (1 - R_1)(1 - R_2)(1 - R_3)(1 - R_4) \cdots (1 - R_n)$.

• The failure rate measures the reliability of products. It can be determined by one of the following ratios:

$$\text{Failure rate (\%)} = \frac{\text{Number of products which failed}}{\text{Total number of products tested}}$$

$$\text{Failure rate (N)} = \frac{\text{Number of products which failed}}{\text{Number of unit hours of operating time}}$$

• The mean time between failures (MTBF) is the reciprocal of the failure rate (N):

$$\text{MTBF} = \frac{1}{\text{Failure rate (N)}}$$
$$= \frac{\text{Operating time for units}}{\text{Number of products which failed}}$$

• The failure rate profile can be expressed by a bathtub curve showing high failure rates at the beginning and the end, and normal failure between these extremes.

• Poka yoke is the principle to make products, process, or services failsafe by incorporating mistake-proof techniques into the design.

• A failure mode, effect and criticality analysis (FMECA) is the detailed study of a system to determine which features are critical to various modes of failure.

• Maintenance is all those operations, such as monitoring, inspecting, adjusting, and repairing, used to keep machines, equipment, or vehicles in proper working order.

• Emergency maintenance, or run-to-breakdown maintenance, is repairing machines or equipment after a failure has occurred.

• Preventive maintenance is programmed on a regular basis to inspect and to make necessary repairs to ensure that the system does not fail during normal operation.

• Total productive maintenance (TPM) places a high value on teamwork, consensus building, and continuous improvement, or kaizen. It places emphasis on bringing equipment to 'a like new condition'.

• Reliability-centred maintenance (RCM) determines what must be done to ensure that any physical asset continues to fulfil its present operating context.

• Failures occur and firms must be prepared to respond quickly. Just-in-time has built-in failure recovery, as does a good supplier/subcontractor network.

• Crisis management is a function in place by major corporations and governments to respond to failure that may be on a large scale.

Notes and references

1. COLEMAN, Brian, 'Daimler-Benz buys out Smart-car partner SMH', *Wall Street Journal Europe*, 5 November 1998
2. 'Car safety: Mercedes bends', *The Economist*, 15 November 1997
3. SCHMID, John, 'Daimler hits brakes on second flawed model', *International Herald Tribune*, 19 December 1997
4. MITCHENER, Briandon, 'Daimler's "Swatchmobile" faces delays', *Wall Street Journal Europe*, 19/20 December 1997
5. 'More dark news for Auckland', *International Herald Tribune*, 5 March 1998, p. 5
6. WALD, Mathew L., 'Accelerating toward near-disaster: A series of missteps left a jet gliding powerless over the Atlantic', and 'Linkage of two engines violated aviation principle', *International Herald Tribune*, 11 September 2001, p. 1 and 4
7. 'The Millennium Bug: Please panic early', *The Economist*, 4 October 1997, pp 23–7
8. Based on an idea by Renault VI, Bridge and axle Division, Lyon, France, 1995
9. 'Challenger, explose en plein vol' (Challenger explodes in mid-flight), *Chronique du 20e siècle*, Larousse, 1990
10. Confidential report

11. *Wall Street Journal Europe*, 31 July 1997

12. 'Un DC-10 perd un réacteur au décollage' (A DC-10 loses an engine on takeoff), *Chronique de l'aviation*, Editions Chronique, Paris, 1992, p. 768

13. 'Reprise des vols sur DC-10 autorisée' (Flying for the DC-10s is authorized), *Chronique de l'aviation*, Editions Chronique, Paris, 1992, p. 769

14. SIVALINGAM, Y. (Raj), 'Applying best practices to maintenance: A 12-step program for moving down the road to recovery', *Plant Engineering*, vol 51, issue 6, June 1997, p. 120 continued on p. 114

15. MOORE, Ron, 'Combining TPM and reliability-focussed maintenance', *Plant Engineering*, vol 51, issue 6, June 1997, pp 88–90

16. MCCARTHY, Dennis, 'Total productive maintenance', *Works Management*, vol 48, issue 4, April 1995, pp 14–15

17. MOUBRAY, John, 'Reliability centred maintenance: Making a positive contribution to asset management strategy', *Works Management*, vol 48, issue 3, March 1995, pp 14–15

18. SMOCK, Robert W., 'A comprehensive look at reliability-centred maintenance', *Power Engineering*, vol 97, issue 10, October 1993, p 12

19. PUJADAS, W. and CHEN, F. Frank, 'A reliability centered maintenance strategy for a discrete part manufacturing facility', *Computers and Industrial Engineering*, vol 31, issue 1, 2, October 1996, pp 241–4

20. ARNOLD, Richard D. and LEVASSEUR, Reginald, 'Reliability centred maintenance becomes strategic asset at Fraser's Madawaska mill', *Pulp and Paper*, vol 71, issue 2, February 1997, pp 55–8

21. GERAGHTY, Tony, 'Maintenance Matters', *The Chemical Engineer*, pp 14–16

22. LEARMOUNT, David, 'Poor repair to DC-10 was cause of Concorde crash', *Flight International*, 24–30 October 2000, p. 4

23. http//www.concordesst.com

24. Machine operator at British Oxygen, Edmonton Works, UK, June 1962

25. 'To the rescue: Toyota's recovery from factory fire shows firm's clout', *Wall Street Journal Europe*, 12 May 1997

26. 'London scurries to restore flights', *International Herald Tribune*, 13/14 December 1997

27. Crisis Corp. Ltd: http://www.crisiscorp.com/services.htm, Crisis Management Services

Review and discussion topics

1. Unexpected occurrences
List unexpected occurrences that have occurred in business in the last five years. Can you describe the reasons for these occurrences, and what steps were taken to minimize subsequent damage?

2. Backup or parallel systems
Other than the examples given in the text, list situations where operations would have in place backup or parallel systems in case of failure of the main system.

3. Failure rate
In your opinion would you consider that tangible products produced today have a 'longer life' than similar products produced, say, 15 years ago? Justify your arguments giving illustrations.

4. Poka yoke
Other than the illustrations given in the text, give other examples of where the concept of poka yoke is used, either in manufacturing or services.

5. Human error
Not infrequently, failure in systems is due to human error. What do think are some of reasons for individuals being the cause of failures? Justify your arguments with examples.

6. Failure mode, effect, and criticality analysis
Develop the framework of items of consideration in a FMECA analysis for:
  (a) an automobile
  (b) a house
  (c) a degree programme (MBA, for example).

7. Run-to-breakdown maintenance
Give illustrations where the philosophy of run-to-breakdown maintenance is employed. In these instances, what are the advantages and disadvantages of this approach in operations?

Demonstrating the concept 19.1 Toilet systems

Situation

Boeing Aircraft Company is interested in learning something about the reliability of its toilets on its long haul 747s, having been notified of passenger complaints. On average, the flight time of these long haul planes is 11 hours. It tested 12 toilet units for a duration of 50 hours each. During the test, one unit failed after 20 hours, one after 25 hours, and one after 45 hours.

Required

Determine the following:

1. the failure as a percentage, FR(%)
2. the number of failures during a period of time FR(N)
3. the mean time between failures
4. estimated toilet failures per 747 trip.

Solution

1. Failure rate $(\%) = \dfrac{\text{Number of products which failed}}{\text{Total number of products tested}}$

$$= \frac{3}{12} = 25.00\%.$$

2. The number of failures during a period of time FR(N): total unit hours of operating time are $12 * 50 = 600$.

   Non-operating time is the total time the three units were not operating for the full 50 hours of the test. For the first unit this is $(50 - 20)$ or 30 hours, the second unit $(50 - 25)$ or 25 hours, and the third unit this is $(50 - 45)$ or 5 hours. Thus total non-operating time is $30 + 25 + 5 = 60$ hours.

   Operating time is $600 - 60 = 540$ hours.

   The failure rate in units per total unit operating time is:

   Failure rate $(N) = \dfrac{\text{Number of products which failed}}{\text{Number of unit hours of operating time}}$

   $$= \frac{3}{540} = 0.005556$$

3. Mean time between failures is the reciprocal of FR(N) or $1/0.005556 = 180$ hours.
4. Average toilet failures per trip is average flight time $* FR(N) = 11 * 0.005556 = 0.06111$.

Demonstrating the concept 19.2 Copying machine

Situation

A consulting company in London has a copying machine that it uses to copy contractual material for its clients. The firm currently operates the machine in a run-to-breakdown mode. The company estimates that on average, each time the copier machine breaks down, the cost due to lost time for client work is £500. Based on historical information over the last 2½ years the number of breakdowns, and the number of months that this level occurred are shown in Table 19.4.

A service company in the area has proposed a preventive maintenance contract at a cost of £900 a month and with this contract it guarantees that the breakdowns will, on average, be one every two months.

Required

Determine whether or not the company should change its policy and purchase the preventive maintenance service contract.

Solution

This problem can be resolved using expected values (discussed in more depth in Chapter 23).

The expected, or average value of the breakdowns is determined by taking the weighted average of the historical data as shown in Table 19.5.

- The total months of the study are 30. The frequency of occurrence for each breakdown is the number per month divided by 30. This frequency is given in column 3.
- Each frequency is multiplied by each of the number of breakdowns. This is given in column 4.
- The total of column 4 is 2.77 or the average or expected number of breakdowns a month.

The expected cost of breakdowns a month is then the average multiplied by the monthly cost or:

$$2.77 * £500 = £1383.33$$

The monthly cost of the preventive maintenance contract is the cost of the contract itself plus the

Table 19.4 Copying machine breakdowns

N° of breakdowns	0	1	2	3	4	5
N° a month	2	5	4	9	7	3

Table 19.5 Average value of breakdowns

N° of breakdowns	N° a month	Frequency	Frequency* breakdowns
0	2	6.67%	0.00
1	5	16.67%	0.17
2	4	13.33%	0.27
3	9	30.00%	0.90
4	7	23.33%	0.93
5	3	10.00%	0.50
Total	30	100.00%	2.77

costs when a breakdown occurs, in this case. Since one breakdown every two months is equivalent to 0.50 per month then the total cost is:

$$£900 + £500 * 0.25 = £1150$$

This amount is less than the run-to-breakdown policy, and so the firm would be best to take out a preventive maintenance contract.

Application exercise 19.1 Bicycle rental

Situation

A company in Switzerland rents out all-terrain bicycles during the summer months for use in the Alps. At one location, the firm has just one employee who devotes his time to the rental arrangement. Since he is alone, he has no time to perform preventive maintenance, but can only repair a bike if a client brings it back having broken it. If this happen, the firm estimates it loses $30 each time because of customer irritation and it is also obliged to let the client have more rental time for longer than the time he has actually paid for. Based on data for the last summer period, Table 19.6 gives a breakdown frequency for the bikes.

The firm is thinking of employing another person on a part-time basis whose sole function will be to perform preventive maintenance on the fleet of bikes. This would cost the firm $280 per month. Even with this preventive

Table 19.6 Bicycle breakdown frequency

Number of bikes broken down	1	2	3	4	5	6	7
Number of weeks when this level occurred	2	3	5	4	6	2	2

maintenance, however, there is still expected to be, on average, one bike broken down a week.

Required

Should the firm hire a second person part time to perform preventive maintenance or should it stay with its present policy? Justify your response.

Application exercise 19.2 Bindings for skis

Situation

A manufacturer of ski equipment wants to learn something about the reliability of its racing ski bindings. It tested 25 units over a period of harsh treatment for 2000 hours each. One unit failed after 200 hours, one after 300 hours, one after 800 hours, one after 1200 hours, and one after 1550 hours. The firm estimated that these bindings were used on average for 200 hours before being replaced.

Required

Determine the following:
1. the failure as a percentage, FR(%)
2. the number of failures during a period of time FR(N)
3. the mean time between failures
4. the estimated failures per use of the bindings.

Application exercise 19.3 Smith Co.

Situation

Smith Co. makes electronic circuit boards that are used in automatically controlled drilling machines. In one particular circuit board the present design has nine components connected in series. The reliability of these nine components is as shown in Table 19.7.

Table 19.7 Smith Co.: Circuit board component reliability

Component	1	2	3	4	5	6	7	8	9
Reliability	0.99	0.98	0.97	0.96	0.99	0.98	0.99	0.96	0.98

Required

1. What is the reliability of this circuit board with the nine components in a series arrangement?
2. How would the reliability change if Smith were able to redesign the system so that the first three components were in series, but these were then connected in parallel to the other five components that were themselves connected in series according to the scheme shown in Figure 19.7?
3. With a much more detailed modification, Smith Co. was able to put components 1 through 3 in series, this

combination in parallel with components 4 through 6 themselves in series, and, finally, this combination in parallel with components 7 through 9, themselves in series as illustrated in Figure 19.8. What would the reliability of the circuit board be then?

Figure 19.8 Smith Co.: Component connection series (2)

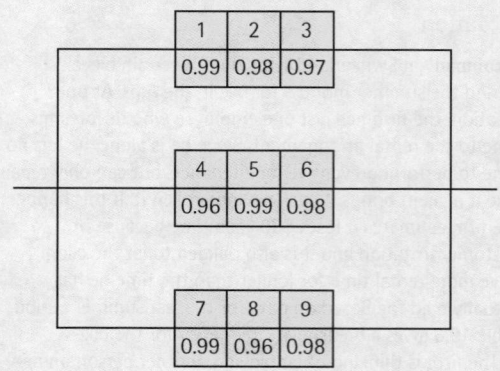

Figure 19.7 Smith Co.: Component connection series (1)

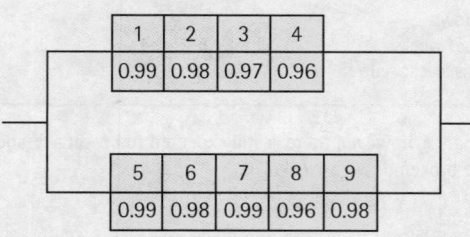

Case study 19.1 A ski resort

Situation

Serre Chevalier, dubbed 'the ski station where all the world descends', is a ski resort in the southern French Alps, very close to the Italian border. The resort is, in fact, four separate ski villages: Briançon, named Serre Che 1200; Chantemerle (Serre Che 1350); Villeneuve La Salle (Serre Che 1400); and Montier les Bains (Serre Che 1500). From the base of these villages you can ski up to an altitude of 2800 metres. The following are the ski lifts for the four villages:

Briançon
- Prorel (cc)
- Serre Blanc (cl)
- Rocher Blanc (cl)
- Croix de la Noire (tb)
- Serre Pelat (tb)
- Stade de slalom (cl)

Chantemerle
- Aiguilette (cl)
- Bois des coqs 1 (tb)
- Grand Alps (cl)
- Combes 2 (tb)
- Bletonet 1 (tc)
- Bletonet 2 (cl)
- Prorel 1 (tb)
- Bois des coqs 2 (tb)
- Grand Serre (cl)
- Grand Alp 1 (cc)
- Bletonet 2 (tc)
- Orée du bois (tb)
- Prorel 2 (tb)
- Replat (tb)
- Combes 1 (tb)
- Grand Alps 2 (cc)
- Bletonet 1 (cl)

Villeneuve
- Contillas (tc)
- Forêt 1 (tb)
- Côte Chevalier (cl)
- Clot Mea (cl)
- Aravet (tc)
- Forêt 2 (tb)
- Pré du bois (tb)
- Balme (cl)
- Tremplin (cl)
- L'Echaillon (tb)
- Clot Gauthier (cl)

Montier
- Yret (cl)
- Corvaria (cl)
- Charmettes (tb)
- Cibouit (cl)
- Étoile (tb)
- Pre Charbert (tb)
- Lauzieres (cl)
- Chanteloubbe (cl)
- Cucumelle (cl)

[cc = cable car   cl = chairlift   tb = towbar   tc = telecabin (60 people)]

At Briançon, the chairlift Serre Blanc is the connection to the neighbouring Chantemerle and Cucumelle is the connecting chairlift between Villeneuve and Montier. All the lift systems runs are driven by electric motors from the same electric power supply that serves the community of Serre Chevalier. The reliability of all the motors driving the lifts is 95%. Each of the lifts has a backup motor driven by an oil-driven generator. These backup systems have a reliability of 90%.

As Serre Chevalier faces south, the snow on the lower slopes thaws easily, exposing rocks and wood stumps. For this reason, and when the snow for the season is poor, at the intermediary level of each of the four villages, there are snow-making machines, operated electrically from the community power supply and fed by water from the respective villages. There are no backup systems to these snow-making machines. At night time a fleet of ten snow cats serve the four villages, grooming the slopes.

Access to the village is from the west over the Col du Lautaret at 2058 metres, or, coming east from Turin, over the Col de Montgenèvre. For the convenience of skiers there is a bus shuttle service between the four villages, plus bus services from Lyon, Grenoble, and Turin to serve both foreign and French tourists.

Required

1. As the manager responsible for the whole Serre Chevalier ski resort, what would you expect from your maintenance programme, from the point of view of both customer service and safety?
2. Develop a scheme for an FMECA covering the ski lifts.

Selected further reading

AUGUST, Jim (2000) *Applied Reliability Centered Maintenance*, Pennwell.

GERTSBAKH, I.B. and GERTSBAKH, Eliahu (2000) *Reliability Theory With Applications to Preventive Maintenance*, Springer Verlag.

KUMAR, U. Dinesh, CROCKER, John, KNEZEVIC, J. and EL-HARAM, M. (2001) *Reliability, Maintenance and Logistic Support: A Life Cycle Approach*, Kluwer Academic Publishers.

MOUBRAY, John (2001) *Reliability-Centered Maintenance*, 2nd edition, Industrial Press.

PHILLIPS, Todd, 'What's your maintenance strategy?', *Plant Engineering and Maintenance*, vol. 21, issue 4, September 1997, pp 22–6.

An extensive listing of other further reading can be found on the website.

What's on the web?

Further learning resources are available to lecturers and students at www.supplychain-online.com, including the following which are specific to *Reliability and maintenance*:

Resource	Subject
Chapter overview	Reliability and maintenance
More further reading	Reliability and maintenance

20 *Statistical quality control*

Elements of statistical quality control

Introduction

As mentioned in Chapter 4, statistical quality control covers the analytical procedures for verifying the conformity of a process or a product, either in manufacturing or services. Non-conforming units, or activities, anywhere in the supply chain will lead to client dissatisfaction because of the poor quality, delays as a result of the time necessary to remedy quality problems, and additional cost to repair the faulty product or remedy the faulty service.

A good total quality management system, either in the purchasing, transformation, or the distribution phase of the supply chain will attempt to correct faults at an early stage using control charts or statistical process control (SPC). This is the philosophy behind the ISO-9000 quality certification (see Chapter 4) where one should ensure that the process that is making the product or performing the service is operating correctly as correcting the fault after the product has been made, or the service has been performed, is often too late. In statistical process control, samples are taken to see whether characteristics of the units or the process lie within specified ranges. If so, the process is operating correctly. If not the process is stopped and corrective measures are taken.

Acceptance sampling is another practice in statistical quality control that some firms use as an alternative to SPC or in addition to it. This is where a series, or lot of goods which have already been produced, are inspected and either accepted or rejected according to some predetermined criteria. The drawback with acceptance sampling is that all the value-added activity has already been performed and that if a lot is rejected, the costs can be exceedingly high. Since most firms have total quality management programmes in place and many are certified ISO-9000, the emphasis is on statistical process control rather than acceptance sampling. In the supply chain, when a supplier is providing components or a service to a downstream client and the supplier is certified ISO-9000 this implies (but doesn't guarantee) that the goods or services are at specification quality and in theory acceptance sampling should not be necessary. However, even with all the quality programmes in place, and all the quality certifications possible, errors do occur and firms still resort to acceptance sampling as appropriate to be quite sure of the quality of their supplied products.

Lots, series, or batches

In a manufacturing or production operation, units are often made in discrete groups called lots or series for tangible units or a batch for liquid products. These groups of units will have been produced under the same operating conditions such as the following:

- on the same machine
- with the same operators
- using raw material from the same batch
- in the same time period
- during the same shift
- under the same process conditions.

The particular quantity of units in a manufactured lot, series or batch might be:

* an amount simply based on economics
* the amount ordered by a client
* the process is a batch operation where the units are made in fixed quantities because of the particular constraint of the process (this is the case of pharmaceutical products, chemicals, wine, beer, etc. where the size of the batch is limited by the volume of the production vessel)
* that quantity of units which is the most practical to produce at any one time given the equipment, raw materials, and operating team available.

Production in discrete quantities occurs in many manufacturing concerns such as the food, automobile, textile, paper, printing, and the chemical industry. Statistical process control attempts to ensure that the process for producing these lots is performing correctly such that when the operation is finished, the lot conforms to specifications. Acceptance sampling would be the inspection of a finished lot and may be performed by a client who has received a lot of units from an upstream supplier or subcontractor.

Quality characteristics

In production, the ultimate goal is to make specification-quality units. The test of quality might be that the product works, or it does not work. This is considered an *attribute*.[1] Alternatively, the test might be that the unit is within a given *variable* range to meet certain specifications such as colour, weight, length, diameter, viscosity, volume, hardness, etc. In the service industry quality characteristics are most often attributes where a service is either good or bad.

Attributes

Attributes are characteristics that can be only one of two outcomes, or a binomial classification. In general terms, examples of binomial outcomes are:

* yes or no
* open or closed
* pass or fail
* go or no go
* clean or dirty
* conforming or non-conforming
* good or bad
* on time or late
* sharp or dull (blades)
* right or wrong.

In production for attribute classification, basically, a product works or it does not:

* a battery generates a current when it is connected to a circuit, or it does not
* a bulb illuminates, or it does not
* a lid closes, or it does not.

In services the attribute classification is that the service is acceptable or it is not:

* the train arrives on time, or it is late
* the bank statement is correct, or it is wrong
* the hotel room is clean, or it is not.

Attribute measures are count data. For example, five of the sample bulbs inspected were found to be defective, or three of the 40 hotel rooms were found to be dirty. For attribute data, a discrete probability distribution such as the binomial, or Poisson serves as the basis for statistical inference (see Chapter 27).

Variables

Variables are characteristics that can be measured on a continuous scale where there is a range of acceptance. For example, a dial micrometer can be used to measure the diameter of a motor shaft and if the diameter is within the minimum and maximum allowable specification, the shaft passes the inspection. When variables are involved it is almost impossible to have exactly the nominal amount specified. The volume of beer in a can is indicated on the label as 33cl. However, it is highly unlikely that the volume will be 33.0000cl but perhaps something like 32.9985cl or 33.0204cl. Both volumes would be acceptable to the consumer or to a weights and measures inspector. For most work, the narrower the specification range, the better the quality of the units produced (see Chapter 4, particularly the section on Taguchi methods). The airline industry considers arrival or departure times somewhat of a variable as in their quality performance measurement times between ±15 minutes is acceptable. For variables, it is the normal distributions that serve as the basis for statistical inference (see Chapter 27).

Origin of statistical quality control

The technique of statistical quality control has its roots in the research work of Walter A Shewart, Harold F Dodge, and H G Romig in the 1920s and 1930s. These three men, who worked at the Bell Telephone Laboratories, USA (since September 1996, as a result of the AT&T de-merger, now part of Lucent Technologies), developed analytical methods using random samples, statistical control charts, and statistical acceptance of products based on sampling from lots.

Goal of statistical quality control

It is statistical process control that is, or should be, the dominant practice of statistical quality control.

In manufacturing the ultimate objective is not to find out if units conform but to avoid the production of non-conforming items in the first place. Similarly, in the airline industry, retailing, banking, medical and other service industries it is not to establish after the fact that quality is poor but to avoid problems before they become widescale. It is always more economical to manufacture products or perform services that are acceptable rather than having to repair damages later. In addition to measurable costs, there is often the intangible customer damage.

Basic concepts of statistical process control

Definition of statistical process control

Statistical process control, SPC, is the periodic sampling and analysis of units, items, or activity, to determine if the system is performing, as expected, according to some predetermined target, or within design limits. The primary purpose of SPC is to analyze the process to verify that it is operating correctly. It is not to analyze the produced units to see if they conform to specifications. This is the objective of acceptance sampling discussed later in the chapter.

Manufacturing

Statistical process control in manufacturing is the periodic sampling of production units from the operating line to determine if processes, such as drilling, soldering, bottle filling, assembly, etc., are performing according to the required conditions. If the units are acceptable, no action is taken as the process is considered in control. If the output is not acceptable then the process is stopped and the necessary corrective action is taken.

Services

Statistical process control in services is the periodic sampling of activities such as:

• on-times arrivals and departures of airplanes
• quality of a professor's teaching
• accuracy of bank statements or other financial records
• room service, restaurant facilities, and cleanliness in the hotel business
• delivery conditions for merchandise in distribution and transportation
• quality of medical services, measured, perhaps, by the accuracy of diagnosis.

The purpose is to determine if the activity is according to some acceptable level. If not, corrective action is taken.

Variations in a process

The objective of statistical process control is to determine if there is variation in a process. There are two types of variation.

Random variations

Random variations are also referred to as common causes, or inherent variations. For example, in the filling operation of a 33cl can of beer the nominal or average value would be 33cl. However, because of slight differences, say in the viscosity of the beer, its foaming characteristics, the velocity of fluid in the pipe, the diameter of the filling nozzles, the rotational speed of the filling platform, etc., every can will not contain exactly 33.0000cl of beer. Some beer cans will have slightly more than 33cl, say between 33.0000 and 33.8250 and some slightly less, say between 32.1750 and 33.0000. However, if one measured the volume of a large quantity of cans of beer, most observations would lie near the nominal or average value of 33cl, with some being below this value and some above. The result would produce a symmetrical or normal distribution centred on the mean value of 33cl, as shown in Figure 20.1. Since random variations are unavoidable this spread of data would be acceptable giving specifications for the volume of beer in the can of, say, 33 ± 0.8250cl. If this distribution remains constant over a satisfactory operating time period, as shown in Figure 20.2, then the process is considered to be operating satisfactorily or in control.

Figure 20.1 Normal distribution centred on a mean of 33cl

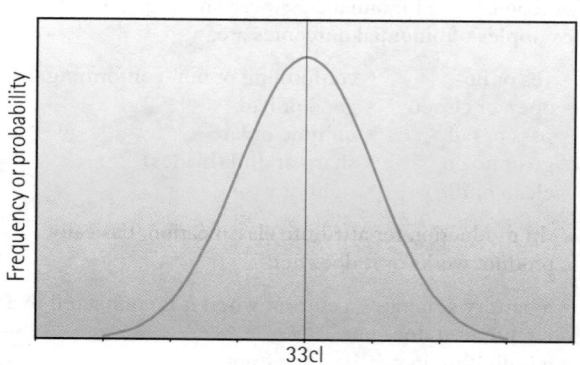

Assignable variations

In the filling operation, after time, the bearings on the rotating filling platform become sloppy, the diameter of the filling nozzles decreases slightly owing to the deposit of a small film of beer, or wear on the feed valve causes the fluid velocity to change, etc. In this case, the average volume of the beer in the can may change from 33cl to some upper or lower value, as illustrated in Figure 20.3. Alternatively, the distribution, or spread, of the volumes in the can may change, but the average volume remains the same, as illustrated in Figure 20.4. Thus, over an operating time period the distribution profiles obtained might be as shown in Figure 20.5. In this case, the variation would be assignable as one can detect or pinpoint the source of the problem. In this case, the process would be considered out of control and so the filling operation would be shut down and appropriate action taken.

In quality control, the emphasis is always on continuous improvement (kaizen). However, for a given process,

little can be done for random variations unless the production operation is changed. The purpose of statistical process control is to detect the assignable variations. When such variations occur, the process is considered out of control.

In services such as measuring, quality of teaching, bank statement errors, hotel quality, ideally there should be no variation, although, since people perform these services sometimes have their 'off days' a small amount of variation may be tolerated and this would be considered random variations. However, if the error problem were consistent, these would be assignable variations.

The control chart

The control chart is the evaluation tool in statistical process control and has already been introduced in Chapter 10. The elements of control are the same, whether the objective is to control, costs, absenteeism,

Figure 20.2 Distribution profile remains fixed over time: Process is in control

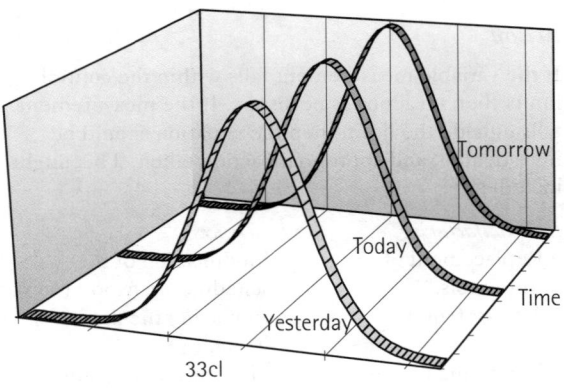

Figure 20.3 Average volume has changed: Process is out of control

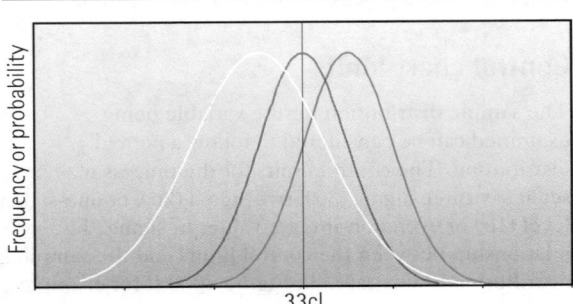

Figure 20.4 Distribution has changed: Process is out of control

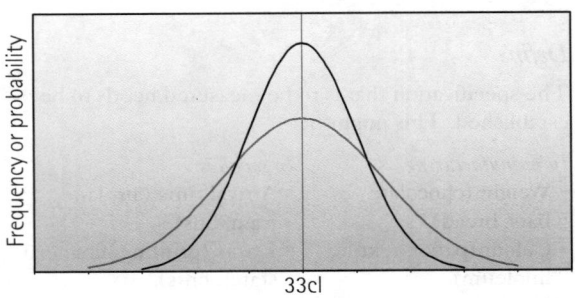

Figure 20.5 Distribution profile changes over time: Process is out of control

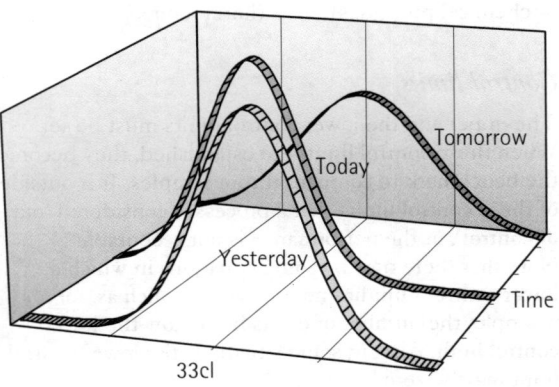

Figure 20.6 Control chart with centreline and upper and lower control limits

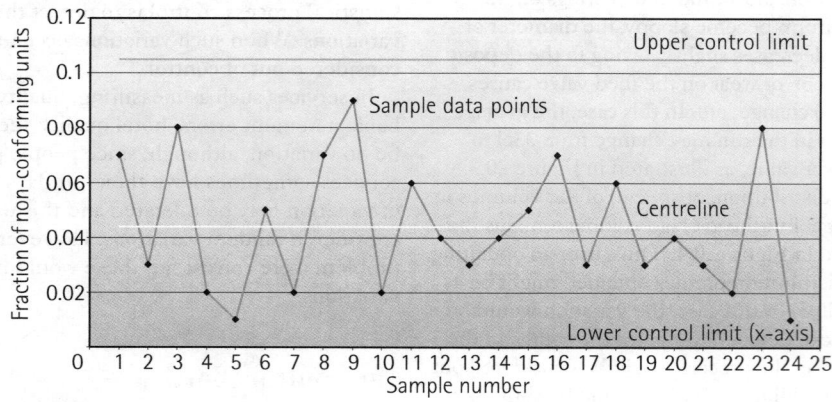

accidents, temperature, weight, time, colour, etc.
A control chart includes:

- a lower control limit (LCL)
- a centreline (CL)
- an upper control limit (UCL).

The steps in quality control using charts are as follows.

Define

The specification that is to be measured needs to be established. This might be:

In manufacturing
- Weight (chocolate bars, bread).
- Colour (paper, textile, linoleum).
- Hardness (gear wheels, metal surfaces).
- Viscosity (oil, ointments).
- Temperature (chemical processes).

In services
- Arrival time (airplane, train, bus).
- Errors (printing, financial statements).
- Evaluation level (teaching).
- Absenteeism (personnel).
- Cleanliness (hotel rooms).

Control limits

The upper and the lower control limits must be set. When these control limits are established, they become the benchmark to compare future samples. It is outside of these control limits that a process is considered 'out of control', or the performance is not acceptable. Note that there may be some situations in which a lower control limit has no importance, such as, for example, the number of errors lies below the lower control limit. Also, in some situations the lower control limit may be zero.

Measure

The variable in question must be measured. This might be the average weight of a sample of 25 chocolate bars, the quality of a professor's teaching by the 30 students in the class or the absentee level out of 600 employees. This variable is compared to the standard.

Action

If the variable measurement falls within the control limits then no action is necessary. If the measurement falls outside the limit, then the situation should be investigated, and appropriate action taken. This might include:

In manufacturing
- Replacement of worn tools.
- Adjustment of machines.
- Retraining of operating staff.

In services
- Modification of the schedule (transportation).
- Replacing the professor (teaching).
- Motivation programmes (personnel).

A typical control chart is illustrated in Figure 20.6. In this chart, all the sampling data points are within limits and so the process is considered in control.

Control chart limits

The sample distribution for the variable being examined can be considered to follow a normal distribution. The control limits for the process may be set at say three-sigma (3σ), two-sigma (2σ), or one-sigma level (1σ) or even non-integer values of sigma. The relationship between the control limits and the sampling distribution is illustrated in Figure 20.7. If for example 3σ limits are being used and sample data lie between

Figure 20.7 Control limits as they relate to the normal distribution

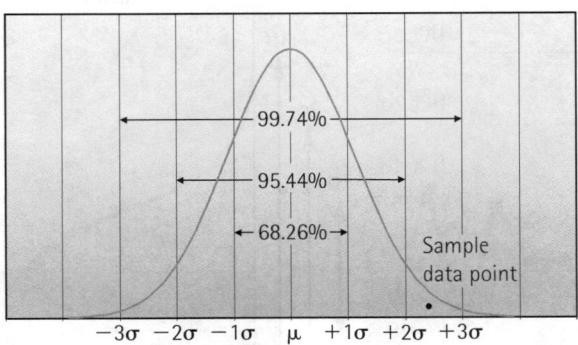

Figure 20.8 Average has shifted: There is a risk of making a Type II error

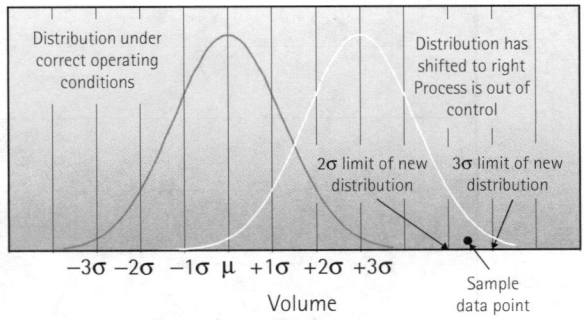

the ±3σ the process is exhibiting inherent or random variation and the process can be considered in control. If sample data lie outside of this range, then the process would be exhibiting assignable causes of variation and would be considered out of control. In interpreting sample data in control charts two types of error are possible.

Type I error

A Type I error occurs when a process is considered out of control when this is not in fact the case. Assume that a given process is in control and that 3σ limits are used to set the boundaries for the process. This is illustrated in Figure 20.7 and a sample data point, exhibiting a random variation, is shown. Since this falls inside the +3σ limit the process would be considered, quite correctly, in control. However, now assume that 2σ limits are put in place, then the indicated data point is now outside the 2σ. Thus, the assumption would be that the process is out of control but it is known that this is not true. The conclusion is that the tighter the control limits, or the smaller the number of standard deviations, the higher the probability, or risk of making a Type I error that a process is considered out of control when this is, in fact, false.

Type II error

A Type II error occurs when a process is considered in control when this is not, in fact, the case. Assume that a process is out of control and that, again, 3σ control limits are used. This is illustrated by Figure 20.8. If we consider the shown sample data point, relative to the normal curve on the left, then this is outside the 3σ limit. This would signal that the process is out of control, which is, in fact, the case. Now if the process is really out of control the distribution will move and shifts

to the right as shown. Now the data point falls within the 3σ limits of this curve and the assumption would be that the process is in control when this is not, in fact, the case. However, if tighter 2σ control limits were used, then according to the right-hand curve, the process would now be considered out of control, which is, in fact, true. Thus the conclusion here is that the tighter the control limits, or the smaller the number of standard deviations, the lower the probability or risk of making a Type II error or the risk of concluding a process is in control, when, in fact, this is not the case.

In the pharmaceutical industry, such as the production of vaccine, the control limits would be tight in order to avoid making a Type II error, as it would be too risky and the costs too high to have a poor quality vaccine on the market. This happened in the 1950s when a contaminated polio vaccine was commercialized and caused the death of several children. Contrary to this is, say, in the manufacture of washing soap where the control limits could be broader as the risk involved of using soap not exactly according to specifications is low.

The relationship with the control limits and the conclusion that a process is out of control is illustrated in Figure 20.9.

Statistical process control for attribute characteristics

The two important control charts for attributes are the p-chart and c-chart as now discussed.

P-chart

A p-chart is to indicate the percentage, or fraction, of defective units in a sample. The value of p is given by

Figure 20.9   Conclusion of out of control situation depends on limits

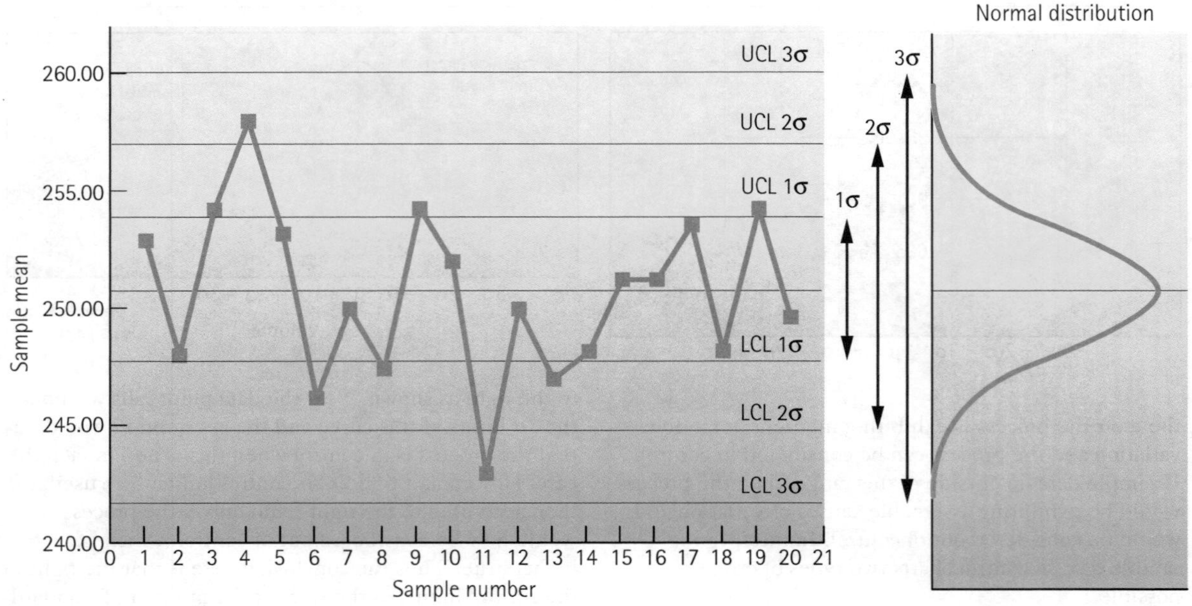

the relationship:

$$p = \frac{\text{Number of defective units}}{\text{Total number of units examined}}$$

A p-chart is a measure of discrete data and thus a binomial distribution is the correct probability function. However, for large sample sizes, the normal distribution can be approximated for the binomial distribution. The control limits in the p-chart are:

Centreline (CL) = p
Upper control limit (UCL) = p + zσ_p
Lower control limit (LCL) = p − zσ_p

where:

- p is the targeted fraction, or percentage, of defective units in the sample. If there is no target level, then the value of p is given by p = $\bar{p}$ where $\bar{p}$ is the average fraction defective in many samples
- z is the number of standard deviations
- σ_p is the standard deviation of the sampling distribution, and can be estimated from the relationship:

$$\sigma_p = \sqrt{\frac{\bar{p}(1-\bar{p})}{n}}$$

where n is the sample size. Thus, in a situation where the centreline is $\bar{p}$, the control limits would be

given by:

Centreline (CL) = $\bar{p}$

Upper control limit (UCL) = p + z$\sqrt{\dfrac{\bar{p}(1-\bar{p})}{n}}$

Lower control limit (LCL) = p − z$\sqrt{\dfrac{\bar{p}(1-\bar{p})}{n}}$

Very often, control charts with a value of z = 3 are used and from the normal distribution relationship, this would cover 99.74%, or essentially all the data (but see the section on six-sigma quality). As discussed previously, these limits are quite loose. Control limits for z = 2 (95.44% of the data) or even for z = 1 (68.26% of the data) are more rigid (this is behind Taguchi's idea of quality; see Chapter 4). The development of p-charts, and the effect of tighter limits, is illustrated in Demonstrating the concept 20.1.

C-chart

A c-chart might be used where counting the number of errors makes more sense than a percentage, or fraction value. For example:

- number of imperfections on a one square metre sample of fabric
- number of blemishes on given surface area of a bobbin of paper

- number of imperfections on a piece of wooden furniture
- number of typing errors in one type-set page.

The Poisson distribution, which has a variance equal to its mean, is the basis developing for c-charts. In this case $\bar{c}$ is the mean number of defects per unit, or:

$$\frac{\sum c}{n}$$

The limits in the c-chart are:

Centreline $(CL) = \bar{c}$

Upper control limit $(UCL) = \bar{c} + z\sqrt{\bar{c}}$

Lower control limit $(LCL) = \bar{c} - z\sqrt{\bar{c}}$

where $\sqrt{\bar{c}}$ is the standard deviation.

The use of c-charts is illustrated in Demonstrating the concept 20.2.

Statistical process control for variable characteristics

X–bar chart and a range chart

Variables are those characteristics that can take on a range of values such as kilograms, decibels, metres, litres, km/hour, gallons, etc. In quality control for variables, samples are withdrawn from populations of products and are described by the sample mean, $\bar{x}$, and the sample range, R. The sample mean is the average of all the values in a specific sample and the sample range is the difference between the greatest and smallest value in the sample. For correct quality control of products, an $\bar{x}$ (x-bar) chart, and an R chart need to be used together as now explained.

Range chart is necessary

Consider a chocolate manufacturer who purchases sacks of sugar by truckload from a local supplier. The weight of each sack is indicated as 25 kg. From a supplied lot, a sample of ten sacks is removed and weighed. These weights in kilograms are:

21	27
24	28
23	25
29	22
25	26

The average weight of these ten samples, $\bar{x}$, is then:

$$\frac{21+24+23+29+25+27+28+25+22+26}{10} = 25\,\text{kg}$$

That is, according to specifications. However, the range is 8 kg (29 − 21) or 32% of the average value, which is very high. Obviously, there is a problem. Having dual monitoring, with both an x-bar and range chart, controls both the average values and the variation of values from their means. It cannot be concluded that a process is in control by just monitoring sample means but the variation or range within a sample must also be monitored.

Sample mean control chart

The control limits in the x-bar chart are:

Centreline $(CL) = \bar{\bar{x}}$ or the average of all the sample averages

Upper control limit $(UCL) = \bar{\bar{x}} + z\sigma_{\bar{x}}$

Lower control limit $(LCL) = \bar{\bar{x}} - z\sigma_{\bar{x}}$

In cases where the standard deviation is unknown, or difficult to determine, it can be replaced with the average range of values, $\bar{R}$ as the range is a measure of deviation (see Chapter 4). Then the control limits become:

Upper control limit $(UCL) = \bar{\bar{x}} + A\bar{R}$

Lower control limit $(LCL) = \bar{\bar{x}} - A\bar{R}$

where A is a factor given in Table 20.1. These values of A are a function of sample size.[2]

Sample range control chart

The control limits in the R-chart are:

Centreline $(CL) = \bar{R}$

Lower control limit $(LCL) = B\bar{R}$

Upper control limit $(UCL) = C\bar{R}$

B and C are factors given in Table 20.1. Sample ranges, R, are compared with the R-chart, which monitors the variation of range among the items within samples.

The control limits are based on the sampling distribution. Each sample mean and sample range are plotted on the appropriate control chart, which provides the information of whether the process is in control. This type of control chart is illustrated in Demonstrating the concept 20.3.

Table 20.1 Control chart factors for variables

| Sample size (n) | Control limit factors | | |
| | Sample means | Sample ranges | |
	A	B	C
2	1.880	0.000	3.269
3	1.023	0.000	2.574
4	0.729	0.000	2.282
5	0.577	0.000	2.114
6	0.483	0.000	2.004
7	0.419	0.076	1.924
8	0.373	0.136	1.864
9	0.337	0.184	1.816
10	0.308	0.223	1.777
11	0.285	0.256	1.744
12	0.266	0.283	1.717
13	0.249	0.308	1.692
14	0.235	0.328	1.672
15	0.223	0.347	1.653
16	0.212	0.363	1.637
17	0.203	0.378	1.622
18	0.194	0.391	1.609
19	0.187	0.403	1.597
20	0.180	0.414	1.586
21	0.173	0.425	1.575
22	0.167	0.434	1.566
23	0.162	0.443	1.557
24	0.157	0.452	1.548
25	0.153	0.460	1.540
>25	$0.751/\sqrt{n}$	$0.45 + 0.001n$	$1.55 - 0.001n$

(For sample sizes greater than 25 the given expressions are linear approximations for constructing control charts.)

Considerations in statistical process control

No guarantees with SPC

As in all analytical work using statistics there are no guarantees:

- Even if all observations are within limits, it does not guarantee that assignable variations are not present. That means that the process may be out of control even though the chart indicates otherwise.
- Even if some observations are outside the control limits, this does not guarantee that assignable variations are present. That means that the process may be in control even though the chart indicates otherwise.

Effects of sigma limits

The following summarizes the effects on the sigma limits used in the process control charts:

- If 3-sigma limits are used, 99.74% of sample means should be within limits, and 0.26% outside limits when only random variations are present.
- If 2-sigma limits are used, 95.44% of sample means should be within limits, and 4.56% outside limits when only random variations are present.
- If 1-sigma limits are used, 68.26% of sample means should be within limits, and 31.74% outside limits when only random variations are present.
- Using 3-sigma limits will reduce the risk of concluding that a process is out of control when only random variations account for points outside the control limits. However, wider limits make it more difficult to detect non-random variations when they are present.

Possibilities in the outcome of control charts

The following summarizes possible outcomes of sampling results from any of the control charts presented: p-chart, c-chart, and an x-bar in conjunction with an R-chart.

Sample means lie close to, or 'hug', the centreline

Figure 20.10 indicates the process is well in control. This is the expectation in the Taguchi methods of quality control (Chapter 4) where the philosophy is to tighten up the control limits or bring them closer to the centreline).

Figure 20.10 Sample means lie close to, or hug the centreline

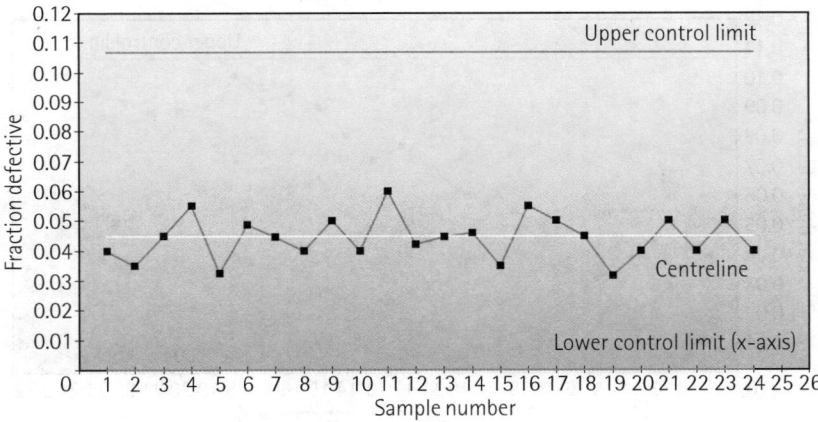

Sample means within limits, but wide variation

Figure 20.11 indicates the process is in control, but the variation is too much and the process is sloppy. An analysis should be made to find out why this is happening.

Sample means within limits, but there is an alarming trend

Figure 20.12 indicates the samples are at present within the limits, but there is an upward trend and it seems the process will soon be out of control. The process should be stopped and investigated.

Sample out of control

Figure 20.13 shows that, from the beginning, the process is out of control. The system should be shut down and investigated.

Change in the process

Figure 20.14 shows that although data points are within limits, there has been a sharp change in the process operation. At first, sample data are between the centreline and the upper control limit. Then, suddenly, the performance of the process improved and data points begin to hug the lower limit. This situation is worthy of investigation.

Online statistical process control

With the advancement of technology, many firms now have online statistical process control instruments measuring data directly. For example, in the filling of toothpaste tubes, after the filling process each tube is automatically weighed, and this weight is incorporated into the average weight of all the tubes that have been

Figure 20.11 Sample means within limits, but wide fluctuation

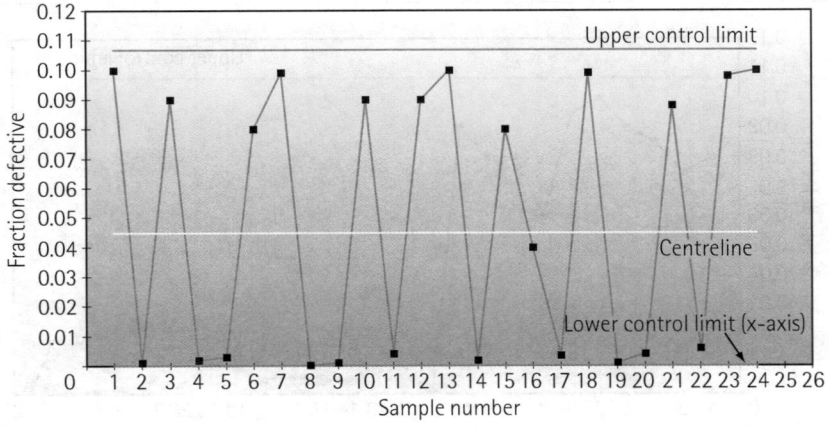

Figure 20.12 Sample means within limits, but an alarming trend

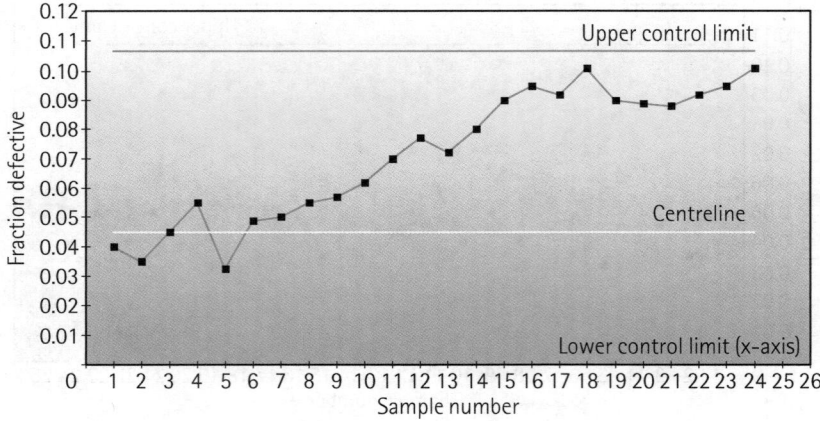

Figure 20.13 Sample means beyond upper limit, out of control

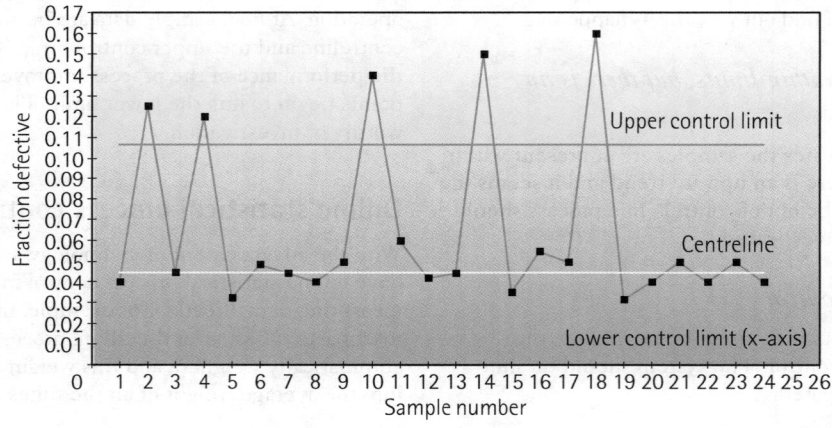

Figure 20.14 Within limits, but there has been an abrupt change in the operation

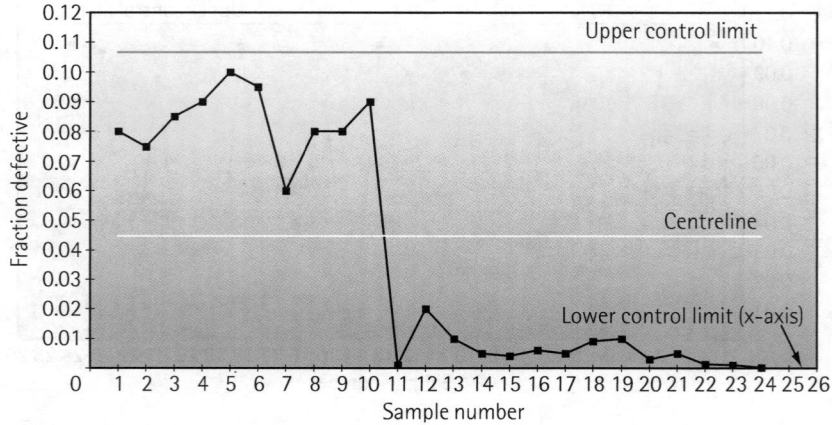

measured since the start of the operation. The average tube weight, the range, and sometimes a graphical distribution of all the units is displayed on an instrument adjacent to the process line. The operator can see directly, in real time, if the process is operating correctly and, if not, take necessary action. Previous to this, an operator had to take samples from the production line, make the appropriate measurement (sometimes in a laboratory away from the production area) and then plot this information on the control chart. If the process was indicated to be out of control then appropriate action was taken. Of course, during the time that the analysis was being carried out either the process was still running, and perhaps producing fault units. Alternatively, the production line was stopped waiting for feedback regarding the quality test. In this case, valuable production time was lost.

Process capability

Product design specifications and the process

The purpose of statistical process control is to monitor the distribution of a process to verify that it remains constant in terms of the mean value of the variable, and its variation around the mean. Data that exceed the control limits on the process control chart indicate when the mean or the variability has changed. However, a process that is in statistical control may not necessarily be producing products or services according to the specified design because the control limits are based on the mean and dispersion of the sampling distribution from the process and not on the product design specifications.

The process capability is the ability of the process to consistently meet the design specifications of the product or service. Where variables are concerned, the design specification is expressed in terms of a nominal, or target value and because of random variables there is a tolerance with an acceptable upper and lower limit. For example, the diameter of a bolt may have a design specification of 10 ± 0.05 cm. The target value is a nominal diameter of 10 mm but one of 10.05 mm (the upper limit) down to one of a diameter 9.95 mm (the limit) would be acceptable. The process producing the bolts, usually a lathe machine, must be capable of turning bolts of this design specification. If this were not the case, some of the bolts would be defective. The process is capable if it has a process distribution whose extreme limits lie inside the upper and lower specification of the product or service. Consider the three process distributions in Figure 20.15, which illustrates the upper and lower specification of the

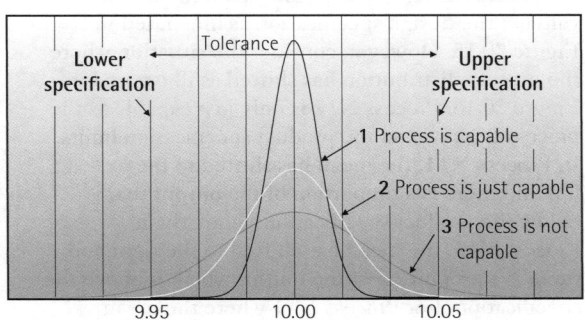

Figure 20.15 Process capability and specifications

bolt and the nominal value of 10.00 mm. Process N° 1 is capable because its extreme values lie well within the specifications of the bolt. Process N° 2 is only just capable because its extreme values lie at the specification limits of the bolt. Process N° 3 is not capable because its extreme limits lie outside the specifications of the product and it would produce too many bolts whose diameters lie above and below the specification limits.

Process capability ratio

A general rule is that most values of a process distribution lie within plus or minus three standard deviations of the mean or a range of six standard deviations, 6σ. The process capability ratio, C_p, is defined as:

$$C_p = \frac{\left[\begin{array}{c}\text{Upper product} \\ \text{specification}\end{array}\right] - \left[\begin{array}{c}\text{Lower product} \\ \text{specification}\end{array}\right]}{6\sigma}$$

where the difference between the upper and lower specification is the tolerance range or also referred to as the design specification width. Thus, considering Figure 20.15 again:

Process N° 1 $C_p > 1.00$
Process N° 2 $C_p = 1.00$
Process N° 3 $C_p < 1.00$

Note that for each of the process distributions, there is a different value of the standard deviation. Often firms choose a critical value of C_p of about 1.33 as a target for reducing process variability. However, the larger the value of C_p, the higher the performance of the process, or machine.

Process capability index

A process is capable, or is able to produce acceptable products, when the value of C_p is greater than 1.00 and preferably at least a critical value of 1.33 and when the process distribution is centred on the nominal value of the design specification as illustrated in Figure 20.15. However, consider the situation where the process distribution has shifted as illustrated in Figure 20.16. Process N° 2 is only just capable as the process limits lie on the product specification limits. In Process N° 1, the mean has shifted to the left and there is a proportion of the output that is below the product specification. Similarly in Process N° 3, the mean has shifted to the right and there is a proportion of the output which is above the specification. For Process N° 1 where the mean output has fallen and is closer to the lower product specification, the process capability index, C_{pk}, is defined as:

$$C_{pk} = \frac{\bar{\bar{x}} - \text{Lower specification}}{3\sigma}$$

For Process N° 3, where the process mean has increased and is closer to the upper product specification, the process capability index, C_{pk}, is defined as:

$$C_{pk} = \frac{\text{Upper specification} - \bar{\bar{x}}}{3\sigma}$$

In both cases $\bar{\bar{x}}$ is the mean of the process distribution. If the capability index is less than 1.00 (the numerator is less than 3σ) for either situation then the process will be not capable and defective units will be produced. In practice, the minimum, or the worst case, would define the process capability index. If the minimum were greater than 1.00 then the process would be capable. Again, a critical value of C_{pk} of about 1.33 would be desirable.

The concept of process capability is illustrated in Demonstrating the concept 20.4.

Figure 20.16 Process capability and specifications: A shift in the process distribution

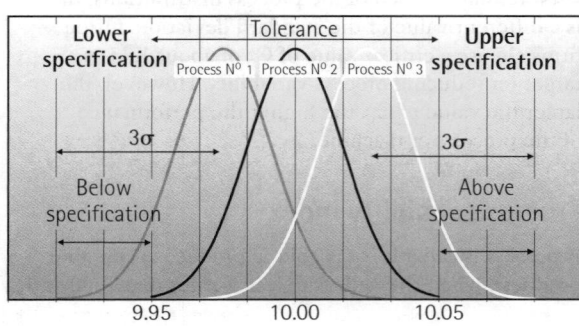

Six-sigma quality

Introduction

Six sigma is a quality management concept adopted by Motorola in the mid-1980s, now used extensively by other leading manufacturing firms such as GE (General Electric) USA, ABB (Asea Brown Boveri), Texas Instruments, Black & Decker, Caterpillar and others.

Product performance

The performance of a product or service is determined by how much margin exists between its design specifications and the actual value of the specifications. Processes or machines at the producer's facility, and/or from subcontractors upstream in the supply chain produce these actual values. Ideally, each process should produce actual specifications identical from unit to unit but within any process, variation occurs. This variation, measured by the standard deviation, may be very small particularly in processes where there is real-time feedback to control the output, but in other situations the variation might be more significant.

Six sigma is based on the sigma, σ, concept of dispersion where the higher the level of sigma, the better the quality of the process, service, or product. This can be illustrated quantitatively by Table 20.2 and illustrated on the sampling distribution of Figure 20.17. If one accepts a $\pm 3\sigma$ level of quality from the sampling distribution then one can say that on average 0.27% of the products or process are non-conforming. This translates into approximately 2700 parts per million non-conforming products being produced. Further, assume that the finished product in the supply chain is assembled from 1200 parts or operating steps, then on the $\pm 3\sigma$ criterion there would be, on average, 3.24 defects per unit (1200*2700/1,000,000). Alternatively, this is saying that of 1000 produced products, only about 32 units would be completely defect free. An even worse situation occurs at a 2σ quality level, where there is 4.55% of defects or 45,500 defective units per million. Increasing the quality limits reduces the error level significantly. At a 4σ limit there would be 63 non-conforming units per million, less than one at 5σ limits, and 0.002, or essentially zero, at a 6σ level. This is what six-sigma quality is driving at: Perfect quality.

Process shift

The process shift is the deviation of the process from the target mean. The defects per million shown in Table 20.2 for various sigma limits assume that there is no process shift during the operation. This may be true in the short term but, in the long term, a process shift

Table 20.2 Six-sigma limits on the normal distribution

Sigma control limits	Percentage conforming	Percentage non-conforming	Defects per million
6.00	99.9999998	0.0000002	0.0020
5.50	99.9999962	0.0000038	0.0381
5.00	99.9999426	0.0000574	0.5742
4.50	99.9993198	0.0006802	6.8016
4.00	99.9936628	0.0063372	63.3721
3.50	99.9534653	0.0465347	465.3467
3.00	99.7300066	0.2699934	2,699.9344
2.50	98.7580640	1.2419360	12,419.3597
2.00	95.4499876	4.5500124	45,500.1241
1.50	86.6385542	13.3614458	133,614.4576
1.00	68.2689480	31.7310520	317,310.5195
0.50	38.2924935	61.7075065	617,075.0653
0.00	0.00000000	100.0000000	1,000,000.0000

Figure 20.17 Six-sigma limits on the normal distribution

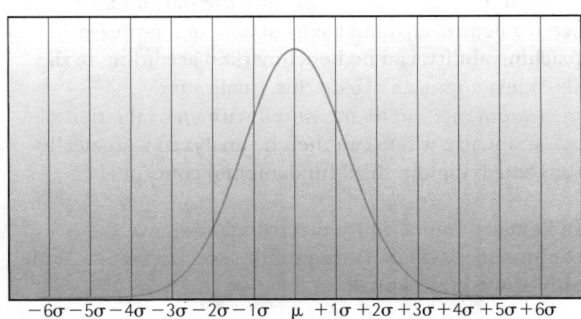

$-6\sigma\ -5\sigma\ -4\sigma\ -3\sigma\ -2\sigma\ -1\sigma\quad \mu\quad +1\sigma\ +2\sigma\ +3\sigma\ +4\sigma\ +5\sigma\ +6\sigma$

can probably be expected and one needs to have a high quality level in the presence of a process shift.

From the preceding, the process capability ratio is given by:

$$C_p = \frac{\left[\begin{array}{c}\text{Upper product}\\\text{specification}\end{array}\right]-\left[\begin{array}{c}\text{Lower product}\\\text{specification}\end{array}\right]}{\text{Process width}}$$

$$= \frac{\text{Specification width}}{\text{Process width}}$$

Figure 20.18 Six-sigma process capability with no process shift

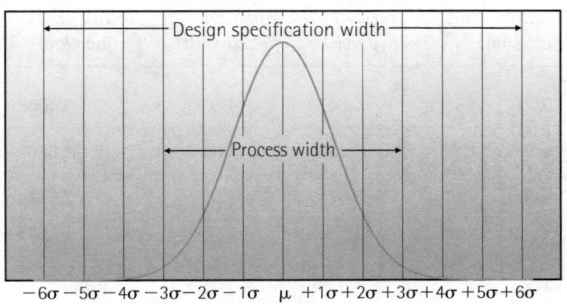

$-6\sigma\ -5\sigma\ -4\sigma\ -3\sigma\ -2\sigma\ -1\sigma\quad \mu\quad +1\sigma\ +2\sigma\ +3\sigma\ +4\sigma\ +5\sigma\ +6\sigma$

Figure 20.19 Six-sigma process capability with a process shift

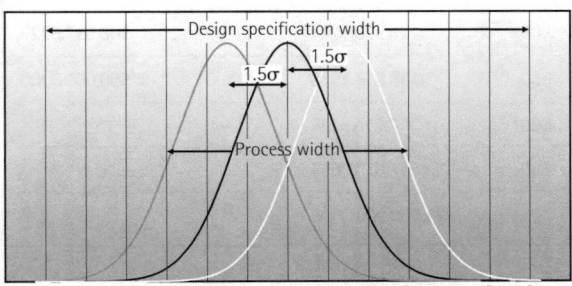

$-6\sigma\ -5\sigma\ -4\sigma\ -3\sigma\ -2\sigma\ -1\sigma\quad \mu\quad +1\sigma\ +2\sigma\ +3\sigma\ +4\sigma\ +5\sigma\ +6\sigma$

If there is no process shift, and the specification width is set at $\pm6\sigma$ or 12σ with a process width of $\pm3\sigma$, or 6σ, as illustrated in Figure 20.18, then the process capability, C_p, is $12/6 = 2.00$. At this level, the process would be very high performing.

When the process mean has shifted with respect to the design mean, as illustrated in Figure 20.19, then the process capability ratio is adjusted by a factor k to give then the process capability index, C_{pk}, presented in the previous section:

$$C_{pk} = C_p(1 - k)$$

where:

$$k = \frac{\text{Process shift}}{0.5 * \text{Design specification width}}$$

If there is a process shift of $\pm1.5\sigma$ (an often accepted value of the process shift), then the value of k is:

$$k = \frac{1.5\sigma}{0.5 * 12\sigma} = \frac{1.5}{6.0} = 0.25$$

Thus:

$$C_{pk} = C_p(1 - k) = 2.00(1 - 0.25) = 1.50$$

It is this level of process capability that is aimed at in six-sigma quality. Note, this value of the process

Table 20.3 Six–sigma quality with a process shift

Sigma control limits (no shift)	Defects/million no shift (two tails)	Corresponding sigma value at 1.5σ shift	Defects/million with 1.5σ shift (one tail)
6.00	0.0020	4.50	3.4008
5.50	0.0381	4.00	31.6861
5.00	0.5742	3.50	232.6734
4.50	6.8016	3.00	1,349.9672
4.00	63.3721	2.50	6,209.6799
3.50	465.3467	2.00	22,750.0620
3.00	2,699.9344	1.50	66,807.2288
2.50	12,419.3597	1.00	158,655.2598
2.00	45,500.1241	0.50	308,537.5326
1.50	133,614.4576	0.00	500,000.0000
1.00	317,310.5195		
0.50	617,075.0653		
0.00	1,000,000.0000		

capability index, for a process shift of $\pm 1.5\sigma$, would be the same value using the relationship from the previous section. Here, for a shift to the right, the process capability index is given by the relationship:

$$C_{pk} = \frac{\text{Upper specification} - \bar{\bar{x}}}{3\sigma}$$

Here, the upper product specification is 6σ. Since the mean has shifted to the right, $\bar{\bar{x}}$ now has a value of 1.5. (Before the shift the value of $\bar{\bar{x}}$ was considered as 0.) Thus:

$$C_{pk} = \frac{\text{Upper specification} - \bar{\bar{x}}}{3\sigma}$$
$$= \frac{6.0\sigma - 1.5\sigma}{3\sigma} = \frac{4.5}{3.0} = 1.5$$

With a process shift of $\pm 1.5\sigma$, there is a change of the probability of non-conforming products as the 6σ limit with no process shift now corresponds to the defect values given by a dispersion of 4.5σ ($6.0\sigma - 1.5\sigma$) with a shift to the right. Also, since one is considering a shift, and for a shift to the right, one is only considering one side (one tail) of the distribution. Thus, the defects per million would now be according to Table 20.3.

Thus the six-sigma quality with a process shift is 3.4 parts per million. Referring again to a product that has 1200 parts or process steps this would give 0.0041 defects per unit (3.4 * 1200/1,000,000). This would mean that out of a production of 1000 units there would, on average, be about 996 units that would be free of defects.

Philosophical extension of six–sigma quality

Although six-sigma quality is based on a quantitative logic, it goes further to translate into a philosophy in the way that people work in business. This is to work smarter, and not necessarily harder, to be rigorous and to make as few mistakes as possible. This includes any activity such as in the manufacture of a product, the delivery of an item, or the simple completion of a purchase order.

Six sigma is also a work tool based on the concept that there is full knowledge of the product, process, and service. It is premised on the five fundamental concepts of knowledge:

1. You do not know what, in fact, you do not know.
2. If you do not benchmark, you will never start to know.
3. If you cannot express what you know in the form of numbers, you really do not know much about it.
4. If you do not know much about it, you cannot control it.
5. If you cannot control it, you are at the mercy of chance.

Even qualitative situations like the performance of a service centre, customer satisfaction, or a professor's teaching ability, can be benchmarked according to the six-sigma approach. To do this, qualitative measurements can be measured with an evaluation questionnaire which can then be analyzed statistically thus satisfying the third fundamental concept.

In financial terms, a firm practising six-sigma conformance will increase profits, asset utilization, and reduce working capital.

Six–sigma black belt

Six-sigma quality has led to the development of a six-sigma black belt award, perhaps best known at General Electric Co (USA).[3] The aim of this black belt programme is to develop technical leaders of the six-sigma method who are able to produce highly credible breakthroughs and ideas and then, through instruction, to subsequently transfer these methods to their peers and customer-focused teams. The focus of the award is an in-depth understanding of the six-sigma philosophy and theory as well as advanced application in the areas of descriptive statistics, inferential statistics, non-parametric methods, quantitative benchmarking, process control, diagnostic tools, design of experiment, as well as organizational and group dynamics and the change process. The intent of the programme is to develop and lead people or teams to improvement, to work with and advise management on the formulation and implementation of improvement plans, and to disseminate the six-sigma tools and methods. Usually the target population for black belt training are those who are technically oriented, are highly regarded in their respective discipline or work area, and who are actively involved in the process of organizational change and development.

Sampling

In manufacturing, lots of materials, assemblies, and finished products are sampled at random to see if these pieces conform to appropriate specifications. If they do, under statistical inference, it is assumed that the entire lot from which these samples are taken meet desired quality control standards. If they do not, it is assumed that the entire lot is defective. This is where probabilities are involved. If a sample of, say, 25 units has more than 3% defective units one might say that the probability is that the entire lot has more than 3% defective units. However, this may not be the case as the 25 units in the sample may not have been representative of the lot.

Random sample

A random sample is one where each unit in the lot has an equal chance of being selected. It is because of this randomness that the sample is considered representative of the lot. In random sampling, either attributes, or variables can be measured and compared to standards.

Central limit theory

The foundation of sampling is based on the central limit theory. This states that in sampling, as the size of the sample increases, there becomes a point when the sampling distribution of the means can be approximated by the normal distribution, even though the distribution of the population is not necessarily normal.

Sampling distribution of the mean

The sampling distribution of the mean is a probability distribution of all the possible means of samples taken from a population. Assume an analysis of the water quality of the river Thames is being made to determine the level of phosphates. Ten 1 litre samples are taken each day, over a period of 120 days, and the phosphate level in parts per million is measured. Thus, each day, ten phosphate measurements are obtained and from these, a mean value is calculated. Repeating this exercise for each day of the 120-day period gives 120 averages, or mean, values. Plotting these data in a frequency distribution (see Chapter 27) gives a sampling distribution of the mean.

Sample size

- For most population distributions, regardless of shape, the sampling distribution of the means will be approximately normally distributed if samples of at least 30 units each are withdrawn from the population.
- If the population distribution is symmetric, the sampling distribution of the means will be approximately normal if samples of at least 15 units are withdrawn from the population.
- If the population is normally distributed, the sampling distribution of the means will be normally distributed, regardless of sample size withdrawn.

Mean of the sample means, and the population mean

The mean of a sample is $\bar{x}$ (x-bar). The mean of all the samples withdrawn from the population is $\bar{\bar{x}}$ (x double-bar). From the central limit theory, the mean of the sample means can be considered equal to the population mean, μ_x. That is:

$$\bar{\bar{x}} = \mu_x$$

Standard error of the sample

By the central limit theory, the standard deviation of the sampling distribution, $\sigma_{\bar{x}}$, also known as the standard error of the sample means, is related to the population standard deviation, σ_x, and the sample size, n, by the following relationship:

$$\sigma_{\bar{x}} = \frac{\sigma_x}{\sqrt{n}}$$

This indicates that, as the size of the sample increases, the standard error decreases, or the sample means lie closer to the population mean.

The practicality of the central limit theory is that by taking samples, either sampling from non-normal populations, or sampling from normal populations, inferences can be made about the population parameters without having any information about the

Figure 20.20 Sampling and the central limit theory

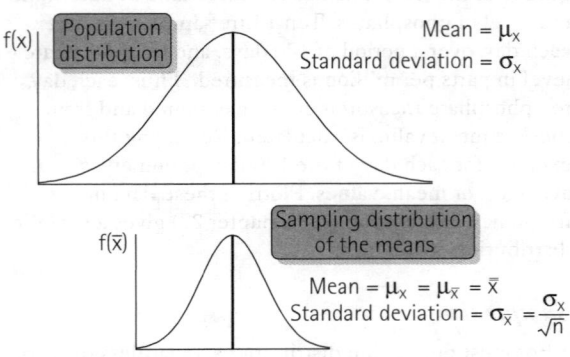

shape of the population distribution other than the information obtained from the sample, as illustrated in Figure 20.20.

Sampling techniques

Three techniques for sampling to see whether a lot conform are, single sampling, double sampling and sequential sampling as described as follows.

Single sampling

In single sampling (see Figure 20.21), there is one upper limit of c defective units in the sample. A random sample is withdrawn from the lot and tested for conformity. If the number of defective units, c' in the sample does not exceed c, the lot is considered good, and accepted. If the number of defective units, c', exceeds c, the lot is considered bad, and rejected.

Double sampling

In double sampling (see Figure 20.22), there are two limits of non-conformity, a lower limit, c_1, and an upper limit, c_2. In this plan, a random sample is taken from the lot and tested:

- If the number of defective units, c', is less than, or equal to c_1, then the lot is accepted.
- If the number of defective units, c', in the sample is greater than c_2 upper limit, the lot is rejected.
- If the number of defective units, c', lies between c_1 and c_2, then a second random sample, c'', is taken

Figure 20.21 Single sampling plan

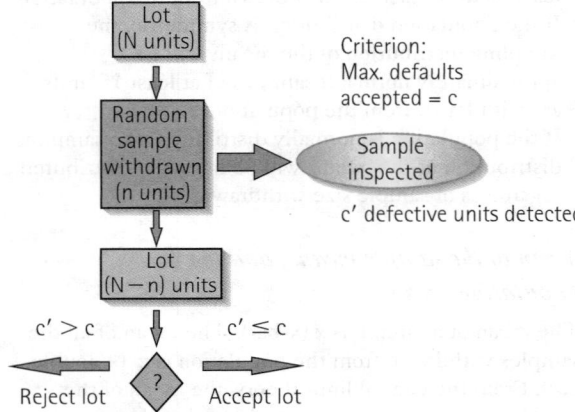

Figure 20.22 Double sampling plan

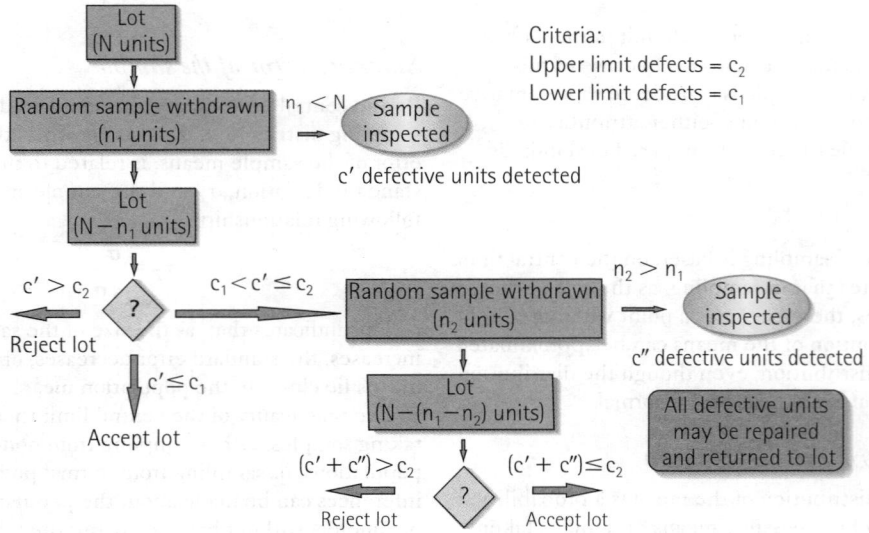

Figure 20.23 Sequential sampling plan (1)

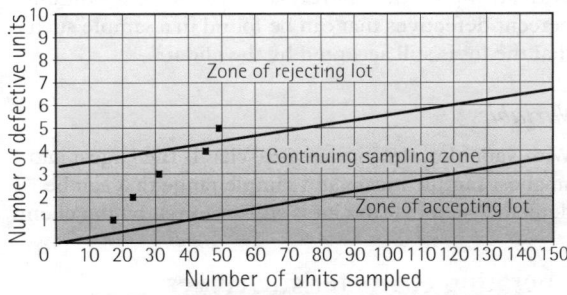

1st defective unit is 17th: Continue sampling
2nd defective unit is 23rd: Continue sampling
3rd defective unit is 31st: Continue sampling
4th defective unit is 45th: Continue sampling
5th defective unit is 49th: Reject lot

Figure 20.24 Sequential sampling plan (2)

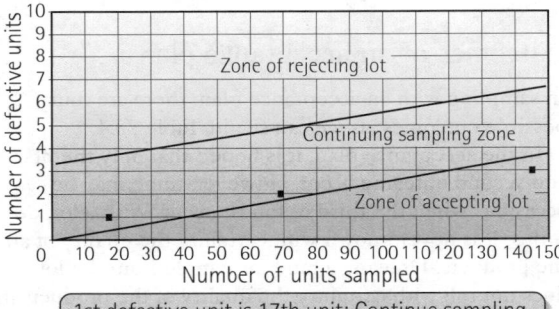

1st defective unit is 17th unit: Continue sampling
2nd defective unit is 69th unit: Continue sampling
3rd defective unit is 145th unit: Accept lot

from the lot and tested. If the sum of the defective units from both samples ($c' + c''$) is greater than c_2, the lot is rejected. If the sum of the defective units is less than c_2, the lot is accepted.

Double sampling is more rigorous than a single sampling plan, and as such is more time consuming and costly.

Sequential sampling

In sequential sampling, lots are rejected (see Figure 20.23) or accepted (see Figure 20.24) according to a pre-established sampling programme. Units are randomly selected from the lot and tested one by one. After each unit has been tested, a reject, accept, or continue sampling decision is made according to the sample plan and the region where the total number of

units that have been tested. If it is in the continuous sampling zone, the process continues until a decision has been reached as to whether to accept, or reject the lot. In the sequential sampling approach, it is conceivable that an entire lot could be tested.

Acceptance plans

Acceptance sampling

Acceptance sampling applies to whether to accept, or reject, a lot of units that has already been made. This is as opposed to inspecting items that are part of an ongoing production process, which is the already presented statistical process control (SPC). Consider a company which purchases a lot of 1000 electrical switches from an external supplier, which are to be installed in refrigerator units.

Switches: Case 1

To be certain that all the switches work, the purchaser tests all of them. Of the 1000 units tested, 80, or 8.0%, are found to be defective. These 80 are sent back to the supplier, who promptly replaces them with good units. In summary:

• The purchaser has spent his time, and money, in verifying the quality of the suppliers units.
• The supplier has avoided any expense for quality control. The purchaser has done it all for him!

Switches: Case 2

The purchaser now takes a random sample of 50 switches from the lot and tests them. Of the 50, four, or 8.0%, are found to be defective. Based on this sampling, the purchaser does not consider the lot acceptable, and he sends the whole lot of 1000 units back to the supplier. In summary:

• The purchaser has only expended about 5% of his time and cost compared to Case 1 (50/1000).
• The supplier, probably irritated, now has the burden on him and he is obligated to spend his time and money on rechecking the quality of his switches (assuming he wants to keep business with his client).

Case 2 illustrates the idea of acceptance sampling, which is to decide whether to accept lots of units (parts, raw materials, or finished products), that have already been delivered to the client, or are at the supplier's facility being prepared for delivery.

Rejected lots

Acceptance sampling is to decide if a lot satisfies predetermined standards. The lot is either rejected or accepted. If a lot is rejected:

- The entire lot may be inspected and faulty items repaired (when the supplier/consumer are the same firm).
- If the lot was purchased, it may be returned to the supplier.
- If it is not possible to repair the lot it may be sold as a down-graded item of inferior quality, such as textiles that are not exactly the right colour, paper that does not have the exact surface finish, or ceramic products which have some imperfection.

Criteria for acceptance sampling

Acceptance sampling procedures are usually employed when:

- A large number of items have been supplied, produced, or prepared ready for shipment.
- Unit cost is relatively low, and the cost consequence of passing a defective unit is not excessively high.
- Destructive testing is required.

High-value goods

Units that have a high added value such as engines, refrigerators, or computers exhibit attribute characteristics (they either work or they do not). However, in light of their high value they are usually 100% inspected before they leave the production or assembly operation. A faulty unit such as these could have severe and costly consequences downstream and could impair customer relations. Hewlett-Packard, for example, checks each computer unit before it leaves the factory.

Acceptance plan

An acceptance plan is the programme, mutually agreed to by a supplier and the purchaser, regarding whether to accept an entire lot of goods based on simply testing a random sample from the lot. As an illustration, if an acceptance plan permits a maximum of 5% defective items, and the sample tested shows that 7% of the items are defective, then under the acceptance plan, the entire lot would be rejected and returned to the supplier. The goal in the development of the acceptance plan is to have one that passes good lots, and fails bad lots. Acceptance sampling programmes can be applied to both attributes, and variable criteria.

Attributes

With attributes, the interest is: 'What is the maximum percent defectives that can be found in a sample such that the lot is still accepted by the client?'

Variables

With variables, the interest is: 'What is the largest and smallest sample mean, and sample range that can be detected such that the lot is still accepted by the client?'

Operating characteristic curves

An operating characteristic curve (OC) is a graphical relation illustrating how well an acceptance plan discriminates between *good* and *bad* lots. The discriminating ability depends on the shape of the curve, which is a function of:

- the sample size, n, withdrawn from the lot
- the acceptance level, c, or the number of allowable defective units found in the sample.

Outcomes of an acceptance plan

In sampling with an acceptance plan, there are four possible outcomes, as we can see in Table 20.4.

In the acceptance plan, it is hoped that only the first and second outcome occur. However, there may be occasions when the third or fourth occur. With a lot, or series, it is never known with certainty the quality of all the products. Drawing a random sample from the lot does not tell with certainty the quality of the products in the lot. The only thing that is known with certainty is the quality of the products in the sample.

Rejected good lot

Assume that there is a lot of 20,000 units of stainless steel rods. In these 20,000 units, 15, or 0.075%, have diameters that are outside the required specifications. This percentage defect is low and, normally, the lot would be accepted. However, in a sample of 20 rods, this included eight off-specification units. That is, eight of the total of 15 defective units appeared in this sample. This number of eight is 40% and, based

Table 20.4 Outcomes of an acceptance plan

Desirable	Undesirable
1. A *good* lot can be accepted	3. A *good* lot can be rejected
2. A *bad* lot can be rejected	4. A *bad* lot can be accepted

on the sample, the lot would be rejected. In fact, it is a 'good' lot.

Accepted bad lot

Assume in another situation there are 20,000 rods of which 1000 are defective. This represents 5% and is probably sufficiently high to reject the lot. If a sample of 20 rods is taken, there could be no off-specification units. The 'bad' lot would then be accepted.

From information about the small proportion of the products in the sample, the quality of all the products in the lot must be inferred and this is both the nature and the risk in acceptance plans. For attribute sampling, where lots are considered either good or bad, the operating characteristic curve is developed from the binomial distribution, or, under certain conditions, the Poisson distribution. These both describe discrete distributions.

Perfect discriminating operating curve

Figure 20.25 illustrates an ideal discriminating operating curve with an acceptance level of 2%. Here, all lots with a 2%, or less, defective units would be accepted. All those lots with greater than 2% defective units would be rejected. This curve is only theoretical, since to obtain perfect discrimination, we would have to inspect all the units in the lot and for products of relative low unit value this would be uneconomical.

Practical operating characteristic curves

Practical operating characteristic curves are illustrated in Demonstrating the concept 20.5.

Inspection and quality

Ideally, the client would like to receive from the producer a lot with zero percent defectives, one of the goals in just-in-time management. However, this might involve 100% inspection of the lot, which would be costly (the cost being passed on to the consumer in the unit price). If the client accepts that, because of the type of operation by the producer, there might be some defective units in the lot, then there are two levels accepted by both parties. One is the acceptable quality level and the other is the lot tolerance percent defective.

Acceptable quality level

The acceptable quality level (AQL) is the level of quality of a product, often expressed as a percentage,

Figure 20.25 Ideal discriminating operating characteristic curve

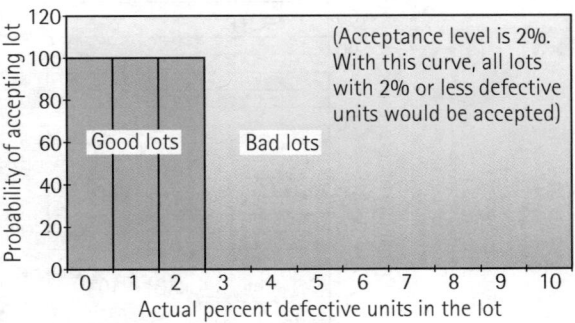

which is considered acceptable for the production. Broadly, it defines the maximum defective level, which is still considered a 'good' lot. For example, in the production of computer chips, an AQL might be one defective unit in 10,000, or 0.01%. For the manufacture of light switches, the AQL may be, say, 2% or 40 units in a lot of 2000. The AQL is a standard established by the product manufacturer, or by the purchaser of the product. The lower the value of the AQL the more rigorous the production process, and the higher the cost of quality. This is a cost that is passed on to the purchaser.

Lot tolerance percent defective

Lot tolerance percent defective (LTPD) is the level of quality considered unacceptable, or bad. Lots at this level, or more, need to be rejected by the acceptance plan. Broadly speaking, the LTPD is the lower level of defects that still constitutes a 'bad' lot. In the production of computer chips, a LTPD might be ten defective units in 10,000, or 0.1%. In the case of the light switches, the LTPD might be 5%, or 100 units in a lot of 2000.

Producer and consumer risk

In the agreed sampling plan, even though the AQL and the LTPD have been defined, there is a risk for both parties concerned.

Producer's risk

The producer or supplier of the units wants to avoid having a good lot rejected by the acceptance plan. The producer's risk, α, involves the taking of a random sample that results in a higher portion of defects in the sample than is actually present in the lot. For example, a good lot of 10,000 units with only

Figure 20.26 Operating characteristic curve showing level of risk (1)

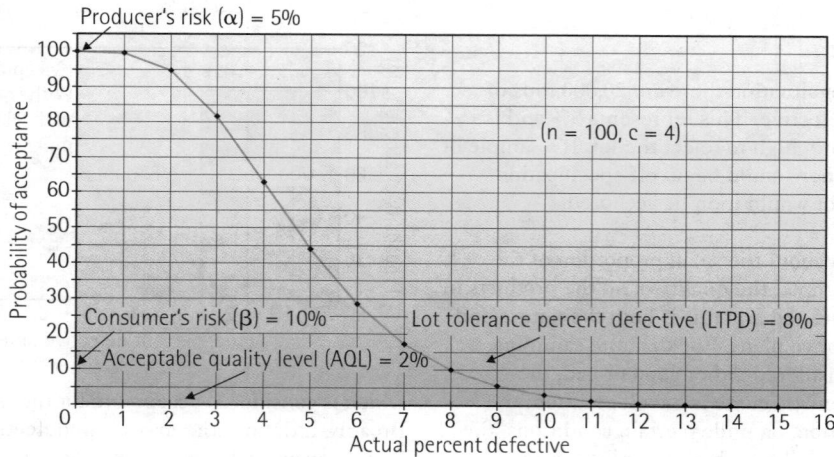

10 defectives or 0.1% could conceivably result in a sample of 100 containing all ten defectives units, or 10%. This lot would be rejected even though in reality it has only 0.1% defective units. Thus, a lot with a given AQL still has a risk of being rejected. In this case, the producer would suffer the loss, having to inspect the whole lot at his expense, discarding the whole batch, or perhaps selling it at a discount.

The producer's risk is considered a Type I error, rejecting a null hypothesis when it is true. (A Type I error has already been discussed earlier in this chapter.) The acceptance plan would reject the lot, when it is, in fact, good. A sampling plan might be designed to have the producer's risk, α, set at 5%, or 0.05.

Consumer's risk

The consumer wants to avoid accepting a bad lot since if the lot were accepted he would be responsible for rectifying faulty units. The consumer's risk (β) involves the taking of a random sample that results in a much lower portion of defects in the sample than is actually present in the lot. For example, a lot of 10,000 units with 2000 defectives could produce a sample of size 100 with no defectives. The lot would be accepted. Thus, a lot with a given LTPD still has a risk of being accepted.

The consumer's risk is a Type II error, accepting a null hypothesis, when it is false. (A Type II error has already been discussed earlier in this chapter.) A sampling plan might be designed to have the consumer's risk, β, set at 10%, or 0.10.

Sample size of 100

Figure 20.26 shows an operating characteristic curve with:

- the producer's risk at 5%
- consumer's risk at 10%
- an acceptable quality level (AQL) of 2%
- lot tolerance percent defective (LTPD) of 8%.

Here, there is a 5% risk of rejecting a good lot (95% probability of accepting the good lot), and a 10% risk of accepting a bad lot (90% chance of rejecting a bad lot). The development of this curve is shown in Table 20.5 (column sample size = 100, c = 4).

Sample size of 200

If the sample size were increased to 200, and a value of c = 8, then the risk levels are decreased for the same values of AQL, and LTPD (see Figure 20.27).
In this situation:

- the producer's risk is 2.2%
- consumer's risk is 2.7%
- an acceptable quality level (AQL) is 2%
- lot tolerance percent defective (LTPD) is 8%.

The development of this curve is shown in Table 20.5 (column sample size = 200, c = 8).

Average outgoing quality

Acceptance plans in statistical quality control provide managers with some assurance that the average quality level, or percent defective items, will not exceed a

Table 20.5 Operating characteristic curve showing risk levels

					Probability of acceptance			
					Sample size			
					25	50	100	200
	Lamda (np/100)					Value of c		
	Sample size							
Percent defective units	25	50	100	200	1	2	4	8
0.00	0.00	0.00	0.00	0.00	100.00	100.00	100.00	100.00
1.00	0.25	0.50	1.00	2.00	97.35	98.56	99.63	99.98
2.00	0.50	1.00	2.00	4.00	90.98	91.97	94.73	97.86
3.00	0.75	1.50	3.00	6.00	82.66	80.88	81.53	84.72
4.00	1.00	2.00	4.00	8.00	73.58	67.67	62.88	59.25
5.00	1.25	2.50	5.00	10.00	64.46	54.38	44.05	33.28
6.00	1.50	3.00	6.00	12.00	55.78	42.32	28.51	15.50
7.00	1.75	3.50	7.00	14.00	47.79	32.08	17.30	6.21
8.00	2.00	4.00	8.00	16.00	40.60	23.81	9.96	2.20
9.00	2.25	4.50	9.00	18.00	34.25	17.36	5.50	0.71
10.00	2.50	5.00	10.00	20.00	28.73	12.47	2.93	0.21
11.00	2.75	5.50	11.00	22.00	23.97	8.84	1.51	0.06
12.00	3.00	6.00	12.00	24.00	19.91	6.20	0.76	0.02
13.00	3.25	6.50	13.00	26.00	16.48	4.30	0.37	0.00
14.00	3.50	7.00	14.00	28.00	13.59	2.96	0.18	0.00
15.00	3.75	7.50	15.00	30.00	11.17	2.03	0.09	0.00
16.00	4.00	8.00	16.00	32.00	9.16	1.38	0.04	0.00
17.00	4.25	8.50	17.00	34.00	7.49	0.93	0.02	0.00
18.00	4.50	9.00	18.00	36.00	6.11	0.62	0.01	0.00
19.00	4.75	9.50	19.00	38.00	4.97	0.42	0.00	0.00
20.00	5.00	10.00	20.00	40.00	4.04	0.28	0.00	0.00

certain limit. In a sampling procedure, if a lot is rejected because the AQL does not meet the criteria, then the whole lot might be inspected and all the defective items replaced. By replacing the defective items in the lot, then the average outgoing quality (AOQ) in terms of defective units is improved. In a sampling plan that replaces all encountered defective items, and knowing the percent defective items for the lot at the beginning, the average outgoing quality (AOQ) can be determined from the following relationship:

$$AOQ = \frac{P_t \cdot P_a (N - n)}{N}$$

where:

- P_t is percent defective items in the incoming lot
- P_a is the probability of accepting the lot
- N is the lot size
- n is the sample size used in the inspection plan.

Figure 20.27 Operating characteristic curve showing level of risk (2)

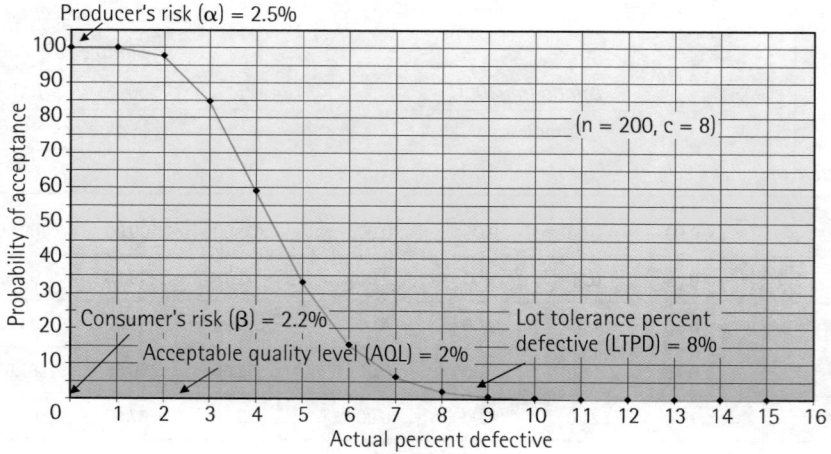

Figure 20.28 Average outgoing quality curve

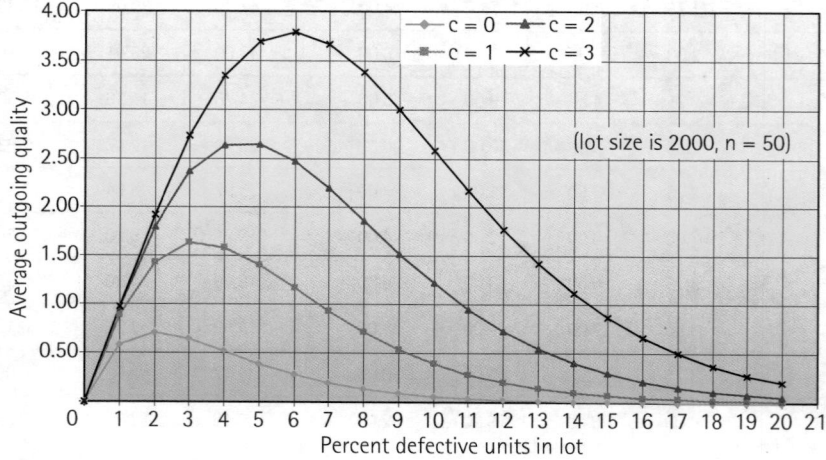

Development of AOQ curves

Normally in the AOQ relationship, the values of P_t and P_a are not known. However, for a particular sampling plan, an AOQ curve can be developed by assuming different values of P_t and calculating the value of P_a from the Poisson relationship. Figure 20.28 gives four AOQ curves for different acceptance plans. These curves were developed as follows:

- Lot size, N, is assumed as 2000 units.
- Sample size, n, is 50 random units.
- Values of defective units in the lot, p (equal to P_t), were considered from 0 to 20.
- Four acceptance plans are considered for values of c (defective units in the sample) of 0, 1, 2, and 3.

- The value of λ, lamda, is calculated from the relationship n * p (divided by 100 since the value of p is a percentage).
- The probability of acceptance, P_a, is calculated from the Poisson relationship for each value of p for the value of c = 0:

$$P_a(c) = \frac{(np)^x e^{-(np)}}{c!}$$

- The value of P_a is calculated, at each level of p, for values of c = 0, 1, 2, and 3.
- The average outgoing quality is then calculated from the relationship:

$$AOQ = \frac{P_t \cdot P_a(N-n)}{N}$$

- As the actual percent defectives in a production lot increases – moves along the horizontal axis from left to right – the effect, initially, is for lots to be passed, even though the number of defective units has increased. Consequently, the number of defective units passed along to the customer increases.
- If the trend continues, however, the acceptance plan begins to reject lots. When lots are rejected, the lots are usually 100% inspected. The defective units are replaced with non-defective ones. Thus, the net effect of rejecting lots is to improve the average quality of the outgoing lots, because the rejected lots, that are ultimately shipped, contain all non-defective units.
- As the actual percent defectives increases, the average outgoing quality improves because more and more lots are rejected. They are 100% inspected, and the defective units replaced. The extreme condition is when all lots are rejected, and thus the percent defectives going to customers approaches zero.

The maximum value of the AOQ curve (average outgoing quality limit, AOQL) gives the highest average percent defective, or the lowest average quality for a particular sampling plan. For example, consider the sampling plan when the value of c = 3 defective units in a sample of 50:

- The highest average percent defective (AOQL) is about 3.8% for an incoming quality in the lot of 6%.
- This means that units are about 96.2% good when the incoming quality in the lot is equal to 6%.

Summary of key elements

- Statistical quality control covers the analytical procedures for verifying the conformity of a process or a product, either in manufacturing or services.

- In many production operations units are made in discrete groups of lots, series, or batches. These units are made perhaps on the same machine, with the same operator, on the same shift, using from the same supply of raw materials, or under the same process conditions.

- Attribute characteristics can be either one of two outcomes, or a binomial classification. Generally, this characteristic is that a product is good or bad, it works or it does not work.

- Variables are characteristics that can be measured on a continuous scale where there is a range of acceptance.

- Statistical process control (SPC) is the periodic sampling and analysis of units, items, or activity, to determine if the system or process is performing according to some predetermined target, or within design limits.

- The two types of variation in a process are random or assignable. The objective of SPC is to detect assignable variations.

- The control chart is the evaluation tool in statistical process control. It has a centreline, an upper control limit, and a lower control limit. When sample data points lie outside the upper or lower control limit the process is considered out of control.

- A Type I error occurs when a process is considered out of control when this is not the case. A Type II error is when a process is considered in control when this is not true.

- Control charts for attributes are p-charts that show the percentage of defective units in a sample, and c-charts for the number of defective units in a sample.

- There are two control charts for measuring variable characteristics, an x-bar chart for sample means, $\bar{x}$, and a sample range chart, R. They must be used in conjunction.

- In SPC, if all observations are within limits, it does not guarantee a process is in control, and, if observations are outside, neither does it guarantee a process is out of control.

- Using broader control limits will reduce the risk of concluding that the process is out of control when only random variations account for points outside the control limits. However, wider limits make it more difficult to detect non-random variations when they are present.

- Online statistical process control is now common in firms and this reduces the delay in taking remedial action should a process be out of control.

- Process capability is the ability of the process consistently to meet the design specifications of the product or service.

- The process capability ratio, C_p, defined as follows, should have a value of the order of 1.33 for a process consistently to produce conforming products:

$$C_p = \frac{\left[\begin{array}{c}\text{Upper product}\\\text{specification}\end{array}\right] - \left[\begin{array}{c}\text{Lower product}\\\text{specification}\end{array}\right]}{6\sigma}$$

- The process capability index, C_{pk}, is a measure of the process capability when there has been a process shift. It is calculated from the following relationships and again its minimum value should be of the order of 1.33 for a process giving high performance:

$$C_{pk} = \frac{\bar{x} - \text{Lower specification}}{3\sigma}$$

$$C_{pk} = \frac{\text{Upper specification} - \bar{\bar{x}}}{3\sigma}$$

• Six-sigma quality, when there is a process shift, implies only 3.4 defects per million. Six sigma is qualitatively also to work smarter, to be rigorous, making few mistakes.

• Sampling in statistical quality control is based in the Central Limit Theory, which states that as the size of the sample increases, the sampling distribution of the means can be approximated by the normal distribution. From this theory the mean of the sample means can be considered equal to the population mean and the standard error of the sample means is the population standard deviation divided by the square root of the sample size.

• Three sampling techniques include single sampling, double sampling, and sequential sampling.

• Acceptance sampling is whether to accept or reject a lot of units that have already been produced. The supplier and the purchaser mutually agree to the acceptance plan whether to accept the lot based on sampling and testing from the lot.

• An operating characteristic curve shows how well an acceptance plan discriminates between good and bad lots. Discriminating ability depends on the shape of the curve and is a function of sample size, and the number of defective sample units considered for the sampling plan.

• With an acceptance plan four things can happen. A good lot can be accepted, a good lot can be rejected, a bad lot can be rejected, or a bad lot can be accepted. Sampling from the lot gives no guarantee of the quality of the lot, only the quality of the sample.

• The acceptable quality level (AQL) is the level of product quality considered acceptable. It is a standard established by the manufacturer, or by the purchaser. The lower the value of AQL the more rigorous is the process, and thus the higher the cost of quality.

• Lot tolerance percent defective is the level of quality considered unacceptable, or bad. Lots at this level, or more, need to be rejected by the acceptance plan.

• The producer of units wants to avoid having a good lot rejected by the acceptance plan. The producer's risk, α, involves the taking of a random sample that results in a higher portion of defects in the sample than is actually present in the lot.

• The consumer wants to avoid accepting a bad lot by the acceptance plan. The consumer's risk, β, involves the taking of a random sample that results in a much lower portion of defects in the sample than is actually present in the lot.

• The average outgoing quality of units (AOQ) will be improved if defective items in rejected lots are replaced.

The AOQ level can be calculated from the following relationship where P_t is the % defectives in the incoming lot, P_a is the probability of accepting the lot, N is the lot size, and n is the sample size:

$$AOQ = \frac{P_t \cdot P_a (N - n)}{N}$$

Notes and references

1. BAILLARGEON, Gérald, *Plans d'Echantillonnage en Contrôle de la Qualité: Contrôle par Attributs* (Sampling plans in quality control: Control by attributes), Editions SMG, Eclipse Marketing, Paris 1990
2. *Economics Control of Manufactured Products*, Bell Telephone Laboratories, Litton Educational Publishing, Van Nostrand Reinhold Co. 1931
3. 'General Electric: The house that Jack built', *The Economist*, 18 September 1999, p. 23

Review and discussion topics

1. Acceptance sampling and SPC
Acceptance sampling and statistical process control are different concepts. However, if improvements were made through statistical process control, what might be the impact on the acceptance plan?

2. Attributes and variables
Which of the following would fall into the category of attributes, and which into that of variables? Are your responses completely black and white?
  (a) the quality of a German shepherd (Alsatian) in a dog show
  (b) the volume of wine in a ¾ litre bottle of Bordeaux
  (c) a soft-boiled egg, ordered in a restaurant for breakfast
  (d) exam results such as A-level physics, or the French Baccalaureate
  (e) an incandescent light bulb
  (f) a neon light bulb
  (g) the weight of a pound of beef
  (h) making a plane connection at London Heathrow after taking a flight from Paris to London.

3. Lots and series
The following products are usually made in lots. Discuss some of the factors that dictate manufacture of these products by lots, rather than individual units:
  (a) flu vaccine
  (b) chocolate
  (c) cotton fabric for shirts
  (d) paper for printing
  (e) screws.

4. Control limits

Which of the following products would have tight control limits, and which would be somewhat looser? Discuss, in general terms, the criteria that establish control limits:

(a) penicillin
(b) gasket seals on a rocket booster for space flight
(c) five-inch nails
(d) surface finish on an automobile
(e) grading of an essay in an English literature exam
(f) thickness of icing on a wedding cake.

5. Standards or control charts

What do you think would be some of the variables measured, and compared to standards, or to control charts:

(a) a brewery
(b) an airline company such as British Airways, Air France, or Lufthansa
(c) an automobile company
(d) a blood test
(e) pharmaceutical ointment
(f) distribution of a consignment of goods from one location to another.

Demonstrating the concept 20.1   Printed circuits

Situation

A company makes small inexpensive printed electrical circuits, a process in which a few of the complex soldered connections are performed by hand. The company wants to develop a process control chart to see if the operation is under control. Samples of size 100 are withdrawn over a 24-hour period and inspected. This information is shown in Table 20.6.

Required

1. Develop a 3-standard deviation p-chart.
2. Would you conclude that the process is under control?
3. What comments do you have regarding random sampling for printed circuits?

Table 20.6 Printed electrical circuit production

Sample number	Nº of defective circuits	Sample number	Nº of defective circuits
1	7	13	3
2	3	14	4
3	8	15	5
4	2	16	7
5	1	17	3
6	5	18	6
7	2	19	3
8	7	20	4
9	9	21	3
10	2	22	2
11	6	23	8
12	4	24	1

Solution

1. Table 20.7 gives the calculation for developing the p-chart with 3σ limits, while Figure 20.29 shows the 24 sample data. The lower control limit is at 0 because, in practice, the calculation indicates a negative value of p, which is impossible.
2. Since all the samples fall within the limits, the process is considered to be under control.
3. One caution is that, even though the process is under control according to the company's requirements, having even one faulty printed circuit for use in downstream use can have serious consequences for the company (faulty products, poor customer relationship, expensive rework operations). One consideration is that all printed circuits should be tested.

Table 20.7 Developing the p-chart with 3σ limits

Sample number	Nº of defective circuits	Fraction defective circuits	CL	UCL	LCL
0					
1	7	0.07	0.0438	0.1051	0.0000
2	3	0.03	0.0438	0.1051	0.0000
3	8	0.08	0.0438	0.1051	0.0000

(Continued)

Table 20.7 (Continued)

Sample number	Nº of defective circuits	Fraction defective circuits	CL	UCL	LCL
4	2	0.02	0.0438	0.1051	0.0000
5	1	0.01	0.0438	0.1051	0.0000
6	5	0.05	0.0438	0.1051	0.0000
7	2	0.02	0.0438	0.1051	0.0000
8	7	0.07	0.0438	0.1051	0.0000
9	9	0.09	0.0438	0.1051	0.0000
10	2	0.02	0.0438	0.1051	0.0000
11	6	0.06	0.0438	0.1051	0.0000
12	4	0.04	0.0438	0.1051	0.0000
13	3	0.03	0.0438	0.1051	0.0000
14	4	0.04	0.0438	0.1051	0.0000
15	5	0.05	0.0438	0.1051	0.0000
16	7	0.07	0.0438	0.1051	0.0000
17	3	0.03	0.0438	0.1051	0.0000
18	6	0.06	0.0438	0.1051	0.0000
19	3	0.03	0.0438	0.1051	0.0000
20	4	0.04	0.0438	0.1051	0.0000
21	3	0.03	0.0438	0.1051	0.0000
22	2	0.02	0.0438	0.1051	0.0000
23	8	0.08	0.0438	0.1051	0.0000
24	1	0.01	0.0438	0.1051	0.0000

Mean fraction defectives	0.0438
Sample size, n	100
Mean fraction good	0.9563
std. dev, $\sqrt{(p\,q)/n}$	0.0205
3σ	0.0614
Centreline (CL)	0.0438
Upper control limit (UCL)	0.1051
Lower control limit (LCL)	−0.0176
Lower control limit (LCL) (practice)	0

Figure 20.29 Printed circuits: p–control chart

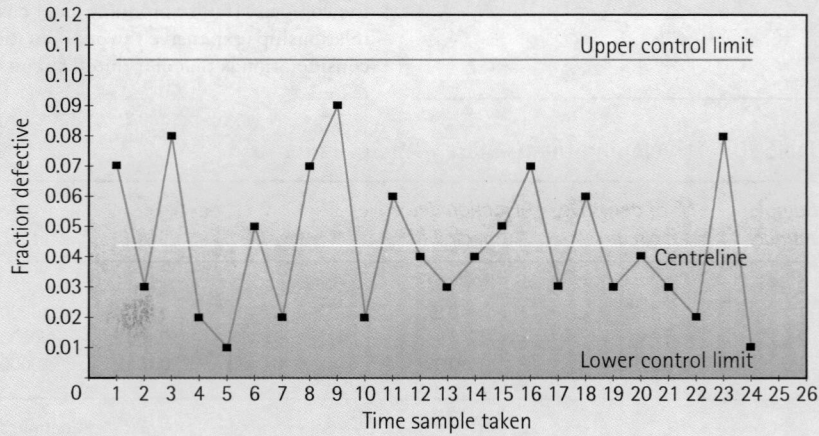

Demonstrating the concept 20.2 Paper making

Situation

A company proposes to modify its paper-making process, using pulp from a foreign supplier, rather than its normal domestic suppliers. It wants to be sure that it can use this raw material in its paper-making operation and obtain the same quality paper as it does with domestic pulp. Prior to running the foreign pulp, it makes paper from its normal suppliers for one week and analyzes the blemishes on the paper. On a total of 32 square metres of paper tested during one week it found 350 blemishes. The company then ran the paper-making machines with the foreign pulp and in five bobbins of paper tested it obtained average blemishes per square metre of paper as shown in Table 20.8.

Required

1. Develop a c-control chart for 3σ control limits using the domestic paper test.
2. Show the information from the foreign paper on the control chart. What are your comments about the foreign paper? Do you have any suggestions?

Solution

1. Table 20.9 gives the calculation for the control limits for the test data and Figure 20.30 shows the five sample data on the control chart.
2. The quality of paper seems erratic. Two averages are outside the limit, one is pretty close to the upper limit, and two are below the centreline. The company should analyze the quality of the raw material, and perhaps re-evaluate the operating procedures such as drying time, tension etc. for paper making using this new raw material.

Table 20.8 Average blemishes per square metre of paper

Sample number	Average blemishes per square metre
1	30
2	19
3	6
4	25
5	3

Figure 20.30 Paper making: c-control chart

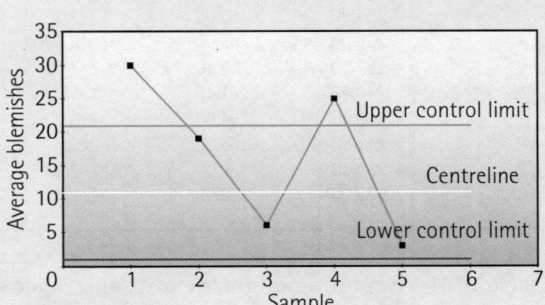

Table 20.9 Control limits for paper-making test data

Sq metres tested	32
Total blemishes	350
Average faults/sq m^2	10.9375
Standard deviation	3.31
z value	3
z*σ	9.92
Centreline (CL)	10.9375
Upper control limit (UCL)	20.8591
Lower control limit (LCL)	1.0159

Sample number	Blemishes per m^2	CL	UCL	LCL
0		10.9375	20.8591	1.0159
1	30	10.9375	20.8591	1.0159
2	19	10.9375	20.8591	1.0159
3	6	10.9375	20.8591	1.0159
4	25	10.9375	20.8591	1.0159
5	3	10.9375	20.8591	1.0159
6		10.9375	20.8591	1.0159

Demonstrating the concept 20.3 Filling machine

Situation

A candy factory has an automatic filling machine which allows 250 grams of candies to be put into plastic bags before they are sealed. The company is concerned about the reliability of this machine and decides to carry out a statistical process control study. First, the filling line is shut down, and adjusted according to specifications. The line is then put into operation and 20 random samples of size 25 units are taken during eight hours of operation. For each of the samples taken, the average weight is determined, and the maximum, and minimum weight is recorded. This information is given in Table 20.10.

Required

1. Develop the two appropriate control charts to analyze this filling operation.
2. What are the conclusions to be drawn from these control charts?

Solution

1. The average value for the weights and the range are calculated as shown in Table 20.11 and the coefficients A, B, and C according to the sample size are taken from Table 20.1 and the two charts are constructed as given in Figures 20.31 and 20.32.

Table 20.10 Filling machine statistical process control results

Sample number	Sample average	Maximum weight	Minimum weight	Sample number	Sample average	Maximum weight	Minimum weight
1	253.00	262.00	232.00	11	246.10	278.00	237.00
2	248.00	261.00	232.00	12	250.00	265.00	235.00
3	254.20	269.00	242.00	13	247.00	265.20	241.00
4	256.00	265.00	248.00	14	248.20	263.20	242.10
5	253.20	262.40	247.00	15	251.30	270.20	247.20
6	246.20	261.40	235.00	16	251.30	265.20	248.10
7	250.00	254.00	230.00	17	253.60	257.20	248.80
8	247.50	265.00	229.00	18	252.70	259.20	248.20
9	254.30	275.00	242.00	19	254.30	259.00	247.90
10	252.00	258.00	241.00	20	255.20	260.10	251.00

Table 20.11 Average value for weights and ranges

		X-bar chart		Range chart	
Sample size, n	25.00	Centreline (CL)	251.21	Centreline (CL)	22.54
Average of sample mean	251.21	Lower control limit (LCL)	247.76	Lower control limit (LCL)	10.37
Average of sample range	22.54	Upper control limit (UCL)	254.65	Upper control limit (UCL)	34.71
For sample size of 25					
A	0.153				
B	0.460				
C	1.540				

Sample number	Sample average	Maximum weight	Minimum weight	Sample range	X-bar chart CL	X-bar chart LCL	X-bar chart UCL	Range chart CL	Range chart LCL	Range chart UCL
1	253.00	262.00	232.00	30.00	251.21	247.76	254.65	22.54	10.37	34.71
2	248.00	261.00	232.00	29.00	251.21	247.76	254.65	22.54	10.37	34.71
3	254.20	269.00	242.00	27.00	251.21	247.76	254.65	22.54	10.37	34.71
4	256.00	265.00	248.00	17.00	251.21	247.76	254.65	22.54	10.37	34.71

(Continued)

Table 20.11 (Continued)

Sample number	Sample average	Maximum weight	Minimum weight	Sample range	X-bar chart			Range chart		
					CL	LCL	UCL	CL	LCL	UCL
5	253.20	262.40	247.00	15.40	251.21	247.76	254.65	22.54	10.37	34.71
6	246.20	261.40	235.00	26.40	251.21	247.76	254.65	22.54	10.37	34.71
7	250.00	254.00	230.00	24.00	251.21	247.76	254.65	22.54	10.37	34.71
8	247.50	265.00	229.00	36.00	251.21	247.76	254.65	22.54	10.37	34.71
9	254.30	275.00	242.00	33.00	251.21	247.76	254.65	22.54	10.37	34.71
10	252.00	258.00	241.00	17.00	251.21	247.76	254.65	22.54	10.37	34.71
11	246.10	278.00	237.00	41.00	251.21	247.76	254.65	22.54	10.37	34.71
12	250.00	265.00	235.00	30.00	251.21	247.76	254.65	22.54	10.37	34.71
13	247.00	265.20	241.00	24.20	251.21	247.76	254.65	22.54	10.37	34.71
14	248.20	263.20	242.10	21.10	251.21	247.76	254.65	22.54	10.37	34.71
15	251.30	270.20	247.20	23.00	251.21	247.76	254.65	22.54	10.37	34.71
16	251.30	265.20	248.10	17.10	251.21	247.76	254.65	22.54	10.37	34.71
17	253.60	257.20	248.80	8.40	251.21	247.76	254.65	22.54	10.37	34.71
18	252.70	259.20	248.20	11.00	251.21	247.76	254.65	22.54	10.37	34.71
19	254.30	259.00	247.90	11.10	251.21	247.76	254.65	22.54	10.37	34.71
20	255.20	260.10	251.00	9.10	251.21	247.76	254.65	22.54	10.37	34.71
Mean	251.21			22.54						
Count	20									

Figure 20.31 Filling machine: x-bar chart

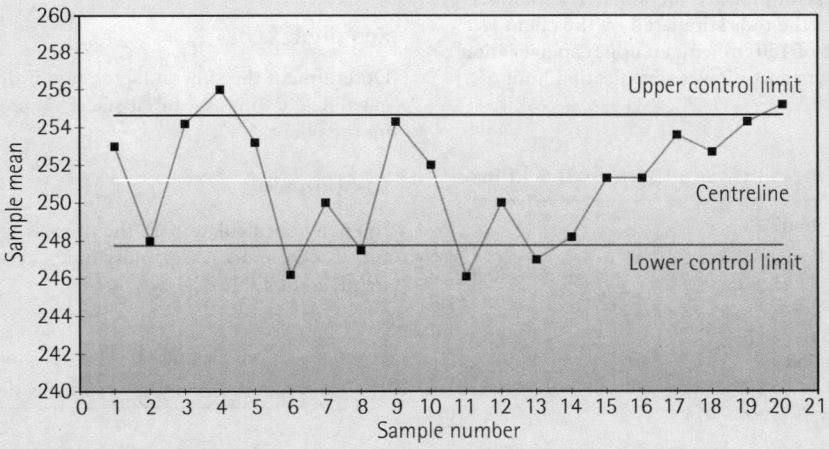

2. Both charts illustrate that there is a problem with the filling machine. In the x-bar chart the early results are erratic, some falling within the range, and sample 4 and 6 falling outside. As the sampling proceeds the average weights are erring on the high side and the 20th sample indicates that the average weight is outside the limit. Although this would be of no concern to the consumer, it is costing more than is necessary to the producer.

The conclusion is that the machine should be shut down and the operating conditions checked.

Figure 20.32 Filling machine: Range chart

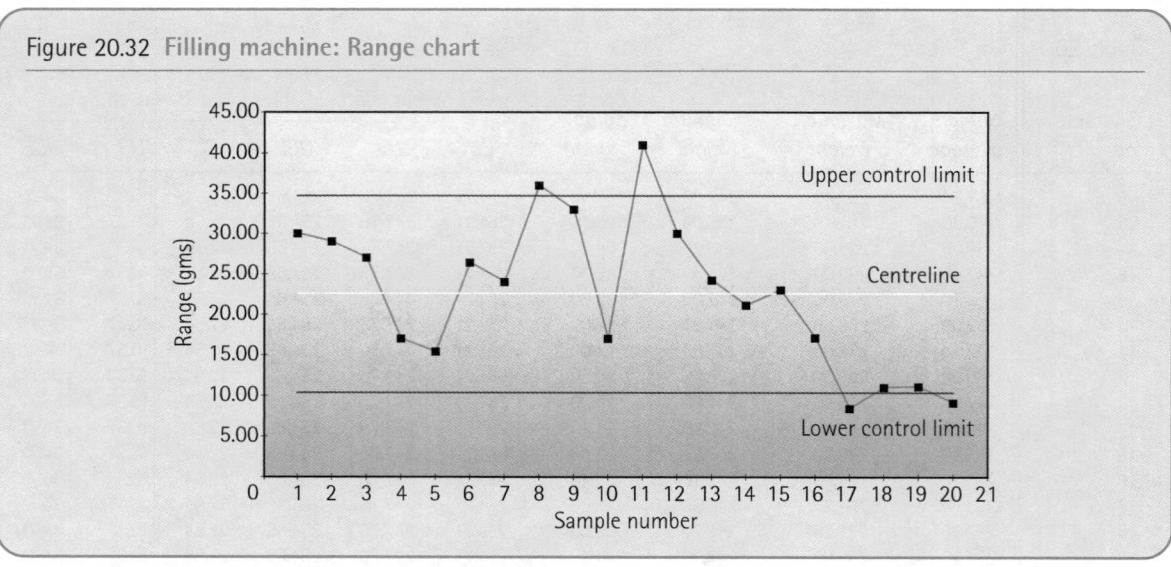

Demonstrating the concept 20.4 Fixation rods

Situation

A client who builds engines destined for shipbuilding has a need for fixation rods for which the firm has asked that a subcontractor produce the units. The product specification for the rods stipulated by the client is a nominal length of 150 cm with an upper specification limit of 150.05 cm and a lower specification limit of 149.95 cm.

Table 20.12 Process capability ratio and index

Product specification	
Nominal length of rods, cm	150.00
Upper specification, cm	150.05
Lower specification, cm	149.95
Tolerance, cm	0.10
Process specification	
Mean length of rods	150.02
Standard deviation of process (σ), cm	0.012
C_p = Tolerance/6σ	1.39
C_{pk} (Lower specification) = (Mean − Lower spec)/3σ	1.94
C_{pk} (Upper specification) = (Upper spec − Mean)/3σ	0.83
Process specification (after adjustment)	
Mean length of rods	150.002
Standard deviation of process (σ), cm	0.012
C_p = Tolerance/6σ	1.39
C_{pk} (Lower specification) = (Mean − Lower spec)/3σ	1.44
C_{pk} (Upper specification) = (Upper spec − Mean)/3σ	1.33

The subcontractor who will produce the rod has a lathe machine that can produce rods of a mean length of 150.02 cm and a standard deviation, based on a normal distribution, of 0.012 cm.

Required

Determine if the subcontractor, under the current machine conditions, can satisfactorily produce the rods for the client.

Solution

You need to calculate both the process capability ratio and also the process capability index. These calculations are given in Table 20.12.

$$C_p = \frac{\begin{bmatrix} \text{Upper product} \\ \text{specification} \end{bmatrix} - \begin{bmatrix} \text{Lower product} \\ \text{specification} \end{bmatrix}}{6\sigma} = 1.39$$

$$C_{pk} = \frac{\bar{\bar{x}} - \text{Lower specification}}{3\sigma} = 1.94$$

$$C_{pk} = \frac{\text{Upper specification} - \bar{\bar{x}}}{3\sigma} = 0.83$$

The process capability ratio is acceptable as it is greater than 1.00 and greater than the critical value of 1.33. Although the process capability index on the lower specification is acceptable, it is not on the upper specification, as it is less than 1.00. The process mean is too close to the upper product specification, which means that too many rods will be produced that are greater in length than the customer product specification.

The subcontractor must reassess the settings on the lathe machine. For example, as shown in the lower part of the table, if the subcontractor can readjust the lathe such that it produces rods with a mean length of 150.002 cm, with the same standard deviation, then both the process capability ratio and the process capability index for the upper and lower product specification will be acceptable. All are greater than or equal to 1.33.

Demonstrating the concept 20.5 Switches

Situation

A small electrical manufacturing company in Chicago, USA, makes a variety of electrical switches in lot sizes of 2000 units used in domestic power circuits, batteries, and for automobile use. The company wants to develop a statistical quality control programme for testing the attribute function of its products. The first step was to develop operating characteristic curves for its sampling programme to see what effect sampling limits and sample sizes would have on the probability of accepting good lots, and rejecting bad lots.

Required

1. Develop operating characteristic curves for a fixed sample size of 50 units, for the number of defective units in the sample of zero, one, two, and three units.
2. Using the operating characteristic curves developed in (1), what is the probability of accepting the lot when the actual percent defective units in the lot are 2, 4, 6, and 8%? What are the conclusions from this information?
3. Develop operating characteristic curves for a sample sizes of 25, 50, 75, and 100 units, for a level when the percent defects in the sample is always at 4%.
4. If the acceptance plan is to reject all lots where the actual percent defective units in the lot is 2%, using the operating characteristic curves developed in (3) what is the probability of accepting the lot when the actual percent defective units in the lot is 1, 2, 3, 4, 6, and 8%? What are the conclusions from this information?

Solution

1. The operating characteristic curve is developed from the modified Poisson distribution:

$$P(x) = \frac{(np)^x e^{-(np)}}{x!}$$

where

- P(x) is the probability of accepting the lot

- n is the sample size (number of units in the sample)
- p is the actual percent defective units in the lot
- x is the number of defective units permitted in the sample
- np is the mean value of defective units in the sample.

  Here n = 50:

- p is given selected values of 0 through 15% in increments of 1%
- four separate curves are developed for values of x (= c) = 0, 1, 2, and 3.

  The data are shown in Table 20.13 and Figure 20.33.
2. The probability of accepting the lot for the given values of the actual percent defective units in the lot is given in Table 20.14. The operating characteristic curve with the tighter limits (low value of c) is less likely to accept the lot (more likely to reject the lot) at whatever the actual percent defect units in the lot. At the lower end, for small value of the actual percent defective units in the lot it is less likely to accept the lot (even though it is a good lot). Thus, except for low values, the best discriminating curve is the one that has smaller values of c in the sample.
3. In order to keep the value at 4% defective units in the sample, Table 20.15 shows the number of defective units at each sample size.

    The modified Poisson distribution is used in the same way to develop the operating characteristic curves. The data for these four operating characteristic curves are shown in Table 20.16 and Figure 20.34.
4. Probability of accepting the lot at the given actual percent defective units in the lot is shown in Table 20.17.

    When the actual percent in the lot is 1 or 2%, there is a higher probability of accepting the lot (a good lot) than with the large sample size. When the actual percentage defective units in the lot are 3% or more (a bad lot) the operating characteristic curve at the larger sample size is less likely to accept the lot (more likely to reject lot). Thus, for a given % defectives, the larger the sample size, the more discriminating is the operating characteristic curve.

Table 20.13 Fixed sample size of switch: Changing values of c

Size 50

Percent defective units	Lamda (np/100)	Operating characteristic curve Probability of acceptance Value of c (= x)			
		0	1	2	3
0.00	0.00	100.00	100.00	100.00	100.00
1.00	0.50	60.65	90.98	98.56	99.82
2.00	1.00	36.79	73.58	91.97	98.10
3.00	1.50	22.31	55.78	80.88	93.44
4.00	2.00	13.53	40.60	67.67	85.71
5.00	2.50	8.21	28.73	54.38	75.76
6.00	3.00	4.98	19.91	42.32	64.72
7.00	3.50	3.02	13.59	32.08	53.66
8.00	4.00	1.83	9.16	23.81	43.35
9.00	4.50	1.11	6.11	17.36	34.23
10.00	5.00	0.67	4.04	12.47	26.50
11.00	5.50	0.41	2.66	8.84	20.17
12.00	6.00	0.25	1.74	6.20	15.12
13.00	6.50	0.15	1.13	4.30	11.18
14.00	7.00	0.09	0.73	2.96	8.18
15.00	7.50	0.06	0.47	2.03	5.91
16.00	8.00	0.03	0.30	1.38	4.24
17.00	8.50	0.02	0.19	0.93	3.01
18.00	9.00	0.01	0.12	0.62	2.12
19.00	9.50	0.01	0.08	0.42	1.49
20.00	10.00	0.00	0.05	0.28	1.03

Figure 20.33 Switches: Operating characteristic curve (1)

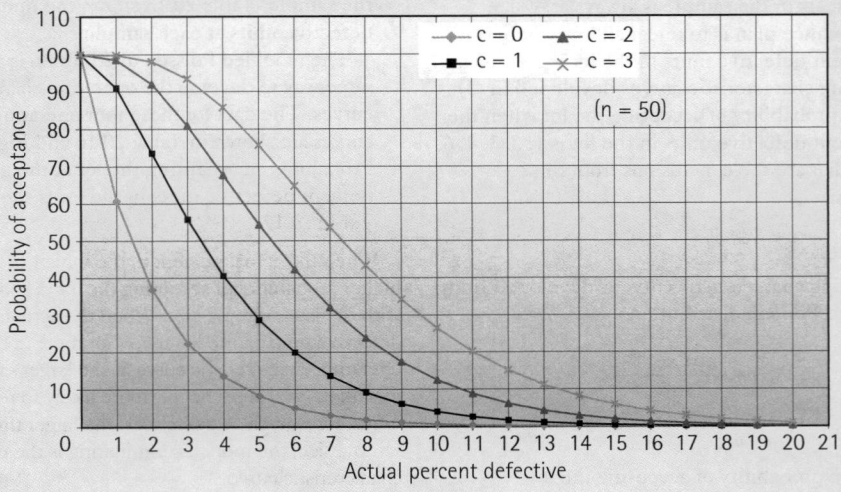

Table 20.14 Probability of accepting lot

Actual % defective units in lot	Probability (%) of accepting lot (curve: c = 0)	Probability (%) of accepting lot (curve: c = 1)	Probability (%) of accepting lot (curve: c = 2)	Probability (%) of accepting lot (curve: c = 3)
1	60.65	90.98	98.56	99.82
2	36.79	73.58	91.97	98.10
4	13.53	40.60	67.67	85.71
6	4.98	19.91	42.32	64.72
8	1.83	9.16	23.81	43.35

Table 20.15 Defective units in each sample size

Sample size	Number of defective units
25	1
50	2
75	3
100	4

Table 20.16 Fixed 4% defectives in switches: Changing sample size

Percent defective units	Lamda (np/100) Sample size = n				Operating characteristic curve Probability of acceptance Sample size			
					25	50	100	200
					Value of c (= x in Poisson)			
	25	50	100	200	1	2	4	8
0.00	0.00	0.00	0.00	0.00	100.00	100.00	100.00	100.00
1.00	0.25	0.50	1.00	2.00	97.35	98.56	99.63	99.98
2.00	0.50	1.00	2.00	4.00	90.98	91.97	94.73	97.86
3.00	0.75	1.50	3.00	6.00	82.66	80.88	81.53	84.72
4.00	1.00	2.00	4.00	8.00	73.58	67.67	62.88	59.25
5.00	1.25	2.50	5.00	10.00	64.46	54.38	44.05	33.28
6.00	1.50	3.00	6.00	12.00	55.78	42.32	28.51	15.50
7.00	1.75	3.50	7.00	14.00	47.79	32.08	17.30	6.21
8.00	2.00	4.00	8.00	16.00	40.60	23.81	9.96	2.20
9.00	2.25	4.50	9.00	18.00	34.25	17.36	5.50	0.71
10.00	2.50	5.00	10.00	20.00	28.73	12.47	2.93	0.21
11.00	2.75	5.50	11.00	22.00	23.97	8.84	1.51	0.06
12.00	3.00	6.00	12.00	24.00	19.91	6.20	0.76	0.02
13.00	3.25	6.50	13.00	26.00	16.48	4.30	0.37	0.00
14.00	3.50	7.00	14.00	28.00	13.59	2.96	0.18	0.00
15.00	3.75	7.50	15.00	30.00	11.17	2.03	0.09	0.00
16.00	4.00	8.00	16.00	32.00	9.16	1.38	0.04	0.00
17.00	4.25	8.50	17.00	34.00	7.49	0.93	0.02	0.00
18.00	4.50	9.00	18.00	36.00	6.11	0.62	0.01	0.00
19.00	4.75	9.50	19.00	38.00	4.97	0.42	0.00	0.00
20.00	5.00	10.00	20.00	40.00	4.04	0.28	0.00	0.00

▶ Figure 20.34 Switches: Operating characteristic curve (2)

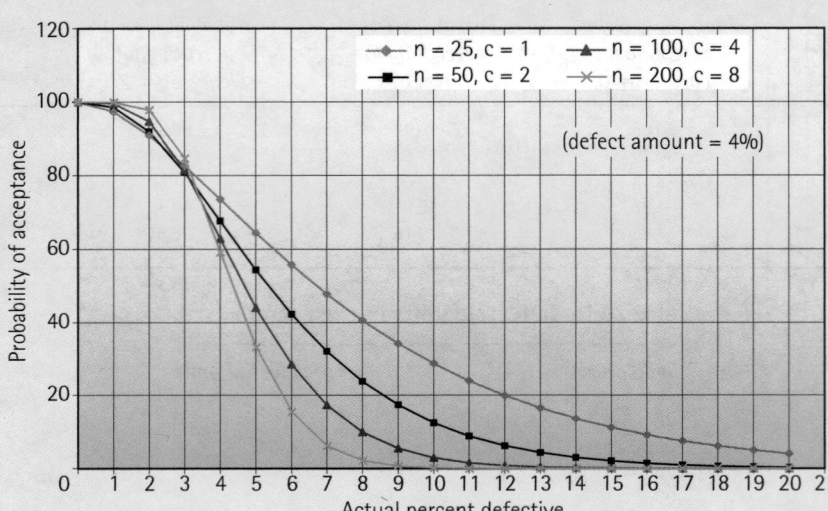

Table 20.17 Probability and actual percent defective units

Actual % defective units in lot	Probability (%) of accepting lot (n = 25: c = 1)	Probability (%) of accepting lot (n = 50: c = 2)	Probability (%) of accepting lot (n = 75: c = 3)	Probability (%) of accepting lot (n = 100: c = 4)
1	97.35	98.56	99.27	99.63
2	90.98	91.97	93.44	94.73
3	82.66	80.88	80.94	81.53
4	73.58	67.67	64.72	62.88
6	55.78	42.32	34.23	28.51
8	40.60	23.81	15.12	9.96

Thus, in summary, the better discriminating operating characteristic curve is either:

- having a very low tolerance of defect units in the sample (low value of c)
- for given fraction defective units in the sample, having a larger sample size.

In either case, the cost will be higher. The first indicates that the process producing the lots must be very reliable (avoid producing defect units). In the second case, the cost of sampling is higher.

Application exercise 20.1 Bearings

Situation

A manufacturing company has a product specification from its design engineers to produce a large quantity of stainless steel bearings for use in the aircraft industry. The specification calls for a nominal diameter of 0.7500 inches, an upper specification of 0.7525 inches and a lower specification of 0.7475 inches.

The production engineer in the firm has a suitable machine that can produce bearings with a mean diameter of 0.7490 inches and a standard deviation of 0.0006 inches.

Required

Determine if the proposed machine will be able to produce the required bearings satisfactorily.

Application exercise 20.2   Carpet making

Situation

A carpet maker in India wishes to install a quality control programme for the production of its carpets. It takes 250 carpets of similar size at random and counts the total number of faults on this sample. The number was 970.

Then for one week, Monday to Friday, the producer takes one carpet at random each from its two work centres and counts the number of blemishes on the carpet. This information is given in Table 20.18. The number in parenthesis after each day indicates the work centre.

Required

1. Establish a c-control chart for three-sigma control limits.
2. Present the test data on the control chart. What conclusions might you draw?

Table 20.18 Carpet blemishes

Day	Number of faults
Monday (1)	2
Monday (2)	12
Tuesday (1)	3
Tuesday (2)	13
Wednesday (1)	3
Wednesday (2)	10
Thursday (1)	2
Thursday (2)	8
Friday (1)	2
Friday (2)	11

Application exercise 20.3   Hotel

Situation

A large 250-room hotel in a major European city has just changed ownership. The new management wants to be sure that things are near perfect at the new hotel and, for that reason, a quality control check is carried out on the rooms. Each time the room is prepared by the hotel cleaning staff, there is an inspection to see if everything conforms to management's expectation. A non-conforming room may mean that the telephone is not properly connected, there are marks on the windows, no extra toilet paper, no shower soap, dust under the bed, the curtains are not drawn properly, there are no flowers in the room, etc.

The quality control check was carried out over a 30-day consecutive period starting on Monday and including weekends. The number of non-conforming rooms is given in Table 20.19, according to the day the inspection was performed. Day 1 is a Monday and Day 30 is a Tuesday.

Required

1. Construct a p-chart for this operation, using a z value of 3.
2. What would you conclude from this control chart?
3. What might be an explanation for your conclusions from question 2?

Table 20.19 Quality control check and non-conforming rooms

Day of inspection	N° of non-conforming rooms	Day of inspection	N° of non-conforming rooms
1	6	16	9
2	5	17	8
3	3	18	9
4	6	19	15
5	11	20	25
6	27	21	27
7	28	22	12
8	4	23	8
9	8	24	7
10	6	25	9
11	2	26	11
12	9	27	22
13	24	28	20
14	23	29	9
15	11	30	7

Application exercise 20.4 The Internet

Situation

A consulting firm in France is considering modifying its information systems network due to problems with the present arrangement. Before any action is taken, a control was made over a three-week period, Monday to Friday, for the time taken to access the first search screen on the Internet. During one-hour periods throughout the day, consultants were asked to record the response time for connecting to the Internet. For each hour period data for 12 consultants picked at random were tabulated. This information is given in seconds in Table 20.20 for the mean of the 12 response times, plus the range.

Required

1. Construct the appropriate control charts to see if the response time of the process is 'in control' according to the information provided.
2. What conclusions might you draw from your control charts?
3. What were your reasons for selecting the control chart you used for your interpretations?

Table 20.20 Internet connection time data

Week 1			Week 2			Week 3		
Period	Mean	Range	Period	Mean	Range	Period	Mean	Range
8–9am	8.25	5.20	8–9am	2.25	14.50	8–9am	5.20	23.60
9–10am	10.65	12.20	9–10am	5.86	26.20	9–10am	4.60	45.20
10–11am	9.45	22.90	10–11am	13.25	15.20	10–11am	3.50	12.60
11–midday	9.86	18.00	11–midday	10.56	32.00	11–midday	3.60	23.60
Midday–1pm	12.24	14.60	Midday–1pm	13.46	14.60	Midday–1pm	4.50	25.40
1–2pm	20.25	23.70	1–2pm	20.45	41.20	1–2pm	13.60	25.60
2–3pm	32.40	21.00	2–3pm	30.25	12.60	2–3pm	9.50	12.60
3–4pm	40.20	25.00	3–4pm	35.21	23.50	3–4pm	12.60	18.60
4–5pm	45.70	26.30	4–5pm	40.56	18.50	4–5pm	13.50	21.60
5–6pm	55.23	30.20	5–6pm	47.50	19.60	5–6pm	20.60	23.60
6–7pm	56.20	23.60	6–7pm	48.60	21.30	6–7pm	25.60	5.60

Application exercise 20.5 Santa Claus

Situation

The Cusin Company in New Jersey is a family-owned toy business. One of its products for Christmas is a Santa that walks, rings a bell, and sings 'Merry Christmas'. Cusin assembles the final product but they import the electrical/mechanical movement from the Chang Company in Seoul in South Korea.

A shipment of 4000 movements has just been received in the Cusin warehouse. Chang and Cusin have jointly agreed to an acceptance plan where the producers' risk is 5%, the consumers' risk is 10%, the acceptable quality level (AQL) is 1%, and the lot tolerance percent defective (LTPD) is 6%.

Required

1. Develop an operating characteristic curve for a sample size of 100, with three or fewer defective units (value of c) in the sample using a value of p from 0 to 15% in 1% intervals. Would this satisfy the acceptance plan of Chang and Cusin?
2. Redo the operating characteristic curve for a sample size of 200, and a value of c of 6 or under. What are your observations?
3. Develop an average outgoing quality level (AOQ) curve for the sampling situation given in question 1.
4. If the actual percentage of defective units from an incoming lot is 3%, given the AOQ curve developed in the answer to question 3, what is the average outgoing quality (AOQ) in percent defectives for the Santa movement?

Application exercise 20.6 Watch manufacture

Situation

The Picasso Company on the outside of Barcelona, Spain, assembles inexpensive watches for sale in the European market. Most of its watches are aimed at children, or young adolescents. The company imports the printed circuit from Singapore, and then assembles the watches with frames made in its own factory. The watches are sold through distributors situated across Europe.

Assembly is quite straightforward. It involves laying the printed circuit into the watch frame then making six solder connections. The battery is then inserted, and the back is snapped onto the frame. The company works seven days a week. The weekend employees are a mixture of temporary and permanent staff.

Of late, Picasso has been receiving complaints from its distributors about defective watches being sold. As a result, Picasso decides to investigate its assembly operation. Picasso carries out sampling over a continuous 28-day period starting on a Monday. Each day it takes a random sample of 150 finished watches from that day's assembled lot, and tests them simply to see if they work. The criterion is that the watches operate, or they do not. The data for this sampling are given in Table 20.21.

Table 20.21 Watch defect sampling results

Day	Quantity of defective watches	Day	Quantity of defective watches
1	3	15	1
2	2	16	4
3	5	17	3
4	4	18	2
5	1	19	9
6	12	20	13
7	16	21	19
8	3	22	5
9	0	23	3
10	2	24	1
11	0	25	0
12	7	26	5
13	11	27	13
14	14	28	18

Required

1. Construct a p-chart for this operation, using a z value of 3 (99.7% confidence limit).
2. What are your observations from this p-chart?
3. Construct a new p-chart just using the Monday through Friday data (i.e., 20 pieces of data).
4. What are your observations from new this p-chart?

Case study 20.1 Candy Co.

Situation

The Candy Co. outside Berlin, Germany, manufactures a large variety of candies. One of its principal products is Gumbo Bears (jelly candies in the shape of the German bear). After production, the Gumbo Bears are cooled and packed in 250-, 500-, and 1000-gram plastic bags. The Gumbo Bears are fed automatically into the bags, which are then sealed by a hot press. Lately, the manager of production has noticed that there have been problems with the hot press sealer and he wonders if this has something to do with the filling operation. This has occurred particularly with the 500-gram bags.

The company decides to investigate the operation of the automatic filling machine and asks Michael Grand to undertake the analysis. The filling machine was first shut down and checked to see if was operating properly. This was just a very quick check, and no extensive adjustments were made. Next, Michael randomly sampled bags of Gumbo Bears and weighed the contents. Sample sizes were 20 bags of each, and in total 200 samples were taken. The average of the 200 sample means was 502.50 grams. The average of the sample range was 24.20 grams. Michael used this information to construct control charts for sample means, and sample ranges.

The following week Michael, together with his assistant, Anne Box, carried out a detailed analysis of the filling machine. Each hour, they took random samples of the 500-gram bags of Gumbo Bears. Michael took samples for the first eight hours, and Anne took samples for the next eight. Thus in total, they took 16 samples. As before, there were 20 bags in each sample. The mean weight of the sample was determined, and also the heaviest, and the lightest bag in each sample were recorded. The data can be found in Table 20.22.

Table 20.22 Candy Co.: Random sampling weights

Sample number	Sample average	Maximum weight	Minimum weight	Sample number	Sample average	Maximum weight	Minimum weight
1	504.00	508.00	499.20	9	498.20	509.60	499.20
2	502.00	510.00	485.50	10	499.80	507.60	499.60
3	501.00	512.60	496.50	11	500.90	503.20	498.40
4	501.30	514.90	498.60	12	501.30	514.60	486.50
5	499.20	520.20	487.20	13	501.90	521.00	498.60
6	501.00	504.90	489.50	14	501.70	521.20	485.60
7	502.10	508.60	489.60	15	502.10	521.90	475.60
8	499.20	512.50	475.60	16	503.20	512.80	498.20

Required

1. Analyze the situation regarding the performance of the filling machine and the operation of the facility in general.

2. Discuss how the effectiveness of these types of statistical process control system might improve with new technology.

Selected further reading

DOTY, Leonard A. (1996) *Statistical Process Control*, 2nd edition, Industrial Press.

HRYNIEWICZ, Olgierd, 'Statistical process control with the help of international statistical standards', *Human Systems Management*, vol. 16, issue 3, 1997, pp 20–6.

LODEWICK, EUGENE L. and LEAVENWORTH, Richard S. (1996) *Statistical Quality Control*, 7th edition, McGraw-Hill.

MAMZIC, C. L. (ed.) (1995) *Statistical Process Control (Practical Guides for Measurement and Control)*, ISA – The Instrumentation, Systems, and Automation Society.

STUART, Michael, MULLINS, Eamonn and DREW, Eileen, 'Statistical quality control and improvement', *European Journal of Operational Research*, vol. 88, issue 2, 20 January 1996, pp 203–14.

An extensive listing of other further reading can be found on the website.

What's on the web?

Further learning resources are available to lecturers and students at www.supplychain-online.com, including the following which are specific to *Statistical quality control*:

Resources	Subject
Chapter overview	Statistical quality control
Detailed chapter summary	Statistical quality control
Exam topics	Statistical quality control
Application exercise: Bolts	Statistical quality control (x-bar and range chart)
Application exercise: Meters	Statistical quality control (x-bar and range chart)
Application exercise: Record keeping	Statistical quality control (p-chart)
More further reading	Statistical quality control

21 *Waiting lines*

Chapter overview

- **Waiting lines in practice**
- **Reasons for waiting lines**
- **Service systems in waiting lines**
- **Single channel, single phase queuing models**
- **Simulation of a waiting line**
- **Managing the waiting line**

Waiting lines in practice

In the supply chain goods often flow sequentially from one entity to another. For example sacks of polypropylene pellets from a supplier *arrive* at a manufacturer's site where they are stored before being processed into plastic wheels for roller blades. The manufacturer is the *service area* for this raw material. In the opposite sense in the supply chain, a piece of information requesting a quantity of polypropylene pellets flows via the Internet from a manufacturer and *arrives* at the supplier's facility. This order has to wait before the supplier can handle or *service* this item of information. In travelling, passengers *arrive* at an airport terminal and form a queue before they are *serviced* by immigration officers. One telephones for a medical appointment and the call *arrives* at the medical centre. The call is put on hold before it is *serviced*. Waiting lines, or queues, that occur in these and similar activities, illustrate a bottleneck situation. Waiting lines are a non-value-added 'activity', are an indicator of inefficiency, result in lost time, and have a subsequent cost. The following gives some specific examples but there are infinitely more. (See also Chapter 22.)

Retail stores

A checkout counter at a super- or hypermarket, for example, where customers are waiting to pay for purchases. The length of the waiting line depends on the time of day and for most stores is greater during lunchtime and early evening when working people come to do their shopping. Waiting lines may be non-existent in the morning or late evening. The 'cost'

of the waiting line is the lost time of the customers who could be doing other things (working, for example!).

Airline industry

The airline industry, both in the USA and Europe, is notorious for delays either at departure or arrival. At major airports such as Heathrow, London, or Chicago and New York in the USA there are constantly rows of airplanes on the tarmac waiting for takeoff clearance. Alternatively, arriving at a busy period at these major airports one can find oneself circling the airport perhaps for more than an hour waiting for landing clearance. The cost of this waiting to the service provider is the airplane fuel being burnt, flight crew salaries, and 'lost' use of the airplane during the waiting period. (Airlines like to have their airplanes flying for the maximum amount of time in order to contribute to the high capital cost.) To the airline customer, there is the 'cost' of the lost time in waiting. To society, there is the 'cost' of the environmental damage of pollution from the fuel being burnt during idling before takeoff or in a holding pattern before landing.

Road networks

Road networks worldwide are becoming very heavily congested with prime examples being roads around Paris, London, New York, Los Angeles, Singapore, Istanbul, and Tokyo. Waiting is a result simply of heavy traffic, or waiting at a tollbooth to entering a bridge, tunnel, ferry, or motorway (as in France or Italy). Again, the cost is the lost time of people in the waiting line, lost use of vehicles, and pollution from exhausts. (The level of NOX (nitrogen oxide gases) emission when a vehicle is running at low speed, or the engine is idling, is greater than when the vehicle is travelling at normal speed.)

Medical centres

In most countries patients spend a lot of time waiting for medical help at hospitals, at the doctor's office, or dentist surgery. Here the premium time is put on the medical profession with the patients' 'lost' time considered much less important.

Government owned or managed

Government-owned or government-managed systems can be notorious for causing waiting lines such as the following:

- Waiting to pass through customs or passport control at major international airports such as London's Heathrow, Los Angeles International, or Kennedy, New York. If three 747s arrive within several minutes of one another then the waiting line can be very long. This waiting time is a concern when the Airbus A-380 comes into service in 2006 with an expected passenger load of 550.
- Customers waiting at a post office.
- Passport office to obtain a passport or a visa. (On one occasion, I arrived at the Los Angeles passport office at 2am and left at 3pm!!)
- Waiting to obtain documents from a tax office.

Sports and entertainment facilities

This might be, for example, skiers waiting for a chair lift, people waiting for an attraction at a theme park, or waiting for the cinema. People may not count the cost here, since the waiting is for entertainment purposes.

Manufacturing

In manufacturing, there can be waiting of material or components to be machined, assembled, or finished products waiting to be delivered to clients. The cost here is the inventory carrying cost. There can also be waiting or idle time for operators to receive component parts. Here the cost is the wages to the operators who are not performing added-value work.

Distribution

In the distribution function there is the waiting of inventory to be loaded or unloaded at the docks, which again results in an inventory carrying cost. There is also the waiting time for trucks to deliver and unload their merchandise or, alternatively, the waiting time to load and depart.

Benefits of waiting lines to the operator

There may be some benefits and 'added value' to a service operator when customers are waiting such as the following.

Additional time to buy

A limited queue in a supermarket gives customers time to buy display items at the checkout counter such as candies, magazines, and batteries. At major airports and train stations there are giftshops and restaurants and waiting passengers will browse these facilities and perhaps make a purchase.

Quality perception

A line in a restaurant may give the impression to prospective clients that the food must be good. Thus, the total customers serviced may be greater and hence revenues higher. The same perception may be applied to a cinema and theatre.

Dissuasive element

A long line in an immigration office may dissuade individuals seeking residency papers.

Customers' behaviour in waiting lines

Not all customers who see a queue accept to wait in line. They may baulk or renege.

Baulk

Long lines in a system might cause customers to *baulk*. This is when they refuse to join the queue because they don't like to wait under any circumstances, or the particular queue is too long. In ski resorts, entertainment centres, retail outlets and the like these can represent a lost opportunity cost to the operator. (This is not a problem in the travel industry, as one often may not have a choice.)

Renege

Reneging is when a customer enters a waiting line but becomes impatient and leaves. Thus, for a part of the time they form the waiting line, but never become serviced. Reneging customers can be detrimental to the operator because if one customer leaves the line it can have a snowball effect and other customers may decide to leave.

Reasons for waiting lines

Waiting lines are caused because there is insufficient capacity of a system to handle a given load at a certain point of time. It might be that with better scheduling the load can be reduced which will balance the system, and thus avoid the waiting line. However, it might be that the capacity of the system is permanently below the load and waiting lines are unavoidable. If there were infinite resources such as money, land, and people, waiting lines could perhaps be eliminated.

Load and capacity

The concept of load and capacity in a waiting line situation might be illustrated by a seesaw arrangement where the load is on the left side of the seesaw, and the capacity of the system on the right side. The capacity is fixed and pivots according to the different loads on the system.

Load is greater than capacity

When the load is greater than the capacity, the seesaw is unbalanced and tips to the left (see Figure 21.1). This represents a bottleneck and people, inventory units, or transportation equipment are waiting.

Load is less than capacity

When the load is less than the capacity then the seesaw is still unbalanced but this time tips to the right (see Figure 21.2). There is no bottleneck but the capacity resources are under-utilized, meaning an unnecessary cost to the operator. There are more machines, transportation equipment, or cashiers in the system than is needed at this time.

Load and capacity balanced

When the load and capacity are balanced the seesaw is horizontal (see Figure 21.3). The system is balanced and there are essentially no waiting lines. In a manufacturing organization this would approach a just-in-time operation. (See Chapter 15.)

Poor scheduling

A system may have sufficient capacity but waiting lines occur because of poor scheduling. For example, a doctor schedules more patients than can be treated in a certain time period. If it is a regular occurrence it means that the doctor is not able, or does not want to balance the load with his service capacity. Waiting lines may be the result of poor scheduling in the airline industry, in

manufacturing, or in the scheduling of the arrival and trucks in a distribution centre.

Badly designed systems

A system may be badly designed such that it never had the capacity to serve the load because the allocated funds were insufficient. This is sometimes the case in government facilities, such as offices for issuing passports, tax documents, and the like.

Figure 21.1 Seesaw: Load greater than capacity

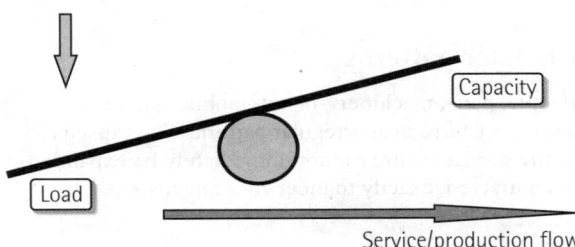

- Bottleneck situation
- Upstream inventory build-up
- People queuing
- Transportation equipment waiting

Figure 21.2 Seesaw: Load less than capacity

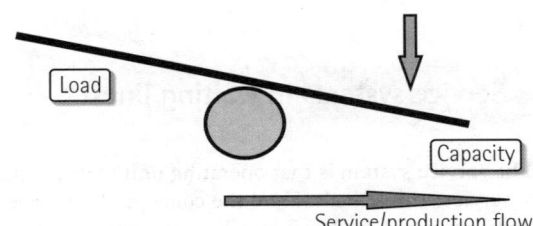

- No bottleneck
- No inventory build-up
- No people queuing
- No transporation equipment waiting
- *But, resources underutilized (people, equipment, investment...)*

Figure 21.3 Seesaw: Load and capacity equal

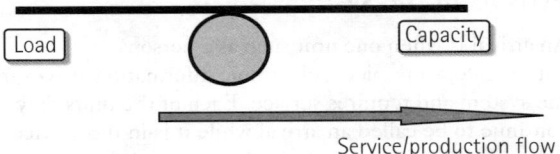

- No bottleneck
- No inventory build-up
- No people queuing
- No transportation equipment waiting
- *And* system is optimized

System has reached saturation

The system used to be able to handle the load, but the capacity is now saturated as for example:

- the London, Paris, or Tokyo underground system at peak periods
- road networks (M25 in England, the Santa Monica Freeway in Los Angeles, or the Fourvière Tunnel in Lyon, France)
- a machine shop's orders have increased but the machines available to perform the work remain the same
- most major airports.

Irregular patterns

People, parts, machinery, or automobiles arrive at a service centre in an irregular pattern. The capacity of the service centre cannot immediately be expanded, or contracted, exactly to meet client needs.

Unknown service time

The time it takes to service a customer is not known with certainty. In a supermarket, some people may have a lot of products to buy, while others may have few. Some pay by cheque, some with cash, or some with a credit card. The times for these types of transaction are different.

Service systems in waiting lines

The service system is that operating unit which handles or services the arrivals. Here the concept of a service system is very broad as it may be a machine cutting sheet steel, a cashier at a retail store, an automatic teller machine (ATM), or a tutor giving individual advice to a number of students. The service system would, for the most part, add value to these arriving units. The following explains some characteristics and terms.

Arrivals in the system

An arrival is when one unit such as a person, automobile, work piece, electronic information arrives in the system and requires service. Each of the units may continue to be called an arrival while it is in the service system. Most often arrival patterns are irregular, as it is not known how many arrivals there will be in a specific time period. However, the average number of arrivals per time period may be known, such as 25 every hour.

The average daily number of customers in a post office can be reasonably estimated from past data, but is not known if they will arrive in the morning, afternoon, or early evening.

Arrival rate to the system

The arrival rate, λ, is the frequency at which the units arrive, or the average units per period. The units might be persons per hour, components per minute, or automobiles per day. For analytical purposes, the arrival rate is usually considered to follow a Gauss (normal) or a Poisson distribution. (See Chapter 27.)

Variable service systems

Depending on the system the service rate may vary with the arrivals. For example, a client in a supermarket may have five articles, 25, or a whole basketload; a medical patient may just want a repeat prescription, or may require an X-ray of a broken arm; a customer at an after-sales service outlet may just be looking for a yes/no answer, whereas another may want details of how a household appliance works. Thus one often does not know in advance how long it will take to service each arrival but one can determine from past data the average time necessary to service arrivals.

Fixed service systems

Automated systems have a fixed service rate that is known in advance as, for example, the following:

- an automatic car wash
- a park attraction at a theme park as, for example, The Matterhorn Ride at Disneyland
- drilling a standard part using a numerically controlled drilling machine
- a soft drink machine that furnishes Coke, Sprite, Perrier and the like
- a coffee machine providing a specific product, say, black coffee with sugar
- an ATM machine (although the service time is also dependent on how quickly the customer pushes on the keys)
- an automatic washing machine for a given cycle, such as cotton at 40°C.

Service rate

The service rate, μ, is the mean rate that arrivals are serviced or helped expressed in arrivals per time unit such as two a minute, 120 per hour, etc. For variable service systems the rate is considered to follow a normal, Poisson, or exponential distribution. For fixed service systems the rate is constant.

Service time

The service time, t_h, is the time it takes to service or help an arrival, and is expressed in time per arrival such as 30 seconds per arrival. This time does not include waiting time. The average service time is given by the reciprocal of the service rate:

$$\bar{t}_h = \frac{1}{\mu}$$

Waiting line in the service system is unlimited

For some systems, the length of the waiting line is unlimited or infinite during the opening hours of the system. This could be the case for automobiles at a tollbooth, skiers waiting for a chair lift, or even customers at a popular supermarket.

Waiting line in the service system is limited

For some systems, the length of the waiting line, in terms of units is a maximum or a finite value defined by the available capacity of the system. This might be the case for cars waiting for a cross-channel ferry, passengers for a train when only seating is allowed, or for a cinema or hotel.

Queue discipline

A queue discipline is the scheduling rule that determines the order in which arrivals in a waiting line are serviced. (See also Chapter 14.) This might include, for example:

- first come, first served, which is perhaps the most common queue discipline
- shortest processing time
- longest processing time
- critical ratio (time to completion/processing time)
- most valuable customer.

The queue discipline can be modified by emergencies, which might be the case for a medical centre or rush orders for a client.

Channels

The channels are the number of waiting lines, N, which are entering a service system. The system may be single channel or multi-channel as follows.

Single channel service system

A single channel system service system gives rise to only one waiting line as, for example:

- a single booth theatre ticket sales office
- a medical centre where there is only one doctor
- one cash register servicing a food line
- one automatic cash dispensing machine.

Multiple channel service system

A multi-channel system is one that has several service areas that provide exactly the same service but would give rise to two or more waiting lines as, for example:

- in a supermarket checkout area there are several cashier counters for clients
- at a tollbooth on a motorway or bridge there are often several areas to obtain or to pay for a ticket
- at major railway stations, New York Central, Waterloo, London, or the Gare de Lyon, Paris, there are several booths from which to buy tickets.

Service phases

The service phases are the number of steps necessary to service an arrival. These phases can be incorporated into a single or multiple channel system, which then gives rise to the following four scenarios.

Single channel, single phase service system

A single channel, single phase service system is where there is only one waiting line for only one service area. This might be the case in a small grocery store where there is only one cashier or in a job shop where there is only one drilling machine for component parts. This concept is illustrated in Figure 21.4.

Single channel, multiple phase service system

A single channel, multiple phase service system is where there is one waiting line but the arrivals are serviced at two or more different functions. For example, at a medical centre a patient would first give medical information to the nurse at the first phase, have a check-up by the doctor at the second phase, and, finally, pay the bill to the secretary at the last phase. Another would be at the drive-in of a fast food restaurant where one first places the food order and then drives forward to receive the order. This concept is illustrated in Figure 21.5.

Multiple channel, single phase service system

A multiple channel, single phase service system would be the case at a supermarket where there are several

Figure 21.4 Queuing: Single channel, single phase system

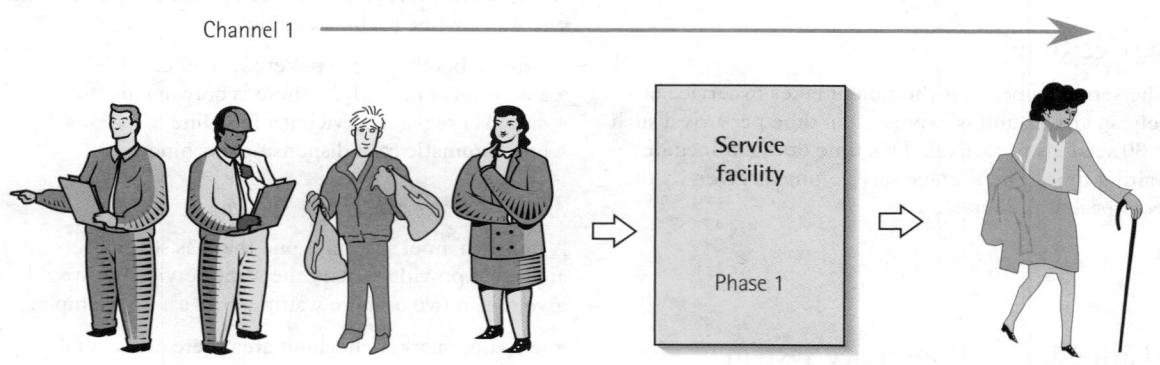

Figure 21.5 Queuing: Single channel, multiple phase system

Figure 21.6 Queuing: Multiple channel, single phase system

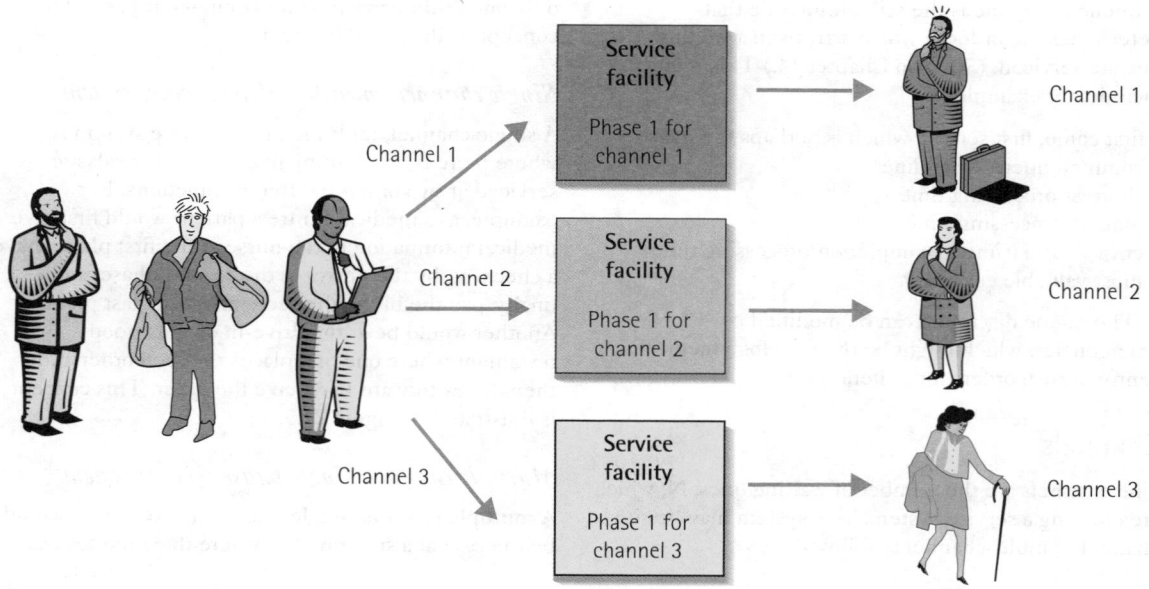

Figure 21.7   Queuing: Multiple channel, multiple phase system

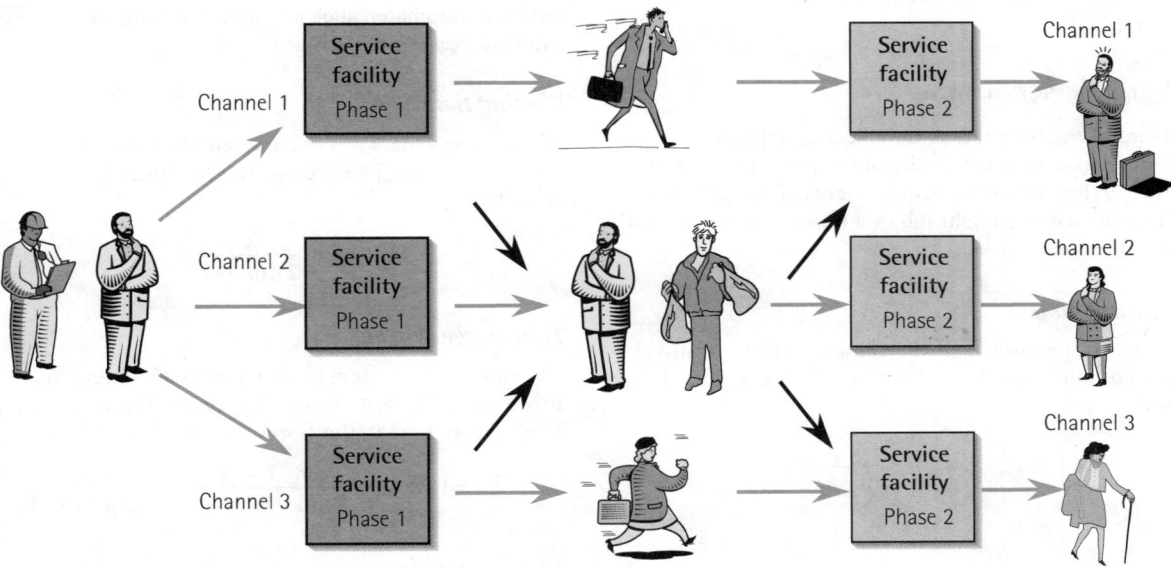

waiting lines or channels waiting to pay the cashier. Another illustration would be waiting to be serviced by a country passport office where there are several passport officers to serve the line of customers. This concept is illustrated in Figure 21.6.

Multiple channel, multiple phase service system

A multiple channel, multiple phase system is where there are at least two channels and two service areas, such as might be the case at an airport terminal where passengers pass first through the immigration control where there are several officers, and then through customs inspection where there are several inspectors. This concept is illustrated in Figure 21.7.

Single channel, single phase queuing models

The purpose of defining queuing systems is to develop models, which can be a useful tool in managing the waiting line with the objective of improving the system. (See Chapter 1 for more information on modelling.) Single channel and single phase models can be analyzed by relatively simple mathematical formulae, which is illustrated in this section.[1] (Modelling of the other systems is not covered here but more information can be found in the further reading at the end of this chapter.)

Conditions

In single channel, single phase queuing models arrivals form a single line and wait to be serviced at a single station. These models apply under the following conditions:

- Arrivals are served on a first come, first served basis.
- Every arrival waits to be served regardless of the length of the queue.
- Arrivals are independent of previous arrivals.
- Arrivals come from a population that is considered infinite.
- The average arrival rate does not change over time.
- Arrivals are described by a Poisson probability distribution.
- Service times may vary from one arrival to the next and are independent of each arrival. However, the average service time is known.
- Service times vary according to an exponential or Poisson distribution.
- The service rate is faster than the arrival rate.

Utilization of service system

- Utilization (P_n) is the probability that the service system is occupied by an arrival or λ/μ. Thus, if the mean number of arrivals is eight an hour, and the service rate on average is ten an hour, then the utilization is 8/10 or 80%.
- By corollary, the probability that the system is idle, or there are no units in the system is $1 - (\lambda/\mu)$.

With the data given, the probability that the system is idle is $100 - 80 = 20\%$.

- Probability of more than k units in the system is $(\lambda/\mu)^{k+1}$.

Variable service rate

Here, the service rate is variable as it depends to a certain extent on the ability of the person performing the service, and to the requirements of the arrival. The service rate might follow a Poisson or exponential distribution.

Waiting time

The waiting time, t_w, is the amount of time an arrival spends in queue. The average waiting time is $\bar{t}_w$. It is given by:

$$\bar{t}_w = \frac{\lambda}{\mu(\mu - \lambda)}$$

Time in the system

The time in the system $(t_w + t_h)$ is the total time that arrivals spend in system (waiting time + service time). The average time in the system is given by:

$$\bar{t}_w + \bar{t}_h = \bar{t}_s = \frac{\lambda}{\mu(\mu - \lambda)} + \frac{1}{\mu} = \frac{1}{(\mu - \lambda)}$$

Number waiting

The average number of arrivals waiting (the length of the queue) is given by the relationship:

$$\bar{n}_w = \frac{\lambda^2}{\mu(\mu - \lambda)}$$

Number being serviced

The average number of arrivals being serviced is given by the relationship:

$$\bar{n}_h = \frac{\lambda}{\mu}$$

Number in system

The average number of arrivals in the system (waiting + being serviced) is given by:

$$\bar{n}_s = \bar{n}_w + \bar{n}_h = \frac{\lambda^2}{\mu(\mu - \lambda)} + \frac{\lambda}{\mu} = \frac{\lambda}{(\mu - \lambda)}$$

This model is illustrated in Demonstrating the concept 21.1.

Constant service rate

In this model, the service rate is fixed as the service station is automated such as coffee, washing, or automatic car wash machines.

Waiting time

The waiting time, t_w, is the amount of time an arrival spends in queue. The average waiting time, $\bar{t}_w$, is given by:

$$\bar{t}_w = \frac{\lambda}{2\mu(\mu - \lambda)}$$

Time in the system

The time in the system $(t_w + t_h)$ is the total time that arrivals spend in system (waiting time + service time). The average time in the system is given by:

$$\bar{t}_w + \bar{t}_h = \bar{t}_s = \frac{\lambda}{2\mu(\mu - \lambda)} + \frac{1}{\mu} = \frac{2\mu - \lambda}{2\mu(\mu - \lambda)}$$

Number waiting

The average number of arrivals waiting is given by the relationship:

$$\bar{n}_w = \frac{\lambda^2}{2\mu(\mu - \lambda)}$$

Number being serviced

The average number of arrivals being serviced is given by the relationship:

$$\bar{n}_h = \frac{\lambda}{\mu}$$

Number in system

The average number of arrivals in the system (waiting + service) is given by:

$$\bar{n}_s = \bar{n}_w = \bar{n}_h = \frac{\lambda^2}{2\mu(\mu - \lambda)} + \frac{\lambda}{\mu} = \frac{\lambda(2\mu - \lambda)}{2\mu(\mu - \lambda)}$$

This model is illustrated in Demonstrating the concept 21.2.

Simulation of a waiting line

Defining simulation

Simulation, like modelling, is to try and create the real environment using smaller systems. Airline pilots use flight simulators in training to aid them in flying the real airplane. Wind tunnel simulators are used to mimic the atmospheric conditions to which aircraft might be exposed. Whirlpool Co. simulates conditions for testing its washing machines for quality control purposes. In waiting lines, simulation means using usually computer-based systems to create the real environment so that scheduling and capacity can be better optimized for situations where mathematical models, such as presented earlier, are not appropriate for the waiting line situation.

Parameters in the waiting line

In a waiting line system there are parameters that are constant and normally cannot be changed. These might have been established by economics, management policy, and technology and would include elements such as the number of service phases, the number of channels, or the service time in automated systems.

Variables in the waiting line

The variables in the waiting line are those that vary randomly in the system and would include the customer arrival rate, the service rate, and the time of arrival.

Monte Carlo process

Some operating systems may be difficult to solve analytically, because variables are random and are better represented by probability distributions. The Monte Carlo process is a technique using random numbers to simulate arrival patterns and service rates in an operation based on probability distributions.[2] When a system has been satisfactorily simulated, variables can be managed by adjusting the parameters of the system.[3] The Monte Carlo concept originates from the casinos in Monaco where clients attempt to select the correct sample from a population. For example, three oranges in a one-armed bandit spun at random, or the correct numbers from the throw of two dice, or numbers from a roulette wheel. The use of the Monte Carlo process using random numbers is detailed in Demonstrating the concept 21.3.

Computer packages

There are many commercial computer packages as management tools for simulating waiting line situations. These are particularly useful when the system is complex such as the multiple channel and single phase system, or the multiple channel and multiple phase system, handling a large number of clients. As an

illustration, Carrefour, a hypermarket in Ecully, France, has 69 checkout stands that handle on average 50,000 customers during a six-day week. Their computer simulator gives information on the store arrivals, service rates, the loading on each cashier, which provides the criteria for opening a new checkout, or closing an open one. Carrefour's checkout stands are of three types: Normal (any customer), fast (those with ten articles or fewer), membership card (those that possess the Carrefour store card). The basis for the computer simulator is similar to that described in Demonstrating the concept 21.3.

Managing the waiting line

The purpose behind analyzing waiting lines is to improve the system and attempt to minimize the non-value added activity. The following are some considerations to better 'manage' a waiting line.

Need to analyze waiting line situations

A service system is designed to service on average a certain number of arrivals per time period (hour, for example). Some questions that may be asked in analyzing the system include:

- What is the average number of units waiting?
- What is the average time each unit spends waiting?
- What is the average number of units in the system?
- What is average time each unit spends in the system?
- What percentage of time is the system empty or not used?
- What is probability that n units will be in the system?

Good management policy

Management should attempt to have the following attitude towards waiting lines:

- Limit the number of units waiting.
- Limit the number of units in the system.
- Limit the time each unit waits.
- Limit the time each unit is in the system.
- Maximize utilization of the service system. That is, minimize the percentage of time the system is empty.

In waiting lines there are 'costs', both to the operator of the service area and the arrivals or customers. The operator may increase the number of service areas, which will increase his cost and reduce the 'cost' of the arrivals. If the service level is too low then customers will baulk or renege, which will also increase

Figure 21.8 Balance between service level and cost

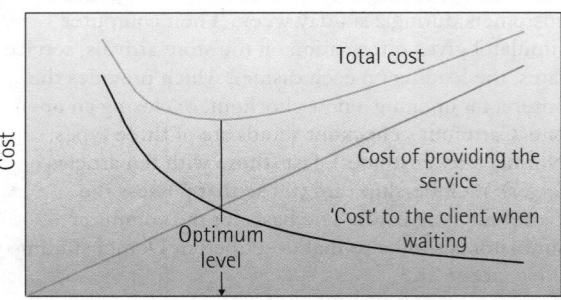

It doesn't actually *reduce* the waiting time but it might make the time *seem* less long.
- Use just-in-time in the system (see Chapter 15), which will minimize the waiting time of raw materials, work-in-process, and finished goods.
- If you are expecting to be caught in a waiting line, have with you a book or something else to read to minimize the impact of this lost time. (Peter Ueberroth, the organizer of the financially successful 1984 Olympics in Los Angeles, always had a book in his pocket so he could read whenever he had to wait.)

his 'cost'. There will be an optimum level as illustrated in Figure 21.8.

Approaches to reduce waiting lines or to minimize their negative impact

Certain approaches to reduce waiting lines or to minimize their negative impact might include the following:

- In grocery stores, when waiting lines occur, managers, shelvestockers, and even warehouse people can help at the checkout stands.
- Some supermarkets have a policy that no more than, say, five people wait in line before another checkout is opened (Ralphs of the USA). In 1994 Tesco, of the UK, adopted the policy 'One in front', meaning it opened a new checkout whenever the line exceeded two trolley carts.[4]
- Part-time workers are used for weekend and evening operations.
- Express checkout counter for, say, fewer than five articles in a supermarket.
- Special checkout counters for those that use the store's own in-store card.
- Appointment schedules for, say, a hairdresser, doctor, or dentist.
- New technology helps to speed up the flow of waiting lines such as the bar code readers in retail stores, or the automatic readers at ski lifts, which avoid a lift operator having to punch or visually check the ski pass.
- 'Take a number' at customer service desk. It will reduce waiting lines if customers holding a number can do other things, such as shop elsewhere in the store. This assumes they are able to estimate the time by which their number will be called.
- Entertain those waiting in line, or inform them of the waiting time. This is the case of customers waiting in line in Disney attractions at Disneyland, Paris.

Summary of key elements

- Waiting lines of people, inventory, or transportation equipment represent a non-value-added 'activity', are an indicator of inefficiency, result in lost time, and have a subsequent cost.

- Some benefits of a waiting line to a system operator is that it may give customers 'more time to make impulse purchases', it may give a quality perception in the case of restaurant, theatre or film, or it might dissuade people from seeking a government service.

- Not all customers accept standing in a waiting line. They may *baulk*, and refuse to join the waiting line. Alternatively, they may *renege*, and leave the waiting line after a certain time.

- Waiting lines are the result of insufficient system capacity to handle a given load and this creates a bottleneck. If the capacity is greater than the load, there is no bottleneck but the system is over-designed. The ideal is when the capacity matches the load on the system.

- Associated reasons for waiting lines might be the result of poor scheduling, a badly designed system, from the start, the system has reached saturation, the arrival pattern of customers is irregular, or the service time is unknown.

- The arrival rate, λ, is the frequency at which units arrive, or the average units per period. The units may be persons an hour, components a minute, or automobiles a day, etc. The arrival rate is usually considered to follow a Gauss (normal) or a Poisson distribution.

- Service systems may be variable when the service rate is unknown in advance or they may be fixed such as for a coffee machine, car wash, or ATM machine.

- The service rate, μ, is the mean rate at which arrivals are serviced expressed in arrivals per time unit. For variable service systems the rate is considered to follow a normal, Poisson, or exponential distribution. For fixed service systems the rate is constant. The service time is the reciprocal of the service rate.

- Some systems may have an unlimited or infinite waiting line, such as a ski lift. Alternatively, they may have a fixed, or finite waiting line determined by the capacity of the system, such as a cinema or airplane.

- The most common form of queue discipline in waiting lines is first come, first served, although others might be shortest processing time, longest processing time, the critical ratio, or the most valuable customer. The queue discipline may be modified by emergencies.

- A channel is the number of waiting lines in the service system. There may be a single channel with just one waiting line, or multiple channels with two or more waiting lines.

- The service phases are the number of steps involved in assisting arrivals. The combinations of phases and channels are, single channel and single phase, single channel and multiple phases, multiple channels and single phase, or multiple channels and multiple phases.

- Computer simulations can be used to understand waiting lines better and thus improve their management. A Monte Carlo simulation is one such approach, which uses random numbers to simulate the system variables such as the arrival interval of customers, or the service rate. Knowing the movement of these variables makes it easier to control parameters such as the number of checkout counters to install.

- Waiting lines might be better 'managed' by analyzing the needs of the waiting lines, adopting good management policies, and using certain approaches to reduce waiting lines or to minimize their negative impact.

Notes and references

1. GRIFFIN, W., *Queuing: Basic Theories and Applications*, Grid Publishing, Columbus, Ohio 1978
2. LEE, Sang M. *Introduction to Management Science*, Dryden Press, London, 1983
3. COOPER, B., *Introduction to Queuing Theory*, Elsevier-North Holland, New York, 1980
4. 'Tesco: Leahy's lead', *The Economist*, 11 August 2001, p. 53

Review and discussion topics

1. Airports
Many airports are notorious for waiting lines either for the passengers, or the airplanes (which, in many cases, also include the passengers, who may be sitting inside them).
  (a) What are the reasons for waiting lines at airports?
  (b) How can waiting lines be better managed?
  (c) What is the impact of some of the proposed solutions to reduce the waiting lines at airports?

2. Queuing experience
In the past month you have probably experienced a waiting line situation. If this is the case:
  (a) Describe the circumstances of the waiting line.
  (b) What has been the 'lost time' to you?
  (c) Can you put a financial value to this lost time?
  (d) How do you think the waiting line could have been better managed?

3. Variables in waiting lines
How would the following impact waiting lines in department stores?
  (a) Promotions
  (b) vacation periods
  (c) the four seasons.

4. Technology and waiting lines
How has technology improved the management of waiting lines in:
  (a) transportation systems
  (b) retail stores
  (c) university registration for the next trimester course
  (d) financial services?

5. Fixed capacity systems
Identify some fixed capacity systems. Indicate the parameters as to why they are 'fixed'.

  How does management try to manage the waiting lines in these fixed capacity systems?

Demonstrating the concept 21.1 Town hall

Situation

A town hall has a department for issuing official documents such as residency papers, marriage licences, fishing permits, etc. At any given time there is one employee who handles the customers. On average, the town hall employer takes 12 minutes to service a client and on average one client arrives every 20 minutes.

The arrival and service rate follow the assumptions for a single channel, single phase queuing model.

Required

1. Determine the average time in minutes that a customer spends in the system (waiting and being helped).

2. Determine the average time in minutes waiting in line, but not including being serviced.
3. Calculate the average utilization of the system.
4. Develop a probability histogram of there being more than k units in the system with a value of k from 0 to 10.

5. What is the probability that there will be more than four people in the system?

Solution

The calculation steps and the solutions are given in Table 21.1 and a histogram is illustrated in Figure 21.9.

Table 21.1 Typical waiting lines in a town hall

Average service rate, mins/unit		12	Given
Average arrival rate, mins/unit		20	Given
Average service rate, units/hr	μ	5	
Average arrival rate, units/hr	λ	3	
Average units in system	$\lambda/(\mu - \lambda)$	1.50	
Average time in system, hours	$1/(\mu - \lambda)$	0.50	
Average time in system, minutes		**30.00**	**Question 1**
Average units waiting	$\lambda^2/[\mu(\mu - \lambda)]$	0.90	
Average time waiting in line, hours	$\lambda/[\mu(\mu - \lambda)]$	0.30	
Average time waiting in line, minutes		**18.00**	**Question 2**
Average utilization of the system	λ/μ	**60.00%**	**Question 3**
Idle percentage	$1 - (\lambda/\mu)$	40.00%	
More than k in system given by	$(\lambda/\mu)^{\kappa+1}$		

	Value of k	Probability (%)	
More than	0	60.00	
More than	1	36.00	
More than	2	21.60	
More than	3	12.96	
More than	4	**7.78**	**Question 5**
More than	5	4.67	
More than	6	2.80	
More than	7	1.68	
More than	8	1.01	
More than	9	0.60	
More than	10	0.36	

Figure 21.9 Town hall

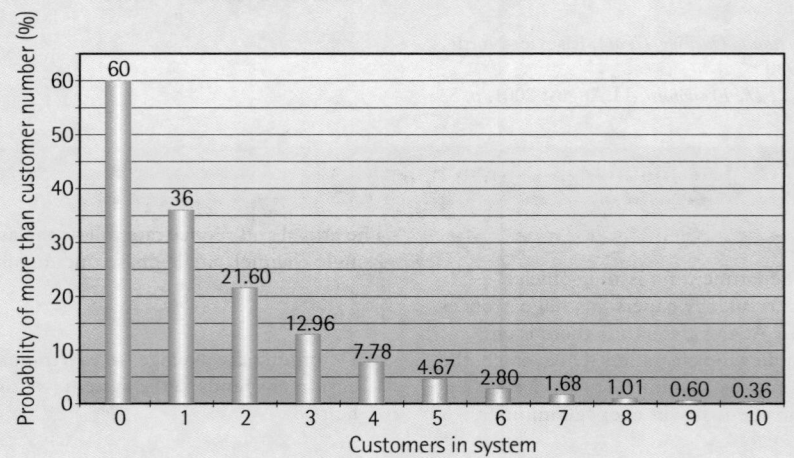

Demonstrating the concept 21.2 Coffee

Situation

A company restaurant has an area where it serves coffee to its employees. The present arrangement is that one person both makes and pours the coffee. The average arrival rate at the coffee area is ten people an hour, and the average service rate is 14 per hour. This activity is assumed to follow the single phase, single channel model with a variable service rate. The cost to the company for every hour an employee is in the system is estimated at £20,000.

Management is considering replacing the server person with an automatic coffee machine which has a fixed rate for making and distributing the coffee. In this case, the model would now be a single phase, single channel model with a fixed service rate.

Required

1. How much would the company save on waiting time in the system if the automatic coffee machine were installed? Assume that the average arrival and service rate remain unchanged.
2. Illustrate the utilization rate on a histogram for up to 15 people using the machine.

Solution

The solution is given in Table 21.2. The savings would be an estimated £1786. The utilization histogram is shown in Figure 21.10. The histogram is the same whether the machine is automatic, or there is a server.

Table 21.2 Waiting for a cup of coffee

Variable rate, person makes and serves coffee		
Average service rate, units/hr	μ	14
Average arrival rate, units/hr	λ	10
Average units in system	$\lambda/(\mu - \lambda)$	2.50
Average time in system, hours	$1/(\mu - \lambda)$	0.25
Average units waiting	$\lambda^2/[\mu(\mu - \lambda)]$	1.79
Average time waiting, hours	$\lambda/[\mu(\mu - \lambda)]$	0.18
Utilization rate	λ/μ	71.43%
Idle percentage	$1 - (\lambda/\mu)$	28.57%
Each hour unit is system costs, £/yr		20,000.00
Total cost being in system, £		5,000.00
Fixed service time with an automatic machine		
Average service rate, units/hr	μ	14
Average arrival rate, units/hr	λ	10
Average units in system	$[\lambda(2\mu - \lambda)]/[2\mu(\mu - \lambda)]$	1.61
Average time in system, hours	$(2\mu - \lambda)/[2\mu(\mu - \lambda)]$	0.1607
Average units waiting	$\lambda^2/[2\mu(\mu - \lambda)]$	0.89
Average time waiting, hours	$\lambda/[2\mu(\mu - \lambda)]$	0.0893
Utilization	λ/μ	71.43%
Idle percentage	$1 - (\lambda/\mu)$	28.57%
Each hour unit is system costs, £/yr		20,000.00
Total cost being in system, £		3,214.29
Difference in cost (variable − fixed), £		1,785.71
More than k in system	$(\lambda/\mu)^{\kappa + 1}$	
	k	**Probability (%)**
Value of k	0	71.43
	1	51.02
	2	36.44
	3	26.03
	4	18.59
	5	13.28
	6	9.49
	7	6.78

(Continued)

Table 21.2 (Continued)

k	Probability (%)
8	4.84
9	3.46
10	2.47
11	1.76
12	1.26
13	0.90
14	0.64
15	0.46

Figure 21.10 Coffee: Probability of utilization

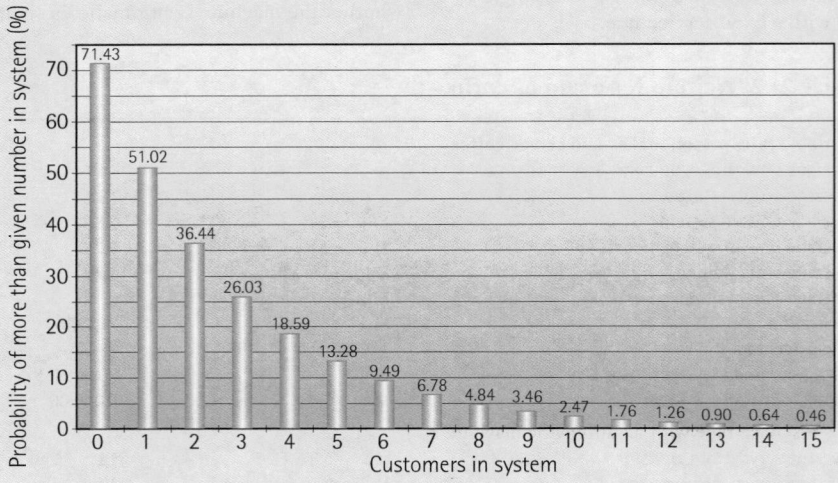

Demonstrating the concept 21.3 Motorway

Situation

A company owns a gasoline station on a major motorway in Europe. In addition to selling gasoline and diesel fuel, the store also sells products that customers may purchase for a trip including candy, food, maps, small gift items and the like. There is currently one person at the cash register who handles payment for gasoline purchases and other items that are bought. Most of the transactions are either by credit card or cash, although occasionally a cheque may be presented. The owner of the retail outlet wants to understand more about the loading on the cashier. That is, is she occupied most of the time with customers, probably resulting in customers waiting, or are their long periods of idle time for the cashier?

Required

Use the Monte Carlo random number approach to simulate the waiting line situation for this motorway outlet for 50 customers. What are your conclusions? The following information is provided.

Arrival time

Based on historical data, Figure 21.11 gives the probability distribution of arrivals at the cashier. This graph is interpreted as saying, for example, that for 22% of the time customers arrive in one-minute intervals, for 30% of the time customers arrive in two-minute intervals, etc. For the purpose of this simulation, discrete time data have been assumed. (In reality customers will arrive in fractions of minutes.)

Service time

Based on historical data, Figure 21.12 gives the probability distribution of the service times with the cashier. This graph is interpreted as saying, for example, that for 1% of the customers the service time is 0.50 minutes, for 6% of the customers the service time is one minute, etc. Again, for the purpose of this simulation, discrete time data have been assumed. (In reality customers will be serviced in fractions of minutes.)

Random numbers

Table 21.3 gives a printout of 500 random numbers ranging from 0 to 99 generated from Microsoft Excel.

Solution

The first step in generating the simulation is to establish the range of random numbers that correspond to the probability distributions for the arrival patterns, and the service rates.

Arrival intervals

Table 21.4 gives the probability distribution for the arrival intervals as presented in the histogram. The range of possible random numbers is from 0 to 99, or a total of 100. Thus, considering the arrival interval of 1.00 minute, with a probability of 22%, the random

Figure 21.11 Motorway: Arrival patterns

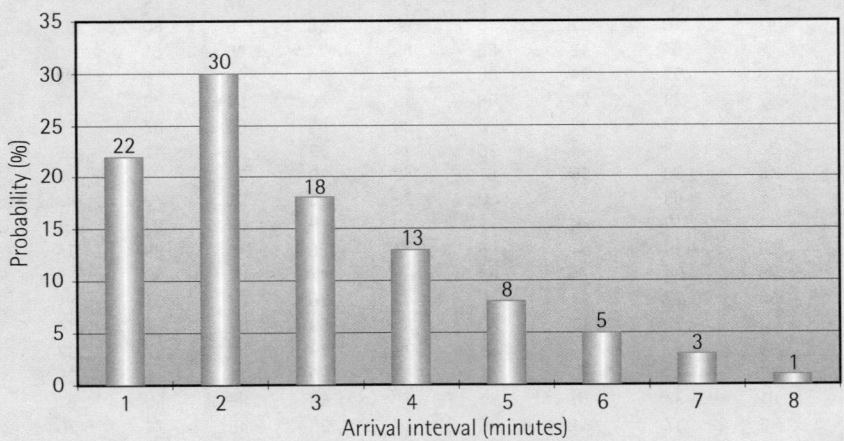

Figure 21.12 Motorway: Service time patterns

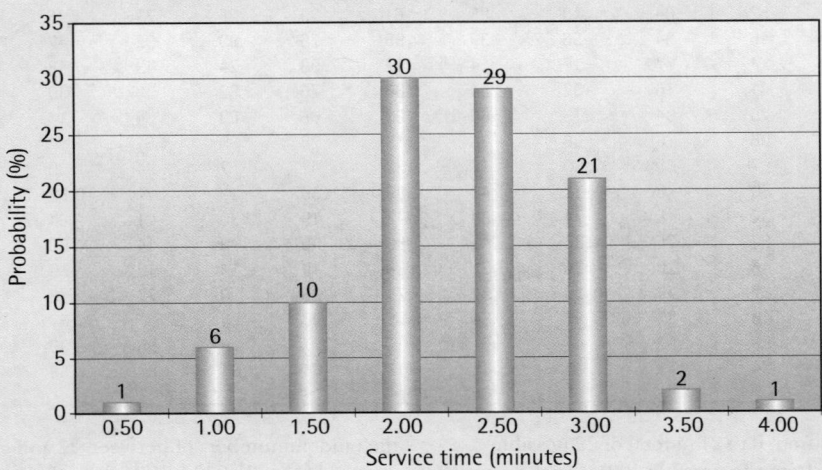

Table 21.3 Motorway: Table of random numbers

	A	B	C	D	E	F	G	H	I	J
1	76	39	63	41	88	35	98	45	64	11
2	5	98	42	22	57	60	90	14	4	6
3	91	58	55	8	71	2	37	68	98	88
4	20	58	59	30	81	2	50	18	8	32
5	7	50	52	50	12	48	83	27	83	71
6	85	65	60	76	48	79	88	73	29	80
7	67	31	29	82	59	40	36	10	78	29
8	5	51	84	77	65	66	9	59	88	71
9	59	90	40	20	69	33	57	30	77	94
10	41	62	30	19	65	93	26	53	1	61
11	80	80	53	5	57	68	75	51	42	48
12	15	48	59	21	9	99.	48	31	61	21
13	87	37	82	83	3	59	71	64	83	36
14	94	91	67	18	52	85	82	74	60	87
15	42	70	37	13	60	38	6	80	94	18
16	6	64	42	86	83	23	46	51	10	64
17	3	92	94	86	23	15	95	8	98	92
18	47	29	23	96	13	80	54	79	77	61
19	23	23	32	6	30	45	65	87	9	9
20	36	38	44	75	24	22	33	42	85	85
21	48	80	55	61	52	19	24	71	33	13
22	5	65	8	0	32	5	92	2	83	45
23	44	19	89	71	60	9	99	63	1	69
24	56	19	94	8	24	56	9	68	74	55
25	79	94	71	63	66	43	67	50	83	36
26	60	77	43	79	42	26	63	31	91	36
27	3	27	42	89	51	59	87	1	4	7
28	88	32	4	65	29	79	34	27	93	7
29	47	83	35	1	68	90	21	76	35	87
30	61	37	20	99	71	63	86	50	61	21
31	6	37	64	95	44	90	45	74	70	19
32	40	64	12	8	21	50	67	21	79	47
33	83	84	25	93	41	70	33	39	83	40
34	38	50	99	13	61	50	73	36	95	23
35	97	99	5	27	29	70	52	95	38	33
36	52	84	13	85	61	29	25	73	6	6
37	46	34	56	32	95	76	89	92	42	88
38	4	7	17	4	12	98	24	49	48	3
39	31	16	32	54	86	76	82	38	39	18
40	25	84	15	86	93	66	89	4	14	58
41	96	6	48	76	13	28	50	61	7	4
42	7	65	80	17	23	11	7	54	30	54
43	80	8	10	48	89	59	22	71	89	71
44	32	8	74	88	18	19	30	1	64	33
45	82	75	30	41	80	80	49	14	60	38
46	46	20	35	31	86	19	14	13	59	4
47	67	79	50	92	73	26	0	77	18	48
48	48	32	99	54	5	93	33	67	67	29
49	69	52	5	61	31	7	16	56	80	54
50	54	41	7	85	7	64	84	87	68	96

number range is from 0 to 21 (a total of 22 possible numbers or 22% from the possible 100). For the arrival interval of 2.00 minutes, the probability is 30% and so the random numbers of between 22 and 51 have been assigned (a total of 30 or 30% from the possible 100). This is repeated for the complete distribution.

Table 21.4 Probability distribution for arrival intervals

Arrival intervals (minutes)	Probability (%)	Cumulative probability (%)	Lower limit of random number	Upper limit of random number
1.00	22.00	22.00	0	21
2.00	30.00	52.00	22	51
3.00	18.00	70.00	52	69
4.00	13.00	83.00	70	82
5.00	8.00	91.00	83	90
6.00	5.00	96.00	91	95
7.00	3.00	99.00	96	98
8.00	1.00	100.00	99	99

Table 21.5 Probability distribution for service rates

Service times (minutes)	Probability (%)	Cumulative probability (%)	Lower limit of random number	Upper limit of random number
0.50	1.00	1.00	0	0
1.00	6.00	7.00	1	6
1.50	10.00	17.00	7	16
2.00	30.00	47.00	17	46
2.50	29.00	76.00	47	75
3.00	21.00	97.00	76	96
3.50	2.00	99.00	97	98
4.00	1.00	100.00	99	99

Service Rates

Table 21.5 gives the probability distribution for the service rates as presented in the histogram. Again, the range of possible random numbers is from 0 to 99, or a total of 100. Thus, considering the service time of 0.50 minutes, with a probability of 1%, the random number range is just the number 0 (a total of 1 possible numbers or 1% from the possible 100). For the service time of 1.00 minute, the probability is 6% and so the random numbers of between 1 and 6 have been assigned (a total of 6 or 6% from the possible 100). Again, this is repeated for the complete distribution.

Simulation

The completed simulation is shown in Table 21.6. The explanation of each column is as follows.

Client number
This is the sequential number of customers who arrive from 1 to 50.

Random number (1)
This is the random number that is used to determine the arrival time for each of the customers. In this illustration the random numbers from column A of the random number table have been used starting from Cell A-1. Any column could have been used.

Arrival interval
This is the arrival interval in minutes, corresponding to the random number for that client, and taken from the arrival interval table (21.4). For example:

- For client 2, the random number is 5, and this corresponds to an arrival interval of 1 minute.

Table 21.6 Motorway: Monte Carlo simulation

Client number	Random no. (1)	Arrival interval (mins)	Time entering (mins)	Random no. (2) (mins)	Service time (mins)	Waiting time (mins)	Time leaving (mins)	Time in system (mins)	Queue length (people)	System status
1			0	39	2.00	0.00	2.00	2.00	0	
2	5	1	1	98	3.50	1.00	5.50	4.50	1	Occupied
3	91	6	7	58	2.50	0.00	9.50	2.50	0	Empty
4	20	1	8	58	2.50	1.50	12.00	4.00	1	Occupied
5	7	1	9	50	2.50	3.00	14.50	5.50	2	Occupied
6	85	5	14	65	2.50	0.50	17.00	3.00	1	Occupied
7	67	3	17	31	2.00	0.00	19.00	2.00	0	Occupied
8	5	1	18	51	2.50	1.00	21.50	3.50	1	Occupied
9	59	3	21	90	3.00	0.50	24.50	3.50	1	Occupied
10	41	2	23	62	2.50	1.50	27.00	4.00	1	Occupied
11	80	4	27	80	3.00	0.00	30.00	3.00	0	Occupied
12	15	1	28	48	2.50	2.00	32.50	4.50	1	Occupied
13	87	5	33	37	2.00	0.00	35.00	2.00	0	Empty
14	94	6	39	91	3.00	0.00	42.00	3.00	0	Empty

(Continued)

Table 21.6 (Continued)

Client number	Random no. (1)	Arrival interval (mins)	Time entering (mins)	Random no. (2) (mins)	Service time (mins)	Waiting time (mins)	Time leaving (mins)	Time in system (mins)	Queue length (people)	System status
15	42	2	41	70	2.50	1.00	44.50	3.50	1	Occupied
16	6	1	42	64	2.50	2.50	47.00	5.00	1	Occupied
17	3	1	43	92	3.00	4.00	50.00	7.00	2	Occupied
18	47	2	45	29	2.00	5.00	52.00	7.00	2	Occupied
19	23	2	47	23	2.00	5.00	54.00	7.00	2	Occupied
20	36	2	49	38	2.00	5.00	56.00	7.00	3	Occupied
21	48	2	51	80	3.00	5.00	59.00	8.00	3	Occupied
22	5	1	52	65	2.50	7.00	61.50	9.50	3	Occupied
23	44	2	54	19	2.00	7.50	63.50	9.50	3	Occupied
24	56	3	57	19	2.00	6.50	65.50	8.50	3	Occupied
25	79	4	61	94	3.00	4.50	68.50	7.50	3	Occupied
26	60	3	64	77	3.00	4.50	71.50	7.50	2	Occupied
27	3	1	65	27	2.00	6.50	73.50	8.50	3	Occupied
28	88	5	70	32	2.00	3.50	75.50	5.50	2	Occupied
29	47	2	72	83	3.00	3.50	78.50	6.50	2	Occupied
30	61	3	75	37	2.00	3.50	80.50	5.50	2	Occupied
31	6	1	76	37	2.00	4.50	82.50	6.50	2	Occupied
32	40	2	78	64	2.50	4.50	85.00	7.00	3	Occupied
33	83	5	83	84	3.00	2.00	88.00	5.00	1	Occupied
34	38	2	85	50	2.50	3.00	90.50	5.50	1	Occupied
35	97	7	92	99	4.00	0.00	96.00	4.00	0	Empty
36	52	3	95	84	3.00	1.00	99.00	4.00	1	Occupied
37	46	2	97	34	2.00	2.00	101.00	4.00	1	Occupied
38	4	1	98	7	1.50	3.00	102.50	4.50	2	Occupied
39	31	2	100	16	1.50	2.50	104.00	4.00	2	Occupied
40	25	2	102	84	3.00	2.00	107.00	5.00	2	Occupied
41	96	7	109	6	1.00	0.00	110.00	1.00	0	Empty
42	7	1	110	65	2.50	0.00	112.50	2.50	0	Occupied
43	80	4	114	8	1.50	0.00	115.50	1.50	0	Empty
44	32	2	116	8	1.50	0.00	117.50	1.50	0	Empty
45	82	4	120	75	2.50	0.00	122.50	2.50	0	Empty
46	46	2	122	20	2.00	0.50	124.50	2.50	1	Occupied
47	67	3	125	79	3.00	0.00	128.00	3.00	0	Empty
48	48	2	127	32	2.00	1.00	130.00	3.00	1	Occupied
49	69	3	130	52	2.50	0.00	132.50	2.50	0	Occupied
50	54	3	133	41	2.00	0.00	135.00	2.00	0	Empty

- For client 3, the random number is 91, and this corresponds to an arrival interval of 6 minutes.

For the first client, random numbers are not used. It is assumed that the client arrives as soon as the simulation starts.

Time entering
This is the time at which a client enters the system, where the system is either in the line waiting to be served, or directly being served by the cashier.

Numerically the time entering is the sum of all the arrival times. For example:

- Arrival time of the sixth customer is the sum of the arrival intervals of customers 1 through 6 or $(0 + 1 + 6 + 1 + 1 + 5) = 14$.

Random number (2)
This is the random number that is used to determine the service time for each of the customers. In this illustration, the random numbers from column B of the random number table have been used starting from Cell B-1. Any column could have been used.

Service time

This is the service time, in minutes, for the client. The value corresponds to the random number for that client, taken from the service time table (21.5) For example:

- For client 1, the random number is 39, and this corresponds to a service time of 2 minutes.
- For client 2, the random number is 98, and this corresponds to a service time of 4 minutes.

Waiting time

This is the waiting time, in minutes, that the client stands in the queue waiting to be assisted by the cashier. It is calculated by the relationship:

$$WT_n = WT_{n-1} + ST_{n-1} - AI_n$$

where WT are waiting times, ST is the service time, AI is the arrival interval, and n is client in question. If the value of the WT_n is negative, there is no waiting time and the client is immediately served. For example:

- For client 7, $WT_7 = WT_6 + ST_6 - AI_7 =$ 0.50 + 2.50 − 3.00 = −0.50 and so there is no waiting time.
- For client 8, $WT_8 = WT_7 + ST_7 - AI_8 =$ 0.00 + 2.00 − 1.00 = 1.00 and so the client stands in line for one minute.

The waiting time for each client is given by the histogram in Figure 21.13.

Time leaving

This is the time at which the client leaves the system, or the service area. It is the sum of the time entering plus waiting and service time.

Time in system

The time in the system is the sum of the waiting time, plus the service time.

Queue length

The queue length is given in terms of the number of people waiting. It is a function of the service time necessary to serve the people. For example:

- Client 14 arrives, there is no waiting time, so the queue length is zero.
- Client 15 arrives, there is a waiting time of 1.00 minute and so the queue length is one unit.
- Client 16 arrives, there is a waiting time given by $WT_{16} = WT_{15} + ST_{15} - AI_{16} = 1.00 + 2.50 - 1.00 =$ 2.50 minutes while client 15 is being served. Thus the queue length is one unit.
- Client 17 arrives, there is a waiting time given by $WT_{17} = WT_{16} + ST_{16} - AI_{17} = 2.50 + 2.50 - 1.00 =$ 4.00 minutes. In this case, client 16 still has not been serviced since client 16 still has a wait time given by WT_{16} (when client 17 arrives) $= WT_{16} - AI_{17} =$ 2.50 − 1.0 = 1.50 minutes. Thus the queue length is two units (clients 16 and 17).

Figure 21.13 Motorway: Client waiting time

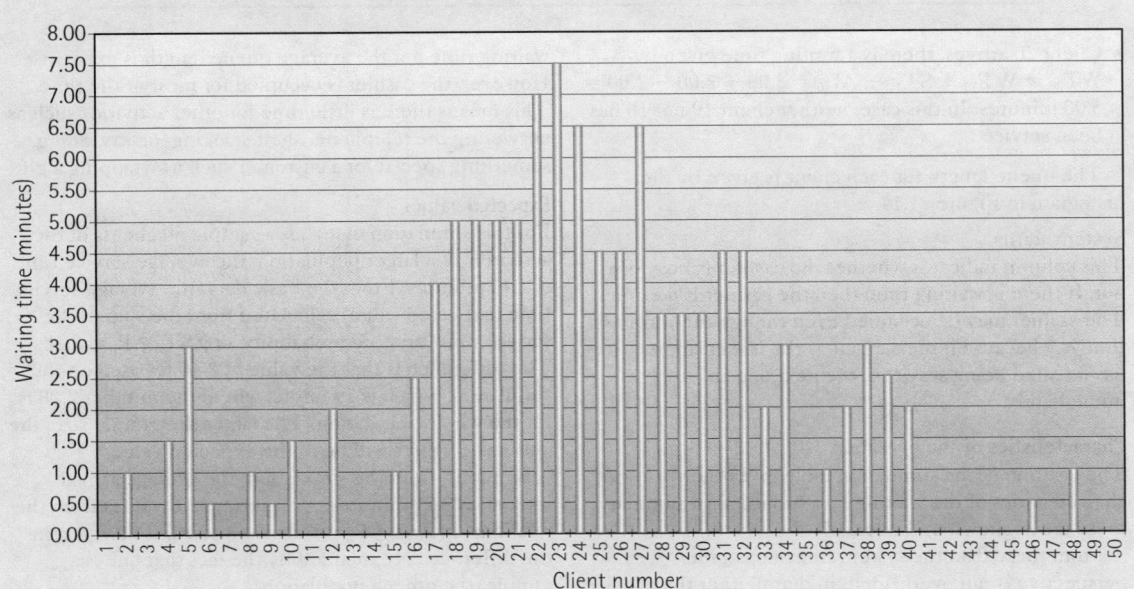

Figure 21.14 Motorway: Queue length

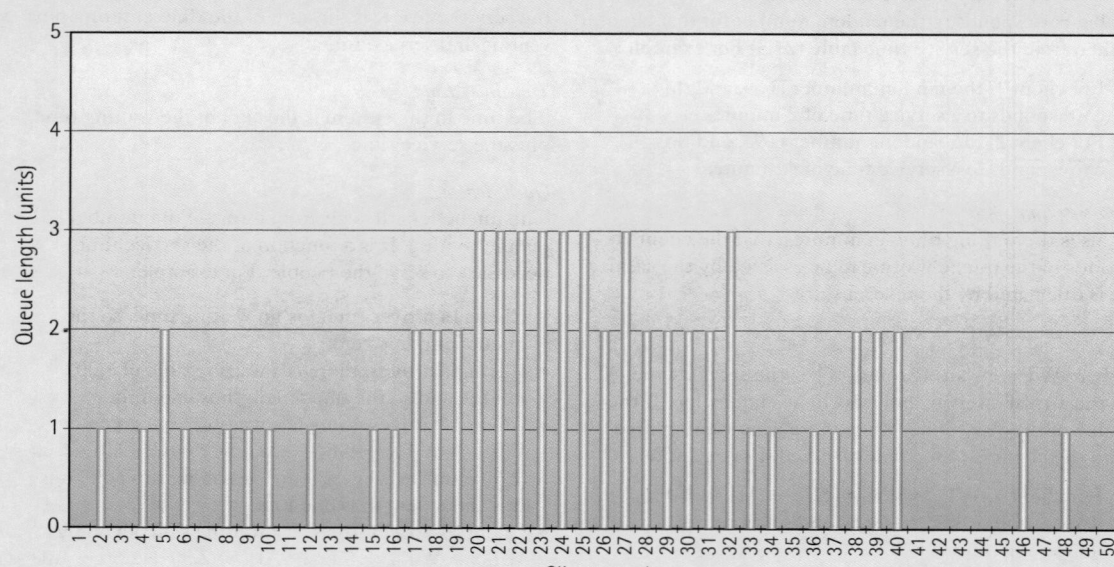

Table 21.7 Characteristics of waiting line situation

Average arrival interval (mins)	Average service time (mins)	Average waiting time (mins)	Average time in system (mins)	Average queue length (units)
2.71	2.40	2.23	4.63	1.26

- Client 20 arrives, there is a waiting time given by $WT_{20} = WT_{19} + ST_{19} - AI_{20} = 5.00 + 2.00 - 2.00 = 5.00$ minutes. In this case, neither client 19 nor 18 has been serviced.

The queue length for each client is given by the histogram in Figure 21.14.

System status

This column indicates whether the cashier is busy or not. If there is waiting time then the cashier is occupied. The cashier may be occupied even though the waiting time is 0 because it means that as the last customer has finished being serviced, the next one arrives immediately.

Characteristics of the operation

The last line of the simulation table gives the characteristics of the waiting line situation. In summary these are as shown in Table 21.7.

From these data the system from a customer perspective is not overloaded, in that neither the average waiting time nor the average queue length is excessive. However, the cashier is occupied for most of the time. This means there is little time for other activities such as answering the telephone, shelf stacking, or, say, doing something special for a customer such as wrapping a gift.

Expected values

For this simulation, which is a sample 50 clients of the activities of a larger population, the average service time is 2.40 minutes. From the basic data, the average service time (expected value) calculated from the sum of the service time, and the probability, or $\Sigma ST_n * P_n$ is 2.28. The difference is that the value of 2.40 is based on the simulation, which is a sample, where the number 2.28 is for the whole population. The larger the sample size, the closer the values will be to the expected value.

Similarly, from the simulation, the average arrival interval is 2.71 minutes. Using expected values from the relationship $\Sigma AI_n * P_n$ the arrival interval is 2.87. Again, the difference is explained by the fact that one is a sample, the other a population.

In this simulation the data will vary according to the random numbers obtained. This can be demonstrated using Excel where the random numbers are continuously changing. (By repeated pressing on the key F9 the random numbers change.) This is the very nature of probabilities. Another consideration is that the simulation was started with no one in the system, so that, in reality, the simulation has to function for a while before the real conditions are obtained. Alternatively, it could have been generated by assuming that there was already a load on the system.

Application exercise 21.1   Camping

Situation

A small camp site has one automatic washing machine for client use. It takes 50 minutes to do a complete wash. The average arrival time for campers to use the machine is one per hour. The proprietor of the campsite is considering installing a second, identical washing machine in the washing area.

Required

1. Develop the waiting line characteristics for one machine showing the queuing time, waiting time in the system, average people queuing, and average number of people in the system.
2. Develop a probability histogram of the utilization of the single washing machine.
3. How would the profile of waiting times change with the addition of the second machine?
4. Show a new probability of utilization of two machines, alongside that for one machine.

Application exercise 21.2   Gravel

Situation

A company is building an underground carpark in the centre of London. Part of the construction work involves dumping gravel at the concrete preparation area at the site. When a lorry arrives, it has to wait in line while the first lorry is dumping its load. The dumping process involves the driver raising the back of the lorry to dump the gravel with the aid of construction workers who rake the gravel from the lorry. The average time taken to unload the lorry is 7.5 minutes/unit and a lorry arrives every 12 minutes. Lorry drivers are paid on average £9 an hour. The arrival and service rate of the lorry follows the assumption of single channel, single phase queuing model.

Required

1. The average time a truck spends in the system (waiting and unloading).
2. The average time waiting in line.
3. Average utilization of the system.
4. What is the average hourly cost for trucks waiting and unloading based on the drivers' wages?
5. Develop a probability histogram of there being more than k trucks in the system with a value of k from 0 to 10.
6. What is the probability that there will be more than three trucks in the system?

Case study 21.1   Motorway (2)

Situation

The basic data for this problem are identical to those given in Demonstrating the concept 21.3. Redo the simulation on the following basis, assuming that as soon as the simulation starts, the first customer arrives. In these Questions, the random number table used is the same as that presented in Demonstrating the concept 21.3.

Required

1. In the random number tables, use column C for the arrival patterns, and column D for the service time (instead of columns A and B), and recreate the simulation. What are your conclusions? Why is there a difference?
2. In the random number tables, use column E for the arrival patterns, and column F for the service time (instead of columns A and B), and recreate the simulation. What are your conclusions? Why is there a difference?
3. In the random number tables, use column G for the arrival patterns, and column H for the service time (instead of columns A and B), and recreate the simulation. What are your conclusions? Why is there a difference?
4. In the random number tables, use column I for the arrival patterns, and column J for the service time (instead of columns A and B), and recreate the simulation. What are your conclusions? Why is there a difference?
5. In the random number tables, use column B for the arrival patterns, and column A for the service time (instead of columns A and B), and recreate the simulation. What are your conclusions? Why is there a difference?
6. Recreate the simulation using your own generated random numbers and leave these numbers floating. Thus, each time you press F9 in Excel, the simulation will change and the graphs will indicate changing queue lengths and waiting times. This is what is expected in a simulation for a waiting line.

Selected further reading

DANIEL, Joseph I., 'Congestion pricing and capacity of large hub airports: A bottleneck model with stochastic queues', *Econometrica*, vol. 63, issue 2, March 1995, pp 327–70.

KLEINROCK, Leonard and Gail, Richard (1996) *Queueing Systems: Problems and Solutions*, Wiley.

PAPADOPOULOS, H.T., HEAVEY, C. and BROWNE, J. (1993) *Queueing Theory in Manufacturing Systems Analysis and Design*, Chapman & Hall.

PROCTOR, Robert A., 'Queues and the power of simulation: Helping with business decisions and problems', *Management Decision*, vol. 32, issue 1, 1994, pp 50–5.

WANG, P. Patrick, 'Optimally scheduling n customer arrival times for a single-server system', *Computers and Operations Research*, vol. 24, issue 8, August 1997, pp 703–16.

An extensive listing of other further reading can be found on the website.

What's on the web?

Further learning resources are available to lecturers and students at www.supplychain-online.com, including the following which are specific to *Waiting lines*:

Resource	Subject
Chapter overview	Waiting lines
More further reading	Waiting lines

22 *Theory of constraints*

Chapter overview

- Concepts
- System throughput
- Bottlenecks and non-bottlenecks
- Transfer batch, process batch, and lot size
- Scheduling and constraints
- Non-manufacturing systems

Concepts

Constraint

A constraint is anything that limits an organization, operation, or a system from maximizing its output or meeting its goals or stated objectives. Constraints may be physical in nature such as insufficient plant capacity, labour, capital, raw materials, or land. If these types of constraint are in the short-term insurmountable then optimizing techniques like linear programming can be used to arrive at a satisfactory output (see Chapter 24). Constraints may be also non-physical and arise because in an organization there are poorly motivated employees, absenteeism among the workforce, lack of training, poor operating procedures, lack of flexibility on the part of unions, bad scheduling, etc.

Bottleneck

A bottleneck is a constraint (it limits the flow of wine from the bottle) and for some is synonymous with the term constraint. However, its common usage in the supply chain is often to describe a situation when there is material or units accumulating upstream because the next operation has insufficient capacity to accept the load (see Figure 22.1). Visually, this might be component parts building up ahead of an assembly operation, people lining up for a service, or trucks waiting to unload at a distribution centre. These are also queuing situations and this type of analysis is discussed in Chapter 21. In this chapter, the term constraint and bottleneck are considered interchangeable.

Drum, buffer, and rope

The theory of constraints (TOC) is sometimes referred to as the drum, buffer, and rope concept. As a result of the bottleneck in the system, a factory or operation is obligated to beat to the rhythm of the *drum* (the bottleneck), which sets the pace for the factory and all the non-bottleneck systems. It is at this pace than units are pulled through the system by a *rope*. As the bottleneck drives the system it should always be working at full capacity and thus inventory *buffers* should always be immediately upstream to ensure that the bottleneck is never starved for work.

The *drum* concept is in contrast to *Takt* time referred to in Chapter 15, where *Takt* time is the rhythm of the conductor, or the client who sets the pace for the operation (or should be) in a finely tuned system. The *Takt* time is an external 'constraint' and perhaps more difficult to control whereas the *drum* is an internal

Figure 22.1 Bottleneck situation

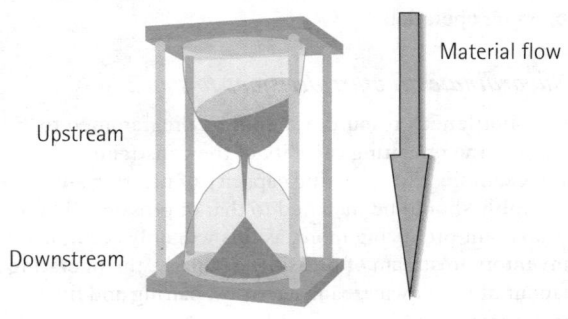

A capacity–constrained resource

constraint and, with good management, should be more controllable.

Focusing on constraints

The presence of constraints in a system have evolved the Theory of Constraints (TOC) put forward by Eliya M Goldratt in his book, *Theory of Constraints*.[1] Here he proposes focusing on five steps for managing system constraints.

Identify the constraint in the system

This is the analytical step to find out why the goal of the system cannot be achieved. Say, for example, a firm makes a certain model of parabolic skis, LW-1942X, whose basic production process is as follows:

- Printing of the top and bottom design of the ski.
- Assembly of the laminated components.
- Pressing by heat treatment of the components and designs.
- Machine finishing of the edges, toe and heel.
- Pairing the skis (that is, matching a left and right).
- Final inspection and packaging in plastic covers.

The demand for this model of ski is for 5000 a week. The producer is only able to supply 4000 a week, as there is a bottleneck in the pressing process.

Exploit methods to overcome the constraint

This step is seeing what actions can be taken to overcome the system constraint. In the ski example, this might be verifying that only model, LW-1942X, currently goes though the pressing step. Other models going through pressing will saturate the capacity and reduce the throughput of model LW-1942X. Perhaps there should be an inspection before pressing to be sure that only 'good' products are being processed at the pressing section. Non-conforming products will add to the load of pressing unit but add nothing to customer demand as they will be rejected downstream of the pressing operation.

Subordinate all other decisions to step 2

Non-bottleneck resources should be programmed to support the operating capacity of the constraint. For example, the operating capacity of printing and assembly should be matched to that of pressing. There is no point producing more, as this will only accumulate inventory upstream of pressing. Similarly, the operating labour of the downstream activities, pairing and final inspection should be matched to the bottleneck capacity of pressing.

Elevate the bottleneck

Once all the activities from steps 2 and 3 have been implemented, if a bottleneck at pressing still exists, management should consider increasing the capacity of the bottleneck. In this case, perhaps by adding another shift in the pressing process or investing in new pressing equipment.

Do not let inertia set in but go back to step 1

Once the constraint has been overcome in pressing this might elevate another function to a bottleneck situation, such as assembly or design. In which case since the system constraint has shifted the firm should repeat the study to the new constraint.

Optimized production technology

Optimized production technology (OPT) is a direct offshoot of the Theory of Constraints and is a computerized production, planning, and scheduling tool developed in 1979 by Creative Output of Milford, Connecticut in the USA. It is useful for coordinating engineering, manufacturing, and marketing operations in a job shop, or a work centre where there is repetitive manufacturing. The OPT software gives a detailed description of the network-defining variables of the resources used such as setup times, production run times, inventory levels, lot sizes, lead times, order quantities, and due dates.

Optimized production technology is based on a set of nine related rules, which principally revolve around the concept of bottlenecks. The nine rules are as follows:

1. Balance material flow through a system, rather than the capacity.
2. Use of a non-bottleneck is determined by other system constraints.
3. Utilization and full employment of a resource are not synonymous.
4. An hour lost on a bottleneck is an hour lost on all the system.
5. An hour saved on a non-bottleneck is a mirage.
6. Bottlenecks govern both throughput and inventory accumulation.
7. The transfer and process batch need not be equal in size.
8. Lot sizes should be variable and not fixed.
9. Establish schedules by considering all system constraints.

These nine rules are discussed in detail in the following sections.

System throughput

Market demand

An operations manager is very conscious of cost. His management approach might be to ensure that all operators are fully occupied so they are paid for carrying. If there are expensive robots in the system he wants to be sure that they are working 24 hours a day in order that their activity contributes to their allocated depreciation. Inventory would be kept low to minimize carrying cost. However, the operations manager should not lose sight of the real issue in the supply chain, which is to provide that quantity of units demanded by the client, at the right time, and, of course, according to quality specifications. It is the end products that generate the revenue for the firm and offset the firm's operating cost. Thus, the operations manager should pay attention to create a smooth and consistent flow of units through the system, adapted to the requirements of the downstream market, rather than to try and keep all resources fully occupied. As illustrated in Figure 22.2, this is the first rule of OPT: Balance material flow through the system, rather than the capacity.

Random occurrences

Each work centre in a manufacturing operation is subjected to different random occurrences such as unplanned machine breakdowns, absentee operators, or raw materials or parts that do not conform to specification. These random occurrences will lead to delays and very often accumulate the delays. This concept of random occurrences and the accumulating effect in the supply chain is illustrated in Demonstrating the concept 22.1, which is based on a situation from *The Goal.*[2]

Bottlenecks and non-bottlenecks

Optimized production technology is governed by the presence of bottlenecks. This is the principal criterion of the next five rules, which are very closely related.

Use of a non-bottleneck is determined by other system constraints (rule N°. 2)

In any production system, the loading of any resource such as a work post, a machine, or a production centre can be described as a bottleneck or non-bottleneck:

- A bottleneck is a resource where the available capacity is less than downstream demand or the upstream load.
- A non-bottleneck resource is where the available capacity is greater than the upstream load or the downstream demand.

 Figure 22.3 illustrates the concept where the system is considered equivalent to two Work posts N° 1 and N° 2 with available capacities of respectively 200 units/hr and 300 units/hr. The client demand is 250 units/hr.

Figure 22.2 OPT rule N° 1: Balance material flow rather than capacity

Each post is subjected to different random occurrences:

- Machine breakdown
- Operator absence
- Component parts' defects

These variables can accumulate and lead to increased delays

Aim for continuous flow

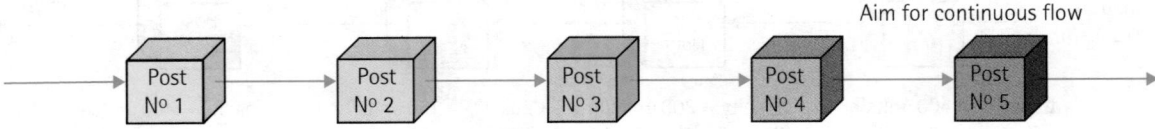

Design capacity of each work post is 6 units/hr

Do not concentrate on keeping work posts fully occupied but use them to create a throughput to meet market demand
If necessary use operators who are multi-skilled, working in teams

Figure 22.3 OPT rule Nº 2: Use of a non-bottleneck is determined by other system constraints

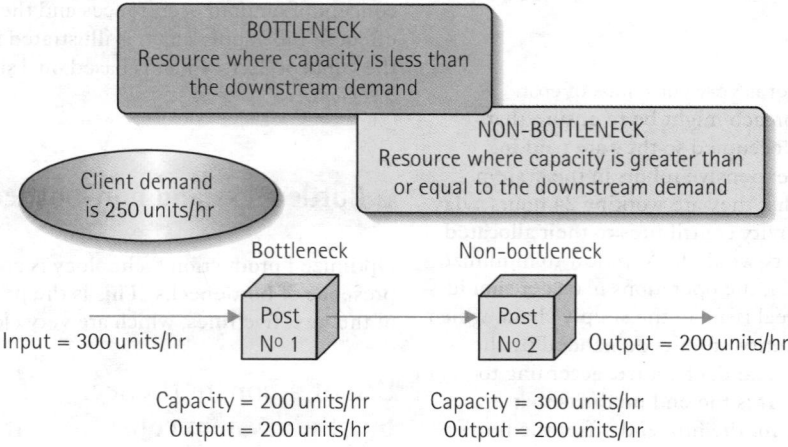

The feed rate to the system is 300 units/hr or the same as the available capacity of Work post Nº 2:

- Work post Nº 1 is the bottleneck to the system because its available capacity of 200 units/hr is less than the upstream load 300 units/hr. In addition, its available capacity is less than the client's demand of 250 units/hr.
- Work post Nº 2 is the non-bottleneck to the system as it has an available capacity of 300 units/hr which is greater than the client demand of 250 units/hr and is equal to the 300 units/hr load entering the system.

Thus, the production level of the system is neither the customer demand of 250 units/hr nor the load into the system of 300 units/hr but just 200 units/hr as governed by the capacity of the bottleneck resource at Work post Nº 1. The level of use of the non-bottleneck is determined by the bottleneck and in this situation the customer service level is only 80% because of the bottleneck.

Utilization and full employment of a resource are not synonymous (rule Nº. 3)

This rule is illustrated in Figure 22.4, where the four work posts are considered the system and the incoming quantity is 400 units/hr. Here Work post Nº 3, with a capacity of 150 units/hr, is the bottleneck to the system. Work post Nº 2, with a capacity of 300 units/hr is a bottleneck to Work post Nº 1:

- Work post Nº 1 is being used to its full capacity.
- Work post Nº 2 is being used to its full capacity, although it is presenting a bottleneck to Work post Nº 1.

Figure 22.4 OPT rule Nº 3: Utilization and full employment of a resource are not synonymous

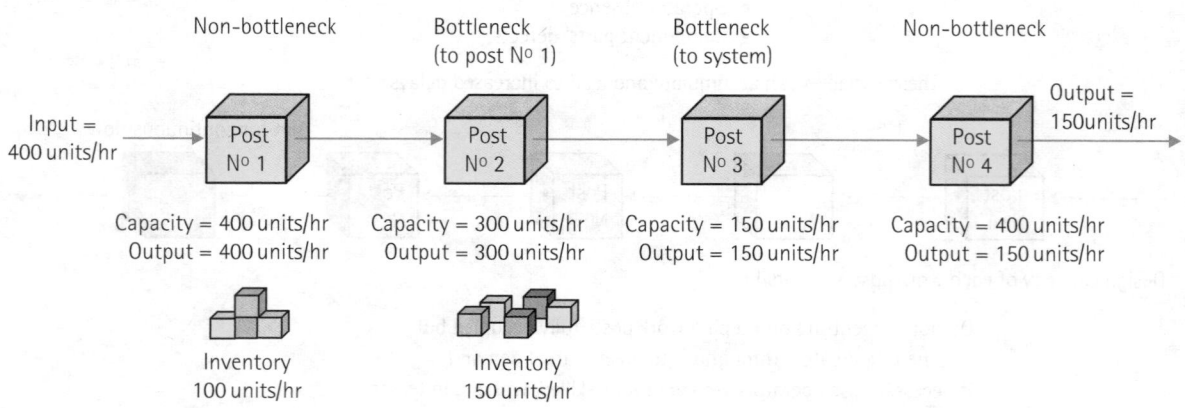

Figure 22.5 OPT rule Nº 4: An hour lost on a bottleneck is an hour lost on all the system

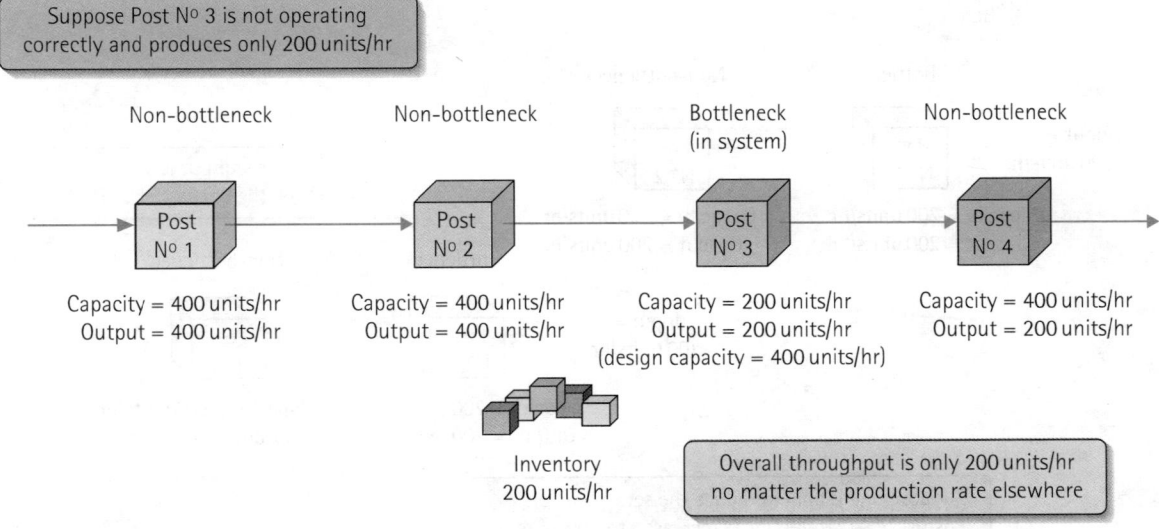

Suppose Post Nº 3 is not operating correctly and produces only 200 units/hr

Non-bottleneck | Non-bottleneck | Bottleneck (in system) | Non-bottleneck

Post Nº 1 | Post Nº 2 | Post Nº 3 | Post Nº 4

Capacity = 400 units/hr
Output = 400 units/hr

Capacity = 400 units/hr
Output = 400 units/hr

Capacity = 200 units/hr
Output = 200 units/hr
(design capacity = 400 units/hr)

Capacity = 400 units/hr
Output = 200 units/hr

Inventory
200 units/hr

Overall throughput is only 200 units/hr no matter the production rate elsewhere

- Work post Nº 3 is being used to its full capacity, although it is a bottleneck to Work post Nº 2 and a bottleneck to the system.
- Work post Nº 4 with a capacity of 400 units/hr is not being fully employed as it is only producing 150 units/hr or 37.50% of its capacity. Its effective capacity is directly constrained by Work post Nº 3.

An hour lost on a bottleneck is an hour lost on all the system (rule Nº 4)

Consider the system in Figure 22.5, which is a system made up of four work posts and where the customer demand is 400 units/hr. All four work posts have a design capacity of 400 units/hr and, initially, the system is perfectly balanced such that the rate of finished products for the customer leaving Work post Nº 4 is 400 units/hr:

- Suppose now that a problem occurs at Work post Nº 3 and its effective capacity drops to 200 units/hr, or half its design capacity. It becomes a bottleneck to the system and both the input and output at Work post Nº 4 are now only 200 units/hr.
- In order to make up the other 200 units, Work post Nº 3 would now have to produce for another hour. One hour has been lost on the bottleneck resource but an hour has also been lost on all the system. If we were only considering 400 units, after one hour has passed with Work post Nº 3 below capacity, Work posts Nº 1 and 2 can be shutdown for

one hour and just run Work posts Nº 3 and 4 for one more hour.

An hour saved on a non–bottleneck is a mirage (rule Nº 5)

Since the capacity of the system is governed by the bottleneck resource, saving time on a non-bottleneck resource does nothing for the throughput in the whole system. This concept is illustrated in Figure 22.6. The system is again two work posts where initially Nº 1 has an effective capacity of 200 units/hr and Nº 2 an effective capacity of 250 units/hr. The client demand is 250 units/hr which is the feed to Work post Nº 1. Work post Nº 1 is the bottleneck to the system:

- Suppose now that changing setup procedures and modifying the schedule double the capacity of the non-bottleneck to 500 units/hr. That is, effectively saving an hour on the non-bottleneck.
- This saving on the non-bottleneck does nothing for the system, as the system output still remains at 200 units/hr.

Bottlenecks govern both throughput and inventory accumulation (rule Nº 6)

This rule is illustrated in Figure 22.7 and is an extension of the previous rules. Here Work post Nº 2 is

Figure 22.6 OPT rule N° 5: An hour saved on a non-bottle resource is a mirage

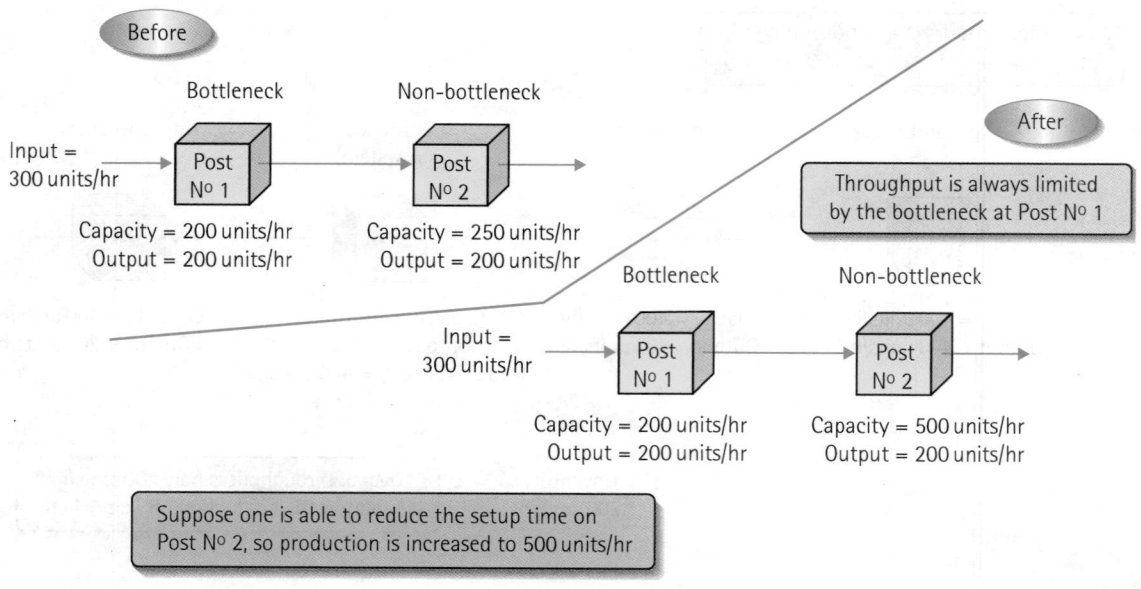

a bottleneck to Work post N° 1 and Work post N° 3 is the bottleneck to the system:

- The system throughput is governed by Work post N° 3 at a rate of 150 units/hr.
- Inventory accumulates at a rate of 100 units/hr between Work posts N° 1 and N° 2 (400 − 300).

- Inventory accumulates at a rate of 150 units/hr between Work posts N° 2 and N° 3 (300 − 150).
- Total inventory accumulation is 250 units/hr caused by the bottlenecks.
- Even if Work post N° 2 were taken out of the system, with no other changes, the inventory accumulation would still be 250 units/hr (400 − 150).

Figure 22.7 OPT rule N° 6: Bottlenecks govern both system throughput and inventory accumulation

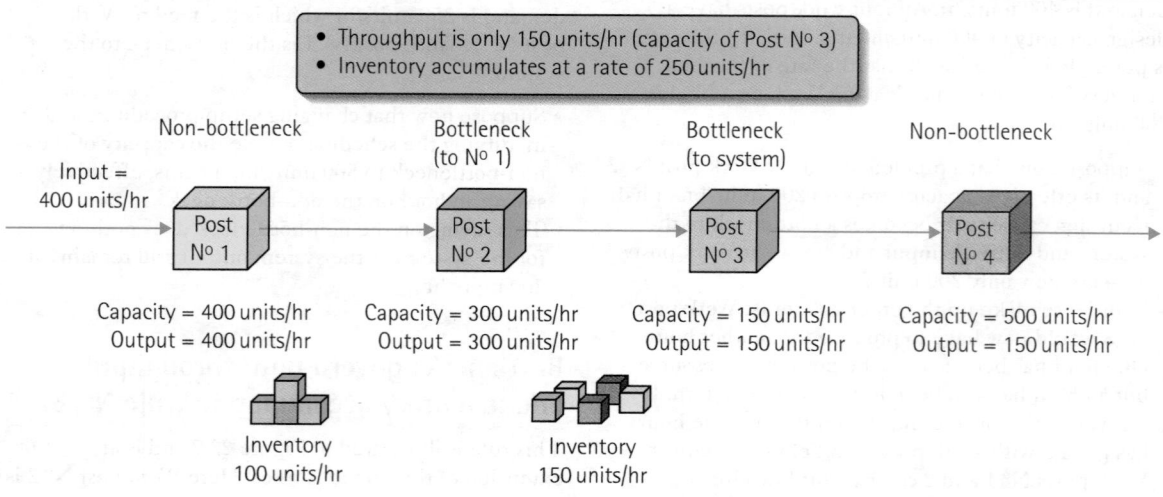

Transfer batch, process batch, and lot size

Transfer batch

The transfer batch is the quantity of material moved from one operating sector to another. For example, in manufacturing this might be cast aluminium pieces that are transferred by trolley from the foundry to the machine shop in another part of the factory. Or the transfer batch might be the quantity of parts moved from one operating line to another in the same work centre. In distribution it might be the quantity of units transferred from the packaging to the labelling department.

Process batch

The process batch, or the production lot or simply lot size, is that quantity of material that is produced between each planned operation at a work centre or the quantity of material produced between each machine setup. This quantity of material might be that dictated by customer requirements, the maximum amount that can be produced before a machine requires adjusting, or perhaps the amount that can be produced before the operating team is changed by a new shift.

Savings in inventory carrying cost

Consider the situations in Figure 22.8:

- A quantity of 1000 units are produced at Work post N° 1 before all these units are transferred to Work post N° 2. Thus the transfer batch is equal to the process batch. In this case there is an accumulation of a maximum of 1000 units of in-process inventory sitting just downstream of Work post N° 1. If the inventory carrying cost were estimated at $5 a unit then the maximum carrying cost would be $5000 or an average of $2500.
- Assume now that for transfer purposes the process batch of 5000 units is broken into transfer batches of 200 units each. That is, each time 200 units are produced these are transferred to the downstream Work post N° 2. Thus the maximum in-process inventory between the two is limited to a maximum of 200 units. In terms of inventory carrying cost this would be a maximum of $1000 or an average of $500.

Reduction in lead times

In addition to the reduction in inventory costs, lead time can be saved in the supply chain by applying this rule. Consider a situation where a client requires 800 units, the process batch, of a certain finished product. These units are produced in a sequential assembly

Figure 22.8 OPT rule N° 7: Transfer batch and process batch need not be equal

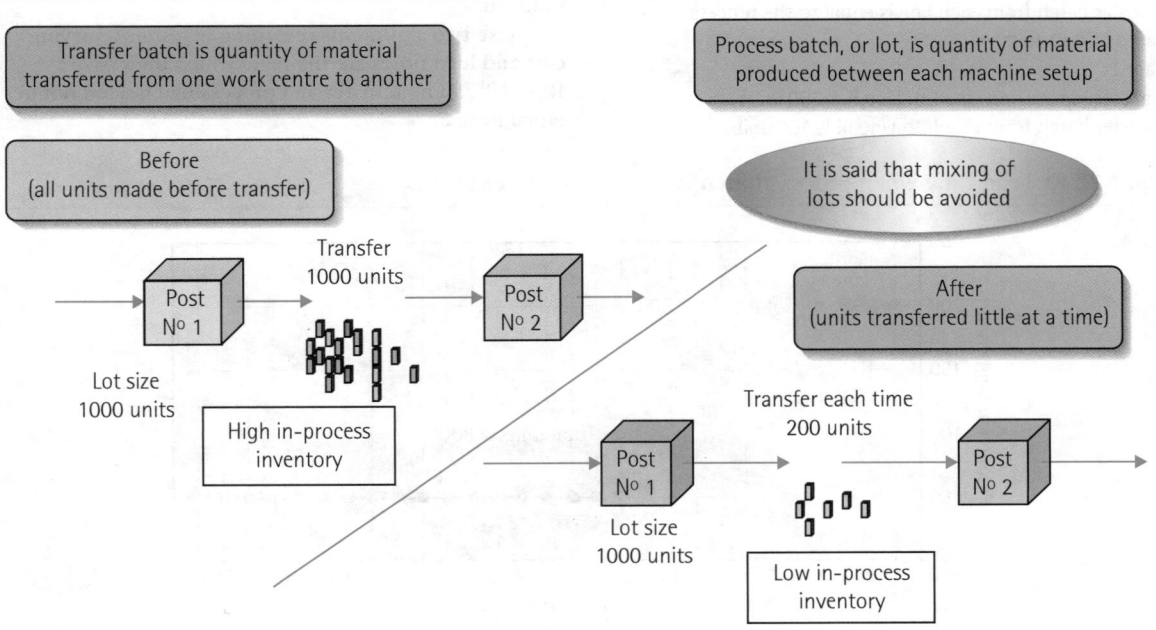

Transfer batch is quantity of material transferred from one work centre to another

Process batch, or lot, is quantity of material produced between each machine setup

It is said that mixing of lots should be avoided

Before (all units made before transfer)

After (units transferred little at a time)

Transfer 1000 units

Post N° 1

Post N° 2

Lot size 1000 units

High in-process inventory

Transfer each time 200 units

Post N° 1

Post N° 2

Lot size 1000 units

Low in-process inventory

operation on three production lines as illustrated in Figure 22.9:

- Line I has a production rate of 200 units per hour.
- Line II a production rate of 100 units per hour.
- Line III a production rate of 50 units per hour.

Transfer batch equals process batch

- On Line I, at a rate of 200 units per hour, it takes four hours to complete the 800 units (800/200). These 800 units are then transferred to Line II.
- On Line II, at a production rate of 100 units per hour, it takes eight hours to complete this phase of the operation (800/100), a total time of 12 hours from the start of the operation. After this period, the 800 units are transferred to Line III.
- On Line III, at a production rate of 50 units per hour, it takes an additional 16 hours (800/50) to complete this phase for the 800 units.
- Thus, ignoring the transfer time between each line, these 800 units will be completed after a total delay of 28 hours (4 + 12 + 16). This planning schedule is shown in Figure 22.10.

Transfer batch does not equal process batch

In this case the transfer batch from Line I to Line II is 200 units and the transfer batch from Line II to Line III is 100 units:

- On Line I, at a production rate of 200 units per hour, it still takes four hours to complete the 800 units. However, each time 200 units are ready this quantity is transferred to Line II. Thus, Line II receives 200 units each hour for a four-hour period.
- On Line II, production starts after a delay of one hour, rather than four hours. The production rate is still 100 units per hour but the batch of 800 is completed after a total delay of nine hours (1 + 8). From Line II, the transfer batch to Line III is 100 units each hour. The first batch is transferred to Line III after a time lapse from the start of the initial operation of two hours.
- On Line III, at a production rate of 50 units per hour, the first 50 units are completed after a total elapsed time of three hours. The total 800 units are completed at the end of an elapsed time of 18 hours (1 + 1 + 16).
- Thus, ignoring the transfer time between each line, the total lead time from the start of the operation is 18 hours or the operating time of Line III plus the lead time for units to pass from Line I to Line II and from Line II to Line III. This planning schedule is shown in Figure 22.11.

Thus, in summary, the reduction in lead time for this part of the supply chain is ten hours (28 − 18) or 35.71%. Another advantage in applying this rule is that idle time for operators on Line II and Line III is considerably reduced.

These two arguments regarding inventory carrying cost and lead times are the logic which underscore Rule N° 7: The transfer and process batch need not be equal in size.

Figure 22.9 Lead times in OPT rule N° 7

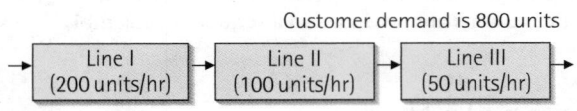

Customer demand is 800 units

Case 1:
Transfer batch from each line is equal to the process batch of 800 units
Case 2:
Transfer batch from Line I to Line II is 200 units
Transfer batch from Line II to Line III is 100 units

Figure 22.10 Lead time when process batch is equal to transfer batch

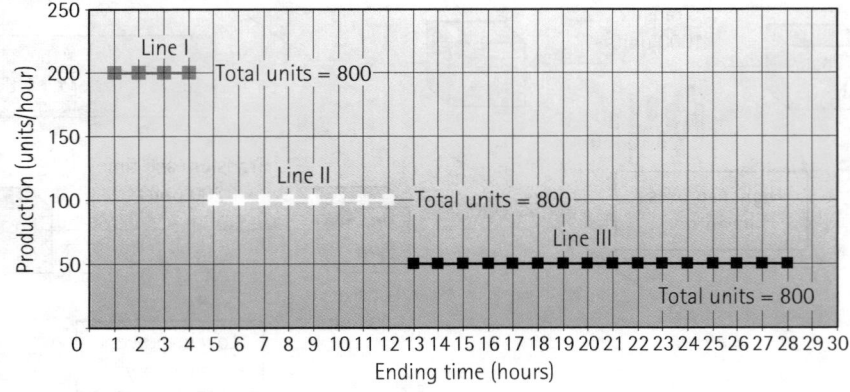

Figure 22.11 Lead time when process batch is not equal to transfer batch

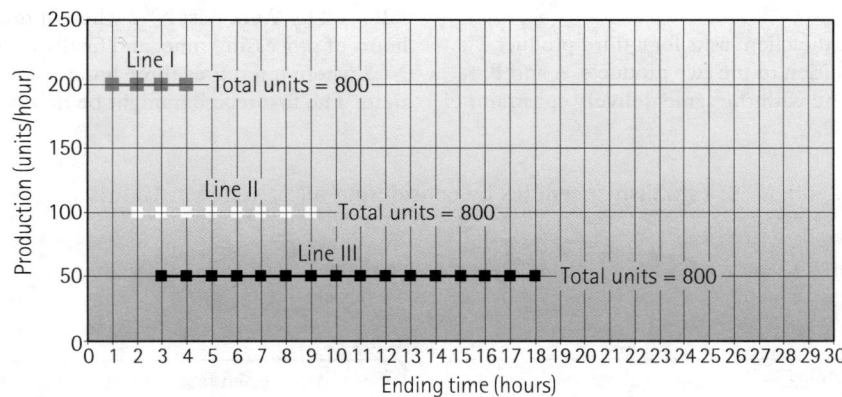

Lot sizes should be variable and not fixed (rule N° 8)

The lot sizes in optimized production technology are a function of the schedule, and thus should not be fixed over time, or from operation to operation. When different components are manufactured on different machines, the lot size should be varied in order to achieve a smooth, and timely flow of materials to the customer.

Scheduling and constraints

Lead times should not be considered fixed

In the supply chain for any manufacturing or service operation a client is given a delay time for the delivery or servicing of a product which is often a function of the established times for all the activities necessary to produce the finished product. These are considered fixed. As an example, in developing an overall delivery time using an MRP planning tool (see Chapter 13), the lead times for producing or making the component parts are considered known beforehand and fixed. However, the OPT Rule N° 9: Establish schedules by considering all system constraints, indicates that perhaps by adjusting the schedule, client lead times in the supply chain may be improved. The following illustrates.

Production of two products and three work posts

Consider the scheme in Figure 22.12, where there are two products destined for the same client which must

be processed on three work posts. Product A has to pass through Work post N° 1 and then Work post N° 2. Product B has to pass through Work post N° 1 followed by Work post N° 3. It takes nine hours to process A on Work post N° 1 and six hours on Work post N° 2. It takes five hours to process B on Work post N° 1 and 14 hours on Work post N° 3. The client due date for these two products is at 22 hours.

Assume that Product A is processed first followed by Product B:

- It takes 9 hours to work on Product A at Work post N° 1 followed by 6 hours at Work post N° 2 or a total of 15 hours before Product A is finished.
- Product B has to wait 9 hours at Work post N° 1, while A is being processed, and it then it takes 5 hours to work on B followed by 14 hours at Work post N° 3. Thus Product B would be completed after a delay of 28 hours (9 + 5 + 14).
- Thus, these two products would be 6 hours late in delivery (28 − 22).

Assume that Product B is now processed first, followed by Product A:

- It takes 5 hours to work on Product B at Work post N° 1 followed by 14 hours at Work post N° 3, or a total of 19 hours before Product B is finished.
- Product A has to wait 5 hours at Work post N° 1, while B is being processed, and it then it takes 9 hours to work on A followed by 6 hours at Work post N° 2. Thus, Product A would be completed after a delay of 20 hours (5 + 9 + 6).

Thus these two products would be delivered on time with a margin of two hours (22 − 20).

Production of three products at three work posts

Assume now that the client asks for a third product, C, to be made in addition to the two products, A and B, already ordered and with the same delivery constraint of 22 hours. Product C must pass through Work post N° 1 where it takes one hour of processing time, followed by Work post N° 2 where it requires nine hours of processing time, and finally on Work post N° 3 where it requires three hours of processing time. The first reaction might be that it would be

Figure 22.12 OPT rule N° 9: Establish schedules by considering all system constraints

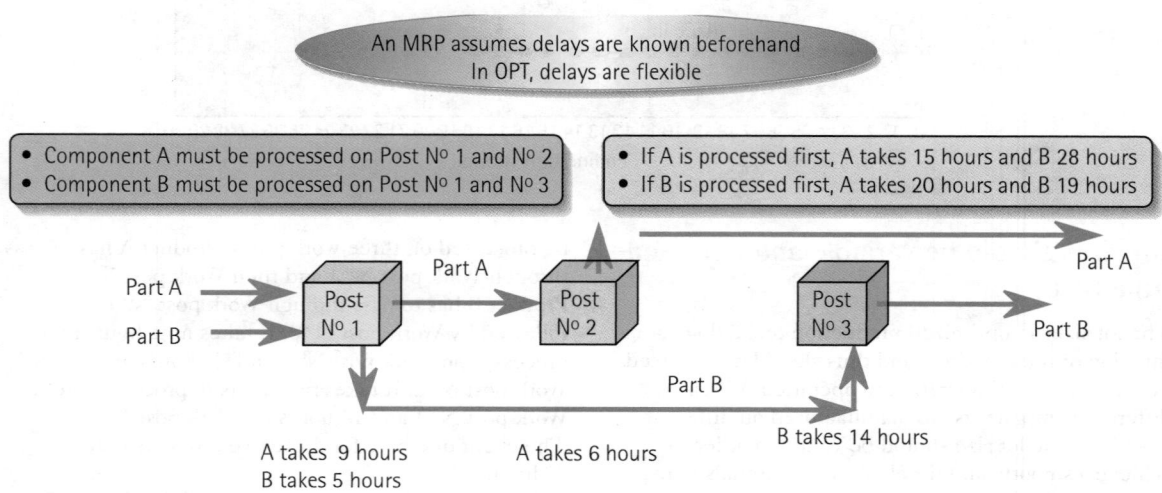

Table 22.1 Rule N° 9: Planning schedules

ORDER	A	B	C	Total	B	A	C	Total	C	B	A	Total
Post 1												
Process time	9	5	1	**15**	5	9	1	**15**	1	5	9	**15**
Start	0	9	14		0	5	14		0	1	6	
Finish	9	14	15		5	14	15		1	6	15	
Post 2												
Process time	6	0	9	**15**	0	6	9	**15**	9	0	6	**15**
Start	9	0	15		0	14	20		1	0	15	
Finish	15	0	24		0	20	29		10	0	21	
Post 3												
Process time	0	14	3	**17**	14	0	3	**17**	3	14	0	**17**
Start	0	14	28		5	0	29		10	13	0	
Finish	0	28	31		19	0	32		13	27	0	
Job finished	**15**	**28**	**31**		**19**	**20**	**32**		**13**	**27**	**21**	
Due date	22	22	22		22	22	22		22	22	22	
Days late	0	6	9	**15**	0	0	10	**10**	0	5	0	**5**

(Continued)

Table 22.1 (Continued)

ORDER	C	A	B	Total	A	C	B	Total	B	C	A	Total
Post 1												
Process time	1	9	5	15	9	1	5	15	5	1	9	15
Start	0	1	10		0	9	10		0	5	6	
Finish	1	10	15		9	10	15		5	6	15	
Post 2												
Process time	9	6	0	15	6	9	0	15	0	9	6	15
Start	1	10	0		9	15	0		0	6	15	
Finish	10	16	0		15	24	0		0	15	21	
Post 3												
Process time	3	0	14	17	0	3	14	17	14	3	0	17
Start	10	0	15		0	24	27		5	19	0	
Finish	13	0	29		0	27	41		19	22	0	
Job finished	13	16	29		15	27	41		19	22	21	
Due date	22	22	22		22	22	22		22	22	22	
Days late	0	0	7	7	0	5	19	24	0	0	0	0

Figure 22.13 Production of three products and three work posts

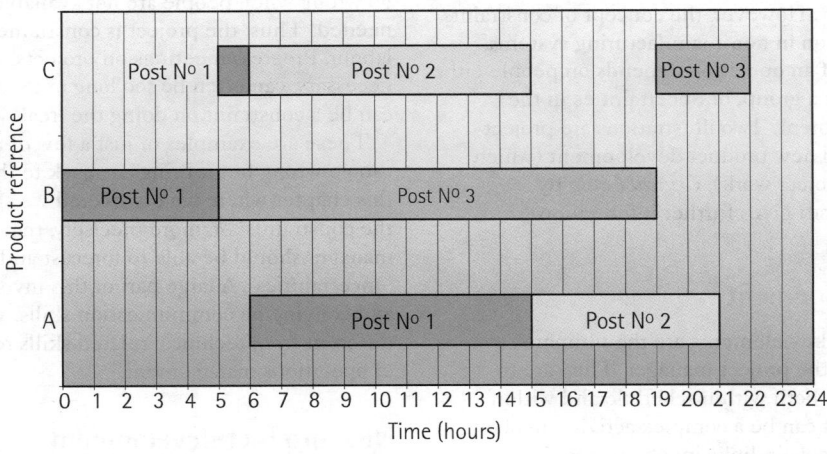

impossible to meet this client's schedule when for products A and B the schedule was already tight. However, this schedule is also possible if processing is in the order B, C, and A. The various combinations are given in Table 22.1, where the last combination, B, C, A is the optimum and is explained as follows:

- Product B is processed first as previously. There are no delays and it is finished after 19 hours.
- Product C is then processed at Work Post N° 1 starting after 5 hours (the delay time for Product B) and finished after 6 hours (5 + 1).
- Since Work post N° 2 is not used for Product B then Product C can start immediately at this post

at a time of 6 hours. The ending time is 15 hours (6 + 9).

- Since Work post N° 3 is still processing Product B and is not finished until 19 hours, work cannot start on Product C until after 19 hours. It is finished at 22 hours (19 + 3).
- Product A starts at Work Post N° 1 when Product C has finished or at 6 hours. Since Work post N° 2 is still working on Product C and is not finished until 15 hours, Product A has to wait until 15 hours before work can be started.
- Product A is finished at Work Post N° 2 after 21 hours (15 + 6). It does not pass through Work post N° 3.

Thus, all three products can be delivered by the deadline of 22 hours in accordance with the client's requirements. The schedule bar chart for this operation is given in Figure 22.13.

This is the logic behind Rule N° 9: Establish schedules by considering all system constraints.

Non-manufacturing systems

Most of this chapter has dealt with constraints as they apply to the delivery of physical goods in the supply chain, particularly as the result of bottlenecks caused by machinery or manufacturing work posts being below a desired capacity. However, the concept of constraints also has application in non-manufacturing systems, where the flow of an operation depends on people either individually or as a group, or uncertainties in the external environment. Two illustrations are project management and new product development (which in essence is a project work). *Critical Chain* by Eliyahu M Goldratt gives further information.[3]

Project management

In a project, two key elements are the ultimate responsibility of the project manager. They are to execute a project both within schedule and within budget. A project can be a complex activity involving numerous supply chain links involving people, governments, subcontractors, suppliers and the client. Within these links there are constraints in the system or subsystem that can cause a project to run over budget and over schedule. (See also Chapter 18.)

On major international projects, government intervention or changes of government can constrain the progress of a project and increase its cost and schedule. This was partly the case with the building of the Sydney Opera House (completed in 1973), the Tunnel

under the English Channel (completed in 1993 – see Chapter 18), or the development of alternative energy resources in the USA in the early 1970s. Weather can be another constraint in the completion of a project. Unexpected rain or cold weather can delay work such was the case of Alaska pipeline (completed in 1977). Very often the completion of housing or office complexes is delayed by bad weather. (See also Industry insight 2.1.)

Vendors or suppliers can be late in their delivery of equipment, which can have a compounding effect on the overall project schedule. This can be demonstrated by the CPM or PERT chart. Vendor delays can be the result of many reasons. During the course of executing a certain piece of work for Client A, a vendor may receive a more lucrative contract from Client B, which now gets priority attention. As a result, the work for Client A gets pushed aside. Government organizations, including, for example, NASA (North American Space Administration) often select the cheapest vendor on product price. These vendors can be unreliable when it comes to schedules. I worked on a project that was severely delayed because the ship that was transporting the vendor's heat exchangers and reactors sank.

Executing a major project involves hiring people. Project managers want to hire people just when they are needed to minimize the costs. This needs careful synchronization with scheduling which sometimes can go wrong when people are not available when really needed. Thus, the project is constrained by lack of labour. Progress meetings on projects, although necessary, can often be too long or too frequent which can be a constraint on doing the 'real' work.

These are examples of just a few of the things that can go wrong but it brings us back to the beginning of this chapter where we discovered we should 'focus on the constraints' or, more precisely, that a good project manager should be able to forecast and manage the 'uncertainties'. A large part of this involves dialogue and convincing communication skills, which are a lot different from technical related skills required in areas of operations management.

New product development

New product development often means exploring unknown areas and these uncertainties can be a constraint on the progress of new development. Again, scheduling is important because it is the smallest time-to-market which can make a firm a winner. Texas Instruments was a winner in the 1970s when it was the first to bring out electronic calculators overcoming constraints in the development with new technology. Apple Computer was a winner in 1984 with the introduction of its new desktop computer, although Microsoft's products later overtook this. Now Microsoft's near monopoly has constrained development work by other software firms.

In the area of life sciences, governments, or government agencies can be a constraint in the introduction of new drugs. The US FDA (Federal Drug Administration) was strongly criticized in the 1980s/1990s for delaying the progress of new drugs for AIDS when many people were dying from the disease. Governments are very much involved (either rightly or wrongly) in controlling genetic engineering, cloning, and stem cell research using embryos. For example, in August 2001 the German and French governments formally presented the United Nations with an initiative to ban human cloning[4] and related developments. These development areas were very much brought to public notice by the birth of Dolly the sheep in Scotland in 1999 – the first cloned animal.

Thus, because of these types of uncertainty a good new product manager (sometimes also known as a project manager, since firms might call new product development a project) must have a vision of potential constraints, and, like a project manager, be a good communicator.

Summary of key elements

- A constraint is anything that limits an organization, operation, or a system from maximizing its output or meeting its stated objectives. Constraints may be physical such as insufficient labour or plant capacity or non-physical such as poor scheduling or lack of motivation.

- A bottleneck is also a constraint but its common usage in the supply chain is to describe a situation when the material, trucks or units accumulate upstream because the downstream operation has insufficient capacity to accept the upstream load.

- System constraints are sometimes referred to as the drum, buffer and rope situation. The system beats to the rhythm of the *drum* (the constraint), products are pulled by the *rope*, and inventory *buffers* must be positioned upstream of the bottleneck to ensure it is never starved for work.

- The drum analogy is in contrast to *Takt* time. Both dictate the rhythm of the system but the drum is an internal constraint and the *Takt* time is an external 'constraint' or more precisely the customer requirement.

- Constraints in a system have evolved the Theory of Constraints (TOC). In this theory one should focus on five steps to manage constraints. **1** Identify the constraint in the system. **2** Exploit methods to overcome the constraint. **3** Subordinate all other decisions to the second step. **4** Elevate the bottleneck. **5** Do not let inertia set in but go back to the first step.

- Optimized production technology (OPT) is a direct offshoot of the Theory of Constraints and is a computer-based scheduling tool with a set of nine rules revolving principally around the concept of bottlenecks. It is useful for coordinating engineering, manufacturing, and marketing operations when there are repetitive operations.

- In the supply chain one should concentrate on a smooth and regular flow of material though the system rather than attempting to balance the capacity. This is the first rule in OPT.

- Bottlenecks govern the system throughput, the loss of operating time, and the accumulation of inventory. Attention should always be focused on the bottlenecks and not the non-bottlenecks, as they have no impact on the system flow. These concepts are the criteria behind rules 2 to 6 in OPT.

- If the transfer batch is less than the process batch both inventory-holding costs and lead times in the supply chain can be reduced. This is the essence of the seventh rule in OPT.

- Rule 8 in OPT stipulates that lot sizes should be variable in size and not fixed, as this can help to achieve a smooth and timely flow of material to the customer.

- Lead times should not be considered fixed but variable and they can be modified according to how an operation is scheduled. This is the essence of the ninth rule in OPT.

- The Theory of Constraints has application in non-manufacturing aspects of management, for example, project management and new product development. Here constraints often involve uncertainties in the environment, governments, and other links such as vendor or supplier activity.

Notes and references

1. GOLDRATT, Eliyahu, *Theory of Constraints*, North River Press, Massachusetts, 1990
2. GOLDRATT, Eliyahu and COX, Jeff, *The Goal*, Gower, UK, 2000
3. GOLDRATT, Eliyahu M., *Critical Chain*, North River Press, Massachusetts, USA, 1997
4. 'Germany, France urge UN to ban human cloning', *Wall Street Journal Europe*, 9 August 2001, p. 2

Review and discussion topics

1. Constraints or bottlenecks
What constraints or bottlenecks do you experience in the following situations?
- (a) Travelling to university or work
- (b) doing your homework or performing your task at work
- (c) having a smooth relationship with your girl/boyfriend, or husband/wife, or children
- (d) making a satisfactory or objective income
- (e) living where you would really like
- (f) having a career that would please you the most.

2. Focusing on constraints
Using the five steps outlined in the Theory of Constraints, how would you apply these to the situations outlined in Question 1?

3. Random occurrences
In your daily activity over the last 12 months, what random occurrences have you experienced that have impeded your progress or attainment of objectives? How did you 'manage' these random occurrences?

4. Non-bottlenecks
In the situations outlined in Question 1, what are the non-bottlenecks? Justify your response by illustrating that modifying these non-bottlenecks will not increase throughput.

5. Project management
Either using projects that you have been involved with or projects that you have studied in the literature, indicate some of the constraints that have occurred, and how these were 'managed'.

6. New product development
Either using new product development work that you have been involved with or new product development work that you have studied in the literature, indicate some of the constraints that have occurred, and how these constraints were 'managed'.

7. Bottleneck situations
In the following, what would raise a red flag to indicate bottlenecks were occurring?
- (a) Retail food store
- (b) restaurant
- (c) highway
- (d) a machine shop producing automobile parts
- (e) border control.

If bottlenecks are occurring, what steps could be taken to reduce them?

Demonstrating the concept 22.1   Production operation

Situation

A production operation consists of five work posts as illustrated in Figure 22.2. Each work post has a design capacity of six units an hour, and in order for a finished product to be assembled units must pass successively through each of the five work posts. Thus, if the operation is finely tuned with no machine breakdowns, no operators absent, all the operators perfectly trained, all the material used conforms to specification etc., the system would be able to produce six finished products an hour and there would be no inventory build-up between work posts.

   Now assume that the operation is not tuned and there are random occurrences due to machine failures, poor quality material, operators unavailable, etc. As a result of this randomness the capacity of each work post varies between integer values of one and six units an hour (the same as the faces of a die). This means that the average production rate of each work post is 3.5 units/hr. Consider that there are ten production runs where each is of one hour duration. When units are processed at one work post, which takes one hour, they then flow to

the next work post. For example, in the first hour units are processed at Work post N° 1 and then processed at Work post N° 2 in the second hour.

Required

Simulate this production operation, taking into account random occurrences. Determine the production levels and inventory movements and present this information graphically. What are your conclusions?

Solution

The random occurrences can be generated by using Excel to generate the random numbers or they can be obtained by simply throwing a die. An illustrative situation with these random occurrences is presented in Table 22.2. Each line is explained as follows.

Location
This is location of each work post. There are five work posts, the furthest upstream is N° 1 and the furthest downstream is N° 5.

Table 22.2 Production operation

Possible production levels, units/hr	
Minimum production level, units/hr	1
	2
	3
	4
	5
Maximum production level, units/hr	6
Average production level, units/hr	3.5

Location	Work post Nº 1											Total
Production run (also number of hours)	0	1	2	3	4	5	6	7	8	9	10	
Elapsed time after start	0	1	2	3	4	5	6	7	8	9	10	
Capacity available (affected by randomness), units/hr		2	6	4	2	5	3	6	4	5	2	
Upstream inventory before production, units		0	0	0	0	0	0	0	0	0	0	
Actual production, units in one hour		2	6	4	2	5	3	6	4	5	2	39
Upstream inventory after production, units		0	0	0	0	0	0	0	0	0	0	
Downstream inventory after production, units		2	6	4	2	5	3	6	4	5	2	39
Production level compared to average level, units/hr		−1.5	1.0	1.5	0.0	1.5	1.0	3.5	4.0	5.5	4.0	

Location	Work post Nº 2											Total
Production run (also number of hours)	0	1	2	3	4	5	6	7	8	9	10	
Elapsed time after start	1	2	3	4	5	6	7	8	9	10	11	
Capacity available (affected by randomness), units/hr		4	6	1	5	2	5	4	6	3	3	
Upstream inventory before production, units		2	6	4	5	5	6	7	7	6	5	
Actual production, units in one hour		2	6	1	5	2	5	4	6	3	3	37
Upstream inventory after production, units		0	0	3	0	3	1	3	1	3	2	
Downstream inventory after production, units		2	6	1	5	2	5	4	6	3	3	37
Production level compared to average level, units/hr		−1.5	1.0	−1.5	0.0	−1.5	0.0	0.5	3.0	2.5	2.0	

Location	Work post Nº 3											Total
Production run (also number of hours)	0	1	2	3	4	5	6	7	8	9	10	
Elapsed time after start	2	3	4	5	6	7	8	9	10	11	12	
Capacity available (affected by randomness), units/hr		4	3	2	2	5	6	1	5	6	5	
Upstream inventory before production, units		2	6	4	7	7	7	5	10	8	5	
Actual production, units in one hour		2	3	2	2	5	6	1	5	6	5	37
Upstream inventory after production, units		0	3	2	5	2	1	4	5	2	0	
Downstream inventory after production, units		2	3	2	2	5	6	1	5	6	5	37
Production level compared to average level, units/hr		−1.5	−2.0	−3.5	−5.0	−3.5	−1.0	−3.5	−2.0	0.5	2.0	

Location	Work post Nº 4											Total
Production run (also number of hours)	0	1	2	3	4	5	6	7	8	9	10	
Elapsed time after start	3	4	5	6	7	8	9	10	11	12	13	
Capacity available (affected by randomness), units/hr		1	6	3	5	1	2	2	1	3	2	
Upstream inventory before production, units		2	4	2	2	5	10	9	12	17	19	
Actual production, units in one hour		1	4	2	2	1	2	2	1	3	2	20
Upstream inventory after production, units		1	0	0	0	4	8	7	11	14	17	
Downstream inventory after production, units		1	4	2	2	1	2	2	1	3	2	20
Production level compared to average level, units/hr		−2.5	−2.0	−3.5	−5.0	−7.5	−9.0	−10.5	−13.0	−13.5	−15.0	

(Continued)

Table 22.2 (Continued)

Location	Work post Nº5											Total
Production run (also number of hours)	0	1	2	3	4	5	6	7	8	9	10	
Elapsed time after start	4	5	6	7	8	9	10	11	12	13	14	
Capacity available (affected by randomness), units/hr		1	3	2	4	1	4	5	3	4	2	
Upstream inventory before production, units		1	4	3	3	1	2	2	1	3	2	
Actual production, units in one hour		1	3	2	3	1	2	2	1	3	2	20
Upstream inventory after production, units		0	1	1	0	0	0	0	0	0	0	
Downstream inventory after production, units		1	3	2	3	1	2	2	1	3	2	20
Production level compared to average level, units/hr		−2.5	−3.0	−4.5	−5.0	−7.5	−9.0	−10.5	−13.0	−13.5	−15.0	

Production run (also the number of hours)
This is the number of production operations carried out. Here, ten operations are illustrated. The system is based on rate per hour, thus the first production run is the activity for one hour, the second production run for the second hour, etc.

Elapsed time after start
This is the time after the start of the operation. Since, at the beginning, Work post Nº 2 has to wait one hour for inventory units to come from Work post Nº 1, Work post Nº 3 has to wait one hour for units to come from Work post Nº 2 etc., there is a delay of one hour between each work post. Thus Work post Nº 5 will have an elapsed time of 14 hours.

Capacity available
This is the actual capacity of each work post, which is now a function of the randomness at each of the work posts. This capacity will vary according to the random number obtained, which can vary between one and six.

Upstream inventory before production
This is the inventory which has accumulated upstream of the work post. It is equal to the inventory units upstream after production from the previous production run at the same work post plus the downstream inventory after production from the preceding work post. For example, consider the situation at Work post Nº 2:

- At the third production run there are 0 units of inventory upstream after the second production run and four units of inventory downstream at Work post Nº 1 after its third production run. Thus, the inventory upstream of Work post Nº 2 is 4 (0 + 4).
- At the fourth production run, there are three units upstream after the third production run

plus two units downstream at Work post Nº 1 after its fourth production run, or a total of 5 units (3 + 2).

Actual production
This is the production level of each work post. Except for Work post Nº 1, this level is a function of the capacity available and the inventory of units immediately upstream of each post. At Work post Nº 1, since this is the start of the operation, the actual production is always the same as the capacity available. However, consider the situation for the first production run:

- At Work post Nº 2 the actual production is only two units an hour, even though the capacity available is four units an hour. This is because there are only two units of inventory upstream of this work post which came from Work post Nº 1.
- At Work post Nº 3 the actual production is only two units an hour, even though the capacity available is four units an hour. The reason is, again, that there are only two units of inventory upstream of this work post.
- At Work post Nº 4 the capacity available is one unit an hour, even though there are two units upstream of this post before production and the actual production is only one unit an hour. This logic of actual production follows for all the production runs at all the work posts.

Upstream inventory after production
This is the inventory of units upstream of the work post after production. It is the difference between the upstream inventory before production and the actual production.

Downstream inventory after production
This is the inventory amount that has been produced at a specific work post and is equal to the actual production

at a work post. This downstream inventory becomes part of the upstream inventory at the next work post.

Production level compared to average level

This is the cumulative production compared to average production level of 3.5 units/hr. For example, at Work post N° 1 for the first production run two units have been produced. Thus the production level compared to the average is −1.5 units (2 − 3.5). After the second production run, the total units produced from run N° 1 and N° 2 is 8 (2 + 6). The average for two runs is 7.0 (2 * 3.5). Thus the difference is 8 − 7 = 1.0. For the third production run, the total units produced for the first three runs (or 3 hours) is 12 (2 + 6 + 4). The average production for three runs is 10.5 (3 * 3.5). Thus the difference is 12 − 10.5 = 1.5.

Result after ten runs

- After ten hours, for a system operating at design capacity of six units an hour there should have been 60 units finished. Alternatively, if the system were running according to the average production level of 3.5 units/hr there should have been 35 units finished (10 * 3.5) In this illustration, from the total column at Work post N° 5, only 20 units have been finished. This represents only 33.3% of the design capacity or 57.1% of the average capacity.
- With a perfectly tuned system, there should be no accumulation of upstream inventory after production. This is not the case here as is illustrated in the table, with Work post N° 4 showing a considerable bottleneck situation with 19 units upstream before the tenth production run. This situation is illustrated in Figure 22.14, which shows that as time moves on after successive production runs, the upstream inventory starts to accumulate and the production compared to the average level seriously deteriorates.

Conclusion

From the simulation it is evident that random occurrences can seriously impact the smooth running of an operation. Good management should be employed to minimize such events as machine stoppages, poor quality material, operators absent, etc. When there are fluctuations in demand and 'unavoidable' random occurrences, multi-skilled operators should help in smoothing out fluctuations.

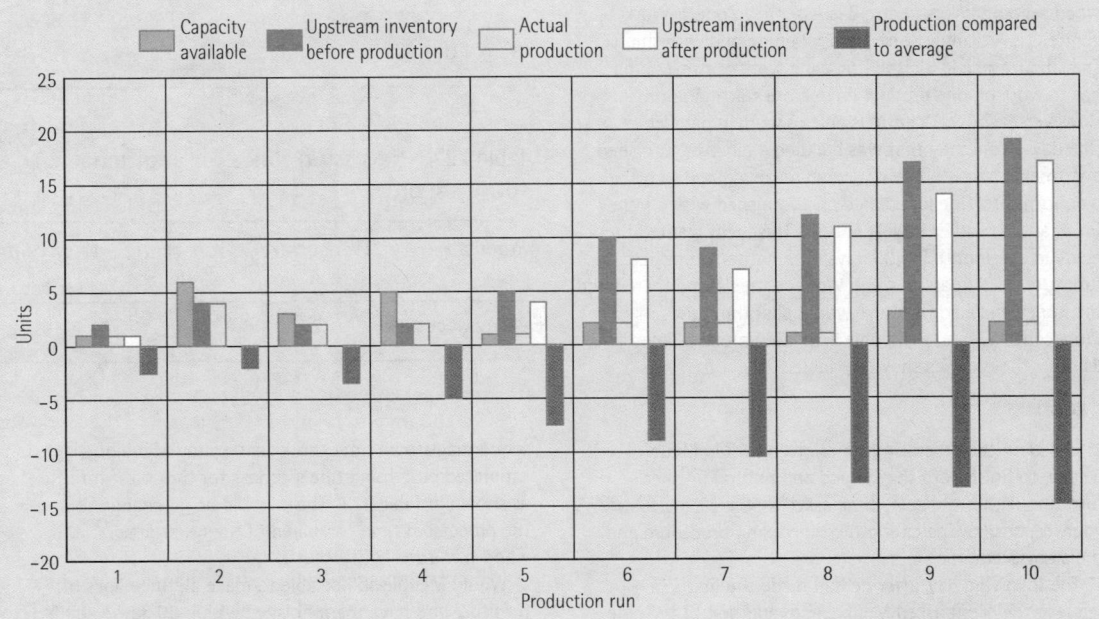

Figure 22.14 Production operations: Work post N° 4

Application exercise 22.1 Computers

Situation

A firm assembles desktop computers from components that are purchased from outside. The assembly operation consists of three basic sequential steps, which allows the firm to customize the computers according to client needs. Currently the assembly operation is carried out at three different sites and when a process batch is finished it is transferred to the next assembly site. Each assembly site is able to process 120 computers an hour and the transfer time between sites for any quantity of units is one hour. Each site works three shifts enabling it to have an uninterrupted production time of 24 hours/day. The firm has an order for 1800 computers.

Required

1. If the transfer batch were equal to the process batch what would be the elapsed time after which the complete order for the client would be finished?

2. If now the transfer batch were 120 units, what would be the elapsed time and what would be the savings in time compared to the first situation?

3. The firm is considering transferring the whole of its operation to another site where all the assembly operation would be under one roof. In this case, the firm would be able to work in a continuous flow operation such that when a computer is finished at one assembly operation it would be passed directly to the next, i.e., the transfer batch = process batch = 1 unit. There would essentially be no transfer time. In this case, what would be the elapsed time to finish the order of computers for the client?

Application exercise 22.2 Furniture

Situation

The Meuble Co. is a small family firm that makes custom-made furniture out of oak, teak, cherry wood and pine. The production site comprises three work centres. The Work centre A is the cutting and shaping of the wood sections. Work centre B is Assembly Zone 1. Work centre C is Assembly Zone 2 plus staining and varnishing. The labour force is such that in each work centre, Meuble has to work on one product line before starting another. However, each work centre is able to work in parallel. One day, a company that was building a block of furnished apartments asks Meuble if it could make a quantity of pine furniture. One lot stained and varnished with a honey finish and the other lot left natural. The client wanted them ready in one month (= 30 days). The naturally finished furniture would pass through Work centres A and then B and the honey-finished furniture would pass through Work centres A and C. Meuble estimated process times in days for the order as shown in Table 22.3.

Required

1. Based on the processing times given, would Meuble be able to finish both the stained and natural finished furniture within the delay time asked by the client? Justify your response by indicating the scheduling procedure and the associated times.

2. The following day, after he had made the first request, the client asked Meuble if, in addition to the pine wood furniture, they could make another quantity of furniture out of cherry wood and have this ready within the same 30-day period. Cherry wood furniture is processed sequentially in all three work centres and Meuble estimated processing times in days for this lot of furniture as shown in Table 22.4. There would be no change to the processing time compared of the other pine wood furniture.

Would Meuble still be able to make all three lines of furniture and have them finished within 30 days? Justify your response by indicating the scheduling procedure and the associated times. Show the schedule on an appropriate bar chart.

Table 22.3 Processing times for furniture order

Product	Work centre A	Work centre B	Work centre C
Natural finished	12	7	–
Stained and varnished	8	–	17

Table 22.4 Processing times for additional furniture order

Product	Work centre A	Work centre B	Work centre C
Cherry wood	2	10	4

Application exercise 22.3   Washing machine

Situation

A firm assembles washing machines that go through a five-step operation at successive work posts. Each work post has a design capacity of six units an hour. However, because of a poorly managed operation, the assembly line is subjected to random occurrences including machine stoppages, poor quality material, and operator absence. These occurrences limit each work post to production levels at integer values between one and six units an hour. (This is similar to the situation in Demonstrating the concept 22.1.)

Required

1. Using the same criteria as in Demonstrating the concept 22.1 and identical table formats, simulate this situation by generating, and then fixing, random numbers using Excel. Plot histograms for each of the five work posts. What are your conclusions?
2. Redo the simulation but this time leave the random numbers floating. This time, the table and the histograms will change each time F9 is pressed. This illustrates a type of situation that may be found in a real operation.

Case study 22.1   Compressor units

Situation

The James Co. is a subcontractor to a major aircraft manufacturer located some 3000 kilometres distant from the client. The company currently works one eight-hour shift a day (8am–midday and 1–5pm), but does work a seven-day week. No work is performed during the lunch period. It receives a special order from the client to produce a lot of 780 precision compressor parts made from a special alloy. These parts will be made in a five-step process as follows.

Work centre Nº 1

This is the cutting operation, where the alloy is cut to the required shape from alloy blocks that James receives pre-cut from its supplier.

Work centre Nº 2

This is the drilling operation, where the rough-cut alloy is drilled with holes of varying dimensions, some of which are screw tapped to receive screwed attachments.

Work centre Nº 3

This is the shaping operation, where the units are turned on a lathe, then shaped into an S form in a heat-treating operation.

Work centre Nº 4

This is the cleaning and polishing operation, where all the burrs from the previous operations are removed by hand. Then the units are individually polished in a rotating tumbler containing small ball bearings that give the units a smooth finish.

Work centre Nº 5

This is the assembly and inspection operation where rubber gaskets are fitted, and other pre-purchased attachments are fitted into the screwed-tapped holes made at Work centre Nº 2. Then each unit is pressure tested.

When the James Co. had first laid out its production site, each work centre had a capacity equal to the design capacity of 40 units a day. However, since that time some of the machinery has become old and also staff turnover has been high, such that the productivity of the operators is not what it used to be. As such only Work centre Nº 1 operates at the design capacity. Work centre Nº 2 operates at 80% of design capacity, Work centre Nº 3 at 85% of design capacity, Work centre Nº 4 at 90% of design capacity, and Work centre Nº 5 operates at a poor 75% of design capacity. These work centres are different buildings on the James production site, which covers several acres. Each work centre produces a quantity of units during a day's operation according to its actual capacity. At the end of the day a handler transfers the units to the next work centre, where they are ready for the next day's operation. The handlers have a special contract and finish work at 7pm. They are always able to move semi-finished products from one work centre to another before the end of their workday. No transfer of units is made during the day. Since this is a special order, James will order just 780 pre-cut blocks from its supplier. Any more than this will not be useable for other work. When all the units are completed they will be loaded onto a truck and delivered to the client. Loading and delivery time is estimated at three days.

Required

What delivery schedule is James able to promise the client? Develop the loading schedules for each of the work centres showing production and inventory movements. What are your comments about this supply chain operation? What are your proposals for improvement, indicating the changes that need to be made? Justify your proposals with work centre loading charts.

Selected further reading

DETTMER, William H. (1997) *Goldratt's Theory of Constraints: A Systems Approach to Continuous Improvement*, American Society for Quality.

SIMONS, Jacobs, Jr and SIMPSON, Wendell P. III, 'An exposition of multiple constraint scheduling as implemented in the goal system', *Production and Operations Management*, vol 6, no. 1, Spring 1997, pp 3–22.

SMITH, Debra A. (1999) *The Measurement Nightmare: How the Theory of Constraints Can Resolve Conflicting Strategies, Policies, and Measures*, St. Lucie Press.

WOEPPEL, Mark J. (2000) *Manufacturer's Guide to Implementing the Theory of Constraints*, Lewis Publishers.

YENRADEE, Pisal, 'Application of optimized production technology in a capacity constrained flow shop: A case study in a battery factory', *Computers and Industrial Engineering*, vol. 27, issues 1–4, September 1994, pp 217–20.

An extensive listing of other further reading can be found on the website.

What's on the web?

Further learning resources are available to lecturers and students at www.supplychain-online.com, including the following which are specific to *Theory of Constraints*:

Resource	Subject
Chapter overview	Theory of Constraints
Detailed chapter summary	Theory of Constraints

23 *Decision making and risk*

The element of risk

Making decisions is part of life and there is no exception in business. The decisions to be made may be at a strategic level involving, perhaps, a large capital investment such as the following:

- What products should we produce for the market?
- Which geographic markets should be pursued?
- When should we invest in the new technology?
- Should we launch this new product onto the market?
- Should be build a new operating facility overseas?
- Should we acquire another company?

Alternatively, the decisions may be at the operating level involving situations such as:

- How much raw material should we purchase?
- When should we start a production run?
- When should we install the new equipment?
- How many new people should we hire?
- How much safety stock should we carry?
- Should we use subcontracting?

The operating decisions obviously directly impact the operations and supply chain. However, as pointed out in Chapter 2, because of the strong synergy between operations and strategy, a strategic decision will, at some point, have an impact on operations.

Whenever a decision is made, there is always an element of risk. Plans may not proceed as desired,

markets may alter, technology may change, or the cost of materials increase unexpectedly. The more systematic the analysis of all the variables involved in a decision, the less likely the downside risk. A decision is usually made from a combination of quantitative analysis such as cost, price information, statistics, historical data, and market factors plus subjective reasoning based on the experience of persons involved in the decision-making process.

Wrong decisions

A Wrong Decision can be costly and some classic examples related to manufacturing are described in the following sections[2] and Industry insight 23.1 is a recent example for a service firm.

Ford Motor Company and the Edsel

In 1957 Ford, USA, launched a new medium priced automobile, the Edsel. This decision was taken after ten years in R&D. Some $50 million was spent in establishing new independent dealers, advertising, and promotion the year it was launched. Ford's market analysis indicated that this project was almost risk free. In fact, the Edsel was a financial disaster. In three years, only 109,466 Edsels were sold, which was far below forecast. In 1959 the production was halted after an estimated loss of $100 million on the original investment, and another $100 million in

Burger King's wrong decision

Burger King is the world's N° 2 hamburger chain with some 11,400 restaurants worldwide including 8400 in the USA. McDonald's, the undisputable N° 1 in the fast food restaurant business, has close to 16,000 restaurants worldwide with some 12,400 in the USA. For years Burger King beat out McDonald's in taste tests for its hamburgers but McDonald's always came out ahead regarding the taste of its French fries. As such, Burger King made a decision that it was also going to be first in the category of fries. French fries are an important product in the fast food market as the profit margin is up to a hefty 80 cents on the dollar making them the most lucrative food on the menu. Further, since 1996, American per capita consumption of frozen French fries, the type served at most fast food restaurants, increased by almost 30% to about 12 kg a year.

Market research showed that people wanted a fry that was both crispy and remained hot. Burger King seized on the idea that crunchiness would distinguish its fry from McDonald's popular version and thus inspire a mass loyal following. Burger King began developing a new French fry in 1996 which was a potato stick coated with a layer of starch designed to help retain heat and add crunch to the product. It developed a 19-page French-fry specification for the product which included that the degree of crispiness should be determined by an audible crunch that must be present for seven or more chews and loud enough to be audible to an evaluator. This seven-audible crunch mandate was considered way outside the norms of the fry business as evaluators had to eat the product and grade it by listening and hearing crunches. The other element in the specification was the starch coating to retain the heat. Burger King assembled a French-fry team of 100 marketing executives, food scientists, franchises, potato suppliers, and others, to test a coated fry. With help from the potato-processing company Lamb Weston, a division of ConAgra Foods Inc., Burger King developed a clear-coated fry that required a complicated preparation formula. Further, the product had to meet staple requirements of length, colour, tenderness, mouth feel, 'toothpack', or the degree to which a fry sticks to the surface of the tooth, and the avoidance of 'marriage' that is two full fry units bonding together by one-third of their surface. In addition to all this, there were numerous suppliers handling different ingredients and preparatory steps. These many players and complex specifications made quality control difficult.

Before Burger King commercialised its fry, the product went through numerous tests. In the testing stage, it was agreed that the fries, cooked carefully under test kitchen conditions, were a tremendous success. For the product launching, each Burger King fry supplier was outfitted with new equipment and about 300,000 restaurant managers and crew were 'certifried' in the new operations including mastering new frying procedures and differing salting techniques. On Friday 2 January 1998 it launched its 'Free Fryday' by giving away 15 million orders of French fries throughout the United States. Governors in three states officially welcomed the new product and Burger King promoted children's meal toys in the likeness of Mr Potato Head, the new fries official emblem or 'spokespud'. The company booked expensive TV commercial time during the 1998 Super Bowl and as part of its 'Decision 98: Try the Fry America' it had a 15-metre advertising trailer crisscrossing the country. Over $70 million was spent on marketing the product. In 1999 Burger King repeated the 'Free Fryday' by promoting its new product in London.

After its introduction, consumers ranked Burger King's fries better than McDonald's for the first time. In an independent national test 57% preferred Burger King's fries compared to 35% for McDonald's, with 8% with no opinion. In the six months following the US 'Free Fryday', Burger King had sold 150 million more orders of fries than in the same period the previous year. At its headquarters in Miami, Burger King management basked in its assault on McDonald's. However, less than one year later consumers started avoiding the new fry in droves and franchises and suppliers complained of drastically falling sales. By the end of 1999 Burger King confirmed that sales of fries had fallen 14% from the year before. Consumers and franchises said the fry's taste was subject to change, they often seemed under-salted, they clumped easily, and when the potatoes cooled they became tough and bitter. Fast food thrives on consistency and this new fry was proving too complicated to get right under anything less than ideal conditions. It was unforgiving in the cooking process and its flavour and consistency varied widely if it was not thawed and cooked exactly to the letter. The crunchy fry was also getting crunchier. As sales started to drop, suppliers, mindful of the 'seven-crunch minimum', started to add more batter to give more crunch. However, as the crunch increased, flavour suffered and with little to hold in the heat, the fry grew colder much faster. Then the fry was so brittle that it snapped like a potato crisp.

Finger pointing for the poor sales extended from the Burger King Company, the franchises, and the potato suppliers. Burger King blamed the cooking procedures of the franchises and even said that a poor potato crop in 1998 may have been a factor. At this comment, a Burger King franchises operator said that in this case McDonald's must have got its potatoes from the planet Mars! In the summer of 2000, some 30 months after the launch of the new French fry, Burger King's executives conceded they had a big problem and something needed to be done. They agreed that the new fry would be replaced by one with less coating, more potato taste, and, further, the supply chain would be simplified and product specifications reassessed. In the annals of consumer product flops, Burger King's 1996 decision turned out to be a whopping and costly mistake.

Adapted from: 'Burger King sought the perfect fry, but got burned', *Wall Street Journal Europe*[1]

operating losses. Some of the reasons for this poor decision are:

- The competition, particularly from General Motors, was very strong.
- A recession in 1958 affected automobile sales.
- The horsepower and performance of the Edsel were under extreme criticism by the National Safety Council, and the Automobile Manufacturing Association.
- The demand for smaller cars was taking hold, and the size and style of the Edsel did not have the expected consumer demand.
- Ford tried to 'push' as many Edsels onto the market immediately after its introduction and as a result quality suffered.
- The network of controllers, dealers, marketing managers, and industrial relations people created within Ford to launch the Edsel was complicated, and inefficient.

Dupont and Corfam

In 1964 Dupont, USA, introduced a synthetic leather, Corfam, as a substitute material for shoe manufacture. Corfam was promoted as a light material, breathed and flexed easily, kept its shape, was water resistant, stood up well to abrasion, and did not have to be polished. Dupont took some 13 years to develop the product and spent $2 million in advertising in the first year of introduction. After seven years of losses ranging from $80 to $100 million, and even after the introduction of a new version of Corfam in 1970, Dupont abandoned the product in 1971. Some of the reasons for this poor decision were considered as follows:

- The leather industry attacked Corfam as a poor substitute for leather.
- Quality control problems occurred in production causing costs to rise. These higher costs put Corfam in the $15 to $20 shoe price range that comprised only 10% of the shoe market. A lower price might have enabled Corfam to capture a larger market share.
- In 1969 less expensive vinyl and fabric materials also entered the market. The leather industry began to promote soft leather. Further, imports infiltrated the USA market, and Corfam's sales declined by 25%.

Coca-Cola and New Coke

Coca-Cola decided in 1984 that it must act boldly to reverse its 20-year market share decline against Pepsi. Coca-Cola decided that the correct strategy was to replace the 98-year-old coke with a better tasting cola, and to label it 'New Coke'. With a loud fanfare, New Coke was launched onto the market in April 1985. It was a flop. One reason for the poor decision was that in launching the new product, the company decided not to present the option of keeping 'old coke' on the market. (Only 79 days after the launch of New Coke, the old formula coke was brought back).[3]

System

A business can be considered a system, comprising principally three subsystems: Marketing, operations, and finance. (See Chapter 1.) Decisions made at the level of one subsystem will impact the other subsystems. A decision that seems logical for one subsystem may not appear so for the other. For example, the marketing department wishes to introduce another product line. However, there is a risk this would saturate the capacity of the production department and a further risk that it would strain the financial situation of the company. In arriving at the final decision, the system has to be considered in its entirety, not only at subsystem level.

Trade-off

In decision making, trade-offs occur. A trade-off is making a choice between one decision and another. With both there is a risk and both have advantages, and disadvantages:

- The finance department wants production to keep inventories at the lowest possible level, to reduce the financial investment and level of working capital. Production wants to keep levels reasonably high because of the uncertainty of supplier deliveries, and fluctuations in final product demand. There is trade-off between what levels of inventories should be held.
- In quality control there is a trade-off between the extent of product inspections, an internal cost, and the number of defects that slip through the production process (an external cost). Thus there is a trade-off between the levels of inspection.

Priority recognition

Managers at all levels are confronted with numerous decisions. One task is to sort the decisions in order that priority is given to the most important:

- Should the problem of quality control in the plant in Europe be dealt with now, or should the new client in Japan be contacted?
- Should the purchase decision of raw materials be made now, in order to get a preferential price, or should the sales negotiations be finalized first?
- Should we start hiring now to meet the expected market demand, or should we wait and see if the market expands as forecast?

Magnitude of the decision-making process

The depth of analysis for making decisions depends on its complexity, the costs involved, and the time horizon as, for example:

- A decision on purchasing a new quantity of raw material may be relatively short term, and simple to make. (The raw material should be consumed within a few days under just-in-time operation.)
- Deciding on the purchase of a new printing press may take three months to finalize with a long-term impact on the outcome (five to ten years' use of the equipment).
- The decision by a German company to build a new production centre in the USA has long-term consequences.

Figure 23.1 Magnitude (and cost) of making a decision

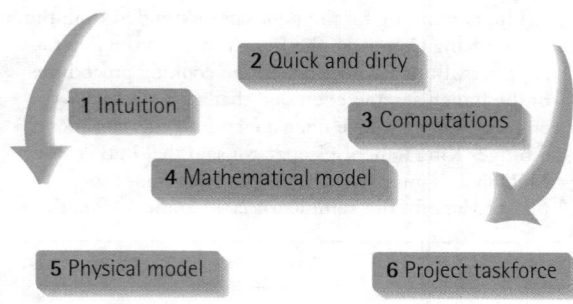

The following illustrates concepts in the magnitude of decision making, which are also summarized in Figure 23.1.

Intuition

The sales vice-president (VP) of a fashion company in Paris receives a telephone call from a prospective client in the USA. He decides to leave that night for New York to meet the customer even though it means cancelling other critical appointments. He goes because, intuition tells him, knowing this particular customer, he is likely to gain a substantial order.

Quick and dirty

The vice-president is on the plane back from New York. The customer has given him a large order for ladies' apparel at a price lower than usual. The vice-president is not immediately clear of the profit margin. The customer wants an answer quickly to know if his order has been accepted and preferably as soon as the vice-president arrives back in Paris. Thus, the VP does some 'quick and dirty' calculations on the flight back to Paris.

Computations

The sale is a bit more complicated, as it involves potential future sales on other clothing items. The vice-president spends a day at the office doing some additional computations and talking with design and production people.

Model building

A model represents a simplified version of the real thing and is used as a tool to aid in decision making (see Chapter 1):

- An oil company is deciding on whether to drill for oil in Ukraine. Before a final decision is made, financial models are developed looking at costs, expected revenues, and the probability of locating oil.
- A food company is considering acquiring a small chocolate manufacturer. Before a decision on the acquisition is made, financial models are developed to analyze the expected revenues from the acquisitions, market forecasts, and additional debt on net returns.
- A construction company develops a proposal for constructing a new hotel in Las Vegas. Three physical scale models are constructed as an aid to the client to make a decision on the final design.
- A boat builder is developing a new sailboat as an entrant to the America's Cup. A model is built to decide on the final aerodynamic design.

Task force

A company is deciding whether to build a large petrochemical facility in Kuwait. A team comprising a project manager, a market analyst, an estimator, a scheduler and two engineers are sent over to Kuwait to analyze the proposition. This taskforce then returns to the home office with a recommendation based on their work in Kuwait city. (In this real illustration, the author was the market analyst.)

The decision process

The process of decision making depends on the magnitude of the decision being made, and the extent of the risk should the wrong decision be made. Steps in the decision process might include the following and are summarized in Figure 23.2.

What is the reason for requiring a decision?

Perhaps markets have changed, the competition has increased, or new technology has been developed. These situations apply to computer hardware companies such as IBM, Dell, Hewlett-Packard, Compaq, Bull, and the like:

- The market has increased as personal computers become more accepted both for business and for personal use.

Figure 23.2 Decision-making process

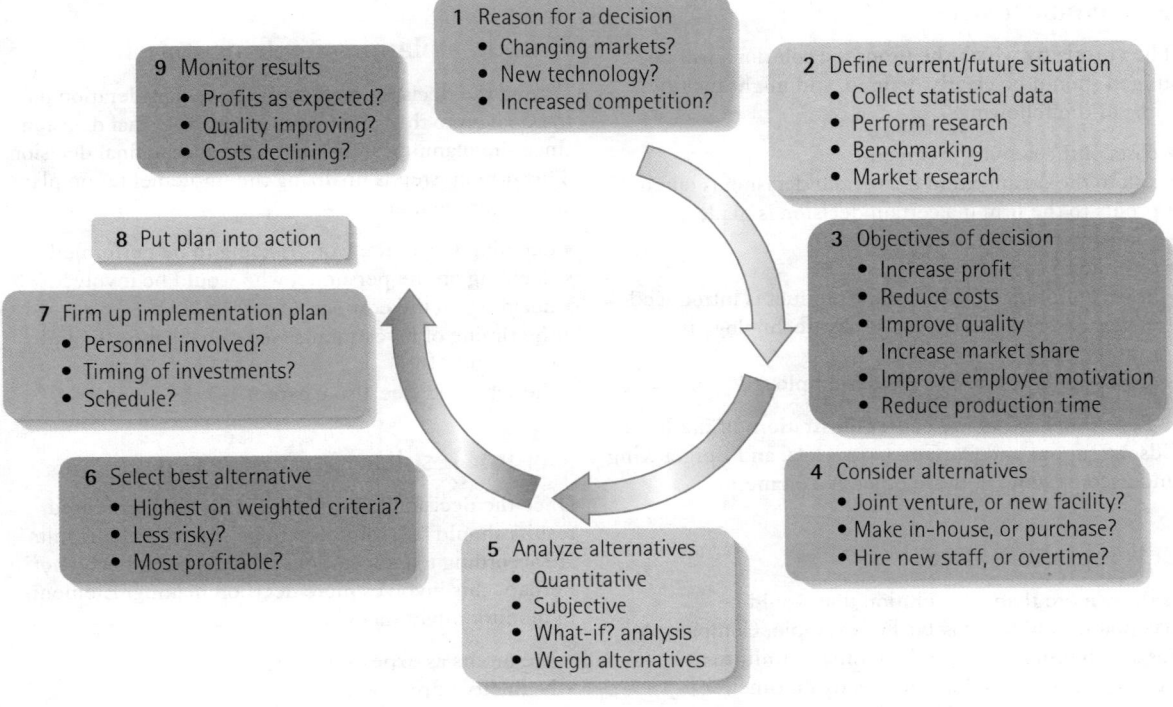

- The use of the Internet has increased the demand for computer hardware.
- Portable computers or laptops are become more in demand for certain sectors such as the business traveller, teaching profession, and consultants.
- Technology is constantly changing with new software offered by Microsoft, and more powerful computer chips.
- The competition is extremely strong among computer manufactures in price, styling, weight, features, etc.

In a production operation, perhaps a reason for the decision is that there are continuing complaints from customers regarding product quality.

Define the current and future situation

This would involve analyzing the situation by gathering cost, price, market data, performing research, interviewing personnel, benchmarking, analyzing the competition, etc. (See also Chapters 4 and 26.)

The current situation might be for example a problem of the poor quality of end products. Here the decision should not be to remove the symptoms, leaving the basic problem unresolved. That is, the non-conforming products are repaired rather than investigating the cause of the poor quality. (See also Chapter 20.)

Define objectives

The criteria by which the proposed solutions will be judged should be clearly defined, and might include some of the following:

- costs of the activity involved
- risk to the organization if a certain decision is taken
- profits to the firm if a certain decision is made
- company image
- return on investment
- impact of demand say if a new product is introduced
- increased productivity, say, if new technology is introduced
- quality level if a new process is employed.

Referring back to the earlier illustrations of the Ford Edsel, Dupont and Corfam, Coca-Cola, and Burger King underscores some of these objective elements.

Develop alternatives

Is there more than one solution that would be acceptable, and less costly? For example, Company A has a rush order for a supply of office furniture to a customer. If the order is not ready on time for

the customer the order will be lost, and quite possibly repeat business from this customer will also be lost. The possible alternative ways of tackling this problem might be:

- putting the factory on overtime
- hiring additional workers
- renting additional factory space
- subcontracting the work – but perhaps sacrificing quality
- purchasing semi-finished units from elsewhere, and then finishing them in the factory of Company A
- promising the customer the furniture, but with a penalty clause in the contract so that if deliveries are not on time, you pay a penalty.

Analyze alternatives

Quantitative methods, as well as subjective analyses, may be used to look at the other options in the decision process. Probability analysis is a useful tool, as is using some other forms of weighting for all the possible decision criteria.

Select the best alternative

The best alternative may be the one that scores best on a weighting criterion. It might be the less risky alternative or it might be the alternative that is the most profitable.

Firm up a plan for implementation

During the decision-making process, consideration has to be given to the implementation of the final decision since the planning steps might impact the final decision. This firm up step is finalizing the implementation plan and might include:

- deciding where the work is going to be performed
- deciding on the personnel who would be involved
- deciding on the equipment
- the timing of investments (see also Chapter 18 and Case study 18.1)
- the schedule (see also Chapter 14).

Monitor results

Once the decision has been made and implemented, results should be monitored to be sure that the results are according to expectations. If they are not, why not? Perhaps this involves more decision making. Elements to monitor might include:

- Are profits as expected?
- Is quality improving?

- Are costs declining?
- Is productivity improving?
- Has delivery time been reduced?

The environment for decision making

Decision making under certainty

Decision making under certainty implies that all relevant parameters in the decision such as cost, capacity, market demand, price, style have values that are known in advance and will not change during the time frame to which the decision is applied. For example:

- A production decision is required concerning the manufacture of 500 engine parts. If the units are made in house, the production costs per unit will be $20. Thus for certainty the total cost will be $10,000 (500 * $20). If the parts are purchased outside, the price paid, or the cost per unit to firm, will be $19.50 or a total cost of $9750 (500 * $19.50).
- An investment decision is required. US government certificate of deposits are currently giving an annual yield of 7.5%. Thus, $200,000 invested for one year will give a return of $15,000 ($200,000 * 0.075).
- A marketing decision is required concerning 750 office desks that a manufacturer has in stock that cost $960 per unit to produce. One client wishes to purchase all these office desks and has agreed to pay $1100 per unit. Thus, the profit to be realized is $140 per unit or a total of $105,000. Another client wishes to purchase 700 of these desks at a price of $1117 per unit. This would yield a profit of $109,900 [700 * (1117 − 960)].

All the parameters are known, and the decision most likely to be taken is the one that maximizes the final outcome.

Decision making under risk

In decision making under risk there is no certainty of the final outcome. However, a probability of success can be estimated and this implies that certain parameters have probabilistic outcomes. The following are illustrations:

- The selling price per unit of an item is $40. Based on previous experience, there is a 75% probability of selling all the 500 units made. What is the expected revenue?
- A contractor is 70% certain that it will receive a building contract that has a value of $23 million.

- A software dealer is 90% certain that this year's profits will exceed the forecast.
- A production manager is 10% sure a machine can exceed capacity.

Here the probabilities would be taken into account in order to try and maximize the benefits of expected outcomes.

Decision making under uncertainty

In decision making under uncertainty it is extremely difficult, or even impossible to assess the likelihood of various possible future events. In this case, assigning probabilities would be wild such as for example:

- The selling price is $40 per unit. However, the sales demand is unknown and thus the revenue is uncertain.
- In ten years what will be profits realized in the former East German market?
- If a new chemical is found to replace chlorofluorocarbons in refrigeration systems, will the new product eventually prove hazardous to the environment?
- If new investments are made in new nuclear technology, would this industry be profitable for the next 30 years?
- In 15 years' time will the income from the investment in Stock A be more than that from Stock B?
- Will Hong Kong under Chinese rule maintain the same spectacular growth?

Decisions made under uncertainty are often long term, complex, involve many players, and sometime involve governments and politics. If the last is involved, the outcome can be extremely unpredictable!

Decision theory

Some of the decisions characterized previously in this chapter lend themselves to an approach called decision theory. Decision theory is an aid to managers to decide on the most attractive alternative. The elements of decision theory are now discussed and then illustrated later in detail.

Characteristics

In decision theory, the following characteristics exist:

- There are several possible future external conditions that will influence the final decision. Usually, these future conditions are beyond the manager's control.

- There are one or several alternatives from which to choose and which are within the decision-maker's control.
- For each alternative, there is a financial payoff under each future condition.

Stages

The stages in using decision theory include the following.

Identify future conditions

The future conditions are those that are likely to impact the final outcome, for example:

- The product demand is expected to be high, low, or unchanged.
- A competitor will introduce a new product, or there is not expected to be any new competition.
- Interest rates are expected to increase, decrease, or remain about the same.

These future conditions are known as states of nature. They are external events and usually those over which one has little control.

Possible alternatives

Develop a list of possible alternatives in the decision-making process. There will always be alternatives even if the alternative means not doing anything.

Payoff

Most business decisions are based on financial returns. Thus, this stage involves estimating the payoff, or financial return such as net income, associated with each alternative for every possible future condition.

Probability

Estimate the probability or the chance of each of the possible future conditions.

Analyze alternatives

Evaluate alternatives according to some decision criterion. This might be maximum profit, minimum cost, maximum market share, a certain growth rate, etc.

Decision making under certainty

In decision making under certainty it is known for certain which of the possible future conditions will actually happen. In this case, the decision is relatively straightforward in that the choice is the alternative with the highest payoff under that given state of nature.

Decision making under uncertainty

In decision making under uncertainty there is no clear information on the likelihood of the states of nature. There are no probability values (see Chapter 27). The following are some criteria for making a decision under conditions of uncertainty.

Maximin

The maximin approach implies selecting the maximum of all the minimum possibilities. The concept requires first selecting the worst, or the minimum possible payoff for each alternative. This might be the lowest profit, the highest cost, or the lowest market share. The final decision made is to choose that alternative that has the best or the maximum of all of the worst payoffs. This is considered a pessimistic approach and although the actual outcome may not be as bad as selected, the maximin criterion establishes a guaranteed minimum level assuming the given base information is correct.

Maximax

The maximax approach implies selecting the maximum of all the maximum possibilities. This concept requires selecting the best or the maximum possible payoff for each alternative. This might be the highest profit, the lowest cost, or the highest market share. The final decision is made to choose the alternative that has the highest or the maximum of all of the best payoffs. This is an optimistic approach as the decision maker has targeted what appears to be the best payoff.

Equally likely

In the equally likely approach, first the arithmetic average of each payoff is determined for each alternative. The decision is made to choose the alternative with the highest average payoff. This approach treats the states of nature as equally likely and would be an approach for someone who is middle of the road in nature.

Minimax regret

The minimax regret is the 'regret' or disappointment resulting from making a decision that is wrong, or not the best. The degree of regret is the difference between what is the best choice and the choice that is made.

In decision making under uncertainty, there are criteria, but no firm basis for preferring one decision to another. Each decision is a function of the 'feeling' of the decision maker. Setting up the matrix does not create certainty where none exists, neither does it attempt to include an element of risk. What it does is to organize the various outcomes so that decision makers can organize thoughts, crystallize prejudice about caution, and highlight information that is needed to improve the decision.

Decision making under risk

Under the case of risk there are probabilities of occurrence and the states of nature are mutually exclusive (see Chapter 27). For example, interest rates will increase, decrease, or remain the same. They cannot do all three! If all the possible probability outcomes are considered, then they must add up to unity. In decision making under risk, the concept of expected value (EV) is used which is a result obtained by weighting the outcomes according to the provided probability data. The decision, which has the highest expected value in, say, the case for profit, or the lowest in the case of cost, would then be the preferred decision. In this approach, the expected value is only a quantitative theoretical value used for decision making. This calculated value cannot be the actual payoff because of the mutual exclusivity of the states of nature, as only one of the states of nature can occur. (The market will increase, decline, or remain stable but cannot do all three.)

Decision trees

A decision tree is a schematic representation of the alternatives involved in decision making and is particularly useful in a situation of decision under risk. By convention, a decision tree has nodes, branches, and payoffs as explained as follows and illustrated in Figure 23.3.

Square nodes

There are square nodes (1, 4, and 5 in the figure), which denote a decision point. This is where the decision maker has control. The manager makes the decision.

Circular nodes

There are circular nodes (2 and 3 in the figure) that denote an external chance event or the states of nature. Here the decision maker has little, if any, control.

Figure 23.3 Decision tree layout

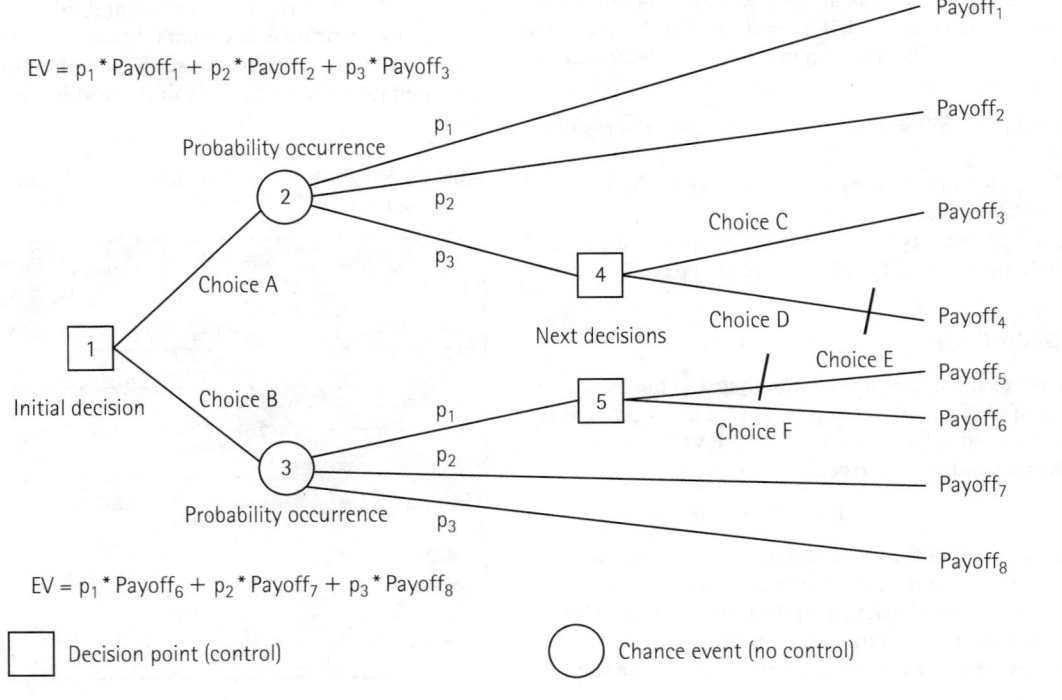

$$EV = p_1 * Payoff_1 + p_2 * Payoff_2 + p_3 * Payoff_3$$

$$EV = p_1 * Payoff_6 + p_2 * Payoff_7 + p_3 * Payoff_8$$

☐ Decision point (control)   ◯ Chance event (no control)

Branches

There are branches (the straight lines in the figure) that indicate the direction the decision is being made. The lengths of the branches themselves have no bearing on the decision process.

Payoffs

All the possible financial outcomes, or payoffs, in the decision-making process are listed on the right of the tree for each alternative, and probability of occurrence.

From the decision tree, branches are cut (de-branched) by drawing a single or double line across the branch if an alternative is less attractive than another:

- Consider decision point 4. If payoff 3, for choice C, is greater than payoff 4 for choice D, then the branch for choice D is de-branched as shown.
- Consider decision point 5. If payoff 6, for choice F, is greater than payoff 5 for choice E, then the branch for choice E is de-branched as shown.

The expected values (EV) for each node are then calculated as follows:

$$EV \text{ (node 2)} = p_1 * Payoff_1 + p_2 * Payoff_2 + p_3 * Payoff_3$$

$$EV \text{ (node 3)} = p_1 * Payoff_6 + p_2 * Payoff_7 + p_3 * Payoff_8$$

Assume that the expected value at node 2 is greater than the expected value at node 3, then the branch for choice B is de-branched. The preferred decision route is then choice A. The decision made is then described as follows for choice A:

- If the probability turns out to be p_1, then the result would be payoff 1.
- If the probability turns out to be p_2, then the result would be payoff 2.
- If the probability turns out to be p_3, then decide on alternative choice C. This would give payoff 3.

Expected value of perfect information

A concept that arises in decision theory is the expected value of perfect information (EVPI). This is given as by the expected value under certainty (EVUC) less the expected value under risk (EVUR) or:

$$EVPI = EVUC - EVUR$$

The purpose of determining the EVPI is that in decision making it would not make sense to pay more than the expected value of perfect information to be more certain of an alternative. For example, one is deciding whether to launch a new product onto the market. The success of the product launch will be based on whether there is a high, low, or medium market demand. Conceivably, one could spend more money on market research in order to be 'more certain' of the outcome. However, it would not make sense to spend more than the EVPI value on the market research in order to be more certain of the outcome.

In calculating the expected value of perfect information, the expected value under certainty is the weighted outcome, based on the probabilities, of all the best possibility outcomes. The expected value under risk is the expected value calculated by taking into account the normal risk situation.

The concept of EVPI is illustrated in Demonstrating the concept 23.1 and Demonstrating the concept 23.2.

What–if and sensitivity analysis

In making a decision, the final outcome can be sensitive to the assumed future external events. This always leads to the question, 'What if this happens?' or, 'What if that occurs?' The following is an example.

Construction of cruise ships

The demand for holiday cruises increased at an annual average rate of 9% between 1980 and 1993. Based on this rapid growth, major cruise line companies such as Carnival, Royal Caribbean Cruises, and Princess Cruises (owned by Peninsular & Oriental Steam Navigation Co. (P&O)) were adding new cruise ships to their fleet, as indicated in Table 23.1. Some of these ships have

Table 23.1 What–if analysis and cruise liner construction

Cruise line	1 April 1995	Net estimate 1998 (includes retirements)	Growth (%)
Carnival	23,995	40,041	67
Royal Caribbean Cruises	13,216	24,724	87
Princess Cruises	10,070	16,570	65
Kloster Cruise	9,539	9,735	2
Cunard Line	6,896	5,319	−23
Celebrity Cruises	4,760	10,150	113

casinos, 18-hole miniature golf courses, and wedding chapels. They cost up to $400 million.[4]

In 1994 passenger growth dropped to 2.2%. Thus, there was a big risk in constructing new lines. Demand is very sensitive to passenger growth and the question asked in the industry is, 'What if the passenger growth fails to materialize?' All this extra capacity will be under-utilized at enormous cost (see Table 23.1).[5]

Under decision making with conditions of risk, the choice of the decision is a function, or is sensitive to the probability values. Probabilities are difficult to quantify exactly, and thus there is a risk in making a decision based on precise probabilities. A sensitivity analysis will show how the final decision might change, with various probabilities.

Payoff tables

Payoff tables are another way of using expected values to analyze the various alternatives available in decision making. Their use was considered in Chapter 11, covering long and short costs.

Method

A matrix is prepared showing all the possible outcomes for the various options available, according to the likely external events. These outcomes are then weighted according to the given probabilities to determine the expected values. The alternative is chosen which has the highest expected value.

Analysis

Again, since only one state of nature is possible, the expected value is only a quantitative measure to determine the best path to take. The real outcome will be only one of the external events or states of nature, since the states of nature are mutually exclusive.

When a situation is a recurring event, such as an inventory stocking, using payoff tables may not give the optimum result each time. What the payoff tables do is to optimize the best alternative in the long run, on the assumption that the probability data remain constant. Again, there is the question of sensitivity in that the chosen decision is based on the probability estimates. If these change, then the decision alternative may be modified.

The use of payoff tables is illustrated in Demonstrating the concept 23.2.

Marginal analysis

Decision making using marginal analysis is an evaluation involving probabilities, and expected values, to consider the additional benefit of taking some particular action, compared to the outcome if that action is not taken.

Probability relationship

Consider the situation of a company that makes standardized products for sale.

- MP is the marginal profit obtained from making an additional item of inventory and which is subsequently sold.
- ML is marginal loss from making an additional item of inventory and which remains unsold in inventory.
- p is the probability of selling this additional unit.
- Thus $(1 - p)$ is the probability of not selling this additional unit since it is a binomial situation.
- The expected marginal profit is the probability that the unit will be sold multiplied by the marginal profit, or $p*MP$.
- The expected marginal loss is the probability of not selling that unit multiplied by the marginal loss, or $(1 - p)*ML$.

Using a marginal analysis approach in decision making, an additional unit would only be produced if the subsequent marginal profit were greater than or equal to the marginal loss. Mathematically, this is given by:

$$p*MP \geq (1 - p)*ML$$

Reorganizing to make p the subject:

$$p*MP \geq (1 - p)*ML$$
$$p*MP \geq ML - p*ML$$
$$p*(MP + ML) \geq ML$$

Which gives:

$$p \geq \frac{ML}{MP + ML}$$

- The value of p given by these expressions is now the minimum required probability of selling at least one additional unit of stock, which would justify the making of that additional unit.
- It would only make sense to make additional units as long as the probability of selling at least an additional unit is greater than p.

Figure 23.4 Normal distribution

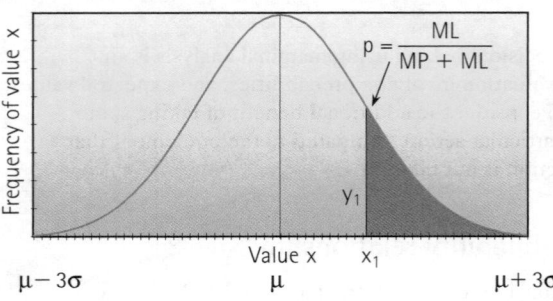

The use of marginal analysis is illustrated in Demonstrating the concept 23.3.

Normal probability distributions and marginal analysis

If the assumption can be made that the distribution of the sale, or stocking of a product follows a normal distribution, then marginal analysis can be used in conjunction with the normal distribution. (See Chapter 27 for more on the normal distribution.)

A normal distribution is given in Figure 23.4. Shown on this distribution is:

- The mean value μ and a standard deviation σ.
- The value of x at the extreme left of the curve is $(\mu - 3\sigma)$.
- The value of x at the extreme right of the curve is $(\mu + 3\sigma)$.

Applying the normal distribution, the probability of occurrence:

- Probability of selling $(\mu - 3\sigma)$ units or more is 100%.
- Probability of selling μ units or more is 50%.
- Probability of selling $(\mu + 3\sigma)$ units or more is 0%.

Thus, the more one moves from left to right on the curve, the probability of selling a certain quantity of units declines. Alternatively putting it another way, the area to the right of any particular point is the probability of selling that quantity of units, or more.

On the curve is a vertical line y_1 at a value of X of x_1. The probability of selling this quantity, or more, is given by the area of the curve to the right of the line y_1. As one moves more to the right, the probability diminishes. In marginal analysis this probability value is given by the following relationship:

$$p \geqslant \frac{ML}{(MP + ML)}$$

This idea is illustrated in Demonstrating the concept 23.4.

When expected values are not the decision-making criteria

Utility

To use expected values, the probability of each outcome is multiplied by the payoff or net return of that outcome. The alternative, which produces the highest expected value, is then the selected option. However, because of fear, gut feeling, or risk-averse personalities, decisions are not always made according to the expected value. This anomaly gives rise to the concept of utility. Utility can be considered as the satisfaction, the disappointment, or even nervousness, as the result of a certain outcomes.

Gambling

Consider a gambler at a casino. In a certain blackjack game, the probability of winning is 70%. Alternatively, since the outcome is binomial, the probability of losing is 30% (100 − 70). Table 23.2 illustrates the expected gains for gambling when placing bets of $5, $50, $500, $5000, $50,000, $100,000 and $1,000,000.

In all cases, the 'expected gain' is greater than the 'expected loss', or greater than the level of bet. Thus, if expected value were the decision criteria used, the gambler would always play. However, in reality this is not the case:

- Placing a bet of $5 causes little concern, even if one loses. The payoff, if the gambler wins, is $500 with an expected outcome of $350 (500 × 70%).
- In the next situation, one might be a more cautious of putting down $50, even though the potential winnings are $5000 with an expected gain of $3500.

As the value of the bet placed becomes higher, a gambler (usually!) becomes more and more cautious about placing a bet, and may refuse to place bets at the $50,000 and $100,000 levels, even though the expected gain is greater than both the expected loss and the value of the bet. In this case, the prospect, or the utility in the mind of the gambler of losing $50,000 or $100,000 outweighs the prospect of winning.

The utility concept is illustrated in Figure 23.5. Utility is given an arbitrary index number ranging from 0 to 200 (satisfaction) and 0 to −500 (disappointment, or fear). The satisfaction or utility of winning up to

Table 23.2 Gambling and probability of winning

Level of the bet ($)	Potential winnings or payoff ($)	Probability of winning (%)	Probability of losing (%)	Expected gain ($)	Expected loss ($)
5	500	70	30	350	150
50	5,000	70	30	3,500	1,500
500	50,000	70	30	35,000	15,000
5,000	500,000	70	30	350,000	150,000
50,000	5,000,000	70	30	3,500,000	1,500,000
100,000	10,000,000	70	30	7,000,000	3,000,000
1,000,000	100,000,000	70	30	70,000,000	30,000,000

Figure 23.5 Utility of profit and loss

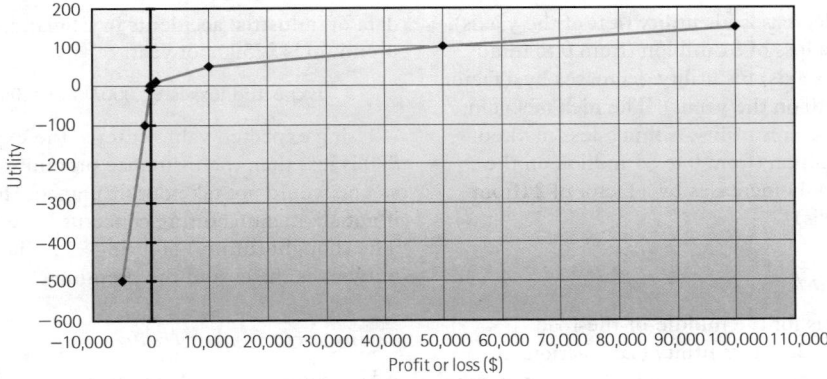

$100,000 increases with the amount of gain. However, the fear or utility of losing decreases at a much sharper rate. There are different utility curves, for different individuals as some people fear loss greater than others.

Managers with different personalities

Figure 23.6 illustrates the concept of utility and risk. Here, utility has been given an index of 0 to 10 (positive utility, or satisfaction) and 0 to −10 (negative utility, or disappointment).

Risk taker

The lower curve, Manager C, is for the risk taker. For this person, taking a great risk is a big challenge. He gets a 'high'. Thus, his satisfaction of reaping great

rewards such as an acquisition, succeeding with a new product, or making a stock investment, increases sharply. Thus, with high profits, the slope of his utility curve is high (the portion of the curve to the right of the y axis). For example, if his profit increases by $1 million (from 0 to $1 million on the x axis), then his utility increases by a factor of 18 (from −8 to 10 on the y axis). In contrast, his disappointment, or loss, is relatively less intense as illustrated by the smaller slope to the left of the y axis. For a loss of $1 million (from 0 to minus $1 million on the x axis) his utility, or disappointment only changes by a factor of 2 (from −8 to −10 on the y axis).

Risk averse

The upper curve, Manager A, is for the risk-averse individual. Here the situation is reversed. The thought

Figure 23.6 Utility for managers' different personalities

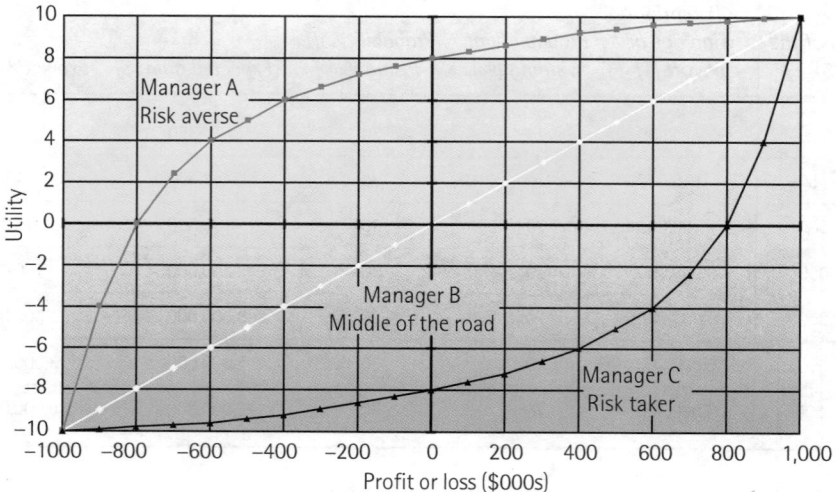

of a loss sharply decreases his utility (left of the y axis). For example, for a loss of $1 million (from 0 to minus $1 million on the x axis) his utility decreases by a factor of 18 (from 8 to −10 on the y axis). The idea of a gain, although it increases his utility, is much less marked. For a gain of $1 million (from 0 to $1 million on the x axis) his utility only increases by a factor of 2 (from 8 to 10 on the y axis).

Middle of the road

The centre curve is for the middle-of-the-road manager, Manager B, where utility (satisfaction, or disappointment) is of equal value whether the outcome is a gain or a loss. Here for a gain of $1 million his utility increases tenfold (from 0 to plus 10 on the curve). For a loss of $1 million his utility decreases tenfold (from 0 to −10 on the curve).

Insurance

The insurance industry makes its fortune on risk. (Insurance is a bad investment if one never has a claim.)

Industrial insurance

A company operates a small manufacturing operation producing steel and aluminium aircraft components. The facility is constructed of brick. The company is valued at £2 million. The probability of the company being destroyed by fire is 0.001% based on historical

data of industrial accidents in England. The insurance premium is £2500 per year:

$$\text{Expected loss is } £2,000,000 * 0.00001 = £20$$

Using expected value criteria, the expected loss of £20 is less than the insurance premium of £2500 and so one would not take out insurance. However, most, if not all, manufacturing concerns have insurance. The thought (utility) of losing £2 million in assets far outweighs the cost of the premium.

Transportation insurance

A US manufacturer of compressors sends a new installation to Germany for use in a pharmaceutical operation. The value of the equipment is $4 million.

The probability of the equipment being damaged, or lost, is 1 in 10,000, or 0.01%:

$$\text{Expected loss is } \$4 * 0.0001 = \$400$$

$$\text{Insuring the equipment cost} = \$2000$$

Since $2000 is greater than the $400, then using expected value criteria, one would not insure the merchandise. However, losing $4 million would be very heavy for the company, and thus it takes out insurance.

Earthquake insurance

Some homes in southern California (especially in Beverly Hills, Brentwood, and San Marino) have market values in excess of $1 million. The possibility of a home being completely destroyed by an earthquake is small (although not remote according to geologists' reports on the San Andreas Fault). Many people have earthquake insurance that can cost upwards of $1000 every year. This is greater than the expected loss. The thought (utility) of losing one's home greatly outweighs the insurance cost.

Flight insurance

Some insurance companies (Travellers in the USA is one) have 'do-it-yourself' insurance booths at major airports. Here, for example, for $10 one is able to take out a life insurance of say $100,000 in the event the airplane crashes:

Probability of the plane crashing is 1 in 500,000 or 0.0002%

Expected loss, if an accident, is $100,000 * 0.000002 = 0.20

This expected loss is less than the insurance premium, and under expected value criteria one would not take out life insurance. However, many travellers do since if there were an accident, the loss of the family breadwinner would be disastrous.

Overall life insurance is a bad investment (the probability of dying prematurely is low) but with the concept of utility many people have life insurance. (With good returns to the insurance companies!!)

Cost–benefit analysis

A cost–benefit analysis is an analytical tool used to decide whether expenditures for a certain project are greater than or less than the 'financial' benefits which would be obtained if the project were executed. If the costs are less, then the decision should be made to go ahead with the project; the reverse if the costs are greater.

Governments

A cost–benefit analysis is a decision tool often used in government agencies. In the USA it was popular under the administrations of Presidents Kennedy and Johnson in the 1960s. It is often used related to environmental situations as the following illustrates.

Phelps Dodge

Phelps Dodge Corporation operated a copper smelter in Douglas, Arizona, for nearly 80 years. For nearly a decade, in the 1970s, and early 1980s the facility failed to meet US Environmental Clean Air laws. After a

cost–benefit analysis, the Company decided to close the facility permanently in 1987. It was felt that the benefits to the operation by the installation of new pollution control equipment to reduce sulphur dioxide emissions were far outweighed by the millions of dollars that would be required to do the work. The plant closure put 347 people out of work, and removed $10 million from the local economy.[6]

Demonstrating the concept 23.5 illustrates the use of cost–benefit analysis.

Summary of key elements

- Any aspect of business (and, indeed, life) involves making a decision. A corollary to this is that decision making invokes risk. The more systematic one is analyzing the variables involved in the decision, the less likely is the downside risk.

- A trade-off is making a choice between one outcome and another where both have advantages and disadvantages.

- When there are several decisions to make it is helpful to prioritize them.

- The magnitude and cost of decision making can range from intuition, quick and dirty, mathematical computations, model building, to implementing a taskforce.

- The decision process involves understanding reasons for a decision, analyzing the situation, defining objectives, developing and analyzing alternatives, selecting the best alternative, executing plans, and, afterwards, monitoring the results.

- The environment for decision making includes decision making under certainty, decision making under risk, and decision making under uncertainty.

- In decision theory there are changes in the environment, or states of nature, over which a manager has no control. Each of these states of nature can produce some financial payoff.

- In decision making under certainty, the future outcomes are known with certainty.

- In decision making under uncertainty, there is no clear information on the external environment, so it is difficult to establish probabilities. Some decision approaches under uncertainty include maximin, maximax, equally likely, and minimax regret.

- In decision making under risk, probabilities can be assigned to outcomes. Then expected values can be determined which can be used as criteria for making a decision.

• A decision tree is a pictorial representation of decision alternatives. Square nodes indicate a decision point where management has control and circular nodes represent the states of nature where probabilities can be assigned but where management has no control. Lines or 'branches' give the direction of the decision. Payoffs for the possible outcomes are shown for all possible decisions that can be made according to each state of nature.

• The expected value of perfect information is the difference between the expected value under certainty and the expected value under risk. It would not make sense to pay more than the expected value of certain information to be more certain of an outcome.

• Many decisions are dependent on the external environment. A 'what-if' analysis looks at the sensitivity of the decision with assumed changes in the external environment.

• A payoff table is a matrix showing all the possible outcomes for various options available, according to the likely external events. These outcomes are then weighted according to the given probabilities to determine expected values.

• Marginal analysis uses probabilities and expected values to consider the benefit of some action, as opposed to the outcome if that action is not taken. The minimum probability is the ratio of marginal loss to (marginal loss plus marginal profit).

• Utility is the satisfaction, or disappointment, derived from certain outcomes. People have different utility levels and this can impact the apparent logic of a decision.

• A cost–benefit analysis is a decision tool used to decide whether the expenditures for a certain project are greater than the perceived financial benefits if the project were to be executed.

Notes and references

1. ORDONEZ, Jennifer, 'Burger King sought the perfect fry but got burned: Sales soon went limp for crispier potato stick', *Wall Street Journal Europe*, 17 January 2001, p. 1
2. HISRICH, Robert D. and PETERS, Michael P., *Marketing Decisions for New and Mature Products*, Merrill, Columbus, Ohio, 1984
3. 'So you fail: Now bounce back', *Fortune*, 1 May 1995, p. 45
4. *Business Week*, 1 May 1995
5. 'The Love boats are brawling: They're launching lush new ships – and small lines may sink', *Business Week*, 8 May 1995, p. 64
6. SHIELDS, Tom, 'Smelter's billows depart Arizona sky', *USA Today*, 15 January 1987, p. 3A

Review and discussion topics

1. Personal decision making
What are some of the biggest decisions you have made in your life? What was the element of risk? Did you make an in-depth analysis before you took the decision? Did the result turn out as planned?

2. Cost–benefit analysis
What are some of the elements you would consider in a cost–benefit analysis for the following situations? Indicate those elements that you believe are difficult to quantify. What are some of the elements which should be taken into account, but which probably don't enter into the decision process?
(a) tree cutting in the Brazilian rainforest
(b) recycling programme for plastic bottles
(c) building a new town hall in your community
(d) closing hospitals in Britain.

3. Magnitude of decision making
Considering the magnitude of decision making, under which category would you put the following decisions?
(a) purchasing a new suit
(b) building an express train link between Berlin and Paris
(c) deciding whether to take early retirement
(d) deciding whether to give your child a university education at a private institution in the United States.

4. Decision trees
Develop a decision tree showing the various paths in your professional career up to retirement. Indicate on the tree the decisions over which you believe you have control, and the states of nature over which you have little control. Attempt to put in probabilities on the decision tree. How sensitive is your plan to the environment?

5. Utility
In the concept of utility, would you consider yourself a risk taker, risk averse or middle of the road? Give examples to justify your classification. If you are not satisfied with your analysis, what might you be able to do to change?

6. E-learning and a cost–benefit analysis
The concept of e-learning or learning at a distance is becoming more and more popular. Universities and business schools are developing their own customized distance learning programmes. Industry is very interested, since they believe in the long run it will be more cost effective for them. Use the concept of a cost–benefit analysis and highlight all the 'costs' and 'benefits' associated with e-learning. Do you think the benefits outweigh the costs?

Demonstrating the concept 23.1   Polyethylene

Situation

An international chemical company is considering increasing its worldwide polyethylene capacity. Polyethylene is a plastic common in the manufacture of packaging materials, automobile components, kitchen utensils, etc. The following are the possible alternatives that management is reviewing for this project:

- build a new grassroots facility
- expand an existing plant
- establish a joint venture with an overseas company.

After some extensive studies, and initial designs, the estimated net present values of the payoff (net return) in $millions for the three alternatives, at three different scenario levels of future polyethylene demand, are as shown in Table 23.3.

Required

1. What would be the preferred decision if management were:
   (a) pessimistic in its decision approach
   (b) optimistic in its decision approach
   (c) middle of the road in its decision approach
   (d) of the opinion to use the minimax regret approach to decision making?
2. After a further market study was performed, the company developed some probability estimates for the market outcome, shown in Table 23.4.
   Using this information what would be the preferred decision?
3. What is the expected value of perfect information (EVPI)? How is this interpreted?
4. Management believes that, although the probability of a stable market at 35% is a reasonable estimate, there is uncertainty of the probabilities for the low and high market demand. Some people involved in the analysis believe that the value of 20% for a low market demand is too high. Others believe it is too low. Illustrate on a graph, the sensitivity of the decision process for all possible ranges of a low demand. (Since the stable market probability is considered fixed at 35%, the possible range of the low probability is 0 to 65%. Correspondingly, the ranges of high demand will then be from 65% to 0%, since the total probabilities must add up to unity.)
5. Develop a decision tree to illustrate the situation and solution, under a condition of risk as presented in question 2. How would the decision be interpreted?

Table 23.3 Estimated net present values of payoff ($ millions)

Project decision	Low market demand	Stable market demand	High market demand
Grassroots	−50	30	100
Expansion	−25	50	75
Joint venture	10	30	45

Table 23.4 Probability estimates for market outcome

Future market	Low market demand	Stable market demand	High market demand
Probability (%)	20	35	45

6. After further discussion, management came up with the following modified situation:
   - If the grassroots alternative were selected, and the market demand were high, the company had an option to expand the capacity. In this case, the estimated payoff would be $125 million instead of $100 million.
   - If the joint venture alternative were selected, and the market demand were high, the company had an option to increase its percentage share in the joint venture. In this case, the estimated payoff would be $65 million instead of $45 million.

   Use decision trees to illustrate the preferred decision for management.
7. What is the expected value of perfect information for the modified situation presented in question 6?

Solution

1. In this first situation, no estimates of probability are given and so this is decision making under uncertainty. The details of the decisions to make are given in Table 23.5. An explanation follows.
   (a) Pessimistic is a maximin approach. Here, the decision would be to select the joint venture alternative, since $10 million is 'best' of the worst alternatives.

Table 23.5 Decision making under uncertainty

	Payoff ($millions according to market)		
	Low	Stable	High
Grassroots	−50	30	100
Expansion	−25	50	75
Joint venture	10	30	45

Maximin	Minimum	
Grass roots	−50	
Expansion	−25	
Joint venture	**10**	
Maximum	10	**Select joint venture**

Maximax	Maximum	
Grassroots	**100**	
Expansion	75	
Joint venture	45	
Maximum	100	**Select grassroots**

Average	Maximum	
Grassroots	26.67	
Expansion	**33.33**	
Joint venture	28.33	
Maximum	33.33	**Select expansion**

Minimax regret

	Payoff ($millions according to market)		
	Low	Stable	High
Grassroots	−50	30	**100**
Expansion	−25	**50**	75
Joint venture	**10**	30	45

Bold text are 'best results' according to market

Regret matrice

	'Best' minus the selected option		
	Low	Stable	High
Grassroots	60	20	0
Expansion	35	0	25
Joint venture	0	20	55

Maximum regret

Grassroots	60	
Expansion	**35**	
Joint venture	55	
Min of max	35	**Select expansion**

Table gives the maximum 'regret' or disappointment in not selecting the best decision.
The minimum of this gives the least painful regret.

(b) Optimistic is a maximax approach. Here, the decision would be to select the grassroots facility, since $100 million is the maximum possible outcome.
(c) Middle of the road is an equally likely approach. Here, expansion would be the preferred alternative, as the average value of the outcome is the highest, at $33.33 million.

$$\text{Average of grassroots option} = \frac{-50 + 30 + 100}{3}$$
$$= \$26.67 \text{ million}$$

$$\text{Average of expansion option} = \frac{-25 + 50 + 75}{3}$$
$$= \$33.33 \text{ million}$$

$$\text{Average of joint venture option} = \frac{10 + 30 + 45}{3}$$
$$= \$28.33 \text{ million}$$

In practice, if all the payoff values are realistic numbers, the $33.33 million is not a realizable value since the future market can only be low, stable, or high, but not all three. The equally likely calculated value is just a quantitative indicator used as a form of hedging to 'optimize' the best decision.
(d) From the payoff tables, the 'best' outcome is determined:
  • The difference between the best outcome, and the selected option according to the environment is calculated. This is the regret in financial terms of not deciding on the choice.
  • The maximum regret for each decision is determined.
  • The minimum of the maximum is determined, which is the least painful regret.
2. Since there is now an estimate of the probability of the outcomes, this represents decision making under risk. To decide on the preferred alternative, the expected value of the outcome is determined by weighting using the probability values.

Expected values

Grassroots $= -50 * 0.20 + 30 * 0.35 + 100 * 0.45$
$= \$45.50$ million

Expansion $= -25 * 0.20 + 50 * 0.35 + 75 * 0.45$
$= \$46.25$ million

Joint venture $= 10 * 0.20 + 30 * 0.35 + 45 * 0.45$
$= \$32.75$ million

The expansion project has the highest expected value and thus, this represents the best alternative. The expected value is not a realizable value (only one

Table 23.6 Decision making under risk

| | Payoff ($millions according to market) | | | |
	Low	Stable	High	EV
Grassroots	−50	30	100	45.50
Expansion	−25	50	75	46.25
Joint venture	10	30	45	32.75
Probability (%)	20.00	35.00	45.00	
Maximum				**46.25 Select expansion**

Table 23.7 Expected value of perfect information

Expected value under certainty	64.50
Expected value under risk	46.25
Expected value of perfect information	18.25

of the future market conditions is possible). The expected value is a quantitative indicator used as a type of hedging to minimize risk by taking into account all the possibilities. The calculation on an Excel spreadsheet is given in Table 23.6.

3. The expected value of perfect information is the difference between the expected value under certainty, and the expected value under risk.

Expected value under certainty

• If it were known in advance that the market for polyethylene would be high, the decision would be to build a grassroots facility, giving a net payoff of $100 million.
• If it were known in advance that the market for polyethylene would be stable, the decision would be to expand an existing facility, giving a net payoff of $50 million.
• If it were known in advance that the market for polyethylene would be low, the decision would be to go into a joint venture, giving a net payoff of $10 million.

The expected value under certainty is thus the weighted probability of best payoff for each alternative:

$$10 * 0.20 + 50 * 0.35 + 100 * 0.45 = \$64.50 \text{ million}$$

Expected value under risk

This is the best outcome considering probabilities for each alternative. The value was calculated in answer to question 2 and is $46.25 million for the expansion option. Thus:

$$EVPI = 64.50 - 46.25 = \$18.25 \text{ million}$$

This means that $18.25 million is the maximum amount one should be willing to spend to obtain perfect information. It would not make sense to spend more than $18.25 million to develop a more detailed market survey, or to sign contracts with prospective clients to guarantee future sales of

polyethylene. More than $18.25 million would mean that it is better to take the risk and choose the project with the highest expected value (the expansion project in this case).

In this situation, obtaining perfect information for a future market is impossible. However, the example illustrates that there is a limit to how much one should be willing to spend to minimize risk. Expected value of perfect information is a value to be taken into consideration when contracts are being considered for 'guaranteeing' a certain sales level.

These calculations in the Excel format are also given in Table 23.7.

4. The probability data for the future market demand are given as precise figures. Probabilities in reality may be different from that which is assumed and as such, a decision is sensitive to the external environment.

Figure 23.7 shows the change in expected values as the probability of a low market increases from 0 to 65% (this means that correspondingly, the probability of a high market decreases from 65 to 0%) on the assumption that the probability of a stable market rests fixed at 35%. The graph illustrates that:

• At a probability of low demand between 0 and 18.50% the decision to build a grassroots facility would be the preferred decision.
• At a probability of low demand between 18.50% and 40.77% the decision to expand an existing facility would be the preferred decision.
• At a probability of low demand between 40.77 and 65.00% the decision to establish a joint venture would be the preferred decision.

The values 18.50% and 40.77% are the breakeven probabilities between the grassroots and expansion option and the expansion, and joint-venture options respectively. The breakeven values are determined as follows:

$$EV(\text{grassroots}) = p_L * GR_L + p_S * GR_S + p_H * GR_H$$

$$EV(\text{expansion}) = p_L * EX_L + p_S * EX_S + p_H * EX_H$$

$$EV(\text{joint venture}) = p_L * JV_L + p_S * JV_S + p_H * JV_H$$

where GR, EX, and JV refer to the payoff values for the grassroots, expansion, and joint venture options respectively, and p_L, p_S, and p_H are the probability values for low, stable, and high market demand.

Figure 23.7 Polyethylene project: Sensitivity

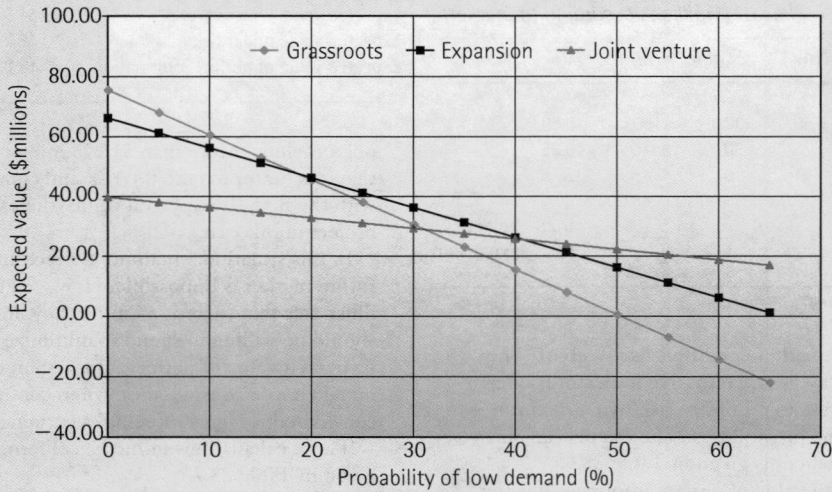

The breakeven point between the grassroots decision and expansion is given when their expected values are equal or:

$$p_L * GR_L + p_S * GR_S + p_H * GR_H = p_L * EX_L + p_S * EX_S + p_H * EX_H$$

since:

$$p_H = 1 - p_L - p_S$$

then:

$$p_L * GR_L + p_S * GR_S + p_H * GR_H = p_L * EX_L + p_S * EX_S + p_H * EX_H$$

$$p_L * GR_L + p_S * GR_S + (1 - p_L - p_S) * GR_H = p_L * EX_L + p_S * EX_S + (1 - p_L - p_S) * EX_H$$

$$p_L * GR_L + p_S * GR_S + GR_H - p_L * GR_H - p_S * GR_H = p_L * EX_L + p_S * EX_S + EX_H - p_L * EX_H - p_S * EX_H$$

giving:

$$p_L = \frac{p_S * (EX_S - EX_H - GR_S + GR_H) + EX_H - GR_H}{GR_L - GR_H - EX_L + EX_H}$$

In a similar manner, the probability at breakeven between the expansion and joint venture options is given by the following relationship:

$$p_L = \frac{p_S * (EX_S - EX_H - JV_S + JV_H) + EX_H - JV_H}{JV_L - JV_H - EX_L + EX_H}$$

And, for the grassroots and joint venture options:

$$p_L = \frac{p_S * (JV_S - JV_H - GR_S + GR_H) + JV_H - GR_H}{GR_L - GR_H - JV_L + JV_H}$$

The computations for the data are given in Table 23.8.

The information illustrates the sensitivity of the decision to the probability. If the probability of low demand drops from 20% and high demand increases from 45% (the given values) to, say, 18% and 47% respectively (a small variation) then the best decision would be to build a grassroots facility.

5. Figure 23.8 gives the decision tree for this situation. The square node N° 1 is the starting point for the decision process. The circular nodes, N° 2, N° 3, and N° 4, represent the states in the environment. The payoff for each possible alternative is indicated on the right of the diagram.

Figure 23.9 is the analysis for this situation. The expected value calculations (already developed in question 2) are presented above each of the circular nodes. The branches for the grassroots and joint venture options are crossed with a double line (debranched), illustrating that these are not the preferred decision since their expected values are lower, $45.50 and $32.75 million respectively, compared to the expansion option (the preferred decision) with an expected value of $46.25 million. The interpretation of the decision to expand an existing facility is:

• The company will realize a net payoff of $75 million if the market change is high

• $50 million if the market remains stable.

• a loss of $25 million if the market demand is low.

6. Figure 23.10 gives the decision tree for this problem. The new square nodes N° 5 and N° 6 are the additional decisions to be made if either the grassroots option is selected, and the market demand

Table 23.8 Sensitivity

| | Payoff ($millions according to market) | | |
	Low	Stable	High
Grassroots	−50	30	100
Expansion	−25	50	75
Joint venture	10	30	45

| Probability of market conditions (%) | | | Expected value | | | |
Low	Stable	High	Grassroots	Expansion	Joint venture	Maximum
0	35	65	**75.50**	66.25	39.75	75.50
5	35	60	**68.00**	61.25	38.00	68.00
10	35	55	**60.50**	56.25	36.25	60.50
15	35	50	**53.00**	51.25	34.50	53.00
20	35	45	45.50	**46.25**	32.75	46.25
25	35	40	38.00	**41.25**	31.00	41.25
30	35	35	30.50	**36.25**	29.25	36.25
35	35	30	23.00	**31.25**	27.50	31.25
40	35	25	15.50	**26.25**	25.75	26.25
45	35	20	8.00	21.25	**24.00**	24.00
50	35	15	0.50	16.25	**22.25**	22.25
55	35	10	−7.00	11.25	**20.50**	20.50
60	35	5	−14.50	6.25	**18.75**	18.75
65	35	0	−22.00	1.25	**17.00**	17.00

Breakeven points

| | | | | Expected value | |
Between	Low (%)	Stable (%)	High (%)	Grassroots	Expansion
Grassroots and expansion	18.50	35.00	46.50	47.75	47.75

| | | | | Expected value | |
Between	Low (%)	Stable (%)	High (%)	Expansion	Joint venture
Expansion and joint venture	40.77	35.00	24.23	25.48	25.48

| | | | | Expected value | |
Between	Low (%)	Stable (%)	High (%)	Grassroots	Joint venture
Grassroots and joint venture	31.09	35.00	33.91	28.87	28.87

is high, or the joint venture option is selected, and the demand is high.

Figure 23.11 gives the analysis and path for the preferred decision. The grassroots option is now the preferred decision with an expected value of $56.75 million. This is arrived at as follows:

• Debranch the path 'maintain capacity' for the alternative at node 5 for the grassroots option

Figure 23.8 Polyethylene project: Initial situation

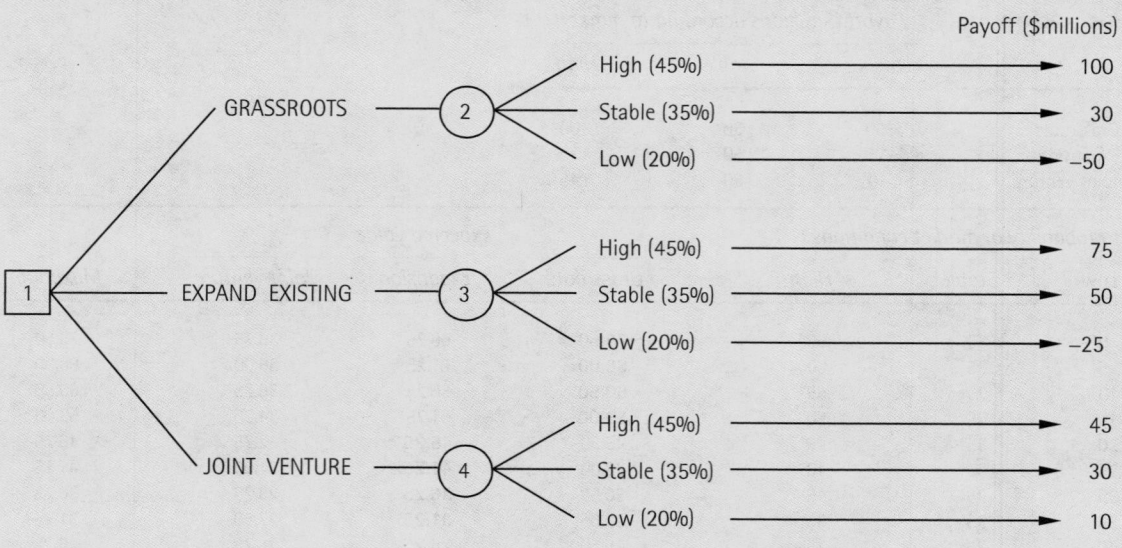

Figure 23.9 Polyethylene project: Solution to initial situation

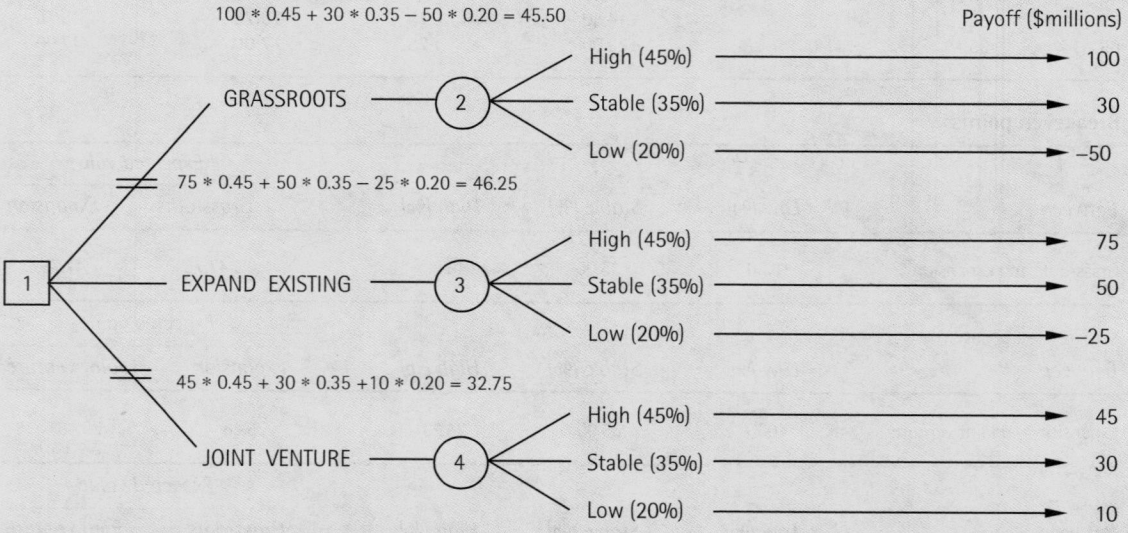

since 'maintain capacity' has a lower payoff than 'expand'.

• Debranch the path 'maintain share' for the alternative at node 6 for the joint venture option since 'maintain capacity' has a lower payoff than 'increase share'.

• Calculate the expected value at each of the three circular nodes, 2, 3, and 4, using the payoff value of

$125 million for the payoff if there is high demand for the grassroots option, and $65 million for the payoff if there is high demand after the joint venture option has been selected.

7. The EVPI is the difference between the expected value under certainty, and the expected value under risk.

Figure 23.10   Polyethylene project: Modified situation

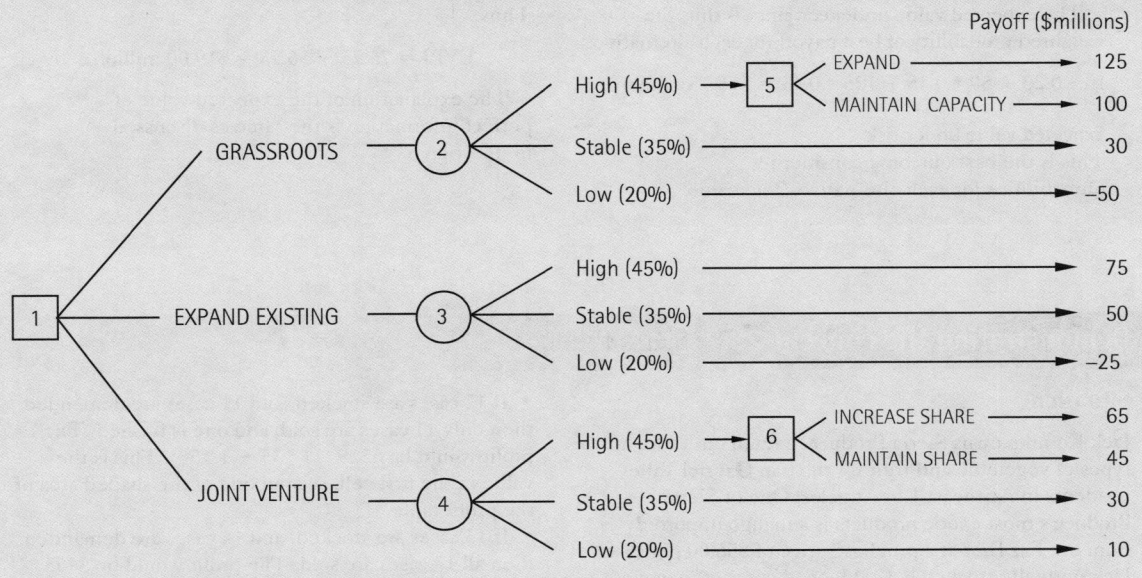

Figure 23.11   Polyethylene project: Solution to modified situation

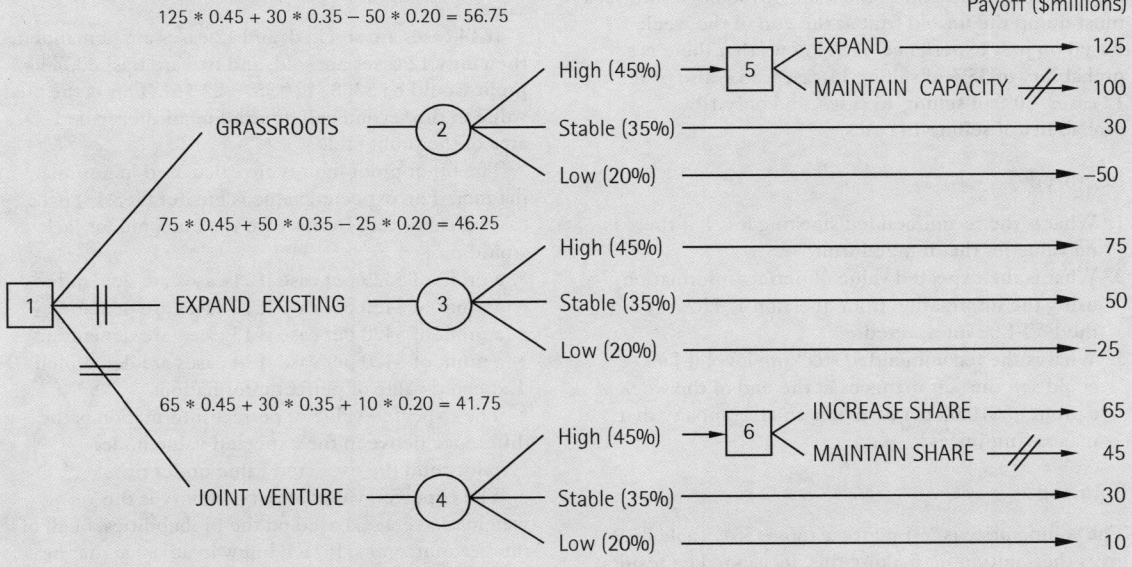

Expected value under certainty
- If it were known in advance that the market for polyethylene would be high, the decision would be to build a grassroots facility and then expanding it, giving a payoff of $125 million.

- If it were known in advance that the market for polyethylene would be stable, the decision would be to expand an existing facility, giving a net payoff of $50 million.
- If it were known in advance that the market for polyethylene would be low, the decision would

be to go into a joint venture giving a net payoff of $10 million.

The expected value under certainty is thus the weighted probability of best payoff for each alternative:

$$10 * 0.20 + 50 * 0.35 + 125 * 0.45 = \$75.75 \text{ million}$$

Expected value under risk
This is the best outcome considering probabilities for each alternative. The value

was calculated in answer to question 6 and is $56.75 million for the grassroots option. Thus:

$$EVPI = 75.75 - 56.75 = \$19.00 \text{ million}$$

The explanation of the expected value of perfect information is the same as discussed in question 3.

Demonstrating the concept 23.2 Sierra Produce

Situation

Jack Komiko owns Sierra Produce, a retail outlet for all types of vegetable and fruit for the San Gabriel Valley residents in northeast Los Angeles. One of Sierra Produce's most exotic products is a mango imported from the Far East at a purchase price of $56.00 per case. Jack normally stocks 11, 12, 13, or 14 cases of mangoes each week. For each case that he sells, he realizes a profit of $35.00. However, since Jack always wants to sell fruit of top quality, and as the mangoes soon go soft, Jack must dump the unsold fruit at the end of the week. Based on past experience, Jack knows that there is a probability of 35% of selling 11 cases, 35% also of selling 12 cases, 20% of selling 13 cases, and only 10% probability of selling 14 cases.

Required

1. What is the recommended stocking level, if there is no value for the dumped fruit?
2. What is the expected value of perfect information using the information from question 1? How would the EVPI be interpreted?
3. What is the recommended stocking level if Jack could sell the soft mangoes at the end of the week at a profit of $10.00 per case, to a small company that makes fruit juices?

Solution

The selling price is $91 per case (56 + 35). Table 23.9 gives the solution for making this decision. The results are arrived at as follows.

1. No value for dumped fruit:
   • If 11 cases are stocked, and 11 cases are demanded, then the entire inventory is sold and the profit would be $385 (11 * 35). This is the value in the top left cell of the shaded area of the profit table.

• If 12 cases are stocked, and 11 cases are demanded, then only 11 cases are sold, and one is trashed. The profit would be $329 (11 * 35 − 1 * 56). This is the value in the first cell, second line of the shaded area of the profit table.
• If 13 cases are stocked, and 14 cases are demanded, then all 13 cases are sold. The profit would be $455 (13 * 35). This is the value in the fourth cell, third line of the shaded area of the profit table. In this case, no consideration is given for opportunity costs (lost sales).
• If 14 cases are stocked, and 12 cases are demanded, then only 12 cases are sold, and two are trashed. The profit would be $308 (12 * 35 − 2 * 56). This is the value in the second cell, fourth line of the shaded area of the profit table.

The other profit figures are calculated in a similar manner. The expected value is greater (388.15) if 12 cases are stocked. In this case the outcome for Jack would be:
• a profit of $329 per case if 11 cases are demanded
• a profit of $420 per case if 12 cases are demanded
• a profit of $420 per case if 13 cases are demanded
• a profit of $420 per case if 14 cases are demanded.

2. Expected value of perfect information:
• The expected value of perfect information is the difference between the expected value under certainty and the expected value under risk.
• The expected value under certainty is the weighted average, based on the probabilities, of all of the best outcomes. If Jack knew in advance that he was going to sell 11 cases, he would only stock 11 cases, giving a profit of $385. If he knew in advance that he was going to sell 12 cases, he would only stock 12 cases, giving a profit of $420. If he knew in advance that he was going to sell 13 cases, he would only stock 13 cases, giving a profit of $455. Finally, if he knew in advance that he was going to sell 14 cases,

Table 23.9 Sierra Produce: Selling price and decision

Selling price, $/case	91
Purchase cost, $/case	56
Profit, $/case	35
Profit on soft mangoes, $/case	10

PROFIT TABLES

Case 1: End of week mangoes dumped

		Cases demanded				
		11	12	13	14	Exp value
Stocking level in number of cases	11	385.00	385.00	385.00	385.00	385.00
	12	329.00	420.00	420.00	420.00	388.15
	13	273.00	364.00	455.00	455.00	359.45
	14	217.00	308.00	399.00	490.00	312.55
Probability		0.35	0.35	0.20	0.10	1.00

Best expected value under risk, $	388.15
Optimum stocking level, cases	12
Expected value under certainty, $	421.75
Expected value of perfect information, $	33.60

Case 2: End of week mangoes sold for fruit juice

		Cases demanded				
		11	12	13	14	Exp value
Stocking level in number of cases	11	385.00	385.00	385.00	385.00	385.00
	12	395.00	420.00	420.00	420.00	411.25
	13	405.00	430.00	455.00	455.00	428.75
	14	415.00	440.00	465.00	490.00	441.25
Probability		0.35	0.35	0.20	0.10	1.00

Best expected value under risk, $	441.25
Optimum stocking level, cases	14

he would only stock 13 cases, giving a profit of $490. Since this information is still subject to probabilities, the expected value under certainty weighting them according to the probabilities is $421.75. The EVPI is the difference between this value and the expected value under risk from question 1, or $33.60. Jack should not spend more than this amount, say on a market study, to be sure of the future market.

3. Sells mangoes for fruit juice:
   • If 11 cases are stocked, and 11 cases are demanded, then the entire inventory is sold, and the profit would

be $385 (11 * 35). This is the value in the top left cell of the shaded area of the profit table.
   • If 12 cases are stocked, and 11 cases are demanded, then 11 cases are sold for their full profit, and one is sold for juice manufacture. The profit would be $395 (11 * 35 + 1 * 10). This is the value in the first cell, second line of the shaded area of the profit table.
   • If 13 cases are stocked, and 14 cases are demanded, then all 13 cases are sold. The profit would be $455 (13 * 35). This is the value in the fourth cell, third line of the shaded area of the profit table. In this case,

no consideration is given for opportunity costs (lost sales).

• If 14 cases are stocked, and 12 cases are demanded, then 12 cases are sold for their full profit and two are sold for juice manufacture. The profit would be $440 (12 * 35 + 2 * 10). This is the value in the second cell, fourth line of the shaded area of the profit table.

The other profit figures are calculated in a similar manner. The expected value is greater ($441.25) if 14 cases are stocked. In this case the outcome for Jack would be:

• a profit of $415 per case if 11 cases are demanded
• a profit of $440 per case if 12 cases are demanded
• a profit of $465 per case if 13 cases are demanded
• a profit of $490 per case if 14 cases are demanded.

Demonstrating the concept 23.3   Adhesive product

Situation

Jameyson Brothers is a small company specializing in carpet laying. Jameyson purchases the organic-based adhesive it uses for carpet-laying drums from a large chemical company. This adhesive dries very quickly, allowing a newly carpeted room to be used within two hours after use. However, the adhesive product has a disadvantage in that if the drums, even unopened, are not used within a week, the adhesive is unusable because it hardens in the drums. In this case, it is sold back to the supplier, which recycles the material. Looking at past data, Jameyson develops Table 23.10, showing drums of adhesive demanded, against the probability of these levels being demanded.

Also, in costing the carpet-laying operation Jameyson calculates that the marginal profit on stocking an additional drum of adhesive as $1.7 and the marginal loss as $2.9.

Required

1. What is the optimum stocking level for Jameyson? At this level, what is the expected marginal profit, and the expected marginal loss?
2. Illustrate the expected marginal loss and expected marginal profit as a graph against stocking level.

Table 23.10 Drums demanded against probability of levels

Drums of adhesive demanded	Probability of this level being demanded	Drums of adhesive demanded	Probability of this level being demanded
0	0.02	6	0.16
1	0.06	7	0.13
2	0.08	8	0.10
3	0.10	9	0.07
4	0.12	10	0.02
5	0.14		

Solution

Table 23.11 gives the solution for this problem.

Column 3 gives the probability values when the probability is equal to, or greater than the amount at a particular demand level. For example:

• At a demand of 0 units, the probability is 0.02. Any demand greater, or equal to zero, must have a probability of all that is left, or 1 or 100%.
• At a demand of 1 unit, the probability is 0.06. Any demand greater, or equal to 1 unit, must have a probability of $(1 - 0.02)$ or 0.98.
• At a demand of 2 units, the probability is 0.08. Any demand greater, or equal to 2 units, must have a probability of $(1 - 0.02 - 0.06)$ or 0.92.
• At a demand of 3 units, the probability is 0.10. Any demand greater, or equal to 3 units, must have a probability of $(1 - 0.02 - 0.06 - 0.08)$ or 0.84.
• Etc.

Column 4 gives the expected marginal profit according to the demand level. It is calculated by $p *$ Marginal profit.

Column 5 gives the expected marginal loss according to the demand level. It is calculated by the relationship $(1 - p) *$ Marginal loss.

The minimum probability to optimize the stocking level is given by:

$$p \geq \frac{ML}{(MP + ML)}$$

where p is the probability, ML is the marginal loss, and MP is the marginal profit

$$p \geq \frac{2.9}{(1.7 + 2.9)}$$

or p must be greater or equal than 0.6304. In this case, this would mean stocking four drums of adhesive where the probability of using four or more drums is 0.74.

The calculation is shown for the marginal loss and marginal profit if four or five drums are stocked.

Table 23.11 Marginal profit and loss for an adhesive product

1 Demand units	2 Prob. of this demand	3 Prob. of this or greater (p)	4 Expected MP	5 Expected ML	6	7
0	0.02	1.00	1.7000	0.0000	Marginal profit, $/drum	1.7
1	0.06	0.98	1.6660	0.0580	Marginal loss, $/drum	2.9
2	0.08	0.92	1.5640	0.2320	Minimum probability	0.63
3	0.10	0.84	1.4280	0.4640		
4	0.12	0.74	1.2580	0.7540	Optimum stocking level in drums	4
5	0.14	0.62	1.0540	1.1020	**If four drums are stocked**	
6	0.16	0.48	0.8160	1.5080	Expected marginal profit	1.258
7	0.13	0.32	0.5440	1.9720	Expected marginal loss	0.754
8	0.10	0.19	0.3230	2.3490		
9	0.07	0.09	0.1530	2.6390	**If five drums are stocked**	
10	0.02	0.02	0.0340	2.8420	Expected marginal profit	1.054
Total	**1.00**		**0.0000**	**2.9000**	Expected marginal loss	1.102

Figure 23.12 Adhesive product: Expected marginal loss and expected marginal profit

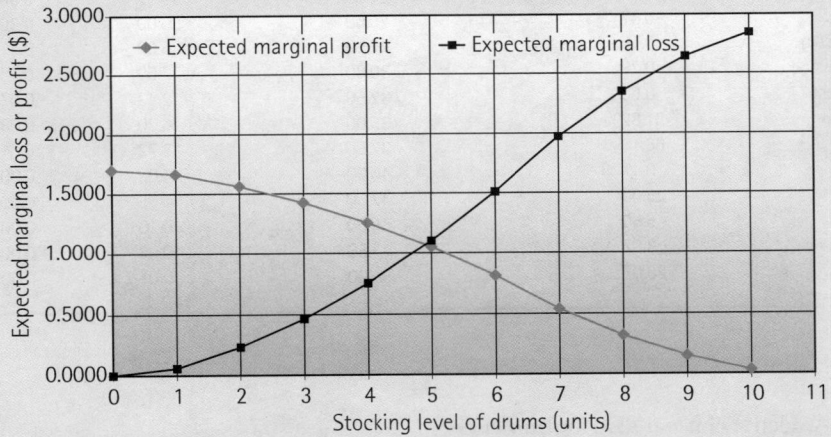

If 4 drums are stocked:

- Marginal profit = 1.7 * 0.74 = $1.258.
- Marginal loss = 2.9 * (1 − 0.74) = $0.754.

or the marginal profit is greater than the marginal loss.
  If 5 drums are stocked:

- Marginal profit = 1.7 * 0.62 = $1.054.

- Marginal loss = 2.9 * (1 − 0.62) = $1.102.

or the marginal profit is less than the marginal loss.
  The change of the expected loss and expected profit with the demand level is given in Figure 23.12.

Demonstrating the concept 23.4 Ardèche

Situation

The Cervelin family, in Ardèche, France, make cheese from the milk they obtain from their cows. The cheese-making process is simple. To the milk is added rennet, which makes the milk curdle. Additives are added for flavour and then the product is air dried and cut into portions. The cheese is sold at the local market.

From past data the average daily sales of cheese is 25 kg with a standard deviation of 6.5 kg. The cheese is sold at €1.07 per kg and costs €0.47 per kg to make.

The customers who buy the cheese want it fresh so that any taken to the market and not purchased is sold to the local farmer for pig feed for €0.19 per kg.

Required

1. Determine the optimum cheese production level in kgs for the Cervelin family.
2. Validate this production level by plotting expected profit against expected loss.

Solution

1. The calculation procedure is given in Table 23.12. This is explained as follows.

   The marginal loss is the difference between the production cost and the pig feed price, or
   $0.47 - 0.19 = €0.28$.

Table 23.12 Optimum cheese production levels

Sales price, €/kg	1.07
Cost, €/kg	0.47
Pig food price, €/kg	0.19
ML = Cost − Salvage	0.28
MP = Price − Cost	0.60
p limit	31.82%
(1 − p)	68.18%
z	0.4728
Mean	25.00
σ	6.50
σ*z	3.07
Kg to make	28.07

The marginal profit is the difference between the sales price and the production cost, or
$1.07 - 0.47 = €0.60$.

Table 23.13 Expected profit and loss table

Cheese demanded (kg)	Probability (p) of selling this amount or more (%)	Expected marginal profit	Expected marginal loss
0.00	99.99	0.6000	0.0000
2.50	99.97	0.5998	0.0001
5.00	99.90	0.5994	0.0003
7.50	99.65	0.5979	0.0010
10.00	98.95	0.5937	0.0029
12.50	97.28	0.5837	0.0076
15.00	93.80	0.5628	0.0174
17.50	87.57	0.5254	0.0348
20.00	77.91	0.4675	0.0618
22.50	64.97	0.3898	0.0981
25.00	50.00	0.3000	0.1400
27.50	35.03	0.2102	0.1819
30.00	22.09	0.1325	0.2182
32.50	12.43	0.0746	0.2452
35.00	6.20	0.0372	0.2626
37.50	2.72	0.0163	0.2724
40.00	1.05	0.0063	0.2771
42.50	0.35	0.0021	0.2790
45.00	0.10	0.0006	0.2797
47.50	0.03	0.0002	0.2799
50.00	0.01	0.0000	0.2800

Figure 23.13 Ardèche: Normal distribution curve

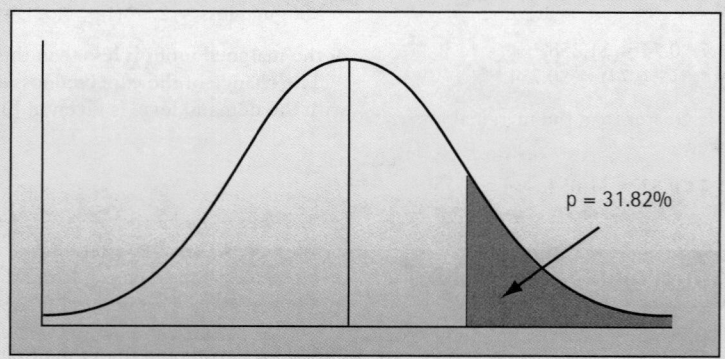

p = 31.82%

Figure 23.14 Ardèche: Cheese production

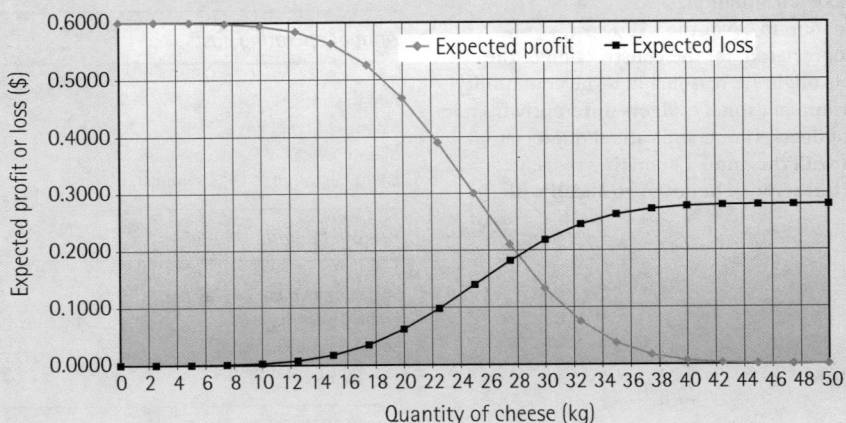

The probability limit is calculated by the ratio ML/(MP + ML) = 31.82%. This is the minimum probability of selling at least another small amount of cheese as shown in Figure 23.13.

From the normal probability tables this gives a z value of 0.4728 and from the transformation formula:

$$z = \frac{X - \mu_x}{\sigma_x}.$$

The quantity of cheese to make is 28.07 kg. (Alternatively this value can be calculated directly from the Excel normal function.)

2. The change of the expected profit and expected loss against the quantity of cheese sold is given in Figure 23.14. This illustrates that above a level of

28.07 kg the marginal loss exceeds the marginal profit. The derivation of this graph is given in Table 23.13:
• The first column in this table is a range of quantities of cheese.
• The second column is the probability of selling this amount of cheese. It is determined from the transformation formula or directly from the Excel normal function. Note, on the normal curve, at the extreme left, the probability of sale is 100% and this declines to 50% at the centre of the curve and drops to zero at the extreme right.
• The third column is the expected marginal profit given by p * MP.
• The fourth column is the expected marginal loss given by (1 − p) * ML.

Demonstrating the concept 23.5 Tennis

Situation

A community is under pressure from its residents to construct several tennis courts in the town. A cost–benefit approach to the project, in pounds, yields the following data on an annual basis (see Table 23.14).

Required

1. Based on a cost–benefit analysis, using the information provided, should the tennis facility be constructed?
2. How could the costs be adjusted to make the project more feasible?
3. What major cost is missing from the data?

Solution

1. The cost–benefit calculation is shown in Table 23.15, which also shows the percentage amount of the costs. Based on the given data, the tennis courts should not be constructed since the costs outweigh the benefits as indicated by the cost–benefit ratio of 1.53.
2. In order to make the project feasible, according to the cost–benefit criterion, the operating costs need to be reduced. In particular, employee salaries are high, at some 53% of the total operating costs. Perhaps these can be reduced by having volunteer labour instead of salaried people. In this case, as is shown in the 'After' column, if the salaries were

reduced to £14,000 a year the cost–benefit ratio would be unity and in which case the project would be at a breakeven situation.

3. There is no item to cover the fixed cost, annually depreciated, for the construction of the facility. This might be reasonable if the community handles its annual capital budgets differently from its operating budgets. If not, and capital depreciation is included with the annual operating costs, it would add further weight not to go ahead with the project.

Table 23.14 Cost–benefit approach to tennis court construction

Annual operating costs	£
Administration	15,000
Salaries of employees (3)	40,000
Maintenance	12,500
Energy (lighting in the evenings)	7,500

Annual benefits	£
Social (enjoyment of playing)	8,000
Community image	6,000
Social (occupies youth)	15,000
Income to restaurant/shops	20,000

Table 23.15 Cost–benefit calculations for tennis court construction

	Present		After	
	Cost	Percent	Cost	Percent
Item				
Administration	15,000	20.00	15,000	20.00
Salaries of employeees (3)	40,000	53.33	14,000	18.67
Maintenance	12,500	16.67	12,500	16.67
Energy	7,500	10.00	7,500	10.00
Total	**75,000**	**100.00**	**49,000**	**65.34**
Benefit				
Social (enjoyment of playing)	8,000	16.33	8,000	16.33
Community image	6,000	12.24	6,000	12.24
Social (occupies youth)	15,000	30.61	15,000	30.61
Income to restaurant/shops	20,000	40.82	20,000	40.82
Total	**49,000**	**100.00**	**49,000**	**100.00**
Cost–benefit ratio	**1.53**		**1.00**	

Application exercise 23.1 Bovine

Situation

Britain has been preoccupied with the possibility of an outbreak of Creutzfeldt-Jakob disease, caused by exposure to beef carrying bovine spongiform encephalopathy (BSE). A major government decision was a major and extensive cull of cattle in order to minimize contamination. Reaction in other European countries was total destruction of herd of cattle. For Britain this brought horrendous costs, and financial ruin for many farmers.

Assume that the ability of BSE to infect humans can be categorized at the levels of zero, low, medium, and high. Further, the government's policy to the crisis could be either to do nothing, mild intervention, which would be selective killing of cattle, or strong intervention, which means complete destruction of all cows.

The basis for a cost matrix, using arbitrary units, is considered by saying that the 'cost', if the government does nothing, under the four possible assumptions would be as shown in Table 23.16.

Table 23.16 Cost matrix for BSE

Cost matrix	Assumptions about infection			
	Zero	Low	Medium	High
Do nothing	0	3,000	6,000	10,000

Further, the cost of action by the government, under the zero assumption of infection is considered as demonstrated in Table 23.17.

Table 23.17 Cost of action by the government

Cost matrix	Zero infection
Do nothing	0
Mild intervention	1,500
Strong intervention	4,500

Further, the assumption is that selective culling reduces the rate of infection by 45% and the total destruction reduces it by 85%.*

Required

1. Develop the complete cost matrix for this situation.
2. Under the maximax criteria, what would the proposed action be?
3. Under the maximin criteria, what would the proposed action be?
4. Develop a regret matrix. Using this evaluation, what would the proposed action be?

* Based on 'Apocalypse maybe: Sometimes governments must respond to unknown probabilities of extremely unpleasant outcomes. Can economic theory help?', *The Economist*, 30 March 1996, p. 84.

Application exercise 23.2   Construk Inc.

Situation

Construk Inc., in southern California, performs engineering, design, and construction work for international and domestic clients. Next year it has a potential project from a French/Chinese consortium to perform design work on the reactor system of a nuclear power plant. The work is very specialized and Construk will need to hire engineers trained in this area. The extent of the design work has not been completely defined but is expected to be between 19,600 hours and 27,440 hours. This is indicated in Table 23.18, with the estimated probabilities for the work being released.

Engineers are paid an average $35/hour on a 2080 hours a year basis. However, included in these 2080 hours are three weeks' paid vacation. (The workweek is 40 hours.) If engineers are hired, and the work level does not materialize, they will be retained by the company, and assigned to developing equipment specifications (indirect work). This indirect work is not billed to the client. That is, these engineers are paid their hourly salary, and this represents a cost to Construk. It is budgeted that the work is finished within the year.

The customer is billed at a rate of $42/hour but only for the time that the engineers work on the project.

Required

1. Using the concept of expected values, without any financial considerations, estimate how many engineers should be hired.
2. Using an expected profit table (taking into account the financial information), how many engineers should be hired to maximize the expected profit? What is this expected profit?
3. What is the expected value of perfect information (EVPI)?
4. How might the concept of EVPI be interpreted in this particular situation?

Table 23.18 Construk Inc.: Extent of design work for nuclear power plant

Customer job hours	19,600	21,560	23,520	25,480	27,440
Probability of this level (%)	20.00	45.00	30.00	4.00	1.00

Application exercise 23.3 Cruise

Situation

A boat construction company on the East Coast of the USA is considering adding to its fleet of cruise ships for the Caribbean region. It is considering four options:

- building a large luxury boat
- building a medium boat
- building a smaller boat
- building in a joint venture with a French company.

The estimated net present value (NPV) of the return in dollars, according to the market demand as defined by the company, for cruise vacations is given in Table 23.19.

Required

1. If a manager were pessimistic in his approach, what decision would be taken?
2. If a manager were optimistic in his approach, what decision would be taken?
3. If a manager were middle of the road in his approach, what decision would be taken?
4. Using the concept of regret, what decision would be taken?
5. If there was a 50% chance of an increase in market, and a 50% chance of a declining market, what decision would be made based on the concept of expected values? (In this risk situation, a stable market is not an option.)
6. In the case of the 50/50 probability from question 4, what would need to be the NPV for the large boat in order that the expected value of returns for the large boat, and medium boat gives a breakeven situation? Show the results graphically.

Table 23.19 Market change for cruise vacations

	Increase	Stable	Decline
Large boat	2,750,000	750,000	−1,500,000
Medium boat	1,500,000	500,000	−100,000
Small boat	1,000,000	400,000	−10,000
Joint venture	550,000	150,000	0

Application exercise 23.4 Hanson

Situation

John Hanson is the Operations Manager of a manufacturing facility that makes automobile engine parts. The facility uses flexible manufacturing and John is able to change from one product range to another relatively easily. The capacity of John's facility is now saturated and he has to make a decision on adding new machines to handle the combined drilling, milling, and welding operations. This automated equipment is expensive.

John knows he wants to purchase equipment manufactured by Brown Boveri and he has narrowed his requirements down to one or, perhaps, two machines. If just one machine is purchased now, and demand for engine parts turns out to be more than expected, a second machine can be purchased at a later date. However, in this case, purchasing a second machine later would cost more than if both machines were purchased together, due to higher unit transportation, and installation costs.

Based on knowledge of the business, John estimates that the probability of low demand is about 40%, and high demand about 60%.

If John purchases two machines at the same time, and demand for engine parts is high, then the net present value (NPV) of profits associated with the machines would be $520,000. If demand turns out to be low, then the NPV of profits will be only $300,000, as one machine would be running below capacity.

If John purchases only one machine now, and demand is low, then the NPV of profits is estimated at $360,000. However, if the demand turns out to be high, then John has three options:

1. Do nothing. This means losing potential business, and the NPV of profits would stay at $360,000.
2. Subcontract the additional business, which would yield a NPV of profits to John of $440,000.
3. Purchase another machine, which would result in a NPV of $400,000.

Required

1. Draw a decision tree showing the various options available to John Hanson.
2. On the decision tree, show the value of all the expected outcomes.
3. Based on the data given, what decision should John make concerning the purchase of machines?
4. If the estimated NPV of profits for the subcontracting option were $480,000 instead of $440,000 what impact would this have on your decision?

Application exercise 23.5 Ipras

Situation

Tugrul Osmal is the Chief Engineer at the Ipras oil refinery in Izmit, Turkey. He is considering adding a new Unit A to the present catalytic cracking unit to upgrade gasoline production. It is not certain that this Unit A will work because the crude used at Ipras is high in sulphur and excessive sulphur levels in the Unit A would poison the catalyst. However, if Unit A works, Ipras could realize a return of $350,000 a year. If the unit does not work, the company stands to lose $150,000 a year. Tugrul estimates that, currently, there is a 40% chance that the Unit A will work.

An alternative option for Tugrul is to build a pilot plant to first test a smaller version of the Unit A. Based on the results of that, Tugrul could then decide whether to build a commercial version of Unit A. Constructing, and operating, the pilot plant would cost an annualized $45,000. There is a 50% chance that the pilot plant would work. If the pilot plants

work, there is then a 90% probability that the commercial Unit A, if subsequently built, would perform correctly. If the pilot unit does not work, there is only a 20% chance that the commercial plant, if constructed, would work.

Required

1. Develop a decision tree based on this information.
2. Show quantitatively on the decision tree, and explain, the best strategy for Tugrul to adopt.
3. After discussing the project with a US engineer, Tugrul decides that the probability of the commercial facility working with no pilot plant could be increased to 55% from the original 40%. In this case, would this cause a change in Tugrul's decision? Justify your response.
4. What can you say about the sensitivity of this decision situation?

Application exercise 23.6 Piller

Situation

Ron Piller is a baker in Normandy. One of Ron's specialities is Black Forest gateau that he sells in his bakery shop for €21.00. The cost of making the cake, including his time, and the ingredients, is €10.80. Ron bakes his cakes in the morning before 7am and hopes to sell them the same day before he closes the store at 7pm. Any Black Forest gateaux remaining at the end of the day are sold to the local retirement home for €4.00. There is never a problem selling his cakes to the retirement home.

Based on past data, the probability of selling the cakes fresh (that is, the same day it is baked) is given in Table 23.20.

Required

1. Using marginal analysis, determine the minimum required probability in order to justify Ron's making an additional cake.
2. At the probability level in question 1, what would be the number of cakes he should make?

3. Verify your answer with a table showing expected marginal loss, and expected marginal profit for each level of cake demanded.
4. Convert the table in question 3 into a histogram.

Table 23.20 Probability of selling cakes fresh

Cakes demanded	Probability of this demand
20	0.02
21	0.05
22	0.07
23	0.09
24	0.12
25	0.14
26	0.18
27	0.20
28	0.10
29	0.02
30	0.01

Case study 23.1 Grivel Foundry

Situation

The Grivel Foundry, established in 1937 in Portugal, is a combination foundry and machinery operation turning out flanges, elbow joints, and cooling block parts for the refinery, chemical and food industries. The basic operation is that pieces are forged in alloyed materials of zinc, copper, and nickel before passing to machinery where the units are cleaned, drilled, polished and assembled. From here, they are dispatched to the final customer. There are 55 people employed in the foundry, and 73 people in machinery. Machinery adds about 80% of the net income to the company, and 20% comes from the foundry operation.

As a result of a directive from the European Union, Grivel has to clean up considerably the pollution emanating from the foundry operation. This work centre uses oil-fired units, which are old and inefficient. To bring the foundry within conformity, and, particularly, to reduce the sulphur dioxide and nitrogen oxide emissions, will involve the installation of some rather expensive equipment. Management at Grivel are wondering whether installing the equipment is really worth the additional cost. They are considering closing the foundry and concentrating on the machining part of the business. Rough-forged components would be purchased from subcontractors and the machinery work would continue as before. This decision would involve terminating the 55 foundry workers. A disadvantage with this approach is that they would lose some flexibility in planning, as they would be entirely dependent on the subcontractors. In addition, they would have to rely on the subcontractors for quality control of forged pieces.

Before management made a final decision, they performed an internal analysis on the cost and benefits involved in installing the new equipment. These data can be seen in Tables 23.21 and 23.22, and are on an annual basis over five years. The following is an explanation.

Table 23.21 Grivel Foundry: Annual costs associated with installing new equipment

	€s
Capital cost (depreciated annual amount)	2,200,000
Annual operating cost	100,000
Increased energy costs	20,000
Lost revenue (a shutdown is necessary to install the equipment)	10,000

Employee relations

Avoiding laying off the foundry workers would maintain morale and thus productivity in machinery. Plus it would avoid the possibility of a strike by machinery personnel.

Company image (increased sales)

If the company maintained the foundry operation it would project a good image to clients who would feel that Grivel was able to give them complete service.

Table 23.22 Grivel Foundry: Annual benefits associated with installing new equipment

	€s
Employee relations	1,200,000
Company image (increased sales)	150,000
Gain to local community	250,000
Specification control	250,000
Flexibility	350,000

Gain to local community

It was felt unlikely that the 55 foundry workers would be able to find other employment in the community. Thus, if employed by Grivel, they were add purchasing power, and tax revenue.

Specification control

Keeping the foundry would mean that Grivel would have better control on the specification, and quality of the units produced.

Flexibility

Planning would be much easier if Grivel were to continue with the foundry operation.

Required

1. Using the criterion of cost–benefit analysis, what decision should be Grivel take, based on the original data provided?
2. Assume now that a member of the Grivel management, who was somewhat out of touch with human relations at the foundry, felt that the €1,200,000 a year allocated for employee relations was far too high. He believed that since there was little other work in the community, there might be a loss of productivity, but the threat of industrial action was slight. On this basis, the 'benefit' of employee relations could be reduced to €80,000 a year, instead of the original €1,200,000. Further, on discussing the project with union leaders, Grivel learns that if the foundry operation were closed, there would be a high risk of prolonged industrial action. If this information were true then, by not having a strike, a more realistic 'benefit' to Grivel concerning employee relations would be €4,000,000 a year rather than €1,200,000. What impact would this new information have on the decisions to be made?
3. Sensitivity is an important consideration in decision making. Discuss the sensitivity of this project by using, in addition to the amounts given for 'employee relations', values of €1, €1.4, €1.6, and €2 million. What are your comments regarding sensitivity and making decisions of the type illustrated by this case?

Selected further reading

ANSELL, J. and WHARTON, F. (1992) *Risk: Analysis, Assessment and Management*, Wiley.

HILLER, Frederick S. (2001) *Introduction to Management Science: A Modeling and Case Studies Approach With Spreadsheets*, McGraw-Hill Education.

RIVETT, Patrick (1994) *The Craft of Decision Modelling*, Wiley.

TARGETT, David (1996) *Analytical Decision Making*, Financial Times Management.

WINSTON, Wayne L. and ALBRIGHT, Christian, (2000) *Practical Management Science* (with CD-ROM), 2nd edition, Duxbury Press.

An extensive listing of other further reading can be found on the website.

What's on the web?

Further learning resources are available to lecturers and students at www.supplychain-online.com, including the following which are specific to *Decision making and risk*:

Resource	Subject
Chapter overview	Decision making and risk
Application exercise: Bed and breakfast	Decision trees
Application exercise: Drilling	Uncertainty
Application exercise: Navajo	Decision trees
More further reading	Decision making and risk

24 *Linear programming*

Chapter overview

- The linear programming tool
- Restrictions in linear programming
- Formulating a linear programme
- Linear programming with only two variables
- Linear programming with more than two variables

The linear programming tool

Background

Linear programming is a quantitative tool for decision making that can be used to optimize decisions both at the operating and strategic level of organizations. George B Dantzig first conceived the concept in 1947. At that time he was head of the US Air Force, Statistical Controls Combat Analysis Branch at the Pentagon, USA. In military operations there were plans covering personnel training, supplying equipment and food, and deploying combat troops and Dantzig developed a management method called 'programming in a linear structure'. This was later renamed linear programming.[1]

The technique of linear programming is to determine the best values of given variables in order to achieve a particular objective such as the following:

- maximize sales revenues
- maximize operating income
- minimize production costs
- minimize operating time
- maximize market share
- minimize labour needs.

Linear programming is a deterministic tool, that is to say, the solution is considered reliable as the analysis is based on accepted input data. This is different from probability outcomes, which are based on statistical sampling analysis (see Chapter 27).

Applications

The following are specific applications in business where linear programming might be applied and

Industry insight 24.1 gives specific applications of linear programming related to the energy industry.

Product mix

In product mix situations, linear programming can be used to select the required formulation of product components, or services that results in maximizing profits, or minimizing cost, but at the same time satisfying required specifications such as the following:

- Gasoline mix in order to satisfy *knock* requirements (the performance of gasoline in the combustion chamber).
- Preparation of aviation fuel mix from kerosene to satisfying *gum* specifications (the avoidance of gum deposits during flight).
- Concrete composition to satisfy building codes.
- Food compositions, such as ingredients in chocolate, margarine, or jam.
- Animal feed composition in order to satisfy minimum protein requirements.
- A range of products to manufacture in order to satisfy forecast client demand.
- Placement of investments, to maximize return but at the same time to minimize risk, such as the proportion in stocks, certificates of deposits, or government bonds.

Transportation

In transportation, this would be the design of a distribution network for delivery of products that would minimize total transportation costs, for example, the selection of the best network for truck delivery of goods from a central warehouse to retail stores. A special network application is the travelling salesman problem, which is to find the shortest tour that visits a given collection of cities or other locations.

Shell Global Solutions and decision–support tools

Refinery blending in South Africa
A linear programming-based blending–scheduling optimization tool, developed by Shell Global Solutions (SGS) brought benefits of around $1.5 million in its first year of operation at the SAPREF (Shell-BP-Amoco) refinery in Durban, South Africa. This amounted to a payback time of less than two months. The tool called MPMP (multi-period, multi-product) realized the savings through innovative refinery studies, reducing working capital by improving monthly planning of crude and refined products inventories, and optimizing blending of motor gasoline (mogas) and fuel oil. A scheduler can simultaneously optimize any combination of refinery cuts such as mogas, gas oil, and fuel oil that exploits the best synergy between the cuts.

Gas distribution in The Netherlands
The Netherlands obtains a large portion of its energy supplies from indigenous onshore and offshore gas fields. The operator of these fields, Nederlands Aardolie Maatschappij (NAM) and its customer Gasunie, have been able to reduce the time needed for evaluating alternative plans to meet fluctuating market demand for gas from weeks to hours using an innovative decision-support optimization tool developed in collaboration with SGS.

Gas demand fluctuates wildly from some $700\,m^3$ a day in the winter down to $100\,m^3$ a day in the summer months. Even within these seasonal fluctuations there are marked daily changes. The most effective operations strategy for meeting this demand is to provide cheap, onshore balancing capacity close to the market that simultaneously allows small peripheral gas fields to have uninterrupted production at maximum capacity. The options available to generate such balancing capacity include compression on the large onshore

Groningen field, infill drilling, facility de-bottlenecking, or seasonal gas storage projects such as underground stores, liquefied gas storage, or salt caverns. Finding the right mix of options is complex particularly because of the varying costs, production capacities, and gas volume limitations of the different projects. This is where the optimizer is used where it is able rapidly to assess different scenarios and find the optimum solution. It can evaluate a set of capacity measures for any new scenario within 8–15 hours using a standard PC. This previously took a month of engineering time. In addition, the tool has helped to identify reductions in development costs of over $137 million.

Production and revenue optimization in Australia
Woodside Energy Ltd (WEL) operates a complex off- and onshore gas and oil complex on the North West Shelf project in Australia. A production and revenue optimization tool (PRO) models the entire gas supply chain including liquefied natural gas (LNG), domestic gas, condensate and liquefied petroleum gas (LPG), such that production levels and revenues are optimized. The three main constraints within the system are physical, product specifications, and gas demand and the tool models the integrated system to reflect all these constraints, saving considerable time and indicating options available. In its major use PRO defines the optimal production plan over a 120-day period, and the plan can be updated weekly giving the opportunity to analyze shutdown synergies, well priorities, and production strategies. Cost savings with this optimization tool are estimated to be in the order of $A10 million per year.

Adapted from: 'Fast payback from blending optimization in South Africa', 'Stepping on the gas', and 'Optimization pays off in Australia'[2]

Production plan

In a production plan linear programming would determine the best combination of normal time, overtime, subcontracting, part-time employees, inventory levels, backlog, etc., in order to minimize cost but at the same time provide the maximum customer service level.

Assignment

In assignment situations, this might cover which machines to assign to a certain production operation, salespeople to various sales regions, or products to

assemble on various operating lines. Linear programming would optimize the assignment so that total costs are minimized, or profits are maximized during the planning period.

Methods for linear programming

When linear programming was introduced in the 1940s following Dantzig's work, computers, as we know them today, did not exist. At that time the Simplex method was the common tool.[3] This is a relatively complex mathematical procedure, which, at that time, was executed manually. As computers were developed, computer software was written based on the Simplex procedure. An alternative to Simplex is Karmarkar's algorithm that was developed by Narendra Karmarkar in 1984.[4] Compared to Simplex, this algorithm usually takes significantly less computer time to solve complex linear programming situations. In transportation, and assignment linear programming, methods include, the North West Corner Rule, Vogel's Approximation Method, and the MODI method.[5] Initially, these were performed manually and many texts still present the manual approach but these again have been adapted for computer use. Today with the advances in computing including memory capacity, computers can solve almost all linear programming problems, containing perhaps thousands of variables in just a few minutes. Linear programming packages can be purchased and used without the user understanding the tedious arithmetical gymnastics involved in their compilation. Microsoft Excel is a well-known spreadsheet computer program that incorporates a linear programming tool called Solver. It is that which is used for the various activities in this text. It should be noted that Solver has limited capacity for solving problems compared to many other commercial packages. (See the Optimization Technology Center of the Northwestern University and Argonne National Laboratory for further information.[6])

Restrictions on linear programming

Decision making can be complex and often there are restrictions, or constraints, which have to be taken into account in arriving at a desired objective. These restrictions might be related to the resources available, to legal or governmental regulations, or to product or process specification requirements as the following illustrates.

Resource availability

Examples on resource availability include the following.

Raw materials

- Crude oil for refining in order to meet heating oil requirements.
- Plastic feedstock to produce plastic bottles for bottled water.
- Blood for transfusion, particularly in a catastrophe situation.

Time

- Time in order to meet a project completion schedule.
- Time available to produce a product in order to satisfy a client's need date.

- Transportation time available in transportation to deliver units from location to another.

Surface area

- The surface area for the installation of a new park of production machines.
- The surface area for the creation of staff office space.
- The surface area for storage of finished goods or raw materials.

Labour

- Labour necessary for construction.
- The labour necessary for a production operation.
- The necessary salesforce personnel for a geographic territory.
- The appropriately trained labour for certain technical activities (developing a website, for example).

Financial

- Capital investment for plant construction.
- Capital available for equipment purchases.
- Cash available to meet employee salaries.
- Cash available to meet budget requirements (often a constraint at the government level).

Land

- Land for constructing a new facility.
- Land for farming.
- Land available for expanding a new facility.

Design specifications

Design specifications related to products include those related to the following:

- To meet the composition of fertilizers regarding the correct percentage of nitrogen, phosphate, and potassium.
- To meet the minimum vitamin requirements in food.
- To meet the specification of construction material regarding the proportion of sand, cement, and gravel in order to satisfy building codes to comply with earthquake or other safety measures. (Sadly overlooked in earthquake regions of developing countries.)

Legal requirements

The legal requirements vary from country to country but they might cover the following:

- The number of hours an employee may work a week. For example, it is 35 hours in France but there is no legal maximum in the USA. Also, in employment there are limits to the maximum overtime, a legal requirement to the minimum vacation days, etc.
- The maximum age at which a person must retire. Thus, this limits the labour availability.
- The maximum driving speed permitted on a highway. (This has an impact on delivery time.)

Quantitative with limitations

Linear programming solves situations when there are quantitative data involved. However, what might be an optimal solution quantitatively may not necessarily be optimum when other qualitative factors are taken into consideration, such as capability of labour, motivation level, or productivity.

Formulating a linear programme

In order to set up the framework for a linear programme the situation must be presented in the form of a mathematical model and the objectives and the constraints of the programme must be identified.

Objective

In linear programming, there must be a well-defined single objective in the decision to be made. This might be to maximize revenues, minimize cost or the objective can be predefined. For example the objective is to have a budget equal to $100,000, or a labour utilization of a total of 4000 hours. Also, in the linear programming problem, there must be alternative ways to arrive at the stated objective.

Constraints

In achieving the objective there are constraints, or limitations, on the resources available. These constraints might take on the following forms.

Less than

Here, the variable must be less than, or equal to ($\leqslant$) the upper limit. For example:

- less than, or equal to 100 machine hours
- less than, or equal to $900 worth of raw materials
- less than, or equal to 40 hours of labour hours per week.

Greater than

The variable must be greater than, or equal to ($\geqslant$) the lower limit. For example:

- greater than, or equal to 12% alcohol content (wine, for example)
- greater than, or equal to 25% of the RDA (recommended daily allowance) of protein
- greater than, or equal to $50 earnings per share next quarter.

Equal to

The variable must be equal ($=$) to a required amount:

- equal to 400 kg in total weight
- equal to 900 machine hours
- equal to a surface area of 1000 square metres.

Integer values

In certain situations, only integer values are acceptable in the linear programme as, for example, the number of people in a work centre, the number or trucks, or the number of machines. Fractions for these types of variables are not meaningful. However, in other situations, continuous variables, giving arise to fractions, might be allowed as, for example, 10.25 machine hours, $5.75 per unit price, or 2.90 labour hours. When the constraints are integer values usually the linear programme takes longer to solve.

Non-negative values

In linear programming, negative values in the solution are not permitted, since they make no sense in an optimization problem. The constraint would then be written as $x \geqslant 0$ where x is the variable and the assumption is that zero is acceptable.

Mathematical function

In formulating the decision to be optimized, the objective and the variables, together with their appropriate constraints, must be expressed as linear mathematical functions. The objective will be a linear function either set to maximize, to minimize, or to equal some predetermined value. The constraints greater than, less than, or equal to, must be represented as linear functions in terms of the variables. The functions are linear which implies the following:

- No variable can have an exponent more than unity. The variables x, y, z, etc., are allowed but not x^2, x^3, y^3, z^4, etc.

- No combinations of variables are allowed. For example, if x and y denote two of the variables, then x * y is not permitted.

Microsoft Solver

Microsoft Solver is a built-in linear programming tool found in the Tools menu of Excel. When the Solver is used it makes the necessary iterations in order to develop an optimum solution. In Solver the following are some of the requirements.

Cell to define

This requires the target cell to be specified and whether the value is to be maximized, minimized, or equal to some given value. This defined cell must be expressed in terms of a mathematical formula.

Variable cells

The variable cell, or cells, must be defined. Again, they must be represented in terms of mathematical formulae.

Constraints

The constraints of the variable values must be specified according to less than or equal to, more than or equal to, equal to, or a whole number.

Options

Here there is an option regarding the time to execute the simulation, and the number of iterations to be made.

It could be that the capacity of the computer in terms of either live memory or hard disk capacity may be a restriction on the size of the linear programming problem that can be solved with Excel Solver.

Linear programming with only two variables

If there are only two variables for a given situation then a linear programme can be presented as a two-dimensional graph and the optimum solution can be determined from the graph as well as by using Excel Solver or some other linear programming package. The ability to present the information graphically is useful in that it gives a clear illustration of the interconnection between the constraints and the objective. This idea is illustrated in Demonstrating the concept 24.1, which is

a profit maximization situation with 'less than'-type constraints, and Demonstrating the concept 24.2 is a cost minimization problem with 'greater than' constraints.

Feasible area and boundary limits

In linear programming, for the solution to be valid all constraints must be satisfied. When there are two variables and the linear functions are presented on a graph then there are feasible areas for a solution and boundary limits. The feasible area is where all the constraints are satisfied but within the feasible area, the solution is probably not optimum. It is on the boundary of the feasible area that the optimum solution is found. In a linear programming situation which has 'less than or equal to' constraints, as illustrated in Demonstrating the concept 24.1, the boundary for acceptability will lie below and to the left of the intersection of the constraint functions and between the origin of the graph and the x and y axis. The optimum solution is situated at one of the intersections of the boundary lines. In a problem where the constraints are 'greater than or equal to', as illustrated in Demonstrating the concept 24.2, then the feasible area lies above and to the right of the intersection of the constraint functions. Again, the optimum solution is found on the boundary of the intersection of the lines representing the constraint function.

Iso-profit line

As illustrated in these two samples when there are only two variables the profit function can also be presented graphically. This straight line is called the iso-profit line where the profit remains constant at any point on this line and intersects the optimum solution point.

Surplus resources

In a linear programme, when an optimum solution is obtained it is likely that there will be unused resources. In this case, a management decision is what to do with these excess resources. For example, in the case of the Braun example (Demonstrating the concept 24.1), there are surplus resources in using the computer time. This may not be critical as the time can perhaps be used elsewhere. However, in the case of Volger (Demonstrating the concept 24.2), there is excess production of both dark and milk chocolate. This could be a problem if there is no market for the product as inventory holding costs could be high and there is a relatively short shelf life for food products such as chocolate.

Sensitivity

Linear programming is a deterministic decision-making tool. However, as in all decision-making processes, one may not always be certain in the linear programme of given parameters (the known values). For example, the cost per unit of a product may be estimated as $10.00. But this is only an estimate. What if the cost were $11.00? Or, it may be given that 2000 machine hours are available. What if, in fact, 2500 machine hours were available? For this reasons, managers often ask what the effect on the solution would be, given different values of the parameters. This would be a sensitivity analysis, which is the sort of situation illustrated by the second part of Demonstrating the concept 24.1.

Limits of two variable linear programmes

When there are only two variables in a decision process the information can be presented visually, which is always a great advantage to explain a situation to people who may not be totally familiar with analytical methods used. However, in practice most business decision involve more than two variables and so the linear programming is somewhat more complex as illustrated in the next section.

Linear programming with more than two variables

Multiple variable linear programming models are the most common situations encountered in business and if the objective and constraints can be defined by linear relationships then a solution can be conveniently obtained using linear programming. The areas of use are almost infinite, ranging from investment, budgeting, marketing, production planning, transportation, personnel assignments, scheduling, and the like. If one uses commercial linear programming packages to solve these problems, and even with Excel, it is usually not necessary to develop the details of the equations showing the constraints and the objective function since the packages simplify the input of the data. However, if the appropriate equations are formulated one can have a clearer understanding of the logic involved and it is perhaps easier to identify errors or inconsistencies. The following describes, with appropriate examples, problems related to transportation networks, refinery blending, job assignments, and personnel scheduling.

Transportation networks

Linear programming can be used to obtain the least cost plan for the distribution of goods from multiple origins to multiple destinations during a particular planning period, such as daily, weekly, or monthly, for example. The characteristics of the transportation method of linear programming are:

• A finite and homogeneous set of discrete units is shipped from several sources to several destinations in a certain time period.
• Each source has a quantified number of units to be shipped in the time period.
• Each destination has a quantified required number of units to be received in the time period.
• Each unit has a unit transportation cost from each source to each destination. The unit cost remains constant regardless of the quantity shipped.
• There is only one transportation route between source and destination.
• The variables in the linear programme are the number of units to be shipped from each source to each destination during the time period.
• The objective is to minimize the total transportation cost for the time period.

Linear transportation methods are very appropriate when the product is homogeneous, as in the case of liquid product such as beer, wine, and petroleum products. If there are several different products to be shipped then an average shipping cost per unit can be determined. The transportation method using the linear programme of Microsoft Solver is illustrated in Demonstrating the concept 24.3.

Blending or mixing

Blending or mixing are situations encountered in refinery blending, in food processing, and diet formulation, where the objective is often to minimize the cost but at the same time develop products that conform to specifications and/or customer requirements. This type of linear programme construction is illustrated in Demonstrating the concept 24.4.

Assignment method

The assignment method of job allocation is a way of assigning tasks when there are several possibilities. For example:

• There are several jobs waiting to be processed that can be assigned to one of various work centres.

- There are drilling jobs waiting to be processed that can be assigned to one of several numerically controlled drilling machines.
- There are many engineers in a design department who can be assigned to one of several design projects.
- There are several salespeople who can be assigned to one of several sales territories.

The objective of the assignment method is either to minimize the cost, such as in an operation that is a cost centre, or to maximize the profit in a marketing or sales situation. In the assignment method, the assumption is that each individual is multi-skilled and can perform any of the tasks (design or sales function) to which they would be assigned. Further, it is assumed that there are n assignments that need to be assigned to n work centres. Demonstrating the concept 14.3, presented in Chapter 14, illustrates the assignment method of job allocation.

Personnel scheduling

Personnel scheduling is a planning activity in all organizations. Service operations, such as the airline industry, a full service restaurant, highway tollbooths, government offices, and supermarket checkouts, are by their very nature heavily people oriented, and scheduling is a major activity. In manufacturing firms, besides the functions that deal with tangible goods, there are support services involving personnel scheduling such as the employee restaurant, the medical centre, customer billing, computer services, or the printing department. Since the operation of a service function is heavily labour intensive, one challenge is to optimize labour costs, although that is not to say that service industries, with heavy capital investment (such as airlines, leisure cruises, and hotels) should not have a first priority to maximize facility utilization. In the service function, the demand often varies according to the time of day, time during the week, or season of the year. And, unlike manufacturing there is no buffer of inventory to smooth out fluctuations. Demonstrating the concept 14.5 (in Chapter 14) also illustrates the development of a personnel scheduling using Excel.

Notes and references

1. DANTZIG, George B., *Linear Programming and its Extensions*, Princeton University Press, Princeton, New Jersey, 1963
2. http://www.aimms/AIMMS-for.ADS/Articles/Shell, updated 2001
3. A good presentation can be found in Chapter 5 of ANDERSON, David R., SWEENEY, Dennis J. and

Summary of key elements

- Linear programming is a quantitative decision-making tool used to optimize an operating or strategic decision such as maximizing revenues, minimizing costs, minimizing labour needs, maximizing market share, etc.

- The areas of use of linear programming are enormous and include transportation, scheduling, product mix, marketing, production planning, and finance.

- Constraints in linear programming might include resources such as land, raw materials and labour. Alternatively, the constraints might be government requirements or customer design specifications.

- In formulating a linear programme the objective has to be defined. This could be a maximum or minimum value or it could be equal to some specific value. In addition, the constraints have to be stipulated which are greater than or equal to a lower limit, less than or equal to an upper limit, or equal to certain values.

- A linear programme may have fractional solutions or integer values. Integer linear programming usually takes more time and more computer memory to solve.

- Negative values are normally not acceptable in linear programming, and this fact has to be defined in the constraints.

- In linear programming, powers of the variables must always be unity and combinations of the form $x*y$ where x and y are variables are not permitted.

- In linear programming with only two variables, the situation can be illustrated, and solved graphically.

- The most common business situation for linear programming is when there are more than two variables. In this case, the problem cannot be presented by a two-dimensional graph.

- In the solution of linear programmes there are usually surplus resources. These are resources that have not been used to solve the problem. These surplus resources also enter the decision-making environment for management.

WILLIAM, Thomas A., *An Introduction to Management Science*, 9th edition, South Western, Cincinnati, Ohio, 2000, p. 217
4. FERRIS, M. C. and PHILPORT, A. B., 'On the performance of Karmarkar's Algorithm', *Journal of the Operational Research Society*, March 1988, pp 257–70
5. TAYLOR III, Bernard W., *Introduction to Management Science*, WCB, 1996
6. http://www-unix.mcs.anlgov/otc/Guide/faq/linear programming-faq.html

Review and discussion topics

1. Linear programming for improvement
In your work, at university or another situation, can you indicate where using linear programming would improve the operation? Indicate the objective and possible constraints. The situation could involve planning, scheduling, distribution, organization, transport, etc.

2. Payback
In the Industry insight 24.1, concerning Shell Global Solutions it refers to payback related to linear programming. How do think the payback would be calculated in these situations?

3. Financing
What are the drawbacks of using linear programming in financing situations, when parameters such as interest rates, stock returns, and bond values are used?

4. Assignment in linear programming
The assignment method can be used to assign individuals to various tasks, taking into account various assumptions. What may some of the pitfalls of this approach be?

Demonstrating the concept 24.1 Braun Engineering

Situation

The Braun Engineering Services Company in Alhambra, California uses senior and junior engineers on its design projects. Senior engineers are the more experienced, and command higher salaries than junior engineers. However, senior engineers require less supervision and less computer assistance than junior engineers. Senior engineers cost Braun $16.00 an hour compared to $7.50 an hour for junior engineers. Each hour of senior engineering time requires, on average, five minutes of supervision by the project manager and requires 15 minutes of computer time. Every hour of junior engineers requires, on average, 30 minutes of supervision from the project manager and requires 25 minutes of computer time. It is the junior engineers who do the bulk of the computer work.

The Braun Company has just been awarded a design project, and needs to decide on the mix of senior and junior engineers to execute the project. In bidding for the project, it budgeted a maximum total labour cost of $75,000 for senior and junior engineers. There is available for the project a maximum of 1000 hours of supervision by the project manager, and 2500 hours computer time. The project will be billed on an hourly rate, such that the time of senior engineers will yield a profit of $2.50 an hour, whereas junior engineers' time will yield a profit of $3.75 an hour.

Required

1. What is the maximum profit attainable for this project within the constraints given and what is the corresponding mix of senior and junior engineers? Illustrate the optimum solution on a graph including the linear relationship for the profit.

2. How would the solution change if the cost for senior engineers were $17.00/hour and 7.00/hour for junior engineers?
3. In both cases, what are the surplus resources?

Solution

1. Let:

$$P = \text{Profit}$$
$$X_s = \text{Number of senior engineer hours}$$
$$X_j = \text{Number of junior engineer hours}$$

The objective function is to maximize profits and this is given by the following relationship:

$$P = 2.50X_s + 3.75X_j$$

The constraints on the project are:

$16.00X_s + 7.50X_j \leq 75,000$ Cost of senior and junior engineers

$5/60X_s + 30/60X_j \leq 1000$ Hours of supervision

$15/60X_s + 25/60X_j \leq 2500$ Computer time

Table 24.1 gives the arrangement to solve using Microsoft Solver.

- Cell [B-3] is the maximum cost possible.
- Cell [B-4] is the maximum supervision hours available.
- Cell [B-5] is the maximum computer hours available.
- Cell [B-6] contains the following formula for calculating the profit objective and this is the cell to maximize in Solver. [C-6] * [C-8] + [D-6] * [D-8].

- Cell [C-3] is the cost per hour for senior engineers.
- Cell [C-4] is the hours of supervision time for each hour of a senior engineer's time.

Table 24.1 Braun Engineering: Layout of problem

Case 1: Framework using Microsoft Solver

	A	B	C	D	E	F
1			Senior engineers	Junior engineers		
2		Maximum			Actual	Surplus
3	Cost	75,000.00	16.00	7.50	75,000.00	0.00
4	Supervision	1000.00	0.0833	0.5000	1000.00	0.00
5	Computer time	2500.00	0.2500	0.4167	1567.80	932.20
6	Profit	0.00	2.50	3.75	Maximize	
7						
8	Hours required		0.00	0.00		

Table 24.2 Braun Engineering: Solution to the problems using Microsoft Solver

Case 1: Solution using Microsoft Solver

	A	B	C	D	E	F
1			Senior engineers	Junior engineers		
2		Maximum			Actual	Surplus
3	Cost	75,000.00	16.00	7.50	75,000.00	0.00
4	Supervision	1000.00	0.0833	0.5000	1000.00	0.00
5	Computer time	2500.00	0.2500	0.4167	1567.80	932.20
6	Profit	15,127.12	2.50	3.75	Maximize	
7						
8	Hours required		4067.80	1322.03		

Case 2: Solution using Microsoft Solver

	A	B	C	D	E	F
1			Senior engineers	Junior engineers		
2		Maximum			Actual	Surplus
3	Cost	75,000.00	17.00	7.00	75,000.00	0.00
4	Supervision	1000.00	0.0833	0.5000	1000.00	0.00
5	Computer time	2500.00	0.2500	0.4167	1528.95	971.05
6	Profit	14,723.68	2.50	3.75	Maximize	
7						
8	Hours required		3852.63	1357.89		

- Cell [C-5] is the hours of computer time for each hour of a senior engineer's time.
- Cell [C-6] is the profit per hour for senior engineers.
- Cell [C-8] is the senior engineering hours to maximize profit. This is a variable value in Solver and is initially set at 0 at the start of the iteration.

- Cell [D-3] is the cost per hour for junior engineers.
- Cell [D-4] is the hours of supervision time for each hour of a junior engineer's time.
- Cell [D-5] is the hours of computer time for each hour of a junior engineer's time.
- Cell [D-6] is the profit per hour for junior engineers.
- Cell [D-8] is the junior engineering hours to maximize profit. This is a variable value in Solver and is initially 0 at the start of the iteration.

- Cell [E-3] contains the formula for calculating the actual cost by the formula [C-3] * [C-8] + [D-3] * [D-8]. The maximum value of this constraint is given in cell [B-3].
- Cell [E-4] contains the formula for calculating the actual supervision hours by the formula [C-4] * [C-8] + [D-4] * [D-8]. The maximum value of this constraint is given in cell [B-4].
- Cell [E-5] contains the formula for calculating the actual computer hours by the formula [C-5] * [C-8] + [D-5] * [D-8]. The maximum value of this constraint is given in Cell [B-5].

Figure 24.1 Braun Engineering

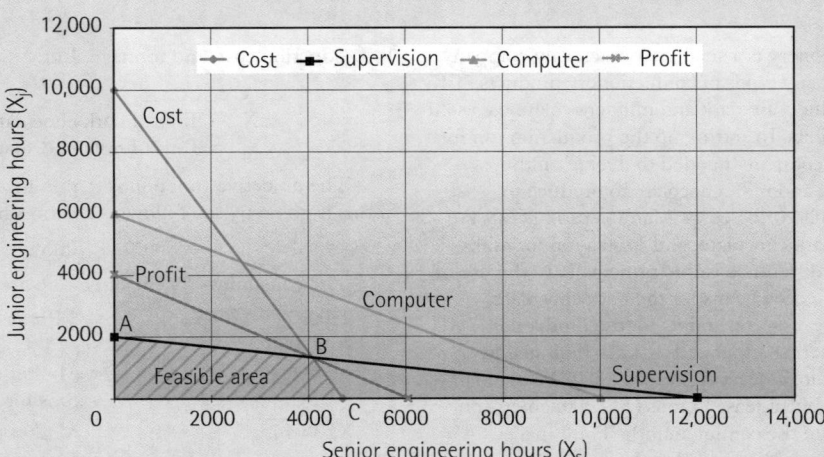

Table 24.2 gives the solution for this linear programming problem with the profit and corresponding senior and junior engineering hours in bold type.

Figure 24.1 gives the graphical presentation of this problem. The three straight lines are arrived at as follows.

Cost of senior and junior engineers

The constraint function is converted to an equation or $16.00X_s + 7.50X_j = 75,000$, when:

$$X_s = 0, \text{ then } X_j = 75,000/7.50 = 10,000$$
$$X_j = 0, \text{ then } X_s = 75,000/16.00 = 4687.50$$

This gives two points to construct the cost curve.

Supervision hours

The constraint function is converted to an equation or $5/60X_s + 30/60X_j = 1000$. Simplifying, $0.08X_s + 0.50X_j = 1000$, when:

$$X_s = 0, \text{ then } X_j = 1000/0.50 = 2000$$
$$X_j = 0, \text{ then } X_s = 1000/0.08 = 12,000$$

This gives two points to construct the supervision curve.

Computer time

The constraint function is converted to an equation or $15/60X_s + 25/60X_j = 2500$. Simplifying, $0.25X_s + 0.42X_j = 2500$, when:

$$X_s = 0, \text{ then } X_j = 2500/0.42 = 5999.52$$
$$X_j = 0, \text{ then } X_s = 2500/0.25 = 10,000$$

This gives two points to construct the computer time curve.

Profit

The profit curve is given by the objective function $P = 2.50X_s + 3.75X_j$, when:

$$X_s = 0, \text{ then } X_j = 15,127.12/3.75 = 4033.90$$
$$X_j = 0, \text{ then } X_s = 15,127.12/2.50 = 6050.85$$

The solution is when all three constraints are satisfied, that means, in this case, the solution must lie within the boundary of the quadrangle, ABCO, since this is a 'less than or equal to' situation. Any values outside ABCO will not satisfy all the constraints, because some of the values are 'greater than' according to the constraints.

The optimum solution is point B, the intersection of the supervision and cost curve, and the profit line goes through this point. This corresponds to the results given by Solver. At this point the cost of the project is at the limit of the constraint, $75,000, the value in Cell [E-3]. The supervision also is at the limit of the constraint, 1000 hours, the value in Cell [E-4]. However, the computer time is not at the maximum of 1567.80 hours, Cell [E-5], as opposed to a maximum possible of 2500 hours, Cell [B-5]. This is also illustrated by the fact that point B does not lie on the curve for computer time.

2. If the hourly cost of senior hours was $17.00 rather than $16.00 and that of junior engineers was $7.00 instead of $7.50, then the profit drops from $15,127 to $14,724 or about 3%.

3. The surplus resources are shown in column F.

Demonstrating the concept 24.2 Vogler Confectionery

Situation

Vogler Confectionery is a small manufacturing company that produces many types of confectionery products. Two of its main products are dark and milk chocolate bars sold in 100-gram tablets. In setting up the production run for the month, the company needed to decide on the quantity of dark and milk chocolate to produce to minimize manufacturing costs. Manufacturing costs are $800 a ton for dark chocolate, and $700 a ton for milk chocolate. The difference is due principally to the use of superior quality cocoa beans for the dark chocolate.

There were several constraints for the production operation. Marketing stipulated that, for their needs, they would require at least eight tons (80,000 tablets) of dark chocolate, and at least 14 tons (140,000 tablets) of milk chocolate for the coming month. The Finance Department set the objective that the profit made on this month's production should be at least $60,000. The profit per ton of chocolate was $2500 for dark and $1200 for milk chocolate. Finally, for scheduling purposes, Production wanted to be sure that at least 2400 hours of total labour time be used in this section of the work centre. Historical data indicated that labour time for dark chocolate was 50 hours/ton, and 75 hours/ton for milk chocolate. The difference was due principally to the additional mixing and controlling needed for the milk chocolate.

Required

1. What is the minimum production cost for Vogler and what are the corresponding production levels for dark and milk chocolate to optimize this problem? Assume that production tonnage can take on non-integer values.
2. Illustrate the optimum solution on a graph, including the constant cost line.
3. How would the situation change if management wanted integer values for the production levels?

Solution

1. Production cost, and tonnage. Let:

$$C = \text{Cost}$$
$$X_b = \text{Tons of dark chocolate}$$
$$X_m = \text{Tons of milk chocolate}$$

The objective function is to minimize the cost and this is given by the following relationship:

$$C = 800X_b + 700X_m$$

The constraints for the operation are as follows:

$2500X_b + 1200X_m$ $\geqslant 60,000$	$ Profit
$X_b \geqslant 8$	Market demand in tons for dark chocolate
$X_m \geqslant 14$	Market demand in tons for milk chocolate
$50X_b + 75X_m \geqslant 2400$	Production time, hours

Table 24.3 gives the layout arrangement and solution using Microsoft Solver.

- Cell [B-3] is the minimum profit required.
- Cell [B-4] is the minimum required market demand for dark chocolate.
- Cell [B-5] is the minimum required market demand for milk chocolate.
- Cell [B-6] is the minimum production time needed.
- Cell [B-7] contains the formula [C-7] * [C-9] + [D-7] * [D-9] for calculating the cost objective. This is the cell to minimize in Solver.

- Cell [C-3] is the profit/ton in $ for dark chocolate.
- Cell [C-4] is the coefficient in the equation for the market demand for dark chocolate. It has a value of unity.
- Cell [C-5] is the coefficient in the equation for the market demand for milk chocolate. It has a value of zero since this column does not concern milk chocolate.

Table 24.3 Vogler Confectionery: Solution 1

	A	B	C	D	E	F
1 2		Minimum needs	Coefficient dark	Coefficient milk	Actual	Excess
3	Profit	60,000.00	2,500.00	1,200.00	60,000.00	0.00
4	Market, dark	8.00	1.00	0.00	12.71	4.71
5	Market, milk	14.00	0.00	1.00	23.53	9.53
6	Production	2,400.00	50.00.00	75.00	2,400.00	0.00
7	Cost	26,635.29	800.00	700.00		
8						
9	Production, tons		12.71	23.53		

- Cell [C-6] is the labour hours/ton for dark chocolate.
- Cell [C-7] is the cost/ton in $ for dark chocolate.
- Cell [C-9] is the tons of dark chocolate to produce to optimize the problem. This is a variable in Solver.

- Cell [D-3] is the profit/ton in $ for milk chocolate.
- Cell [D-4] is the coefficient in the equation for the market demand for dark chocolate. It has a value of zero since this column does not concern dark chocolate.
- Cell [D-5] is the coefficient in the equation for the market demand for milk chocolate. It has a value of unity.
- Cell [D-6] is the labour hours/ton for milk chocolate.
- Cell [D-7] is the cost/ton in $ for milk chocolate.
- Cell [D-9] is the tons of milk chocolate to produce to optimize the problem. This is a variable in Solver.

- Cell [E-3] contains the formula [C-3] * [C-9] + [D-3] * [D-9] for calculating the actual profit. This is one of the constraints in the problem with the minimum constraint value given in cell [B-3].
- Cell [E-6] contains the formula [C-6] * [C-9] + [D-6] * [D-9] for calculating the production time. This is another constraint with the minimum constraint value given in Cell [B-6].

- Cost is $26,635.29.
- Tons of dark chocolate to produce is 12.71.
- Tons of milk chocolate to produce is 23.53.

2. Figure 24.2 gives the graphical presentation of this problem. The four straight lines are arrived at as follows.

Profit

The constraint function is converted to an equation or $2500X_b + 1200X_m = 60,000$, when:

$$X_b = 0, \text{ then } X_m = 60,000/1200 = 50.00$$
$$X_m = 0, \text{ then } X_b = 60,000/2500 = 24.00$$

This gives two points to construct the cost curve.

Market demand for dark chocolate

The constraint function is converted to an equation or $X_b = 8 =$ Market demand for dark chocolate.

No matter what, the market demand for dark chocolate is a line vertical to the y axis.

Market demand for milk chocolate

The constraint function is converted to an equation or $X_m = 14 =$ Market demand for milk chocolate.

No matter what, the market demand for milk chocolate is a line horizontal to the x axis.

Production time

The constraint function is converted to an equation or $50X_b + 75X_m = 2400 =$ Production time, hours, when:

$$X_b = 0, \text{ then } X_m = 2400/75 = 32.00$$
$$X_m = 0, \text{ then } X_b = 2400/50 = 48.00$$

This gives two points to construct the production time curve.

To satisfy the constraints of this situation all four must be satisfied. In this case, the solution must lie to the right and above the area denoted by ABCDE since this is a 'greater than or equal to' situation.

Figure 24.2 Vogler Confectionery

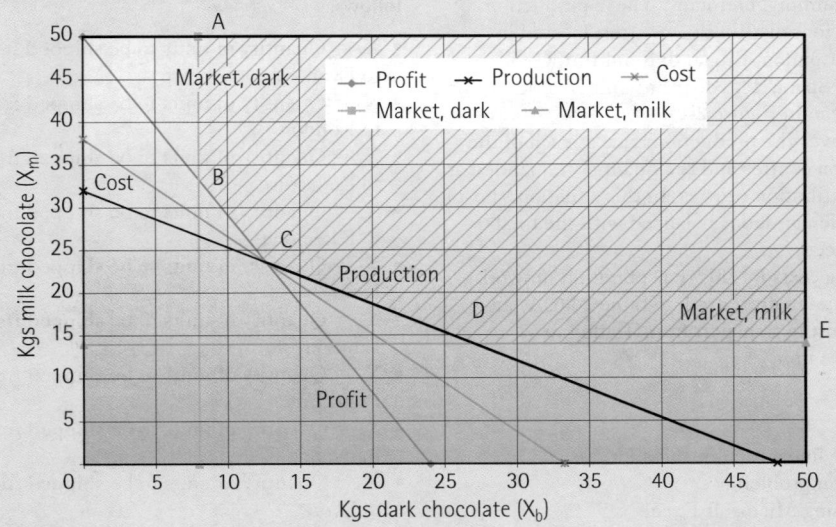

The optimum solution is the intersection of the market demand for dark chocolate and the profit curve, or point C, which corresponds to the results given by Solver. At this point, the production cost is at the limit of the constraint $60,000, the value in Cell [E-3]. The production of dark chocolate, 12.71 tons, is above the minimum market demand, Cell [B-4], and the tonnage of milk chocolate, 23.53 tons, is above the minimum amount of 14 tons, Cell [B-5]. Further, the labour time,

2400 hours, Cell [E-6], is at the minimum requirement of 2400 hours, Cell [B-6].

3. This solution is shown in Table 24.4. The procedure is identical to question 1, except that a new constraint is added to indicate that the production levels, Cells [C-9] and [D-9], are integer values. For this situation the production levels are 12 tons of dark chocolate and 25 tons of milk chocolate with a new cost of $27,100. The labour hours have increased to 2475.

Table 24.4 Vogler Confectionery: Solution 2

	A	B	C	D	E	F
1		Minimum	Coefficient	Coefficient		
2		needs	dark	milk	Actual	Excess
3	Profit	60,000.00	2,500.00	1,200.00	60,000.00	0.00
4	Market, dark	8.00	1.00	0.00	12.00	4.00
5	Market, milk	14.00	0.00	1.00	25.00	11.00
6	Production	2,400.00	50.00	75.00	2,475.00	75.00
7	Cost	27,100.00	800.00	700.00		
8						
9	Production, tons		12.00	25.00		

Demonstrating the concept 24.3 Machine tools

Situation

A company which manufactures machine tools has production centres in Liverpool, England; Toulon, France; and Hamburg, Germany. These production centres supply four distribution centres, located in Lyon, France; London, England; Frankfurt, Germany; and Barcelona, Spain. The distribution network for this operation is given in Figure 24.3.

Table 24.5 gives the production rates at each of the three production centres and the quantity demanded at each of the distribution centres. In this situation, the total quantity demanded is balanced with the total quantity produced.

The shipping costs for this transportation network in euros per unit are presented in Table 24.6. As an example, the cost to transport from Toulon to Frankfurt is €8 a unit.

Required

1. Develop the linear relationships for this transportation problem.
2. Optimize using Microsoft Excel.

Solution

Decision variables

There are 12 decision variables, which are designated as follows:

- X_1 = Quantity of units to be shipped from Liverpool to Lyon
- X_2 = Quantity of units to be shipped from Liverpool to London
- X_3 = Quantity of units to be shipped from Liverpool to Frankfurt
- X_4 = Quantity of units to be shipped from Liverpool to Barcelona
- X_5 = Quantity of units to be shipped from Toulon to Lyon
- X_6 = Quantity of units to be shipped from Toulon to London
- X_7 = Quantity of units to be shipped from Toulon to Frankfurt
- X_8 = Quantity of units to be shipped from Toulon to Barcelona
- X_9 = Quantity of units to be shipped from Hamburg to Lyon

Figure 24.3 Distribution network for machine tools

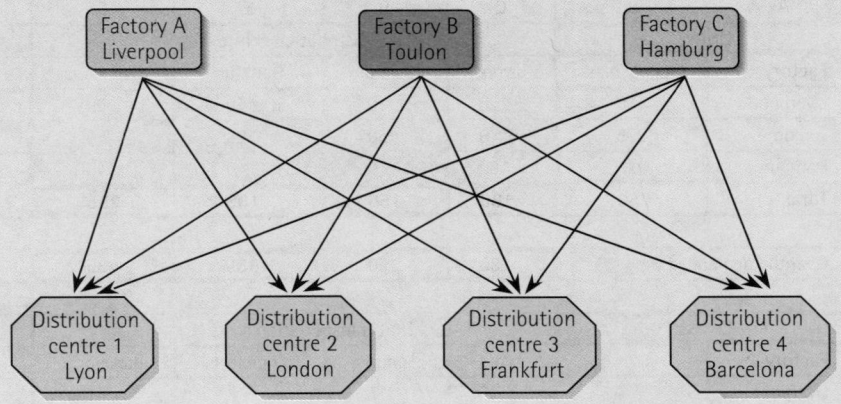

Table 24.5 **Production rates and quantities demanded**

Factory	Production rate (units/day)	Distribution centre	Daily demand (units/day)
Liverpool	150	Lyon	180
Toulon	275	London	150
Hamburg	325	Frankfurt	185
Total	**750**	Barcelona	235
		Total	**750**

- X_{10} = Quantity of units to be shipped from Hamburg to London
- X_{11} = Quantity of units to be shipped from Hamburg to Frankfurt
- X_{12} = Quantity of units to be shipped from Hamburg to Barcelona.

Objective function

The objective is to minimize the total transportation costs. Minimize:

- $Z = 5X_1 + 7X_2 + 7X_3 + X_4 + 12X_5 + 4X_6 + 8X_7 + 9X_8 + 8X_9 + 11X_{10} + 15X_{11} + 5X_{12}$

Constraints

- $X_1 + X_2 + X_3 + X_4 \leq 150$
- $X_5 + X_6 + X_7 + X_8 \leq 275$
- $X_9 + X_{10} + X_{11} + X_{12} \leq 325$
- $X_1 + X_5 + X_9 \geq 180$
- $X_2 + X_6 + X_{10} \geq 150$
- $X_3 + X_7 + X_{11} \geq 185$
- $X_4 + X_8 + X_{12} \geq 235$
- $X_1, X_2, X_3, X_4, X_5, X_6, X_7, X_8, X_9, X_{10}, X_{11}, X_{12} \geq 0$

Table 24.6 **Shipping costs for a transportation network**

	Lyon	London	Frankfurt	Barcelona
Liverpool	5	7	7	1
Toulon	12	4	8	9
Hamburg	8	11	15	5

- $X_1, X_2, X_3, X_4, X_5, X_6, X_7, X_8, X_9, X_{10}, X_{11}, X_{12}$ = integer value.

Excel Solver

The optimum distribution network is solved by using the macro 'Solver' in Excel and Table 24.7 gives the framework and the solution, which is now described.

Value to optimize

Here it is to minimize the total distribution costs for all the sites (Cell [G-16]). This cell contains the formula:

$$[G-16] = [G-11] + [G-12] + [G-13]$$

and

$$[G-12] = [C-3] * [C-12] + [D-3] * [D-12] \\ + [E-3] * [E-12] + [F-3] * [F-12]$$
$$[G-13] = [C-4] * [C-13] + [D-4] * [D-13] \\ + [E-4] * [E-13] + [F-4] * [F-13]$$
$$[G-14] = [C-5] * [C-14] + [D-5] * [D-14] \\ + [E-5] * [E-14] + [F-5] * [F-14]$$

Variables to calculate

These are the 12 values contained in the matrix from Liverpool–Lyon (Cell [C-3]) to Hamburg–Barcelona (Cell [F-5]).

Table 24.7 Distribution network solution

	A	B	C	D	E	F	G
1	Units		Distribution centre				
2	Factory	Supply max	Lyon	London	Frankfurt	Barcelona	Total
3	Liverpool	150	0	0	60	90	150
4	Toulon	275	0	150	125	0	275
5	Hamburg	325	180	0	0	145	325
6	Total	750	180	150	185	235	750
7							
8	Quantity demanded		180	150	185	235	750
9							
10	Costs		Unit transportation costs (€)				
11	Factory		Lyon	London	Frankfurt	Barcelona	Total cost
12	Liverpool		5	7	7	1	510
13	Toulon		12	4	8	9	1600
14	Hamburg		8	11	15	5	2165
15							
16	Total cost		1440	600	1420	815	4275

System constraints

- The values of the variables (Cells [C-3] through [F-5]) must be greater than or equal to zero. Before starting the iteration, these cells should be given an arbitrary value of 0.
- The totals of the quantity demanded for each distribution centre (Cells [C-8] through [F-8]) must be greater than or equal to the quantity delivered (Cells [C-6] through [F-6]).
- The total supplied (Cells [G-3] through [G-5]) must be less than or equal to the given maximum supply (Cells [B-3] through [B-5]).

Optimum network

Here the minimum cost is €4275 with the following distribution:

- 60 units shipped from Liverpool to Frankfurt
- 90 units shipped from Liverpool to Barcelona
- 150 units shipped from Toulon to London
- 125 units shipped from Toulon to Frankfurt
- 180 units shipped from Hamburg to Lyon
- 145 units shipped from Hamburg to Barcelona.

Demonstrating the concept 24.4 Blending

Situation

A refinery company produces three grades of motor oil, super, premium, and regular, from three components. The company wants to determine the optimal mix of these three components in each grade of motor oil in order to maximize profit. The maximum quantities available of each component, and their cost per barrel, are given in Table 24.8.

In order to ensure the appropriate blend to satisfy specifications each grade must contain certain general specifications. Each grade must have a minimum amount of component XL-11, plus a combination of other components as shown in Table 24.9.

Table 24.8 Maximum quantities of motor oil

Component	Maximum bbl available/day	Cost/bbl ($)
XL-11	7000	13.50
ST-21	4200	11.50
BF-31	5100	15.00

The customer demand indicates that the refining company should produce at least 4500 bbl/day of super, 5000 bbl/day of premium, and 3700 of standard grade.

Required

Using Microsoft Excel, determine the optimum blending mix to maximize the profit. Determine the revenues, costs, and profit for the operation. The volumes of products XL-11, ST-21, BF-31 must be integer values.

Solution

The optimum solution using Excel is given in Table 24.10 and this is explained as follows with the cell reference indicating where the mathematical formula is contained or in the case of the variables in which cell the value will be generated.

Variables

There are nine variables in the matrix [B-3:D-5] the individual cells:

- X_{1S} is quantity of product XL-11 in super Cell [B-3]
- X_{2S} is quantity of product ST-21 in super Cell [B-4]
- X_{3S} is quantity of product BF-31 in super Cell [B-5]

Table 24.9 Specifications required for appropriate blends

Grade	Component specification	Selling price/bbl
Super	• At least 40% of XL-11 • Not more than 25% of ST-21	25.00
Premium	• At least 45% of XL-11 • Not more than 20% of BF-31	22.00
Regular	• At least 50% of XL-11 • At least 15% of ST-21	21.50

- X_{1P} is quantity of product XL-11 in premium Cell [C-3]
- X_{2P} is quantity of product ST-21 in premium Cell [C-4]
- X_{3P} is quantity of product BF-31 in premium Cell [C-5]
- X_{1R} is quantity of product XL-11 in regular Cell [D-3]
- X_{2R} is quantity of product ST-21 in regular Cell [D-4]
- X_{3R} is quantity of product BF-31 in regular Cell [D-5].

Objective is to maximize profit

Revenues
- Revenues for super are given by the relationship $25.00(X_{1S} + X_{2S} + X_{3S})$ and this is the formula in Cell [B-11]. This value is $181,250.
- Revenues for premium are given by the relationship $22.00(X_{1P} + X_{2P} + X_{3P})$ and this is the formula in Cell [C-11]. The value is $110,000.
- Revenues for regular are given by the relationship $21.50(X_{1R} + X_{2R} + X_{3R})$ and this is the formula in Cell [D-11]. The value is $79,550.
- The formula in Cell [E-11] is the total revenues and this value is $370,800.

Cost
- Costs for product XL-11 are given by the relationship $13.50(X_{1S} + X_{1P} + X_{1R})$ and this is the formula in Cell [G-3]. This value is $94,500.
- Costs for product ST-21 are given by the relationship $11.50(X_{2S} + X_{2P} + X_{2R})$ and this is the formula in Cell [G-4]. This value is $48,300.
- Costs for product BF-31 are given by the relationship $15.00(X_{3S} + X_{3P} + X_{3R})$ and this is the formula in Cell [G-5]. This value is $71,250.

Table 24.10 Optimum blending mix solution to maximize profit

	A	B	C	D	E	F	G	H
1	Component	Finished product				Component	Component	Component
2	reference	Super	Premium	Regular	Total	unit cost/bbl	total cost	max bbls/day
3	XL-11	2900.00	2250.00	1850.00	7000.00	13.50	94,500.00	7000
4	ST-21	1583.00	1750.00	867.00	4200.00	11.50	48,300.00	4200
5	BF-31	2767.00	1000.00	983.00	4750.00	15.00	71,250.00	5100
6	Total	7250.00	5000.00	3700.00	15,950.00		214,050.00	
7	Min volume, bbl	4500.00	5000.00	3700.00				
8	Constraints	40.00%	45.00%	50.00%				
9		25.00%	20.00%	15.00%				
10	Unit price, $/bbl	25.00	22.00	21.50				
11	Revenue, $	181,250.00	110,000.00	79,550.00	370,800.00			
12	Profit, $				156,750.00			

- The total cost is $13.50(X_{1S} + X_{1P} + X_{1R}) - 11.50(X_{2S} + X_{2P} + X_{2R}) - 15.00(X_{3S} + X_{3P} + X_{3R})$. This value of $214,050 is in Cell [G-6].

$$\text{Profit (Z)} = \text{Revenues} - \text{Cost}$$

The optimum profit is in Cell [E-12], which contains the formula Cell [E-11] − [E-6] to give a value of $156,750 ($370,800 − $214,050).

The complete relationship for calculating the profit is:

$$\begin{aligned} Z = &\ 25.00(X_{1S} + X_{2S} + X_{3S}) \\ &+ 22.00(X_{1P} + X_{2P} + X_{3P}) \\ &+ 21.50(X_{1R} + X_{2R} + X_{3R}) \\ &- 13.50(X_{1S} + X_{1P} + X_{1R}) \\ &- 11.50(X_{2S} + X_{2P} + X_{2R}) \\ &- 15.00(X_{3S} + X_{3P} + X_{3R}) \end{aligned}$$

Reorganizing

$$\begin{aligned} Z = &\ 11.50X_{1S} + 13.50X_{2S} + 10.00X_{3S} + 8.50X_{1P} \\ &+ 10.50X_{2P} + 7.00X_{3P} + 8.00X_{1R} + 10.00X_{2R} \\ &+ 6.50X_{3R} \end{aligned}$$

This could be an alternative formula in Cell [E-12] for calculating the profit but in this example the calculation has been broken up into its individual components.

Constraints

The following are the constraints for the components available:

- $(X_{1S} + X_{1P} + X_{1R}) \leq 7000$ Cell [E-3]. The optimum value is 7000 bbl.
- $(X_{2S} + X_{2P} + X_{2R}) \leq 4200$ Cell [E-4]. The optimum value is 4200 bbl.
- $(X_{3S} + X_{3P} + X_{3R}) \leq 5100$ Cell [E-5]. The optimum value is 4750 bbl.

The following are the constraints for the proportion of components present in the final products. These proportions are in the matrice [B-8:D-7].

Super
- $X_{1S}/(X_{1S} + X_{2S} + X_{3S}) \geq 0.40$, or $0.60X_{1S} - 0.40X_{2S} - 0.40X_{3S} \geq 0$.
- $(X_{2S})/(X_{1S} + X_{2S} + X_{3S}) \leq 0.25$, or $0.75X_{2S} - 0.25X_{1S} - 0.25X_{3S} \leq 0$.

Premium
- $(X_{1P})/(X_{1P} + X_{2P} + X_{3P}) \geq 0.45$, or $0.55X_{1P} - 0.45X_{2P} - 0.45X_{3P} \geq 0$.
- $(X_{3P})/(X_{1P} + X_{2P} + X_{3P}) \leq 0.20$, or $0.80X_{3P} - 0.20X_{2P} - 0.20X_{1P} \leq 0$.

Regular
- $(X_{1R})/(X_{1R} + X_{2R} + X_{3R}) \geq 0.50$, or $0.50X_{1R} - 0.50X_{2R} - 0.50X_{3R} \geq 0$.
- $(X_{2R})/(X_{1R} + X_{2R} + X_{3R}) \geq 0.15$, or $0.85X_{2R} - 0.15X_{1R} - 0.15X_{3R} \geq 0$.

Production quantities
- $X_{1S} + X_{2S} + X_{3S} \geq 4500$: Cell [B-7]. The actual value of 7250 bbl is in Cell [B-6].
- $X_{1P} + X_{2P} + X_{3P} \geq 5000$: Cell [C-7]. The actual value of 5000 is in Cell [C-6].
- $X_{1R} + X_{2R} + X_{3R} \geq 3700$: Cell [D-7]. The actual value of 3700 is in Cell [D-6].

Not negative
- $X_{1S}, X_{2S}, X_{3S}, X_{1P}, X_{2P}, X_{3P}, X_{1R}, X_{2R}, X_{3R} \geq 0$.

Integer values
- $X_{1S}, X_{2S}, X_{3S}, X_{1P}, X_{2P}, X_{3P}, X_{1R}, X_{2R}, X_{3R} =$ integer values.

Application exercise 24.1   Desks

Situation

A company produces two types of wooden desk, Product 1 and Product 2. These are produced on two assembly lines, Line 1 and Line 2. Line 1 has 178.00 hours available and Line 2 has 78.00 hours available.

Product 1 requires 10.00 hours of production time on Line 1 and 6.00 hours of production time on Line 2. Product 2 requires 8.00 hours on Line 1 and 3.00 hours on Line 2.

The unit profit for Product 1 is $6.00, and the unit profit for Product 2 is $4.00.

Required

1. Solve this situation using linear programming. What is the optimum profit, and what are the corresponding production levels?
2. Determine the excess resources under the optimum situation.
3. Illustrate the production situation on a two-dimensional graph. Indicate the feasible area for the solution.
4. Show the iso-profit line on the graph.

Application exercise 24.2   Quarry

Situation

The Winterberger Quarry Company owns two quarries used for providing aggregate material for the building industry. At both of these two quarries the firm is able to provide a coarse, medium, and fine-grade aggregate.

The company has a contract to supply a large construction site each day with at least 76 cubic metres of coarse grade, 68 cubic metres of medium grade and 64 cubic metres of fine-grade material.

The capacity of Quarry N° 1 is such that it can produce 8 cubic metres of coarse grade material an hour, 10 cubic metres of medium grade and 14 cubic metres of fine grade. The capacity of Quarry N° 2 is such that it can produce 10 cubic metres of coarse grade material, 8 cubic metres of medium grade and 6 cubic metres of fine grade material an hour.

The operating cost of Quarry N° 1 is £220.00 an hour and £160.00 for Quarry N° 2.

Required

1. Solve this situation using linear programming. What is the optimum cost, and what are the corresponding hourly production levels of each quarry?
2. Determine the excess resources under the optimum situation.
3. Illustrate the production situation on a two-dimensional graph. Indicate the feasible area for the solution.
4. Show the iso-cost line on the graph.

Application exercise 24.3   Transformers

Situation

Serge Company produces electrical transformers for the heavy manufacturing industry. All the components are purchased from outside and Serge assembles the components, which is the strategic element for the firm. For two particular relatively standard transformers, reference D-137 and W-731, the assembly is performed in two stages in two different workshops. For a particular production plan there are a maximum of 400 hours available in each workshop. For product D-137 the labour standard is 2.25 hours/unit in Workshop 1, and 2.85 hours/unit in Workshop 2. For product W-371 the labour standard is 5.75 hours/unit in Workshop 1, and 3.25 hours/unit in Workshop 2. The profit from D-137 is calculated at $220.00/unit and $340.00/unit for W-731.

Required

1. Based on the given information, optimize this linear programming problem in order to maximize profits. Determine the profit and the corresponding number of units for each of the two products. Assume that only whole number units are made. Are there any excess resources?
2. Show the solution graphically including the profit line at the optimum number of units. Indicate the feasible area.
3. A slight redesign of product reference D-137 was later made which increased the labour standard for this unit in both workshops to 3.00 hours/unit. All the other conditions remain the same. What impact would this have on the optimum solution? What are your comments?

Application exercise 24.4   Advertising

Situation

A large department store is planning a yearend sale at its city stores of which it has many branches. It has set a budget of $250,000 in order to advertise the sale and is planning to use as its media television commercials, radio announcements, the daily newspaper, a free newspaper that is circulated in the city, and billboard advertising. An advertising consultant has indicated that the department store can expect an exposure to the public of 30,000 people per advertisement for television commercials, 28,000 for radio, 10,000 for the daily newspaper, 8000 for the free newspaper, and 15,000 for the billboard.

The estimated cost per advertisement for the television is $20,000, $18,000 for the radio commercial, $8000 for the daily newspaper, $2000 for the free newspaper, and $3000 for each billboard advertisement. As the yearend sale is fast approaching, the store has only time to prepare a total of 24 advertisements for all five types of media, but it does want to have at least one advertisement on TV, radio, the daily newspaper, the free newspaper, and the billboard.

Required

1. Develop the linear relationships for this problem showing the objective of maximizing the exposure to the public, and corresponding constraints.
2. Solve this investment problem using Excel Solver.
3. What will be the estimated total exposure, and what will be the cost of the advertising campaign?

Application exercise 24.5 Beer distribution

Situation

A brewing company has four breweries located in Marseille, France; Newcastle, UK; Tarragona, Spain; and Cologne, Germany. It supplies eight distribution centres in Porto, Portugal; Madrid, Spain; Birmingham, England; Bonn, Germany; Paris, France; Lille, France; Brussels, Belgium; and Milan, Italy.

One product, which is transported either by truck, or train is canned beer. Before being shipped, the beer is stacked on pallets 100 × 150 cm. A full pallet is considered a unit for shipping purposes.

Table 24.11 shows the weekly supply of canned beer, in units, available from the four breweries, and the units demanded by the eight distribution centres.

Transportation costs in dollars per unit are as shown in Table 24.12.

Required

1. Develop the optimum transportation network.
2. What are the total weekly transportation costs?

3. If the distribution centres are billed for their actual transportation costs, what will be their individual costs?
4. If this situation were on average the regular supply and delivery pattern, what changes would you propose?

Table 24.11 Weekly supply of canned beer

Brewery	Weekly supply (units)	Distribution centre (units)	Weekly demand (units)
Marseille	3,250	Porto	1,750
Newcastle	5,380	Madrid	2,350
Tarragona	7,750	Birmingham	2,480
Cologne	5,845	Bonn	2,200
Total	**22,225**	Paris	3,785
		Lille	1,980
		Brussels	3,150
		Milan	3,250
		Total	**20,945**

Table 24.12 Transportation costs of canned beer

	Porto	Madrid	Birmingham	Bonn	Paris	Lille	Brussels	Milan
Marseille	4.2	3.5	5.2	4.2	1.2	1.4	2.2	2.5
Newcastle	7.5	6.0	2.5	5.0	4.0	3.0	3.5	7.4
Tarragona	1.2	1.5	5.6	4.8	4.0	4.7	4.8	5.2
Cologne	6.2	6.1	2.7	1.7	3.1	3.2	3.0	4.7

Application exercise 24.6 Investment

Situation

Bob Cozzi has just sold one of his real estate properties for $200,000. Of this amount, $50,000 will be used to cover various costs, and the remainder he plans to invest in stocks, bonds and certificates of deposit. For the coming year, certificates of deposit have a yield rate of 5.00%, municipal bonds 7.50% and Bob estimates that technical stocks listed on the NASDAQ will yield 15.00% and blue chip stocks listed on Wall Street 12.50%.

From a risk point of view, Bob is going to use the following guidelines for his investment, but with the objective of maximizing his return:

- No more than 10% of the total investment will be in certificates of deposit.

- The amount invested in the total of municipal bonds, technical stocks and blue chip stocks is to be more than the amount invested in certificates of deposit.
- The total amount invested in stocks will be more than 50% of the total sum invested.
- The amount invested in technical stocks will be no more than 40% of the amount listed in blue chip stocks.

Required

1. Develop the linear relationships for this problem showing the objectives and constraints.
2. Solve this investment problem using Excel Solver.
3. If the yield rates are correct for the various investments, what will be the value of Bob's investments after one year?

Case study 24.1 Easthope

Situation

The Easthope Co. in southern California manufactures and assembles heart-monitoring equipment for hospitals and the medical profession. Easthope designed the equipment and the production operation is relatively straightforward. The company prepares a six-month planning programme in advance and for each month the company has a policy always to have a 100% client service level, that is, no orders for the month are put on backlog. A monthly planning schedule is considered to be four weeks.

The company has 50 permanent employees who work 40 hours a week and are able to work up to ten hours a week overtime. The labour cost for the normal workweek is $24.00 an hour and they receive time and a half for overtime work. The labour hours per unit for this heart-monitoring equipment are 2.50. They remain the same for overtime work.

If there is insufficient permanent labour to meet customer requirements Easthope can use part-time labour that costs $16 an hour but their labour hours a unit are 3.20. Easthope has a policy to use only up to 10% of the permanent labour force for part-time work in order not to jeopardize quality or to upset the team spirit in the organization. In addition the company can use a reliable subcontractor in the area for which the subcontracting costs are $55.00 a unit. The contractor is promised a maximum of 300 units each month from Easthope. The inventory holding costs are estimated at $2.50 a unit a week and the total inventory holding costs are calculated on a monthly linear average. Any units made by the subcontractor are calculated into

Easthope's inventory carrying cost since the subcontractor delivers the units to Easthope as soon as they are made.

At the end of December one particular year estimated customer demand for the next six months stood as shown in Table 24.13. At the end of the previous December, there were 250 units of the heart-monitoring equipment in Easthope's finished goods storage.

Required

1. Using linear programming, develop a production plan for Easthope, showing, on a monthly basis, the units to be produced by the permanent labour force, overtime, part-time labour, and subcontracting. Also show the costs for these production activities.

2. If Easthope were able to negotiate with the subcontractor that he would promise the subcontractor a minimum of 500 units a month if the unit cost were reduced to $50 a unit, how would this change the production plan? What would the financial impact be to Easthope? What qualitative impact do you think it would have on the permanent employees of Easthope? Justify your reasoning.

Table 24.13 Easthope: Estimated customer demand

Month	Jan	Feb	Mar	Apr	May	Jun
Demand	3,800	3,500	2,450	4,100	5,000	4,400

Selected further reading

CHVATAL, Vasek (1983) *Linear Programming*, W H Freeman & Co.

DANTZIG, George B. (1998) *Linear Programming and Extensions*, Princeton University Press.

MURTY, Katta G. (1983) *Linear Programming*, Wiley.

SCHRIJVER, Alexander (1998) *Theory of Linear and Integer Programming*, Wiley.

SOFER, Ariela and NASH, Stephen G. (1995) *Linear and Nonlinear Programming*, McGraw-Hill.

An extensive listing of other further reading can be found on the website.

What's on the web?

Further learning resources are available to lecturers and students at www.supplychain-online.com, including the following which are specific to *Linear programming*:

Resource	Subject
Chapter overview	Linear programming
Application exercise: Braun Engineering	Two variables
Application exercise: Farming	Two variables
Application exercise: Vogler	Two variables
Application exercise: Blending	More than two variables
Application exercise: Machine tools	More than two variables
Application exercise: Religious organization	More than two variables
More further reading	Linear programming

25 *Financial analysis*

Chapter overview

- **Product pricing**
- **Variable costs**
- **Fixed costs**
- **Financial treatment of fixed assets**
- **Traditional cost accounting**
- **Activity–based costing**
- **Breakeven analysis**
- **Short run production costs**
- **Long run production costs**

Product pricing

Profit motive

A market-driven firm is in business to make money. In its particular segment of the supply chain, whether it is business to business or business to consumer a firm generates its income from the sale of its end products either goods or services. From an accounting point of view the firm's operating income is essentially the difference between sales revenues and costs where the sales revenue is the product of the units sold and the product price. The economic basis of profit is different in that profits are realized when sales and production continue to expand for as long as marginal revenue is higher than or equal to marginal cost. The marginal revenue is not the normal accounting price a unit but assumes that the price/demand relationship shows an increase in demand with a reduction in price. This concept is illustrated in Demonstrating the concept 25.1. Here under normal accounting the firm continues to make a profit until almost 9000 units are sold. However, under the economic marginal analysis the marginal profit is zero at 5000 units.

Product price and the operations manager

Although the operations manager may not be directly involved in product pricing, an awareness of a company's pricing strategy will facilitate effective cost management

of the associated operations function. Further, knowing a product price will give the operations management an indication of how much leverage there is with the price of raw materials since they are a component of the product cost. As illustrated in Chapter 2, cost reductions, for given sales revenues, can have significant impact on net income. Although some firms may consider that the client is king, others say that cost is king!

For a given product price, lower product costs translate into a higher profit margin. Thus, in establishing a product price, the strategy of the firm would be to maximize the total profit margin over a certain time horizon. Prices should not be set too high so that the firm's market share is low. Neither should the price be too low so that costs are barely recuperated unless perhaps a low price of one product helps the sales of another product. The following are some approaches to product pricing.

Market price

The market price, or the price the market would bear, is the amount customers are willing to pay. It is often the market that determines the product price because of such factors as the number of competing products, the price of alternatives that have similar functions, or the quality and value perception of the product. Thus, the cost to produce a product may not be a factor in finally determining its price. For products that are a monopoly in the market, the price may have little relationship to cost as is illustrated in Industry insight 25.1.

Scotch whisky

The production operation of whisky is relatively simple. The raw material is barley, which is first steeped in water before it is passed to the malting floors. Here it is agitated and turned continuously to prevent heat build-up during the germination process which turns it into malt. At this stage the starch has been converted to maltose (a sugar). The malt is then dried in a peat kiln that gives the malt a smoky flavour that is eventually imparted to the whisky. After drying, the malt is ground into grist and this is mixed with water in a mash tun. Here at progressively hotter temperatures, with different infusions of water, the sugar is extracted from the grist. The spent grist, after all the sugar has been removed, is called draff and this is used for animal feed. The sugar liquid, or worts, is mixed with yeast to facilitate fermentation. This mixture of yeast and worts is successively distilled where the middle cut eventually produces a spirit of 70% alcohol, or 140 proof. This alcohol is then transferred to wooden casks where the whisky is aged. Under Scottish law the minimum period for aging is three years in order that the whisky can be classified as 'Scotch' whisky. The last process is bottling before the Scotch whisky is distributed worldwide.

The production, distillation and maturation process is estimated to cost $5.00 for a fifth of whisky (a fifth is a unit of measure equal to one-fifth of a US gallon). On the same basis, the distribution costs, over mostly 5400

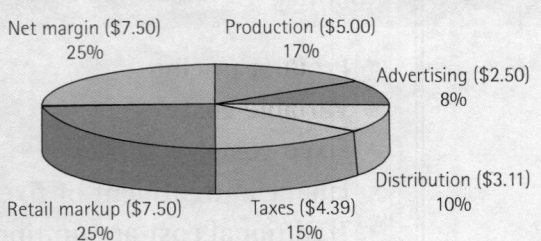

Figure 25.1 Price breakdown of a fifth of Johnnie Walker Scotch whisky

kilometres of ocean, to New York City are estimated at $3.11, which gives a total supply chain cost of $8.11. However, the price of a fifth of Scotch whisky in New York is $30, which has little relationship to the supply chain costs as illustrated in Figure 25.1.

In the $30 price there is a $15 mark-up, with an estimated one-half of this going to the retailer and one-half to Guinness (now Diageo plc), the producer. There is about 15% in Federal and local taxes. Finally, there is about 8% in advertising to convince the purchaser that he is paying a price of $30 for the Scotch whisky because it is a premium brand!

Adapted from: 'Why whisky costs so much', *Fortune*[1]

For new products introduced into the market, prices may be very high at first in order to recoup earlier development costs (see Chapter 6). As more competitors enter the market, companies are forced to lower prices in order to keep customers and this sometimes explains the eventual similarities of product prices as the following illustrates:

• When Texas Instruments introduced their calculators in the early 1970s the prices were very high at over $250. However they dropped to below $100 in a period of only a few months. Now, with other competitors such as Hewlett-Packard and Casio, calculators, even the most sophisticated, are relatively inexpensive.
• When personal computers came on the market in the late 1980s, notably from IBM, the prices were high. However they dropped dramatically in the 1990s and now in the 2000s, with competitors such as Dell, Compaq, and Hewlett-Packard, they are reasonably priced.
• The price of airfares in real terms, particularly in the USA, has fallen since the 1980s partly as a result of deregulation as new competitors entered the market.

The price decline in Europe has not been so steep as deregulation is still not completely in force.

When there are many competitors offering similar products, and the product is quite standard, the price level, or range is usually already established and will lie between close limits, for example:

• Services such as restaurants, hotels, and airlines have similar prices for equivalent products.
• Consumer products such as blue jeans, washing machines, or food products.
• Industrial products such as stainless steel tubing, moulded plastic units, or pumps.

Some companies may choose to have lower profits on some products in order to increase their market share or visibility in the market. Alternatively, similar products may be sold at different prices in different markets.

Catalogue price

A catalogue price is similar to the market price in that it is a price already published in a catalogue. A company

Figure 25.2 Product price based on cost plus margin

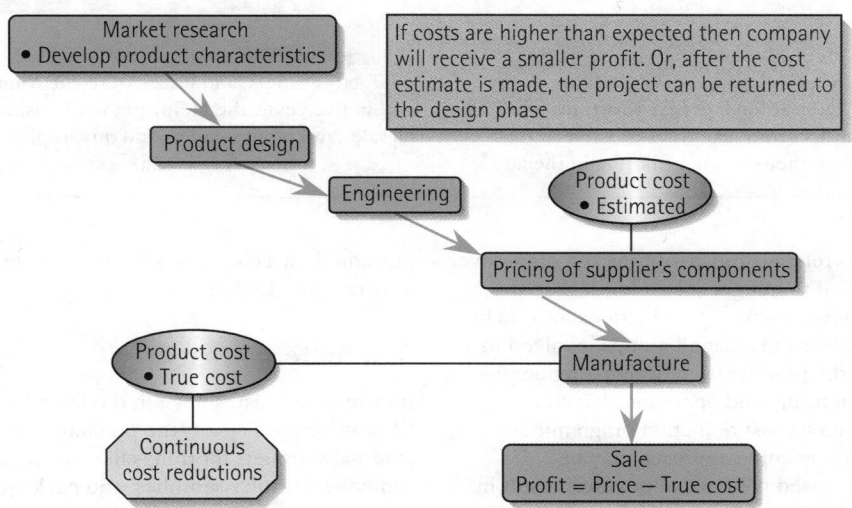

bringing out a similar product that cannot be differentiated from competitive products would likely follow the catalogue price. Examples of standard industrial goods for which catalogue prices exist may be screws, bolts, nails, PVC pellets for making plastic, corrugated cardboard, etc.

Price equal to cost plus margin

Here a company would add up all the costs going into the product and then add a profit margin (say, 15%) to

give the market price. This approach is illustrated in Figure 25.2.

Price based on target cost

The target cost, as illustrated in Figure 25.3,[2] is a market-driven cost in competitive industries determined from the sales price necessary to capture a predetermined market share:

Target cost
 = Sales price (for expected market share) − Profit

Figure 25.3 Product price based on target cost

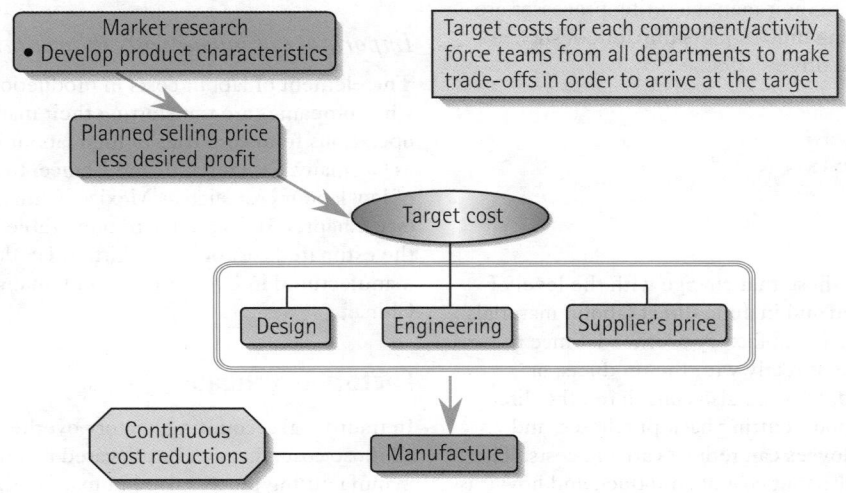

Thus, from this relationship, assuming the profit level is pre-established, if the target cost is lower than the standard, or budgeted costs, cost reductions have to be implemented. This means that all groups involved in commercializing the product from design, engineering, suppliers, manufacturing and operations have to implement continuous cost reduction programmes. Here again, a learning curve approach may be appropriate as increased volumes of products result in lower unit costs. An illustration can be found in Industry insight 25.2.

Exchange rates

Companies that export may find that, as a result of changes in exchange rates, the sales price of their products rises on foreign markets making them less attractive to consumers. This has been the case for Japanese and German products where the Yen and the Mark have strengthened in relation to the US dollar. To counteract this, companies are pushed to drop their prices, and if the same profit level is desired, this means a drop in target cost. For example, to achieve this, Japanese automobile companies such as Toyota, Nissan, and Honda, are cutting out extras on their vehicles such as heated mirrors, leather seats, and all-round disc brakes. In addition, their manufacturing processes are changing by leaving hidden parts unpainted, such as the fuel tanks and drive shafts.[3]

Variable costs

Definition

Variable costs are those that change with the level of products produced and include direct labour, materials used in the product, and factory overhead. Since these costs are identified directly with the products, or services produced, they are also considered the direct costs. In slow periods, cutting back purchases, and terminating employees can reduce variable costs. The development of the unit cost of a product, and how it is presented on a company's financial statement, is illustrated in Table 25.1.

Raw material cost

Raw material cost, shown in the table by the line item 'Raw materials', covers the purchase price paid to external suppliers for things like raw materials, components, subassemblies, and packaging. For components made in one work centre of the same company, and then used by another work centre the 'price' or material cost would be an established transfer cost.

Direct labour cost

Direct labour cost, shown in the table by the line item 'Direct labour', is that which can be directly accounted for in the production of products in question. It would cover things like labour employed for operating machines, performing assembly operations, or packaging. The direct labour cost is not only paid wages but also the burden. The burden is the mandatory social charges such as medical insurance, retirement, unemployment, holiday pay, etc.

Importance of labour costs in product cost

The element of labour costs in production is a reason why companies are transferring their manufacturing operations from countries of high labour cost such as Germany, Switzerland, and France, to regions of low labour cost such as Mexico, China, Brazil (see Chapter 3). As an illustration, Table 25.2 gives the estimated cost of a silk shirt, in US dollars, manufactured in Lyon, France and Shanghai, China.[5]

Factory overhead

In traditional accounting, factory overhead includes all those costs that can be allocated to a particular manufacturing process used in making the product.

Table 25.1 Cost of goods sold (yearend 31 December 2001)

Work-in-process, 1 January 2001		$5,176,000
Raw materials		
Inventory, 1 January 2001		$2,943,500
Purchases	$4,712,500	
Less: Purchase returns and allowances	214,100	
Net purchases		4,498,400
Total cost of materials available		$7,441,900
Less: Inventory, 31 December 2001		3,532,200
Cost of materials put into production		$3,909,700
Direct labour		$2,079,000
Factory overhead		
Indirect labour	$184,800	
Repairs	72,150	
Energy (heating, light, power)	5,780	
Water	1,500	
Depreciation – machinery and equipment	24,150	
Factory supplies (oil, cleaning fluids, gloves)	1,800	
Patents expense	2,750	
Insurance	5,780	
Total factory overhead		$298,710
Total manufacturing costs		$6,287,410
Work-in-process during 2001		$11,463,410
Less: Work-in-process inventory, 31 December 2001		7,246,400
Costs of goods sold		$4,217,010
Units sold in 2001	27,400	
Unit cost price of manufactured goods in 2001		$153.91

Table 25.2 Cost of a silk shirt

Item	Shanghai	Lyon
Raw materials	5	7
Labour	1	18
Margin	5	6
Transportation to Europe	1	0
Total product cost	12	31
Labour as % product cost	8	58

It might include energy costs, lubricating fluids, maintenance costs, and a portion of machinery depreciation used in the manufacture. This is shown in the line item 'factory overhead'.

Value of inventory

In the table there are line items for inventory. As discussed in Chapter 11, the amount of inventory to hold depends on:

- the needs for a production run
- how often the material is used
- the cost of placing an order
- the lead time for delivery of the materials
- deterioration or obsolescence
- discounts for bulk purchases
- price fluctuations.

Holding inventory ties up capital, uses storage space, requires personnel for its administration, risks being stolen, becoming obsolete, or deteriorating. The price paid for inventory items changes with time. As an example, in paper manufacture, the raw pulp, purchased in one period may increase in price when the identical raw material is purchased six months later. Physically, the component is the same and makes no difference in the operation of the manufactured end product. However, the question arises as to what the value is of inventory to be used to calculate the final cost of goods sold. Methods used include the following.

First in, first out

In first in, first out (FIFO), the first items of inventory obtained are charged against sales. Since the first items will probably have cost less than later items, the cost of goods sold will be the lowest possible. The effect on the income statement will to indicate a higher gross profit. The value of inventory remaining will be accounted at a relatively high value.

Last in, first out

In last in, first out (LIFO), the last items of inventory obtained are charged against sales. Since the last items will probably have cost more than earlier items, the cost of goods sold will be the highest possible. The effect on the income statement will to indicate a lower gross profit. The value of inventory remaining will be accounted at a relatively low value.

Weighted unit average cost

In weighted unit average cost (WUAC), the average value of the inventory items obtained is charged against sales. This will balance out the value of the cost of goods sold, and the value of inventory remaining.

In the USA, the LIFO or FIFO methods of accounting are permitted for reporting financial results. The FIFO method would be very optimistic in determining profits and would report high in-process inventory values that could impact insurance or taxation levels. With LIFO, profit figures are conservative with low value of inventory remaining. In other countries such as France, the weighted average unit cost is the accepted accounting method for inventory valuation. Demonstrating the concept 25.2 illustrates these three methods of valuing inventory.

Fixed costs

Definition

Fixed costs are derived from the capital assets used for running a business and normally have a useful life of over one year. (Chapter 11 differentiates capital assets from inventory.) Capital assets include machinery, computers, transportation equipment, buildings, office

furniture, etc. In operations planning, the need, and timing, of acquiring capital assets is important as these are charged as a cost to the operation in the form of depreciation.

The need for additional capital assets may arise as a result of expansion due to increased sales or new markets, or existing capital equipment needs to be replaced as it is worn, becomes obsolete, or technological sophistication necessitates replacement. Normally, top management makes the decision to purchase capital assets but those in operations are very often required to justify their acquisition. Capital assets are being used proportionately more and more, relative to labour, in flexible manufacturing systems. Land is a capital asset but its financial treatment is different from that of equipment, as it does not 'wear out'.

Depreciation

Depreciation is the accounting method by which a capital asset is charged to the business. Although payment for the capital asset is normally made at the time the asset is acquired (though this depends on terms with the supplier), depreciation is a periodic non-cash charge. It indirectly impacts the cash flow or profits through its income tax effect as illustrated in Table 25.3.

Since tax rates and depreciation methods vary from country to country, the magnitude of the tax advantage will not be the same in every country.

Calculation of depreciation

The way depreciation is calculated and applied for the cost of a capital asset affects the annual cash flow. Three accounting methods are straight line, the sum of year's digits, and the declining balance method.

Table 25.3 Impact of depreciation

Financial entry	No depreciation allowance	Depreciation allowance
Income, before depreciation and taxes	500,000	500,000
Less depreciation	0	35,000
Taxable income	500,000	465,000
Taxes payable @ 45%	225,000	209,250
Income after taxes	275,000	255,750
Tax advantage with depreciation	0	19,250

Straight line method

The straight line method divides in equal portions the cost of the fixed asset, C, over the period of its estimated life, n years. If there is a salvage value, S, then the amount of depreciation applied each year is:

$$\frac{C - S}{n}$$

Assume that an asset is purchased for $510,000. The life of the asset is seven years, and the salvage value is $20,000:

$$\text{Depreciation amount} = \frac{510,000 - 20,000}{7}$$

$$= \frac{490,000}{7} = \$70,000/\text{year}$$

The amounts charged to depreciation each year are shown in Table 25.4.

Sum of the year's digits

Here, the sum of the year's digits is used to give the denominator to proportion the depreciation amount. For an asset with a seven-year life, the sum of the year's digits is:

$$7 + 6 + 5 + 4 + 3 + 2 + 1 = 28$$

The numerator is the year in question. For example, for the asset with a cost price of $510,000 and a salvage value of $20,000, the depreciation amounts are:

Year 1 = (7/28) * (510,000 − 20,000) = $122,250.

Table 25.4 Amounts charged to depreciation

Year	Depreciation amount ($)
1	70,000
2	70,000
3	70,000
4	70,000
5	70,000
6	70,000
7	70,000
Total	490,000

Year 2 = (6/28) * (510,000 − 20,000) = $105,000.
Year 3 = (5/28) * (510,000 − 20,000) = $87,500.
Year 4 = (4/28) * (510,000 − 20,000) = $70,000.
Year 5 = (3/28) * (510,000 − 20,000) = $52,500.
Year 6 = (2/28) * (510,000 − 20,000) = $35,000.
Year 7 = (1/28) * (510,000 − 20,000) = $17,500.

Total depreciation is $490,000. With this method, higher rates are charged in the earlier years, and less in the later periods.

Declining balance

This method applies a constant depreciation rate to a gradually reducing balance. It applies a higher depreciation rate in early years, and lower amounts in later years. A common used rate is twice the straight line rate, or double declining balance. The rate is applied to cost and not the cost less salvage. The following is an illustration.

In the straight line method the rate used is 1/7. In the double declining balance the rate is 2/7. Depreciation amounts are thus as follows:

Year 1 = (2/7) * (510,000) = $145,714
    Remaining is ($510,000 − $145,714) = $364,286
Year 2 = (2/7) * (364,286) = $104,082
    Remaining is ($364,286 − $104,082) = $260,204
Year 3 = (2/7) * (260,204) = $74,344
    Remaining is ($260,204 − $74,344) = $185,860
Year 4 = (2/7) * (185,860) = $53,103
    Remaining is ($185,860 − $53,103) = $132,757
Year 5 = (2/7) * (132,757) = $37,931
    Remaining is ($132,757 − $37,931) = $94,826
Year 6 = (2/7) * (94,827) = $27,093
    Remaining is ($94,826 − $27,093) = $67,733
Year 7 = (2/7) * (67,733) = $19,352
    Remaining is ($67,733 − $19,352) = $48,381

Total depreciation is $461,619.

Financial treatment of fixed assets

Payback method

The payback method gives an indication how long it takes to recover the initial investment for the purchase of an asset taking into account operating cost savings, or other financial expenses. The payback period is dependent on the depreciation method employed and it should be considered on an after-tax basis to give meaningful results otherwise the time period determined may be quite wrong. The method does not consider the time value of money but its calculation is straightforward and the results are easy to understand. The payback method of financial analysis is illustrated in questions 1 to 3 of the Demonstrating the concept 25.3.

Net present value

Net present value analysis (NPV) considers the time value of money and discounts the value of all after-tax cash flows back to the present time. Investments in the asset are outflows, or a negative value. Savings, as a result of improved operations, are positive flows. A positive net present value indicates that the value of the investment has been recuperated during the life of the investment considered. The basis of the net present value calculation is that an amount of money today invested, say, in a certificate of deposit, will be worth more in the future because of the interest on the investment. Assume:

- P is the initial investment
- i the interest rate
- n is the period of investment
- F is the future value of the initial investment after n years.

Future values

For annual compounding, $F = P(1 + i)^n$, and for daily compounding, $F = P(1 + [i/365])^{n*365}$.

Some financial institutions may use 360 instead of 365 days.

Assume £2500 is invested for a period of six years at a rate of 5%. The value of the investment at the end of the period for annual compounding is:

$$F = 2500(1 + 0.05)^6 = 2500 * 1.3401 = £3350.24$$

For daily compounding the value is:

$$F = 2500[1 + (0.05/365)]^{6*365} = 2500 * 1.3498 = £3374.58$$

Present values

By corollary in the NPV concept, the present value of a future sum of money is less in absolute terms because future values implies accrued interest. To bring it to its present value, all accrued interest has to be removed. Thus, reversing the previous relationships, for annual compounding, $P = F/(1 + i)^n$ and for daily compounding, $P = F/(1 + [i/365])^{n*365}$.

Thus, the present value of £3350.24 to be received six years from now would have a present value of £2500 at an interest rate of 5% compounded annually.

The present value of £2500 to be received six years from now at a rate of 5% is:

$$P = \frac{F}{(1 + i)^n} = \frac{2500}{(1 + 0.05)^6} = \frac{2500}{1.3401} = £1865.54$$

The net present value method of financial analysis is illustrated in question 4 of Demonstrating the concept 25.3.

Internal rate of return

The internal rate of return method computes the discount rate or true interest rate that equates the present value of all net cash inflows (positive values), with the cost of the capital asset (a negative value). In other words, it is the discount rate that will cause the net present value of an investment to be zero. The calculation approach is similar to the net present value method except that in the NPV approach the discount, or interest rate is specified. The concept is illustrated in the Demonstrating the concept 25.4.

Traditional cost accounting

Assigning costs

In manufacturing, traditional cost accounting involves first assigning to the product the direct costs such as labour and the materials used and then attributing to this a proportion of the production overhead. Depending on the size of the firm, this is usually a two-step procedure. The first stage is to allocate the overhead to cost centres according to some basis such as surface area of the cost centres, the number of employees, or book value of the capital equipment. The second stage is to assign the overheads allocated to each cost centre to the products produced in these cost centres. This might be on the basis of labour or machine hours used. Finally, to each product cost is then added a proportionate amount of general overhead that includes sales and marketing and administrative expenses in order to arrive at a global product cost. This cost can then provide a basis for product pricing. In this way of allocation the overheads are absorbed by the cost centres. This principle of this traditional cost accounting approach is illustrated in Demonstrating the concept 25.5.

Production overhead

The overhead costs in production are those costs associated with the manufacturing and assembly process but which cannot be directly assigned to a particular product. This may include the salaries of supervisors, the cost of machine maintenance, the wages of quality control inspectors, the rent of the facility, depreciation charges on machinery and buildings, energy costs such as power, lighting, and water, and administration of the production facility. Some of these costs may be fixed costs independent of the production output, such as depreciation and rent. Alternatively, they may be variable such as power and cooling fluids that are related to the time the machinery or the operation is in use. In this case, if it is feasible to track these costs, then they should be allocated directly to the products in question.

The following are the general procedures used to analyze production overhead:

1. Each expense item must be traced to the department or the cost centre, from which it originates.
2. If the department is not a production department where value is added to a product but is used by the production personnel then these costs must be reallocated to the various production departments. Such 'non-value'-added departments might include the restaurant, storage centre, maintenance facility, or human resource facility for the production people.
3. An overhead rate must be calculated for each production department based on the total costs of the department and the expected use of the department during the period in question.

Under- or over-absorption of overhead

As overhead absorption rates need to be calculated before a period of production activity starts, it is normal to base them on budgeted costs at a predetermined capacity level. In doing this, firms are later often confronted with under- or over-absorption of overheads once the actual production activity has finished. As an illustration, assume that annual fixed overheads are $300,000 and that the budgeted annual direct labour hours are 120,000. Thus, the estimated allocation rate for the overhead is $2.50 per hour ($300,000/120,000). Assume now that, at the end of the year, there was no change in the overhead amount but that the actual labour hours used was 100,000. Thus using the allocated rate only $250,000 of overhead will be charged to production (2.50 * 100,000). The balance of $50,000 (300,000 − 250,000) will be under-recovered. Alternatively, assume that the actually hours used were 135,000, then the overhead charged would be $337,500 ($2.50 * 135,000). This means an over-absorption of $37,500 (337,500 − 300,000). Thus the question arises how to handle an over- or under-absorption of overhead.

One way is to treat them as a period cost and write them off against the profit and loss statement in the current accounting period.

Activity-based costing

Operating changes

Many companies today produce a multitude of different products. In addition, they increasingly rely on computer-based information systems, numerically controlled machines, robots, CAD/CAM equipment, The Internet and the web. Work centres have been reorganized to incorporate these new technologies, and to adapt to just-in-time operation. These changes have considerably reduced the amount of labour input to operations and, as such, there is justification for modifying how costs are allocated thus moving away from traditional cost accounting. In modern automated organizations, the variable elements of cost have now become a small part of total costs and the direct labour is very small or perhaps non-existent. In addition, resources consumed by products are not only the production facilities as reflected in traditional absorption costing but includes, for example, the purchasing activity to place an order, negotiations to outsource the work, the use of the ERP system to manage the operation, monitoring quality with lasers or other equipment, etc.

The need for a more responsive system was highlighted by the fact that low volume, products that required high setup, or perhaps required extensive sales efforts were not being fairly charged with a proportion of these costs. This was distorting not only product pricing and abandonment decisions, but in some cases the selling effort and the amount of commission attributed to salespeople. Figure 25.4, which is based on a study by the Tokyo Metropolitan University of Japan, illustrates how over the last 50 odd years manufacturing costs have changed.[6] Of significance are the reduction in proportion of labour and materials and the increase in the proportion of subcontracting and automation. Thus, proportioning overhead in the traditional cost accounting way may give a false interpretation of product cost.

Principle of activity-based costing

The principle of activity-based costing is to analyze in depth actual product costs by specifically identifying all those activities associated with the product at each step in the flow of the product through the manufacturing or service centre supply chain. In manufacturing, these

Figure 25.4 Breakdown of manufacturing costs in Japan

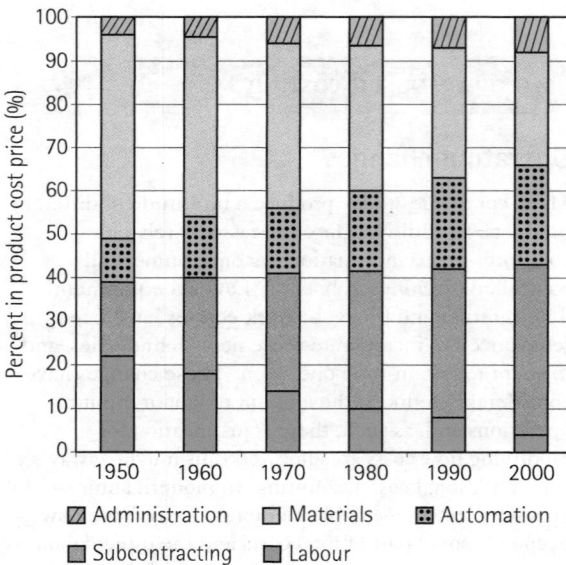

- ▨ Administration
- ▨ Subcontracting
- ▨ Materials
- ▨ Labour
- ▨ Automation

include not only the production, or transformation step, but the technology used and non-value activities that take time such as setups, material transfer, inspection, rework, bottlenecks, material delays, inventory in storage, etc. Then like conventional costing, ABC analysis is based on a two-stage approach. The overhead cost is charged to an activity pool such as setup, quality, handling, receiving, packaging, etc. These costs are then assigned to the product, which thus keeps the allocated overhead proportion to a minimum. Thus, activity-based costing is an absorption costing system that incorporates into the product a direct charge for:

- use of resources which were previously included in an all purpose overhead rate, such as material handling, machine setup times, inspection, quality control, etc.
- activities that were not previously included at all such as material procurement, personnel costs, selling activities, etc.

The use of activity-based costing highlights all the activities in the operating process, including inefficiencies whereas traditional accounting does not take this into consideration.

Non–value added

A non-value-added activity is one that involves the expenditure of time, money, and other resources but to the client there is no apparent improvement in quality,

performance, function, or perceived value to the product. The following is what Henry Ford is quoted as saying in 1921 about time:

Time waste differs from material waste in that with time there can be no salvage. The easiest of all wastes, and the hardest to correct, is the waste of time, because wasted time does not litter the floor like wasted material.

A particular non-value-added activity is holding inventory, either raw materials, in-process, or finished goods. Financing this inventory must be made though internal cash, or external debt and equity. Costs associated with holding assets are often buried in overhead and ignored in real product costing. Activity-based costing identifies, these non-value-added activities to provide a basis for their reduction, and/or elimination. In Chapter 11 the activities (times) globally associated with the transformation of a product were:

$$\text{Activity time} = \text{Processing} + (\text{Waiting} + \text{Transfer} + \text{Queuing} + \text{Setup})$$

If we combine these non-value activities then the equation reduces to:

$$\text{Activity time} = \text{Processing} + \text{Non-value-added time}$$

Then the efficiency of the operation can be represented by:

$$\text{Operating efficiency} = \frac{\text{Processing time}}{(\text{Processing time} + \text{Non-valued-added time})}$$

Reducing the non-value-added time such as by the following can increase the operating efficiency:

- improving equipment effectiveness
- a SMED analysis to reduce setup times
- implementing just-in-time kanban systems
- minimizing idle time as a result of worker pause and lunch breaks by staggering these times
- improving layout to have a more streamlined flow
- simplifying product design to reduce operating time
- working closely with suppliers to reduce delays.

Reducing the non-value-added time by better balancing the operation by continuous flow increases the efficiency and reduces the wasted time. Schematically, the concept is illustrated in Figure 25.5.

The difference in product costs between traditional accounting and activity-based costing is illustrated in Demonstrating the concept 25.6.

Depreciation charges

In the traditional accounting for depreciation the assumption is that technology becomes obsolete over

Figure 25.5 Reducing non–value–added activities

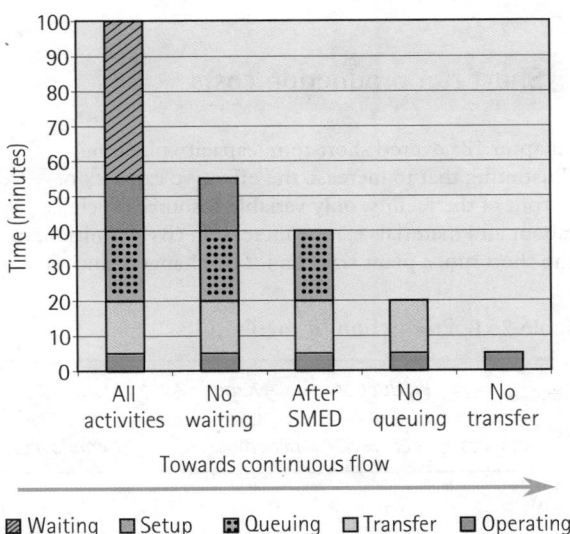

Towards continuous flow

☒ Waiting   ▦ Setup   ▣ Queuing   ☐ Transfer   ▨ Operating

time and that the costs are recovered over a fixed period. The depreciation of the equipment is part of the overhead charge but it can distort product costs if the technology is lumped into overhead when it is not evenly used for all products. This concept is illustrated in Demonstrating the concept 25.7.

Customer focus

Users of activity-based costing have extended their analysis to collect costs by customer as well as by product. This can show that particular customers are more demanding in terms of expecting priority, delivery distances, frequency, price discounts, after-sales service etc. Then, with this information available there is justification for charging higher prices to these customers to take into account the activity associated with their order.

Service industries

Other than the capital costs, one of the principal costs in service industries such as financial centres, insurance agencies, and retail stores, are labour charges. Staff members in these service centres are often expected to perform a wide variety of functions for different types of customer. The philosophy of activity-based costing can also be applied here by analyzing in detail staff activities and resources according to the different products. This can lead to improved job rationalization and better correlated product pricing.

Breakeven analysis

Breakeven analysis has already been treated in Chapters 3 and 16. The purpose of this section is now to go deeper into the actual analytical procedures.

Contribution margin

In any operation in the long term a firm needs to earn a sufficient contribution in the operation to cover fixed costs such that it breaks even. Any contribution above the breakeven point is profit. The analytical approach to determine the contribution margin and breakeven point is to use a cost–volume–profit analysis that determines a contribution margin for each sales unit. The process may not be straightforward and one needs to analyze alternatives and perhaps make short run decisions to use surplus capacity and to forecast future costs and revenues. The relevant costs and revenues should be analyzed by behaviour in order to make the correct decision and, in which case, product costs calculated by full absorption costing may not be appropriate. The costs used in a contribution analysis should include all organizational costs including administration, sales, and finance. Any variable element of these costs should be included as part of the variable product cost.

Terms and definitions

Table 25.5 contains definitions and most commonly used symbols in breakeven analysis.

Graphical analysis

In analyzing the breakeven point and the contribution margin the following three types of graph might be presented according to the production or sales quantities (assuming these are the same):

- a breakeven chart which emphasizes the fixed costs in the operation
- a contribution chart which emphasizes the total contribution or the difference between total sales and the total variable cost
- a profit–volume graph which highlights the profit or loss at different values.

These types of graphical presentations are illustrated and explained in Demonstrating the concept 25.8.

Assumptions in breakeven analysis

- The activities being considered are within relevant ranges. If, for example, it is based on activities between 20 and 85% production levels then the analysis should only be used within these ranges.

- Fixed and variable costs are correctly separated over the whole range of output since fixed costs and to a certain extent variable costs may not be same for different output levels.
- Variable costs may not necessarily be linear. As an illustration, distribution costs may increase at a faster rate than activity as higher sales further away from the production area may result in higher transportation costs.
- Selling price per unit is fixed regardless of output. This is very often not always true as at higher levels purchasers are offered lower unit prices.

Table 25.5 Terms and symbols used in breakeven analysis

Expression	Symbol or equation
Unit price	P
Quantity of units sold	Q
Fixed costs	FC
Variable cost per unit	VC
Revenues are (Unit price*Quantity)	P * Q
Total variable cost is Units*Variable cost	Q * VC
Total costs are fixed costs plus variable costs	FC + Q * VC
Net profit is Revenues − Costs	P * Q − (FC + Q * VC) or Q(P − VC) − FC
Contribution margin	Q(P − VC)
Contribution margin per unit	P − VC
Breakeven point is when revenues equal total cost	P * Q = FC + Q * VC
Breakeven point quantity, Q	Q = FC/(P − VC)
Breakeven point in financial terms, £	P * Q = P * FC/(P − VC)
Profit: Volume ratio is (Contribution margin per unit)/(Sales price per unit)	(P − VC)/P
Margin of safety	Expected sales − Breakeven sales
Percent margin of safety	Margin of safety/Expected sales

- Production and sales are equal such that inventory cost changes do not enter into the equation.

Short run production costs

Chapter 12 covered short-term capacity planning, illustrating that to increase the effective capacity or output of the facility, only variable resources such as labour and materials can be increased. (By definition, in the short run, a plant size cannot be changed, and so

Table 25.6 Production of men's suits

Employees	Production units per week	Average units per employee	Marginal units per employee
0	0	–	–
1	6	6.00	6.00
2	13	6.50	7.00
3	22	7.33	9.00
4	34	8.50	12.00
5	50	10.00	16.00
6	68	11.33	18.00
7	81	11.57	13.00
8	92	11.50	11.00
9	102	11.33	10.00
10	110	11.00	8.00
11	116	10.55	6.00
12	120	10.00	4.00
13	123	9.46	3.00
14	126	9.00	3.00
15	126	8.40	0.00
16	122	7.63	−4.00
17	112	6.59	−10.00
18	100	5.56	−12.00
19	88	4.63	−12.00
20	75	3.75	−13.00

fixed costs such as depreciation of the building and machines employed are independent of the output.) However, increasing labour has limitations as illustrated as follows using as an example the short-term production of men's suits.

Increasing labour

In the short run, to increase output, labour can be increased to work on the machines in the fixed physical plant. This can be accomplished by, say, adding a second, and even a third shift. In addition, people can be put on overtime and more workers, either full or part time, can be hired. At first, hiring more people will increase output, as this is the objective. However, as the facility and machines become fully utilized there becomes a point that increasing labour does not result in a corresponding output. The physical building space becomes saturated, as there are not enough machines for all the employees so that some employees become idle. As hiring continues, a situation arises when the total output actually decreases because additional workers have no machines on which to work, and also the presence of these new hires hinders other operators. This type of situation is quantified in Table 25.6.

Total production output

Figure 25.6 shows the weekly production output in terms of the number of employees. The output increases up to a maximum of 126 suits per week with 14 employees, although not at the same rate. There is an increasing rate up to six employees and then output

increases but at a declining rate until there are 14 employees. Between 14 and 15 employees the output is the same and then output declines to 75 units a week at 20 employees. The changing slope and the decline are the result of adding more employees to the work centre.

Average production

The average production in units/employee, as presented in Table 25.6, is given by the ratio:

$$\frac{\text{Total output}}{\text{Number of employees}}$$

The average production increases to a maximum with seven employees and then declines. This is illustrated in Figure 25.7.

Marginal production

The marginal production, as presented in Table 25.6, is the extra output, obtained by adding an extra employee and is calculated by:

Unit output with (n + 1) employees
− Unit output with (n) employees

The marginal output increases up to six employees and then declines to zero with 15 employees. After that the marginal output is negative. The marginal production is also illustrated in Figure 25.7. The marginal production curve is greater than the average production curve until eight employees are reached, when it becomes less than the average production.

Figure 25.6 Total production of men's suits

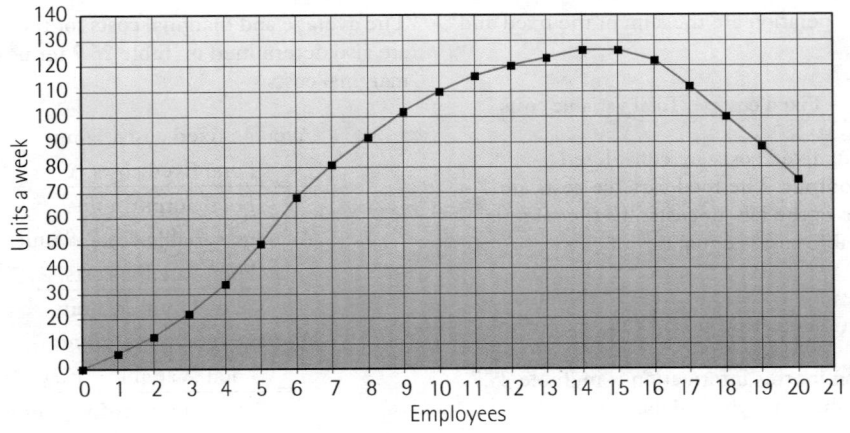

Figure 25.7 Production of men's suits: Average and marginal output

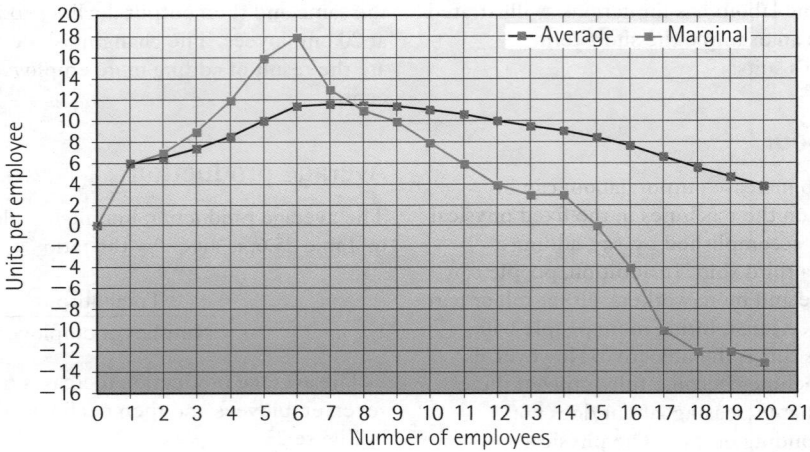

Figure 25.8 Production cost curves for suit manufacture

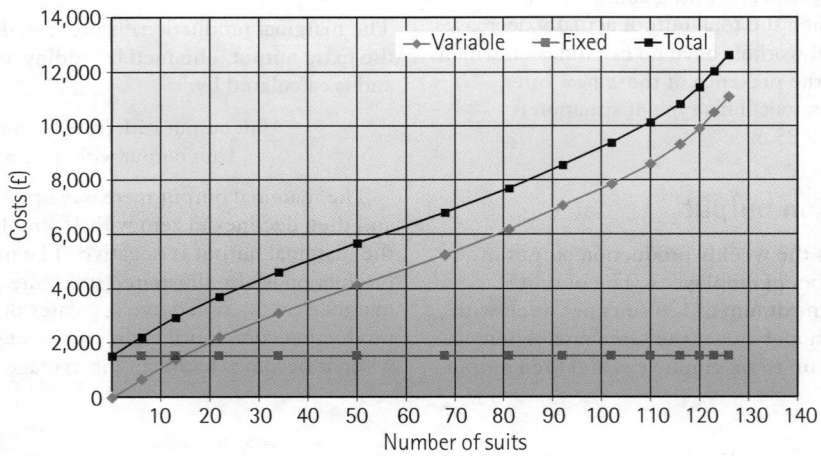

Total costs

The costs for an operation are the sum of the fixed and variable costs:

Total costs = Fixed costs + Total variable costs

In the short run, fixed costs are considered independent of output. The total variable costs are given by the sum of the labour costsplus the material costs, or the variable cost is equal to:

(Labour rate, £/hour) * (Hours/week) * (Number of employees) + (Material cost/unit) * (Number of units)

The calculation for this information is in Table 25.7 and Figure 25.8 illustrates these data.

Average and marginal costs

The average and marginal costs for the suit production are also determined in Table 25.7 for positive values of marginal costs:

Average fixed costs, £/unit

$$= \frac{\text{Total fixed costs, £}}{\text{Total output, units}}$$

Average variable costs, £/unit

$$= \frac{\text{Total variable costs, £}}{\text{Total output, units}}$$

Average total costs, £/unit

$$= \frac{\text{Total (Variable + Fixed) costs, £}}{\text{Total output, units}}$$

Table 25.7 Costs for suit manufacture

						Wages, £/hour		12.00	
						Material costs, £/unit		35.00	
						Hours/week		40.00	

Employees	Production per week	Variable costs (£/week)	Fixed costs costs (£/week)	Total costs (£/week)	Avg variable costs (£/unit/week)	Avg fixed costs (£/unit/week)	Avg total costs (£/unit/week)	Marginal costs (£/unit/week)
0	0	0	1,500	1,500	–	–	–	
1	6	690	1,500	2,190	115.00	250.00	365.00	115.00
2	13	1,415	1,500	2,915	108.85	115.38	224.23	103.57
3	22	2,210	1,500	3,710	100.45	68.18	168.64	88.33
4	34	3,110	1,500	4,610	91.47	44.12	135.59	75.00
5	50	4,150	1,500	5,650	83.00	30.00	113.00	65.00
6	68	5,260	1,500	6,760	77.35	22.06	99.41	61.67
7	81	6,195	1,500	7,695	76.48	18.52	95.00	71.92
8	92	7,060	1,500	8,560	76.74	16.30	93.04	78.64
9	102	7,890	1,500	9,390	77.35	14.71	92.06	83.00
10	110	8,650	1,500	10,150	78.64	13.64	92.27	95.00
11	116	9,340	1,500	10,840	80.52	12.93	93.45	115.00
12	120	9,960	1,500	11,460	83.00	12.50	95.50	155.00
13	123	10,545	1,500	12,045	85.73	12.20	97.93	195.00

Marginal cost, £/unit

$$= \frac{\text{Change in total cost}}{\text{Change in units produced}}$$

These costs are illustrated in Figure 25.9.

Diminishing marginal returns

The average variable cost (AVC), and the average total cost (ATC) decrease at first to a minimum value and then start to increase because of the law of diminishing marginal returns. As more people are hired the costs per unit initially decreases. They reach a minimum point at which both the AVC and the ATC start to increase.

The marginal cost (MC) is that cost required to produce an additional unit of output. Like the variable cost curve, it declines at first, reaches a minimum, and then starts to increase. Again, the increase reflects the law of diminishing marginal returns. As more and more variable input is used, the extra output obtained becomes smaller as it eventually takes more and more of the variable input to produce each extra unit of output. The marginal cost depends only on changes in variable costs, not fixed costs. The fixed cost is independent of output.

The marginal cost curve intersects the average total cost curve, and the average variable cost curve at their respective minimum points since the marginal cost is the last number added to both the average total cost and the average variable cost when these values are calculated. When the marginal cost is below the average variable cost and the average total cost, these values will continue to decline. Conversely, when the marginal cost

Figure 25.9 Average and marginal costs for suits

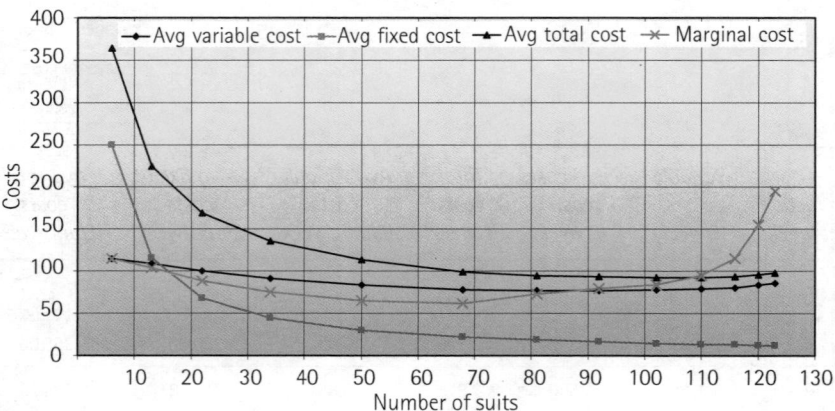

is above the average total cost and the average variable cost these costs will increase. The marginal cost curve intercepts the average variable cost first since it is below the average total cost curve by an amount equal to the average fixed cost.

The marginal cost is not a value that is accounted for in the firm. Total costs are presented on financial statements, and average costs can be easily deduced. However, it is the marginal cost that an operations manager should take into account before adding extra input such as labour. If the marginal cost increases when extra input is added, then the wrong decision would have been made. This concept re-emphasizes the difference between the accountants' and economists' view of operations, as discussed at the beginning of this chapter, regarding product pricing.

Long run production costs

In the long run, management can expand, or indeed contract, the capacity of the physical plant and the corresponding number of machines to accommodate demand requirements. In this case, all costs can be considered variable in the long run. However, of course, since capacity plant expansion is a step-wise process at any specific time period, an operation would be confined to a plant of a certain physical size or capacity and in which case the short-term criteria for costs would apply.

Long run cost curves

Figure 25.10 shows the average cost curves for manufacturing suits in five possible different plants.

For each plant there is a minimum average cost corresponding to a certain production level.

Plant 1

In Plant 1, the minimum average cost is about £108/unit at a production level of 75 suits. As the output increases beyond this amount the average cost rises. At an output of about 125 suits, the average cost per unit is the same in Plant 1 as in Plant 2. Beyond 125 units the average cost per unit is lower in Plant 2 than in Plant 1.

Plant 2

In Plant 2, the minimum average cost is about £90/unit at an output of 220 suits. Beyond this point, the average cost rises until at an output of 255 suits, when the average cost at £138/unit is again a trade-off between Plant 2 and Plant 3. Beyond 255, the lowest average cost lies on the production at Plant 3.

Plant 3

In Plant 3, the minimum average cost is about £80/unit at an output of 470 suits. Beyond this point, the average cost rises until at an output of 490 suits, the average cost of £90/unit is the same in both Plants 3 and 4.

Plant 4

In Plant 4, the minimum average cost is about £73/unit at an output of 620 suits. Beyond this point, the average cost rises until at an output of 710 suits, the average cost of £95/unit is the same in both Plant 4 and Plant 5.

Plant 5

In Plant 5, the minimum average cost is about £90/unit or higher than the minimum average cost in Plant 4.

Figure 25.10 Suit production: Long run costs

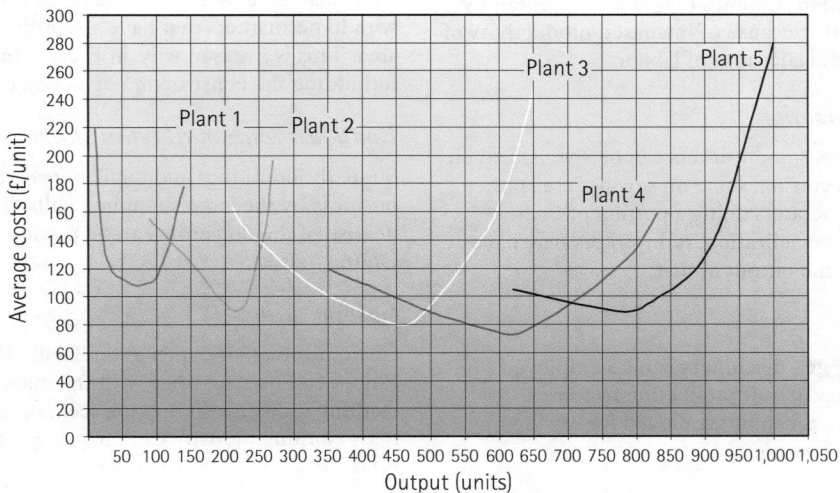

Figure 25.11 Smooth long run average cost curve

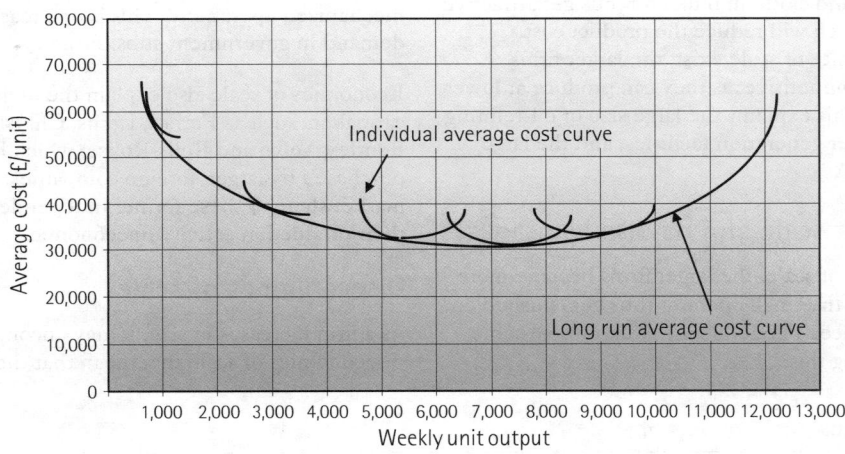

Flexibility

In the long run, the optimum long run cost is the minimum cost when all the inputs including labour, material, and physical plant capacity are variable. The difference between the long run and short run operation is flexibility, as in the long run management has the option not only of modifying the people and materials but also the size and the number of physical plants. There is the phenomenon of economies of scale.

A smooth long run cost curve exists when there is the flexibility to vary plant size so that the output corresponding to the minimum possible average unit cost for each plant is just one unit greater than output

from the previous plant. This would occur when one is able to add, say, an additional square metre to the plant surface area, and/or a fraction of a machine hour, whenever necessary. This is different from the example with the five specific plants when there is only a step-wise, rather than a smooth transition. A smooth long run cost curve is illustrated in Figure 25.11, when there is continually variable plant size and the long run cost curve is made up of the minimum of many average cost curves. Moving to the right on the curve corresponds to a slightly large plant. In the graph, for an output of about 7000 units, the plant size would be the one which has a minimum average cost of £20,750/units.

Economies of scale and its benefits

As a firm's operation becomes bigger it can benefit by economies of scale because of increased productivity of inputs and the specialization of labour.

Labour specialization

In suit production, some workers can be specialized on dyeing, some on cutting, some on sewing, etc., rather than having all operators doing a portion of each. Thus, with this specialization, ten workers may have more than twice the output of five.

Automation

As a firm gets bigger, machinery can be employed, rather than labour. As suit production increases, automatic machines can be employed for sewing, rather than hand sewing.

Bulk purchases

With increase in size, the firm can purchase the raw materials, fibre and cloth, in bulk and thus get attractive price breaks, which will reduce the product cost.

When economies of scale exist, the larger firms become more competitive, as they can produce at lower average costs. This explains the large size of oil-refining operations, power generation facilities, and the large farms in the USA.

Economies of scale and its disadvantages

With economies of scale, the larger firms become more competitive but the small operator thus gets pushed out of the marketplace. The following situations go some way to explaining this.

Village grocery store

The small grocery store is unable to compete on price with hypermarkets that have a significant larger surface area. This is a reason why, in France, there is now a law forbidding the construction of any more hypermarkets.

Boutiques and small retail stores

Similarly, boutiques and retail stores are forced out of business by the large shopping malls. This explains the demise of the downtown areas, particularly in the United States.

Custom tailors

Customized tailors, such as on Saville Row in London, cannot compete on price with the mass-produced clothing industry. Production technology used in the mass clothing industry can provide good quality products at much lower prices.

Farming

Small farmers cannot compete with the larger mechanized operations. This is one reason for their demand in government subsidies.

Economies of scale also explain the demise of exclusive carmakers such as Ferrari, Lotus, Chrysler, Jaguar, Bentley, Volvo and Rolls-Royce, which have all been purchased by larger, foreign companies. The small market share of these former independent firms made their production activity uneconomic.

Diseconomies of scale

As a firm increases in size, it may encounter diseconomies of scale that mean that the average cost is

Figure 25.12 Constant economy of scale

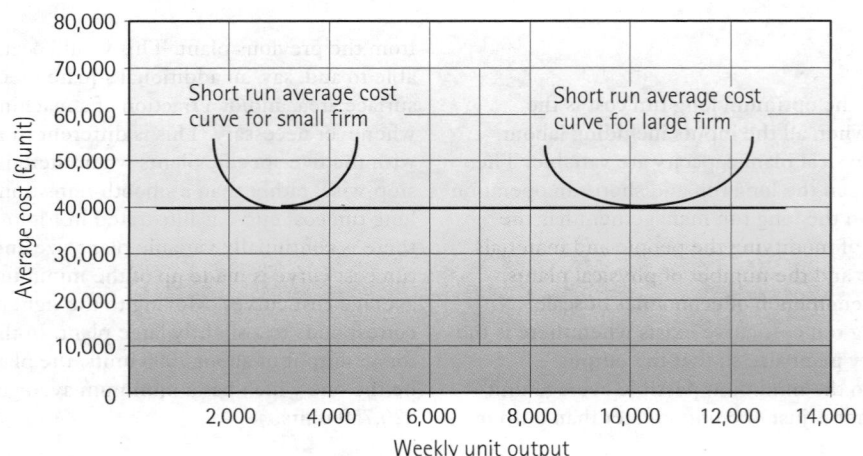

increasing with output. This might arise because there are too many people and management becomes difficult, workers are lost in the size and become lazy or avoid doing their work. Diseconomies of scale depend on the industry, and in fact may never occur for some firms. Diseconomies of scale are part of the reason why some job shop operations, such as a car repair, dry cleaning, and bakeries such as in France, remain relatively small. It also explains in part why firms are now outsourcing or subcontracting activity as they find that the specialized firm can do the work at a lower cost.

Constant economy of scale

It may be that the long run average cost curve is horizontal, or near horizontal (see Figure 25.12), so that the minimum on the average cost curve is the same for the small firm as it is for the large firm. In this case, the large firm would have no significant economic advantage over the small firm, as the average cost remains essentially constant regardless of the output.

Summary of key elements

- Although an operations manager may not be involved in product pricing, an awareness of a firm's pricing strategy greatly facilitates the effective cost management of operations.

- The market price, or price the market would bear, is the amount customers are willing to pay for the product. For products that are a monopoly in the market, the price may have little relationship to cost.

- A catalogue price is similar to the market price in that it is a price that is already published. A company bringing out a similar product that cannot be differentiated from competitive products would likely follow the catalogue price.

- A product price equal to cost plus margin is where a firm would add up all the costs going into the product and then add a profit margin to give the market price.

- The target cost is a market-driven cost in competitive industries determined from the sales price necessary to capture a predetermined market share. Target cost is given by the sales price less profit.

- Variable, or direct, costs are those that change with the level of products produced. They include direct labour, materials used in the product, and factory overhead.

- FIFO inventory management puts a low value on product cost, but a high value on remaining inventory. LIFO puts a high value on product costs, but a low value on

inventory. The weighted unit average cost balances out the cost of goods and the value of inventory.

- Fixed costs are the capital assets for running a business such as buildings, machines, and equipment, and normally have a life over one year. Depreciation is a way of accounting for fixed assets.

- Three methods for calculating depreciation are the straight line method, sum of the year's digits, and the declining balance methods.

- The payback, net present value, or the internal rate of return methods can be used to analyze the effectiveness of fixed assets.

- Traditional cost accounting is essentially assigning fixed costs to the product and then attributing to this a portion of the production overhead.

- Activity-based costing is to analyze in depth actual product costs by identifying all those activities associated with the product at each step in the supply chain. In particular, this includes non-value-added time.

- When capital equipment is used in an operation at the expense of labour, the way in which this fixed cost is allocated can impact the value put on the product cost.

- Breakeven is the point after which profits are generated. Ways of presenting a breakeven analysis is a chart which emphasizes the fixed costs in the operation, a contribution chart, and a profit–volume graph, which highlights profit or loss for different production levels.

- In the short run, increasing labour can increase the capacity of an operation. However, there comes a point when the marginal cost declines. The marginal cost is not an accounted cost but a value that should be taken into account in short-term capacity planning.

- In the long run, plant capacity can be increased so that all resources, including labour, material, and physical plant are variable. This gives an economy of scale where some firms benefit by labour specialization, automation, and bulk purchases.

Notes and references

1. 'Why whisky costs so much', *Fortune*, 25 November 1996, p. 18
2. 'Japan's smart secret weapon: It's a unique cost-management system, and it helps Japanese companies to cut costs, undersell Western competitors, and beat them with new products', *Fortune*, 12 August 1991, p. 48
3. 'Lean enough? Japan's car makers are cutting costs by simplifying their cars rather than slimming their workforces. This could prove a costly mistake', *The Economist*, 10 February 1996, pp 61–2

4. *Wall Street Journal Europe*, 11 March 97
5. ICBT Company, Rhône-Alps, France
6. 'Costing the factory of the future: Factories run by numbers. Numbers to calculate profit and losses to analyse the costs of new products; and to chart corporate strategy. But a lot of managers are relying on the wrong numbers', *The Economist*, 3 March 1990

Review and discussion topics

1. Product pricing

What do you think are the main elements in price structure that differentiate the price of the following products? Indicate which is normally the least expensive to purchase:

(a) diapers carrying the label Procter & Gamble and diapers carrying a store's own label (Tesco, Carrefour, Safeway, etc.)

(b) an 18-ct gold chain necklace and an identical 14-ct gold chain

(c) a silk shirt made in France, a similar silk shirt made in China

(d) a compact disc purchased in Germany, and the same compact disc purchased in the United States

(e) a 1996 Bordeaux, and a similar wine bottled in 1985.

2. Retail stores

In the United States, the small boutiques and the small grocery store have almost disappeared in large urban areas. In Britain, France, and other European countries the same is happening, such that governments are enacting laws to 'prevent the decimation of small communities'. Discuss in terms of product prices, fixed, and variable costs why the small store is having difficulty surviving.

3. Service industries

What are the principal variable costs in the following types of service industry? Why is it difficult to control these costs? What are some of the trends in these industries to reduce these variable costs?

(a) Financial services
(b) medical centre
(c) education establishment
(d) film industry
(e) department store.

4. International operations

Discuss some of the major differences in a cost analysis for a television manufacturer in the Netherlands and a television manufacturer in China. Consider both the variable and fixed costs, plus overhead allowances.

5. Marginal costs

How would you use the concept of marginal costs to describe the following activities? What action is often taken in these situations which is a result of marginal impacts?

(a) Increasing the level of finished goods inventory
(b) increasing the class size for a university course in operations management
(c) increasing the number of skiers permitted to use a certain ski area
(d) increasing the number of grape harvesters in a given vineyard.

6. Economies of scale

Give some real examples, and justify, where the economy of scale has:

(a) benefited industry and, as a corollary, the consumer and society
(b) benefited industry but to the detriment of some consumers and society.

Demonstrating the concept 25.1   Lindsey Co.

Situation

The Lindsey Co. assembles and sells pocket calculators. For one particular inexpensive model the estimated variable costs per unit are €7.00 and the fixed costs are €1800. The demand is a function of the sales price and is as shown in Table 25.8.

Required

1. Under normal accounting procedures where the profit is equal to revenues less total costs, at what level should the company stop making the product?

2. Using the concept of marginal values, at what level should the company stop making the product?

Solution

The calculated data are given in Table 25.9.

1.

- Total revenues are calculated by the relationship Price * Quantity.
- Total costs by the relationship Variable cost * Quantity + Fixed cost.
- Profit = Total revenues − Total costs.

Table 25.8 Lindsey Co.: Demand as a function of sales price

Sales price (€/unit)	15	14	13	12	11	10	9	8	7	6	5	4	3	2	1
Demand (units)	1,000	2,000	3,000	4,000	5,000	6,000	7,000	8,000	9,000	10,000	11,000	12,000	13,000	14,000	15,000

Table 25.9 Lindsey: Calculated data

| Fixed costs, € | 1,800.00 |
| Variable costs, €/unit | 7.00 |

Sales price (€/unit)	Demand (units)	Total revenues (€)	Variable costs (€)	Fixed costs (€)	Total cost (€)	Profit (€)	Total revenue per 1000 units (€)	Total cost per 1000 units (€)	Total profit per 1000 units (€)	Marginal revenue per 1000 units (€)	Marginal cost per 1000 units (€)	Marginal profit per 1000 units (€)
16	0	0	0	1,800	1,800	−1,800						
15	1,000	15,000	7,000	1,800	8,800	6,200	15,000	8,800	6,200	15,000	7,000	8,000
14	2,000	28,000	14,000	1,800	15,800	12,200	14,000	7,900	6,100	13,000	7,000	6,000
13	3,000	39,000	21,000	1,800	22,800	16,200	13,000	7,600	5,400	11,000	7,000	4,000
12	4,000	48,000	28,000	1,800	29,800	18,200	12,000	7,450	4,550	9,000	7,000	2,000
11	5,000	55,000	35,000	1,800	36,800	18,200	11,000	7,360	3,640	7,000	7,000	0
10	6,000	60,000	42,000	1,800	43,800	16,200	10,000	7,300	2,700	5,000	7,000	−2,000
9	7,000	63,000	49,000	1,800	50,800	12,200	9,000	7,257	1,743	3,000	7,000	−4,000
8	8,000	64,000	56,000	1,800	57,800	6,200	8,000	7,225	775	1,000	7,000	−6,000
7	9,000	63,000	63,000	1,800	64,800	−1,800	7,000	7,200	−200	−1,000	7,000	−8,000
6	10,000	60,000	70,000	1,800	71,800	−11,800	6,000	7,180	−1,180	−3,000	7,000	−10,000
5	11,000	55,000	77,000	1,800	78,800	−23,800	5,000	7,164	−2,164	−5,000	7,000	−12,000
4	12,000	48,000	84,000	1,800	85,800	−37,800	4,000	7,150	−3,150	−7,000	7,000	−14,000
3	13,000	39,000	91,000	1,800	92,800	−53,800	3,000	7,138	−4,138	−9,000	7,000	−16,000
2	14,000	28,000	98,000	1,800	99,800	−71,800	2,000	7,129	−5,129	−11,000	7,000	−18,000
1	15,000	15,000	105,000	1,800	106,800	−91,800	1,000	7,120	−6,120	−13,000	7,000	−20,000

Figure 25.13 gives this information. From this, the profit falls to zero at about 8800 units and so this is the quantity at which the firm should stop making the product.

2.

- Marginal revenues per 1000 units is the difference in revenues between successives increase in demand.

- Marginal cost per 1000 units is Variable cost * Production quantity.
- Marginal profit is the difference between the marginal revenue and the marginal cost.

Figure 25.14 illustrates this information. Here, the marginal profit is zero at 5000 units and so this is the level at which the firm should stop making the product.

Figure 25.13 Lindsey Co.: Total revenues, costs, and profit

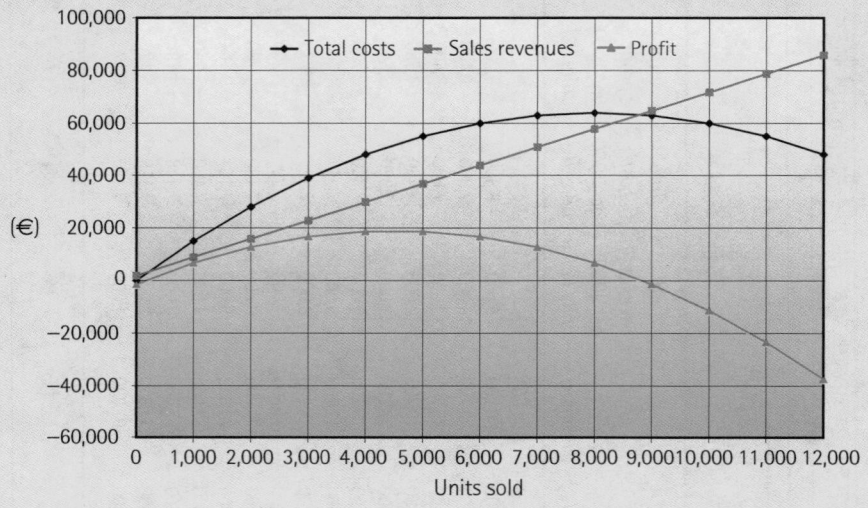

Figure 25.14 Lindsey Co.: Marginal revenues, costs, and profit per 1000 units

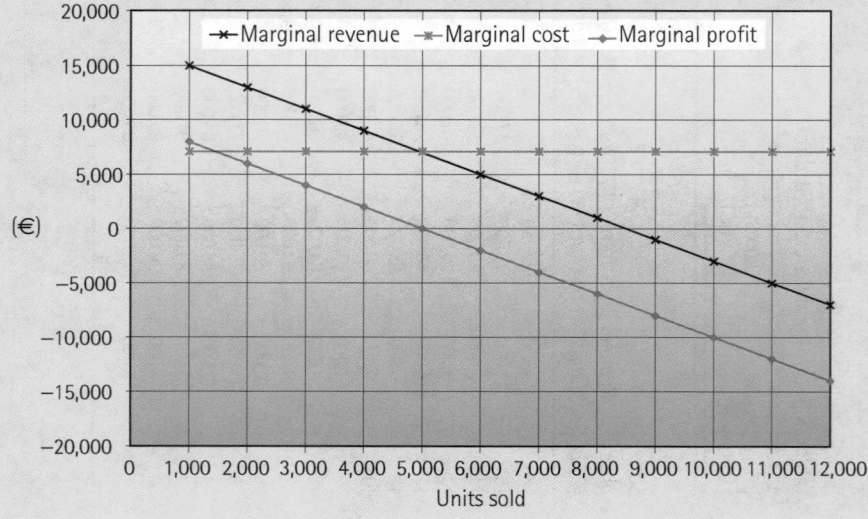

Demonstrating the concept 25.2   Rosehead Co.

Situation

The Rosehead Co. in England makes specialized electric pumps for which it buys the electrical winding units from an outside supplier. At the end of July 2001 it has 1000 inventory items of these electrical windings. The quantity, date acquired, and the unit cost paid for these units is as shown in Table 25.10.

During August 2001, the company uses 300 of the electrical windings to make pump units. None of the 1000 units has been used before this period. Each pump unit is sold for £10.00.

Required

Determine the gross margin for Rosehead, and the value of the inventory remaining using:

(a) first in, first out inventory valuation
(b) last in, first out inventory valuation
(c) weighted unit average method of inventory evaluation.

Solution

Table 25.11 gives the solutions for the inventory valuing methods. A summary is shown in Table 25.12.

Table 25.10 Rosehead Co.: Electrical windings inventory held

Quantity	Date acquired	Unit cost (£)
400	1 January 2001	4.00
300	1 April 2001	6.00
300	1 July 2001	8.00

Table 25.12 Rosehead Co.: Inventory valuation methods – summary

Method	Gross margin (£)	Value of inventory remaining (£)
FIFO	1,800	4,600
LIFO	600	3,400
WUAC	1,260	4,060

Table 25.11 Rosehead Co.: Inventory valuation methods (All financial figures in £s)

	Quantity	Date acquired	Unit cost	Value
	400	01 Jan 01	4.00	1,600
	300	01 Apr 01	6.00	1,800
	300	01 Jul 01	8.00	2,400
Total	1,000			5,800
Weighted unit average cost			5.80	
Quantity end products sold, units	300			
Price per unit, £	10.00			
Revenues generated	3,000.00			
Inventory units remaining	700			
(a) FIFO				
Cost per unit of inventory	4.00			
Revenues		3,000.00		
Cost of inventory units		1,200.00		
Gross margin		1,800.00		
Value of inventory remaining	4,600			
(b) LIFO				
Cost per unit of inventory	8.00			
Revenues		3,000.00		
Cost of inventory		2,400.00		
Gross margin		600.00		
Value of inventory remaining	3,400			
(c) WUAC				
Cost per unit of inventory	5.80			
Revenues		3,000.00		
Cost of inventory		1,740.00		
Gross margin		1,260.00		
Value of inventory remaining	4,060			

Demonstrating the concept 25.3 OTL Co.

Situation

The OTL Co., in the north of England, is a small printing company that prints brochures, catalogues, and posters for a wide variety of customers. It is planning to purchase a new offset printing machine at a cost of £375,000 to replace an existing printing press. The economic life of the new machine is considered ten years, after which the salvage value is expected to be £35,000. The old machine currently has a salvage value of £12,500. For financial analysis purposes, the discount rate is considered fixed at 9% and the tax rate is 40%, and straight line depreciation is considered. Operating cost savings with the new machine are estimated as shown in Table 25.13.

Required

1. Determine the payback period in years if income taxes are taken into consideration.

Table 25.13 OTL Co.: Operating cost savings

Year	Operating cost saving (£)	Year	Operating cost saving (£)
1	41,000	6	82,000
2	51,250	7	82,000
3	61,500	8	82,000
4	82,000	9	82,000
5	82,000	10	82,000

2. Determine the payback period without tax considerations.
3. Illustrate the cumulative cash flow movements for both payback methods graphically.
4. What is the net present value of the investment? Based on the NPV does the investment seem sound?

Solution

Table 25.14 gives the calculation methods.

1. Table 25.15 gives the calculation with tax considerations. The payback is between six and seven years. By the following linear interpolation the exact period is 6.1 years or 6 years and 5 weeks:

$$6 + \frac{6050}{56,750 + 6050} = 6.10$$

2. Table 25.16: The payback is between three and four years. By the following linear interpolation the exact period is 3.62 years or about 3 years and 32 weeks:

$$3 + \frac{71,750}{71,750 + 44,250} = 3.62$$

3. The graph for the two payback approaches is given in Figure 25.15.
4. The net present value flows are shown in Table 25.17. Yes, the NPV is positive when all the cash flows are considered, so on this basis it would seem a sound investment.

Table 25.14 OTL Co.: Supplied data and tax savings with depreciation

Supplied data

Purchase price of asset, £	375,000
Economic life of asset, years	10
Tax rate, %	40.00
Cost saving, £	
Year 1	41,000
Year 2	51,250
Year 3	61,500
Year 4	82,000
Year 5	82,000
Year 6	82,000
Year 7	82,000
Year 8	82,000
Year 9	82,000
Year 10	82,000
Total	**727,750**
Salvage value new equipment, £	35,000
Salvage value old equipment, £	12,500
Asset cost less salvage	327,500
Discount rate, %	9.00

Tax savings with depreciation

Year	Annual depreciation	Accumulated depreciation	Annual tax savings
1	34,000	34,000	13,600
2	34,000	68,000	13,600
3	34,000	102,000	13,600
4	34,000	136,000	13,600
5	34,000	170,000	13,600
6	34,000	204,000	13,600
7	34,000	238,000	13,600
8	34,000	272,000	13,600
9	34,000	306,000	13,600
10	34,000	340,000	13,600
Total	**340,000**		**136,000**

Table 25.15 OTL Co.: Cash flows taking into account taxes

Year	After tax operating cost savings (1 − rate)*savings	After tax savings from depreciation	After tax savings total	After tax savings and outgoings	Cumulative cash flows
0				−327,500	−327,500
1	24,600	13,600	38,200	38,200	−289,300
2	30,750	13,600	44,350	44,350	−244,950
3	36,900	13,600	50,500	50,500	−194,450
4	49,200	13,600	62,800	62,800	−131,650
5	49,200	13,600	62,800	62,800	−68,850
6	49,200	13,600	62,800	62,800	−6,050
7	49,200	13,600	62,800	62,800	56,750
8	49,200	13,600	62,800	62,800	119,550
9	49,200	13,600	62,800	62,800	182,350
10	49,200	13,600	62,800	62,800	245,150

Payback period 6.10 years

Table 25.16 OTL Co.: Cash flows not taking into account taxes

Year	Cost savings	Annual depreciation	Savings + Depreciation	Outgoings and savings	Cumulative outgoings and savings
0				−327,500	−327,500
1	41,000	34,000	75,000	75,000	−252,500
2	51,250	34,000	85,250	85,250	−167,250
3	61,500	34,000	95,500	95,500	−71,750
4	82,000	34,000	116,000	116,000	44,250
5	82,000	34,000	116,000	116,000	160,250
6	82,000	34,000	116,000	116,000	276,250
7	82,000	34,000	116,000	116,000	392,250
8	82,000	34,000	116,000	116,000	508,250
9	82,000	34,000	116,000	116,000	624,250
10	82,000	34,000	116,000	116,000	740,250
Total depreciation		**340,000**			

Payback period, 3.62 years

Figure 25.15 OTL Co.: Payback period

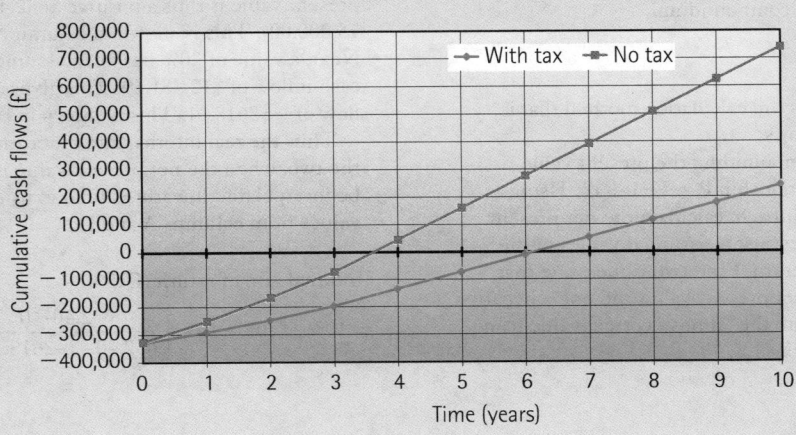

Table 25.17 OTL Co.: Net present value

| | After tax cash flows | | | | | |
Year	Purchase price	Salvage value	Operating savings	Savings from depreciation	Total flows	Present value
0	−375,000	12,500			−362,500	−362,500
1			24,600	13,600	38,200	35,046
2			30,750	13,600	44,350	37,329
3			36,900	13,600	50,500	38,995
4			49,200	13,600	62,800	44,489
5			49,200	13,600	62,800	40,816
6			49,200	13,600	62,800	37,446
7			49,200	13,600	62,800	34,354
8			49,200	13,600	62,800	31,517
9			49,200	13,600	62,800	28,915
10		35,000	49,200	13,600	97,800	41,312
				Net present value		7,718

Demonstrating the concept 25.4 Bergery Co.

Situation

The Bergery Co. is planning to invest in a new automatically controlled labelling machine. This machine has a capital cost of $15,000. The estimated cash inflows in using this machine are shown in Table 25.18.

Required

Determine the internal rate of return for this project assuming annual compounding.

Solution

Table 25.19 gives the calculation method that is explained as follows.

For annual compounding the present value is given by the relationship $P = F/(1 + i)^n$. Using a trial and error approach, calculate the net present value of the project using assumed values of the internal rate of return. Find two values: one that gives a positive net present value and one a negative value and calculate the 'almost' correct value using linear interpolation:

Table 25.18 Bergery Co.: Cash inflows

Year	1	2	3	4	5
Cash inflows ($)	3,500.00	4,000.00	6,000.00	5,000.00	2,000.00

- Here, first a value of 10% has been assumed and the present value of each cash flow has been calculated to give a total for the five years of $15,652.40. The net present value is thus a positive $652.40 ($15,652.40 − 15,000.00). This is shown in column A.
- Next, a value of 20% has been assumed to give a total cash inflow of $12,381.69. This gives a negative cash flow of −$2618.31. This is shown in column D.

Thus the real internal rate of return lies between the two, when the net present value is zero. This can be interpolated linearly as follows using the numerical values from columns A and D:

Internal rate of return (IRR)

$$= 10\% + (20\% - 10\%)\left[\frac{652.40 - 0}{652.40 - (-2618.31)}\right] = 11.9947\%$$

Table 25.19 Bergery Co.: Internal rate of return with annual compounding

Inital outlay	15,000.00			
		A	**B**	**C**	**D**

Year	Cash inflows ($)	Present value in $ at rate of 10.0000%	Present value in $ at rate of 11.9947%	Present value in $ at rate of 11.7200%	Present value in $ at rate of 20.0000%
1	3,500.00	3,181.82	3,125.15	3,132.83	2,916.67
2	4,000.00	3,305.79	3,189.08	3,204.78	2,777.78
3	6,000.00	4,507.89	4,271.29	4,302.87	3,472.22
4	5,000.00	3,415.07	3,178.19	3,209.57	2,411.27
5	2,000.00	1,241.84	1,135.12	1,149.15	803.76
Total	**20,500.00**	**15,652.40**	**14,898.84**	**14,999.20**	**12,381.69**
Net present value		652.40	−101.16	−0.80	−2,618.31
IRR estimate	11.9947%				

- The internal rate of return calculation is then repeated using this value. This gives a net present value of −$101.16. This is shown in column B.

- A linear interpolation is not quite correct and the closest value is 11.72%, as shown in column C. (Using the 'target value' function in Excel the exact value is 11.7128%.)

Demonstrating the concept 25.5 Maxell (1)

Situation

Maxell Co. manufactures three main products using basically the same production methods and the same equipment for each. Currently, a conventional product costing system is used for accounting purposes. The manufacturing conditions for the three products are given in Table 25.20.

Direct labour costs are $14.00 an hour and production overheads are absorbed on a machine-hour basis. The rate for the period is $32.00 a machine-hour. The firm determines the selling price of the products by applying percentages to the determined product cost as shown in Table 25.21.

Required

1. Determine the cost per unit for each product using the conventional accounting method.
2. From the conventional accounting method determine the unit selling price and the total net income from the sale of the three products.

Solution

Table 25.22 gives the calculation procedure for pricing using traditional cost accounting. The sales prices for this method are shown in Table 25.23.

Table 25.20 Maxell: Manufacturing conditions (1)

Basic data	Product X	Product Y	Product Z
Units produced	850	1,750	8,000
Labour hours/unit	0.75	1.75	1.25
Machine hours/unit	1.75	1.25	3.25
Materials, $/unit	25.00	14.00	29.00

Table 25.21 Maxell: Selling price determined by product cost

Basic data	Product X	Product Y	Product Z
Expected margin on cost (%)	35.00	40.00	25.00

Table 25.22 Maxell: Traditional costing

	Product X	Product Y	Product Z	Total
Expected margin on cost (%)	35.00	40.00	25.00	
Units produced	850	1,750	8,000	
Labour hours/unit	0.75	1.75	1.25	
Machine hours/unit	1.75	1.25	3.25	
Materials, $/unit	25.00	14.00	29.00	
Labour costs, $/hour	14.00	14.00	14.00	
Overhead absorption rate, $/machine hour	32.00	32.00	32.00	
Material cost, $/unit	25.00	14.00	29.00	
Direct labour, $/unit (Labour cost * Labour hours/unit)	10.50	24.50	17.50	
Overhead absorption, $/unit (Machine hours * Overhead absorption rate)	56.00	40.00	104.00	
Total product cost (Material cost + Direct labour + Overhead absorption)	91.50	78.50	150.50	
Total values				
Total cost, $ (Product cost * Units produced)	77,775	137,375	1,204,000	**1,419,150**
Total margin, $ (Total cost * % margin)	27,221	54,950	301,000	**383,171**
Total revenues, $ (Total cost + Total margin)	104,996	192,325	1,505,000	**1,802,321**
Sales price, $ per unit (Total revenues/Units produced)	123.53	109.90	188.13	

Table 25.23 Maxell: Sales price using traditional cost accounting

	Product X	Product Y	Product Z
Sales price, $ per unit	123.53	109.90	188.13

Demonstrating the concept 25.6 Maxell (2)

Situation

The Maxell Co. is now proposing to implement an activity-based costing system into the firm. The basic data remain the same (see Table 25.24).

Direct labour costs are $14.00 an hour and production overheads are absorbed on a machine-hour basis at a rate for the period is $32.00 a machine hour. The firm determines the selling price of the products by applying percentages to the determined product cost as shown in Table 25.25.

However, now it believes that the total production overheads can be divided as shown in Table 25.26.

Activity volumes are associated with the product line for the period as shown in Table 25.27.

Required

1. Calculate the cost per unit for each product using ABC principles.

Table 25.24 Maxell: Manufacturing conditions (2): Basic data

Basic data	Product X	Product Y	Product Z
Units produced	850	1,750	8,000
Labour hours/unit	0.75	1.75	1.25
Machine hours/unit	1.75	1.25	3.25
Materials, $/unit	25.00	14.00	29.00

Table 25.25 Maxell: Selling price determined by product cost (2)

Basic data	Product X	Product Y	Product Z
Expected margin on cost (%)	35.00	40.00	25.00

Table 25.26 Maxell: Production overheads (%)

Cost related to setups	30.00
Cost related to machinery	23.00
Cost related to material handling	15.00
Cost related to inspection	32.00
Total	**100.00**

Table 25.27 Maxell: Activity volumes

	Product X	Product Y	Product Z	Total
N° of setups	70	120	490	**680**
N° of movement of materials	14	23	90	**127**
N° of inspections	160	190	700	**1,050**

Table 25.28 Maxell: Activity-based costing

	Product X	Product Y	Product Z	Total	Portion of total
Expected margin on cost (%)	35.00	40.00	25.00		
Units produced	850	1,750	8,000		
Labour hours/unit	0.75	1.75	1.25		
Machine hours/unit	1.75	1.25	3.25		
Materials, $/unit	25.00	14.00	29.00		
Labour costs, $/hour	14.00	14.00	14.00		
Overhead absorption rate, $/machine hour	32.00	32.00	32.00		
Material cost, $/unit	25.00	14.00	29.00		
Direct labour, $/unit (Labour cost * Labour hours/unit)	10.50	24.50	17.50		
Overhead absorption, $/unit (Machine hours * Overhead absorption rate)	56.00	40.00	104.00		
Overhead from traditional basis, $ (Absorbtion rate/Unit * Units produced)	47,600	70,000	832,000	**949,600**	
Cost related to setups, $ (% Cost * Total overhead)				**30.00%**	284,880
Cost related to machinery, $ (% Cost * Total overhead)				**23.00%**	218,408
Cost related to material handling, $ (% Cost * Total overhead)				**15.00%**	142,440
Cost related to inspection, $ (% Cost * Total overhead)				**32.00%**	303,872
Total				**100.00%**	949,600
Activity volumes					
N° of setups	70	120	490	**680**	
N° of movement of materials	14	23	90	**127**	
N° of inspections	160	190	700	**1,050**	
Machinery hours used (Machine hours per unit * Units produced)	1,488	2,188	26,000	**29,675**	
Total costs					
Cost related to setups, $ (N° setups * $ total cost related to setups/Total setups)	29,325.88	50,272.94	205,281.18	**284,880**	
Cost related to machinery, $ (Machine hours * Total machine cost/Total machine hours)	10,948.00	16,100.00	191,360.00	**218,408**	
Cost related to material handling, $ (N° movements * $ Total cost related to movement/Total movements)	15,702.05	25,796.22	100,941.73	**142,440**	
Cost related to inspection, $ (N° of inspections * $ Total cost related to inspection/Total inspections)	46,304.30	54,986.36	202,581.33	**303,872**	
Per unit					
Cost related to setups, $/unit	34.50	28.73	25.66		
Cost related to machinery, $/unit	12.88	9.20	23.92		
Cost related to material handling, $/unit	18.47	14.74	12.62		
Cost related to inspection, $/unit	54.48	31.42	25.32		
Total overhead, $/unit	120.33	84.09	87.52		
Material cost, $/unit	25.00	14.00	29.00		
Direct labour, $/unit (Labour cost * Labour hours/unit)	10.50	24.50	17.50		
Total product cost per unit (Total overhead + Material cost + Direct labour)	155.83	122.59	134.02		
Total cost, $ (Cost per unit * N° units)	132,455.23	214,530.52	1,072,164.24	**1,419,150.00**	
Total margin, $ (Total cost * % margin)	46,359.33	85,812.21	268,041.06	**400,212.60**	
Total revenues, $ (Total cost + Total margin)	178,814.57	300,342.73	1,340,205.30	**1,819,362.60**	
Sales price per unit, $ (Revenues/Units produced)	210.37	171.62	167.53		
Difference from traditional costing (%)	70.31	56.16	−10.95		

Table 25.29 Maxell: Unit sales prices

	Product X	Product Y	Product Z
Sales price by activity-based costing, $/unit	210.37	171.62	167.53
Sales price by traditional costing, $/unit	123.53	109.90	188.13
Difference compared to traditional costing, %	+70.31	+56.16	−10.95

2. Determine the unit selling price and the total net income from the sale of the three products.
3. What is the difference between the sales prices calculated by activity-based costing and those calculated by traditional costing in Maxell (1)?

Solution

Table 25.28 gives the calculation procedure for pricing using activity-based costing. The unit sales price and the differences are given in Table 25.29.

Demonstrating the concept 25.7 Techno Co.

Situation

Techno Co. is a manufacturer of electric appliances. It has two assembly lines, I and II, that can both be used for assembly of similar products. Line II is a much newer, and more automated line using computers, and automated equipment. Line I, in operation since the company got started, is much more labour intensive.

The cost data for the two production lines are given in Table 25.30.

Required

1. Based on the data, determine a unit product cost for Line I and Line II by allocating the factory overhead, according to direct labour hours used.
2. If the depreciation charge for Line II is $8325 a month for the automatic equipment and there is no depreciation charge for Line I, what would be a new product cost? Again, all factory overhead is allocated according to direct labour hours.

Solution

Tables 25.31 and 25.32 gives the calculation method and the cost prices for the two approaches. Table 25.33 gives a summary.

Table 25.30 Techno Co.: Cost data for two production lines

	Line I	Line II	Total
Units produced per month	700	1,000	1,700
Labour cost, $/hour	15.00	15.00	
Labour hours/unit	3.25	0.25	
Material cost, $/unit	17.50	17.50	
Monthly factory O/H			8,750
Total direct labour hours/month	2,275	250	2,525

Table 25.31 Techno Co.: Product cost by traditional accounting

	Line I	Line II	Total
Units produced per month	700	1,000	1,700
Labour cost, $/hour	15.00	15.00	
Labour hours/unit	3.25	0.25	
Labour cost, $/unit (Cost per hour * Hours per unit)	48.75	3.75	
Material cost, $/unit	17.50	17.50	
Monthly factory O/H			8,750
Total direct labour hours/month (Units/Month * Hours/Unit)	2,275	250	2,525

(Continued)

Table 25.31   (Continued)

Total costs	Line I £	Line I % of total	Line II £	Line II % of total	Line I + Line II £	Line I + Line II % of total
Labour	34,125.00	62.89	3,750.00	16.96	37,875.00	49.59
Material	12,250.00	22.58	17,500.00	79.13	29,750.00	38.95
Monthly factory O/H*	7,883.66	14.53	866.34	3.92	8,750.00	11.46
Total costs	54,258.66	100.00	22,116.34	100.00	76,375.00	100.00
Cost per unit	**77.51**		**22.12**			

*Allocated by direct labour hours

Table 25.32   Techno Co.: Product cost by activity-based costing

	Line I	Line II	Total
Units produced per month	700	1,000	**1,700**
Labour cost, $/hour	15.00	15.00	
Labour hours/unit	3.25	0.25	
Labour cost, $/unit	48.75	3.75	
Material cost, $/unit	17.50	17.50	
General factory O/H			**425**
Technology component			**8,325**
Monthly factory O/H			**8,750**
Total direct labour hours/month	2,275	250	**2,525**

Total costs	Line I £	Line I % of total	Line II £	Line II % of total	Line I + Line II £	Line I + Line II % of total
Labour	34,125.00	72.98	3,750.00	12.66	37,875.00	49.59
Material	12,250.00	26.20	17,500.00	59.09	29,750.00	38.95
General factory O/H (a)	382.92	0.82	42.08	0.14	425.00	0.56
Technology component of O/H (b)	0.00	0.00	8,325.00	28.11	8,325.00	10.90
Total costs	46,757.92	100.00	29,617.08	100.00	76,375.00	100.00
Cost per unit	**66.80**		**29.62**			

(a) Allocated by direct labour hours
(b) Allocated by direct labour hours and technology component

	£	%
Decrease in unit cost in Line I	10.72	13.82
Increase in unit cost in Line II	7.50	33.91

Table 25.33   Techno Co.: Summary of costings

	Line I Cost price/unit	Line II Cost price/unit
1. All O/H allocated by direct labour	$77.51	$22.12
2. O/H for equipment separated	$66.80	$29.62
Change	About 14% decrease	About 34% increase

Demonstrating the concept 25.8 James Co.

Situation

James Co. manufactures a certain product that has a sales price of $14.00 a unit. The variable cost is $7.50 a unit and the monthly fixed costs are $32,500. The estimated sales revenues for this operation are $100,000. Assume that all costs remain constant between these ranges.

Required

1. Calculate the breakeven point for this situation and the margin of safety.
2. Using a production range of from zero to 10,000 units a month develop the following cost–volume–profit graphical presentations and explain their significance:
   (a) a breakeven chart
   (b) a contribution graph
   (c) a profit–volume graph.

Solution

1. The calculation is shown in Table 25.34.
   - The contribution margin per unit is price − variable cost = $14.00 − 7.50 = $6.50.
   - The breakeven point is the ratio of the fixed costs to the contribution margin = 32,500/6.50 = 5000 units.
   - The sales revenue at the breakeven point is price * breakeven sales = 5000 * 14,000 = $70,000.
   - The percent margin of safety is the ratio (expected sales − breakeven sales)/expected sales or (100,000 − 70,000)/100,000 = 30%.

2. (a) Breakeven chart
   This is shown in Figure 25.16. It gives the curve for the total costs, fixed cost and total revenues. The breakeven point is where the sales revenues cut the total cost curve. The area to

Table 25.34 James Co.: Breakeven and margin of safety

	$/unit	Total at breakeven
Sales price, $/unit	14.00	70,000
Variable cost, $/unit	7.50	37,500
Fixed cost per month, $	32,500	32,500
Contribution margin/unit	6.50	32,500
Breakeven units	5,000	
Estimated sales, $	100,000	
Margin of safety (%)	30.00	

Units	Revenues	Total VC	Fixed cost	Total cost	Profit
0	0	0	32,500	32,500	−32,500
500	7,000	3,750	32,500	36,250	−29,250
1,000	14,000	7,500	32,500	40,000	−26,000
1,500	21,000	11,250	32,500	43,750	−22,750
2,000	28,000	15,000	32,500	47,500	−19,500
2,500	35,000	18,750	32,500	51,250	−16,250
3,000	42,000	22,500	32,500	55,000	−13,000
3,500	49,000	26,250	32,500	58,750	−9,750
4,000	56,000	30,000	32,500	62,500	−6,500
4,500	63,000	33,750	32,500	66,250	−3,250
5,000	70,000	37,500	32,500	70,000	0
5,500	77,000	41,250	32,500	73,750	3,250
6,000	84,000	45,000	32,500	77,500	6,500
6,500	91,000	48,750	32,500	81,250	9,750
7,000	98,000	52,500	32,500	85,000	13,000
7,500	105,000	56,250	32,500	88,750	16,250
8,000	112,000	60,000	32,500	92,500	19,500
8,500	119,000	63,750	32,500	96,250	22,750
9,000	126,000	67,500	32,500	100,000	26,000
9,500	133,000	71,250	32,500	103,750	29,250
10,000	140,000	75,000	32,500	107,500	32,500

Figure 25.16 James Co.: Breakeven chart

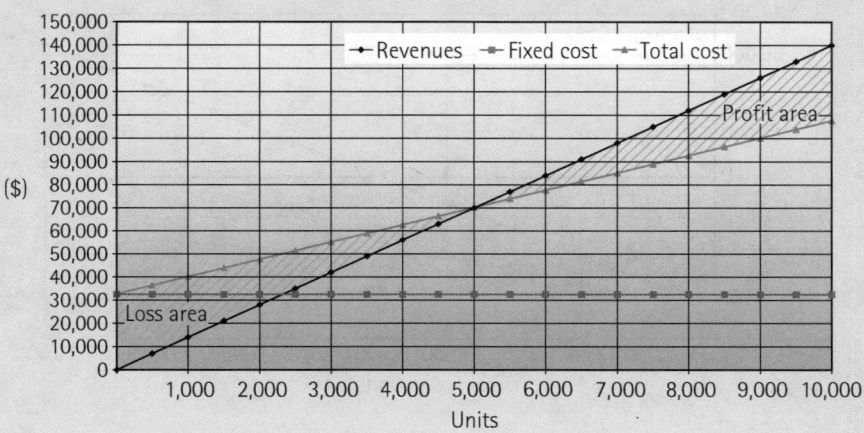

Figure 25.17 James Co.: Contribution chart

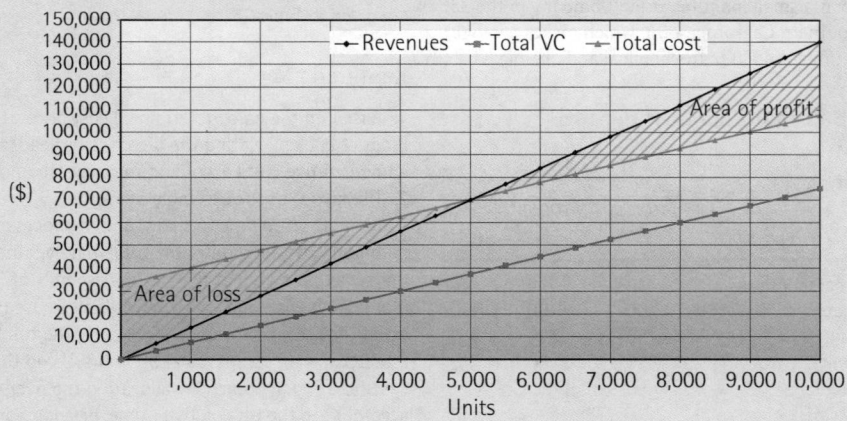

the right of the intersection is the profit area and to the left it is the loss area.

(b) Contribution chart
This is shown in Figure 25.17. It gives the curve for the total variable costs, total cost and total revenues. Here the total variable cost is parallel to and below the total cost. The difference is equal to the fixed costs. The advantage with this chart is that the total contribution of the operation is apparent, as it is the difference between the total sales revenues and the total variable costs. As before, the breakeven point is indicated, as are the profit and loss areas.

(c) Profit–volume chart
This is shown in Figure 25.18. It gives the impact on profit or loss with a change in production levels. The breakeven point is where the curve cuts the x axis at zero profit. For zero unit sales the curve intersects the y axis at a value equal to the fixed costs.

It should be emphasized that in this type of analysis all costs and revenues are considered a linear function of output and they are only valid within the production range given. This may not always be the case. Furthermore, the analysis would only apply to a short-range planning horizon.

Figure 25.18 James Co.: Profit–volume chart

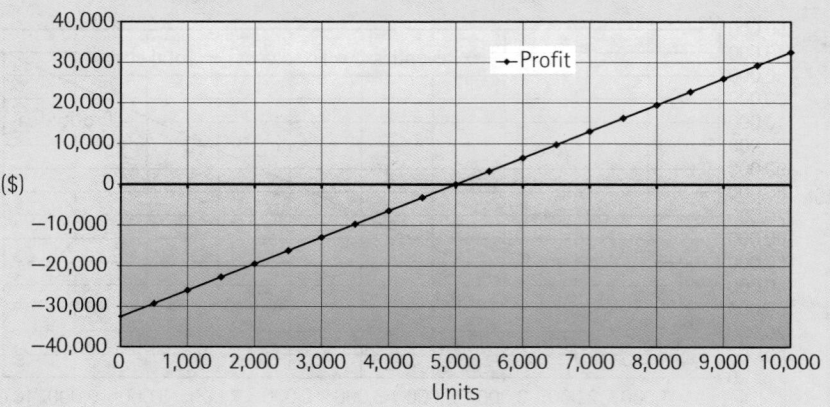

Application exercise 25.1 Balekjian Co.

Situation

The Balekjian Co. is a small manufacturing Company in the San Gabriel Valley, southern California, USA, which makes a variety of small control units used in petrochemical and chemical facilities. In one particular month, 240 each of two models, A and B, were assembled. The cost data for these two products are given in Table 25.35.

Table 25.35 Balekjian Co.: Cost data for control units

	Product A	Product B	Total
Units produced per month	240	240	480
Labour cost, $/hour	15.00	15.00	
Labour hours/unit	0.50	2.50	
Labour cost, $/unit	7.50	37.50	
Material cost, $/unit	17.50	17.50	
Monthly factory O/H			500
Sales and Administrative, $/month			5,000
Total direct labour hours/month	120	600	720

Required

1. Based on the data, determine a cost price of Product A, and Product B, by allocating the factory overhead, and sales and administrative costs according to direct labour hours used.
2. The layout of the assembly of Product B is very linear, equipment setup times are low, and in-process inventory a minimum. For the month, the total inactive time for the 240 units was estimated at five hours. Assembly of Product A was more batch wise, and with the equipment used there were significant setup times. For the month, the total delays for Product A were estimated at 90 hours. Using the activity-based costing approach, by allocating the overhead costs according to the total activity time, develop a product cost for A and B.

Application exercise 25.2 Garen Co.

Situation

Garen Co. makes metal cabinets for control systems that are sold to industrial users in Manchester, England. The cabinets are standard products and are published in Garen Co's. catalogue. The average operating data for two of Garen's principal products are given in Table 25.36.

Garen Co. adds 15% to the product cost to establish the price for its products. The catalogue price for Product STA-3 is £36/unit, and that for product DIS-8 is £53/unit.

Table 25.36 Garen Co.: Average operating data

	Product STA-3	Product DIS-8
Units produced per month	720	800
Labour cost, £/hour	9.50	9.50
Labour hours/unit	0.75	2.75
Material cost, £/unit	17.50	17.50
Monthly factory O/H, £	1,500	
Sales and administrative, £/month	5,000	

Required

1. If Garen allocates both the overhead quantities according to direct labour hours, how would product prices compare to competitors' catalogue prices?
2. In addition to direct labour hours, there are other activity times associated with the products including machine time, waiting, and storage time as shown in Table 25.37.

If the overhead were now allocated according to total hours for the product (labour hours + other activity hours), how

Table 25.37 Garen Co.: Other activity times

	Product STA-3	Product DIS-8
Other activity times for total monthly units, hours	250	50

would this change the proposed product prices for the two products? Would they be competitive in others' catalogues of similar articles?

Application exercise 25.3 Lorain Co.

Situation

Lorain Co. is a small English business that assembles electronic components. It has two principal products, reference DW-1705 and CW-1905. In 1995 the production quantity of these two products was 85,000 units each. The unit cost of raw materials and components was £13.75 for DW-1705 and £14.25 for CW-1905. Other costs associated with the two products in 1995 are as shown in Table 25.38.

The production time (elapsed time) a unit for DW-1705 was 6.50 hours and 1.50 hours for product CW-1905. A major reason for the difference in time was that DW-1705 was produced on an old, poorly organized assembly line with machines that required long setup times. However, CW-1905

was produced in a newer part of the factory where machines were more recent and a just-in-time kanban organization was in effect. The sales price for product DW-1705 was £36.00 a unit and £21.00 for CW-1905.

Required

1. Determine a contribution margin for each product by allocating:
   - purchasing costs according to the value of raw material
   - manufacturing costs according to the manufacturing time
   - sales and administrative costs according to total costs less administration costs.
   What conclusions might be drawn from these results?
2. Develop an income statement for the organization based on the two products. What is the annual profit?
3. What would be the profit for the organization:
   (a) if only product, DW-1705, were produced
   (b) if only product, CW-1905, were produced?
   Assume that all other costs remain unchanged, and that the total time used for manufacturing is the same as that used in question 1.
4. What is the added value for the two products?

Table 25.38 Lorain Co.: Production costs

Other costs	Purchasing	Manufacturing	Sales and administration
Salaries	45,000	550,000	650,000
Expenses	25,000	105,000	150,000
Depreciation	45,000	750,000	55,000

Application exercise 25.4 Motors

Situation

After a technical study, a company that manufactures large industrial motor units established that the variation of the total daily costs, in $ according to the end use of the units produced (Q), could be represented by the following function:

$$CT = 100Q^3 - 2000Q^2 + 5000Q + 5000$$

Required

1. What type of cost does the last term represent? What is represented by the sum of the three first terms?
2. From the equation, which gives the total cost, develop a function for the average cost.
3. From Table 25.39 for the average cost, show on a graph the evolution as a function of the motors produced.

Table 25.39 Average cost of small motor units

Units	Average cost, $	Units	Average cost, $
1	9,810	11	4,465
2	7,140	12	4,457
3	6,157	13	4,475
4	5,610	14	4,517
5	5,250	15	4,583
6	4,993	16	4,673
7	4,804	17	4,784
8	4,665	18	4,918
9	4,566	19	5,073
10	4,500	20	5,250

4. Market conditions, because of competitors, impose a unit sales price of $5,000. Above what production level will the firm start to make a profit? Does the shape of the average cost curve show there is always a profit made above the breakeven point?

5. At what units sold will the profit be a maximum at a unit sales price of $5,000?

6. Calculate the total profit that corresponds to a maximum unit profit.

7. Calculate the marginal cost for the 12th unit, and also for the 13th unit. Compare these values to the average cost. What are your observations?

8. What is the shape of the average cost curve when the marginal cost is less? When it is greater? How does the level relative to the marginal cost compared to the average cost explain the evolution of the latter?

9. Calculate the total profit for the company if it can sell 13 units at $5,000/unit. Compare this profit with that obtained for a sale of 12 units. Why does a maximum unit profit not necessarily correspond with a total maximum profit? Can the firm continue to increase its total profit in producing and selling 14 units instead of just 13?

Application exercise 25.5 Pumps

Situation

A company makes industrial pumps for the pharmaceutical, food, and chemical industries principally out of stainless steel.

Table 25.40 Processing and financial data for industrial pumps

	DIW-17	GDW-14
Labour rate, £/hour	15.00	15.00
Labour hours/unit	3.75	17.25
Average material cost, £/unit	4.25	6.75
Quantity of material, kg	5.5	3.5
Machine cost, £/hour	25.00	25.00
Machine time, hours/unit	12.25	3.75
Sales and administration for firm, £12,250		

There is both a labour and machining operation for the pumps. Machining is carried out on automatic, numerically controlled units. Table 25.40 gives processing and financial data for two major models, DIW-17 and GDW-14.

There are 125 units of each model produced every month.

Required

1. The firm wishes to establish a product cost based on allocating sales and administrative costs according to labour time and then adding 20% for profit. On this basis, what would be the quoted sales price of the pumps?

2. If the firms allocated sales and administrative costs according to machine time, and then added 20% for profit, would this change the quoted price of the units?

3. What do you believe is the better method? Do you believe the firm should take another approach?

Application exercise 25.6 Stamping

Situation

A company which makes aluminium parts for the automobile and aircraft industry is considering replacing one of the stamping presses it has in its work centre. This new stamping press is faster, and almost completely automated so that, if purchased, there would be a big savings in labour. Prior to the commitment of purchase the company has established financial information as shown in Table 25.41.

Table 25.41 Financial data for aluminium parts production

Purchase price of asset, £	1,572,500
Economic life of asset, years	10
Tax rate, %	38.00
Cost saving, £	
Year 1	175,800
Year 2	219,750
Year 3	263,700
Year 4	351,600
Year 5	351,600
Year 6	351,600
Year 7	351,600
Year 8	351,600
Year 9	351,600
Year 10	351,600
Total	**3,120,450**
Salvage value new equipment, £	550,000
Salvage value old equipment, £	148,000
Asset cost less salvage	874,500
Discount rate, %	12.00

Required

1. Based on this information, determine the payback period in years if income taxes are taken into consideration.
2. What would be the apparent payback period if income taxes were not taken into consideration?
3. Illustrate on a graph the cumulative cash flow movements for the two payback methods.
4. What is the net present value of the investment? Based on the NPV, does the investment seem sound?

Case study 25.1 Manning

Situation

Frank Manning, who lives in the Wasdale area of the Lake District in England, is a carpenter who makes handmade good-quality wooden benches from oak. There are no nails and screws in the assembly; they are all dovetail joints secured by horse-based resin waterproof glue. Frank's principal costs are the raw materials, which include the oak slats that he purchases from a supplier in Gosforth, the glue, varnish, stain, and his tools for which he needs to replace the cutting blades from time to time. When Frank's production increases beyond a certain level he uses the services of Willie Greenup, who lives just down the road from Frank. Willie is not too efficient, but he helps Frank out with some of the woodcutting work and, as such, he is able to help Frank keep up with the scheduled delivery dates. The costs for making the benches according to the number made are given in Table 25.42. Frank proposes to sell the benches for £200 each.

Table 25.42 Manning: Cost of benches according to number made

Quantity	Cost	Quantity	Cost	Quantity	Cost
1	464.48	11	1,624.96	21	2,961.92
2	660.08	12	1,700.08	22	3,223.52
3	829.84	13	1,780.00	23	3,520.64
4	976.72	14	1,867.84	24	3,856.40
5	1,103.92	15	1,966.64	25	4,233.60
6	1,214.48	16	2,079.52	26	4,655.84
7	1,311.52	17	2,209.52	27	5,125.84
8	1,397.92	18	2,359.68	28	5,646.64
9	1,476.96	19	2,533.04	29	6,229.25
10	1,551.60	20	2,732.80	30	6,898.23

Required
Discuss in detail the operating cost and profit situation based on this information, including developing the appropriate financial curves. What decisions should be made based on this information? What would be the impact on the operation, and how would decisions change, if Frank sold the benches for £160? If he sold them for £240?

Selected further reading

ALNESTIG, Peter and SEGERSTEDT, Anders, 'Product costing in ten Swedish manufacturing companies', *International Journal of Production Economics*, vol. 46–7, December 1996, pp 441–57.

DRURY, Colin (1998) *Costing: An Introduction*, 4th edition, International Thomson Business Press.

HICKS, Douglas T. (1999) *Activity-Based Costing: Making it Work for Small and Mid-Sized Companies*, 2nd edition, Wiley.

SEDGLEY, Dawn J. and JACKIW, Christopher, F. (2001) *The 123s of ABC in SAP: Using SAP R/3 to Support Activity-Based Costing*, Wiley.

SHIM, Eunsup and SUDIT, Ephraim, F., 'How manufacturers price products', *Management Accounting*, vol. 76, issue 8, Feb 1995, pp 37–9.

An extensive listing of other further reading can be found on the website.

What's on the web?

Further learning resources are available to lecturers and students at www.supplychain-online.com, including the following which are specific to *Financial analysis*:

Resource	Subject
Chapter overview	Financial analysis
Depreciation tables	Fixed costs
Demonstrating the concept: Smiley	Breakeven analysis
Application exercise: Alumni	Costs and breakeven
Application exercise: Lamps	Inventory accounting
More further reading	Financial analysis

26 Auditing the operations and supply chain

Introduction

A firm's operations must be optimized if it is to remain competitive. The purpose of this chapter is to bring together many of the concepts, tools, and analytical measures that have been discussed in earlier chapters, illustrating how they can be effectively and pragmatically used to fine-tune the operations and supply chain of the firm.

The operations audit

An operational audit, or diagnostic, is a detailed analysis of the firm, the operation, or the supply chain to obtain an in-depth understanding of current performance. An audit is conducted because there is a perception that improvements can be made and the audit would give a baseline from which to start making these changes. Often when one talks of an audit, one thinks in terms of a financial audit. However, this is only part of the story as a thorough operations audit will examine customer relations, planning, quality levels, employee working environment as well as an objective accounting for all of the costs in the operation.

Auditor

Who performs the audit depends on the resources available to the firm. A competent external auditing firm, or consultants, can often provide an unbiased opinion of a firm's business. They are able to 'see the wood for the trees'. However, external auditors can be very expensive and often take time to understand the firm in question. An internal audit undertaken by current staff members is less costly and has the advantage that those involved know the firm. However, it can be biased in that individuals cannot recognize their own difficulties. To avoid this, an internal audit is perhaps best carried out with the aid of at least one outside competent consultant. The duration of an audit, again, depends on the size of the company, and what is being targeted. It might be a few days or up to several months.

Starting point

Performing an audit, or diagnostic, of an operation takes time and is thus expensive. One approach for starting is to take a global look at the supply chain from purchasing through transformation to delivery particularly noting the level of customer satisfaction (discussed in the next section). Then, once a global viewpoint has been established, break the whole operation into manageable 'blocks' and conduct a detailed audit sequentially on each.

Analytical tools

Analytical tools are the methods and instruments available to carry out the audit. They may be quantitative, or qualitative in nature. Except for benchmarking, which is presented at the end of this chapter, they have all been treated in previous chapters. For summary purposes, they are given in alphabetical order in Table 26.1, indicating in which chapter details of the methods can be found.

Table 26.1 Check sheet: Analytical tools

Procedure	Description	In which chapter
ABC analysis	Type of Pareto presentation useful for classifying inventory or suppliers according to their financial importance	11 Inventory management 16 Purchasing and subcontracting
Activity-based costing	Technique that measures costs at each step of the supply chain and uncovers inefficiencies and non-value-added activities	25 Financial analysis
Benchmarking	Comparison of one firm's business practices with others	26 Auditing operations
Brainstorming	Searching out new ideas in a group environment without any preconceived notions	4 Quality management 6 Design of the product
Failure mode, effect, and criticality analysis (FMECA)	Detailed studies of a product design, manufacturing operation, or distribution network to determine which features are critical to various modes of failure	19 Reliability and maintenance
Frequency check sheet	Indicates how often a certain problem occurs with a product or process. The data can be presented graphically as a Pareto analysis	4 Quality management
Hoshin	Searching for simple practical solutions to improve efficiency and reduce waste in an operation	4 Quality management
Improvement monitoring charts	Charts indicating if improvements have been obtained in certain analytical procedures	4 Quality management
Ishikawa diagram	A fishbone diagram highlighting causes that might contribute to quality-related problems	4 Quality management
Just-in-time	Managing such that the exact quantity of inventory is delivered at the right time	15 Lean production and just-in-time
Keep designs simple	With simple designs, and reducing the number of component parts helps to minimize the probability of errors	19 Reliability and maintenance for control
Kaizen, or continuous improvement	Continuously improving quality and efficiency by isolating and analyzing sources of problems	4 Quality management
Overall equipment effectiveness	Analyzing whether a machine or work post is optimum concerning the value-added activities	15 Lean production and just-in-time
Pareto analysis	A frequency distribution of problems associated with an operation. Often a graphical representation of a frequency check sheet	4 Quality management
Phantom customer	In reality the customer is a company employee checking to see the quality of a service operation	4 Quality management
Pipeline map	Histogram illustrating relationship of inventory levels with operating time	17 Managing the integrated supply chain

(Continued)

Table 26.1 (Continued)

Procedure	Description	In which chapter
Poka yoke	Failsafe approach to increase reliability and quality	**4** Quality management **19** Reliability and maintenance
Process flow chart	Illustrates the movement of material between successive functions in order to highlight non-value-added activities	**7** Process design and the operations network
Quality circles	A small group of employees who meet regularly on a voluntary basis to discuss problems occurring in their operating centre	**4** Quality management
Quality function deployment	Focuses on designing products and services which are desired by the customer	**6** Design of the product
Reengineering	The complete re-evaluation and modification of a firm with the objective of improving performance	**7** Process design and the operations network
Scatter diagram	A chart illustrating if there is a correlation between an independent and a dependent variable	**10** Forecasting: The trigger in the supply chain
Spider web	A form of Pareto analysis showing the occurrence of certain criteria in the form of a spider web	**4** Quality management
Statistical process control charts	Analytical charts in manufacturing or services to ascertain if a process is operating according to defined specifications	**20** Statistical quality control
Taguchi methods	Specific concepts on improving product and process quality based on developing a robust design	**6** Design of the product

Audit checklists

There are audit check-sheets, together with detailed explanations, in each section of this chapter, which are useful for carrying out an audit. With all the checklists it is important to make an analysis over time to see whether improvements are being made. This is the concept illustrated by the improvement monitoring chart explained in Chapter 4.

Customer satisfaction

A key starting area in an audit should be at the customer level. The client is king! Firms are in business to make a profit, providing there is a satisfactory return on capital employed, and this implies satisfying the customer with desired products, expected quality, and meeting promised delivery dates. It is the customer who is

pulling the products through the supply chain, or is demanding the services of the firm. Satisfied customers, either for industrial products, or consumer products, increase market share and thus increase activity at the operational level.

Customer analysis

The following are considerations for an analysis at the customer level, presented in question form with the corresponding reasoning. A summary audit sheet of these criteria can be found in Table 26.2. As indicated on the sheet, the response to these questions can be on a qualitative scale such as:

1. Never.
2. Rarely.
3. Sometimes.
4. Most of the time.
5. All the time.

Table 26.2 Check sheet: Are you customized?

Criteria	1 Never	2 Rarely	3 Sometimes	4 Most of the time	5 All the time
1 Do you have all the customers you would like?					
2 Are the customers as loyal as you would like?					
3 Do you generate as much business from each customer as you would like?					
4 Do you always know what your customers want?					
5 Does your entire organization know what your customers want?					
6 Is your information network focused on helping you to understand what customers and markets are trying to tell to?					
7 Can your organization respond quickly to what your customers and markets are telling?					
8 Does your information network enable the proactive delivery of information to your customers?					
9 Are the full capabilities of your organization accessible to your customers at all your regional locations?					
10 Does your information network reflect the bottom line importance of customer service?					

- Having a binomial yes or no response may simplify this check sheet
- It is useful if the analysis is performed periodically, say, once a quarter, or once every six months, to see if improvements are being obtained
- A quantitative measurement can be made by using the numerical scale indicated (1 = Never, 2 = Rarely, etc.)

Alternatively, they can be simply binomial *yes* or *no*. If the answer is at the low end of the scale, or no, then there are obvious rooms for improvement.[1]

Customer levels

Do you have as many customers as you would like?

- The bottom line, or profit, can never be too healthy.
- A growth-oriented company can never have too many customers.
- Customers are the engine that generate revenues.

Customer loyalty

Are the customers as loyal as you would like?

- It is one thing to gain customers. It is another thing to keep them!
- The strength of a firm depends very much on the ability to sustain a strong relationship with customers.

Business volume

Do you generate as much business from each customer as you would like?

- Critical to business growth is continually increasing sales.
- To maximize each business opportunity the total organization needs to be leveraged to bring it to bear at the point of customer contact.

Comprehension

Do you really know what your customers want?

- Are you alert to every product your customers could use?
- Do you understand every service that might be of interest to them?
- Are you aware of every transaction the customer is prepared to make?

- Do you appreciate every sale that your customer would allow you to follow through?
- Are you completely tuned into your market?

Teamwork

Does your entire organization know what your customers want?

- Customer orientation has limited value unless it is embedded into the very heart of the enterprise. This means at all levels, and at every place that directly or indirectly involves the customer.

Communication

Is your information network focused on helping you hear what customers and markets are trying to tell you?

- The next best thing to reading your customers' mind is listening to what there are saying.
- Unless you are constantly tuned into your customers' signals, you might be missing messages that could guide you to greater results for your business.

Lead time

Can your organization respond quickly to what customers and markets are telling you?

- If the flow lines of your information system are not within your customer reach, you may not always sense when opportunity knocks.
- Even if customers are getting the message, it may not be enough if you cannot reply rapidly to market signals with information, products, and services. In this case, important revenues will be lost.

Proactive response

Does the information network enable a proactive delivery of information to customers?

- Some business plans underestimate the power of information to build customer relationships.
- There is tremendous advantage of using information technology to transform customer information into customers who are generating revenue for your business.

Accessibility

Are the full capabilities of the organization accessible to customers at all locations?

- An office, a branch, a retail site, or a representative are all part of your company to a customer. They are part of the subsystem of which your whole organization is the system.
- It is strategically important to leverage your entire organization by extending its capabilities to each, and every point of customer contact.

Service

Does your information network reflect the bottom line importance of customer service?

- Business is built on customers.
- Without customers, there is no business. There is no bottom line.
- Government is also built on customers: The public.
- Whether one is in business, commerce, or the business of government, no objective of an information network is more fundamental than enhanced customer service.

The customer is not always the final purchaser of the product. It is any group, organization, or person downstream of the operation such as the next work post, the adjacent work centre, the parent company, or the final consumer.

Customer satisfaction index

In the automobile industry, a firm that makes extensive customer surveys using a customer satisfaction index is J D Power and Associates of Agoura Hills, California. A high rating from this firm can turn a car into an enormous hit. As an illustration, in November 2000 the J D Power survey, using a matrix of 137 possible vehicle problems, found that for the sixth consecutive year the Lexus (Toyota) ranked highest in long-term vehicle dependability with less than one-half of the number of vehicle problems of the average manufacturer. Others high on the list included Porsche, Infiniti (Nissan) and Accura (Honda). According to J D Power, manufacturers that understand the importance of long-term durability and produce vehicles that experience fewer problems in the later years of ownership are rewarded with higher customer retention. Fewer vehicle problems also translate into greater satisfaction with dealer service, better brand reputation and a greater likelihood of making recommendations to friends and family.[2] In a more global survey covering the seven major automobile firms J D Power found that Ford Motor, including its European luxury brands, Jaguar, Volvo and Land Rover, ranked last, as illustrated in Figure 26.1.[3]

Figure 26.1 Problems per 100 automobiles in model year (2001)

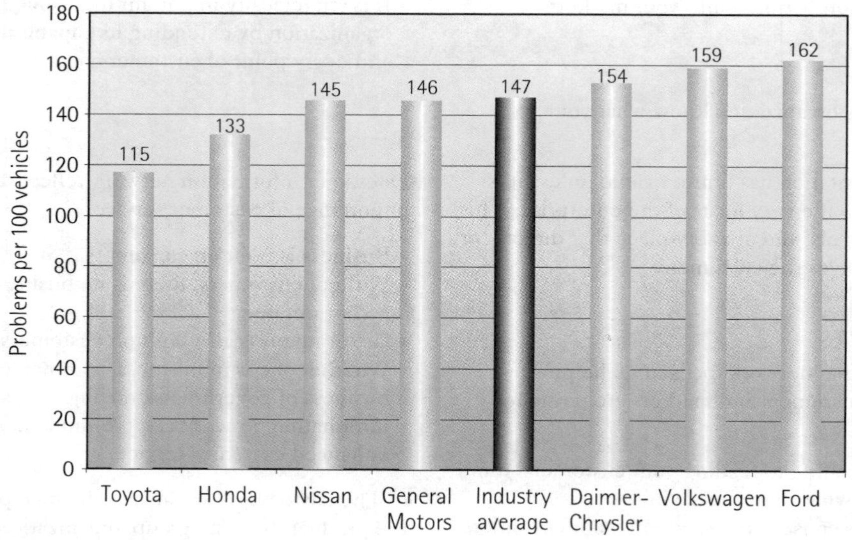

Customer service level

The customer service level is a measure of customer satisfaction regarding delivery of specific identified goods, or services. The service level might be measured by a qualitative or a quantitative approach.

Qualitative measurement of service level

The following are qualitative measures of the customer service level, again in question form. A summary audit sheet of these criteria can be found in Table 26.3 and again, as indicated on the sheet, the response to these questions can be on a qualitative scale or simply binomial *yes* or *no*. If the answer is at the low end of the scale, or no, then there is obvious room for improvement.

Delivery completeness

When a delivery is made does it exactly correspond to what the customer has ordered?

Delivery reliability

When a delivery date is fixed, are you able to keep the date, and the time?

Delivery frequency

Are you able to delivery frequently in small lot sizes such that the client can operate in a just-in-time mode?

Order status information

This is the ability of a firm's information system to respond in a timely and accurate manner to customer's request for information about a product, or a service. For example, can the customer make contact directly through e-mail or other electronic information system?

Minimum order quantity

Are you prepared to provide service to your small clients who might only ask for few items or even just one item?

Delivery flexibility

Are you flexible to respond to special, and/or unexpected needs of customer by expediting the required order in a timely manner?

Recovery from a system malfunction

Are you well equipped with reliable procedures to recover in a timely manner from a system malfunction, such as billing errors, wrong shipment, shipping damage claims, etc.?

Table 26.3 Check sheet: Qualitative delivery service attributes

Delivery service criteria	1 Never achieved	2 Rarely achieved	3 Achieved sometimes	4 Achieved most of the time	5 Achieved all the time
1 Delivery completeness					
2 Delivery reliability					
3 Delivery frequency					
4 Order status information					
5 Minimum order quantity					
6 Delivery flexibility					
7 Recovery from a system malfunction					
8 Ability to make emergency orders					
9 Responsive after-sales service					

- This check sheet may be simplified by having a binomial yes or no response
- It is useful if the analysis is performed periodically; say, once a quarter, or once every six months, to see if improvements are being obtained
- A quantitative measurement can be made by using the numerical scale indicated (1 = Never, 2 = Rarely, etc.)

Ability to fill emergency orders

Are you willing and able to supply units outside normal working hours, such as at night, weekends, and vacation periods?

Responsive after-sales service

Are you efficient and quick in providing product support, technical help, after delivery of product has been made?

Quantitative measurement of service level

The following are quantitative measures of the customer service level. A summary audit sheet of these criteria can be found in Table 26.4.

Service level according to availability of the number orders

This is the product availability in terms of the orders demanded by the customer as a percentage. It is given by:

$$\frac{\text{Total orders demanded} - \text{Number of incomplete orders}}{\text{Total orders demanded}}$$

For example, a food company may have given a producing firm 25 orders for different products. How many of these orders can be filled out of existing inventory, or produced in time to meet the required delivery date? And, how many of the orders have to be put on backorder? If two out of the 25 were incomplete, the customer service level would be 92%:

$$\frac{25 - 2}{25} = 92\%$$

Service level according to availability of units of finished products

This indicator is similar to the previous except that it measures the service level as a percentage according to the number of units supplied:

$$\frac{\text{Total units demanded} - \text{Number of units unavailable}}{\text{Total units demanded}}$$

If a client puts in an order for 250 units, maybe many different references, and out of these only 240 can be supplied or a stockout of ten units, then the customer service level would be 96%:

$$\frac{250 - 10}{250} = 96\%$$

Table 26.4 Check sheet: Quantitative delivery service attributes

Indicator	Calculation	Today	In three months	In six months	In nine months	In one year
1 Service level according to availability of the number of orders, %	$\dfrac{\text{Total orders demanded} - \text{Number of incomplete orders}}{\text{Total orders demanded}}$					
2 Service level according to availability of the number of units, %	$\dfrac{\text{Total units demanded} - \text{Number of units unavailable}}{\text{Total units demanded}}$					
3 Delivery service level, %	$\dfrac{\text{Total Shipments ordered} - \text{Number of shipments late or early}}{\text{Total shipments ordered}}$					
4 Order cycle time or production lead times	Delivery date — date order was placed					
5 Availability and order cycle time	Combined service level with order cycle time					

Delivery service level

Delivery service level to the client can be measured by:

$$\frac{\left[\begin{array}{c}\text{Total shipments} \\ \text{ordered}\end{array}\right] - \left[\begin{array}{c}\text{Number of shipments} \\ \text{late or early}\end{array}\right]}{\text{Total shipments ordered}}$$

A client makes an order for 20 shipments of items, which are promised on a certain, or certain dates. One is not delivered on time and thus the service level is 95%.

$$\frac{20-1}{20} = 95\%$$

Order cycle time

The order cycle time, or the production lead time, is the elapsed time from the customer placing the order, to when the customer receives the order. It is an indicator of the flexibility of an organization. One of the challenges of the industry is to reduce lead times.

Product availability combined with order cycle time

This quantitative measure might be, for example, 95% of orders can be delivered within one week.

Inventory management

Inventory management is a key indicator of how efficiently a manufacturer or a distribution company is operating. Holding unnecessary inventory is costly and it is a major component of a firm's working capital. Inventory can quickly become obsolete for high-tech products or when model designs change rapidly and if goods are perishable they can spoil when kept too long. Further, any inventory may be damaged or be stolen.

Quantitative measurements of inventory

The following are some quantitative indicators, which may be used to measure how inventories are being managed, and they are summarized in Table 26.5. As shown on this sheet, it is useful if the indicators are measured over a period of time, say, every three months to see if improvements are being made.

Average inventory level during a cycle

During the inventory cycle (the period between one order and the next) the average inventory is:

$$\frac{\left[\begin{array}{c}\text{Beginning value of} \\ \text{inventory}\end{array}\right] + \left[\begin{array}{c}\text{Ending value of} \\ \text{inventory}\end{array}\right]}{2}$$

The average inventory for each reference item should be measured and not the total inventory.

Order-processing cost per cycle

The order-processing cost per cycle is given by the relationship:

$$\frac{(\text{Total demand in units}) * (\text{Cost of each order})}{\text{Units per order}}$$

Table 26.5 Check sheet: Inventory management – quantitative measures

Indicator	Calculation	Today	In three months	In six months	In nine months	In one year
1 Average inventory level during a cycle	$\dfrac{\text{Beginning value} + \text{Ending value of inventory}}{2}$					
2 Order processing cost per cycle	$\dfrac{\text{Total demand in units} * \text{Cost of each order}}{\text{Units per order}}$					
3 Inventory carrying cost, per unit	$\dfrac{\text{Cost of financing, warehousing, insurance, waste, etc.}}{\text{Total quantity of inventory}}$					
4 Inventory turnover	$\dfrac{\text{Cost of goods sold}}{\text{Value of inventory}}$					
5 Inventory to sales ratio	$\dfrac{\text{Value of inventory held during a period}}{\text{Sales value during the period}}$					
6 Record accuracy in a cycle, %	$\dfrac{\text{Number of items counted} - \text{Number of inaccurate records}}{\text{Number of items counted}}$					
7 Average value of working inventory	$\dfrac{\text{Number of items ordered} * \text{Value}}{2}$					
8 Value of safety stock	Total inventory value − Value of working inventory					
9 Inventory as a percent of assets	$\dfrac{\text{Total value of inventory}}{\text{Value of inventory} + \text{Value of fixed assets}}$					
10 References of raw material, in-process, and finished goods	Number of product references managed					
11 Value of raw materials inventory	Sum of (Units of each type of raw material * Unit cost)					
12 Value of in-process inventory	Sum of (Units of each type of in-process inventory * Unit cost)					
13 Value of in-finished goods inventory	Sum of (Units of each type of finished goods inventory * Unit cost)					
14 Value of packaging material	Sum of (Units of each type of packaging * Unit cost)					

This ordering cost can be applied if orders are purchased from outside or if they are ordered from inside, where setup and other preparation costs would be incurred.

Inventory carrying cost

This covers the total cost of financing, warehousing, insurance, theft, waste, obsolescence, etc., and if this number is divided by the total quantity of inventory would give the carrying cost per unit.

Inventory turnover

The inventory turnover is expressed by the ratio:

$$\frac{\text{Cost of goods sold}}{\text{Value of inventory}}$$

The greater the inventory turnover, the more efficient the operation, and the lower the inventory carrying cost.

Inventory to sales ratio

This is expressed by the ratio:

$$\frac{\text{Value of inventory}}{\text{Sales volume}}$$

This measure gives, for example, the value of the finished goods inventory relative to the sales for a given time period. The lower the value, the more efficient the firm is in turning over the inventory. It is a similar measure to inventory turnover but in the reciprocal sense.

Record accuracy

Mistakes can be made in the recording of inventory. Records might indicate that there is more inventory in stock than is, in fact, the case. Thus, when the time comes to use this inventory for a production operation, it is not available. Alternatively, when it comes to supplying the customer with the finished goods, the products are not there. Record accuracy as a percentage for a given cycle can be measured by the following:

$$\frac{\left[\begin{array}{c}\text{Number of items}\\\text{counted}\end{array}\right] - \left[\begin{array}{c}\text{Number of inaccurate}\\\text{records}\end{array}\right]}{\text{Number of items counted during cycle}}$$

Record accuracy is improved by using bar coding on items either at purchase, in-process, or the finished goods stage.

Average value of working inventory

This is the amount of money invested in the inventory that goes to make up the working material of the organization. To keep this value to a minimum, quantity discounts would be an advantage. However, if this means buying in large quantities it may not, in effect, reduce the value of the working inventory. The value is calculated by:

$$\frac{(\text{Number of items ordered})*(\text{value})}{2}$$

Value of safety stock
This is:

Total inventory value − Value of working inventory

Obviously, the closer this value is to zero, the better. Safety stock is dead stock and only adds to the cost of doing business. Minimizing the uncertainty of the operation can reduce safety stock. For example, choosing suppliers who are reliable in delivery dates and material quality, fine-tuning the production operation so that unplanned shutdowns are minimized, or trying to anticipate customer needs.

Inventory as a percentage of assets

This is expressed by the ratio:

$$\frac{\text{Value of inventory}}{\text{Value of total assets (Inventory + Equipment)}}$$

The lower this ratio, again the better the performance. This value can be benchmarked with other firms but care has to be taken in drawing conclusions because of different types of capital equipment used in the operations.

Product references

This is the total number of product references managed during the operation and includes raw materials, work-in-process and finished goods. Customer demands may result in many different item references even so some products may be very similar, such as fasteners which have similar lengths and diameter, plastic components of varying colours, chassis frames of many different sizes, etc. The higher the number of different references means:

• greater inventory
• increased ordering costs
• larger carrying costs
• more management attention
• greater the possibility of errors.

Henry Ford (Chapter 1) had this in mind in the production of the Model T automobile. His operating approach was that: 'A customer can have any colour car he likes as long as it is black!' Thus, with this very standard product, the references of automobile components were kept very low. An audit should ask the question, 'Can the number of references be reduced without jeopardizing customer satisfaction?'

Value of raw materials inventory, in-process inventory, and finished goods inventory

These three measurements give the value of inventory held at the various stages of the supply chain. When they are measured on a sequential basis they give a measure of how the value chain is progressing.

Value of packaging material

Packaging is necessary for protecting material in transport and also as a marketing tool in the case of finished products. Packaging is not part of the finished product but could represent a significant cost in the operation.

Table 26.6 Check sheet: Why is inventory being held?

Criteria	Today	In three months	In six months	In nine months	In one year
1 Customer uncertainty					
2 Lack of confidence in suppliers					
3 Long supplier delivery times					
4 Insufficient production capacity					
5 Insufficient transportation					
6 Poor scheduling					
7 Long setup times					

Qualitative evaluation of why inventory is being held

In addition to quantitative measurement of inventory one might also ask why inventory is being held in the first place. This might be for some of the following reasons a summary of which is given in Table 26.6.

Customer uncertainty

A high level of finished goods inventories is being held because there is considerable uncertainty of the client needs. Sometimes they are higher than forecast, and sometimes they are lower. If this is the case, one should examine the forecast methods being used or perhaps the salespeople should have more contact with the customer better to understand their future needs. The supplier firm might consider having an electronic linkup with its customers so that it has real-time information of customer needs so that it can plan inventory levels accordingly.

Lack of confidence in suppliers

If one is uncertain about supplier delivery dates, and whether the exact quantity of goods are going to be delivered, one might be inclined to keep high levels of raw materials inventory to minimize the risk of a stockout. If this is the case, one should examine how the supplier manages its activity and try to improve the reliability. If not, consider looking for another supplier. Again, an electronic network linkup with the supplier may improve the situation.

Long supplier delivery times

This might be because a supplier is a long distance from your firm. For example, you are in the USA and

the supplier is in Singapore and shipment is by boat. It might be because you are not a preferred client to the supplier and not much attention is given to the delivery of your product. Again, work with your supplier and see if times can be reduced. Alternatively, if it is cost effective, choose a supplier that is closer to your user facility.

Insufficient production capacity

Perhaps somewhere in the production line there is a bottleneck resource (see Chapter 22) and work-in-process inventory is building up ahead of this resource. In this case attention should be considered to balance the capacity of this resource with other resources in the system.

Insufficient transportation

Here there is insufficient transportation to deliver the finished goods inventory when it is made. This is costly, as the finished goods inventory has the highest value to your firm. Consider subcontracting more transportation needs. If transportation is by train and this is the bottleneck, work with the rail companies to see if better train schedules can be developed. If this is not feasible, consider transferring from shipping by truck instead of by train where there is more flexibility.

Poor scheduling

Here the scheduling is not made in conjunction with the production activity such that when products are made, the schedule does not require these products at the next stage of the operation. A more coordinated schedule should be developed. This is where an ERP system is beneficial (see Chapter 13).

Figure 26.2 Inventory to sales ratio for Dell and Cisco systems

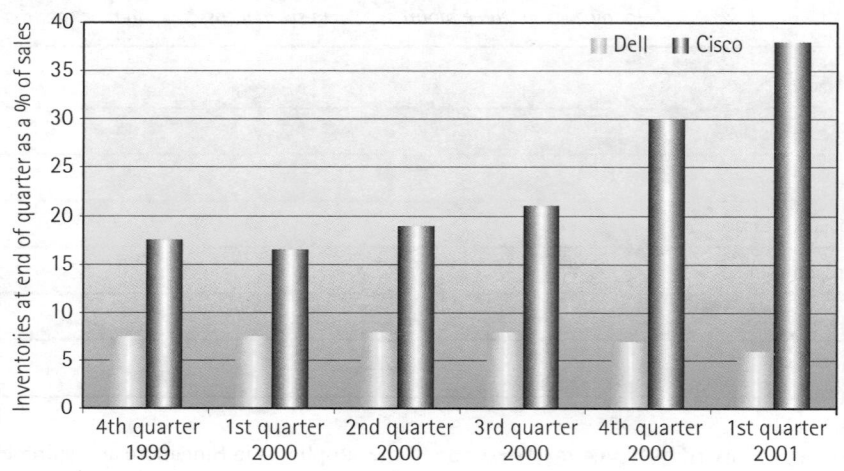

Long setup times

At some part of the production operation setup times are long, such that high levels of work-in-process inventory is being held so that production can continue while a machine or work post is being set up. In this case the application of SMED should be considered. (See Chapter 15.)

Company performance and inventory

Dell Computer Company sells PCs direct to customers rather than indirectly through dealer networks like IBM and Compaq. It is one of the most successful computer companies and, as Figure 26.2 illustrates, Dell keeps a very low level of inventory. In the first quarter of 2001 it was 6% compared to nearly 40% for Cisco Systems, the firm that makes routers for Internet systems.[4]

Efficiency and quality measurements

Manufacturing

The following are efficiency and quality indicators for an operation not including inventory measurements. A summary of these is in Table 26.7.

Production costs

Production costs are the total unit cost for producing a product. If production costs can be reduced, then for the same sales price, margins can be increased.

Alternatively, lower production costs may allow a reduced sales price, which could increase market share. (See Chapter 2.)

Use of data processing

Verbal orders, paper commands, or checkboards can be misread, or misinterpreted. Using data processing can increase speed and reduce errors thus responding better to customer needs. The indicator as a percentage is:

$$\frac{\text{Oders sent by EDI in a certain period}}{\text{Total orders dispatched in the same period}}$$

Waste

Material lost is money thrown out of the window. The waste can be accounted for as follows. Every effort is needed to keep this value as low as possible:

$$\frac{\text{Cost of material lost in period}}{\text{Average value of material in the same period}}$$

Support services

Support personnel are the total number of support services such as maintenance, subcontractors, inspectors, part-time labour, administration etc. Of these services, those that are not adding value to the production operation should be kept to a bare minimum. Operators should be their own inspectors and, where possible, perform maintenance. Using data processing can reduce record keepers. Some of the support services, such as subcontracting, may, of course,

Table 26.7 Check sheet: Efficiency and quality (not including inventory)

Indicator	Calculation	Today	In three months	In six months	In nine months	In one year
1 Production costs	Total unit cost for producing order					
2 Use of data processing, %	$\dfrac{\text{Orders made by data processing}}{\text{Total orders made}}$					
3 Waste, %	$\dfrac{\text{Cost of material lost in period}}{\text{Average value of material in the same period}}$					
4 Level of support services, %	$\dfrac{\text{Support services not adding value in the operating unit}}{\text{Total labour in the same operating unit}}$					
5 Product quality of received lots, %	$\dfrac{\text{Total number of lots received} - \text{Lots rejected}}{\text{Total number of lots received}}$					
6 Product quality of components, %	$\dfrac{\text{Total number of components received} - \text{Components rejected}}{\text{Total number of components received}}$					
7 Product quality (financial), %	$\dfrac{\text{Total value of shipments received} - \text{Value of rejected items}}{\text{Total value of shipments received}}$					
8 Purchasing or ordering costs per order	$\dfrac{\text{Total purchasing department operating and administrative costs}}{\text{Total number of purchase orders}}$					
9 Setup time of a machine, %	$\dfrac{\text{Total time taken for setup}}{\text{Operating time} + \text{Setup times}}$					
10 Time loss due to machine breakdowns, %	$\dfrac{\text{Total time machines are down due to breakdowns}}{\text{Operating time} + \text{Downtime due to breakdowns}}$					
11 Time loss due to rework of components, %	$\dfrac{\text{Time spent on rework}}{\text{Total time taken for producing units}}$					
12 Level of manual labour to automation	$\dfrac{\text{Labour time per unit}}{\text{Labour time per unit} + \text{Automation time per unit}}$					
13 Level of subcontracted work	$\dfrac{\text{Cost of subcontracted work in a product}}{\text{Cost of subcontracted work in a product} + \text{In-house cost for the product}}$					

be adding value to the operation (see the subcontractor ratio later). The indicator is:

$$\frac{\text{Number of support personnel not adding value in the operating unit}}{\text{Total personnel in the same operating unit}}$$

Product quality in terms of lots

The following is an indicator for the quality of the lots received:

$$\frac{\text{Total number of lots received} - \text{Lots rejected}}{\text{Total number of lots received}}$$

Product quality in terms of components rejected

The following is an indicator for the quality of the units received:

$$\frac{\left[\begin{array}{c}\text{Total number of components}\\ \text{received}\end{array}\right] - \left[\begin{array}{c}\text{Components}\\ \text{rejected}\end{array}\right]}{\text{Total number of components received}}$$

Product quality in financial terms

The following is an indicator for the quality of shipments in financial terms:

$$\frac{\left[\begin{array}{c}\text{Total value of shipments}\\\text{received}\end{array}\right] - \left[\begin{array}{c}\text{Value of rejected}\\\text{items}\end{array}\right]}{\text{Total value of shipments received}}$$

Purchasing costs

A measure of the efficiency of the purchasing department can be determined by:

$$\frac{\begin{array}{c}\text{Total purchasing department operating}\\\text{and administrative costs}\end{array}}{\text{Total number of purchase orders}}$$

This indicator considers the cost of running the department, rather than the costs tied to the products purchased. This indicator can be manipulated by issuing more orders for smaller quantities whereas the real purchasing efficiency may be in the opposite direction (issuing fewer orders for larger quantities).

Setup time of a machine

In a given period, say, one week, the percent of time for setups is:

$$\frac{\text{Total time taken for setup}}{\text{Operating time} + \text{Setup times}}$$

Time loss due to machine breakdowns

In a given period, say, one week, the percent of time for breakdowns is:

$$\frac{\text{Total time machines are down due to breakdowns}}{\text{Operating time} + \text{Downtime due to breakdowns}}$$

Time loss due to rework of components

In a given period, say, one week, the percent of time for rework is:

$$\frac{\text{Time spent on rework}}{\text{Total time taken for production units}}$$

Level of manual labour to automation

This is a measure of how the firm is automated. On a unit basis it can be measured by the ratio:

$$\frac{\text{Labour time per unit}}{(\text{Labour time per unit} + \text{Automation time per unit})}$$

Level of subcontracted work

This is a measure of the percentage of subcontracted work in a product. It may be more cost effective to subcontract certain activities rather than to perform the

Table 26.8 **Check sheet: Quality of restaurant service**

Criteria	1 Very poor	2 Poor	3 Good	4 Very good	5 Excellent
1 Friendliness of the personnel					
2 Speed of the service					
3 Quality of the food					
4 Quantity of food served					
5 Presentation of the food					
6 General cleanliness of the restaurant					
7 Relationship quality/price					
8 Are you staying at the hotel?	Yes	No			
9 Are you here for the first time?	Yes	No			
10 Do you come to the region for:	Tourism	Business			

- It is useful if the analysis is performed periodically, say, once a quarter, or once every six months, to see if improvements are being obtained
- A quantitative measurement can be made by using the numerical scale indicated (1 = Very poor, 2 = Poor, etc.)

work in-house. Automobile firms may have up to 80% of the product cost subcontracted. The percentage can be measured by the ratio:

$$\frac{\text{Cost of subcontracted work in a product}}{\left[\begin{array}{c}\text{Cost of subcontracted}\\\text{work in a product}\end{array}\right]+\left[\begin{array}{c}\text{In-house cost for}\\\text{the product}\end{array}\right]}$$

Services

The quality measurements for a service firm depend on the type of service. Table 26.8 gives one illustration.

Working environment

A good audit also includes analyzing the work environment. A poor work environment can be the reason for poor quality, high cost, and low morale. Some considerations regarding the work environment are now given according to the generic headings of management, personnel involvement, documentation, and the physical environment. Many of these underscore the human relations discussion in Chapter 8. Then, Table 26.9 provides a summary audit sheet covering these criteria. Again, as for some of the other audit sheets the response to these questions can be according to the following qualitative scale:

1. Never.
2. Rarely.
3. Sometimes.
4. Most of the time.
5. All the time.

Alternatively, a simple binomial *yes* or *no* can be employed. If the answer is at the low end of the scale, or no, then there is obvious room for improvement.

Management

Good management is the driving force for a successful operation in order that it can respond to market needs.

Absenteeism

If the absentee level is high in a company, there is a problem. Perhaps personnel are unhappy with the management organization, the working environment and/or the decision-making process.

Turnover

In a vibrant economy, a low turnover (1–2%) is an indicator of motivated employees.

Training

Personnel cannot improve, or be motivated, if management does not make available the appropriate training programmes.

Changes

Are changes accepted as a way of improvement? If so, this means that management encourages new ideas, input, and recommendations from employees.

Communication with peers

Does management create the environment such that there is free and easy communication between operators and peer-level employees? Do people 'trust' each other and work as a team?

Management communication

Is there free and easy communication between operators and management? Does management have an open door policy so that employees are free at any moment to discuss problems?

Objectives

Has management defined a common objective in the organization? A common objective improves motivation and encourages teamwork.

Customers

Has management ensured that everyone's attention is focused to satisfy customers? All employees must have the customer in mind, whether it is the final client, or the downstream workstation.

Promotion

Does management make their best efforts to see that career movement, and promotion is from within? When there are new opportunities in the firm, effort should be made to promote from the existing workpool. If this is not possible, reasons should be clearly explained.

Performance measurements

Is performance judged by objectives? Setting objectives, and measuring against this baseline is an equitable way of managing, and is what everyone understands.

Table 26.9 Check sheet: Working environment of an organization

Criteria	1 Never	2 Rarely	3 Sometimes	4 Most of the time	5 All the time
1 Are changes accepted as a way of improvement?					
2 Are operators encouraged to be multi-skilled?					
3 Are operators motivated at all levels in their work?					
4 Are personnel motivated to do quality work?					
5 Can operators stop a facility if there is a problem?					
6 Is attention focused to satisfy customers?					
7 Are career movement and promotion made from within the organization?					
8 Is decision making by consensus?					
9 Is operation documentation easily available?					
10 Is operation documentation easy to use?					
11 Is operation documentation sufficiently detailed?					
12 Is operation documentation up to date?					
13 Is performance judged by objectives?					
14 Is plant always well organized?					
15 Is plant always clean?					
16 Is absenteeism low?					
17 Is the facility neat and organized?					
18 Is the noise level low?					
19 Is there adequate training for personnel?					
20 Do peer members communicate easily?					
21 Does management have an open door policy?					
22 Is there is a common objective in the organization?					

- This check sheet may be simplified by having a binomial yes or no response
- It is useful if the analysis is performed periodically, say, once a quarter, or once every six months, to see if improvements are being obtained
- A quantitative measurement can be made by using the numerical scale indicated (1 = Never, 2 = Rarely, etc.)

Decision making

Is decision making by consensus? If a large number of people are involved in the decision process, it is more easy to put that decision into effect. (See the section about attitude towards employees in Chapter 8.)

Personnel involvement

Management leads, and the employees follow that lead. The measure of management's success can, to a certain extent, be measured by the ease of the personnel involvement.

Motivation

Are personnel motivated at all levels in their work? Everyone in the organization must be motivated. This includes those that take care of cleaning, warehouse managers, up to the supervisory and middle management level. All employees must be made to feel they are part of a team.

Quality

Are personnel encouraged to do the job right the first time? Quality the first time minimizes waste, and hence cost. Quality training programmes need to be available.

Stopping the facility

In any production, can operators stop the facility if there is a problem? Giving operators this responsibility lets them know they are part of the bigger picture. This is enriching and motivating.

Multi-skills

Are personnel encouraged to be multi-skilled? To be multi-skilled involves providing additional training, and there has to be a motivational reason to take this training. For example, the prospects of a more interesting job, more security of employment, international assignments, a higher salary, etc.

Documentation

Firms today work with a variety of different technologies. If they are international, different languages may be used at one site. Further, most organizations have to conform to certain standards which may be client specifications, government requirements or specifications demanded by the ISO-9000 quality standards (see Chapter 4) or the ISO-14000 environmental standards (see Chapter 5). Whatever the situation, relevant documentation is always needed. The following gives considerations in relation to this documentation.

Availability

Is the documentation easily available? Instruction manuals should always be near the workstation. This is a specific requirement of both the ISO-9000 quality certification and the ISO-14000 environmental standards.

Ease of use

Easy language should be used so that operators can easily follow instructions. If necessary, it should be available in all languages of the employees present at the site.

Detail

The documentation should be sufficiently detailed. Any missing information can cause problems and cause delays.

Up to date

Documentation should be up to date and correspond to the system or equipment in use. Out-of-date documentation wastes time and might be a safety problem.

Physical environment

Is the work facility organized, clean, pleasing, efficient, with a low noise level, and safe? The Japanese are very rigorous in this respect. (See Chapter 15, 'The five S rules').

The supply chain

The integrated supply chain includes the purchasing of raw materials, manufacturing/assembly, and distribution (see Chapter 17). A global audit of the integrated supply chain might be carried out by analyzing the various costs relative to revenues.

Financial measurements

Table 26.10 gives an example for analyzing some financial measurements for a supply chain for several products in a certain period. The first column are the revenues and costs, the second gives the ratio of the financial data as a percent of revenues, and the third column the results either as a percent of the total distribution costs or as a percentage of the total production cost. This is not a statement that would be found in a normal accounting document as it includes items such as special delivery costs, storage costs and stockout costs. These are a measure of customer service level and operating costs and should be a consideration in an operational audit.

Figures 26.3, 26.4 and 26.5 give a graphical analysis of these financial data, where one can readily see what the important cost elements in the supply chain are. Here, for example, raw material costs are almost 50% of revenues, or 61% of production costs. In distribution, it is the external warehouse costs and stocking costs that constitute some 70% of costs for this activity. The

Table 26.10 Financial measurement analysis

Monthly items	Results ($)	As percent of revenues (%)	As percent of distribution costs (%)
Total sales revenue	40,906,939	100.00	
Distribution costs			
Special delivery costs	80,900	0.19	2.18
Stockout costs	1,431,960	3.50	38.54
Kilometres travelled	198,685	0.48	5.35
Normal truck hours	398,125	0.97	10.72
Overtime truck hours	48,110	0.12	1.30
Stocking costs at distribution site	298,158	0.73	8.03
External warehouse costs	1,258,324	3.08	33.88
Total distribution costs	3,714,262	9.08	**100.00**
Margin distribution	**37,192,677**	**90.92**	
Production costs			*As percent of production costs (%)*
Stocking costs at production site	3,799,118	9.29	11.50
Labour costs	8,540,277	20.88	25.85
Hiring and termination costs	372,600	0.91	1.13
Transfer costs	110,254	0.27	0.33
Raw material cost	20,145,587	49.25	60.99
Subcontracting costs	64,254	0.16	0.20
Total production costs	**33,032,090**	**80.75**	**100.00**
Operating income	**4,160,587**	**10.17**	

Figure 26.3 Costs and operating margin as a percentage of revenues

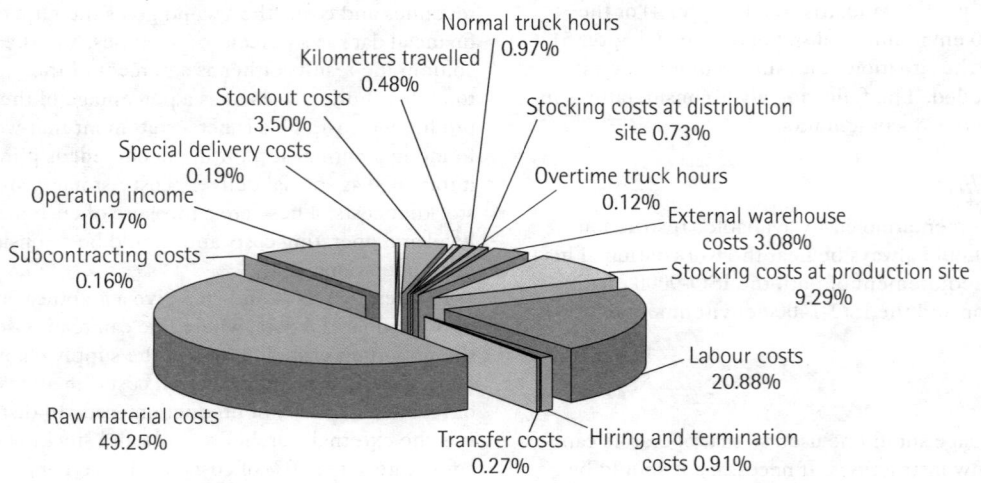

Figure 26.4 Distribution activity as a percentage of total distribution costs

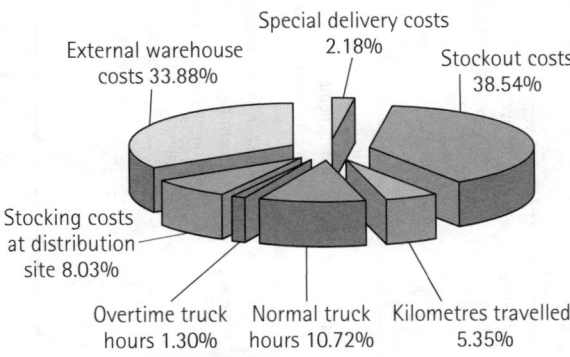

Special delivery costs 2.18%

External warehouse costs 33.88%

Stockout costs 38.54%

Stocking costs at distribution site 8.03%

Overtime truck hours 1.30%

Normal truck hours 10.72%

Kilometres travelled 5.35%

Figure 26.5 Production–related costs as a percentage of total production costs

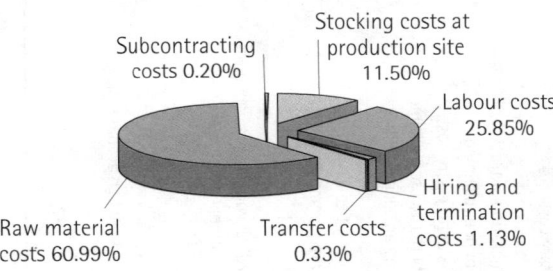

Subcontracting costs 0.20%

Stocking costs at production site 11.50%

Labour costs 25.85%

Hiring and termination costs 1.13%

Raw material costs 60.99%

Transfer costs 0.33%

explanation of these activities together with considerations for improvement are given in Tables 26.11 and 26.12. Finally, Table 26.13 is a qualitative check sheet to understand fully some of the operating activities in the supply chain.

Benchmarking

Benchmarking is an analytical tool but is somewhat special in that it involves comparison of firms rather than a stand-alone internal analysis of the same firm. Benchmarking is the continuous process of measuring a firm's products, services, and operating practices against competitors, or those recognized as leaders. Benchmarking may include not only direct competitors but also how a company compares to other firms even when the products are not the same. For example, a food company might compare its indicators with a computer firm, or a furniture

manufacturer. US companies used benchmarking to analyze the production methods of Japanese automobile producers, which then ultimately led them to implement just-in-time production and other forms of lean manufacturing in many types of industries. (See Chapter 15.)

Operating level

Specific areas to benchmark at the operating level might include the following:

- customer service levels
- inventory management
- inventory control (extent of automation)
- purchasing
- billing and collection
- production operations
- purchasing practices
- quality process
- warehousing and distribution
- transportation.

European firms

As an illustration of benchmarking, Table 26.14 compares major European manufacturing and service firms with their competition on the bases of revenue growth, profitability, stock price increase, international business, and perceived company image.[5]

Petroleum industry

The following are ten conclusions of a benchmark study on the purchasing practices of the petroleum industry in 1988:[6]

1. The amount of money spent with vendors accounted for 9% of sales revenues.
2. It cost less than $0.01 to purchase $1 worth of goods or services.
3. Purchasing staff represented 0.6% of total employees.
4. There was one purchasing employee per $104 million of sales.
5. There were $8.5 million in purchases made by the purchasing department/employee in purchasing.
6. There were 102 active suppliers per purchasing employee.
7. Each supplier received $96,000 in company orders in 1988.
8. Inventory of purchased items accounted for 1% of sales revenues.

Table 26.11 Check sheet: Analysis of financial indicators in the supply chain – distribution centre

Indicator	Measures	Comments	Impact	Considerations
Special deliveries	• For unplanned or urgent deliveries to satisfy client demand	• Poor delivery planning to distribution centre • Underestimated forecast • Not confident of clients' needs • Client has last minute changes	• High cost (additional planning, special truck, driver at last minute)	• Work closer with client • Integrated MRP/DRP system • Modify forecasting methods
Stockout	• Inability to satisfy client demand at the right time	• Production plan not matching forecast • Unforeseen occurrence in production • Last minute client needs	• Loss of revenues • Loss of clients	• Work closer with client • Integrated MRP/DRP system • Modify forecasting methods • Higher level of safety stock
Distance travelled by trucks	• Charge for distance travelled between work centre and distribution outlet	• Normal charge but may be high as a result of poor route planning	• Cost higher than normal eats into margin	• Improve route planning (computer tools) • Ensure trucks are full
Weekly charge for trucks	• Fixed charges for a normal week • Additional costs for overtime use • Includes loading and unloading time	• Normal charge • Under-utilization of truck because of poor planning engenders unnecessary cost	• Cost higher than normal eats into margin	• Improve planning • Subcontract transportation
Overtime charge for trucks	• Fixed charge for truck based on the allowed overtime • Includes loading and unloading time	• Under-utilization of truck because of poor planning engenders unnecessary cost • Perhaps better to use overtime rather than an additional truck	• Cost higher than normal eats into margin	• Improve planning • Subcontract transportation
Storage costs at distribution site	• Costs associated with holding inventory at distribution centre	• Poor planning tied in with customer requirements	• Ties up capital • More capacity than really needed	• Use just-in-time management • Delivery direct to client
Storage costs at external distribution site	• Costs associated with holding inventory at an external or subcontracted distribution centre	• If repeatedly incurred costs consider adding additional warehouse space	• Ties up capital • More capacity than really needed	• Just-in-time management might help • Consider delivery direct to client
Margin from delivery	• Contribution to final profit (revenues less total business logistics costs)	• Stockout cost not an accountable cost		

Table 26.12 Check sheet: Analysis of financial indicators in the supply chain – production site

Indicator	Measures	Comments	Impact	Considerations
Storage costs	• Costs for holding raw materials, in-process, and finished goods inventory	• Some inventory usually necessary for unplanned occurrences • Raw materials may be higher than normal because of discounts	• Ties up capital • Increases storage area • Increased management	• Just-in-time planning reduced this cost • Reduce product references
Labour costs	• Normal labour time, and overtime to perform the work	• Regular hours a normal cost but attention should be made to keep idle time to a minimum • Overtime, in the short term, usually cheapest way to handle excess load	• High labour translates into high production costs	• Move to low labour areas • Automate labour intensive operations • Keep idle time to a minimum • Reduce setup time (SMED)
Hiring and termination	• Costs associated with increasing or reducing employment levels • Includes interviewing and training for new hires • Social and outplacement costs in the case of termination	• Hiring policies should be well planned to ensure that growth is sustained • Layoffs de-motivate remaining employees • May include the learning curve concept as new hires are not immediately operational	• Under normal accounting, not a direct charge to the operation but an overhead charge • Activity-based cost treats this as a direct cost	• Improve forecasting, planning to minimize labour fluctuations • Use temporary/part-time labour
Transfer of personnel	• Charges for transferring employees between work centres • Includes training (learning curve)	• Employees motivated if they change work type from time to time • Cost kept to a minimum if employees are multi-skilled	• May not always translate into costs as transferred employees may be highly motivated	• Optimize to maintain employee morale but keep costs to a minimum
Raw materials	• Payment for raw materials. Whether payment is paid on reception, or other terms (2/10 net 30)	• Raw material should be received only when needed • Timing payment depends on terms and conditions	• Ties up capital • More capacity than really needed	• Use JIT purchasing
Subcontracting costs	• Price paid for outsourcing activity in order to maintain a required client service level	• If subcontracting is unplanned it could be expensive • However, subcontracting certain activities may be cost effective	• Frees up resources in the firm to undertake strategic activities • Transfers knowhow to a third party • One way of not adding additional capacity to the firm	• Good network needed if used on a regular basis • Are subcontractors certified quality and/or environment? • Some subcontractors may have shorter lead times
Stockout costs	• Costs for not having materials to meet production requirements	• Results from poor planning • Assembly line shut down, labour idle • Not a normal accountable cost	• Inactive production line costly • Snowballs into stockouts of finished products	• Optimize MRP system • Reliable suppliers for lead times • Include a safety stock
Production costs	• Distribution margin less production costs gives operating income	• In accounting includes labour, raw materials and variable overhead	• Low production costs a key to maintaining profit margins	

Table 26.13   Check sheet: Planning considerations in the supply chain

Considerations	Yes	No	Action
PURCHASING			
Have lead times for raw materials, component parts, and packaging been considered in client delivery dates?			
If there are several purchased components, have their delivery dates been considered in scheduling production?			
Have times for unloading, controlling, and storage of raw materials been taken into account in the planning?			
Are payments for raw materials being delayed to as late as possible?			
Has the timing and amount been taken into consideration in production costs?			
Are the delivered quantities of raw materials and component parts appropriate for a just-in-time operation?			
Is the number of suppliers kept to a bare minimum to avoid unnecessary management activity from the purchasing staff?			
Are all the suppliers' quality certified (ISO-9000) or other certification such as ISO-14000 as required by your organization?			
Is the quality of received goods always perfect and according to specifications?			
PRODUCTION			
Is the labour sufficient in each work centre to meet production requirements?			
Are finished goods made to order, or made to stock? Producing to order simplifies the production forecast			
Have setup times between each product been considered in planning?			
Is labour multi-skilled such that it can be transferred between assembly posts or different sites?			
Is hiring necessary to meet the planned production level?			
Have inventory storage costs been considered in production costs?			
Is production capacity sufficient?			
If normal capacity is tight, what overtime possibilities exist?			
Are production quantities made as an economic batch, or just-in-time?			
Is there an integrated planning system for production?			
Are there frequent machine changeovers to satisfy important clients?			

Is the production cycle time as short as possible?

Can the production operation respond quickly to change in customer requirements?

Is the facility layout optimum for the production operation?

If products are perishable, is the production cycle time optimum to permit a satisfactory shelf life of the end products?

Has optimum use of subcontracting been made?

Are customer complaints of your produced products close to zero?

DISTRIBUTION

Is the delivery by company-owned transport?

Has consideration been given to subcontracting delivery?

Is the truck weight sufficient?

Is the truck volume sufficient?

Has loading and unloading time been taken into consideration in planning?

Is there sufficient transportation?

Is the capacity of the distribution centre sufficient?

Has consideration been given to subcontracting the warehouse activity?

If activity is seasonal, are there periods when additional warehouse capacity is needed?

FORECASTING

Are the sales forecasts consistent with the actual demand?

Are the sales forecasts based on past data?

Are the sales forecasts timely, such that the production operation can respond accordingly?

Is the forecasting model sufficiently responsive to actual customer needs, especially when changes occur?

Table 26.14 Benchmarking comparison of some leading European companies

Company	Country	Activity	Revenue growth	Profitability	Stock price increase	International	Company image	Score
Elf	France	Oil					X	1
Shell	UK/Netherlands		X	X	X	X		4
Rhône-Poulenc*	France	Chemicals Pharmaceuticals				X		1
Hoechst*	Germany		X	X	X		X	4
Groupe PSA	France	Automobiles	X					1
Volkswagen	Germany			X	X	X	X	4
L'Oréal	France	Cosmetics and beauty products	X	X	X		X	4
Benckiser	Germany					X		1
Aérospatiale	France	Airplanes and components	X			X		2
British Aerospace	Britain			X	X		X	3
Schneider	France	Heavy equipment				X		1
ABB	Sweden/Switzerland		X	X	X		X	4
Usinor-Sacilor	France	Steel and steel products	X			X	X	3
British Steel	Britain			X	X			2
Lafarge	France	Cement	X	X			X	3
Holderbank	Switzerland				X	X		2
Bull	France	Computers		X		X	X	3
Olivetti	Italy		X		X			2
Alcatel	France	Electronic telecommunications					X	1
Siemens	Germany		X	X	X	X		4
LVMH	France	Drinks	X	X	X	X	X	5
Vendome	Switzerland							0
Danône	France	Food	X					1
Nestlé	Switzerland			X	X	X	X	4
Carrefour	France	Retail distribution	X	X	X	X	X	5
Metro	Germany							0
Accor	France	Hotels				X		1
Granada	Britain		X	X	X		X	4
UAP	France	Insurance	X					1
Allianz	Germany			X	X	X	X	4

*Now merged to become Aventis
X, indicates the best

9. Inactive inventory, or that which had not moved in at least 3 years, was 21% of total purchased inventory.
10. The number of suppliers decreased by 7% from 1987 to 1988.

Guidelines to benchmarking

Companies have different approaches to benchmarking. IBM has a four-phase step approach, AT&T has a nine-step approach, and Xerox a ten-step method. In all these, however, there are some general guidelines.[7]

Do not go on a fishing expedition

When one prepares a benchmark study, pick a specific area in the organization that needs improving. This might be quality, customer satisfaction, accounts payable, or delivery time, for example. Then do your homework, including thoroughly reviewing your own process and procedures before picking a company which excels in the particular area chosen.

Use company people

The people who are going to implement changes need to see and understand for themselves so it is them who make the site visits and discuss with people concerned. It is difficult to implement changes if senior management or outside consultants do the benchmarking and return to tell the process operators what to do. Further, keep site visits short, and working teams small.

Exchange information

You should be ready to exchange information and answer any questions that you might ask another company.

Legal concerns

Avoid legal problems that might arise due to discussions that might imply price fixing, market allocation, or other illegal activities. This could lead to problems. Do not expect to learn much about new products. Most benchmarking missions focus on existing products, business practices, human resources, and customer satisfaction.

Confidentiality

Respect the confidentiality of data obtained. Companies that agree to share information with you may strongly object if that information leaks out to a competitor.

Summary of key elements

- An operational audit, or diagnostic, is an analysis to obtain an in-depth understanding of performance of the firm. It is performed because there is a perception that improvements can be made and the audit gives a baseline from which to start making these changes.

- Analytical tools for performing an audit include pipeline maps, process flow charts, Ishikawa diagrams, frequency checklists coupled with a Pareto analysis, ABC inventory analysis, improvement monitoring charts, statistical quality control charts, scatter diagrams, quality function deployment, quality circles, failure mode effect and criticality analysis, and an overall equipment effectiveness analysis.

- A starting area in an audit should be at the customer level. The client is king! Firms are in business to make a profit and to provide a satisfactory return on investment. This implies satisfying the customer with desired products, expected quality, and promised delivery.

- The customer service level can be measured both quantitatively and qualitatively. The firm should strive for 100% service level in all areas. Service indicators include service according to order or unit availability, order cycle time, product availability combined with order cycle time, system flexibility, use of information systems, speed to recover from a system malfunction, after-sales service, minimum order size, emergency orders, delivery frequency, and delivery reliability.

- Good inventory management is important to minimize carrying costs and associated working capital. Audit indicators include average inventory levels, order-processing cost, inventory turnover, inventory to sales ratio, record accuracy, value of working inventory, value of safety stock, inventory to asset ratios, and the number of product references.

- Efficiency measurements should concentrate on the non-value-added activities in the operation such as production setup time, time loss due to breakdown, time loss due to rework, and level of support services. Steps should be taken to minimize these activities.

• Tangible goods product quality may be measured in terms of non-conforming components rejected, or in financial terms. Service level quality is more on a qualitative basis.

• A work environment should be established such that absenteeism and turnover is low, training is provided, communication is transparent, company objectives are identified, promotion is from within, there are appropriate performance measurements, and that the work environment is agreeable. These are all management's responsibility.

• In the integrated supply chain, financial performance measures of a distribution centre include special delivery costs, stockout costs, transportation cost, external warehouse costs, storage costs of finished goods, and the operating margin. Financial measures at the production site include costs associated with storage, direct and indirect labour, hiring and termination, personnel transfer, subcontractor costs, and costs of purchased raw materials.

• Benchmarking involves comparison with other firms' products, services, operating practices, against competitors or other firms recognized as leaders. Guidelines for benchmarking include: be objective, use company personnel, exchange information, be aware of legal concerns, and respect confidentiality.

Notes and references

1. Adapted from advertising announcements of Unisys in *International Management*, May 1994
2. J. D. Power and Associates Reports: http://www.jdpa.com/studies/Pressrelease.asp?Study ID = 486&CatID = 1
3. 'Ford Motor falls behind the pack on quality control: Auto maker seeks to bring US plants up to speed', *Wall Street Journal Europe*, 28 May 2001, pp 1 and 9
4. 'A revolution of one', *The Economist*, 14 April 2001, p. 67
5. *Le Nouvel Economiste*, France, 7 June 1996, p. 44
6. Center for Advanced Purchasing Studies, PO Box 22160, Tempe, Arizona, 85285-2160
7. 'How to steal the best ideas around. Benchmarking is a perfectly legal way of copying the smartest business practices. Ford Motor, Xerox, AT&T, Motorola, Du Pont, and others are using it to bound ahead', *Fortune*, 19 October 1992, pp 86–9

Review and discussion topics

1. Customer satisfaction
Consider the last purchase, or purchases, you made. Were you satisfied with the service, and the product you bought? If yes, indicate why you came to this conclusion. If the answer is no, discuss how the supplying organization could improve its customer service.

2. Working environment
You work or study (or have worked or studied) in some organization. Evaluate the working environment. Are (were) the considerations satisfactory? Consider ease of communication (with the professor!), training, possibilities, physical conditions, motivation, etc. If there was dissatisfaction, what improvements would you propose?

3. Ishikawa diagram
In the following situations, the system is not operating or performing as expected by the customer or user. The effect is that the product, process, or service is of poor quality or below expected standards. Develop a detailed Ishikawa diagram, after brainstorming, with what you believe might be possible causes grouped in the fishbone branches according to generic causes:
  (a) university or business school
  (b) supermarket, hypermarket, or grocery store
  (c) road system around where you live and work (or study)
  (d) your residence (house, apartment, or hall of residence)
  (e) ski resort
  (f) a Club Méditerranée resort
  (g) a manufacturer of running shoes
  (h) a rail transportation network
  (i) a hospital.

4. Benchmarking
Perform a benchmarking analysis, using literature, or the Internet, of the following:
  (a) your university, with others
  (b) the lifestyle in your country of residence or birth, compared with the countries where you live, are familiar with, and the USA (thus, several 'benchmarks')
  (c) an automobile company in your country, with others not in your country
  (d) environmental standards where you live compared with other countries on the same continent, and the USA
  (e) the transportation network where you live, compared with other countries on the same continent, and the USA
  (f) the government system where you live compared with other countries.

5. Audit of an operation
Using Figure 26.6, and the elements discussed in the text, develop an operational audit of either a manufacturing, or a services firm.

Figure 26.6 Operational audit of a firm

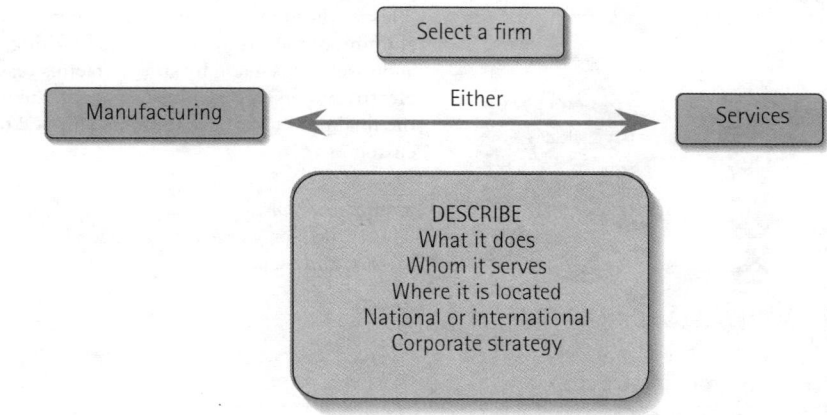

Then perform an audit of the operations, considering:

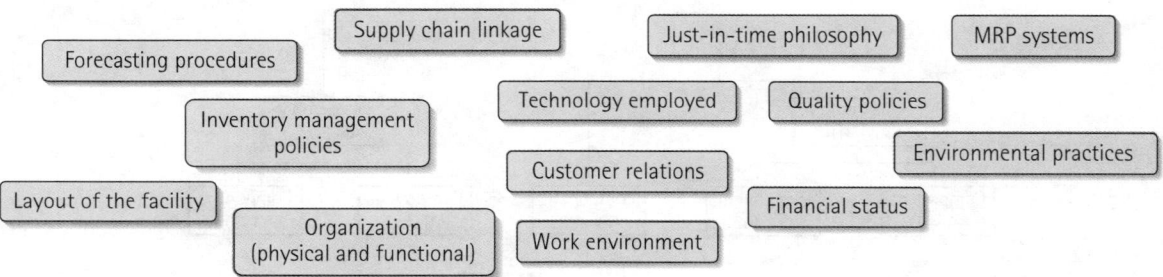

Case study 26.1 Berger Co.

Situation

Berger Co. near Birmingham, England, is a subsidiary of a major US conglomerate that makes electrically operated metering instruments used for flow measurement for gas, oil, and water. Berger's clients are utility companies, the oil industry, and chemical firms such as Esso, EDF of France, Texaco, Total, and British Petroleum.

Product

The metering instruments are similar in their basic design in that they have a casing made of stainless steel, cast iron, ordinary carbon steel, or aluminium. The choice of material depends on the service in which the instrument is to be used. For all corrosive conditions, stainless steel is employed. The dimensions of the meters depend on the volume of fluid flow, and the operating pressure. For most

of the meters the casings are purchased from outside subcontractors. The operating and strategic part of the instrument is a rotating piston arrangement that is manufactured by Berger. The piston arrangement is made of stainless steel, aluminium, or in a few cases, carbon steel. Electronic motors control the meters. All these are purchased from subcontractors.

There are three principal models manufactured by the company. These are shown in Figure 26.7. The product structure of these three meters is given in Figure 26.8. The product structure illustrates how the meters are assembled from the various machined or purchased parts.

Work centre

Figure 26.9 shows the work centre arrangement. The following is a description.

Figure 26.7 Berger Co.: Meters

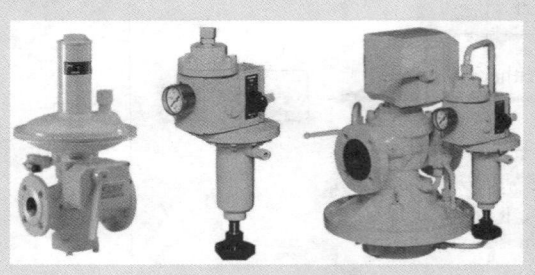

Model I   Model II   Model III

Receiving and shipping

This is where the raw materials (sheet steel, aluminium rods, rubber for gaskets, wiring, paint, etc.) and assemblies made by subcontractors (casings, and electric motors) are received. It is also the area where the final product is packaged and shipped to the customer.

Storage raw materials

This is the storage area for all received materials, except motors, and casing.

Figure 26.8 Berger Co.: Product structure

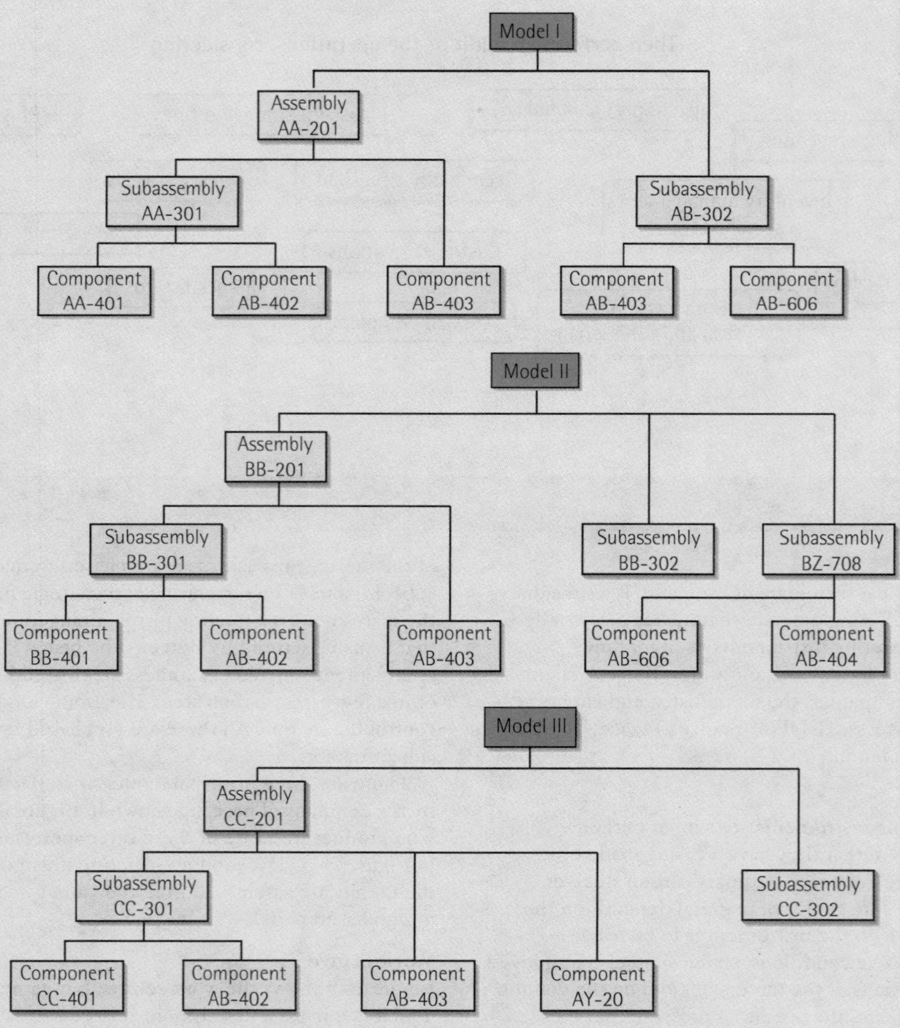

Model I
- Assembly AA-201
  - Subassembly AA-301
    - Component AA-401
    - Component AB-402
    - Component AB-403
  - Subassembly AB-302
    - Component AB-403
    - Component AB-606

Model II
- Assembly BB-201
  - Subassembly BB-301
    - Component BB-401
    - Component AB-402
    - Component AB-403
  - Subassembly BB-302
    - Component AB-606
  - Subassembly BZ-708
    - Component AB-404

Model III
- Assembly CC-201
  - Subassembly CC-301
    - Component CC-401
    - Component AB-402
    - Component AB-403
    - Component AY-20
  - Subassembly CC-302

Figure 26.9 Berger Co.: Layout

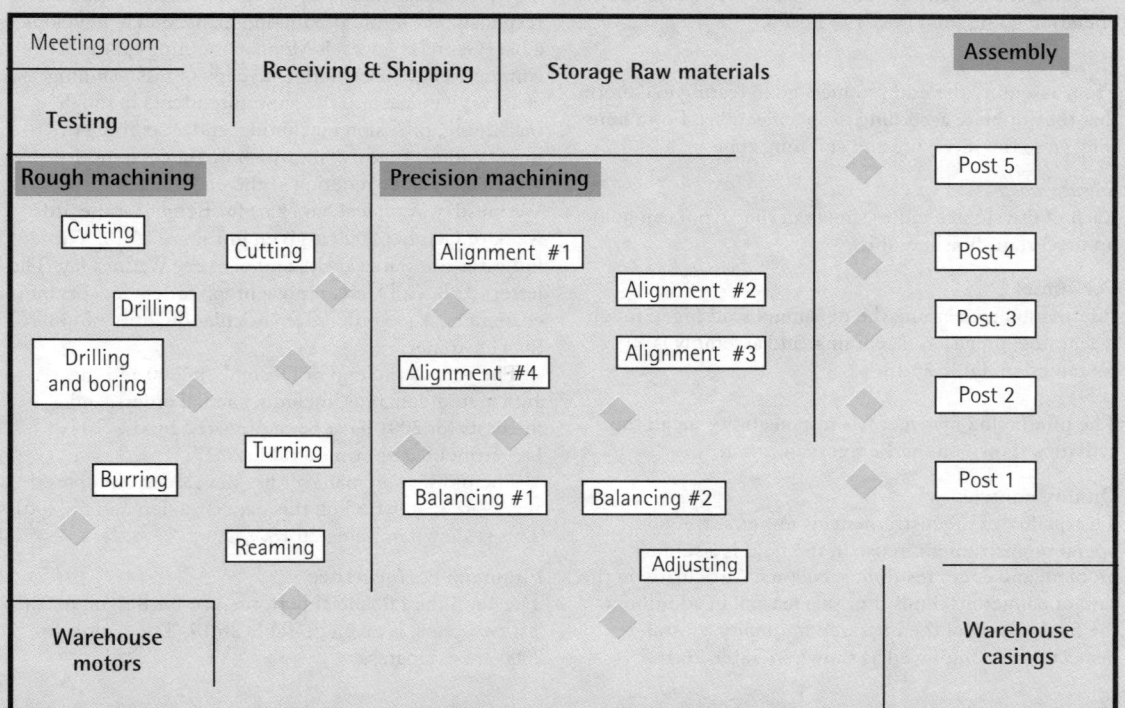

Storage tables   Scale: 1 cm = 4 metres

Rough machining

This is the first machinery operation for the preparation of the meters. The various operations in sequence are as follows.

Cutting: Here the aluminium and steel is cut to shape and length. There are two cutting work posts.

Drilling: Here holes of varying dimensions are cut into the metal pieces according to specifications. There is one drilling work post.

Drilling and boring: This step is a specialized step for certain models when the drill holes are much smaller. The boring operation puts a high tolerance on the units. There is one combined drilling–boring operation.

Turning: This is where appropriate meter components are reduced to the correct diameter on a lathe machine. There is one lathe machine.

Burring: Here all the rough edges are removed from the cut pieces.

Reaming: This is another operation for giving fine tolerances on the meters. Not all models pass through this step. There is one reaming work post.

Precision machining

This work area is where the working parts of the meters are closely matched, aligned, and adjusted before final assembly.

Alignment: There are four work posts.

Balancing: Here the meters are balanced so that they will respond correctly to whatever media they will be measuring. There are two balancing work posts.

Adjusting: Final adjustments are made at this work post. There is one work post here, and all the meters pass through this work area.

Assembly

This is where the final product is assembled. The assembly involves installing the piston unit in the casing, bolting and sealing with gaskets, and then attaching the electric motor. Assembly is a sequential operation going from Post 1 to Post 5.

Testing
From assembly the end products go to testing to confirm that they operate according to specifications. From here they go to the receiving and shipping zone.

Storage tables
Each of the storage tables shown in the layout can hold up to 35 semi-finished units.

Personnel
Information concerning the personnel working in rough machining, precision machining, and assembly is contained in Table 26.15.

The production manager has responsibility for all the activities shown on the Berger plan layout.

Quality control
The quality of the instruments is important. A poor operation instrument in use in the field is a serious problem and could result in accidents, particularly in the case of dangerous fluids. For this reason, in addition to the final testing of the instrument, quality control inspectors are employed as shown in Table 26.16.

Planning
The planning of the production operation is also the responsibility of the production manager. He develops a bar (Gantt) chart each Monday morning for the coming week's operation. One copy of this planning chart is given each to the superintendents in rough machining, precision machining, and assembly. Any modifications to the plan, which might occur mid-week, are discussed at a meeting at the end of each Wednesday. A typical bar chart for Berger for the 3rd week of October 2000 is given in Figure 26.10. This indicates the status at the end of every Wednesday. The letters A, B, C, D, etc. represent job orders for specific customers. A job order is a particular quantity of units for a customer.

The time is the end of December 2000 and the anticipated demands, including actual orders, and forecasts for 2001 have been prepared by the Sales Department as shown in Table 26.17.

The production manager has developed a proposed aggregate plan based on this expected demand for 2001. This is shown in Table 26.18.

Financial performance
The simplified financial performance for Berger, for the last two years, is given in Table 26.19. The figures for 2000 are estimates.

Table 26.15 Berger Co.: Employee information

	Name	Year of birth	Start date		Name	Year of birth	Start date
1	Framer	1942	1958	19	Arce	1945	1966
2	Berge	1937	1952	20	Boldon	1939	1957
3	Jones	1936	1953	21	Barish	1961	1980
4	Seidel	1952	1972	22	Cusin	1964	1983
5	Forgeon	1948	1966	23	Cornford	1975	1992
6	Caumont	1961	1976	24	Nicholson	1947	1978
7	Wilson	1935	1960	25	Schmitz	1942	1982
8	Stanford	1947	1972	26	Brown	1941	1960
9	Zukowski	1951	1968	27	Jacobs	1958	1990
10	Manfred	1938	1968	28	Harold	1959	1988
11	Duong	1965	1987	29	Alision	1955	1976
12	Faseil	1958	1977	30	Wheeler	1952	1982
13	Revault	1942	1967	31	Atmal	1950	1975
14	Abdulla	1959	1989	32	Olson	1940	1980
15	Hannan	1948	1973	33	Heath	1957	1978
16	Ringe	1961	1993	34	Cerder	1959	1978
17	Joffrey	1971	1989		Production	1942	1961
18	Fagiano	1958	1974		manager		

Required

Based on the information given, make an audit (diagnostic) of Berger Co.

1. What improvements would you suggest?
2. What are some of the areas where attention should be directed?
3. If appropriate, add any other ideas even though they may not be directly referred to in the case

Table 26.16 Berger Co.: Quality control responsibilities

Work area	Time spent on quality control (job hours/week)
Receiving and shipping	32
Rough machining	16
Precision machining	24
Assembly	48
Testing	Ongoing operation

Table 26.17 Berger Co.: Actual and forecast demand

Month	Model I	Model II	Model III	Total
January	380	785	560	1,725
February	325	645	450	1,420
March	310	870	158	1,338
April	380	821	489	1,690
May	420	745	753	1,918
June	280	610	489	1,379
July	290	845	167	1,302
August	410	879	962	2,251
September	385	960	523	1,868
October	345	450	895	1,690
November	386	562	991	1,939
December	325	876	451	1,652
Total	**4,236**	**9,048**	**6,888**	**20,172**
Average/month	353	754	574	1,681

Figure 26.10 Berger Co.: Gantt chart

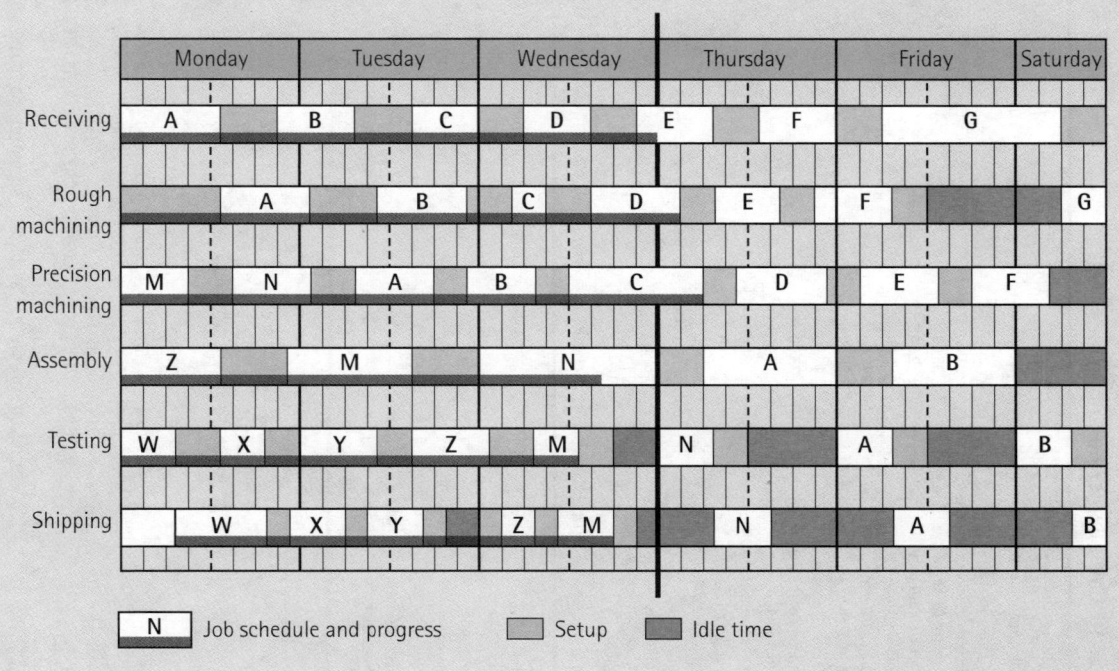

Table 26.18 Case: Berger Co.: Aggregate plan

Month	Jan	Feb	Mar	Apr	May	Jun	Jul	Aug	Sep	Oct	Nov	Dec	Total
Aggregate demand (units)	1,725	1,420	1,338	1,690	1,918	1,379	1,302	2,251	1,868	1,690	1,939	1,652	20,172

Ending December inventory, units	2,000
Stockout costs, £/unit	35.00
Holding cost, £/unit/week	2.50
Hiring cost/employee, £	350.00
Termination cost/employee	275.00
Labour cost, £/hour	8.00
Overtime cost, £/hour	12.00
Subcontracting cost £/unit	35.00
Labour hours/unit	3.20
Production December	1,800
Work week, hours	40
Max overtime/week, hours	10
Weeks/month	4
Units/month/person (normal hours)	50.00
Units/month/person (overtime hours)	12.50

Month	Dec	Jan	Feb	Mar	Apr	May	Jun	Jul	Aug	Sep	Oct	Nov	Dec	Total
Demand		1,725	1,420	1,338	1,690	1,918	1,379	1,302	2,251	1,868	1,690	1,939	1,652	20,172
Labour														
Production, units		1,681	1,681	1,681	1,681	1,681	1,681	1,681	1,681	1,681	1,681	1,681	1,681	20,172
Labour hours		5,379.20	5,379.20	5,379.20	5,379.20	5,379.20	5,379.20	5,379.20	5,379.20	5,379.20	5,379.20	5,379.20	5,379.20	64,550
Staff		33.62	33.62	33.62	33.62	33.62	33.62	33.62	33.62	33.62	33.62	33.62	33.62	403
Staff (rounded)	34	34	34	34	34	34	34	34	34	34	34	34	34	408
Actual production		1,700	1,700	1,700	1,700	1,700	1,700	1,700	1,700	1,700	1,700	1,700	1,700	20,400
Hiring		0	0	0	0	0	0	0	0	0	0	0	0	0
Termination		0	0	0	0	0	0	0	0	0	0	0	0	0
Inventory														
Beginning	2000	2,000	1,975	2,255	2,617	2,627	2,409	2,730	3,128	2,577	2,409	2,419	2,180	
Ending		1,975	2,255	2,617	2,627	2,409	2,730	3,128	2,577	2,409	2,419	2,180	2,228	
Average		1,987.50	2,115.00	2,436.00	2,622.00	2,518.00	2,569.50	2,929.00	2,852.50	2,493.00	2,414.00	2,299.50	2,204.00	
Stockouts		0	0	0	0	0	0	0	0	0	0	0	0	
Costs														
Production		43,520.00	43,520.00	43,520.00	43,520.00	43,520.00	43,520.00	43,520.00	43,520.00	43,520.00	43,520.00	43,520.00	43,520.00	522,240.00
Hiring		0.00	0.00	0.00	0.00	0.00	0.00	0.00	0.00	0.00	0.00	0.00	0.00	0.00
Termination		0.00	0.00	0.00	0.00	0.00	0.00	0.00	0.00	0.00	0.00	0.00	0.00	0.00
Carrying		19,875.00	21,150.00	24,360.00	26,220.00	25,180.00	25,695.00	29,290.00	28,525.00	24,930.00	24,140.00	22,995.00	22,040.00	294,400.00
Stockouts		0	0	0	0	0	0	0	0	0	0	0	0	0.00
Total		63,395.00	64,670.00	67,880.00	69,740.00	68,700.00	69,215.00	72,810.00	72,045.00	68,450.00	67,660.00	66,515.00	65,560.00	816,640.00

Table 26.19 Berger Co.: Financial performance (1999–2000)

Income statement	2000	1999	Balance sheet	2000	1999
Net sales	8,350	6,852	ASSETS		
Cost of goods sold			Current assets		
Direct labour	1,008	715	Cash	18	121
Materials	3,124	2,540	Accounts receivable	1,470	1,274
Manufacturing O/H	1,212	1,105	Inventory	3,025	2,012
Total cost of goods	5,344	4,360	Other	42	54
			Total current assets	4,555	3,461
Gross profit	3,006	2,492	Net fixed assets	521	520
			TOTAL ASSETS	5,076	3,981
G&A	442	359			
Marketing	1,090	989	LIABILITIES		
R&D	1,208	902	Current liabilities		
Total	2,740	2,250	Notes payable	1,800	845
			Accounts payable	934	672
Profit before taxes	266	242	Accruals	356	570
Tax provision	95	108	Total current liabilities	3,090	2,087
			Long-term debt	600	542
Net profit	171	134			
			Capital stock and surplus	602	654
			Earned surplus	784	698
				1,386	1,352
			Total liabilities	5,076	3,981

Case study 26.2 Cardoso

Situation

The Cardoso company is a small manufacturing firm based in Belgium that makes compressed air drilling equipment used in road and building construction. The products are made in three work centres as illustrated in Figure 26.11. There are two principal products, N° 1 which is a smaller unit principally used for breaking up softer material, and Product N° 2 which is a larger unit suitable for heavy concrete agglomerate. The products are distributed by company-owned trucks to five distribution centres as shown in the figure. The product structure is given in Figures 26.12 and 26.13.

The operating cost data are shown in Table 26.20. In addition to the lead times for the raw materials shown, another week is needed to carry out quality control of the raw materials material and to put it into storage. At all the work centres, when the material is produced, it is available one week later in the downstream work centre. The finished goods from Work centre N° 1 are placed the same week in finished goods storage. They can then be delivered to the distribution centres one week later.

At the end of one particular year, the inventory situation at the production site, at the distribution centres and on order was as shown in Table 26.21.

In addition, at the end of the same year, the financial results were as shown in Table 26.22.

Required

1. Analyze the costs in the integrated supply chain as a percentage of revenues. What are your comments?
2. For the business logistics section of the supply chain, develop a pie chart for all the costs. What are your comments on the actual situation and what improvements do you think could be made?

3. For the materials management section of the supply chain, develop a pie chart for all the costs. What are your comments on the actual situation and what improvements do you think could be made?

4. Develop a pipeline map in terms of cost, and also in terms of units for the complete supply chain. What are your comments?

5. Summarize improvements that you feel could be made in the various phases of this supply chain.

Figure 26.11 Cardoso: Production site

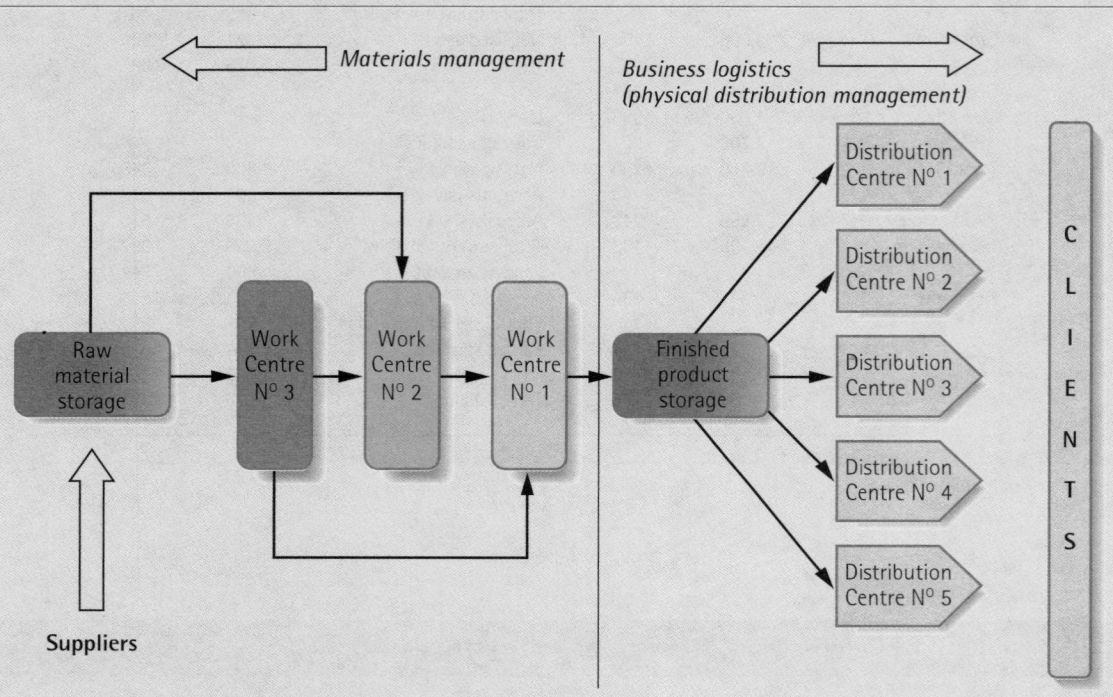

Figure 26.12 Cardoso: Structure for Product N° 1

Figure 26.13 Cardoso: Structure for Product N° 2

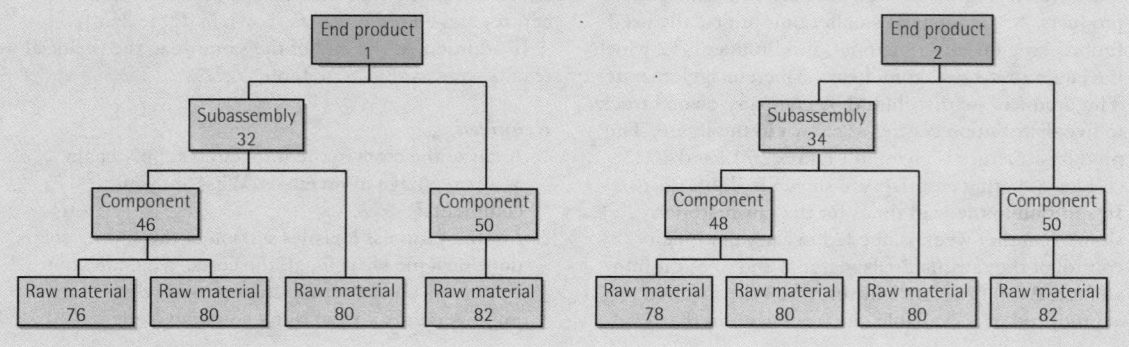

Table 26.20 Cardoso: Cost data ($)

Work centre Nº 1

Work centre wages per hour	13.50	
End product reference in work centre	**1**	**2**
Production time, min/unit	2.67	24.00
Labour cost per unit	0.60	5.40

Unit cost of components

Article 32	24.80	
Article 50	4.60	
Labour component	0.60	
Total cost of Product 1	**30.00**	
Article 34		170.00
Article 50		4.60
Labour component		5.40
Total cost of Product 2		**180.00**

Work centre Nº 2

Work centre wages per hour	15.00	
End product reference in work centre	**32**	**34**
Production time, min/unit	3.20	48.00
Labour cost per unit	0.80	12.00

Unit cost of components

Article 46	20.00	
Article 80	4.00	
Labour component	0.80	
Total cost of product 16	**24.80**	
Article 48		154.00
Article 80		4.00
Labour component		12.00
Total cost of product 34		**170.00**

Work centre Nº 3

Work centre wages per hour	12.50		
End product reference in work centre	**46**	**48**	**50**
Production time, min/unit	4.80	240.00	9.60
Labour cost per unit	1.00	50.00	2.00

Unit cost of components

Article 76	15.00		
Article 80	4.00		
Labour component	1.00		
Total cost of Product 46	**20.00**		
Article 78		100	
Article 80		4	
Labour component		50.00	
Total cost of Product 48		**154.00**	
Article 82			2.60
Labour component			2.00
Total cost of Product 50			**4.60**

Raw materials

Product reference	76	78	80	82
Unit price	15.00	100.00	4.00	2.60
Lead time to production site, weeks	2	3	1	1

Table 26.21 Cardoso: Inventory situation at yearend

Product	76	78	80	82
Raw materials storage	3,289	596	720	640

Product	1	2
Work centre Nº 1	3,700	681

Product	32	34
Work centre Nº 1	4,177	900

Product	46	48	50
Work centre Nº 1	2,958	1,505	2,985

Product	1	2
Distribution centre Nº 1	70	35
Distribution centre Nº 2	200	150
Distribution centre Nº 3	30	80
Distribution centre Nº 4	120	140
Distribution centre Nº 5	90	50

Product	76	78	80	82
For delivery in one week	1,335	1,000	16,000	15,000
For delivery in two weeks	1,250	300		
For delivery in three weeks		600		

Table 26.22 Cardoso: Financial results at yearend

Item ($)	Results
Total sales revenue	2,579,320
DISTRIBUTION COSTS	
Special delivery costs	6,000
Stockout costs	500
Kilometres travelled	8,690
Normal truck hours	22,400
Overtime truck hours	702
Stocking costs at distribution site	8,847
External warehouse costs	2,000
Total distribution costs	49,139
Margin distribution	2,530,181
PRODUCTION COSTS	
Stocking costs at production site	193,483
Labour costs	267,840
Hiring and termination costs	75,600
Transfer costs	5,400
Raw material cost	1,144,608
Subcontracting costs	64,254
Total production costs	1,751,185
Operating income	778,996

Selected further reading

CHAMBERS, Andrew and RAND, Graham (1997) *The Operational Auditing Handbook: Auditing Business Processes*, Wiley.

FITZ-ENZ, Jac (1993) *Benchmarking Staff Performance: How Staff Departments Can Enhance Their Value to the Customer*, Jossey-Bass.

REIDER, Harry R. (1996) *The Complete Guide to Operational Auditing: 1997 Cumulative Supplement*, Wiley.

TOROK, Robert M. (1997) *Operational Profitability: Conducting Management Audits*, Wiley.

ZAIRI, Mohamed (1996) *Effective Benchmarking*, Chapman & Hall.

An extensive listing of other further reading can be found on the website.

What's on the web?

Further learning resources are available to lecturers and students at www.supplychain-online.com, including the following which are specific to *Auditing the operations and supply chain*:

Resource	Subject
Chapter overview	Auditing operations
More further reading	Auditing operations

27 *Statistical concepts*

Chapter overview

- The role of statistics
- Common terms
- Summation rules
- Probability
- Central tendency
- Dispersion
- Exponential distribution
- Normal distribution
- Binomial distribution
- Poisson distribution
- Student t distribution
- Beta distribution

The role of statistics

Areas of use

As the earlier chapters of this book have illustrated, the operations and supply chain environment is quantitative. There are costs, profits, sales revenues, units sold, productivity levels, flow rates, capacity factors, inventory quantities, waiting times, delivery periods, etc., all of which require periodic evaluation. Statistical analysis is an important tool, which uses as a base, historical or measured data, to examine quality conditions, or to make estimates, or forecasts about actual, or future events. Banks and insurance companies use statistics to estimate the evolution of interest rates, or to calculate financial risk. (See Chapter 23.) Manufacturing and service firms use statistical control on their products and activity (see Chapter 20) and pharmaceutical firms use statistics to test the effectiveness of their products before launching them onto the market. The use of statistics is extensive.[1] The purpose of this final chapter is to give an overview of some of the basic statistical terms and concepts with the objective to complement methods referred to earlier in this book, and perhaps refresh the reader's

knowledge of earlier studies. It is an effort to 'close the loop' for the quantitative elements of operations and supply chain management.

No guarantee

Statistics is for the most part probabilistic (as opposed to linear programming, for example, which is deterministic) and using statistics in analysis is never a guarantee of a situation or a future outcome, as analysis is often based on sampling. However, if data measurements are performed correctly, the sampling experiment is appropriately designed, and future conditions can be considered similar to the past, statistical analysis for decision making can be used with a certain degree of confidence.

Black belt in statistics

General Electric Co. USA (GE), one of the world's most successful companies, strongly emphasizes the importance of statistics. The firm has in place a quality programme (borrowed from Motorola, USA), involving training black belts for four months in statistical and other quality-enhancing measures. After the training, the black belts spend all of their time roaming the plants of GE and set up quality-improvement projects. John F Welch, a former chairman of the company, told young managers that they did not have much future at GE unless they were selected to become black belts in statistics and quality control. The company has so far trained 2000 and planned to increase that number to 4000 by the end of 1997, and to 10,000 by the year 2000. In all, it is investing hundreds of millions of dollars in training, in specific projects, and in computer systems to analyze and run the statistical-based quality control programmes.[2] (See Chapter 20.)

Microsoft Excel

Almost all statistical terms described in this chapter, and used throughout this book, including central tendency, dispersion, random variables, and normal, binomial, Poisson, beta, and t distributions etc., can be generated, or calculated by using the built-in statistical functions in Microsoft Excel. This avoids going through the sometimes laborious mathematical calculations.

Common terms

Data characteristics

Data characteristics are the units of measurement that describe weight, volume, length, production rate, viscosity, etc.

Raw data

Raw data are collected data that have not been organized into any order. Raw data are sometimes referred to as a data set.

Data array

A data array is raw data that have been sorted in either ascending, or descending order.

Class

A class is a grouping into which data are arranged. The following age groups would constitute four classes:

- 20 to 29 years
- 30 to 39 years
- 40 to 49 years
- 50 to 59 years.

Discrete data

Discrete data consist of distinct or unconnected information usually obtained from the counting process:

- Four finished units are defective.
- Seven machine operators are absent.
- Five bottles of wine have been sold.
- Nine assembly machines are shut down.

It is not possible to have $4\frac{1}{4}$ defective units, $7\frac{1}{2}$ operators absent, $5\frac{1}{2}$ bottles sold, or $9\frac{3}{4}$ machines shut down. Discrete data do not progress from one class or another.

Continuous data

Continuous data are information that progresses from one class to another. For example, the exact volume of beer in a bottle, which is nominally indicated as 33cl, might, in fact, be any of the following, where there is progression from one value to another:

- 32.7954cl
- 33.0094cl
- 32.9271cl
- 33.1000cl

A statistic

A statistic describes the characteristic of a sample, taken from a population, such as the weight, volume length, etc.

Descriptive statistics

Descriptive statistics is the analysis of sample data in order to describe the characteristics of that particular sample.

Inferential statistics

Inferential statistics is the analysis of sample data for the purpose of describing the characteristics of the population from which that sample is taken. That is, the population characteristics are inferred from the analysis of the sample. This is the most common practical usage of statistical analysis.

Population

The population is all the elements being studied, and about which conclusions need to be drawn. The following are examples:

- The total employees worldwide working for General Motors Corporation.
- The population of China.

- The volume of water in the Rhône in France.
- The number of sheep in Australia.

Parameter

A parameter describes the characteristic of a population such as the weight, height, or length. A parameter is the opposite of a statistic, which describes a sample.

Sample

A sample is the collection of a portion of population elements:

- A blood sample is used to describe the total blood in the body, and, by corollary, the health of the individual.
- A sample of ten slabs of chocolate taken from a batch of 50,000 to understand the quality of the batch.
- A sample of 15 piston rods taken from the production line in an automobile firm to ascertain the quality of the product from the assembly line.

Random sample

A random sample is where each item in the sample has an equal chance of being selected. In random sampling, the selection of one item from the sample has no impact on the chance that any other item is chosen.

Sampling with replacement

Sampling with replacement is taking a sample from a population, and after analysis, the sample is returned to the population. One reason for this would be not to change the probability outcome of future selections. For example, one card is selected from a pack:

- The probability of this card being the ace of spades is 1/52 or 1.92%.
- Assume this chosen card is not the ace of spades and is not replaced.
- Another card is chosen. The probability of this second card being the ace of spades is 1/51 or 1.96%, or a slightly higher probability.
- If the first card were replaced, there would be no change in the probability outcome for the second card.

Sampling from an infinite population

Sampling from an infinite population means that even if the sample were not replaced, the probability outcome for a subsequent sample would not significantly change. For example, in a population of 5000 bottled chemical samples, one is believed to be toxic. If one sample is taken, the probability of this sample being toxic is 1/5,000 or 0.02%. If the first sample is good, and a second is taken, without replacing the first, the probability of this being toxic is 0.020004%. This is not much different from the first sampling experiment.

Distribution

A distribution is a tabular or graphical display of the progressive movement or grouping of data. Common graphical displays include the exponential, normal, binomial, Poisson, Student t, and beta distributions presented later in this chapter.

Frequency distribution

A frequency distribution is a display, either in tabular, or graphical form, that illustrates the number of observations, or the frequency of occurrence, that fall into each set of mutually exclusive classes. The more frequently certain data occur, the higher the probability that these data will occur again. Frequency distributions are more manageable than raw data and demonstrate trends more easily. The normal, binomial, Poisson, and beta distributions are examples of frequency distributions.

Ogive

An ogive is a special form of frequency distribution that illustrates the cumulative number of observations, or the cumulative percentage of data, which lie above or below certain values. There is a *less than* ogive, which has a positive slope (increases in value from left to right) and indicates data below certain values. A *more than* ogive which has a negative slope (decreases in value from left to right) is one that illustrates data above certain values.

Pie chart

A pie chart shows data according to the percentage of certain occurrences. The presentation of waiting times in Chapter 11 is an example of a pie chart.

Histogram

A histogram is a vertical bar chart with the length of the vertical bar proportional to the data value. Histograms are used extensively in Chapter 3.

Bar chart

A bar chart is a horizontal histogram. Gantt charts (Chapters 14 and 18) are forms of bar chart.

Polygon

A polygon is a line graph representing a frequency distribution.

Summation rules

The following are some rules governing the calculation of the sum of data sets. Using these rules can sometimes simplify calculations.

Mean value

The mean of a value is equal to the sum of the values divided by the number of observations:

$$\overline{X} = \frac{\sum X}{n}$$

If X has values of 1, − 5, 9, − 2, 6, then n = 5 and:

$$\overline{X} = \frac{(1-5+9-2=6)}{5} = 1.80$$

Addition of two variables

The total of the addition of two variables is equal to the total of the individual sum of each variable:

$$\sum (X + Y) = \sum X + \sum Y$$

Assume the five values:

(1, 6), (−5, −2), (9, −8), (−2, 5), (6, 4)

$$\sum (X + Y) = (1 + 6) + (-5 - 2) + (9 - 8) + (-2 + 5) + (6 + 4)$$

$$\sum (X + Y) = 7 - 7 + 1 + 3 + 10 = 14$$

$$\sum X + \sum Y = (1 - 5 + 9 - 2 + 6) + (6 - 2 - 8 + 5 + 4)$$

$$\sum X + \sum Y = 9 + 5 = 14$$

Difference of two variables

The sum of the difference of two variables is equal to the sum of the individual differences of each variable:

$$\sum (X - Y) = \sum X - \sum Y$$

Assume the five values:

(1, 6), (− 5, − 2), (9, − 8), (− 2, 5), (6, 4)

$$\sum (X - Y) = (1 - 6) + (-5 + 2) + (9 + 8) + (-2 - 5) + (6 - 4)$$

$$\sum (X - Y) = -5 - 3 + 17 - 7 + 2 = 4$$

$$\sum X - \sum Y = (1 - 5 + 9 - 2 + 6) - (6 - 2 - 8 + 5 + 4)$$

$$\sum X - \sum Y = 9 - 5 = 4$$

Constant multiplied by a variable

The sum of a constant times a variable is equal to the constant times the sum of the variables:

$$\sum (kX) = k \sum X$$

If k = 5, and X has values of 1, − 5, 9, − 2, 6:

$$\sum (kX) = 5 * 1 - 5 * 5 + 5 * 9 - 5 * 2 + 5 * 6 = 45$$

$$k \sum X = 5(1 - 5 + 9 - 2 + 6) = 45$$

Constant summed n times

A constant summed n times is equal to n times the constant:

$$\sum k = n * k$$

If n = 6, and k = 5:

$$\sum k = 5 + 5 + 5 + 5 + 5 + 5 = 30 = 5 * 6$$

Summation of a random variable around the mean

Summation rules can be used to demonstrate that the summation of a random variable around the mean of the random variable is equal to zero, or:

$$\sum (X - \overline{X}) = 0$$

From the difference of two variables rule this equation becomes:

$$\sum X - \sum \overline{X} = 0$$

For any fixed set of data, $\overline{X}$, is a constant. Further, from the constant summed n times rule:

$$\sum \overline{X} = n\overline{X}$$

Thus:

$$\overline{X} = \frac{\sum X}{n} \quad \text{or} \quad n\overline{X} = \sum X$$

Thus the equation for the sum of a random variable about the mean becomes as follows:

$$\sum X - \sum \overline{X} = \sum X - n\overline{X} = \sum X - \sum X = 0$$

(See in the section on dispersion later in this chapter.)

Probability

Probability means the chance that something will or will not happen. Probabilities might be expressed subjectively, based on the frequency of past events, or by the application of certain rules, which are the roots of classical probability.

Subjective probabilities

Subjective probabilities are based on the feelings of the person making the judgment. This might be a function of that person's experience in a particular situation:

- A good salesperson may be able to say: '*I am 90% certain the customer will buy that product.*'
- A competent manager may be able to say: '*I am 95% certain John will finish that project by the end of the week.*'

Relative frequency probability

Relative frequency probability assumes that an activity has occurred many times before and that this information has been recorded such that a frequency distribution can be developed. As an illustration, historical data indicate that, in a sample of 3000 bronze castings made, 24 had hairline cracks. This implies that 0.80% of the castings (24/3000) were of poor quality. By extrapolating these data it can be estimated that, in future activity, 0.8% of the castings will be defective. Thus, knowing the frequency of occurrence from past data, necessary action can be taken. In this case, for example, by putting into production 101 castings for every 100 demanded since about eight in 1000 castings were found to be defective. In relative frequency probabilities, the larger the number of observations, the greater the reliability of the relative frequency measurement. However, the larger the sample size, the more expensive the analysis.

Classical probability rules

In classical probability, determining the probability outcome of events can be obtained by applying certain rules. Classical probability is often known as *a priori* probability as one knows the probability outcome in advance before any experiment or test has been performed.

Marginal or unconditional probability

In marginal, or unconditional probability, there is only a single occurrence, which assumes that every outcome has an equal possibility. It can be determined by the relationship:

$$\frac{\text{Number of outcomes where the event occurs}}{\text{Total number of possible outcomes}}$$

A simple illustration applies in gambling. For example, the chance of drawing the ace of spades from a full pack of cards would be:

$$\frac{1}{52} = 1.92\%$$

This probability outcome is known even before a card is drawn from the deck.

Mutually exclusive or independent events

Mutually exclusive or independent is when two or more events are not related. In a card-drawing situation, the outcome of drawing of one card is independent of the outcome of drawing a second card. Similarly in the tossing of a coin, if heads is obtained on the first throw, this result has no bearing on the second throw of the coin.

Probability of independent events occurring together

The probability of two independent events, A and B, occurring together, or in succession, is given by the product of their marginal probabilities:

Probability(A and B) = Probability(A) × Probability(B)

For example, in two packs of cards, the probability of drawing the ace of spades from both packs is:

$$\frac{1}{52} * \frac{1}{52} = 0.04\%$$

When joint probabilities are being considered, the probability outcome is always less than the individual probabilities. Joint probabilities occur in PERT distributions in determining the probability of a project being finished on time when there is more than one project path to be considered (see Chapter 18).

Probability of only one independent event occurring

The probability of one, or the other, of two independent events, A and B, occurring can be expressed by the addition rule:

Probability(A or B) = Probability(A) + Probability(B)

From a pack of cards, the probability of drawing the ace of spades, or the queen of hearts is:

$$P(\text{Ace of spades or Queen of hearts}) = \frac{1}{52} * \frac{1}{52} = 3.85\%$$

When the probability outcome of one or the other is being considered the probability is always greater than the individual probabilities.

Non-mutually exclusive events

Two events, A and B, are not mutually exclusive when it is possible for both events to occur. For example, in the probability of selecting either an ace, or a spade, from a deck of cards, an ace and spade can occur together since the ace of spades could be drawn. Thus, drawing an ace and a spade are not completely mutually exclusive events. In this case, the addition rule is adjusted to avoid double accounting by the probability of drawing the ace of spades:

$$\text{Probability}(A \text{ or } B) = \text{Probability}(A) + \text{Probability}(B) - \text{Probability}(AB)$$

where probability(AB) is the probability of A and B occurring together:

- The probability(A) of drawing an ace is 4/52.
- The probability(B) of drawing a spade is 13/52.

Thus:

$$P(\text{Ace or Spade}) = \frac{4}{52} + \frac{13}{52} - \frac{4}{52} * \frac{13}{52} = \frac{17}{52} - \frac{1}{52}$$
$$= \frac{16}{52} = 30.77\%$$

Application of probability rules to relative frequency occurrences

Probability rules can be applied to situations whose historical probability is derived from frequency distributions. For example, in a supply chain, based on the analysis of a large amount of data, the probability of a delivery truck containing raw materials arriving late is 5%, a breakdown of a machine which uses these raw materials is 6%, and an operator on this machine being absent is 8%. These are independent events.

Events occurring together

In this supply chain, the probability of the three events occurring together is the product of their individual probabilities, or 0.024%:

$$0.05 \times 0.06 \times 0.08 = 0.00024 = 0.024\%$$

That is to say, a probability occurrence less than the individual probabilities.

One or the other occurring

In this supply chain, the probability of the truck arriving late, or the machine breaking down, or the operator being absent, is the addition of its independent probabilities, or 19.00%:

$$0.05 + 0.06 + 0.08 = 0.19 = 19.00\%$$

That is to say, a probability occurrence greater than the individual probabilities.

See Chapter 19 for use of these probability relationships.

Central tendency

Most data cluster, or group, around a central point. This central point is often used to describe the data, or the population, and is used as a reference. The mean (average), median, midrange, and mode are often used as measures of central tendency.

Mean

The mean, also referred to as average, arithmetic average, or arithmetic mean, is the sum of all values, ΣX, divided by n, the number of elements in the observations:

$$\overline{X} = \frac{\Sigma X}{n}$$

For example, the recorded temperatures, in °C, at midday at a certain location for one week are:

Mon	15
Tue	14
Wed	13
Thu	16
Fri	14
Sat	16
Sun	17.

The arithmetic mean for the week is thus 15°C (105/7) or one would say that the average daily temperature was 15°C. The value of the mean can be distorted by extreme values, which are high or low relative to others in the data set. For example, if on the following Monday the recorded temperature was 39°C then one would say that the average daily temperature was 18°C (144/8), which is somewhat exaggerated. The number of values may not affect the value of the mean. If, for example, the temperature the Sunday before the data were recorded was 15°C, and the following Monday's temperature was not included, then for eight readings the average daily temperature is still unchanged at 15°C (120/8).

Median

The median is the middle value of an ordered set of data. The following raw data set must be rearranged in descending, or ascending order:

9
13
12
7
6
11
12.

In ascending order this gives:

6
7
9
11
12
12
13.

This shows 11 is the median value. The following is the rule to calculate the median.

Odd number of values

If n, the number of values, is odd, the median is calculated from (n + 1)/2. If there are seven values, the median is (7 + 1)/2, or the fourth value.

Even number of values

If n, the number of values, is even, the median is the average of the values n/2 and (n + 2)/2 . If there are six values, the median is the average of the 6/2 and (6 + 2)/2 value or the average of the third and fourth values.

The median value indicates that half of the data lie above the median, and half below. For example, in early 2001 the median price of a house in San Francisco, was $550,000, according to figures from the California Association of Realtors.[3] This meant that half of the number of houses in San Francisco was priced above $550,000 and the other half were priced below. (San Francisco is one of the most expensive cities in the country to live in, and only 10% of the population can afford this median price tag.) The median is not affected by extreme values but it is affected by the number of values.

Mode

The mode is that value that occurs most frequently in data. Consider the following data:

9
13
17
19
7
3
13
8
22
4
10.

The mode is 13 since it occurs twice. The mode is of interest because that value that occurs most frequently is probably a response that deserves further investigation. The mode is unaffected by extreme values but may be affected by the number of values if these new values introduce another modal value.

Mode in a qualitative sense

The mode can also be used for qualitative data. In the listing:

Yellow	Red
Green	Blue
Brown	Purple
Mauve	Blue
Violet	Grey
Green	Blue

the modal value is blue since it occurs three times. Thus, if this were a survey of customer preference for a fabric, a manufacturer might carry more inventory of blue stock.

Bimodal

If there are two values in a data set that occur most frequently then it is bimodal. In the following data set, the values 9 and 13 occur most frequently and so the data set is bimodal. When a data set is bimodal it indicates that two pieces of data are of particular interest:

9
13
17

19
7
3
13
8
22
4
10
9.

Midrange

The midrange is the average of the smallest and largest observation in a data set. In the following data set the midrange is $(6 + 13)/2 = 9.5$:

9
13
12
7
6
11
12.

Like the average, the midrange can be distorted by extreme values. Further, the distortion may be high because unlike the average, the midrange only considers extremes values. In this example, if the highest value were 26 then the midrange would be $(6 + 26)/2 = 16.0$. This is the disadvantage with the midrange as a measure of central tendency.

Geometric mean

The geometric mean is a special measure of central tendency when data are changing over a period of time. Examples might be the growth of investments, the inflation rate, or the growth rate of the gross national product (see Chapter 25).

Consider the growth of an initial investment of $1000 in a savings account that is deposited for a period of five years. The interest rate, which is accumulated annually, is variable. Table 27.1 gives the interest and the growth of the investment.

The growth rate, or geometric mean, is given by the relationship:

$$\sqrt[n]{\text{Product of growth rates}}$$

In this case the geometric mean is:

$$\sqrt[5]{1.060*1.075*1.082*1.079*1.051} = 1.0693$$

Table 27.1 Interest and growth on investment

Year	Interest rate (%)	Growth factor	Value yearend
1	6.0	1.060	$1,060.00
2	7.5	1.075	$1,139.50
3	8.2	1.082	$1,232.94
4	7.9	1.079	$1,330.34
5	5.1	1.051	$1,398.19

That is, an average growth rate of 6.93% per year. Thus, the value of the $1000 investment at the end of five years is:

$$\$1000 * 1.0693^5 = \$1398.19$$

the same value as given in the last cell of the last column of Table 27.1.

If the arithmetic average of the growth rates were used then the mean growth rate would be:

$$\frac{1.060+1.075+1.082+1.079+1.051}{5} = 1.0690$$

That is, a growth rate of 6.90% per year.

Using this mean interest rate, the value of the initial deposit after five years would be:

$$\$1000 * 1.0690^5 = \$1396.01$$

This is less than calculated using the geometric mean. Although the difference is small, in cases where interest rates are fluctuating widely, and deposit amounts are large, the difference could be significant.

Dispersion

Dispersion is a measure of the spread of the data. Data that lie close to the central point have a low dispersion and are more reliable for analysis. On the other hand, data that lie far from the central point, or are highly dispersed, are less reliable for analysis. Data sets may have the same measure of central tendency, such as for example the same mean, but have different dispersions. Measures of dispersion are the range, variation, standard deviation, and fractiles as now given.

Range

The range is the difference between the maximum, and minimum value in a data set. In the following data set, the range is 13 − 6 = 7:

$$9$$
$$13$$
$$12$$
$$7$$
$$6$$
$$11$$
$$12.$$

Since only extreme values are used to calculate the range, changes in these can distort the value. The conclusion, that the larger the range in a data set, the greater the dispersion or uncertainty, should be treated cautiously because of distortion from extreme values. The number of values may not affect the range. These are the same arguments already presented for the use of the midrange as a measure of central tendency.

Variance

The variance is the average of the squared difference between each of the observations in a data set, and the mean value.

Sample variance

The sample variance is the sum of the squared difference between each observation and the mean, divided by the number of observations minus one:

$$s^2 = \frac{\sum (x - \bar{x})^2}{(n-1)}$$

where:

- $\bar{x}$ is the sample mean
- s^2 is the sample variance
- s is the sample standard deviation
- x is a data value
- n is the number of values.

Using $(n-1)$ in the denominator removes the bias.

Population variance

The population variance is the sum of the squared difference between each observation and the mean, divided by the number of observations:

$$\sigma^2 = \frac{\sum (X - \mu_x)^2}{N}$$

where:

- μ_x is the population average
- σ^2 is the population variance
- X is a data value
- N is the number of values.

In either the population, or sample variance:

- Subtracting the mean from each value indicates how far the observation is from the central point or the mean.
- Squaring each difference removes the negative sign.
- Summing, and dividing by N, for the population, or $(n-1)$ for the sample gives an average value.

In the following data set the sample variance is 7.333, and the population variance is 6.286:

$$9$$
$$13$$
$$12$$
$$7$$
$$6$$
$$11$$
$$12.$$

Both the sample and population variance are affected by extreme values but, in contrast to the range, as each value in the data set is taken into consideration, the effect is less pronounced.

Standard deviation

The standard deviation is the square root of the variance. It is more useful than the variance because, as a measure of dispersion, it has the same units as the data from which it was calculated. For example, the units for determining the variance in grams, of sample weights would be grams². Taking the square root of this gives the units as grams. The standard deviation is the most common measure of dispersion in statistical analysis. It is useful because it takes into account all items in the data set. Like the variance, the sample and population standard deviation are affected by extreme values.

Sample standard deviation

This is given by:

$$s = \sqrt{s^2} = \sqrt{\frac{\sum (x - \bar{x})^2}{(n-1)}}$$

Population standard deviation

This is given by:

$$\sigma_x = \sqrt{\sigma^2} = \sqrt{\frac{\sum (X - \mu_x)^2}{N}}$$

In the following data set the sample standard deviation is 2.708 and the population standard deviation is 2.507:

9
13
12
7
6
11
12.

Deviations about the mean

The variance and standard deviation measure the average scatter of data around the mean of this data. The deviation shows how larger observations in the data fluctuate above the mean and how smaller observations fluctuate below. Mathematically, the sum of the deviation of all the data about their mean value must be zero since the mean is derived from all these data:

$$\sum (x - \bar{x}) = 0$$

In:

9
13
12
7
6
11
12.

The mean of the data set is 10. And:

$$(9 - 10) + (13 - 10) + (12 - 10) + (7 - 10)$$
$$+ (6 - 10) + (11 - 10) + (12 - 10) = 0$$

This logic has already been presented in the summation rules section earlier in this chapter.

Bienayme–Chebyshev rule

The Bienayme-Chebyshev rule (named after the two Russians) relates to the variability of data about the mean point. It states that regardless of how a set of data is distributed, the percentage of observations that are contained within a distance, k standard deviations, around the mean, must be at least

Table 27.2 Estimation of probabilities

N° of standard deviations	Observations between mean and given standard deviation
2	At least 75.00%
3	At least 88.89%
4	At least 93.75%
5	At least 96.00%
6	At least 97.22%

the value calculated by:

$$\left(1 - \frac{1}{k^2}\right) * 100$$

where k takes on values greater than 1. For example, for k = 2 standard deviations, the percentage of observations must be greater than:

$$\left(1 - \frac{1}{2^2}\right) * 100 = 75\%$$

In summary, for any type of distribution, Table 27.2 is useful for estimating probabilities.

Fractiles

Fractiles are the division of data into well-defined parts such that a given fraction, or proportion, of the data lies at, or below, a fractile. The most common fractiles are as follows.

Quartiles

Quartiles are fractiles that divide data into four equal parts. There are three quartiles.

Deciles

Deciles are fractiles that divide data into ten equal parts. There are nine deciles.

Percentiles

Percentiles are fractiles that divide data into 100 equal parts. There are 99 percentiles.

Fifty percent fractile, or the 50th percentile

The 50% fractile, or the 50th percentile is also the median, because half the data are less than or equal to this value.

Table 27.3 Data set for interquartile range

0	8	19	27	37	51	58	68	78	89
2	8	19	30	37	52	58	68	80	90
2	9	20	31	38	54	59	69	81	91
2	13	21	33	38	55	59	73	81	93
3	15	22	34	41	56	62	74	84	93
3	16	22	35	41	56	63	74	85	94
5	16	22	35	41	57	66	75	88	94
7	18	22	35	46	57	67	75	88	95
7	19	22	36	49	57	67	76	89	95
8	19	27	36	51	58	68	77	89	98

Interfractile range

The interfractile range is a measure of the spread between two fractiles in a data set.

Interquartile range

The interquartile range, or midspread, is the difference between the third and first quartiles in a data set. Consider the data set shown in Table 27.3.

- The 1st quartile, Q_1, is 22 and 25% of the data lie at, or below 22 and 75% above.
- The 2nd quartile, Q_2, is 51 and 50% of the data lie at, or below 51 and 50% above.
- The 3rd quartile, Q_3, is 74 and 75% of the data lie at, or below 74 and 25% above.
- The 50th percentile, the median is 51.
- The interquartile range is:

$$Q_3 - Q_1 = 74 - 22 = 52$$

The interquartile range considers the spread in the middle 50% of the data.

Note that, in using Excel for determining fractiles, the values may be slightly different from observed values determined from sorting the data, as Excel takes the average at the cut-off point.

Exponential distribution

The exponential distribution is a mathematical function for which a dependent variable increases or decreases according to the power, or exponent, of a given independent value. The general form of the exponential equation is as follows where the value of x can be either positive or negative. (For the examples given here, the constants a and b are assumed to be positive and greater than unity.) For example:

$$y = ab^x$$

The exponential distribution is sometimes referred to as the 'function of natural growth' as it is the distribution that often explains the events such as:

- product sales of a new product in the introduction phase (see Chapter 6)
- learning rate (see Chapter 8)
- technological inventions (see Chapter 1)
- population expansion
- growth of a forest
- spread of disease.

Growth

The exponential increase is illustrated in Figure 27.1. In this equation, the constants a = 1 and b = 3. This exponential format would illustrate, say, the growth of portable telephones in the late 1990s (see Chapter 10) or population. It implies that there is really no limit but, in actual practice, an exponential growth cannot be sustained. New products soon saturate the market. Even the population cannot increase indefinitely as, at some point, food supplies would be insufficient, or needed land surface would become exhausted.

Decline

This change is illustrated in Figure 27.2. In this equation, the constants a = 1 and b = 3. This exponential format would illustrate, say, the learning rate of new ideas (see Chapter 8) or average cost curves (see Chapter 11) when there is at first a very rapid decrease but the rate of change slows down although it never becomes completely horizontal.

Increase to a maximum

This change is illustrated in Figure 27.3. In this equation, the constants a = 1 and b = 3. Here the value of y reaches a maximum value of unity, or 100%. The form of this curve is similar to the ABC inventory analysis (see Chapter 11).

Figure 27.1 Exponential curve when x is positive: $y = ab^x$

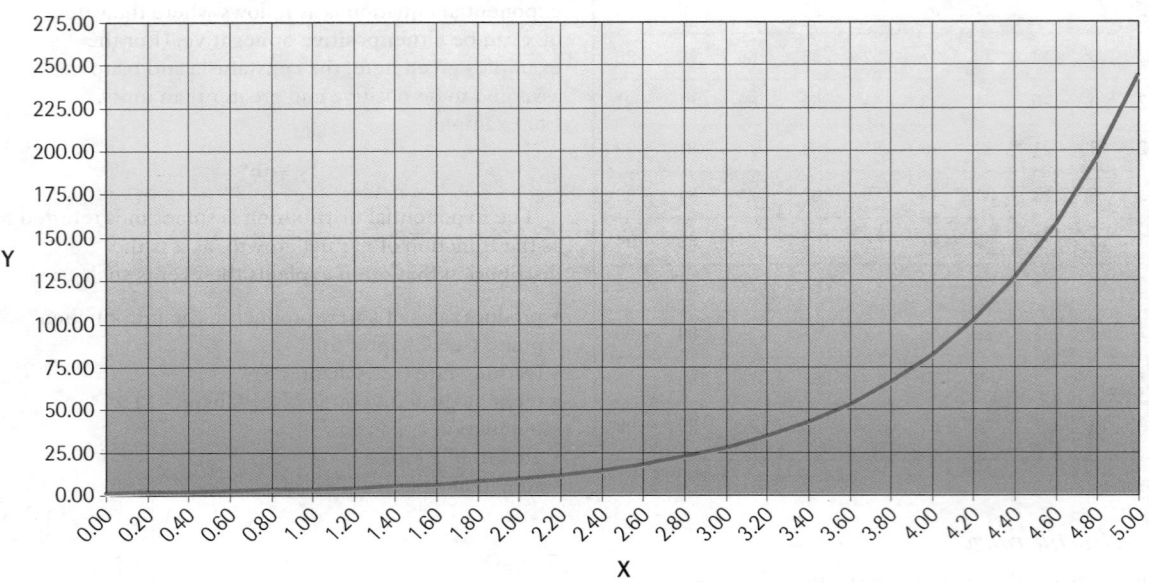

Figure 27.2 Exponential curve when x is negative: $y = ab^{-x}$

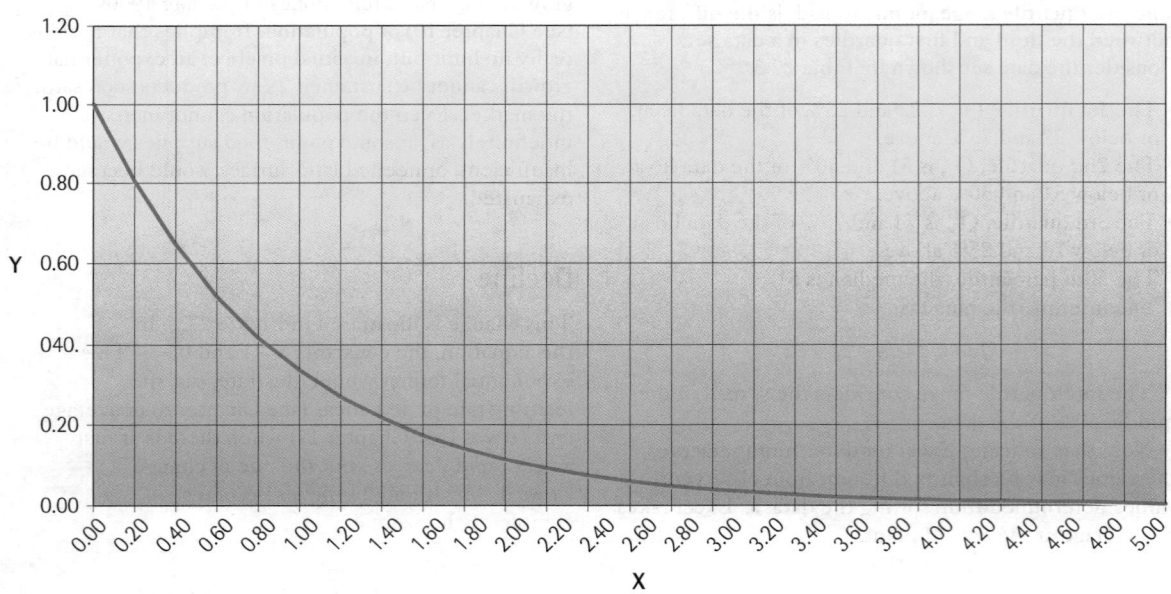

Natural logarithm

Other exponential distribution curves may be based on some form of using e, the natural logarithm, where e = 2.718281. Three general forms would be as follows:

$$y = e^x \quad y = e^{-x} \quad y = 1 - e^{-x}$$

Figure 27.3   Exponential curve for the function y = 1 − ab $^{-x}$

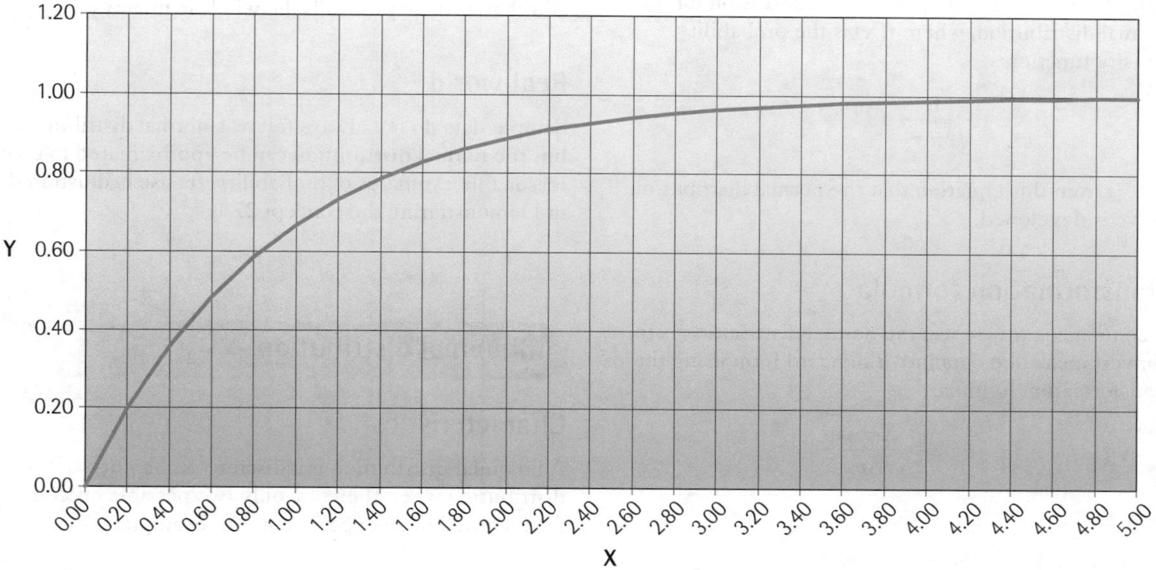

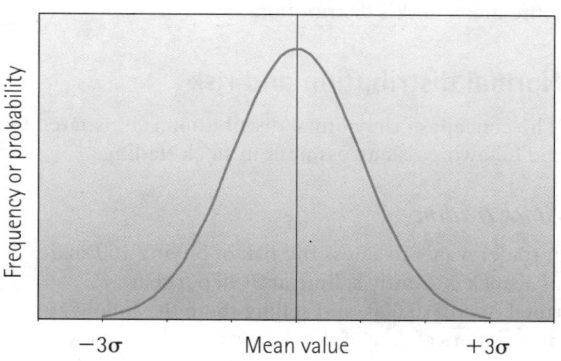

Normal distribution

Definition

A normal distribution, as illustrated in Figure 27.4, is a continuous probability distribution illustrating the frequency of occurrence of a random variable. It was developed by the German, Karl Friedrich Gauss (1777–1855) and is thus also known as the Gaussian distribution. The characteristics of the normal distribution are:

• It is a continuous distribution.
• It is bell shaped, and symmetrical.
• The mean, median, mode, and midrange lie at the centre, and all have the same value.
• The two tails of the normal distribution extend indefinitely, meaning that the associated random variable has an infinite range: $(-\infty < x < +\infty)$.

Area under the normal distribution

The following are quantitative measures regarding the area under the normal distribution:

• No matter what the values of the mean, or the standard deviation, the area under the curve is 1.00 or the area under the curve represents 100% of all the data values.

Figure 27.4   Shape of the normal distribution

Frequency or probability

−3σ   Mean value   +3σ

• In the distribution, there are 68.26% of all data values falling within ±1 standard deviations from the mean.
• In the distribution, there are 95.44% of all data values falling within ±2 standard deviations from the mean.
• In the distribution, there are 99.74% of all data values falling within ±3 standard deviations from the mean.
• All intervals containing the same number of standard deviations from the mean will contain the same proportion of the total area under the curve for any normal probability distribution.

Mathematical expression

The following is the mathematical expression for the normal distribution, where f(X) is the probability density function:

$$f(X) = \frac{1}{\sqrt{2\pi}\sigma_x} e^{-(1/2)[(X - \mu_x)/\sigma_x]^2}$$

It is from this equation that the normal distribution curve is developed.

Transformation formula

A convenient way to use the normal distribution is to convert measured data into a standard form using the transformation formula:

$$z = \frac{X - \mu_x}{\sigma_x}$$

where:

- X is the value of the random variable
- μ_x is the mean of the distribution of the random variables
- σ_x is the standard deviation of the distribution
- z is the number of standard deviations from X to the mean of this distribution.

Normal distribution and risk

The concept of the normal distribution is illustrated by the following risk assessment in stock trading.[4]

Stock trading

A trader wants to assess the risk of buying 100 shares of a stock currently selling at $100 per share (total price $10,000) and selling them the following day. Historical data of the daily price of the stock measured over the past 12 months show that it follows a normal distribution with an average price of $100 per share. This normal distribution curve, and its associated standard deviation, represents the volatility of the stock. An overnight volatility of 1% means that the price can swing $1 in either direction (1% of $100 is $1).

Two standard deviations mean that the swing of the price of the stock will cover 95% (actually 95.5%) of the possible movements or a swing between $98 and $102. This also means that there is a 5% chance that the price will be more than $102 or less than $98. Since the curve is symmetrical there is a 2.5% chance that the price will be less than $98 and 2.5% chance that the price will be more than $102. Thus, if the trader

buys the share at $100 there is a 2.5% chance (risk) that the price will be less than $98 the following day and that, if the trader sells, he will lose money.

Real world

Sample data do not always follow a normal distribution, but the normal distribution can be approximated to give reasonable estimates of probability. Its use is illustrated in Demonstrating the concept 27.1.

Binomial distribution

Characteristics

A binomial distribution is a discrete probability distribution when there are only two possible outcomes for each trial of an experiment. For example:

- In tossing a coin, the only two possible outcomes are heads or tails. The probability of obtaining one, two, three, four, or five heads in successive throws of a coin would follow a binomial distribution.
- In the manufacture of a product, quality control might be to test whether an inspected item is either good, or defective. These probability outcomes for analyzing several products would follow a binomial distribution. These are attribute characteristics and were presented in Chapter 20.
- In a market survey a client might be asked if he liked or disliked a product. The response under this criterion would follow a binomial distribution.
- On electrical appliances there is an on/off switch which is designated '0' for off and '1' for on. This is a binomial designation.

Validity

The following rules apply in order for the binomial distribution to be valid:

Rule 1   Each observation is considered as having been selected from an infinite population, without replacement. Alternatively from a finite population, with replacement.

Rule 2   Each sample, or trial, has two possible outcomes:

Success, or failure	Present, or absent
Win, or lose	On time, or late
Good, or bad	Open, or closed

Rule 3   The probability, p, of obtaining the desired result (success) remains fixed over time. Since the sum of the probabilities is unity (there are only two possible outcomes) the probability of failure, q, is (1 − p). In the case of tossing a coin, the distribution is symmetrical. Here p = q = 0.5.

Rule 4   The outcome of any observation is independent of the outcome of any other observation. In tossing a coin for the first time, the outcome of the toss has no bearing on the outcome of the second toss. Tosses are mutually independent.

Deviations

Meeting conditions for a binomial distribution are not always evident as the following illustrates.

Fixed over time

Rule 3 requires that the probability of success remains fixed over time. In, say, a drilling operation, each time a hole is drilled, there is wear on the machine, and the drill. Thus, in time, the hole drilled may not be according to specifications.

Observations are independent

Rule 4 requires that the outcome of any observation is independent of the outcome of other observations. In personnel evaluations, a positive evaluation of one person can cause a less positive evaluation of another, and vice versa. Assume candidates are being interviewed for a senior job position. Candidate A is rated negatively. The next candidate, B, is rated more positively because B is compared with A. Interviewers often make a subliminal comparison of competing candidates.

Mathematical expression

The following equation, which is the probability of r successes, in n trials describes the binomial distribution. It was developed by experiments carried out by the Swiss mathematician, Jacques Bernoulli (1654–1705):

$$P(X) = \frac{n!}{r!(n-r)!} p^r q^{(n-r)}$$

where:

- p is the characteristic probability, or probability of success (0.5 for toss of a coin)
- q = (1 − p) = probability of failure (equals 0.5 for the coin toss experiment)
- r = number of successes desired
- n = number of trials undertaken.

If p = 0.5, the distribution is symmetrical, regardless of the values of n. When p is not equal to 0.5 the distribution is skewed.

Dissecting the binomial equation

The expression:

$$p^n q^{(n-r)}$$

is the probability of obtaining exactly r successes out of n observations in a particular sequence.

The relationship:

$$\frac{n!}{x!(n-x)!}$$

indicates how many combinations of the r successes, out of n observations are possible.

Mean value of the binomial distribution

The mean value, also known as the expected value, E(x), is given by the product of the number of trials and the characteristic probability:

$$\text{Mean} = \mu_x = E(x) = np$$

Standard deviation of the binomial distribution

The standard deviation is the square root of the variance. The variance is the product of the number of trials, the characteristic probability of success, and the characteristic probability of failure:

$$\text{Standard deviation}, \sigma_x = \sqrt{\text{var}(x)} = \sqrt{np(1-p)} = \sqrt{npq}$$

Binomial distribution situations

1. In gambling, what is the probability that an ace and a jack will occur once in 50 rounds of black jack (twenty-one)?
2. In quality control, what is the probability that, in a sample of 1000 computer cards, none will be defective? Historically, it is known that 0.02% of all cards produced are defective.
3. In finance, what is the probability that the price of Texaco stock increases next week, if price changes are random?
4. In education, what is probability that a student will pass a 100 question multiple-choice exam, each with five choices, if the student guesses each question? Passing is considered obtaining a score greater than 70%.

Approximating to the normal distribution

The binomial distribution can be approximated to the normal distribution when:

- The product of sample size and probability of success is greater or equal to five, or $n * p \geqslant 5$.

- The product of sample size and probability of failure is greater or equal to five, or $n * q \geqslant 5$.

In the binomial distribution, the mean $\mu = n \cdot p$ and the standard deviation $\sigma = \sqrt{n \cdot p \cdot q}$.

From the transformation formula, $z = (X - \mu)/\sigma$.

Substituting from the binomial relationships, $z = (X - n \cdot p)/(\sqrt{n \cdot p \cdot q})$.

Demonstrating the concept 27.2 illustrates the use of the binomial distribution.

Poisson distribution

Characteristics

The Poisson distribution, named after the Frenchman, Denis Poisson (1781–1840), is another discrete probability distribution. It is often used to describe waiting line situations, such as the number of patients arriving at a doctor's surgery, the arrival of vehicles at a tollbooth, or the number of customers arriving at a credit card/cash distribution machine (see Chapter 21).

Requirements

The number of vehicles arriving at a road tunnel at rush hour would be an example of a Poisson distribution. The requirements and conditions would be:

1. The mean number of vehicles arriving per hour can be estimated from past data.
2. If the rush hour period is divided into single seconds, the following would be approximately true:
   - The probability that exactly one vehicle will arrive at the tunnel mouth every second is a very small number and is constant for every one-second interval.
   - The probability that two or more vehicles will arrive within a one-second interval is so small that it can be considered zero.
   - The number of vehicles that arrive in a given one-second interval is independent of the time at which that one-second interval occurs during the overall prescribe time period.
   - The number of arrivals in any one-second interval is independent on the number of arrivals in any other one-second interval.

Mathematical expression

The equation describing the Poisson probability of occurrence, P(x) is:

$$P(x) = \frac{\lambda^x e^{-\lambda}}{x!}$$

where:

- λ (lambda) is the mean number of occurrences
- e is the base of the natural logarithm, or 2.71828
- P(x) is the probability of exactly x occurrences.

Poisson distribution as an approximation of the binomial distribution

The Poisson distribution can be a reasonable approximation of the binomial distribution if the sample size, n, is greater than or equal to 20, and p, the characteristic probability, is less than or equal to 0.05.

If this requirement is true then the mean of the binomial distribution, which is given by the product $n * p$, can be substituted for the mean of the Poisson distribution, λ. The probability function then becomes:

$$P(x) = \frac{(np)^x e^{-(np)}}{x!}$$

The use of the Poisson distribution is illustrated in Demonstrating the concept 27.3.

Student t distribution

Characteristics

A t distribution is another continuous probability distribution similar to the normal distribution in that it is bell shaped, and symmetrical. However, the t distribution is lower at the mean, and higher in the tails than the normal distribution. The t distribution was developed by William Gossett of the Guinness Brewery, in Dublin, Ireland in the early 1900s. He referred to it as the Student's t distribution as Guinness would not let him use his own name for the discovery.

Degrees of freedom

There is a different t distribution for each possible degree of freedom. Consider the following equation that contains five variables:

$$\frac{A + B + C + D + E}{5} = 13$$

If the four variables A, B, C, and D are given the values 14, 16, 12, and 18, then automatically the fifth variable, E is fixed at a value of 5 in order to retain the validity of the equation. Thus, in general terms for a sample size of n units, the degrees of freedom are (n − 1).

Using a t distribution

A t distribution, rather than a normal distribution, is used when the sample size, n, is ⩽30, and the population standard deviation is unknown. There is a different t distribution for each sample size. As the sample size increases, the t distribution approaches the normal distribution. When n > 30, the normal distribution can be used. In this case, the sample standard deviation, s, approaches the population standard deviation, σ.

The use of the t distribution is illustrated in Demonstrating the concept 27.4.

Beta distribution

Definition

A beta distribution is commonly used to describe the inherent variability between various samples such as the time certain groups take to perform a specific activity. For example, students completing an exam, the time sample groups watch television, or the time people sleep. Unlike the normal distribution, the beta distribution has the properties of being entirely contained within finite limits because there is always a lower limit and an upper limit. The beta distribution can be symmetrical or skewed to the right or the left according to the nature of the activity.

Network diagrams

The beta distribution is used in PERT project management network diagrams (see Chapter 18) where three time estimates are considered and a mean value is calculated. For example if:

b = pessimistic time
a = optimistic time
m = most likely time.

then mean or expected time, t, for an activity is given by:

$$t = \frac{a + 4m + b}{6}$$

Variance is given by the relationship:

$$\sigma^2 = \left[\frac{(b - a)}{6}\right]^2 = \frac{(b - a)^2}{36}$$

The standard deviation for the activity is the square root of the variance or:

$$\sigma = \sqrt{\sigma^2} = \left[\frac{(b - a)}{6}\right]$$

The value of six is used in the denominator is there is an equivalence to the ±3σ (or six sigma) used in the normal distribution. Examples of using the beta distribution are given in Chapter 18.

Summary of key elements

- Discrete data are distinct information usually obtained from counting. These are in contrast to continuous data that progress from one class to another.

- Inferential statistics is the analysis of sample data for the purpose of describing the characteristics of the population from which that sample is taken.

- A random sample is where each sample item has an equal chance of being selected, and the selection of one item from the sample has no impact on the chance that any other item is chosen.

- A frequency distribution is a display that shows the number of observations that fall into each set of mutually exclusive classes. The more frequently certain data occur, the higher probability that these data will be repeated in the future.

- Some simple summation rules include the following:

$$\Sigma(X + Y) = \Sigma X + \Sigma Y$$

$$\Sigma(X - Y) = \Sigma X - \Sigma Y$$

$$\Sigma k = n * k$$

$$\Sigma(X - \overline{X}) = \Sigma X - \Sigma \overline{X} = 0$$

- Probability is the chance that something will or will not happen. It might be subjective, based on the frequency of past events, or by the application of certain probability rules.

- Most data cluster around a central point. This central point is often used to describe the data, or the population, and is used as a reference. The mean, median, midrange, mode, and geometric mean are central tendency measures.

- Dispersion is a measure of the spread of data. Data that lie close to the central point have a low dispersion and are more reliable for analysis whereas data that lie far from the central point are more dispersed and are less reliable.

- An exponential distribution is where a dependent variable changes according to the power, or exponent, of an independent value. Population expansion, sales of a new product in the introduction phase, the learning rate, growth of a forest, or the spread of disease often follow an exponential distribution.

- A normal distribution is symmetrical and bell shaped. No matter the values of the mean, or the standard deviation, the area under the curve is 1.00. Approximately 68.26% of all values lie within ±1 standard deviations from the mean, 95.44% within ±2 standard deviations, and 99.74% of all values lie within ±3 standard deviations from the mean.

- A binomial distribution is a discrete probability distribution with only two possible outcomes for each trial such as success or failure, present or absent, win or lose, on time or late, good or bad, or open or closed.

- The Poisson distribution is a discrete distribution used to describe waiting lines such as the number of patients arriving at a doctor's surgery, the arrival of vehicles at a tollbooth, or the number of customers arriving at a cash register.

- A Student t distribution is another continuous probability distribution similar to the normal distribution in that it is bell shaped, and symmetrical. There is a different t distribution for each possible degree of freedom.

- A beta distribution, used in PERT network diagrams, describes inherent variability between various samples such as the time to perform a specific activity. It has the properties of being entirely contained within finite limits and can be symmetrical or skewed to the right or the left according to the nature of the activity.

Notes and references

1. 'Les statisticiens montent en puissance dans les entreprises', (Statisticians increase their power in businesses). *Le Monde*, 22 October 1997
2. 'Charging ahead: To keep GE's profits rising, Welch pushes quality control plan. "Black Belts" are roaming its plants to weed out foul ups and slash costs. Some gripes at high levels', *Wall Street Journal Europe*, 14 January 1997
3. NIEVES, Evelyn, 'Dot-crash: San Francisco feels it', *International Herald Tribune*, 27 March 2001, p. 15
4. MARK, Robert, 'Chemical bank', *The Economist*, 10 April 1993

Review and discussion topics

1. Distributions

What type of probability distributions might apply to the following situations:

(a) delivery vehicles waiting to unload at a hypermarket on a Monday morning

(b) a passenger driving to the airport trying to get the midday flight from Los Angeles to London

(c) the lengths of 50,000 screws in a lot, which have a nominal length of 5 cm

(d) the test to see if a watch works

(e) the estimated chance to see if a construction project will be completed on time when there are four activity paths leading to the completion

(f) stock market prices as they are currently quoted on the New York Stock Exchange

(g) stock market prices as they are presented on dividend investment statements.

2. Probability

What type of probability might be used in the following situations? Justify your reasons:

(a) whether a client will sign a contract for the purchase of a line of clothing

(b) that an aircraft engine may at the same time, lose an impeller blade, and break away from its wing mounting (two unrelated events)

(c) the rolling of two fair dice such that 12 comes up the first time

(d) an insurance company's estimation of the life expectancy of men in the United Kingdom.

3. Life and death

Even as the European Union (EU) gets ready to enlarge by taking in new member states, the existing members are slowly shrinking. Eurostat, the EU's statistical branch, predicts that the bloc's share of the global population could drop to just 3% in the year 2050 compared with 7% today and 12% in 1950. As women have fewer children, or are put off motherhood, fertility rates in the EU are at an all-time low of 1.45 children per women. Eurostat also says that women are living longer than ever before, with the current life expectancy at 87 years.[*]

(a) What type of probabilities is this information based on?

(b) The life expectancy of 87 years is what type of statistical term? How would this statement apply to a sample of 5000 women? What type of distribution might it represent?

(c) What impact does this information have globally on operations and the supply chain?

4. Percentiles

Statistical analysis indicates that US high school students are in a lower percentile on maths scores than some European and Asian Countries:

(a) In simple words what does this mean?

(b) On what type of statistical analysis is this based?

(c) What might be the impact of this fact on future international business?

'EU notebook', *Wall Street Journal Europe*, 26 June 1997.

Demonstrating the concept 27.1   Drive shaft

Situation

A company has a factory where it machines drive shafts used in the manufacture of motors. The production manager wants to know the probability that a randomly selected shaft will last more than 12,000 hours before failure so that she can better define its warranty requirements.

Required

Determine the probability that a shaft will last more than 12,000 hours if it is known from historical data that the average life of a drive shaft is 11,000 hours, the standard deviation of the life is 500 hours, and the life of a drive shaft follows a normal distribution.

Solution

From the transformation formula:

$$z = \frac{x - \mu_x}{\sigma_x}$$

where:

- x is 12,000 hours
- μ_x is 11,000 hours
- σ_x is 500 hours

Therefore:

$$z = \frac{12,000 - 11,000}{500} = 2.00$$

From the Microsoft Excel function menu, or standard distribution tables, this value of z gives a value of 0.47725. This means that the area of the curve between 11,000 and 12,000 hours is 0.47725. However, the question asks 'more than 12,000 hours' so the area of the curve of interest is that portion to the right of 12,000 hours. Since the area of the curve to the right of the mean is 0.5, then the area of the curve to the right of 12,000 hours is:

$$0.5 - 0.47725 = 0.02275$$

Thus, the probability of the drive shaft lasting longer than 12,000 hours is about 2.275 or about 2%. This information is illustrated in Figure 27.5.

Figure 27.5 Drive shaft

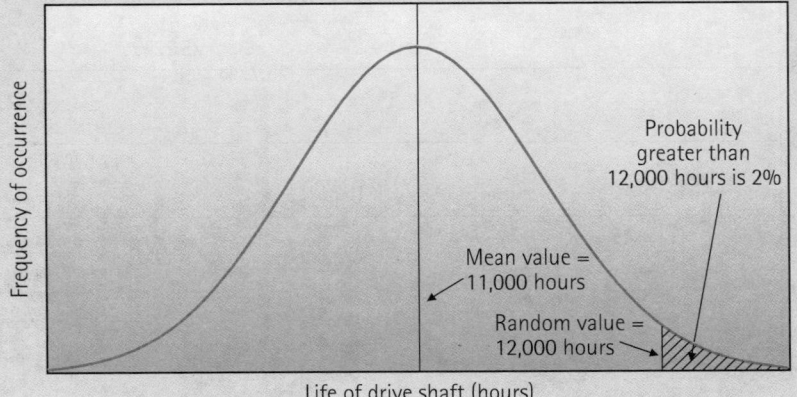

Probability greater than 12,000 hours is 2%

Mean value = 11,000 hours

Random value = 12,000 hours

Frequency of occurrence

Life of drive shaft (hours)

Demonstrating the concept 27.2 Hair dryers

Situation

Historical data indicate that simply by replacing the heating coil, 65% of defective hairdryers assembled by an electrical company can be repaired. Since the units can either be repaired or not, the probability of success is considered to follow a binomial distribution.

Required

1. Develop a distribution of the probability of repairing a hairdryer if there are ten units defective.
2. What is the probability that six of the defective units can be repaired?
3. What is the probability that at least seven can be repaired?
4. What is the probability that no more than six can be repaired?

Solution

- The characteristic probability is 0.65 or 65%.
- The number of trials is ten.
- The outcome of units that can be repaired ranges from 0 to 10.

1. The probability distribution using the binomial distribution function for a sample size of ten using Microsoft Excel is given in Table 27.4 and the histogram for this distribution is given in Figure 27.6.
2. Probability that six of the defective units can be repaired is 23.77%.

3. Probability that at least seven can be repaired (seven through ten units) is 51.38% (100 − 48.62).
4. Probability that no more than six (0 through six) can be repaired is 48.62%.

Table 27.4 Probability distribution applied to hairdryer repairs

Characteristic probability, p	0.65	Given
Sample size	10	Given
Mean	6.5	n*p
Std dev	1.5083	$\sqrt{n*p*q}$

Nº that can be repaired	Probability this number can be repaired (%)	Cumulative probability this number can be repaired (%)
0	0.00	0.00
1	0.05	0.05
2	0.43	0.48
3	2.12	2.60
4	6.89	9.49
5	15.36	24.85
6	23.77	48.62
7	25.22	73.84
8	17.57	91.40
9	7.25	98.65
10	1.35	100.00

Figure 27.6 Hairdryers

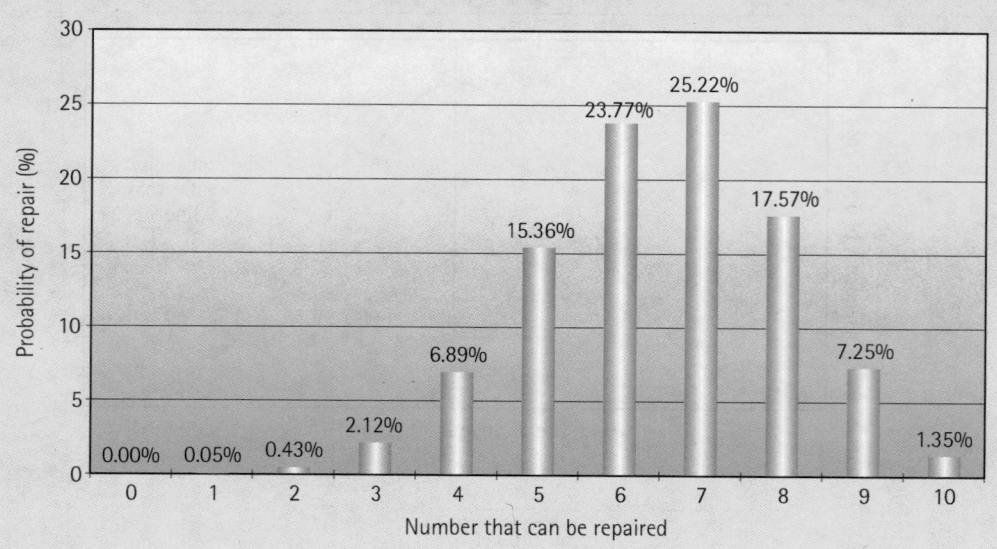

Demonstrating the concept 27.3 Gas pump

Situation

A service station is interested to learn about the utilization of its single automatic gasoline pump that is operated by the insertion of a credit card. In order to know if he is recuperating his investment, the franchise owner of this service station wants some assurance that there is a probability of greater than 50% that ten or more customers in any hour use the automatic pump. Past data indicate that, on average, eight customers an hour use the automatic pump.

Required

1. Develop a Poisson distribution for the utilization of this gasoline pump.
2. Should the franchise be satisfied with the utilization, based on the data given?

Solution

1. Using the Poisson distribution, where $\lambda = 8$, the probability of customers using this machine during any hour is given in Table 27.5 where the distribution is determined from the Microsoft Excel function. Figure 27.7 gives the histogram of these data.
2. The table shows that the probability of ten or more people using the pump in any hour is 28.34% (100 − 71.66). Thus, the utilization is below the requirements of the franchise. Appropriate steps should be taken to increase usage, such as by publicity, price or other incentives.

Table 27.5 Probability of customers using a gas pump (Poisson distribution)

$$\lambda = 8$$

Customers	P(X) exactly (%)	P(X) cumulative (%)
0	0.03	0.03
1	0.27	0.30
2	1.08	1.38
3	2.86	4.24
4	5.73	9.97
5	9.16	19.13
6	12.21	31.34
7	13.96	45.30
8	13.96	59.26
9	12.41	71.67
10	9.93	81.60
11	7.22	88.82
12	4.81	93.63
13	2.96	96.59
14	1.69	98.28
15	0.90	99.18
16	0.45	99.63
17	0.21	99.84
18	0.09	99.93
19	0.04	99.97
20	0.02	99.99
21	0.01	100.00

Figure 27.7 Gas pump

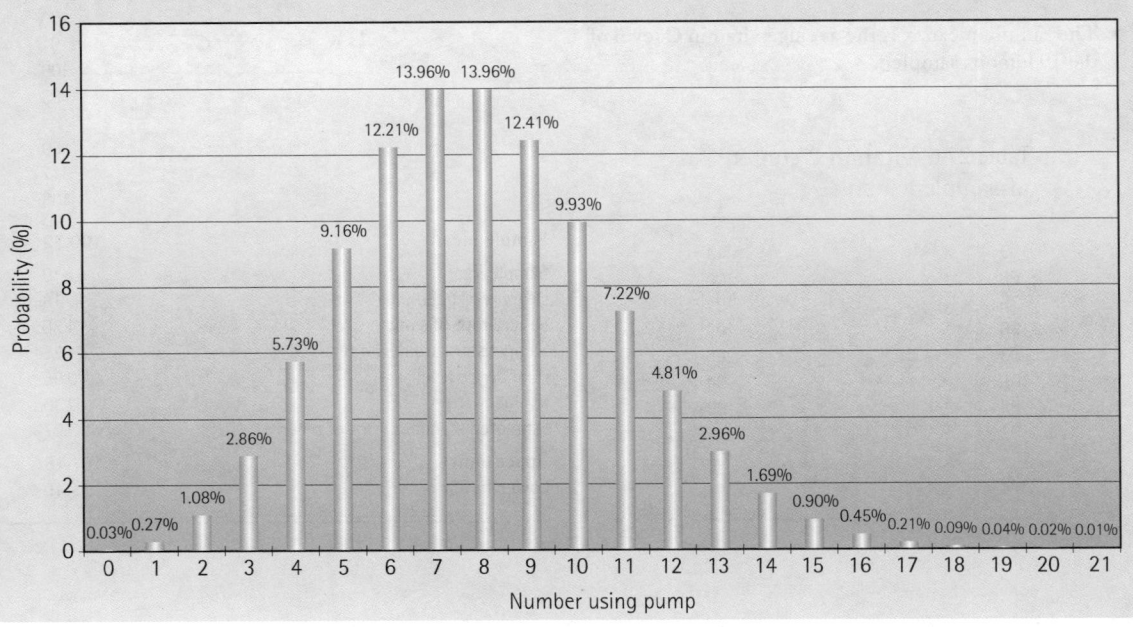

Demonstrating the concept 27.4 Lemons

Situation

The Nomel Company, in the East End of London, imports citrus fruits from Israel. This particular year, the level of sunshine in Israel has been less than usual. As a result, Nomel is interested in learning about the vitamin C content in its imported lemons.

With the aid of an analyst, the company takes a random sample of 19 lemons from a shipload, and determines the milligrams of vitamin C they contained. This information is set out in Table 27.6.

Required

1. What is an estimate of the mean amount of vitamin C in each lemon?
2. Determine a 95% confidence interval for the mean amount of vitamin C in lemons imported by the Nomel Company. This means that you are 95% confident that the mean amount of vitamin C in these lemons lies within this range.

Solution

1. The estimated mean level of vitamin C in the lemons is 100.32.
2. The 95% confidence level is between a vitamin C level of 107.18 and 93.45.

The solution is given in Table 27.7; which is a Microsoft Excel spreadsheet. The elements are explained as follows:

- The sample mean, $\bar{x}$ is the average vitamin C level of the 19 lemons sampled.

Table 27.6 Vitamin C content of sample lemons

109	114
88	106
76	91
136	109
93	85
101	94
89	89
97	117
115	105
92	

- The sample size, n is the number of lemons sampled. As this is less than 30 a t distribution is considered.
- The degrees of freedom are the sample size minus one (n − 1).
- Square root of sample size is $\sqrt{n}$.
- Sample standard deviation is determined directly from Excel, which is based on the equation from the 'Dispersion' section in this chapter.
- The confidence level is given as 95%.
- The t-value is determined from the corresponding Excel function.
- The estimated standard error of the mean is $s/\sqrt{n}$.
- The upper confidence limit is $\bar{x} + t*s/\sqrt{n}$.
- The lower confidence limit is $\bar{x} - t*s/\sqrt{n}$.

Table 27.7 Mean vitamin C level and confidence level in sample lemons

	Vitamin C level
	109
	88
	76
	136
	93
	101
	89
	97
	115
	92
	114
	106
	91
	109
	85
	94
	89
	117
	105
Sample mean	**100.32**
Sample size	19
Degrees of freedom	18
Square root of sample size	4.36
Sample standard deviation	14.25
Confidence level	0.95
t value	2.10
Estimated standard error of mean	3.27
Upper limit	**107.18**
Lower limit	**93.45**

Application exercise 27.1 Airports

Situation

The data given in Table 27.8 give information on the flight delays at selected European airports.* Consider this as a sample of all the commercial airports in the European Union.

Required

1. What is an estimate of the average delay, of delayed flights, at all commercial airports in Europe? (Data for this are in last column.)
2. Determine a 95% confidence interval for the average delay of delayed flights at all commercial airports in Europe. This would mean that you would be 95% confident that the

average delay of delayed flights at all commercial airports in Europe lies within this range.
3. Determine an 85% confidence interval for the average delay of delayed flights at all commercial airports in Europe. This would mean that you would be 85% confident that the average delay of delayed flights at all commercial airports in Europe lies within this range.
4. What is your explanation of the difference between the interval data developed in questions 2 and 3?

*James, Barry, 'Routing Europe's flights in a fragmented system: Network struggles with 68 air traffic centers', *International Herald Tribune*, 1 and 2 April 2000.

Table 27.8 Flight delays at selected European airports

Departure airport	N° of flights delayed (%)	N° of flights delayed more than 60 minutes	Average delay of delayed flights (min)
Athens, Greece	24	1,755	30.2
Barcelona, Spain	27	3,286	30.0
Basel/Mulhouse, Switzerland	32	1,122	26.1
Bologna, Italy	47	2,200	34.5
Brussels, Belgium	31	2,109	23.3
Dusseldorf, Germany	33	1,969	25.1
Geneva, Switzerland	40	1,987	26.7
Hanover, Germany	28	715	25.6
Lisbon, Portugal	28	854	25.7
Lyon/Satolas, France	36	1,283	24.0
Madrid/Barajas, Spain	31	3,477	26.9
Malaga, Spain	34	1,159	30.2
Milan/Linate, Italy	39	1,407	27.7
Milan/Malpensa, Italy	42	4,897	30.5
Munich, Germany	27	2,826	25.5
Nice, France	33	2,215	28.1
Palma Mallorca, Spain	35	4,199	34.9
Stuttgart, Germany	26	1,283	26.4
Tenerife Sur/Reina Sofia, Spain	30	606	29.4
Zurich, Switzerland	41	2,945	23.8

Application exercise 27.2 Cola

Situation

A food manufacturing company has a bottling process for making its own recipe of cola. The cola is made in large mixing vessels, and then sent to the filling area where one-litre PET bottles are filled. The bottling line moves very rapidly and sometimes a bottle, after filling, is ejected from the moving line and splits open on impact with the floor. Past data

indicate that 0.25% of the bottles are ejected from the line. This type of operating problem follows a Poisson distribution.

Required

1. For 1500 filled bottles, develop a probability histogram from 0 to 20 bottles falling from the line.

2. What is the probability that in 1500 filled bottles none is ejected from the line?
3. What is the probability that in 1500 filled bottles five are ejected from the line?

4. What is the probability that in 1500 filled bottles at least six are ejected from the line?
5. What is the probability that in 1500 filled bottles fewer than four bottles are ejected from the line?

Application exercise 27.3 Delivery vehicles

Situation

A food distribution company has a fleet of 1500 trucks that it uses for delivering products from its distribution centre to retail outlets. Based on records, the trucks travel an average 120,000 km a year with a standard deviation of 25,000 km. The distance travelled by the trucks approximates a normal distribution.

Required

1. Estimate what proportion of trucks can be expected to travel between 75,000 and 130,000 km a year.

2. What is the probability that a randomly selected truck travels under 60,000 km a year?
3. What percentage of trucks can be expected to travel more than 145,000 km a year?
4. How many of the trucks in the fleet are estimated to travel between 40,000 and 90,000 km a year?
5. How many kilometres will be travelled by at least 90% of the trucks?

Application exercise 27.4 Diploma

Situation

A certain business school has a double diploma programme for its students. In this programme, participants are able to spend a year studying at universities such as INSEAD in France; Bocconi in Italy; Lancaster in England; Texas and Connecticut in USA; and Toronto in Canada.

The competition for this programme is high. Candidates are selected on their language ability, motivation, and GMAT (graduate management admission test) score. Past data indicate that 60% of the candidates are accepted for this programme. Acceptance, or rejection follows a Bernoulli process.

Required

1. Develop a table showing all the possible exact probabilities of acceptance if 15 candidates apply for this programme.

2. Develop a table showing all the possible cumulative probabilities of acceptance if 15 candidates apply for this programme.
3. Illustrate, on a histogram, all the possible exact probabilities of acceptance if 15 candidates apply for this programme.
4. If 15 candidates apply, what is the probability that exactly five candidates will be accepted?
5. If 15 candidates apply, what is the probability that exactly ten candidates will be accepted?
6. If 15 candidates apply, what is the probability that at least ten candidates will be accepted?
7. If 15 candidates apply, what is the probability that fewer than eight candidates will be accepted?

Application exercise 27.5 Snow

Situation

The data array in Table 27.9 is the level of snow in metres at a certain ski resort taken every ten days during a four-month period, December through March, over five years. There are 60 measurements: 12 per year times for five years.

Required

1. From these data determine the:
   (a) maximum value
   (b) minimum value
   (c) range

Table 27.9   Snow levels as a data array

3.24	4.72	3.48	4.24	3.80	3.72	4.60	1.91	4.25	4.64
3.12	5.92	3.04	7.18	3.56	1.32	3.44	2.71	4.08	8.19
3.96	3.92	8.20	1.25	7.20	6.04	9.27	0.40	2.60	3.00
8.75	5.70	3.68	4.26	6.80	9.80	7.80	5.75	0.75	6.78
5.93	4.27	6.14	5.78	5.78	1.91	8.37	2.68	7.25	6.10
0.95	6.90	4.12	5.48	5.12	7.20	2.92	1.91	2.12	5.00

(d) midrange
(e) average
(f) median
(g) mode
(h) standard deviation if the data were considered a sample of snow levels (which they are)
(i) standard deviation if the data were considered a population of snow levels.
2. Develop a closed-limit frequency distribution for these data using a data range of one metre and a logical lower and upper limit for the data. Convert this frequency distribution into a relative frequency distribution.
3. Plot the relative frequency distribution as a histogram. At any moment, what is the probability that the snow level will be between three and four metres? What can you say about this probability?
4. Convert the relative frequency distribution into a greater than and less than ogive and plot these two line graphs on the same axis.
5. Using the appropriate ogive:
    (a) What is the probability that the snow level will be less than three metres?
    (b) From the appropriate ogive, what is the probability that the snow level will be greater than seven metres?
6. Assume that the data follow a normal distribution, and the measured snow levels are sample data, calculate:
    (a) the probability that the snow level will be less than three metres
    (b) the probability that the snow level will be more than seven metres.

Selected further reading

ANDERSON, David R., SWEENEY, Dennis J. and WILLIAMS, Thomas A. (1999) *Statistics for Business and Economics*, 7th edition, South-Western.

KOHLER, Heinz (2001) *Statistics for Business and Economics with Excel CD-ROM*, South-Western.

LEVIN, Richard I. and RUBIN, David S. (1998) *Statistics for Management*, 7th edition, Prentice-Hall.

LEVINE, David M., BERENSON, Mark L., KREHBIEL, Timothy C. and STEPHAN, David (2001) *Statistics for Managers Using Microsoft Excel*, 3rd edition, Prentice-Hall.

SANDERS, Donald H. and SMIDT, Robert (1999) *Statistics: A First Course with Data CD-Rom*, 6th edition, McGraw-Hill.

An extensive listing of other further reading can be found on the website.

What's on the web?

Further learning resources are available to lecturers and students at www.supplychain-online.com, including the following which are specific to *Statistical concepts*:

Resource	Subject
Chapter overview	Statistical concepts
Application exercise: Children	Binomial distribution
Application exercise: Salaries	Dispersion and normal distributions
More further reading	Statistical concepts

Appendix

Technical Discoveries, Inventions and Developments

The following are key discoveries inventions, and developments, beginning with the Industrial Revolution, which have had a big impact on the operations environment in both manufacturing and services.*

1733 Flying shuttle loom for weaving invented in Britain by John Kay

1747 Rubber tree discovered in Guyana by François Fresneau of France

1751 Nickel discovered by Cronstedt of Sweden

1754 Aluminium discovered in Germany by Andreas Sigismund Marggraf

1759 First factory for printed linen, Jouy-en-Josas, France, by Christophe Philippe Oberkampf

1764 First mechanical weaving machine, spinning jenny, by James Hargreaves of Britain

1765 Steam engine of Newcomen perfected by the Scotsman James Watt

1774 Magnesium and chlorine discovered by C W Scheele

1783 First manned flight (in a balloon) in France by François Pilâtre de Rozier and François d'Arlandes

1785 Mechanical weaving machine perfected by Edmund Cartwright of Britain

1789 Uranium and zirconium discovered by Martin Heinrich Klaproth of Germany

1790 Preserving jars for food perfected in France by Nicolas Appert

1793 Cotton gin to quickly comb the seed from cotton invented in Britain by Eli Whitney

1794 First graphite pencil developed by Nicolas Jacques Conté of France

1804 First steam locomotive put into service in Britain by Richard Trevithick

1807 First steam boat, *Clermont*, on the Hudson River between New York and Albany, USA (Robert Fulton)

1813 First steam locomotive to utilize traction by friction, the *Puffing Billy*, by William Hedley of Britain

1814 The steam locomotive, the *Rocket*, developed by George Stevenson in Britain

1816 Principle of photography invented in France by Nicéphore Niepce

1819 First Atlantic crossing by a steam boat, the *Savannah*

1824 Composition of Portland cement established by Joseph Aspdin in Britain for which a patent is obtained

1826 Benzene discovered by Michael Faraday in Britain

1828 First train put into service in France between Saint-Etienne and Andrézieux, France

1830 First patent for the sewing machine deposited by the Frenchman Barthélemy Thimonnier

1836 Discovery of acetylene by Edward Davy in Britain

1837 First commercial demonstration of the telegraph using dots and dashes by Samuel Morse in the USA

1839 Vulcanization of rubber discovered by Charles Goodyear in the USA

1839 The world's first commercial telegraph system starts in Britain

1840 First electric transformer constructed Antoine Masson and Louis Brégue of France

1841 Invention of the rheostat by Johann Christian Poggendorff in Germany

1843 First steel boat driven by propeller, the *Great Britain*, launched by Isambard Kingdom Brunel of Britain

1844 First inter-city telephone call (Washington and Baltimore, USA) using Samuel Morse's system

1845 Rotating printing press developed Richard Marsh Hoe of the USA

1845 Inflatable rubber tyre developed Robert William Thompson of Britain

1847 Invention of photography on a glass plate by Abel Niepce de Saint-Victor of France

1851 Sewing machine perfected by Isaac Merrit Singer of the USA

1851 First undersea cable (between Dover, UK, and Calais, France)

1852 First steam driven war ship built, the *Napoléon*, by Henri Dupuy de Lôme of France

1853 Discovery of aspirin by Charles Gerhardt of France

1854   First tar road surfacing by Henri Sainte-Claire-Deville of France

1855   Discovery of isopropyl alcohol by the French chemist, Pierre Berthelot

1856   The Bessemer process for making steel developed by Henry Bessemer in Britain

1857   First elevator (lift) installed in New York, USA, by Elisha Graves Otis

1859   First oil drilling and production operation, Titusville, Pennsylvania, USA (Edwin Laurentine Drake)

1860   Manufacture of linoleum perfected by J Walton of Britain

1861   Development of the process for producing sodium carbonate by Ernest Solvay of Belgium

1861   First large hydraulic press constructed by John Haswell of Austria

1861   The transcontinental telegraph system essentially kills the Pony Express in the United States

1862   Patent deposited for the 4-cycle internal combustion engine by Alphonse Beau de Rochas of France

1864   The existence of electromagnetic waves demonstrated by James Clerk Maxwell, a British physicist

1865   Commercialization of the first rotating printing press (front and back) by William A Bullock of the USA

1865   First patent of a railway sleeping carriage in USA by George Mortimer Pullman and Ben Field

1866   Invention of dynamite by Alfred Nobel of Sweden

1866   Introduction of automatic train signals (automatic blocks) by Thomas Hall of the USA

1866   The first telegraph cable is laid across the Atlantic Ocean linking the USA and Europe

1867   Principle of antiseptic discovered aiding surgical procedures by Joseph Lister of Britain

1867   First typewriter built by Christopher Latham Sholes of the USA

1869   First skin graft by Jacques Louis Reverdin of Switzerland

1869   Margarine discovered by Hippolyte Mège-Mouriès of France

1869   Invention of the vacuum cleaner by I G McGaffe of the USA

1869   Invention of the ball bearing by J Suriray of France

1871   Invention of the pneumatic hammer by Simon Ingersoll of the USA

1871   Invention of the photographic gelatine emulsion bromine/silver by Richard Leach Maddox of Britain

1872   First use of compressed air brakes on trains by George Westinghouse of the USA

1872   Patent for the gasoline engine by George B Brayton of the USA

1872   Laying of first transatlantic cable between Europe and South America

1873   First transmission of electric energy at Vienna by Hippolyte Fontaine

1873   Perfection, and assembly line production of the typewriter by Philio Remington of the USA

1875   Transport long distance of refrigerated meat (Buenos Aires/Le Havre) Ferdinand Carré of France

1875   Remington launches the production of the typewriter from the invention of L Sholes

1876   The Scottish-born American, Alexander Graham Bell, invents the telephone (US patent N° 174,465)

1876   4-stroke internal combustion engines, Nikolaus Otto/Gottlieb Daimler/Wilhelm Maybach of Germany

1877   Invention of the record player by Thomas Alva Edison of the USA

1877   A telephone line is established in Boston which begins US commercial service

1878   Construction of the 2-stroke gas engine by Carl Benz of Germany

1878   First photographic plates of silver bromide emulsion by George Eastman of the USA

1878   Invention of the incandescent light bulb by Thomas A Edison of the USA

1878   Invention of the centrifuge by Gustaf De Laval of Sweden

1879   First vaccination experiments on animals by Louis Pasteur of France

1879   First electric locomotive built by Werner von Siemens of Germany

1880   First electrical distribution system on a transatlantic boat (*Columbia*), Thomas A Edison of the USA

1882   Construction of the first industrial alternator by Sebastiano Ziani de Ferranti of Britain (originally Italian)

1882   Invention of the electric fan by Schuyler Skoats Wheeler of the USA

1883   First internal combustion engine automobile driven by Edouard Delamare-Deboutteville

1884   Discovery of the bacterial nitrification of soil by Jean-Jacques Schloesing of France

1884   Invention of the transformer by Lucien Gaulard of France

1884   Invention of the steam turbine by Charles Parson of Britain

1884   Invention of the first artificial textile fibre by Hilaire Bernigaud of France

1884   Invention of the first fountain pen by Edson Waterman of USA

1884   Invention of the first photographic film by George Eastman of the USA

1885   Invention of the first adding machine, William Steward Burroughs of the USA

1886   First automobile driven by a 4-stroke gasoline engine (three wheels) by Carl Benz of Germany

1886   First offshore drilling in California

1887   Carburettor and 2-stroke gasoline engine invented by Gottlieb Daimler and Wilhelm Maybach of Germany

1887   The number of telephone subscribers reaches more than 100,000 worldwide

1888   First special steels developed by Robert Abbot Hadfield of Britain

1888   Pneumatic tyre developed by John Boyd Dunlop of Scotland

1888   Electromagnetic waves transmitted by the German Heinrich Hertz. Name used for frequency measure

1890   First tube (metro) line in London, England

1891   First gasoline driven automobile by René Panhard and Emile Levassor of France

1891   Invention of the replaceable inflatable tyre for the bicycle by Edouard Michelin of France

1892   First patent for the internal combustion engine by Rudolf Diesel of Germany

1892   Refinement of the electric oven by Henri Moissan of France

1893   Invention of the thermos flask for liquefied gases by James Dewar of Scotland

1893   Invention of the radio antenna by Aleksandr Stepanovitch Popov of Russia

1894   Invention of the replaceable inflatable tyre for the automobile by Edouard Michelin of France

1894   A prototype of the wireless telegraph developed by Guglielmo Marconi in Italy

1895   Discovery of the X-ray by Wilhelm Conrad Röntgen of Germany

1895   Invention of cinematography by Louis and Auguste Lumière (brothers) of France

1895   First use of the electric train in Baltimore, USA

1896   Discovery of natural occurring uranium by Henri Becquerel of France

1896   Wireless telegraphy that uses airwaves instead of wires patented by Guglielmo Marconi in London

1896   First electrical record player, or pick-up by Frantz Dussaud of Switzerland

1896   The telephone dialler is invented. Operators are no longer needed to connect all calls

1897   Demonstration that yeast from beer is the fermentation agent for alcohol by Edouard Buchner of Germany

1897   Invention of the cathode ray oscilloscope by Karl Ferdinand Braun of Germany

1898   Hydrogen gas liquefied in Scotland by James Dewar

1898   Radium and polonium discovered by Pierre and Marie Curie of France

1898   Louis Renault, of France, develops the direct-drive transmission revolutionizing the automobile industry

1899   First morse code sent over a long distance (40km) by Gugliemo Marconi of Italy

1899   First bus built by Gottlieb Daimler in Germany

1899   First electrified rail line in Europe (Switzerland) by Burgdorf-Thourne

1900   The human voice broadcast over a distance of one mile by Reginald Fessenden

1901   Battery with electrodes of iron and nickel invented by the German, Junger

1901   First transatlantic radio transmission in Morse code by Marconi

1902   Synthesis of methane realized by Paul Sabatier in France

1902   Invention of electric lighting using a magneto by Robert Bosch in Germany

1903   First powered airplane flight, *Kitty Hawk* by Orville and Wilbur Wright, in N Carolina, USA

1904   Invention of the electric vacuum tube by John Ambrose Fleming in England

1904   Invention of colour photography by Auguste and Louis Lumière of France

1905   First industrial production of offset printing in the USA by Ira W Rubel

1906   Ammonia synthesized in Germany by Fritz Haber

1906   AM radio created by Reginald Fessenden with voice and music broadcast

1906   Two-way telegraphic transmission, by voice not code between Massachusetts and Scotland by Fessenden

1909   First flight across the English Channel by the Frenchman, Louis Blériot

1910   Work on first car telephone by Lars Magnus Ericsson and his wife in Sweden

1913   First flight across the Mediterranean by the Frenchman, Roland Garros

1913   Invention of the cathode ray tube for the production of x-rays by Hans Geiger of Germany

1913   Invention of the first gas filled electric bulb by the American, Irving Langmuir

1913   Opening of the first assembly line car production operation by Henry Ford of the USA

1915   First airplane constructed entirely of metal by Hugo Junkers of Germany

1915   First radio transmission of voices across the Atlantic between Virginia and Paris

1916   Stainless steel invented by Brealey in England

1918   First hybrids of corn developed by the American, Donald Jones

1920   Opening of the first radio station in Pittsburgh, Pennsylvania, USA

1920   Invention of steel–nickel alloy for manufacture of clock springs by Charles Guillaume of Switzerland

1920   Commercialization of isopropyl alcohol by Exxon giving birth to the petrochemical industry

1923   Invention of the bulldozer in the USA

1925   First automobile made with a single body of metal by André Citroën of France

1925 First short-wave intercontinental radio–telephone contact between Sydney and London by Marconi

1926 First demonstration of colour television by the Englishman, John Logie Baird

1926 Invention of pre-stressed concrete by Eugène Freyssinet of France

1926 First two-way transatlantic wireless telephone conversation takes place from New York to London

1927 First talking movie by Warner and Fox, USA

1927 Non-stop transatlantic crossing by Charles Lindbergh of the USA

1928 Penicillin discovered by Alexander Fleming of Britain

1928 Invention of the electric razor by the American, Schick

1930 Invention of the particle accelerator by Robert Jemison van de Graff

1931 Invention of the synthetic rubber, neoprene, by Wallace Hume Carothers of the USA

1932 Discovery of heavy water and deuterium by Harold Urey of the USA

1932 Installation of the talking clock at the Paris observatory by Ernest Esclangon

1933 Development of the insecticide, DDT, by Herman Müller of Switzerland

1934 Development of nuclear fission by the Italian, Enrico Fermi

1934 Invention of the iconoscope for television by Vladimir Zworykin of the USA (originally Russian)

1935 Invention of radar by Robert Alexander Watson-Watt

1935 Invention of the fountain pen with a refillable reservoir

1938 Uranium fission discovered by the Germans, Otto Hahn and Friedrich Strassmann

1939 First flight in Germany a turbine driven airplane (Heinkel He-78)

1939 First helicopter with a propeller *anti-couple* by Igor Sikorsky of the USA

1939 Ball point pen invented by the Hungarian L Biro and put into production by the firm Reynolds of the USA

1941 Plutonium discovered by the Americans, Ewin Mattison McMillan and Glenn Seaborg

1941 Discovery of silicones by Frederick Stanley Kipping

1941 First flight of a turbine-driven airplane perfected by Frank Whittle

1941 Cellular telephones created in US military research labs during World War II

1941 System patented in US for guiding torpedoes by radio signals. Forms basis for satellite communication

1942 First atomic pile built at the University of Chicago by the Italian, Enrico Fermi

1943 Commercialization of the first polyacrylic fibres

1944 Production of electro-mechanical calculator by Howard Aiken and IBM

1945 First atomic bomb explosion in New Mexico, USA

1945 Atomic bombs dropped on Hiroshima and Nagasaki, Japan

1946 Computer ENIAC (Electronic Numerical Integrator and Calculator) invented by John Ecket/John Mauchy of the USA

1946 First commercial radio–telephone service in St Louis Missouri, USA, by Southwestern Bell and AT&T

1947 Cellular network idea proposed by Bell Labs, USA, in an internal memorandum

1948 Transistor invented by John Barden, Walter Brattain, William Shockley at the Bell Laboratories, USA

1948 Development of the instantaneous photographic camera by Edward Herbert Land of the USA

1950 First numerically controlled machine tool (milling machine), USA

1951 Colour movies (Eastman Color) launched by Eastman Kodak

1951 First electronic calculator, UNIVAC, for management applications by Remington Rand

1951 Largest European oil refinery by Esso Petroleum opened in September in Fawley, UK

1951 First stored-program computer developed by Lyons, a UK catering firm (Lyons Electronic Office)

1952 First computers (IBM 701)

1952 First television link between Britain and France

1953 Cinemascope developed by 20th Century Fox

1954 First nuclear powered submarine, *Nautilus*, launched in USA

1955 Polymerization of ethylene (polyethylene) achieved in Germany by Karl Ziegler

1955 Technique for making artificial diamonds discovered by Percy William Bridgman of the USA

1955 First automobiles with hydraulic suspension (DS 19 Citroën)

1955 Two locomotives in France reach the speed of 331 km/hr

1955 First flight of the French Caravelle jet with rear engines

1955 First nuclear power plant put into service (Calder Hall, UK)

1956 FORTRAN becomes the first computer programming language by John Backus of IBM

1956 Laying of first undersea telephone cable between the USA and Britain

1956 General Electric (US) begins producing industrial diamonds

1956 Lever Brothers launches Wisk, Americas first liquid laundry detergent

1956 First portable pager developed by Motorola in the USA

1957 First satellite put into orbit by the Russians (*Sputnik 1*)

1957 Ford introduces the Edsel (loses more than $250 million in 2 years)

1958 First automobile with an automatic gear box by Dutch firm DAF

1958 Launching of the first nuclear powered ice-breaker

1958 Pan American Airways (USA) inaugurates New York to Paris commercial jet service

1958 Integrated circuit developed by Kilbey at Texas Instruments and Noyce at Fairchild in the USA

1958 Bank of America issues BankAmericard (later called Visa)

1959 Hovercraft put into service by C Cockerell of Britain

1959 Haloid Xerox introduces plain paper copier in the USA

1960 The FDA approves Searle's Enovid as the first oral contraceptive

1960 Development of the first laser by Theodore Harold Maiman at the Hughes Research Labs, California

1962 *Telstar-1*, a communications satellite that receives, amplifies and sends signals is launched by AT&T

1962 First transatlantic TV satellite emission (Andover USA and Plemeur-Bodou, France)

1962 First industrial robot commercialized in USA

1962 Philips, Holland, introduces the compact cassette

1963 Pepsi Cola introduced

1964 Blue Ribbon Sports (Nike) introduces its first running shoes

1964 First typewriter with a memory (IBM)

1964 Ford introduces the Mustang

1966 Carbon fibres developed in Britain by W Watt, L N Phillips and W Johnson

1967 Amana introduces countertop microwave oven

1967 First flexible factories, Sundstrand Aviation, Rockford, USA and IBM, Deptford, Britain

1967 Approximately 200 million phones in service worldwide with over 50% in the USA

1968 First supersonic transport plane, Tupolev Tu-144, USSR

1968 Cameron printing press for large volumes in the USA

1968 Burroughs produces first computers (B2500 and B3500) using integrated circuits

1968 A cellular phone system design and technical standard by Bell Labs accepted by the FCC of the USA

1969 Integrated circuit (CDD charge coupled device) of silicon by Boyle and Smith at Bell Labs, USA

1969 Citroën, France commercializes fuel injection systems

1969 Moon landing (Neil Armstrong and Edwin Aldrin of the USA)

1969 Dept of Defense ARPA connects four US universities in an online network system. Start of the Internet

1970 Pan Am inaugurates wide-body jet service with flights from New York to London

1971 Intel, USA, commercialize first microprocessor (2300 transistors on 7 sq mm of silicon)

1971 Intel produces microprocessor

1972 Fibre optics developed by Corning Glassworks, USA

1972 Pong, the first home video game is introduced

1972 First colour home VCR is produced by Philips, Holland

1972 First pocket calculators, Texas Instruments, USA

1972 EMI of the UK introduces the CT scanner

1972 Colour TV outnumbers black and white sets

1972 Kevlar, artificial fibre commercialized by Dupont, USA

1972 Electronic mail is introduced

1973 Sharp introduces calculators with LCDs (liquid crystal displays)

1973 10,000 components are placed on a 1-square centimetre chip

1973 Invention of the scanner for medical work by Godfrey Newbold Hounsfield of Britain

1973 Transmission control protocol/Internet protocol (TCP/IP) is designed for the Internet

1974 The first international fax standard transmits one page in six minutes

1974 Intel's second-generation microprocessor makes personal computers possible

1974 First programmable calculators

1975 Development of computer-aided design (CAD)

1976 Super-computer, Cray 1, capable of performing 250 million operations/sec

1976 Queen Elizabeth of Britain sends her first e-mail

1977 Apple II by Apple, first PC able to generate colour graphics, has a keyboard and power supply

1977 CompuServe, a computer information service, goes online

1978 Genentech clones first recombinant DNA product, human insulin

1978 A commercial cell phone system is put into operation by the Bahrain Telephone Co.

1978 A cellular network system is tested by the Bell Labs in Chicago

1979 First laser printers by IBM

1979 Compact disc developed by Philips, Holland

1979 IBM PC launched

1979 Commercial cell phone network opens in Tokyo, Japan

1980 First experiments at video conferencing

1980 First phone cards introduced

1981 Development of interferon an antiviral protein

1981 IBM adopts Microsoft's industry standard disk operating system (DOS)

1981 Xerox PARC introduces graphical user interface

1981 First systems of computer-aided design and computer-aided manufacturing (CAD/CAM), USA

1982 First compact discs introduced

1983 First cellular telephone system introduced in Chicago, USA, by Motorola and AT&T

1983 Sega introduces a three-dimensional video game

1983 MCI orders first big fibre optic system from Corning and Siecor

1983 Chrysler introduces the minivan

1983 File transfer protocol (FTP) allows Internet users to log onto a remote computer and download its files

1984 Philips (Holland) and Sony (Japan) develop the compact disc read-only memory (CD-ROM)

1984 Commercialization by Seiko, Japan, of the first colour portable TV with a flat screen

1984 Apple introduces the Macintosh, a powerful, and user-friendly desktop computer

1984 Phones are introduced on commercial aircraft by Airfone

1985 A single optical fibre transmits the equivalent of 300,000 simultaneous phone calls

1985 Cell phone service begins in Britain, France, Italy, Spain, Austria, and Ireland

1985 Forensic use of DNA (deoxyribonucleic acid) testing begins

1986 First laser robots used in a mechanical production centre

1986 Motorola cellular systems set up in Beijing and Shanghai, China

1987 First virtual reality products sold commercially

1988 Hewlett-Packard develops DeskJet printer in just 22 months

1989 Lotus introduces Notes groupware

1990 Internet's World Wide Web set up by Tim Berners-Lee at European Particle Physics Lab, Switzerland

1990 Saturn, GM's first new car division since 1919, rolls out first car

1990 Iridium satellite phone system developed designed to reach every point on the globe

1991 Compact discs outsell cassettes

1991 GSM cellular standard digital system for telephones adopted in Europe

1991 TDMA cellular standard digital system for telephones adopted in the USA

1991 Gopher, the first user-friendly web interface, created at the University of Minnesota

1993 Intel's Pentium microprocessor enables personal computers to run thousands of programs

1993 Mosaic, a software program developed by Marc Andreeson, can be used to surf the World Wide Web

1993 First auctions of spectrums for mobile phones authorized by US Congress

1994 Netscape creates its Navigator software for browsing the Internet

1994 Digital satellite system provides up to 175 TV channels using an 18-inch satellite dish

1994 Mobile phone auctions net $600 million in the USA

1994 Initial commercial websites are established

1995 FCC begins auctioning broadband spectrum licences for personal communications services

1995 Microsoft introduces Windows 95, an upgrade of its operating system

1995 Mobile phone auctions net $10 billion in the USA

1995 Personal Handy-phone System (PHS), a cordless home phone for citywide use, introduced in Japan

1997 Dolly, a sheep, is the first animal to be born by cloning as a result of the work by Ian Wilmut in the UK

1998 Wireless Application Protocol 1.0 specifications introduced to give Internet access to mobile phones

1999 I-mode Internet service for cell phones by NTT DoCoMo launched in Japan. 4 m subscribers in first year

2000 Commercial WAP launched by UK's BT Cellnet

2000 European companies bid over $100 billion in auctions to license third-generation mobile phone service

2001 UK establishes the world's first embryo stem cell bank

2001 Solar-powered craft, *The Helios*, with 14 propellers, soars to altitude record of 29,410 metres in Hawaii

2001 More than 1 billion cell phone subscribers by yearend

2001 NTT DoCoMo (Japan) launches world's first third generation mobile phones with video/audio connection

2002 On 1 January, the euro becomes the common currency for 300 million Europeans replacing 12 national currencies

*Various sources including:

- *Chronique du 20e siècle*, Larousse 1990
- *Economist*
- *Fortune*
- *History of the World*, Odhams Press Ltd, 1951
- *Pears Cyclopaedia*, 1993–94, Pelham Books, 1993
- *International Herald Tribune*
- *Petit Larousse illustré 1986*, Libraire Larousse, Paris 1980
- *Petit Robert*, 2, Universel des Noms Propres, Dictionnaires Le Robert, Paris 1989
- *Sunday Times Makers of the 20th Century*, Times Newspapers Ltd, London, UK, 1991
- *Time*, 13 November 1995, 'Computers can do a great job – yours', pp 22–3
- *Wall Street Journal*
- *International Herald Tribune*, 26 September 2001, pp 17–18
- The Lamp, Exxon Mobil Corporation, Autumn 2001

Glossary

NOTE: words in *italics* are defined elsewhere.

A

A priori probability in statistics means knowing the likelihood of an event in advance without any previous experimentation. For example, it is known in advance that the probability of obtaining heads on the toss of a coin is 50% even before the coin is tossed. Or, the probability of obtaining a five, on the throw of a single die, is 16.67% (1/6) even before the die is thrown. By way of contrast, one doesn't know in advance the exact probability of whether it will rain, whether a client will accept a new contract, or whether a student will pass a certain exam.

ABC inventory management is a way of classifying *inventory* components. It is based on a *Pareto analysis* grouping units according to annual cost. Inventory having a high total annual cost is considered in the 'A' classification, inventory with the lowest cost in the 'C' classification, and inventory with costs in between, in the 'B' classification.

A-classification, part of the *VAT classification*, means that from a multitude of raw materials, parts, and components (the base of the A) is made a single or a few products (the apex of the A) such as a cruise ship, or a jumbo jet.

Abscissa is the horizontal, or x axis of a two-dimensional graphical presentation.

Absentee management is when executives of corporations have their offices in one location but the facilities for which they are responsible are located elsewhere.

Absolute advantage is an economic basis for the development of international trade because one country possesses a resource that the other does not, which gives that country an absolute advantage. South Africa has an absolute advantage over England in the trade of gold, Saudi Arabia over Switzerland in the trade of crude oil, and France over Argentina in the trade of nuclear engineers.

Acceptable quality level (AQL), is the level of product quality, often expressed as a percentage, considered acceptable. It is a standard established by the manufacturer, or by the purchaser of the product. The lower the value of the AQL the more rigorous the production process, and the higher the *cost of quality*.

Acceptance plans are the agreed programmes between suppliers and purchasers for *random sampling* and testing, of a quantity of goods to decide whether to accept the entire *lot* based on the quality of a tested sample.

Accommodation endorser is a financial instrument that may be required when an individual, or a sole proprietorship (the maker), is granted a bank loan (note). If there is doubt as to the ability to repay the loan, either from business income, or personal assets the bank which is granting the loan may require the borrower to secure a third party, in whom it has confidence, to also sign the note. If the third party signs the face of the note, along with the borrower, the third party is known as the co-maker, or co-signer. If the third party signs on the back he is considered an *accommodation endorser*. The difference between the two is that the co-signer is equally liable, along with the maker, for repayment. An accommodation endorser is not liable until after the maker has defaulted on his obligation.

Accountability is when a subordinate accepts a manager's delegation of authority such that the subordinate is responsible for the outcome of any associated action. Accountability is the extent by which the individual has fulfilled that responsibility. Being accountable implies that the manager might confer either reward or punishment depending on how well the *responsibility* for the delegated authority has been exercised.

Accounting in a financial sense, is the recording, classifying, analyzing, and summarizing of business transactions. Financial accounting data are typically recorded in *income statements*, *balance sheets*, *cash flow statements*, and other financial tabulations. These accounting records provide a financial record of a company's activities.

Accounts payable are the financial amounts owed to suppliers of goods, or services. Time allowed for payment depends on the supplier but is usually in the range 30–60 days. Accounts payable are a short-term obligation and appear in current liabilities in a firm's *balance sheet*.

Accounts receivable are the financial amounts due to a company as a result of the sale of goods or services that were provided on credit terms. Accounts receivable are reported under *current assets* of a company's financial balance sheet. They might include an allowance for bad debts based on historical information.

Acid rain is principally derived from fossil fuels, particularly oil and coal, which produce sulphur dioxide and sulphur trioxide when burnt. These gases, dissolved in atmospheric moisture, constitute acid rain a constituent of air pollution.

Acid test ratio, also known as the *quick ratio*, is a financial ratio that illustrates the ability of a firm to meet its current debt at very short notice. It is calculated by dividing the sum of the cash and accounts receivable (current assets less inventory) by the current liabilities. A ratio equal to, or greater than 1.00 indicates a firm can readily repay its current debt. A value less than 1.00 indicates a firm would have difficulties. From the following data a company would have problems because the acid test ratio is only 0.80. ($200,000/250,000):

Cash, and cash equivalents	$75,000
Accounts receivable	$125,000
Current liabilities	$250,000

Acquisition strategy is a corporate strategy of buying other firms to expand its business volume, territory, or product mix. Companies which in the past have used an acquisition strategy include Groupe Schneider (France) which purchased Square D (USA) in 1992 to increase its presence in North America, Bank of America which purchased Security Pacific Bank (both of the USA) in 1991 to expand its business portfolio, and Ford (USA) which purchased Jaguar (UK) in 1991 to give it an automobile in the high price market.

Active strategy in aggregate planning is one that attempts to modify client demand in order to smooth out demand changes over the production planning period. Active strategies might include modifying demand by advertising, promotion, or price changes. For example, in France, electricity is cheaper between 10.30pm and 6.30am to encourage customers to use major appliances during this period. This is in an effort to smooth out electricity production and ultimately avoid additional capital expenditure. Another active strategy includes using backordering during heavy demand periods. Some companies that are heavily dependent on seasonal effects have an active strategy of developing a product mix of counter-seasonal items – lawn mowers in the summer, snow blowers in the winter or winter skiing equipment and summer mountaineering/backpacking items for example.

Activity in a project would be an identifiable, and well-defined task. For example, in the design and construction of an oil refinery, activities might include, design of the crude oil distillation column, the shipment of the water treatment unit, or the construction of the catalytic cracker. In house construction activities might include, the laying of foundations, frame construction, and electrical connections.

Activity-based costing is analyzing the cost of an operation at each processing step. In addition to measuring direct costs like materials, and labour, it covers rework, bottlenecks, delays, and other time-related activities. In this way, activity-based costing highlights areas of inefficiencies in an operation.

Activity chart is a tool used to analyze the activity of an operator and machine or a combination of a crew of operators with a park of machines with the objective to improve the utilization of man/machine.

Activity direct costs are those that can directly be assigned to a project. They might include labour costs, overtime premiums, hiring additional labour, leasing or purchasing construction equipment, or purchasing costs.

Activity on arrow in a *PERT* or *CPM* chart is a way for representing the various stages of a project, where arrows indicate activities and the direction of flow. The duration of the activity is shown on the arrow though the length of the arrow is not necessarily to the time of the activity. The nodes give the stage of the activity – either starting, or finishing. This is the most common form of representing a project network.

Activity on node in a *PERT* or *CPM* chart is where a node indicates an activity.

Activity ratios, or *asset ratios*, indicate how well an organization is selling its products, or services, in relationship to its available *assets*. The three main activity ratios are *inventory turnover* (sales/inventory), *fixed assets turnover* (sales/fixed assets), and *total assets turnover* (sales/total assets).

Activity scheduling chart is an alternative name for a *Gantt* or *bar chart*.

Activity time estimate is the estimated time to complete a project activity in a *PERT* or *CPM* network diagram.

Actuary is an individual employed by an insurance company who is experienced at computing risks and the size of life insurance premiums deemed appropriate to be issued by his company.

Ad hoc committees are composed of groups of people who are put together on an as needed basis for a specific purpose. Once that purpose has been resolved, ad hoc committees are disbanded, that is they have no permanency. Their function is similar to that of a *taskforce*.

Ad valorem duties are tariff duties on products based on some aspect of the value of the goods in question.

Adaptive smoothing is a type of *exponential smoothing* forecast where the smoothing constant is automatically adjusted to keep forecasting errors to a minimum.

Added-value tax is the amount of tax added to each phase of the production of a product, or part of a service to give an added value.

Addition rule in statistics is used to calculate the probability that one or the other of two events will happen. Events can either be mutually exclusive or not mutually exclusive. For example, if a die is thrown and produces a six, it is impossible to obtain a five in the same throw. Thus, the two events, obtaining a five, or a six, are mutually exclusive. Using the addition rule to calculate the probability (P) of obtaining a five or a six gives:

$$P(5 \text{ or } 6) = 1/6 + 1/6 = 2/3 = 66.7\%.$$

Adjustable capacity is the resource in operating a firm that is relatively easily changeable in the short term and so gives capacity flexibility. It includes labour, materials, tools, packing, and supplies. Resources such as plant and equipment which have high capital cost take time to install, and so are considered fixed in the short term.

Administered price is when a seller, often the producer of the product or service, establishes a sales price of a product at a predetermined level. This price may have no correlation with the cost of manufacturing, or providing, the product but may be a predetermined level based on similar competing products, or services. In this case, price is not a strong factor in the appeal for sales. Administered prices are also known as judgment pricing.

AFL-CIO is the biggest US labour movement formed by the merger of the American Federation of Labor and the Congress of Industrial Organizations in 1955.

Agency shop is a labour management agreement where workers who refuse to join the union representing the firm are expected to pay the union for the benefits derived through collective bargaining. In this condition of employment, non-union workers cannot be criticized for 'getting a free ride' even though they are not union members.

Agile manufacturing implies the ability to be flexible in a manufacturing operation when there is a high demand uncertainty on the part of clients.

Aggregate demand is the total client demand of a product, or service as opposed to the demand of the individual products.

Aggregate inventory is the total inventory maintained by a firm rather than specific quantities of the different materials and products that are contained in a storage area.

Aggregate planning is the development of a production plan to use available resources efficiently, such as labour, machines, and subcontractors in order to satisfy expected demand.

Airfreight is merchandise that is transported by air. It is the most expensive way to expedite goods and is usually reserved for perishable, or urgently required items.

Air pollution is caused by chemicals or solid particles in the air, principally from industry and transportation. In humans this leads to respiratory or other health problems, is destructive to plant and animal life, and corrosion on buildings and equipment.

Alpha risk, in statistics also known as a *Type I error*, is the risk of rejecting a null hypothesis, when it is, in fact, true.

American Production and Inventory Control Society (APICS), is a US-based professional organization associated with operations management activities.

Analogue computer carries out calculations by taking measurements of *continuous variables* such as temperature, pressure, or flow rates which are then translated into understandable mechanical or electrical values. Analogue devices are often used in the *process industries*.

Analysis of variance (ANOVA), is a technique useful in *statistical quality control*, enabling the testing of significance of the difference between two or more sample means.

Annual operating plan, developed from the firm's *strategic plan*, details the actions to be taken, the budget to be allocated, and a forecast of expected results.

Annual report is a document which, by law, is published every year by corporations or those whose shares are publicly traded. The report includes financial data of the corporation and also information covering the company's activities, personnel, achievements, environmental record, and perhaps future strategies.

Annuity is a series of payments, or receipts, of equal amounts, which usually occur at the end of a period. A life insurance policy when matured, or activated, can pay an annuity to the beneficiary a fixed sum of money each month, or each year.

Appointment book is a planning document often used in the service industry, for example, in medical centres as a master schedule for patient appointments. It is analogous to the master production schedule in manufacturing.

Apprentice system is where inexperienced workers are assigned to master craftsmen, or experienced workers, who supervise and monitor the apprentice's activity for a certain period. During this time it is expected the student will become knowledgeable of his trade, and at the end be able to obtain the appropriate apprentice certification.

Approved list is those suppliers that have been preselected by a purchasing authority. Preselection may have been based on such factors as price, reliability, service, or quality. When a supplier is selected from an approved list there is assurance that the supplier meets the organization's requirements.

Approved supplier is one providing raw materials, or parts, who is given preferential treatment in purchasing activities because the supplier scores high on price, quality, reliability, delivery, service, and stability of business.

Arbitration is negotiation and conflict resolution where an impartial third party is involved to hear and settle the dispute. This arbitrator decides the evidence that can be heard and how the dispute should be resolved. Binding arbitration is often used in labour disputes where both parties agree to abide by the decision of the arbitrator.

Area of feasibility in two-dimensional linear programming is the region bounded by the graphs and the axes containing feasible solutions to the linear programming model.

Arrival notice is an import document sent by the carrier and informs the customer of the estimated arrival date of the vessel and gives information regarding the nature of the goods.

Arrivals are the number of units or people arriving at a service area and forming a *waiting line* or *queue*. Knowledge of the pattern of arrivals, size, service time, and the like, is necessary in order to design the service centre handling the arrivals.

Artificial intelligence is an aspect of information technology and is broadly the use of computers to mimic or copy aspects of human intelligence such as learning languages, making decisions, and performing physical actions.

Assembly chart, also known as a *Gozinto chart* after the Italian mathematician, Zepartzat Gozinto, uses information from an *assembly drawing* to indicate how parts fit together, order of assembly, and perhaps the material flow pattern.

Assembly drawing is an exploded view of a product showing component parts, and where they are interconnected. It is used to facilitate the final assembly of the product.

Assembly line is a plant layout where a product is progressively assembled at successive work posts where components might be transferred from one work post to another on belt or roller conveyers, or overhead cranes. An assembly line is designed using *assembly line balancing*.

Assembly line balancing is the assignment of tasks, or activities on an *assembly line* operation so that each workstation is balanced with its immediate upstream and downstream post. The objective is to optimize the assembly operation avoiding bottlenecks, excessive accumulation of inventory, and minimizing employee idle time.

Assembly operation is that part of the manufacturing process where subassemblies, or the end product, are put together.

Assembly time chart is a planning document indicating when to order, or manufacture, component parts in order to meet scheduled completion dates for finished products. The assembly time chart is derived from the *material requirements plan*.

Asset ratios are a group of measurements that indicate the speed at which a firm is turning over, or utilizing its assets. The ratios include *inventory turnover*, *fixed asset turnover*, *total asset turnover*, and the average time it takes to collect *accounts receivable*.

Assets are all the tangible and non-tangible items that belong to an organization or an individual. They include *current assets* – cash, *accounts receivable*, and *inventory*; and fixed assets – land, machines, equipment and buildings. Goodwill, patents, and intellectual property are also assets.

Assignable variations in an operation are those that can usually be identified or assigned to a specific cause. They might be due to worn tools, badly adjusted equipment, defective materials, or human error.

Assignment method is a linear programming method which assigns jobs, or functions to resources such as machine operation, territories to specific representatives, or tasks to various employees. The objective is to match the task with the resource to optimize performance according to criteria such as cost, profit, efficiency, or rate.

Associative forecasts are estimates of future demands that rely on identification of related variables for prediction. Sales of a particular computer may be directly related to its price, or the price of a competing model, or to the capacity of the model. The essence of associative forecasting is to develop an equation, or model, to predict future demands.

Attribute inspection involves controlling according to the desired *attribute* rather than the degree of failure. The inspection of a light bulb would be attribute inspection as it either works or does not work.

Attributes are the classification of products where there are only binomial or two possible states such as it works or it does not work, good or bad, pass or fail, fits or doesn't fit. A watch works or it doesn't, a student passes an exam or he fails.

Authorized requisition is a purchase agreement where certain persons, or situations, allow its execution. The requisition may be authorized because the activity is below a certain budget, below a certain quota, or the purchasing manager may automatically have signature authorization.

Autocratic leader is a manager who makes most of the decisions himself rather than depending on a consensus opinion.

Automated guided vehicles (AGVs), are computer-controlled chariots often used in manufacturing to move parts and equipment between workstations or storage areas.

Automated storage and retrieval systems are computed-controlled systems in warehouses where inventory is automatically added or withdrawn and forklifts, bins, conveyers, and inventory records are managed by a central control system.

Automated teller machine (ATM), is a computer-controlled cash dispenser.

Automated warehouse is a storage facility managed and operated principally using computers, automatic equipment, robots, and conveyers rather than a lot of manual labour.

Automatic vending is the sale of products using automatic controlled machines rather than salespeople, for items such as food, beverages, newspapers, and stamps.

Automation is the manufacture of products, or the distribution of services, using computer-operated equipment rather than human labour. In the long term, automated production produces more uniform products, and unit costs are generally lower.

Autonomous production or assembly is when all work on a certain product is performed at a single workstation, rather than being processed at successive workstations. Artisans may be autonomous in producing wood furniture, for example.

Average forecasting models average or smooth past data in order to develop a forecast. The models might be *simple moving averaging* or *weighted moving averaging*.

Average inventory is the mean quantity maintained during a certain period and can be calculated by the simple arithmetic mean of the beginning and ending inventory.

Average outgoing quality (AOQ), is the percentage of defective items in an average lot size of products, which have been inspected through acceptance sampling.

B

Baan is a Netherlands-based company, founded in 1978, specializing in the development of computer-based *material resource planning* or *enterprise resource planning* tools.

Backlog is customer orders not yet shipped and may be expressed in units, or in financial terms. Backlog is usually encountered for custom, or produce-to-order goods.

Backorder is when an out of stock item has been re-ordered from the supplier but has not been delivered.

Backup systems are in place when the failure of the principal system would be of concern. The backup, or *parallel system*, cuts in if the principal system fails. Hospitals have backup electrical generators, and airplanes have backup control systems.

Backward integration is when a company purchases, or merges with another who is a supplier of its raw materials. This would be a strategy that helps to ensure a continued supply of those raw materials as in the case of a paper company purchasing forestry land.

Backward scheduling determines when to start production or to place purchase orders to meet client needs. Scheduling begins with the product due date and then subtracts the various lead times from this to determine when production or purchasing should begin.

Balance sheet is the financial statement that indicates what *assets* the organization or individual owns, and how these assets are financed in the form of liabilities or ownership interest.

Baldrige, Malcolm, was the US Secretary of Commerce under President Reagan from 1981 until his death in a rodeo accident in 1987. That year congress created an internationally recognized award entitled the Malcolm Baldridge Quality Award.

Baulking occurs in systems where *waiting lines* are present, such as at a bank or grocery checkout stands. Arriving customers see the length of the line and refuse to wait. They leave without ever becoming part of the waiting line.

Bar chart, also called a *Gantt chart*, indicates scheduling activities. Horizontal bars show the various activities, the start and finish times, with the length of the bar proportional to the time taken for execution of a particular activity.

Bar code scanner is used for reading the bar code stamped onto an article. The scanner is often integrated with a computer program to record inventory movements.

Bar coding uniquely identifies a product by a series of wide and narrow strips, or bars, stamped onto the product label. The bar code has incorporated symbols, letters, and numbers to identify a product, which can be identified by a *bar code scanner*. Bar coding is common in retail stores where the code incorporates the product price.

Bargaining is negotiating a work contract, such as for salaries or other conditions. If unions are involved, collective bargaining replaces individual bargaining where the union is the bargaining agent between company management and its members. In some cases, the union may be the agent for some or all of the non-union employees.

Base stock system is where inventory is replenished at a scheduled shipment date at the quantity equal to the actual usage for the previous period.

Batch processing is the manufacture or processing of products, or units, in bulk, or large lots. Examples would include the preparation of a batch of dye in the textile industry, printing a certain quantity of a book, or the seating of passengers according to a block of seat numbers in a Boeing-747.

BATNEEC principle, or the best available technology not entailing excessive cost, is the principle that if the costs of technology are reasonable and also would make a product more environmentally acceptable, then this should be the chosen production technology.

Bayesian decision theory is the concept of revising one's decision as more information related to that decision becomes available as, with more information, the probability of making the correct decision becomes more likely.

Behavioural approaches to management emphasize the understanding of people in increasing performance and productivity. The belief is that if managers understand their people, and adapt their organizations to them, company success usually follows.

Bell curve for projects is the profile of financial expenditures over time. The initial phase of a project is design and costs rise slowly being related just to personnel charges. When major equipment is purchased, earthwork and construction starts costs rise rapidly. Towards completion, costs decline being associated again with personnel such as operators, painters, and startup crews.

Benchmarking is rating a firm's products, processes, and policies with other companies in the same, or another business. The objective is to see how the company is performing, particularly relating to quality, service, and unit cost.

Bernoulli equation is an expression used to describe a *binomial distribution*. It was developed by experiments carried out by the 17th-century Swiss mathematician, Jacob Bernoulli. The tossing a coin a fixed number of times is a Bernoulli process.

Beta distribution, which has the properties of being entirely contained within a finite interval, is a probability distribution commonly used in *PERT* network diagrams. The mean and variance of the distribution can be determined by the estimated *optimistic*, *pessimistic*, and *most likely times*.

Bhopal is a site in India which suffered a catastrophic accident in 1984, as the result of the release of toxic methyl isocyanate gas in a pesticide facility owned by Union Carbide.

Bienayme-Chebyshev rule concerns the variability of data about the mean point. The rule says that regardless how a set of data is distributed, the percentage of observations contained within a distance of 2 standard deviations around the mean are at least 75.00%, at least 88.89% for 3 standard deviations, and at least 93.75% for 4 standard deviations.

Bill of labour is the labour requirements for producing an end item tangible product, or service specifying the labour specialization required, quantity, and hourly rate.

Bill of material is a listing of the parts, subassemblies, assemblies, and raw materials that go into making a finished product.

Bill of sale is a legal document, signed by the seller, giving evidence of the transfer of the title or ownership of a product, real estate, or other asset.

Bimodal is when there are two values in a data set that occur most frequently.

Binary code, the arithmetic of computers, is based on two digits, zero and one. A digit, either the 0 or the 1 in the binary code is called the *bit*, or binary digit. When a binary digit is moved one space to the left, and a zero is placed after it, the resulting number is twice the original number.

Binary digit is another term for a bit.

Binomial distribution is the probability distribution of discrete probabilities when there are only two possible outcomes for each trial of an experiment, such as yes or no, good or bad, open or closed.

Biodegradable materials are those which will break down under natural conditions to become harmless substances. Vegetable matter, and to some extent paper, are biodegradable.

Biodiversity refers to the earth's multitude of plant and animal species. Human activity, population growth, and economic progress contribute to the reduction of biodiversity.

Biotechnology is producing products through recombinant genetics, or gene splicing.

Bit, or *binary digit* is either the 0 or the 1 in the *binary code*.

Blacklist in labour circles it is a secret list of union organizers and members that is compiled by employers' associations and circulated among the members for the purpose of denying employment to the listed persons. It is regarded as an unfair labour practice under a ruling of the US National Labor Relations Board.

Blanket orders are used when a company has a continuous, but perhaps varying need for relatively low cost items. This purchase order usually covers a given time, and deliveries are arranged by sending a simple release notice to the supplier. Price and other specifications have previously been established in the principal blanket order contract.

Blister pack is transparent plastic packaging, made up of a matrix of air pockets, which gives added protection by preventing a transported product being directly in contact with the outside packing container. Blister packaging is not biodegradable.

Block models are a scale representation of a construction project, such as a chemical plant. These plastic blocks, built during the project's design stage, aid *facility layout*.

Blue-collar workers are those in a manufacturing environment who work in the factory.

Board of directors is that group of people ultimately responsible for directing the affairs of a corporation, elected typically for a three-year period.

Bonus payments are a form of incentive pay given by firms to employees in addition to normal wages. These bonuses are frequently paid on a yearly basis and may be related to length of service, and company profitability.

Bottleneck is when some equipment, facility, or other resource reduces the normal operating rate of a process, as it does not have the capacity to meet the upstream load.

Bottom round management is a consensus approach to management often employed in Japanese firms where all parties are involved in the decision making. It is also known as consensus management, committee management, or bottom up management.

Brainstorming is a process where a small group of people in the company, often from different departments, meet, and without any inhibitions or preconceived notions, put forward their ideas related to company issues, such as new products.

Breakeven is the point at which there is a balance between costs and revenues, or the point at which two or more operating centres exhibit equal costs.

Breaking the china expresses what occurs when a firm applies business process reengineering, starting all over again by being brave enough to ignore, or even destroy the process design activities that went on before.

Buffer stock is inventory kept to smooth out an irregular operation, or to avoid stockouts with clients. If there were uncertainty in the delivery of raw materials, a buffer stock may be held to avoid a possible shutdown of a production operation.

Building codes are rules, usually legally enforceable, on the conditions for construction of buildings, bridges, and the like. Codes differ from region to region and may be based on safety regulations, or aesthetic considerations.

Bulk products are those quoted, sold, or transported in significantly large quantities such as coal, wood, and plastic fibre.

Business cycle is the period of prosperity, or depression for business activity. In periods of economic prosperity, the volume of production, employment, company profits, and price rises. The reverse is true during depression. When the downward movement of the business cycle is short, the period is referred to as recession, rather than depression.

Business ethics is the standard of conduct for doing business. The standards of conduct vary for companies, countries, and people, which often create difficulties for firms involved in international business.

Business game is a simulation of an actual business activity, maybe computerized, and often used as an aid to teaching in universities, and business schools.

Business process reengineering is the means by which an organization may achieve radical change in performance as measured by cost, cycle time, service and quality by applying tools and techniques that focus on the business as a set of related customer-oriented core business processes rather than a set of organizational functions.

Business to business is the relationship between one firm and another firm in the supply chain before the final customer is reached. For example, Firm A supplying polypropylene pellets to a plastics manufacturer would be business to business. This would concern *intermediate products*.

Business to consumer is the relationship in the supply chain between the firm and the final consumer. An example would be the sale of a travel package to an individual, or the sale of an automobile from a dealer to a customer.

Buyer's expectation is a qualitative approach to sales forecasting by soliciting opinions from prospective buyers. It is more commonly used for *industrial goods*.

Buying is the purchasing of goods and services from external sources. Often buyers are specialized according to a commodity such as copper, steel, valves, ladies' clothing, floor coverings, or other unique items. This specialization allows buyers to become experts at purchasing their particular commodity.

C

C&F is the abbreviation for *cost and freight*.

C-chart is a control tool in *statistical process control* to monitor the number of defects found on a surface area, or unit such as on woven fabric, paper, the surface of an item of furniture, or the errors on a page of newsprint.

Cabotage is a European Union system which decides the conditions under which domestic road transport in one member state may be undertaken by a haulier registered in another member state.

Capacity is the ability of an operating system to handle a certain load.

Capacity-constrained resource is one whose utilization is very close to capacity such that bottlenecks could occur if work centre scheduling is not properly managed.

Capacity control is the management of a work centre such that equipment, people, and materials are being fully utilized, but not overloaded.

Capacity cushion is the amount of capacity of a resource in excess of its planned charge. If a work centre has a monthly production capacity of 12,000 units, and the planned charge is 10,000 units then the capacity cushion is (12,000 − 10,000)/10,000 or 20%.

Capacity planning is the management of resources, such as labour, equipment, and material typically over a medium-term planning horizon such as a few weeks to perhaps 18 months.

Capacity requirements planning is the management of resources such as labour, equipment, and material that tests the *master production schedule* to see if sufficient capacity is available for the operation.

Capacity utilization rate is the extent to which an organization uses its available capacity and given by the ratio, capacity used/design capacity.

Capital assets include equipment, buildings, fixtures, patents, and land.

Capital investment is the amount of funds used to purchase *capital assets*.

Carbon dioxide is an odourless, colourless gas under normal conditions, formed by the burning of hydrocarbon fuels and considered a contributor to the *greenhouse effect*.

Carload lots in train shipments are that quantity of material that completely fill a railroad car. In this way, the unit shipping costs are less than if the wagon were only partly full.

Carousel is an inventory storage or retrieval system that rotates in a horizontal plane. In manufacturing, carousels are used to move inventory from storage to the working area and in airport terminals to move passenger luggage from the airplane to the client.

Carrier's certificate and release order is an import document to advise customs of the details of the shipment, its ownership, port of loading, etc. This document is certification of the owner or consignee of the cargo.

Carrying costs are those associated with holding of inventory including borrowing costs for purchasing the stock, warehouse rent or depreciation, operating cost of the warehouse, inventory insurance, warehouse taxes, taxes on the inventory, losses due to theft, damage, or obsolescence, and labour costs concerned with storing and handling.

Cash budget is a series of monthly or quarterly schedules showing cash receipts, cash payments, and the borrowing requirements for meeting financial obligations. The cash budget is developed from the *pro-forma financial statement* and other supporting data.

Cash discounts allow a reduction in price of goods if payment is made within a specified period. A 2/10, net 30 cash discount means that the price is 2% less if payment is made within ten days after billing otherwise the full amount must be made within 30 days.

Cash flow statement is the presentation of the cash movement of an organization, which is the income, after taxes have been deducted, plus non-cash expenses, which in capital budgeting is usually the depreciation expense.

Causal forecasting incorporates into the forecast model factors which could influence the forecast. For kitchen appliances, the forecast could be a function of housing construction; car sales a function of interest rates; or housing a function of immigration.

Cause and effect chart is another name for a *fishbone chart* or *Ishikawa diagram*.

Cellular layout is the arrangement of a work centre such that many different operations can be performed on one product.

Cellular manufacturing is production using a *cellular layout*.

Central limit theorem in statistical sampling says that as the sample size increases there is a point when the sampling distribution of the mean can be approximated by the normal distribution, even though the distribution of the population is not necessarily normal.

Central tendency implies that most *data sets* cluster around a central point. The mean, median, mode, and midrange are measures of central tendency.

Centralized purchasing is the buying of goods and services from a common location rather than each individual user making his own purchases.

Centre of gravity method for site selection determines the central location at which total transportation costs to and from that site to other locations are minimized.

Centred moving average in forecasting is the average of data around a middle point.

Changeover time is the requirement to switch from one operation to another.

Chi-square test in statistics indicates whether the difference between several sample analyses is just due to chance, or there is a justifiable reason for the difference.

Chlorinated fluorocarbons (CFCs), and sometimes referred to as *freons*, are chemical compounds containing chlorine, fluorine and carbon. The chlorine in these is the constituent that damages the ozone in the upper atmosphere.

CIF is the abbreviation for *cost, insurance and freight*.

CIP is a shipping term similar to *OCP* meaning that the seller pays all transport insurance in addition to paying for the cost of freight and transport. Again, it is similar to CIF but is appropriate for modes of transport other than ships.

Clayton Act is a 1914 US law related to *purchasing*, extending the earlier *Sherman Act* covering price discrimination, tying clauses requiring the purchase of another item with the purchase of the desired item, and exclusive dealings.

Client is not just the end user, but also the immediate downstream work post.

Client is king is the philosophy that the client, or customer, must receive the best service and is always right. The idea being this is that in business the object is to serve the customer and if not there will be a problem. This concept is very dominant in the USA.

Client–server systems are where one computer acts as a central repository for files and programs (server) that can be shared by a number of personal computers (clients) connected by a network. This system replaces the mainframe centric arrangement.

Cloning is the creation of an animal or a person that derives its genes from a single other individual.

Closed-loop material requirements planning manage material movement, *production planning*, *master production scheduling*, and *capacity requirements planning*. An execution function covers *shop floor* control, scheduling, dispatching, and delay reports. Being closed loop provides feedback and control between the execution and planning.

Closed system is where machines, organizations, or programmes are not constrained or do not interact with the external environment. In the short run, a manufacturing assembly operation could be considered a closed system.

Cluster sampling is the division of the population into clusters and sampling one or more clusters. If London is targeted for analysis it could be divided into clusters using a city map and then an appropriate number of clusters selected for study.

Coefficient of correlation (r), in *regression analysis* explains the relative importance of the association between the independent variable, x, and the dependent variable, y. It can take a value between ±1 where −1 indicates a perfect negative relationship and +1 a perfect positive relationship. Zero would mean there is no relationship between x and y.

Coefficient of determination (r^2), measures the variation in the *dependent variable*, y, which is explained by the fitted simple *regression equation*. It is the square of the *coefficient of correlation* and thus always has a positive value.

Coefficient of variation is the relative analysis of the standard deviation of a distribution, σ, and its mean, μ, given by the ratio, σ/μ.

Coincident indicators, or simultaneous indicators, are ones in harmony with the associated economic activity such as GNP, unemployment rate, retail store sales, or index of industrial production.

Commercial invoice is an export document and is a bill for the goods from the seller to the buyer. It is often used by governments to determine the true value of goods for the assessment of customs duties and is used to prepare consular documents.

Completely knocked down (CKD), is a term used for companies that export their products in a disassembled, or kit form. In this way, products can be purchased at a lower price, shipping costs are less as the product can be packaged more precisely, and customs duties are lower as there is often a reduced tariff on components rather than finished goods.

Compound sum is the future value of a single amount of money, or an annuity, when compounded at a given interest rate for a specified time period.

Computer-aided design (CAD), is the use of computer software to aid engineers to design products, or process schemes using graphic and three-dimensional displays.

Computer-aided manufacturing (CAM), is the technology where, in manufacturing, CAD provides tooling departments with data and generates codes for numerically controlled machines. The two concepts are thus integrated resulting in CAD/CAM systems.

Computer-integrated manufacturing (CIM), is a flexible system connecting engineering, production, and inventory control where computers generate electronic codes to control numerically controlled machines and material handling equipment.

Concurrent engineering is the practice where design engineers work closely, or in parallel, with production people to ensure a product can be easily, and cost effectively manufactured avoiding costly design changes, and waste, at a later stage.

Consignee is the person, or firm, to which goods have to be shipped.

Consular invoice is an export document used to control and identify goods shipped to a country. It usually must be prepared on special forms and may require legalization by the country's consul.

Consumer price index, a measures of the inflation rate, or an indicator of the level of consumer prices, estimates how much it costs to buy a market basket of goods by urban middle-class families, in comparison to the purchase of the same goods a year earlier.

Consumer risk (β), is taking a random sample that shows a lower portion of defects in the sample than actually present in the lot. A lot of 10,000 units with 2000 defectives could produce a sample with no defects, in which case the lot would be accepted.

Consumer surveys are analyses of consumer wants and tastes often used by marketing departments to determine future product needs.

Contact–distance analysis is a *facility layout* method when there is contact with various functional departments. This approach is to adopt a department layout where the product of the total number of physical contacts and distance travelled is a minimum. The logic is similar to the *load–distance analysis* except that material flow is not involved.

Contingency table is a cross-classification of data in statistical analysis to determine if data exhibit a pattern and, if so, to determine the reasons.

Continuous flow manufacturing is the term used to describe *just-in-time* production.

Continuous improvement is always looking for ways to improve a process or product, but not necessarily making radical changes. The idea is that if the basic idea is sound, then building on this will improve quality. The Japanese refer to this as *kaizen*.

Continuous process is an operation having a very long and continuous cycle where output volumes are high, but the product variety is usually low. Oil refining is a continuous process operating continuously for, perhaps, 350 days a year. The product range is limited to propane or butane gas, gasoline, kerosene, diesel, and heavy oils.

Continous variables are those that do not have a well-defined cut off point and progress from one class to another. The volume of beer in a can is nominally 33 cl. but the actual value may be 33.7896, 32.5487 or 33.9857 cl.

Contribution margin is the financial contribution to fixed costs. It is given by the difference between sales revenues and total variable costs. Alternatively, on a unit basis, it is the sales price per unit minus variable costs per unit.

Control limits, in statistical quality control, are the upper and lower barriers of variables such as temperature and length outside which a process is considered to be malfunctioning.

Corporate towns are those which grew up, or were established, by a corporation which located in that area such as Bourneville, UK, established by Cadbury chocolate.

Cost and freight is a shipping-related term, meaning that it is the seller who must pay the costs and freight necessary to bring the goods to the named destination. However, the risk is transferred from the seller to the buyer when the goods pass the ship's rail in the port of shipment.

Cost–benefit analysis is a decision method showing whether expenditures for a project are greater, or less than, the financial benefits that would be ultimately realized. In the analysis, if the costs were less, then the decision would be to proceed. The reverse would be true if costs were greater than the benefits.

Cost insurance freight is *cost and freight*, but with the addition that the seller has to buy marine insurance against the risk of loss or damage to the goods during transport.

Cost of non-quality is that associated to items produced below specification and discovered internally, or externally, leading to a product recall.

Cost of quality is that to attain a certain quality level. It might include employee training programmes, systems development for quality improvement, pilot plants, costs related to the quality assurance, and those connected to detection and/or evaluation.

Counting rules are the mathematical relationships that describe the number of possible outcomes, or results, of various types of experiments, or trials.

Crisis management is a function often put in place by major corporations and governments, to respond to and to recover from a failure or accident usually on a large scale.

Critical path is the longest path in a project *network diagram*.

Critical path method (CPM) is a *network diagram* analysis technique, originally developed to schedule maintenance projects in chemical plants. The method is useful for projects which have many activities and where on-time completion is imperative.

Critical ratio, time to due date/remaining process time, is an *order sequencing* rule where the next job processed among those waiting is that with the lowest critical ratio.

Crosby, Philip B of the USA, is a quality management expert recognized for his 1979 book, *Quality is Free*, in which where he contends that any level of defects is too high and companies should have programmes that will lead them towards the goal of zero defects.

Cross–classification table is an alternative name for a *contingency table*.

Crossdocking is the practice when goods arrive at a warehouse, rather than being unloaded, logged in, broken down into smaller units, and reloaded onto a truck, they simply 'cross the dock' to be shipped out, thus minimizing labour costs of handling.

Cumulative frequency distribution is a tabular, or graphical display of data showing how many observations lie above, or below certain values.

Current assets are those items such as cash, *accounts receivable*, and *inventory* that can (except for cash) be converted into cash within one year.

Customer relationship management (CRM) is the development of all the tools and strategies necessary to have the maximum client relationships in terms of such elements as quality, cost, reliability and responsiveness.

Customer service level related to inventory is a measure of the probability with which a client can be supplied goods immediately from stock.

Customs entries are import forms required by countries of entering goods into that country. It provides information about the goods, their origin, and estimated customs duties.

Customs invoice is an import document usually prepared by the exporter or forwarder and used by customs to determine the value of the shipment.

Cutting fluid is a liquid used to cool and lubricate a work piece and tool in a machining. These fluids, which are difficult to purify, are potential pollutants.

Cycle time is the elapsed period between two successive operations, or when products come off a production line.

D

Data array is the arrangement of *raw data* in either ascending, or descending order.

Datamining is finding appropriate patterns in data so that business decisions can be improved. This might be in the modelling data for sales forecasting, finding patterns in data for solving criminal cases, detection of disease, transportation planning, etc.

Data set is a collection of data not necessarily in order.

Database is a set of records, perhaps computerized, containing specific information on such things such as clients, subcontractors, employees, inventory, etc.

Decentralized purchasing is where individual sites of the same firm make their own purchase decisions and transactions.

Deciles are special forms of *fractiles* that divide data into ten equal parts.

Decision environment is the conditions under which decisions are made.

Decision making under certainty is the situation knowing for certainty which of the possible future conditions will actually happen. In this case, decision making is straightforward: choosing the alternative with the highest payoff under that state of nature.

Decision making under risk implies probabilities of occurrence exist such as

60% the market conditions will be favourable, thus 40% they will not.

Decision making under uncertainty is when there is no clear information on the likelihood of the states of nature which may occur, or one is not able to assess probabilities for each possible outcome.

Decision tree is a pictorial representation of the possible outcomes, and alternatives in decision making. The tree has nodes and branches where a square node denotes a decision point, a circular node denotes an external chance event. The branches indicate the direction of the next decision point, state of nature, or outcome.

Deforestation is the massive destruction of forests for economic development. Trees are an inventory of oxygen, and absorb the *greenhouse gas*, carbon dioxide. Further, destroying trees reduces the ability of soil to absorb rain causing flooding, and erosion.

Degrees of freedom are the choices available for making a decision. In a two variables linear equation there is only one degree of freedom as, if one variable is given, the other is automatically fixed.

Delay is the time lag between starting and finishing an operation. In inventory management it is the elapsed time, or *lead time*, between making and receiving an order.

Delivered at frontier is a shipping term meaning that the seller's obligations are fulfilled when the goods have arrived at the frontier, but before the customer's borders of the country named in the sales contract.

Delivered duty paid, followed by words naming the buyer's premises, is a shipping term indicating the maximum obligation a seller can accept. The seller takes all risks and expenses in delivering the goods.

Delivery instructions is an export document which provides specific information to the inland carrier concerning the arrangement made by the forwarder to deliver the merchandise to a particular pier or steamship line.

Delivery order is an import order issued by the *consignee*, or his customs broker, to the ocean carrier as authority to release the cargo to the inland carrier. It includes all data necessary to ascertain that the cargo can be released.

Delphi method is for long-range forecasting, and was developed by the Rand Corporation of Santa Monica, California, USA. It was originally used to assess the potential impact of a nuclear bomb attack on the USA but since has had uses in forecasting. The method involves three key groups: decision makers, staff, and the respondents.

Demand during lead time is the quantity of a product demanded during *lead time*. This amount demanded is critical because it is when inventory levels are low, and an unexpected surge in demand might result in stockouts.

Demand management is the correct interpretation regarding the timing and quantity of orders slotted into the MPS. It may also involve price adjustments when sales are slow or the inventory of finished goods is increasing.

Deming, W Edwards, who died in 1994, was a quality guru known for his 14 criteria for quality improvement. By training he was a statistician, and a professor at New York University, as well a consultant. He worked with Japanese industries so successfully that the Japanese established the annual Deming Prize for innovation in quality management.

Dependent inventory is material whose quantity demanded is a function of a finished product such as the number of wheels demanded for an automobile is five.

Dependent variable is one that is related, or dependent on another sometimes an *independent* variable. For example, the sugar content of grapes is dependent on the number of days of sunshine; hotel revenues in the summer are dependent on the amount of disposable income; or the consumption of certain goods and services is dependent on price.

Descriptive statistics is the collection, and analysis of a *data set* in order to describe that set of data and not the *population* from which the data were drawn.

Design review is a formal, documented, comprehensive, and systematic examination of a design to evaluate the design requirements, its capability to meet these requirements, and to identify problems and thence to propose appropriate solutions.

Discrete data are normally obtained from the counting process and which do not progress from one class to the next without a break.

Discrete distribution is a probability distribution of *discrete data* such as the *binomial* or *Poisson* distribution.

Dispersion is a measure of the spread of data such as given by the *range*, or *standard deviation*.

Distribution requirements planning (DRP), is the planning step in the supply chain to move finished goods from the production or storage source to the client. The DRP is very often a computerized module in an overall *enterprise resource planning* system.

Dock receipt is an export document used to transfer accountability between domestic and international carriers at the ocean terminal. It is the document prepared by the shipper or forwarder, which the ocean carrier signs and returns to the delivering inland carrier, acknowledging receipt of the cargo.

Double sampling plan is where two samples may be taken from a lot and there is an upper and lower defective limit. If in the first sample defective units are below the lower limit the lot is accepted, and rejected if above the upper limit. If the results are between the two limits a second sample is withdrawn, and tested, combining the results from both samples.

Drucker, Peter, a specialist in human relations, wrote extensively on employee motivation and the role of management in organizations. He was responsible for establishing the idea of *management by objectives*.

Dummy activity is a fictitious activity included in a *network diagram* to indicate a precedence relationship, although for this activity no time span is involved.

E

Earliest due date in *order sequencing* is when the next job to be processed among those waiting is that which has the next earliest date at which the job is promised to a client.

Earliest finish in network diagrams for *project management* is the earliest date by which an activity can be completed.

Earliest start in network diagrams for *project management* is the earliest date by which an activity can begin.

Eco-labelling is affixing a label to a product, or its packaging, to indicate the product is environmentally acceptable. For the producer this helps to enhance the sale of its product and to a consumer it gives some assurance that the product is less environmentally damaging.

Economic order quantity (EOQ), in inventory management, is the amount of material to order which has the least overall cost taking into account inventory carrying costs, inventory ordering costs, and stockout costs.

Economies of scale is the concept that as a production facility increases in size, the average production costs per unit fall, because each new unit absorbs part of the fixed cost of the plant implying that larger firms would be more efficient than smaller ones.

Effective capacity is another expression for *capacity utilization rate*.

Efficiency in operations is another way of expressing *productivity*.

Elastic product is one whose quantity demanded changes markedly with price, such as expensive goods like perfume, certain wines, or expensive cars.

Elasticity of demand refers to the change in the quantity of a product demanded relative to its price. Products might be classified as *elastic*, or *inelastic*.

Electronic data interchange (EDI), is communication using computer networks employing fibre optic cables, or other relay sources.

Emergency maintenance involves repairs when a facility unexpectedly breaks down.

Emission is the discharge of materials that may pose an environmental hazard.

Employee benefits include health insurance, retirement, vacation and the like which have to be added to employee wages to determine the total labour costs.

Empowerment is an extension of *job enrichment*, giving complete employee trust, and responsibilities not originally associated with the job.

End item is the finished unit in an operating function.

Enterprise resource planning (ERP) is the extension of MRP-II systems to the management of the complete business function.

Entitlement is a legal obligation for governments to pay certain benefits to employees such as healthcare, retirement, or unemployment. They are a reason why balancing the budget is difficult since entitlements have to be paid regardless of tax revenues collected and, demographically, the proportion of retirees to active employees is increasing.

Environmental auditing is a management tool comprising a systematic, documented, periodic and objective evaluation of how well environmental organization, management and equipment are performing with the aim of helping to safeguard the environment.

Environmental balance implies balancing economic or production output with safeguarding the environment by minimizing pollution.

Environmental Protection Agency (EPA), is the USA government environmental watchdog.

Environmentally friendly product is one that is designed, produced, or used in such a manner that it minimizes the adverse impact on the environment.

Equally likely is a decision-making process under uncertainty where the arithmetic average of all possible outcomes is considered.

Ergonomics is balancing the work of the employee with the machine or the task at hand in order to minimize human effort and to make the work as comfortable as possible.

Ethics in buying refers to situations in which buyers may feel obligated to salespersons who have given them gifts and thus may not act in the best interest of their own organization.

European Telecommunications Standards Institute (ETSI) is the organization that sets the standards in telecommunications in Europe. ETSI took a lead role in the development of *GSM* telephone standards.

Event is an activity often used in statistical experiments. For example, the tossing of a coin, to see whether it falls heads or tails, is an event.

Ex-quay is a shipping term where the seller makes the goods available to the buyer on the quay at the destination named in the sales contract. It is the seller who bears the full cost and risk of getting the goods to that point.

Ex-ship is a shipping term where the seller makes the goods available to the buyer to the destination named in the sales contract. It is the seller who bears the full cost and risk of getting the goods to that point.

Ex-works is a shipping term where the only responsibility of the seller responsibility is to make the goods available at his premises. It is the buyer who bears the full cost and risk involved in moving the goods from the seller's location to their final destination.

Expected demand during lead time (EDDLT), is the mean value of inventory consumed during the time between when a new order is placed and its being delivered.

Expected value is the weighted average of all possible outcomes.

Expected value of perfect information (EVPI), is the difference between the *expected value under certainty* and the *expected value under risk*.

Expected value under certainty is the weighted average of the probability of best payoff for each alternative.

Expected value under risk is the weighted average using the probabilities of all the possible outcomes.

Expediting is the delivery of a product under an urgent situation.

Experience curve is another name for the *learning curve*.

Expert systems are knowledge-based systems that emulate expert thinking, or human logic, to solve complex problems in a particular domain, such as the design of a process network.

Explained variation is the variation in the regression equation relating y to x.

Exponential smoothing in forecasting uses a single smoothing factor, alpha, to forecast the next period's activity where alpha takes on a value between 0 and 1.

Export declaration is an export form required for controlling exports and acts as a source document for export statistics and includes complete particulars of the shipment.

External faults in quality control are those that occur when a product has left the production site and is in the hands of the consumer.

F

Facility layout is the arrangement of machines, workstations, storage areas, etc., to enable an operation to function efficiently, safely, and in a cost-effective manner.

Facility location is the site selection for a manufacturing facility, retail store, warehouse, office or other facility to optimize the supply chain of that organization.

Failure is when a product or service ceases to function according to requirements.

Failure mode effect and criticality analysis (FMECA), developed originally for military equipment, is the detailed study of a product design, manufacturing operation, or distribution network to determine which features are critical to various modes of failure.

FAS is the abbreviation for *free alongside ship*.

Feasibility studies are detailed analyses of a product design, process or other system to see if it is reasonable in terms of design, operating capability, acceptability, and cost.

Feasible region in linear programming is the area in which all the constraints and objectives are met.

Federal Communications Commission (FCC) is an independent US government agency, responsible directly to Congress. The FCC was established by the Communications Act of 1934 and is charged with regulating interstate and international communications by radio, television, wire, satellite and cable. The FCC's jurisdiction covers the 50 states, the District of Columbia, and US possessions.

Feigenbaum, Armond V, a proponent of quality management, in 1983 published a book called *Total Quality Control* in which he emphasized that the responsibility for quality has to rest with the people who perform the associated work, or *quality at the source*.

Financial accounting is the financial analysis of a firm with the objective of providing information to those external to the firm. Financial accounting usually applies to the whole firm. The annual report gives the financial accounts of a firm. (As a comparison see *management accounting*.)

Finite population is a collection of data that have a stated or limited size.

First come, first served is an *order-sequencing* rule in which the next job to be processed among the jobs waiting is the one that arrived first.

First in, first out (FIFO), in inventory accounting, is where the first items acquired are charged against sales. As these probably will have cost less than the last items, the income statement will indicate a higher gross profit. However, this method causes the value of the inventory remaining to be higher.

Fishbone chart, another name for an *Ishikawa diagram*, or *cause and effect* chart, is referred to in this way, as it resembles the skeleton of a fish.

Fixed assets turnover is a financial measure of the ratio of sales to fixed assets (plant and equipment).

Fixed capacity refers to systems that have little flexibility to increase capacity. Cinemas, restaurants, or airplanes have fixed capacity limited by seat availability.

Fixed costs are derived from *capital assets* usually in the form of depreciation. These costs are charged to operations and are thus independent of the level of production.

Fixed order interval in inventory planning means that new orders of inventory are made at regular intervals, such as every two days, every week, etc.

Fixed order period model for inventory is based on ordering at *fixed order intervals*. The quantity ordered is determined from the amount remaining so that with a new order, the inventory

in storage is brought up to some pre-established level. The quantity ordered each time is usually not the same since consumption between each order period varies.

Fixed order quantity model for inventory is based on the criterion that the same quantity is ordered each time material is requisitioned. Orders would be placed when the inventory in storage falls to a certain pre-established minimum level.

Fixed position layout is an arrangement of a work centre where the product being produced, because of its weight, size, or character, such as a bridge or cargo vessel, does not move. The workers, machines, and tool areas rotate around the stationary product.

Flexi time is when employees have variable hours regarding starting and finishing, although normally they have to be present during a certain core period of the day.

Flexible manufacturing systems are clusters of computer-controlled machines that produce a variety of products. The computers give instructions, robots handle materials, and machine settings are automatically changed to produce the different products.

FOB is the abbreviation for *free on board* applying to transportation by a seagoing vessel.

FOB airport is the abbreviation for *free on board* but applies to transportation by airplane.

Focused factory is one that is dedicated to one, or a few types of product.

FOR is the abbreviation for *free on board rail*.

Ford, Henry, developed one of the first major assembly line operations in the USA in 1913 for the manufacture of the Ford Model T automobile.

Forecast error is the difference between actual data and that estimated from the forecast.

Forecast horizon is the time span of the forecast where the longer the span, the more unreliable the estimates.

Forecasting is estimating future outcomes using statistical data or a qualitative approach.

FOT is the abbreviation for *free on board truck*.

Fractile is a division of data into well-defined parts, such that a given fraction, or proportion, of the data lie at, or below, a fractile. The *median* is the 50% fractile, or the 50th *percentile*, because half the data are less or equal to this value.

Fraction defective in a lot is that proportion of products that do not conform.

Free alongside ship is a shipping term where the obligation of the seller is fulfilled when the goods have been placed alongside the ship in lighters (barges used for loading or unloading). In this case the buyer bears all costs and risks of loss or damage after this activity has been fulfilled. Unlike FOB, FAS means that it is the buyer's responsibility to clear the goods for export.

Free carrier is a shipping term which meets the requirements of multimodal transport, such as containers, or roll on roll off traffic by trailers and lorries. It is based on the same main principle as FOB and the seller's obligation are fulfilled when the goods are delivered to the carrier at a named point.

Free on board is the abbreviation *FOB* and is the same as *free on board price* meaning included in the price of the goods are the costs paid by the seller, including transportation, insurance, and handling to place them on board a ship at a port of shipment named in the sales contract. The risk of loss or damage to the goods is transferred from the seller to the buyer when the goods pass the ship's rails.

Free on board airport is similar to the ordinary *FOB* term but applies to goods sent by air.

Free on board price is an alternative to *free on board*.

Free on rail is the abbreviation *FOR* and is similar to the ordinary *FOB* but applies to rail transport.

Free on truck is the abbreviation *FOT* and is similar to the ordinary *FOB* but applies to transport by truck (lorry).

Freight release is an import document and is evidence that the freight charges for the cargo have been paid.

Freons are a generic group of fluorinated hydrocarbons used as refrigerants, propellants, blowing agents, fire extinguishing agents, cleaning fluids and solvents. Their release into the atmosphere is considered to increase the destruction of the *ozone layer*.

Frequency distribution is a table or graph in which data are arranged into unique class groupings that are more manageable than *raw data* and demonstrate easily recognizable trends.

Frequency polygon is a line graph of a *frequency distribution*.

Functional layout is the organization of a work centre according to specialty, such as a manufacturing firm organized according to cutting, grinding, drilling, and assembly.

Fuzzy logic deals with approximate values, influences, or ambiguous data to make decisions. Chefs with years of experience know when to add ingredients in order to make meals taste good, although their logic for modifications may be ill defined.

G

Gantt chart, after *Henry L Gantt* is a horizontal bar chart, used in operations or project scheduling. It shows when activities need to be completed and their start and finish times.

Gantt, Henry L, an American engineer (1861–1919), was interested in both the human and scientific approach to management. His perception of managers was that they were slave-drivers forcing workers to do jobs in which they had little interest, under poor conditions. On the scientific side he was responsible for developing the *Gantt chart* for scheduling.

Gaussian distribution, after Karl Gauss, is an alternative name for the *normal distribution*.

Geometric mean is a measure of *central tendency*, used for data that change over time, such as the growth of investments, inflation rate, or the GNP. Over a period of n years, the geometric mean is given by the relationship $\sqrt[n]{\text{Product of growth rules}}$.

Global system for mobile (GSM) is the de facto global standard for mobile phones. As of early 2000 the standard had not been adopted either by the USA or Japan.

Gilbreth, Frank and Lilian, were the USA husband and wife team who analyzed operations management as a science in the period 1900–1910. Their primary research tool was motion studies in order to reduce a job to its most basic movements and was used to establish performance standards, and to eliminate unnecessary physical movements.

Gozinto chart is another name for an *assembly chart*.

Grade is an indicator of category, or rank, applied to products, processes, or services that are intended for the same functional use, but for an otherwise different set of needs. Hotels and restaurants have grades, as do clothing and work tools like sandpaper.

Grassroots is a term used in *project management* for a project that is built from scratch on virgin land or 'grassroots'.

Graveyard shift is one that starts around midnight and finishes around 8am.

Green product is one that is considered environmentally friendly or at least one less damaging to the environment that perhaps a product that has similar uses.

Greenhouse effect is the accumulation of gases, principally carbon dioxide, in the upper atmosphere preventing heat to escape thus causing the earth's temperature to increase.

Gross national product (GNP), is the total value of goods and services usually during one year, and used as an economic indicator as a measure of the well-being of a country.

Group technology identifies components by a code that specifies the type of processing, such as milling, and the parameters of processing such as shape. Machines then process families of parts as a group minimizing setups, materials handling, and routing.

Growth stage refers to the period when a new product has been introduced onto the market and is growing in acceptance by consumers and expanding in market share.

H

Halons are gaseous chlorine, and bromine compounds which, when emitted alone, or combined with other chemicals, attack and destroy the upper atmosphere ozone layer.

Hard copy is a printed version on paper of computer-based information.

Hardware is the physical equipment used in information technology such as the computers, printers, terminals, scanners, etc.

Hawthorne Studies, by Elton Mayo and others, between 1927–1932 at the US Western Electric plant, studied human relations in the work environment. They look at the effect of lighting on productivity and the human side. They concluded that the role of individuals was more important to productivity than physical elements such as lighting.

Herzberg, Frederick, on human motivation at work in the 1960s, concluded there were two different types of variable that influenced people. One was hygiene, or maintenance factors that impacted job dissatisfaction and related to the work environment. The other included motivating factors that affected job satisfaction and was connected to the work itself.

Heuristic methods, from the Greek 'heuris' 'I have found', are those methods that provide a plausible solution to a problem, but may not necessarily be optimum. They can be based on mathematical algorithms, practical approaches, or sometimes 'seat of the pants' analysis. Heuristic methods may not be optimum but they work.

Hierarchy of needs are those five human desires developed by *Abraham Maslow* and from first to last include physiological, security, social, esteem, and self-actualization.

Histogram is a graph of a *data set*, of rectangles where each is proportional in width to the range of values in a class, and proportional in height to the number, or fraction of items falling in the class. A histogram may represent a *frequency distribution*.

Holdback provision is a proportion, or amount of money not paid to a supplier of services until there is assurance that the work performs according to specifications.

Horizontal integration is fusion of firms that have similar products, and compete in the same markets. Integration may give the combined organization bigger market clout.

Hoshin is the Japanese idea of searching for simple practical solutions for improving an operation by working at the shop floor level with operators familiar with the work.

Hoteling is an open plan office at its very extreme where private offices are eliminated to provide temporary space for employees, such as consultants, only when they are in town. This saves money on rent and gets employees out spending more time with customers.

House of quality is another name for *quality function deployment*.

Human resource management is the management of all personnel in an organization including work assignments, salaries, promotion, training, etc.

Hydrocarbons contain the atoms of carbon and hydrogen and are a natural product of plantlife. They are also a constituent of gasoline and thus one of the components in automobile exhaust *emissions*. By the action of sunlight, hydrocarbons react with other substances causing smog, an environmental concern in large cities.

Hypermarkets are those retail stores with a very large surface area that sell just about everything from food, clothing, appliances, books, garden tools, plants, furniture, etc.

Hypertext markup language (HTML) is the standard for the Internet that formats documents and pictures and links them in the same computer or remote installations.

Hypothesis testing is when decisions are made about population characteristics based only on information from a sample. A hypothesis is called the null hypothesis for which there will always be an alternative hypothesis.

I

IBM compatible is a personal computer (PC) whose programs like DOS and Windows can be used interchangeably with an IBM machine.

Income statement indicates the profitability (or loss) of an organization over a period of time. All costs and expenses are subtracted from sales to arrive at the net income.

Independent inventory is one whose quantity demanded is not a function of other units and is most often finished products. A bicycle would be independent inventory and the wheels *dependent inventory*. Spares also constitute independent inventory.

Independent variable in forecasting is the one that has no direct relationship to the one being estimated and graphically it is always plotted on the *x axis*.

Industrial goods are those manufactured by one firm destined to another firm such as engine parts. They are sometimes referred to as intermediary goods.

Industrial park is a zone established often outside a town, purely for industrial firms.

Industrial Revolution, 1733–1878, is considered to have heralded the beginning of technological inventions and industrial growth. It started with the invention of the flying shuttle for weaving textiles by John Kay of Britain in 1733.

Inelastic product is one whose quantity sold does not vary much with price. Usually, they are basic products such as milk, cheese, and margarine.

Infant mortality is the early stages of product life where components are fragile as they have not been 'run in', or operators are not familiar with equipment and because of bad use it breaks down. The term relates to infants who are fragile at this point in their life.

Inferential statistics is the estimation of the *population* characteristics based on sampling. The population characteristic such as weight is inferred from the sample.

Infinite population is one whose size is so large that, for analytical purposes, taking a sample from the population does not change the characteristics of that population.

Information systems are the network and architecture for communicating including databases, computer links with purchasing, manufacturing, distribution, and with clients.

Infrastructure for a project is all the support facilities enabling a project to operate. The infrastructure for an airport would include parking, restaurants, access roads, etc.

Inspection in *quality control* covers measuring, examining, testing, or gauging the characteristics of a product, process, or service, and comparing these with specifications.

Institute of Industrial Engineers is a US-based professional group.

Insurance certificate is an export document and assures the *consignee* that insurance is provided to cover loss or damage to the cargo while in transit.

Interfractile range measures the spread between two fractiles in a *data set*.

Intermediate products, sometimes called *industrial goods*, are tangible items that are sold to other companies in a business-to-business transaction and then converted into other products. Polypropylene granules produced by a chemical company would be an intermediate product used in the manufacture of plastic products by another firm.

Internal faults are those occurring before the product or service has left the facility.

International Organization for Standardization (ISO), is a Swiss-based non-governmental group founded in 1947, with a goal of decreasing trade barriers by promoting worldwide product standardization. *ISO-9000* series for quality and *ISO-14000* for the environment are two.

International Telecommunications Union, ITU, is the organization that studies telecommunications at an international level.

Internet, the **Inter**connection of **net**works, is a sophisticated form of *electronic data interchange* where one is able to communicate by a worldwide network on literally thousands of topics.

Interquartile range is a measure of dispersion and the difference between the third and the first *quartile* in a data set. The *midspread* is another name for interquartile range.

Inventory is material consumed during the normal course of business including raw materials, *work-in-process*, finished goods, packing, spares, supplies, and small tools.

Inventory carrying costs is an alternative for *carrying costs*.

Inventory management involves keeping inventory costs to a minimum, but at the same time providing the most economic service level to clients and to the production centre.

Inventory models are mathematical expressions used to describe the movement of inventory.

Inventory ordering costs are those associated with obtaining inventory-like salaries of purchasing staff, communication costs, receiving, handling and inspection costs. For inventory produced by the same company the costs include preparation of production orders, preparation of materials and tools, and setup of machines.

Inventory records file is a *database* of information about the status of inventory.

Inventory stockout costs occur by having insufficient inventory to satisfy demand, and may include loss of revenues, loss of clients, and expediting to make up for the stockout.

Inventory turnover is a measure of how a firm uses its inventory. The greater the inventory turnover, the more efficient the operation, and the lower inventory carrying cost. It is calculated by the ratio cost of goods sold/value of inventory.

Irregular components in a time series analysis refer to changes that are the result of infrequent activities such as machine failure, truck strike, and absence in the workforce.

Ishikawa diagram, named after its inventor, is a tool used to determine the causes of quality-related problems. It is also known as a *cause and effect diagram* or a *fishbone analysis*.

ISO-14000 is the international standard covering environmental concerns.

ISO-9000 is the international series covering quality standards. The basic standard is ISO-9001:2000.

J

Jidoka is the Japanese word that means to stop everything if something has gone wrong.

Job enlargement avoids an employee being trapped in *job specialization* by improving the variety within a certain

sphere of a person's ability, and interest. Adding shaping and forming which would constitute horizontal expansion of the job could enlarge a cutting operation.

Job enrichment is expanding the job vertically such as by adding design and planning elements. A purchasing secretary whose basic job is the correspondence for the department could have the job enriched by planning work assignments, being an intermediary in customer contacts, and maybe helping in proposal evaluation.

Job lot is a batch of parts or units that have been produced together.

Job rotation is moving from one activity to another to add interest and avoid boredom.

Job shop is a *functional organization* where departments are organized around special equipment or operations such as cutting, drilling, milling, or heat treatment in manufacturing. Products flow through departments in batches often corresponding to individual orders as stock for inventory or for specific customer orders.

Job specialization relates to the knowledge and training in just one particular job activity, such as mining or typing.

Johnson's rule is a method for scheduling jobs through two, or in special circumstances three, work centres giving an order sequence that minimizes the total processing time.

Joint probability is when two or more independent events occur together, or in succession, and is calculated by the product of the individual marginal probabilities.

Joint venture is when two or more firms work together on a project to minimize the individual risk, pool financial or other resources, or perhaps for governmental reasons.

Juran, Joseph M, in the 1970s and 1980s was another pioneer in helping the Japanese to improve product quality. Like *Deming* he believed in top management commitment, and involvement in quality and also in teamwork continually to strive to raise standards.

Jury of executive opinion is consolidating the opinions of top management or executives in order to develop a forecast of future activity for the firm.

Just-in-time (JIT), is a management practice where the exact quantities of a product are produced, purchased, or delivered only when needed. Delays and inventory levels are kept to an absolute minimum, the philosophy being that unnecessary inventories, or delays, are inefficient use of resources. Practising JIT enforces adherence to quality.

K

Kaizen is the Japanese word meaning *continuous improvement*.

Kanban, from the Japanese meaning card or ticket, refers to the technique for managing the flow of materials principally in manufacturing. Kanbans are used to communicate the needs for parts from one work centre to another, replacing written work orders. The card 'pulls' the needed parts from the upstream supply post to the downstream client post.

Kanban square is an area marked out on the floor, or bench, which represents the storage area for a specified referenced component part. A supplying workstation has authority to furnish more parts only if there is space available in this kanban square.

Karmarkar's algorithm is a mathematical expression in linear programming.

Keiretsu is the Japanese approach for firms to integrate suppliers and/or subcontractors into their supplier chain. These firms provide financial support to the suppliers and/or subcontractors by providing loans or perhaps part-ownership. The subcontractor and/or supplier then become part of the firm's coalition known as a keiretsu. Participating subcontractors or suppliers are assured long-term relationships with the firm and in turn are expected to provide technical assistance coupled to a reliable and quality service. Keiretsu is an alternative to complete *vertical integration*.

KISS principle meaning, keep it simple, stupid implies the less sophisticated a product or service, the less likely there will be quality problems.

Kurtosis is the characteristic of the peak, of a frequency distribution curve. Distributions may have the same mean, but different standard distributions that changes the sharpness of the peak. Three classifications are *leptokurtic, platykurtic,* or *mesokurtic*.

L

Labour is the human resources of a firm and includes current employees, new hires, workers on recall, part-time employees, and overtime labour.

Labour costs are those associated with employing human resources including basic salary or wages plus social and other charges paid to the employee, or paid by the employer for the employee. Social charges include medical insurance, social security, paid vacations, retirement benefits, unemployment benefits, and paid education.

Labour organizations are unions that represent the workers in a firm.

Labour standard is the basic hours needed to carry out a task and this standard is often used both to plan and price a job.

Labour turnover is a measure of the change of employment in a firm where a repeat high level is probability associated with motivational factors.

Lagging indicators in the economy are those that reach a high, or low, after the economic activity has occurred such as labour cost per unit of production, commercial and industrial loans, and book value of inventories.

Laser scanner is the instrument used to read *bar code* charts.

Last in, first out (LIFO), is an inventory policy where the last items of inventory acquired are charged against sales. As these normally cost more than earlier items, the cost of goods sold will be high indicating a lower profit on the *income statement*. And the value of inventory remaining will be accounted at a relatively low value.

Layout refers to *facility layout*.

Lead time is an alternative for *delay*.

Leading indicators are those that reach a high, or a low, before a related economic activity and thus are useful in forecasting. Construction contracts, equipment orders, new business incorporation, capital appropriation, and manufacturing orders are examples.

Lean production means having the most efficient operation possible, avoiding waste, and giving employees maximum responsibility.

Learning curve, or *experience curve*, shows labour hours against the quantity of products produced. It decreases exponentially meaning that when starting with a new operation, as the number of units produced increase, hours/unit decrease as an operator becomes familiar with the task.

Least changeover cost is an *order-sequencing rule* where the next job processed among those waiting is the one that involves the least machine setup cost. Some jobs are better suited to this sequencing operation because of the similarities of machine settings.

Least slack rule is an *order-sequencing rule* where the next job processed among those waiting is the one where the difference between due date and operating time is the least.

Least squares method is for determining the best straight line from a set of data. The method minimizes the error between the estimated points from the calculated line, and the actual observed points used to draw the line.

Leptokurtic is a measure of *kurtosis* in a frequency distribution curve meaning the peak is sharp, so data dispersion is small, or the standard deviation is low (lepto = slender).

Letter of credit is a financial document, for exporting goods, issued by a bank at the request of the consignee guaranteeing payment to the shipper of the cargo.

Level of analysis refers to the depth of decision making and might range from intuitive analysis, quick-and-dirty, computations, to model building, or project teams.

Level production is the production of goods, or services, at a relatively constant output from period to period thus simplifying planning and perhaps minimizing costs.

Lifecycle analysis is the evaluation of the life of a product from conception, through design, production, distribution, use, and disposal at the end of its useful life. The objective is to manage so that environmental damage from the product is minimal.

Line balancing is a *facility layout* procedure that determines which tasks each employee will perform and how they are grouped at workstations to optimize the system.

Line function is one that has direct responsibility over operations.

Linear programming is a mathematical technique for optimization.

Linear regression is the development of a straight line relationship between a dependent variable, for which future values need to be forecast, and another independent variable.

Load–distance analysis is a facility layout procedure used to identify the one with the least product or material travel per time period.

Long cost is the cost of stocking one inventory unit that is not demanded, meaning the unit is in inventory but there is no client need. This cost is associated with carrying costs, handling, and other expenses involved in carrying a unit from one period to another.

Longest processing time is an *order-sequencing rule* where the next job processed among those waiting is the one that has the greatest processing time.

Lot is the label given to a discrete quantity of tangible goods that have been produced under similar operating conditions such as on the same machine; in the same time period; using the same operators; during the same shift; using raw material from the same supply batch; under the same process conditions, etc. In this way the units in the lot should have similar characteristics.

Lot sizing is determining the optimum quantity of units to make or purchase.

Lot tolerance percent defective (LTPD), in *statistical quality control* is the level of quality considered unacceptable, or bad, such that a lot should be rejected.

Lot for lot means producing or purchasing exactly that quantity of material that is required by the client, or the downstream work post.

Love Canal is an abandoned canal along the Niagara River, in New York State, into which between 1942 and 1953, Hooker Chemical and Plastics dumped tons of toxic chemicals. This material contaminated a housing zone constructed later, resulting in a major environmental disaster costing the US government millions of dollars.

Low-level coding in a bill of materials is coding an item at the lowest level at which it appears.

M

Macroeconomic factors include GNP, interest rates, inflation rates all of which can impact the forecast of future sales and business activity.

Make or buy is the decision whether to buy a component or to make the part. Sometimes firms can make parts for less, at better quality, faster delivery, than purchasing. Generally for small or specialized orders, it is more cost effective to purchase. A *breakeven analysis* is useful for deciding whether to make or buy a product.

Management accounting is financial analysis of the operations of a firm enabling persons within that firm to make responsible decisions concerning costs and productivity. It may be applied just to one segment of the firm. (As a comparison see *financial accounting*.)

Management by objectives, the concept of *Peter Drucker*, is where employees mutually agree to goals that they attempt to achieve in a reasonable time. Performance reviews are conducted periodically to see how near the individual is to achieving these objectives and rewards are given on the basis of how close they are to reaching their objectives.

Manufacturing resource planning (MRP-II), is the expansion of *materials requirement planning* to include other functions such as marketing, finance, engineering, distribution, and human resource planning. Commercially, MRP-II is now referred to as *enterprise resource planning*.

Marginal cost is the cost to produce an additional product.

Maslow, Abraham, of the USA, is best known for his 1943 publication *A Theory of Human Motivation*, in which he theorized that people have five basic requirements, which he put into a pyramid as a *hierarchy of needs*.

Mass production is the production in high volume of standard-type products in an *assembly line* operation.

Master production schedule (MPS) is a planning tool in operations, with a time horizon in weeks, or months, showing what *end items*, and timing are needed to satisfy client demands.

Material requirements planning (MRP), is a computer-based tool for materials management in manufacturing used when there is *dependent demand*.

Materials management refers to the purchasing of raw materials and components through to transformation to the storage of the finished product.

Maximax is an optimistic approach to *decision making under uncertainty* when management selects the maximum of the best of the possible outcomes.

Maximin is a pessimistic approach to *decision making under uncertainty* when management selects the maximum of the worst of the possible outcomes.

McGregor, Douglas, studying human relations, identified people as Theory X type who usually had negative assumptions about other people, and Theory Y who had positive ideas. In the management environment the implications were that Theory X managers were bad, and Theory Y managers were good and made the best managers.

Mean absolute deviation is a measure of the forecast error given as the average of the absolute deviation between the actual and forecast values for all the data points.

Mean squared error for forecasting is the average of the sum of the squared difference between the actual and the forecast value.

Mean time between failure in product *reliability* is the average time between when a product fails.

Median is the middle value in a *data array* or an ordered set of data. One half of the data lies below the median and one half above.

Mesokurtic is qualitative measure of the characteristic or *kurtosis* of the peak of a frequency distribution curve. It means that the peak is intermediate (*meso* means intermediate) between a sharp peak, where the data dispersion is small, and a flat peak where the data dispersion is large.

Midspread, or the *interquartile range*, is the difference between the third and first quartiles in a data set. It gives the dispersion or spread in the middle 50% of the data.

Minimax regret is a method for *decision making under uncertainty* when management selects the minimum of the worst regret, or disappointment, of an outcome.

Mission statement globally defines the business and objectives of an organization and is the start point of the strategic plan.

Modelling is the development of a mathematical or physical representation of the real thing used as a tool in planning, management, and decision making.

Monte Carlo simulation in queuing systems uses random numbers as an approach to model the waiting times and queue length.

Most likely time in a *PERT* network is the time that would occur most frequently if the activity were repeated many times.

Motion study is analyzing the time to perform a specified activity and is often the basis for developing *labour standards*.

Moving average forecasting is developing a forecast model based on the average of past data, say three periods, and then dropping the oldest data point as one moves on in time.

Multi-skilled, or polyvalent, applies to people who have the expertise to perform several tasks.

Multiple regression is when there is more than one independent variable to estimate a value for the dependent variable. Sales might be dependent on the sales budget, number of salespeople, and the number of sales contacts, or three independent variables.

N

Naive approach to forecasting assumes that the forecast activity for the next period is equal to the actual immediate past period's result.

Net present value is the value of a future stream of incomes recalculated to the present, taking into account the time value of money.

Net requirements in an inventory situation are the gross requirements required by the customer less the amount of inventory in stock.

Network diagrams in *project management* are flow schemes that show the various activities and their beginning and end points.

Neural networks are computer-based programs patterned on the human brain's mesh-like network of interconnecting cells, programmed to recognize patterns for problem solving.

Nitrogen is a gas that makes up 78% of air. When nitrogen is heated, such as in the engine of an automobile, it reacts with oxygen to give nitrogen oxide and nitrogen dioxide. These gases, which are collectively known as No_x, react with moisture in the atmosphere to give nitric acid or acid rain.

Noise pollution is the nuisance or pollution caused by excess noise. Sound levels are measured in decibels and the addition of ten decibels doubles the sound level, with 85 decibels considered the maximum level safe for the human ear. Continuous exposure to noise leads to health problems and in a work environment lowers *productivity*.

Normal distribution, or *Gaussian distribution*, is a graph of the frequency of occurrence of a random variable. The distribution is continuous, bell shaped, symmetrical, and the two tails extend indefinitely. The mean, median, mode, and midrange are equal and lie at the centre of the distribution.

Not-for-profit organizations are those that do not declare a profit and often have a preferential tax status.

Numerically controlled machines have control systems that read instructions and translate these into machine operations. Machines are pre-programmed with

computer commands to perform repeat cycle of operations that replace manual machine settings.

O

Objective function in linear programming defines the goal of the decision process such as maximizing profits or minimizing costs.

Ocean bill of lading is an export document and is a receipt for the cargo and a contract between a shipper and the ocean carrier. It may also be used as an instrument of ownership that can be bought, sold or traded while the goods are in transit.

OCP is used in shipping goods and means that the seller pays freight and transport to a named destination. It is equivalent to *C&F* but is appropriate for modes of transport other than ships.

Office layout is the efficient arrangement of workers, equipment, and offices.

Ogive is a *cumulative frequency distribution* useful in decision making. It shows how many observations, or the percentage of data, lie above or below certain values.

Open system is an organization, programme, department, or machine that, under normal operation, has continuous interaction with the external environment such as marketing.

Operating budget is that money allocated in advance, or forecast, for a business operation such as for sales activity, a building project, or research and development.

Operating characteristic curve in quality control is a graph illustrating how well an *acceptance plan* discriminates between good and bad lots. The discriminating ability depends on the shape of the curve that is a function of the sample size withdrawn from the lot, and acceptance level or the number of allowable defective units in the sample.

Operations management is the effective planning, organizing, and control of all resources and activities necessary to provide the market with tangible goods and services. It applies to manufacturing, service industries and *not-for-profit organizations*.

Optimized production technology (OPT), is a planning and scheduling tool for coordinating engineering, manufacturing, and marketing for a job shop, or repetitive manufacturing. It is based on nine rules that revolve around the concept of *bottlenecks*.

Optimistic time in a *PERT* network is the shortest possible time within which an *activity* could be completed if everything went right.

Oracle is a California-based company developing enterprise resource planning tools.

Order point is the time at which a new order is placed for additional inventory.

Order sequencing is the timing in which a group of orders such as assembling machine parts, packing of items, or machining operations are processed at a work centre.

Ordering costs are those associated with purchasing, or making a new inventory of goods.

Organization for Economic Cooperation and Development (OECD), established in 1961, is a grouping of 30 countries that provides governments with a forum for developing and setting economic and social policies. The members are some of the world's richest countries which provide two-thirds of the world's goods and services. The original 20 members are Austria, Belgium, Canada, Denmark, France, Germany, Greece, Iceland, Ireland, Italy, Luxembourg, Netherlands, Norway, Portugal, Spain, Sweden, Switzerland, Turkey, UK, and the USA. Since the original 20, the following ten countries (and the year of their becoming a member) are: Australia (1971), Finland (1969), South Korea (1996), Czech Republic (1995), Hungary (1996), New Zealand (1973), Japan (1964), Mexico (1994), Poland (1996), and Slovakia (2000).

Organization of Petroleum Exporting Countries (OPEC), was formed in 1960 by 13 oil-producing countries (Algeria, Ecuador, Gabon, Indonesia, Iran, Iraq, Kuwait, Libya, Nigeria, Qatar, Saudi Arabia, United Arab Emirates and Venezuela) for the purpose of controlling world oil production and thus inventory levels with the ultimate intent of determining oil prices.

Outsourcing, or *subcontracting*, is contracting work to another firm.

Overall equipment effectiveness is the real output of a machine. It is given by the theoretical output less downtime due to operator pauses, machine breakdowns, unplanned interruptions, machine setup, low performance, and material non-conforming.

Ozone, a gas comprising three atoms of oxygen, is formed from the action of sunlight on vehicle emissions. At ground level it causes respiratory problems.

Ozone layer in the upper atmosphere is a barrier to the sun's ultraviolet rays. Ozone is destroyed by chlorine compounds like *chlorofluorocarbons* allowing higher concentrations of ultraviolet rays to penetrate the earth's surface. This leads to higher incidence of skin cancer, glaucoma, and other health and environmental problems.

P

P-chart in *statistical process control* indicates the proportion or percentage of defective products in an operation.

Parallel system is an alternative to a *backup system*.

Parameter is a measure that describes the characteristics of a population.

Pareto analysis, after the Italian, Vilfredo Pareto, is a tool based on a frequency distribution for quality control and also in *ABC analysis* for inventory management.

Part-period balancing is a lot-sizing method that balances setup costs with holding costs. It is dynamic as it reflects requirements for future demand requirements.

Payback period is the time taken to recover an original investment made for a capital project, machine, equipment, or other *capital asset*.

Percentiles are special forms of *fractiles* that divide data into 100 equal parts.

Periodic order quantity is a *lot-sizing* method where a quantity of parts is produced at regular periods. This simplifies planning, as setup needs are known in advance.

Pessimistic time in a *PERT* network is the longest possible time the activity would require to be completed, assuming everything went wrong.

Physical distribution management concerns the delivery, storage, and other activities of delivering finished goods to clients.

Pictogram is a picture, or sketch, representing quantitative data.

Pie chart is a circle representing data, divided into segments (portions of a pie), where segments are proportional to the data represented. The circle is 100% of the data.

Piecework is where employees are paid based on the volume of work they produce.

Piggybacking is a transportation mode where container trucks can be directly loaded onto the wagons of trains avoiding unloading and repackaging.

Pipeline is another term for the *supply chain*.

Pipeline map is a linear flow scheme of the *supply chain*, highlighting each operation by processing time and holding time that material stays in the supply chain.

Piping and instrument diagram (P&I), is the engineer's drawing of a facility showing pipelines, instruments, valves, and other key control equipment.

Planned ordered deliveries are those quantities of material that are scheduled to be delivered at a defined date.

Planned ordered receipts are those quantities of material that are scheduled to be received at a defined date.

Planned ordered release is that material to be released to meet a planned delivery date.

Planning horizon is the time period for an organization's various planning programmes.

Platykurtic describes the peak of a frequency distribution that is relatively flat. This distribution has a large dispersion, or a high standard deviation (platy = broad, or flat).

Point estimate is a single figure, or statistic, to estimate the true population parameter.

Poisson distribution, after the Frenchman, Simeon Denis Poisson, is a *discrete* probability distribution often used to describe *waiting line* situations.

Poka yoke is a failsafe approach, incorporating devices to make products, processes, or services mistake proof to avoid errors, and at the same time to maintain quality.

Polygon is a line graph representing a *data set*.

Polynomial regression is the relationship between the dependent value, y, and the independent value, x, when there are values of x in the equation other than unity, for example x^2.

Population is a collection of all the elements being studied.

Portal, in the Internet, is the gateway or central destination point, through which users normally pass for e-mail transmission, shopping information and data searches. Yahoo! (yet another hierarchical officious oracle) is one of the biggest portals on the Internet. Ford Motor Company has created its own corporate portal, which users must pass to obtain other Internet services. The portal also provides access to segmented information on Ford's markets, products, distributors, etc., or important players in the supply chain.

Power, J D, is a California-based firm which regularly carries out quality-based surveys on automobiles using a customer satisfaction index.

Preventive maintenance is the work activity that has been programmed on a regular basis to inspect a system, uncover potential problems, and to make whatever repairs are necessary to ensure that the system does not fail during normal operation.

Pro-forma financial statements are those that are an estimate of future performance.

Probabilistic time estimates are those used in *PERT* network diagrams to estimate the duration of the various activities.

Process capability is the ability of a process, such as a machine, consistently to produce products that are within the design specifications of the product being manufactured.

Process capability ratio is a measure of the *process capability*. It is defined by the ratio:

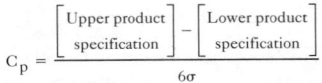

$$C_p = \frac{\left[\begin{array}{c}\text{Upper product} \\ \text{specification}\end{array}\right] - \left[\begin{array}{c}\text{Lower product} \\ \text{specification}\end{array}\right]}{6\sigma}$$

where 6σ is the process width. If the value of $C_p < 1.00$, the process is not capable of satisfactorily meeting the product design specifications. If $C_p = 1.00$ it is just capable of producing according to design specifications. For a high-performing operation the value of C_p should be greater than 1.00 and often a value of 1.33 is considered acceptable.

Process control charts in quality control indicate the performance of an operation.

Process flow chart shows the flow of materials between successive operating units whose usefulness is to locate the value and non-value-added activities.

Process flow diagram shows sequentially all the activities in a production operation.

Process-focused factories are facilities equipped to produce non-standard products in relatively small batches. They are sometimes referred to as *job shops*.

Process industries historically are those organizations, which deal with fluid flow and have a process, formula or recipe for making a particular product. Oil, chemical, and pharmaceutical firms are part of the process industry. The term is becoming somewhat blurred as sometimes one hears of an automobile firm being part of the process industry as it is active in the process of making cars.

Process liability is the risk a producer or others take regarding the responsibility for the personal injury, or harm resulting from the use of a process that they have supplied.

Produce to order is supplying goods or services, often non-standard items, only when requested by the customer.

Produce to stock is making products, often of standard design, which go into inventory.

Producer risk (α) involves the taking of a random sample that results in a higher portion of defects in the sample than is actually present in the lot.

Product analysis matrix is a tool using weighting to evaluate viability of new products.

Product-focused factories are facilities arranged to produce many products of a relative standard design using a *product layout*. Usually the *assembly line* is the layout arrangement of a product-focused factory where the finished items go into inventory.

Product layout describes the arrangement for a *product-focused factory*.

Product liability is the risk that a producer or others take regarding the responsibility for the personal injury, or harm resulting from the use of a product that they have supplied.

Product lifecycle is the duration of the life of products ranging from development, birth or introduction, growth, maturity, decline and death.

Product structure shows the make-up of a product from its various components.

Production permit, or deviation permit, is written authorization, prior to production, to depart from specified requirements, a specified quantity, or for a specified time.

Production planning is all the activity involved in preparing for the making of a tangible product or service.

Productivity measures *efficiency* and can be calculated by the ratio of outputs to inputs.

Program evaluation and review technique (PERT), is technique in *project management* using network diagrams to determine the critical path. It relies on three times estimates for the activity duration and is thus a probabilistic method.

Project acceleration is employing resources necessary to reduce the time of a project.

Project management involves the planning, scheduling, budgeting, and control of a project using an integrated team of workers and specialists. A project is a unique item of work for which there is a financial budget and a defined schedule. A project may be large – the tunnel under the channel between England and France; or small – the refurbishing of an office.

Pull system is one where a product moves through the *supply chain* as a result of the customer demand or 'pulling' the item.

Purchasing is the selection, and ultimate acquisition of raw materials, components, or equipment for a manufacturing or service organization.

Purchasing managers' index measures the level of purchasing activity. It is related to economic activity as a high index signals an increase in manufacturing and vice versa.

Push system is where the producer 'pushes' his products through the *supply chain*, relying on marketing to sell them to the client.

Q

Qualitative data are categorical, or subjective information.

Qualitative forecasting is based on subjective opinions.

Quality is the totality of features and characteristics of a product, process, or service that bear on its ability to satisfy stated or implied needs.

Quality assurance covers those planned and systematic actions necessary to provide confidence that a product, process, or service, will satisfy given quality requirements.

Quality at the source implies that all those persons responsible for an activity are also responsible for its quality thus avoiding non-value quality inspection.

Quality audit is a systematic, and independent, examination to determine whether quality activities and results comply with planned arrangements and also whether these arrangements are effectively implemented, and are suitable to achieve objectives.

Quality circle is a small group of employees who voluntarily meet regularly to analyze work-related projects with the objective of improving company operations. There are no direct cash incentives and the principal reason for participation is personal satisfaction.

Quality control covers the operational techniques and activities that are used to satisfy quality requirements such as inspection, measuring, and testing.

Quality function deployment (QFD), is a method to ensure a new product or service satisfies clients. Its goal is to develop an appropriate design and then translate this into targets throughout product development and production. QFD is also known as the *house of quality*, because of its shape, or the *voice of the customer*, because of its purpose.

Quality loop is a conceptual model of interacting activities that influence the quality of a product, process, or service, in the various stages ranging from identification of needs to the assessment of whether these needs have been satisfied.

Quality loss function, an element of *Taguchi's* robust design, is a relationship that identifies costs, L, associated with poor quality. It shows how costs increase as the product deviates from specifications and is given by $L = D^2 \cdot C$, where D is deviation from the target specification and C is cost of avoiding the deviation.

Quality management, the responsibility of top executives, is that aspect of the overall management function that determines and implements the quality policy.

Quality plan is a document setting out the specific quality practices, resources, and activities, relevant to a particular product, process, service, contract, or project.

Quality policy is the programme or course of action an organization has in place to design, control and monitor its activities related to ensuring that the quality of its products and processes is according to requirements.

Quality robust refers to products designed to function under adverse conditions.

Quality spiral is an alternative name for a *quality loop*.

Quality surveillance is the continuing evaluation of the status of procedures, methods, conditions, products, processes, services, and analysis of records in relation to stated references to ensure that quality requirements are being met. Customers, or third parties often perform quality surveillance independently to ensure that contractual requirements are met.

Quality system is the organizational structure, responsibilities, procedures, activities, capabilities, and resources, aimed at ensuring that products, processes, or services, will satisfy stated, or implied needs.

Quality system review is a formal management evaluation of the status and adequacy of the *quality system* in relation to *quality policy*, and new objectives, arising from changing circumstance.

Quantitative data are numerical information that can be rigorously analyzed.

Quantitative forecasting is that using *quantitative* or *statistical data*.

Quantity discount is a reduction offered per unit in buying bulk purchases.

Quartile deviation is one-half of the *interquartile range*.

Quartiles are special forms of *fractiles* that divide data into four equal parts.

Queuing is an alternative to *waiting lines*.

Quick ratio or *acid test ratio* is the total cash and *accounts receivables* divided by the current liabilities. It is a measure of the ability of a firm to meet its current debt on a very short notice.

R

Random sample is where each item has the same chance of being selected.

Random variations are those for which there are no assignable causes.

Range chart is an analytical tool in *statistical process control* to monitor the sample range of continuous variables. They are used in conjunction with *x-bar charts*.

Range is a measure of the dispersion of data.

Raw data are pieces of information before they are arranged, or analyzed by statistical, or other methods.

Reengineering is used as an alternative to *business process reengineering*.

Regression analysis indicates how to determine the nature and the strength of the relationship between variables. *Linear regression* is perhaps the most common but *multiple regression* is another possibility.

Regression equation is the equation that indicates the relationship between the dependent variable and the independent variable or variables.

Relative frequency distribution is the display of a data set that shows the fraction, or percentage, of the total data set that falls into each set of mutually exclusive classes.

Reliability is the ability of an item to perform a required function, under stated conditions, for a specified period of time.

Reliability-centred maintenance focuses on function and equipment by establishing what is meant by the right maintenance rather than just very frequent overhauls. It determines what must be done to ensure that physical assets continue to fulfil its operating context ensuring that systems work as designed with minimal problems.

Renege relates to *waiting lines*, when a customer enters the queue but becomes impatient and leaves. Thus, for a part of the time they form part of the queue, but never receive service.

Reorder point is the level of inventory in storage at which another order is placed.

Repatriation of earnings refers to the transfer of income from a foreign operation back to the home office.

Request for proposal (RFP), is the formal demand from a user to suppliers of services or goods to present a technical and financial proposal of their proposed offer.

Responsibility in a business context is the obligation of the employee when that person accepts a manager's delegation of authority.

Reverse osmosis is a filtering process where very small molecules are removed.

Robot is an automatic, computer-driven, flexible machine that can hold, turn, lift, and perform other activities according to electronic impulses.

Run length is an alternative to the *lot size*.

Run-out method of scheduling is a procedure based on when a product's stock would be depleted. For production in fixed lot sizes this is the ratio of current inventory to demand. Alternatively, inventory can be aggregated to determine at what point in time inventory will be depleted, or 'run out'.

S

Safety stock is inventory for unplanned purposes such as transport strikes, delivery delays due to bad weather, unreliable suppliers, or unexpected increase in demand. Safety stock reduces the probability of stockouts, but increases *inventory carrying costs*.

Salesforce composite is a judgmental forecast where opinions are solicited from line sales at the regional level and then these sales forecasts are compiled at headquarters.

Salvage value is the value of equipment at the end of its life when it is sold for scrap.

Sample is a collection of some, but not all, of the elements of a population being studied.

Sampling distribution of the mean is a probability distribution of all the possible means of samples taken from a population.

Sampling with replacement is taking an item from a population for analysis, and then putting this sample back into the population. For a *finite population* the probability of a sample being selected is then always the same.

Sampling without replacement is taking an item from a population for analysis, and not putting this sample back into the population. For an *infinite population* the probability would not change but for a *finite population* it would.

Sandoz, now Novartis, has a chemical plant in Basel, Switzerland, that, as a result of a fire in 1986, caused an environmental disaster. Water used for the fire's containment flowed into the Rhine carrying with it tons of toxic chemicals killing fish and contaminating drinking water in Switzerland, France, Germany, and the Netherlands.

Scatter diagram is a graph showing the x and y measurements of various observations.

Scheduled receipt is that planned quantity of inventory due to arrive at a given date.

Scheduling is the preparation of a timetable, and sequencing order, for activities that have to occur in order to achieve a set of objectives.

Scientific management was an approach by theorists in the period from around 1875 to 1925, whose objectives were to treat the activity of workers in a logical, scientific way by using time, motion, and methods study. The ultimate goal of this analytical approach was to increase worker output, efficiency, productivity, and to reduce production costs.

Seasonal index is a factor in a time series showing the magnitude of seasonal effects.

Segmentation is the separation of consumer and industrial markets into identifiable groupings for the ultimate purpose of increasing a company's marketing success.

Seiketsu is a Japanese word meaning to standardize. Applied to operations it means that with standardization, jobs and activities are performed in a consistent manner.

Seiro is a Japanese word meaning to remove. It means in operations, remove from the work area unneeded tools, materials, equipment, or documents. The idea is that if it's not needed, don't have it cluttering the area because it gets in the way and could slow down activity.

Seiso is a Japanese word meaning to keep clean, which, in a manufacturing environment, means keeping the working area clean, which is appropriate from a health and safety point of view.

Seiton is a Japanese word meaning to organize. In operations, it means organize materials, tools, pencils, papers, computer diskettes, and documents. Classification of these work items will help to reduce search time for these when they are needed.

Sensitivity analysis is determining how a given solution reacts to changes in values. In decision making, the best result might be chosen but it can be sensitive to small changes.

Sequencing rules are those that govern the order for scheduling work.

Sequential sampling in *statistical quality control* is where lots are rejected or accepted according to a pre-established programme. Units are randomly selected from the lot and tested after which a reject, accept, or continue sampling decision is made according to the sample plan, and the region where the total number of units that have been tested fall.

Service industries are those that do not transform materials in the classic sense. The term applies to such industries as transportation, financial services, retailing, and leisure.

Service level is that proportion of customer orders that can be completed from existing inventory. A 95% service level means that 95% of customers can be supplied out of existing inventory, while 5% will not, or the probability of a stockout is 5%.

Setup time is the *delay* involved in regulating a machine such that it can work on a component part. Incorporating SMED ideas or automating procedures may reduce setup times.

Sherman Act is an 1890 US law that forbids price fixing among competitors, group boycotts, allocation of customers or markets, or agreements between a manufacturer and customers such that they will not buy competitor's products.

Shitsuke is a Japanese word meaning to respect the rules. In business it underscores that firms and society function through teamwork and cooperation or respecting rules.

Shop floor refers to the area where the manufacturing and assembly activities occur.

Short cost in inventory management is the cost of not stocking a unit demanded, meaning there is a customer need but that the unit is not in inventory. This cost is associated with stockouts such as lost revenue, or special handling and expediting to satisfy the customer.

Short run production costs relate to labour, materials, variable overhead that can change in the short run. Not included is physical capacity that is fixed in the short run.

Shortest processing time is an *order-sequencing rule* where the next job to be processed among the jobs waiting is the one that involves the shortest operating time.

Simple moving averaging is a method in forecasting to predict a future value by using the simple, straight, or linear average of past data. If sales in January,

February, and March were $10,750, $9,500 and $12,750 respectively then using simple moving average, the estimate for April would be $10,000 (10,750 + 9,500 + 12,750)/3.

Simple moving averaging approach is forecasting using the method of *simple moving averaging*.

Simplex method is a tool for linear programming.

Simulation is duplicating activity that occurs in the real world often using computers.

Single channel, multiple phase in queuing is where there is one line but several phases, such as a medical centre where a patient sees first a nurse, the doctor, and then pays the bill to the cashier.

Single channel, single phase in queuing is where there is one line and one service area, such as a grocery store when with only one cashier.

Single minute exchange of die (SMED) from Toyota is a procedure to try and reduce machine setup times to less than ten minutes (a single minute).

Single sampling in *statistical quality control* has one upper limit of permitted defective units. A random sample is withdrawn from the lot and tested. If the defective units in the sample do not exceed the limit the lot is accepted and, if not, it is rejected.

Site selection is the decision involving establishing the location for an operating facility.

Six-sigma quality is a concept originated by Motorola, and rigorously enforced by General Electric, implying very high quality of products, processes, or services. Quantitatively six-sigma quality indicates that there will only be 3.4 defective components per million even when considering a process shift of 1.5 sigma.

Smith, Adam (1723–1790), an early theorist of scientific management suggested in his book, *The Wealth of Nations*, that labour specialization could reduce labour costs.

Smoothing constant is the alpha factor in forecasting using exponential smoothing.

Solid waste pollution is dumping untreated commercial, consumer, or industrial waste on land. Besides being an eyesore, toxic products from waste can percolate into water sources.

Sourcing is the activity in purchasing to locate, or 'source', the best raw material, component, service, or supplier at the optimum cost/quality ratio. The sourcing activity is worldwide.

Specification is the document that describes in detail the requirements with which a product, process, or service, has to conform.

Staff functions are those that have no direct responsibility in production output such as a *quality control* inspector.

Standard deviation is a measure of the dispersion of a data set either applied to a population or a sample and is given by the square root of the variance.

Standard error of estimate measures variability or scatter around a regression line.

Standard error of the mean measures variability of the means of each sample.

Standard time is the practical time needed to perform work and on which labour costs are often based.

State of nature is the condition in the external environment governing decision making.

Statistic is a measure that describes a characteristic of a sample such as weight.

Statistical data is sample information data that has been taken from a *population* in order to make some analysis of the characteristics of the population. A sample of the weight in grams of bars of chocolate from a production line would be statistical data to make an analysis about the weight of the *lot* of chocolate bars produced.

Statistical process control is the procedure used to verify that a process operates correctly.

Statistical quality control covers all the quantitative analytical procedures to verify that a process, product, or service is according to specifications.

Stem cells are non-specialized cells that have the capacity to self-renew and to differentiate into more mature cells.

Stem and leaf display is a method of data presentation highlighting which data occur most frequently. The stem shows the principal value of the *data set*, and the leaf intermediate values. It is useful when dealing with a large quantity of *raw data*.

Stockkeeping units (SKUs), is a common term denoting the amount of inventory items being carried.

Stockout costs are those associated with being unable to satisfy demand. They include lost sales, lost customers, or activities needed eventually to satisfy the customer.

Straight line depreciation is the allocation of depreciated costs linearly over the life of the *capital asset*.

Strategic plan is the detail of how an organization proposes to arrive at its desired objectives. The plan is often long term, although firms may have short-term strategies, and gives the timeframe, the *mission statement* or charter for *not for profit organizations*.

Stratified sampling is a survey approach where the population is divided into homogeneous groups or strata such as according to age.

Student t distribution is an alternative for *t distribution*.

Sub–optimality is the condition that exists when optimization of a component, or subsystem, gives a less than optimal performance of the larger system and vice versa.

Subcontracting is giving work to another firm, enforced by a legal contract.

Subcontractor networks cover the contacts, services, relationships and availability of third parties to perform work. The network, called *keiretsu* in Japan, can be critical to the flexibility and the performance of the firm.

Sum of year's digits is a depreciation method where the sums of the year's digits are totalled to give the denominator to proportion the depreciation amount.

Supply chain is a network that for tangible goods covers purchasing of raw materials, manufacturing, assembly, and distribution of finished goods to the client.

Sustainable development is the management of economic growth, avoiding irreparable damage to the environment.

By balancing economic demands with ecological concerns, people's needs are satisfied without jeopardizing the prospects of future generations.

SWOT analysis is a management planning tool used for analyzing a company's future strategy and an acronym for the firm's internal strength and weaknesses, and the external opportunities and threats. A SWOT analysis assumes that, if managers carefully review such elements, an appropriate long-term programme for success will emerge.

Synchronized production is producing a product at the rate at which it is demanded.

System is a group of interdependent components, variables, activities, or departments.

Systematic layout planning rates relative importance of the closeness of departments considering factors such as types of customer, ease of supervision, common personnel, and common equipment, and then selecting a layout according to the closeness importance.

Systematic sampling is where elements are selected and analyzed from a population at a uniform interval of time, order, or space. Analyzing the surface condition of a motorway, by sampling every half-mile, would be systematic sampling.

T

T-classification, part of the *VAT classification*, is where products are similar in their functionality, but used in different services or applications. Components may be common in each product but towards the end of assembly, combining certain subassemblies produces different products, such as flow control valves for water, gas, and other fluids.

t distribution is a continuous probability distribution, like the *normal distribution*, in that it is bell shaped, and symmetrical, except that it is lower at the mean, and higher in the tails. A t distribution is used when the sample size, n, is small and the population standard deviation is unknown. There is a t distribution for every sample size.

Taguchi methods are aimed at quality improvement, based on making designs robust by building in tolerances for manufacturing variables known to be unavoidable. Taguchi's philosophy is that missing the quality target in a consistent manner can be better than hitting it a few times with the rest being scattered all over the board.

Takt time, from the German and meaning in rhythm with the conductor, is synonymous in operations for being in rhythm with client demands.

Taskforce is a group of specialized people who have an objective to solve a particular problem or make a decision concerning a certain activity. A taskforce might decide on the development of a new product, the construction of a new project, or a new market direction for example.

Taylor, Frederick Winslow of the USA (1856–1915), is considered the father of scientific management. He rigorously examined the field of operations as a science proposing to increase worker efficiency by job design. His logic was that there was one best way to work and it was this way that should be developed and put into action.

Taylorism is the scientific approach to management based on *Taylor*'s theories. For many, it is synonymous with rigidity, inflexibility, and loss of motivation.

Technology is the application of science and engineering to achieve a practical purpose.

Theory X is a concept proposed by *Douglas McGregor*, wherein these types of people have negative opinions about others and are considered to make poor managers.

Theory Y is a concept proposed by *Douglas McGregor*, wherein these types of people have positive opinions about others and are considered to make good managers.

Time fences in the *master production schedule* refer to the frozen, fixed, full and open time periods, which is a scale of rigidly for planning purposes.

Time series is historical data, such as sales revenues, GNP, or cash flow, which have been compiled over a regular period of time and might be used to forecast future values.

Time value of money refers to the fact that value declines over time. A £100 bill today will not have the same value five years from now.

Time-to-market is the time delay for a product after start of the purchasing of the raw materials until it reaches the client. For some firms, it is the time from conception of the product to commercialization.

Tolerance limits refer to the upper and lower values, for example, the length in which a unit or work piece is considered acceptable.

Total assets turnover is a financial ratio given by sales to total assets and is a measure of the performance of the firm.

Total productive maintenance is a well-defined and organized programme, which places a high value on teamwork, consensus building, and continuous improvement, or *kaizen*.

Total quality management (TQM), is where attention to quality pervades the whole operation, not just one particular sector, with the driver being top management.

Total sum of squares in a regression equation, also called the *total variation*, measures the variation of the observed Y values around the mean value of Y.

Total variation in the forecasting *regression equation* is a measure of the variation between actual and forecast data. It is made up of the explained variation, or that which is attributable to the relationship between the independent and dependent variable and the unexplained variation, or that which is attributable to factors other than the relationship between the independent and dependent variable.

Traceability is the ability to trace the history, application, or location of an item or activity, or similar items or activities, by means of recorded identification.

Tracking signal in forecasting indicates how well the forecast is predicting actual data.

Trade-off in decision making is choosing between two or more possibilities when there are advantages and disadvantages attached to all of them.

Trading pollution rights is a market-based approach for firms involving buying, or selling the right to pollute, with the objective of reducing overall pollution level.

Transmittal letter is an export document listing the particulars of the shipment of goods and a record of the documents being transmitted, together with instructions for disposition of documents. Any special instructions are also included.

Transportation method is a linear programme technique to determine the lowest cost plan for the distribution of goods from multiple origins to multiple destinations.

Two-bin system is a *fixed order* inventory management approach where inventory is held in two bins. The first, the principal storage container, has a large capacity. The capacity of the second is based on *demand during lead time*. When the first is empty, a new order is placed; meanwhile withdrawal is from the second.

Two-dimensional template is a technique for *facility layout* where cutouts, of the same scale as the floor plan, are made to scale of equipment to be located. These cutouts are moved around by trial and error until the desired floor plan is achieved.

Type I error (α) is rejecting a null hypothesis when, in fact, it should be accepted. In *statistical process control*, this is concluding that a process is out of control when, in fact, it is under control.

Type II error (β) is accepting a null hypothesis when, in fact, it should be rejected. In *statistical process control*, this is concluding that a process is under control when, in fact, it is out of control.

U

UK Best Factory Awards is a quality awards programme operated by Cranfield Business School and the publication, *Management Today*, which annually identifies those plant sites in the UK according to industry sector considered to be 'the best'.

Unbalanced transportation problem in linear programming is when the total supply of a product is greater than total demand, or total product demand is greater than total supply.

Uncertainty in decision making implies that probabilities cannot be assigned to outcomes.

Universal mobile telecommunications system (UMTS) is a set of standards defining the next generation of mobile telephony expected to be in widespread commercial use in 2002.

Utilization rate is the time by which a production unit must be on line to produce required output. It is given by the ratio of total operating time divided by the total time available.

Utility in decision making refers to the pleasure, or displeasure, as the result of a certain outcomes. Managers are not the same and might make different decisions for the same situation that, in part, is related to their utility.

V

V-classification, part of the *VAT classification* is where from one, or few raw materials (the base of the V), a variety of different end products can be produced. From petroleum a vast range of chemicals can be made.

Vacation days are the number of holiday days a year allotted to an employee, and paid by the employer. The greater the number of days given the higher the labour costs which, in part, explains the differences in labour costs between Europe and the USA.

Valdez principle, after the *Exxon Valdez* oil spill, calls on companies to make organizational changes and appoint an environmentalist to the corporate board, and also to conduct an annual public audit of the company's environmental progress.

Value-added tax (VAT), is a surcharge added to the sales price, or the cost of goods or services in theory based on the 'value added' to that product.

Value analysis, or *value engineering*, very often a practice in purchasing, is the evaluation of the expected performance of a product relative to its price.

Value engineering is similar to *value analysis*.

Variable costs are those that change with output such as labour, materials, and variable overhead.

Variety funnel illustrates the reduction of flexibility with raw materials and components as the operation moves through the supply chain.

VAT classification is grouping items according to the type of end product, and, to a certain extent, by the manufacturing process employed.

Vendor analysis is the comparison of vendors, or suppliers, based on criteria such as price or global cost, delivery time, quality, availability of spares, and after-sales service.

Venn diagram is a rectangular scheme used to illustrate visually the probability outcomes of events that are or are not mutually exclusive.

Vertical integration in the supply chain is the combination, under single ownership, of two or more stages of production and/or distribution of entities that are normally separate. An example would be an oil refiner (BP, ExxonMobil, or Texaco) that own the crude, pipelines, oil refinery, oil tankers, and retail outlets.

Virtual systems are those that perform a function but don't physically exist, or that exist only at the instant they are needed.

Voice of the customer is another name for *quality function deployment*.

W

Waiting line or *queue* is people or units in a system waiting to be serviced.

Water pollution is the discharge of toxic products directly into rivers, lakes, and the sea, or the dumping on land because the toxic chemicals can percolate into water sources.

Web page is a block of information that can be called up across the *World Wide Web*. It is a way of organizing data on the web. Individuals, manufacturers, universities, publishers, hospitals, restaurants, etc., prepare web pages as a means of advertising their activities.

Weighted moving average forecasting is applying a weighting factor to each period rather than using the straight average as in the *simple moving average approach*.

Weighted unit average cost for inventory accounting is when the average value of inventory items is charged against sales. This gives a 'fair' value of the cost of goods sold, and the value of inventory remaining.

What–if analysis in decision making looks at alternative outcomes by posing the question: 'What if this happens', 'What if this decision is made?'

White-collar worker is a term referring to managers or supervisory people.

Wireless application protocol (WAP) is a specification intended to define an open standard architecture and set of protocols for wireless Internet access. It has been designed to ensure interoperability between vendors and service providers and has the cooperation of such firms as IBM, Nokia, Hewlett-Packard, Ericsson, Lucent, Motorola, and major network operators.

Wireless markup language (WML) is a presentation standard for mobile Internet applications. It is a modified subset of the web mark-up language, *HTML*, scaled appropriately to meet the physical constraints and data capabilities of mobile devices primarily *GSM* phones. The HTML served by a website passes through a WML gateway to be scaled and formatted for the mobile device.

Work-in-process is that raw material inventory to which some processing has been applied but it is still not a finished product.

Work order is the instruction for producing a given quantity of items, usually according to a required schedule.

Working capital is the difference between current assets and current liabilities and represents the funds used for running a firm such as the investment in inventories, money for paying outstanding bills, and wages and salaries. The management of working capital is one of the functions of the treasurer or controller.

Working week is the number of hours a week that an employee works usually according to law. A longer workweek usually results in lower unit product costs.

World Wide Web (the web, or WWW) is a set of standards on the Internet for storing, retrieving, formatting, and displaying information using a client/server architecture. Using the web one can be connected to information at another site, perhaps many kilometres away.

X

X axis is the horizontal axis, or *abscissa*, of a graph and in forecasting is for the independent variable.

X-bar chart is a graph in *statistical process control* for monitoring the average value of continuous variables such as hardness, height, temperature, and weight. *Range charts* are used in conjunction with x-bar charts to give correct monitoring.

Y

Y axis is the vertical axis, or ordinate, of a graph that in forecasting contains the dependent variable.

Yield rate in a production process is the percentage of starting material that actually ends up in the product taking into account scrap. It is calculated by (100 − scrap percentage).

Z

Z value, in a *normal distribution*, is the number of standard deviations a random variable, x, lies from the mean, μ. It is calculated by $(x - \mu)/\sigma$, where σ is the standard deviation.

Zero inventories are the ultimate objective of an operation whose approach can be obtained using *just-in-time*. Zero breakdowns, zero defects, zero delays, and zero paper are other related goals. Together they are known as the five zeros targeting ultimate efficiency. By corollary, 'zero accidents' is a sixth.

Index